GREENLAND

ALASKA
151

CANADA
152

ICELAND
61

EUROPE
52

NORWAY

London
53

Paris
53

NORTH AMERICA
145

156

160

167
• Metropolitan
New York

UNITED STATES
154

Metropolitan Los Angeles •
164

158

162

Azores
75

Madeira 75

MOROCCO

NORTHERN
AFRICA
124

Canary Is.
75

ALGERIA

146
MEXICO

150 BAHAMAS

Oahu
154

154

Distrito
Federal
147

Mexico City — Veracruz
CUBA

122
CAPE VERDE

MAURITANIA

MALI

NIG

HAWAII

147

JAMAICA

GUAT.

HON.

NICAR.

148

HAITI

DOM.
REP.
150

SEN.

128

B.F.

BENIN

GUINEA

CÔTE
D'IV.

TOGO
GHANA

NIG
ER

Costa Rica

PANAMA

LIBR.

NORTHERN
SOUTH AMERICA
136

VENEZUELA

COLOMBIA

138

SUR.
GUYANA

FR. GUIANA

AFRICA
122

GAB

144

Galapagos Is.

ECU.

CENTRAL
PACIFIC OCEAN
120

144
PERU

BRAZIL

140

BOLIVIA

SOUTHERN
AFRICA
126

121
Samoa

121
Tahiti

SOUTH AMERICA
134

141
São Paulo —
Rio de Janiero
141

PAR.

ARGENTINA

142
Santiago —
Valparaiso
142

UR.
143

Río de la
Plata

SOUTHERN
SOUTH AMERICA
135

CHILE

143

UNITED STATES/CANADA

CANADA

AB.

SK.

MB.

BC

156

QU.

ON.

Montréal
161

BC

Seattle —
Tacoma
165

WA.

MT.

ND

MN.

Chicago —
Milwaukee
165

Toronto —
Buffalo
161

NB

OR.

ID.

WY.

SD

WI.

Detroit
165

MI.

160

ME.

NS

IA.

NE.

IL.

IN.

OH.

168

NY

168

NV.

UT.

CO.

KS.

MO.

UNITED STATES

PA.
166

CA.

158

AZ.

NM

OK.

AR.

KY.

WV

VA.

TN.

162

NC

Sacramento —
San Francisco —
San Jose
165

TX.

MS.

AL.

GA.

SC

LA.

FL.

MEXICO

KEY TO ATLAS MAPS

1:14,000,000 ASIA 90
AND SMALLER SCALES

1:7,000,000 162

1:1,170,000 165

1:10,500,000 106

1:3,500,000 100

1:587,000 • London 53

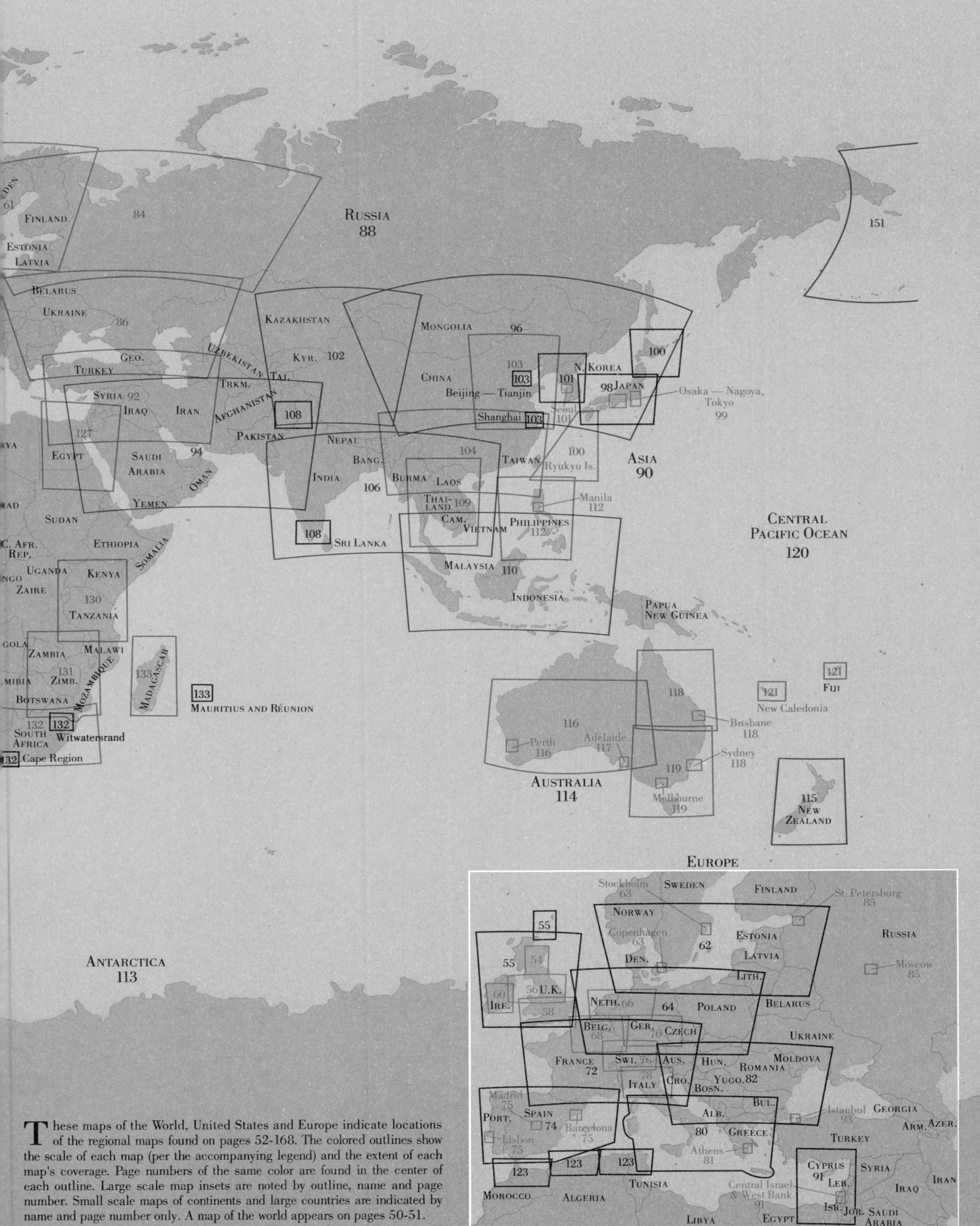

These maps of the World, United States and Europe indicate locations of the regional maps found on pages 52-168. The colored outlines show the scale of each map (per the accompanying legend) and the extent of each map's coverage. Page numbers of the same color are found in the center of each outline. Large scale map insets are noted by outline, name and page number. Small scale maps of continents and large countries are indicated by name and page number only. A map of the world appears on pages 50-51.

HAMMOND

Atlas of the World

CONCISE EDITION

HAMMOND

Atlas of t

CONCISE
EDITION

HAMMOND INCORPORATED, MAPLEWOOD, NEW JERSEY

MAPMAKERS AND PUBLISHERS FOR THE 21ST CENTURY

he World

Contents

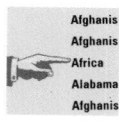

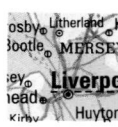

INDEX

68/B3 **Flixecourt** A 60,000-entry Master Index
69/D4 **Flize, Fran** lists places and features appear-
69/D4 **Floing, Fra** ing in this atlas, complete with
69/H4 **Flonheim,**
69/F5 **Florange, I** page numbers and easy-to-use
69/D3 **Floreffe, B**
69/D2 **Florennes** alpha-numeric references.

LIBRARY OF CONGRESS
CATALOGING-IN-PUBLICATION DATA

Hammond Incorporated.
    Hammond Atlas of the World. – Concise Edition.
        p.   cm.
    Includes index.
    ISBN 0-8437-1178-7
    ISBN 0-8437-1179-5 (pbk.)
    1. Atlases. I. Title. II. Title: Atlas of the world.
G1021. H2667   1996   <G&M>
912--dc20   96-27532
                                            CIP
                                            MAP

Evolution of Cartography

Early cartographers used optical instruments and mathematical analysis to survey and measure distances on the ground. Map-making was slow and time consuming, though accuracy was impressive.

Hot air balloons were occasionally used by military observers to map battle areas not accessible by land. More importantly, the application of photography by cartographers ushered in a new age of map-making.

Airplanes permitted aerial reconnaissance at higher altitudes, greatly reducing surveying time. Meanwhile, advances in photography allowed sharp images of increasingly larger areas.

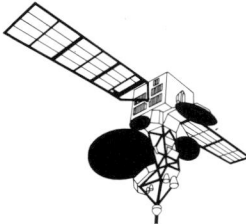

Satellites gave cartographers a global vantage point beyond the earth's atmosphere. Technological advances, many derived from military and aerospace research, permitted images to be systematically sent from space to sophisticated computers, where they were organized and enhanced.

Digital geographic databases are revolutionizing map-making. As this brief history of cartography reveals, maps can now be created and updated with greater accuracy and speed than ever before.

The foundation of modern-day cartography was laid by the ancient Greeks, who recognized the spherical shape of the earth, developed our system of longitude and latitude, designed the first map projections and calculated the size of the earth — with surprising accuracy. Claudius Ptolemy's Geographia, produced in the 2nd century A.D., was the first bound collection of maps designed to serve both scholarship and administration.

During the Middle Ages, mapmakers made little attempt to show the world as it was. The typical medieval map represented a Christian ideal, usually placing Jerusalem in the center of the world. At the same time, however, Arab scholars were improving on Ptolemy's work, making significant advances in map presentation and accuracy.

At the end of the 13th century, the compass came into general use, and with it came a new kind of map, called a portolan chart, created by the Genovese fleet for navigational purposes. Based on compass surveys, these outline maps depicted the Mediterranean and Black seas with great accuracy. An elaborate system of lines indicating compass directions crisscrossed the maps' surfaces. In 1375, the Catalan Atlas used portolans to depict most of the world, following the text of Marco Polo.

Three key events contributed to the renaissance of cartography. First was the rediscovery of Ptolemy's Geographia in the West. Carefully preserved by devotees, the text eventually reached the Moorish rulers in Spain.

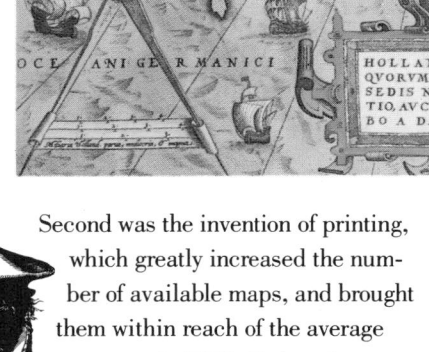

An eminent cartographer of the Age of Exploration, Gerardus Mercator, produced his first world map in 1538. As an aid to seamen, Mercator's map was unsurpassed, because all compass directions appeared as straight lines.

Second was the invention of printing, which greatly increased the number of available maps, and brought them within reach of the average person. In 1478, Ptolemy's Geographia became the first of the classical Greek works to be printed.

Third, and perhaps most important, was the age of the great discoveries, which was itself made possible by the development of new three-masted sailing vessels.

THE AGE OF EXPLORATION

European mariners set sail across the Atlantic beginning in the late 15th century. The great sea-going explorers of this era — Columbus, Cabot, Amerigo Vespucci, Magellan and Sir Francis Drake — all owed much to Ptolemy's ancient text, and to the refinements made at the navigational school founded by Prince Henry the Navigator. Ptolemy and others, however, considerably exaggerated the Eurasian landmass, showing it to occupy nearly half the globe. This error led Columbus to underestimate the distance to Asia; thus he failed to realize that he had reached the new world.

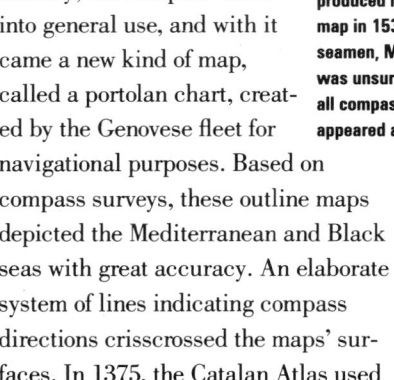

In 1572 a volume of maps published in Rome added the figure of Atlas holding up the world—hence the name "Atlas".

This map of Holland was reproduced from an original version of Theatrum Orbis Terrarum. (Courtesy of Federico Canobbio-Codelli)

Gerardus Mercator, an important cartographer of his age, was the first to produce a true world navigational chart on a flat surface. It became the favored depiction among map publishers.

Many new maps followed as great explorers, and later traders, returned to correct and fill in the blank spaces of the expanding world. The first modern atlas, Theatrum Orbis Terrarum, was published in 1570.

The first successful marine chronometer, in use by 1761, offered a reliable means of measuring longitude. By the late 18th century, mapmakers were already producing a reasonable picture of the world as we know it today.

With the invention of photography in the 19th century, cartographers could at last record the landscape with photo-realistic precision and detail. Then, in the early 1900's, airplanes dramatically extended the scope of our view. Advances in photography kept pace, permitting crisp images of ever expanding areas. Aerial reconnaissance became the standard method for gathering cartographic data. Infrared and ultra-violet photography extended the range of

A satellite view of the area shown on the map at left. Note the addition of Dutch "polders" or land reclaimed from the sea. perception beyond the visible spectrum, while radar penetrated visual obstacles such as clouds and fog.

IMAGES FROM SPACE

But a quantum leap forward occurred in the 1970's, when remote sensing satellites launched a new age of cartography, giving us a vantage point beyond the earth's atmosphere. Satellites provided the first exact measurements of the earth's diameter and the distances between continents, and showed the earth to be flattened at the poles by precisely 26.6 miles (42.8 km.).

Today, satellites are mapping the globe. Landsat digital images of the earth are systematically broadcast from space to sophisticated computers, where the images are assembled and enhanced. This marriage of computers and satellites has given birth to radically new geographic information systems.

COMPUTER-ASSISTED MAPS

Computers were quickly employed in the everyday production of maps. In computer-assisted map-making systems, computers function as electronic versions of traditional drafting tools. Hand-drawn maps are scanned into a computer, where revisions such as name and color changes can be made quickly and easily. However, because these systems must use existing maps as their source material, their ability to output maps at various scales, projections or with different levels of detail is seriously limited.

CREATING A DIGITAL DATABASE

The Hammond Atlas of the World is the first world atlas created directly from a digital database, and its computer-generated maps represent a new phase in map-making technology.

To build the database capable of generating this world atlas, the latitude and longitude of every significant town, river, coastline, natural and political border, transportation network and peak elevation was researched and digitized.

Engineering the complex data structure was critical to the success of the system, which relies on powerful computers and enormous data storage

Traditional craftsmanship still plays a vital role. To vividly represent a region's topography, hand-sculpted TerraScape™ relief models created by master cartographer Ernst Hofmann are married to the computer-generated world maps.

capacity. Hundreds of millions of data points describing nearly every important geographic feature on earth are organized into over 1,000 different map feature codes.

HOW COMPUTER-GENERATED MAPS ARE MADE

There are no maps in this unique system. Rather, it consists entirely of coded points, lines and polygons. To create a map, cartographers determine what city, region or continent they want to show and select specific information to include, based on editorial considerations such as scale, town size, population density, and the relative importance of different features. How does a computer plot irregular rivers and mountains — at many different scales? Using fractal geometry to describe natural forms such as coastlines, mathematical physicist Mitchell Feigenbaum developed software capable of reconfiguring coastlines, borders and mountain ranges to fit a multitude of map scales and projections.

Even map labeling has finally given way to new technology. Dr. Feigenbaum also created a new computerized type placement program which places thousands of map labels in minutes, a task which previously required days of tedious labor. The program insures that the type carefully follows the curve of the graticule, or map grid, for maximum legibility and aesthetic appeal. After these steps have been completed, the computer then draws the final map. The benefits of such a system go far beyond producing more timely and accurate maps. For the first time, geographers possess a uniquely creative map-making tool. Map projections can be changed at whim. Revisions that once took months can be completed in hours. Because the maps are digitally created, they can be utilized in a wide variety of electronic media.

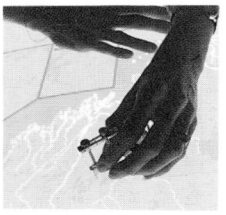

A traditionally-produced map may require ten to forty film overlays, each containing a portion of the final map. Updating city names and political boundaries in the conventional manner is a tedious manual effort requiring light tables, ink pens and opaquing brushes.

The computer-generated maps in this atlas represent a new phase in cartography. They are derived from a digital world database that contains the precise latitude and longitude coordinates for every significant point on the globe. A single change with a computer control can alter the entire look of a map.

Once the map design is approved, a sophisticated laser plotter prints the final artwork onto film, producing a complete set of film positives for the standard four-color printing process in close to an hour — a savings of many days over conventional methods. Or, the image can be electronically transmitted anywhere in the world.

Map Projections

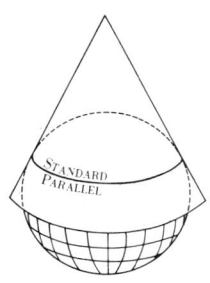

Simply stated, the mapmaker's challenge is to project the earth's curved surface onto a flat plane. To achieve this elusive goal, cartographers have developed map projections — equations which govern this conversion of geographic data.

This section explores some of the most widely used projections. It also introduces a new projection, Hammond's Optimal Conformal.

GENERAL PRINCIPLES AND TERMS

The earth rotates around its axis once a day. Its end points are the North and South poles; the line circling the earth midway between the poles is the equator. The arc from the equator to either pole is divided into 90 degrees of latitude. The equator represents 0° latitude. Circles of equal latitude, called parallels, are traditionally shown at every fifth or tenth degree.

The equator is divided into 360 degrees. Lines circling the globe from pole to pole through the degree points on the equator are called meridians, or great circles. All meridians are equal in length, but by international agreement the meridian passing through the Greenwich Observatory near London has been chosen as the prime meridian or 0° longitude. The distance in degrees from the prime meridian to any point east or west is its longitude.

While meridians are all equal in length, parallels become shorter as they approach the poles. Whereas one degree of latitude represents approximately 69 miles (112 km.) anywhere on the globe, a degree of longitude varies from 69 miles (112 km.) at the equator to zero at the poles. Each degree of latitude and longitude is divided into 60 minutes. One minute of latitude equals one nautical mile (1.15 land miles or 1.85 km.).

HOW TO FLATTEN A SPHERE: THE ART OF CONTROLLING DISTORTION

There is only one way to represent a sphere with absolute precision: on a globe. All attempts to project our planet's surface onto a plane unevenly stretch or tear the sphere as it flattens, inevitably distorting shapes, distances, area (sizes appear larger or smaller than actual size), angles or direction.

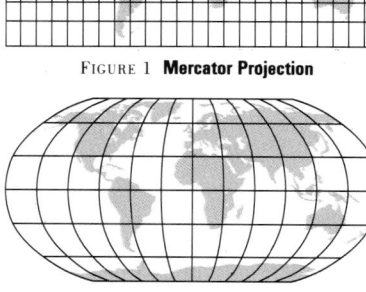

FIGURE 1 **Mercator Projection**

FIGURE 2 **Robinson Projection**

Since representing a sphere on a flat plane always creates distortion, only the parallels or the meridians (or some other set of lines) can maintain the same length as on a globe of corresponding scale. All other lines must be either too long or too short. Accordingly, the scale on a flat map cannot be true everywhere; there will always be different scales in different parts of a map. On world maps or very large areas, variations in scale may be extreme. Most maps seek to preserve either true area relationships (equal area projections) or true angles and shapes (conformal projections); some attempt to achieve overall balance.

PROJECTIONS: SELECTED EXAMPLES

Mercator (Fig. 1): This projection is especially useful because all compass directions appear as straight lines, making it a valuable navigational tool. Moreover, every small region conforms to its shape on a globe — hence the name conformal. But because its meridians are evenly-spaced vertical lines which never converge (unlike the globe), the horizontal parallels must be drawn farther and farther apart at higher

latitudes to maintain a correct relationship. Only the equator is true to scale, and the size of areas in the higher latitudes is dramatically distorted.

Robinson (Fig. 2): To create the thematic maps in Global Relationships and the two-page world map in the Maps of the World section, the Robinson projection was used. It combines elements of both conformal and equal area projections to show the whole earth with relatively true shapes and reasonably equal areas.

Conic (Fig. 3): This projection has been used frequently for air navigation charts and to create most of the national and regional maps in this atlas. (See text in margin at left).

HAMMOND'S OPTIMAL CONFORMAL

As its name implies, this new conformal projection presents the optimal view of an area by reducing shifts in scale over an entire region to the minimum degree possible. While conformal maps generally preserve all small shapes, large shapes can become very distorted because of varying scales, causing considerable inaccuracy in distance measurements. The concept underlying the Optimal Conformal is that for any region on the globe, there is an ideal projection for which scale variation can be made as small as possible. Consequently, unlike other projections, the Optimal Conformal does not use one standard formula to construct a map. Each map is a unique projection — the optimal projection for that particular area.

In practice, the cartographer first defines the map subject, then, working on a computer, draws a band around the region to be mapped. Next, a sophisticated software program evaluates the size and shape of the region to determine the most accurate way to project it. The result is the most distortion-free

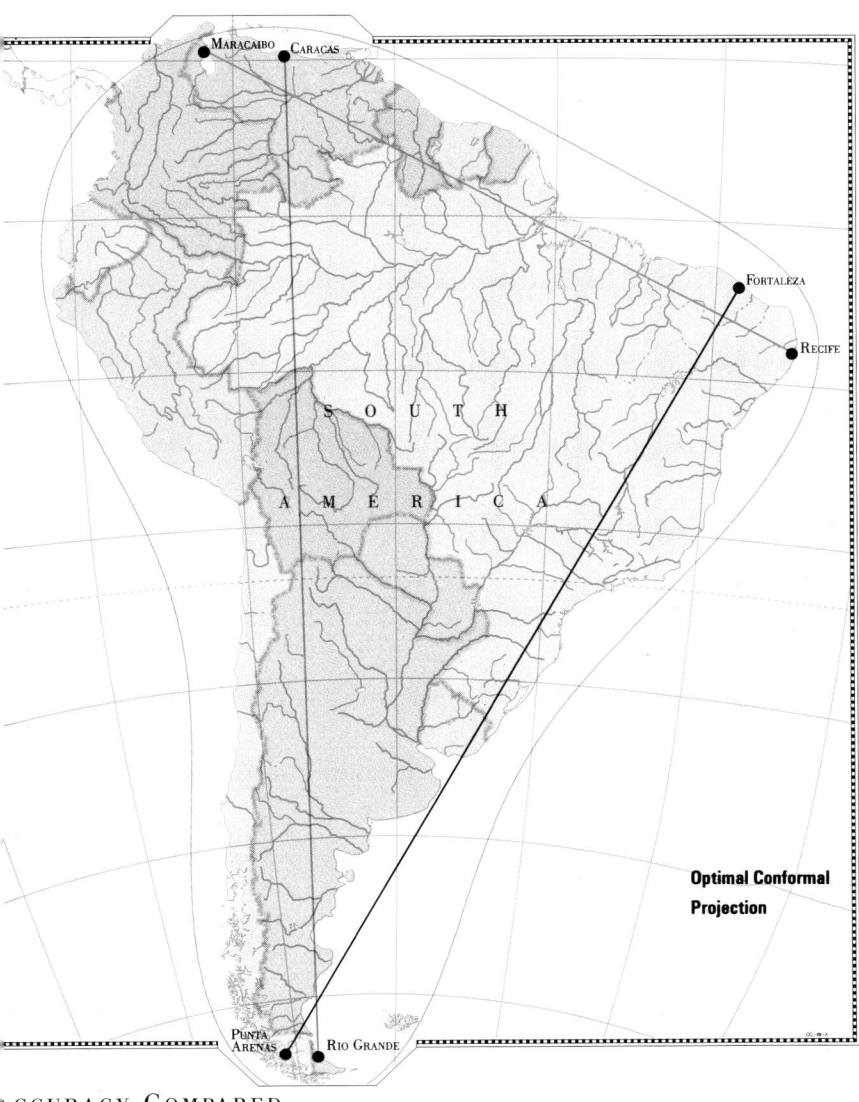

Optimal Conformal Projection

ACCURACY COMPARED

CITIES	SPHERICAL (TRUE) DISTANCE	OPTIMAL CONFORMAL DISTANCE	LAMBERT AZIMUTHAL DISTANCE
CARACAS TO RIO GRANDE	4,443 MI. (7,149 KM.)	4,429 MI. (7,126 KM.)	4,316 MI. (6,944 KM.)
MARACAIBO TO RECIFE	2,834 MI. (4,560 KM.)	2,845 MI. (4,578 KM.)	2,817 MI. (4,533 KM.)
FORTALEZA TO PUNTA ARENAS	3,882 MI. (6,246 KM.)	3,907 MI. (6,266 KM.)	3,843 MI. (6,163 KM.)

continent maps drawn using the Lambert Azimuthal Equal Area projection (Fig. 4) contain distortions ranging from 2.3 percent for Europe up to 15 percent for Asia. The Optimal Conformal cuts that distortion in half, improving distance measurements on these continent maps. Less distortion means greater visual fidelity, so the shape of a continent on an Optimal projection more closely represents its True shape. The table above compares measurements on the Optimal projection to those of the Lambert Azimuthal Equal Area projection for selected cities.

conformal map possible, and the most accurate projections that have ever been made. All of the continents maps in this atlas (with the exception of Antarctica) have been drawn using this projection.

PROJECTIONS COMPARED

Because the true shapes of earth's landforms are unfamiliar to most people, distinguishing between various projections can be difficult. The following diagrams reveal the distortions introduced by several commonly used projections. By using a simple face with familiar shapes as the starting point (The Plan), it is easy to see the benefits — and drawbacks — of each. Think of the facial features as continents. Note that distortion appears not only in the features themselves, but in the changing shapes, angles and areas of the background grid, or graticule.

Figure 5: The Plan
The Plan indicates that the continents are either perfect concentric circles or are true straight lines *on the earth.* They should appear that way on a "perfect" map.

Figure 6: Orthographic Projection
This view shows the continents on the earth as seen from space. The facial features occupy half of the earth, which is all that you can see from this perspective. As you move outward towards the edge, note how the eyes become elliptical, the nose appears larger and less straight, and the mouth is curved into a smile.

Figure 7: Mercator
This cylindrical projection preserves angles exactly, but the mouth is now smiling broadly, and shows extreme distortion at the map's outer edge. This rapid expansion as you move away from the map's center is typified by the extreme enlargement of Greenland found on Mercator world maps (also see Fig. 1).

Figure 8: Peters
The Peters projection is a square equal area projection elongated, or stretched vertically, by a factor of two. While representing areas in their correct proportions, it does not closely resemble the Plan, and angles, local shapes and global relations are significantly distorted.

Figure 9: Hammond's Optimal Conformal
As you can see, this projection minimizes inaccuracies between the angles and shapes of the Plan, yielding a near-perfect map of the given area, up to a complete hemisphere. Like all conformal maps, the Optimal projection preserves every angle exactly, but it is more successful than previous projections at spreading the inevitable curvature across the entire map. Note that the sides of the triangle appear almost straight while correctly containing more than 180°. And though the eyes are slightly too large, it is the only map with eyes which appear concentric. Both mathematically and visually, it offers the best conformal map that can be made of the ideal Plan.

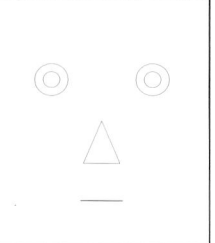

FIGURE 5
The Plan

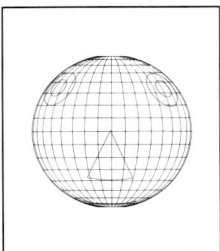

FIGURE 6
Orthographic Projection

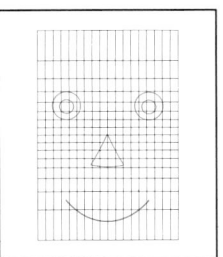

FIGURE 7
Mercator Projection

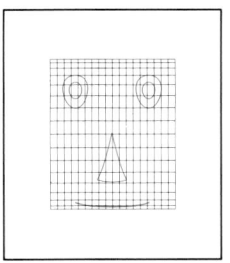

FIGURE 8
Peters Projection

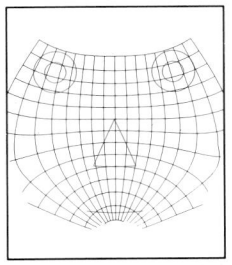

FIGURE 9
Optimal Conformal Projection

Using This Atlas

How to Locate Information Quickly

For familiar locations such as continents, countries and major political divisions, the Quick Reference Guide helps you quickly pinpoint the map you need. For less familiar places, begin with the Master Index.

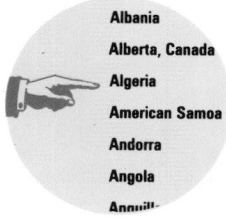

Albania
Alberta, Canada
Algeria
American Samoa
Andorra
Angola
Anguilla

Quick Reference Guide

This concise guide lists continents, countries, states, provinces and territories in alphabetical order, complete with the size, population and capital of each. Red page numbers and alpha-numeric reference keys are visible at a glance.

Merlimont, Fran.
.3/F4 Mersch, Luxembou.
68/A3 Mers-les-Bains, France
69/F4 Mertert, Luxembourg
69/F4 Mertesdorf, Germany
69/G6 Mertzwiller, France
68/B5 Méru, France
68/B2 Merville, France
69/F2 Merzenich, Germany
69/F5 Merzig, Germany
F4 Messancy, Belgi
Mottet, Bel

Master Index of the World

When you're looking for an unfamiliar place or physical feature, your quickest route is the Master Index. This 60,000-entry alphabetical index lists both the page number and alpha-numeric reference key for places and features in Maps of the World.

The Hammond Atlas of the World, Concise Edition has been thoughtfully designed to be easy and enjoyable to use, both as a general reference, and for armchair exploration of the globe. A short time spent familiarizing yourself with its organization will help you to benefit fully from its use.

GLOBAL RELATIONSHIPS

This section highlights key social, cultural, economic and geographic factors. Together, these seven succinct chapters — from Population to Standards of Living— provide a fresh perspective on the world today. In the case of complex and rapidly evolving topics such as Environment, data analysis is in a relatively early stage, and projected outcomes are sometimes controversial.

THE PHYSICAL WORLD

These relief maps of the continents and major regions of the world depict the topography of the earth's surface, and represent our most current knowledge of the ocean floor. Because the maps are actual photographs of three-dimensional TerraScape™ models, they present the relationships of land and sea forms and the rugged contours of the terrain with startling realism.

GEOGRAPHIC COMPARISONS

World Statistics lists the dimensions of the earth's principal mountains, islands, rivers and lakes, along with other useful geographic information. The Time Zones map shows all standard time zones as well as those areas using half hour deviations. All countries plus selected major cities are included. Population of Major Cities contains the latest population figures for the world's largest cities, organized by country in alphabetical order. You'll find the size, population and location of major geographical areas, from countries, states and territories to continents, in the Quick Reference Guide.

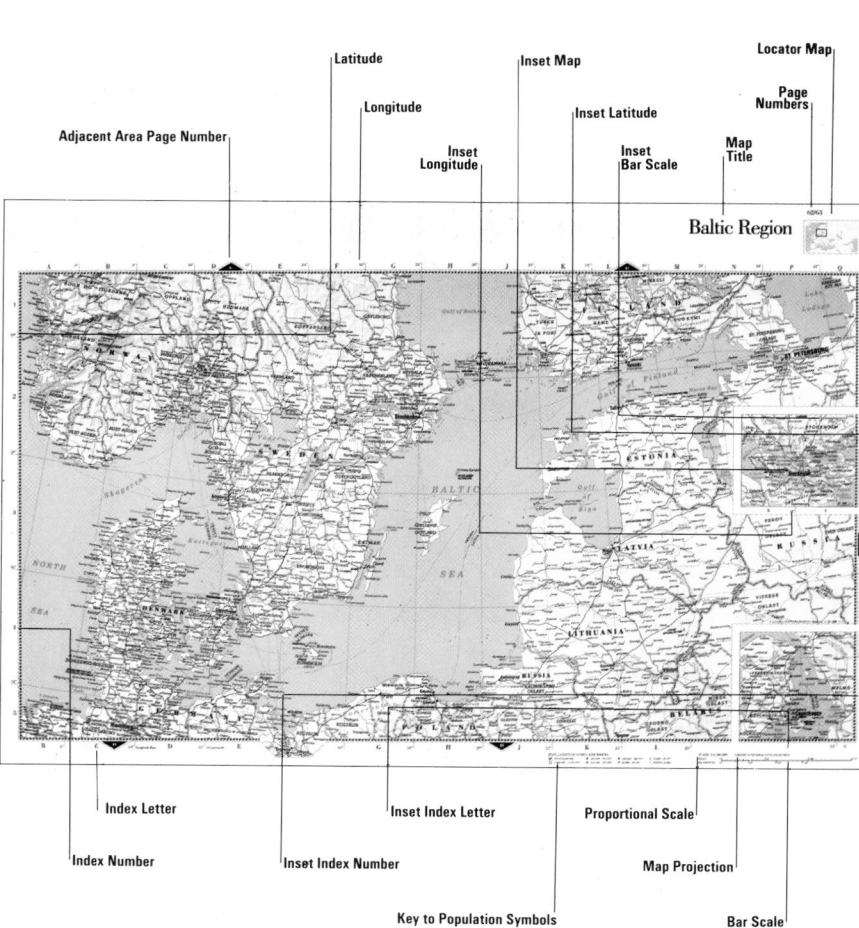

SYMBOLS USED ON MAPS OF THE WORLD

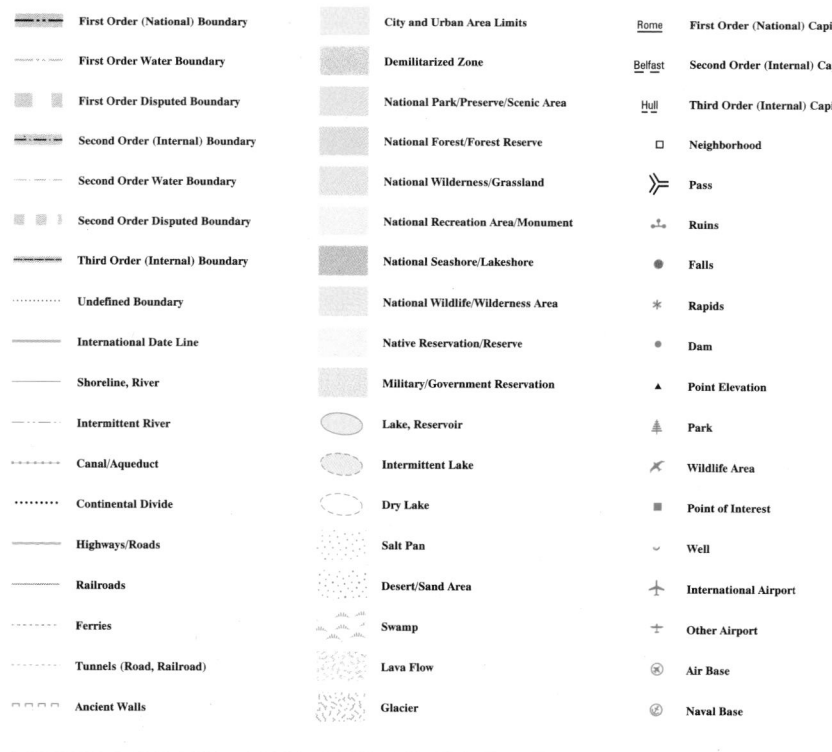

First Order (National) Boundary	City and Urban Area Limits	Rome — First Order (National) Capital
First Order Water Boundary	Demilitarized Zone	Belfast — Second Order (Internal) Capital
First Order Disputed Boundary	National Park/Preserve/Scenic Area	Hull — Third Order (Internal) Capital
Second Order (Internal) Boundary	National Forest/Forest Reserve	□ Neighborhood
Second Order Water Boundary	National Wilderness/Grassland	⫞ Pass
Second Order Disputed Boundary	National Recreation Area/Monument	⸬ Ruins
Third Order (Internal) Boundary	National Seashore/Lakeshore	● Falls
Undefined Boundary	National Wildlife/Wilderness Area	⁎ Rapids
International Date Line	Native Reservation/Reserve	◉ Dam
Shoreline, River	Military/Government Reservation	▲ Point Elevation
Intermittent River	Lake, Reservoir	⛺ Park
Canal/Aqueduct	Intermittent Lake	✗ Wildlife Area
Continental Divide	Dry Lake	■ Point of Interest
Highways/Roads	Salt Pan	‿ Well
Railroads	Desert/Sand Area	✈ International Airport
Ferries	Swamp	✢ Other Airport
Tunnels (Road, Railroad)	Lava Flow	⊗ Air Base
Ancient Walls	Glacier	⊘ Naval Base

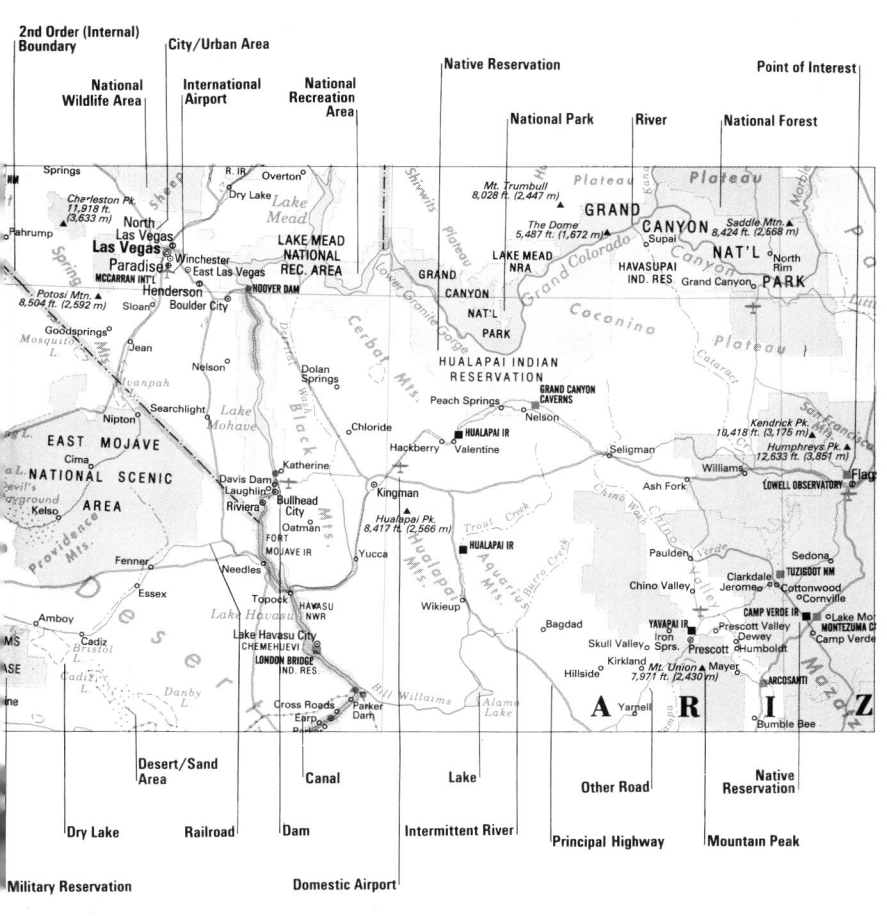

2nd Order (Internal) Boundary

City/Urban Area

National Wildlife Area

International Airport

National Recreation Area

Native Reservation

Point of Interest

National Park

River

National Forest

Desert/Sand Area

Canal

Lake

Other Road

Native Reservation

Dry Lake

Railroad

Dam

Intermittent River

Principal Highway

Mountain Peak

Military Reservation

Domestic Airport

PRINCIPAL MAP ABBREVIATIONS

ABOR. RSV.	ABORIGINAL RESERVE	IND. RES.	INDIAN RESERVATION	NWR	NATIONAL WILDLIFE
ADMIN.	ADMINISTRATION	INT'L	INTERNATIONAL		RESERVE
AFB	AIR FORCE BASE	IR	INDIAN RESERVATION	OBL.	OBLAST
AMM. DEP.	AMMUNITION DEPOT	ISTH.	ISTHMUS	OCC.	OCCUPIED
ARCH.	ARCHIPELAGO	JCT.	JUNCTION	OKR.	OKRUG
ARPT.	AIRPORT	L.	LAKE	PAR.	PARISH
AUT.	AUTONOMOUS	LAG.	LAGOON	PASSG.	PASSAGE
B.	BAY	LAKESH.	LAKESHORE	PEN.	PENINSULA
BFLD.	BATTLEFIELD	MEM.	MEMORIAL	PK.	PEAK
BK.	BROOK	MIL.	MILITARY	PLAT.	PLATEAU
BOR.	BOROUGH	MISS.	MISSILE	PN	PARK NATIONAL
BR.	BRANCH	MON.	MONUMENT	PREF.	PREFECTURE
C.	CAPE	MT.	MOUNT	PROM.	PROMONTORY
CAN.	CANAL	MTN.	MOUNTAIN	PROV.	PROVINCE
CAP.	CAPITAL	MTS.	MOUNTAINS	PRSV.	PRESERVE
C.G.	COAST GUARD	NAT.	NATURAL	PT.	POINT
CHAN.	CHANNEL	NAT'L	NATIONAL	R.	RIVER
CO.	COUNTY	NAV.	NAVAL	RA	RECREATION AREA
CR.	CREEK	NB	NATIONAL	RA.	RANGE
CTR.	CENTER		BATTLEFIELD	REC.	RECREATION(AL)
DEP.	DEPOT	NBP	NATIONAL	REF.	REFUGE
DEPR.	DEPRESSION		BATTLEFIELD PARK	REG.	REGION
DEPT.	DEPARTMENT	NBS	NATIONAL	REP.	REPUBLIC
DES.	DESERT		BATTLEFIELD SITE	RES.	RESERVOIR,
DIST.	DISTRICT	NHP	NATIONAL HISTORICAL		RESERVATION
DMZ	DEMILITARIZED ZONE		PARK	RVWY.	RIVERWAY
DPCY.	DEPENDENCY	NHPP	NATIONAL HISTORICAL	SA.	SIERRA
ENG.	ENGINEERING		PARK AND PRESERVE	SD.	SOUND
EST.	ESTUARY	NHS	NATIONAL HISTORIC	SEASH.	SEASHORE
FD.	FIORD, FJORD		SITE	SO.	SOUTHERN
FED.	FEDERAL	NL	NATIONAL LAKESHORE	SP	STATE PARK
FK.	FORK	NM	NATIONAL MONUMENT	SPR., SPRS.	SPRING, SPRINGS
FLD.	FIELD	NMEMP	NATIONAL MEMORIAL	ST.	STATE
FOR.	FOREST		PARK	STA.	STATION
FT.	FORT	NMILP	NATIONAL MILITARY	STM.	STREAM
G.	GULF		PARK	STR.	STRAIT
GOV.	GOVERNOR	NO.	NORTHERN	TERR.	TERRITORY
GOVT.	GOVERNMENT	NP	NATIONAL PARK	TUN.	TUNNEL
GD.	GRAND	NPP	NATIONAL PARK AND	TWP.	TOWNSHIP
GT.	GREAT		PRESERVE	VAL.	VALLEY
HAR.	HARBOR	NPRSV	NATIONAL PRESERVE	VILL.	VILLAGE
HD.	HEAD	NRA	NATIONAL	VOL.	VOLCANO
HIST.	HISTORIC(AL)		RECREATION AREA	WILD.	WILDLIFE,
HTS.	HEIGHTS	NRSV	NATIONAL RESERVE		WILDERNESS
I., IS.	ISLAND(S)	NS	NATIONAL SEASHORE	WTR.	WATER

MAPS OF THE WORLD

These detailed regional maps are arranged by continent, and introduced by a political map of that continent. The continent maps, which utilize Hammond's new Optimal Conformal projection, are distinguished by individual colors for each country to highlight political divisions.

On the regional maps, different colors and textures highlight distinctive features such as parks, forests, deserts and urban areas. These maps also provide considerable information concerning geographic features and political divisions. The realistic topography is achieved by combining the computer-generated political maps with the hand-sculpted TerraScape™ relief maps.

MASTER INDEX

This is an A-Z listing of names found on the political maps. It also has its own abbreviation list which, along with other Index keys, appears on page 170.

MAP SCALES

A map's scale is the relationship of any length on the map to an identical length on the earth's surface. A scale of 1:3,000,000 means that one inch on the map represents 3,000,000 inches (47 miles, 76 km.) on the earth's surface. Thus, a 1:1,000,000 scale is larger than 1:3,000,000, just as 1/1 is larger than 1/3.

The most densely populated areas are shown at a scale of 1:1,170,000, while selected metropolitan areas are covered at either 1:587,000 or 1:1,170,000. Other populous areas are presented at 1:3,500,000 and 1:7,000,000, allowing you to accurately compare areas and distances of similar regions. Remaining regions are scaled at 1:10,500,000. The continent maps, as well as the United States, Canada, Russia, Pacific and World have smaller scales.

Quick Reference Guide

This concise alphabetical reference lists continents, countries, states, territories, possessions and other major geographical areas, complete with the size, population and capital or chief town of each. Blue page numbers and alpha-numeric reference keys (which refer to the grid squares of latitude and longitude on each map) are visible at a glance. The population figures are the latest and most reliable figures obtainable.

Place	Square Miles	Square Kilometers	Population	Capital or Chief Town	Page/Index Ref.
A Afghanistan	250,775	649,507	21,251,821	Kabul	95/H 2
Africa	11,707,000	30,321,130	705,924,000	....	122
Alabama, U.S.	51,705	133,916	4,040,587	Montgomery	163/G 3
Alaska, U.S.	591,004	1,530,700	550,043	Juneau	151
Albania	11,100	28,749	3,413,904	Tiranë	81/F 2
Alberta, Canada	255,285	661,185	2,545,553	Edmonton	152/E 3
Algeria	919,591	2,381,740	28,539,321	Algiers	124/F 2
American Samoa	77	199	57,366	Pago Pago	121/J 6
Andorra	188	487	65,780	Andorra la Vella	75/F 1
Angola	481,351	1,246,700	10,069,501	Luanda	126/C 3
Anguilla, U.K.	35	91	7,099	The Valley	150/F 3
Antarctica	5,500,000	14,245,000.	....	....	113
Antigua and Barbuda	171	443	65,176	St. John's	150/F 3
Argentina	1,072,070	2,776,661	34,292,742	Buenos Aires	135/C 4
Arizona, U.S.	114,000	295,260	3,665,228	Phoenix	158/D 4
Arkansas, U.S.	53,187	137,754	2,350,725	Little Rock	162/E 3
Armenia	11,506	29,800	3,557,284	Yerevan	87/H 4
Aruba, Netherlands	75	193	65,974	Oranjestad	150/D 4
Ascension Island, St. Helena	34	88	719	Georgetown	52/J 6
Ashmore & Cartier Islands, Australia	61	159	....	(Canberra, Austr.)	114/C 2
Asia	17,128,500	44,362,815	3,407,967,000	....	90
Australia	2,966,136	7,682,300	18,322,231	Canberra	114
Australian Capital Territory	927	2,400	280,132	Canberra	119/D 2
Austria	32,375	83,851	7,986,664	Vienna	*73/L 3
Azerbaijan	33,436	86,600	7,789,886	Baku	87/H 4
Azores, Portugal	902	2,335	237,000	Ponta Delgada	75/R12
B Bahamas	5,382	13,939	256,616	Nassau	150/B 2
Bahrain	240	622	575,925	Manama	94/F 3
Baker Island, U.S.	1	2.6	....	....	121/H 4
Balearic Islands, Spain	1,936	5,014	690,000	Palma	75/F 3
Bangladesh	55,126	142,776	128,094,948	Dhaka	106/E 3
Barbados	166	430	256,395	Bridgetown	150/G 4
Belarus	80,154	207,600	10,437,418	Minsk	52/G 3
Belgium	11,781	30,513	10,081,880	Brussels	64/C 3
Belize	8,867	22,966	214,061	Belmopan	148/D 2
Benin	43,483	112,620	5,522,677	Porto-Novo	129/F 4
Bermuda, U.K.	21	54	61,629	Hamilton	145/L 6
Bhutan	18,147	47,000	1,780,638	Thimphu	106/E 2
Bolivia	424,163	1,098,582	7,896,254	La Paz; Sucre	136/F 7
Bonaire, Neth. Antilles	112	291	8,087	Kralendijk	150/D 4
Bosnia & Hercegovina	19,940	51,129	3,201,823	Sarajevo	82/C 3
Botswana	224,764	582,139	1,392,414	Gaborone	126/D 5
Bouvet Island, Norway	22	57	....	....	51/K 8
Brazil	3,284,426	8,506,663	160,737,489	Brasília	134/D 3
British Columbia, Canada	366,253	948,596	3,282,061	Victoria	152/D 3
British Indian Ocean Terr., U.K.	29	75	....	(London, U.K.)	90/G10
British Virgin Islands	59	153	13,027	Road Town	150/E 3
Brunei	2,226	5,765	292,266	Bandar Seri Begawan	112/A 4
Bulgaria	42,823	110,912	8,775,198	Sofia	83/G 4
Burkina Faso	105,869	274,200	10,422,828	Ouagadougou	129/E 3
Burma (Myanmar)	261,789	678,034	45,103,809	Rangoon	107/G 2
Burundi	10,747	27,835	6,262,429	Bujumbura	130/A 3
C California, U.S.	158,706	411,049	29,760,021	Sacramento	158/B 3
Cambodia (Kampuchea)	69,898	181,036	10,561,373	Phnom Penh	109/D 3
Cameroon	183,568	475,441	13,521,000	Yaoundé	124/H 7
Canada	3,851,787	9,976,139	28,434,545	Ottawa	152
Canary Islands, Spain	2,808	7,273	1,495,000	Las Palmas; Santa Cruz	75/X16
Cape Verde	1,557	4,033	435,983	Praia	122/J 9
Cayman Islands, U.K.	100	259	33,192	Georgetown	149/F 2
Celebes, Indonesia	72,986	189,034	12,520,711	Ujung Pandang	111/E 4
Central African Republic	242,000	626,780	3,209,759	Bangui	125/J 6
Chad	495,752	1,283,998	5,586,505	N'Djamena	125/J 4
Channel Islands, U.K.	75	194	133,000	St. Helier; St. Peter Port	72/B 2
Chile	292,257	756,946	14,161,216	Santiago	135/B 3
China, People's Rep. of	3,691,000	9,559,690	1,203,097,268	Beijing	90/J 6
China, Republic of (Taiwan)	13,971	36,185	21,500,583	Taipei	105/J 3
Christmas Island, Australia	52	135	889	Flying Fish Cove	90/K11
Clipperton Island, France	2	5.2	....	....	50/D 5
Cocos (Keeling) Islands, Australia	5.4	14	604	West Island	90/J11
Colombia	439,513	1,138,339	36,200,251	Bogotá	138/C 4
Colorado, U.S.	104,091	269,596	3,294,394	Denver	158/F 3
Comoros	719	1,862	549,338	Moroni	133/G 5
Congo	132,046	342,000	2,504,996	Brazzaville	122/D 5
Connecticut, U.S.	5,018	12,997	3,287,116	Hartford	161/F 3
Cook Islands, New Zealand	91	236	18,000	Avarua	121/J 6
Coral Sea Islands, Australia	8.5	22	....	....	115/J 2
Corsica, France	3,352	8,682	249,737	Ajaccio; Bastia	80/A 1
Costa Rica	19,575	50,700	3,419,114	San José	149/F 4
Côte d'Ivoire	124,504	322,465	14,791,257	Yamoussoukro	128/D 5
Croatia	22,050	56,538	4,665,821	Zagreb	82/B 3
Cuba	44,206	114,494	10,937,635	Havana	149/F 1
Curaçao, Neth. Antilles	178	462	145,430	Willemstad	150/D 4
Cyprus	3,473	8,995	736,636	Nicosia	91/C 2
Czech Republic	30,449	78,863	10,432,774	Prague	65/H 4
D Delaware, U.S.	2,044	5,294	666,168	Dover	160/F 4
Denmark	16,629	43,069	5,199,437	Copenhagen	62/C 4
District of Columbia, U.S.	69	179	606,900	Washington	166/B 6
Djibouti	8,880	23,000	421,320	Djibouti	125/P 5
Dominica	290	751	82,608	Roseau	150/F 4
Dominican Republic	18,704	48,443	7,511,263	Santo Domingo	150/D 3
E Eastern Cape, South Africa	65,858	170,616	6,665,400	Bisho	132/D 3
Eastern Transvaal, South Africa	31,581	81,816	2,838,500	Nelspruit	133/E 2
Ecuador	109,483	283,561	10,890,950	Quito	136/C 4
Egypt	386,659	1,001,447	62,359,623	Cairo	127/B 3
El Salvador	8,260	21,393	5,870,481	San Salvador	148/D 3
England, U.K.	50,516	130,836	48,068,400	London	55/K10
Equatorial Guinea	10,831	28,052	420,293	Malabo	124/G 7
Eritrea	36,170	93,679	3,578,709	Äsmera	125/N 4
Estonia	17,413	45,100	1,625,399	Tallinn	63/L 2
Ethiopia	435,606	1,128,220	55,979,018	Addis Ababa	125/N 5
Europe	4,057,000	10,507,630	732,653,000	....	52
F Falkland Is. & Depdcs., U.K.	6,198	16,053	2,317	Stanley	143/M 8
Faroe Islands, Denmark	540	1,399	48,871	Tórshavn	52/D 2
Fiji	7,055	18,272	772,891	Suva	120/G 6
Finland	130,128	337,032	5,085,206	Helsinki	61/H 2
Florida, U.S.	58,664	151,940	12,937,926	Tallahassee	163/H 4
France	210,038	543,998	58,109,160	Paris	72/D 3
French Guiana	35,135	91,000	145,270	Cayenne	137/H 3
French Polynesia	1,544	4,000	219,999	Papeete	121/M 6
G Gabon	103,346	267,666	1,155,749	Libreville	124/H 7
Gambia	4,127	10,689	989,273	Banjul	128/B 1
Gaza Strip	139	360	813,322	Gaza	91/C 4
Georgia	26,911	69,700	5,725,972	Tbilisi	87/G 4
Georgia, U.S.	58,910	152,577	6,478,216	Atlanta	163/G 3
Germany	137,753	356,780	81,337,541	Berlin	64/E 3
Ghana	92,099	238,536	17,763,138	Accra	129/E 4
Gibraltar, U.K.	2.28	5.91	31,874	Gibraltar	74/C 4
Great Britain & Northern Ireland (United Kingdom)	94,399	244,493	58,295,119	London	55
Greece	50,944	131,945	10,647,511	Athens	81/G 3
Greenland, Denmark	840,000	2,175,600	57,611	Nuuk (Godthåb)	145/N 2

Place	Square Miles	Square Kilometers	Population	Capital or Chief Town	Page/ Index Ref.
Grenada	133	344	94,486	St. George's	150/F 5
Guadeloupe & Dependencies, France	687	1,779	402,815	Basse-Terre	150/F 3
Guam, U.S.	209	541	153,307	Agaña	120/D 3
Guatemala	42,042	108,889	10,998,602	Guatemala	148/D 3
Guinea	94,925	245,856	6,549,336	Conakry	128/C 4
Guinea-Bissau	13,948	36,125	1,124,537	Bissau	128/B 3
Guyana	83,000	214,970	723,774	Georgetown	139/G 3
H Haiti	10,694	27,697	6,539,983	Port-au-Prince	149/H 2
Hawaii, U.S.	6,471	16,760	1,108,229	Honolulu	154/S10
Heard & McDonald Islands, Australia	113	293	....	....	51/P 8
Holland, see Netherlands					
Honduras	43,277	112,087	5,459,743	Tegucigalpa	148/E 3
Hong Kong, U.K.	403	1,044	5,542,869	Victoria	105/G 4
Howland Island, U.S.	1	2.6	....	....	121/H 4
Hungary	35,919	93,030	10,318,838	Budapest	82/D 2
I Iceland	39,768	103,000	265,998	Reykjavík	61/N 7
Idaho, U.S.	83,564	216,431	1,006,749	Boise	156/E 5
Illinois, U.S.	56,345	145,934	11,430,602	Springfield	160/B 4
India	1,269,339	3,287,588	936,545,814	New Delhi	106/C 3
Indiana, U.S.	36,185	93,719	5,544,159	Indianapolis	160/C 3
Indonesia	788,430	2,042,034	203,583,886	Jakarta	111/E 4
Iowa, U.S.	56,275	145,752	2,776,755	Des Moines	157/K 5
Iran	636,293	1,648,000	64,625,455	Tehran	90/E 6
Iraq	172,476	446,713	20,643,769	Baghdad	92/E 3
Ireland	27,136	70,282	3,550,448	Dublin	55/G10
Ireland, Northern, U.K.	5,452	14,121	1,610,000	Belfast	55/H 9
Isle of Man, U.K.	227	588	72,751	Douglas	56/D 3
Israel	7,847	20,324	5,433,134	Jerusalem	91/D 3
Italy	116,303	301,225	58,261,971	Rome	52/E 4
Ivory Coast, see Côte d'Ivoire					
J Jamaica	4,411	11,424	2,574,291	Kingston	149/G 2
Jan Mayen, Norway	144	373	....	....	52/D 1
Japan	145,730	377,441	125,506,492	Tokyo	97/M 4
Jarvis Island, U.S.	1	2.6	....	....	121/J 5
Java, Indonesia	48,842	126,500	107,581,306	Jakarta	110/C 5
Johnston Atoll, U.S.	.91	2.4	327	....	121/J 3
Jordan	35,000	90,650	4,100,709	Amman	92/D 4
K Kampuchea (Cambodia)	69,898	181,036	5,200,000	Phnom Penh	109/D 3
Kansas, U.S.	82,277	213,097	2,477,574	Topeka	159/H 3
Kazakhstan	1,048,300	2,715,100	17,376,615	Aqmola	88/G 5
Kentucky, U.S.	40,409	104,659	3,685,296	Frankfort	160/C 4
Kenya	224,960	582,646	28,817,227	Nairobi	130/C 2
Kermadec Islands, New Zealand	13	33	5	....	120/G 7
Kingman Reef, U.S.	0.1	0.26	....	....	121/J 4
Kiribati	291	754	79,386	Bairiki	120/H 5
Korea, North	46,540	120,539	23,486,550	P'yŏngyang	101/D 2
Korea, South	38,175	98,873	45,553,882	Seoul	101/D 4
Kuwait	6,532	16,918	1,817,397	Al Kuwait	93/F 4
KwaZulu Natal, South Africa	35,312	91,481	8,549,000	Pietermaritzburg	133/E 3
Kyrgyzstan	76,641	198,500	4,769,877	Bishkek	102/B 3
L Laos	91,428	236,800	4,837,237	Vientiane	109/C 2
Latvia	24,595	63,700	2,762,899	Riga	63/L 3
Lebanon	4,015	10,399	3,695,921	Beirut	91/D 3
Lesotho	11,720	30,355	1,992,960	Maseru	132/D 3
Liberia	43,000	111,370	3,073,245	Monrovia	128/C 5
Libya	679,358	1,759,537	5,248,401	Tripoli	125/J 2
Liechtenstein	61	158	30,654	Vaduz	77/F 3
Lithuania	25,174	65,200	3,876,396	Vilnius	63/K 4
Louisiana, U.S.	47,752	123,678	4,219,973	Baton Rouge	162/E 4
Luxembourg	999	2,587	404,660	Luxembourg	69/E 4
M Macau, Portugal	6	16	490,901	Macau	105/G 4
Macedonia	9,889	25,713	2,159,503	Skopje	81/G 2
Madagascar	226,657	587,041	13,862,325	Antananarivo	133/H 8
Madeira Islands, Portugal	307	796	262,800	Funchal	75/V15
Maine, U.S.	33,265	86,156	1,227,928	Augusta	161/G 2

Place	Square Miles	Square Kilometers	Population	Capital or Chief Town	Page/ Index Ref.
Malawi	45,747	118,485	9,808,384	Lilongwe	131/D 2
Malaya, Malaysia	50,806	131,588	11,138,227	Kuala Lumpur	110/B 3
Malaysia	128,308	332,318	19,723,587	Kuala Lumpur	110/C 2
Maldives	115	298	261,310	Male	90/G 9
Mali	464,873	1,204,021	9,375,132	Bamako	124/E 4
Malta	122	316	369,609	Valletta	80/D 5
Manitoba, Canada	250,999	650,087	1,091,942	Winnipeg	152/F 3
Marquesas Islands, French Polynesia	492	1,274	5,419	Atuona	121/M 5
Marshall Islands	70	181	56,157	Majuro	120/G 3
Martinique, France	425	1,101	394,787	Fort-de-France	150/F 4
Maryland, U.S.	10,460	27,091	4,781,468	Annapolis	160/E 4
Massachusetts, U.S.	8,284	21,456	6,016,425	Boston	161/F 3
Mauritania	419,229	1,085,803	2,263,202	Nouakchott	124/C 4
Mauritius	790	2,046	1,127,068	Port Louis	133/S15
Mayotte, France	144	373	97,088	Dzaoudzi	133/H 6
Mexico	761,601	1,972,546	93,985,848	Mexico City	145/G 7
Michigan, U.S.	58,527	151,585	9,295,297	Lansing	160/C 2
Micronesia, Federated States of	....	....	122,950	Kolonia	120/D 4
Midway Islands, U.S.	1.9	4.9	453	....	120/H 2
Minnesota, U.S.	84,402	218,601	4,375,099	St. Paul	157/K 4
Mississippi, U.S.	47,689	123,515	2,573,216	Jackson	163/F 3
Missouri, U.S.	69,697	180,515	5,117,073	Jefferson City	159/J 3
Moldova	13,012	33,700	4,489,657	Kishinev	83/J 2
Monaco	368 acres	149 hectares	31,515	....	78/A 5
Mongolia	606,163	1,569,962	2,493,615	Ulaanbaatar	96/D 2
Montana, U.S.	147,046	380,849	799,065	Helena	156/F 4
Montserrat, U.K.	40	104	12,738	Plymouth	150/F 3
Morocco	172,414	446,550	29,168,848	Rabat	124/C 1
Mozambique	303,769	786,762	18,115,250	Maputo	126/G 4
Myanmar, see Burma					
N Namibia	317,827	823,172	1,651,545	Windhoek	126/C 5
Nauru	7.7	20	10,149	Yaren (district)	120/F 5
Navassa Island, U.S.	2	5	....	....	149/H 2
Nebraska, U.S.	77,355	200,349	1,578,385	Lincoln	159/G 2
Nepal	54,663	141,577	21,560,869	Kathmandu	106/D 2
Netherlands	15,892	41,160	15,452,903	The Hague; Amsterdam	64/C 3
Netherlands Antilles	320	817	203,505	Willemstad	150/D 5
Nevada, U.S.	110,561	286,353	1,201,833	Carson City	158/C 3
New Brunswick, Canada	28,354	73,437	723,900	Fredericton	161/H 2
New Caledonia & Dependencies, France	7,335	18,998	184,552	Nouméa	120/F 6
Newfoundland, Canada	156,184	404,517	568,474	St. John's	153/K 3
New Hampshire, U.S.	9,279	24,033	1,109,252	Concord	161/G 3
New Jersey, U.S.	7,787	20,168	7,730,188	Trenton	166/D 3
New Mexico, U.S.	121,593	314,926	1,515,069	Santa Fe	158/F 4
New South Wales, Australia	309,498	801,600	5,731,906	Sydney	119/C 1
New York, U.S.	49,108	127,190	17,990,455	Albany	160/F 3
New Zealand	103,736	268,676	3,407,277	Wellington	115/Q10
Nicaragua	45,698	118,358	4,206,353	Managua	149/E 3
Niger	489,189	1,267,000	9,280,208	Niamey	124/G 4
Nigeria	357,000	924,630	101,232,251	Abuja	124/G 6
Niue, New Zealand	100	259	1,837	Alofi	121/J 7
Norfolk Island, Australia	13.4	34.6	2,756	Kingston	115/M 5
North America	9,363,000	24,250,170	443,438,000	....	145
North Carolina, U.S.	52,669	136,413	6,628,637	Raleigh	163/H 3
North Dakota, U.S.	70,702	183,118	638,800	Bismarck	157/H 4
Northern Cape, South Africa	140,268	363,389	763,900	Kimberley	132/C 3
Northern Ireland, U.K.	5,452	14,121	1,610,000	Belfast	55/H 9
Northern Marianas, U.S.	184	477	51,033	Capitol Hill	120/D 3
Northern Territory, Australia	519,768	1,346,200	175,876	Darwin	114/E 3
Northern Transvaal, South Africa	46,168	119,606	5,120,600	Pietersburg	131/C 4
North Korea	46,540	120,539	23,486,550	P'yŏngyang	101/D 2
North-West, South Africa	45,822	118,710	3,506,800	Mmabatho	132/D 2
Northwest Territories, Canada	1,304,896	3,379,683	57,649	Yellowknife	152/E 2
Norway	125,053	323,887	4,330,951	Oslo	61/C 3
Nova Scotia, Canada	21,425	55,491	899,942	Halifax	161/J 2

Place	Square Miles	Square Kilometers	Population	Capital or Chief Town	Page/ Index Ref.
O Oceania (Pacific Ocean)	3,292,000	8,526,280	24,436,000	....	120
Ohio, U.S.	41,330	107,045	10,847,115	Columbus	160/D 3
Oklahoma, U.S.	69,956	181,186	3,145,585	Oklahoma City	159/H 4
Oman	120,000	310,800	2,125,089	Muscat	95/G 4
Ontario, Canada	412,580	1,068,582	10,084,885	Toronto	152/H 3
Orange Free State, South Africa	49,963	129,437	2,804,600	Bloemfontein	132/D 3
Oregon, U.S.	97,073	251,419	2,842,321	Salem	156/C 4
Orkney Islands, Scotland	376	974	19,700	Kirkwall	55/N13
P Pakistan	310,403	803,944	131,541,920	Islamabad	95/H 3
Palau	188	487	16,661	Koror	120/C 4
Palmyra Atoll, U.S.	3.85	1	....	....	121/J 4
Panama	29,761	77,082	2,680,903	Panamá	149/F 4
Papua New Guinea	183,540	475,369	4,294,750	Port Moresby	120/D 5
Paracel Islands	....	....	....	....	105/F 5
Paraguay	157,047	406,752	5,358,198	Asunción	134/C 5
Pennsylvania, U.S.	45,308	117,348	11,881,643	Harrisburg	160/E 3
Peru	496,222	1,285,215	24,087,372	Lima	144/C 3
Philippines	115,707	299,681	73,265,584	Manila	112
Pitcairn Islands, U.K.	18	47	73	Adamstown	121/N 7
Poland	120,725	312,678	38,792,442	Warsaw	65/K 2
Portugal	35,549	92,072	10,562,388	Lisbon	74/A 3
Pretoria-Witwatersrand-Vereeniging (PWV), South Africa	7,241	18,760	6,847,000	Johannesburg	132/Q12
Prince Edward Island, Canada	2,184	5,657	129,765	Charlottetown	161/J 2
Puerto Rico, U.S.	3,515	9,104	3,812,569	San Juan	150/E 3
Q Qatar	4,247	11,000	533,916	Doha	94/F 3
Québec, Canada	594,857	1,540,680	6,895,963	Québec	153/J 3
Queensland, Australia	666,872	1,727,200	2,977,813	Brisbane	118/B 3
R Réunion, France	969	2,510	666,067	St-Denis	133/R15
Rhode Island, U.S.	1,212	3,139	1,003,464	Providence	161/F 3
Romania	91,699	237,500	23,198,330	Bucharest	83/F 3
Russia	6,592,812	17,075,400	149,909,089	Moscow	88/H 3
Rwanda	10,169	26,337	8,605,307	Kigali	130/A 3
S Sabah, Malaysia	29,300	75,887	1,790,000	Kota Kinabalu	111/E 2
Saint Helena & Dependencies, U.K.	162	420	6,762	Jamestown	122/B 6
Saint Kitts and Nevis	104	269	40,992	Basseterre	150/F 3
Saint Lucia	238	616	156,050	Castries	150/F 4
Saint Pierre & Miquelon, France	93.5	242	6,757	Saint-Pierre	161/K 2
Saint Vincent & the Grenadines	150	388	117,344	Kingstown	150/F 4
Sakhalin, Russia	29,500	76,405	655,000	Yuzhno-Sakhalinsk	89/Q 4
San Marino	23.4	60.6	24,313	San Marino	79/F 5
São Tomé and Príncipe	372	963	140,423	São Tomé	124/G 7
Sarawak, Malaysia	48,202	124,843	1,648,217	Kuching	110/D 3
Sardinia, Italy	9,301	24,090	1,650,000	Cagliari	80/A 2
Saskatchewan, Canada	251,699	651,900	988,928	Regina	152/F 3
Saudi Arabia	829,995	2,149,687	18,729,576	Riyadh	94/D 4
Scotland, U.K.	30,414	78,772	5,111,200	Edinburgh	55/J 8
Senegal	75,954	196,720	9,007,080	Dakar	128/B 3
Seychelles	145	375	72,709	Victoria	123/H 5
Shetland Islands, Scotland	552	1,430	22,600	Lerwick	55/N 2
Siam, see Thailand					
Sicily, Italy	9,926	25,708	4990,000	Palermo	80/C 3
Sierra Leone	27,925	72,325	4,753,120	Freetown	128/B 4
Singapore	226	585	2,890,468	Singapore	110/B 3
Slovakia	18,924	49,014	5,432,383	Bratislava	65/K 4
Slovenia	7,898	20,251	2,051,522	Ljubljana	82/B 3
Society Islands, French Polynesia	677	1,753	117,703	Papeete	121/K 6
Solomon Islands	11,500	29,785	399,206	Honiara	120/E 6
Somalia	246,200	637,658	7,347,554	Mogadishu	125/Q 6
South Africa	455,318	1,179,274	45,095,459	Cape Town; Pretoria	126/D 6
South America	6,875,000	17,806,250	314,335,000	....	134
South Australia, Australia	379,922	984,000	1,400,630	Adelaide	114/E 5
South Carolina, U.S.	31,113	80,583	3,486,703	Columbia	163/H 3
South Dakota, U.S.	77,116	199,730	696,004	Pierre	157/H 4
South Korea	38,175	98,873	45,553,882	Seoul	101/D 4
Spain	194,881	504,742	39,404,348	Madrid	74/C 2
Spratly Islands	....	....	....	....	110/D 2

Place	Square Miles	Square Kilometers	Population	Capital or Chief Town	Page/ Index Ref.
Sri Lanka	25,332	65,610	18,342,660	Colombo	106/D 6
Sudan	967,494	2,505,809	30,120,420	Khartoum	125/L 5
Sumatra, Indonesia	164,000	424,760	36,505,703	Medan	110/B 4
Suriname	55,144	142,823	429,544	Paramaribo	139/G 3
Svalbard, Norway	23,957	62,049	2,914	Longyearbyen	88/C 2
Swaziland	6,705	17,366	966,977	Mbabane	133/E 3
Sweden	173,665	449,792	8,821,759	Stockholm	61/E 3
Switzerland	15,943	41,292	7,084,984	Bern	76/D 4
Syria	71,498	185,180	15,451,917	Damascus	92/D 3
T Tahiti, French Polynesia	402	1,041	95,604	Papeete	121/X13
Taiwan	13,971	36,185	21,500,583	Taipei	105/J 3
Tajikistan	55,251	143,100	6,155,474	Dushanbe	88/H 6
Tanzania	363,708	942,003	28,701,077	Dar es Salaam	130/B 4
Tasmania, Australia	26,178	67,800	452,851	Hobart	119/C 4
Tennessee, U.S.	42,144	109,153	4,877,185	Nashville	163/G 3
Texas, U.S.	266,807	691,030	16,986,510	Austin	162/C 4
Thailand	198,455	513,998	60,271,300	Bangkok	109/C 3
Tibet, China	463,320	1,200,000	2,196,029	Lhasa	102/D 5
Togo	21,622	56,000	4,410,370	Lomé	129/F 4
Tokelau, New Zealand	3.9	10	1,503	Fakaofo	121/H 5
Tonga	270	699	105,600	Nuku'alofa	121/H 7
Trinidad and Tobago	1,980	5,128	1,271,159	Port-of-Spain	150/F 5
Tristan da Cunha, St. Helena	38	98	251	Edinburgh	50/J 7
Tuamotu Archipelago, French Polynesia	341	883	9,052	Apataki	121/L 6
Tunisia	63,378	164,149	8,879,845	Tunis	124/G 1
Turkey	300,946	779,450	63,405,526	Ankara	92/C 2
Turkmenistan	188,455	488,100	4,075,316	Ashkhabad	88/F 6
Turks and Caicos Islands, U.K.	166	430	13,941	Cockburn Town, Grand Turk	150/D 2
Tuvalu	9.78	25.33	9,991	Funafuti	120/G 5
U Uganda	91,076	235,887	19,573,262	Kampala	130/B 2
Ukraine	233,089	603,700	51,867,828	Kiev	86/D 2
United Arab Emirates	32,278	83,600	2,924,594	Abu Dhabi	94/F 4
United Kingdom	94,399	244,493	58,295,119	London	55
United States	3,536,338	9,159,116	263,814,032	Washington	154
Uruguay	72,172	186,925	3,222,716	Montevideo	135/E 3
Utah, U.S.	84,899	219,888	1,722,850	Salt Lake City	158/E 3
Uzbekistan	173,591	449,600	23,089,261	Tashkent	88/G 5
V Vanuatu	5,700	14,763	173,648	Vila	120/F 6
Vatican City	108.7 acres	44 hectares	830	....	80/C 2
Venezuela	352,143	912,050	21,004,773	Caracas	139/E 3
Vermont, U.S.	9,614	24,900	562,758	Montpelier	161/F 2
Victoria, Australia	87,876	227,600	4,244,282	Melbourne	119/C 3
Vietnam	128,405	332,569	74,393,324	Hanoi	109/D 2
Virginia, U.S.	40,767	105,587	6,187,358	Richmond	160/E 3
Virgin Islands, British	59	153	12,000	Road Town	150/E 3
Virgin Islands, U.S.	132	342	97,229	Charlotte Amalie	150/E 3
W Wake Island, U.S.	2.5	6.5	302	Wake Islet	120/F 3
Wales, U.K.	8,017	20,764	2,886,400	Cardiff	55/J10
Wallis and Futuna, France	106	275	14,499	Mata Utu	120/G 6
Washington, U.S.	68,139	176,480	4,866,692	Olympia	156/C 4
West Bank	2,100	5,439	1,319,991	....	91/D 3
Western Australia, Australia	975,096	2,525,500	1,587,050	Perth	114/B 4
Western Cape, South Africa	49,943	129,386	3,620,200	Cape Town	132/C 4
Western Sahara	102,703	266,000	217,211	....	124/B 3
Western Samoa	1,133	209,360	209,360	Apia	121/R 9
West Virginia, U.S.	24,231	62,758	1,793,477	Charleston	160/D 4
Wisconsin, U.S.	56,153	145,436	4,891,769	Madison	160/B 2
World	(land) 57,970,000	150,142,300	5,733,687,096	....	50
Wyoming, U.S.	97,809	253,325	453,588	Cheyenne	156/F 5
Y Yemen	188,321	487,752	14,728,474	Sanaa	94/E 5
Yugoslavia	38,989	100,982	11,101,833	Belgrade	82/D 3
Yukon Territory, Canada	207,075	536,324	27,797	Whitehorse	152/C 2
Z Zaire	905,063	2,344,113	44,060,636	Kinshasa	122/E 5
Zambia	290,586	752,618	9,445,723	Lusaka	126/E 3
Zimbabwe	150,803	390,580	11,139,961	Harare	131/C 3

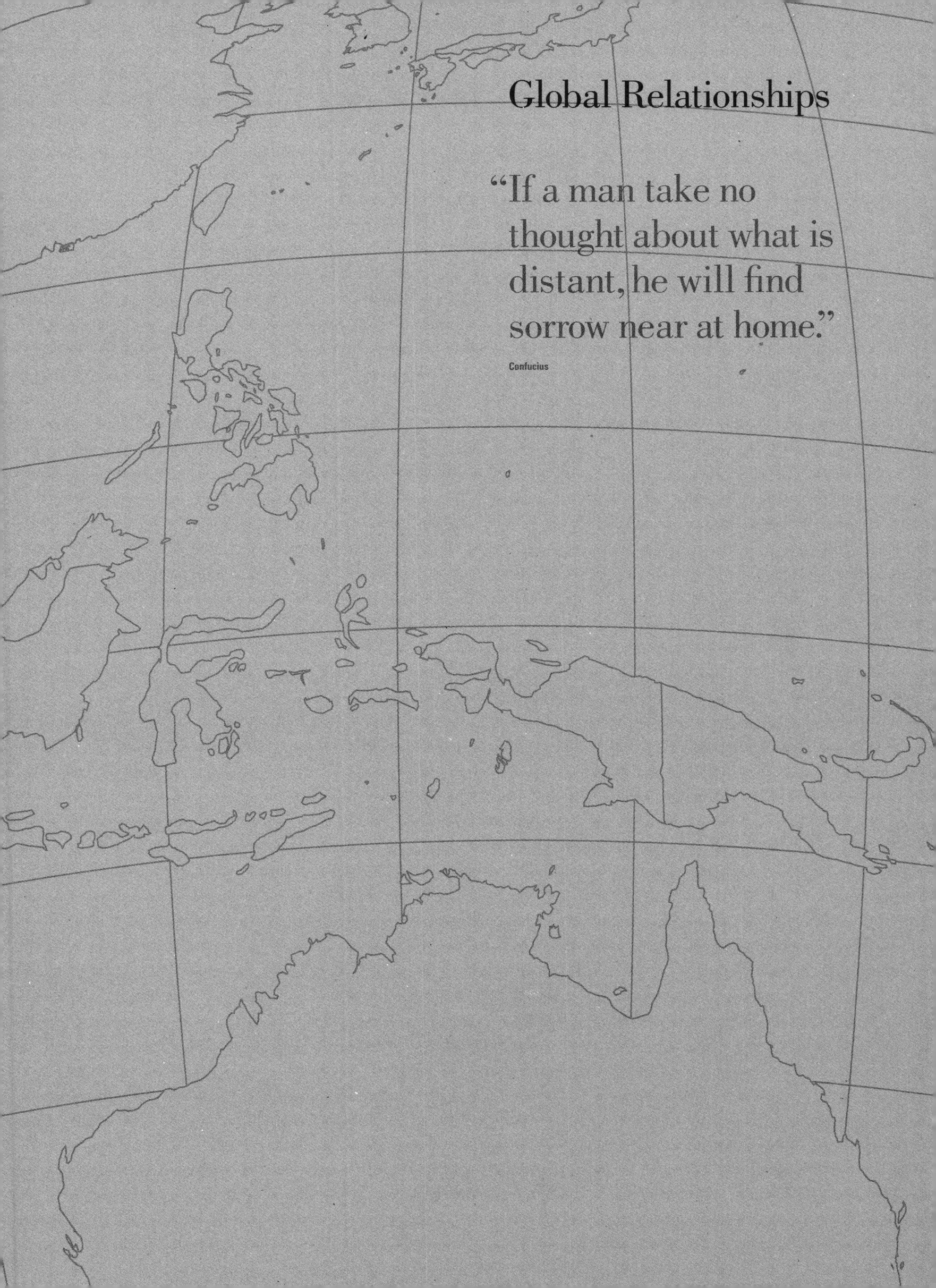

Global Relationships

"If a man take no thought about what is distant, he will find sorrow near at home."

Confucius

Environmental
Concerns

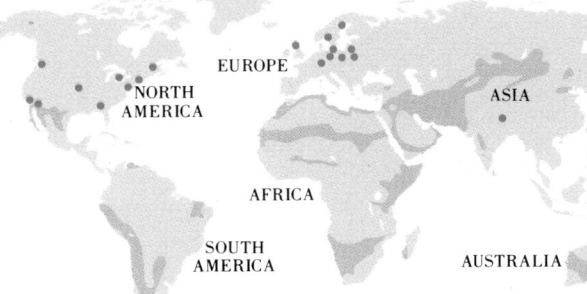

DESERTIFICATION AND ACID RAIN DAMAGE

EUROPE
NORTH AMERICA
ASIA
AFRICA
SOUTH AMERICA
AUSTRALIA

▭ AREAS OF PRODUCTIVE DRYLANDS DESERTIFIED BY EARLY 1980's

● AREAS OF DAMAGE FROM ACID RAIN AND OTHER AIRBORNE POLLUTANTS

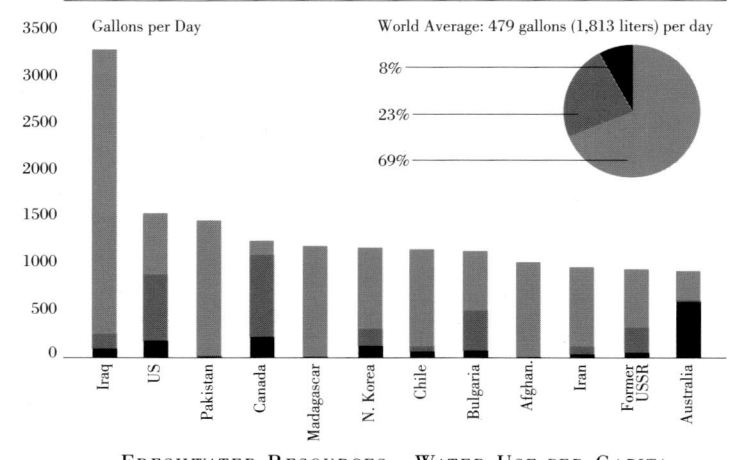

World Average: 479 gallons (1,813 liters) per day

8%
23%
69%

Gallons per Day

3500
3000
2500
2000
1500
1000
500
0

Iraq | US | Pakistan | Canada | Madagascar | N. Korea | Chile | Bulgaria | Afghan. | Iran | Former USSR | Australia

FRESHWATER RESOURCES—WATER USE PER CAPITA

■ DOMESTIC   ■ INDUSTRY   ▭ AGRICULTURE

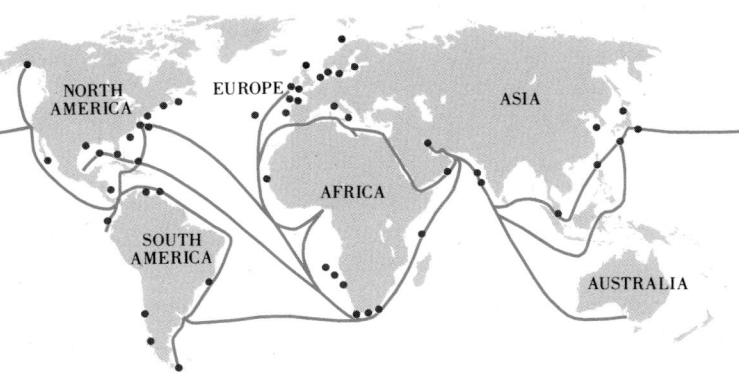

NORTH AMERICA
EUROPE
ASIA
AFRICA
SOUTH AMERICA
AUSTRALIA

MAIN TANKER ROUTES AND MAJOR OIL SPILLS

—— ROUTES OF VERY LARGE CRUDE OIL CARRIERS   ● MAJOR OIL SPILLS

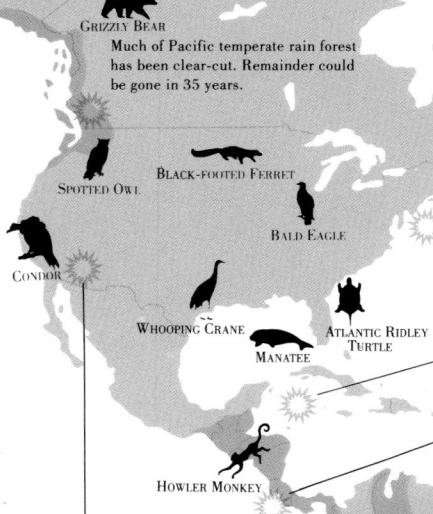

GRIZZLY BEAR
Much of Pacific temperate rain forest has been clear-cut. Remainder could be gone in 35 years.

WOODLAND CARIBOU

HUMPBACK WH[ALE]
Hydroelectric power projec[ts] and development in Quebe[c] are disrupting wildlife habitats.

SPOTTED OWL   BLACK-FOOTED FERRET

Commercial fishing harvest[s] in the northwest Atlantic h[as] declined over 30 percent since 1970.

BALD EAGLE

Fragile barrier beaches of the Atlantic coast have been damaged by agricultural runoff, sewage and overdevelopment.

CONDOR

WHOOPING CRANE   ATLANTIC RIDLEY TURTLE
MANATEE

Ecological balance in coral reefs of the Gulf and Caribbean area is being upset by a booming tourist industry.

At the present rate of clearing, half o[f] Central America's rain forest will dis[-] appear by the year 2000.

HOWLER MONKEY

One-third of Guinea's tropical forest [is] expected to disappear in the next [-] decade.

Erosion, the depletion of water resources for irrigation, and overgrazing have turned range and cropland into desert.

GALÁPAGOS TORTOISE

BLACK CAIMAN

JAGUAR

VICUNA

Every year over 5000 square miles (13,000 sq km) of rain forest is destroyed in Brazil's Amazon Basin.

GOLDEN LION TAMARIN

CHINCHILLA

GIANT ARMADILLO

Southern Chile's rain forest is threatened by development.

The Atlantic waters off Patagonia have suffered fr[om] over-fishing and oil spills.

BLUE WHALE

Acid Rain

Acid rain of nitric and sulfuric acids has killed all life in thousands of lakes, and over 15 million acres (6 million hectares) of virgin forest in Europe and North America are dead or dying.

Deforestation

Each year, 50 million acres (20 million hectares) of tropical rainforests are being felled by loggers. Trees remove carbon dioxide from the atmosphere and are vital to the prevention of soil erosion.

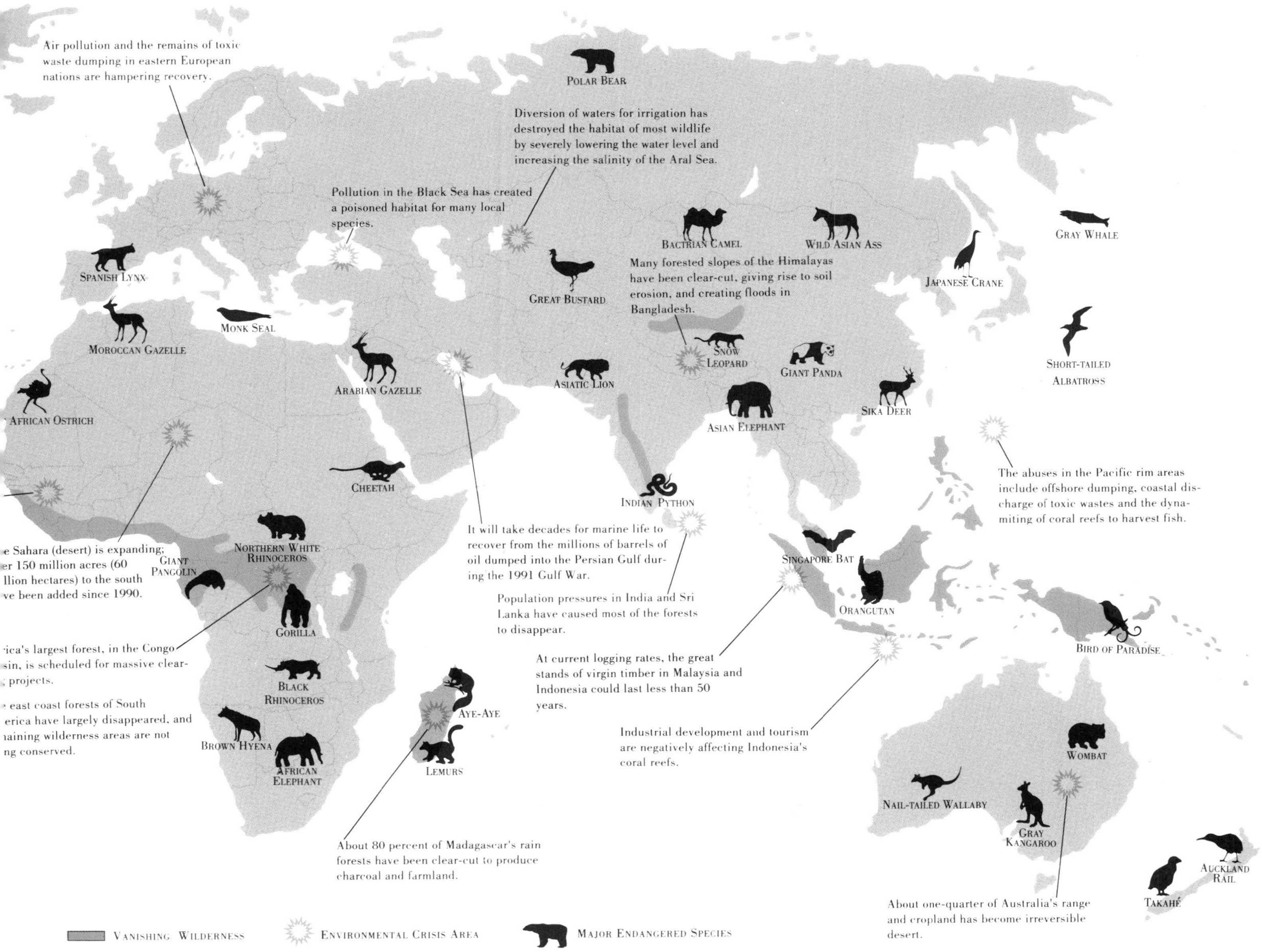

Air pollution and the remains of toxic waste dumping in eastern European nations are hampering recovery.

POLAR BEAR

Diversion of waters for irrigation has destroyed the habitat of most wildlife by severely lowering the water level and increasing the salinity of the Aral Sea.

Pollution in the Black Sea has created a poisoned habitat for many local species.

GRAY WHALE

BACTRIAN CAMEL   WILD ASIAN ASS

Many forested slopes of the Himalayas have been clear-cut, giving rise to soil erosion, and creating floods in Bangladesh.

JAPANESE CRANE

SPANISH LYNX

GREAT BUSTARD

MONK SEAL

MOROCCAN GAZELLE

SHORT-TAILED ALBATROSS

ARABIAN GAZELLE

ASIATIC LION

SNOW LEOPARD

GIANT PANDA

AFRICAN OSTRICH

SIKA DEER

ASIAN ELEPHANT

CHEETAH

The abuses in the Pacific rim areas include offshore dumping, coastal discharge of toxic wastes and the dynamiting of coral reefs to harvest fish.

INDIAN PYTHON

...e Sahara (desert) is expanding; ...r 150 million acres (60 ...llion hectares) to the south ...ve been added since 1990.

GIANT PANGOLIN

NORTHERN WHITE RHINOCEROS

It will take decades for marine life to recover from the millions of barrels of oil dumped into the Persian Gulf during the 1991 Gulf War.

SINGAPORE BAT

GORILLA

Population pressures in India and Sri Lanka have caused most of the forests to disappear.

...rica's largest forest, in the Congo ...sin, is scheduled for massive clear...s projects.

ORANGUTAN

At current logging rates, the great stands of virgin timber in Malaysia and Indonesia could last less than 50 years.

BIRD OF PARADISE

BLACK RHINOCEROS

...e east coast forests of South ...erica have largely disappeared, and ...aining wilderness areas are not ...ng conserved.

AYE-AYE

Industrial development and tourism are negatively affecting Indonesia's coral reefs.

BROWN HYENA

WOMBAT

AFRICAN ELEPHANT

LEMURS

NAIL-TAILED WALLABY

GRAY KANGAROO

About 80 percent of Madagascar's rain forests have been clear-cut to produce charcoal and farmland.

AUCKLAND RAIL

TAKAHÉ

About one-quarter of Australia's range and cropland has become irreversible desert.

▬ VANISHING WILDERNESS   ☼ ENVIRONMENTAL CRISIS AREA   🐻 MAJOR ENDANGERED SPECIES

Extinction

Biologists estimate that over 50,000 plant and animal species inhabiting the world's rain forests are disappearing each year due to pollution, unchecked hunting and the destruction of natural habitats.

Air Pollution

Billions of tons of industrial emissions and toxic pollutants are released into the air each year, depleting our ozone layer, killing our forests and lakes with acid rain and threatening our health.

Water Pollution

Only 3 percent of the earth's water is fresh. Pollution from cities, farms and factories has made much of it unfit to drink. In the developing world, most sewage flows untreated into lakes and rivers.

Ozone Depletion

The layer of ozone in the stratosphere shields earth from harmful ultraviolet radiation. But man-made gases are destroying this vital barrier, increasing the risk of skin cancer and eye disease.

Population

CURRENT POPULATION COMPARISONS

EACH AREA'S SIZE IS PROPORTIONATE TO ITS POPULATION

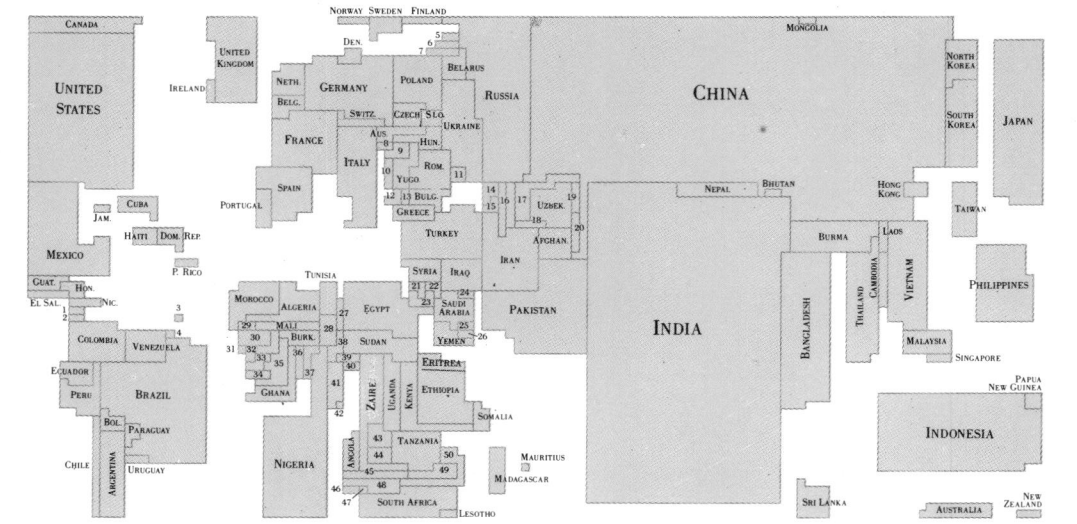

COUNTRIES INDICATED BY NUMBER

1 COSTA RICA	10 BOSNIA AND	20 TAJIKISTAN	30 SENEGAL	40 CONGO	51 CYPRUS
2 PANAMA	HERZEGOVINA	21 LEBANON	31 GUINEA-BISSAU	41 CAMEROON	52 CAPE VERDE
3 TRINIDAD AND	11 MOLDOVA	22 JORDAN	32 GUINEA	42 GABON	53 GAMBIA
TOBAGO	12 ALBANIA	23 ISRAEL	33 SIERRA LEONE	43 RWANDA	54 EQUATORIAL GUINEA
4 GUYANA	13 MACEDONIA	24 KUWAIT	34 LIBERIA	44 BURUNDI	55 BAHRAIN
5 ESTONIA	14 GEORGIA	25 UNITED ARAB	35 CÔTE D'IVOIRE	45 ZAMBIA	56 QATAR
6 LATVIA	15 ARMENIA	EMIRATES	36 TOGO	46 NAMIBIA	57 BRUNEI
7 LITHUANIA	16 AZERBAIJAN	26 OMAN	37 BENIN	47 BOTSWANA	58 SOLOMON ISLANDS
8 SLOVENIA	17 KAZAKHSTAN	27 LIBYA	38 CHAD	48 ZIMBABWE	
9 CROATIÁ	18 TURKMENISTAN	28 NIGER	39 CENTRAL AFRICAN	49 MOZAMBIQUE	
	19 KYRGYZSTAN	29 MAURITANIA	REPUBLIC	50 MALAWI	

PROJECTED POPULATION COMPARISONS - 2020

EACH AREA'S SIZE IS PROPORTIONATE TO ITS POPULATION

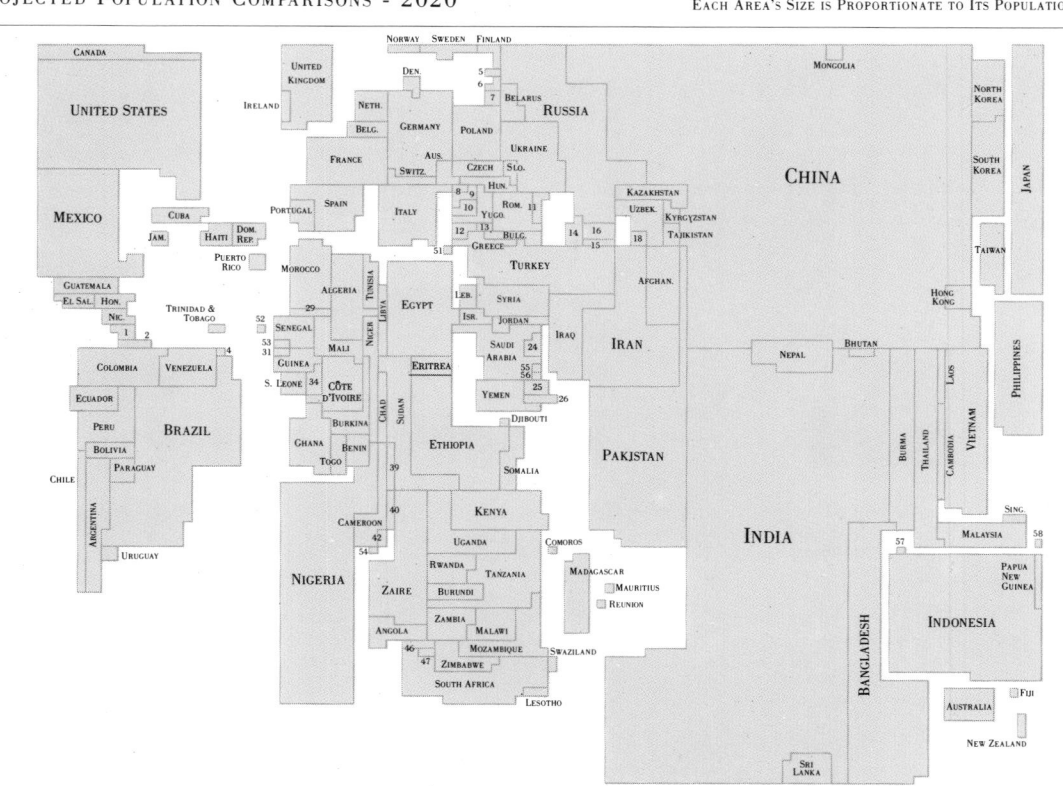

3.5 PERCENT OR MO

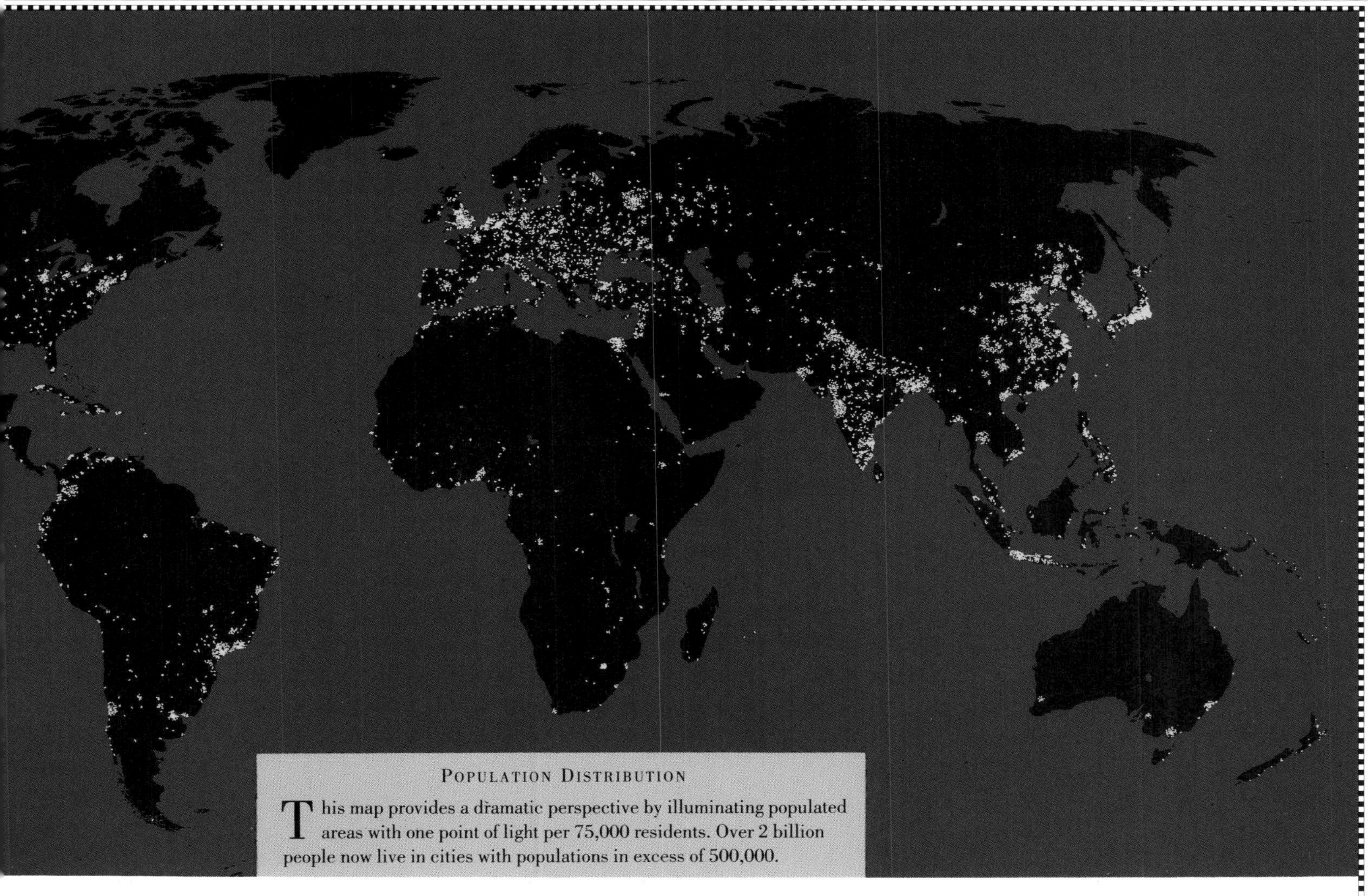

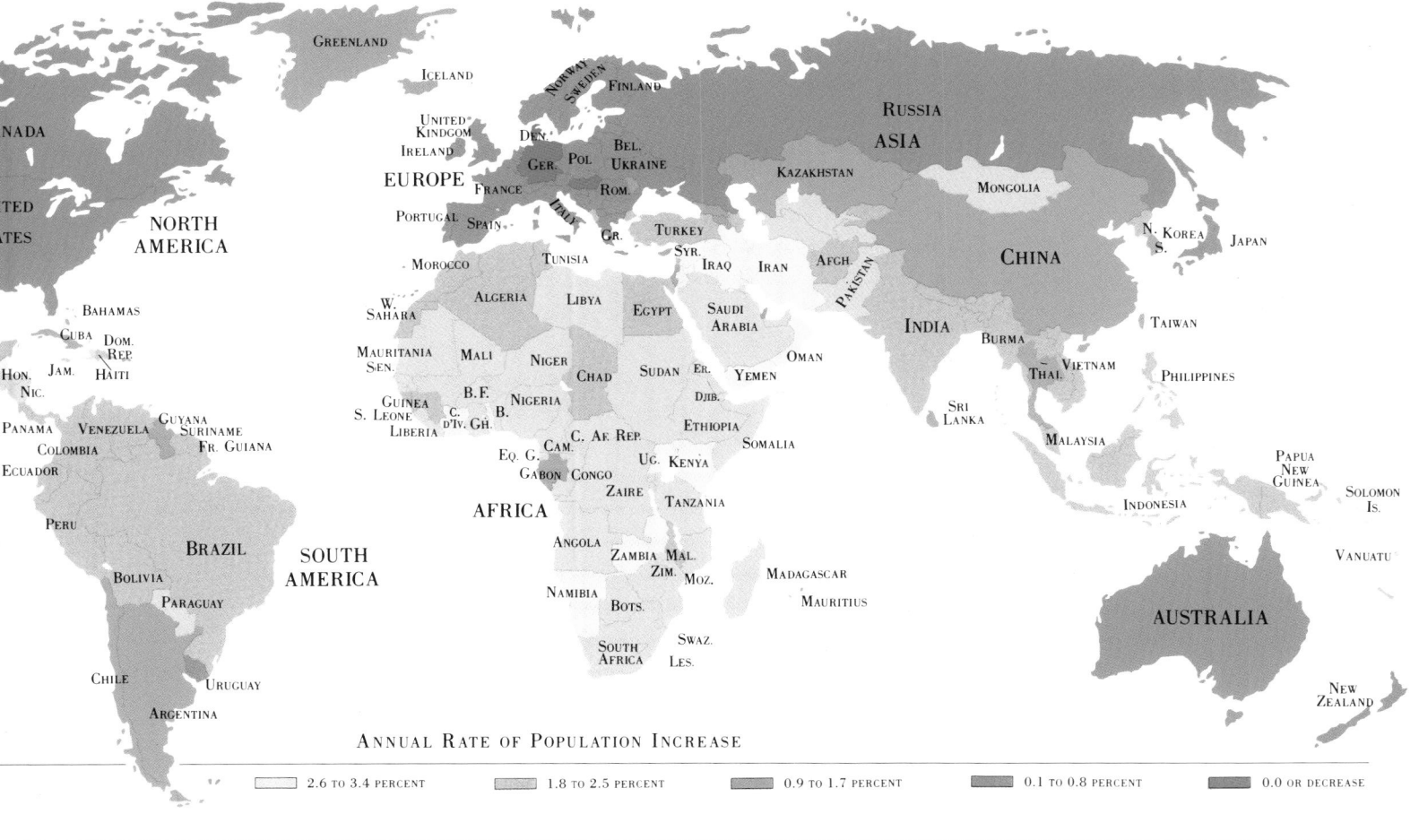

POPULATION DISTRIBUTION

This map provides a dramatic perspective by illuminating populated areas with one point of light per 75,000 residents. Over 2 billion people now live in cities with populations in excess of 500,000.

ANNUAL RATE OF POPULATION INCREASE

| 2.6 TO 3.4 PERCENT | 1.8 TO 2.5 PERCENT | 0.9 TO 1.7 PERCENT | 0.1 TO 0.8 PERCENT | 0.0 OR DECREASE |

Standards of Living

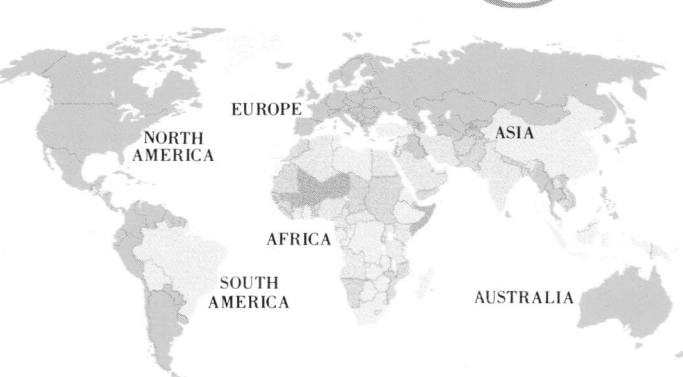

ALASKA

CANADA

UNITED STATES

UNITED STATES
The economic and political influence of women has risen substantially. In a number of fields, women's salaries are now nearly equal to men's.

MEXICO

BAHAMAS

CUBA

JAM. **DOM. REP.**
HAITI

BEL.
HON.
GUAT.
EL. SAL. **NIC.**

C.R.
PANAMA **VENEZUELA** **GUYANA**
SURINAME
COLOMBIA **FR. GUIANA.**

ECUADOR

SOUTH AMERICA
Political unrest, rising inflation and slow economic growth continue to thwart efforts to bring unity and prosperity to the nations of South America

LATIN AMERICA
The gulf between rich and poor continues to widen, despite efforts to reform oppressive governments, increase literacy and relieve overburdened cities.

PERU

BRAZIL

BOLIVIA

PARAGUAY

CHILE

URUGUAY

ARGENTINA

GREE

LITERATE PERCENT OF POPULATION

EUROPE · NORTH AMERICA · ASIA · AFRICA · SOUTH AMERICA · AUSTRALIA

- 80 AND ABOVE
- 60-79
- 40-59
- 20-39
- 0-19

YEARS OF LIFE EXPECTANCY (MEN AND WOMEN)

EUROPE · NORTH AMERICA · ASIA · AFRICA · SOUTH AMERICA · AUSTRALIA

- 70 AND ABOVE
- 60-69
- 50-59
- 40-49
- 0-39

INFANT DEATHS PER 1,000 LIVE BIRTHS

EUROPE · NORTH AMERICA · ASIA · AFRICA · SOUTH AMERICA · AUSTRALIA

© HAMMOND INC.

- 150 AND MORE
- 100-149
- 50-99
- 25-49
- 0-24

COMPARISON OF EUROPEAN, U.S. AND JAPANESE WORKERS

COUNTRY	SCHEDULED WEEKLY HOURS	ANNUAL LEAVE DAYS/HOLIDAYS	ANNUAL HOURS WORKED
GERMANY	39	42	1708
NETHERLANDS	40	43.5	1740
BELGIUM	38	31	1748
AUSTRIA	39.3	38	1751
FRANCE	39	34	1771
ITALY	40	39	1776
UNITED KINGDOM	39	33	1778
LUXEMBOURG	40	37	1792
FINLAND	40	37	1792
SWEDEN	40	37	1792
SPAIN	40	36	1800
DENMARK	40	34	1816
NORWAY	40	30	1848
GREECE	40	28	1864
IRELAND	40	28	1864
UNITED STATES	40	22	1912
SWITZERLAND	41.5	30.5	1913
PORTUGAL	45	36	2025
JAPAN	44	23.5	2116

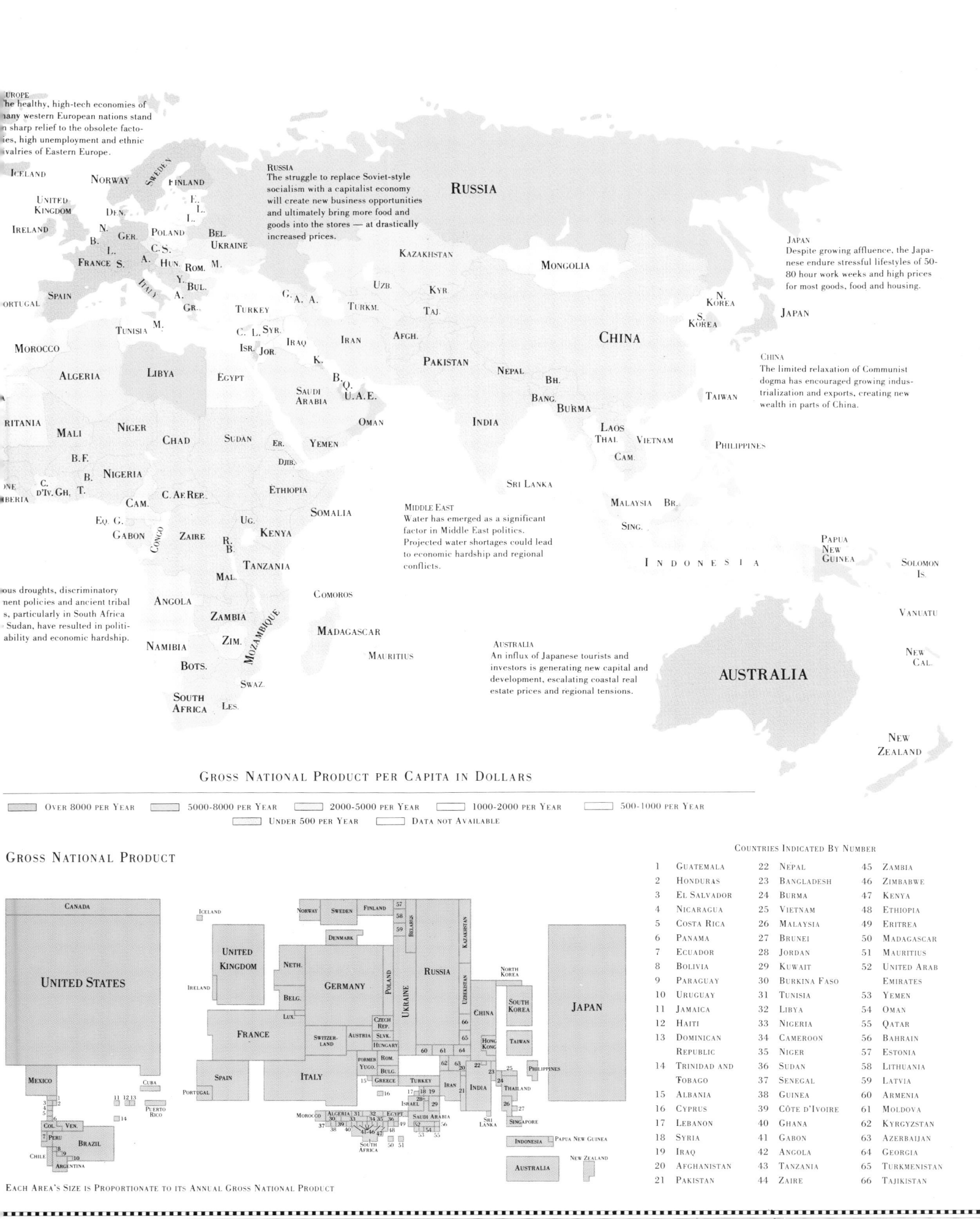

...UROPE
...he healthy, high-tech economies of
...nany western European nations stand
...n sharp relief to the obsolete facto-
...ies, high unemployment and ethnic
...valries of Eastern Europe.

RUSSIA
The struggle to replace Soviet-style socialism with a capitalist economy will create new business opportunities and ultimately bring more food and goods into the stores — at drastically increased prices.

JAPAN
Despite growing affluence, the Japanese endure stressful lifestyles of 50-80 hour work weeks and high prices for most goods, food and housing.

CHINA
The limited relaxation of Communist dogma has encouraged growing industrialization and exports, creating new wealth in parts of China.

MIDDLE EAST
Water has emerged as a significant factor in Middle East politics. Projected water shortages could lead to economic hardship and regional conflicts.

...ous droughts, discriminatory
...nent policies and ancient tribal
...s, particularly in South Africa
... Sudan, have resulted in politi-
...ability and economic hardship.

AUSTRALIA
An influx of Japanese tourists and investors is generating new capital and development, escalating coastal real estate prices and regional tensions.

GROSS NATIONAL PRODUCT PER CAPITA IN DOLLARS

- OVER 8000 PER YEAR
- 5000-8000 PER YEAR
- 2000-5000 PER YEAR
- 1000-2000 PER YEAR
- 500-1000 PER YEAR
- UNDER 500 PER YEAR
- DATA NOT AVAILABLE

GROSS NATIONAL PRODUCT

EACH AREA'S SIZE IS PROPORTIONATE TO ITS ANNUAL GROSS NATIONAL PRODUCT

COUNTRIES INDICATED BY NUMBER

1	GUATEMALA	22	NEPAL	45	ZAMBIA
2	HONDURAS	23	BANGLADESH	46	ZIMBABWE
3	EL SALVADOR	24	BURMA	47	KENYA
4	NICARAGUA	25	VIETNAM	48	ETHIOPIA
5	COSTA RICA	26	MALAYSIA	49	ERITREA
6	PANAMA	27	BRUNEI	50	MADAGASCAR
7	ECUADOR	28	JORDAN	51	MAURITIUS
8	BOLIVIA	29	KUWAIT	52	UNITED ARAB
9	PARAGUAY	30	BURKINA FASO		EMIRATES
10	URUGUAY	31	TUNISIA	53	YEMEN
11	JAMAICA	32	LIBYA	54	OMAN
12	HAITI	33	NIGERIA	55	QATAR
13	DOMINICAN	34	CAMEROON	56	BAHRAIN
	REPUBLIC	35	NIGER	57	ESTONIA
14	TRINIDAD AND	36	SUDAN	58	LITHUANIA
	TOBAGO	37	SENEGAL	59	LATVIA
15	ALBANIA	38	GUINEA	60	ARMENIA
16	CYPRUS	39	CÔTE D'IVOIRE	61	MOLDOVA
17	LEBANON	40	GHANA	62	KYRGYZSTAN
18	SYRIA	41	GABON	63	AZERBAIJAN
19	IRAQ	42	ANGOLA	64	GEORGIA
20	AFGHANISTAN	43	TANZANIA	65	TURKMENISTAN
21	PAKISTAN	44	ZAIRE	66	TAJIKISTAN

Energy & Resources

TOP FIVE WORLD PRODUCERS OF SELECTED MINERAL COMMODITIES

MINERAL FUELS	1	2	3	4	5
CRUDE OIL	RUSSIA	UNITED STATES	SAUDI ARABIA	CHINA	IRAQ
REFINED OIL	UNITED STATES	RUSSIA	JAPAN	CHINA	UNITED KINGDOM
NATURAL GAS	RUSSIA	UNITED STATES	CANADA	NETHERLANDS	UNITED KINGDOM
COAL (ALL GRADES)	CHINA	UNITED STATES	GERMANY	RUSSIA	POLAND
MINE URANIUM	CANADA	SOUTH AFRICA	UNITED STATES	AUSTRALIA	NAMIBIA

METALS					
CHROMITE	SOUTH AFRICA	KAZAKHSTAN	ALBANIA	FINLAND	INDIA
IRON ORE	BRAZIL	UKRAINE	RUSSIA	CHINA	AUSTRALIA
MANGANESE ORE	FORMER USSR	SOUTH AFRICA	CHINA	GABON	AUSTRALIA
MINE NICKEL	CANADA	RUSSIA	NEW CALEDONIA	AUSTRALIA	INDONESIA
MINE SILVER	MEXICO	UNITED STATES	PERU	FORMER USSR	CANADA
BAUXITE	AUSTRALIA	GUINEA	BRAZIL	JAMAICA	FORMER USSR
ALUMINIUM	UNITED STATES	FORMER USSR	CANADA	AUSTRALIA	BRAZIL
GOLD	SOUTH AFRICA	FORMER USSR	UNITED STATES	AUSTRALIA	CANADA
MINE COPPER	CHILE	UNITED STATES	CANADA	FORMER USSR	ZAIRE
MINE LEAD	AUSTRALIA	FORMER USSR	UNITED STATES	CANADA	CHINA
MINE TIN	BRAZIL	INDONESIA	MALAYSIA	CHINA	FORMER USSR
MINE ZINC	CANADA	FORMER USSR	AUSTRALIA	CHINA	PERU

NONMETALS					
NATURAL DIAMOND	AUSTRALIA	ZAIRE	BOTSWANA	FORMER USSR	SOUTH AFRICA
POTASH	FORMER USSR	CANADA	GERMANY	UNITED STATES	FRANCE
PHOSPHATE ROCK	UNITED STATES	FORMER USSR	MOROCCO	CHINA	TUNISIA
ELEMENTAL SULFUR	UNITED STATES	FORMER USSR	CANADA	POLAND	CHINA

Names in Black Indicate More Than 10% of Total World Production

NUCLEAR POWER PRODUCTION

PERCENTAGE OF WORLD TOTAL

United States 27.4
France 15.1
Japan 11.4
Germany 8.6
Canada 4.6
Sweden 4.1
United Kingdom 3.3
Belgium 2.5
Spain 2.5
South Korea 2.4
Czech Republic 1.3
Switzerland 1.3
Finland 1.2

COMMERCIAL ENERGY CONSUMPTION/PRODUCTION

PERCENTAGE OF WORLD TOTAL
☐ 0.0 PRODUCTION ■ 0.0 CONSUMPTION

Former USSR 23.2 / 19.3
United States 19.8 / 24.1
China 8.8 / 8.3
Canada 3.3 / 2.7
United Kingdom 3.3 / 3.0
Saudi Arabia 3.3 / 0.8
Mexico 2.5 / 1.5
Germany 2.5 / 4.9
India 2.1 / 2.3
Australia 1.9 / 1.1
Iran 1.9 / 0.7
Poland 1.8 / 1.9
Venezuela 1.7 / 0.6

ALASKA

UNIT

ME

- ▨ OIL FIELDS
- ▮ NATURAL GAS FIELDS
- ● MAJOR COAL DEPOSITS
- ▲ OIL SANDS
- ◆ OIL SHALE
- ✱ MAJOR URANIUM DEPOSITS
- ■ IMPORTANT PEAT DEPOSITS

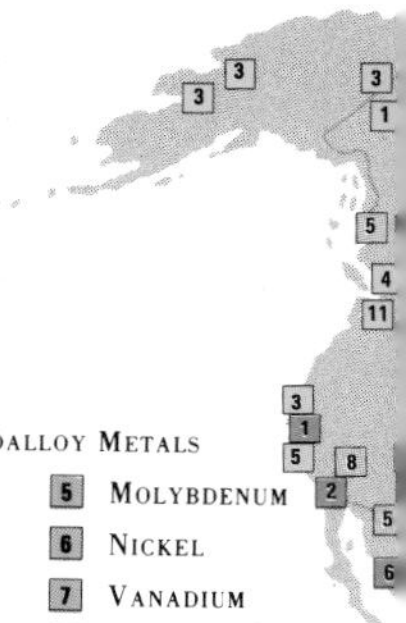

IRON AND FERROALLOY METALS

1	COBALT	5	MOLYBDENUM
2	CHROMIUM	6	NICKEL
3	IRON ORE	7	VANADIUM
4	MANGANESE	8	TUNGSTEN

OTHER METALS

1	SILVER	7	PLATINUM
2	BAUXITE	8	ANTIMONY
3	GOLD	9	TIN
4	COPPER	10	TITANIUM
5	MERCURY	11	ZINC
6	LEAD		

NONMETALS

1	ASBESTOS	10	MICA
2	BORAX	11	NITRATES
3	DIAMONDS	12	OPALS
4	EMERALDS	13	PHOSPHATES
5	FLUORSPAR	14	PEARLS
6	GRAPHITE	15	RUBIES
7	IODINE	16	SULFUR
8	JADE	17	SAPPHIRES
9	POTASH		

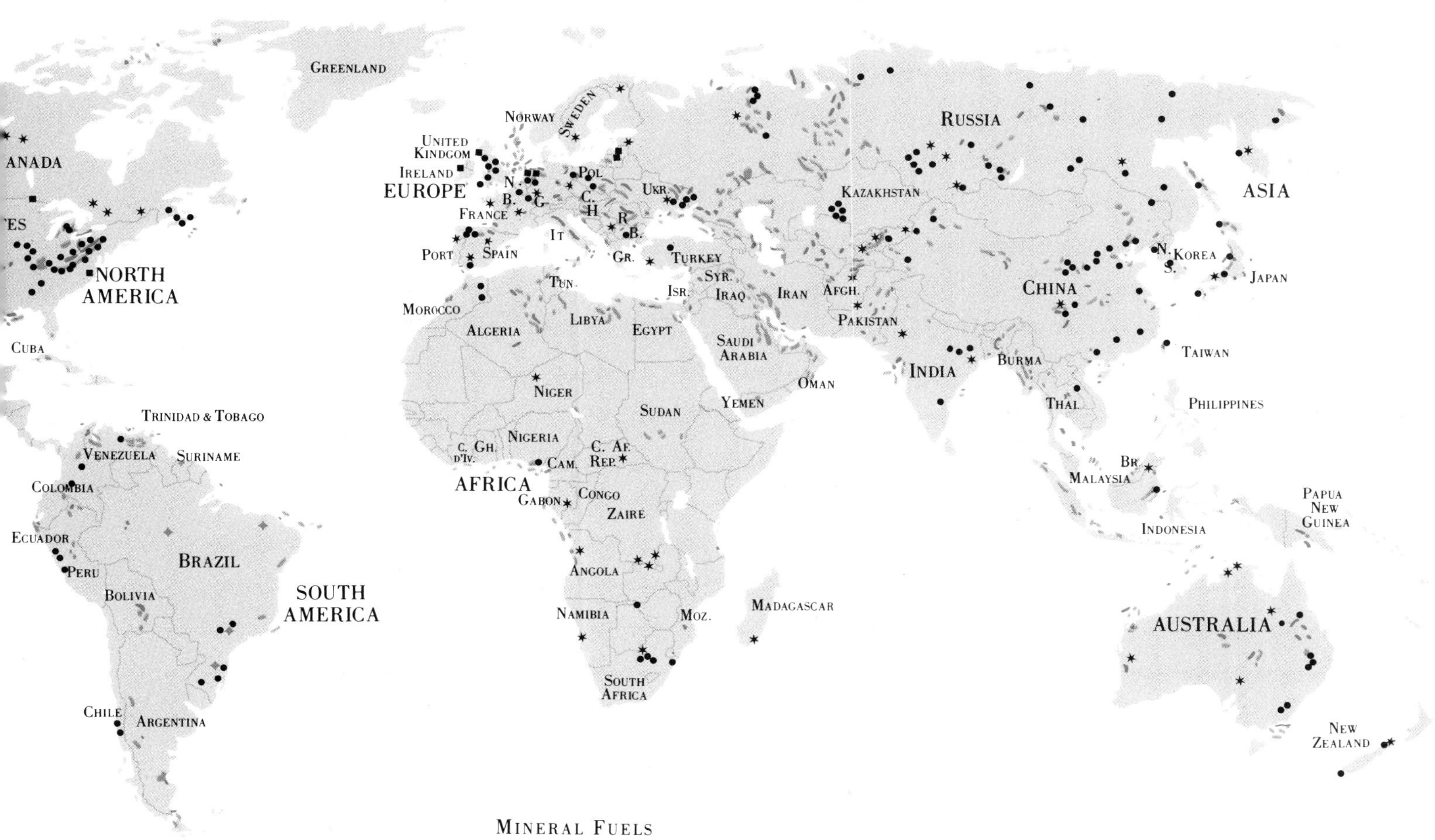

Mineral Fuels

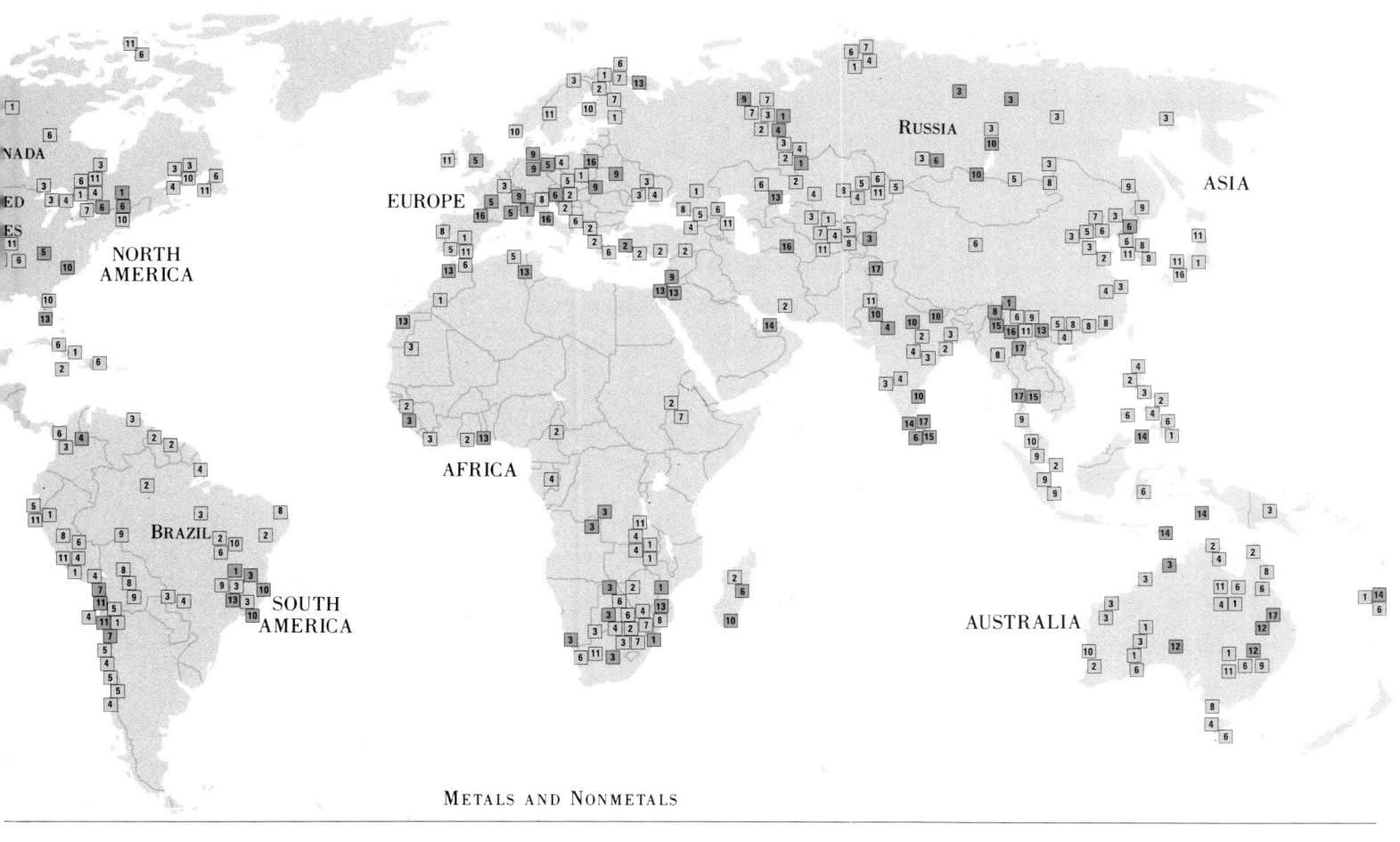

Metals and Nonmetals

Agriculture & Manufacturing

Top Five World Producers of Selected Agricultural Commodities

	1	2	3	4	5
WHEAT	CHINA	FORMER USSR	UNITED STATES	INDIA	FRANCE
RICE	CHINA	INDIA	INDONESIA	BANGLADESH	THAILAND
OATS	FORMER USSR	UNITED STATES	CANADA	GERMANY	POLAND
CORN (MAIZE)	UNITED STATES	CHINA	BRAZIL	ROMANIA	FORMER USSR
SOYBEANS	UNITED STATES	BRAZIL	CHINA	ARGENTINA	CANADA
POTATOES	RUSSIA	POLAND	CHINA	GERMANY	UKRAINE
COFFEE	BRAZIL	COLOMBIA	INDONESIA	MEXICO	CÔTE D'IVOIRE
TEA	INDIA	CHINA	SRI LANKA	KENYA	FORMER USSR
TOBACCO	CHINA	UNITED STATES	INDIA	BRAZIL	FORMER USSR
COTTON	CHINA	UNITED STATES	FORMER USSR	PAKISTAN	INDIA
CATTLE	AUSTRALIA	BRAZIL	UNITED STATES	CHINA	RUSSIA
SHEEP	AUSTRALIA	CHINA	NEW ZEALAND	RUSSIA	INDIA
HOGS	CHINA	UNITED STATES	RUSSIA	GERMANY	BRAZIL
COW'S MILK	UNITED STATES	GERMANY	RUSSIA	FRANCE	POLAND
HEN'S EGGS	CHINA	UNITED STATES	RUSSIA	JAPAN	BRAZIL
WOOL	AUSTRALIA	FORMER USSR	NEW ZEALAND	CHINA	ARGENTINA
ROUNDWOOD	UNITED STATES	RUSSIA	CHINA	INDIA	BRAZIL
NATURAL RUBBER	MALAYSIA	INDONESIA	THAILAND	CHINA	INDIA
FISH CATCHES	JAPAN	FORMER USSR	CHINA	UNITED STATES	CHILE

Names in Black Indicate More Than 10% of Total World Production

Percent of Total Employment in Agriculture, Manufacturing and Other Industries

Legend:
- AGRICULTURE (INCLUDES FORESTRY AND FISHING)
- MANUFACTURING
- CONSTRUCTION
- TRADE AND COMMERCE
- FINANCE, INSURANCE, REAL ESTATE
- SERVICES
- OTHER (INCLUDES MINING, UTILITIES, TRANSPORTATION)

Scale: 0   20   40   60   80   100

- India
- China
- Indonesia
- Pakistan
- Mexico
- Brazil
- Spain
- Argentina
- Italy
- Japan
- France
- Canada
- Australia
- Germany
- United States
- United Kingdom

Finance, Insurance, Real Estate Data Included With "Other" for India, China, Indonesia and Pakistan

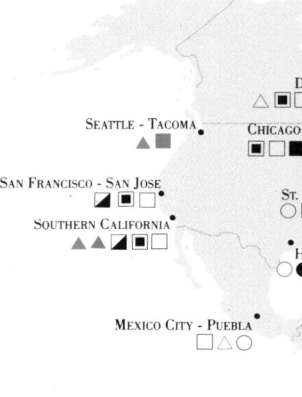

CEREALS, LIVESTOCK

LIVESTOCK RANCHING AND H...

SEATTLE - TACOMA
SAN FRANCISCO - SAN JOSE
SOUTHERN CALIFORNIA
MEXICO CITY - PUEBLA
CHICAGO -
ST. L...
DE...
Ho...

SANTIAGO - VALPA...

- ▲ AIRCRAFT
- △ MOTOR VEHICLES
- ▽ SHIPBUILDING

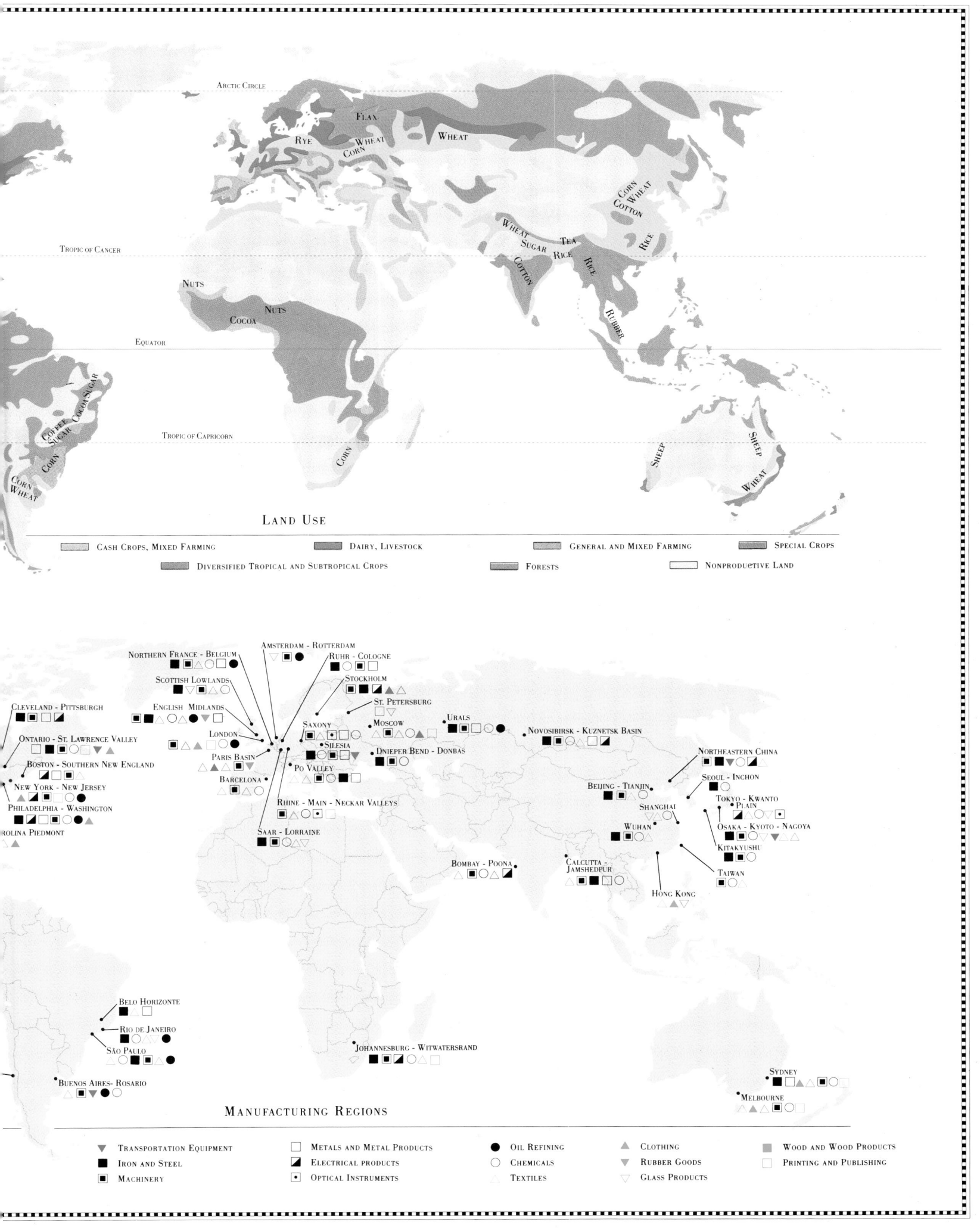

ARCTIC CIRCLE

FLAX

RYE
WHEAT
CORN
WHEAT

CORN
WHEAT
COTTON

TROPIC OF CANCER

NUTS

COCOA
NUTS

WHEAT
SUGAR
RICE
TEA
RICE
RICE
COTTON

RUBBER

EQUATOR

COFFEE
SUGAR
COCOA
SUGAR

CORN
TROPIC OF CAPRICORN

CORN

SHEEP
SHEEP

CORN
WHEAT

WHEAT

LAND USE

CASH CROPS, MIXED FARMING · DAIRY, LIVESTOCK · GENERAL AND MIXED FARMING · SPECIAL CROPS

DIVERSIFIED TROPICAL AND SUBTROPICAL CROPS · FORESTS · NONPRODUCTIVE LAND

AMSTERDAM - ROTTERDAM
NORTHERN FRANCE - BELGIUM
RUHR - COLOGNE
SCOTTISH LOWLANDS
STOCKHOLM
CLEVELAND - PITTSBURGH
ST. PETERSBURG
ENGLISH MIDLANDS
URALS
NOVOSIBIRSK - KUZNETSK BASIN
ONTARIO - ST. LAWRENCE VALLEY
LONDON
SAXONY
MOSCOW
BOSTON - SOUTHERN NEW ENGLAND
PARIS BASIN
SILESIA
NORTHEASTERN CHINA
NEW YORK - NEW JERSEY
BARCELONA
PO VALLEY
DNIEPER BEND - DONBAS
SEOUL - INCHON
PHILADELPHIA - WASHINGTON
BEIJING - TIANJIN
TOKYO - KWANTO
PLAIN
CAROLINA PIEDMONT
RHINE - MAIN - NECKAR VALLEYS
SHANGHAI
OSAKA - KYOTO - NAGOYA
SAAR - LORRAINE
WUHAN
KITAKYUSHU
BOMBAY - POONA
CALCUTTA - JAMSHEDPUR
TAIWAN
HONG KONG

BELO HORIZONTE

RIO DE JANEIRO
SÃO PAULO

JOHANNESBURG - WITWATERSRAND

SYDNEY

BUENOS AIRES- ROSARIO
MELBOURNE

MANUFACTURING REGIONS

TRANSPORTATION EQUIPMENT · METALS AND METAL PRODUCTS · OIL REFINING · CLOTHING · WOOD AND WOOD PRODUCTS
IRON AND STEEL · ELECTRICAL PRODUCTS · CHEMICALS · RUBBER GOODS · PRINTING AND PUBLISHING
MACHINERY · OPTICAL INSTRUMENTS · TEXTILES · GLASS PRODUCTS

Climate

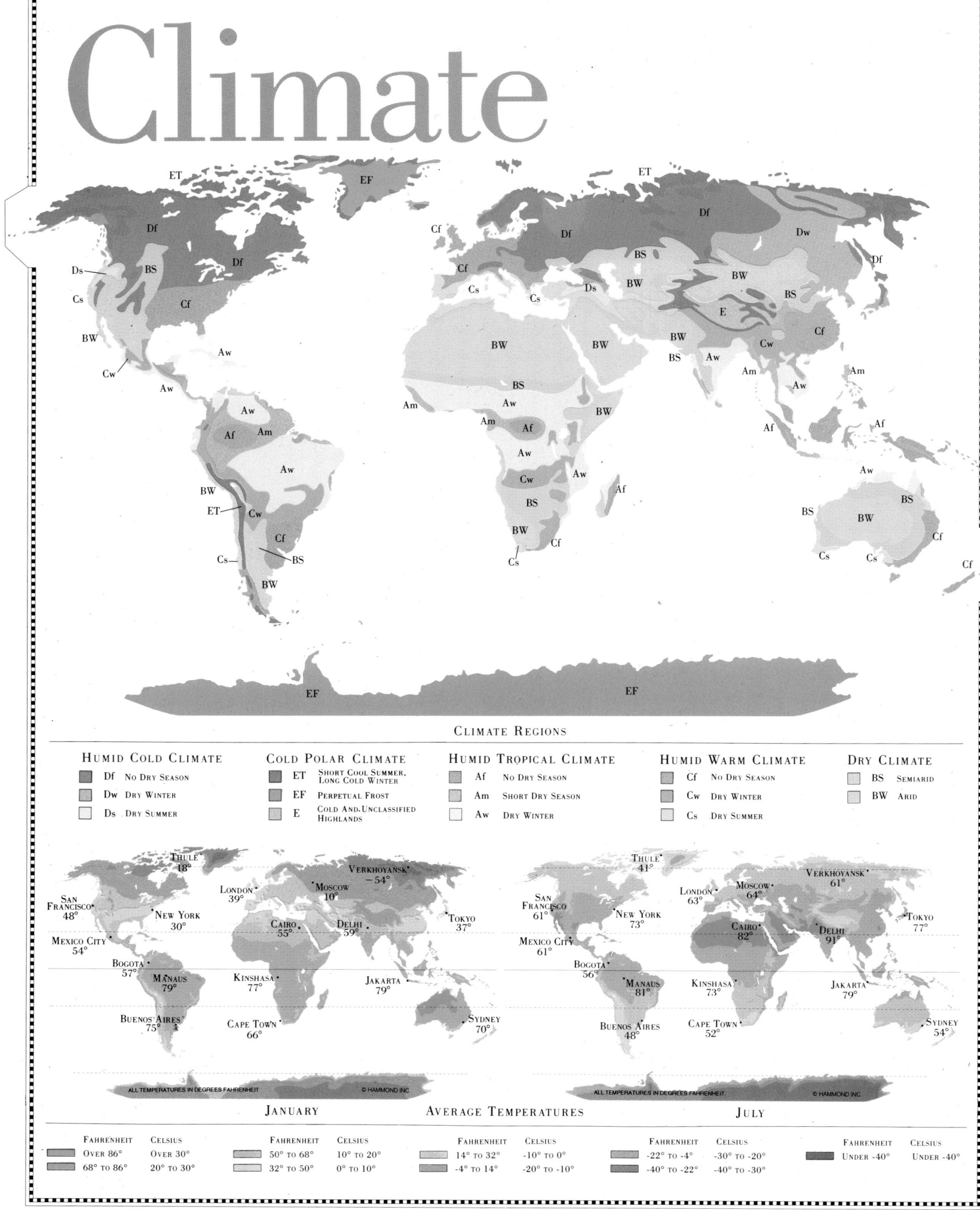

CLIMATE REGIONS

HUMID COLD CLIMATE		COLD POLAR CLIMATE		HUMID TROPICAL CLIMATE		HUMID WARM CLIMATE		DRY CLIMATE	
Df	No Dry Season	ET	Short Cool Summer, Long Cold Winter	Af	No Dry Season	Cf	No Dry Season	BS	Semiarid
Dw	Dry Winter	EF	Perpetual Frost	Am	Short Dry Season	Cw	Dry Winter	BW	Arid
Ds	Dry Summer	E	Cold And Unclassified Highlands	Aw	Dry Winter	Cs	Dry Summer		

JANUARY   AVERAGE TEMPERATURES   **JULY**

ALL TEMPERATURES IN DEGREES FAHRENHEIT   © HAMMOND INC

FAHRENHEIT	CELSIUS	FAHRENHEIT	CELSIUS	FAHRENHEIT	CELSIUS	FAHRENHEIT	CELSIUS	FAHRENHEIT	CELSIUS
Over 86°	Over 30°	50° to 68°	10° to 20°	14° to 32°	-10° to 0°	-22° to -4°	-30° to -20°	Under -40°	Under -40°
68° to 86°	20° to 30°	32° to 50°	0° to 10°	-4° to 14°	-20° to -10°	-40° to -22°	-40° to -30°		

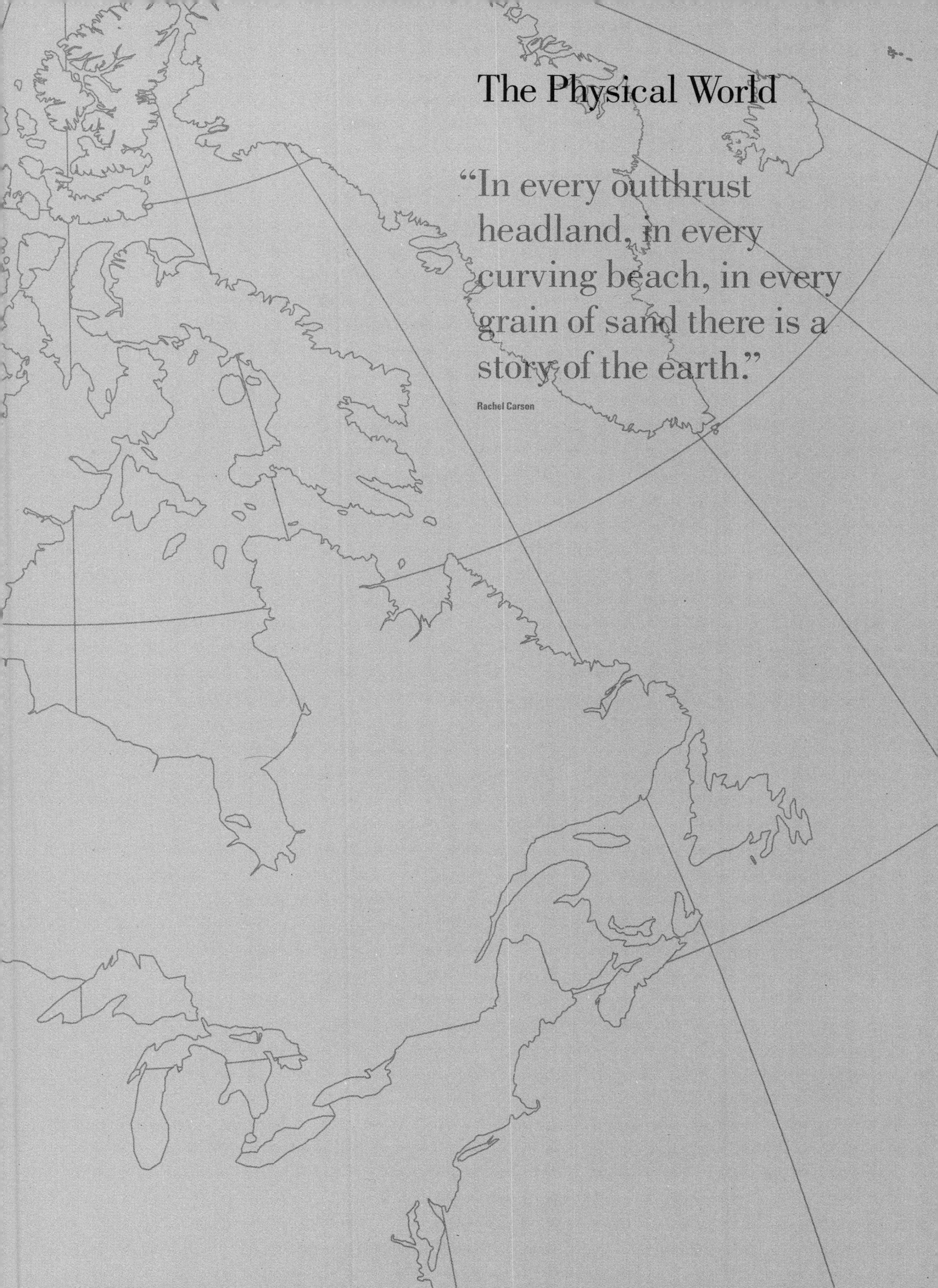

The Physical World

"In every outthrust headland, in every curving beach, in every grain of sand there is a story of the earth."

Rachel Carson

ARCTIC OCEAN

QUEEN ELIZABETH
ISLANDS

Ellesmere I.

GREENLAND

CANADA
BASIN

Beaufort Sea

Devon I.

Baffin

Wrangel I.

Pt. Barrow

Banks I.

Victoria I.

Baffin
Island

Bay

Arctic Circle

Chukchi
Sea

Yukon

Mt. McKinley

Mac Kenzie

Great
Bear L.

Denmark Str.

Iceland

Great
Britain

Bering Sea

ROCKY

Peace

Great
Slave L.

Hudson
Bay

LABRADOR
BASIN

IRMINGER BASIN

ICELAND BASIN

ALEUTIAN
BASIN
ALEUTIAN ISLANDS

Gulf of Alaska

MOUNTAINS

N O R T H

Ireland

ALEUTIAN TRENCH

Great

Plains

A M E R I C A

Great
Lakes

Appalachian Mts.

CHARLIE-GIBBS
FRACTURE ZONE

Newfoundland

C. Race

MENDOCINO FRACTURE ZONE

C. Mendocino

Missouri

Ohio

Mississippi

Colorado

A T L A N T I C

HAWAIIAN
ISLANDS

MOLOKAI FRACTURE ZONE

Lower

Rio

Grande

C. Hatteras

HAWAIIAN RIDGE

Tropic of Cancer

California

Gulf of
Mexico

WEST

▼ -28,232 ft.
(- 8605 m)

Cuba

CENTRAL

CLIPPERTON FRACTURE ZONE

Caribbean
Sea

INDIES

C. Verde

PACIFIC

P A C I F I C

GUATEMALA
BASIN

Orinoco

BASIN

Equator

Negro

Amazon

ROMANCHE FRACTURE ZONE

C. de São Roque

O C E A N

Madeira

PERU-CHILE TRENCH

San Francisco

S O U T H

BRAZIL

MID-ATLANTIC RIDGE

PERU
BASIN

A M E R I C A

BASIN

O C E A

TONGA
TRENCH

Tropic of Capricorn

-26,457 ft.
(- 8064 m)

NAZCA RIDGE

CHILE
BASIN

Paraná

Cerro
Aconcagua

ANDES MOUNTAINS

S O U T H W E S T

KERMADEC
TRENCH

P A C I F I C

ARGENTINE

BASIN

B A S I N

E A S T

P A C I F I C

R I S E

PERU-CHILE TRENCH

Falkland Is.

Tierra del Fuego

-27,313 ft.
(- 8325 m)

SOUTH
SANDWICH
TRENCH

C. Horn

Drake Passage

PACIFIC-ANTARCTIC RIDGE

Antarctic Circle

AMUNDSEN ABYSSAL PLAIN

Antarctic
Peninsula

W E D D E L L

ABYSSAL PLAIN

Bellingshausen
Sea

W e d d e l l

S e a

Ross Sea

A N T A R C T I C A

World

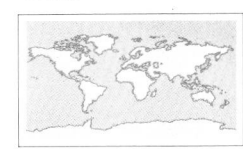

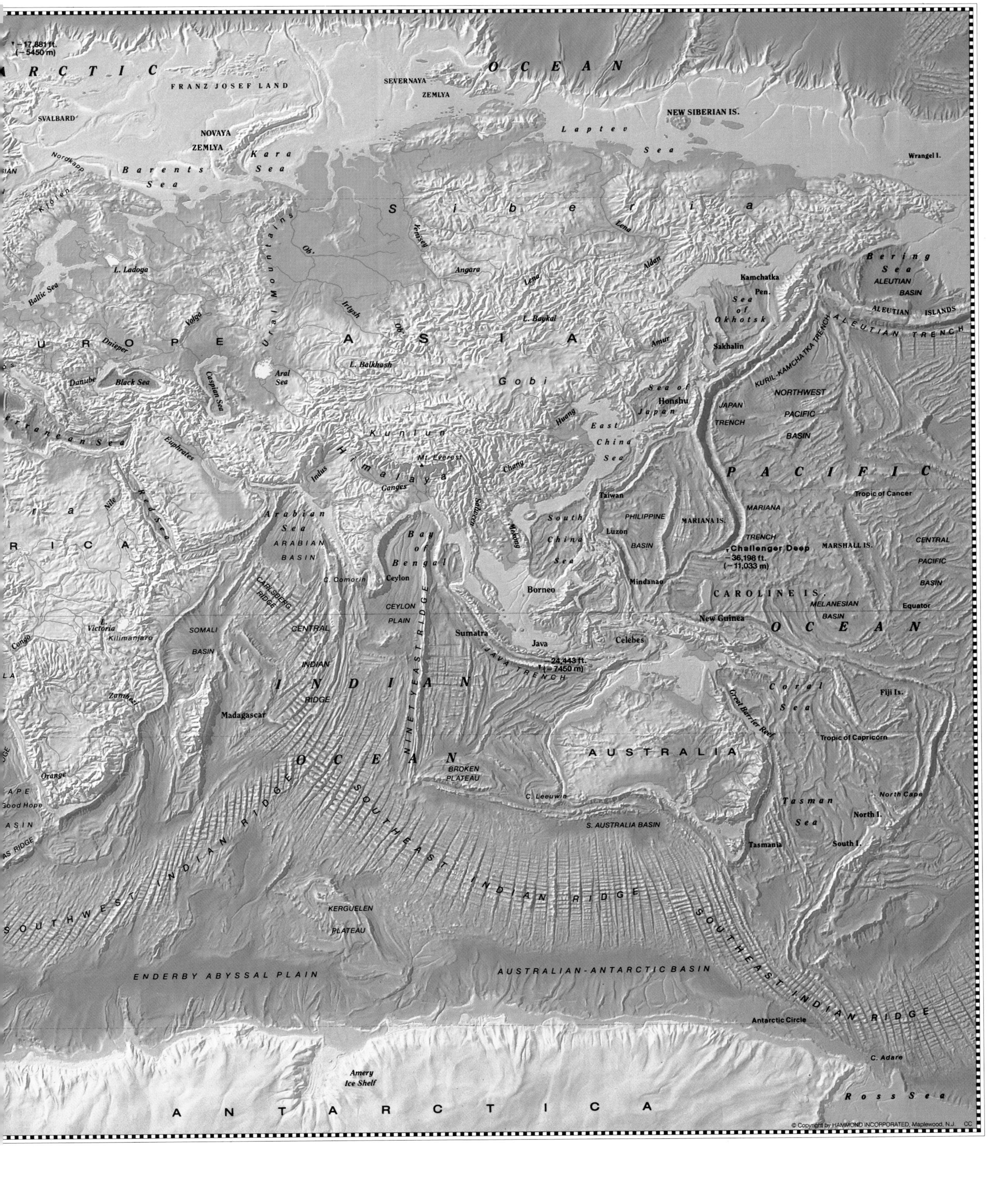

' = 17,881 ft.
(= 5450 m)

A R C T I C — O C E A N

FRANZ JOSEF LAND

SVALBARD

Nordkapp

SEVERNAYA
ZEMLYA

NEW SIBERIAN IS.

Laptev

Sea

Wrangel I.

NOVAYA
ZEMLYA

Kara
Sea

B a r e n t s
S e a

Kjölen

S i b e r i a

B e r i n g
S e a

ALEUTIAN
BASIN

ALEUTIAN   ISLANDS

L. Ladoga

Ob.

Yenisei

Angara

Lena

Aldan

Kamchatka
Pen.

Sea
of
Okhotsk

KURIL-KAMCHATKA TRENCH

ALEUTIAN   TRENCH

Baltic Sea

Volga

Irtysh

Ob.

L. Baykal

Amur

Sakhalin

NORTHWEST

E U R O P E

Dnieper

Caspian Sea

Aral
Sea

L. Balkhash

G o b i

PACIFIC

BASIN

Danube

Black Sea

Euphrates

K u n l u n

Huang

Honshu
Japan

JAPAN
TRENCH

P A C I F I C

A S I A

Nile

Red Sea

H i m
a l a y a

Mt. Everest

Chang

East
China
Sea

Taiwan

MARIANA

Tropic of Cancer

Indus

Ganges

Salween

Mekong

South
China
Sea

Luzon

MARIANA IS.

TRENCH

MARSHALL IS.

CENTRAL

Arabian
Sea

ARABIAN
BASIN

PHILIPPINE
BASIN

Challenger Deep
−36,198 ft.
(−11,033 m)

PACIFIC

A F R I C A

CARLSBERG
RIDGE

C. Comorin

Ceylon

Mindanao

BASIN

R I C A

CEYLON

PLAIN

Borneo

CAROLINE IS.

L.
Victoria
Kilimanjaro

SOMALI

BASIN

CENTRAL

Sumatra

Java

MELANESIAN

New Guinea

Equator

BASIN

Congo

INDIAN

RIDGE

JAVA TRENCH

24,443 ft.
(= 7450 m)

Celebes

O C E A N

Zambezi

I N D I A N

Coral
Sea

Fiji Is.

Madagascar

NINETYEAST RIDGE

AUSTRALIA

Tropic of Capricorn

Orange

O C E A N

BROKEN
PLATEAU

Tasman
Sea

North Cape

Good Hope

S O U T H W E S T   I N D I A N   R I D G E

S O U T H E A S T   I N D I A N   R I D G E

C. Leeuwin

S. AUSTRALIA BASIN

North I.

South I.

Tasmania

KERGUELEN

PLATEAU

S O U T H E A S T   I N D I A N   R I D G E

ENDERBY ABYSSAL PLAIN

AUSTRALIAN-ANTARCTIC BASIN

Antarctic Circle

C. Adare

Amery
Ice Shelf

R o s s   S e a

A N T A R C T I C A

Europe

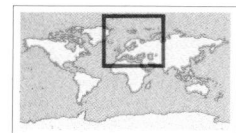

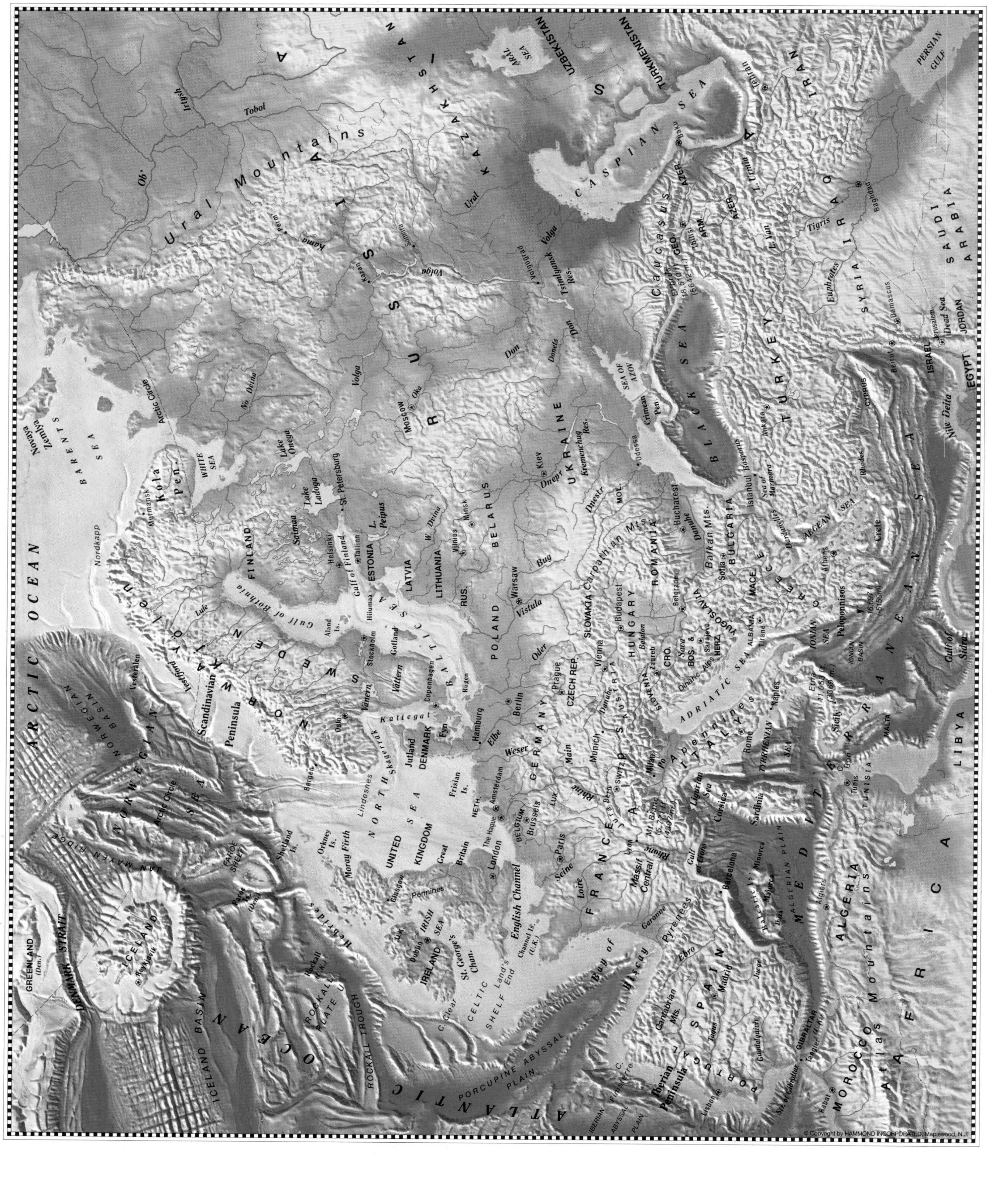

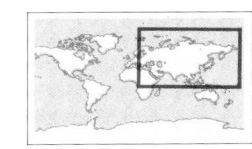

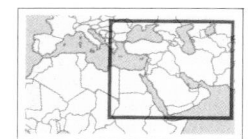

Near and Middle East

RUSSIA

Syrdar'ya

Tashkent

Kyzyl-Kum Desert

UZBEKISTAN

Amudar'ya

Murgab

TURKMENISTAN

Kara-Kum Desert

Ashkhabad

Meshed

Herirud

Harirud

KAZAKHSTAN

Ust'-Urt Plateau

Gulf of Kara-Bogaz

ARAL SEA

Mangyshlak Pen.

CASPIAN SEA

Baku

-3264 ft. (-995 m)

Rasht

Qareh

Tehran

Elburz Mts.

Dom

Damavand 18,376 ft. (5601 m)

Dasht-e Kavir

Plateau

Isfahan

IRAN

AFGHANISTAN

Kabul

Tarnak

Helmand

Farah

PAKISTAN

Indus

Hari Rud

Dasht

Dasht-e Lut

Kerman

Shur

Zahedan

Karachi

MAKRAN RIDGE

INDUS CONE

OWEN FRACTURE ZONE

OMAN BASIN

Gulf of Oman

Ras al Hadd

Masira

Str. of Hormuz

Qeshm

Muscat

Jeb. Akhdar

O M A N

Kuria Muria Is.

Ras Fartak

16,864 ft. (5143 m)

WEST SHEBA RIDGE

Socotra (Yemen)

RUSSIA

Kuban

Terek

Grozny

GEORGIA'S MTS.

El'brus 18,481 ft. (5633 m)

Tbilisi

ARMENIA

AZERBAIJAN

Kura

Sevan

Yerevan

AZER.

Mt. Ararat 16,804 ft. (5165 m)

L. Urmia

Tabriz

L. Van

Zagros Mountains

Karun

Abadan

Shiraz

Wadi

UNITED ARAB EMIRATES

Abu Dhabi

Doha

QATAR

BAHRAIN

Persian Gulf

Al Kuwait

KUWAIT

Riyadh

Tuwaiq

Summan

Rub' al Khali

YEMEN

Aden

ETHIOPIA

ERITREA

Asmara

Dahlak Arch.

Farasan Is.

Ras Dashen 15,157 ft. (4620 m)

L. Tana

DJIBOUTI

BLACK SEA

-7254 ft. (-221 m)

UKR

Yalta

Bosporus

Istanbul

Sea of Marmara

Bursa

Pontic Mts.

Samsun

Sakarya

Plateau of

Ankara

Anatolia

Kizilirmak

Tuz

Kayseri

TURKEY

Taurus Mts.

Murat

Tigris

Euphrates

SYRIA

Gaziantep

Aleppo

Homs

Mosul

Baghdad

Tigris

Euphrates

IRAQ

Al Hasa

Basra

An Nafud

Jebel Shammar

SAUDI ARABIA

Medina

Mecca

8645 ft. (2635 m)

Midian

RED SEA

Port Sudan

ROMANIA

Danube

BULGARIA

YUGOSLAVIA

ALBANIA MACEDONIA

GREECE

Olympus 9570 ft. (2917 m)

Peloponnesos

Athens

Evvoia

AEGEAN SEA

Izmir

RHODES

Crete

16,880 ft. (5150 m)

MEDITERRANEAN RIDGE

CYPRUS BASIN

MEDITERRANEAN SEA

Nicosia

CYPRUS

LEBANON

Beirut

Damascus

ISRAEL

Tel Aviv-Jaffa

Jerusalem

Amman

JORDAN

Dead Sea

Syrian Desert

Gulf of Aqaba

Jebel Musa Muhammad

Sinai Pen.

Gulf of Suez

Suez Canal

Suez

Port Said

Cairo

Alexandria

Qattara Depression

Nile

Asyut

EGYPT

LIBYA

Libyan Desert

Arabian Desert

Aswan

L. Nubia

Lake Nasser

Nubian Desert

Atbara

Nile

Blue Nile

White Nile

Khartoum

SUDAN

CHAD

Tropic of Cancer

Southern Asia

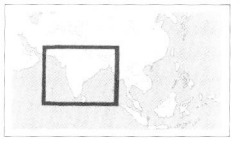

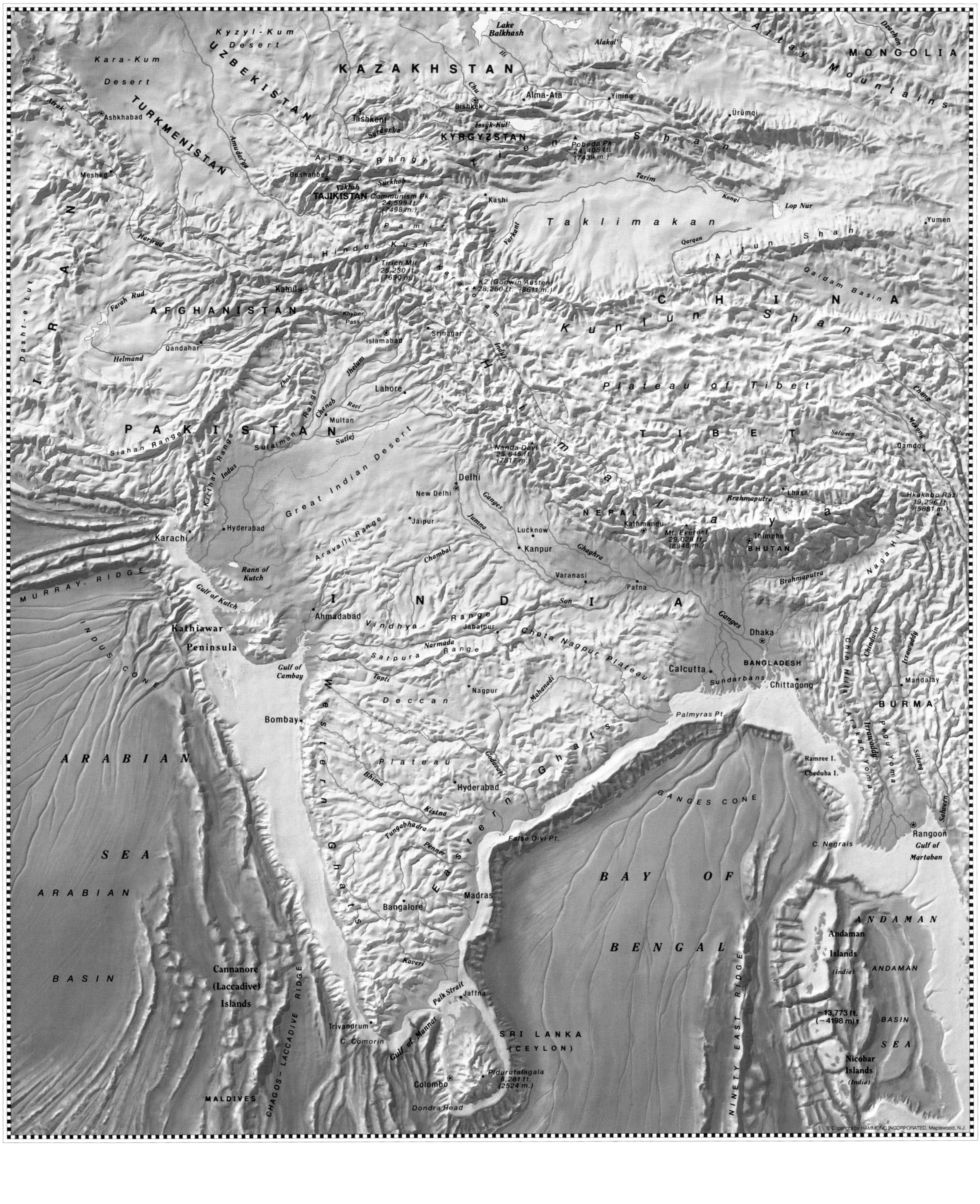

Kyzyl-Kum
Desert

Kara-Kum
Desert

UZBEKISTAN

Lake
Balkhash

Alakol

KAZAKHSTAN

MONGOLIA

Altay Mountains

Dzhun

TURKMENISTAN

Ashkhabad

Il

Alma-Ata

Yining

Bishkek

Issyk-Kul'

KYRGYZSTAN

Tien Shan

Ürümqi

Meshed

Amu darya

Tashkent

Syr darya

Chu

Pobeda Pk.
24,406 ft.
(7439 m.)

Tarim

Lop Nur

Yumen

Alay Range

Surkhob

Kashi

Tarim

Kongi

IRAN

Harirud

Dushanbe

Yakhsh

Surkhob

TAJIKISTAN

Communism Pk.
24,599 ft.
(7498 m.)

Taklimakan

Qarqan

Altun Shan

Qaidam Basin

Dasht-i-Lut

Pamir

Hindu Kush

Yarkent

Kashi

CHINA

Farah Rud

Tirich Mir
25,230 ft.
(7690 m.)

K2 (Godwin Austen)
28,250 ft. (8611 m.)

Kabul

AFGHANISTAN

Khyber
Pass

Srinagar

Islamabad

Kunlun Shan

Plateau of Tibet

Chang

Qandahar

Helmand

Jhelum

Lahore

TIBET

Salween

Damdo

Zhob

Indus

Kabul

Murray Ridge

Siahan Range

Kirthar Range

Sulaiman Range

Multan

Chenab

Ravi

Sutlej

Himalaya

Nanda Devi
25,645 ft.
(7817 m.)

Hkakabo Razi
19,296 ft.
(5881 m.)

PAKISTAN

Great Indian Desert

New Delhi

Delhi

Ganges

NEPAL

Brahmaputra

Lhasa

Karachi

Hyderabad

Jaipur

Jumna

Lucknow

Kanpur

Kathmandu

Mt. Everest
29,028 ft.
(8848 m.)

Thimphu

BHUTAN

Nagahills

INDIA

Chambal

Ghaghra

Son

Varanasi

Patna

Brahmaputra

Chindwin

Irrawaddy

Rann of
Kutch

Aravalli Range

Ganges

Dhaka

Gulf of
Kutch

Kathiawar
Peninsula

Ahmadabad

Vindhya   Range

Jabalpur

Chota Nagpur Plateau

Calcutta

BANGLADESH

Chin Hills

Arakan Yoma

INDUS CONE

Narmada

Satpura   Range

Sunderbans

Chittagong

Gulf of
Cambay

Tapti

Deccan

Nagpur

Mahanadi

Pegu Yoma

BURMA

Mandalay

Bombay

Western Ghats

Plateau

Bhima

Hyderabad

Eastern Ghats

Mohanadi

Palmyras Pt.

GANGES CONE

Ramree I.

Cheduba I.

Salween

ARABIAN

Kistna

Godavari

Sittang

SEA

Tungabhadra

Penner

False Divi Pt.

BAY   OF

C. Negrais

Rangoon

Gulf of
Martaban

ARABIAN

BASIN

Bangalore

Madras

BENGAL

ANDAMAN

Cannanore
(Laccadive)
Islands

Kaveri

Andaman
Islands
(India)

ANDAMAN

NINETY EAST RIDGE

Polk Strait

Jaffna

BASIN

SEA

CHAGOS - LACCADIVE RIDGE

Trivandrum

C. Comorin

Gulf of
Mannar

SRI LANKA
(CEYLON)

-13,773 ft.
(-4198 m.)

Nicobar
Islands
(India)

MALDIVES

Colombo

Pidurutalagala
8,281 ft.
(2524 m.)

Dondra Head

East Asia

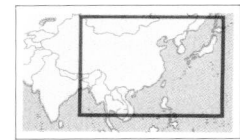

Australia and Pacific Ocean

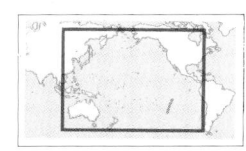

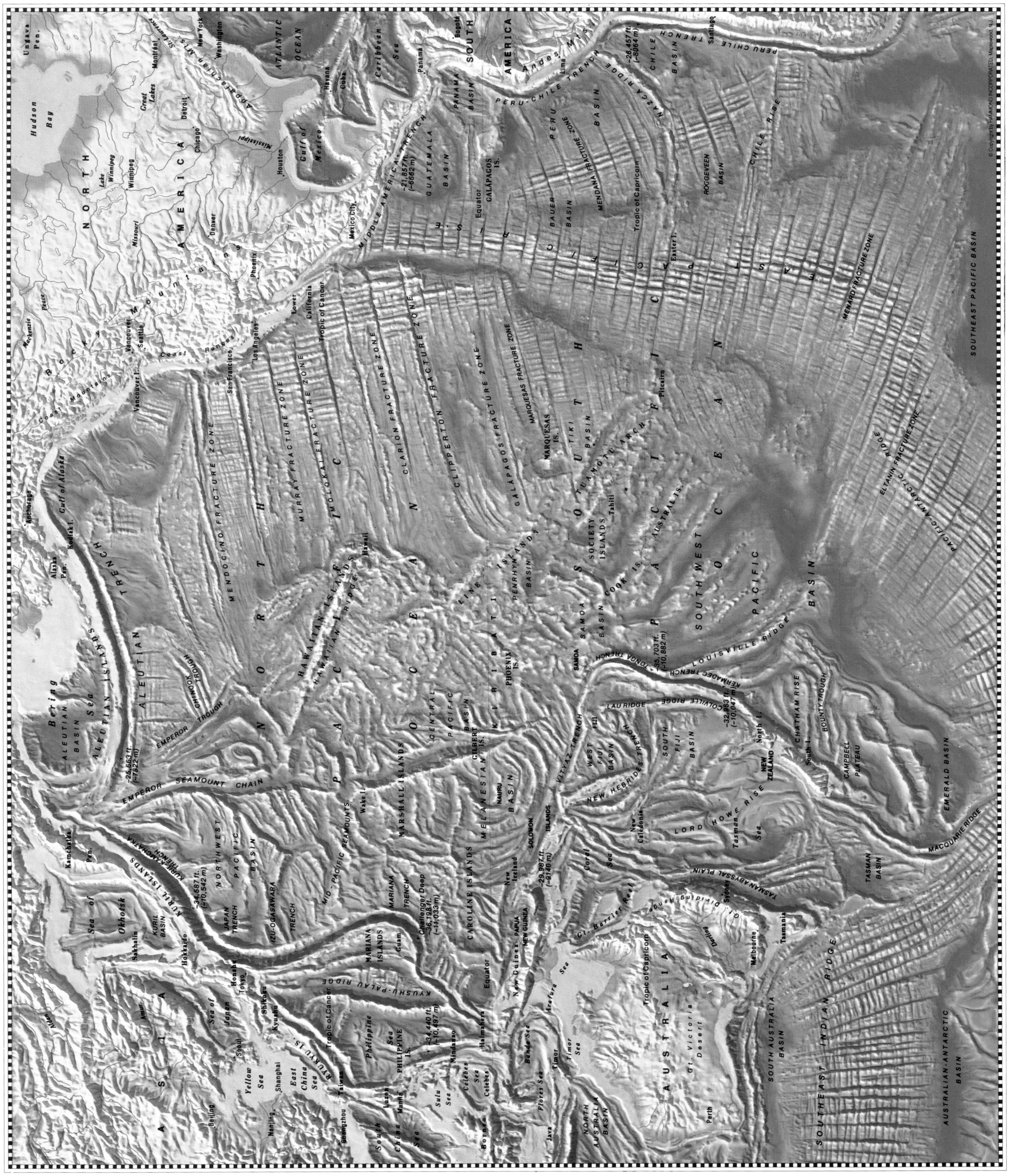

Africa

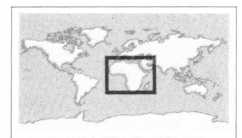

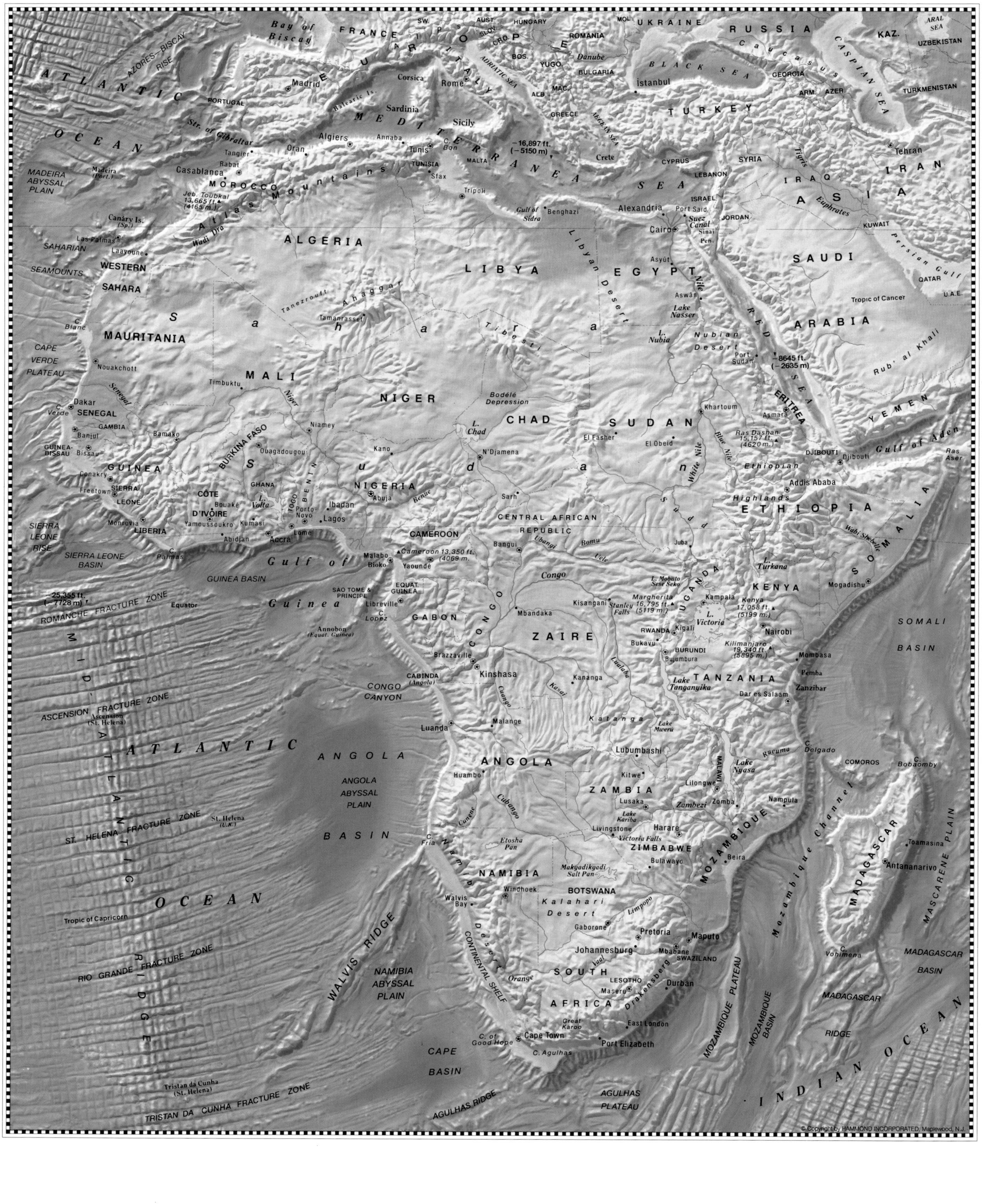

South America

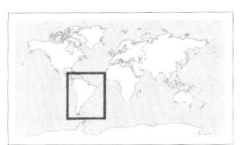

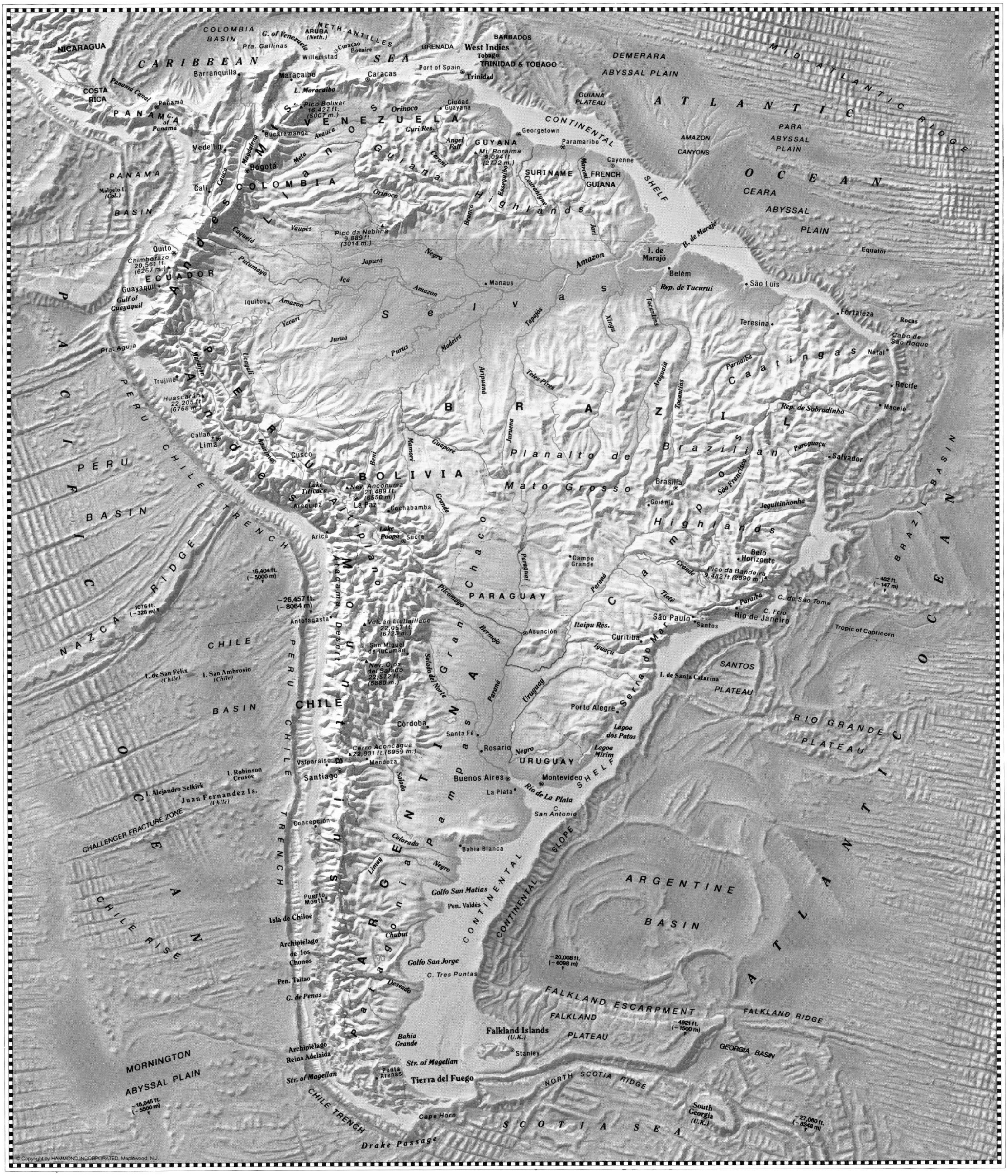

North America

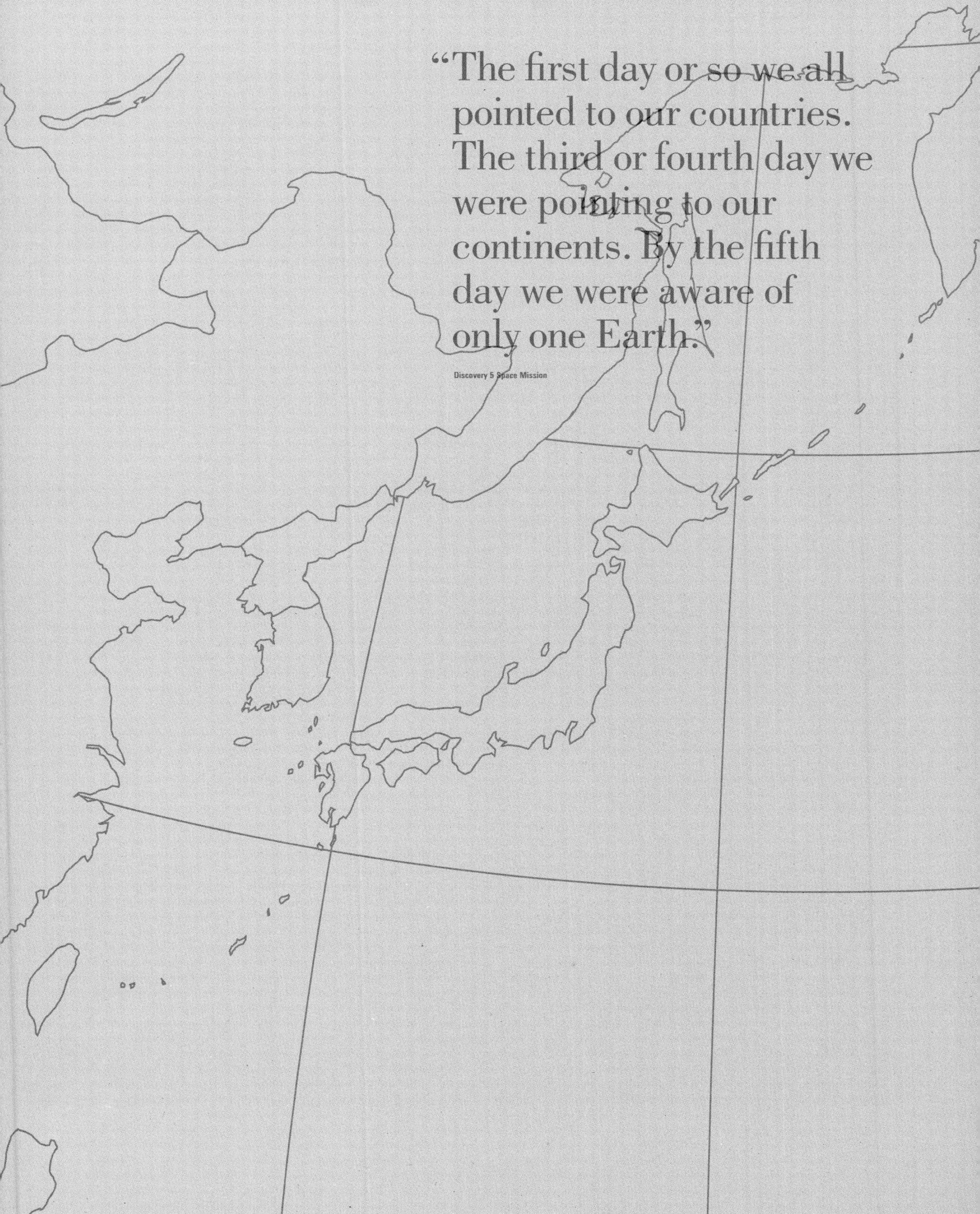

Geographic Comparisons

"The first day or so we all pointed to our countries. The third or fourth day we were pointing to our continents. By the fifth day we were aware of only one Earth."

Discovery 5 Space Mission

World Statistics

ELEMENTS OF THE SOLAR SYSTEM

	Mean Distance from Sun: in Miles	in Kilometers	Period of Revolution around Sun	Period of Rotation on Axis	Equatorial Diameter in Miles	in Kilometers	Surface Gravity (Earth = 1)	Mass (Earth = 1)	Mean Density (Water = 1)	Number of Satellites
Mercury	35,990,000	57,900,000	87.97 days	59 days	3,032	4,880	0.38	0.055	5.5	
Venus	67,240,000	108,200,000	224.70 days	243 days†	7,523	12,106	0.90	0.815	5.25	
Earth	93,000,000	149,700,000	365.26 days	23h 56m	7,926	12,755	1.00	1.00	5.5	
Mars	141,730,000	228,100,000	687.00 days	24h 37m	4,220	6,790	0.38	0.107	4.0	
Jupiter	483,880,000	778,700,000	11.86 years	9h 50m	88,750	142,800	2.87	317.9	1.3	1
Saturn	887,130,000	1,427,700,000	29.46 years	10h 39m	74,580	120,020	1.32	95.2	0.7	2
Uranus	1,783,700,000	2,870,500,000	84.01 years	17h 24m†	31,600	50,900	0.93	14.6	1.3	1
Neptune	2,795,500,000	4,498,800,000	164.79 years	17h 50m	30,200	48,600	1.23	17.2	1.8	
Pluto	3,667,900,000	5,902,800,000	247.70 years	6.39 days(?)	1,500	2,400	0.03(?)	0.01(?)	0.7(?)	

† Retrograde motion

DIMENSIONS OF THE EARTH

	Area in: Sq. Miles	Sq. Kilometers
Superficial area	196,939,000	510,073,000
Land surface	57,506,000	148,941,000
Water surface	139,433,000	361,132,000

	Distance in: Miles	Kilometers
Equatorial circumference	24,902	40,075
Polar circumference	24,860	40,007
Equatorial diameter	7,926.4	12,756.4
Polar diameter	7,899.8	12,713.6
Equatorial radius	3,963.2	6,378.2
Polar radius	3,949.9	6,356.8

Volume of the Earth	2.6 x 10^{11} cubic miles	10.84 x 10^{11} cubic kilometers
Mass or weight	6.6 x 10^{21} short tons	6.0 x 10^{21} metric tons
Maximum distance from Sun	94,600,000 miles	152,000,000 kilometers
Minimum distance from Sun	91,300,000 miles	147,000,000 kilometers

OCEANS AND MAJOR SEAS

	Area in: Sq. Miles	Sq. Kms.	Greatest Depth in: Feet	Meters
Pacific Ocean	64,186,000	166,241,700	36,198	11,033
Atlantic Ocean	31,862,000	82,522,600	28,374	8,648
Indian Ocean	28,350,000	73,426,500	25,344	7,725
Arctic Ocean	5,427,000	14,056,000	17,880	5,450
Caribbean Sea	970,000	2,512,300	24,720	7,535
Mediterranean Sea	969,000	2,509,700	16,896	5,150
South China Sea	895,000	2,318,000	15,000	4,600
Bering Sea	875,000	2,266,250	15,800	4,800
Gulf of Mexico	600,000	1,554,000	12,300	3,750
Sea of Okhotsk	590,000	1,528,100	11,070	3,370
East China Sea	482,000	1,248,400	9,500	2,900
Yellow Sea	480,000	1,243,200	350	107
Sea of Japan	389,000	1,007,500	12,280	3,743
Hudson Bay	317,500	822,300	846	258
North Sea	222,000	575,000	2,200	671
Black Sea	185,000	479,150	7,365	2,245
Red Sea	169,000	437,700	7,200	2,195
Baltic Sea	163,000	422,170	1,506	459

THE CONTINENTS

	Area in: Sq. Miles	Sq. Kms.	Percent of World's Land
Asia	17,128,500	44,362,815	29.5
Africa	11,707,000	30,321,130	20.2
North America	9,363,000	24,250,170	16.2
South America	6,875,000	17,806,250	11.8
Antarctica	5,500,000	14,245,000	9.5
Europe	4,057,000	10,507,630	7.0
Australia	2,966,136	7,682,300	5.1

MAJOR SHIP CANALS

	Length in: Miles	Kms.	Minimum Depth in: Feet	Meters
Volga-Baltic, Russia	225	362	–	–
Baltic-White Sea, Russia	140	225	16	5
Suez, Egypt	100.76	162	42	13
Albert, Belgium	80	129	16.5	5
Moscow-Volga, Russia	80	129	18	6
Volga-Don, Russia	62	100	–	–
Göta, Sweden	54	87	10	3
Kiel (Nord-Ostsee), Germany	53.2	86	38	12
Panama Canal, Panama	50.72	82	41.6	13
Houston Ship, U.S.A.	50	81	36	11

LARGEST ISLANDS

	Area in: Sq. Miles	Sq. Kms.
Greenland	840,000	2,175,600
New Guinea	305,000	789,950
Borneo	290,000	751,100
Madagascar	226,400	586,376
Baffin, Canada	195,928	507,454
Sumatra, Indonesia	164,000	424,760
Honshu, Japan	88,000	227,920
Great Britain	84,400	218,896
Victoria, Canada	83,896	217,290
Ellesmere, Canada	75,767	196,236
Celebes, Indonesia	72,986	189,034
South I., New Zealand	58,393	151,238
Java, Indonesia	48,842	126,501
North I., New Zealand	44,187	114,444
Newfoundland, Canada	42,031	108,860
Cuba	40,533	104,981
Luzon, Philippines	40,420	104,688
Iceland	39,768	103,000
Mindanao, Philippines	36,537	94,631
Ireland	31,743	82,214
Sakhalin, Russia	29,500	76,405
Hispaniola, Haiti & Dom. Rep.	29,399	76,143

	Area in: Sq. Miles	Sq. Kms.
Hokkaido, Japan	28,983	75,066
Banks, Canada	27,038	70,028
Ceylon, Sri Lanka	25,332	65,610
Tasmania, Australia	24,600	63,710
Svalbard, Norway	23,957	62,049
Devon, Canada	21,331	55,247
Novaya Zemlya (north isl.), Russia	18,600	48,200
Marajó, Brazil	17,991	46,597
Tierra del Fuego, Chile & Argentina	17,900	46,360
Alexander, Antarctica	16,700	43,250
Axel Heiberg, Canada	16,671	43,178
Melville, Canada	16,274	42,150
Southampton, Canada	15,913	41,215
New Britain, Papua New Guinea	14,100	36,519
Taiwan, China	13,836	35,835
Kyushu, Japan	13,770	35,664
Hainan, China	13,127	33,999
Prince of Wales, Canada	12,872	33,338
Spitsbergen, Norway	12,355	31,999
Vancouver, Canada	12,079	31,285
Timor, Indonesia	11,527	29,855
Sicily, Italy	9,926	25,708

	Area in: Sq. Miles	Sq. Kms.
Somerset, Canada	9,570	24,786
Sardinia, Italy	9,301	24,090
Shikoku, Japan	6,860	17,767
New Caledonia, France	6,530	16,913
Nordaustlandet, Norway	6,409	16,599
Samar, Philippines	5,050	13,080
Negros, Philippines	4,906	12,707
Palawan, Philippines	4,550	11,785
Panay, Philippines	4,446	11,515
Jamaica	4,232	10,961
Hawaii, United States	4,038	10,458
Viti Levu, Fiji	4,010	10,386
Cape Breton, Canada	3,981	10,311
Mindoro, Philippines	3,759	9,736
Kodiak, Alaska, U.S.A.	3,670	9,505
Cyprus	3,572	9,251
Puerto Rico, U.S.A.	3,435	8,897
Corsica, France	3,352	8,682
New Ireland, Papua New Guinea	3,340	8,651
Crete, Greece	3,218	8,335
Anticosti, Canada	3,066	7,941
Wrangel, Russia	2,819	7,301

PRINCIPAL MOUNTAINS

	Height in : Feet	Meters		Height in : Feet	Meters		Height in : Feet	Meters
Everest, Nepal-China	29,028	8,848	Llullaillaco, Chile-Argentina	22,057	6,723	Blanc, France	15,771	4,807
K2 (Godwin Austen), Pakistan-China	28,250	8,611	Nevada Ancohuma, Bolivia	21,489	6,550	Klyuchevskaya Sopka, Russia	15,584	4,750
Makalu, Nepal-China	27,789	8,470	Chimborazo, Ecuador	20,561	6,267	Fairweather, Br. Col., Canada	15,300	4,663
Dhaulagiri, Nepal	26,810	8,172	McKinley, Alaska	20,320	6,194	Dufourspitze (Mte. Rosa), Italy-Switzerland	15,203	4,634
Nanga Parbat, Pakistan	26,660	8,126	Logan, Yukon, Canada	19,524	5,951	Ras Dashen, Ethiopia	15,157	4620
Annapurna, Nepal	26,504	8,078	Cotopaxi, Ecuador	19,347	5,897	Matterhorn, Switzerland	14,691	4,478
Rakaposhi, Pakistan	25,550	7,788	Kilimanjaro, Tanzania	19,340	5,895	Whitney, California, U.S.A.	14,494	4,418
Kongur Shan, China	25,325	7,719	El Misti, Peru	19,101	5,822	Elbert, Colorado, U.S.A.	14,433	4,399
Tirich Mir, Pakistan	25,230	7,690	Pico Cristóbal Colón, Colombia	18,947	5,775	Rainier, Washington, U.S.A.	14,410	4,392
Gongga Shan, China	24,790	7,556	Huila, Colombia	18,865	5,750	Shasta, California, U.S.A.	14,162	4,317
Communism Peak, Tajikistan	24,590	7,495	Citlaltépetl (Orizaba), Mexico	18,701	5,700	Pikes Peak, Colorado, U.S.A.	14,110	4,301
Pobedy Peak, Kyrgyzstan	24,406	7,439	Damavand, Iran	18,606	5,671	Finsteraarhorn, Switzerland	14,022	4,274
Chomo Lhari, Bhutan-China	23,997	7,314	El'brus, Russia	18,510	5,642	Mauna Kea, Hawaii, U.S.A.	13,796	4,205
Muztag, China	23,891	7,282	St. Elias, Alaska, U.S.A.-Yukon, Canada	18,008	5,489	Mauna Loa, Hawaii, U.S.A.	13,677	4,169
Cerro Aconcagua, Argentina	22,831	6,959	Dykh-tau, Russia	17,070	5,203	Jungfrau, Switzerland	13,642	4,158
Ojos del Salado, Chile-Argentina	22,572	6,880	Batian (Kenya), Kenya	17,058	5,199	Grossglockner, Austria	12,457	3,797
Bonete, Chile-Argentina	22,546	6,872	Ararat, Turkey	16,946	5,165	Fujiyama, Japan	12,389	3,776
Tupungato, Chile-Argentina	22,310	6,800	Vinson Massif, Antarctica	16,864	5,140	Cook, New Zealand	12,349	3,764
Pissis, Argentina	22,241	6,779	Margherita (Ruwenzori), Africa	16,795	5,119	Etna, Italy	10,902	3,323
Mercedario, Argentina	22,211	6,770	Kazbek, Georgia-Russia	16,558	5,047	Kosciusko, Australia	7,310	2,228
Huascarán, Peru	22,205	6,768	Puncak Jaya, Indonesia	16,503	5,030	Mitchell, North Carolina, U.S.A.	6,684	2,037

LONGEST RIVERS

	Length in : Miles	Kms.		Length in : Miles	Kms.		Length in : Miles	Kms.
Nile, Africa	4,145	6,671	Indus, Asia	1,800	2,897	Don, Russia	1,222	1,967
Amazon, S. America	3,915	6,300	Danube, Europe	1,775	2,857	Red, U.S.A.	1,222	1,966
Chang Jiang (Yangtze), China	3,900	6,276	Salween, Asia	1,770	2,849	Columbia, U.S.A.-Canada	1,214	1,953
Mississippi-Missouri-Red Rock, U.S.A.	3,741	6,019	Brahmaputra, Asia	1,700	2,736	Saskatchewan, Canada	1,205	1,939
Ob'-Irtysh-Black Irtysh, Russia-Kazakhstan	3,362	5,411	Euphrates, Asia	1,700	2,736	Peace-Finlay, Canada	1,195	1,923
Yenisey-Angara, Russia	3,100	4,989	Tocantins, Brazil	1,677	2,699	Tigris, Asia	1,181	1,901
Huang He (Yellow), China	2,877	4,630	Xi (Si), China	1,650	2,601	Darling, Australia	1,160	1,867
Amur-Shilka-Onon, Asia	2,744	4,416	Amudar'ya, Asia	1,616	2,601	Angara, Russia	1,135	1,827
Lena, Russia	2,734	4,400	Nelson-Saskatchewan, Canada	1,600	2,575	Sungari, Asia	1,130	1,819
Congo (Zaire), Africa	2,718	4,374	Orinoco, S. America	1,600	2,575	Pechora, Russia	1,124	1,809
Mackenzie-Peace-Finlay,Canada	2,635	4,241	Zambezi, Africa	1,600	2,575	Snake, U.S.A.	1,038	1,670
Mekong, Asia	2,610	4,200	Paraguay, S. America	1,584	2,549	Churchill, Canada	1,000	1,609
Missouri-Red Rock, U.S.A.	2,564	4,125	Kolyma, Russia	1,562	2,514	Pilcomayo, S. America	1,000	1,609
Niger, Africa	2,548	4,101	Ganges, Asia	1,550	2,494	Uruguay, S. America	994	1,600
Paraná-La Plata, S. America	2,450	3,943	Ural, Russia-Kazakhstan	1,509	2,428	Platte-N. Platte, U.S.A.	990	1,593
Mississippi, U.S.A.	2,348	3,778	Japurá, S. America	1,500	2,414	Ohio, U.S.A.	981	1,578
Murray-Darling, Australia	2,310	3,718	Arkansas, U.S.A.	1,450	2,334	Magdalena, Colombia	956	1,538
Volga, Russia	2,194	3,531	Colorado, U.S.A.-Mexico	1,450	2,334	Pecos, U.S.A.	926	1,490
Madeira, S. America	2,013	3,240	Negro, S. America	1,400	2,253	Oka, Russia	918	1,477
Purus, S. America	1,995	3,211	Dnieper, Russia-Belarus-Ukraine	1,368	2,202	Canadian, U.S.A.	906	1,458
Yukon, Alaska-Canada	1,979	3,185	Orange, Africa	1,350	2,173	Colorado, Texas, U.S.A.	894	1,439
St. Lawrence, Canada-U.S.A.	1,900	3,058	Irrawaddy, Burma	1,325	2,132	Dniester, Ukraine-Moldova	876	1,410
Rio Grande, Mexico-U.S.A.	1,885	3,034	Brazos, U.S.A.	1,309	2,107	Fraser, Canada	850	1,369
Syrdar'ya-Naryn, Asia	1,859	2,992	Ohio-Allegheny, U.S.A.	1,306	2,102	Rhine, Europe	820	1,319
São Francisco, Brazil	1,811	2,914	Kama, Russia	1,252	2,031	Northern Dvina, Russia	809	1,302

PRINCIPAL NATURAL LAKES

	Area in: Sq. Miles	Sq. Kms.	Max. Depth in: Feet	Meters		Area in: Sq. Miles	Sq. Kms.	Max. Depth in: Feet	Meters
Caspian Sea, Asia	143,243	370,999	3,264	995	Lake Eyre, Australia	3,500-0	9,000-0	–	–
Lake Superior, U.S.A.-Canada	31,820	82,414	1,329	405	Lake Titicaca, Peru-Bolivia	3,200	8,288	1,000	305
Lake Victoria, Africa	26,724	69,215	270	82	Lake Nicaragua, Nicaragua	3,100	8,029	230	70
Lake Huron, U.S.A.-Canada	23,010	59,596	748	228	Lake Athabasca, Canada	3,064	7,936	400	122
Lake Michigan, U.S.A.	22,400	58,016	923	281	Reindeer Lake, Canada	2,568	6,651	–	–
Aral Sea, Kazakhstan-Uzbekistan	15,830	41,000	213	65	Lake Turkana (Rudolf), Africa	2,463	6,379	240	73
Lake Tanganyika, Africa	12,650	32,764	4,700	1,433	Issyk-Kul', Kyrgyzstan	2,425	6,281	2,303	702
Lake Baykal, Russia	12,162	31,500	5,316	1,620	Lake Torrens, Australia	2,230	5,776	–	–
Great Bear Lake, Canada	12,096	31,328	1,356	413	Vänern, Sweden	2,156	5,584	328	100
Lake Nyasa (Malawi), Africa	11,555	29,928	2,320	707	Nettilling Lake, Canada	2,140	5,543	–	–
Great Slave Lake, Canada	11,031	28,570	2,015	614	Lake Winnipegosis, Canada	2,075	5,374	38	12
Lake Erie, U.S.A.-Canada	9,940	25,745	210	64	Lake Mobutu Sese Seko (Albert), Africa	2,075	5,374	160	49
Lake Winnipeg, Canada	9,417	24,390	60	18	Kariba Lake, Zambia-Zimbabwe	2,050	5,310	295	90
Lake Ontario, U.S.A.-Canada	7,540	19,529	775	244	Lake Nipigon, Canada	1,872	4,848	540	165
Lake Ladoga, Russia	7,104	18,399	738	225	Lake Mweru, Zaire-Zambia	1,800	4,662	60	18
Lake Balkhash, Kazakhstan	7,027	18,200	87	27	Lake Manitoba, Canada	1,799	4,659	12	4
Lake Maracaibo, Venezuela	5,120	13,261	100	31	Lake Taymyr, Russia	1,737	4,499	85	26
Lake Chad, Africa	4,000 –	10,360 –			Lake Khanka, China-Russia	1,700	4,403	33	10
	10,000	25,900	25	8	Lake Kioga, Uganda	1,700	4,403	25	8
Lake Onega, Russia	3,710	9,609	377	115	Lake of the Woods, U.S.A.-Canada	1,679	4,349	70	21

Time Zones of the World

30° E	45° E	60° E	75° E	90° E	105° E	120° E	135° E	150° E	165° E	180°
2 P.M.	3 P.M.	4 P.M.	5 P.M.	6 P.M.	7 P.M.	8 P.M.	9 P.M.	10 P.M.	11 P.M.	MIDNIGHT	1 A.M.

| 2 P.M. | 3 P.M. | 4 P.M. | 5 P.M. | 6 P.M. | 7 P.M. | 8 P.M. | 9 P.M | 10 P.M. | 11 P.M. | MIDNIGHT | 1 A.M. |

Population of Major Cities

The following pages include population figures for all cities with more than 100,000 inhabitants, and for all national capitals, regardless of size. Cities are listed alphabetically, and grouped alphabetically by country. Three dependencies, Hong Kong, Macau and Puerto Rico, follow the country listing. Capitals are indicated with an asterisk (*). The population figures, given in thousands, represent the most current information available.

Country / City	Population in thousands
A Afghanistan	
Herāt	177
Kābul*	1,424
Mazār-e Sharīf	131
Qandahar	226
Albania	
Tiranë*	171
Algeria	
Algiers*	1,688
Annaba	228
Batna	185
Bechar	107
Bejaïa	118
Biskra	130
Blida	132
Chelif	130
Constantine	450
Mostaganem	115
Oran	599
Sétif	186
Sidi Bel-Abbes	155
Skikda	129
Tébessa	108
Tiaret	106
Tlemcen	108
Andorra	
Andorra la Vella*	12
Angola	
Luanda*	1,530
Antigua and Barbuda	
Saint John's*	22
Argentina	
Avellaneda	347
Bahía Blanca	240
Buenos Aires*	2,961
Concordia	116
Córdoba	1,148
Corrientes	258
Formosa	154
General San Martin	408
Godoy Cruz	179
Lanús	467
La Plata	520
La Rioja	104
Lomas de Zamora	573
Mar del Plata	512
Mendoza	122
Merlo	386
Morón	642
Neuquén	167
Paraná	207
Posadas	202
Resistencia	228
Río Cuarto	135
Rosario	895
Salta	367
San Fernando	110
San Juan	119
San Luis	110
San Miguel de Tucumán	471
San Nicolás de los Arroyos	115
San Salvador de Jujuy	181
Santa Fé	343
Santiago del Estero	189
Tigre	254
Vicente López	289
Armenia	
Kirovakan	146
Kumayri	120
Yerevan*	1,199
Australia	
Adelaide	978
Brisbane	1,149
Canberra*	247
Geelong	140
Gold Coast	135
Hobart	175
Melbourne	3,081
Newcastle	256
Perth	994
Sydney	3,656
Wollongong	207
Austria	
Graz	243
Innsbruck	116
Linz	198
Salzburg	138
Vienna*	1,540
Azerbaijan	
Baku*	1,150
Gyandzhe	278
Sumgait	231
B Bahamas	
Nassau*	135
Bahrain	
Manama*	109
Bangladesh	
Barisāl	159
Chittagong	1,388
Comilla	126
Dhākā*	3,459
Jessore	149
Khulna	623
Nārāyanganj	196
Pābna	101
Rājshāhi	172
Barbados	
Bridgetown*	7
Belarus	
Baranovichi	159
Bobruysk	223
Borisov	144
Brest	258
Gomel'	500
Grodno	270
Minsk*	1,589
Mogilëv	356
Mozyr'	101
Orsha	123
Pinsk	119
Vitebsk	350
Belgium	
Antwerp	186
Brugge	118
Brussels*	997
Charleroi	222
Ghent	239
Liège	214
Namur	102
Schaerbeek	107
Belize	
Belmopan*	3
Benin	
Cotonou	383
Porto-Novo*	144
Bhutan	
Thimphu*	12
Bolivia	
Cochabamba	205
La Paz*	635
Oruro	124
Santa Cruz	255
Sucre*	64
Bosnia & Herzegovina	
Banja Luka	184
Mostar	110
Prijedor	109
Sarajevo*	449
Tuzla	122
Zenica	133
Botswana	
Gaborone*	120
Brazil	
Americana	122
Anápolis	161
Aracaju	293
Araçatuba	113
Barra Mansa	123
Baurú	179
Belém	934
Belo Horizonte	2,049
Blumenau	145
Brasília*	1,596
Campina Grande	222
Campinas	567
Campo Grande	291
Campos	174
Canoas	214
Carapicuíba	186
Caruaru	138
Caxias do Sul	199
Contegem	112
Cuiabá	213
Curitiba	1,290
Diadema	229
Divinópolis	108
Duque du Caxias	306
Feira de Santana	225
Florianópolis	188
Fortaleza	1,758
Franca	144
Goiânia	718
Governador Valadares	174
Guarulhos	395
Imperatriz	112
Ipatinga	105
Itabuna	130
Jacareí	104
João Pessoa	330
Joinvile	217
Juazeiro do Norte	125
Juiz de Fora	300
Jundiaí	210
Lages	109
Limeira	138
Londrina	258
Macapá	138
Maceió	400
Manaus	635
Marília	104
Maringá	158
Mauá	206
Mogi das Cruzes	122
Montes Claros	152
Mossoró	118
Natal	420
Nilópolis	103
Niterói	386
Nova Iguaçu	492
Novo Hamburgo	132
Olinda	266
Osasco	474
Passo Fundo	103
Pelotas	197
Petrópolis	149
Piracicaba	179
Ponta Grossa	171
Porto Alegre	1,263
Porto Velho	135
Presidente Prudente	128
Recife	1,290
Ribeirão Preto	301
Rio Branco	117
Rio Claro	103
Rio de Janeiro	5,336
Rio Grande	125
Salvador	2,056
Santa Maria	151
Santarém	102
Santo André	549
Santos	411
São Bernardo do Campo	381
São Caetano do Sul	163
São Carlos	109
São Gonçalo	221
São João de Meriti	211
São José do Rio Preto	172
São José dos Campos	268
São Luís	450
São Paulo	9,480
São Vicente	193
Sorocaba	255
Taguatinga	480
Taubaté	155
Teresina	378
Uberaba	180
Uberlândia	230
Vitória	208
Vitória da Conquista	126
Volta Redonda	178
Brunei	
Bandar Seri Begawan*	64
Bulgaria	
Burgas	183
Pleven	130
Plovdiv	343
Shumen	100
Sofia*	1,122
Stara Zagora	151
Tolbukhin	109
Varna	303
Burkina	
Bobo Dioulasso	231
Ouagadougou*	308
Burma	
Akyab	108
Bassein	144
Insein	144
Mandalay	533
Monywa	107
Moulmein	220
Pegu	151
Rangoon*	2,513
Taunggyi	108
Burundi	
Bujumbura*	141
C Cambodia	
Phnom Penh*	300
Cameroon	
Douala	784
N'Kongsamba	102
Yaoundé*	552
Canada	
Brampton	188
Burlington	117
Burnaby	145
Calgary	671
Edmonton	785
Halifax	114
Hamilton	307
Kitchener	151
Laval	284
London	269
Longueuil	125
Markham	115
Mississauga	374
Montréal	1,018
Oshawa	124
Ottawa*	301
Québec	165
Regina	175
Richmond	108
Saint Catharines	123
Saskatoon	201
Surrey	181
Thunder Bay	112
Toronto	2,276
Vancouver	431
Windsor	193
Winnipeg	625
Cape Verde	
Praia*	57
Central African Republic	
Bangui*	474
Chad	
N'Djamena*	179
Chile	
Antofagasta	203
Arica	158
Barrancas	184
Chillán	127
Concepción	281
Iquique	127
Maipú	118
Osorno	102
Puente Alto	126
Puerto Montt	119
Punta Arenas	107
Rancagua	157
San Bernardo	136
Santiago*	4,100
Talca	138
Talcahuano	218
Temuco	168
Valdivia	105
Valparaíso	273
Viña del Mar	261
China	
Anda	423
Anqing	449
Anshan	1,196
Anshun	201
Anyang	501
Baicheng	276
Baiyin	325
Baoding	495
Baoji	341
Baotou	1,076
Beihai	174
Beijing*	5,531
Beipiao	605
Bengbu	550
Benxi	774
Binzhou	186
Botou	1,076
Cangzhou	280
Changchun	1,747
Changde	214
Changsha	1,066
Changshu	100
Changshun	1,747
Changzhi	450
Changzhou	534
Chaoyang	207
Chaozhou	162
Chengde	327
Chengdu	2,499
Chenzhou	166
Chifeng	293
Chongqing	2,673
Conghua	280
Da Xian	193
Dafang	962
Dalian	1,480
Dandong	545
Daqing	758
Datong	962
Da Xian	193
Dezhou	259
Ding Xian	938
Dongguan	1,230
Dongying	540
Duyun	102
Echeng	119
Fengcheng	996
Foshan	274
Fushun	1,185
Fuxin	647
Fuyang	178
Fuzhou	1,112
Ganzhou	363
Gejiu	353
Guangzhou	3,182
Guilin	432
Guiyang	1,350
Haicheng	992
Haikou	263
Hailar	157
Haining	600
Handan	930
Hangzhou	1,171
Hanzhong	374
Harbin	2,519
Hebi	336
Hefei	795
Hegang	592
Hengshui	101
Hengyang	532
Heshan	112
Hohhot	754
Houma	144
Huaibei	445
Huaihua	436
Huainan	1,029
Huangshi	376
Huaying	321
Huizhou	158
Hunjiang	694
Huzhou	953
Jiamusi	540
Ji'an	168
Jiangmen	212
Jiaojiang	391
Jiaozuo	484
Jiaxing	655
Jilin	1,888
Jinan	1,359
Jingdezhen	611
Jingmen	957
Jinhua	869
Jining (Nei Mong.)	159
Jining (Shandong)	190
Jinzhou	599
Jiujiang	351
Jixi	782
Kaifeng	602
Kaiyuan	223
Karamay	157
Kashi	257
Korla	118
Kunming	1,419
Kuytun	240
Langfang	533
Lanxi	612
Lanzhou	1,364
Laohekou	102
Lengshuijiang	255
Lengshuitan	371
Leshan	958
Lhasa	343
Lianyungang	397
Liaocheng	737
Liaoyang	589
Liaoyuan	772
Lichuan	718
Linchuan	619
Linfen	208
Liuzhou	582
Longyan	347
Loudi	266
Lu'an	158
Luohe	158
Luoyang	952
Luzhou	305
Ma'anshan	352
Manzhouli	104
Maoming	413
Meizhou	111
Mianyang	769
Mudanjiang	581
Nanchang	1,076
Nanchong	228
Nanjing	2,091
Nanning	890
Nanping	408
Nantong	403
Nanyang	288
Neijiang	271
Ningbo	479
Pingdingshan	470
Pingxiang	1,189
Pingyang	510
Qingdao	1,172
Qingjiang	235
Qinhuangdao	394
Qiqihar	1,209
Qitaihe	283
Quanzhou	403
Qufu	545
Quzhou	981
Renqiu	591
Rizhao	988
Sanmenxia	147
Sanming	199
Shanghai	6,293
Shangqiu	187
Shangrao	665
Shantou	718
Shaoguan	371
Shaoxing	1,091
Shaoyang	397
Shashi	239
Shenyang	3,944
Shihezi	564
Shijiazhuang	1,069
Shishou	558
Shiyan	307
Shizuishan	298
Shuangyashan	400
Siping	334
Suizhou	143
Suzhou	192
Tai'an	1,275
Taiyuan	1,746
Taizhou	161
Tangshan	1,408
Tianjin	5,152
Tianshui	185
Tieling	221
Tongchuan	354

Country / City	Population in thousands
Tonghua	360
Tongliao	213
Tongling	184
Ulanhot	174
Ürümqi	961
Wanxian	267
Weifang	393
Weihai	205
Wenzhou	516
Wuhan	3,288
Wuhu	449
Wuxi	798
Wuzhou	245
Xiaguan	117
Xiamen	507
Xi'an	2,185
Xiangfan	323
Xiangtan	492
Xianning	406
Xianyang	502
Xichang	146
Xifeng	237
Xingtai	334
Xining Shi	567
Xinji	532
Xinxiang	525
Xinyang	240
Xinyu	622
Xuchang	219
Xuzhou	777
Ya'an	254
Yangquan	478
Yangzhou	302
Yanji	176
Yantai	385
Yibin	245
Yichang	365
Yichun	756
Yinchuan	354
Yingcheng	546
Yingkou	423
Yingtan	120
Yining	257
Yiyang	165
Yong'an	272
Yuci	271
Yueyang	972
Yumen	195
Yushu	150
Yuyao	778
Zaozhuang	1,244
Zhangjiakou	617
Zhangzhou	283
Zhanjiang	854
Zhaoqing	172
Zhaotong	133
Zhengzhou	1,404
Zhenjiang	346
Zhongshan	135
Zhoukou	214
Zhuhai	132
Zhumadian	150
Zhuo Xian	478
Zhuzhou	383
Zibo	2,198
Zigong	866
Zixing	340
Zunyi	351
Colombia	
Armenia	211
Barrancabermeja	136
Barranquilla	1,000
Bello	260
Bogotá*	5,699
Bucaramanga	403
Buenaventura	187
Cali	1,625
Cartagena	576
Cúcuta	462
Floridablanca	177
Ibagué	336
Itagüí	168
Manizales	341
Medellín	1,485
Montería	182
Neiva	223
Palmira	189
Pasto	244
Pereira	329
Popayán	175
Santa Marta	211
Sincelejo	120
Soacha	181
Soledad	236
Tuluá	104
Tunja	102
Valledupar	209
Villavicencio	190
Comoros	
Moroni*	20
Congo	
Brazzaville*	299
Pointe-Noire	142
Costa Rica	
San José*	241
Côte d'Ivoire	
Abidjan	710
Bouaké	173
Yamoussoukro*	36
Croatia	
Osijek	159
Rijeka	193
Slavonski Brod	106
Split	236
Zadar	116
Zagreb*	681
Cuba	
Bayamo	122
Camagüey	279
Cienfuegos	119
Guantánamo	198
Havana*	2,078
Holguín	223
Marianao	128
Matanzas	112
Pinar del Río	117
Santa Clara	191
Santiago de Cuba	397
Victoria de las Tunas	115
Cyprus	
Limassol	120
Nicosia*	167
Czech Republic	
Brno	371
Olomouc	102
Ostrava	322
Pilsen	171
Prague*	1,182
D Denmark	
Ålborg	155
Århus	182
Copenhagen*	494
Odense	137
Djibouti	
Djibouti*	96
Dominica	
Roseau*	8
Dominican Republic	
Santiago de los Caballeros	279
Santo Domingo*	1,313
E Ecuador	
Ambato	113
Cuenca	157
Guayaquil	1,513
Machala	108
Manta	104
Portoviejo	123
Quito*	890
Santo Domingo de los Colorados	128
Egypt	
Alexandria	3,295
Al Fayyum	167
Al Jīzah	1,247
Al Maḥallah al Kubrá	293
Al Mansūra	258
Al Minyā	146
Aswān	144
Asyūt	214
Az Zaqāzīq	203
Banī Suwayf	118
Cairo*	6,663
Damanhūr	189
Ismailia	146
Kafr ad Dawwār	161
Port Said	263
Shibīn al Kaum	103
Shubrā al Khaymah	394
Suez	194
Tantā	285
El Salvador	
San Miguel	179
San Salvador*	471
Santa Ana	228
Equatorial Guinea	
Malabo*	37
Eritrea	
Asmera*	275
Estonia	
Tallinn*	482
Tartu	114
Ethiopia	
Addis Ababa*	1,413
Dirē Dawa	105
Gonder	108
F Fiji	
Suva*	70
Finland	
Esbo (Espoo)	157
Helsinki*	486
Tampere	169
Turku	161
Vantaa	144
France	
Aix-en-Provence	100
Amiens	130
Angers	135
Besançon	112
Bordeaux	202
Boulogne-Billancourt	103
Brest	154
Caen	112
Clermont-Ferrand	146
Dijon	139
Grenoble	156
Le Havre	199
Le Mans	146
Lille	168
Limoges	138
Lyon	410
Marseille	868
Metz	113
Montpellier	190
Mulhouse	112
Nantes	238
Nice	331
Nîmes	121
Paris*	2,175
Perpignan	108
Reims	176
Rennes	191
Roubaix	101
Rouen	101
Saint-Étienne	194
Strasbourg	247
Toulon	177
Toulouse	345
Tours	131
G Gabon	
Libreville*	105
Gambia	
Banjul*	49
Georgia	
Batumi	136
Kutaisi	235
Rustavi	159
Sukhumi	121
Tbilisi*	1,260
Germany	
Aachen	233
Augsburg	248
Bergisch Gladbach	102
Berlin*	3,434
Bielefeld	312
Bochum	389
Bonn	282
Bottrop	116
Braunschweig	254
Bremen	535
Bremerhaven	127
Chemnitz	314
Cologne	937
Cottbus	127
Darmstadt	136
Dessau	104
Dortmund	587
Dresden	520
Duisburg	527
Düsseldorf	570
Erfurt	217
Erlangen	101
Essen	621
Frankfurt am Main	625
Freiburg	184
Gelsenkirchen	287
Gera	113
Göttingen	118
Hagen	211
Halle	236
Hamburg	1,652
Hamm	174
Hannover	498
Heidelberg	131
Heilbronn	112
Herne	175
Hildesheim	104
Jena	108
Karlsruhe	265
Kassel	189
Kiel	241
Koblenz	107
Köpenick	118
Krefeld	235
Leipzig	551
Leverkusen	157
Lübeck	211
Ludwigshafen	158
Magdeburg	289
Mainz	175
Mannheim	300
Moers	102
Mönchengladbach	253
Mülheim an der Ruhr	175
Munich	1,229
Münster	249
Neuss	144
Nürnberg	249
Oberhausen	221
Offenbach	112
Oldenburg	141
Osnabrück	155
Paderborn	114
Pforzheim	109
Potsdam	141
Recklinghausen	122
Regensburg	119
Remscheid	121
Reutlingen	100
Rostock	249
Saarbrücken	188
Salzgitter	112
Schwerin	128
Siegen	106
Solingen	161
Stuttgart	563
Ulm	197
Wiesbaden	254
Witten	104
Wolfsburg	126
Wuppertal	371
Würzburg	126
Zwickau	121
Ghana	
Accra*	860
Kumasi	349
Tamale	137
Greece	
Athens*	886
Iráklion	102
Kallithéa	117
Lárisa	102
Pátrai	142
Peristérion	141
Piraiévs	196
Thessaloníki	406
Grenada	
Saint George's*	6
Guatemala	
Guatemala*	750
Guinea	
Conakry*	526
Guinea-Bissau	
Bissau*	109
Guyana	
Georgetown*	63
H Haiti	
Port-au-Prince*	461
Honduras	
La Ceiba	104
San Pedro Sula	397
Tegucigalpa*	598
Hungary	
Budapest*	2,017
Debrecen	217
Győr	131
Kecskemét	105
Miskolc	210
Nyíregyháza	119
Pécs	182
Szeged	188
Székesfehérvár	113
I Iceland	
Reykjavík*	96
India	
Ādoni	109
Āgra	747
Agartala	132
Ahmadābād	2,873
Ahmadnagar	181
Ajmer	376
Akola	225
Alīgarh	321
Allahābād	650
Alleppey	170
Alwar	146
Ambāla	121
Amravati	261
Amritsar	595
Amroha	113
Anantapur	120
Arrah	125
Asansol	366
Aurangābād	316
Bīkaner	288
Bally	148
Bālurghāt	113
Bangalore	2,651
Baranagar	170
Bareilly	449
Baroda	745
Barrackpur	116
Batāla	102
Belgaum	300
Bellary	202
Berhampore	102
Berhampur	163
Bhadrāvati	131
Bhāgalpur	225
Bharātpur	105
Bharuch	121
Bhatinda	127
Bhātpāra	265
Bhavnagar	309
Bhilai	376
Bhīlwāra	123
Bhīmavaram	102
Bhiwandi	115
Bhiwāni	101
Bhopāl	671
Bhubaneswar	219
Bhusawal	132
Bīhar	151
Bijāpur	147
Bilāspur	187
Bokaro Steel City	264
Bombay	9,910
Bulandshahr	103
Burdwān	167
Burhānpur	141
Calcutta	4,388
Cannanore	158
Chandannagar	102
Chandigarh	423
Chandrapur	116
Chāpra	112
Cochin	686
Coimbatore	920
Cuddalore	128
Cuddapah	103
Cuttack	327
Darbhanga	176
Dāvangere	197
Dehra Dūn	293
Delhi	7,175
Dhānbād	621
Dhārwār	379
Dhūlia	211
Dindigul	164
Dombivli	103
Durg	115
Durgāpur	312
Elūrū	168
Erode	276
Etāwah	112
Faizābād	143
Farīdābād	331
Farrukhābād	161
Firozābād	202
Firozpur	106
Gadag-Betigeri	117
Garden Reach	191
Gauhāti	152
Gayā	247
Ghaziābād	287
Gondia	100
Gorakhpur	308
Gulbarga	221
Guntūr	368
Gurgaon	101
Gwalior	556
Hābra	130
Hāpur	103
Hardwār	146
Hisār	137
Hooghly-Chinsura	125
Hospet	115
Howrah	744
Hubli-Dhārwār	527
Hyderābād	3,005
Ichalkaranji	134
Imphāl	157
Indore	829
Jabalpur	757
Jaipur	1,015
Jālgaon	145
Jālna	122
Jammu	223
Jāmnagar	317
Jamshedpur	670
Jaridih	102
Jaunpur	105
Jhānsi	284
Jodhpur	506
Jullundur	442
Junāgadh	120
Kākināda	226
Kalyān	136
Kāmārhāti	235
Kānchīpuram	145
Kānpur	1,639
Kāraikkudi	100
Karnāl	132
Katihār	122
Khandwa	115
Kharagpur	233
Kolār Gold Fields	144
Kolhāpur	351
Kota	358
Kozhikode	546
Kumbakonam	142
Kurnool	206
Lātūr	112
Lucknow	1,008
Ludhiāna	607
Machilipatnam	139
Madras	3,795
Madurai	908
Mālegaon	246
Mandya	100
Mangalore	306
Mathurā	159
Meerut	537
Miraj	105
Mirzāpur	128
Monghyr	129
Morādābād	345
Murwāra	123
Muzaffarnagar	172
Muzaffarpur	190
Mysore	479
Nabadwīp	130
Nadiād	143
Nāgercoil	172
Nāgpur	1,302
Naihāti	115
Nānded	191
Nāsik	429
Navsāri	129
Nellore	237
New Delhi*	273
Nizāmābād	183
Pālghāt	118
Pānipat	138
Pānihāti	206
Parbhani	109
Pātan	105
Pathānkot	110
Patiāla	206
Patna	919
Pimpri-Chinchwad	221
Pollāchi	115
Pondicherry	251
Poona	1,686
Porbandar	133
Proddatūr	107
Purī	101
Purnia	110
Quilon	168
Raichūr	125
Raipur	338
Rājahmundry	268
Rājapālaiyam	102
Rājkot	445
Rāmpur	205
Rānchī	503
Rāniganj	119

Country City	Population in thousands
Ratlām	156
Raurkela	321
Rewa	101
Rohtak	167
Sāgar	207
Sahāranpur	295
Salem	498
Sambalpur	162
Sambhal	108
Sāngli	269
Secunderābād	136
Serampore	127
Shāhjahānpur	205
Shillong	175
Shimoga	152
Sholāpur	515
Sīkar	103
Silīguri	154
Sītāpur	101
Sonepat	109
South Dum Dum	230
South Suburban	395
Sri Gangānagar	124
Srīnagar	606
Surat	914
Tenāli	119
Thāna	390
Thanjavur	184
Tiruchchirāppalli	545
Tirunelveli	178
Tirupati	115
Tiruppūr	203
Titāgarh	105
Trichūr	170
Trivandrum	520
Tumkūr	109
Tuticorin	251
Udaipur	233
Ujjain	282
Ulhāsnagar	315
Vālpārai	115
Vārānasi	797
Vellore	247
Verāval	105
Vijayawada	543
Visākhapatnam	604
Vizianagaram	115
Warangal	335
Yamunānagar	160
Indonesia	
Ambon	209
Balikpapan	281
Bandung	1,463
Banjarmasin	381
Bekasi	123
Bogor	247
Ciamis	105
Cianjur	132
Cilacap	119
Cimahi	157
Cirebon	224
Jakarta*	7,886
Jambi	230
Jember	115
Kediri	222
Kuningan	105
Madiun	151
Magelang	123
Malang	512
Manado	217
Medan	1,379
Padang	481
Padangsidempuan	135
Pakanbaru	186
Palembang	787
Pare	108
Pekalongan	133
Pemalang	110
Pematangsiantar	150
Pontianak	305
Probolinggo	100
Purwokerto	125
Samarinda	265
Semarang	1,027
Sukabumi	110
Surabaya	2,028
Surakarta	470
Tanjungkarang	284
Tanjungpriok	148
Tasikmalaya	136
Tegal	132
Ujung Pandang	709
Yogyakarta	399
Iran	
Ābādān	296
Āmol	118

Country City	Population in thousands
Ahvāz	580
Arāk	265
Ardabīl	147
Bābol	115
Bākhtarān	561
Bandar-e `Abbās	202
Borūjerd	184
Būshehr	121
Dezfūl	151
Eşfahān	987
Gorgān	139
Hamadān	272
Karaj	275
Kāshān	139
Kermān	257
Khomeynīshahr	105
Khorramābād	209
Khorramshahr	147
Khvoy	115
Malāyer	104
Marāgheh	101
Mashhad	1,464
Masjed-e Soleymān	105
Najafābād	129
Neyshābūr	109
Orūmīyeh	301
Qā'emshahr	109
Qazvīn	249
Qom	543
Rasht	291
Sabzevār	129
Sanandaj	205
Sārī	141
Shīrāz	848
Tabrīz	971
Tajrīsh	157
Tehrān*	6,043
Yazd	230
Zāhedān	282
Zanjān	215
Iraq	
Al Başrah	313
An Najaf	128
Baghdad*	1,900
Kirkūk	167
Mosul	315
Ireland	
Cork	133
Dublin*	503
Israel	
Bat Yam	129
Beersheba	111
Hefa	226
Holon	133
Jerusalem*	429
Netanya	102
Petaḥ Tiqwa	124
Ramat Gan	117
Rishon LeẔiyyon	102
Tel Aviv-Yafo	327
Italy	
Bari	369
Bergamo	121
Bologna	455
Bolzano	103
Brescia	203
Cagliari	219
Catania	380
Cosenza	101
Ferrara	118
Florence	443
Foggia	150
Genoa	755
La Spezia	111
Livorno	172
Messina	240
Mestre	198
Milan	1,432
Modena	165
Monza	123
Naples	1,210
Padua	228
Palermo	698
Parma	160
Perugia	104
Pescara	131
Piacenza	104
Prato	157
Reggio di Calabria	159
Reggio nell'Emilia	107
Rimini	112
Rome*	2,791
Salerno	150
Sassari	104
Siracusa	109
Taranto	231

Country City	Population in thousands
Trieste	237
Turin	1,115
Udine	102
Venice	317
Verona	239
Vicenza	111
Jamaica	
Kingston*	494
Japan	
Abiko	101
Ageo	166
Aizu-Wakamatsu	115
Akashi	255
Akita	285
Amagasaki	524
Anjō	124
Aomori	288
Asahikawa	353
Ashikaga	166
Atsugi	145
Beppu	136
Chiba	793
Chigasaki	171
Chofu	181
Daitō	117
Fuchū	192
Fuji	206
Fujieda	103
Fujinomiya	108
Fujisawa	300
Fukui	241
Fukuoka	1,089
Fukushima	263
Fukuyama	346
Funabashi	479
Gifu	410
Habikino	103
Hachiōji	387
Hachinohe	238
Hadano	123
Hakodate	320
Hamamatsu	491
Higashikurume	107
Higashimurayama	119
Higashi-Ōsaka	522
Himeji	446
Hino	145
Hirakata	353
Hiratsuka	214
Hirosaki	175
Hiroshima	899
Hitachi	205
Hōfu	111
Ibaraki	234
Ichihara	216
Ichikawa	364
Ichinomiya	253
Ikeda	101
Imabari	123
Iruma	104
Ise	106
Isesaki	106
Ishinomaki	121
Itami	178
Iwaki	342
Iwakuni	113
Izumi	124
Jōetsu	128
Kadoma	139
Kagoshima	505
Kakamigahara	115
Kakogawa	212
Kamakura	173
Kanazawa	418
Kariya	106
Kashihara	107
Kashiwa	239
Kasugai	244
Kasukabe	156
Kawagoe	259
Kawaguchi	379
Kawanishi	130
Kawasaki	1,041
Kiryū	133
Kisarazu	111
Kishiwada	180
Kitakyūshū	1,065
Kitami	103
Kōbe	1,367
Kōchi	301
Kōfu	199
Kōriyama	286
Kodaira	155
Koganei	102
Komaki	103

Country City	Population in thousands
Komatsu	104
Koshigaya	223
Kumagaya	137
Kumamoto	526
Kurashiki	404
Kure	235
Kurume	217
Kushiro	215
Kyōto	1,473
Machida	295
Maebashi	265
Matsubara	136
Matsudo	401
Matsue	136
Matsumoto	192
Matsusaka	113
Matsuyama	402
Mino'o	104
Mitaka	165
Mito	216
Miyakonojō	129
Miyazaki	265
Moriguchi	166
Morioka	229
Muroran	150
Musashino	137
Nagano	324
Nagaoka	180
Nagareyama	107
Nagasaki	447
Nagoya	2,155
Naha	296
Nara	298
Narashino	125
Neyagawa	256
Niigata	458
Niihama	132
Niiza	119
Nishinomiya	410
Nobeoka	137
Numazu	204
Obihiro	154
Odawara	177
Ogaki	143
Ōita	360
Okayama	546
Okazaki	262
Ōmiya	354
Ōmuta	163
Onomichi	102
Osaka	2,624
Ota	123
Otaru	181
Ōtsu	215
Oyama	127
Saga	164
Sagamihara	439
Sakai	810
Sakata	103
Sakura	101
Sapporo	1,672
Sasebo	251
Sayama	124
Sendai	665
Seto	121
Shimizu	242
Shimonoseki	269
Shizuoka	458
Sōka	187
Suita	332
Suzuka	156
Tachikawa	143
Takamatsu	317
Takaoka	175
Takarazuka	184
Takasaki	221
Takatsuki	341
Tokorozawa	236
Tokushima	249
Tokuyama	111
Tōkyō*	8,164
Tomakomai	152
Tottori	131
Toyama	305
Toyohashi	304
Toyokawa	103
Toyonaka	403
Toyota	282
Tsu	145
Tsuchiura	113
Ube	169
Ueda	112
Uji	153
Urawa	358
Utsunomiya	378
Wakayama	401

Country City	Population in thousands
Yachiyo	134
Yaizu	104
Yamagata	237
Yamaguchi	115
Yamato	168
Yao	273
Yatsushiro	108
Yokkaichi	255
Yokohama	3,220
Yokosuka	421
Yonago	127
Jordan	
`Ammān*	624
Az Zarqā'	216
Irbid	113
Kazakhstan	
Aktyubinsk	253
Alma-Ata	1,128
Aqmola*	277
Chimkent	393
Dzhambul	307
Dzhezkazgan	109
Ekibastuz	135
Gur'yev	149
Karaganda	614
Kokchetav	137
Kustanay	224
Kzyl-Orda	153
Pavlodar	331
Petropavlovsk	241
Rudnyy	110
Semipalatinsk	334
Shevchenko	159
Taldy-Kurgan	119
Temirtau	212
Ural'sk	200
Ust'-Kamenogorsk	324
Kenya	
Mombasa	247
Nairobi*	509
Kiribati	
Bairiki*	2
Korea, North	
Ch'ŏngjin	306
Haeju	140
Hamhŭng	484
Kaesŏng	175
Kimch'aek	100
Nampb	140
P'yŏngyang*	1,250
Sinŭiju	300
Wŏnsan	275
Korea, South	
Andong	102
Anyang	254
Cheju	168
Chinhae	112
Chinju	203
Ch'ŏnan	121
Ch'ŏngju	253
Chŏnju	367
Ch'unch'ŏn	155
Ch'ungju	113
Inch'ŏn	1,085
Iri	145
Kangnŭng	117
Kimhae	203
Kimje	221
Kohŭng	217
Kunsan	165
Kwangju	728
Kyŏngju	122
Masan	387
Mokp'o	222
Nonsan	226
P'ohang	201
Puch'ŏn	221
Pusan	3,160
Seoul*	9,639
Sunch'ŏn	114
Suwŏn	311
Taegu	1,607
Taejŏn	652
Ulsan	418
Wŏnju	137
Yanggu	278
Yŏsu	161
Kuwait	
Al Kuwait*	182
As Sālimīyah	153
Ḩawallī	145
Jalīb ash Shuyūkh	115
Kyrgyzstan	
Bishkek*	616

Country City	Population in thousands
Osh	213
Laos	
Vientiane*	377
Latvia	
Daugavpils	127
Liepāja	114
Riga*	915
Lebanon	
Beirut*	475
Tripoli	128
Lesotho	
Maseru*	13
Liberia	
Monrovia*	167
Libya	
Benghāzī	287
Mişrātah	102
Tripoli*	550
Liechtenstein	
Vaduz*	5
Lithuania	
Kaunas	423
Klaipėda	204
Panevėžys	126
Šiauliai	145
Vilnius*	582
Luxembourg	
Luxembourg*	76
Macedonia	
Bitola	138
Gostivar	101
Kumanovo	126
Skopje*	507
Tetovo	162
Madagascar	
Antananarivo*	452
Fandriana	105
Malawi	
Blantyre	332
Lilongwe*	234
Malaysia	
Georgetown	248
Ipoh	294
Johor Baharu	246
Kelang	192
Kota Baharu	168
Kuala Lumpur*	920
Kuala Terengganu	180
Kuantan	132
Seremban	133
Taiping	199
Maldives	
Male*	46
Mali	
Bamako*	404
Malta	
Valletta*	14
Marshall Islands	
Majuro*	9
Mauritania	
Nouakchott*	135
Mauritius	
Port Louis*	134
Mexico	
Acapulco de Juárez	515
Aguascalientes	440
Campeche	151
Celaya	142
Chihuahua	516
Ciudad Juárez	790
Ciudad Madero	132
Ciudad Obregón	166
Ciudad Victoria	195
Coatzacoalcos	127
Colima	107
Cuernavaca	279
Culiacán	415
Durango de Victoria	348
Ecatepec de Morelos	742
Ensenada	120
Gómez Palacio	117
Guadalajara	1,650
Guadalupe	371
Hermosillo	406
Irapuato	265
Jalapa Enríquez	279
La Paz	138
León	758
Los Mochis	123
Matamoros	266
Mazatlán	268

Country / City	Population in thousands
Mérida	529
Mexicali	439
Mexico City*	8,237
Minatitlán	107
Monclova	116
Monterrey	1,069
Morelia	428
Naucalpan de Juárez	724
Netzahualcóyotl	1,341
Nuevo Laredo	202
Oaxaca de Juárez	213
Orizaba	115
Pachuca de Soto	188
Poza Rica	167
Puebla de Zaragoza	1,007
Querétaro	387
Reynosa	195
Saltillo	421
San Luis Potosí	489
San Nicolás de los Garzas	281
Tampico	273
Tepic	207
Tijuana	699
Tlalnepantla de Galeana	778
Tlaquepaque	134
Toluca de Lerdo	328
Torreón	439
Tuxtla Gutiérrez	290
Uruapan del Progreso	123
Veracruz Llave	439
Villahermosa	261
Zacatecas	100
Zapopan	345
Micronesia, Federated States of	
Kolonia*	6
Moldova	
Bel'tsy	159
Bendery	130
Kishinëv*	665
Tiraspol'	182
Monaco	
Monaco*	30
Mongolia	
Ulaanbaatar*	515
Morocco	
Casablanca	1,506
Fès	325
Kenitra	139
Marrakech	333
Meknès	248
Oujda	176
Rabat*	368
Safi	129
Salé	156
Tangier	188
Tétouan	139
Mozambique	
Maputo*	883
Nampula	183
Namibia	
Windhoek*	96
Nepal	
Kāthmāndu*	423
Netherlands	
Amsterdam*	695
Apeldoorn	147
Arnhem	129
Breda	121
Dordrecht	109
Eindhoven	191
Enschede	145
Groningen	168
Haarlem	149
Leiden	109
Maastricht	116
Nijmegen	145
Rotterdam	576
The Hague*	444
Tilburg	155
Utrecht	240
Zaandam	130
New Zealand	
Auckland	149
Christchurch	168
Manukau	177
Wellington*	137
Nicaragua	
Managua*	608
Niger	
Niamey*	225
Nigeria	
Aba	177
Abeokuta	253
Abuja*	1
Ado	213
Benin City	136
Calabar	103
Ede	182
Enugu	187
Ibadan	847
Ife	176
Ilesha	224
Ilorin	282
Iseyin	115
Iwo	214
Kaduna	202
Kano	399
Katsina	109
Lagos	1,061
Maiduguri	189
Ogbomosho	432
Onitsha	220
Oshogbo	282
Oyo	152
Port Harcourt	242
Zaria	224
Norway	
Bergen	207
Oslo*	447
Trondheim	134
Oman	
Muscat*	8
Pakistan	
Bahāwalpur	180
Chiniot	106
Dera Ghāzi Khān	102
Faisalabad	1,104
Gujrānwāla	659
Gujrāt	155
Hyderābād	752
Islāmābād*	204
Jhang Sadar	196
Jhelum	106
Karāchi	5,076
Kasūr	156
Lahore	2,953
Lārkāna	124
Mardān	148
Mīrpur Khās	124
Multān	732
Nawābshāh	102
Okāra	127
Peshāwar	566
Quetta	286
Rahīmyār Khān	119
Rāwalpindi	795
Sāhīwāl	151
Sargodha	291
Shekhūpura	141
Siālkot	302
Sukkur	191
Wāh	127
Palau	
Koror*	9
Panama	
Panamá*	432
Papua New Guinea	
Port Moresby*	124
Paraguay	
Asunción*	388
Peru	
Arequipa	108
Callao	261
Chiclayo	280
Chimbote	216
Comas	287
Huancayo	165
Ica	111
Iquitos	174
Lima*	376
Piura	186
Trujillo	355
Philippines	
Angeles	189
Bacolod City	262
Baguio	119
Batangas	144
Butuan	173
Butuan City	172
Cabanatuan City	138
Cadíz	130
Cagayan de Oro City	227
Calamba	121
Calbayog City	107
Caloocan City	468
Cebu City	490
Davao City	610
General Santos	149
Iligan	167
Iligan City	167
Iloilo	245
Lipa City	121
Lucena	108
Makati	373
Malabon	191
Mandaue	111
Manila City*	1,876
Marikina	212
Olongapo	156
Ormoc City	105
Paranaque	209
Pasay City	288
Pasig	269
Quezon City	1,166
San Carlos	101
San Fernando	111
San Pablo City	132
Silay	111
Tacloban	103
Tarlac	176
Valenzuela	212
Zamboanga City	344
Poland	
Białystok	268
Bielsko-Biała	181
Bydgoszcz	380
Bytom	230
Chorzów	132
Częstochowa	257
Dąbrowa Górnicza	135
Elbląg	126
Gdańsk	462
Gdynia	251
Gliwice	212
Gorzów Wielkopolski	123
Grudziądz	102
Jastrzębie Zdroj	102
Kalisz	106
Katowice	366
Kielce	213
Koszalin	108
Kraków	746
Legnica	104
Łódź	849
Lublin	349
Olsztyn	161
Opole	127
Płock	121
Poznań	587
Radom	226
Ruda Śląska	169
Rybnik	142
Rzeszów	151
Słupsk	100
Sosnowiec	259
Szczecin	411
Tarnów	121
Toruń	201
Tychy	190
Wałbrzych	142
Warsaw*	1,651
Włocławek	121
Wodzisław Śląski	111
Wrocław	641
Zabrze	203
Zielona Góra	113
Portugal	
Lisbon*	818
Porto	330
Qatar	
Doha*	217
Romania	
Arad	188
Bacău	180
Baia Mare	140
Botoşani	109
Brăila	236
Braşov	351
Bucharest*	2,068
Buzău	136
Cluj-Napoca	310
Constanţa	328
Craiova	281
Galaţi	295
Iaşi	313
Oradea	214
Piatra Neamţ	109
Piteşti	157
Ploieşti	235
Reşiţa	106
Satu Mare	130
Sibiu	178
Timişoara	325
Tîrgu Mures	159
Russia	
Abakan	154
Achinsk	122
Al'met'yevsk	129
Angarsk	266
Anzhero-Sudzhensk	108
Archangel	416
Armavir	161
Arzamas	109
Astrakhan'	509
Balakovo	198
Balashikha	136
Barnaul	602
Belgorod	300
Belovo	112
Berezniki	201
Biysk	233
Blagoveshchensk	206
Bratsk	255
Bryansk	452
Cheboksary	420
Chelyabinsk	1,143
Cherepovets	310
Cherkessk	113
Chita	366
Dimitrovgrad	124
Dzerzhinsk	285
Elektrostal'	153
Engel's	182
Glazov	104
Groznyy	401
Irkutsk	626
Ivanovo	481
Izhevsk	635
Kaliningrad (Kalin.)	401
Kaliningrad (Moscow)	160
Kaluga	312
Kamensk-Ural'skiy	209
Kamyshin	122
Kansk	110
Kazan'	1,094
Kemerovo	520
Khabarovsk	601
Khimki	133
Kineshma	105
Kiselevsk	128
Kislovodsk	114
Kolomna	162
Kolpino	142
Komsomol'sk-na-Amure	315
Kopeysk	146
Kostroma	278
Kovrov	160
Krasnodar	620
Krasnoyarsk	912
Kurgan	356
Kursk	424
Leninsk-Kuznetskiy	165
Lipetsk	450
Lyubertsy	165
Magadan	152
Magnitogorsk	440
Makhachkala	315
Maykop	149
Mezhdurechensk	107
Miass	168
Michurinsk	109
Moscow*	8,769
Murmansk	468
Murom	124
Mytishchi	154
Naberezhnye Chelny	501
Nakhodka	165
Nal'chik	235
Neftekamsk	107
Nevinnomyssk	121
Nizhnekamsk	191
Nizhnevartovsk	242
Nizhniy Novgorod	1,438
Nizhniy Tagil	440
Noginsk	123
Noril'sk	174
Novgorod	229
Novocheboksarsk	115
Novocherkassk	187
Novokuybyshevsk	113
Novokuznetsk	600
Novomoskovsk	146
Novorossiysk	186
Novoshakhtinsk	106
Novosibirsk	1,436
Novotroitsk	106
Obninsk	100
Odintsovo	125
Oktyabr'skiy	105
Omsk	1,148
Orekhovo-Zuyevo	137
Orël	337
Orenburg	547
Orsk	271
Penza	483
Perm'	1,091
Pervoural'sk	142
Petropavlovsk-Kamchatskiy	269
Petrozavodsk	270
Podol'sk	210
Prokop'yevsk	274
Pskov	204
Pyatigorsk	129
Rostov	1,020
Rubtsovsk	172
Ryazan'	515
Rybinsk	252
Saint Petersburg	4,456
Salavat	150
Samara	1,257
Saransk	312
Sarapul	111
Saratov	905
Sergiyev Posad	115
Serov	104
Serpukhov	144
Severodvinsk	249
Shakhty	224
Shchelkovo	109
Simbirsk	625
Smolensk	341
Sochi	337
Solikamsk	110
Staryy Oskol'	174
Stavropol'	318
Sterlitamak	248
Surgut	248
Syktyvkar	233
Syzran'	174
Taganrog	291
Tambov	305
Tol'yatti	630
Tomsk	502
Tula	540
T'ver	451
Tyumen'	477
Ufa	1,083
Ukhta	111
Ulan-Ude	353
Usol'ye-Sibirskoye	107
Ussuriysk	162
Ust'-Ilimsk	109
Velikiye Luki	114
Vladikavkaz	300
Vladimir	350
Vladivostok	648
Volgograd	999
Vologda	283
Volzhskiy	269
Vorkuta	116
Voronezh	887
Votkinsk	103
Vyatka	441
Yakutsk	187
Yaroslavl'	633
Yekaterinburg	1,367
Yelets	120
Yoshkar-Ola	242
Yuzhno-Sakhalinsk	157
Zelenograd	158
Zhukovskiy	101
Zlatoust	208
Rwanda	
Kigali*	118
Saint Kitts and Nevis	
Basseterre*	15
Saint Lucia	
Castries*	56
Saint Vincent and the Grenadines	
Kingstown*	17
San Marino	
San Marino*	4
Sao Tome and Principe	
São Tomé*	8
Saudi Arabia	
Ad Dammām	128
Al Hufūf	101
At Ţā'if	205
Jiddah	561
Mecca	367
Medina	198
Riyadh*	667
Senegal	
Dakar*	799
Kaolack	107
Thiès	117
Seychelles	
Victoria*	16
Sierra Leone	
Freetown*	274
Singapore	
Singapore*	2,756
Slovak Republic	
Bratislava*	380
Košice	202
Slovenia	
Ljubljana*	305
Maribor	186
Solomon Islands	
Honiara*	30
Somalia	
Mogadishu*	371
South Africa	
Bloemfontein	104
Boksburg	111
Cape Town*	777
Durban	634
East London	120
Germiston	117
Johannesburg	632
Kimberley	105
Pietermaritzburg	115
Port Elizabeth	273
Pretoria*	443
Roodeport-Maraisburg	142
Soweto	522
Springs	143
Tembisa	149
Wes-Rand	647
Spain	
Albacete	116
Alcalá de Henares	137
Alcorcón	141
Alicante	246
Almería	141
Badajoz	111
Badalona	230
Baracaldo	119
Barcelona	1,668
Bilbao	433
Burgos	153
Cádiz	157
Cartagena	168
Castellón de la Plana	124
Córdoba	279
Elche	165
Getafe	127
Gijón	256
Granada	247
Huelva	128
Jerez de la Frontera	176
La Coruña	232
La Laguna	106
Las Palmas de Gran Canaria	360
Leganés	164
León	127
L'Hospitalet de Llobregat	295
Lleida	107
Logroño	110
Madrid*	3,159
Málaga	502
Móstoles	150
Murcia	285
Oviedo	184
Palma	290
Pamplona	178
Sabadell	186
Salamanca	154
San Sebastián	172
Santa Cruz de Tenerife	186
Santander	180
Saragossa	572
Seville	646
Tarragona	109
Terrassa	156
Valencia	745
Valladolid	320
Vigo	261
Vitoria	190

Country / City	Population in thousands
Sri Lanka	
Colombo*	609
Dehiwala-Mount Lavinia	190
Galle	109
Jaffna	127
Kandy	102
Kotte	107
Moratuwa	165
Sudan	
Khartoum*	334
Khartoum North	151
Omdurman	299
Port Sudan	133
Wad Medanī	107
Suriname	
Paramaribo*	68
Swaziland	
Mbabane*	38
Sweden	
Borås	101
Göteborg	431
Hälsingborg	107
Jönköping	110
Linköping	119
Malmö	232
Norrköping	119
Örebro	120
Stockholm*	669
Uppsala	162
Västerås	118
Switzerland	
Basel	182
Bern*	145
Geneva	157
Lausanne	127
Zürich	370
Syria	
Aleppo	977
Damascus*	1,251
Ḥamāh	177
Ḥimş	355
Latakia	197
Taiwan	
Changhua	186
Chiayi	252
Kaohsiung	1,227
Keelung	348
Pingtung	189
Taichung	565
Tainan	541
Taipei*	2,268
Taoyuan	106
Tajikistan	
Dushanbe*	595
Khudzhand	160
Tanzania	
Dar es Salaam*	757
Mwanza	111
Tanga	103
Zanzibar	111
Thailand	
Bangkok*	5,876
Chiang Mai	102
Chon Buri	116
Nakhon Si Thammarat	102
Songkhla	173
Thon Buri	628
Togo	
Lomé*	370
Tonga	
Nuku'alofa*	18
Trinidad and Tobago	
Port-of-Spain*	60
Tunisia	
Safāqis	232
Tūnis*	597
Turkey	
Adana	778
Adapazarı	152
Ankara*	2,559
Antalya	261
Antioch	108
Balıkesir	150
Batman	110
Bursa	613
Denizli	169
Diyarbakır	306
Elazığ	182
Erzurum	246
Eskişehir	367
Gaziantep	479
İskenderun	152
İsparta	101
İstanbul	6,620
İzmir	1,757
İzmit	233
Kağıthane	164
Kahramanmaraş	210
Kayseri	374
Kırıkkale	208
Konya	439
Kütahya	119
Malatya	243
Manisa	127
Mersin	314
Osmaniye	104
Samsun	241
Sivas	199
Tarsus	147
Trabzon	142
Urfa	195
Van	111
Zonguldak	118
Turkmenistan	
Ashkhabad*	398
Chardzhou	161
Tashauz	112
Tuvalu	
Funafuti*	1,500
Uganda	
Kampala*	479
Ukraine	
Aleksandriya	103
Belaya Tserkov'	197
Berdyansk	132
Cherkassy	290
Chernigov	296
Chernovtsy	257
Dneprodzerzhinsk	282
Dnepropetrovsk	1,179
Donetsk	1,110
Gorlovka	337
Ivano-Frankovsk	214
Kamenets-Podol'skiy	102
Kerch'	174
Khar'kov	1,611
Kherson	355
Khmel'nitskiy	237
Kirovograd	269
Kiev*	2,587
Kommunarsk	126
Konstantinovka	108
Kramatorsk	198
Krasnyy Luch	113
Kremenchug	236
Krivoy Rog	713
Lisichansk	127
Lugansk	497
Lutsk	198
L'viv	790
Makeyevka	430
Mariupol'	517
Melitopol'	174
Nikolayev	503
Nikopol'	158
Odessa	1,115
Pavlograd	131
Poltava	315
Rovno	228
Sevastopol'	356
Severodonetsk	131
Simferopol'	344
Slavyansk	135
Stakhanov	112
Sumy	291
Ternopol'	205
Uzhgorod	117
Vinnitsa	374
Yenakiyevo	121
Yevpatoriya	108
Zaporozh'ye	884
Zhitomir	292
United Arab Emirates	
Abu Dhabi*	243
Ash Shāriqah	125
Dubayy	266
United Kingdom	
Aberdeen	190
Belfast	295
Birkenhead	156
Birmingham	1,014
Blackburn	110
Blackpool	146
Bolton	144
Bournemouth	143
Bradford	293
Brighton	135
Bristol	414
Cardiff	262
Coventry	319
Derby	218
Dudley	187
Dundee	174
Edinburgh	420
Glasgow	765
Gloucester	107
Hillingdon	227
Huddersfield	148
Hull	322
Ipswich	130
Kingston upon Thames	131
Leeds	452
Leicester	324
Liverpool	539
London*	7,567
Luton	163
Manchester	449
Middlesbrough	159
Newcastle upon Tyne	199
Newport	116
Northampton	154
Norwich	170
Nottingham	273
Oldham	107
Oxford	114
Peterborough	113
Plymouth	239
Poole	123
Portsmouth	174
Preston	167
Reading	195
Rotherham	122
Saint Helens	114
Sheffield	471
Slough	106
Southampton	211
Southend-on-Sea	156
Stockport	135
Stoke-on-Trent	272
Sunderland	195
Sutton Coldfield	103
Swansea	172
Swindon	127
Walsall	178
Warley	152
Warrington	129
Watford	110
West Bromwich	154
Wolverhampton	264
York	123
United States	
Abilene	107
Akron	223
Albany	101
Albuquerque	385
Alexandria	111
Allentown	105
Amarillo	158
Amherst	112
Anaheim	266
Anchorage	226
Ann Arbor	110
Arlington (Tex.)	262
Arlington (Va.)	171
Atlanta	394
Aurora	222
Austin	466
Bakersfield	175
Baltimore	736
Baton Rouge	220
Beaumont	114
Berkeley	103
Birmingham	266
Boise	126
Boston	574
Bridgeport	142
Buffalo	328
Cedar Rapids	109
Charlotte	396
Chattanooga	152
Chesapeake	152
Chicago	2,784
Chula Vista	135
Cincinnati	364
Citrus Heights	107
Cleveland	506
Colorado Springs	281
Columbus (Ga.)	179
Columbus (Ohio)	633
Concord	111
Corpus Christi	257
Dallas	1,007
Dayton	182
Denver	468
Des Moines	193
Detroit	1,028
Durham	137
East Los Angeles	126
Elizabeth	110
El Monte	106
El Paso	515
Erie	109
Escondido	109
Eugene	113
Evansville	126
Flint	141
Fort Lauderdale	149
Fort Wayne	173
Fort Worth	448
Fremont	173
Fresno	354
Fullerton	114
Garden Grove	143
Garland	181
Gary	117
Glendale (Ariz.)	148
Glendale (Calif.)	180
Grand Rapids	189
Greensboro	184
Hampton	134
Hartford	140
Hayward	111
Hialeah	188
Hollywood	122
Honolulu	365
Houston	1,631
Huntington Beach	182
Huntsville	160
Independence	112
Indianapolis	742
Inglewood	110
Irvine	110
Irving	155
Jackson	197
Jacksonville	635
Jersey City	229
Kansas City (Kans.)	150
Kansas City (Mo.)	435
Knoxville	165
Lakewood	126
Lansing	127
Laredo	123
Las Vegas	258
Lexington	225
Lincoln	192
Little Rock	176
Livonia	101
Long Beach	429
Los Angeles	3,485
Louisville	269
Lowell	103
Lubbock	186
Macon	107
Madison	191
Memphis	610
Mesa	288
Mesquite	101
Metairie	149
Miami	359
Milwaukee	628
Minneapolis	368
Mobile	196
Modesto	165
Montgomery	187
Moreno Valley	119
Nashville	488
Newark	275
New Haven	130
New Orleans	497
Newport News	170
New York	7,323
Norfolk	261
Oakland	372
Oceanside	128
Oklahoma City	445
Omaha	336
Ontario	133
Orange	111
Orlando	165
Overland Park	112
Oxnard	142
Paradise	125
Pasadena (Calif.)	132
Pasadena (Tex.)	119
Paterson	141
Peoria	114
Philadelphia	1,586
Phoenix	983
Pittsburgh	370
Plano	129
Pomona	132
Portland	437
Portsmouth	104
Providence	161
Raleigh	208
Rancho Cucamonga	101
Reno	134
Richmond	203
Riverside	227
Rochester	232
Rockford	139
Sacramento	369
Saint Louis	397
Saint Paul	272
Saint Petersburg	239
Salem	108
Salinas	109
Salt Lake City	160
San Antonio	936
San Bernardino	164
San Diego	1,111
San Francisco	724
San Jose	782
Santa Ana	294
Santa Clarita	111
Santa Rosa	113
Savannah	138
Scottsdale	130
Seattle	516
Shreveport	199
Simi Valley	100
Sioux Falls	101
South Bend	106
Spokane	177
Springfield (Ill.)	105
Springfield (Mo.)	140
Springfield (Mass.)	157
Stamford	108
Sterling Heights	118
Stockton	211
Sunnyvale	117
Syracuse	164
Tacoma	177
Tallahassee	125
Tampa	280
Tempe	142
Thousand Oaks	104
Toledo	333
Topeka	120
Torrance	133
Tucson	405
Tulsa	367
Vallejo	109
Virginia Beach	393
Waco	104
Warren	145
Washington*	607
Waterbury	109
Wichita	304
Winston-Salem	143
Worcester	170
Yonkers	188
Uruguay	
Montevideo*	1,173
Uzbekistan	
Almalyk	114
Andizhan	293
Angren	131
Bukhara	224
Chirchik	156
Dzhizak	102
Fergana	200
Karshi	156
Kokand	182
Margilan	125
Namangan	308
Navoi	107
Nukus	169
Samarkand	366
Tashkent*	2,073
Urgench	128
Vanuatu	
Vila*	5
Vatican City	
Vatican City*	1
Venezuela	
Barinas	158
Barquisimeto	661
Cabimas	162
Caracas*	1,822
Ciudad Bolívar	241
Ciudad Guayana	459
Cumaná	218
Guarenas	104
Los Teques	149
Maracaibo	1,124
Maracay	497
Maturín	205
Mérida	188
Petare	396
San Cristóbal	235
San Francisco	198
Valencia	856
Valera	132
Vietnam	
Biên Hòa	187
Cam Ranh	118
Can Tho	183
Đà Lat	105
Đà Nang	319
Haiphong	1,279
Hanoi*	2,571
Ho Chí Minh City	3,420
Hong Gai	115
Hue	166
Long Xuyên	112
My Tho	101
Nam Định	160
Nha Trang	173
Qui Nhon	127
Thái Nguyên	110
Vinh	160
Vũng Tàu	108
Western Samoa	
Apia*	32
Yemen	
Aden	240
Sanaa*	135
Yugoslavia	
Belgrade*	1,555
Čačak	111
Kragujevac	165
Kraljevo	122
Kruševac	133
Leskovac	159
Niš	231
Novi Sad	258
Pančevo	124
Peć	111
Priština	210
Prizren	135
Šabac	120
Smederevo	107
Subotica	155
Titograd	132
Uroševac	114
Zrenjanin	139
Zaire	
Bukavu	135
Kananga	429
Kikwit	112
Kinshasa*	2,654
Kisangani	230
Lubumbashi	318
Matadi	110
Mbandaka	108
Mbuji-Mayi	256
Zambia	
Chingola	146
Kabwe	144
Kitwe	315
Luanshya	132
Lusaka*	538
Mufulira	150
Ndola	282
Zimbabwe	
Bulawayo	414
Harare*	656

Dependency

Country / City	Population in thousands
Hong Kong (U.K.)	
Kowloon	2,450
Victoria*	1,183
Macau (Port.)	
Macau*	238
Puerto Rico (U.S.)	
Bayamón	202
Carolina	162
Ponce	159
San Juan*	426

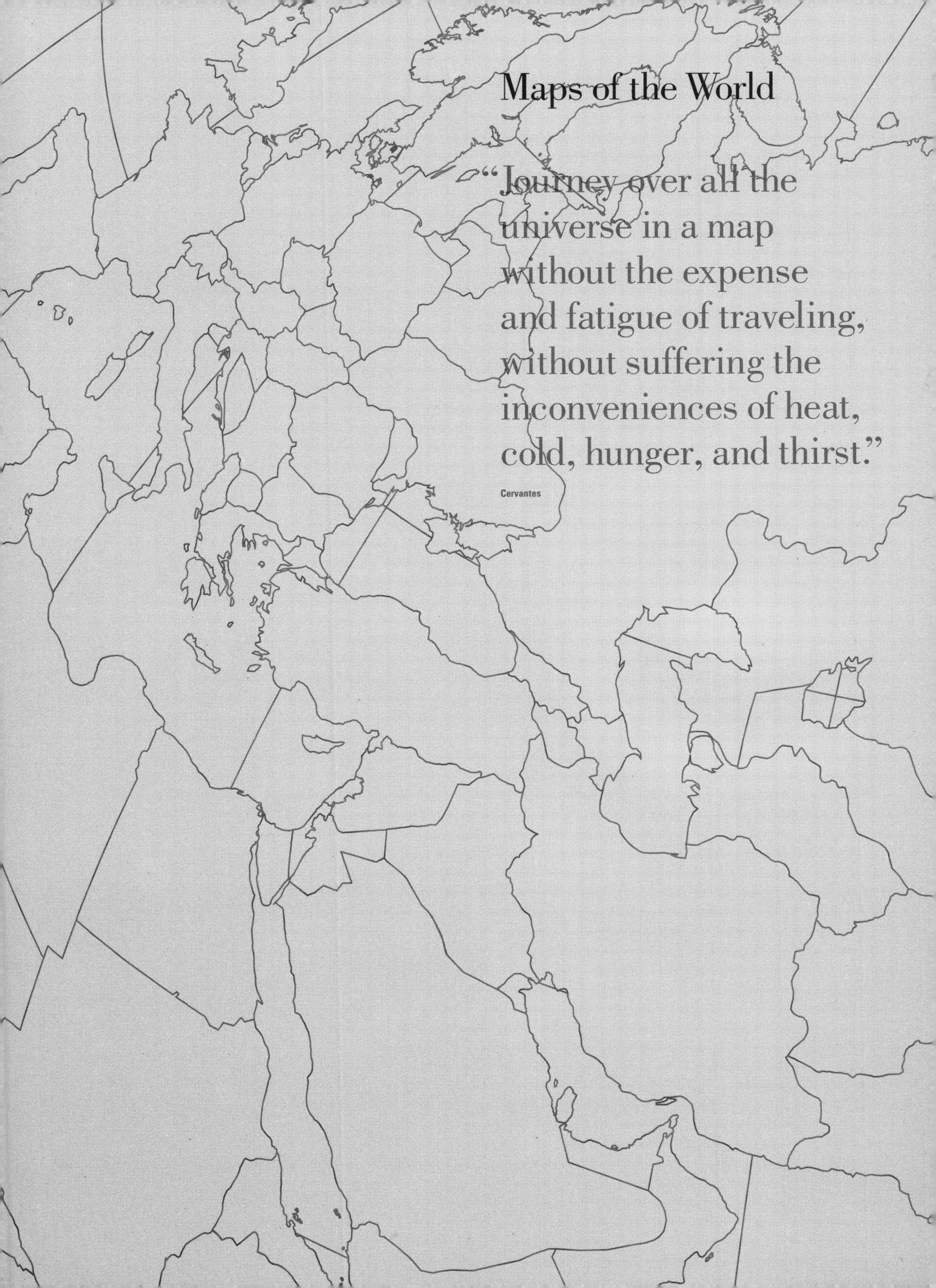

Maps of the World

"Journey over all the
universe in a map
without the expense
and fatigue of traveling,
without suffering the
inconveniences of heat,
cold, hunger, and thirst."

Cervantes

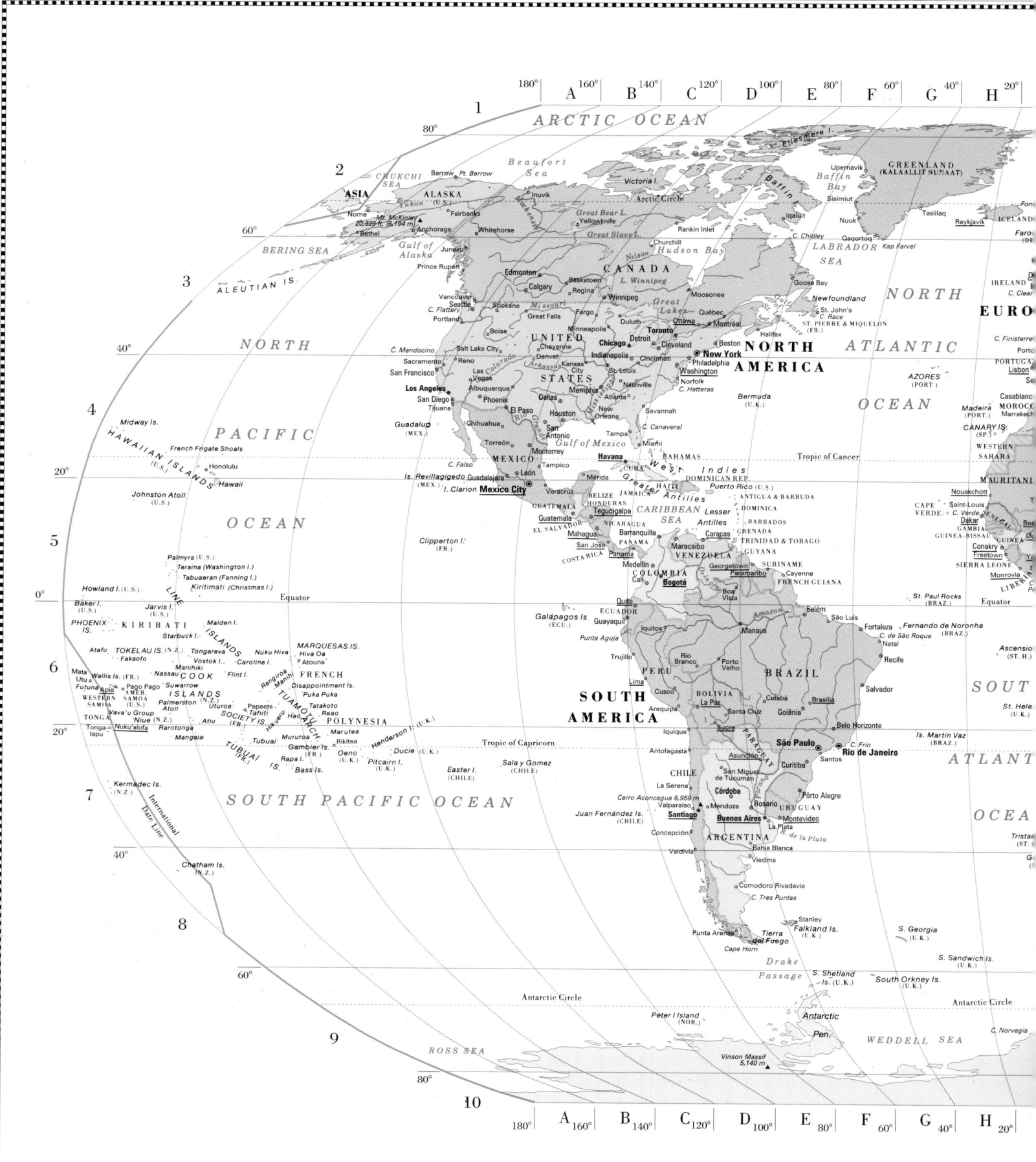

World

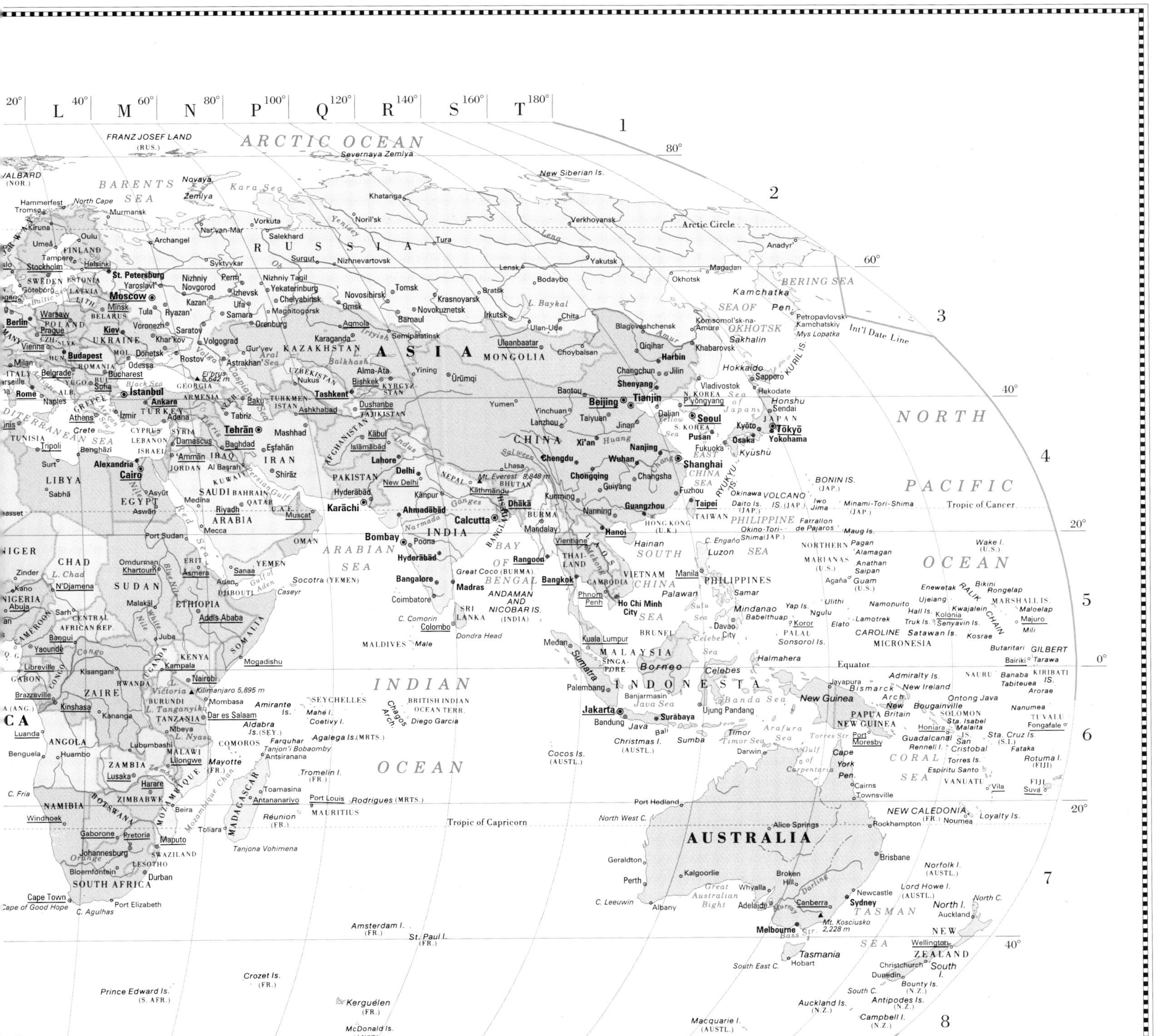

Coordinate borders (top): 20° L 40° M 60° N 80° P 100° Q 120° R 140° S 160° T 180°
Grid numbers (right): 1 2 3 4 5 6 7 8 9 10

ARCTIC OCEAN

FRANZ JOSEF LAND (RUS.)
Severnaya Zemlya
New Siberian Is.
80°

BARENTS SEA
Novaya Zemlya
Kara Sea
Khatanga
Verkhoyansk
Arctic Circle
Anadyr'
60°

VALBARD (NOR.)
Hammerfest
Tromsø
North Cape
Murmansk
Vorkuta
Nar'yan-Mar
Salekhard
Noril'sk
Yenisey
Lena
Yakutsk
Okhotsk
Magadan
BERING SEA
Kamchatka
SEA OF OKHOTSK
Pen.
Petropavlovsk-Kamchatskiy
Mys Lopatka
Int'l Date Line
3

Kiruna
Oulu
Umeå
Tampere
FINLAND
Helsinki
Archangel
Syktyvkar
Surgut
Nizhnevartovsk
Tura
Bratsk
Komsomol'sk-na-Amure
Sakhalin
KURIL IS.
Hokkaido
Sapporo
Hakodate

SWEDEN
Göteborg
Stockholm
ESTONIA
St. Petersburg
Yaroslavl'
Nizhniy Novgorod
Perm
Nizhniy Tagil
Yekaterinburg
Chelyabinsk
Tomsk
Novosibirsk
Krasnoyarsk
L. Baykal
Irkutsk
Chita
Ulan-Ude
Blagoveshchensk
Amur
Khabarovsk
Vladivostok
Changchun
Harbin
Jilin
Shenyang
40°

RUSSIA
Moscow
Tula
Ryazan'
Kazan
Samara
Orenburg
Magnitogorsk
Omsk
Barnaul
Semipalatinsk
Ulaanbaatar
MONGOLIA
Choybalsan
Qiqihar
N. KOREA
Pyŏngyang
Seoul
Pusan
Kyōto
Tōkyō
Yokohama
Honshu
Sendai

Berlin
Warsaw
POLAND
Prague
Vienna
BELARUS
Minsk
Kiev
UKRAINE
Khar'kov
Voronezh
Saratov
Volgograd
Rostov
Astrakhan'
KAZAKHSTAN
Karaganda
Balkhash
Alma-Ata
Bishkek
KYRGYZSTAN
Yining
Ürümqi
Yumen
Baotou
Yinchuan
Lanzhou
Taiyuan
Beijing
Tianjin
Jinan
Dalian
S. KOREA
Osaka
Fukuoka
Kyūshū
JAPAN

Budapest
ROMANIA
Bucharest
Sofia
Black Sea
GEORGIA
ARMENIA
Baku
Nukus
UZBEKISTAN
Tashkent
TURKMENISTAN
Dushanbe
TAJIKISTAN
Kābul
Islāmābād
Lahore
Delhi
CHINA
Xi'an
Chengdu
Chongqing
Wuhan
Nanjing
Shanghai
EAST CHINA SEA

ITALY
Belgrade
YUGO.
Rome
Naples
GREECE
Athens
Crete
Istanbul
Ankara
TURKEY
Adana
CYPRUS
SYRIA
Damascus
LEBANON
ISRAEL
Baghdad
IRAN
Tehrān
Mashhad
Eşfahān
Tabrīz
Shīrāz
AFGHANISTAN
PAKISTAN
New Delhi
NEPAL
Kāthmāndu
BHUTAN
Mt. Everest 8,848 m
Lhasa
Kunming
Guiyang
Changsha
Fuzhou
Taipei
TAIWAN
Okinawa
RYUKYU IS.

MEDITERRANEAN SEA
TUNISIA
Tripoli
Benghazi
Surt
Alexandria
Cairo
EGYPT
Aswān
Sabhā
JORDAN
Amman
Al Başrah
KUWAIT
SAUDI ARABIA
BAHRAIN
QATAR
U.A.E.
Riyadh
Muscat
OMAN
Karāchi
Hyderābad
Ahmadābad
Kānpur
Ganges
Calcutta
BANGLADESH
Dhāka
BURMA
Mandalay
Nanning
Guangzhou
HONG KONG (U.K.)
Hainan
BONIN IS. (JAP.)
VOLCANO IS. (JAP.)
Iwo Jima
Minami-Tori-Shima (JAP.)
Tropic of Cancer
20°

LIBYA
NIGER
CHAD
L. Chad
Zinder
N'Djamena
Omdurman
Khartoum
SUDAN
ERITREA
Asmera
YEMEN
Sanaa
Socotra (YEMEN)
Gulf of Aden
Aden
Mecca
Medina
Port Sudan
Red Sea
ARABIA
ARABIAN SEA
OMAN
Bombay
INDIA
Hyderābad
Narmada
BAY OF BENGAL
Rangoon
THAILAND
Bangkok
Vientiane
LAOS
VIETNAM
Hanoi
SOUTH CHINA SEA
Manila
Luzon
PHILIPPINE SEA
NORTHERN MARIANAS (U.S.)
Pagan
Alamagan
Saipan
Agaña
Guam (U.S.)
Wake I. (U.S.)
OCEAN

NIGERIA
Abuja
Kano
CENTRAL AFRICAN REP.
Sarh
CAMEROON
Yaoundé
Bangui
ETHIOPIA
Addis Ababa
Juba
Malakal
SOMALIA
DJIBOUTI
Caseyr
Bangalore
Madras
Coimbatore
C. Comorin
SRI LANKA
Colombo
Dondra Head
MALDIVES
Male
Great Coco (BURMA)
ANDAMAN AND NICOBAR IS. (INDIA)
CAMBODIA
Phnom Penh
Ho Chi Minh City
Palawan
Mindanao
PHILIPPINES
Samar
Yap Is.
Ulithi
Ngulu
Babelthuap
Koror
PALAU
Elato
Lamotrek
Namonuito
Truk Is.
CAROLINE
MICRONESIA
Kolonia
Ujelang
Enewetak
Bikini
Rongelap
RALIK CHAIN
MARSHALL IS.
Kwajalein
Maloelap
Majuro
Mili
5

GABON
Libreville
CONGO
Brazzaville
ZAIRE
Kinshasa
Kananga
RWANDA
BURUNDI
KENYA
Kampala
Kisangani
Nairobi
UGANDA
Victoria
Kilimanjaro 5,895 m
Mogadishu
INDIAN OCEAN
SEYCHELLES
Mahé I.
Coetivy I.
BRITISH INDIAN OCEAN TERR.
Chagos Arch.
Diego Garcia
MALAYSIA
SINGAPORE
Kuala Lumpur
Medan
BRUNEI
Borneo
Celebes
Sumatra
INDONESIA
Halmahera
Jayapura
Celebes Sea
Equator
NAURU
Banaba
Butaritari
Bairiki
Tarawa
KIRIBATI
GILBERT IS.
Tabiteuea
Arorae
Ontong Java
Nanumea
TUVALU
Funafale
0°

ANGOLA
Luanda
Benguela
Huambo
ZAMBIA
Lubumbashi
Lusaka
MALAWI
Lilongwe
TANZANIA
Dar es Salaam
Mombasa
L. Tanganyika
L. Nyasa
COMOROS
Mayotte
Amirante Is.
Aldabra Is. (SEY.)
Farquhar
Tanjon' Bobaomby
Antsiranana
Tromelin I. (FR.)
Agalega Is. (MRTS.)
Palembang
Java Sea
Banjarmasin
Ujung Pandang
Banda Sea
New Guinea
Bismarck Arch.
New Ireland
New Britain
Bougainville
SOLOMON IS.
Sta. Isabel
Guadalcanal
Honiara
Malaita
San Cristobal
Sta. Cruz Is. (S.I.)
Rennell I.
Rotuma I. (FIJI)
Fataka
6

NAMIBIA
Windhoek
BOTSWANA
Gaborone
Pretoria
Johannesburg
ZIMBABWE
Harare
MOZAMBIQUE
Beira
MADAGASCAR
Antananarivo
Toamasina
Port Louis
MAURITIUS
Réunion (FR.)
Rodrigues (MRTS.)
Tropic of Capricorn
Christmas I. (AUSTL.)
Sumba
Timor
Timor Sea
Arafura Sea
Darwin
Gulf of Carpentaria
Cape York Pen.
Cairns
Townsville
PAPUA NEW GUINEA
Port Moresby
CORAL SEA
Torres Str.
Espiritu Santo
VANUATU
Vila
NEW CALEDONIA (FR.)
Noumea
Loyalty Is.
20°

SOUTH AFRICA
Gaborone
Pretoria
SWAZILAND
Maputo
LESOTHO
Durban
Bloemfontein
Cape Town
Cape of Good Hope
C. Agulhas
Port Elizabeth
Amsterdam I. (FR.)
St. Paul I. (FR.)
North West C.
Port Hedland
North C.
Geraldton
Kalgoorlie
Perth
Great Australian Bight
C. Leeuwin
Albany
Adelaide
AUSTRALIA
Alice Springs
Rockhampton
Brisbane
Whyalla
Broken Hill
Newcastle
Sydney
Canberra
Mt. Kosciusko 2,228 m
Melbourne
Norfolk I. (AUSTL.)
Lord Howe I. (AUSTL.)
North C.
Auckland
TASMAN SEA
NEW ZEALAND
7

Crozet Is. (FR.)
Prince Edward Is. (S. AFR.)
Kerguélen (FR.)
McDonald Is. (AUSTL.)
Macquarie I. (AUSTL.)
Wellington
Bass Str.
Tasmania
Hobart
South East C.
Christchurch
Dunedin
South I.
Auckland Is. (N.Z.)
Bounty Is. (N.Z.)
Antipodes Is. (N.Z.)
Campbell I. (N.Z.)
South C. (N.Z.)
8
40°

C. Batterbee
ANTARCTICA
Antarctic Circle
C. Adare
ROSS SEA
9
80°
10

Coordinate borders (bottom): 20° L 40° M 60° N 80° P 100° Q 120° R 140° S 160° T 180°
60°

© Copyright by HAMMOND INCORPORATED, Maplewood, N.J.   CC-1001-A-A

POPULATION OF CITIES AND TOWNS
- ◉ OVER 5,000,000
- ● 2,000,000 - 4,999,999
- ◉ 500,000 - 1,999,999
- ○ UNDER 500,000

SCALE 1:81,700,000   ROBINSON PROJECTION   STANDARD PARALLELS 38°N AND 38°S
MILES 0   1000   2000   3000   4000
KILOMETERS 0   1000   2000   3000   4000

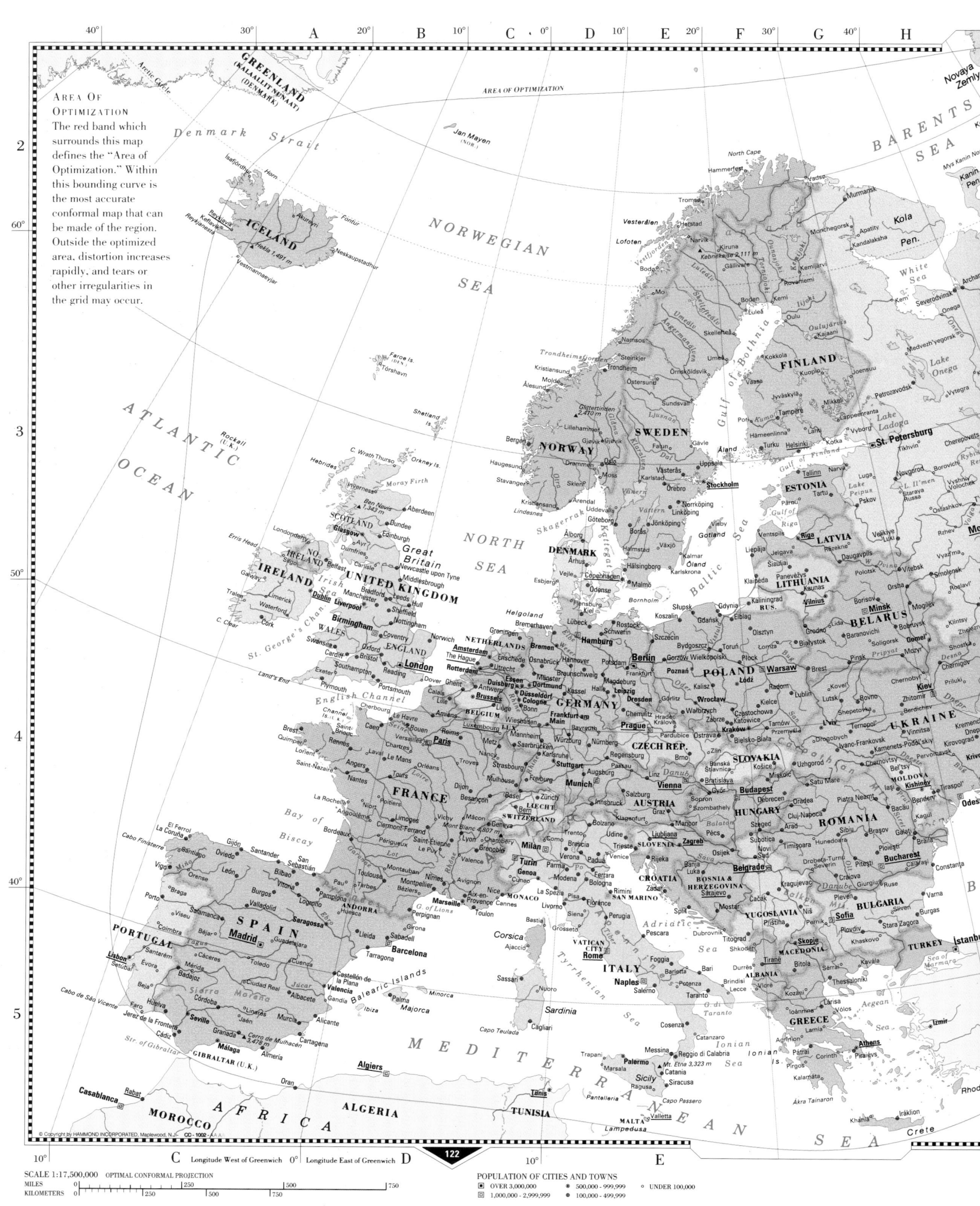

AREA OF
OPTIMIZATION
The red band which
surrounds this map
defines the "Area of
Optimization." Within
this bounding curve is
the most accurate
conformal map that can
be made of the region.
Outside the optimized
area, distortion increases
rapidly, and tears or
other irregularities in
the grid may occur.

AREA OF OPTIMIZATION

SCALE 1:17,500,000   OPTIMAL CONFORMAL PROJECTION

MILES
KILOMETERS

| 0 | 250 | 500 | 750 |

POPULATION OF CITIES AND TOWNS

⊡ OVER 3,000,000   ● 500,000 - 999,999   ○ UNDER 100,000
⊡ 1,000,000 - 2,999,999   ● 100,000 - 499,999

Longitude West of Greenwich 0° Longitude East of Greenwich

© Copyright by HAMMOND INCORPORATED, Maplewood, N.J.   CC-1002

Europe

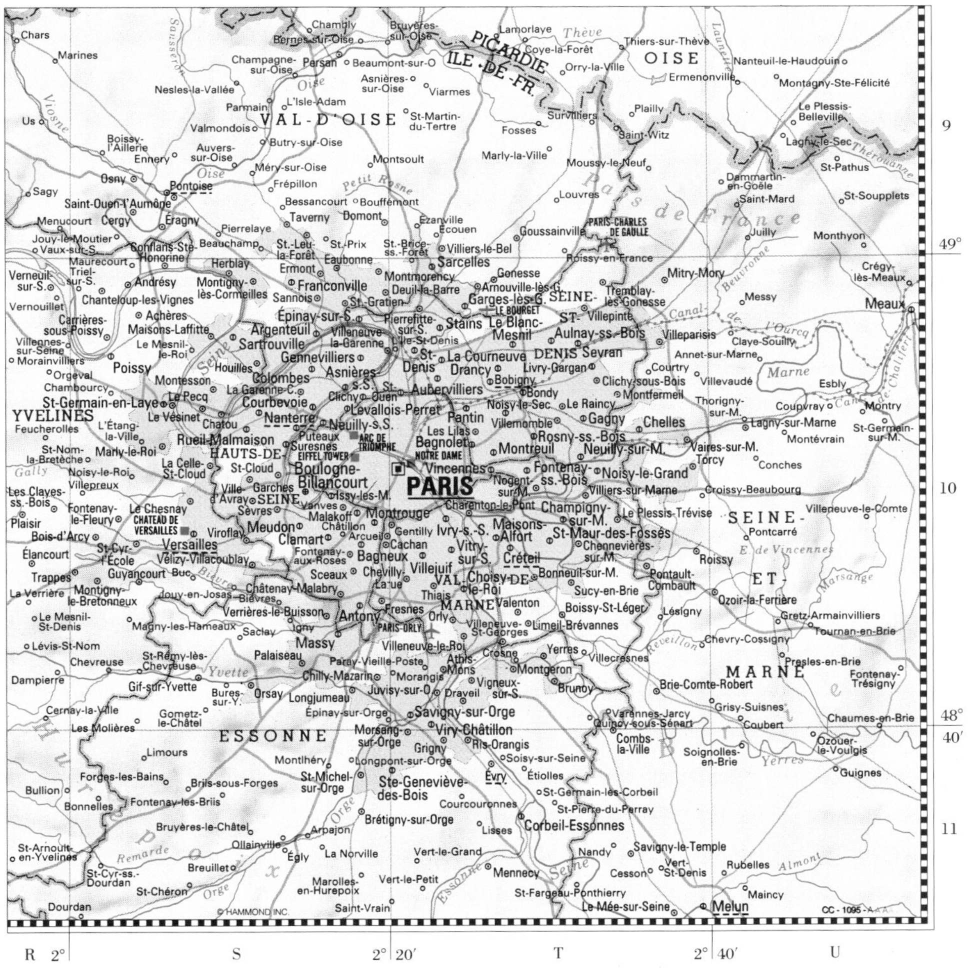

© HAMMOND INC.

SCALE 1:587,000   LAMBERT CONFORMAL CONIC PROJECTION

MILES

KILOMETERS

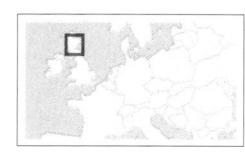

Central Scotland

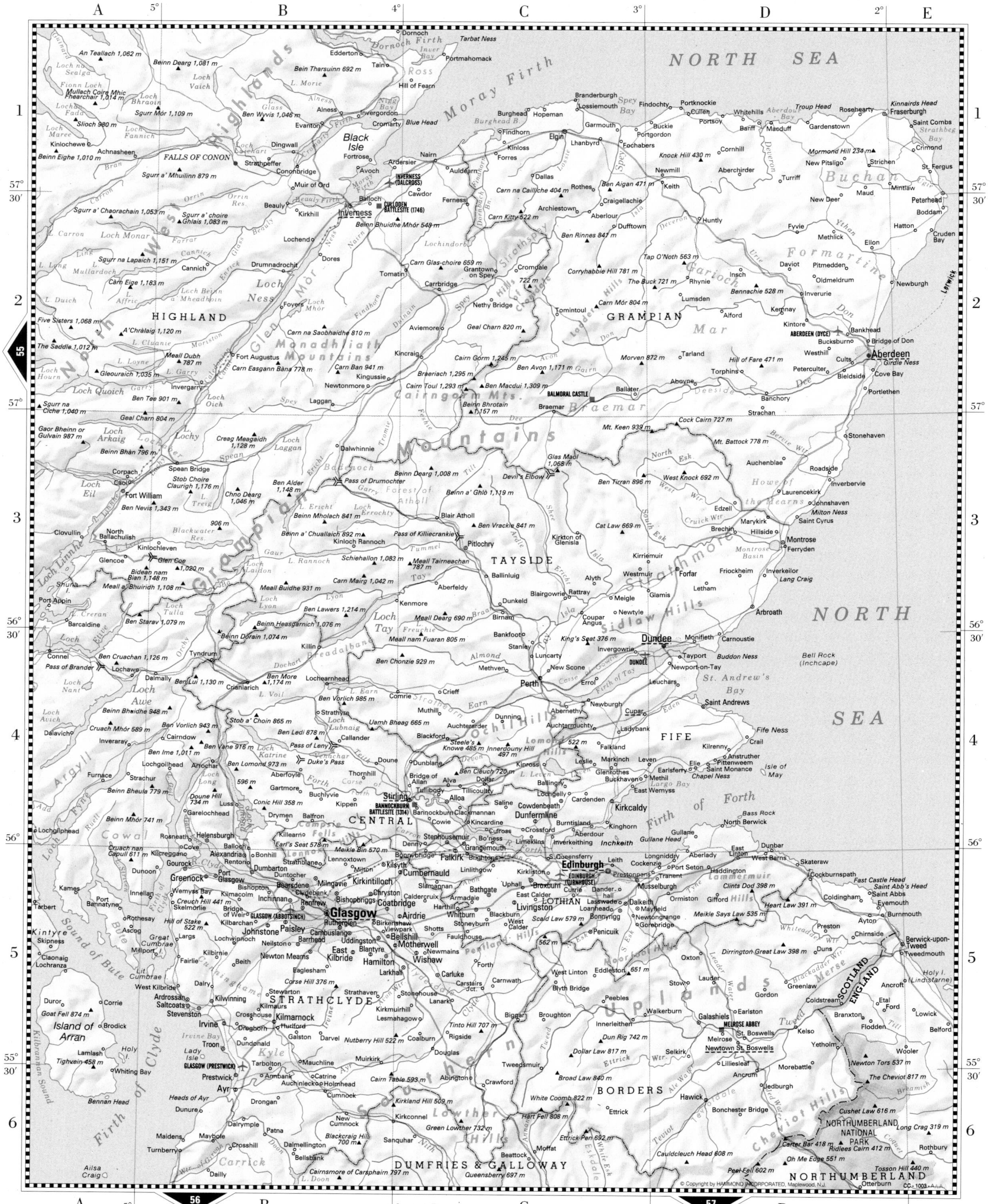

SCALE 1:1,170,000   LAMBERT CONFORMAL CONIC PROJECTION

MILES 0 | 10 | 20 | 30 | 40 | 50

KILOMETERS 0 | 10 | 20 | 30 | 40 | 50

Longitude West of Greenwich

POPULATION OF CITIES AND TOWNS

▪ OVER 2,000,000
▫ 1,000,000 - 1,999,999
● 500,000 - 999,999
◍ 250,000 - 499,999
● 100,000 - 249,999
● 30,000 - 99,999
○ 10,000 - 29,999
○ UNDER 10,000

United Kingdom, Ireland

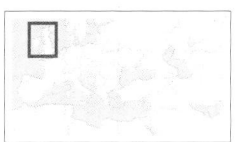

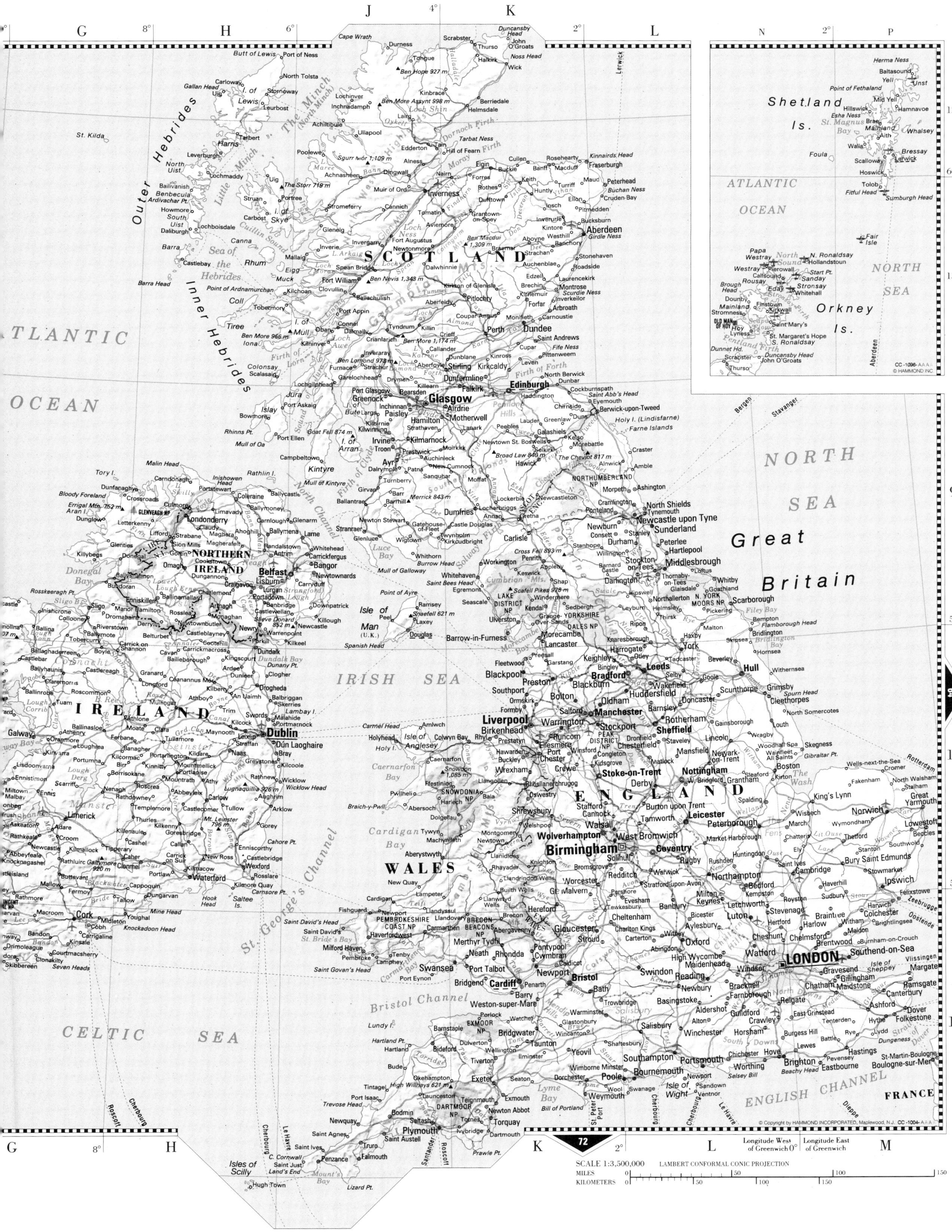

SCALE 1:3,500,000   LAMBERT CONFORMAL CONIC PROJECTION

MILES

KILOMETERS

Longitude West of Greenwich 0°   Longitude East of Greenwich

Northeastern Ireland, Northern England and Wales

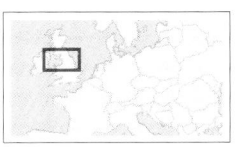

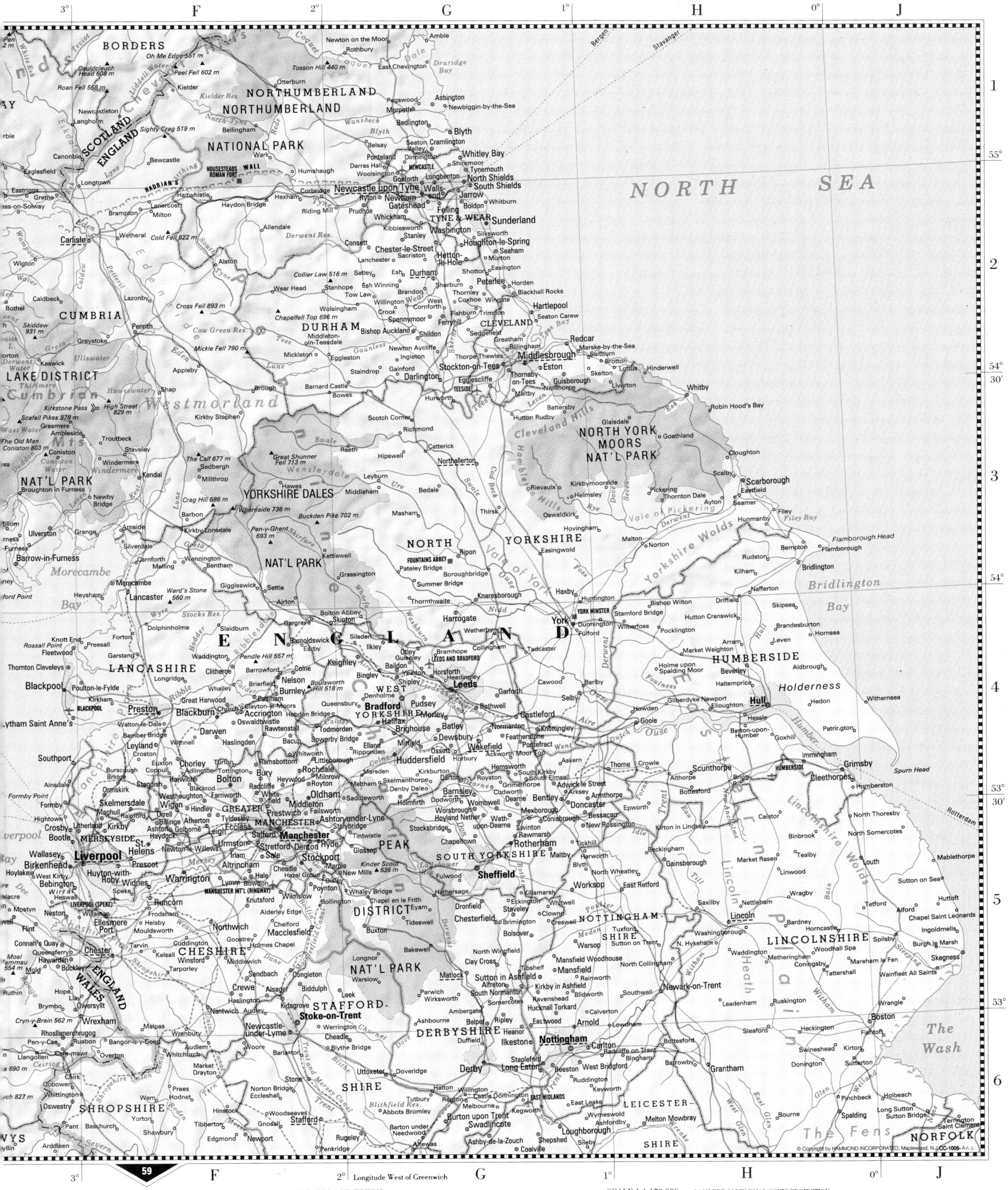

NORTH SEA

SCOTLAND
ENGLAND

BORDERS

NORTHUMBERLAND
NORTHUMBERLAND
NATIONAL PARK

HADRIAN'S WALL

CUMBRIA

LAKE DISTRICT
NAT'L PARK

Cumbrian Mts.

DURHAM

TYNE & WEAR

CLEVELAND

TEESIDE

Newcastle upon Tyne
Gateshead
Sunderland
Durham
Middlesbrough
Darlington
Carlisle
Penrith
Kendal
Lancaster

NORTH YORK MOORS NAT'L PARK

YORKSHIRE DALES NAT'L PARK

Yorkshire Wolds

Vale of Pickering
Vale of York

NORTH YORKSHIRE

Scarborough
Filey Bay
Flamborough Head
Bridlington Bay

WESTMORLAND

Morecambe Bay

LANCASHIRE

Blackpool
Preston
Blackburn
Burnley
Southport

York
YORK MINSTER

Harrogate
Leeds
LEEDS AND BRADFORD
WEST YORKSHIRE
Bradford
Halifax
Huddersfield
Wakefield

HUMBERSIDE
Holderness
Hull
Grimsby
Cleethorpes
Spurn Head

GREATER MANCHESTER
MANCHESTER
Salford
Bolton
Oldham
Stockport
MANCHESTER INT'L (RINGWAY)

MERSEYSIDE
Liverpool
Birkenhead
Wallasey
LIVERPOOL (SPEKE)
St. Helens
Warrington
Widnes
Runcorn

SOUTH YORKSHIRE
Sheffield
Rotherham
Barnsley
Doncaster

Scunthorpe

PEAK DISTRICT NAT'L PARK
Kinder Scout 636 m

CHESHIRE
Chester
Crewe
Macclesfield

LINCOLNSHIRE
Lincoln
Lincolnshire Wolds
Lincoln Heath
Louth
Skegness
Boston

NOTTINGHAMSHIRE
Mansfield
Newark-on-Trent

STAFFORDSHIRE
Stoke-on-Trent
Newcastle-under-Lyme

ENGLAND
WALES
Wrexham

DERBYSHIRE
Derby
Nottingham
Ilkeston
Long Eaton

EAST MIDLANDS

LEICESTERSHIRE

SHROPSHIRE
Shrewsbury

The Wash
The Fens
NORFOLK

Longitude West of Greenwich

POPULATION OF CITIES AND TOWNS

- ■ OVER 2,000,000
- ▣ 1,000,000 - 1,999,999
- ● 500,000 - 999,999
- ◉ 250,000 - 499,999
- ● 100,000 - 249,999
- ○ 30,000 - 99,999
- ○ 10,000 - 29,999
- ○ UNDER 10,000

SCALE 1:1,170,000   LAMBERT CONFORMAL CONIC PROJECTION

MILES   0   10   20   30   40   50
KILOMETERS   0   10   20   30   40   50

Southern England and Wales

A 5° **56** **B** 4° **C** 3° **D**

52°30'
60
52°
51°30'
51°
50°30'

George's Channel · *Saint George's Channel*

Cardigan Bay

GWYNEDD · Llanelltyd · Dolgellau · Barmouth · Cader Idris 892 m · Waun-Oer 670 m · Tir Rhiwiog 545 m · Llyn Efyrnwy · Llanfyllin · ▲540 m · Baschurch · Shawbury · Tibberton · Edgmond · Newport · Gnosall

SNOWDONIA NATIONAL PARK · Corris · Penegoes · Machynlleth · Moelfre 468 m · Esgair Ddu 464 m · Aberangell · Llanfair Caereinion · Welshpool · Guilsfield · Shrewsbury · Wroxeter · The Wrekin 407 m · Telford · Wheaton Aston · St · Shifnal

Tywyn · Aberdyfi · Borth · 560 m · Moel-y-Llyn 521 m · Plynlimon 753 m · Trefeglwys · Newtown · Kerry · Montgomery · Long Mtn. 408 m · Berriew · Dorrington · Much Wenlock · Iron Bridge · Albrighton · Wolverhampton · Wombourne

Aberystwyth · Ponterwyd · Devils Bridge · Llanidloes · Llangurig · Clifaesty Hill 528 m · Church Stretton · The Long Mynd 516 m · Bishops Castle · Brown Clee Hill 540 m · Highley · Kingswinford · Stourbridge · Dudle · Halesow

POWYS · Llanrhystyd · Lledrod · Rhyddhywel 585 m · Geifas 571 m · Moel Hywel 505 m · Bucknell · Knighton · Aston on Clun · Clun · Ludlow · Cleobury Mortimer · Bewdley · Stourport-on-Severn · Hartlebury · Kiddermin

Llanon · Aberaeron · Trawsallt 593 m · Claerwen Res. · Rhayader · Crossgates · New Radnor · Presteigne · Mortimers Cross · Kingsland · Leominster · Tenbury · Clifton-upon-Teme · Great Witley · Ombersley · Worces

New Quay · Tregaron · Gorllwyn 613 m · Caban-Coch Res. · Llandrindod Wells · Newbridge-on-Wye · Kington · Hope-under-Dinmore · Newton · Bromyard · Martley · Worces

Cernaes Head · Llanarth · Aberarth · Lampeter · Bryn Brawd 484 m · Drygarn Fawr 641 m · Llanwrtyd Wells · Garth · Llangammarch Wells · Wellington · Staunton on Wye · Credenhill · HEREFORD & WORCESTER · Gt. Malvern 425 m · Colwall · Pershe

Aberporth · Pen y Gurnos 456 m · Llyn Brianne Res. · Builth Wells · Painscastle · Hay-on-Wye · Hereford · Trumpet · Ledbury

DYFED · Cardigan · Rhydowen · Llandyssul · Mynydd Pencarreg 415 m · Pumpsaint · WALES · Llandovery · Epynt · Glasbury · Bronllys · Talgarth · Pontrilas · Fownhope · Upton upon Severn

Strumble Head · Dinas Head · Newport · Goodwick · Fishguard · PEMBROKESHIRE · 468 m · 536 m · Newcastle Emlyn · Llechryd · Cynwyl Elfed · Carmarthen · Llandeilo · Black Mtn · Sennybridge · BRECON · Brecon · Waun Fach 810 m · Black Mountains · 719 m · Llanthony · ENGLAND WALES · Ross-on-Wye · Mich

St. David's Head · Llanrian · Solva · COAST · Trelech · Llandysul · 633 m · 802 m · 886 m · BEACONS · Sugar Loaf 596 m · Abergavenny · Monmouth · Forest of Dean · Cinderford · Gloucester

Ramsey I. · Saint David's · Clunderwen · Whitland · BRECON 734 m · 763 m · PARK · Llangattock · Crickhowell · Raglan · Coleford · Newnham · Quedgeley · Gl

St. Brides Bay · Haverfordwest · Narberth · Laugharne · St. Clears · Llandybie · 616 m · NAT'L · Brynmawr · Tredegar · Ebbw Vale · Blaenavon · Usk · Llandogo · TINTERN ABBEY · Bream · Stonehouse · Stroud

Skomer I. · Johnston · Ferryside · Ammanford · Glanamman · Ystradgynlais · Rhymney · Cwm · Abertillery · Pontypool · Chepstow · St. Briavels · Lydney · Netherend · Berkeley · 249 m · Nailsworth

Skokholm I. · Milford Haven · Neyland · Kidwelly · Llannon · Pontardawe · Glyn Neath · Resolven · Merthyr Tydfil · MID · New Tredegar · Brynithel · Cwmbran · Wotton-under-Edge

Saint Ann's Head · Pembroke Dock · Saundersfoot · Pontyates · Pontardulais · Clydach · Neath · Hirwaun 620 m · Aberdare · GWENT · Blackwood · Pontypridd · Caerleon · Thornbury · Dursley

Linney Head · Pembroke · Lamphey · Bury Port · Burry Inlet · Whiteford Point · Morriston · GLAMORGAN · Mountain Ash · Rhondda · GLAMORGAN · Ystrad Mynach · Crosskeys · Risca · Machen · Newport · Caldicot · Alveston

Saint Govan's Head · PARK · Crofty · SWANSEA · Baglan · Cwmafan · Gilfach Goch · Maesteg · Porth · Beddau · Caerphilly · Magor · Patchway · Yate · Chipping Sodbury · Castle Combe

Gower Pen. · Rhossili · Port Talbot · Pont-y-Cymmer · Ogmore-by-Sea · Pyle · Pencoed · Pontyclun · Llantrisant · Taffs Well · Whitchurch · Rumney · Saint Mellons · Filton · Winterbourne · Chippenham · Corsham

Port Eynon · Port-Eynon Point · Swansea Bay · Porthcawl · Bridgend · SOUTH GLAMORGAN · Cowbridge · Dinas Powys · CARDIFF · Penarth · Portishead · Clevedon · Nailsea · BRISTOL · Kingswood · Lacock

Nash Point · Saint Athan · Llantwit Major · Barry · Sully · Steep Holm · Weston-super-Mare · Backwell · Keynsham · Saltford · Bath · Melksham · Bradford-on-Avon

CARDIFF-WALES · Flat Holm · Sand Point · Mouth of the Severn · Worle · AVON · BRISTOL (LULSGATE) · Chew · Pensford · Chew Valley L. · Paulton · Radstock · Trowbridge · Westbur

Bristol Channel

Lundy I. · Foreland Point · Lynton · Porlock · Minehead · Watchet · Williton · Burnham-on-Sea · Wedmore · 304 m · Wells · Midsomer Norton · Frome

Morte Point · Ilfracombe · Combe Martin · Brendon · Dunkery Hill 520 m · EXMOOR · Lype Hill 423 m · Bridgwater · Highbridge · 384 m · Shepton Mallet · Evercreech · LONGLEAT HOUSE

Baggy Point · Braunton · 487 m · EXMOOR NAT'L · 493 m · North Petherton · Woolavington · Glastonbury · Street · Brutton · Mere · Tisbur

Barnstaple or Bideford Bay · Barnstaple · Frithelstock · South Molton · PARK · Dulverton · Wiveliscombe · Bampton · Taunton · Milverton · SOMERSET · Somerton · Castle Cary · Wincanton · Gillingham

Hartland Point · Westward Ho! · Northam · East-the-Water · Bideford · Clovelly · Dolton · Witheridge · Wellington · Blackdown · 315 m · Hills · South Petherton · Martock · Ilchester · Milborne Port · Marnhull · Shaftesb

Celtic Sea · Hartland · Great Torrington · Beaford · Tiverton · Cullompton · Ilminster · Yeovil · Sherborne · Stalbridge · Cran b Ch

Bude Bay · Bude · Stratton · Holsworthy · Hatherleigh · DEVON · Silverton · Bradninch · Chard · Crewkerne · Yetminster · 265 m · 274 m · DORSET · Blandford

Week St. Mary · Dolton · Crediton · Honiton · Ottery Saint Mary · Axminster · Beaminster · Cerne Abbas · Maiden Newton · Lytchett · Wool · Is

Tintagel Head · Tintagel · Boscastle · Camelford · Okehampton · High Willhays 621 m · Hangingstone Hill 605 m · Exeter · Exminster · Seaton · Bridport · Bothenhampton · Dorchester · Preston · Pu

Pentire Point · Port Isaac · Brown Willy 419 m · Bodmin Moor · Cut Hill 604 m · DARTMOOR · Moretonhampstead · EXETER · Topsham · Sidmouth · 237 m · Abbotsbury · Wareham

Trevose Head · Padstow · Wadebridge · Kilmar Tor 390 m · Caradon Hill 370 m · Bovey Tracey · Newton Abbot · Budleigh Salterton · Exmouth · *Lyme Bay* · Melcombe Regis · Weymouth · St. Aldhe

Park Head · Colliford Res. · Great Mis Tor 539 m · NAT'L · Kingsteignton · Teignmouth · Dawlish · Chickerell · *Weymouth Bay*

Watergate Bay · NEWQUAY CIVIL · Bodmin · Liskeard · Callington · Tavistock · Horrabridge · Ashburton · Buckfastleigh · Torquay · Fortuneswell · Isle of Portland · Easton

Kelsey Head · Newquay · St. Columb Major · Roche · 313 m · Lostwithiel · Saltash · PLYMOUTH · Yelverton · PARK · South Brent · Paignton · Bill of Portland

Perranporth · Saint Agnes Head · St. Stephen-in-Brannel · Saint Austell · CORNWALL · Fowey · Polperro · Looe · Millbrook · Plymouth · Ivybridge · Totnes · Tor Bay · Berry Head · Brixham

Navax Point · Illogan · Redruth · Truro · Gribbin Head · St. Austell Bay · Torpoint · Newton Ferrers · Modbury · South Hams · Dartmouth · Kingswear

St. Ives · Camborne · Lanner · St. Just-in-Roseland · Dodman Point · Eddystone Rocks · Stoke Point · *Bigbury Bay* · Start Bay · Start Point

St. Just · Penzance · Newlyn · Godolphin Cross · Wendron · Penryn · Saint Mawes · Veryan Bay · Nare Point · Salcombe · Bolt Head · Prawle Point

Land's End · *Mount's Bay* · Marazion · Helston · Gweek · Porthleven · Manacle Point · The Lizard · Black Head · St. Peter Port

Hugh Town · Mullion · Lizard · Lizard Point

B 4° **C** **72** 3° **D**

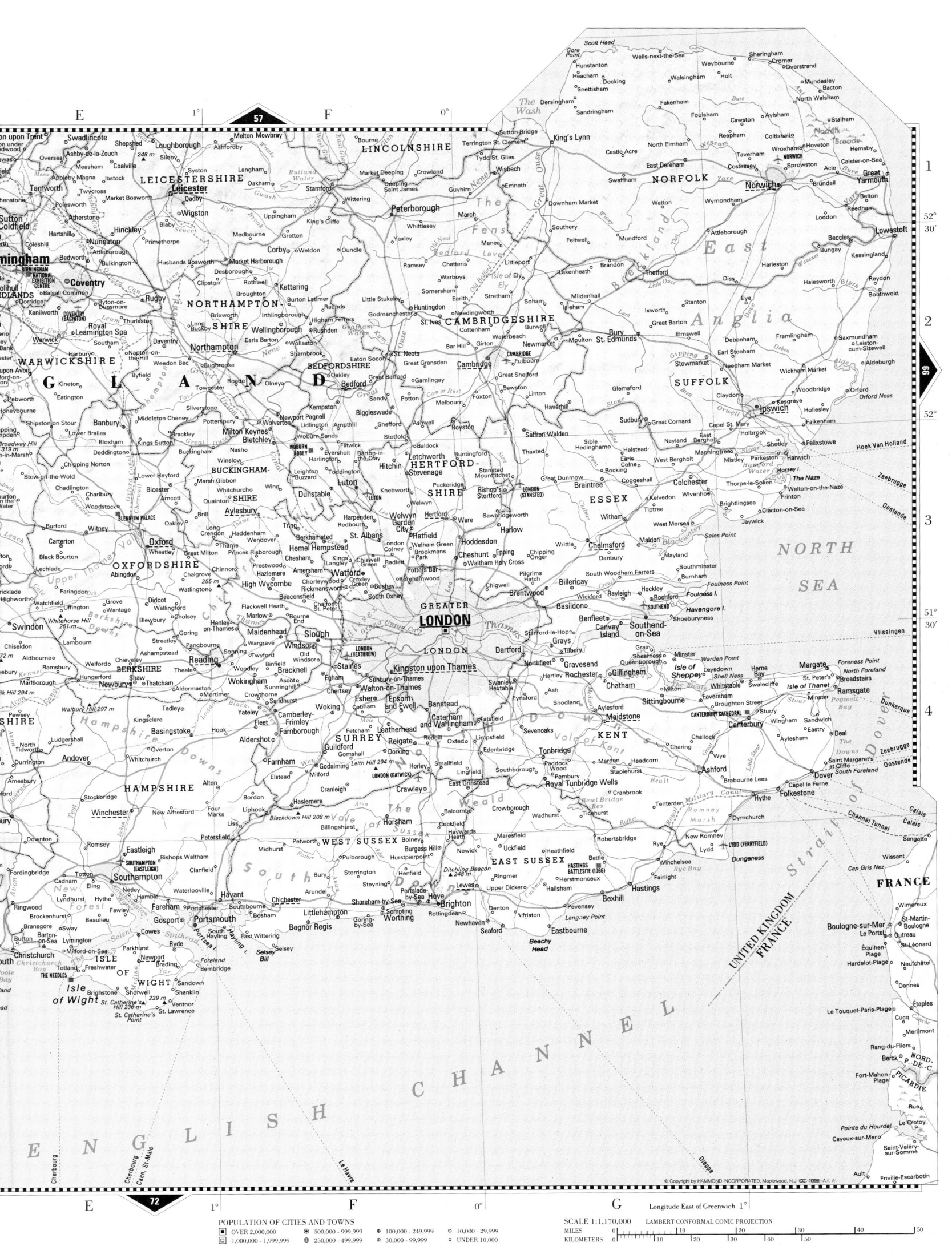

POPULATION OF CITIES AND TOWNS

- ■ OVER 2,000,000
- ◉ 500,000 - 999,999
- ● 100,000 - 249,999
- ◎ 10,000 - 29,999
- ⊡ 1,000,000 - 1,999,999
- ● 250,000 - 499,999
- ● 30,000 - 99,999
- ○ UNDER 10,000

SCALE 1:1,170,000 LAMBERT CONFORMAL CONIC PROJECTION

MILES 0 ⌶⌶⌶ 10 · 20 · 30 · 40 · 50
KILOMETERS 0 ⌶⌶⌶ 10 · 20 · 30 · 40 · 50

Longitude East of Greenwich 1°

Central and Southern Ireland

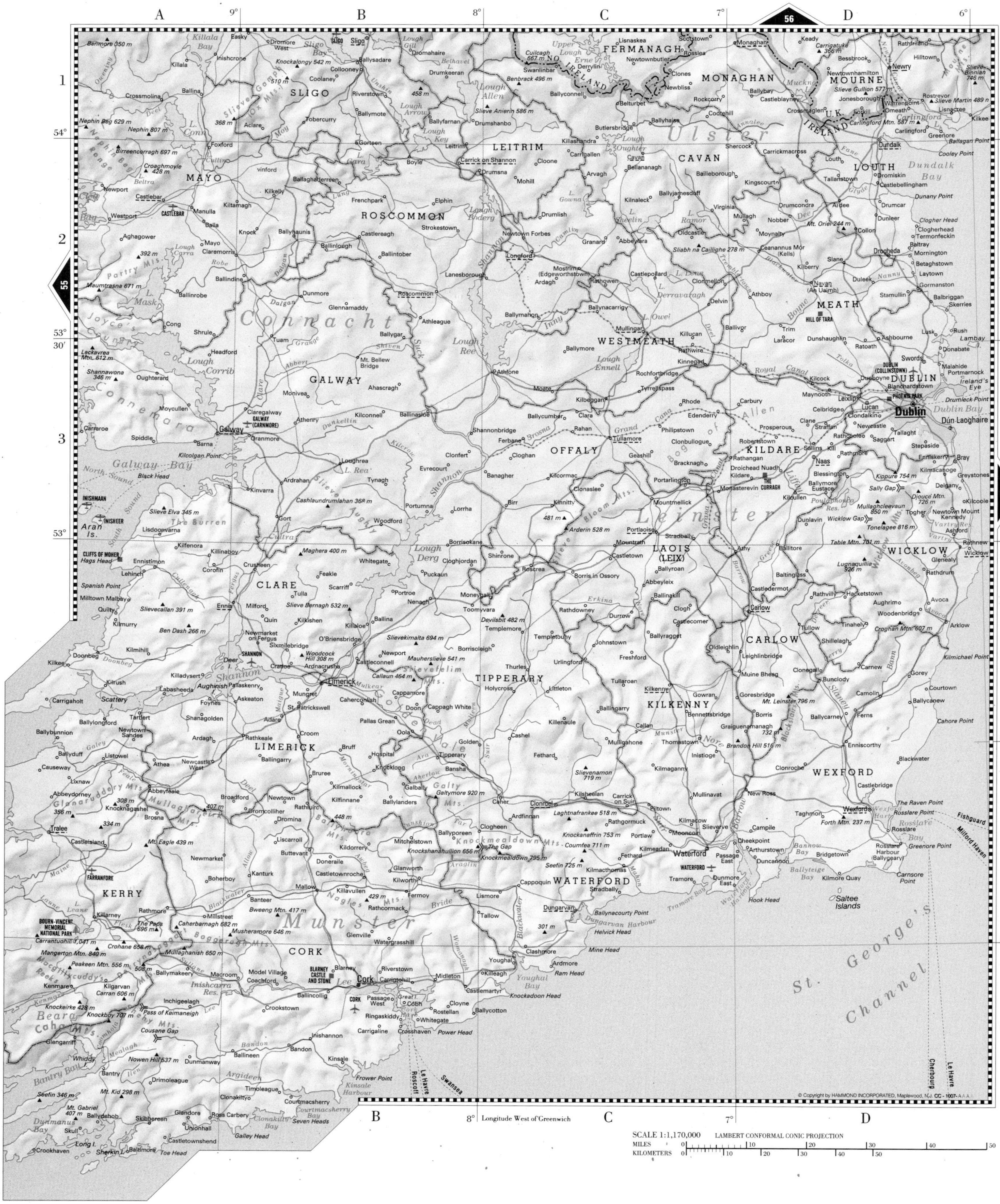

SCALE 1:1,170,000   LAMBERT CONFORMAL CONIC PROJECTION

MILES

KILOMETERS

Longitude West of Greenwich

Scandinavia and Finland, Iceland

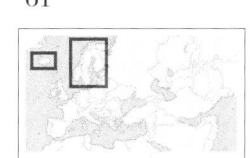

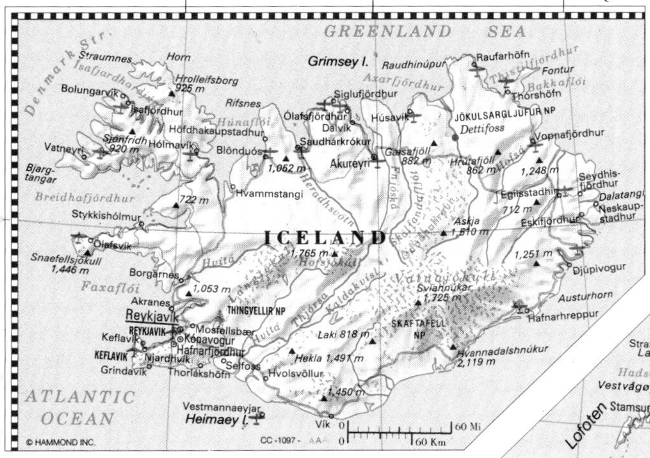

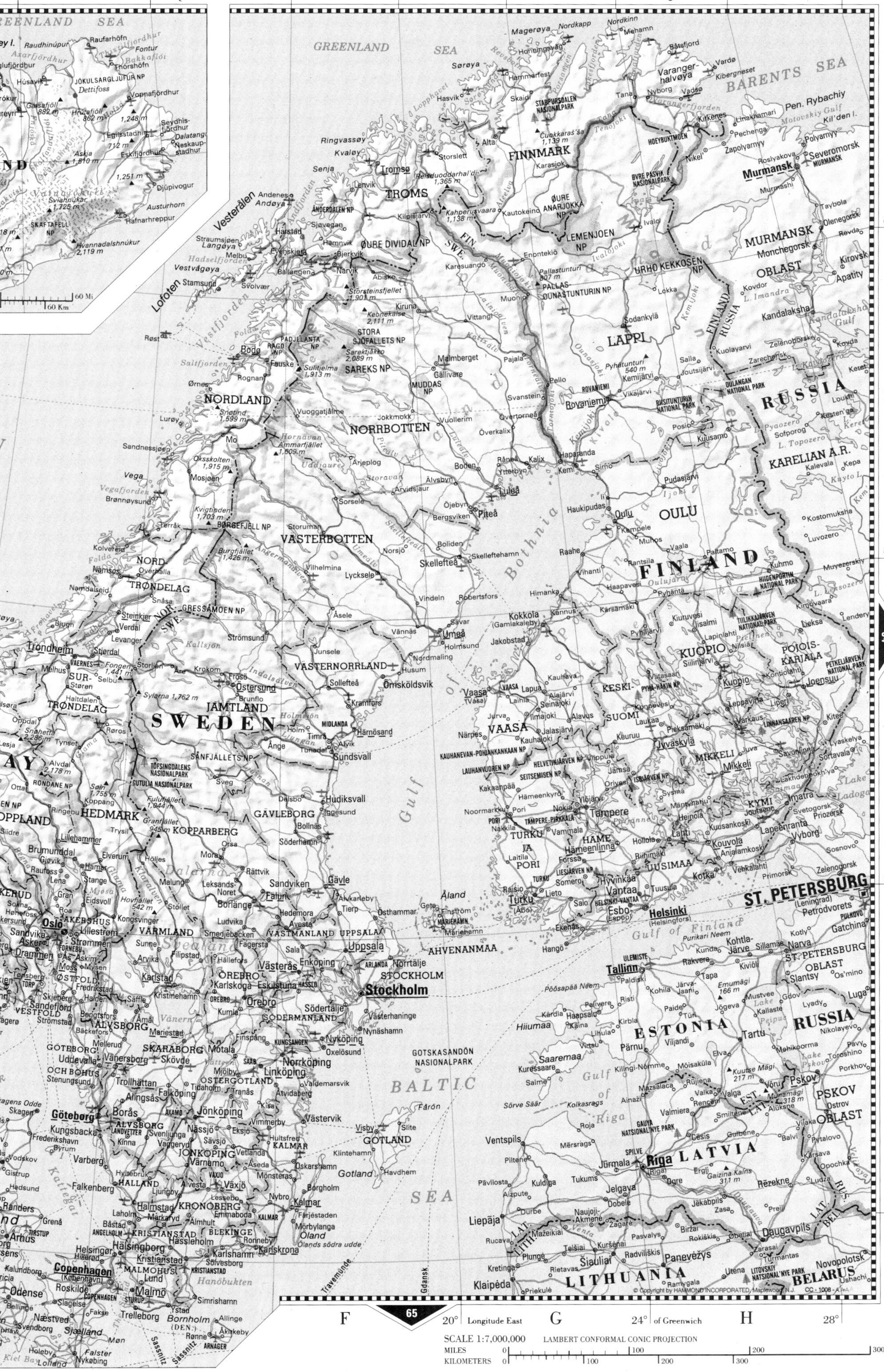

ICELAND

SCALE 1:7,000,000   LAMBERT CONFORMAL CONIC PROJECTION

MILES
KILOMETERS

© HAMMOND INC.

Longitude East   of Greenwich

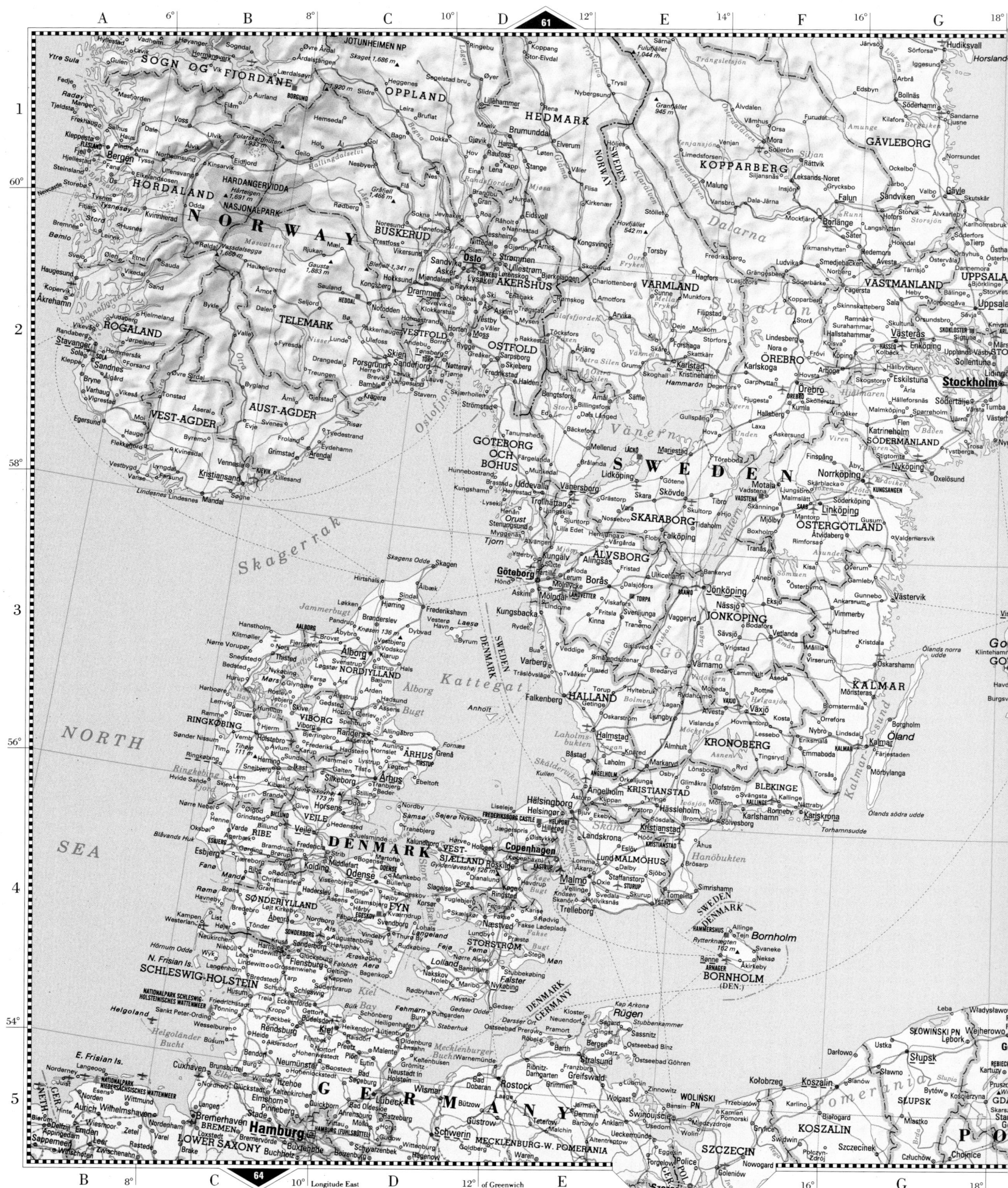

Baltic Region

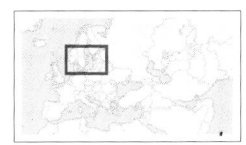

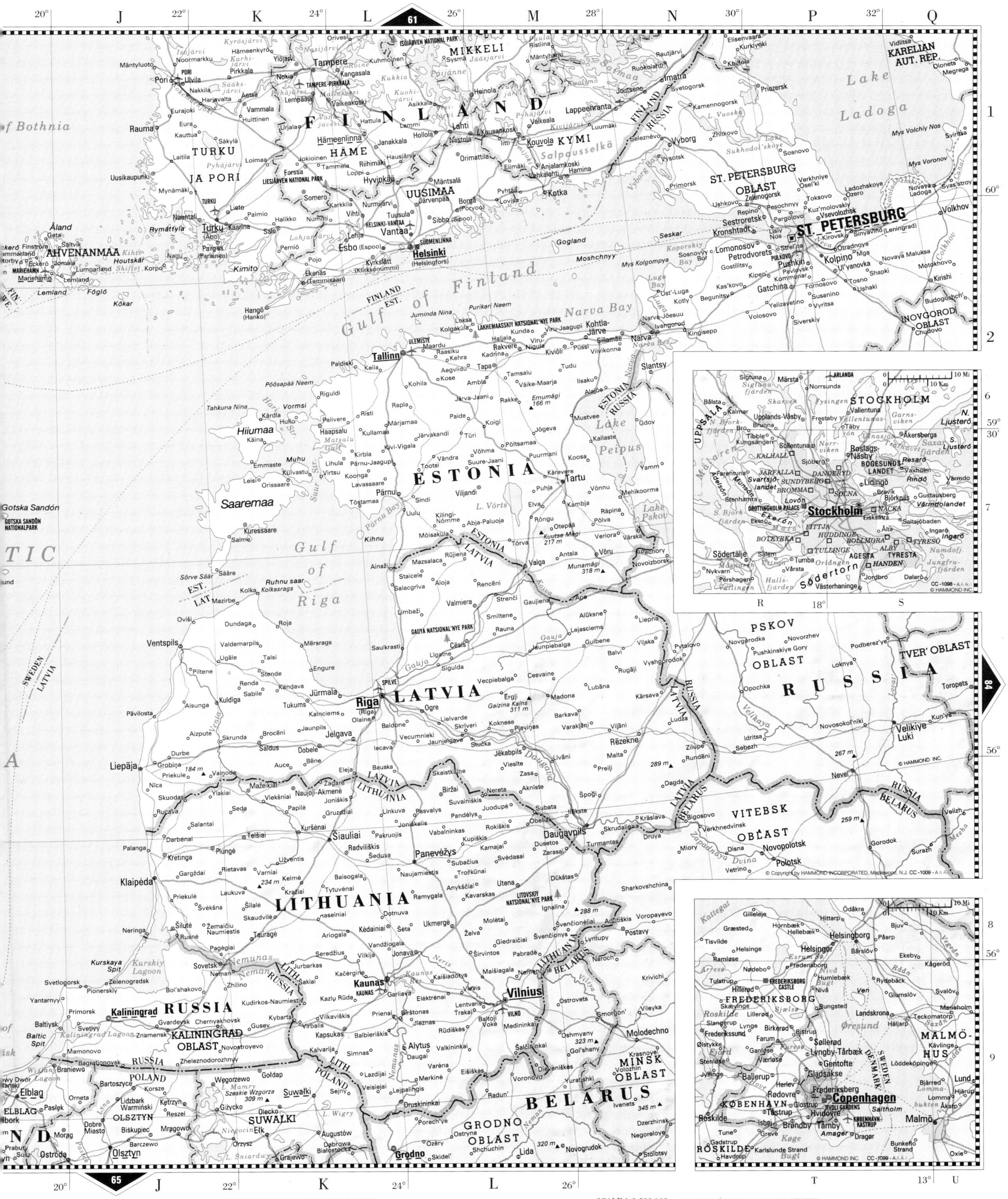

POPULATION OF CITIES AND TOWNS

- ■ OVER 2,000,000
- □ 1,000,000 - 1,999,999
- ◉ 500,000 - 999,999
- ◎ 250,000 - 499,999
- ● 100,000 - 249,999
- ◐ 30,000 - 99,999
- ⊙ 10,000 - 29,999
- ○ UNDER 10,000

SCALE 1:3,500,000 LAMBERT CONFORMAL CONIC PROJECTION

MILES 0 50 100 150

KILOMETERS 0 50 100 150

North Central Europe

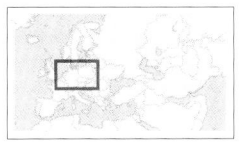

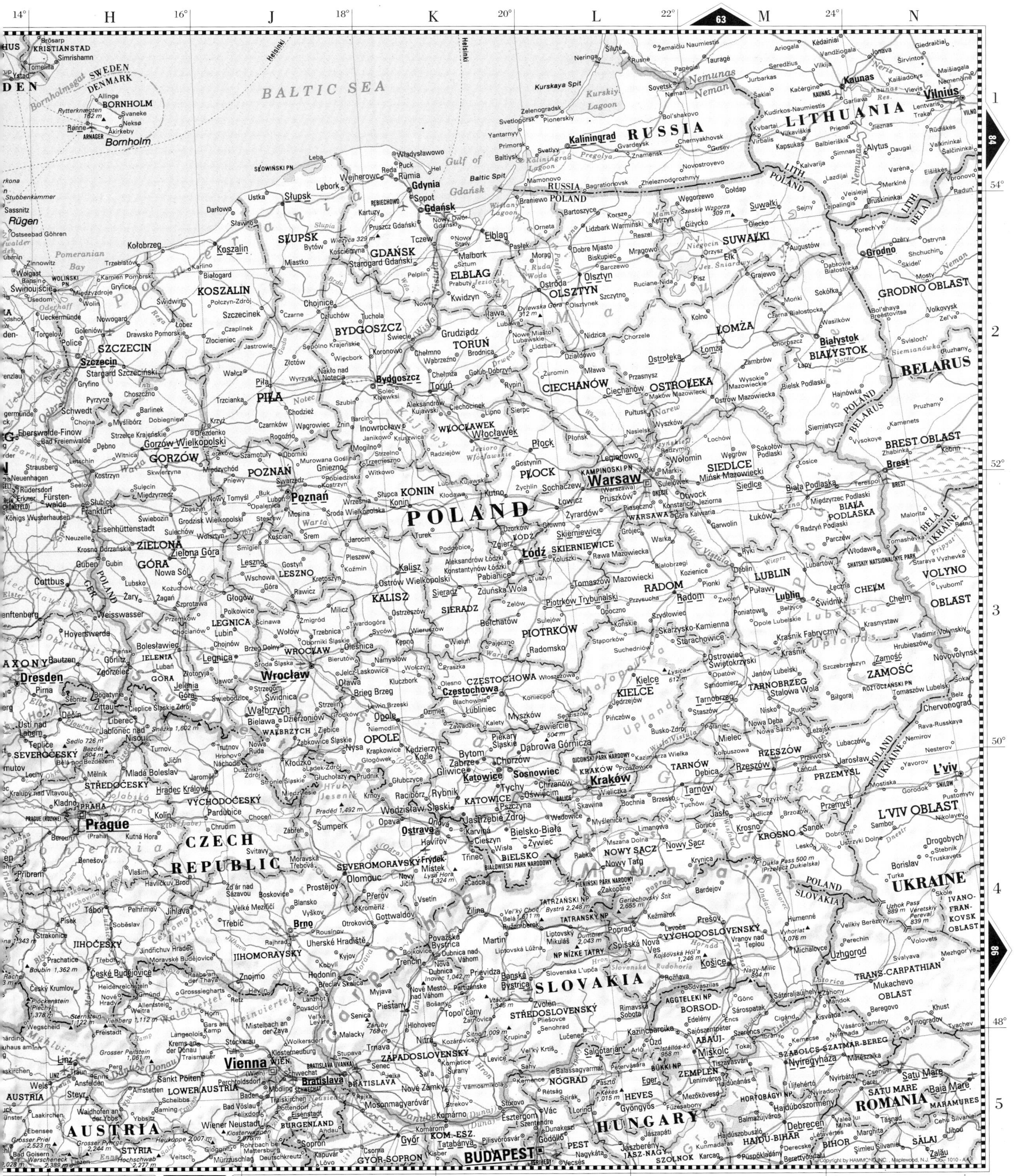

POPULATION OF CITIES AND TOWNS

| ■ OVER 2,000,000 | ● 500,000 - 999,999 | ● 100,000 - 249,999 | ○ 10,000 - 29,999 |
| □ 1,000,000 - 1,999,999 | ◉ 250,000 - 499,999 | ◉ 30,000 - 99,999 | ○ UNDER 10,000 |

SCALE 1:3,500,000   LAMBERT CONFORMAL CONIC PROJECTION

MILES
KILOMETERS

Copyright by HAMMOND INC., Maplewood, N.J.

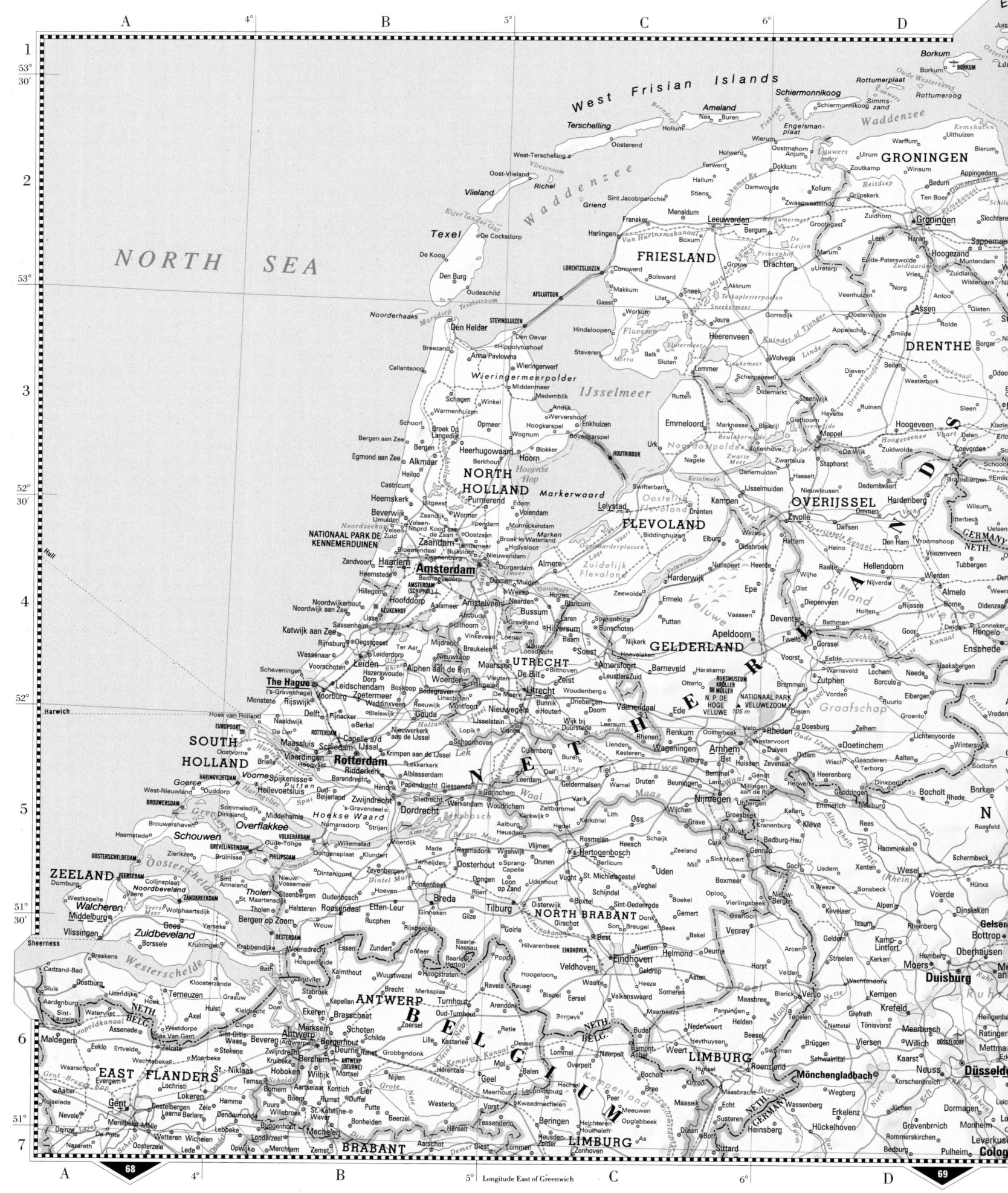

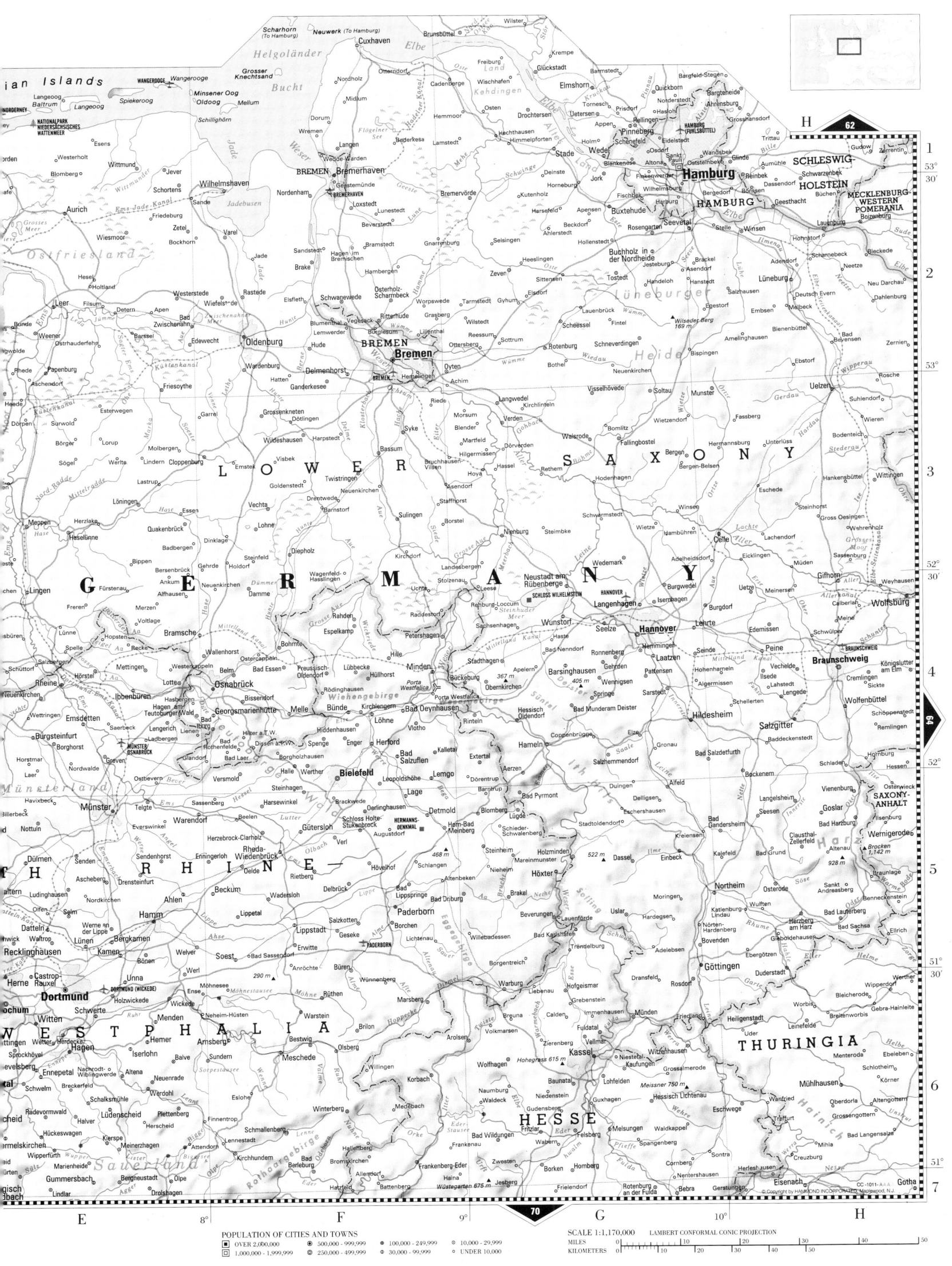

POPULATION OF CITIES AND TOWNS

■ OVER 2,000,000   ● 500,000 - 999,999   ○ 100,000 - 249,999   ○ 10,000 - 29,999
□ 1,000,000 - 1,999,999   ◉ 250,000 - 499,999   ○ 30,000 - 99,999   ○ UNDER 10,000

SCALE 1:1,170,000   LAMBERT CONFORMAL CONIC PROJECTION

MILES   0   10   20   30   40   50
KILOMETERS 0 10 20 30 40 50

© Copyright by HAMMOND INCORPORATED, Maplewood, N.J.
CC-1011-A A A

Belgium, Northern France, Western Germany

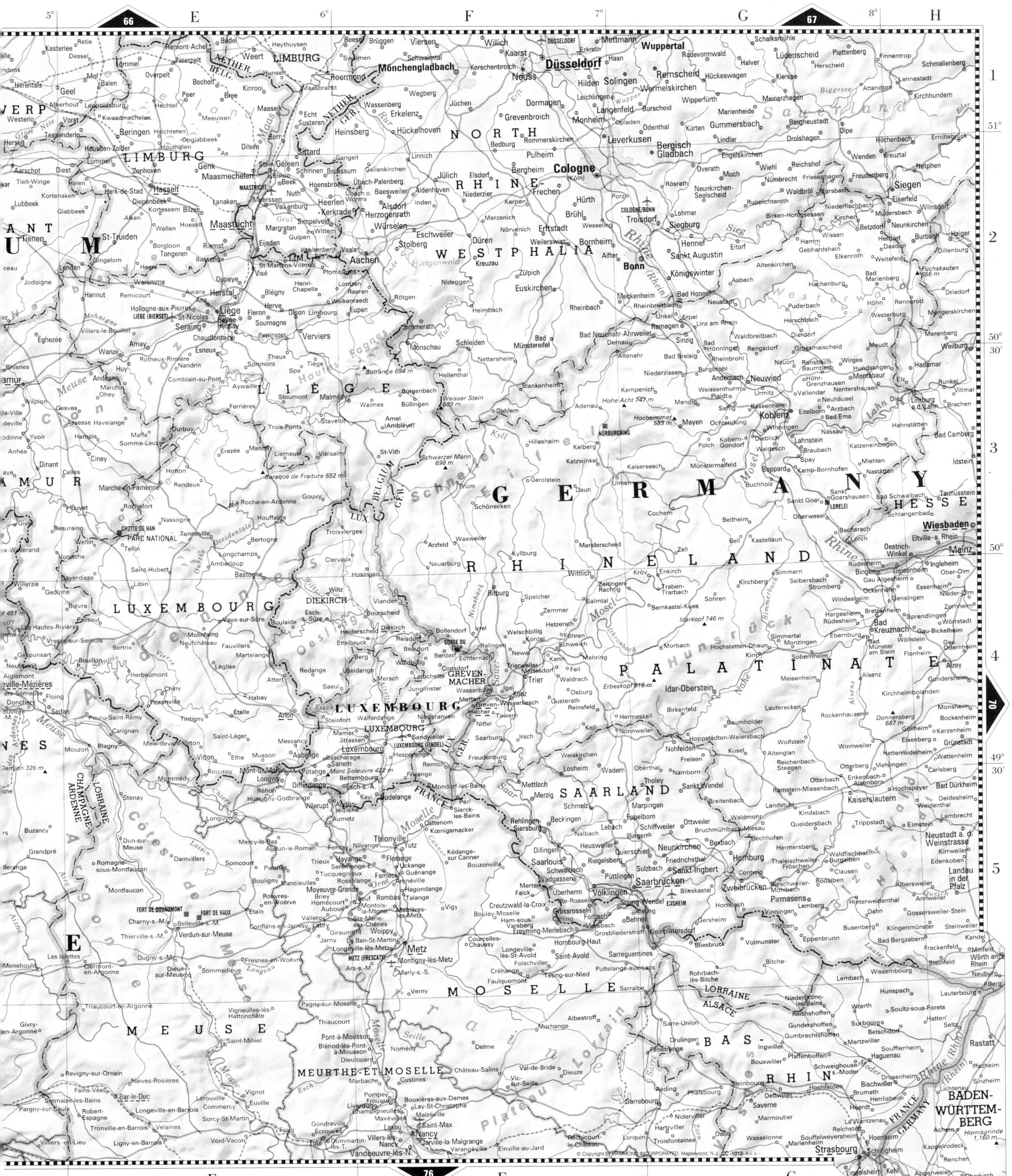

POPULATION OF CITIES AND TOWNS
- ■ OVER 2,000,000
- □ 1,000,000 - 1,999,999
- ● 500,000 - 999,999
- ● 250,000 - 499,999
- ● 100,000 - 249,999
- ○ 30,000 - 99,999
- ○ 10,000 - 29,999
- ○ UNDER 10,000

SCALE 1:1,170,000   LAMBERT CONFORMAL CONIC PROJECTION

MILES 0 10 20 30 40 50
KILOMETERS 0 10 20 30 40 50

Copyright by HAMMOND INCORPORATED, Maplewood, N.J. CC-1012-AA

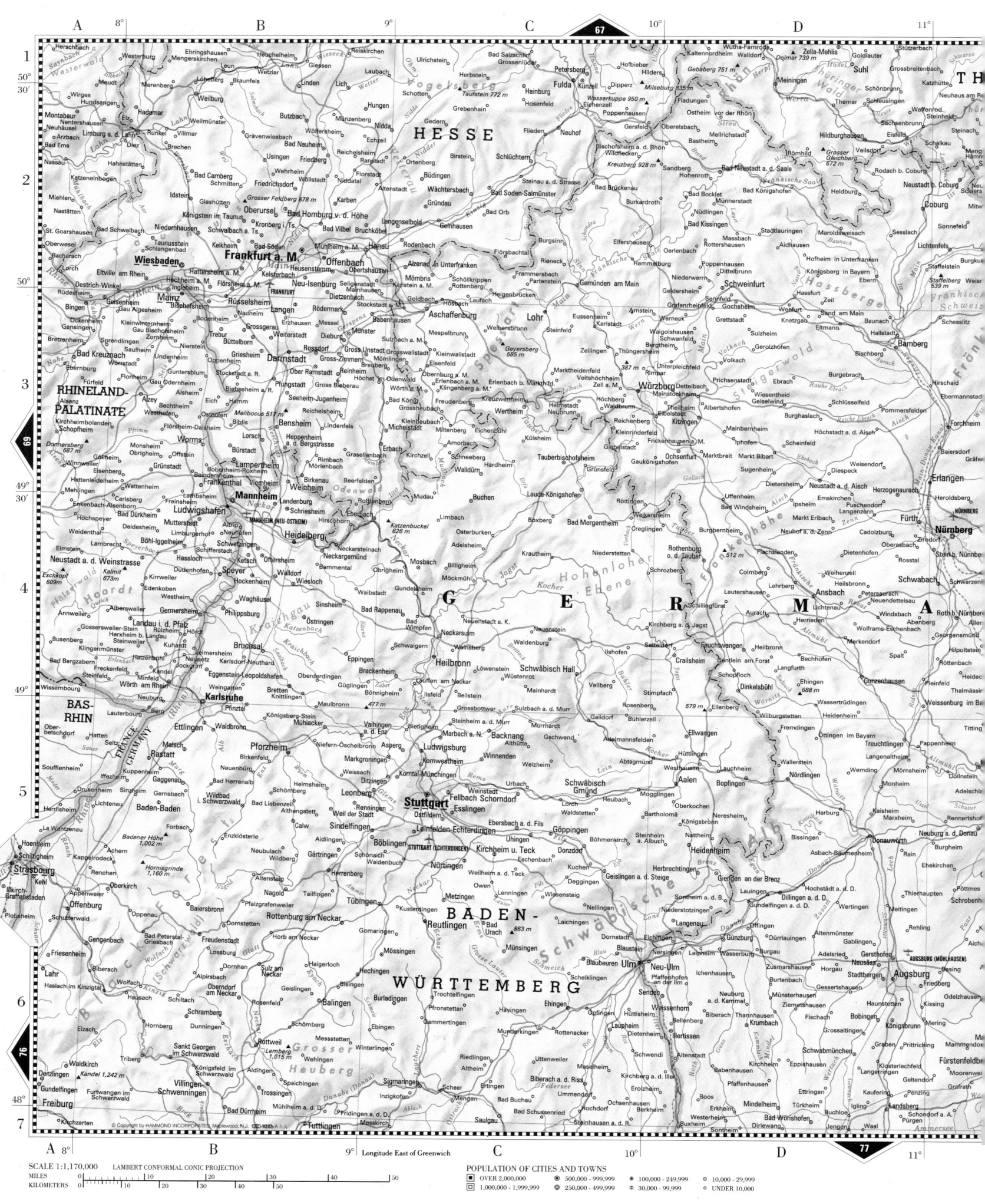

Southern Germany, Czech Republic, Upper Austria

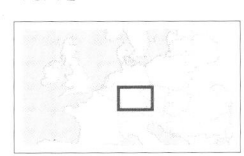

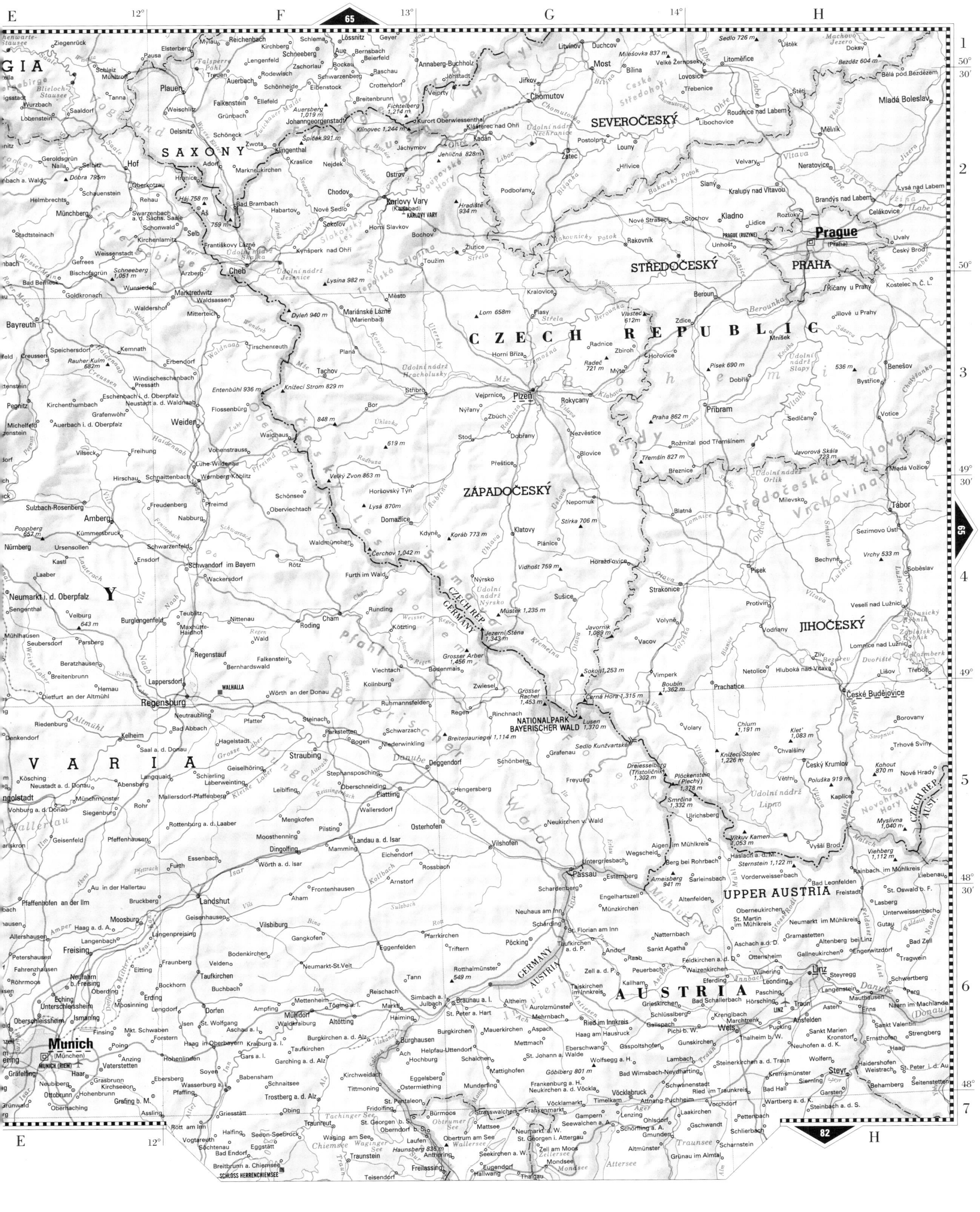

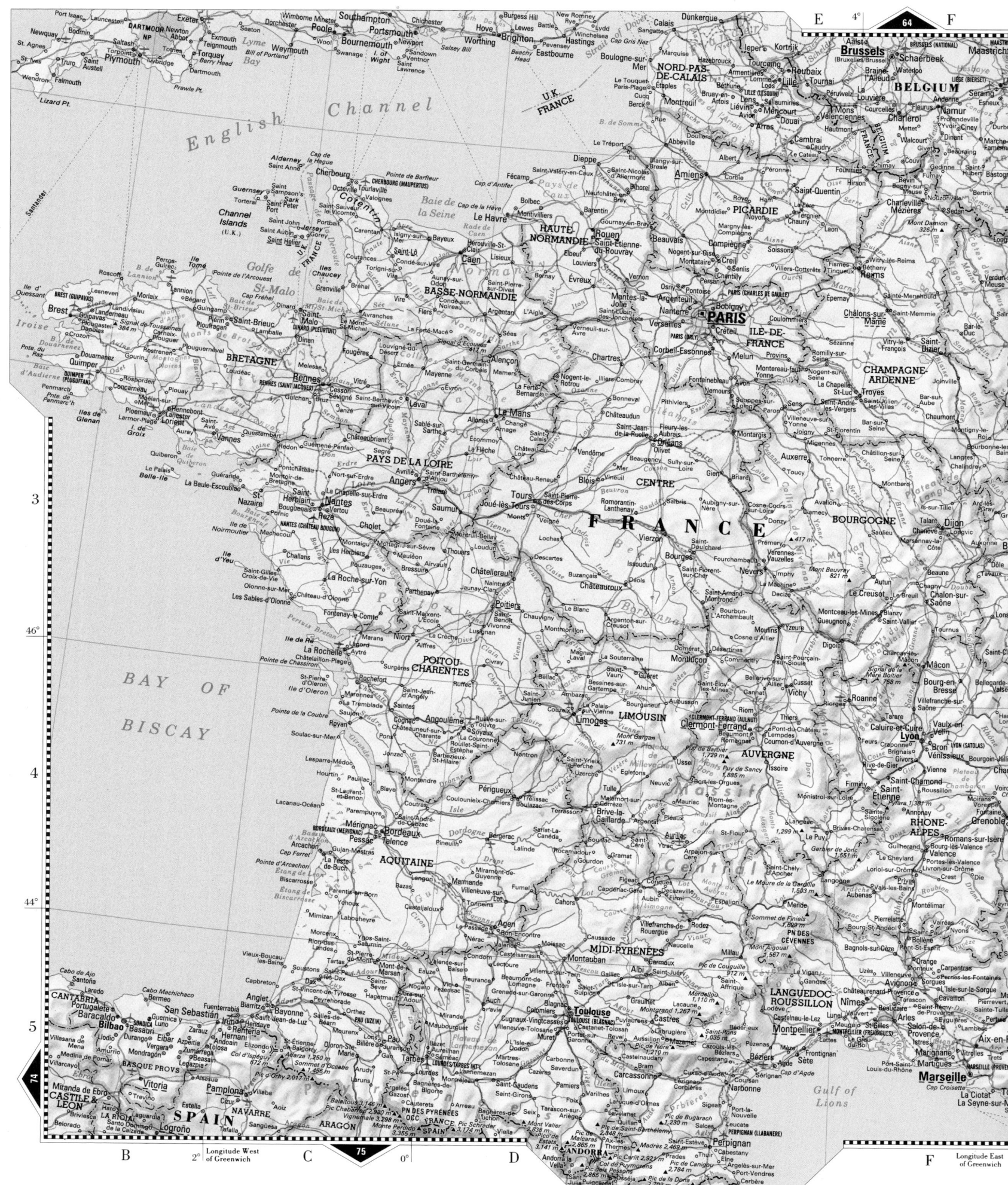

West Central Europe

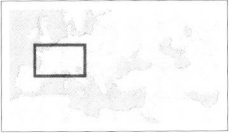

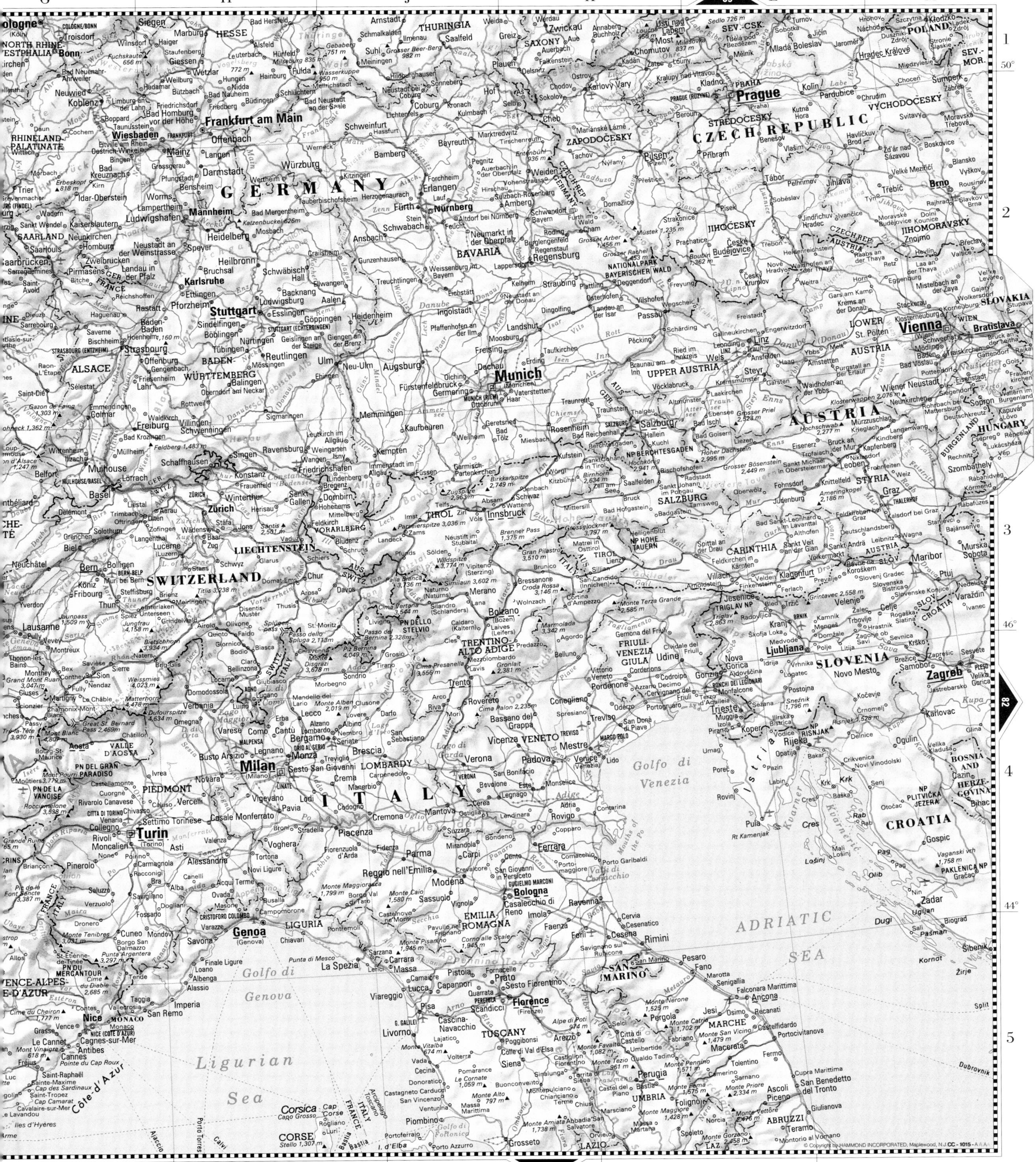

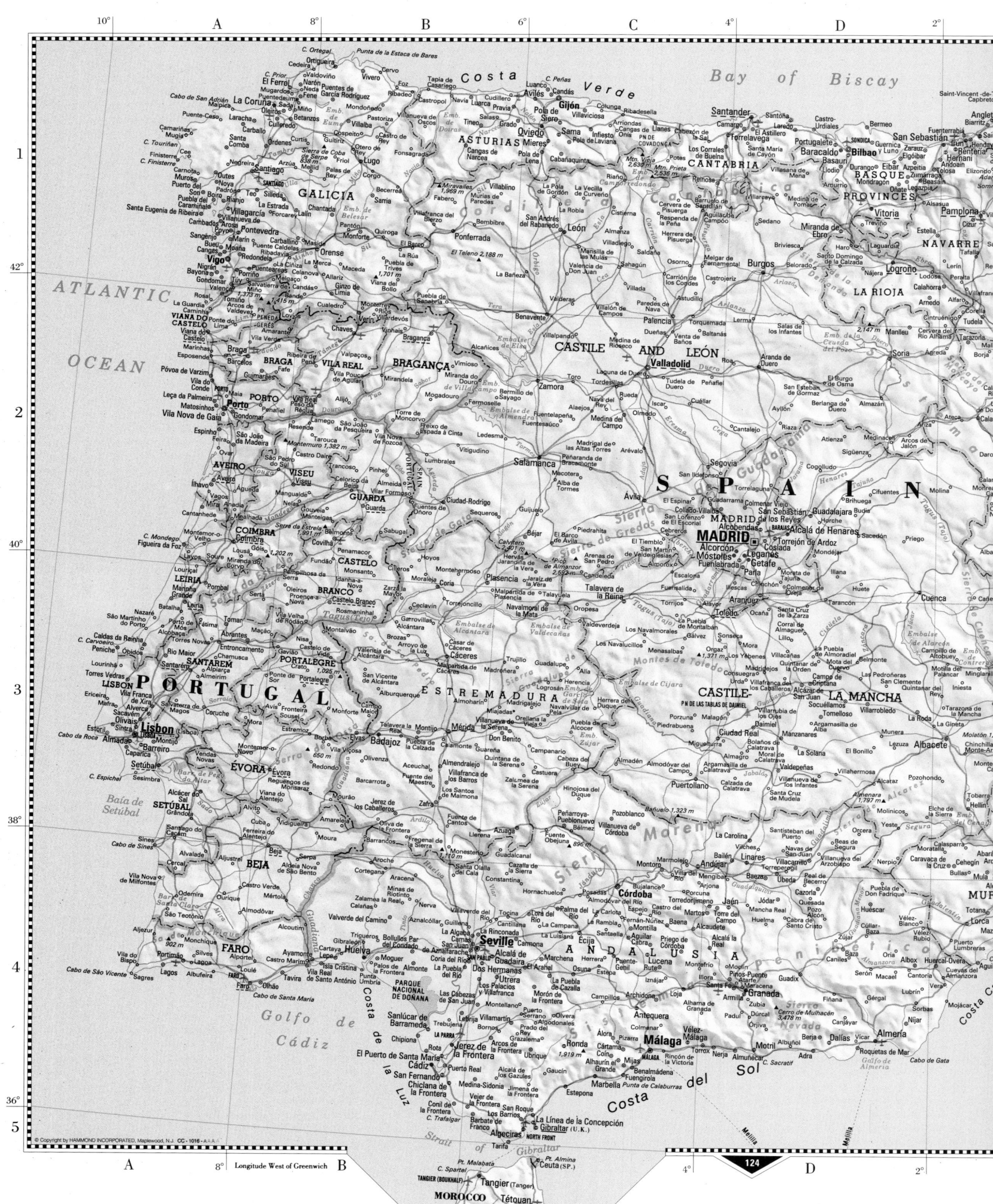

Spain, Portugal

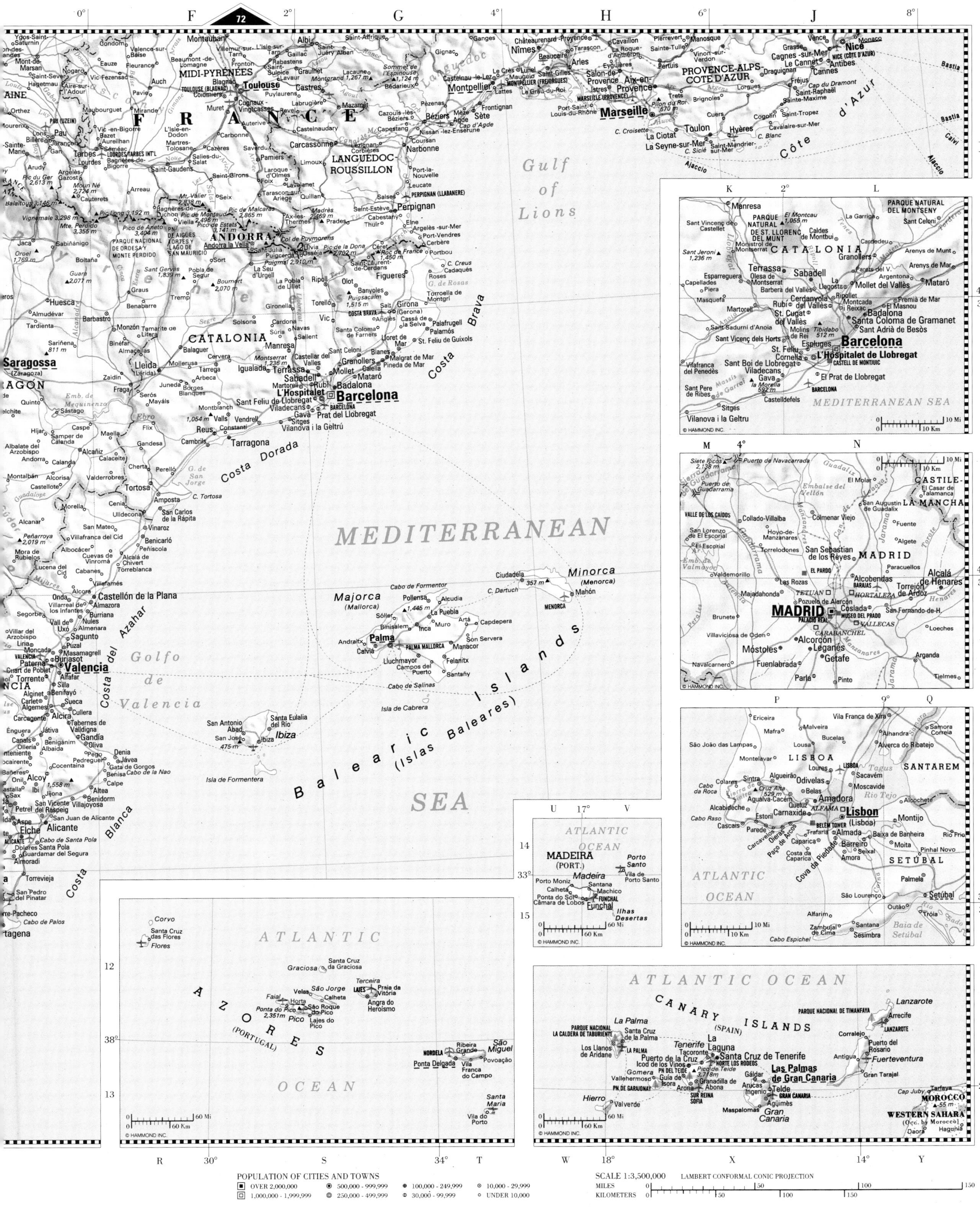

FRANCE

MIDI-PYRÉNÉES
Toulouse
LANGUEDOC ROUSSILLON
ANDORRA
Andorra la Vella
CATALONIA
Saragossa (Zaragoza)
ARAGON
Barcelona
L'Hospitalet
Tarragona
Costa Dorada
Costa Brava

PROVENCE-ALPS-CÔTE D'AZUR
Nîmes
Montpellier
Marseille
Toulon
Nice (CÔTE D'AZUR)
Cannes
Côte d'Azur

Gulf of Lions

MEDITERRANEAN SEA

Valencia
Golfo de Valencia
Costa del Azahar
Castellón de la Plana
Alicante
Costa Blanca
Cartagena

Majorca (Mallorca)
Palma
PALMA MALLORCA
Minorca (Menorca)
Mahón
Ibiza
Balearic Islands (Islas Baleares)

CATALONIA (inset K–L)
Manresa
PARQUE NATURAL DEL MONTSENY
Terrassa
Sabadell
Barcelona
L'Hospitalet de Llobregat
El Prat de Llobregat
Badalona
Santa Coloma de Gramanet
Mataró
MEDITERRANEAN SEA

MADRID (inset M–N)
VALLE DE LOS CAÍDOS
El Escorial
San Lorenzo de El Escorial
MADRID
PALACIO REAL
Alcalá de Henares
Móstoles
Alcorcón
Leganés
Getafe
CASTILE-LA MANCHA

LISBOA (inset P–Q)
Sintra
Lisbon (Lisboa)
BELEM TOWER
ALFAMA
Almada
Barreiro
Amadora
SANTARÉM
SETÚBAL
Setúbal
ATLANTIC OCEAN
Baía de Setúbal

MADEIRA (inset U–V)
ATLANTIC OCEAN
MADEIRA (PORT.)
Funchal
Porto Santo
Ilhas Desertas

AZORES (PORTUGAL)
ATLANTIC OCEAN
Corvo
Flores
Graciosa
São Jorge
Faial
Pico
Terceira
Angra do Heroismo
São Miguel
Ponta Delgada
Santa Maria

CANARY ISLANDS (SPAIN)
ATLANTIC OCEAN
La Palma
Tenerife
Santa Cruz de Tenerife
PN DEL TEIDE
Las Palmas de Gran Canaria
Gran Canaria
Lanzarote
Arrecife
Fuerteventura
PARQUE NACIONAL DE TIMANFAYA
MOROCCO
WESTERN SAHARA (Occ. by Morocco)

POPULATION OF CITIES AND TOWNS
■ OVER 2,000,000
□ 1,000,000 – 1,999,999
● 500,000 – 999,999
○ 250,000 – 499,999
● 100,000 – 249,999
● 30,000 – 99,999
○ 10,000 – 29,999
○ UNDER 10,000

SCALE 1:3,500,000 LAMBERT CONFORMAL CONIC PROJECTION
MILES 0 50 100 150
KILOMETERS 0 50 100 150

© HAMMOND INC.

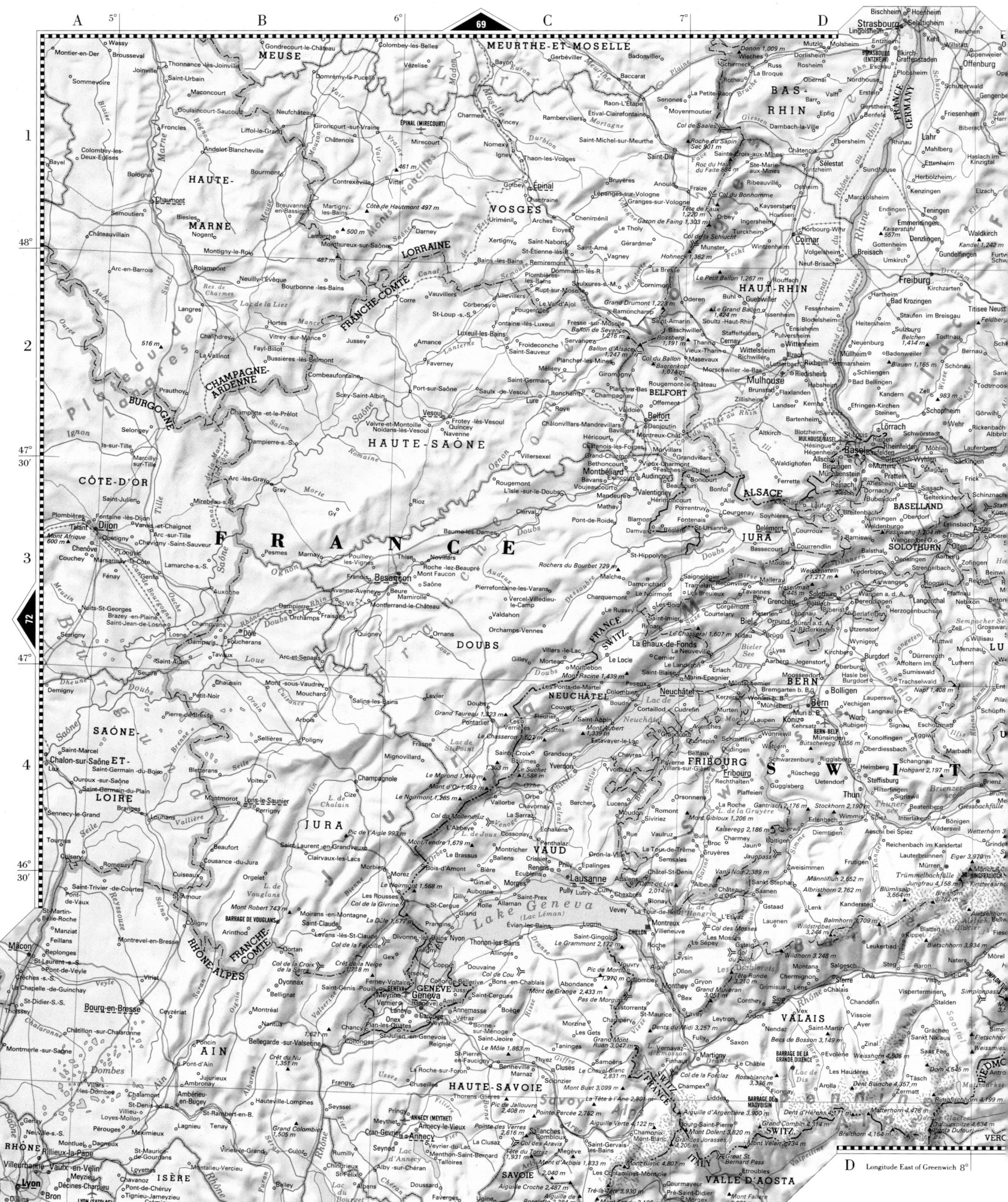

Central Alps Region

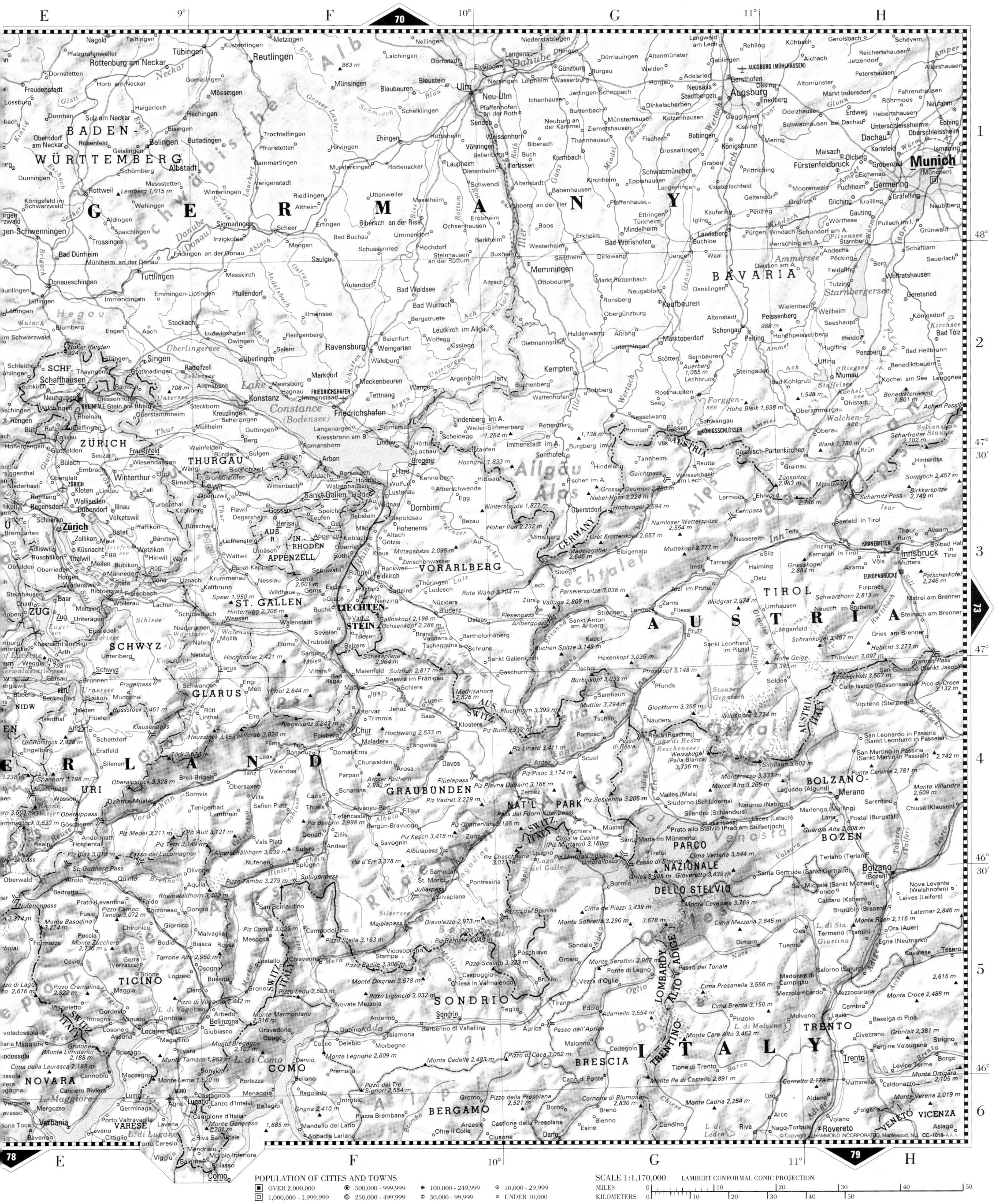

Northern Italy

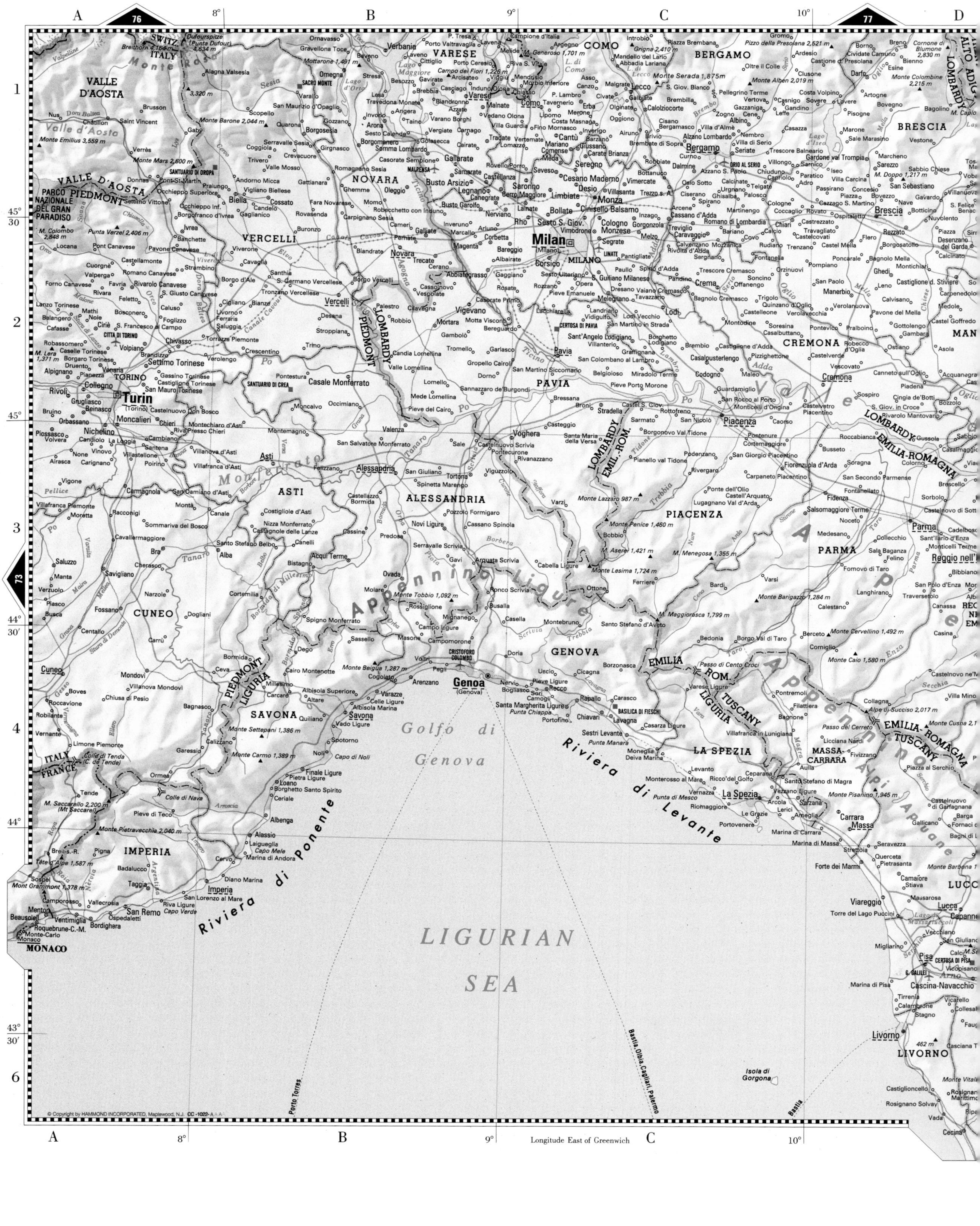

Longitude East of Greenwich

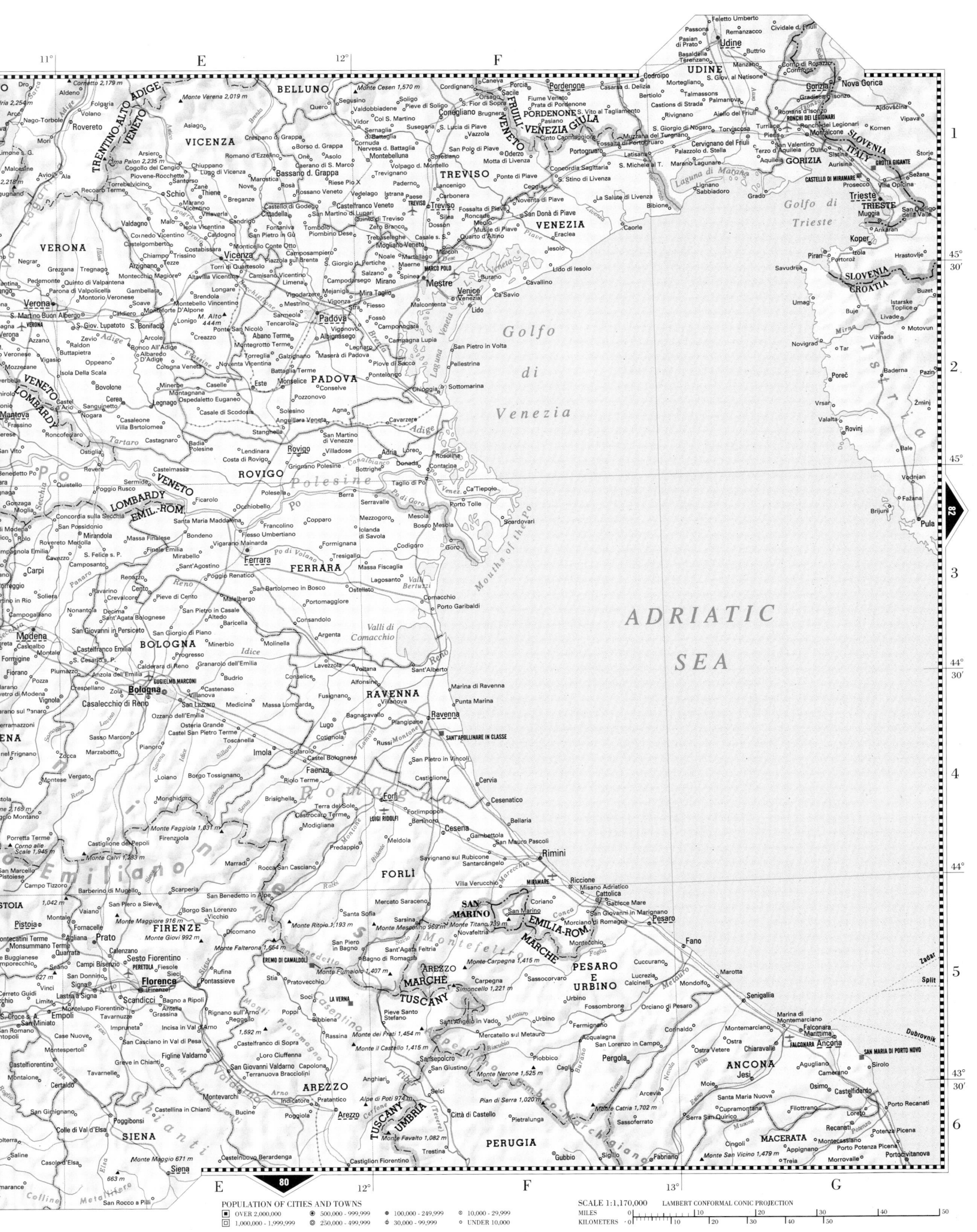

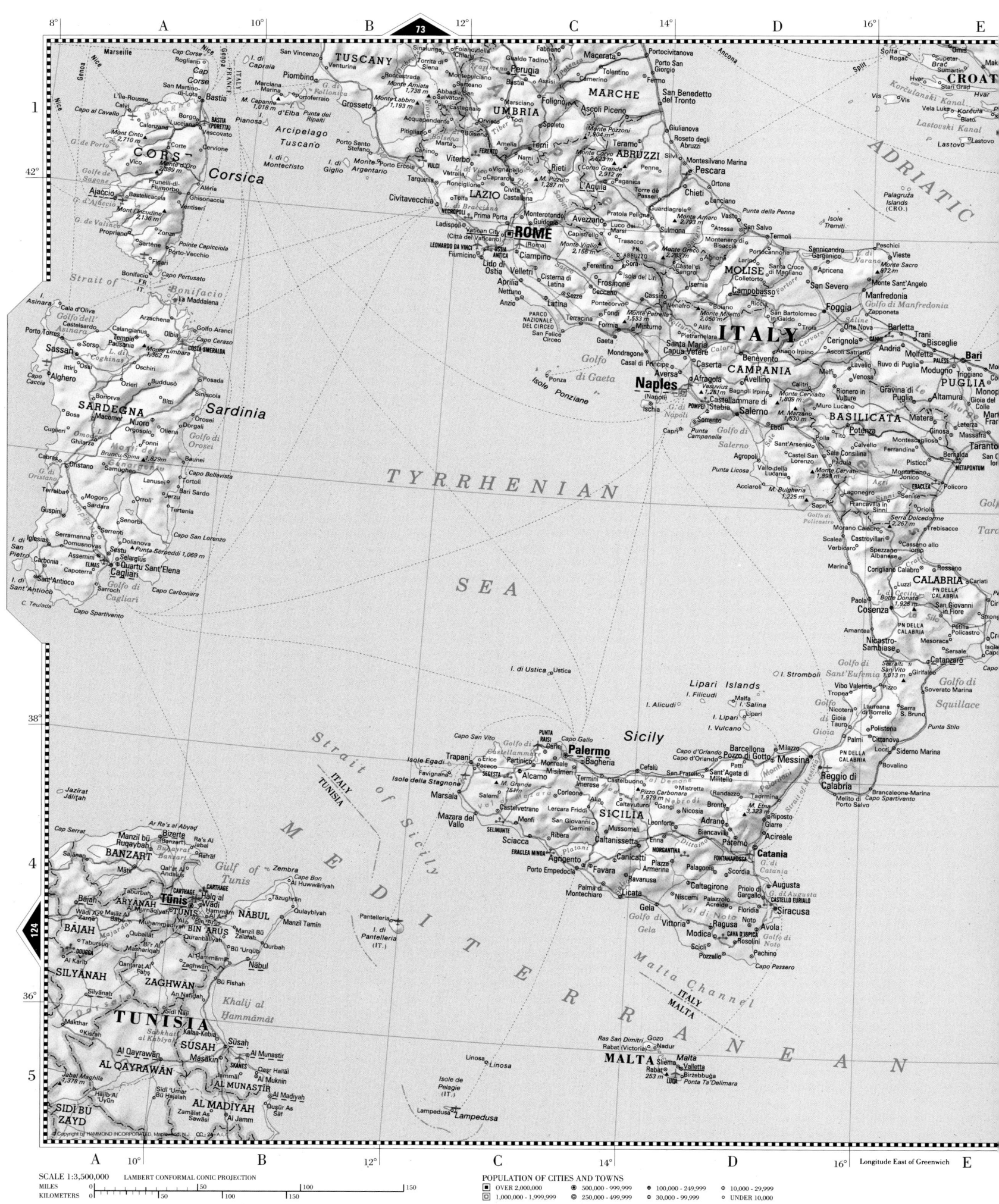

SCALE 1:3,500,000   LAMBERT CONFORMAL CONIC PROJECTION

MILES
KILOMETERS

POPULATION OF CITIES AND TOWNS
- ■ OVER 2,000,000
- ▣ 1,000,000 - 1,999,999
- ◉ 500,000 - 999,999
- ◎ 250,000 - 499,999
- ● 100,000 - 249,999
- ● 30,000 - 99,999
- ● 10,000 - 29,999
- ○ UNDER 10,000

Longitude East of Greenwich

© Copyright by HAMMOND INCORPORATED, Maplewood, N.J.

Southern Italy, Albania, Greece

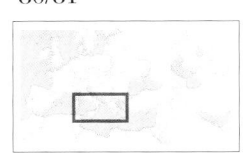

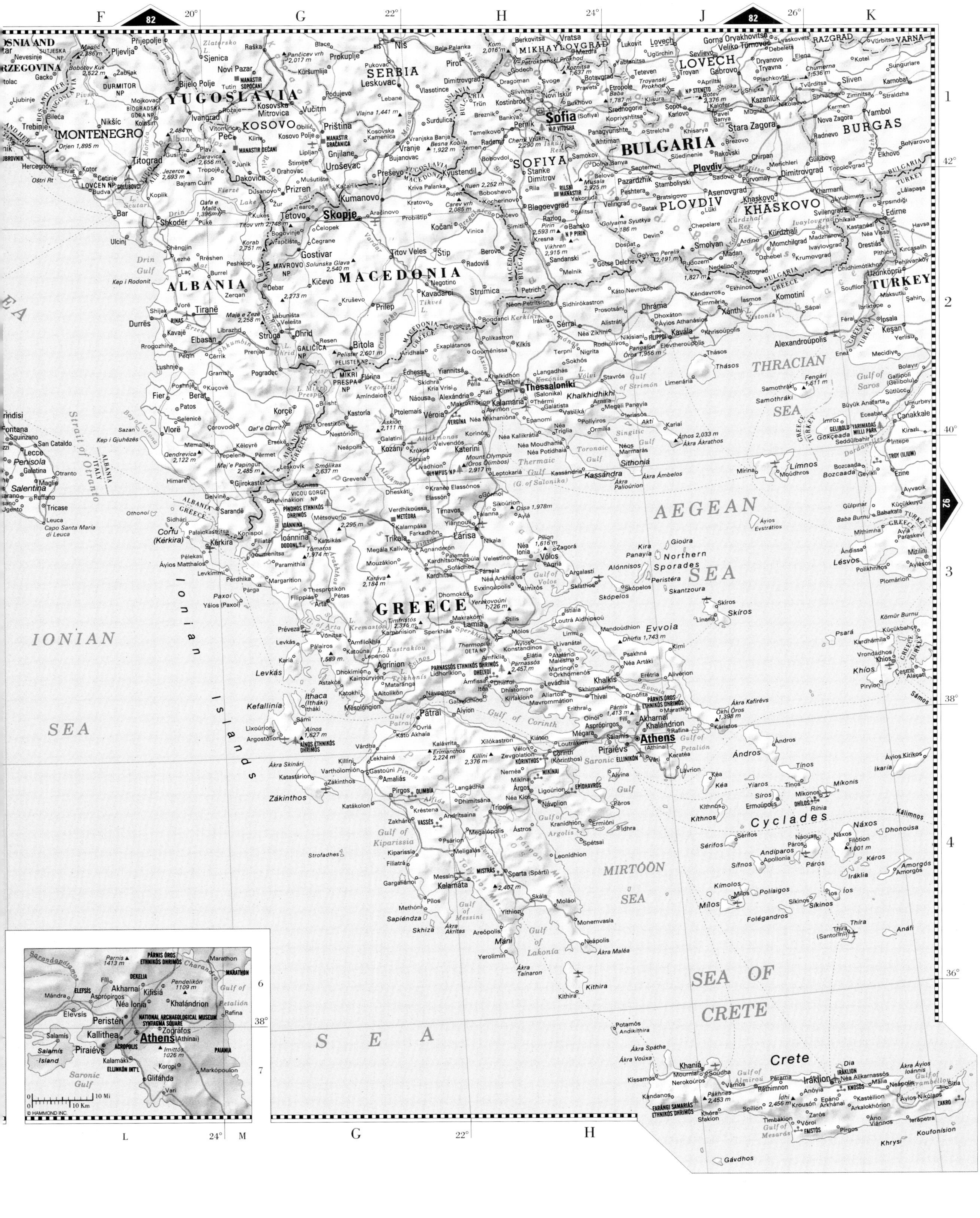

POPULATION OF CITIES AND TOWNS

| ■ | OVER 2,000,000 | ◉ | 500,000 - 999,999 | ◉ | 100,000 - 249,999 | ○ | 10,000 - 29,999 |
| ▣ | 1,000,000 - 1,999,999 | ◉ | 250,000 - 499,999 | ○ | 30,000 - 99,999 | ○ | UNDER 10,000 |

* WHILE THERE IS NO OTHER OFFICIALLY RECOGNIZED NAME FO
AREA, THE NAME "MACEDONIA" DERIVES FROM ITS FORMER S
A YUGOSLAV REPUBLIC, AND IS NOT RECOGNIZED BY MANY NA'

Hungary, Northern Balkan States

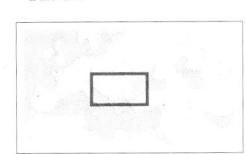

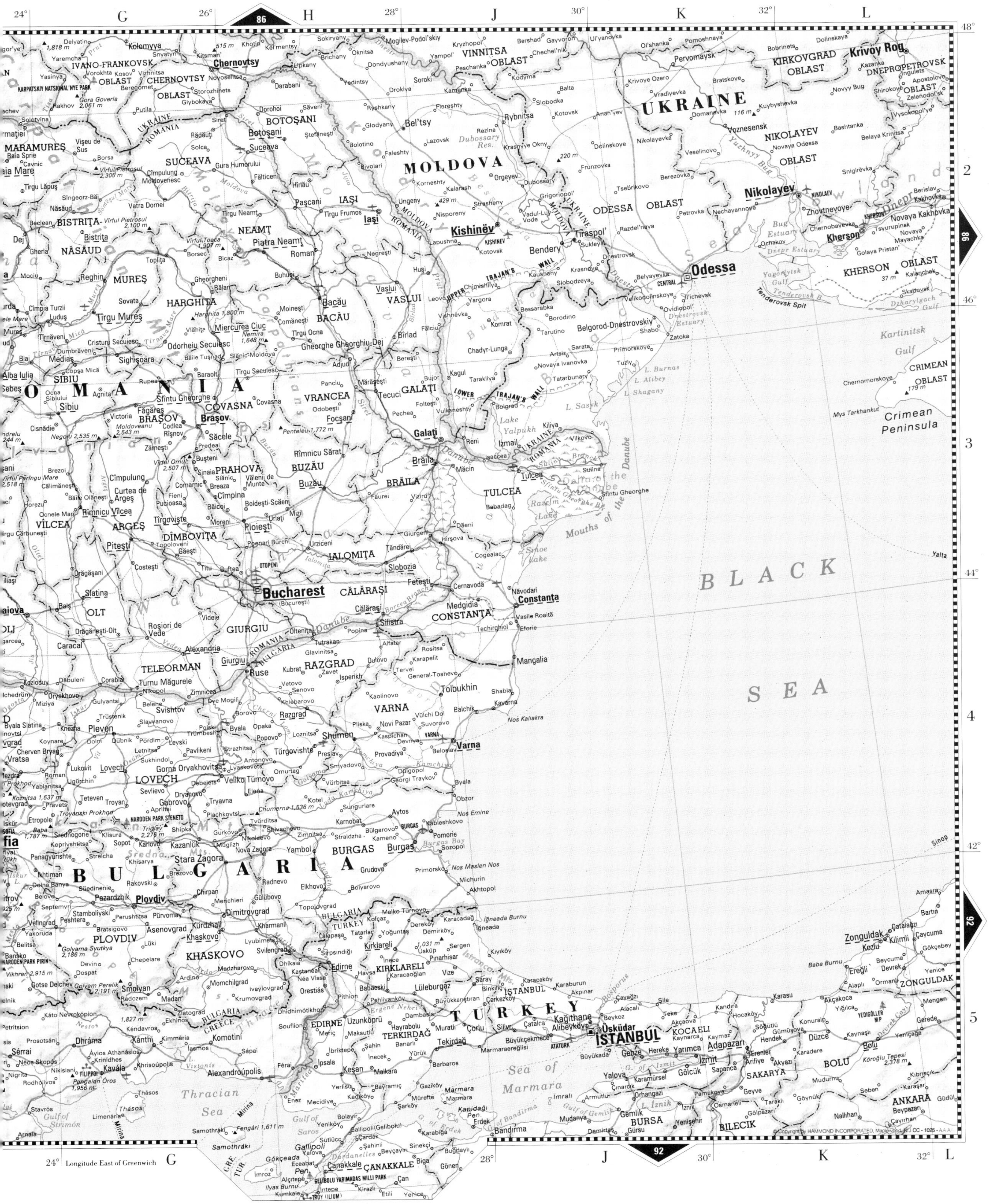

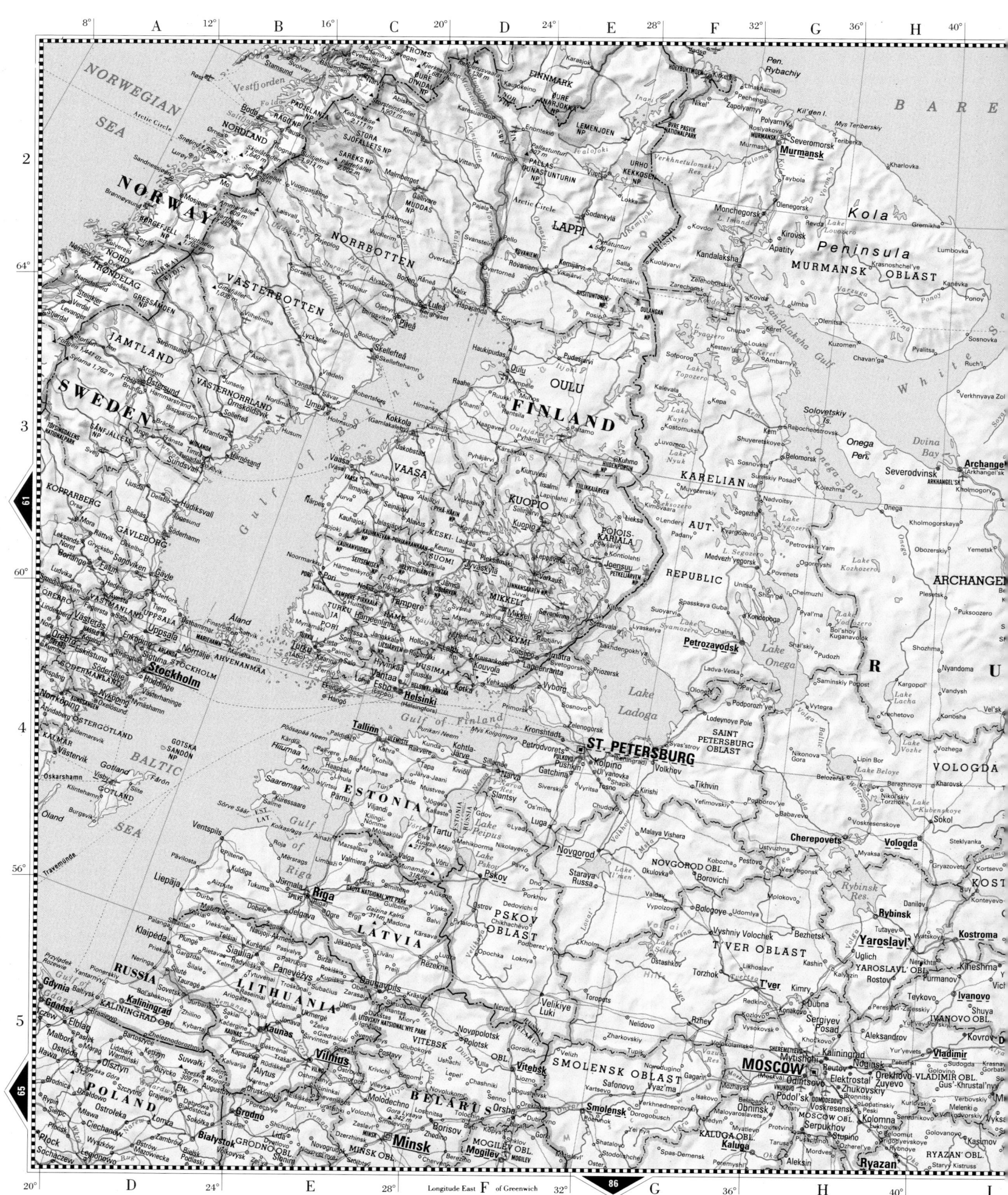

Northeastern Europe

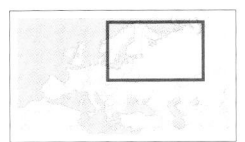

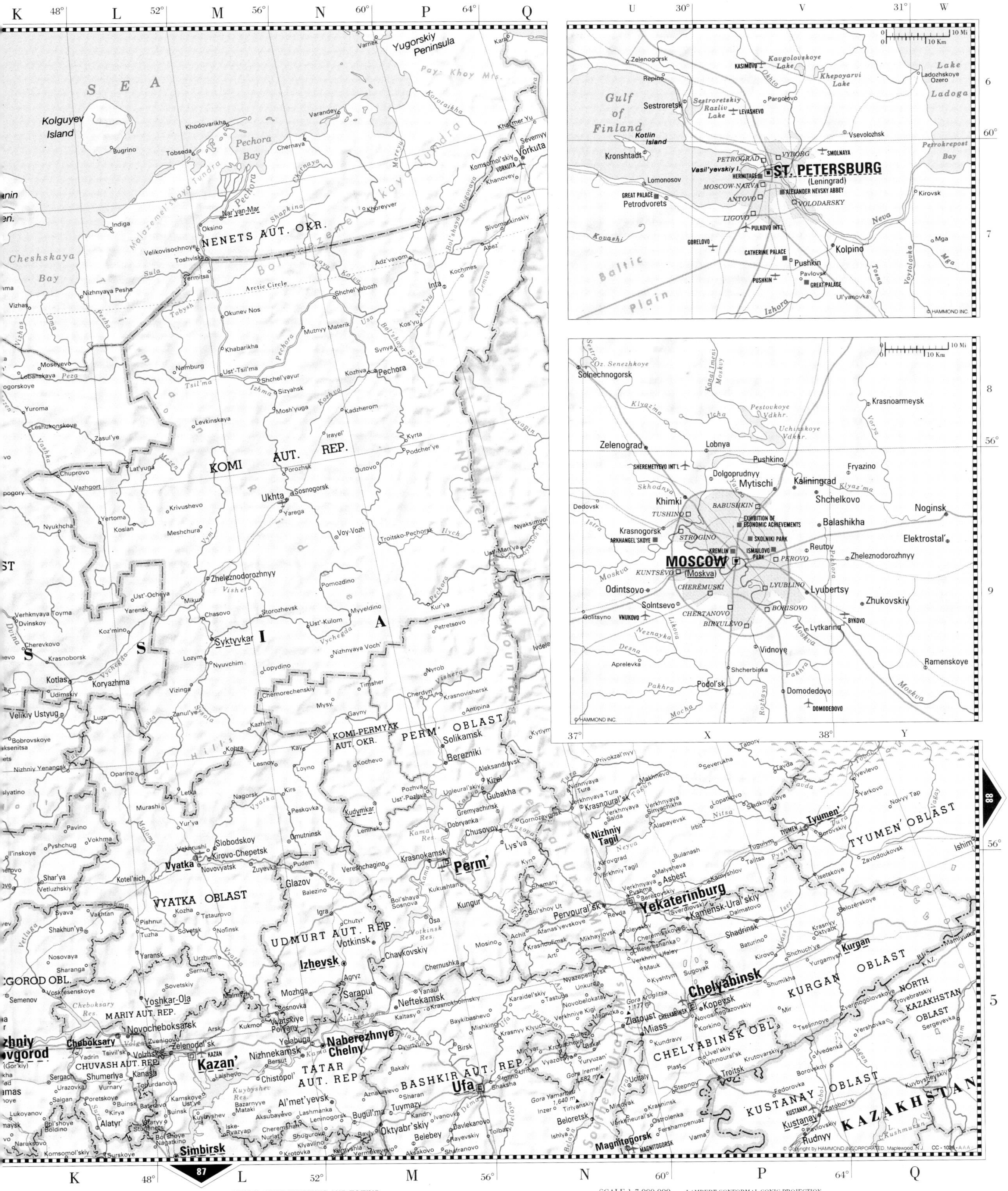

K 48° L 52° M 56° N 60° P 64° Q

S E A

Kolguyev Island

Yugorskiy Peninsula
Pay - Khoy Mts.

Cheshskaya Bay

Pechora Bay

NENETS AUT. OKR.

Nar'yan-Mar

Arctic Circle

KOMI AUT. REP.

Ukhta Sosnogorsk

Syktyvkar

R U S S I A

Kotlas
Koryazhma
Velikiy Ustyug

KOMI-PERMYAK AUT. OKR.

PERM' OBLAST
Solikamsk
Berezniki

Kudymkar

Perm'

Nizhniy Tagil

Tyumen'
TYUMEN' OBLAST

VYATKA OBLAST
Vyatka
Kirov-Chepetsk

UDMURT AUT. REP.
Votkinsk
Izhevsk

Yekaterinburg
Kamensk-Ural'skiy
Kurgan
KURGAN OBLAST

Chelyabinsk
Kopeysk
Miass
Zlatoust
CHELYABINSK OBL.

NORTH KAZAKHSTAN OBLAST

MARIY AUT. REP.
Yoshkar-Ola
Cheboksary
Novocheboksarsk
CHUVASH AUT. REP.
Nizhniy Novgorod (Gor'kiy)

Kazan'
Zelenodol'sk
Nizhnekamsk
Naberezhnye Chelny
TATAR AUT. REP.

BASHKIR AUT. REP.
Ufa

KUSTANAY OBLAST
Kustanay

Simbirsk

Magnitogorsk

KAZAKHSTAN

K 48° L 52° M 56° N 60° P 64° Q
87   88

U 30° V 31° W

Gulf of Finland

KASIMOVO

Sestroretsk
Kronstadt
Kotlin Island

PETROGRAD
ST. PETERSBURG
(Leningrad)

Vasil'yevskiy I.
HERMITAGE
MOSCOW-NARVA
ANTOVO
ALEXANDER NEVSKY ABBEY
VOLODARSKY

Lake Ladoga
Petrokrepost Bay
Kirovsk

Lomonosov
GREAT PALACE
Petrodvorets

Baltic Plain

GORELOVO
PULKOVO INT'L
CATHERINE PALACE
Pushkin
Pavlovsk
GREAT PALACE

Kolpino

© HAMMOND INC.

X 37° Y 38°

Solnechnogorsk
Krasnoarmeysk

Zelenograd
Lobnya
Pushkino
Fryazino

SHEREMETYEVO INT'L
Dolgoprudnyy
Mytischi
Kaliningrad
Shchelkovo
Noginsk

Khimki
BABUSHKIN
Balashikha
Elektrostal'

Krasnogorsk
STROGINO
EXHIBITION OF ECONOMIC ACHIEVEMENTS
ARKHANGEL'SKOYE
SOKOLNIKI PARK
Reutov
Zheleznodorozhnyy

MOSCOW (Moskva)
KREMLIN
ISMAILOVO PARK
PEROVO

Odintsovo
KUNTSEVO
CHERËMUSKI
LYUBLINO
Lyubertsy
Zhukovskiy

Solntsevo
VNUKOVO
CHERTANOVO
BORISOVO
BIRYULEVO
BYKOVO
Lytkarino

Vidnoye
Ramenskoye

Aprelevka
Shcherbinka
Domodedovo

Podol'sk
DOMODEDOVO

© HAMMOND INC.

POPULATION OF CITIES AND TOWNS

- OVER 2,000,000
- 1,000,000 - 1,999,999
- 500,000 - 999,999
- 250,000 - 499,999
- 100,000 - 249,999
- 30,000 - 99,999
- 10,000 - 29,999
- UNDER 10,000

SCALE 1:7,000,000   LAMBERT CONFORMAL CONIC PROJECTION

MILES   0   100   200   300
KILOMETERS 0   100   200   300

© Copyright by HAMMOND INCORPORATED, Maplewood, N.J.   CC - 1026 - A-A-A

Southeastern Europe

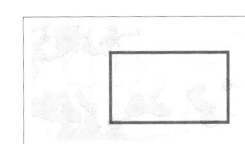

Russia and Neighboring Countries

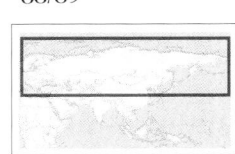

Administrative Divisions bear same names as their respective capitals, except:

Ukraine
1. Crimean Oblast
2. Trans-carpathian Oblast
3. Volyn' Oblast

Georgia
4. Abkhaz Aut. Rep.
5. Adzhar Aut. Rep.
6. South Ossetian Aut. Oblast

Azerbaijan
7. Nakhichevan Aut. Rep.
8. Nagorno-Karabakh Aut. Oblast

Russia
9. Dagestan Aut. Rep.
10. Chechen-Ingush Aut. Rep.
11. North Ossetian Aut. Rep.
12. Kabardin-Balkar Aut. Rep.
13. Karachay-Cherkess Aut. Oblast
14. Adyge Aut. Oblast
15. Kalmyk Aut. Rep.
16. Mordvian Aut. Rep.
17. Chuvash Aut. Rep.
18. Mariy Aut. Rep.
19. Tatar Aut. Rep.
20. Bashkir Aut. Rep.
21. Udmurt Aut. Rep.
22. Komi-Permyak Aut. Okrug
23. Khakass Aut. Oblast
24. Ust'-Ordynsk Buryat Aut. Okrug
25. Aginsk Aut. Okrug
26. Yevrey Aut. Oblast

Kazakhstan
27. North Kazakhstan Oblast

Kyrgyzstan
28. Issyk-Kul' Oblast

Uzbekistan
29. Syrdar'ya Oblast
30. Surkhandar'ya Oblast
31. Kashkadar'ya Oblast
32. Khorezm Oblast

© Copyright by HAMMOND INCORPORATED, Maplewood, N.J. CC-1029-A.A.A.

POPULATION OF CITIES AND TOWNS

■ OVER 2,000,000
▣ 1,000,000 - 1,999,999
● 500,000 - 999,999
◉ 100,000 - 499,999
○ 50,000 - 99,999
· UNDER 50,000

SCALE 1:21,000,000   LAMBERT CONFORMAL CONIC PROJECTION

MILES 0 ... 300 ... 600 ... 900
KILOMETERS 0 ... 300 ... 600 ... 900

Asia

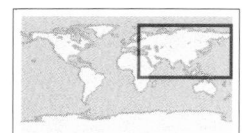

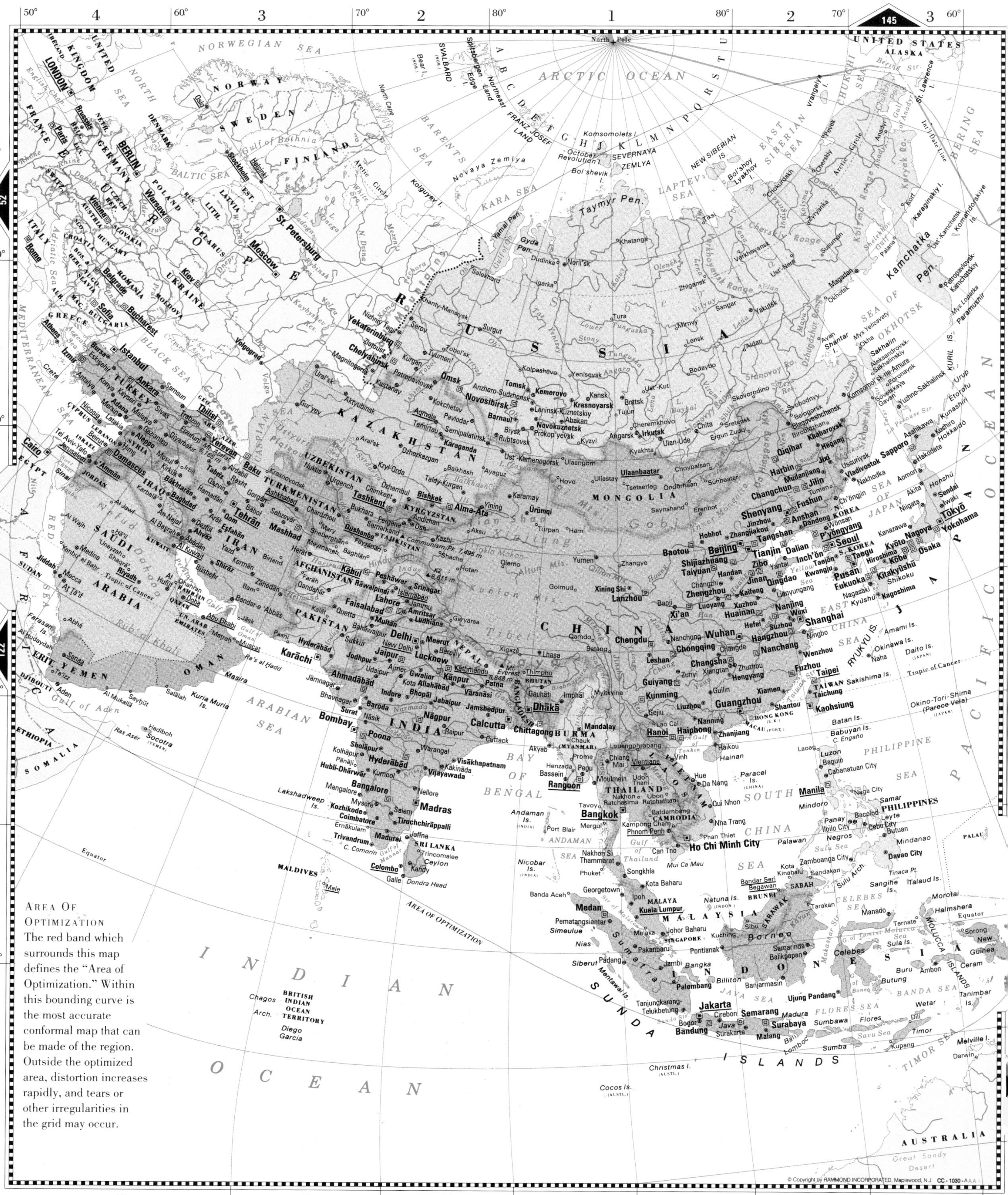

AREA OF OPTIMIZATION
The red band which surrounds this map defines the "Area of Optimization." Within this bounding curve is the most accurate conformal map that can be made of the region. Outside the optimized area, distortion increases rapidly, and tears or other irregularities in the grid may occur.

SCALE 1:49,000,000   OPTIMAL CONFORMAL PROJECTION

Longitude East of Greenwich

MILES   0   700   1400   2100
KILOMETERS   0   700   1400   2100

POPULATION OF CITIES AND TOWNS

▣ OVER 3,000,000	✳ 500,000 - 999,999
▣ 1,000,000 - 2,999,999	● 100,000 - 499,999
	○ UNDER 100,000

Eastern Mediterranean Region

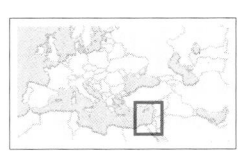

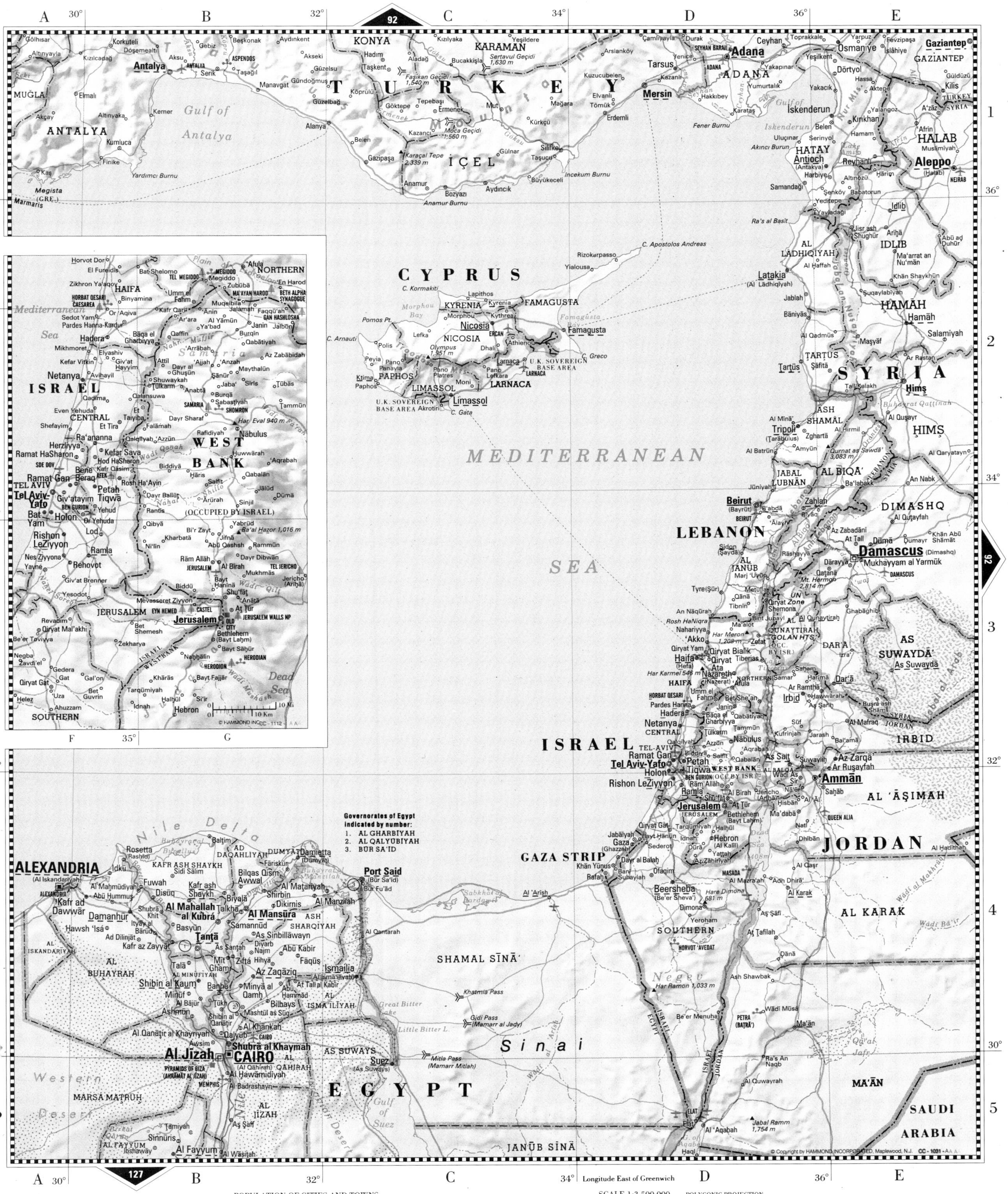

POPULATION OF CITIES AND TOWNS

☐ OVER 2,000,000 ◉ 500,000 - 999,999 ● 100,000 - 249,999 ⊙ 10,000 - 29,999
☐ 1,000,000 - 1,999,999 ● 250,000 - 499,999 ⊙ 30,000 - 99,999 ○ UNDER 10,000

SCALE 1:3,500,000   POLYCONIC PROJECTION

MILES   0   50   100   150
KILOMETERS   0   50   100   150

Longitude East of Greenwich

© Copyright by HAMMOND INCORPORATED, Maplewood, N.J.   CC-1091-A

SCALE 1:7,000,000   LAMBERT CONFORMAL CONIC PROJECTION

MILES

KILOMETERS

POPULATION OF CITIES AND TOWNS

| ■ OVER 2,000,000 | ● 500,000 - 999,999 | ● 100,000 - 249,999 | ● 10,000 - 29,999 |
| ▣ 1,000,000 - 1,999,999 | ● 250,000 - 499,999 | ● 30,000 - 99,999 | ○ UNDER 10,000 |

Longitude East of Greenwich

© Copyright HAMMOND INCORPORATED, Maplewood, N.J. CC-1032-A-A

Northern Middle East

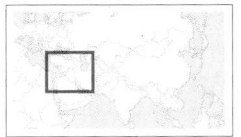

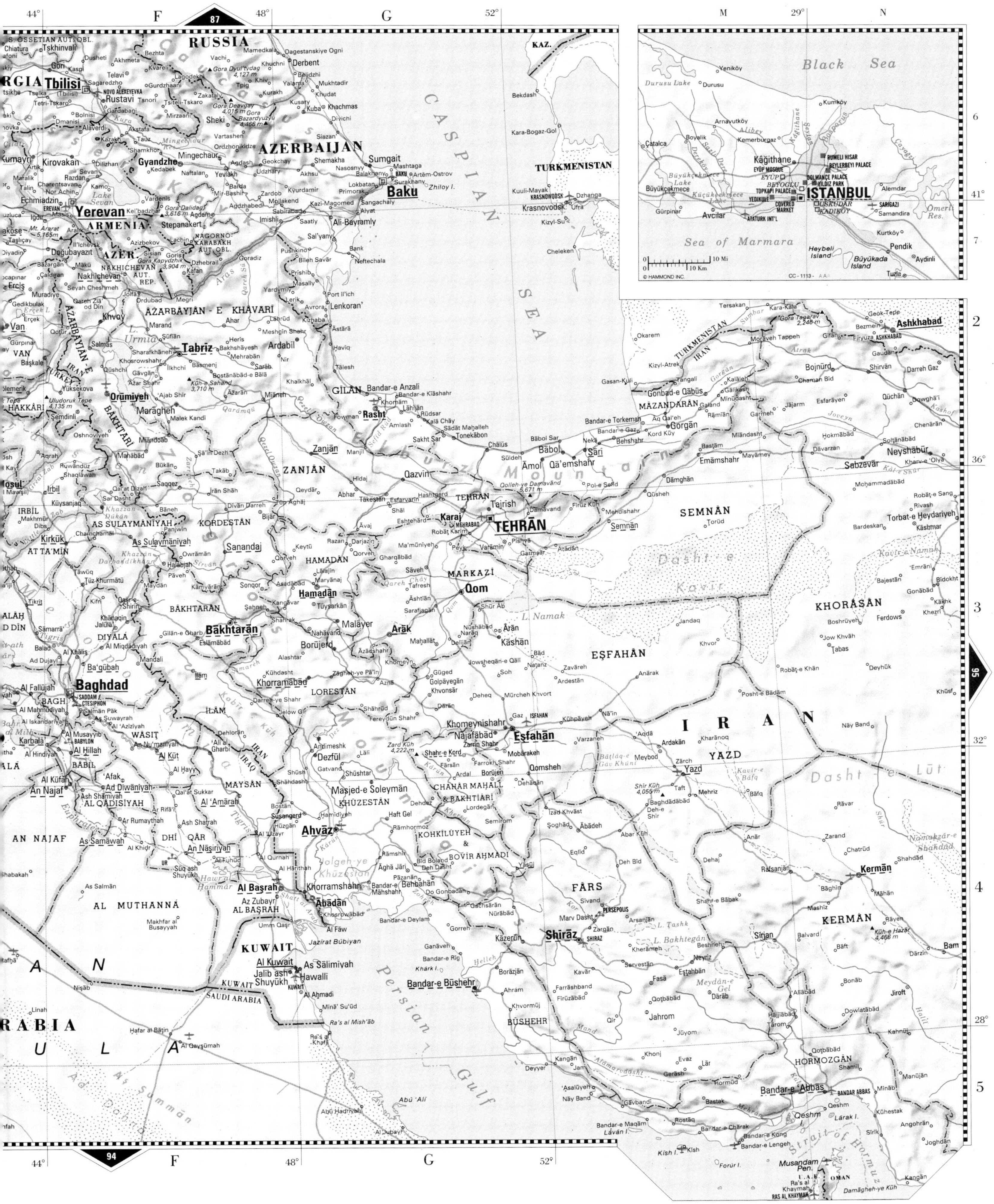

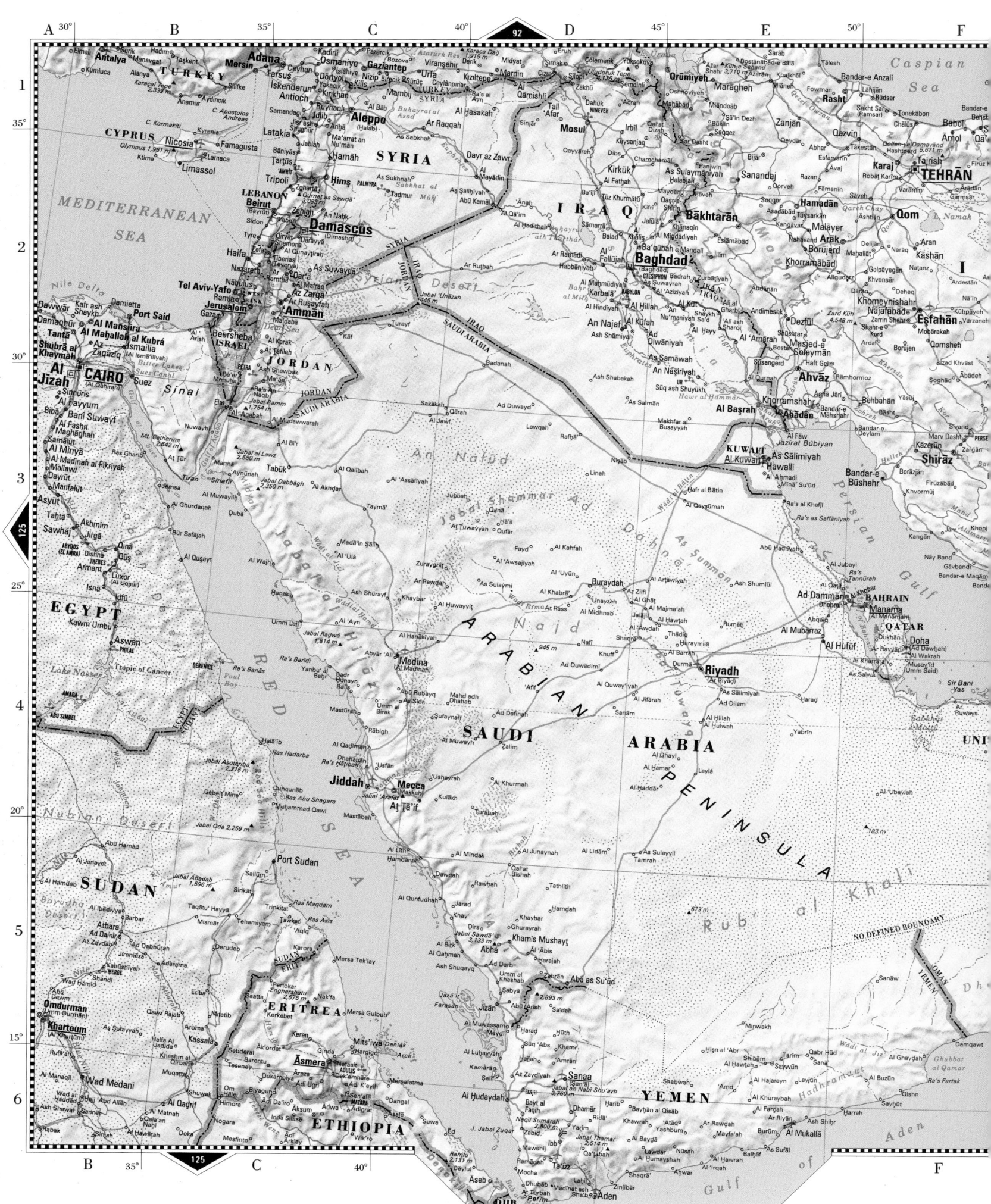

Southwestern Asia

CHINA

TAJIKISTAN

TURKMENISTAN

AFGHANISTAN

IRAN

PAKISTAN

INDIA

OMAN

BALUCHISTĀN

RAJASTHAN

PUNJAB

ARABIAN SEA

Gulf of Oman

Gulf of Masira

Makran Coast

Thar Desert

Hindu Kush

POPULATION OF CITIES AND TOWNS

■ OVER 2,000,000	● 500,000 - 999,999
▣ 1,000,000 - 1,999,999	● 250,000 - 499,999
● 100,000 - 249,999	○ 10,000 - 29,999
● 30,000 - 99,999	○ UNDER 10,000

SCALE 1:10,500,000   LAMBERT CONFORMAL CONIC PROJECTION

MILES 0 ___ 150 ___ 300 ___ 450

KILOMETERS 0 ___ 150 ___ 300 ___ 450

© Copyright by HAMMOND INCORPORATED, Maplewood, N.J. CO-1033 · A·A

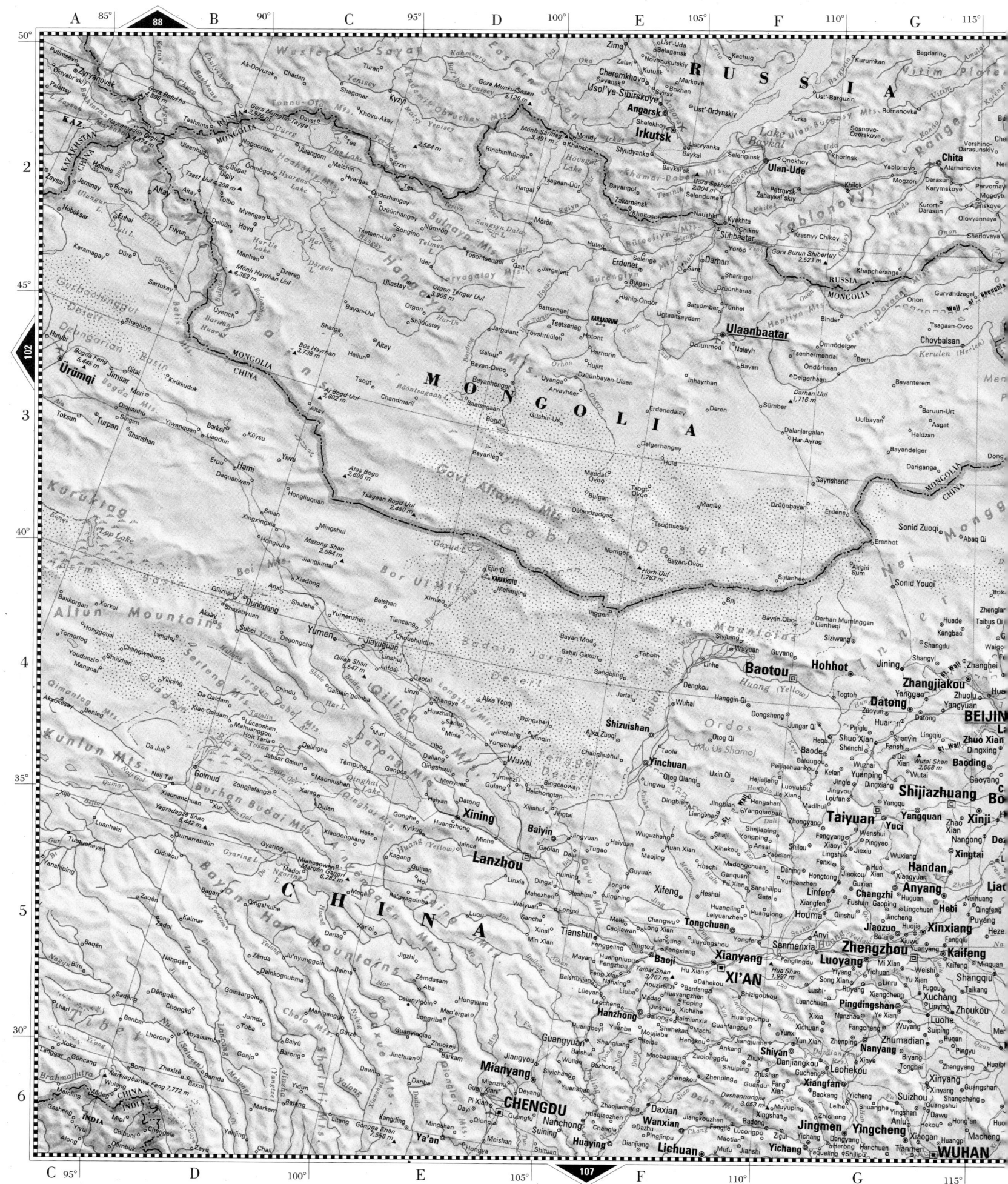

Eastern Asia

POPULATION OF CITIES AND TOWNS

- ■ OVER 2,000,000
- ◻ 1,000,000 - 1,999,999
- ● 500,000 - 999,999
- ◉ 250,000 - 499,999
- ● 100,000 - 249,999
- ● 30,000 - 99,999
- ● 10,000 - 29,999
- ● UNDER 10,000

SCALE 1:10,500,000   LAMBERT CONFORMAL CONIC PROJECTION

MILES   0   150   300   450

KILOMETERS   0   150   300   450

SEA OF JAPAN

KOREA STRAIT

SOUTH KOREA

Taegu

PUSAN

Fukuoka
Kitakyūshū
Shimonoseki

Nagasaki

Kumamoto

Kagoshima

Miyazaki

Kyūshū

JAPAN

EAST CHINA SEA

PACIFIC OCEAN

Shikoku

Matsuyama

Kōchi

Tosa Bay

Tokushima

Takamatsu

ŌSAKA

KYŌTO

Kōbe

Wakayama

Okayama

HIROSHIMA

Fukuyama

TOTTORI

SHIMANE

OKI ISLANDS

Liancourt Rocks
(Disputed between Japan
and South Korea)

Ullŭng I.
(South Korea)

ŌSUMI ISLANDS

KIRISHIMA-YAKU NAT'L PARK

Longitude East of Greenwich

Central and Southern Japan

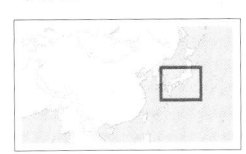

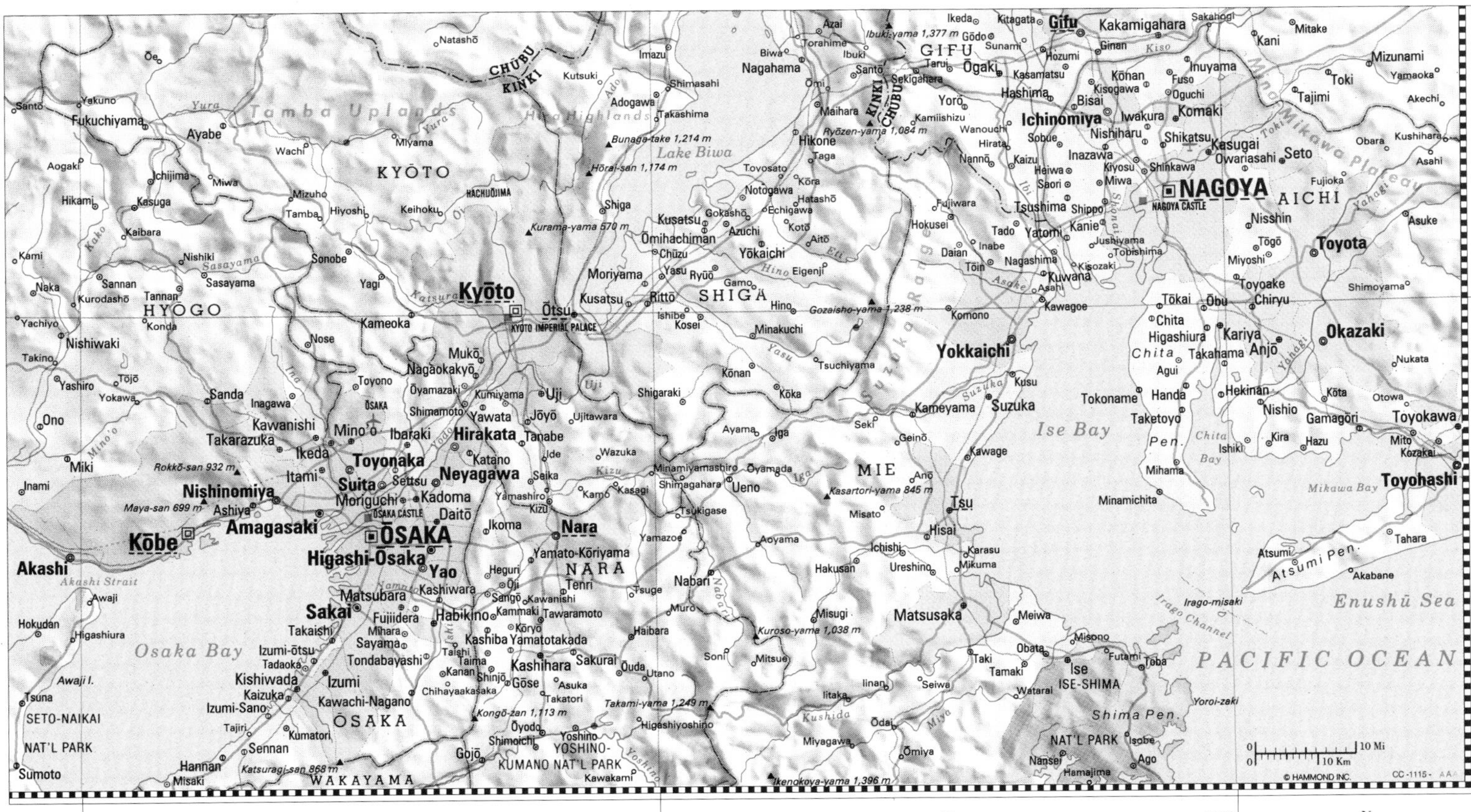

POPULATION OF CITIES AND TOWNS

■ OVER 2,000,000 ● 500,000 – 999,999 ● 100,000 – 249,999 ○ 10,000 – 24,999
▣ 1,000,000 – 1,999,999 ● 250,000 – 499,999 ● 30,000 – 99,999 ○ UNDER 10,000

SCALE 1:3,500,000   LAMBERT CONFORMAL CONIC PROJECTION

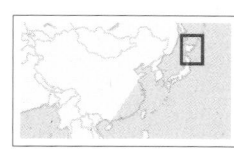

Northern Japan, Ryukyu Islands

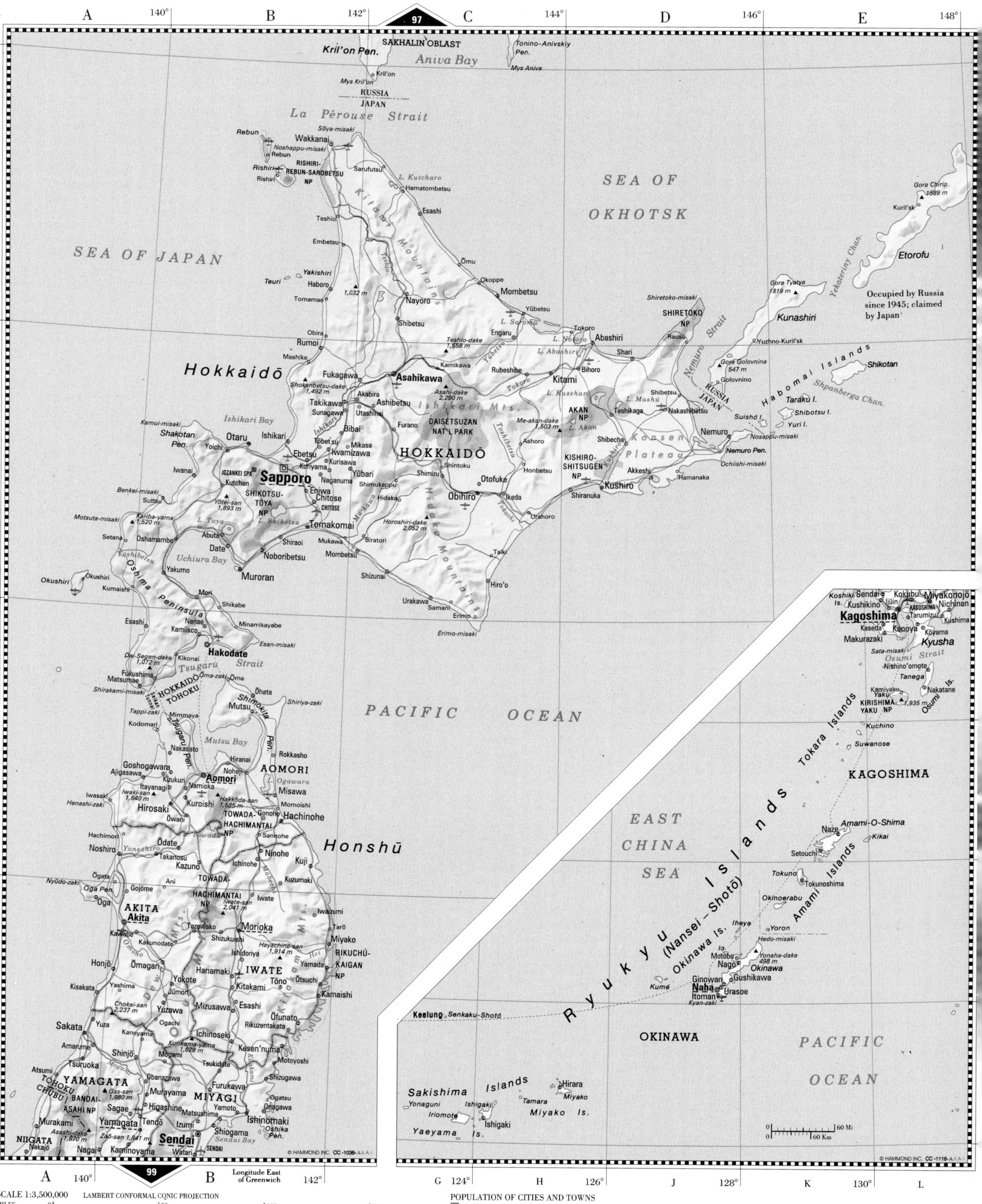

97

A 140° B 142° C 144° D 146° E 148°

46°

44°

42°

40°

SEA OF OKHOTSK

SEA OF JAPAN

PACIFIC OCEAN

EAST CHINA SEA

Kril'on Pen.
Aniva Bay
SAKHALIN OBLAST
Tonino-Anivskiy Pen.
Mys Kril'on
Kril'on
Mys Aniva
RUSSIA
JAPAN
La Pérouse Strait
Sōya-misaki
Rebun
Wakkanai
Noshappu-misaki
Rebun
RISHIRI-REBUN-SAROBETSU NP
Rishiri
Rishiri
Sarufutsu
Teshio
Hamatombetsu
L. Kutcharo
Esashi
Ōmu
Okoppe
Mombetsu
Gora Chirip 1,589 m
Kuril'sk
Etorofu
Gora Tyatya 1,819 m
Occupied by Russia since 1945; claimed by Japan

Embetsu
Teuri
Yakishiri
Haboro
Tomamae
1,032 m
Nayoro
Kitami Mountains
Yūbetsu
Shibetsu
Engaru
Tokoro
Abashiri
Shari
Shiretoko-misaki
SHIRETOKO NP
Rausu
Kunashiri
Gora Golovnina 547 m
Golovnino

Obira
Rumoi
Fukagawa
Shokambetsu-dake 1,492 m
Takikawa
Akabira
Sunagawa
Ashibetsu
Asahikawa
Asahi-dake 2,290 m
Kamikawa
Rubeshibe
Bihoro
L. Noboro
L. Kussharu
Teshikaga
L. Mashu
Shibecha
Shibetsu
Nakashibetsu
Nemuro
Nosappu-misaki
RUSSIA JAPAN
Taraku I.
Suishō I.
Yuri I.
Shikotan
Habomai Islands
Shpanberga Chan.
Yekaterinsy Chan.

Hokkaidō
Kamui-misaki
Shakotan Pen.
Yoichi
Otaru
Ishikari
Ishikari Bay
Ebetsu
Tōbetsu
Mikasa
Iwamizawa
Kurisawa
Kuriyama
Naganuma
Yūbari
DAISETSUZAN NAT'L PARK
Me-akan-dake 1,503 m
AKAN NP
L. Akan
Ashoro
Honbetsu
KISHIRO-SHITSUGEN NP
Akkeshi
Hamanaka
Konsen Plateau
Nemuro Pen.
Ochiishi-misaki

Benkei-misaki
IGZANKEI SPA
Sapporo
SHIKOTSU-TŌYA NP
Yōtei-san 1,893 m
Eniwa
Chitose
CHITOSE
Furano
Shintoku
Otofuke
Obihiro
Ikeda
Shiranuka
Kushiro

Motsuta-misaki
Shakotan
Kutchan
Kariba-yama 1,520 m
Suttsu
Abuta
L. Toya
L. Shikotsu
Shiraoi
Mukawa
Hidaka
Shimukappu
Shimizu
Urahoro
Taiki

Okushiri
Kumaishi
Setana
Oshamambe
Date
Yakumo
Noboribetsu
Tomakomai
Biratori
Mombetsu
Horoshiri-dake 2,052 m
Hidaka Mountains
Shizunai
Urakawa
Samani
Hiro'o
Erimo
Erimo-misaki

Oshima Peninsula
Toshibetsu
Uchiura Bay
Mori
Shikabe
Minamikayabe
Esan-misaki
HOKKAIDŌ
TOHOKU
Esashi
Nanae
Kamiiso
Dai-Segen-dake 1,072 m
Hakodate
Kikonai
Oma-zaki
Oma
Tsugaru Strait

Fukushima
Matsumae
Shirakami-misaki
Tappi-zaki
Mimmaya
Ōhata
Shiriya-zaki
Shimokita Pen.
Mutsu

Kodomari
Nakasato
Mutsu Bay
Hiranai
Rokkasho
Rokkasho
Hiranai
Noheji
AOMORI
Misawa
Momoishi

Goshogawara
Ajigasawa
Kizukuri
Namioka
Aomori
Ogawara
Hachinohe
Iwasaki
Iwaki-san 1,640 m
Itayanagi
Kuroishi
Hakkōda-san 1,585 m
Gonohe
Sannohe
Ninohe
Kuji

Henashi-zaki
Hirosaki
TOWADA-HACHIMANTAI NP
Ōwani
Kazuno
Ichinohe
Hachiman
Odate
Towada
Iwate
Iwaizumi

Honshū

Noshiro
Takanosu
Ani
Gojōme
HACHIMANTAI NP
Iwate-san 2,041 m
Morioka
Hayachine-san 1,914 m
Miyako
RIKUCHŪ-KAIGAN NP
Yamada

Nyūdō-zaki
Oga Pen.
Oga
Tazawako
Shizukuishi
Ishidoriya
Ōtsuchi

AKITA
Akita
Kawabe
Kakunodate
Kamaishi

Honjō
Ōmagari
IWATE
Hanamaki
Tōno
Kitakami
Kawai

Kisakata
Yashima
Yokote
Ichinoseki
Rikuzentakata

Sakata
Yuza
Yuzawa
Mizusawa
Esashi
Ōfunato

Chōkai-san 2,237 m
Sagae
Ogachi
Ichinoseki
Kesen'numa
Motoyoshi

Amarume
Murayama
Shinjō
Mogami
Tsukidate
Shizugawa

Atsumi
Tsuruoka
YAMAGATA
Gas-san 1,980 m
Higashine
Matsushima
Onagawa
Oshika Pen.

TOHOKU
CHŌKAI
BANDAI-ASAHI NP
MIYAGI
Furukawa
Opatsu
Ishinomaki

Murakami
Asahi-dake 1,870 m
Yamagata
Kaminoyama
Shiogama
Watari
Sendai Bay

NIIGATA
Nakajō
Nagai
Zaō-san 1,841 m
Sendai

99

A 140° B 142°
Longitude East of Greenwich

SCALE 1:3,500,000   LAMBERT CONFORMAL CONIC PROJECTION

MILES 0 50 100 150
KILOMETERS 0 50 100 150

G 124° H 126° J 128° K 130° L

Koshiki Is.
Sendai
Kushikino
Kokubu
Miyakonojo
Nichinan
KAGOSHIMA
Kagoshima
Kaseda
Kanoya
Kushima
Makurazaki
Kōyama
Sata-misaki
Osumi Strait
Kyusha
Nishino'omote
Tanega
KIRISHIMA-YAKU NP 1,935 m
Kamiyaku
Yaku
Osumi Is.
Nakatane
Kuchino
Suwanose
Tokara Islands
KAGOSHIMA
Naze
Amami-O-Shima
Kikai
Setouchi
Amami Islands
Tokuno
Tokunoshima
Okinoerabu
Ryukyu (Nansei-Shotō)
Ryukyu Islands (Nansei-Shotō)
Yoron
Hedo-misaki
Iheya
Io
Motobu
Yonaha-dake 498 m
Nago
Okinawa
Okinawa Is.
Kume
Ginowan
Gushikawa
Naha
Itoman
Urasoe
Kyan-zaki
OKINAWA

Keelung
Senkaku-Shotō
Sakishima Islands
Yonaguni
Iriomote
Ishigaki
Ishigaki
Tamara
Hirara
Miyako
Miyako Is.
Yaeyama Is.

EAST CHINA SEA
PACIFIC OCEAN

0 60 Mi
0 60 Km

© HAMMOND INC. CC-1036-A-A-A
© HAMMOND INC. CC-1116-A-A-A

POPULATION OF CITIES AND TOWNS
■ OVER 2,000,000   ◉ 500,000 - 999,999   ● 100,000 - 249,999   ◎ 10,000 - 29,999
□ 1,000,000 - 1,999,999   ⊚ 250,000 - 499,999   ○ 30,000 - 99,999   ○ UNDER 10,000

Korea

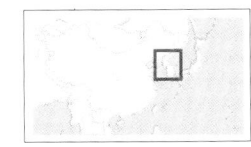

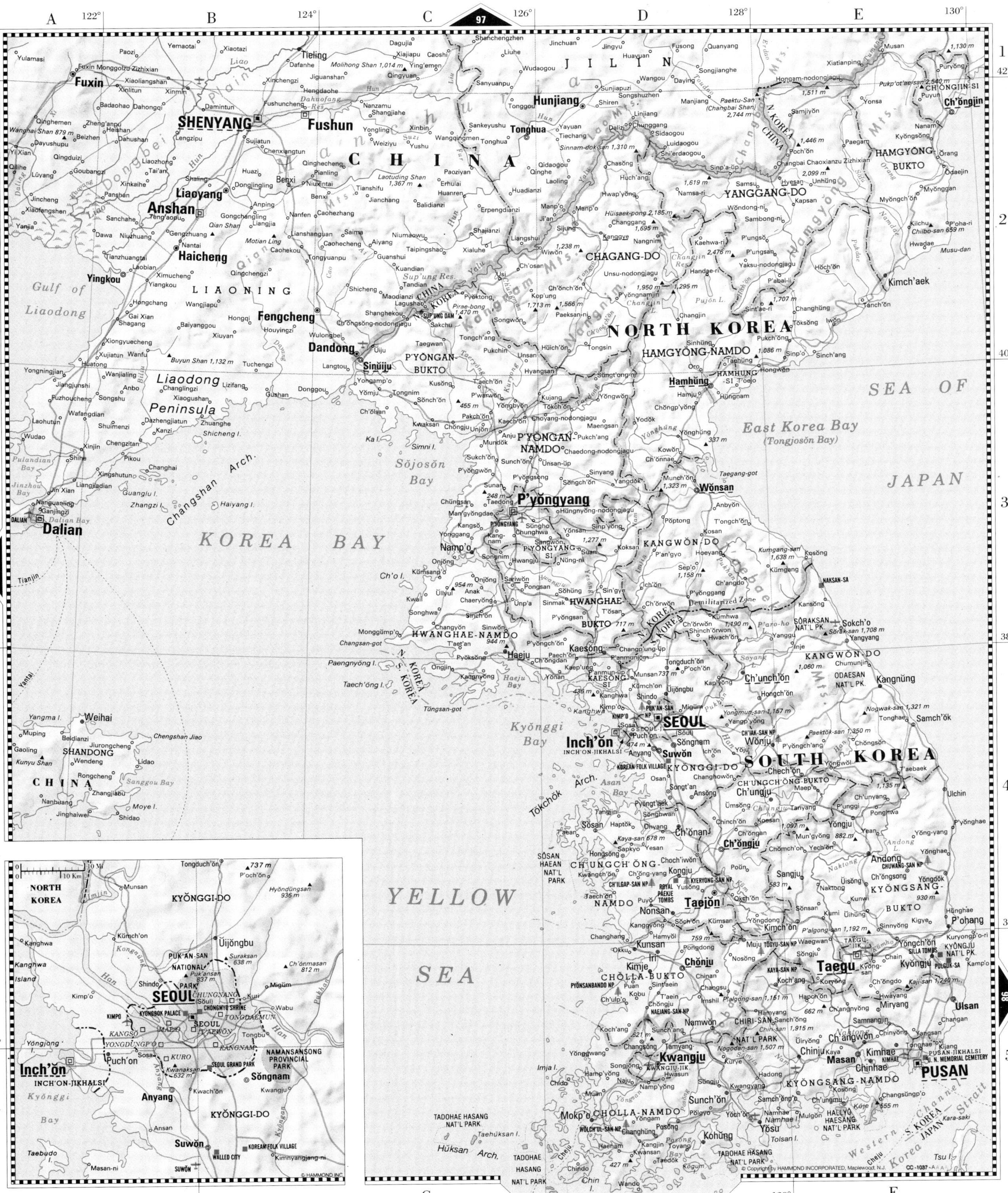

SCALE 1:3,500,000   LAMBERT CONFORMAL CONIC PROJECTION

MILES

KILOMETERS

Longitude East of Greenwich

POPULATION OF CITIES AND TOWNS

■ OVER 2,000,000	◉ 500,000 - 999,999	● 100,000 - 249,999	○ 10,000 - 29,999
▣ 1,000,000 - 1,999,999	◎ 250,000 - 499,999	⊕ 30,000 - 99,999	○ UNDER 10,000

© Copyright HAMMOND INCORPORATED, Maplewood, N.J.   CC-1037

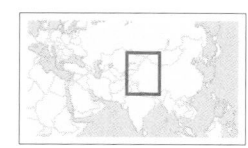

Central Asia

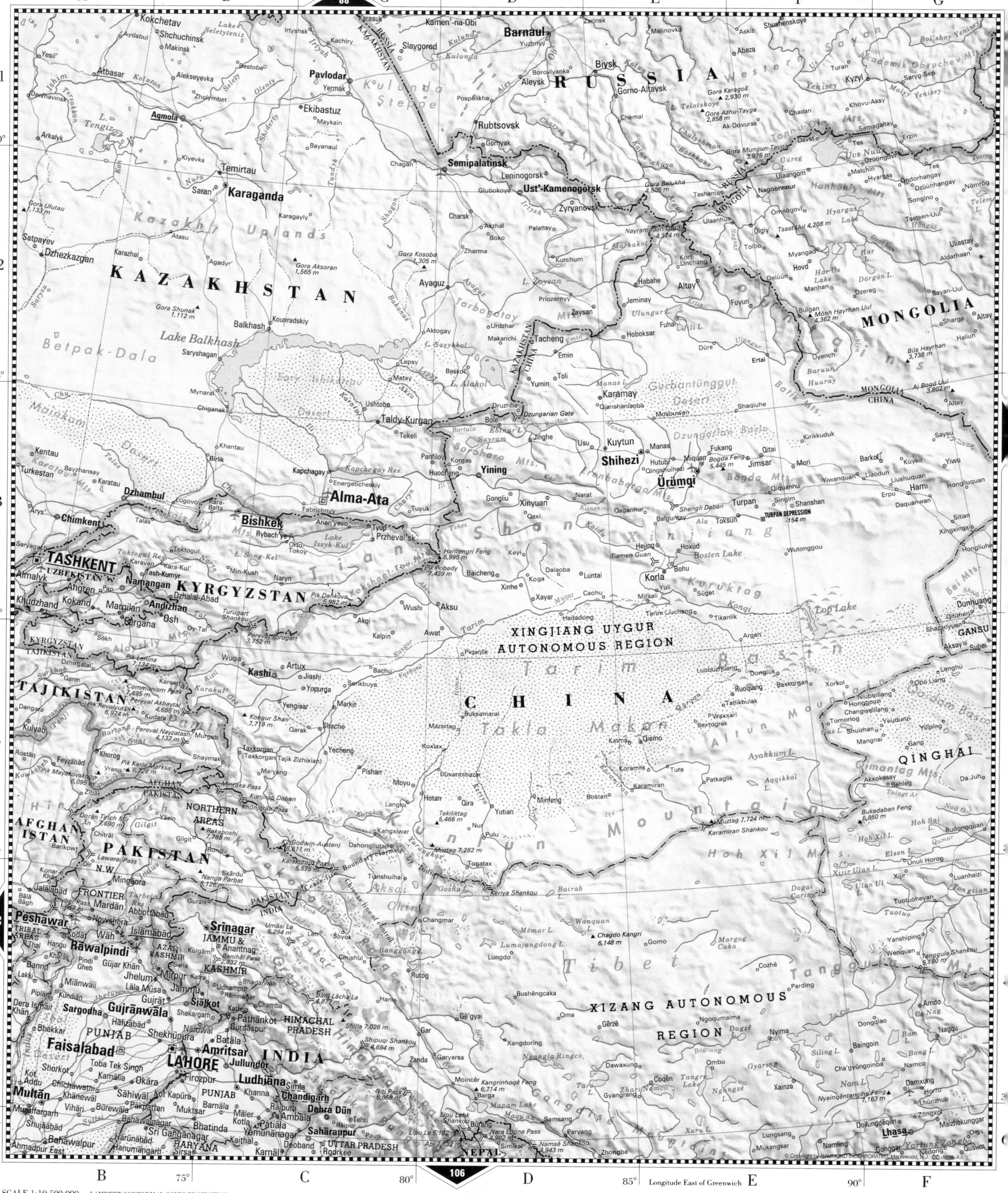

SCALE 1:10,500,000   LAMBERT CONFORMAL CONIC PROJECTION

MILES   0 ___ 150 ___ 300 ___ 450

KILOMETERS 0 __ 150 __ 300 __ 450

POPULATION OF CITIES AND TOWNS

▪ OVER 2,000,000   ● 500,000 - 999,999   ● 100,000 - 249,999   ○ 10,000 - 29,999

▫ 1,000,000 - 1,999,999   ● 250,000 - 499,999   ● 30,000 - 99,999   ○ UNDER 10,000

Longitude East of Greenwich

Northeastern China

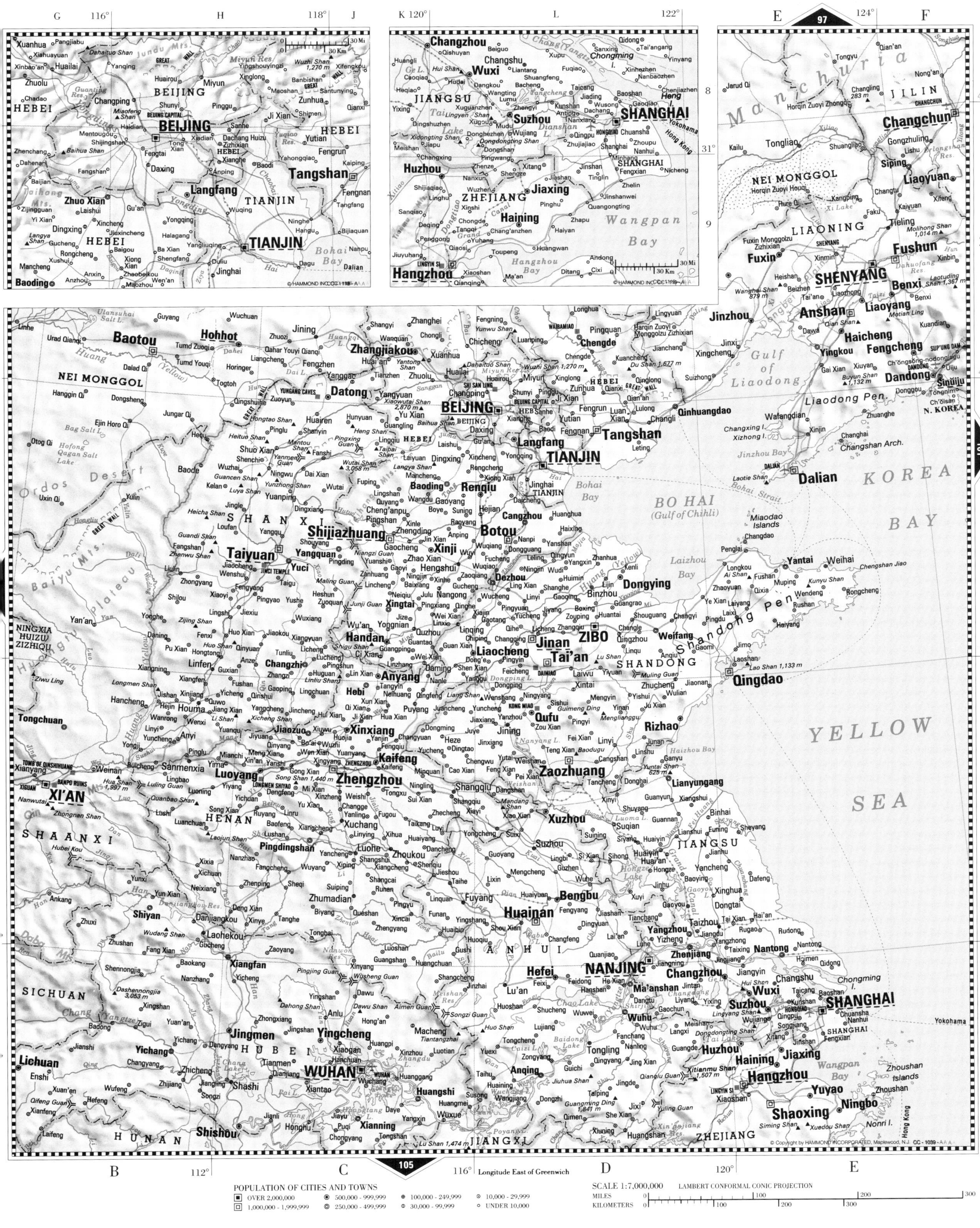

BEIJING
TIANJIN
Tangshan
Langfang
HEBEI
Changzhou
Wuxi
Suzhou
SHANGHAI
Huzhou
Jiaxing
Haining
Hangzhou
JIANGSU
ZHEJIANG
Wangpan Bay
Hangzhou Bay
Changchun
JILIN
Siping
Liaoyuan
Tieling
Fushun
SHENYANG
Benxi
Anshan
Liaoyang
Fuxin
LIAONING
NEI MONGGOL
Manchuria
Baotou
Hohhot
Zhangjiakou
Datong
Chengde
Qinhuangdao
Jinzhou
Yingkou
Haicheng
Fengcheng
Dandong
Gulf of Liaodong
Liaodong Pen.
Dalian
KOREA BAY
N. KOREA
BO HAI (Gulf of Chihli)
Bohai Bay
Baoding
Renqiu
Cangzhou
Botou
Shijiazhuang
Taiyuan
Yuci
SHANXI
Xingtai
Handan
Anyang
Changzhi
Jinan
Tai'an
ZIBO
Dongying
Weifang
Yantai
Qingdao
Rizhao
Shandong Pen.
SHANDONG
Liaocheng
Dezhou
Qufu
Zaozhuang
Lianyungang
Xuzhou
YELLOW SEA
Luoyang
Zhengzhou
Kaifeng
Xinxiang
Jiaozuo
Xi'AN
SHAANXI
HENAN
Pingdingshan
Xuchang
Luohe
Zhoukou
Huainan
Bengbu
Hefei
ANHUI
NANJING
Zhenjiang
Yangzhou
Nantong
Shiyan
Xiangfan
Jingmen
Yingcheng
WUHAN
HUBEI
Yichang
Shashi
Huangshi
Anqing
SICHUAN
HUNAN
JIANGXI
Shaoxing
Ningbo
Zhoushan Islands
Yokohama

POPULATION OF CITIES AND TOWNS

OVER 2,000,000	500,000 - 999,999	100,000 - 249,999	10,000 - 29,999
1,000,000 - 1,999,999	250,000 - 499,999	30,000 - 99,999	UNDER 10,000

SCALE 1:7,000,000 LAMBERT CONFORMAL CONIC PROJECTION

MILES 0 100 200 300

KILOMETERS 0 100 200 300

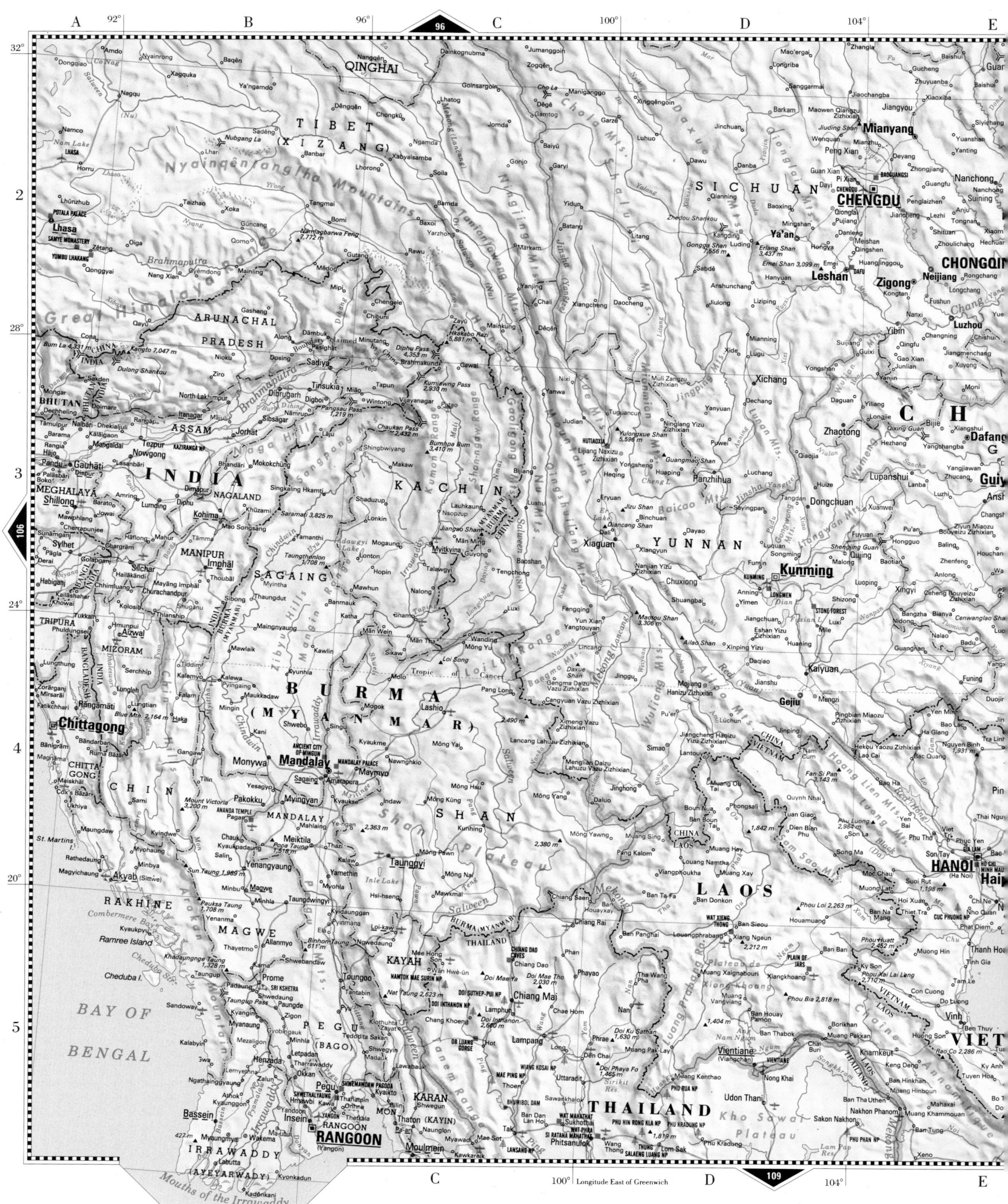

Southeastern China, Burma

POPULATION OF CITIES AND TOWNS

| ■ OVER 2,000,000 | ◉ 500,000 - 999,999 | ● 100,000 - 249,999 | ⊙ 10,000 - 29,999 |
| ▣ 1,000,000 - 1,999,999 | ◉ 250,000 - 499,999 | ● 30,000 - 99,999 | ○ UNDER 10,000 |

SCALE 1:7,000,000   LAMBERT CONFORMAL CONIC PROJECTION

MILES   0 ---- 100 ---- 200 ---- 300

KILOMETERS   0 ---- 100 ---- 200 ---- 300

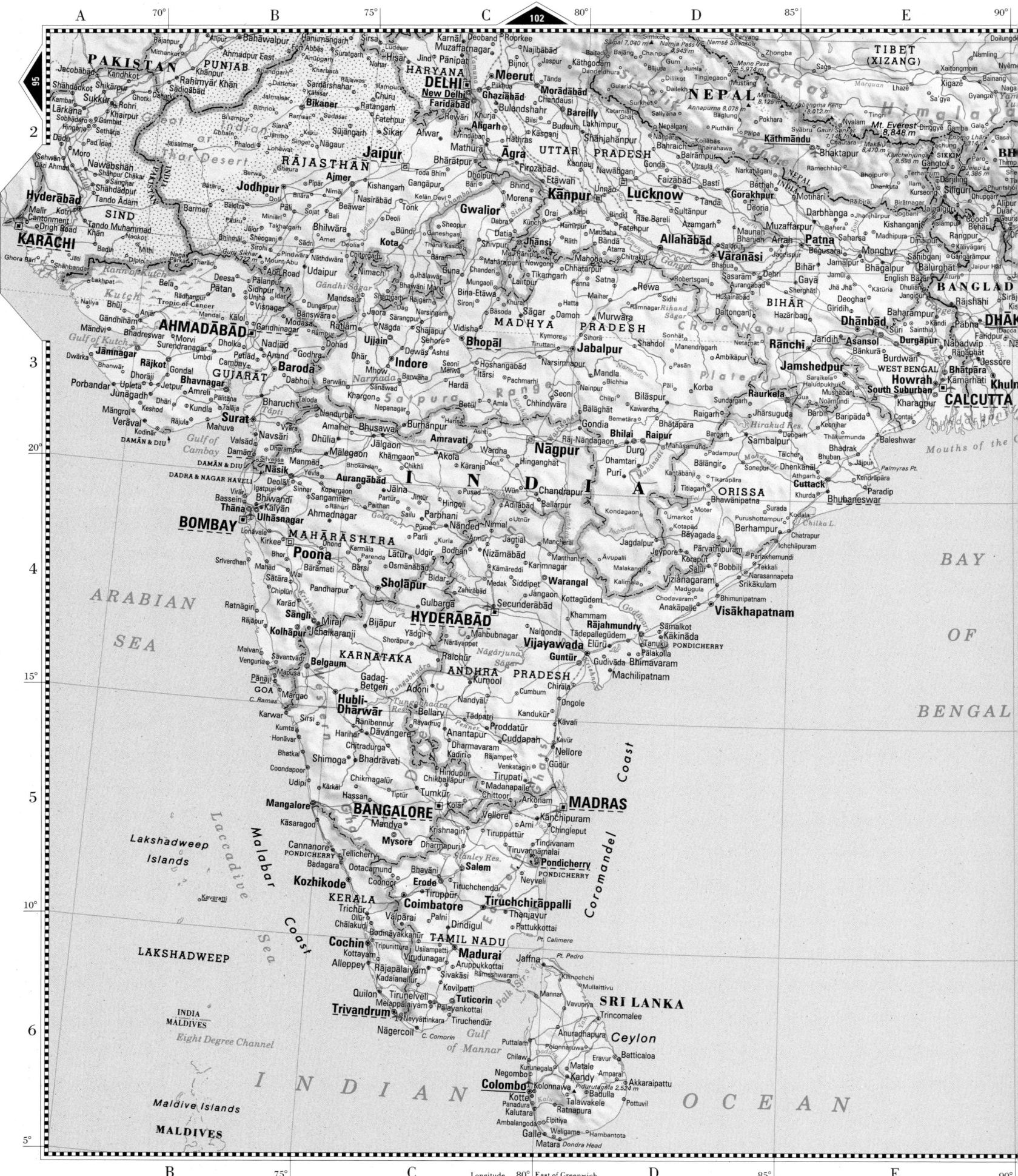

Southern Asia

POPULATION OF CITIES AND TOWNS

■ OVER 2,000,000	● 500,000 - 999,999
□ 1,000,000 - 1,999,999	● 250,000 - 499,999
● 100,000 - 249,999	● 10,000 - 29,999
● 30,000 - 99,999	○ UNDER 10,000

SCALE 1:10,500,000   LAMBERT CONFORMAL CONIC PROJECTION

MILES 0 — 150 — 300 — 450

KILOMETERS 0 — 150 — 300 — 450

Longitude 100° East of Greenwich

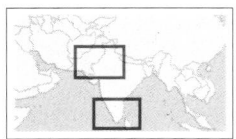

Punjab Plain, Southern India

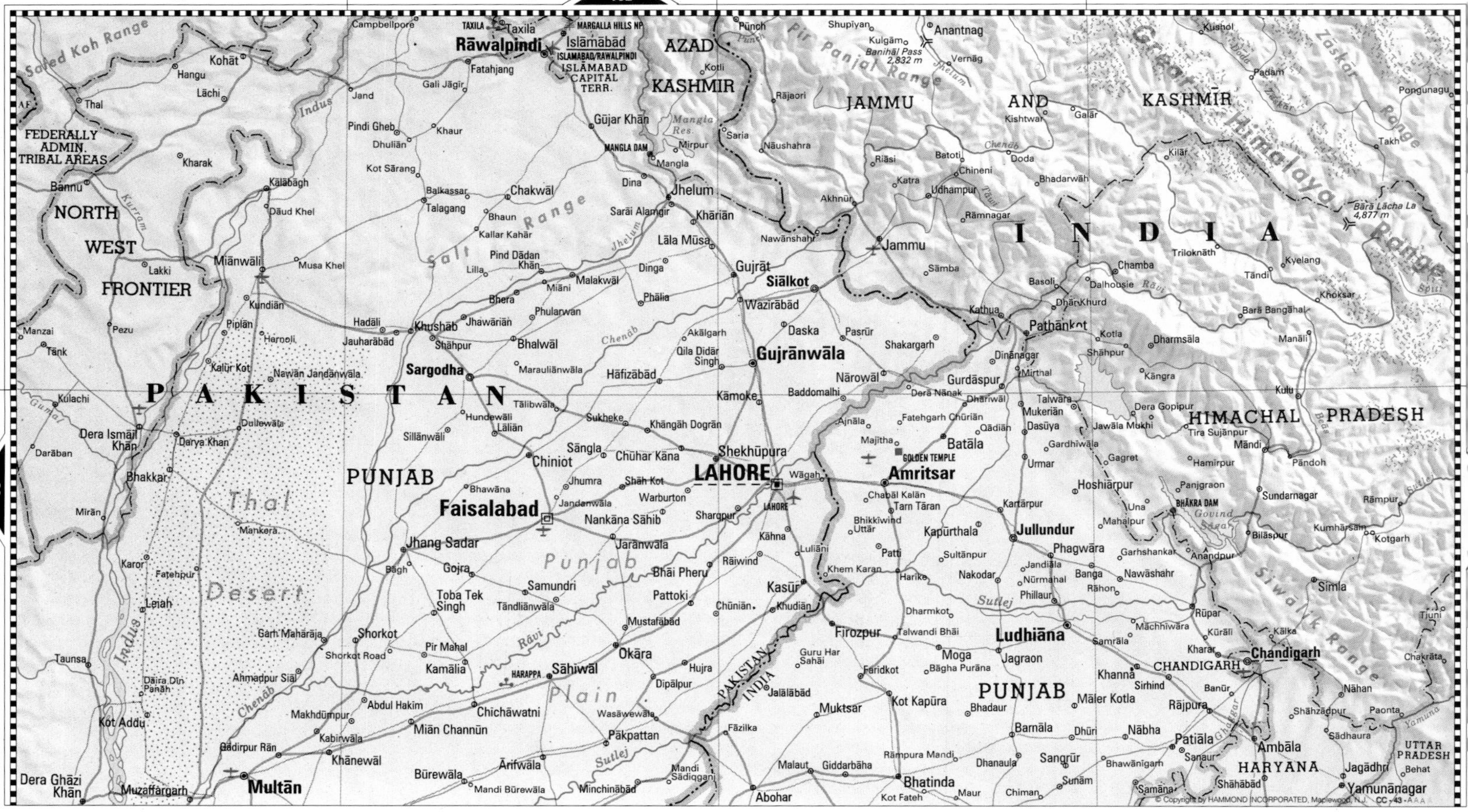

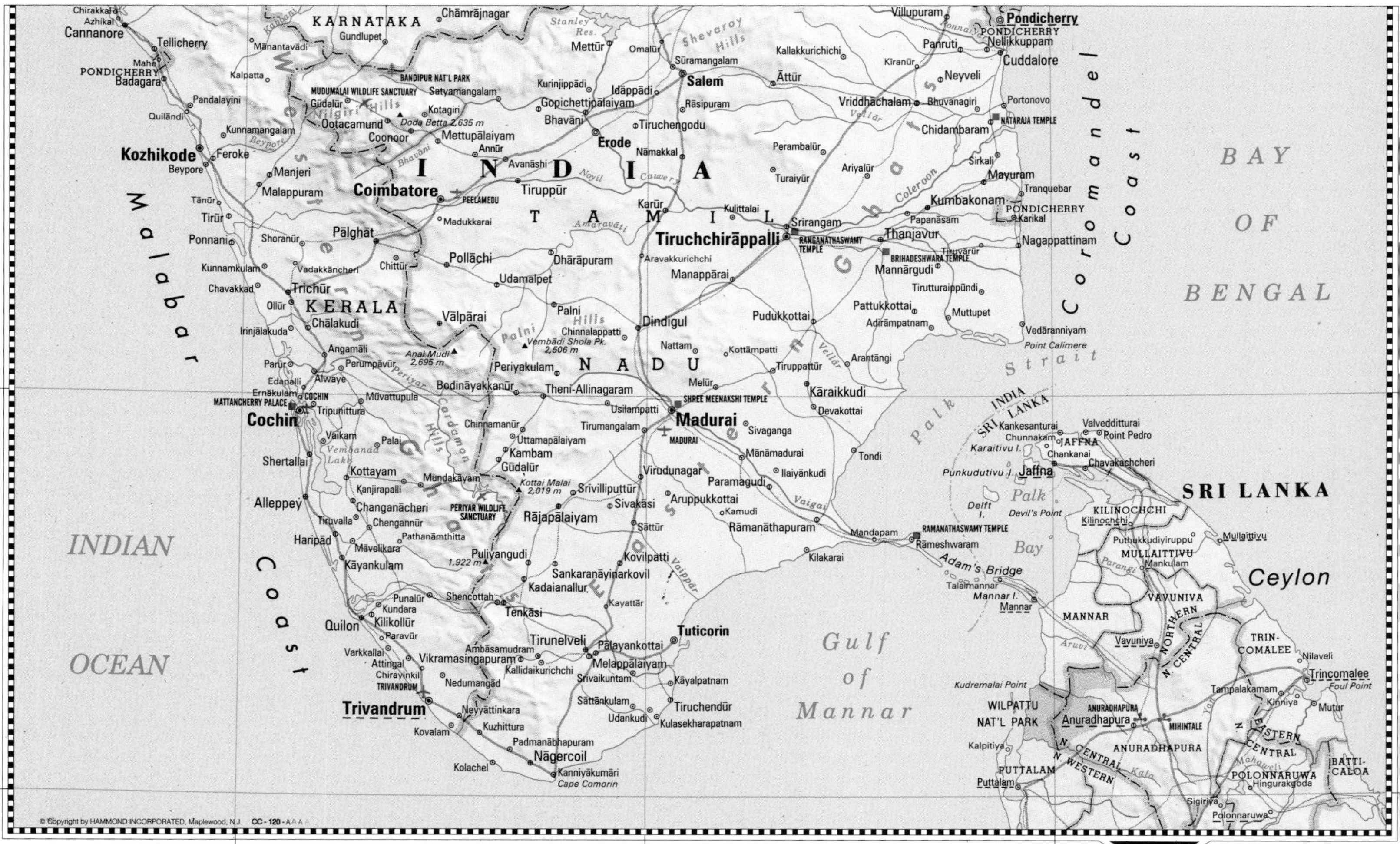

SCALE 1:3,500,000   LAMBERT CONFORMAL CONIC PROJECTION

MILES 0   50   100   150
KILOMETERS 0   50   100   150

POPULATION OF CITIES AND TOWNS

■ OVER 2,000,000	◉ 500,000 - 999,999	● 100,000 - 249,999	● 10,000 - 29,999
▫ 1,000,000 - 1,999,999	◎ 250,000 - 499,999	● 30,000 - 99,999	○ UNDER 10,000

Longitude East of Greenwich 80°

Eastern Burma, Thailand, Indochina

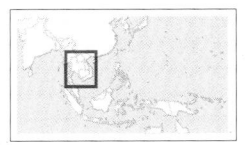

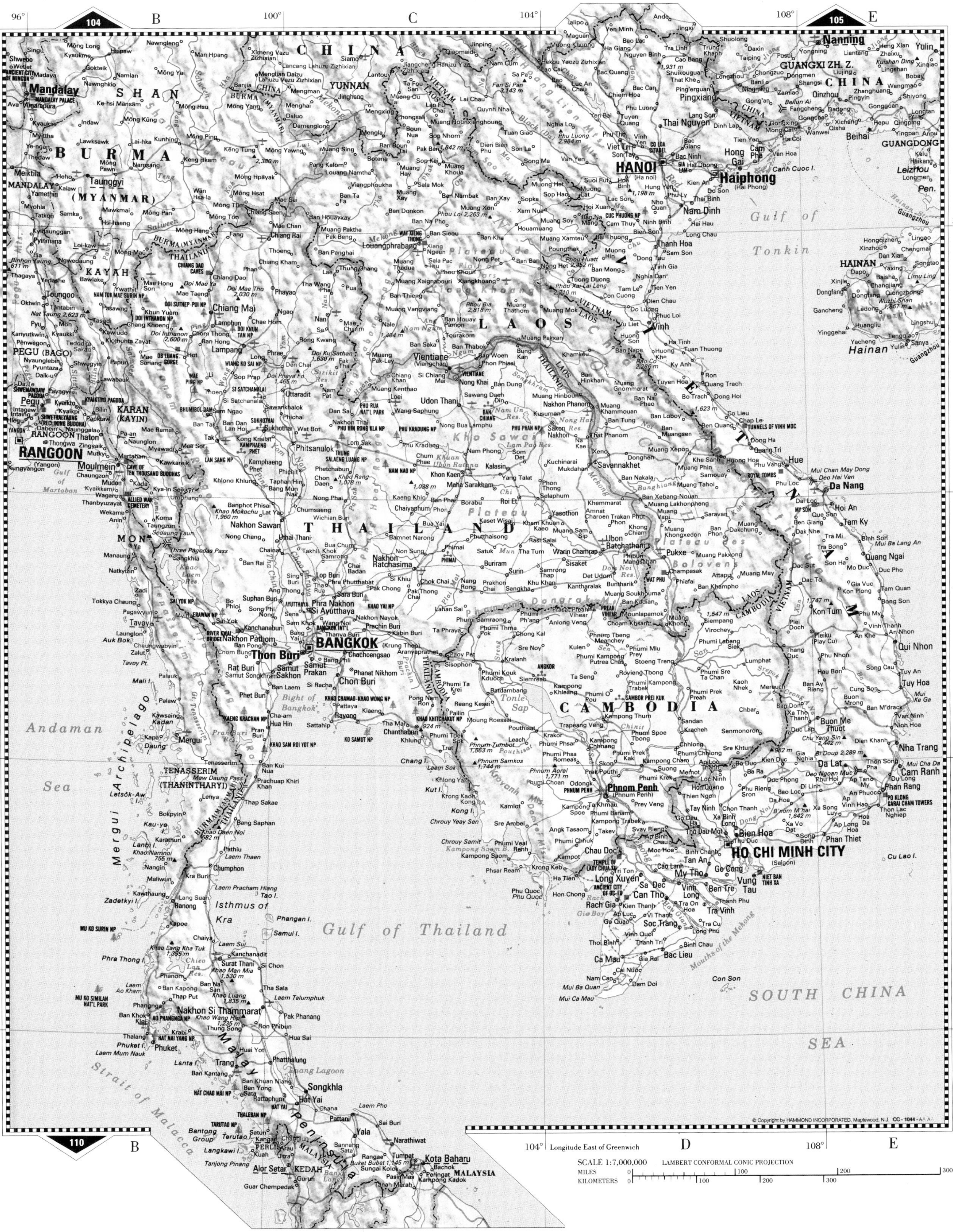

104° Longitude East of Greenwich

SCALE 1:7,000,000   LAMBERT CONFORMAL CONIC PROJECTION

MILES 0 100 200 300
KILOMETERS 0 100 200 300

95°   A   100°   B   105°   C   110°   D   1

Andaman

Sea

Mergui
Archipelago
Mergui

Cha-am
Hua Hin
Tenasserim
Prachuap Khiri
Khan

**BURMA
(MYANMAR)**

Letsók-Aw I.
Lenya
Bokpyin

Khao Daen Noi
852 m

THAILAND

Khao Namnoi
755 m

Kra Buri
Chumphon
Ranong

*Isthmus of
Kra*

Zadetkyi I.
Kapoe

Khao Lang Kha Tuk
1,395 m

Chaiya
Phanom
Phangan I.
Surat Thani
Samui I.

Nakhon Si
Thammarat
Khao Luang
1,835 m

Phangnga
Krabi
Ban Na San
Ban Pak
Phanang

Phuket I.
Phuket
Lanta I.
Trang
Phatthalung

Laem Mum Nauk
Songkhla

Rayong
Chanthaburi
Trat
Chang I.
Kut I.
Krong Kaoh
Kong

Phumi Ta
Krei
Tha Mai
Pouthisat

Phnum Tbong
Kampong
Thum

Batdambang
Tonle Sap

CAMBODIA

Phnum Tumbor
Leach
Chhnang
1,563 m

Phnum Samkos
4,744 m

Chrouy Samit

Kampong Saom B.
Kampong Saom

Phnum Aôral
1,771 m

Prey Veng

Pouthisat
Phumi Phsa
Rumcac

Kampong
Cham

Phnom Penh
(Phnum Penh)

Chau Doc
Svay Rieng

Ban Ay Rieng
Ban Don
Senmonoron

Cung Son
Buon Mrong
Lac Thien

Tuy An
Muï Ké Ga
Van Ninh

Tuy Hoa
Nha Trang

Buon Me Thuot
B'nom M'hai
1,642 m

Dien Khanh
Cam Ranh
Phan Rang

VIETNAM

SOUTH

SEA

Spratly Islands
(Sovereignty disputed)

MALAYSIA

Natuna
Is.

Ranai
Bunguran I.

BRU
Bandar Seri Begaw

Kuala Belait
Tanjong Baram
Lutong
Miri

Sarawak

Bukit Batu
2,012 m

Labang

INDIAN

OCEAN

Southeastern Asia

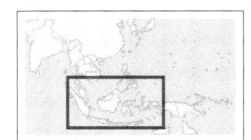

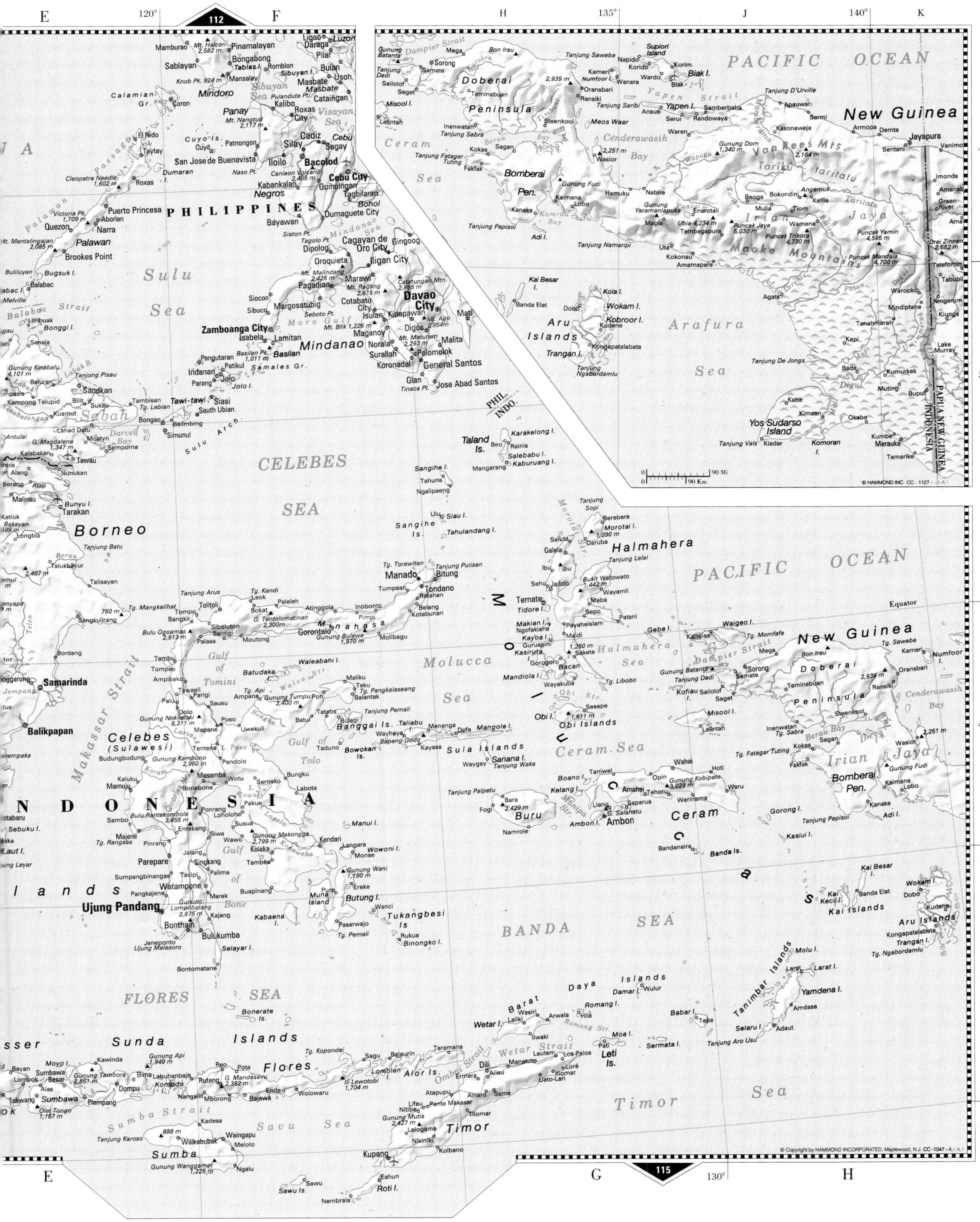

Philippines

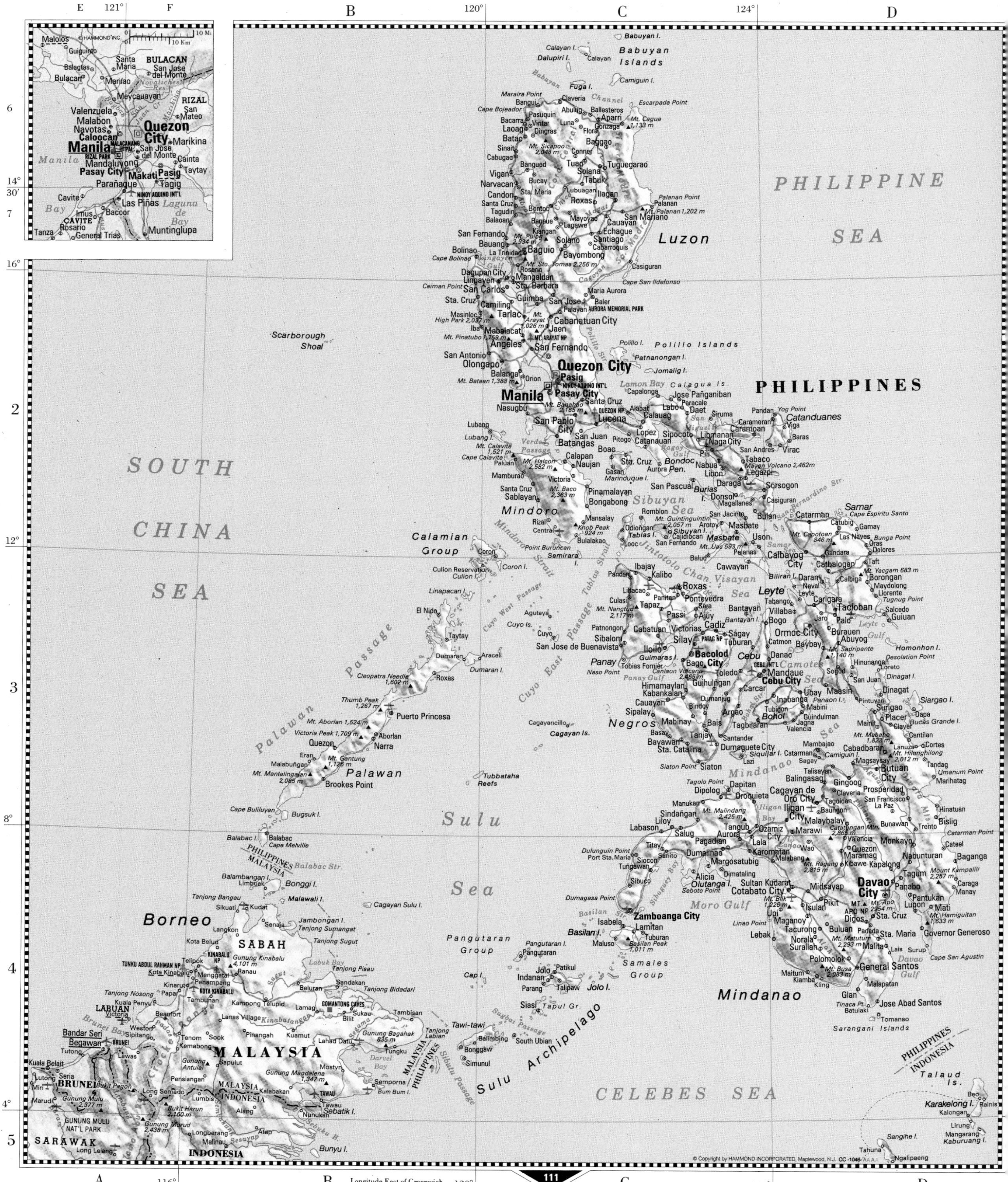

POPULATION OF CITIES AND TOWNS

- ■ OVER 2,000,000
- ▣ 1,000,000 - 1,999,999
- ■ 500,000 - 999,999
- ▢ 250,000 - 499,999
- ● 100,000 - 249,999
- ● 30,000 - 99,999
- ● 10,000 - 29,999
- ○ UNDER 10,000

SCALE 1:7,000,000   LAMBERT CONFORMAL CONIC PROJECTION

MILES 0 ... 100 ... 200 ... 300
KILOMETERS 0 ... 100 ... 200 ... 300

Longitude East of Greenwich

© Copyright by HAMMOND INCORPORATED, Maplewood, N.J. CC-1045-AAAA

Antarctica

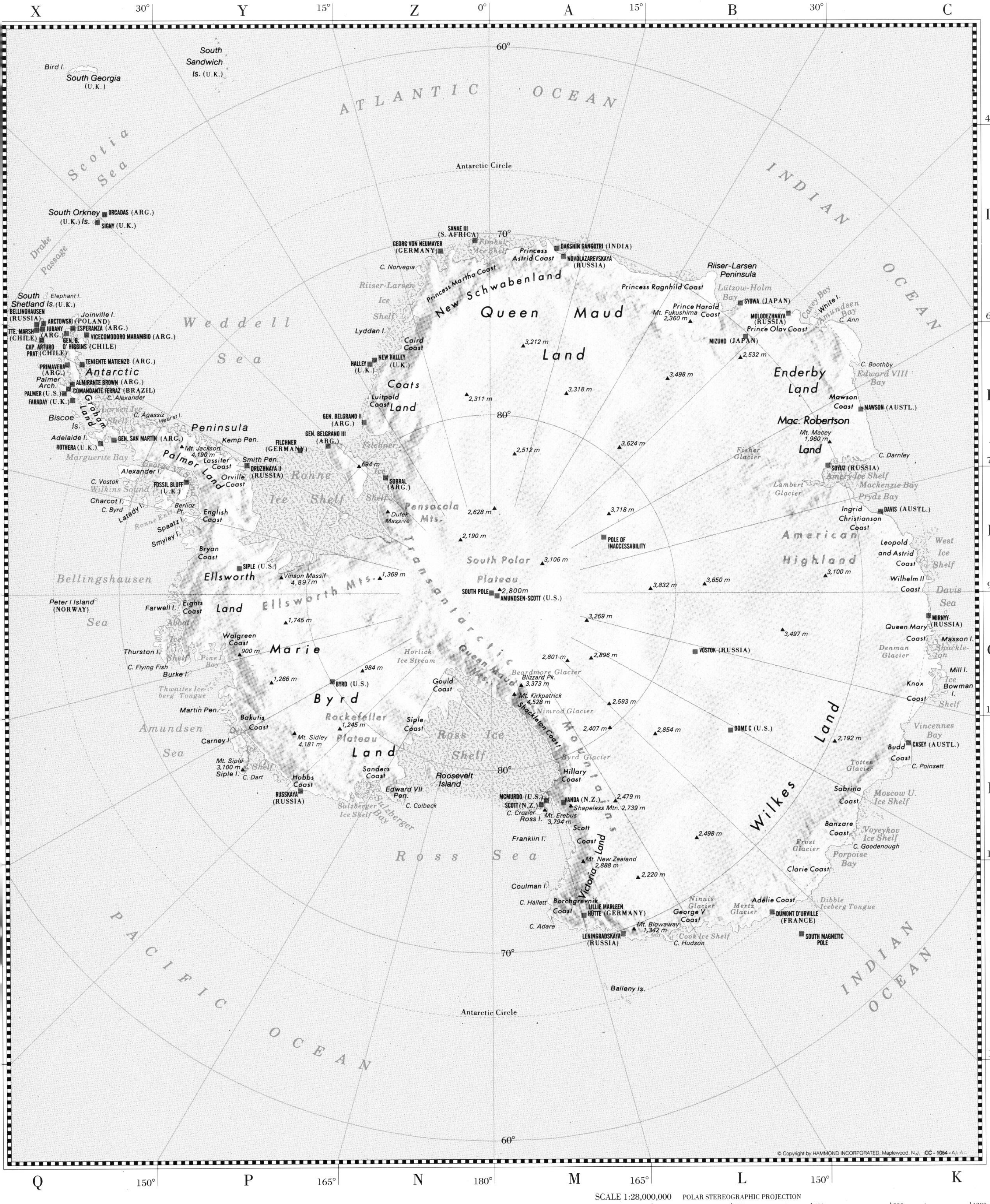

X 30° Y 15° Z 0° A 15° B 30° C

60°

ATLANTIC OCEAN

Antarctic Circle

INDIAN OCEAN

45°

D

Bird I.
South Georgia (U.K.)
South Sandwich Is. (U.K.)

Scotia Sea

South Orkney Is. (U.K.)
ORCADAS (ARG.)
SIGNY (U.K.)

70°

SANAE III (S. AFRICA)
GEORG VON NEUMAYER (GERMANY)
C. Norvegia
DAKSHIN GANGOTRI (INDIA)
NOVOLAZAREVSKAYA (RUSSIA)
Princess Astrid Coast

Riiser-Larsen Peninsula
Princess Ragnhild Coast
Lützow-Holm Bay
Prince Harold Coast
Mt. Fukushima 2,360 m
SYOWA (JAPAN)
MOLODEZHNAYA (RUSSIA)
Prince Olav Coast
Casey Bay
White I.
Amundsen Bay
C. Ann

60°

Drake Passage

South Shetland Is. (U.K.)
BELLINGSHAUSEN (RUSSIA)
Elephant I.
Joinville I.
ARCTOWSKI (POLAND)
TTE. MARSH (CHILE)
JUBANY (ARG.)
ESPERANZA (ARG.)
CAP. ARTURO PRAT (CHILE)
GEN. O. HIGGINS (CHILE)
VICECOMODORO MARAMBIO (ARG.)
TENIENTE MATIENZO (ARG.)
PRIMAVERA (ARG.)
ALMIRANTE BROWN (ARG.)
COMANDANTE FERRAZ (BRAZIL)
PALMER (U.S.)
FARADAY (U.K.)

Weddell Sea

Riiser-Larsen Ice Shelf
New Schwabenland
Princess Martha Coast
Lyddan I.
Caird Coast

Queen Maud Land

3,212 m
2,532 m
MIZUHO (JAPAN)

Enderby Land

E

HALLEY (U.K.)
NEW HALLEY (U.K.)
Coats Land
Luitpold Coast
Brunt Ice Shelf
3,498 m
3,318 m
C. Boothby
Edward VIII Bay

Antarctic Arch.
Palmer
Graham Land
C. Alexander
C. Agassiz
Hearst I.
GEN. BELGRANO II (ARG.)
GEN. BELGRANO III (ARG.)
694 m
SOBRAL (ARG.)
2,311 m

Mawson Coast
MAWSON (AUSTL.)

Biscoe Is.
Adelaide I.
ROTHERA (U.K.)
Marguerite Bay
GEN. SAN MARTIN (ARG.)
Kemp Pen.
Mt. Jackson 4,190 m
FILCHNER (GERMANY)
DROZHNAYA II (RUSSIA)
Smith Pen.
Lassiter Coast
Orville Coast

Peninsula
Palmer Land

Ronne Ice Shelf
Filchner Ice Shelf
80°
2,512 m

3,624 m
Mac. Robertson Land
Mt. Macey 1,960 m
C. Darnley

75°

C. Vostok
Wilkins Sound
FOSSIL BLUFF (U.K.)
Alexander I.
Charcot I.
C. Byrd
Berlioz Pt.
Spaatz I.
Smyley I.
Bryan Coast

Pensacola Mts.
Dufek Massive
2,628 m
2,190 m

3,718 m
SOYUZ (RUSSIA)
Amery Ice Shelf
Lambert Glacier
Mackenzie Bay
Prydz Bay
Ingrid Christianson Coast
DAVIS (AUSTL.)

F

Peter I Island (NORWAY)
Bellingshausen Sea
SIPLE (U.S.)
Ellsworth Land
Farwell I.
Eights Coast

South Polar Plateau
3,106 m
POLE OF INACCESSABILITY

American Highland
Leopold and Astrid Coast
3,100 m
Wilhelm II Coast

West Ice Shelf

90°

Vinson Massif 4,897 m
Ellsworth Mts.
1,369 m
SOUTH POLE 2,800 m
AMUNDSEN-SCOTT (U.S.)
3,832 m
3,650 m
Davis Sea

Thurston I.
Abbot Ice Shelf
Walgreen Coast 900 m
1,745 m
Transantarctic
Marie
3,269 m
3,497 m
Queen Mary Coast
MIRNYY (RUSSIA)
Masson I.
Shackle-ton I.

G

C. Flying Fish
Burke I.
Pine I. Bay
1,266 m
984 m
Horlick Ice Stream
BYRD (U.S.)
Byrd Land
Gould Coast
2,801 m
VOSTOK (RUSSIA)
2,896 m
Denman Glacier
Knox Coast
Mill I.
Bowman I. Ice Shelf

Amundsen Sea
Martin Pen.
Bakutis Coast
Carney I.
1,245 m
Rockefeller Plateau
Siple Coast
Queen Maud Mts.
Beardmore Glacier 3,373 m
Mt. Kirkpatrick 4,528 m
Nimrod Glacier
2,407 m
2,593 m
2,854 m
DOME C (U.S.)
Vincennes Bay
2,192 m
Budd Coast
CASEY (AUSTL.)
C. Poinsett

105°

Mt. Sidley 4,181 m
Ross Ice Shelf
Byrd Glacier
Totten Glacier

Mt. Siple 3,100 m
Siple I.
C. Dart
Hobbs Coast
RUSSKAYA (RUSSIA)
Sanders Coast
Edward VII Pen.
Roosevelt Island
Hillary Coast
Wilkes Land
Sabrina Coast
Moscow U. Ice Shelf

H

Sulzberger Ice Shelf
Sulzberger Bay
C. Colbeck
MCMURDO (U.S.)
SCOTT (N.Z.)
C. Crozier
Ross I.
Mt. Erebus 3,794 m
VANDA (N.Z.)
Shapeless Mtn. 2,739 m
2,479 m
Scott Coast
2,498 m
Banzare Coast
Frost Glacier
C. Goodenough
Porpoise Bay

120°

Franklin I.
80°
Ross Sea
Victoria Land
Mt. New Zealand 2,888 m
2,220 m
Clarie Coast

Coulman I.
C. Hallett
Borchgrevink Coast
C. Adare
LILLIE MARLEEN HÜTTE (GERMANY)
Mt. Blowaway 1,342 m
LENINGRADSKAYA (RUSSIA)
George V Coast
Ninnis Glacier
Mertz Glacier
Adélie Coast
DUMONT D'URVILLE (FRANCE)
Dibble Iceberg Tongue
Cook Ice Shelf
C. Hudson
SOUTH MAGNETIC POLE

J

PACIFIC OCEAN

70°

Balleny Is.

INDIAN OCEAN

Antarctic Circle

60°

© Copyright by HAMMOND INCORPORATED, Maplewood, N.J.   CC-1064-A-A-A

Q 150° P 165° N 180° M 165° L 150° K

SCALE 1:28,000,000   POLAR STEREOGRAPHIC PROJECTION
MILES   0   300   600   900   1200
KILOMETERS   0   300   600   900   1200

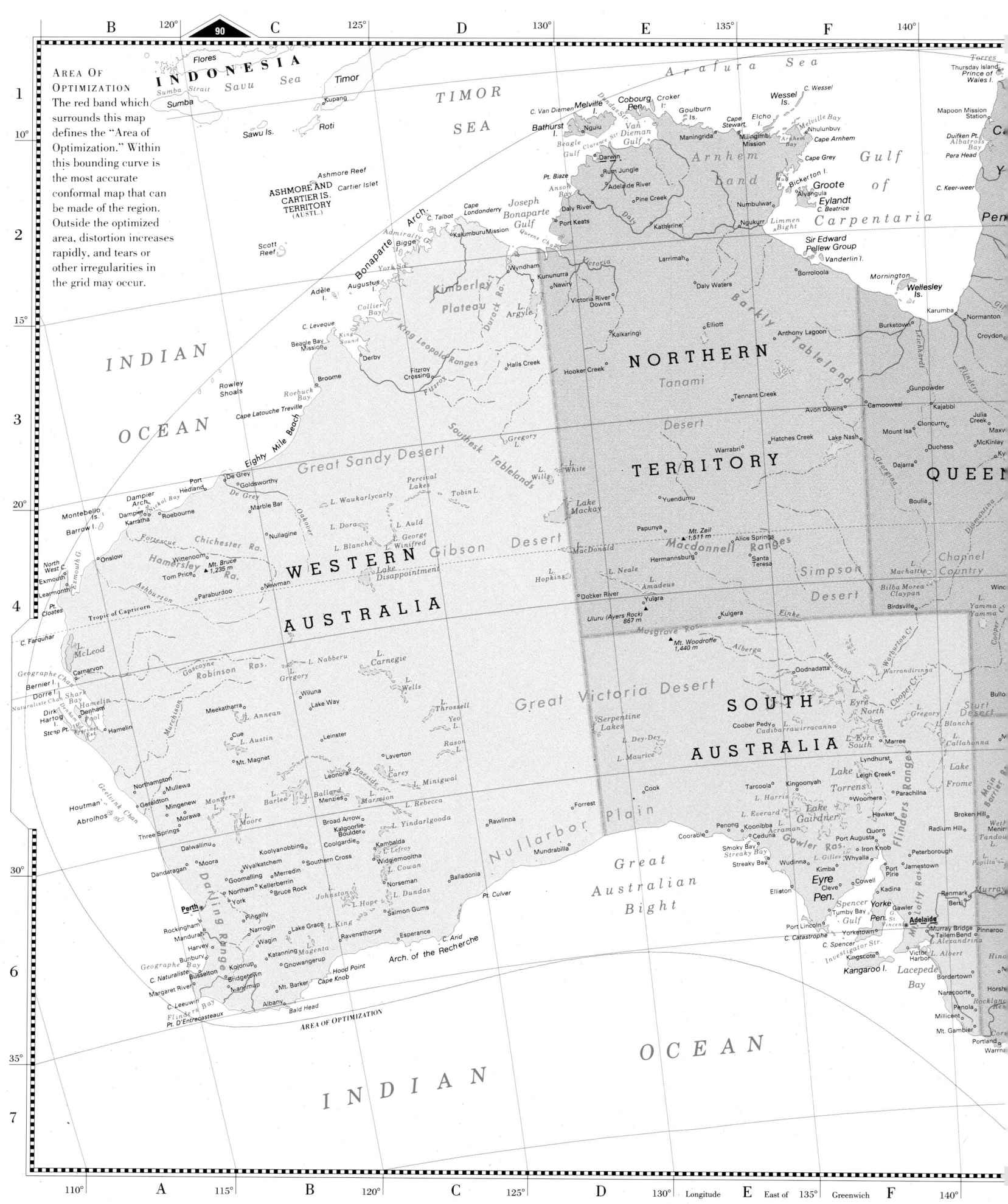

B   120°   C   125°   D   130°   E   135°   F   140°

**AREA OF
OPTIMIZATION**
The red band which
surrounds this map
defines the "Area of
Optimization." Within
this bounding curve is
the most accurate
conformal map that can
be made of the region.
Outside the optimized
area, distortion increases
rapidly, and tears or
other irregularities in
the grid may occur.

INDONESIA

Flores

Timor

Sumba Strait   Savu   Sea

Sumba   Kupang

Sawu Is.   Roti

TIMOR

SEA

Arafura   Sea

Torres
Thursday Island
Prince of
Wales I.

C. Wessel

Wessel
Is.

Mapoon Mission
Station

Duifken Pt.
Albatross
Bay
Pera Head

C. Van Diemen   Melville   Cobourg   Croker
I.   Pen.   I.
Bathurst   Nguiu   Van
Beagle   Clarence   Dieman
Gulf   Sir   Gulf

Ashmore Reef
Cartier Islet

ASHMORE AND
CARTIER IS.
TERRITORY
(AUSTL.)

Scott
Reef

Goulburn   Cape
Is.   Stewart   Elcho
I.
Maningrida   Milingimbi
Mission
Darwin   Rum Jungle
Pt. Blaze   Adelaide River
Ansom   Pine Creek
Bay

Nhulunbuy
Arnhem   Cape Arnhem
Bay
Cape Grey

Melville Bay

Gulf

of

Numbulwar

C. Keer-weer

Cape   Bonaparte
Londonderry   Gulf
C. Talbot   Joseph
Bonaparte
Gulf
Kalumburu Mission   Queens Chan.
Bigge   Wyndham   Victoria
Admiralty   York Sd.
Arch.   Kununurra
Bonaparte   Newry
Adèle   Augustus   Victoria River
I.   I.   Downs
Collier
Bay
C. Leveque   King   L.
Beagle Bay   Sound   Argyle
Mission   King
Derby   Fitzroy
Crossing
Broome   Fitzroy
Roebuck   Halls Creek
Bay   Southesk

INDIAN

OCEAN

Rowley
Shoals

Eighty   Mile   Beach

Daly River
Port Keats
Katherine

Daly Waters

Kalkaringi

Hooker Creek

Dundas Str.

Bickerton I.
Alyangula

Groote
Eylandt
C. Beatrice

Ndukurr   Limmen
Bight

Sir Edward
Pellew Group
Vanderlin I.

Larrimah

Elliott

Arnhem

Land

Borroloola
Mornington
I.

Wellesley
Is.

Barkly

Karumba

NORTHERN
Tanami

Anthony Lagoon

Tableland

Normanton
Burketown

Croydon

CARPENTARIA

Leichhardt

Flinders

Gulf

Camooweal

Gunpowder

Dampier   Port
Arch.   Hedland   De Grey
Goldsworthy
Montebello   Dampier   Nickol Bay
Is.   Arch.
Barrow I.   Karratha   Roebourne   Marble Bar
Onslow   Nullagine
North   Fortescue   Chichester Ra.
West   Hamersley   Wittenoom
Exmouth   Ra.   Mt. Bruce
Learmonth   Ashburton   Tom Price   1,235 m
Pt.   Paraburdoo   Newman
Cloates

TERRITORY

Warrabri

Avon Downs

Hatches Creek   Lake Nash

Tennant Creek

Desert

Gregory
L.

Great Sandy Desert

De Grey

Tablelands

L. Waukarlycarly

Percival
Lakes

Tobin L.

L. Dora

L. Blanche   L. Auld

L. George
Winifred

L. Wills   L.
White

Lake
Mackay

Yuendumu

Papunya   Mt. Zeil
1,511 m

MacDonald

L. Neale

Kajabbi
Mount Isa   Cloncurry

Dajarra

Boulia

Mt. Bruce

WESTERN   Gibson   Desert

Lake
Disappointment

AUSTRALIA

L.
Hopkins

Dobber River

Macdonnell   Ranges

Alice Springs
Hermannsburg   Santa
Teresa

Yulara

QUEEN

Duchess
McKinlay
Maxv

Julia
Creek

Georgina

Simpson

Channel
Country

Desert

Bilba Morea
Claypan

Wind

Tropic of Capricorn

C. Farquhar

McLeod

Carnarvon

Geographe Chan.
Bernier I.
Dorre I.   Naturaliste Chan.

Dirk
Hartog I.   Denham
Steep Pt.

Uluru (Ayers Rock)
867 m

Kulgera

Mt. Woodroffe
1,440 m

Einke

Birdsville

Alberga

Musgrave Ras.

Macumba

Oodnadatta

L. Nabberu

Gascoyne   Robinson Ras.
L.
Gregory
Murchison

Hamelin
Pool   Meekatharra
L. Annean
Cue   L. Austin

L.
Carnegie

Wiluna
Lake Way

L.
Wells

Throssell
Yeo
L.
Rason
L.

Great   Victoria   Desert

Serpentine
Lakes
L. Dey-Dey

L. Maurice

SOUTH

Coober Pedy

Cadibarrawirracanna

Eyre
North

AUSTRALIA

L. Gregory

Warrandirinna

Bullo

Sturt

L. Blanche

L. Callabonna

Yamma
Yamma

Cooper Cr.

Yarra

Lyndhurst

Lake
Frome

Mt. Magnet

Leinster

Leonora

Laverton

Carey
Minigwal
L.

Northampton
Mullewa

Geraldton   Mingenew
Houtman   Morawa
Abrolhos   Three Springs

Dalwallinu

L.
Moore

Rawlinna

L. Raeside
Barlee
Ballard
Menzies
L. Rebecca

L. Yindarlgooda
Broad Arrow
Kalgoorlie-
Boulder
Coolgardie
Kambalda

Forrest

Nullarbor   Plain

L. Everard

Tarcoola   Kingoonya

L. Harris

Penong   Koonibba

L.
Torrens

Kingoonya

L. Acraman   Ceduna

Coorabie

Eyre
South

L. Gilles

Marree

Leigh Creek

Woomera   Parachilna

Hawker

Kimba   Iron Knob

Broken Hill

Radium Hill

Flinders

Ranges

Main
Barrier

Wet
Wening
Tandou

Murray

Dandaragan   Moora
Koolyanobbing
Wyalkatchem
Goomalling   Merredin
Northam   Kellerberrin
Perth   Bruce Rock
York
Rockingham   Pingelly
Mandurah   Narrogin

Southern Cross
Widgiemooltha
L. Cowan
Norseman
L. Dundas
L. Hope
Salmon Gums

Daly   Harvey   Wagin
Range   Bunbury   Kojonup
C. Naturaliste   Busselton   Bridgetown
Margaret River   Nannup   Mt. Barker
C. Leeuwin   Mandurah
Geographe   Flinders Bay
Bay   Pt. D'Entrecasteaux

L. King
Lake Grace
Katanning   Magenta
Gnowangerup
Hood Point
Cape Knob
Bald Head

Mundrabilla

Balladonia

Pt. Culver

Great

Australian

Bight

Coorabie

Smoky Bay
Streaky Bay
Streaky Bay

Wudinna

Whyalla

Cleve
Eyre
Pen.

Cowell

Eliston

Port Lincoln
C. Catastrophe
Kangaroo I.

Tumby Bay

Spencer
Gulf

Kadina

Yorke
Pen.

C. Spencer   Kingscote
Investigator Str.

Jamestown

Port
Pirie

Quorn

Port Augusta

Peterborough

Gawler

Gawler Ras.

Adelaide

Renmark
Berri

Murray Bridge
Tailem Bend
L. Alexandrina
Victor
Harbor   L. Albert
Bordertown

Pinnaroo

Si

Murray

Lacepede
Bay

Naracoorte
Panola   Rockba
Millicent

Mt. Gambier

Cor

Hind

Horsha

Ravensthorpe

Esperance

C. Arid

Arch. of the Recherche

Rawlinna

Rawlinna

INDIAN

OCEAN

AREA OF OPTIMIZATION

110°   A   115°   B   120°   C   125°   D   130°   Longitude   E   East of   135°   Greenwich   F   140°

Australia; New Zealand

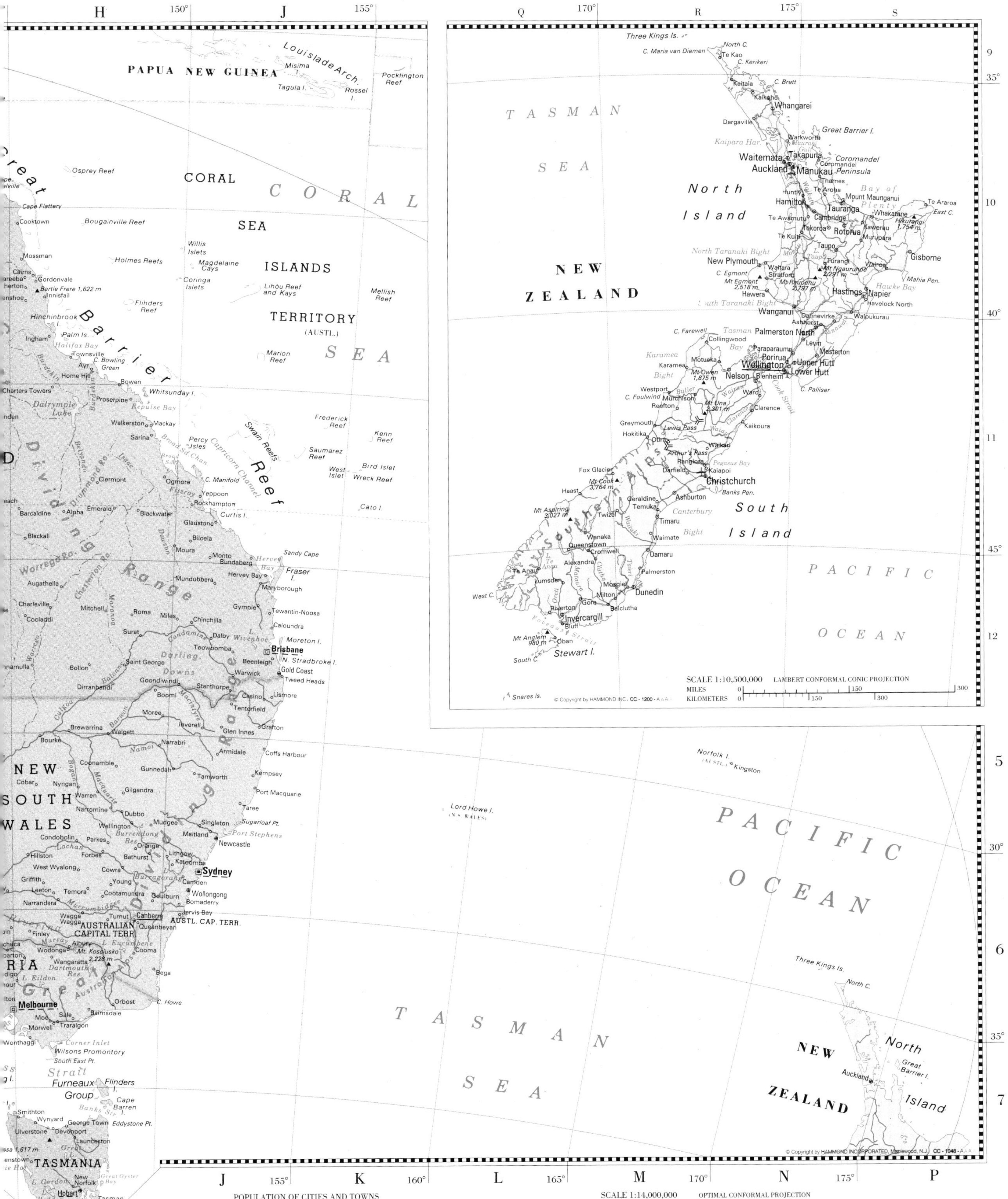

Map labels

PAPUA NEW GUINEA — Louisiade Arch., Misima, Tagula I., Rossel I., Pocklington Reef

CORAL SEA — Osprey Reef, Bougainville Reef, Willis Islets, Holmes Reefs, Magdelaine Cays, Coringa Islets, Lihou Reef and Kays, Mellish Reef

CORAL SEA ISLANDS TERRITORY (AUSTL.) — Marion Reef, Frederick Reef, Kenn Reef, Saumarez Reef, West Islet, Bird Islet, Wreck Reef, Cato I.

Cape Flattery, Cooktown, Mossman, Cairns, Gordonvale, Bartle Frere 1,622 m, Innisfail, Hinchinbrook I., Ingham, Halifax Bay, Palm Is., Townsville, Ayr, C. Bowling Green, Home Hill, Bowen, Whitsunday I., Proserpine, Repulse Bay, Walkerston, Mackay, Sarina, Broad Sd., Percy Isles, Capricorn Channel, C. Manifold, Ogmore, Yeppoon, Clermont, Rockhampton, Curtis I., Blackwater, Gladstone, Biloela, Moura, Monto, Bundaberg, Hervey Bay, Fraser I., Maryborough, Gympie, Tewantin-Noosa, Caloundra, Moreton I., Brisbane, Beenleigh, N. Stradbroke I., Gold Coast, Tweed Heads

Great Barrier Reef, **Great Dividing Range**

Charters Towers, Dalrymple Lake, Alpha, Barcaldine, Emerald, Blackall, Augathella, Charleville, Mitchell, Roma, Miles, Chinchilla, Dalby, Toowoomba, Warwick, Stanthorpe, Goondiwindi, Casino, Lismore, Boomi, Moree, Inverell, Glen Innes, Grafton, Tenterfield, Armidale, Coffs Harbour, Tamworth, Kempsey, Port Macquarie, Taree, Port Stephens, Newcastle

NEW SOUTH WALES — Cobar, Nyngan, Warren, Narromine, Dubbo, Gilgandra, Coonamble, Gunnedah, Wellington, Mudgee, Singleton, Maitland, Condobolin, Parkes, Orange, Bathurst, Lithgow, Katoomba, West Wyalong, Forbes, Cowra, Young, **Sydney**, Camden, Wollongong, Bomaderry, Griffith, Leeton, Temora, Cootamundra, Goulburn, Jervis Bay, Narrandera, Tumut, Canberra, Queanbeyan, **AUSTRALIAN CAPITAL TERR.**, Wagga Wagga, Finley, Albury, Mt. Kosciusko 2,228 m, Cooma

VICTORIA — Wodonga, Wangaratta, Bega, Melbourne, Orbost, C. Howe, Bairnsdale, Sale, Moe, Traralgon, Morwell, Wonthaggi, Corner Inlet, Wilsons Promontory, South East Pt.

TASMANIA — Smithton, Wynyard, Ulverstone, Devonport, George Town, Launceston, Furneaux Group, Flinders I., Cape Barren I., Eddystone Pt., Great Oyster Bay, New Norfolk, Hobart, Tasman Pen., South West C.

NEW ZEALAND — North Island

Three Kings Is., C. Maria van Diemen, Te Kao, North C., Te Araroa, Kaitaia, Kerikeri, C. Brett, Kaikohe, Kaikohe, Whangarei, Dargaville, Kaipara Har., Great Barrier I., Warkworth, Waitemata, Takapuna, Coromandel Peninsula, Auckland, Manukau, Thames, Mount Maunganui, Huntly, Te Aroha, Hamilton, Tauranga, Cambridge, Whakatane, Te Kuiti, Rotorua, Murupara, Hikurangi 1,754 m, Taupo, Gisborne, New Plymouth, C. Egmont, Mt. Egmont 2,518 m, Stratford, Mt. Ngauruhoe 2,291 m, Mt. Ruapehu 2,797 m, Hastings, Napier, Hawera, Wanganui, Mahia Pen., Hawke Bay, Waipukurau, Dannevirke, North Taranaki Bight, South Taranaki Bight

South Island

C. Farewell, Collingwood, Palmerston North, Levin, Masterton, Motueka, Paraparaumu, Porirua, Upper Hutt, Lower Hutt, Wellington, Nelson, Blenheim, Mt. Owen 1,875 m, Ward, C. Palliser, Cook Strait, Westport, Murchison, Reefton, Mt. Una 2,301 m, Clarence, Kaikoura, Greymouth, Hokitika, Otira, Arthur's Pass, Lewis Pass, Rangiora, Pegasus Bay, Fox Glacier, Darfield, Kaiapoi, Christchurch, Mt. Cook 3,764 m, Haast, Darfield, Banks Pen., Geraldine, Ashburton, Temuka, Timaru, Mt. Aspiring 2,027 m, Wanaka, Twizel, Waimate, Canterbury Bight, Queenstown, Cromwell, Alexandra, Oamaru, Te Anau, Lumsden, Palmerston, Gore, Mossburn, Dunedin, West C., Riverton, Invercargill, Milton, Balclutha, Bluff, Mt. Anglem 980 m, Oban, Stewart I., South C., Snares Is.

Southern Alps, **TASMAN SEA**, **PACIFIC OCEAN**

SCALE 1:10,500,000 LAMBERT CONFORMAL CONIC PROJECTION
MILES 0 ... 150 ... 300
KILOMETERS 0 ... 150 ... 300
© Copyright by HAMMOND INC., CC-1200

Norfolk I. (AUSTL.), Kingston, Lord Howe I. (N.S. WALES), Three Kings Is., North C.

NEW ZEALAND — North Island, Auckland, Great Barrier I.

PACIFIC OCEAN, **TASMAN SEA**

© Copyright by HAMMOND INCORPORATED, Maplewood, N.J. CC-1048

POPULATION OF CITIES AND TOWNS

- ■ OVER 2,000,000
- ◉ 500,000 - 999,999
- 50,000 - 99,999
- ☐ 1,000,000 - 1,999,999
- ⊕ 100,000 - 499,999
- ○ UNDER 50,000

SCALE 1:14,000,000 OPTIMAL CONFORMAL PROJECTION
MILES 0 ... 200 ... 400 ... 600
KILOMETERS 0 ... 200 ... 400 ... 600

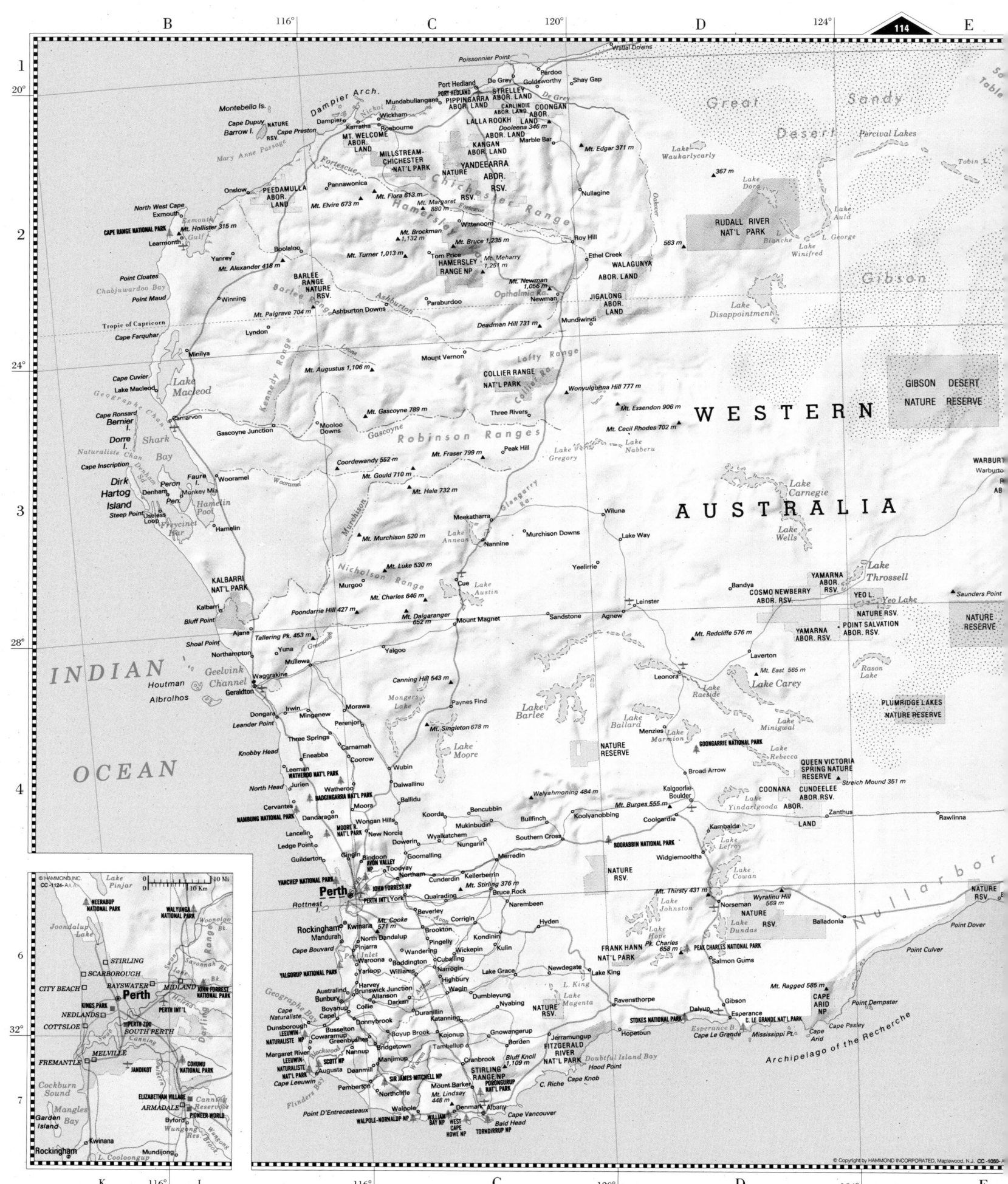

B   116°   C   120°   D   124°   E

20°

Great   Sandy

Poissonnier Point

Wittal Downs

Perdoo

Port Hedland   De Grey   Goldsworthy   Shay Gap

Mundabullangana   STRELLEY

PORT HEDLAND   PIPPINGARRA   CARLINDIE   COONGAN

ABOR. LAND   ABOR. LAND   ABOR.

Montebello Is.   LALLA ROOKH   LAND

Cape Dupuy   NATURE   Dooleens 346 m

Barrow I.   RSV.   Cape Preston   ABOR. LAND   Marble Bar

Dampier   MT. WELCOME   KANGAN

Karratha   Roebourne   ABOR.   ABOR. LAND   Mt. Edgar 371 m

Wickham   LAND

Mary Anne Passage   MILLSTREAM-   YANDEEARRA

CHICHESTER   ABOR.

NAT'L PARK   RSV.   Nullagine   Lake Waukarlycarly   Percival Lakes

Onslow   PEEDAMULLA   Pannawonica   NATURE   367 m   Lake Dora

ABOR.   RSV.   Tobin I.

North West Cape   LAND   Mt. Flora 613 m   L. George

Exmouth   Mt. Elvire 673 m   Lake Auld

RUDALL RIVER

Mt. Margaret   NAT'L PARK   L. Winifred

CAPE RANGE NATIONAL PARK   Mt. Hollister 315 m   880 m   563 m   Lake Blanche

Learmonth   Boolaloo   Mt. Brockman   Wittenoom

1,132 m   WALAGUNYA

Point Cloates   Yanrey   Mt. Turner 1,013 m   Mt. Bruce 1,235 m   Roy Hill   ABOR. LAND   Gibson

Mt. Alexander 418 m   Tom Price   Mt. Meharry   Ethel Creek

HAMERSLEY   1,251 m   JIGALONG

Chabjuwardoo Bay   RANGE NP   Mt. Newman   ABOR.

Point Maud   BARLEE   1,056 m   LAND

Winning   RANGE   Newman

Tropic of Capricorn   NATURE   Paraburdoo

Mt. Palgrave 704 m   RSV.   Ashburton Downs   Mundiwindi

Cape Farquhar   Lyndon   Deadman Hill 731 m

24°   Minilya   *Lake Disappointment*

Cape Cuvier   Lake Mount Vernon   *Lofty Range*

Lake Macleod   Macleod   Mt. Augustus 1,106 m   COLLIER RANGE

Bernier I.   NAT'L PARK   GIBSON   DESERT

Cape Ronsard   Wonyulgunna Hill 777 m   NATURE   RESERVE

Carnarvon   Mt. Gascoyne 789 m   Mt. Essendon 906 m

Dorre I.   Three Rivers

Shark   Gascoyne Junction   Mocloo   Mt. Cecil Rhodes 702 m   WESTERN

Naturaliste Chan.   Downs   *Robinson Ranges*   WARBUR

Cape Inscription   *Bay*   Coordewandy 552 m   Mt. Fraser 799 m   Peak Hill   Warburto

Dirk   Peron   Faure I.   Mt. Gould 710 m   *Lake*   AB

Hartog   Denham   Wooramel   *Gregory*   *Lake Carnegie*

Island   Pen.   Monkey Mia   Mt. Hale 732 m   *Nabberu*

Steep Point   *Hamelin*   AUSTRALIA

Pool   Meekatharra   Wiluna   *Lake Wells*

Hamelin   Mt. Murchison 520 m   Lake Way

Murchison Downs   Lake Throssell

Lake Annean   Nannine

KALBARRI   Yeelirrie   YAMARNA

NAT'L PARK   Mt. Luke 530 m   Bandya   ABOR.   YEO L.

Kalbarri   Murgoo   Cue   Lake Austin   COSMO NEWBERRY   RSV.   Yeo Lake

Bluff Point   Mt. Charles 646 m   ABOR. RSV.   NATURE RSV.   Saunders Point

Poondarrie Hill 427 m   Mt. Dalgaranger   NATURE

Ajana   652 m   Mount Magnet   Sandstone   Agnew   Mt. Redcliffe 576 m   POINT SALVATION   RESERVE

Shoal Point   Tallering Pk. 453 m   YAMARNA   ABOR. RSV.

28°   Northampton   Yuna   Yalgoo   ABOR. RSV.

Mullewa   Laverton

INDIAN   Waggrakine   Mt. East 565 m

Houtman   Geraldton   Canning Hill 543 m   Leonora   *Rason Lake*

Albrolhos   Irwin   Morawa   Paynes Find   *Lake Raeside*   *Lake Carey*

Dongara   Mingenew   *Lake Barlee*   *Lake Ballard*

Leander Point   Perenjori   PLUMRIDGE LAKES

Three Springs   Mt. Singleton 678 m   Menzies   *Lake Marmion*   NATURE RESERVE

OCEAN   Knobby Head   Carnamah   *Lake Moore*   *Lake Minigwal*

Eneabba   Coorow   NATURE   GOONGARRIE NATIONAL PARK   *Lake Rebecca*

Leeman   Wubin   RESERVE   QUEEN VICTORIA

WATHEROO NAT'L PARK   Broad Arrow   SPRING NATURE

North Head   Jurien   Watheroo   Walyahmoning 484 m   Kalgoorlie-   RESERVE   Streich Mound 351 m

BADGINGARRA NAT'L PARK   Dalwallinu   Mt. Burges 555 m   Boulder   COONANA   CUNDEELEE

Cervantes   Moora   Koolyanobbing   ABOR. RSV.   ABOR.   Zanthus

NAMBUNG NATIONAL PARK   Ballidu   Koorda   Coolgardie   *Lake Yindarlgooda*   Rawlinna

Lancelin   Wongan Hills   Bencubbin   Bullfinch   Kambalda   LAND

Ledge Point   New Norcia   Mukinbudin   Southern Cross   BOORABBIN NATIONAL PARK   *Lake Lefroy*

Guilderton   Dowerin   Wyalkatchem   Widgiemooltha

MOORE R.   Goomalling   Nungarin   NATURE

Gingin   NAT'L PARK   Merredin   RSV.   *Lake Cowan*

Bindoon   Northam   Cunderdin   Mt. Thirsty 431 m

YANCHEP NATIONAL PARK   Toodyay   Mt. Stirling 376 m   Widgiemooltha   Wyralinu Hill

AVON VALLEY   Kellerberrin   Bruce Rock   NATURE   569 m

Perth   JOHN FORREST NP   York   Quairading   Norseman   RSV.   Balladonia

Rottnest   PERTH INT'L   *Lake Johnston*

Mt. Cooke   Beverley   Corrigin   *Lake Dundas*   Point Dover

Rockingham   Kwinana   571 m   Hyden   FRANK HANN   Point Culver

Mandurah   North Dandalup   Brookton   Kondinin   NAT'L PARK   PEAK CHARLES NATIONAL PARK

Pinjarra   Pingelly   Kulin   Salmon Gums   Mt. Ragged 585 m

Cape Bouvard   Wandering   Wickepin   Newdegate   Pk. Charles 658 m   CAPE

YALGORUP NATIONAL PARK   Waroona   Baddington   Narrogin   Lake King   Gibson   ARID NP

Yarloop   Williams   Lake Grace   NATURE   Dalyup   Point Dempster

Harvey   Wagin   Highbury   RSV.   Ravensthorpe   Esperance   C. LE GRANDE NAT'L PARK

Australind   Brunswick Junction   Arthur   *L. King*   STOKES NATIONAL PARK   Cape Le Grande

Bunbury   Boyanup   Collie   Darkan   Dumbleyung   *Lake Magenta*   Mississippi Pt.   Cape Pasley

Geographe Bay   Donnybrook   Duranillin   Nyabing   *Esperance B.*   Cape Arid

Cape   Busselton   Kojonup   Gnowangerup   FITZGERALD   Hopetoun   *Archipelago of the Recherche*

Naturaliste   Cowaramup   Boyup Brook   Katanning   RIVER   Jerramungup

LEEUWIN   Greenbushes   Tambellup   NAT'L PARK   Borden

Margaret River   Bridgetown   Cranbrook   *Doubtful Island Bay*

NATURALISTE   SCOTT NP   Manjimup   STIRLING   *Hood Point*

Cape Leeuwin   Nannup   SIR JAMES MITCHELL NP   RANGE NP   PORONGURUP

Deanmill   Mount Barker   Bluff Knoll   C. Riche

Pemberton   Mt. Lindsay   1,109 m   C. Knob

Northcliffe   448 m   Denmark   Albany   Cape Vancouver

Walpole   Point D'Entrecasteaux   WALPOLE-NORNALUP NP   WILLIAM   WEST   Bald Head

Flinders Bay   BAY NP   CAPE   HOWE NP   TORNDIRRUP NP   *© Copyright by HAMMOND INCORPORATED, Maplewood, N.J. CC-1090-P*

32°

K   116°   L

© HAMMOND, INC.   CC-2124-A.A.   *Lake Pinjar*   0   10 Mi   10 Km

WEERABUP   NATIONAL PARK   WALYUNGA NATIONAL PARK

Joondalup Lake   STIRLING

SCARBOROUGH   BAYSWATER   MIDLAND   JOHN FORREST NATIONAL PARK

CITY BEACH   **Perth**   PERTH INT'L

KINGS PARK   NEDLANDS   PERTH ZOO

COTTSLOE   SOUTH PERTH

FREMANTLE   MELVILLE   JANDAKOT   CANNING   COHUNU   NATIONAL PARK

Cockburn Sound   ELIZABETHAN VILLAGE   ARMADALE   PIONEER WORLD

Garden Island   *Mangles Bay*   Byford

Rockingham   Kwinana   Mundijong

Western and Central Australia

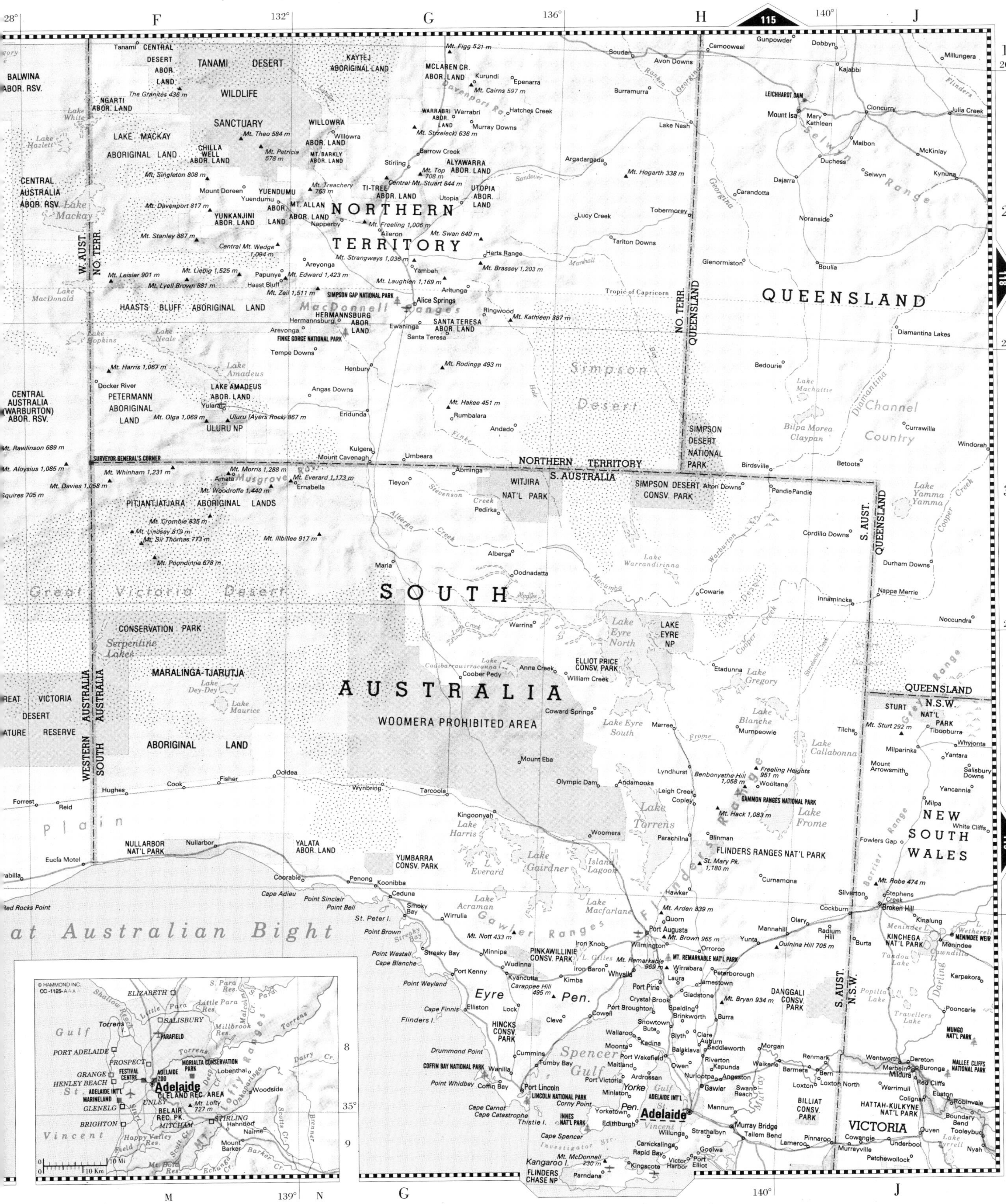

POPULATION OF CITIES AND TOWNS

- ■ OVER 2,000,000
- ◉ 500,000 - 999,999
- ● 100,000 - 249,999
- ⊙ 10,000 - 29,999
- ▣ 1,000,000 - 1,999,999
- ● 250,000 - 499,999
- ● 30,000 - 99,999
- ○ UNDER 10,000

SCALE 1:7,000,000   LAMBERT CONFORMAL CONIC PROJECTION

MILES 0 ─── 100 ─── 200 ─── 300

KILOMETERS 0 ─── 100 ─── 200 ─── 300

Northeastern Australia

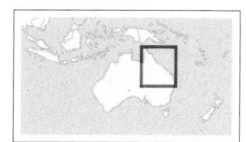

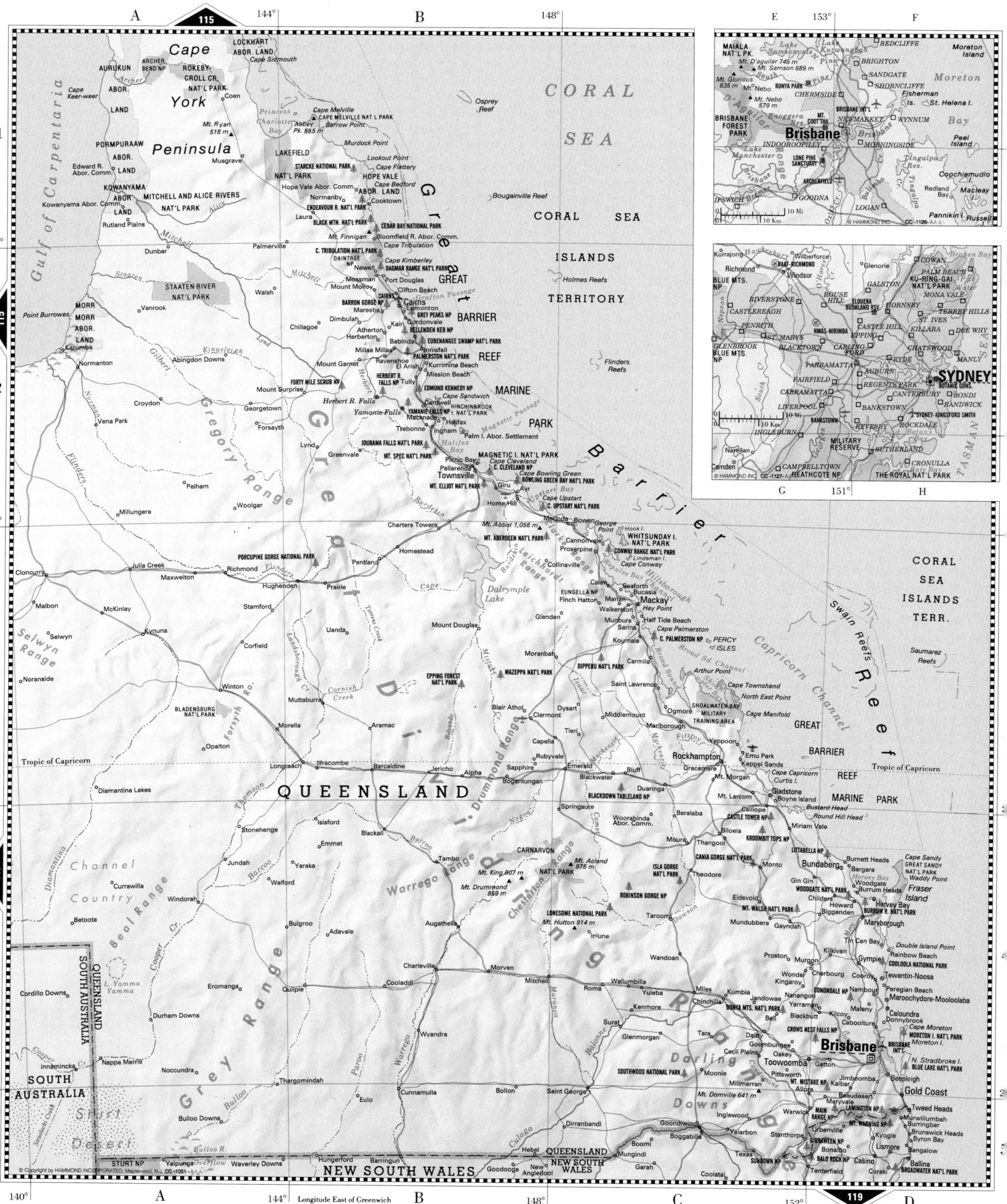

CORAL SEA

CORAL SEA ISLANDS TERRITORY

CORAL SEA ISLANDS TERR.

Cape York Peninsula

Gulf of Carpentaria

QUEENSLAND

SOUTH AUSTRALIA

NEW SOUTH WALES

Tropic of Capricorn

Great Barrier Reef

Great Dividing Range

Grey Range

Cairns

Townsville

Mackay

Rockhampton

Bundaberg

Brisbane

Toowoomba

Gold Coast

Brisbane

SYDNEY

SCALE 1:7,000,000   LAMBERT CONFORMAL CONIC PROJECTION

MILES

KILOMETERS

Longitude East of Greenwich

POPULATION OF CITIES AND TOWNS

▪ OVER 2,000,000	● 500,000 - 999,999
▫ 1,000,000 - 1,999,999	◉ 250,000 - 499,999

● 100,000 - 249,999	○ 10,000 - 29,999
• 30,000 - 99,999	○ UNDER 10,000

© Copyright by HAMMOND INCORPORATED, Maplewood, N.J. CC-1051-AAA

Southeastern Australia

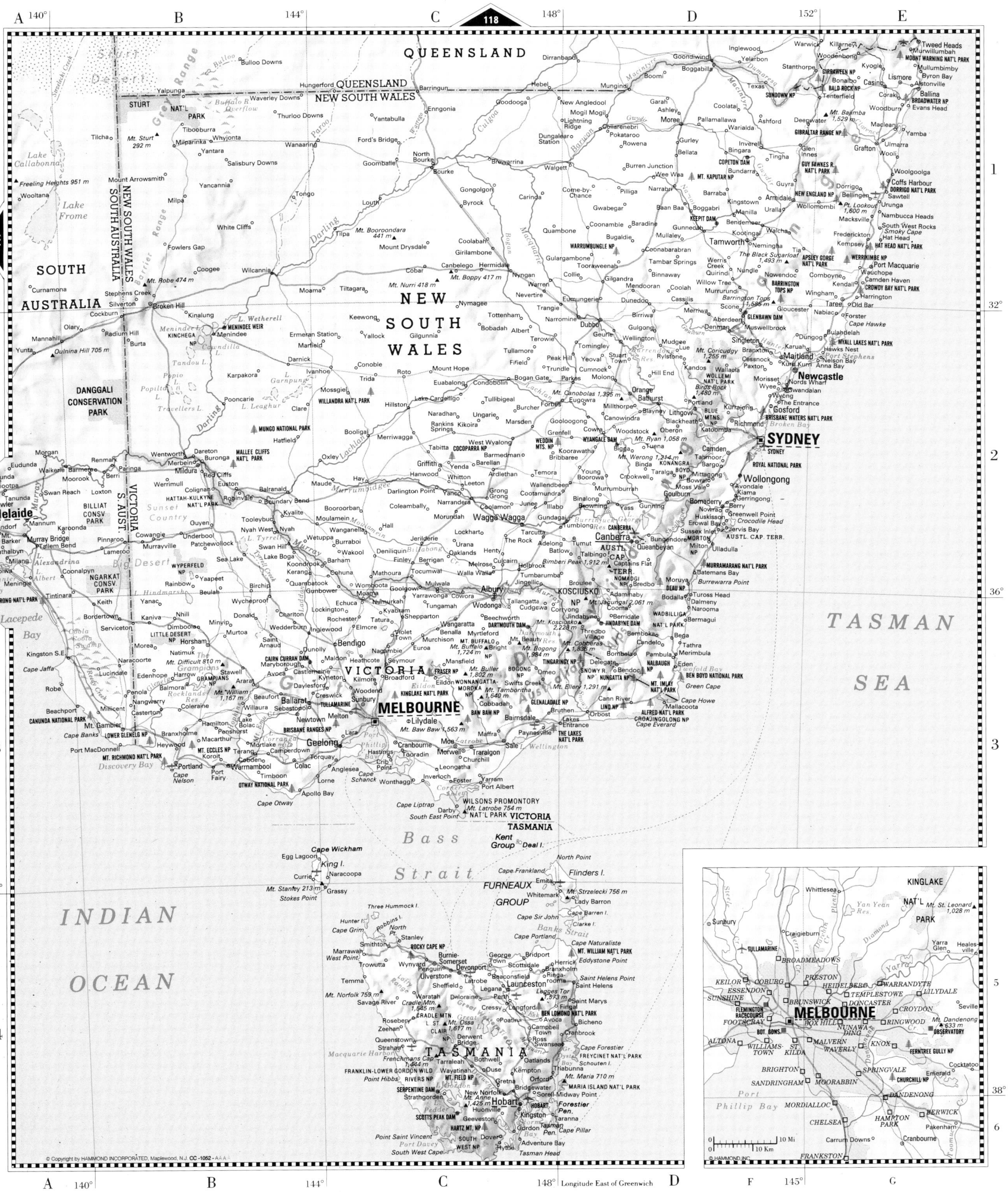

POPULATION OF CITIES AND TOWNS

- ■ OVER 2,000,000
- ▣ 1,000,000 - 1,999,999
- ● 500,000 - 999,999
- ● 250,000 - 499,999
- ● 100,000 - 249,999
- ● 30,000 - 99,999
- ○ 10,000 - 29,999
- ○ UNDER 10,000

SCALE 1:7,000,000 LAMBERT CONFORMAL CONIC PROJECTION

MILES 0   50   100   200   300

KILOMETERS 0   100   200   300

Longitude East of Greenwich

© Copyright by HAMMOND INCORPORATED, Maplewood, N.J. CC-1052

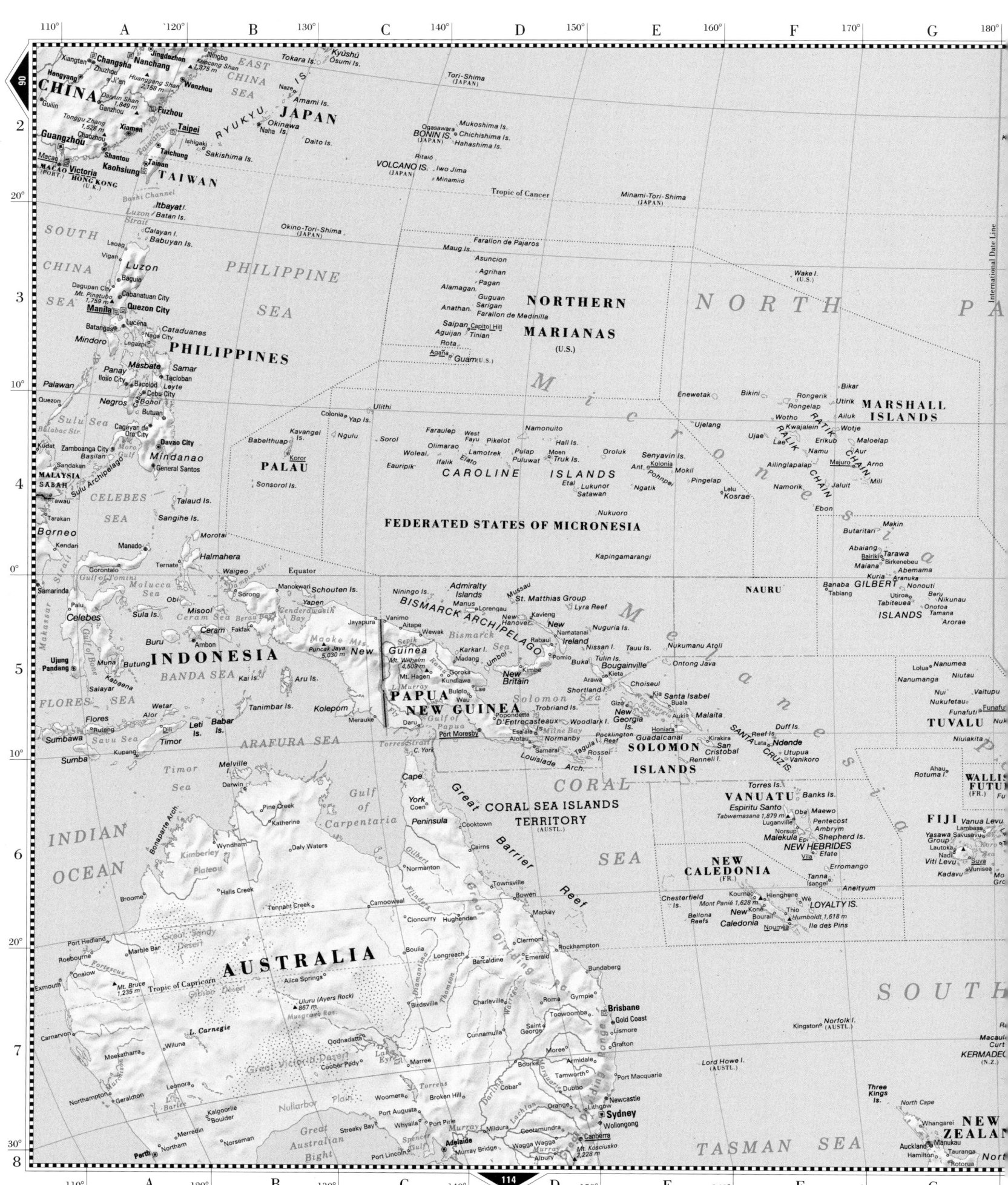

Central Pacific Ocean

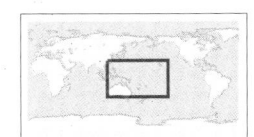

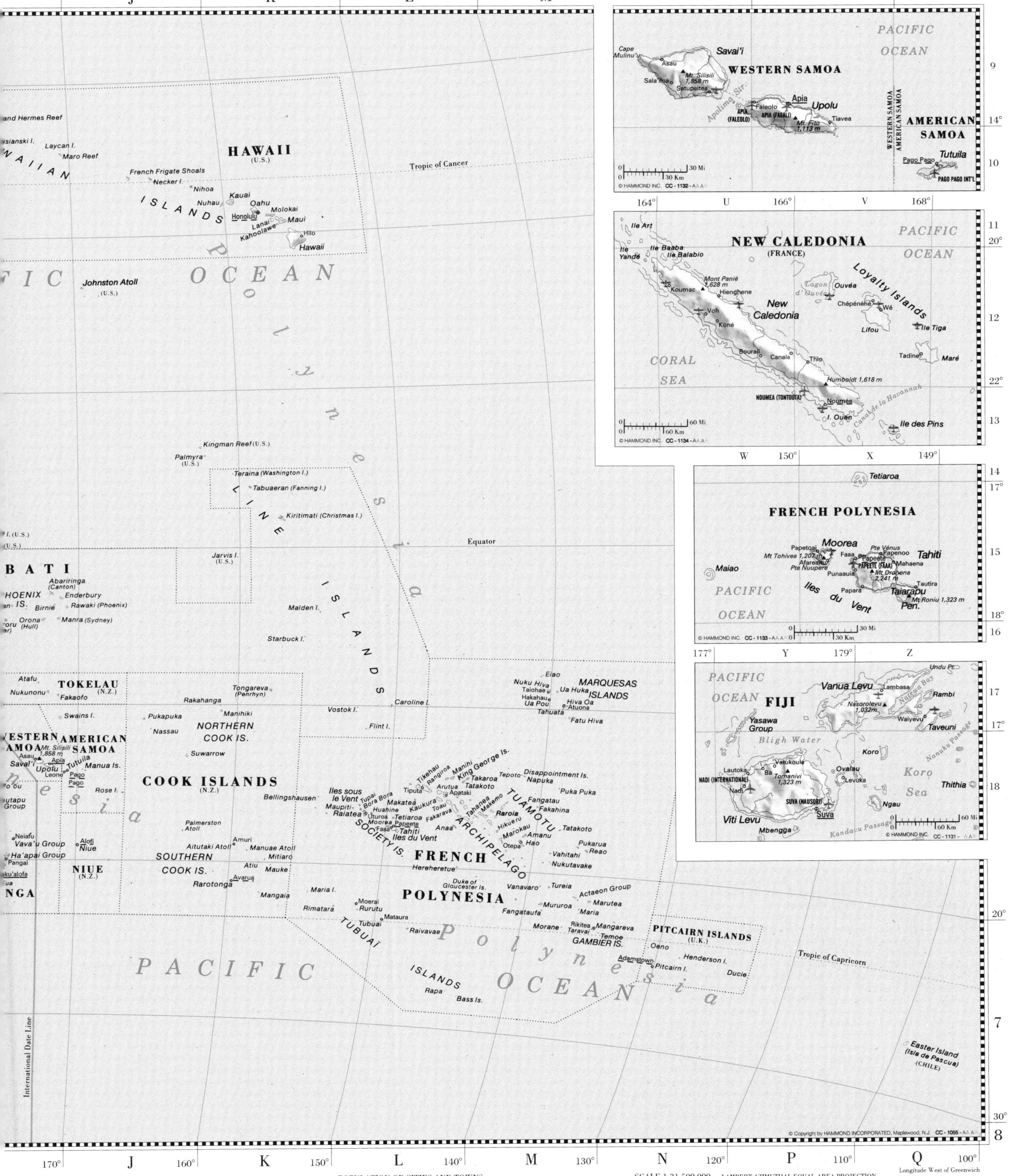

Main map

170° J 160° K 150° L 140° M

and Hermes Reef
wsianski I. · Laycan I.
· Maro Reef
French Frigate Shoals

HAWAII (U.S.)

Tropic of Cancer

· Necker I. · Nihoa
Nuhau · Kauai
Oahu · Molokai
Honolulu · Lanai · Maui
Kahoolawe
Hilo
Hawaii

ISLANDS

Johnston Atoll (U.S.)

OCEAN

Kingman Reef (U.S.)
Palmyra (U.S.)

Teraina (Washington I.)
Tabuaeran (Fanning I.)

Kiritimati (Christmas I.)

Jarvis I. (U.S.)

Equator

LINE ISLANDS

BATI
Abariringa (Canton)
HOENIX · Enderbury
IS. · Birnie
Rawaki (Phoenix)
oru · Orona (Hull) · Manra (Sydney)

Malden I.
Starbuck I.

TOKELAU (N.Z.)
Atafu
Nukunonu · Fakaofo

WESTERN SAMOA
AMOA · Swains I.
Saval'i · Upolu
Mt. Silisili 1,858 m
Pago

Tongareva (Penrhyn)
Rakahanga
Pukapuka · Manihiki
Nassau

NORTHERN COOK IS.
Suwarrow

COOK ISLANDS (N.Z.)

Nuku Hiva
Taiohae · Ua Huka
Hakahau · Hiva Oa
Ua Pou · Atuona
Tahuata · Fatu Hiva

MARQUESAS ISLANDS

Caroline I.
Vostok I.
Flint I.

Eiao

Tikehau · Rangiroa · Manihi
King George's Is.
Takaroa · Tepoto
Tiputa · Arutua · Takaroa · Napuka
Iles sous le Vent · Toau · Fangatau
Bora Bora · Kaukura
Maupiti · Huahine · Apataki
Raiatea · Uturoa · Tetiaroa · Fakarava · Hikueru
Moorea · Papeete · Raroia
Tahiti · Anaa · Marokau
Iles du Vent · Otepa · Hao
Hereheretue · Vahitahi
Nukutavake
Amuri · Pukarua
Reao

Bellingshausen

SOCIETY IS.

TUAMOTU ARCHIPELAGO

Disappointment Is.
Puka Puka
Fangatau
Fakahina
Tatakoto

Aitutaki Atoll
Manuae Atoll
Mitiaro

SOUTHERN COOK IS.
Atiu · Mauke
Palmerston Atoll
Rarotonga · Avarua

NIUE (N.Z.)

FRENCH POLYNESIA

Maria I.
Mangaia
Rimatara · Mataura
Tubuai
Raivavae

TUBUAI ISLANDS
Rapa · Bass Is.

Moerai · Rurutu
Morane · Mururoa · Marutea
Fangataufa · Maria
Rikitea · Mangareva
Taravai · Reao
Temoe

Duke of Gloucester Is.
Vanavaro · Tureia · Actaeon Group
Vahitahi · Marutea

GAMBIER IS.

PITCAIRN ISLANDS (U.K.)
Oeno
Adamstown · Pitcairn I. · Henderson I. · Ducie

Tropic of Capricorn

PACIFIC OCEAN

Polynesia

Easter Island (Isla de Pascua) (CHILE)

International Date Line

170° J 160° K 150° L 140° M 130° N 120° P 110° Q 100°

Longitude West of Greenwich

Western Samoa inset

R 172° S 171° T

PACIFIC OCEAN

Cape Mulinu'u
Savai'i · Asau
Sala'ilua
Mt. Silisili 1,858 m
Setupaitea

WESTERN SAMOA

APIA (FALEOLO)
Faleolo · Apia
APIA (FAGALI) · Upolu
Mt. Fito 1,113 m · Tiavea

WESTERN SAMOA
AMERICAN SAMOA

AMERICAN SAMOA
Tutuila
Pago Pago
PAGO PAGO INT'L

0   30 Mi
© HAMMOND   CC-1132-A-A-A

9
14°
10

New Caledonia inset

164° U 166° V 168°

Ile Art
Ile Yandé · Ile Baaba
Ile Balabio

NEW CALEDONIA (FRANCE)

PACIFIC OCEAN

Koumac · Mont Panié 1,628 m
Hienghene
Voh · Koné
Bourail · Canala · Thio
Humboldt 1,618 m

Lagon d'Ouvéa
Ouvéa
Chépénéhé · Wé
Lifou

Loyalty Islands

Ile Tiga
Tadine · Maré

New Caledonia

CORAL SEA

NOUMEA (TONTOUTA)
Nouméa
I. Ouen
Canale de la Havannah
Ile des Pins

0   60 Km   60 Mi
© HAMMOND INC.   CC-1134-A-A-A

11
20°
12
22°
13

French Polynesia inset

W 150° X 149°

Tetiaroa

FRENCH POLYNESIA

Papetoai · Moorea · Pte Vénus · Papenoo
Mt Tohivea 1,207 m · Faaa · Papeete · Tahiti
Afareaitu · PAPEETE (FAAA) · Mahaena
Maiao · Pte Nuupere · Punaauia · Mt Orohena 2,241 m
Papara · Tautira
Taiarapu Pen.
Mt Roniu 1,323 m

Iles du Vent

PACIFIC OCEAN

0   30 Mi
© HAMMOND INC.   CC-1133-A-A-A   0   30 Km

14
17°
15
18°
16

Fiji inset

177° Y 179° Z   Undu Pt.

PACIFIC OCEAN

Vanua Levu · Lambasa
Nasorolevu 1,032 m · Rambi
Nal=an Bay · Waiyevu · Taveuni

Yasawa Group
Bligh Water

Yatukoule · Koro
Lautoka · Vetukoule · Ovalau
NADI (INTERNATIONAL) · Ba · Tomanivi 1,323 m · Levuka
Nadi · Koro Sea · Thithia
Viti Levu · SUVA (NAUSORI) · Ngau
Suva
Mbengga
Kandavu Passage

FIJI

0   60 Km   60 Mi
© HAMMOND INC.   CC-1131-A-A

17
17°
18

Legend

POPULATION OF CITIES AND TOWNS

■ OVER 3,000,000	★ 500,000 - 999,999 · UNDER 100,000
▣ 1,000,000 - 2,999,999	● 100,000 - 499,999

SCALE 1:31,500,000   LAMBERT AZIMUTHAL EQUAL-AREA PROJECTION

MILES   0   400   800   1200
KILOMETERS   0   400   800   1200

© Copyright by HAMMOND INCORPORATED, Maplewood, N.J.   CC-1055-A-A-A

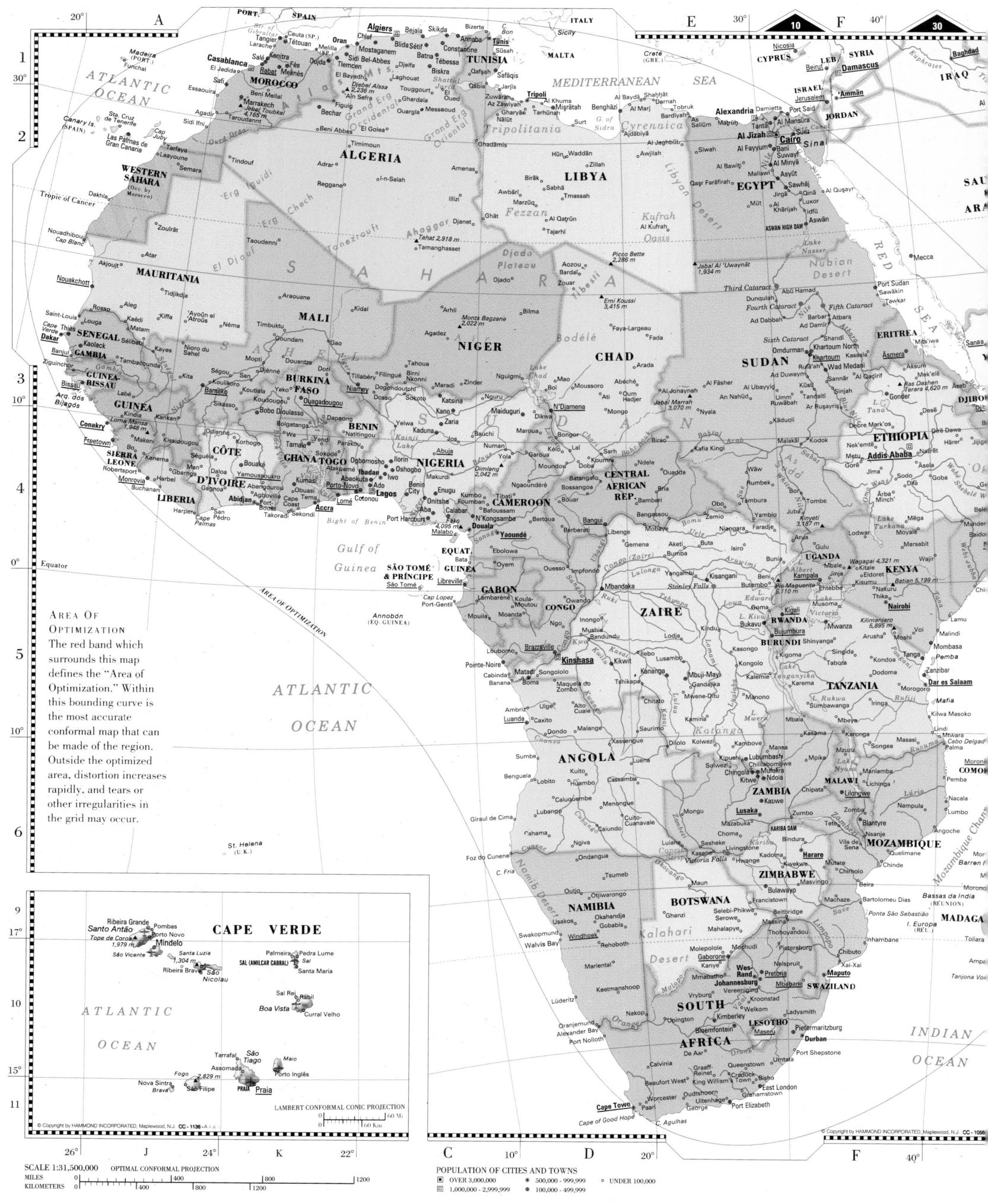

ATLANTIC OCEAN

MEDITERRANEAN SEA

INDIAN OCEAN

AREA OF OPTIMIZATION

The red band which surrounds this map defines the "Area of Optimization." Within this bounding curve is the most accurate conformal map that can be made of the region. Outside the optimized area, distortion increases rapidly, and tears or other irregularities in the grid may occur.

AREA OF OPTIMIZATION

MOROCCO · WESTERN SAHARA · MAURITANIA · SENEGAL · GAMBIA · GUINEA-BISSAU · GUINEA · SIERRA LEONE · LIBERIA · CÔTE D'IVOIRE · GHANA · TOGO · BENIN · NIGERIA · CAMEROON · EQUAT. GUINEA · GABON · CONGO · ALGERIA · TUNISIA · LIBYA · EGYPT · NIGER · CHAD · SUDAN · ERITREA · ETHIOPIA · MALI · BURKINA FASO · CENTRAL AFRICAN REP. · ZAIRE · UGANDA · KENYA · RWANDA · BURUNDI · TANZANIA · ANGOLA · ZAMBIA · MALAWI · MOZAMBIQUE · NAMIBIA · BOTSWANA · ZIMBABWE · SOUTH AFRICA · LESOTHO · SWAZILAND · MADAGASCAR · SÃO TOMÉ & PRÍNCIPE

CAPE VERDE

Santo Antão · Ribeira Grande · Pombas · Porto Novo · Tope de Coroa 1,979 m · Mindelo · São Vicente · Santa Luzia · Ribeira Brava · São Nicolau · Palmeira · Pedra Lume · SAL (AMILCAR CABRAL) · Sal · Santa Maria · Sal Rei · Rabil · Boa Vista · Curral Velho · Tarrafal · São Tiago · Maio · Assomada · Porto Inglés · Nova Sintra · Fogo 2,829 m · Brava · São Filipe · PRAIA · Praia

ATLANTIC OCEAN

LAMBERT CONFORMAL CONIC PROJECTION

© Copyright by HAMMOND INCORPORATED, Maplewood, N.J. CC-1136-A

SCALE 1:31,500,000   OPTIMAL CONFORMAL PROJECTION

MILES   0   400   800   1200
KILOMETERS   0   400   800   1200

POPULATION OF CITIES AND TOWNS

- ◻ OVER 3,000,000
- ◻ 1,000,000 - 2,999,999
- ● 500,000 - 999,999
- ● 100,000 - 499,999
- · UNDER 100,000

© Copyright by HAMMOND INCORPORATED, Maplewood, N.J. CC-1056

Africa

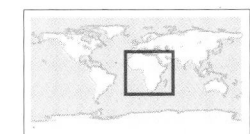

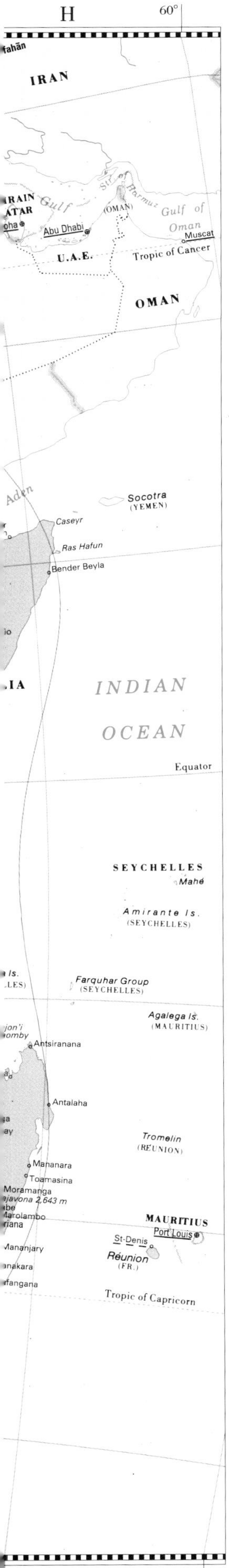

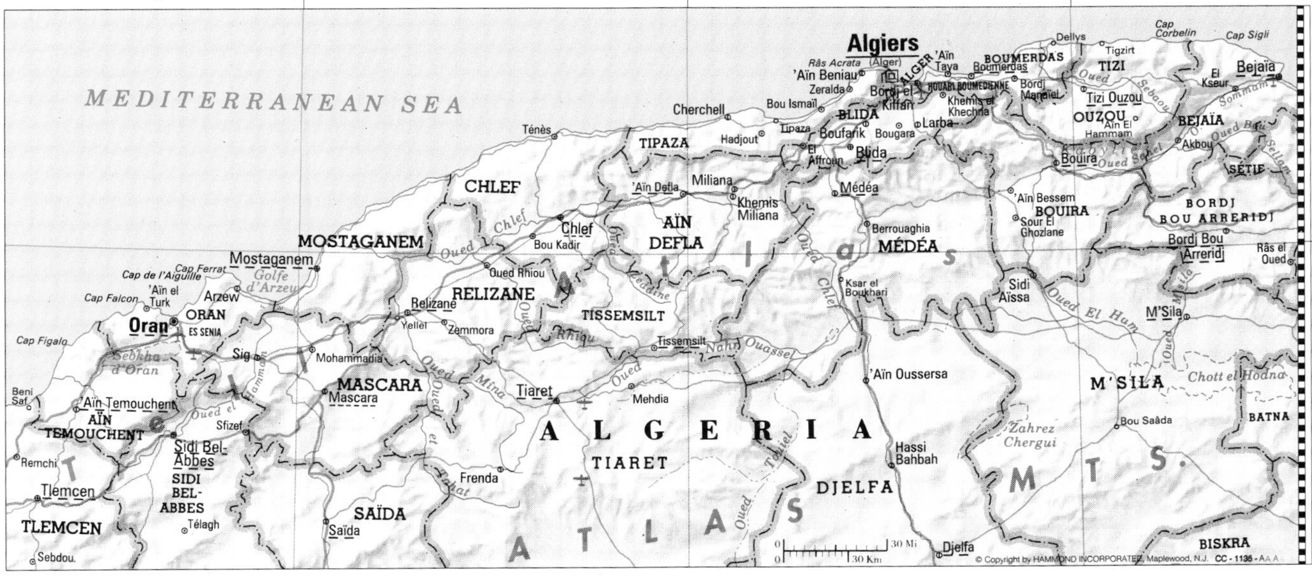

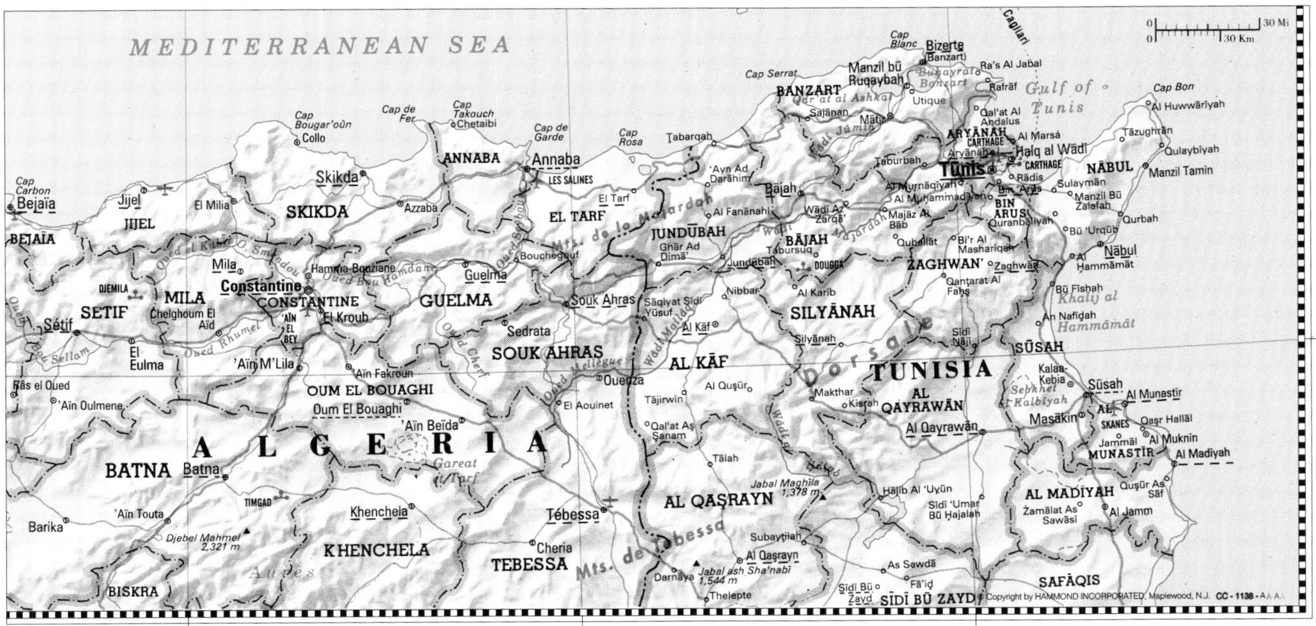

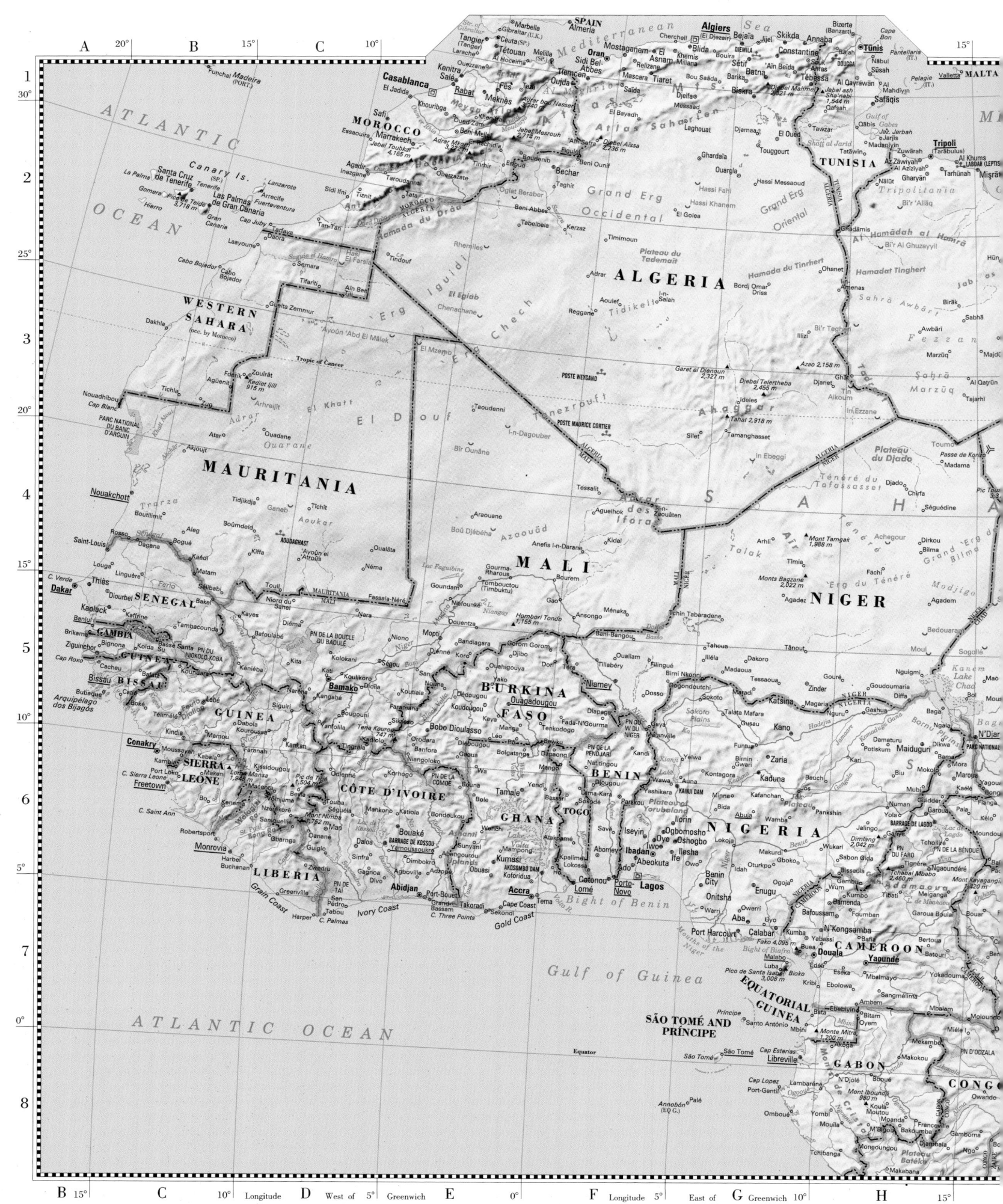

Northern Africa

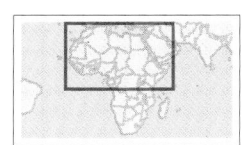

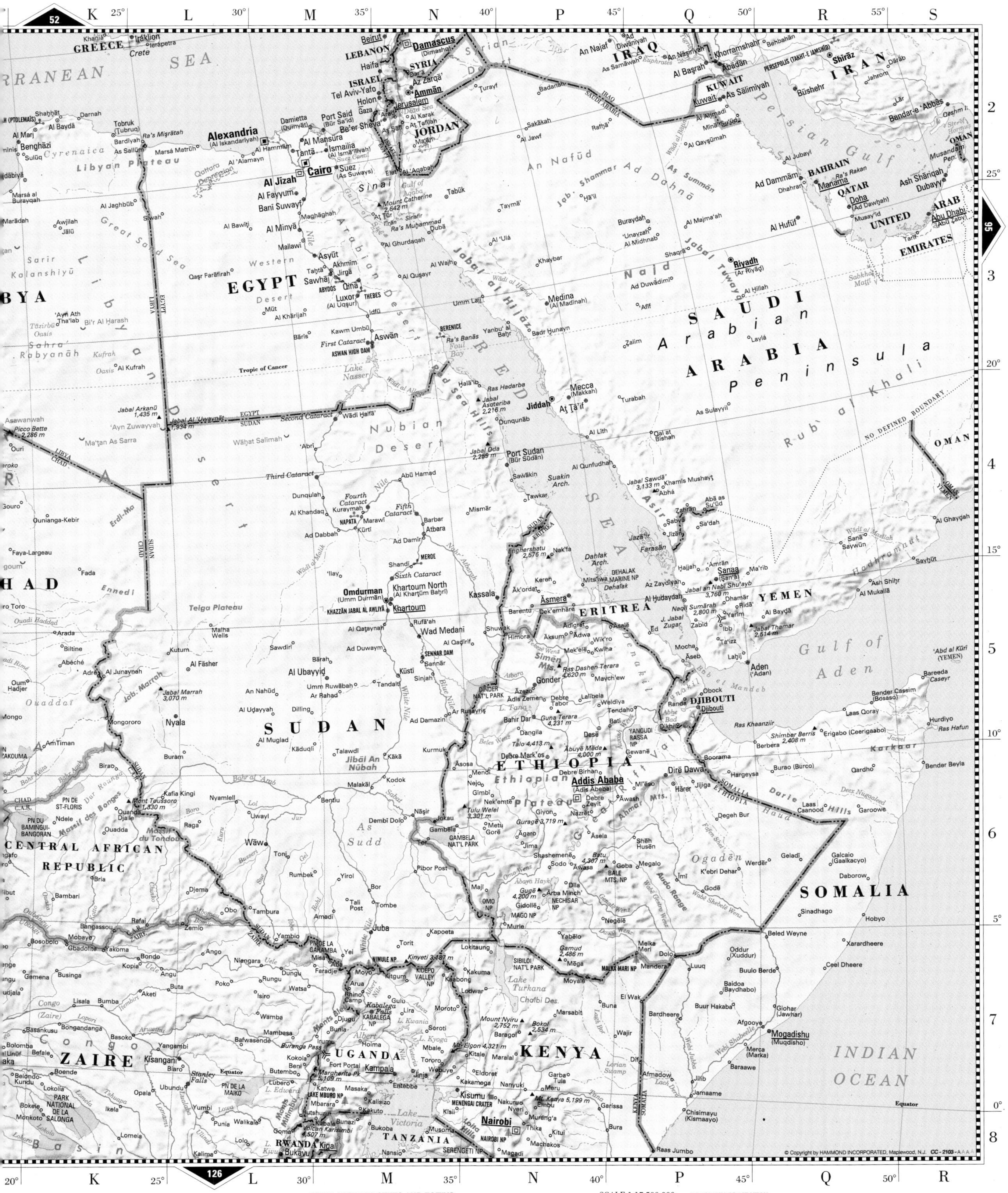

POPULATION OF CITIES AND TOWNS

- OVER 2,000,000
- 1,000,000 - 1,999,999
- 500,000 - 999,999
- 100,000 - 499,999
- 50,000 - 99,999
- UNDER 50,000

SCALE 1:17,500,000 POLYCONIC PROJECTION

MILES 0   250   500   750
KILOMETERS 0   250   500   750

© Copyright by HAMMOND INCORPORATED, Maplewood, N.J.   CC-2103

Southern Africa

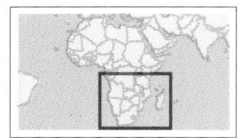

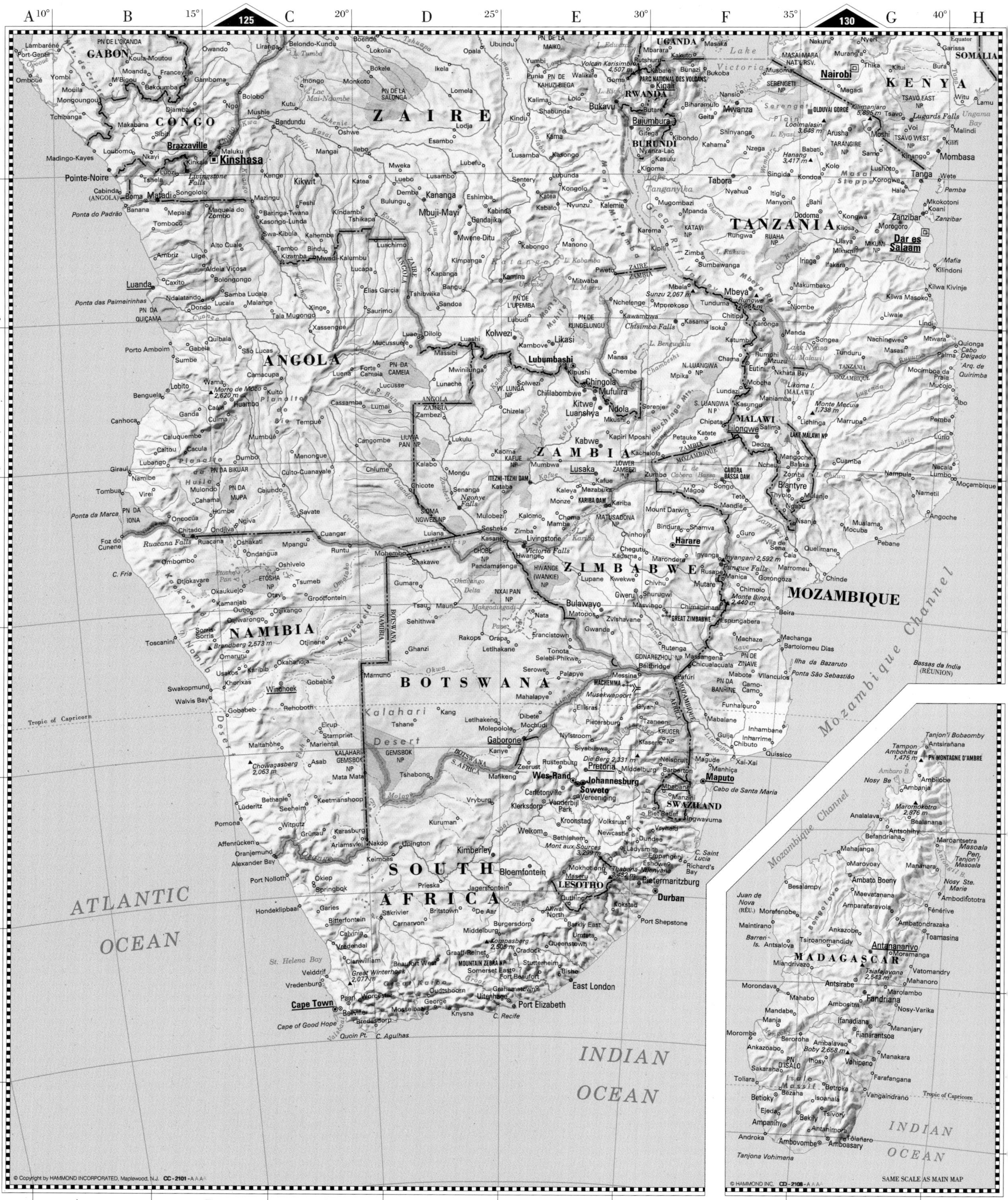

SCALE 1:17,500,000   POLYCONIC PROJECTION

MILES   0   250   500   750
KILOMETERS   0   250   500   750

POPULATION OF CITIES AND TOWNS
- ■ OVER 2,000,000
- ◉ 500,000 - 999,999
- ◉ 50,000 - 99,999
- ▣ 1,000,000 - 1,999,999
- ◉ 100,000 - 499,999
- ○ UNDER 50,000

SAME SCALE AS MAIN MAP

Northeastern Africa

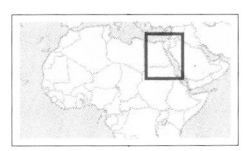

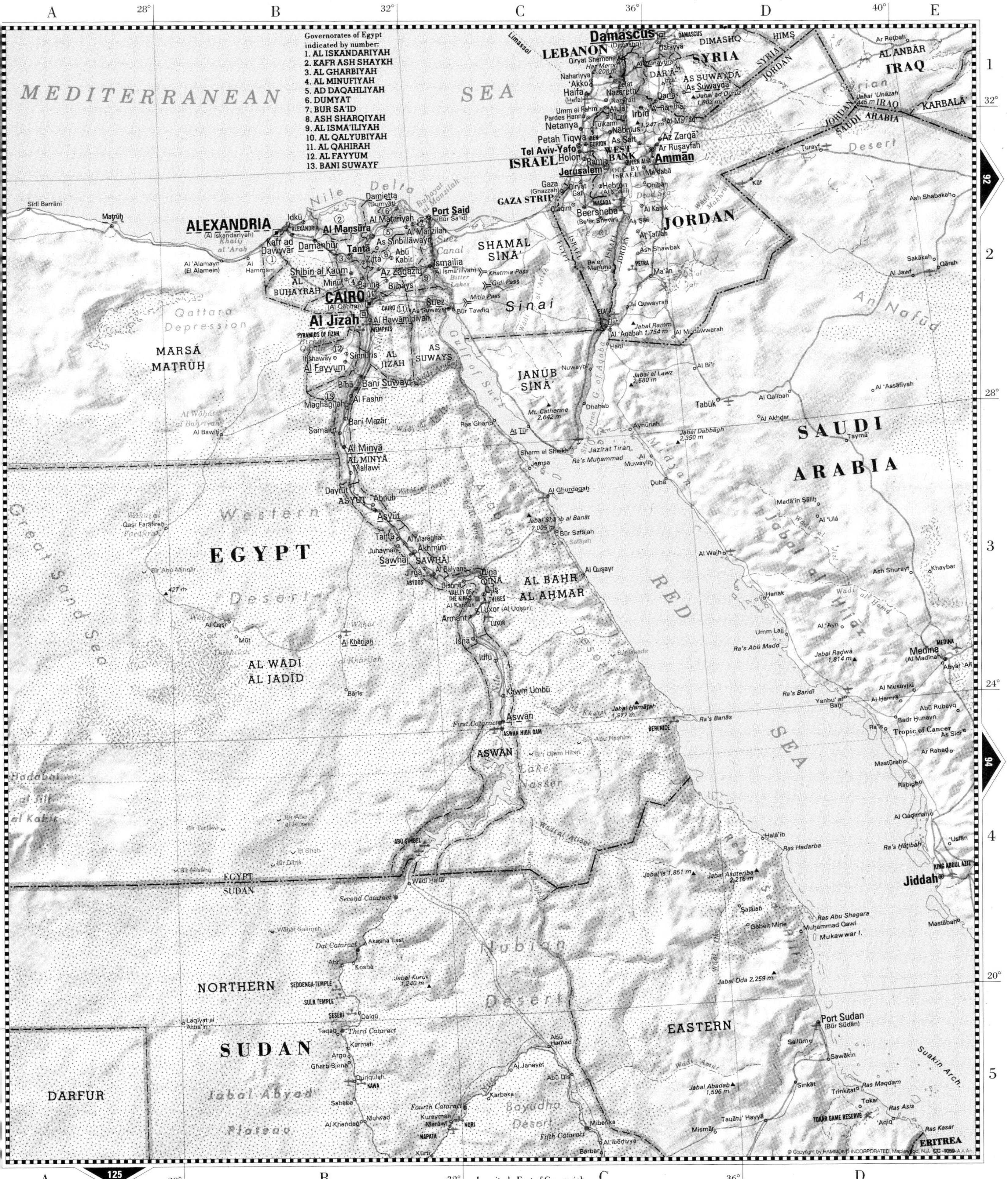

POPULATION OF CITIES AND TOWNS

■ OVER 2,000,000	◉ 500,000 - 999,999	● 100,000 - 249,999	⊙ 10,000 - 29,999
▣ 1,000,000 - 1,999,999	◍ 250,000 - 499,999	○ 30,000 - 99,999	∘ UNDER 10,000

SCALE 1:7,000,000   POLYCONIC PROJECTION

MILES 0 — 100 — 200 — 300
KILOMETERS 0 — 100 — 200 — 300

Longitude East of Greenwich

© Copyright by HAMMOND INCORPORATED, Maplewood, N.J. CC-1059 A A A

Governorates of Egypt indicated by number:
1. AL ISKANDARIYAH
2. KAFR ASH SHAYKH
3. AL GHARBIYAH
4. AL MINUFIYAH
5. AD DAQAHLIYAH
6. DUMYAT
7. BUR SA'ID
8. ASH SHARQIYAH
9. AL ISMA'ILIYAH
10. AL QALYUBIYAH
11. AL QAHIRAH
12. AL FAYYUM
13. BANI SUWAYF

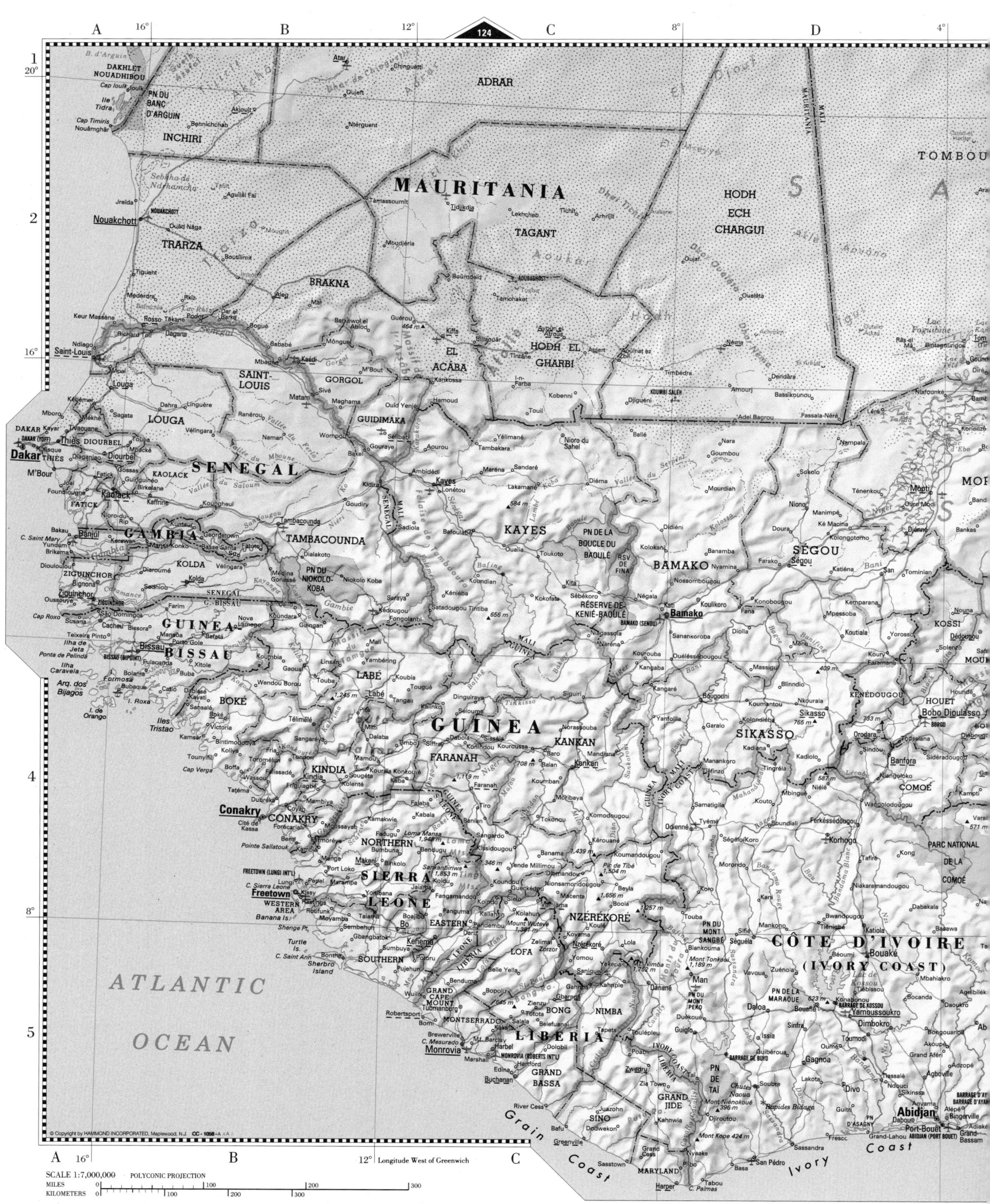

MAURITANIA

ADRAR

TOMBOU

INCHIRI

TRARZA

BRAKNA

TAGANT

HODH
ECH
CHARGUI

HODH EL
GHARBI

EL
ACÁBA

GORGOL

GUIDIMAKA

SENEGAL

LOUGA

KAYES

DAKAR
THIES

KAOLACK

KAYES

SÉGOU

BAMAKO

GAMBIA

TAMBACOUNDA

PN DE LA
BOUCLE DU
BAOULÉ
RSV
DE
FINA

ZIGUINCHOR

KOLDA

SENEGAL
G.-BISSAU

RÉSERVE DE
KENIÉ-BAOULÉ

KOSSI

GUINEA
BISSAU

LABÉ

GUINEA

HOUET
Bobo Dioulasso

BOKÉ

SIKASSO

KÉNÉDOUGOU

KINDIA

GUINEA

KANKAN

KANKAN

COMOE

FARANAH

Conakry
CONAKRY

BANFORA

NORTHERN

PARC NATIONAL
DE LA
COMOÉ

SIERRA
LEONE

KORHOGO

CÔTE D'IVOIRE
(IVORY COAST)

EASTERN

NZÉRÉKORÉ

LOFA

SOUTHERN

BONG

NIMBA

GRAND
CAPE
MOUNT

MONTSERRADO

LIBERIA

Monrovia

GRAND
BASSA

Abidjan

GRAND
JIDE

PN
DE
TAI

SINO

MARYLAND

ATLANTIC

OCEAN

Grain

Coast

Ivory

Coast

SCALE 1:7,000,000
POLYCONIC PROJECTION

MILES 0 · · · 100 · · · 200 · · · 300
KILOMETERS 0 ··· 100 ·· 200 ·· 300

Longitude West of Greenwich

West Africa

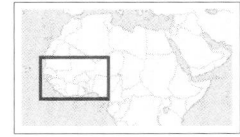

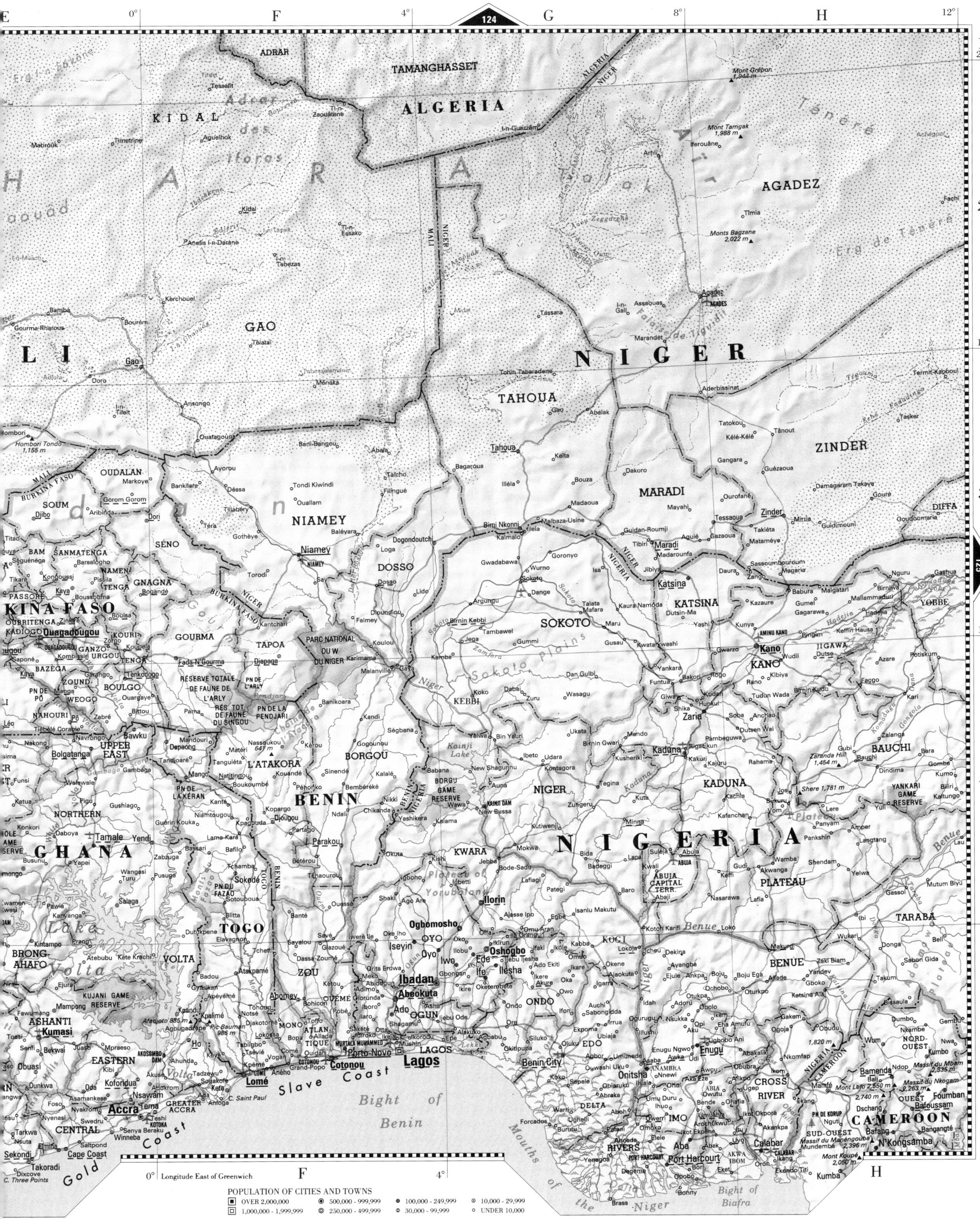

East Africa

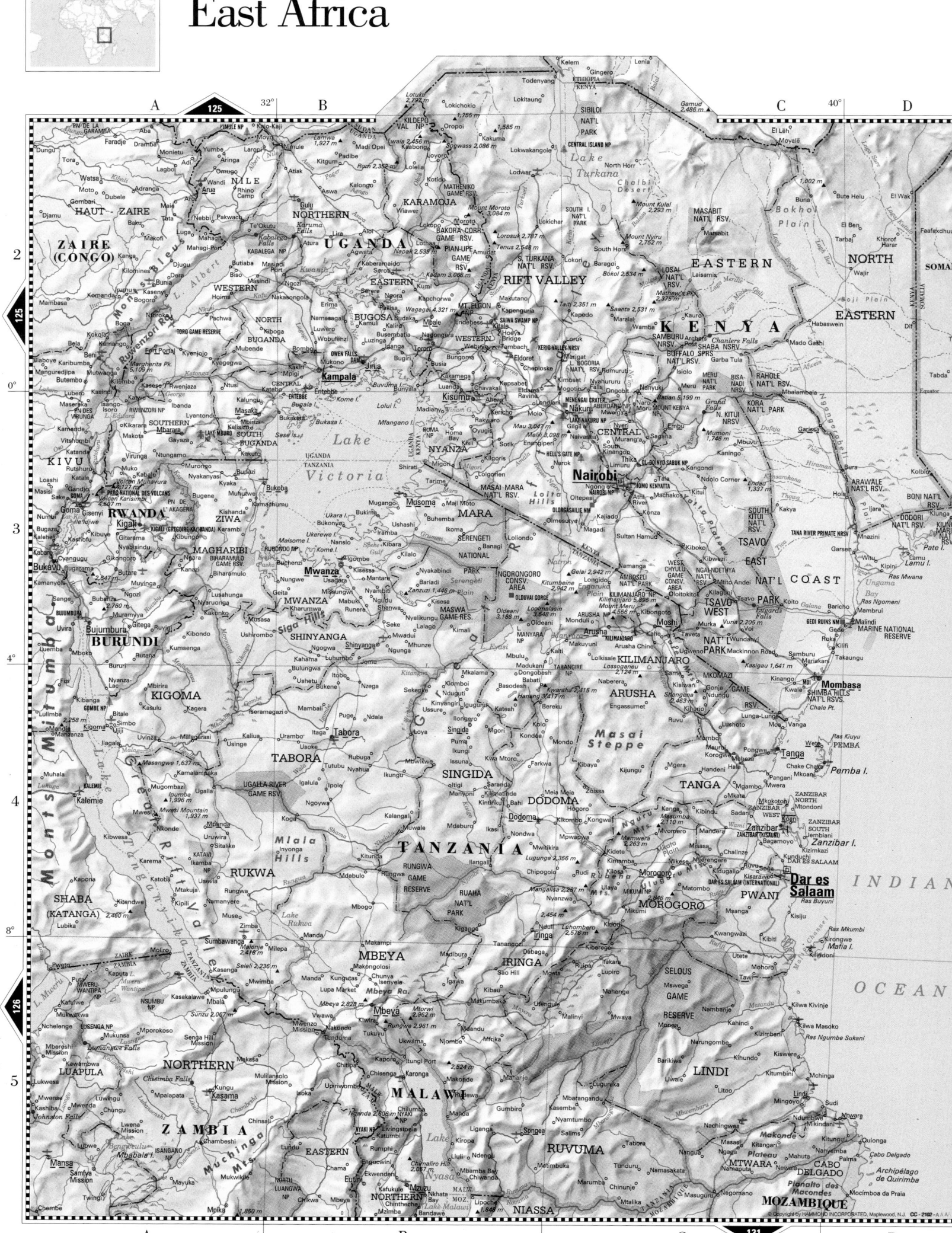

Longitude East of Greenwich

POPULATION OF CITIES AND TOWNS

■ OVER 2,000,000	● 500,000 - 999,999	● 100,000 - 249,999	○ 10,000 - 29,999
◻ 1,000,000 - 1,999,999	◉ 250,000 - 499,999	◦ 30,000 - 99,999	∘ UNDER 10,000

South Central Africa

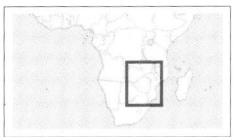

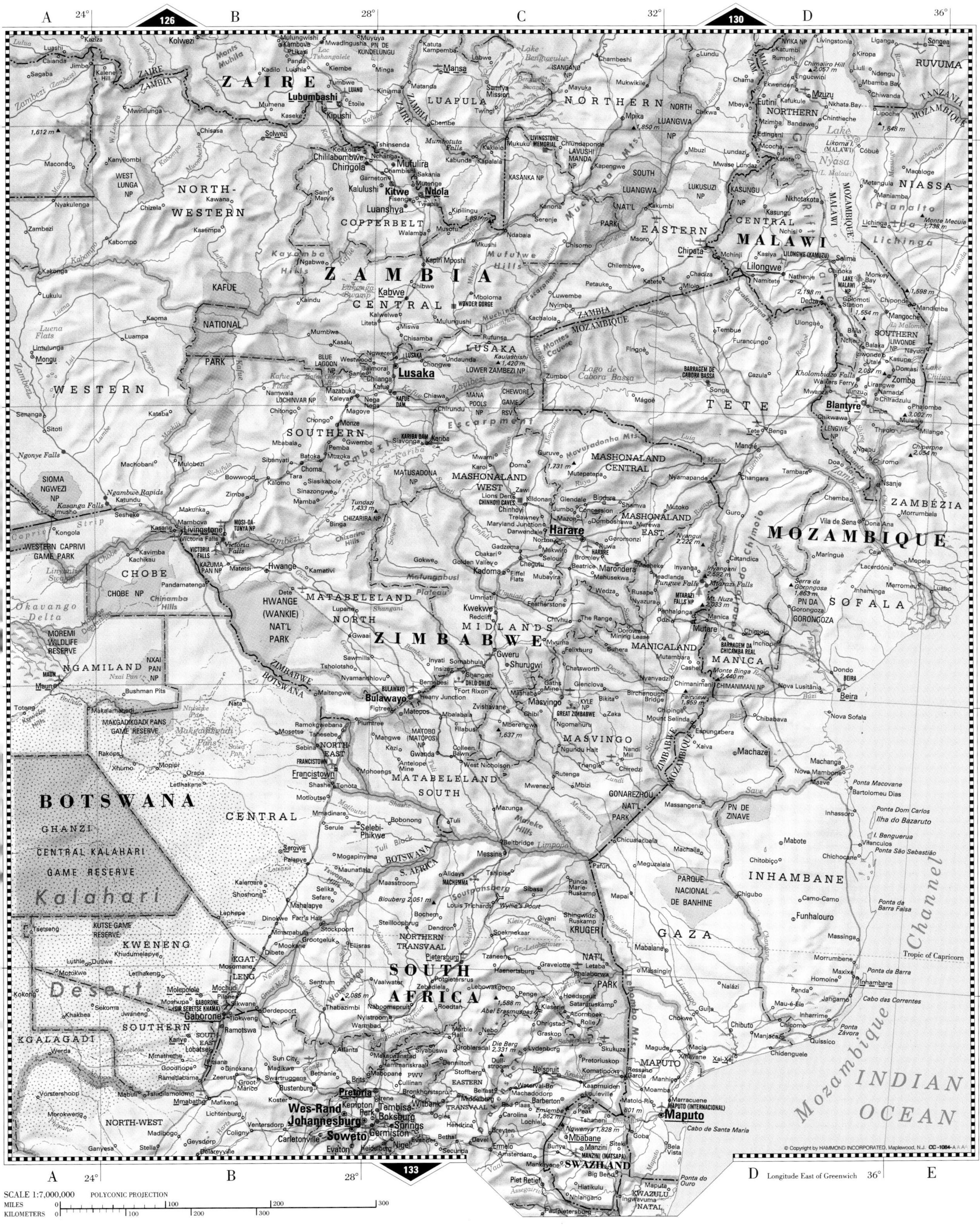

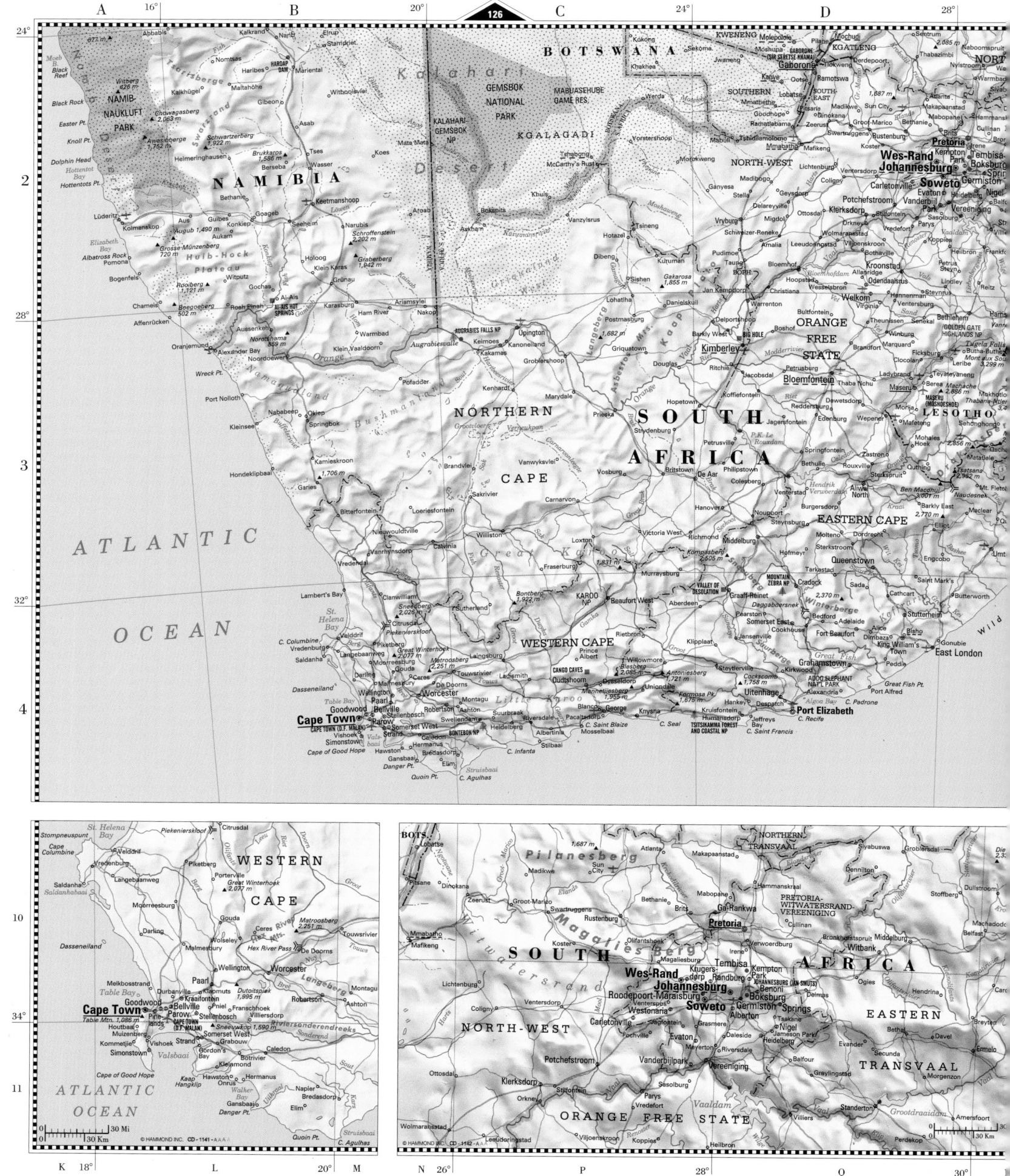

South Africa

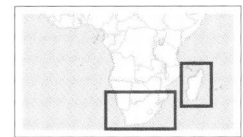

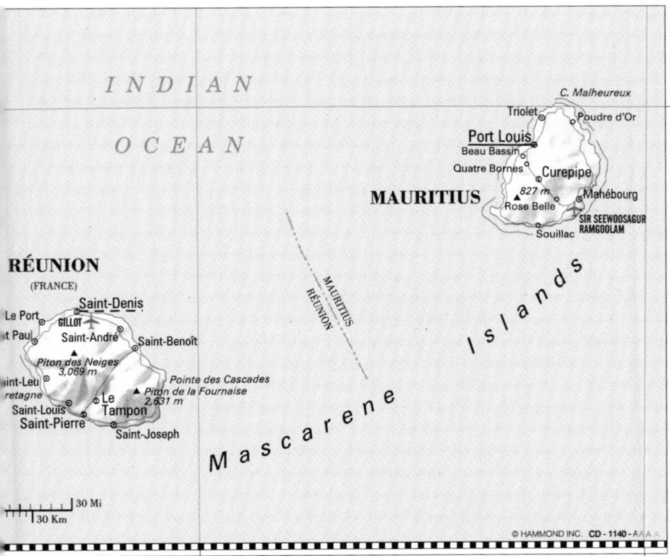

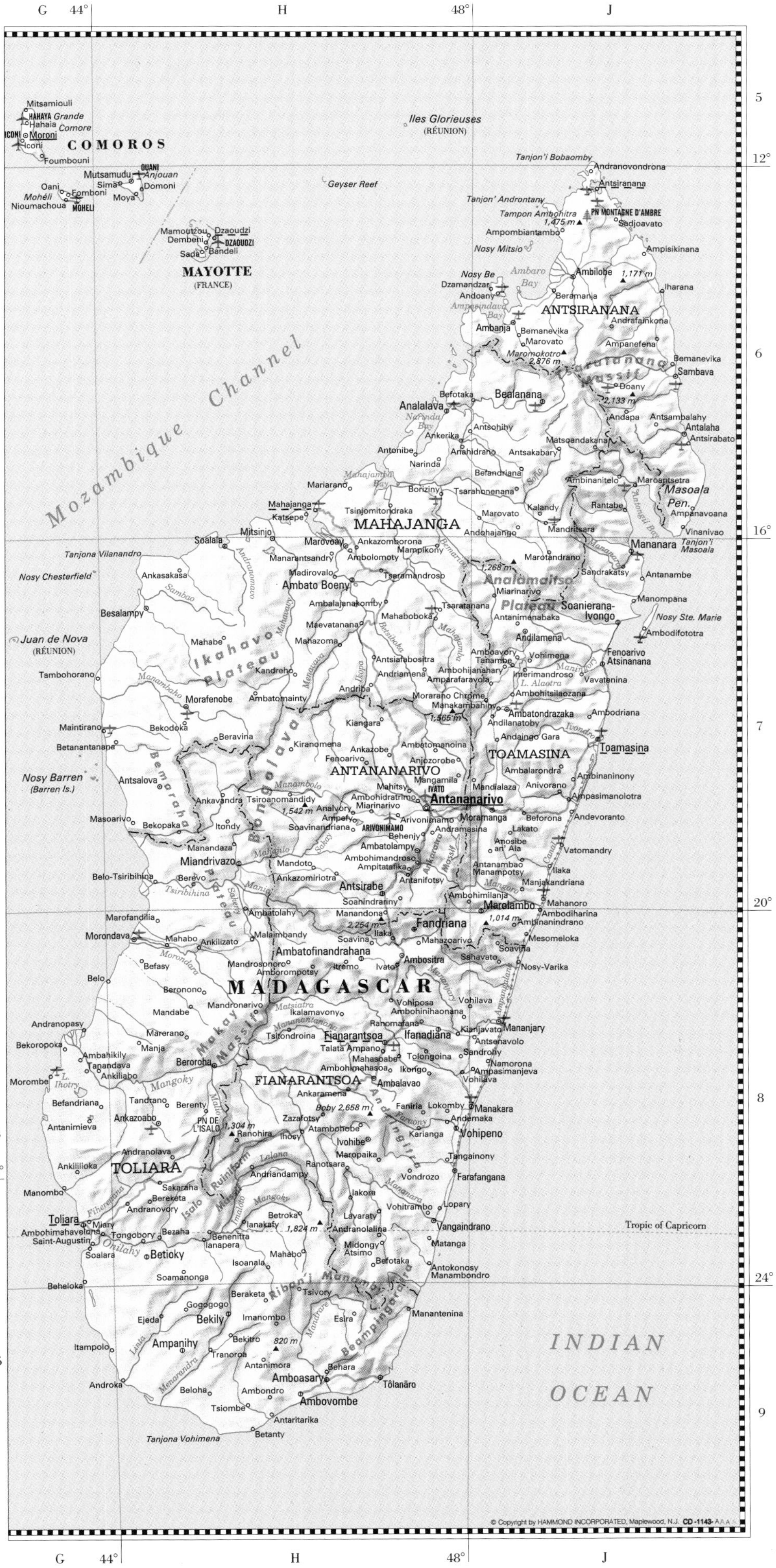

MOZAMBIQUE · GAZA · INHAMBANE

MAPUTO · Maputo · SWAZILAND · AZULU/NATAL · Durban · DURBAN (LOUIS BOTHA)

INDIAN OCEAN

COMOROS · MAYOTTE (FRANCE)

Mozambique Channel

ANTSIRANANA · MAHAJANGA · Mahajanga · ANTANANARIVO · Antananarivo · TOAMASINA · Toamasina · ANTSIRABE · MADAGASCAR · FIANARANTSOA · Fianarantsoa · TOLIARA · Toliara

Tropic of Capricorn

Tanjona Vohimena

INDIAN OCEAN

MAURITIUS · Port Louis · RÉUNION (FRANCE) · Saint-Denis

Mascarene Islands

© Copyright by HAMMOND INCORPORATED, Maplewood, N.J. CD-1055-AAA
© Copyright by HAMMOND INCORPORATED, Maplewood, N.J. CD-1143-AAA
HAMMOND INC. CD-1140-AAA

POPULATION OF CITIES AND TOWNS

■ OVER 2,000,000	● 500,000 - 999,999
□ 1,000,000 - 1,999,999	◉ 250,000 - 499,999
	● 100,000 - 249,999
	○ 30,000 - 99,999
	◦ 10,000 - 29,999
	○ UNDER 10,000

SCALE 1:7,000,000 · LAMBERT CONFORMAL CONIC PROJECTION

MILES 0 · 100 · 200 · 300
KILOMETERS 0 · 100 · 200 · 300

30 Mi
30 Km

South America

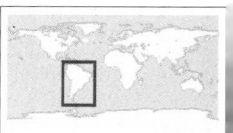

CARIBBEAN SEA

NETH. ANTILLES

ATLANTIC OCEAN

PACIFIC OCEAN

VENEZUELA

COLOMBIA

ECUADOR

PERU

BRAZIL

BOLIVIA

PARAGUAY

CHILE

ARGENTINA

URUGUAY

GUYANA

SURINAME

FRENCH GUIANA

TRINIDAD AND TOBAGO

Guiana Highlands

Mato Grosso

Planalto do Brazilian Highlands

Tropic of Capricorn

Equator

Area of Optimization

The red band which surrounds this map defines the "Area of Optimization." Within this bounding curve is the most accurate conformal map that can be made of the region. Outside the optimized area, distortion increases rapidly, and tears or other irregularities in the grid may occur.

POPULATION OF CITIES AND TOWNS
- ▣ OVER 3,000,000
- ◉ 1,000,000 - 2,999,999
- ★ 500,000 - 999,999
- ● 100,000 - 499,999
- ○ UNDER 100,000

SCALE 1:28,000,000 OPTIMAL CONFORMAL PROJECTION

MILES 0 400 800 1200
KILOMETERS 0 400 800 1200

Longitude West of Greenwich

© Copyright by HAMMOND INCORPORATED, Maplewood, N.J. CC-1069 · A·A

Southern South America

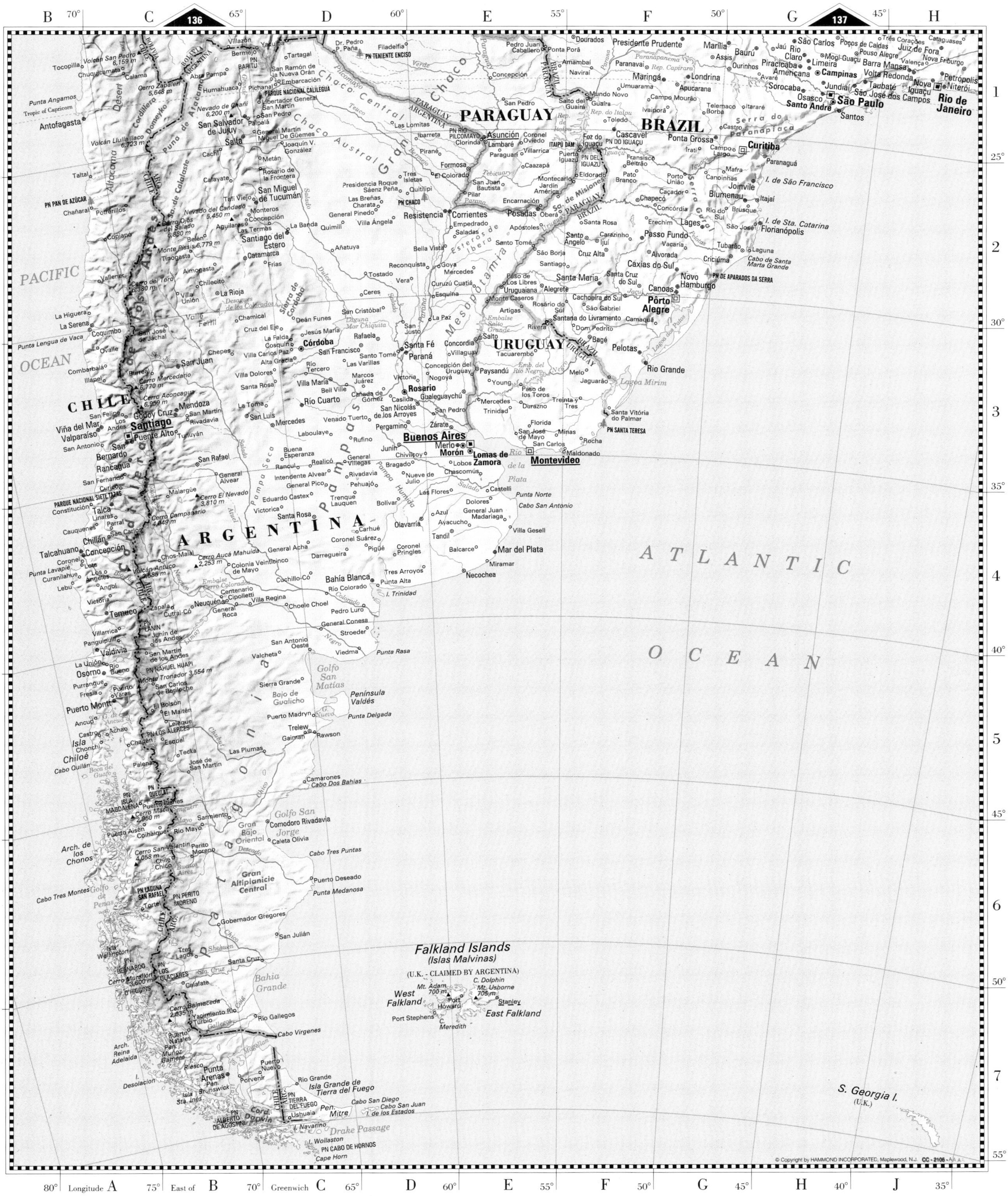

PARAGUAY

BRAZIL

PACIFIC OCEAN

CHILE

ARGENTINA

URUGUAY

ATLANTIC OCEAN

Buenos Aires

Montevideo

São Paulo

Rio de Janeiro

Pôrto Alegre

Curitiba

Santiago

Asunción

Córdoba

Rosario

Mendoza

Falkland Islands
(Islas Malvinas)
(U.K. - CLAIMED BY ARGENTINA)

West Falkland

East Falkland

Stanley

S. Georgia I.
(U.K.)

Drake Passage

Cape Horn

POPULATION OF CITIES AND TOWNS

| ■ OVER 2,000,000 | ● 500,000 - 999,999 | ○ 50,000 - 99,999 |
| ▣ 1,000,000 - 1,999,999 | ● 100,000 - 499,999 | ○ UNDER 50,000 |

SCALE 1:15,000,000   LAMBERT CONFORMAL CONIC PROJECTION

MILES 0 — 200 — 400 — 600

KILOMETERS 0 — 200 — 400 — 600

© Copyright by HAMMOND INCORPORATED, Maplewood, N.J. CC-2106-AA

Northern South America

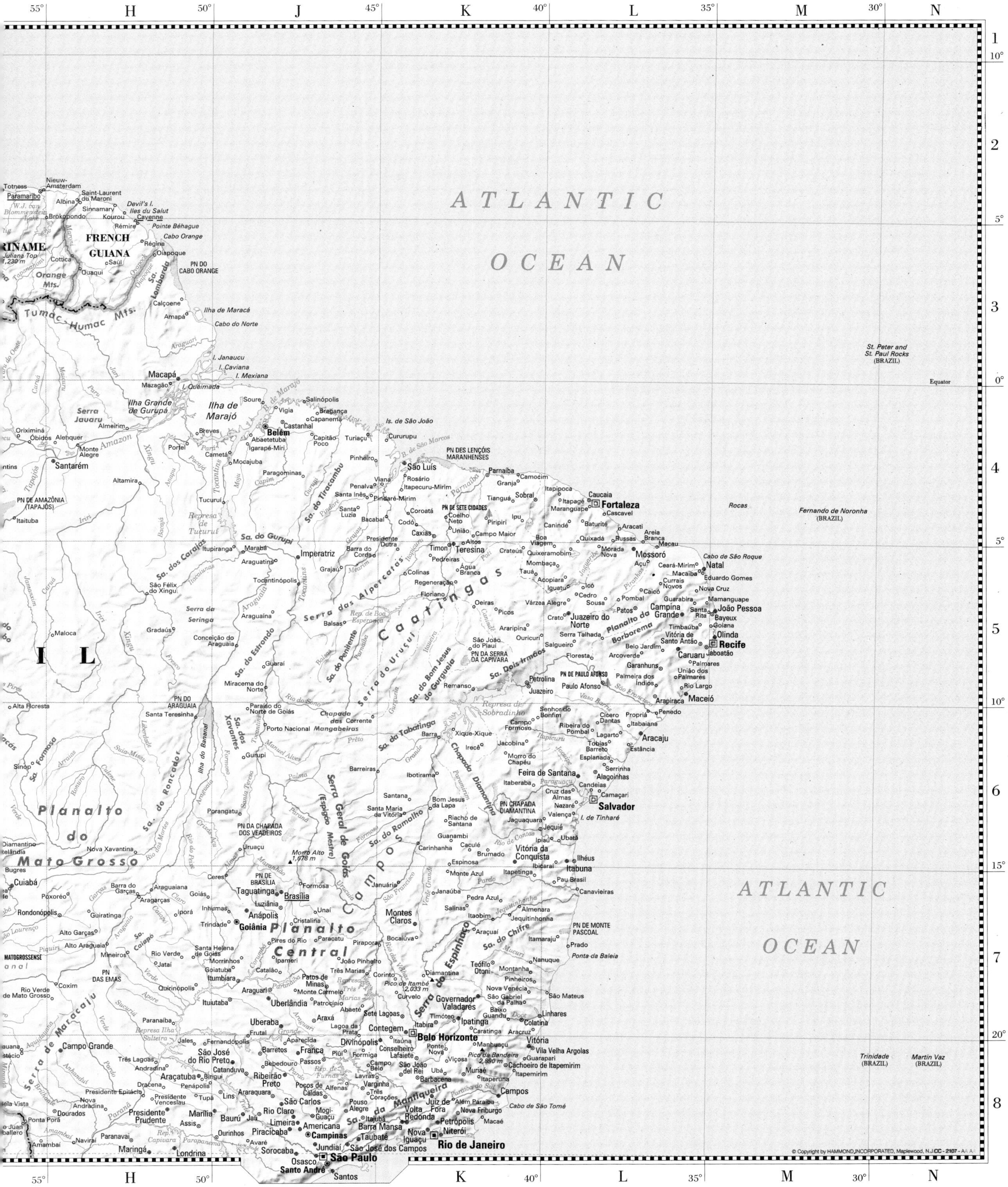

POPULATION OF CITIES AND TOWNS

▣ OVER 2,000,000	◉ 500,000 - 999,999	○ 50,000 - 99,999
◻ 1,000,000 - 1,999,999	● 100,000 - 499,999	○ UNDER 50,000

SCALE 1:15,000,000   LAMBERT CONFORMAL CONIC PROJECTION

MILES   0   200   400   600
KILOMETERS   0   200   400   600

© Copyright by HAMMOND INCORPORATED, Maplewood, N.J.CC - 2107 - A-A

Colombia, Venezuela, Ecuador

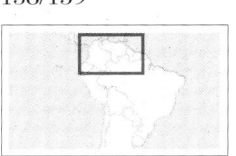

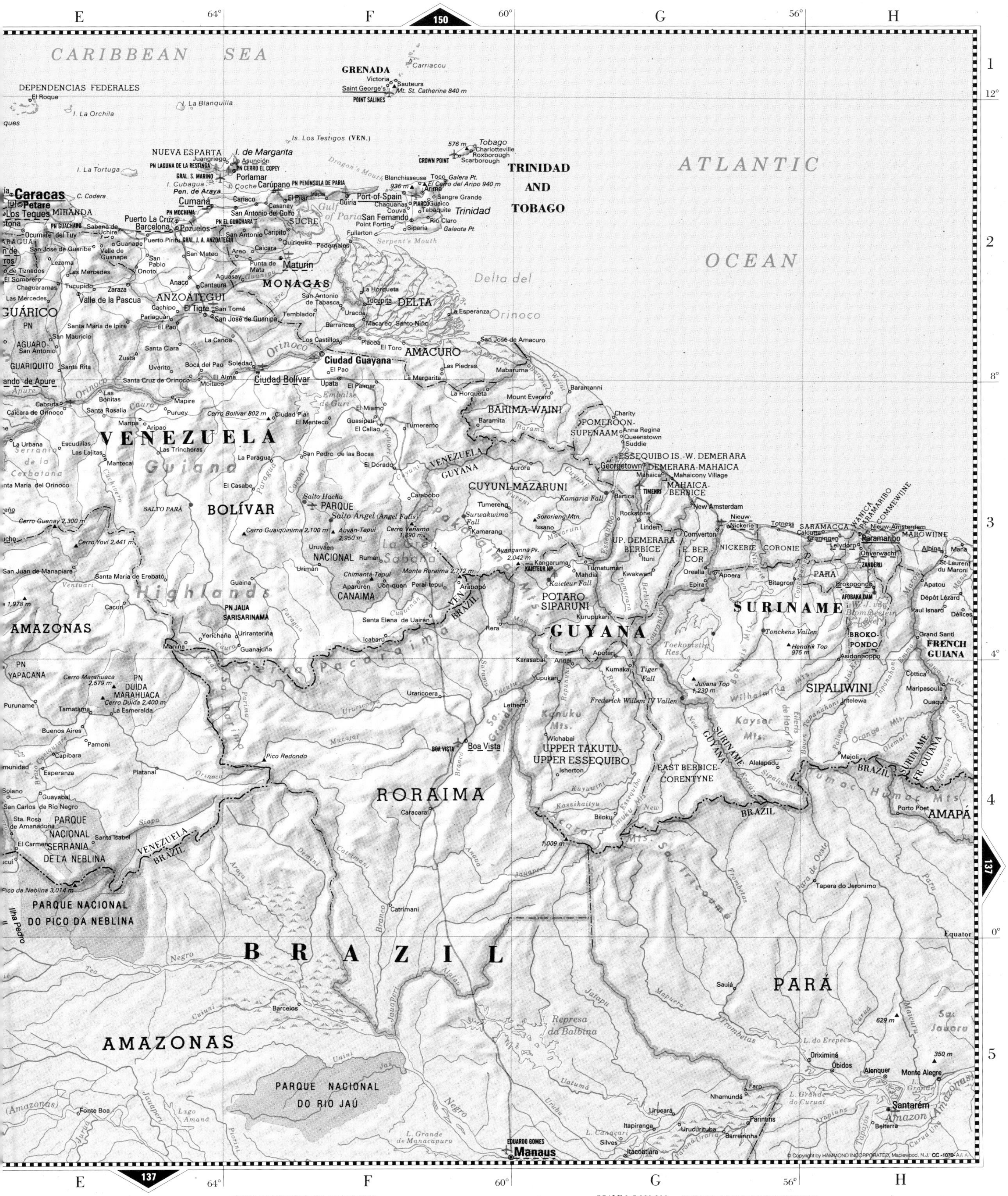

E   64°   **150**   60°   G   56°   H

CARIBBEAN SEA

DEPENDENCIAS FEDERALES

El Roque   I. La Blanquilla

ques   I. La Orchila

1

12°

Is. Los Testigos (VEN.)

GRENADA
Victoria
Sauteurs
Saint George's   *Mt. St. Catherine 840 m*
POINT SALINES   Carriacou

576 m   Tobago
Charlotteville
CROWN POINT   Roxborough
Scarborough

**TRINIDAD
AND
TOBAGO**

ATLANTIC

NUEVA ESPARTA   I. de Margarita
Juangriego
PN LAGUNA DE LA RESTINGA   PN CERRO EL COPEY
Asunción
GRAL. S. MARINO   Porlamar
I. Cubagua   Coche   Carúpano   PN PENÍNSULA DE PARIA
Pen. de Araya   Cariaco   Casanay   El Pilar
Cumaná   936 m   *Dragon's Mouth*
Toco   Galera Pt.
Blanchisseuse   *El Cerro del Aripo 940 m*
Irapa   Güiria   Port-of-Spain
Chaguaramas   PIARCO
Guárico

ia   **Caracas**
Petare   C. Codera
Los Teques   MIRANDA
toria
Ocumare del Tuy   PN GUATOPO   Sabana de
RAGUA   Uchire
San José de Guaribe
de   Guanape   Valle de Guanape
ros   Lezama
de Tiznados   Las Mercedes   San Pablo
El Sombrero   Onoto
Chaguaramas   Tucupido   Anaco
Zaraza   Cantaura

Puerto La Cruz   Barcelona   Pozuelos
Guanta   PN MOCHIMA
San Antonio del Golfo
Casanay
SUCRE
San Antonio de Carípito   Caicara
Quiriquire
Maturín   San Fernando   Sipária   *Trinidad*
Couva   Tabaquite   Río Claro
Fullarton   Galeota Pt.
Point Fortin
Serpent's Mouth
Pedernales

Aguasay   Punta de Mata
Areo   Guanipa
MONAGAS
San Antonio de Tabasca   La Horqueta
Uracoa   Tucupita
DELTA

San Mateo   Temblador
Barrancas   Macareo   Santo Niño
Delta del
La Esperanza
Orinoco

ANZOÁTEGUI
Cachipo   San Antonio
El Tigre   San Tomé
Pariaguán   San José de Guanipa
El Pao   La Canoa   Tigre
Santa María de Ipire
GUÁRICO
PN   Santa Clara
AGUARO   San Mauricio   Zuata
San Antonio   Uverito
GUARIQUITO   Santa Rita   Boca del Pao   Soledad
Santa Cruz de Orinoco
ando de Apure   Las Bonitas   Moitaco
Los Castillos
El Toro
Los Pilacos

San José de Amacuro
AMACURO
Las Piedras   Mabaruma
San José de Amacuro

Ciudad Guayana
El Pao
Ciudad Bolívar   Upata   El Palmar
El Alma   La Marparita

2

8°

La Horqueta
BARIMA-WAINI
Baramita

Apure   La Urbana   Escudillas
Cabruta   Caicara de Orinoco
Santa Rosalía
Maripa   Puruey   Cerro Bolívar 802 m   Ciudad Piar
Aripao   El Manteco
Embalse de Guri
El Miamo   Tumeremo
Guasipati
El Callao   Mount Everard
Baramanni
Charity
POMEROON-
SUPENAAM
Anna Regina
Queenstown
Suddie

VENEZUELA
Guiana
Serranía de la Cerbatana
Santa María del Orinoco
Cerro Guanay 2,300 m
Cerro Yaví 2,441 m
San Juan de Manapiare

Manteca   La Paragua
Las Trincheras
Guiana Highlands
El Casabe
Salto Hacha   PARQUE
SALTO PARÁ   *Salto Ángel (Angel Falls)*
Cerro Guaiquinima 2,100 m   Auyán-Tepui 2,950 m
Uruyén   Cerro Venamo 2,950 m
NACIONAL   Uriman
Chimantá-Tepui   Monte Roraima 2,772 m
Aparurén   Uba-quen Perai-tepui
CANAIMA
Santa Elena de Uairén

BOLÍVAR
San Pedro de las Bocas
El Dorado
VENEZUELA
GUYANA
Carabobo
Tumeremo
CUYUNI-MAZARUNI
Cuyuni
Kamaria Fall
Surwakwima Fall
Kamarang
Avanganna Pk. 2,042 m
KAIETEUR NP.
Kangaruma
Tumatumari
Kaieteur Fall
POTARO-
SIPARUNI
Kurupukari

Aurora
ESSEQUIBO IS.-W. DEMERARA
Georgetown   DEMERARA-MAHAICA
Mahaica   Mahaicony Village
MAHAICA-
BERBICE
Bartica
Rockstone
Linden
Ituni
Kwakwani
New Amsterdam
Nieuw-Nickerie
Totness   SARAMACCA
Calcutta   WANICA   PARAMARIBO
Nieuw-Amsterdam   Groningen   COMMEWIJNE
NICKERIE   CORONIE   Lelydorp   MAROWIJNE
Onverwacht   Albina   Mana
PARA   St-Laurent du Maroni
ZANDERIJ   Apatou
Brokopondo   Dépôt Lézard
AFOBAKADAM   Paul Isnard
W.J. v.d. Blomestein Meer   Grand Santi
BROKO-   Asidonhoppo   **FRENCH GUIANA**
PONDO

3

4°

AMAZONAS
PN YAPACANA
Cerro Marahuaca 2,579 m
PN DUIDA MARAHUACA
Cerro Duida 2,400 m
La Esmeralda
Tamatama

Yerichaña   Uriranterina
Guanajuna
Manina
Serra Parima
Karasabai   Annai
Yupukari   Kumaka
Tiger Fall
Apoteri
SURINAME
GUYANA
Toekomstig Res.
Tonckens Vallen
Juliana Top 1,230 m
Frederick William IV Vallen
Kanuku Mts.
Wichabai
Lethem
Isherton
Hendrik Top 975 m
Wilhelmina Geb.
SURINAME
SIPALIWINI
Kayser Mts.
Tafelberg
Cottica
Mapiri
Mariepasoula
Ouaqui

Venturi   Buenos Aires   Pamoni
Platanal
Boa Vista   **Boa Vista**

comunidad   Capibara
Solano   Guayabal
San Carlos de Río Negro
Sta. Rosa de Amanadona
El Carmen   PARQUE NACIONAL
SERRANÍA DE LA NEBLINA
ucuí   VENEZUELA / BRAZIL

RORAIMA
Caracaraí

UPPER TAKUTU-
UPPER ESSEQUIBO
Kuyuwini
Kassikaityu
Biloku
Kanuku Mts.
Acaraí Mts.
1,009 m
EAST BERBICE-
CORENTYNE
BRAZIL
BRAZIL   SURINAME
FR. GUIANA
Tumuc Humac Mts.
Porto Poet
AMAPÁ

Pico da Neblina 3,014 m   PARQUE NACIONAL DO PICO DA NEBLINA
Ilha Pedro

4

137

Equator   0°

B R A Z I L
Catrimani
Tapera do Jerônimo
Pora do Oeste
Negro
Barcelos
Catrimani

PARÁ
Sauiá
629 m
Maricá

AMAZONAS
Fonte Boa
PARQUE NACIONAL DO RIO JAÚ
Represa da Balbina
Nhamundá
Oriximiná
Óbidos
Faro
Alenquer
Monte Alegre
350 m
5

L. do Erepecu
Amazon
Santarém
L. Grande de Manacapuru
Itapiranga
Urucurituba
Barreirinha
Parintins
EDUARDO GOMES
Manaus
L. Canaçari
Silves
Itacoatiara

E   137   64°   F   60°   G   56°   H

POPULATION OF CITIES AND TOWNS

Symbol	Population
■	OVER 2,000,000
□	1,000,000 - 1,999,999
◉	500,000 - 999,999
◎	250,000 - 499,999
●	100,000 - 249,999
◔	30,000 - 99,999
⊙	10,000 - 29,999
○	UNDER 10,000

SCALE 1:7,000,000   LAMBERT CONFORMAL CONIC PROJECTION

MILES 0   100   200   300
KILOMETERS 0   100   200   300

Northeastern Brazil

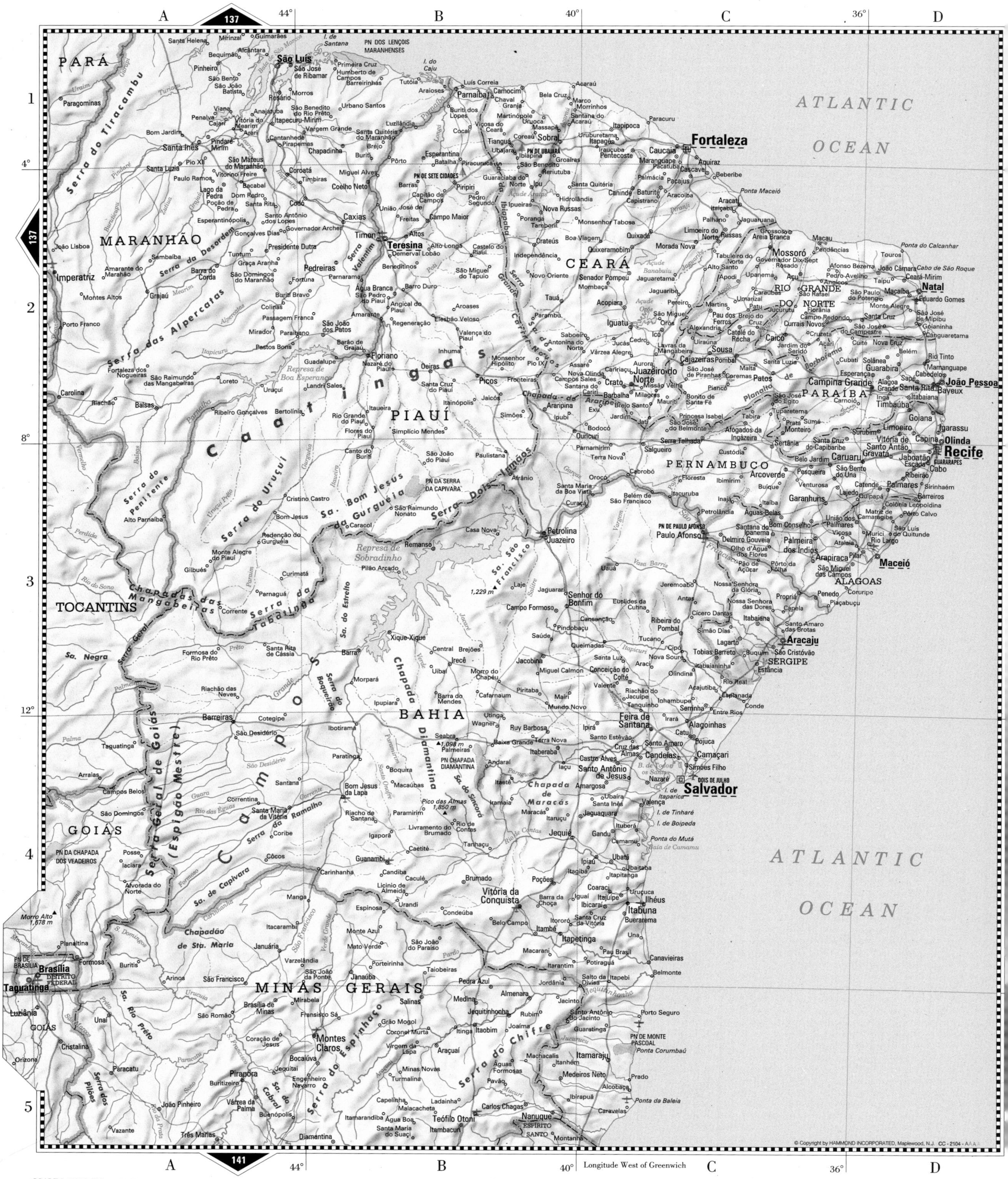

Southeastern Brazil

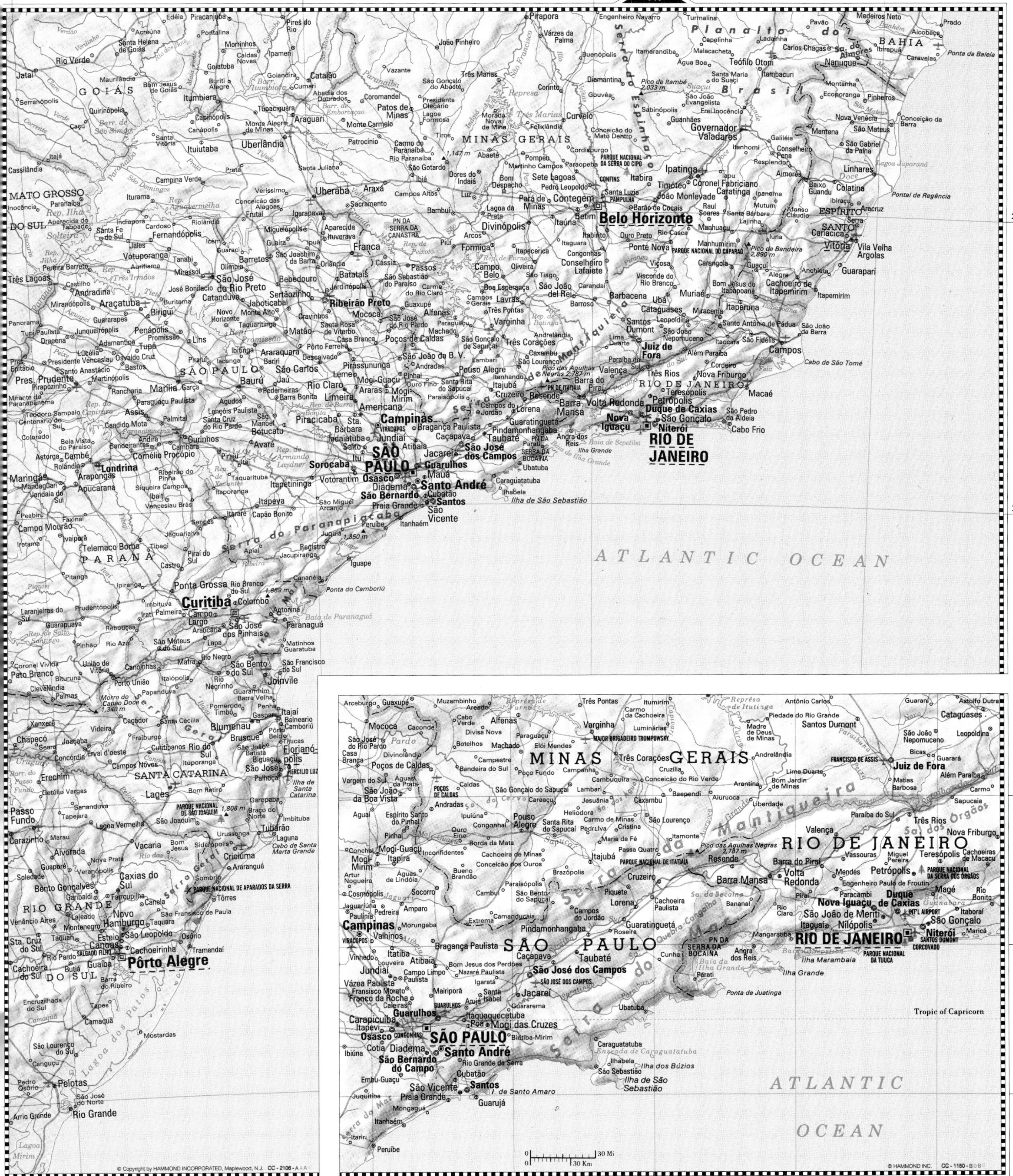

POPULATION OF CITIES AND TOWNS

■ OVER 2,000,000
▣ 1,000,000 - 1,999,999
● 500,000 - 999,999
◉ 250,000 - 499,999
⊕ 100,000 - 249,999
⊖ 30,000 - 99,999
○ 10,000 - 29,999
○ UNDER 10,000

SCALE 1:7,000,000   LAMBERT CONFORMAL CONIC PROJECTION

MILES 0 — 100 — 200 — 300
KILOMETERS 0 — 100 — 200 — 300

© Copyright by HAMMOND INCORPORATED, Maplewood, N.J. CC-2106-A.A.A.

© HAMMOND INC. CC-1150-B.B.B.

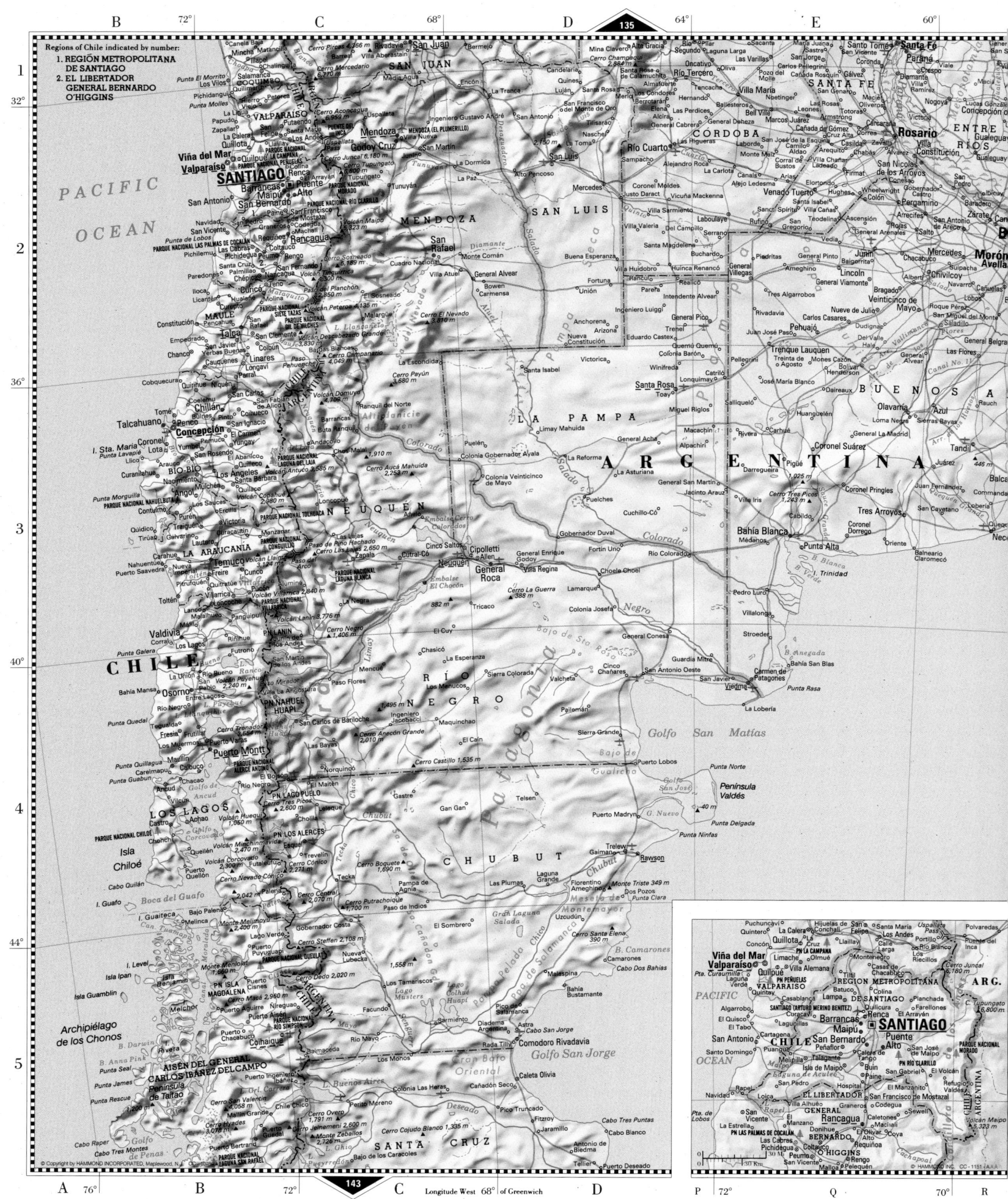

Southern Chile and Argentina

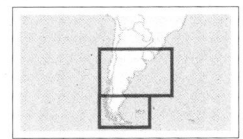

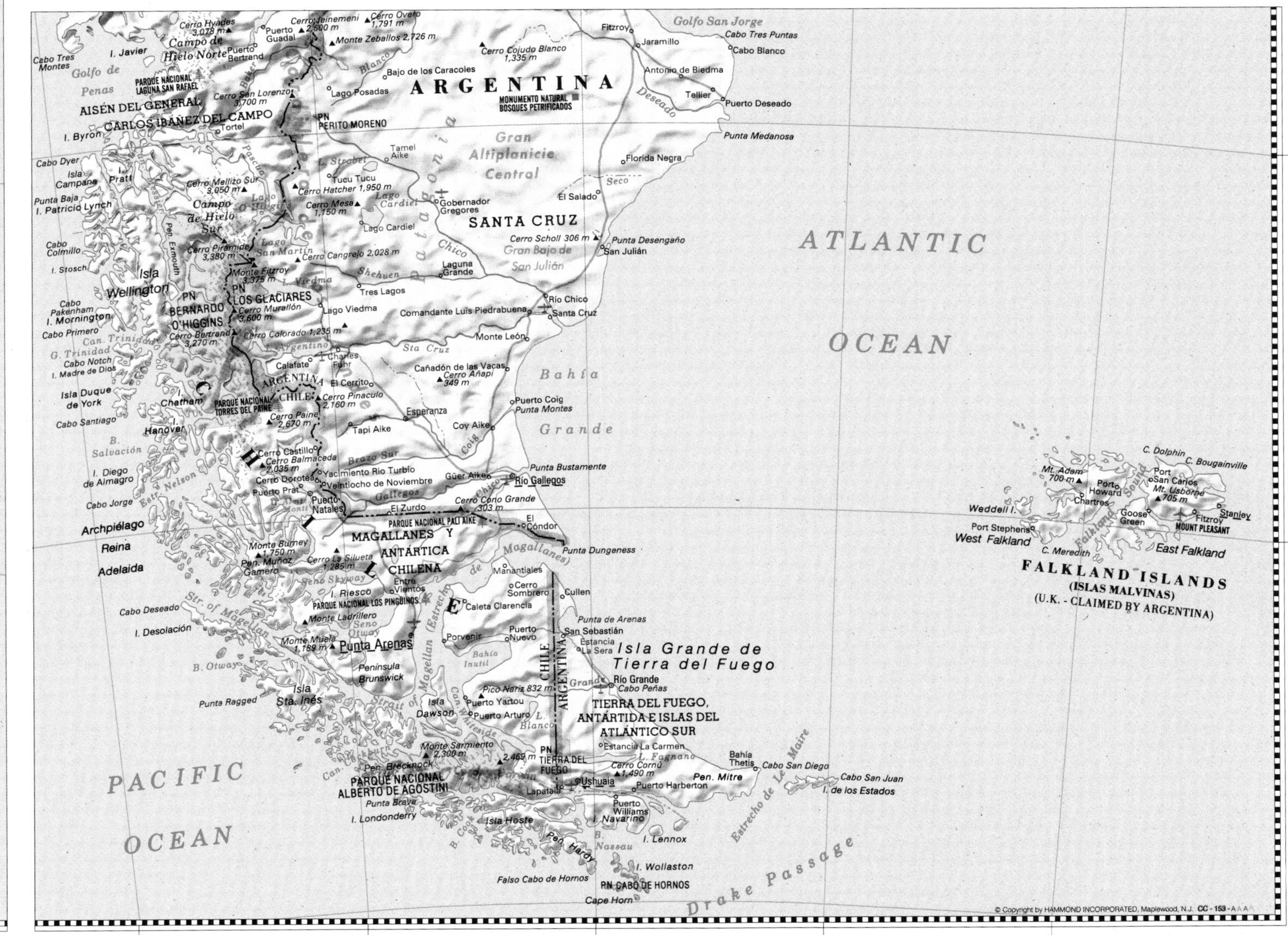

POPULATION OF CITIES AND TOWNS

- ■ OVER 2,000,000
- ▣ 1,000,000 - 1,999,999
- ◉ 500,000 - 999,999
- ⊚ 250,000 - 499,999
- ◎ 100,000 - 249,999
- ⊙ 30,000 - 99,999
- ⊕ 10,000 - 29,999
- ∘ UNDER 10,000

SCALE 1:7,000,000   LAMBERT CONFORMAL CONIC PROJECTION

MILES 0   100   200   300
KILOMETERS 0   100   200   300

© Copyright by HAMMOND INCORPORATED, Maplewood, N.J.   CC-153-AAA

Peru

138

SCALE 1:7,000,000   LAMBERT CONFORMAL CONIC PROJECTION

MILES

KILOMETERS

POPULATION OF CITIES AND TOWNS

■ OVER 2,000,000	● 500,000 - 999,999	● 100,000 - 249,999	○ 10,000 - 29,999
▣ 1,000,000 - 1,999,999	◉ 250,000 - 499,999	● 30,000 - 99,999	○ UNDER 10,000

Longitude West of Greenwich

North America

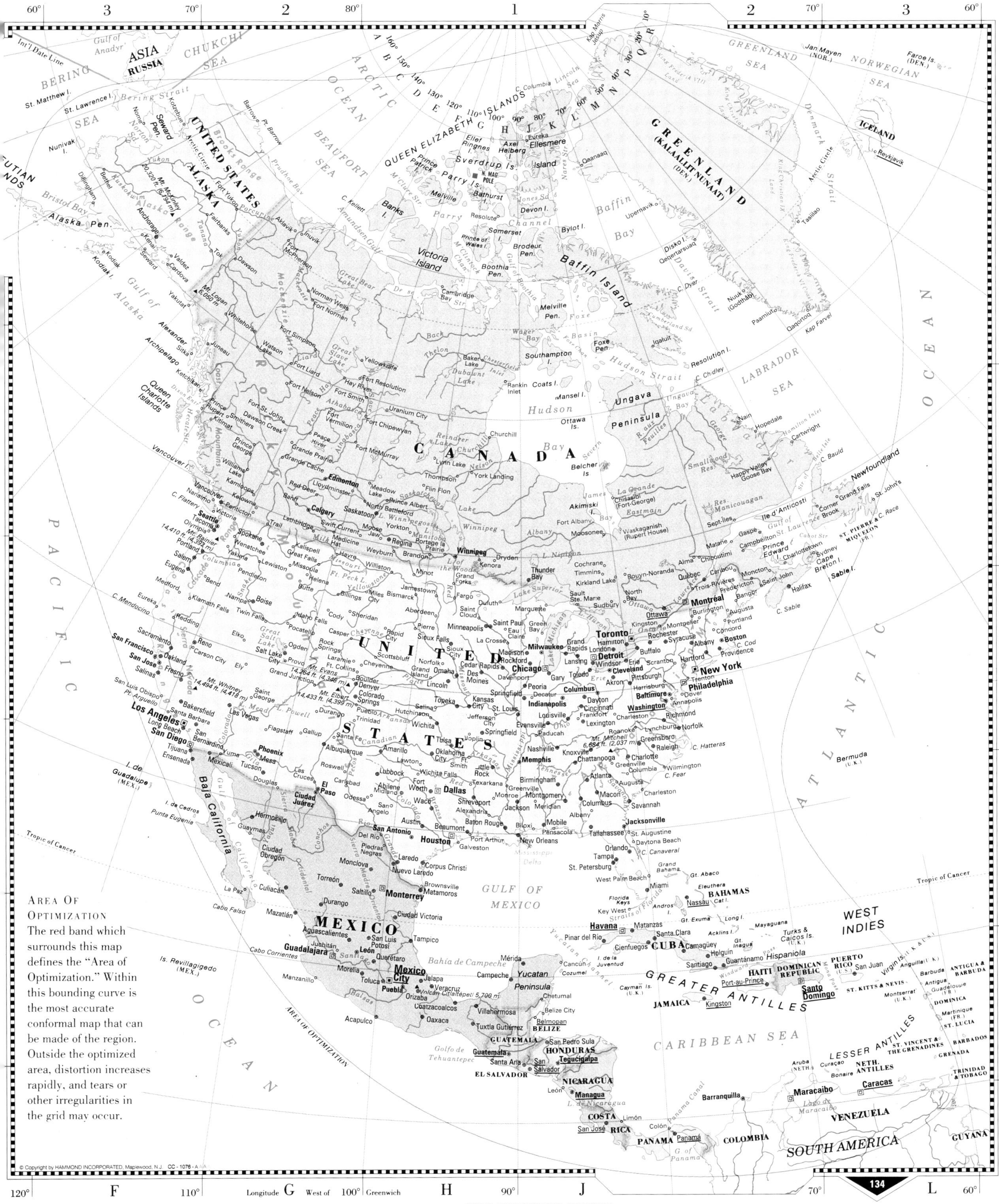

AREA OF OPTIMIZATION
The red band which surrounds this map defines the "Area of Optimization." Within this bounding curve is the most accurate conformal map that can be made of the region. Outside the optimized area, distortion increases rapidly, and tears or other irregularities in the grid may occur.

© Copyright by HAMMOND INCORPORATED, Maplewood, N.J. CC-1076-A

SCALE 1:35,000,000   OPTIMAL CONFORMAL PROJECTION

| MILES | 0 | 500 | 1000 | 1500 |
| KILOMETERS | 0 | 500 | 1000 | 1500 |

Longitude G West of 100° Greenwich

POPULATION OF CITIES AND TOWNS
- ▣ OVER 3,000,000
- ◉ 500,000 - 999,999
- ○ UNDER 100,000
- ▢ 1,000,000 - 2,999,999
- ● 100,000 - 499,999

134

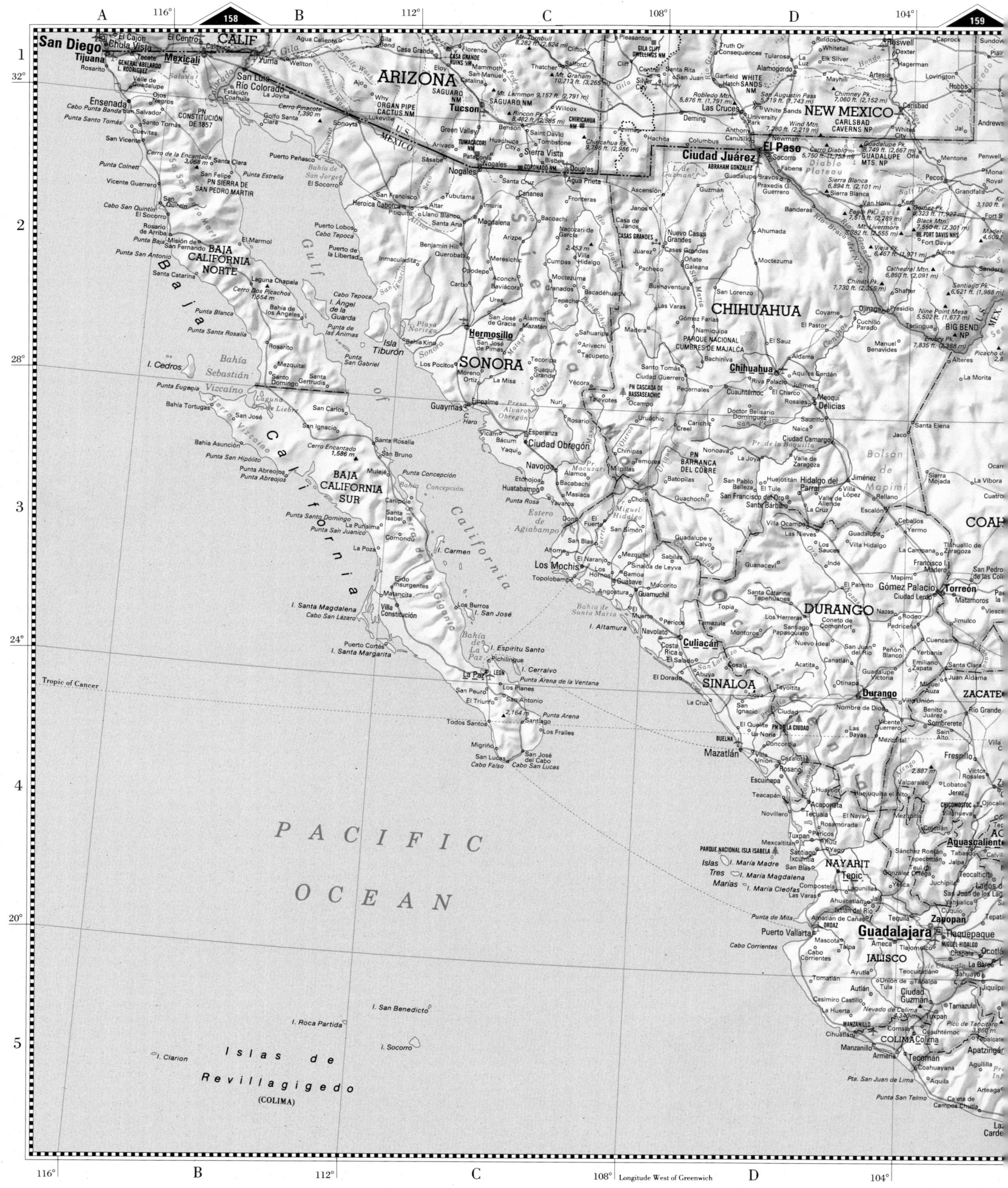

A   116°   B   112°   C   108°   D   104°

1

San Diego · El Cajon · El Centro — **CALIF**
Chula Vista · Tecate · Calexico
Tijuana · **Mexicali** · Yuma

32°

General Abelardo · San Luis
I. Rodríguez · Río Colorado

Ensenada

ARIZONA

Tucson

New Mexico

Ciudad Juárez · El Paso

2

**BAJA
CALIFORNIA
NORTE**

Gulf

SONORA

Hermosillo

CHIHUAHUA

Chihuahua

28°

3

**BAJA
CALIFORNIA
SUR**

California

Guaymas

Ciudad Obregón

Los Mochis

DURANGO

COAH

24°

La Paz

Culiacán

SINALOA

Durango

ZACATE

Tropic of Cancer

San José
del Cabo
Cabo San Lucas

Mazatlán

4

**PACIFIC

OCEAN**

NAYARIT
Tepic

AG

Aguascaliente

20°

Puerto Vallarta

Guadalajara

JALISCO

Ciudad
Guzmán

5

I. Clarion

Islas de
Revillagigedo
(COLIMA)

I. San Benedicto

I. Socorro

COLIMA Colima

116°   B   112°   C   108° Longitude West of Greenwich   D   104°

Northern and Central Mexico

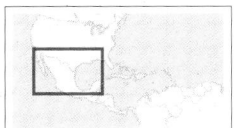

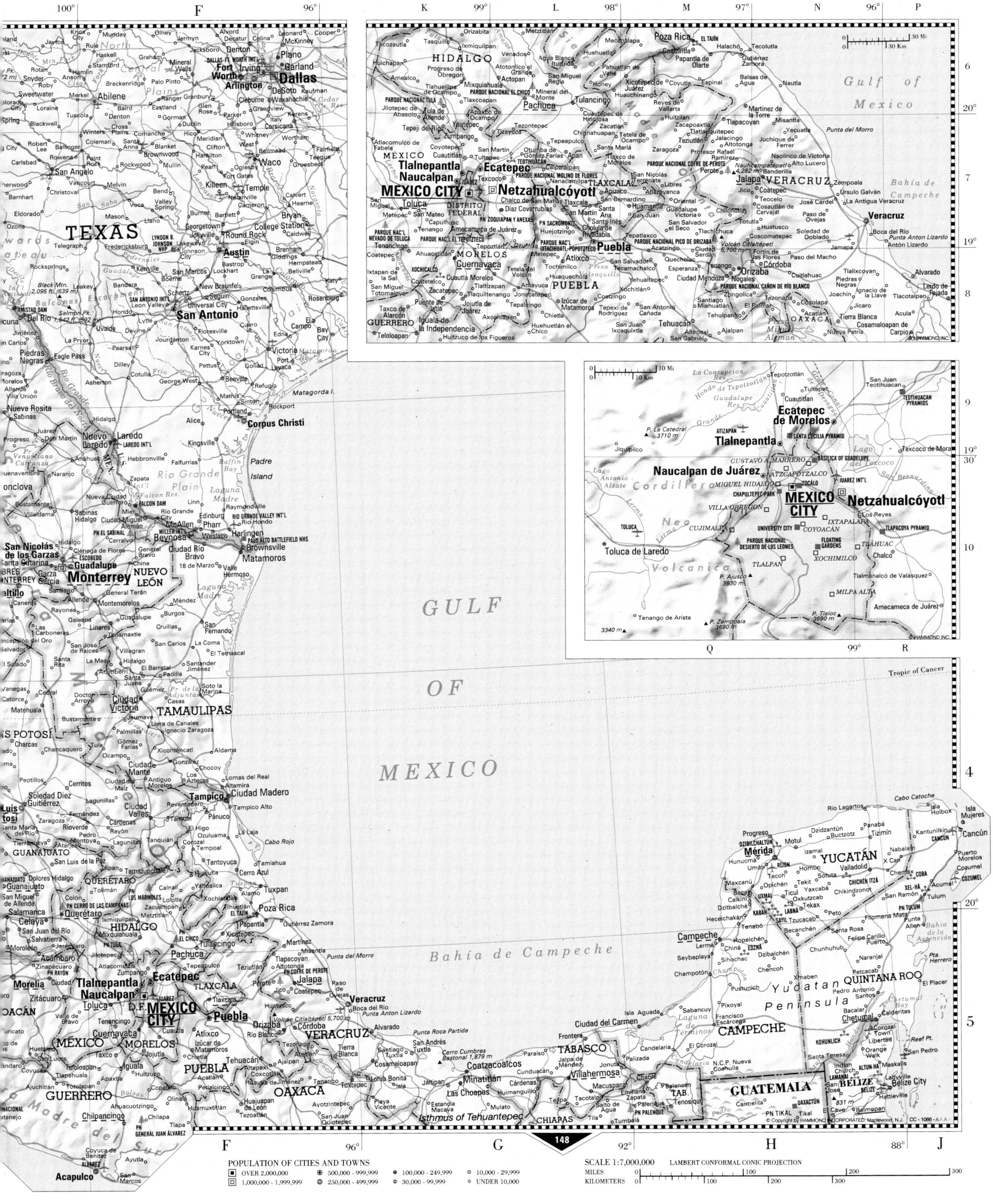

POPULATION OF CITIES AND TOWNS

■ OVER 2,000,000	● 500,000 - 999,999	● 100,000 - 249,999	● 10,000 - 29,999
□ 1,000,000 - 1,999,999	● 250,000 - 499,999	● 30,000 - 99,999	○ UNDER 10,000

SCALE 1:7,000,000   LAMBERT CONFORMAL CONIC PROJECTION

MILES   0   100   200   300

KILOMETERS   0   100   200   300

© Copyright by HAMMOND INCORPORATED, Maplewood, N.J.   CC - 1066 - A A A

A 100°   B   96°   C   92°   D   88°

147

GULF OF MEXICO

TAMAULIPAS

San Luis Potosí
Tampico   Ciudad Madero
GUANAJUATO
QUERÉTARO
Querétaro
HIDALGO
Pachuca
Tlalhepantla Ecatepec
Naucalpan TLAXCALA
Toluca
MEXICO CITY Puebla
Cuernavaca MORELOS
MEXICO
GUERRERO
PUEBLA
Chilpancingo
Acapulco

MEXICO

Bahía de

Campeche

Mérida
YUCATÁN
Campeche
Yucatán
Peninsula
QUINTANA ROO
Chetumal

Cancún

VERACRUZ
Veracruz
Córdoba
Orizaba
OAXACA
Oaxaca
MONTE ALBÁN

TABASCO
Coatzacoalcos
Minatitlán
Villahermosa
Isthmus of
Tehuantepec
CHIAPAS
Tuxtla
Gutiérrez

CAMPECHE

*Golfo de
Tehuantepec*

Tapachula

GUATEMALA
Quezaltenango
Guatemala
San Salvador
EL SALVADOR
San Miguel

BELIZE

HONDURAS
Tegucigalpa

Managua

PACIFIC

OCEAN

© Copyright by HAMMOND INCORPORATED, Maplewood, N.J. CC-1067-AAA

B   96°   Longitude West of Greenwich   C   92°   D   88°

SCALE 1:7,000,000   LAMBERT CONFORMAL CONIC PROJECTION
MILES   0   100   200   300
KILOMETERS 0   100   200   300

POPULATION OF CITIES AND TOWNS
■ OVER 2,000,000   ● 500,000 - 999,999   ⊕ 100,000 - 249,999   ⊙ 10,000 - 29,999
□ 1,000,000 - 1,999,999   ◉ 250,000 - 499,999   ⊘ 30,000 - 99,999   ○ UNDER 10,000

Southern Mexico, Central America, Western Caribbean

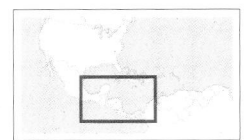

Eastern Caribbean, Bahamas

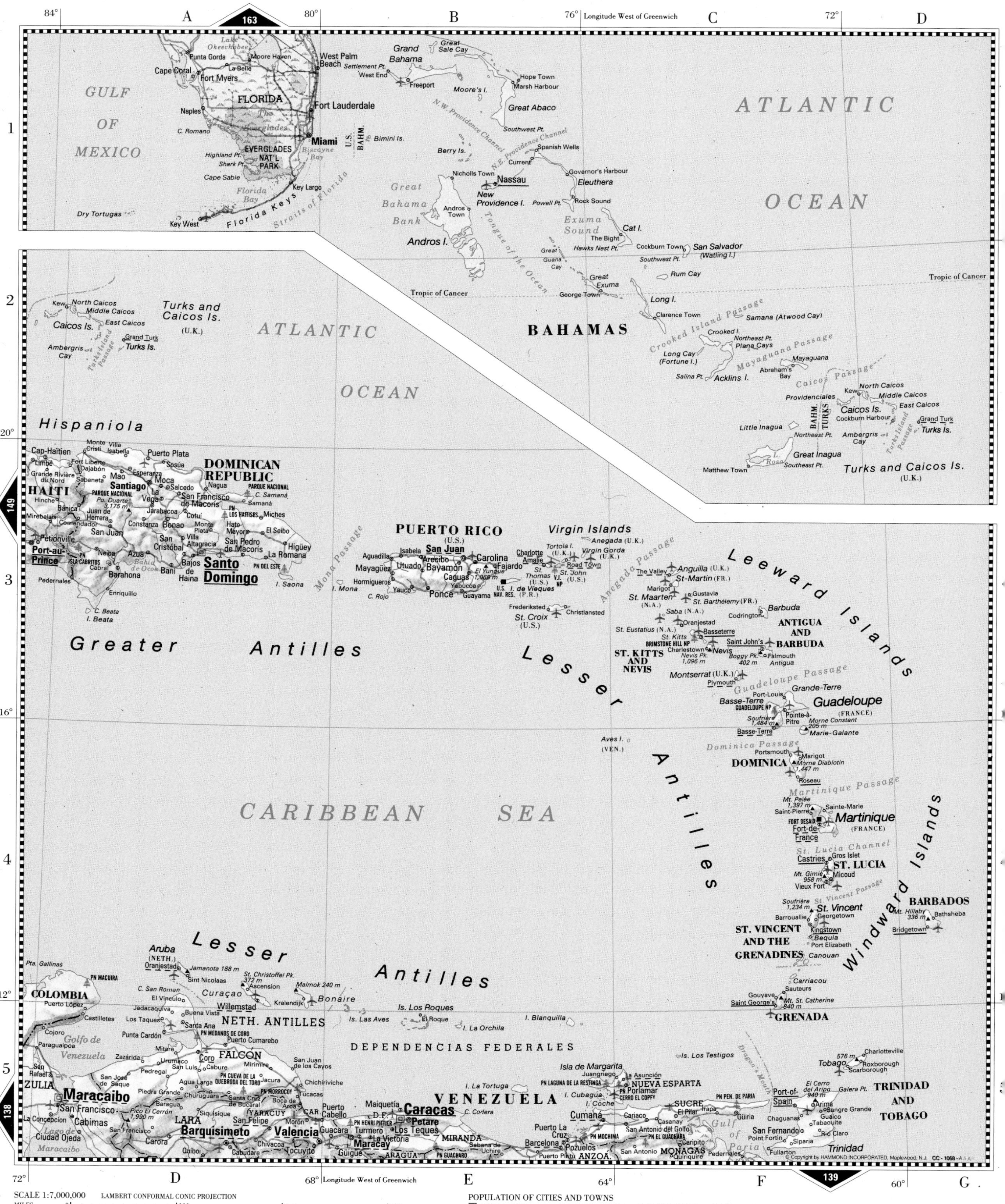

84° A 80° B 76° Longitude West of Greenwich C 72° D

1

GULF OF MEXICO

FLORIDA

Lake Okeechobee
Moore Haven
La Belle
Punta Gorda
Cape Coral
Fort Myers
Naples
C. Romano
Highland Pt.
Shark Pt.
Cape Sable
Dry Tortugas
Key West
Key Largo
Florida Bay
Florida Keys
Straits of Florida
West Palm Beach
Settlement Pt.
West End
Fort Lauderdale
Miami
Biscayne Bay
EVERGLADES NAT'L PARK
The Everglades
U.S. BAHM.
Bimini Is.

Grand Bahama
Great Sale Cay
Freeport
Moore's I.
N.W. Providence Channel
Hope Town
Marsh Harbour
Great Abaco
Southwest Pt.
N.E. Providence Channel
Berry Is.
Spanish Wells
Current
Nicholls Town
Nassau
Governor's Harbour
New Providence I.
Eleuthera
Powell Pt.
Rock Sound

ATLANTIC OCEAN

Andros Town
Great Bahama Bank
Andros I.
Tongue of the Ocean
Great Guana Cay
The Bight
Hawks Nest Pt.
Southwest Pt.
Cockburn Town
San Salvador (Watling I.)
Cat I.
Exuma Sound
Rum Cay
Great Exuma
George Town
Long I.

2

North Caicos
Middle Caicos
Kew
East Caicos
Caicos Is.
Grand Turk
Ambergris Cay
Turks Is.
Turks and Caicos Is.
(U.K.)
Turks Island Passage

ATLANTIC OCEAN

Tropic of Cancer

BAHAMAS

Clarence Town
Long I.
Crooked Island Passage
Samana (Atwood Cay)
Crooked I.
Long Cay (Fortune I.)
Northeast Pt.
Plana Cays
Salina Pt.
Acklins I.
Abraham's Bay
Mayaguana
Mayaguana Passage
Kew
North Caicos
Middle Caicos
East Caicos
Providenciales
Caicos Is.
Cockburn Harbour
BAHM. TURKS
Grand Turk
Ambergris Cay
Turks Is.
Little Inagua
Northeast Pt.
Turks and Caicos Is.
(U.K.)
Matthew Town
L. Rosa
Great Inagua
Southeast Pt.
Caicos Passage
Turks Island Passage
Tropic of Cancer

20°

Hispaniola

3

Cap-Haïtien
Monte Villa
Cristi
Isabela
Limbé
Fort Liberté
Grande Rivière du Nord
Dajabón
Esperanza
Puerto Plata
Sosúa
Santiago
Moca
Salcedo
San Francisco de Macorís
HAITI
PARQUE NACIONAL
Po. Duarte 3,175 m
La Vega
Jarabacoa
Cotuí
Nagua
C. Samaná
PARQUE NACIONAL
LOS HAITISES
Sánchez
Miches
PN LOS HAITISES
Hinche
Banica
Comendador
Juan de Herrera
San Juan
Constanza
Bonao
Monte Plata
Hato Mayor
El Seibo
Higüey
DOMINICAN REPUBLIC
Mirebalais
Port-au-Prince
ISLA CABRITOS
Azua
San Cristóbal
Villa Altagracia
San Pedro de Macorís
La Romana
Pétionville
Neiba
Baní
Bajos de Haina
Santo Domingo
PN DEL ESTE
I. Saona
Pedernales
Barahona
Enriquillo
C. Beata
I. Beata
Bahía de Ocoa

Greater   Antilles

PUERTO RICO
(U.S.)
Aguadilla
Isabela
Arecibo
San Juan
Carolina
Fajardo
Mayagüez
Utuado
Bayamón
Charlotte Amalie
St. Thomas (U.S.)
Tortola (U.K.)
Anegada (U.K.)
Hormigueros
Caguas
El Yunque 1,065 m
Road Town
Virgin Gorda (U.K.)
St. John (U.S.) NP
Yauco
Yabucoa
Virgin Islands
I. Mona
C. Rojo
Ponce
Guayama
U.S. I. de Vieques
NAV. RES. (P.R.)
Mona Passage
Frederiksted
Christiansted
St. Croix (U.S.)
Anegada Passage
Anguilla (U.K.)
The Valley
St-Martin (FR.)
Marigot
St. Maarten (N.A.)
Gustavia
St. Barthélemy (FR.)
Saba (N.A.)
St. Eustatius (N.A.)
Oranjestad
Barbuda
Codrington
ANTIGUA AND BARBUDA
St. Kitts
Basseterre
ST. KITTS AND NEVIS
BRIMSTONE HILL NP
Charlestown
Nevis
Saint John's
Boggy Pk. 402 m
Falmouth
Antigua
Nevis Pk. 1,096 m
Montserrat (U.K.)
Plymouth
Guadeloupe Passage
Port-Louis
Grande-Terre
Basse-Terre
Guadeloupe
GUADELOUPE NP
Pointe-à-Pitre
Soufrière 1,484 m
Morne Constant 205 m
Basse-Terre
Marie-Galante

Leeward   Islands

4

CARIBBEAN   SEA

Lesser   Antilles

Aves I. (VEN.)

Dominica Passage
Portsmouth
Marigot
Morne Diablotin 1,447 m
DOMINICA
Roseau
Martinique Passage
Mt. Pelée 1,397 m
Sainte-Marie
Saint-Pierre
FORT DESAIX
Fort-de-France
Martinique
(FRANCE)
St. Lucia Channel
Castries
Gros Islet
ST. LUCIA
Mt. Gimie 958 m
Micoud
Vieux Fort
Soufrière 1,234 m
St. Vincent Passage
Barrouallie
St. Vincent
Georgetown
Kingstown
ST. VINCENT AND THE GRENADINES
Bequia
Port Elizabeth
Canouan
Carriacou
Sauteurs
Gouyave
Saint George's
Mt. St. Catherine 840 m
GRENADA
Mt. Hillaby 336 m
Bathsheba
BARBADOS
Bridgetown
Windward   Islands

12°

Lesser

5

Pta. Gallinas
PN MACUIRA
Aruba (NETH.)
Oranjestad
Jamanota 188 m
St. Christoffel Pk. 372 m
Ascension
Malmok 240 m
Cojoro
COLOMBIA
Puerto López
Castilletes
San Román
El Vínculo
Curaçao
Kralendijk
Bonaire
Is. Los Roques
I. La Orchila
I. Blanquilla
Los Taques
Santa Ana
Buena Vista
Willemstad
Jadacaquiva
El Roque
I. Las Aves
Antilles
Paraguaipoa
Punta Cardón
PN MEDANOS DE CORO
Puerto Cumarebo
NETH. ANTILLES
DEPENDENCIAS   FEDERALES
Is. Los Testigos
Charlotteville 576 m
Roxborough
Scarborough
Tobago
TRINIDAD AND TOBAGO
Golfo de Venezuela
Mitare
Coro
FALCON
San Juan de los Cayos
Isla de Margarita
Juangriego
Asunción
NUEVA ESPARTA
Porlamar
PN PEN. DE PARIA
Galera Pt.
El Cerro del Aripo 940 m
San Rafael
ZULIA
Ciudad Ojeda
Zaráraga
Drumaco
Pedregal
Agua Larga
Chichiriviche
PN MORROCOY
Tucacas
I. La Tortuga
I. Cubagua
SUCRE
Cariaco
Chaguaramas
Arima
Sangre Grande
Guaico
Sangre Grande
Maracaibo
Cabimas
San Francisco
San José de Seque
Pico El Cerrón 1,990 m
Siquisique
San Felipe
La Victoria
Morón
Guacara
Puerto Cabello
Maiquetía
Chichiriviche
Casanay
Carúpano
El Pilar
Irapa
Güiria
Point Fortin
Siparia
Rio Claro
Maracay
Lago de Maracaibo
La Concepción
Carora
LARA
Barquisimeto
Chivacoa
YARACUY
Valencia
Turmero
Los Teques
D.F.
Caracas
Petare
MIRANDA
Sabana de Uchire
Barcelona
Puerto La Cruz
Cumaná
PN MOCHIMA
San Antonio del Golfo
Cariaco
MONAGAS
Maturín
Caripito
Fullarton
Trinidad
Gulf of Paria
San Fernando
Chivacoa
Cabudare
Quíbor
Ocumare
ARAGUA
PN GUATOPO
Güigue
Guigue
ANZOA.
Pariaguán
Puerto Píritu
Pozuelos
San Antonio
Dragon's Mouths
Port-of-Spain

72° D 68° Longitude West of Greenwich E 64° F 60° G

SCALE 1:7,000,000   LAMBERT CONFORMAL CONIC PROJECTION

MILES 0   100   200   300
KILOMETERS 0   100   200   300

POPULATION OF CITIES AND TOWNS

☐ OVER 2,000,000   ⊛ 500,000 - 999,999   ● 100,000 - 249,999   ⊙ 10,000 - 29,999
☐ 1,000,000 - 1,999,999   ⊛ 250,000 - 499,999   ⊙ 30,000 - 99,999   ○ UNDER 10,000

163
149
138
139

Alaska

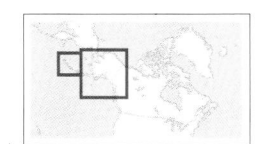

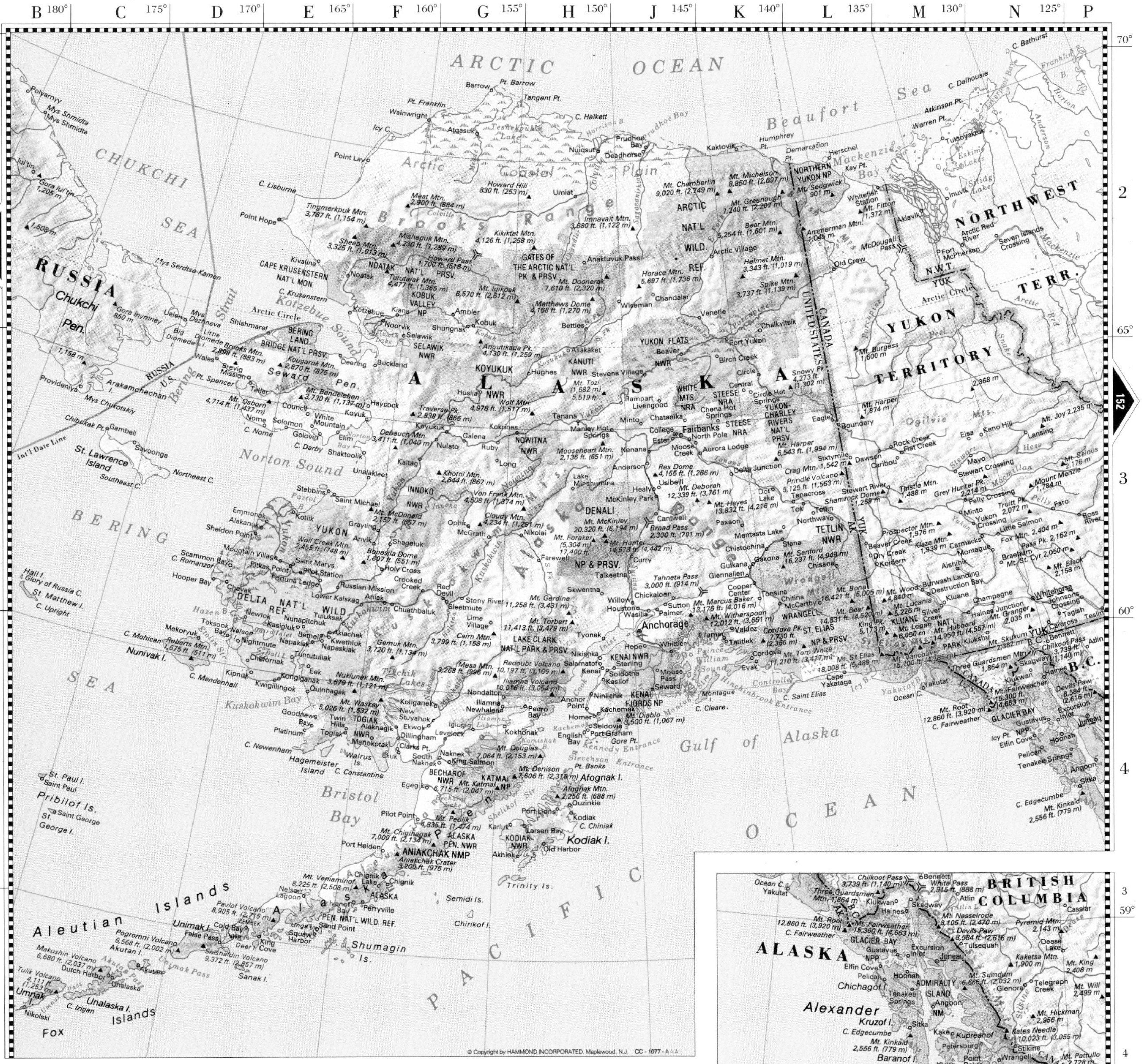

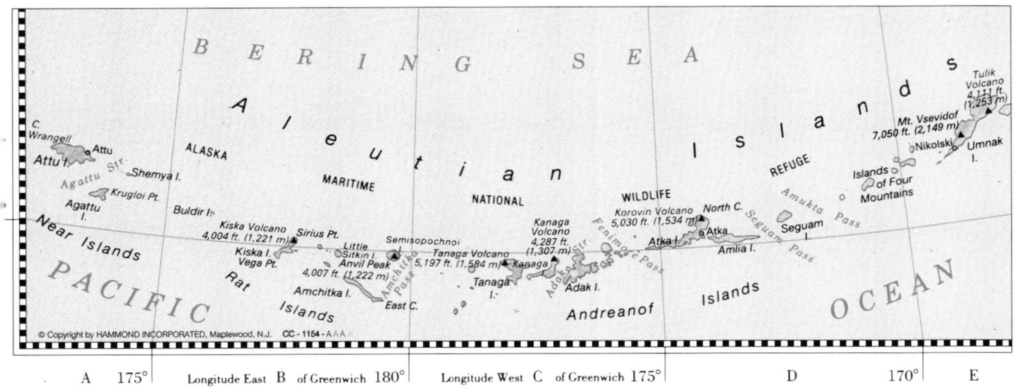

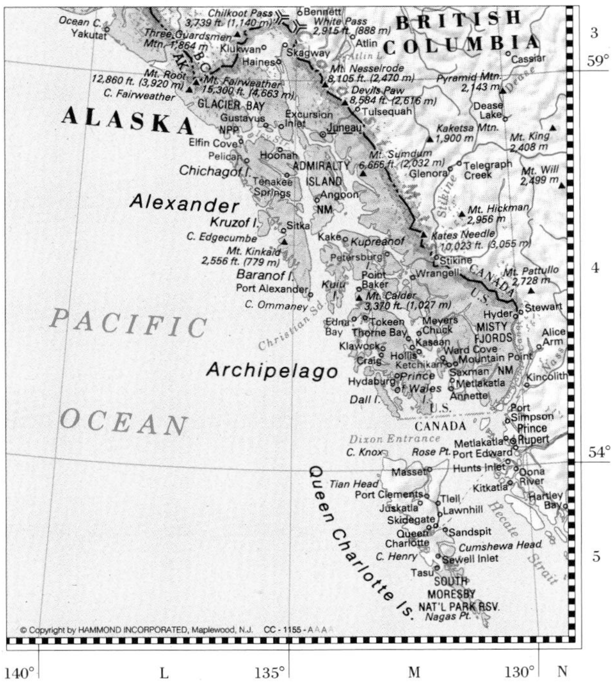

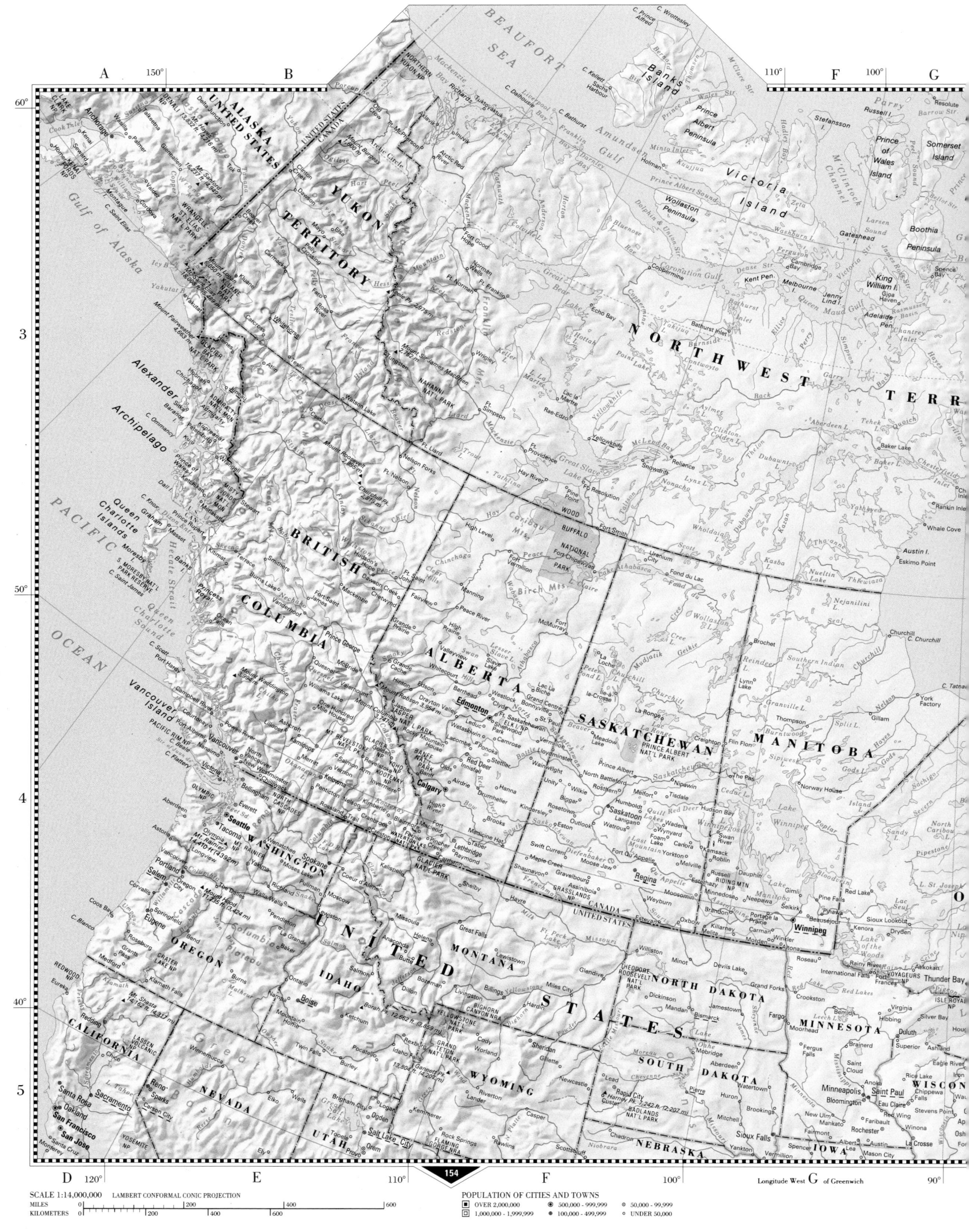

SCALE 1:14,000,000   LAMBERT CONFORMAL CONIC PROJECTION

MILES   0   200   400   600

KILOMETERS   0   200   400   600

POPULATION OF CITIES AND TOWNS

■ OVER 2,000,000   ● 500,000 - 999,999   ○ 50,000 - 99,999
▣ 1,000,000 - 1,999,999   ◉ 100,000 - 499,999   ○ UNDER 50,000

Longitude West **G** of Greenwich

Canada

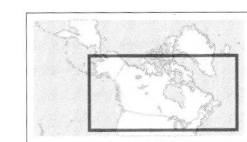

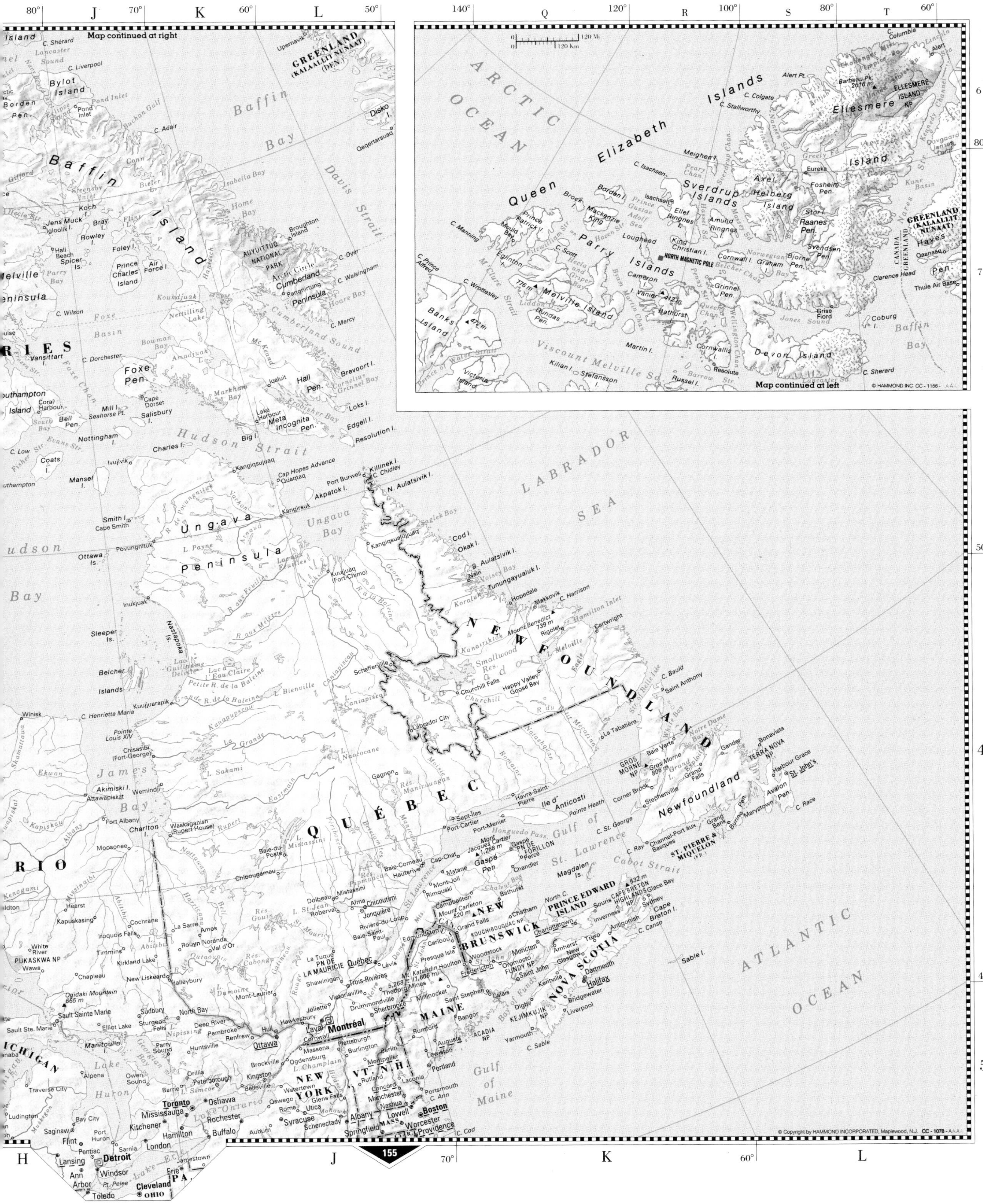

United States

POPULATION OF CITIES AND TOWNS
- ▣ OVER 2,000,000
- ▢ 1,000,000 - 1,999,999
- ● 500,000 - 999,999
- ● 100,000 - 499,999
- ○ 50,000 - 99,999
- ○ UNDER 50,000

SCALE 1:14,000,000   LAMBERT CONFORMAL CONIC PROJECTION

MILES 0   200   400   600
KILOMETERS 0   200   400   600

© Copyright by HAMMOND INCORPORATED, Maplewood, N.J.

CC · 1079 · A·A

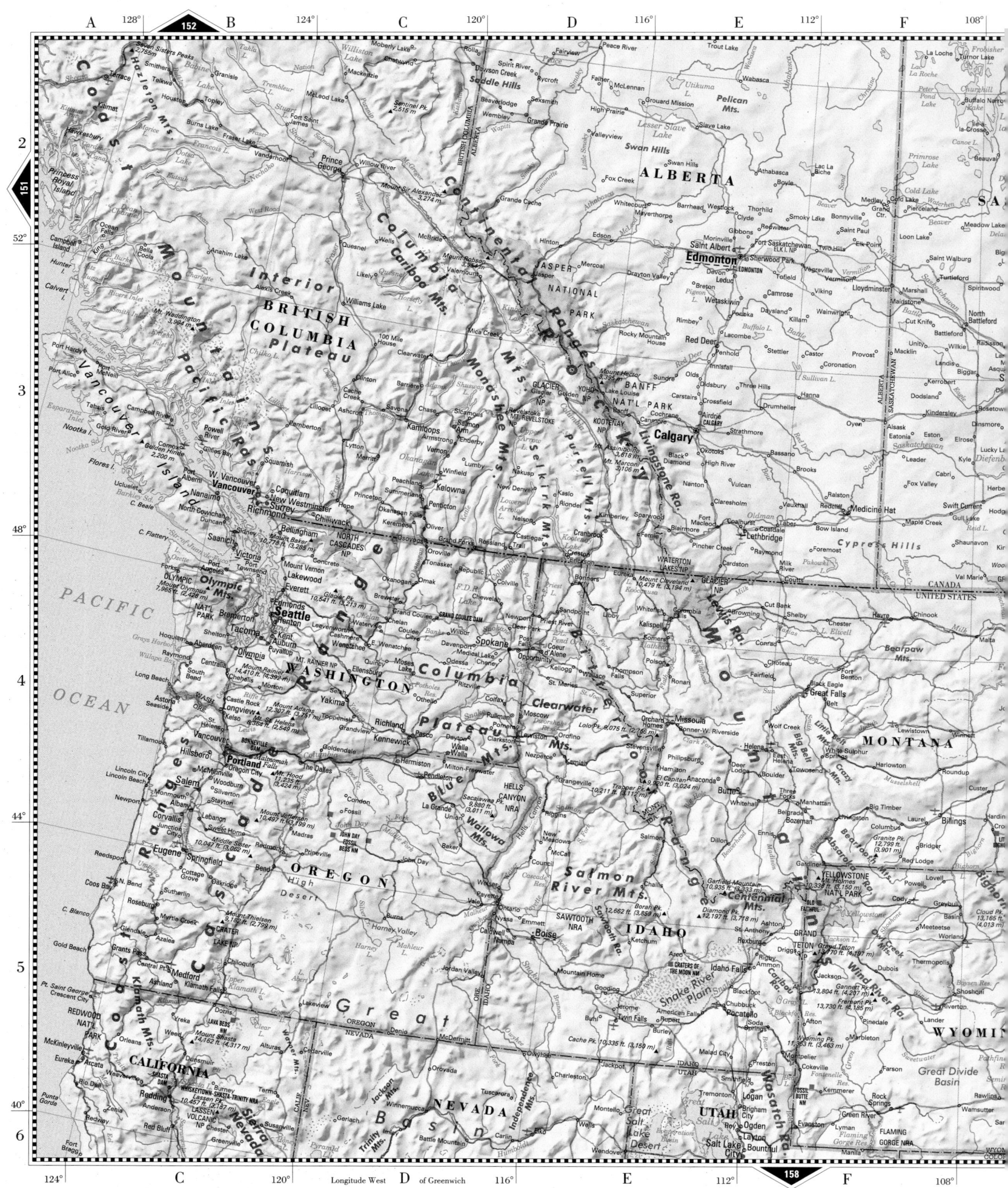

Southwestern Canada, Northwestern United States

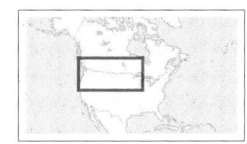

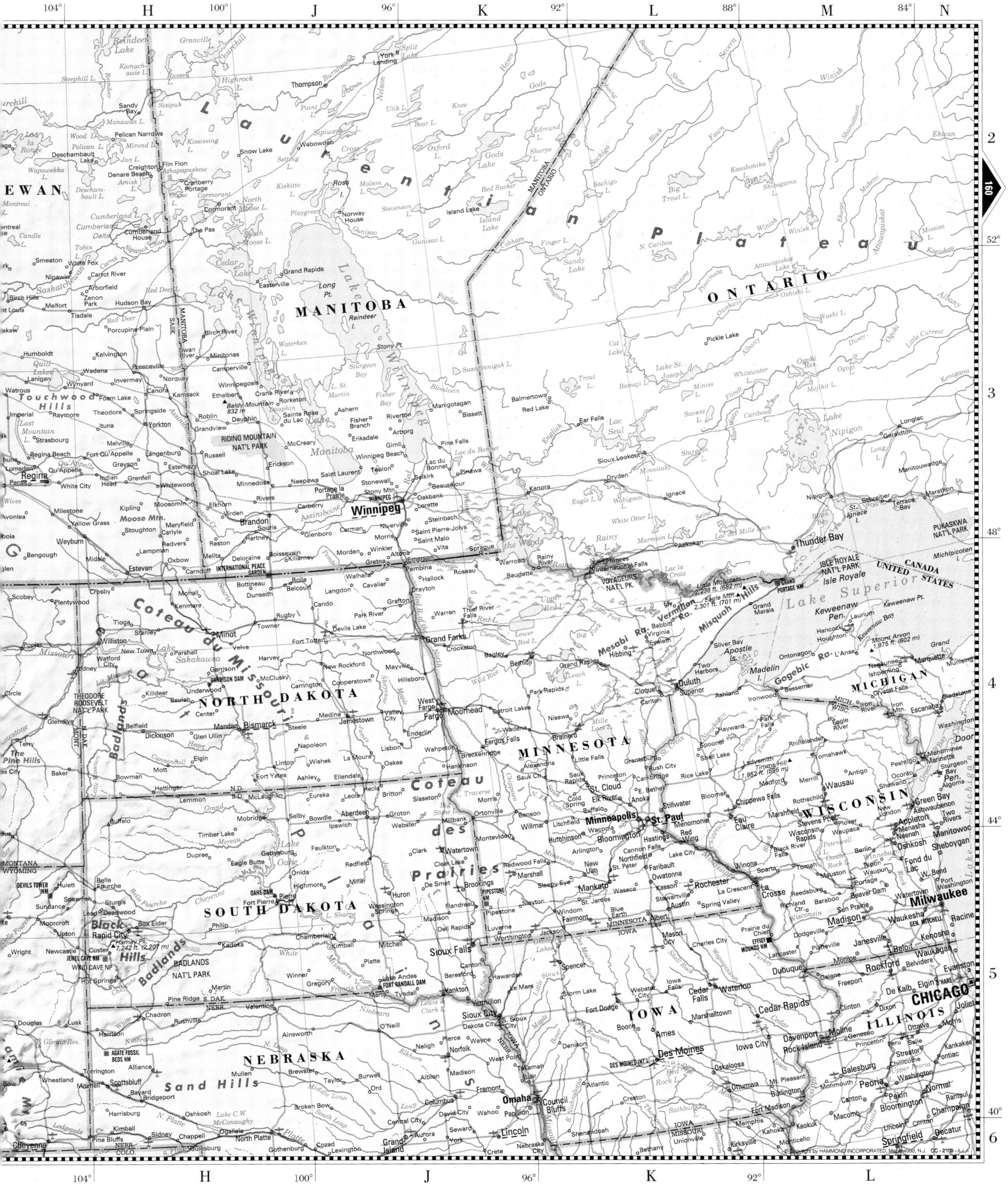

POPULATION OF CITIES AND TOWNS

■ OVER 2,000,000	● 500,000 - 999,999
▣ 1,000,000 - 1,999,999	◉ 250,000 - 499,999
● 100,000 - 249,999	• 10,000 - 29,999
● 30,000 - 99,999	○ UNDER 10,000

SCALE 1:7,000,000   LAMBERT CONFORMAL CONIC PROJECTION

MILES   0   100   200   300

KILOMETERS   0   100   200   300

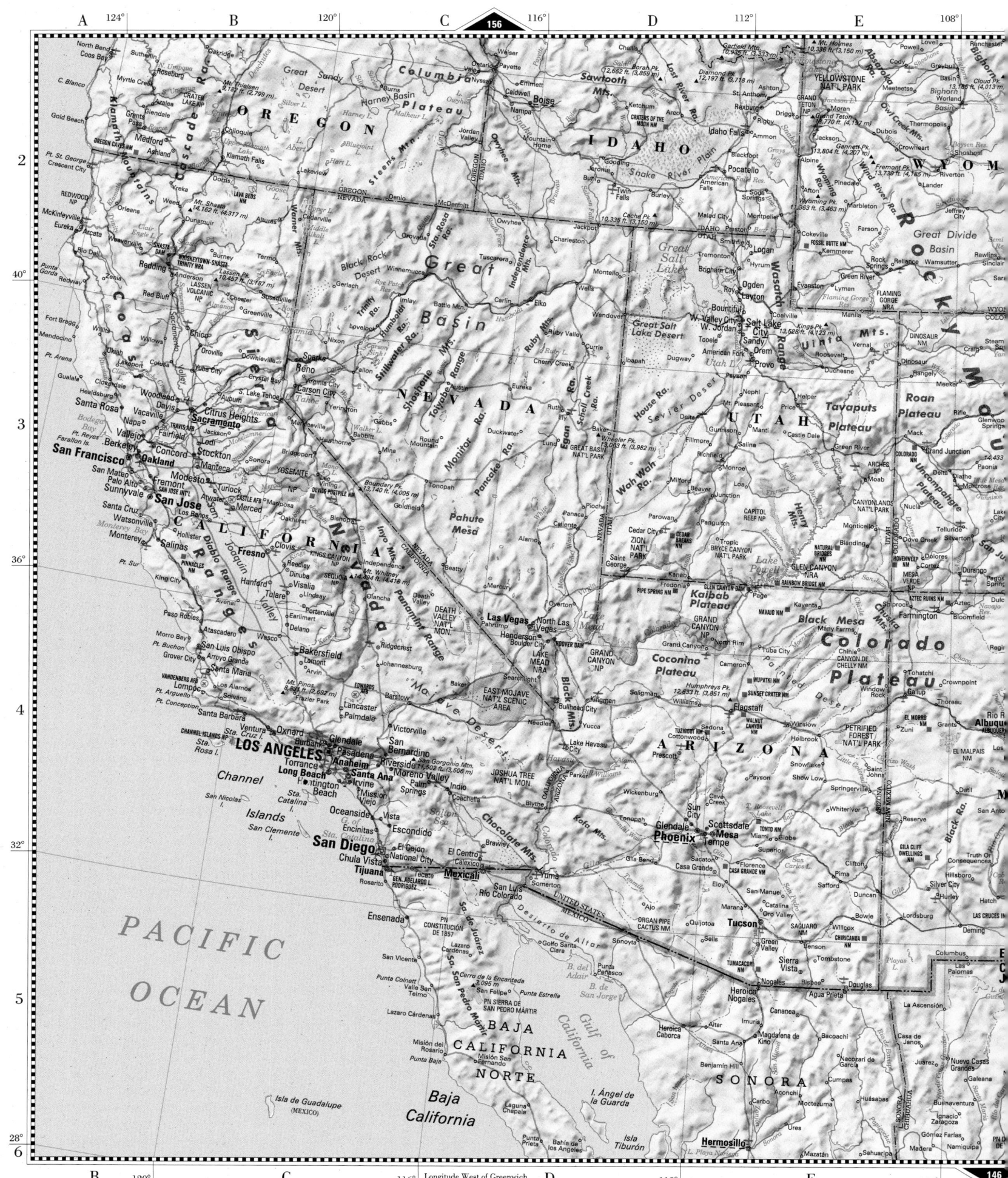

Southwestern United States

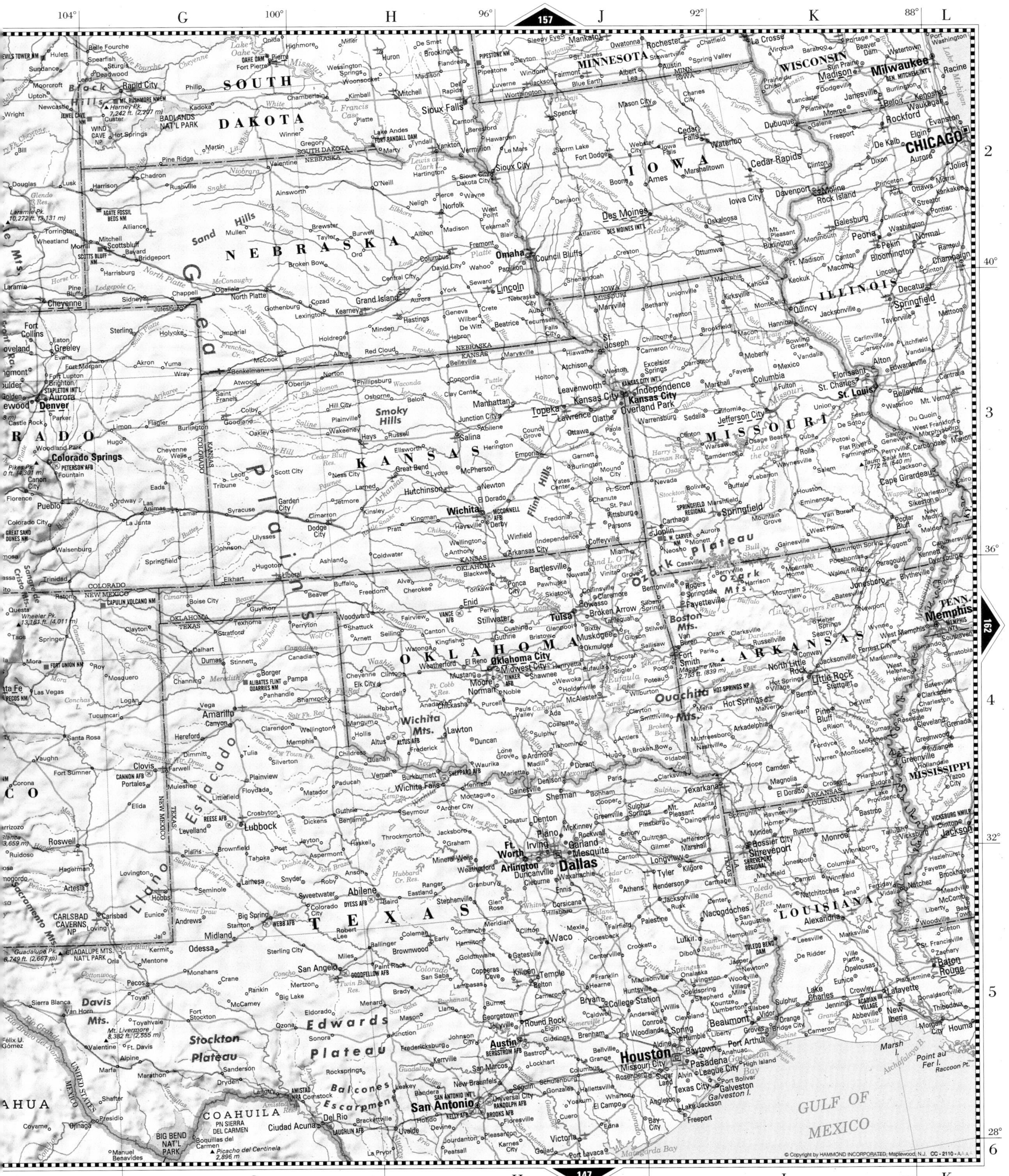

POPULATION OF CITIES AND TOWNS

■ OVER 2,000,000	● 500,000 - 999,999
▣ 1,000,000 - 1,999,999	● 250,000 - 499,999
● 100,000 - 249,999	● 10,000 - 29,999
● 30,000 - 99,999	○ UNDER 10,000

SCALE 1:7,000,000   LAMBERT CONFORMAL CONIC PROJECTION

MILES 0   100   200   300

KILOMETERS 0   100   200   300

© Copyright by HAMMOND INCORPORATED, Maplewood, N.J.   CC - 2110 - A

Southeastern Canada, Northeastern United States

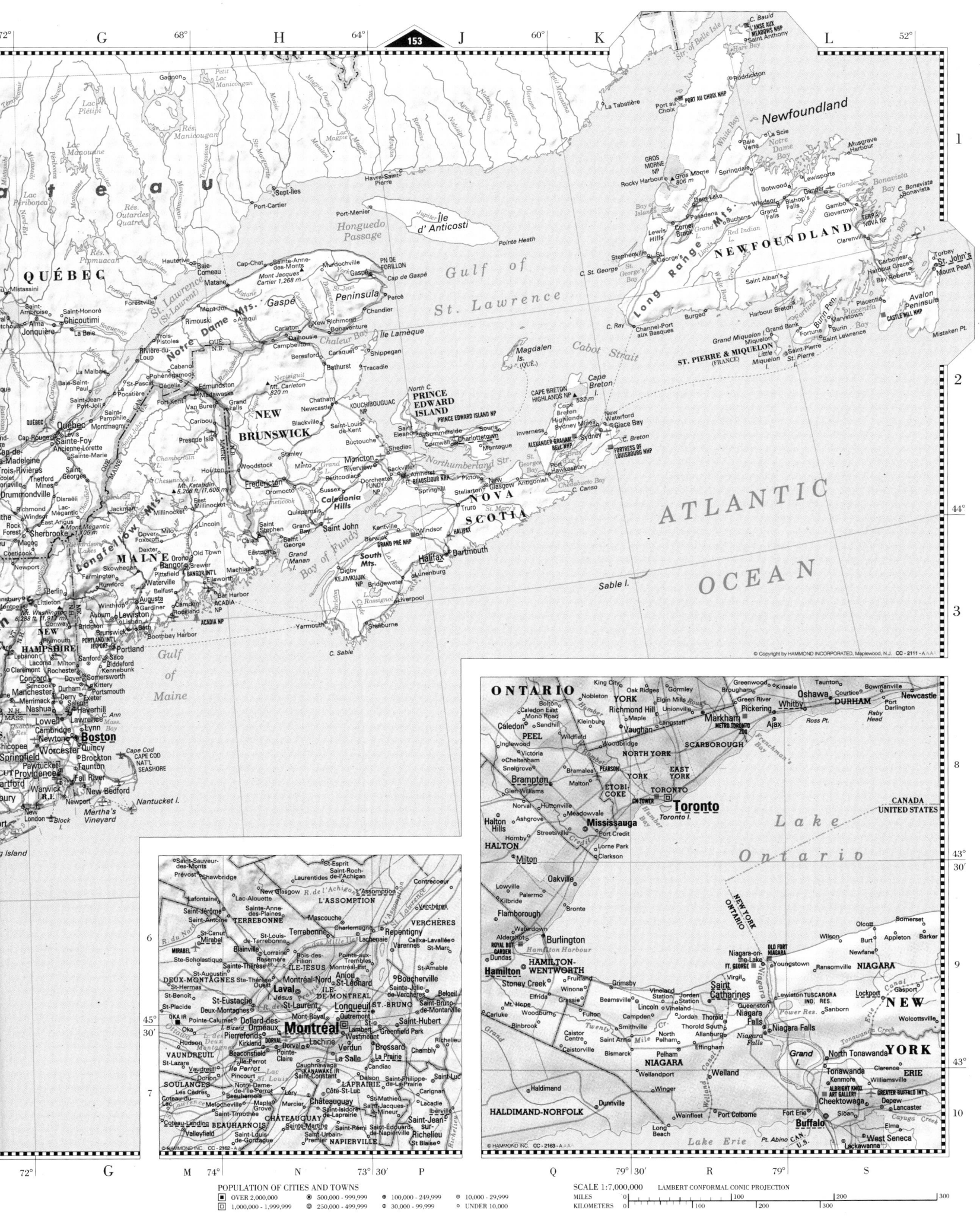

POPULATION OF CITIES AND TOWNS
- ■ OVER 2,000,000
- ▣ 1,000,000 - 1,999,999
- ● 500,000 - 999,999
- ◉ 250,000 - 499,999
- ● 100,000 - 249,999
- ● 30,000 - 99,999
- ● 10,000 - 29,999
- ○ UNDER 10,000

SCALE 1:7,000,000   LAMBERT CONFORMAL CONIC PROJECTION

MILES   0   100   200   300
KILOMETERS   0   100   200   300

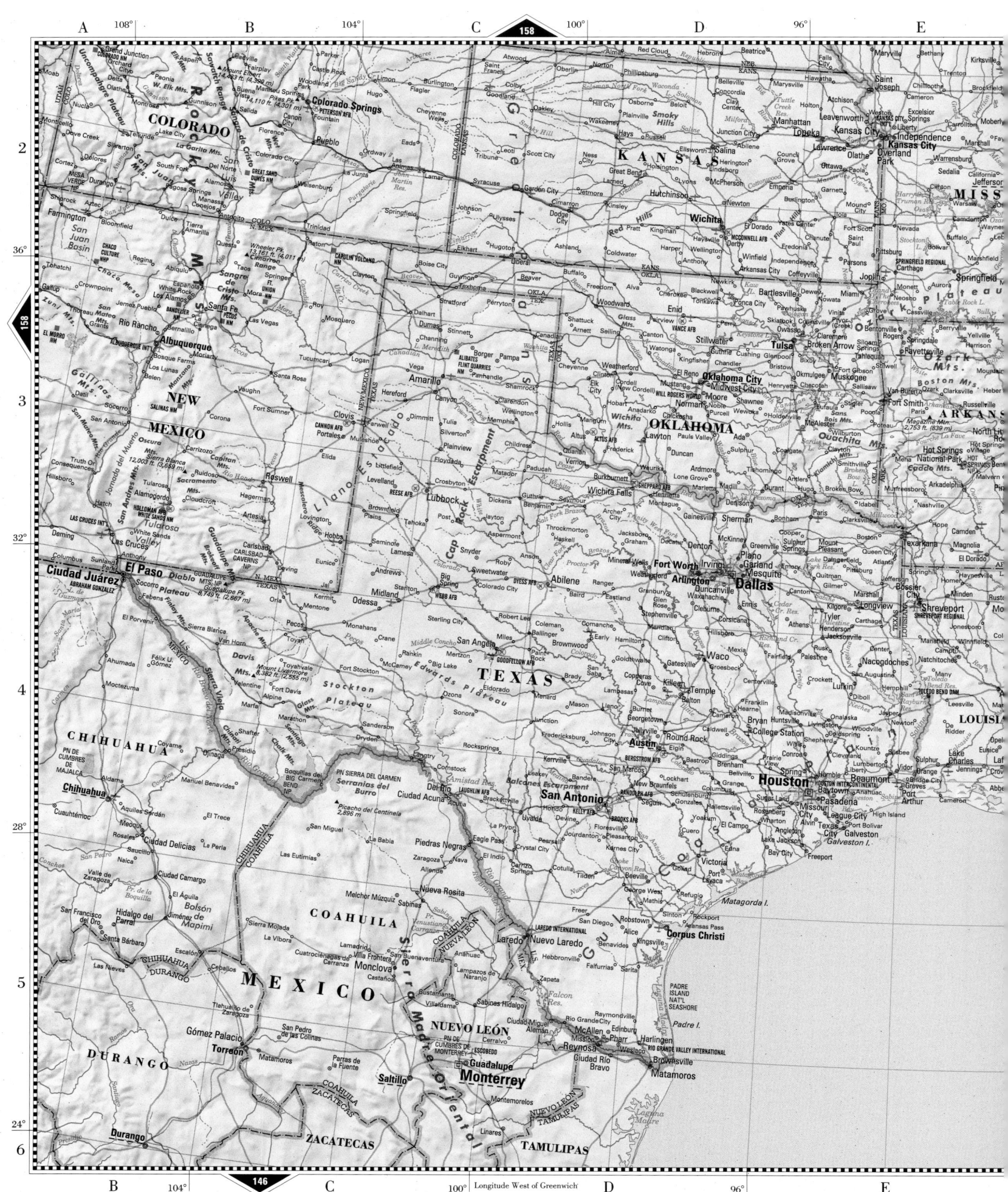

Southeastern United States

POPULATION OF CITIES AND TOWNS

■	OVER 2,000,000
◉	500,000 – 999,999
●	100,000 – 249,999
●	10,000 – 29,999
▣	1,000,000 – 1,999,999
◉	250,000 – 499,999
●	30,000 – 99,999
∘	UNDER 10,000

SCALE 1:7,000,000   LAMBERT CONFORMAL CONIC PROJECTION

MILES 0 — 100 — 200 — 300
KILOMETERS 0 — 100 — 200 — 300

Los Angeles-San Diego

POPULATION OF CITIES AND TOWNS

■ OVER 2,000,000	● 500,000 - 999,999	○ 100,000 - 249,999	● 10,000 - 29,999
□ 1,000,000 - 1,999,999	● 250,000 - 499,999	● 30,000 - 99,999	○ UNDER 10,000

SCALE 1:1,170,000 LAMBERT CONFORMAL CONIC PROJECTION

MILES 0 10 20 30 40 50

KILOMETERS 0 10 20 30 40 50

Longitude West of Greenwich

© Copyright by HAMMOND INCORPORATED, Maplewood, N.J. CC-1091-A·A·A

Seattle, San Francisco, Detroit, Chicago

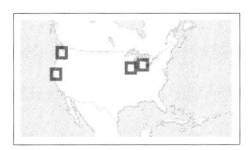

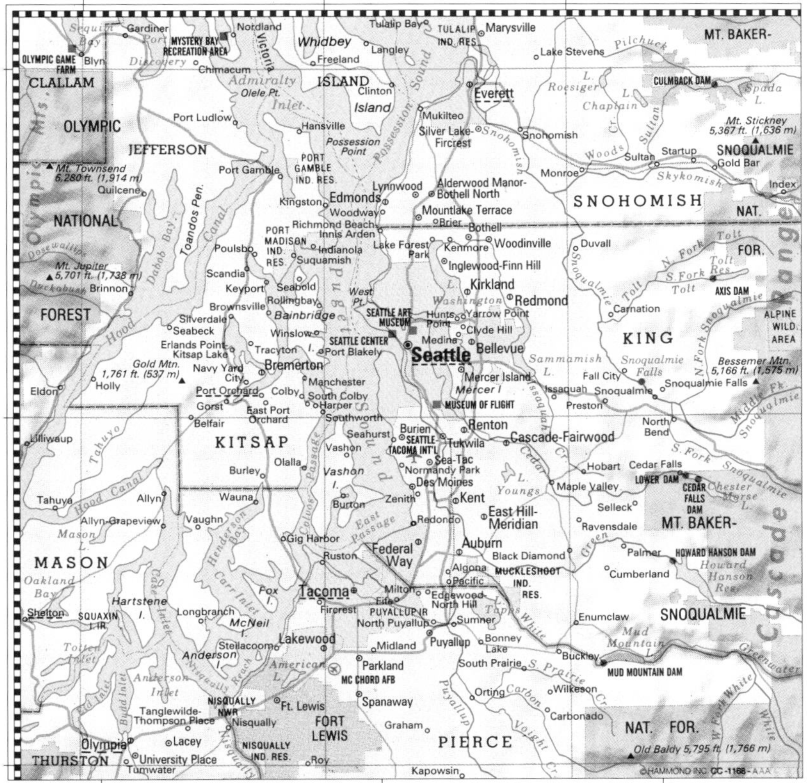

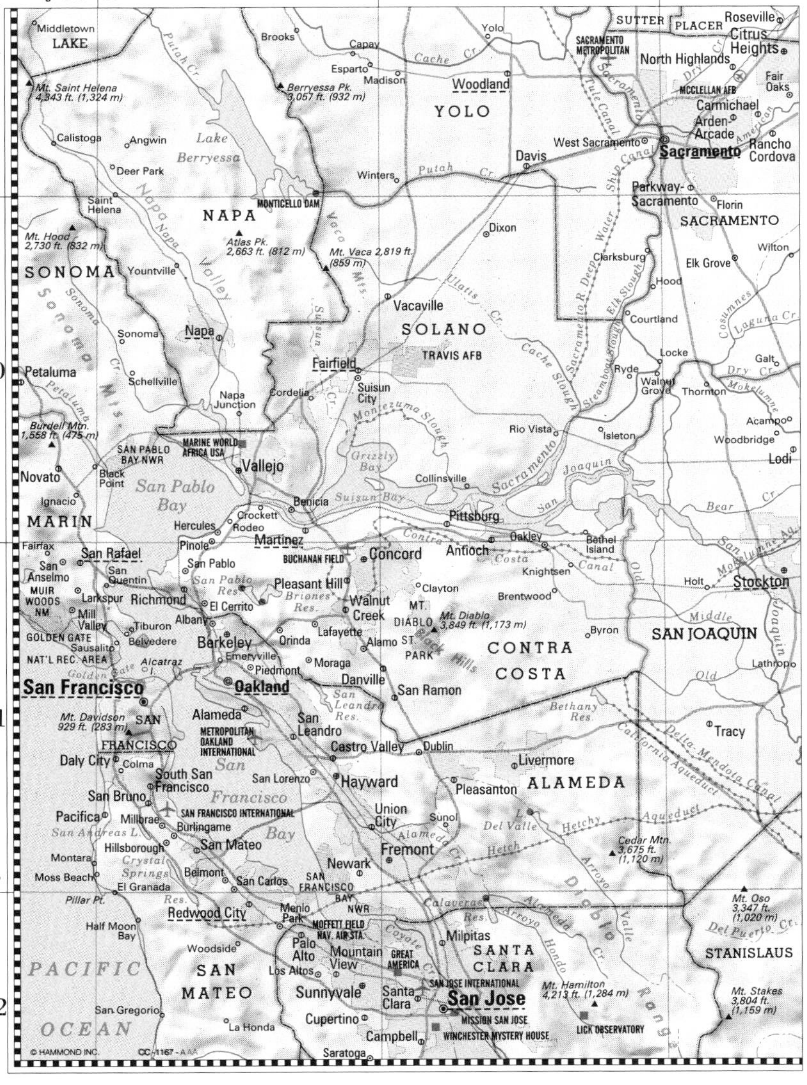

SCALE 1:1,170,000   LAMBERT CONFORMAL CONIC PROJECTION

MILES 0 10 20 30 40 50
KILOMETERS 0 10 20 30 40 50

Longitude West of Greenwich

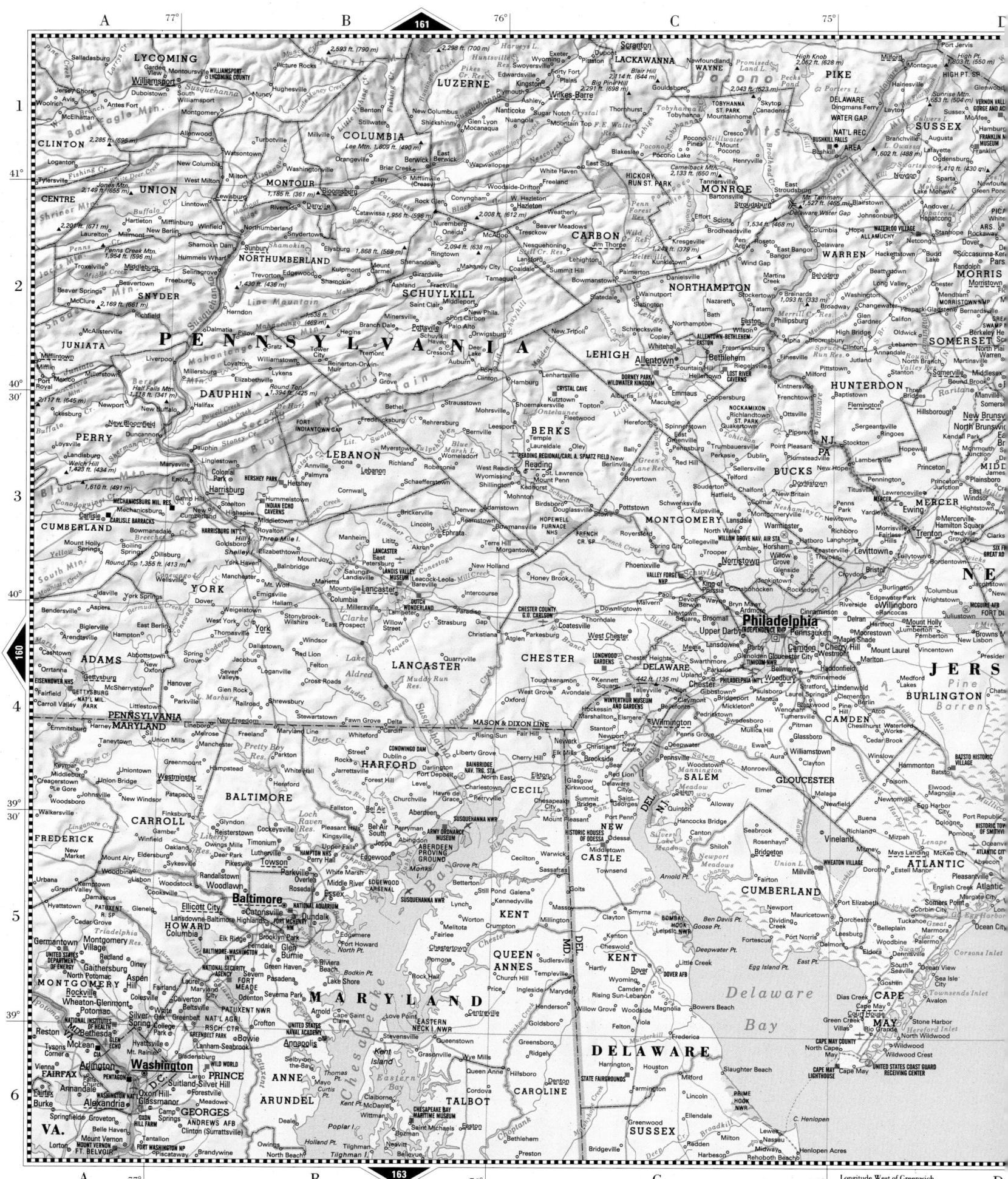

New York–Philadelphia–Washington

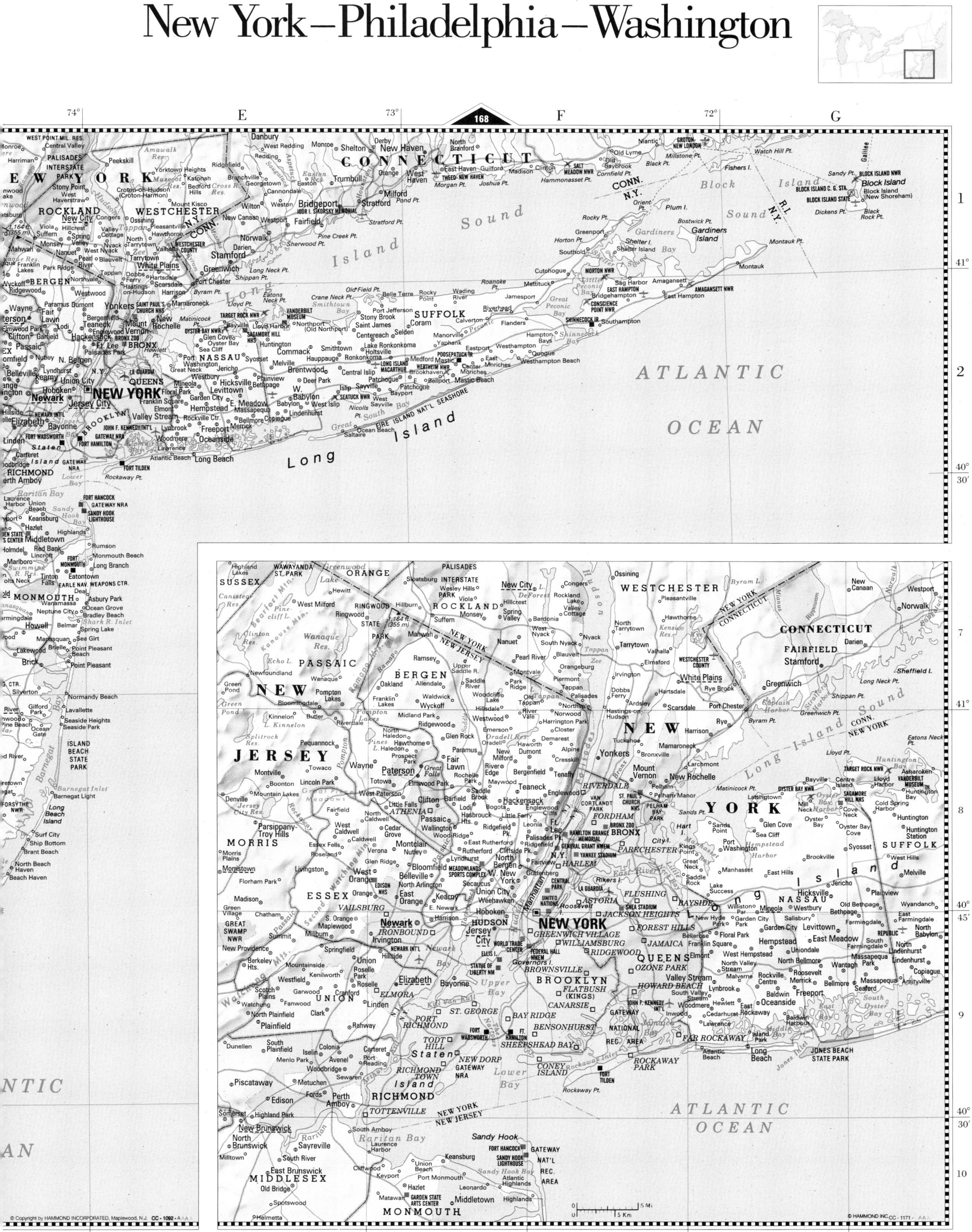

POPULATION OF CITIES AND TOWNS

- ■ OVER 2,000,000
- ▣ 1,000,000 - 1,999,999
- ◉ 500,000 - 999,999
- ◍ 250,000 - 499,999
- ⊕ 100,000 - 249,999
- ⊙ 30,000 - 99,999
- ○ 10,000 - 29,999
- ○ UNDER 10,000

SCALE 1:1,170,000   LAMBERT CONFORMAL CONIC PROJECTION

MILES 0 — 10 — 20 — 30 — 40 — 50
KILOMETERS 0 — 10 — 20 — 30 — 40 — 50

© Copyright by HAMMOND INCORPORATED, Maplewood, N.J.   CC-1092-A
© HAMMOND INC. CC-1171-AA

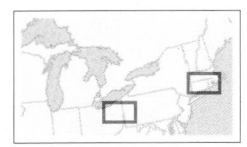

Hartford-Boston, Cleveland-Pittsburgh

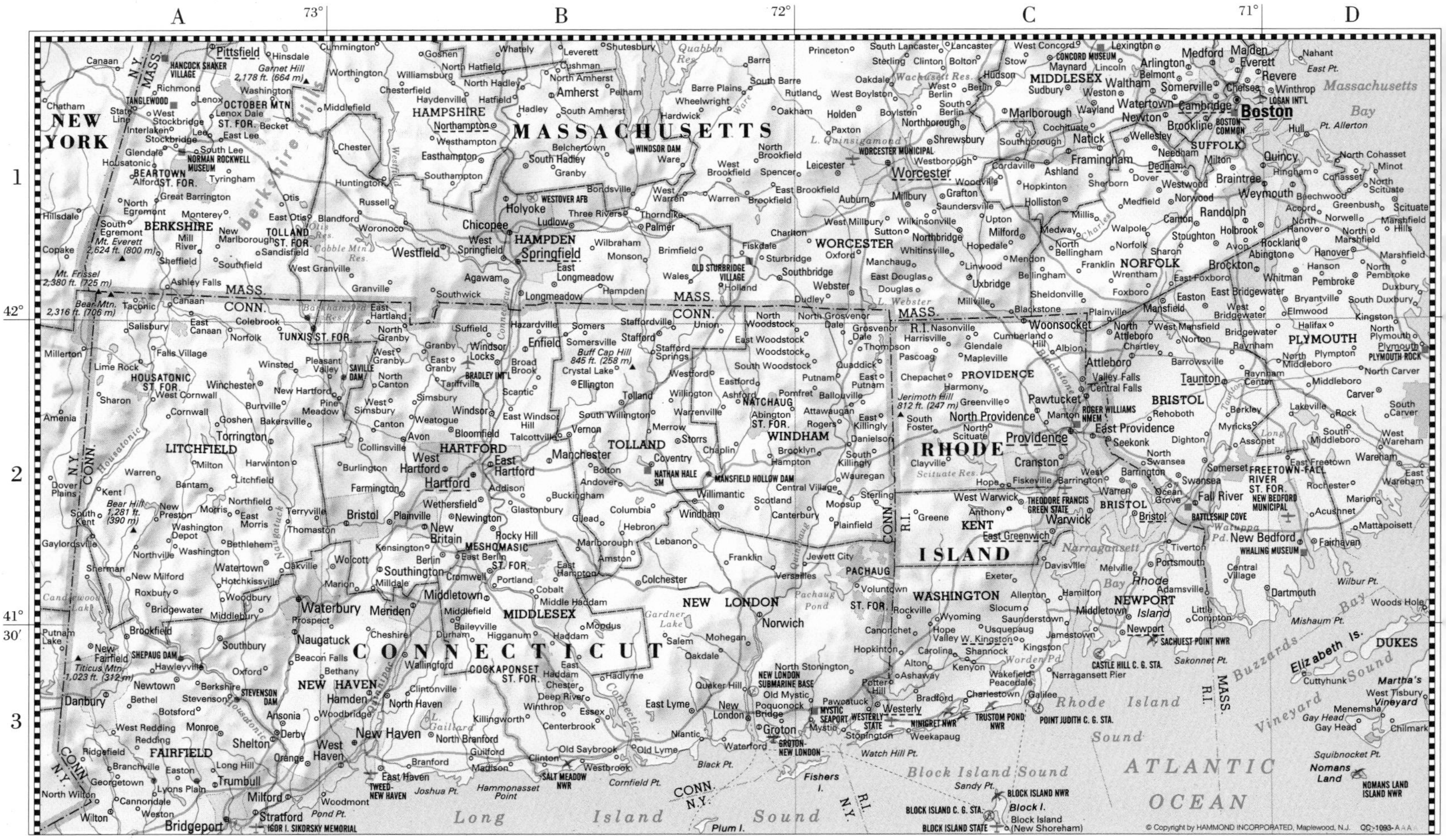

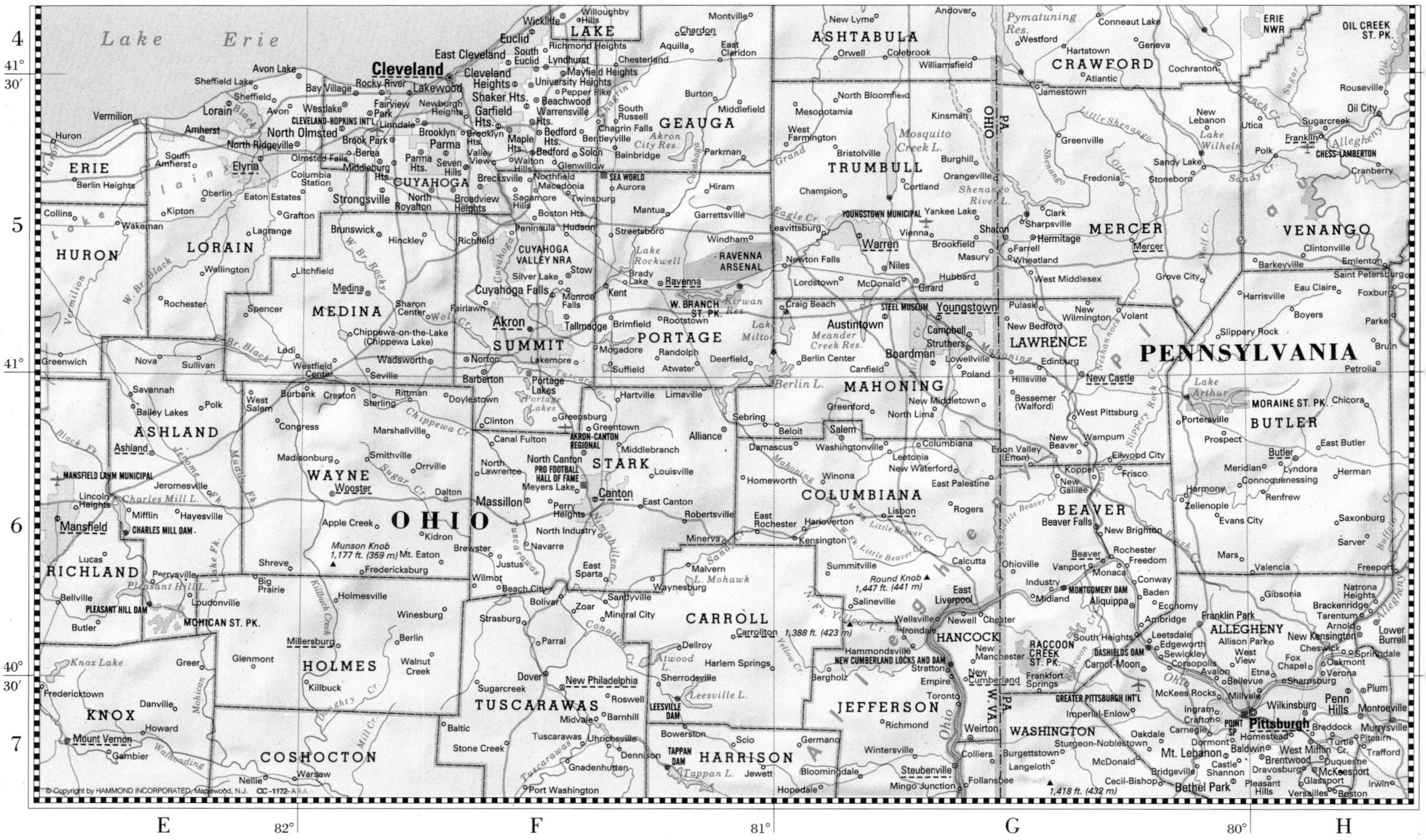

SCALE 1:1,170,000   LAMBERT CONFORMAL CONIC PROJECTION

MILES 0 10 20 30 40 50

KILOMETERS 0 10 20 30 40 50

POPULATION OF CITIES AND TOWNS

■ OVER 2,000,000	◉ 500,000 - 999,999 ⬤ 100,000 - 249,999 ● 10,000 - 29,999
▣ 1,000,000 - 1,999,999	◎ 250,000 - 499,999 ⊙ 30,000 - 99,999 ○ UNDER 10,000

© Copyright by HAMMOND INCORPORATED, Maplewood, N.J. QC-1093-AAA

© Copyright by HAMMOND INCORPORATED, Maplewood, N.J. CC-1172-AAA

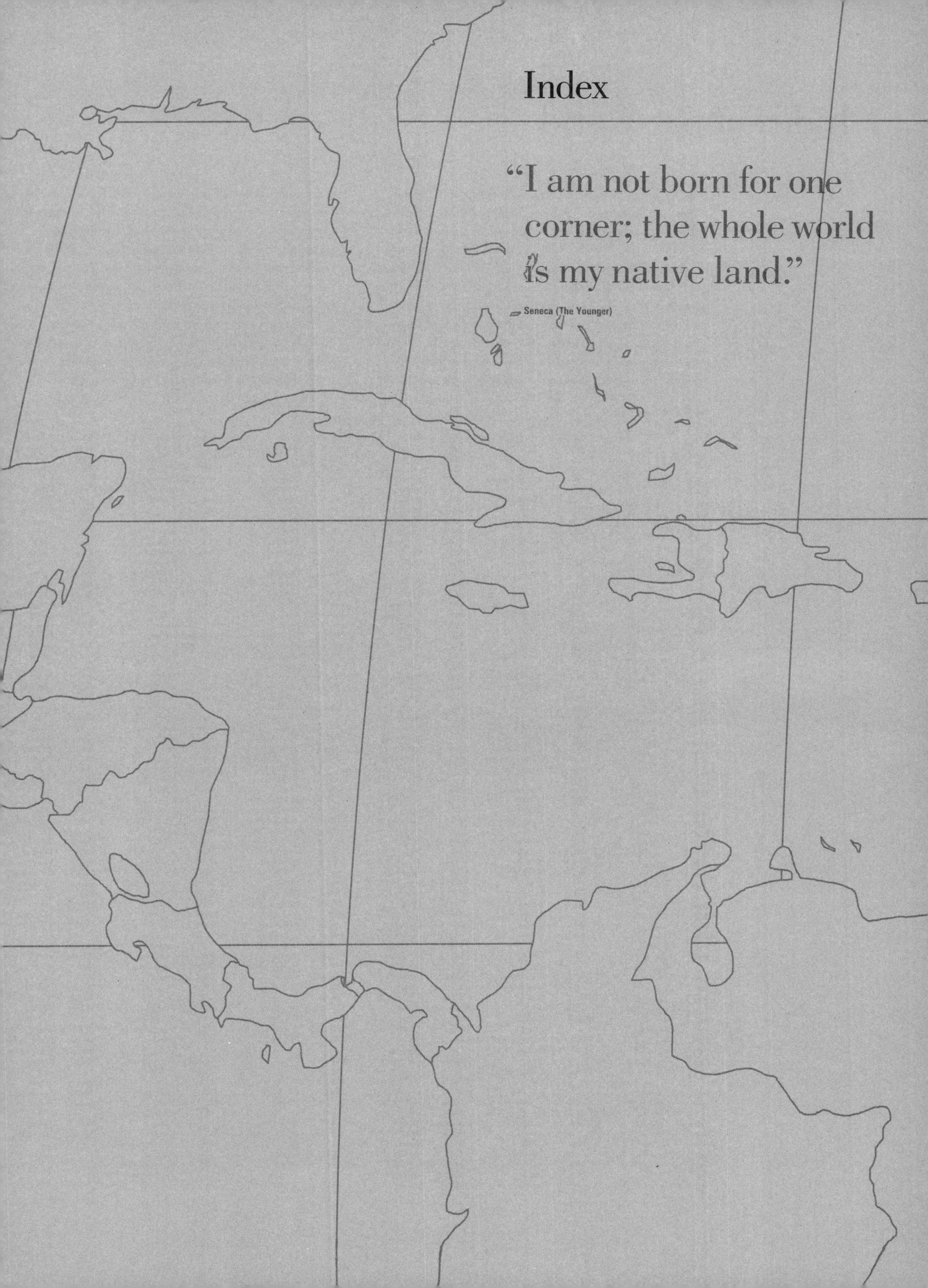

Index

"I am not born for one corner; the whole world is my native land."

— Seneca (The Younger)

Index of the World

This index is a comprehensive listing of the places and geographic features found in the atlas. Names are arranged in strict alphabetical order, without regard to hyphens or spaces. Every name is followed by the country or area to which it belongs. Except for cities, towns, countries and cultural areas, all entries include a reference to feature type, such as province, river, island, peak, and so on. The page number and alpha-numeric code appear in blue to the left of each listing. The page number directs you to the largest scale map on which the name can be found. The code refers to the grid squares formed by the horizontal and vertical lines of latitude and longitude on each map. Following the letters from left to right and the numbers from top to bottom helps you to locate quickly the square containing the place or feature. Inset maps have their own alpha-numeric codes. Names that are accompanied by a point symbol are indexed to the symbol's location on the map. Other names are indexed to the initial letter of the name. When a map name contains a subordinate or alternate name, both names are listed in the index. To conserve space and provide room for more entries, many abbreviations are used in this index. The primary abbreviations are listed below.

Index Abbreviations

Abbrev.	Meaning	Abbrev.	Meaning
A Ab,Can	Alberta	Cap. Terr.	Capital Territory
Acad.	Academy	Cay.	Cayman Islands
ACT	Australian Capital Territory	C.G.	Coast Guard
A.F.B.	Air Force Base	Chan.	Channel
Afld.	Airfield	Chl.	Channel Islands
Afg.	Afghanistan	Co.	County
Afr.	Africa	Co,US	Colorado
Ak,US	Alaska	Col.	Colombia
Al,US	Alabama	Com.	Comoros
Alb.	Albania	Cont.	Continent
Alg.	Algeria	CpV.	Cape Verde Islands
Amm. Dep.	Ammunition Depot	CR	Costa Rica
And.	Andorra	Cr.	Creek
Ang.	Angola	Cro.	Croatia
Angu.	Anguilla	CSea.	Coral Sea Islands Territory
Ant.	Antarctica	Ct,US	Connecticut
Anti.	Antigua and Barbuda	Ctr.	Center
Ar,US	Arkansas	Ctry.	Country
Arch.	Archipelago	Cyp.	Cyprus
Arg.	Argentina	Czh.	Czech Republic
Arm.	Armenia	**D** DC,US	District of Columbia
Arpt.	Airport	De,US	Delaware
Aru.	Aruba	Den.	Denmark
ASam.	American Samoa	Depr.	Depression
Ash.	Ashmore and Cartier Islands	Dept.	Department
Aus.	Austria	Des.	Desert
Austl.	Australia	DF	Distrito Federal
Aut.	Autonomous	Dist.	District
Az,US	Arizona	Djib.	Djibouti
Azer.	Azerbaijan	Dom.	Dominica
Azor.	Azores	Dpcy.	Dependency
B Bahm.	Bahamas	DRep.	Dominican Republic
Bahr.	Bahrain	**E** Ecu.	Ecuador
Bang.	Bangladesh	Emb.	Embankment
Bar.	Barbados	Eng.	Engineering
BC,Can	British Columbia	Eng,UK	England
Bela.	Belarus	EqG.	Equatorial Guinea
Belg.	Belgium	Erit..	Eritrea
Belz.	Belize	ESal.	El Salvador
Ben.	Benin	Est.	Estonia
Berm.	Bermuda	Eth.	Ethiopia
Bfld.	Battlefield	Eur.	Europe
Bhu.	Bhutan	**F** Falk.	Falkland Islands
Bol.	Bolivia	Far.	Faroe Islands
Bor.	Borough	Fed. Dist.	Federal District
Bosn.	Bosnia and Hercegovina	Fin.	Finland
Bots.	Botswana	Fl,US	Florida
Braz.	Brazil	For.	Forest
Brln.	British Indian Ocean Territory	Fr.	France
Bru.	Brunei	FrAnt.	French Southern and Antarctic Lands
Bul.	Bulgaria	FrG.	French Guiana
Burk.	Burkina	FrPol.	French Polynesia
Buru.	Burundi	**G** Ga,US	Georgia
BVI	British Virgin Islands	Galp.	Galapagos Islands
C Ca,US	California	Gam.	Gambia
CAfr.	Central African Republic	Gaza	Gaza Strip
Camb.	Cambodia	GBis.	Guinea-Bissau
Camr.	Cameroon	Geo.	Georgia
Can.	Canada	Ger.	Germany
Can.	Canal		
Canl.	Canary Islands		
Cap.	Capital		
Cap. Dist.	Capital District		

Abbrev.	Meaning	Abbrev.	Meaning
Gha.	Ghana	Me,US	Maine
Gib.	Gibraltar	Mem.	Memorial
Glac.	Glacier	Mex.	Mexico
Gov.	Governorate	Mi,US	Michigan
Govt.	Government	Micr.	Micronesia, Federated States of
Gre.	Greece	Mil.	Military
Grld.	Greenland	Mn,US	Minnesota
Gren.	Grenada	Mo,US	Missouri
Grsld.	Grassland	Mol.	Moldova
Guad.	Guadeloupe	Mon.	Monument
Guat.	Guatemala	Mona.	Monaco
Gui.	Guinea	Mong.	Mongolia
Guy.	Guyana	Monts.	Montserrat
H Har.	Harbor	Mor.	Morocco
Hi,US	Hawaii	Moz.	Mozambique
Hist.	Historic(al)	Mrsh.	Marshall Islands
HK	Hong Kong	Mrta.	Mauritania
Hon.	Honduras	Mrts.	Mauritius
Hts.	Heights	Ms,US	Mississippi
Hun.	Hungary	Mt.	Mount
I Ia,US	Iowa	Mt,US	Montana
Ice.	Iceland	Mtn., Mts.	Mountain, Mountains
Id,US	Idaho	Mun. Arpt.	Municipal Airport
Il,US	Illinois	**N** NAm.	North America
IM	Isle of Man	Namb.	Namibia
In,US	Indiana	NAnt.	Netherlands Antilles
Ind. Res.	Indian Reservation	Nat'l	National
Indo.	Indonesia	Nav.	Naval
Int'l	International	NB,Can	New Brunswick
Ire.	Ireland	Nbrhd.	Neighborhood
Isl., Isls.	Island, Islands	NC,US	North Carolina
Isr.	Israel	NCal.	New Caledonia
Isth.	Isthmus	ND,US	North Dakota
It.	Italy	Ne,US	Nebraska
IvC.	Côte d'Ivoire	Neth.	Netherlands
J Jam.	Jamaica	Nf,Can	Newfoundland
Jor.	Jordan	Nga.	Nigeria
K Kaz.	Kazakhstan	NH,US	New Hampshire
Kiri.	Kiribati	NI,UK	Northern Ireland
Ks,US	Kansas	Nic.	Nicaragua
Kuw.	Kuwait	NJ,US	New Jersey
Ky,US	Kentucky	NKor.	North Korea
Kyr.	Kyrgyzstan	NM,US	New Mexico
L La,US	Louisiana	NMar.	Northern Mariana Islands
Lab.	Laboratory	Nor.	Norway
Lag.	Lagoon	NS,Can	Nova Scotia
Lakesh.	Lakeshore	Nv,US	Nevada
Lat.	Latvia	NW,Can	Northwest Territories
Lcht.	Liechtenstein	NY,US	New York
Ldg.	Landing	NZ	New Zealand
Leb.	Lebanon	**O** Obl.	Oblast
Les.	Lesotho	Oh,US	Ohio
Libr.	Liberia	Ok,US	Oklahoma
Lith.	Lithuania	On,Can	Ontario
Lux.	Luxembourg	Or,US	Oregon
M Ma,US	Massachusetts	**P** Pa,US	Pennsylvania
Macd.	Macedonia	PacUS	Pacific Islands, U.S.
Madg.	Madagascar	Pak.	Pakistan
Madr.	Madeira	Pan.	Panama
Malay.	Malaysia	Par.	Paraguay
Mald.	Maldives	Par.	Parish
Malw.	Malawi		
Mart.	Martinique		
May.	Mayotte		
Mb,Can	Manitoba		
Md,US	Maryland		

Abbrev.	Meaning	Abbrev.	Meaning
PE,Can	Prince Edward Island	Sval.	Svalbard
Pen.	Peninsula	Swaz.	Swaziland
Phil.	Philippines	Swe.	Sweden
Phys. Reg.	Physical Region	Swi.	Switzerland
Pitc.	Pitcairn Islands	**T** Tah.	Tahiti
Plat.	Plateau	Tai.	Taiwan
PNG	Papua New Guinea	Taj.	Tajikistan
Pol.	Poland	Tanz.	Tanzania
Port.	Portugal	Ter.	Terrace
Poss.	Possession	Terr.	Territory
Pkwy.	Parkway	Thai.	Thailand
PR	Puerto Rico	Tn,US	Tennessee
Pref.	Prefecture	Tok.	Tokelau
Prov.	Province	Trg.	Training
Prsv.	Preserve	Trin.	Trinidad and Tobago
Pt.	Point	Trkm.	Turkmenistan
Q Qu,Can	Quebec	Trks.	Turks and Caicos Islands
R Rec.	Recreation(al)	Tun.	Tunisia
Ref.	Refuge	Tun.	Tunnel
Reg.	Region	Turk.	Turkey
Rep.	Republic	Tuv.	Tuvalu
Res.	Reservoir, Reservation	Twp.	Township
Reun.	Réunion	Tx,US	Texas
RI,US	Rhode Island	**U** UAE	United Arab Emirates
Riv.	River	Ugan.	Uganda
Rom.	Romania	UK	United Kingdom
Rsv.	Reserve	Ukr.	Ukraine
Rus.	Russia	Uru.	Uruguay
Rvwy.	Riverway	US	United States
Rwa.	Rwanda	USVI	U.S. Virgin Islands
S SAfr.	South Africa	Ut,US	Utah
SAm.	South America	Uzb.	Uzbekistan
SaoT.	São Tomé and Príncipe	**V** Va,US	Virginia
SAr.	Saudi Arabia	Val.	Valley
Sc,UK	Scotland	Van.	Vanuatu
SC,US	South Carolina	VatC.	Vatican City
SD,US	South Dakota	Ven.	Venezuela
Seash.	Seashore	Viet.	Vietnam
Sen.	Senegal	Vill.	Village
Sey.	Seychelles	Vol.	Volcano
SGeo.	South Georgia and Sandwich Islands	Vt,US	Vermont
Sing.	Singapore	**W** Wa,US	Washington
Sk,Can	Saskatchewan	Wal,UK	Wales
SKor.	South Korea	Wall.	Wallis and Futuna
SLeo.	Sierra Leone	WBnk.	West Bank
Slov.	Slovenia	Wi,US	Wisconsin
Slvk.	Slovakia	Wild.	Wildlife, Wilderness
SMar.	San Marino	WSah.	Western Sahara
Sol.	Solomon Islands	WSam.	Western Samoa
Som.	Somalia	WV,US	West Virginia
Sp.	Spain	Wy,US	Wyoming
Spr., Sprs.	Spring, Springs	**Y** Yem.	Yemen
SrL.	Sri Lanka	Yk,Can	Yukon Territory
Sta.	Station	Yugo.	Yugoslavia
StH.	Saint Helena	**Z** Zam.	Zambia
Str.	Strait	Zim.	Zimbabwe
StK.	Saint Kitts and Nevis		
StL.	Saint Lucia		
StP.	Saint Pierre and Miquelon		
StV.	Saint Vincent and the Grenadines		
Sur.	Suriname		

170/171
Aa – Ale W

A

68/B2 Aa (riv.), Fr.
66/D5 Aa (riv.), Ger.
67/G5 Aa (riv.), Ger.
77/E3 Aabach (riv.), Swi.
77/F2 Aach (riv.), Ger.
69/F2 Aachen, Ger.
70/C3 Aalbach (riv.), Ger.
66/C5 Aalburg, Neth.
70/D5 Aalen, Ger.
66/B4 Aalsmeer, Neth.
68/D2 Aalst, Belg.
66/D5 Aalten, Neth.
68/C1 Aalter, Belg.
70/B2 Aar (riv.), Ger.
76/E3 Aarau, Swi.
76/D3 Aare (riv.), Swi.
76/E3 Aargau (canton), Swi.
69/D2 Aarschot, Belg.
68/D1 Aartselaar, Belg.
96/E5 Aba, China
129/G5 Aba, Nga.
130/A2 Aba, Zaire
94/D5 Abā as Su'ūd, SAr.
136/G5 Abacaxis (riv.), Braz.
127/C5 Abadab, Jabal (peak), Sudan
93/G4 Ābādān, Iran
93/H4 Ābādeh, Iran
141/C1 Abadia dos Dourados, Braz.
82/E2 Abádszalók, Hun.
141/C1 Abaeté, Braz.
137/J4 Abaetetuba, Braz.
120/G4 Abaiang (atoll), Kiri.
154/D4 Abajo (mts.), Ut,US
88/K4 Abakan, Rus.
144/C4 Abancay, Peru
79/E2 Abano Terme, It.
96/G3 Abaq Qi, China
74/E3 Abarán, Sp.
121/H5 Abariringa (Canton) (atoll), Kiri.
93/H4 Abar Kūh, Iran
100/D1 Abashiri, Japan
100/C2 Abashiri (lake), Japan
147/E4 Abasolo, Mex.
88/H5 Abay, Kaz.
125/N6 Ābaya Hayk' (lake), Eth.
102/F1 Abaza, Rus.
80/B1 Abbadia San Salvatore, It.
60/B3 Abbert (riv.), Ire.
68/A3 Abbeville, Fr.
162/E4 Abbeville, La,US
163/H3 Abbeville, SC,US
56/E2 Abbey Head (pt.), Sc,UK
78/B2 Abbiategrasso, It.
113/T Abbot Ice Shelf, Ant.
57/G6 Abbots Bromley, Eng,UK
58/D5 Abbotsbury, Eng,UK
53/M6 Abbots Langley, Eng,UK
95/K2 Abbottābād, Pak.
66/B4 Abcoude, Neth.
92/D2 'Abd al 'Azīz, Jabal (mts.), Syria
108/B2 Abdul Hakīm, Pak.
87/K1 Abdulino, Rus.
125/K5 Abéché, Chad
133/E2 Abel Erasmuspas (pass), SAfr.
120/G4 Abemama (atoll), Kiri.
128/E5 Abengourou, IvC.
62/C4 Åbenrå, Den.
71/E5 Abens (riv.), Ger.
71/E5 Abensberg, Ger.
129/F5 Abeokuta, Nga.
56/D5 Aber, Wal,UK
58/B2 Aberaeron, Wal,UK
58/C1 Aberangell, Wal,UK
58/B2 Aberath, Wal,UK
58/B3 Abercarn, Wal,UK
54/D1 Aberchirder, Sc,UK
58/C3 Aberdare, Wal,UK
130/C3 Aberdare Nat'l Park, Kenya
56/D6 Aberdaron, Wal,UK
152/G2 Aberdeen (lake), NW,Can
54/D2 Aberdeen, Sc,UK
166/B4 Aberdeen, Md,US
163/F3 Aberdeen, Ms,US
157/J4 Aberdeen, SD,US
156/C4 Aberdeen, Wa,US
166/B5 Aberdeen Prov. Gnd. (mil. res.), Md,US
54/C4 Aberdour, Sc,UK
54/D1 Aberdour (bay), Sc,UK
58/B1 Aberdyfi, Wal,UK
54/C3 Aberfeldy, Sc,UK
54/B4 Aberfoyle, Sc,UK
58/C3 Abergavenny, Wal,UK
56/E5 Abergele, Wal,UK
54/D5 Aberlady, Sc,UK
54/D2 Aberlour, Sc,UK
54/C4 Abernethy, Sc,UK
58/B2 Aberporth, Wal,UK
56/D6 Abersoch, Wal,UK
58/C3 Abersychan, Wal,UK
158/B2 Abert (lake), Or,US
58/C3 Abertillery, Wal,UK
58/B2 Aberystwyth, Wal,UK
94/D5 Abhā, SAr.
93/G2 Abhar, Iran
125/P5 Abhe Bad (lake), Djib., Eth.
149/G4 Abide, Serraníade (range), Col.
128/D5 Abidjan, IvC.
99/J7 Abiko, Japan
159/H3 Abilene, Ks,US
162/D3 Abilene, Tx,US
59/E3 Abingdon, Eng,UK
160/D4 Abingdon, Va,US
54/C6 Abington, Sc,UK
168/D1 Abington, Ma,US
161/R10 Abino (pt.), On,Can
159/F3 Abiquiu, NM,US
160/E1 Abitibi (lake), On,Can
160/D1 Abitibi (riv.), On,Can
87/G4 Abkhaz Aut. Rep., Geo.
70/C6 Ablach (riv.), Ger.
127/B3 Abnūb, Egypt
108/C2 Abohar, India
128/E5 Aboisso, IvC.
129/F5 Abomey, Ben.
82/E2 Abony, Hun.
112/B3 Aborlan, Phil.
112/B3 Aborlan (mtn.), Phil.
63/K1 Åbo (Turku), Fin.
54/D2 Aboyne, Sc,UK
112/C1 Abra (riv.), Phil.
160/C4 Abraham Lincoln Birthplace Nat'l Hist. Site, Ky,US
150/C2 Abraham's Bay, Bahm.
74/A3 Abrantes, Port.
135/C1 Abra Pampa, Arg.
146/B3 Abreojos, Punta (pt.), Mex.
127/B4 'Abrī, Sudan
53/P7 Abridge, Eng,UK
82/F2 Abrud, Rom.
80/C1 Abruzzi (reg.), It.
80/C2 Abruzzo Nat'l Park, It.
156/F4 Absaroka (range), Mt, Wy,US
166/D5 Absecon, NJ,US
70/D5 Abtsgmünd, Ger.
94/F4 Abū al Abyaḑ (isl.), UAE
93/G5 Abū 'Alī (isl.), SAr.
95/F4 Abu Dhabi (Abū Ẓaby) (cap.), UAE
127/C5 Abū Dīs, Sudan
127/B4 Abu el-Husein, Bîr (well), Egypt
127/C5 Abū Ḩamad, Sudan
91/B4 Abū Ḩammād, Egypt
127/C4 Abu Hashim, Bi'r (well), Egypt
91/B4 Abū Ḩummuş, Egypt
129/G4 Abuja (cap.), Nga.
129/G4 Abuja Cap. Terr., Nga.
91/B4 Abū Kabīr, Egypt
92/E3 Abū Kamāl, Syria
99/G2 Abukuma (hills), Japan
99/G2 Abukuma (riv.), Japan
112/C1 Abulug, Phil.
127/A3 Abu Minqâr, Bîr (well), Egypt
136/E6 Abuná (riv.), Bol.
136/E5 Abunã (riv.), Braz.
106/B3 Abu Road, India
92/D3 Abu Rujmayn, Jabal (mts.), Syria
127/D4 Abu Shagara, Ras (cape), Sudan
127/B4 Abu Simbel (ruins), Egypt
100/B2 Abuta, Japan
125/N5 Ābuyē Mēda (peak), Eth.
112/D3 Abuyog, Phil.
95/F4 Abū Ẓaby (Abu Dhabi) (cap.), UAE
80/A4 Abyaḑ, Ar Ra's al (cape), Tun.
127/B3 Abydos (ruins), Egypt
138/C4 Acacias, Col.
161/G2 Acadia Nat'l Park, Me,US
162/E4 Acadian Village, La,US
140/C3 Acajutiba, Braz.
147/E4 Acámbaro, Mex.
146/D4 Acaponeta, Mex.
146/D4 Acaponeta (riv.), Mex.
147/E5 Acapulco, Mex.
139/G4 Acarai (mts.), Braz., Guy.
140/B1 Acaraú, Braz.
140/B1 Acaraú (riv.), Braz.
140/C2 Acari, Braz.
136/G5 Acari (riv.), Braz.
138/D2 Acarigua, Ven.
147/F5 Acatlán, Mex.
147/M8 Acatzingo de Hidalgo, Mex.
129/E5 Accra (cap.), Gha.
57/F4 Accrington, Eng,UK
71/G6 Ach (riv.), Aus.
77/H2 Ach (riv.), Ger.
136/E7 Achacachi, Bol.
142/B4 Achao, Chile
129/H2 Achegour (well), Niger
77/H2 Achen (pass), Ger.
97/K2 Acheng, China
53/S10 Achères, Fr.
70/B5 Achern, Ger.
68/B3 Achicourt, Fr.
68/B3 Achiet-le-Grand, Fr.
161/N6 Achigan (riv.), Qu,Can
54/F10 Achill (isl.), Ire.
54/F10 Achill Head (pt.), Ire.
55/J7 Achiltibuie, Sc,UK
88/K4 Achinsk, Rus.
128/D2 Achmîm (well), Mrta.
54/A1 Achnasheen, Sc,UK
54/A2 A'Chràlaig (mtn.), Sc,UK
69/G3 Acht, Hohe (peak), Ger.
148/E3 Achupa, Nic.
144/B1 Achupallas, Ecu.
92/B2 Acıpayam, Turk.
80/D4 Acireale, It.
150/C2 Acklins (isl.), Bahm.
57/G4 Ackworth Moor Top, Eng,UK
118/C4 Acland (peak), Austl.
59/H1 Acle, Eng,UK
142/C2 Aconcagua, Cerro (peak), Arg.
140/C2 Acopiara, Braz.
78/B3 Acqui Terme, It.
117/G5 Acraman (lake), Austl.
144/D3 Acre (state), Braz.
136/E6 Acre (riv.), Braz., Peru
141/B1 Acreúna, Braz.
81/L7 Acropolis, Gre.
121/M7 Actaeon Group (isls.), FrPol.
53/N7 Acton, Eng,UK
147/F5 Actopan, Mex.
140/C2 Açu, Braz.
147/P8 Acula, Mex.
142/Q9 Aculeo (lake), Chile
168/D2 Acushnet, Ma,US
160/D3 Ada, Oh,US
159/H4 Ada, Ok,US
82/E3 Ada, Yugo.
153/J1 Adair (cape), NW,Can
74/C2 Adaja (riv.), Sp.
151/C6 Adak (isl.), Ak,US
151/C6 Adak (str.), Ak,US
143/M7 Adam (peak), Falk.
141/B2 Adamantina, Braz.
129/H5 Adamawa (plat.), Camr., Nga.
77/G5 Adamello (peak), It.
156/D3 Adams (lake), BC,Can
166/A4 Adams (co.), Pa,US
156/C4 Adams (peak), Wa,US
108/G4 Adam's Bridge (shoals), SrL.
91/D1 Adana, Turk.
91/D1 Adana (prov.), Turk.
83/K5 Adapazarı, Turk.
113/M Adare (cape), Ant.
72/C5 Adarza (mtn.), Fr.
54/A4 Add (riv.), Sc,UK
78/C2 Adda (riv.), It.
125/M4 Ad Dabbah, Sudan
93/F5 Ad Dahnā' (des.), SAr.
125/M5 Ad Damazin, Sudan
125/M4 Ad Dāmir, Sudan
94/F3 Ad Dammām, SAr.
91/B4 Ad Daqahlīyah (gov.), Egypt
94/F3 Ad Dawḩah (Doha) (cap.), Qatar
91/B4 Ad Dilinjāt, Egypt
125/N6 Addis Ababa (cap.), Eth.
165/Q16 Addison, Il,US
93/F4 Ad Dīwānīyah, Iraq
53/M7 Addlestone, Eng,UK
132/D4 Addo Elephant Nat'l Park, SAfr.
93/F3 Ad Dujayl, Iraq
125/M5 Ad Duwaym, Sudan
113/V Adelaide (isl.), Ant.
117/H5 Adelaide, Austl.
152/G2 Adelaide (pen.), NW,Can
132/D4 Adelaide, SAfr.
117/M8 Adelaide Zoo, Austl.
164/C1 Adelanto, Ca,US
114/C3 Adèle (isl.), Austl.
67/G5 Adelebsen, Ger.
113/K Adélie (coast), Ant.
63/R7 Adelsön (isl.), Swe.
125/Q5 Aden (gulf), Afr., Asia
94/D6 Aden, Yem.
67/H2 Adendorf, Ger.
111/H4 Adi (isl.), Indo.
130/A2 Adi, Zaire
117/G5 Adieu (cape), Austl.
73/J4 Adige (Etsch) (riv.), It.
125/N5 Ādīgrat, Eth.
106/C4 Adilābād, India
93/E2 Adilcevaz, Turk.
129/E2 Adiora (well), Mali
108/G3 Adirāmpatnam, India
160/F2 Adirondack (mts.), NY,US
125/N6 Ādīs Ābeba (Addis Ababa) (cap.), Eth.
125/N5 Ādīs Zemen, Eth.
92/D2 Adıyaman, Turk.
92/D2 Adıyaman (prov.), Turk.
83/H2 Adjud, Rom.
147/F4 Adjuntas (res.), Mex.
57/F4 Adlington, Eng,UK
77/E3 Adliswil, Swi.
114/D2 Admiralty (gulf), Austl.
153/H1 Admiralty (inlet), NW,Can
120/D5 Admiralty (isls.), PNG
165/B2 Admiralty (inlet), Wa,US
151/M4 Admiralty I. Nat'l Mon., Ak,US
99/L9 Ado (riv.), Japan
129/F5 Ado, Nga.
99/M9 Adogawa, Japan
106/C4 Ādoni, India
72/C5 Adour (riv.), Fr.
74/D4 Adra, Sp.
130/A2 Adranga, Zaire
80/D4 Adrano, It.
124/E2 Adrar, Alg.
129/F1 Adrar (wilaya), Alg.
128/B1 Adrar (reg.), Mrta.
124/E1 Adrar bou Nasser (peak), Mor.
129/F1 Adrar des Iforas (mts.), Mali
125/K5 Adré, Chad
79/F2 Adria, It.
160/C3 Adrian, Mi,US
52/E4 Adriatic (sea)
59/F5 Adur (riv.), Eng,UK
125/N5 Ādwa, Eth.
57/G4 Adwick le Street, Eng,UK
89/P3 Adycha (riv.), Rus.
87/G4 Adzhar Aut. Rep., Geo.
85/N2 Adz'va (riv.), Rus.
81/J3 Aegean (sea), Gre., Turk.
62/D4 Aerø (isl.), Den.
58/B2 Aeron (riv.), Wal,UK
76/D3 Aesch, Swi.
56/E1 Ae, Water of (riv.), Sc,UK
129/F5 Afadjoto (peak), Gha.
93/F3 'Afak, Iraq
121/X15 Afareaitu, FrPol.
91/F7 Afek Nat'l Park, Isr.
72/B3 Aff (riv.), Fr.
54/A2 Affric, Loch (lake), Sc,UK
95/H2 Afghanistan
125/Q7 Afgooye, Som.
125/P7 Afmadow, Som.
139/H3 Afobaka (dam), Sur.
140/C2 Afogados da Ingàzeira, Braz.
151/H4 Afognak (isl.), Ak,US
151/H4 Afognak (mtn.), Ak,US
128/C2 Afollé (reg.), Mrta.
140/C2 Afonso Bezerra, Braz.
141/D2 Afonso Cláudio, Braz.
80/D2 Afragola, It.
140/B3 Afrânio, Braz.
122/* Africa
165/K10 Africa USA (Marine World), Ca,US
91/E1 'Afrīn, Syria
91/E1 'Afrīn (riv.), Syria
91/E1 Afrin (riv.), Turk.
76/A3 Afrique (mtn.), Fr.
92/D2 Afşin, Turk.
66/C2 Afsluitdijk (IJsselmeer) (dam), Neth.
67/F5 Afte (riv.), Ger.
156/F5 Afton, Wy,US
91/D3 'Afula, Isr.
92/B2 Afyon, Turk.
92/B2 Afyon (prov.), Turk.
124/H3 Agadem, Niger
129/G2 Agadez, Niger
129/H2 Agadez (dept.), Niger
124/D1 Agadir, Mor.
130/B2 Agago (riv.), Ugan.
123/H6 Agalega (isls.), Mrts.
129/F2 Agamor (well), Mali
120/D3 Agaña (cap.), Guam
99/F2 Agano (riv.), Japan
125/N6 Āgaro, Eth.
107/F3 Agartala, India
113/V Agassiz (cape), Ant.
153/T6 Agassiz (ice field), NW,Can
159/G2 Agate Fossil Beds Nat'l Mon., Ne,US
151/A5 Agattu (isl.), Ak,US
151/A5 Agattu (str.), Ak,US
168/B1 Agawam, Ma,US
129/G5 Agbor, Nga.
128/D5 Agboville, IvC.
87/H5 Agdam, Azer.
72/E5 Agde, Fr.
72/E5 Agde, Cap d' (cape), Fr.
72/D4 Agen, Fr.
99/H7 Ageo, Japan
71/G7 Ager (riv.), Aus.
62/C4 Agerbæk, Den.
77/E3 Agerisee (lake), Swi.
63/S7 Agesta (reg. park), Swe.
67/E6 Agger (riv.), Ger.
82/E1 Aggteleki Nat'l Park, Hun.
56/B3 Aghagallon, NI,UK
93/G4 Āghā Jārī, Iran
146/C3 Agiabampo (lag.), Mex.
96/G1 Aginskoye, Rus.
56/B1 Agivey, NI,UK
79/E5 Agliana, It.
83/G3 Agnita, Rom.
79/E1 Agno (riv.), It.
77/E6 Agno, Swi.
99/M10 Ago, Japan
78/B2 Agogna (riv.), It.
105/J5 Agoo, Phil.
72/D5 Agout (riv.), Fr.
106/C2 Āgra, India
80/E2 Agri (riv.), It.
93/E2 Ağri (prov.), Turk.
87/H5 Ağri (Ararat) (peak), Turk.
80/C4 Agrigento, It.
120/D3 Agrihan (isl.), NMar.
81/G3 Agrínion, Gre.
142/C3 Agrio (riv.), Arg.
80/D2 Agropoli, It.
85/M4 Agryz, Rus.
147/L6 Agua Blanca Iturbide, Mex.
141/D1 Água Boa, Braz.
140/B2 Água Branca, Braz.
138/C2 Aguachica, Col.
138/C3 Aguadas, Col.
150/E3 Aguadilla, PR
148/C2 Agua Dulce, Mex.
149/F4 Aguadulce, Pan.
164/C4 Agua Hedionda (lag.), Ca,US
141/F7 Aguaí, Braz.
75/P10 Agualva-Cacém, Port.
148/E3 Aguan (riv.), Hon.
161/J1 Aguanus (riv.), Qu,Can
141/B2 Aguapeí (riv.), Braz.
144/B2 Aguarico (riv.), Ecu.
139/E2 Aguaro-Guariquito Nat'l Park, Ven.
141/H6 Águas (hills), Braz.
140/C3 Águas Belas, Braz.
146/E4 Aguascalientes, Mex.
146/E4 Aguascalientes (state), Mex.
141/G6 Águas da Prata, Braz.
141/G7 Águas de Lindóia, Braz.
140/B5 Águas Formosas, Braz.
141/B1 Aguavermelha (res.), Braz.
144/C3 Aguaytía (riv.), Peru
141/B2 Agudos, Braz.
74/A2 Águeda, Port.
74/B2 Agueda (riv.), Sp.
124/C3 Agüenit, WSah.
99/M10 Agui, Japan
120/D3 Aguijan (isl.), NMar.
74/C4 Aguilar, Sp.
74/C1 Aguilar de Campóo, Sp.
135/C2 Aguilares, Arg.
74/E4 Aguilas, Sp.
146/E5 Aguililla, Mex.
75/X17 Agüimes, Canl.,Sp.
144/A2 Aguja (pt.), Peru
132/M11 Agulhas (cape), SAfr.
141/C2 Agulhas Negras (peak), Braz.
111/E5 Agung (vol.), Indo.
112/D3 Agusan (riv.), Phil.
138/C2 Agustín Codazzi, Col.
130/B2 Agwata, Ugan.
124/G3 Ahaggar (plat.), Alg.
93/F2 Ahar, Iran
66/E4 Ahaus, Ger.
69/F3 Ahbach (riv.), Ger.
60/B5 Aherlow (riv.), Ire.
130/B3 Ahero, Kenya
92/E2 Ahlat, Turk.
67/E5 Ahlen, Ger.
106/B3 Ahmadābād, India
106/B4 Ahmadnagar, India
95/K3 Ahmadpur East, Pak.
108/A2 Ahmadpur Siāl, Pak.
125/P6 Ahmar (mts.), Eth.
56/B2 Ahoghill, NI,UK
69/F3 Ahr (riv.), Ger.
91/B5 Ahrāmāt al Jīzah (The Pyramids of Giza), Egypt
67/H1 Ahrensburg, Ger.
67/F5 Ahse (riv.), Ger.
147/K8 Ahuacatitlán, Mex.
148/D3 Ahuachapán, ESal.
154/W13 Ahuimanu, Hi,US
62/F4 Åhus, Swe.
93/G4 Ahvāz, Iran
63/H1 Ahvenanmaa (prov.), Fin.
101/C2 Ai (riv.), China
132/B2 Ai-Ais Hot Springs, Namb.
103/B2 Aibag Gol (riv.), China
70/E6 Aichach, Ger.
99/E3 Aichi (pref.), Japan
70/B5 Aidlingen, Ger.
154/W13 Aiea, Hi,US
76/C5 Aigle, Swi.
76/B4 Aigle, Pic de l' (peak), Fr.
72/E4 Aigoual (mtn.), Fr.
72/F4 Aigues (riv.), Fr.
75/F1 Aigues Tortes y Lago de San Mauricio Nat'l Park, Sp.
123/Q16 Aiguille, Cap de l' (cape), Alg.
99/F1 Aikawa, Japan
163/H3 Aiken, SC,US
104/D3 Ailao (mtn.), China
104/D4 Ailao (mts.), China
149/G4 Ailigandí, Pan.
120/F4 Ailinglapalap (atoll), Mrsh.
54/A6 Ailsa Craig (isl.), Sc,UK
120/G3 Ailuk (atoll), Mrsh.
105/G2 Aimen (pass), China
103/C5 Aimen Guan (pass), China
135/C2 Aimogasta, Arg.
141/D1 Aimorés, Braz.
76/B5 Ain (riv.), Fr.
123/V18 'Aïn Beïda, Alg.
123/S15 'Aïn Beniau, Alg.
124/D2 Aïn Ben Tili, Mrta.
123/S15 'Aïn Bessem, Alg.
123/R15 'Aïn Defla, Alg.
123/R15 'Aïn Defla (wilaya), Alg.
123/Q16 'Aïn el Turk, Alg.
123/V17 'Aïn Fakroun, Alg.
123/Q17 'Aïn M'Lila, Alg.
81/G3 Aínos (peak), Gre.
81/G3 Ainos Nat'l Park, Gre.
123/U18 'Aïn Oulmene, Alg.
123/S16 'Aïn Oussersa, Alg.
57/E4 Ainsdale, Eng,UK
124/E1 'Aïn Sefra, Alg.
159/H2 Ainsworth, Ne,US
123/S15 'Aïn Taya, Alg.
123/Q16 'Aïn Temouchent, Alg.
123/Q16 'Aïn Temouchent (wilaya), Alg.
123/U18 'Aïn Touta, Alg.
129/G2 Aïr (plat.), Niger
156/E3 Airdrie, Ab,Can
54/C5 Airdrie, Sc,UK
68/D5 Aire (riv.), Fr.
57/G4 Aire (riv.), Eng,UK
68/B2 Aire, Canal de (can.), Fr.
57/E5 Aire, Point of (pt.), Wal,UK
68/B2 Aire-sur-la-Lys, Fr.
153/J2 Air Force (isl.), NW,Can
57/F3 Airton, Eng,UK
70/D3 Aisch (riv.), Ger.
68/D3 Aiseau-Presles, Belg.
142/B5 Aisén del General Carlos Ibáñez del Campo (reg.), Chile
103/E3 Ai Shan (mtn.), China
151/L3 Aishihik, Yk,Can
69/E3 Aisne (riv.), Belg.
68/C4 Aisne (dept.), Fr.
68/C5 Aisne (riv.), Fr.
124/E1 Aïssa (peak), Alg.
71/H6 Aist (riv.), Aus.
71/F5 Aiterach (riv.), Ger.
55/P12 Aith, Sc,UK
99/M9 Aitō, Japan
121/J6 Aitutaki (atoll), CookIs.
83/F2 Aiud, Rom.
141/J6 Aiuruoca, Braz.
141/J7 Aiuruoca (riv.), Braz.
72/F5 Aix-en-Provence, Fr.
72/F4 Aix-les-Bains, Fr.
81/H4 Aíyina, Gre.
81/H3 Aíyion, Gre.
99/F2 Aizu-Wakamatsu, Japan
104/B4 Āīzwal, India
80/A2 Ajaccio, Fr.
80/A2 Ajaccio (gulf), Fr.
147/F5 Ajalpan, Mex.
161/R8 Ajax, On,Can
96/D3 Aj Bogd (peak), Mong.
124/K1 Ajdābiyā, Libya
100/B3 Ajigasawa, Japan
127/C5 Aj Janayet, Sudan
82/C2 Ajka, Hun.
106/B2 Ajmer, India
158/D4 Ajo, Az,US
74/D1 Ajo, Cabo de (cape), Sp.
147/E5 Ajuchitlán, Mex.
147/Q10 Ajusco (mtn.), Mex.
112/C3 Ajuy, Phil.
99/F1 Aka (riv.), Japan
99/N10 Akabane, Japan
100/C2 Akabira, Japan
102/F1 Akademik Obruchev (mts.), Rus.
99/F3 Akaishi-dake (mtn.), Japan
100/D2 Akan (lake), Japan
100/D2 Akan Nat'l Park, Japan
127/B4 Akasha East, Sudan
98/D3 Akashi, Japan
99/K10 Akashi (str.), Japan
102/B4 Akbaytal (pass), Taj.
123/T15 Akbou, Alg.
92/D1 Akçaabat, Turk.
92/D2 Akçadağ, Turk.
92/D2 Akçakale, Turk.
83/K5 Akçakoca, Turk.
128/B2 Akchâr (reg.), Mrta.
92/C2 Akdağmadeni, Turk.
94/G4 Akdar, Al Jabal (mts.), Oman
99/N9 Akechi, Japan
62/H2 Åkersberga, Swe.
62/D2 Akershus (co.), Nor.
125/K7 Aketi, Zaire
87/G4 Akhaltsikhe, Geo.
81/H3 Akharnaí, Gre.
81/G3 Akhelóös (riv.), Gre.
92/A2 Akhisar, Turk.
127/B3 Akhmīm, Egypt
87/H3 Akhtuba (riv.), Rus.
87/H2 Akhtubinsk, Rus.
86/E2 Akhtyrka, Ukr.
98/C4 Aki, Japan
99/H7 Aki (riv.), Japan
99/H7 Akigawa, Japan
153/H3 Akimiski (isl.), NW,Can
91/D1 Akıncı (pt.), Turk.
99/H7 Akishima, Japan
100/B4 Akita, Japan
100/B4 Akita (dept.), Japan
128/B2 Akjoujt, Mrta.
106/D6 Akkaraipattu, SrL.
100/D2 Akkeshi, Japan
91/D3 'Akko, Isr.
128/D2 'Aklé 'Aouâna (dune), Mali, Mrta.
98/D3 Akō, Japan
124/H7 Akoga, Gabon
106/C3 Akola, India
125/N4 Āk'ordat, Erit.
92/C2 Akören, Turk.
129/F5 Akosombo (dam), Gha.
153/K2 Akpatok (isl.), NW,Can
102/C3 Akqi, China
81/J2 Ákrathos, Ákra (cape), Gre.
62/A2 Åkrehamn, Nor.
81/G4 Akrítas, Ákra (cape), Gre.
159/G2 Akron, Co,US
168/F5 Akron, Oh,US
168/F5 Akron City (res.), Oh,US
102/C4 Aksai Chin (reg.), China, India
92/C2 Aksaray, Turk.
92/C2 Aksaray (prov.), Turk.
96/C4 Aksay, China
87/K2 Aksay, Kaz.
92/B2 Akşehir, Turk.
92/B2 Akşehir (lake), Turk.
91/B1 Akseki, Turk.
102/C2 Aksoran (peak), Kaz.
102/D3 Aksu, China
102/C3 Aksu (riv.), China
102/C2 Aksu (riv.), Kaz.
91/B1 Aksu (riv.), Turk.
125/N5 Āksum, Eth.
81/J2 Aktí (pen.), Gre.
87/L2 Aktyubinsk, Kaz.
87/L3 Aktyubinsk Obl., Kaz.
98/B4 Akune, Japan
61/N6 Akureyri, Ice.
151/E5 Akutan (isl.), Ak,US
151/E5 Akutan (passg.), Ak,US
129/G5 Akwa Ibom (state), Nga.
104/B4 Akyab (Sittwe), Burma
87/L2 Ak"yar, Rus.
83/K5 Akyazı, Turk.
96/B3 Ala (riv.), China
163/G3 Alabama (state), US
163/G4 Alabama (riv.), Al,US
163/G3 Alabama Space & Rocket Ctr., Al,US
163/G3 Alabaster, Al,US
112/C2 Alabat, Phil.
92/C1 Alaca, Turk.
92/C1 Alaçam, Turk.
163/H4 Alachua, Fl,US
149/F1 Alacranes, Embalse (res.), Cuba
87/H4 Alagir, Rus.
72/E4 Alagnon (riv.), Fr.
140/D2 Alagoa Grande, Braz.
140/C3 Alagoas (state), Braz.
140/C4 Alagoinhas, Braz.
74/B2 Alagón (riv.), Sp.
112/D4 Alah (riv.), Phil.
93/G4 Al Aḩmadi, Kuw.
61/G3 Alajärvi, Fin.
149/E4 Alajuela, CR
102/D2 Alakol' (lake), Kaz.
127/B2 Al 'Alamayn (El Alamein), Egypt
139/F5 Alalaú (riv.), Braz.
120/D3 Alamagan (isl.), NMar.
93/F4 Al 'Amārah, Iraq
93/H5 'Alāmarvdasht (riv.), Iran
165/K11 Alameda, Ca,US
165/L11 Alameda (co.), Ca,US
165/L11 Alameda (cr.), Ca,US
147/F4 Alamo, Mex.
158/D4 Alamo (lake), Az,US
165/K11 Alamo, Ca,US
158/D3 Alamo, Nv,US
159/F4 Alamogordo, NM,US
144/A2 Alamor, Ecu.
159/F3 Alamosa, Co,US
92/E3 Al Anbār (gov.), Iraq
63/H1 Åland (isls.), Fin.
64/F2 Åland (riv.), Ger.
91/C1 Alanya, Turk.
133/J7 Alaotra (lake), Madg.
163/H4 Alapaha (riv.), Ga,US
83/K5 Alaplı, Turk.
91/D5 Al 'Aqabah, Jor.
74/D3 Alarcón (res.), Sp.
92/B2 Alaşehir, Turk.
91/E4 Al 'Āsimah (gov.), Jor.
151/* Alaska (state), US
151/J4 Alaska (gulf), Ak,US
151/F4 Alaska (pen.), Ak,US
151/H3 Alaska (range), Ak,US
151/B5 Alaska Maritime Nat'l Wild. Ref., Ak,US
151/G4 Alaska Pen. Nat'l Wild. Ref., Ak,US
78/B5 Alassio, It.
85/K5 Alatyr', Rus.
87/H4 Alaverdi, Arm.
61/G3 Alavus, Fin.
56/D5 Alaw (riv.), Wal,UK
56/D5 Alaw, Llyn (lake), Wal,UK
102/B4 Alayskiy (mts.), Kyr.
89/R3 Alazeya (riv.), Rus.
93/E3 Al 'Azīzīyah, Iraq
124/H1 Al 'Azīzīyah, Libya
70/B5 Alb (riv.), Ger.
78/B3 Alba, It.
83/F2 Alba (co.), Rom.
92/D2 Al Bāb, Syria
74/E3 Albacete, Sp.
91/B5 Al Badrashayn, Egypt
127/C3 Al Baḩr al Aḩmar (gov.), Egypt
83/F2 Alba Iulia, Rom.
91/B4 Al Bājūr, Egypt
91/B4 Al Balqā' (gov.), Jor.
127/C3 Al Balyanā, Egypt
161/F1 Albanel (lake), Qu,Can
81/F2 Albania
116/C5 Albany, Austl.
153/H3 Albany (riv.), On,Can
165/K11 Albany, Ca,US
163/G4 Albany, Ga,US
160/C4 Albany, Ky,US
160/F3 Albany (cap.), NY,US
156/C4 Albany, Or,US
76/B6 Albarine (riv.), Fr.
93/F4 Al Başrah, Iraq
93/F4 Al Başrah (gov.), Iraq
114/G2 Albatross (bay), Austl.
132/A2 Albatross (pt.), Namb.
127/B2 Al Bawīţī, Egypt
125/K1 Al Bayḑā, Libya
77/E2 Albbruck, Ger.
144/J6 Albemarle (pt.), Ecu.
163/H3 Albemarle, NC,US
163/J2 Albemarle (sound), NC,US
78/B4 Albenga, It.
78/C1 Alben, Monte (peak), It.
76/B6 Albens, Fr.
74/C2 Alberche (riv.), Sp.
114/E5 Alberga (riv.), Austl.
119/A2 Albert (inlet), Austl.
114/F7 Albert (lake), Austl.
69/E2 Albert (can.), Belg.
68/B4 Albert, Fr.
130/A2 Albert (lake), Ugan., Zaire
152/E3 Alberta (prov.), Can.
142/E2 Alberti, Arg.
82/D2 Albertirsa, Hun.
157/K5 Albert Lea, Mn,US
130/A2 Albert Nile (riv.), Ugan.
143/J8 Alberto de Agostini Nat'l Park, Chile
132/Q13 Alberton, SAfr.
73/G4 Albertville, Fr.
163/G3 Albertville, Al,US
72/E5 Albi, Fr.
79/E2 Albignasego, It.
78/C1 Albino, It.
160/C3 Albion, Mi,US
159/H2 Albion, Ne,US
91/E2 Al Biqā' (gov.), Leb.
91/D3 Al Biqā' (Bekaa) (val.), Leb.
91/D4 Al Bīrah, WBnk.
78/B4 Albisola Superiore, It.
66/B5 Alblasserdam, Neth.
62/C3 Ålborg, Den.
62/D3 Ålborg (bay), Den.
74/D4 Albox, Sp.
161/S10 Albright Knox Art Gallery, NY,US
58/D1 Albrighton, Eng,UK
76/D5 Albristhorn (peak), Swi.
77/F1 Albstadt, Ger.
74/A4 Albufeira, Port.
91/B4 Al Buḩayrah (gov.), Egypt
77/F4 Albula (riv.), Swi.
77/F4 Albulapass (pass), Swi.
158/F4 Albuquerque, NM,US
74/B3 Alburquerque, Sp.
119/C3 Albury, Austl.
63/S7 Alby, Swe.
75/P10 Alcabideche, Port.
74/A3 Alcácer do Sal, Port.
74/C4 Alcalá de Guadaira, Sp.
74/D2 Alcalá de Henares, Sp.
74/D4 Alcalá la Real, Sp.
80/C4 Alcamo, It.
75/E2 Alcanadre (riv.), Sp.
75/E2 Alcanar, Sp.
75/E2 Alcañiz, Sp.
140/A1 Alcântara, Braz.
74/B3 Alcántara (res.), Sp.
74/E4 Alcantarilla, Sp.
74/D3 Alcarez (range), Sp.
165/K11 Alcatraz (isl.), Ca,US
74/C4 Alcaudete, Sp.
74/D3 Alcázar de San Juan, Sp.
59/E2 Alcester, Eng,UK
75/E3 Alcira, Sp.
163/H3 Alcoa, Tn,US
140/C5 Alcobaça, Braz.
74/D2 Alcobendas, Sp.
75/Q10 Alcochete, Port.
75/E2 Alcora, Sp.
74/D2 Alcorcón, Sp.
163/H3 Alcovy (riv.), Ga,US
75/E3 Alcoy, Sp.
123/G5 Aldabra (isls.), Sey.
162/B4 Aldama, Mex.
89/N4 Aldan, Rus.
89/N4 Aldan (plat.), Rus.
89/P3 Aldan (riv.), Rus.
102/G2 Aldarhaan, Mong.
59/E4 Aldbourne, Eng,UK
57/H4 Aldbrough, Eng,UK
59/H2 Alde (riv.), Eng,UK
59/H2 Aldeburgh, Eng,UK
126/B2 Aldeia Viçosa, Ang.
69/F2 Aldenhoven, Ger.
56/B2 Aldergrove, NI,UK
57/F5 Alderley Edge, Eng,UK
59/E4 Aldermaston, Eng,UK
72/B2 Alderney (isl.), Chl,UK
161/Q9 Aldershot, On,Can
59/F4 Aldershot, Eng,UK
165/C2 Alderwood Manor-Bothell North, Wa,US
70/B6 Aldingen, Ger.
166/B4 Aldred (lake), Pa,US
59/E1 Aldridge, Eng,UK
128/B2 Aleg, Mrta.
141/D2 Alegre, Braz.
135/E2 Alegrete, Braz.
134/A6 Alejandro Selkirk (isl.), Chile
86/E2 Aleksandriya, Ukr.
84/H4 Aleksandrov, Rus.
85/N4 Aleksandrovsk, Rus.
97/N1 Aleksandrovsk-Sakhalinskiy, Rus.
65/K2 Aleksandrów Kujawski, Pol.
65/K3 Aleksandrów Łódzki, Pol.
102/B1 Alekseyevka, Kaz.
86/F2 Alekseyevka, Rus.
84/H5 Aleksin, Rus.
82/E4 Aleksinac, Yugo.
93/N6 Alemdar, Turk.
141/L6 Além Paraíba, Braz.
72/D2 Alençon, Fr.
139/H5 Alenquer, Braz.
154/T10 Alenuihaha (chan.), Hi,US
91/E2 Aleppo (Ḩalab), Syria
142/B4 Alerce Andino Nat'l Park, Chile
153/S6 Alert (pt.), NW,Can
82/F2 Aleşd, Rom.
78/B3 Alessandria, It.
78/B3 Alessandria (prov.), It.
61/C3 Ålesund, Nor.
76/D5 Aletschhorn (peak), Swi.
151/E5 Aleutian (isls.), Ak,US
151/G4 Aleutian (range), Ak,US
54/D6 Ale Water (riv.), Sc,UK

113/V **Alexander** (cape), Ant.
113/V **Alexander** (isl.), Ant.
116/B2 **Alexander** (peak), Austl.
151/L4 **Alexander** (arch.), Ak,US
163/G3 **Alexander City**, Al,US
161/J2 **Alexander Graham Bell Nat'l Hist. Park**, NS,Can
115/Q12 **Alexandra**, NZ
140/C2 **Alexandra**, Braz.
81/H2 **Alexándria**, Gre.
83/G4 **Alexandria**, Rom.
54/B5 **Alexandria**, Sc,UK
162/E4 **Alexandria**, La,US
157/K4 **Alexandria**, Mn,US
166/A6 **Alexandria**, Va,US
127/B2 **Alexandria** (Al Iskandarīyah), Egypt
119/A2 **Alexandrina** (lake), Austl.
81/J2 **Alexandroúpolis**, Gre.
156/C2 **Alexis Creek**, BC,Can
102/D1 **Alev** (riv.), Rus.
102/D1 **Aleysk**, Rus.
75/E3 **Alfafar**, Sp.
93/E3 **Al Fallūjah**, Iraq
75/P10 **Alfama**, Port.
75/P11 **Alfarim**, Port.
74/E1 **Alfaro**, Sp.
125/L5 **Al Fāsher**, Sudan
127/B2 **Al Fashn**, Egypt
93/E3 **Al Fathah**, Iraq
93/G4 **Al Fāw**, Iraq
91/B5 **Al Fayyum**, Egypt
91/B5 **Al Fayyūm** (gov.), Egypt
69/F3 **Alfbach** (riv.), Ger.
67/G5 **Alfeld**, Ger.
141/H6 **Alfenas**, Braz.
81/G4 **Alfiós** (riv.), Gre.
79/F4 **Alfonsine**, It.
57/J5 **Alford**, Eng,UK
54/D2 **Alford**, Sc,UK
119/D3 **Alfred Nat'l Park**, Austl.
57/G5 **Alfreton**, Eng,UK
59/G5 **Alfriston**, Eng,UK
69/G2 **Alfter**, Ger.
87/L2 **Alga**, Kaz.
62/A2 **Algård**, Nor.
74/C4 **Algeciras**, Sp.
75/E3 **Algemesí**, Sp.
123/S15 **Alger** (wilaya), Alg.
123/S15 **Alger** (Algiers) (cap.), Alg.
124/F2 **Algeria**
67/G4 **Algermissen**, Ger.
75/N8 **Algete**, Sp.
93/F4 **Al Ghammās**, Iraq
127/B2 **Al Gharbī yah** (gov.), Egypt
80/A2 **Alghero**, It.
127/C3 **Al Ghurdaqah**, Egypt
123/S15 **Algiers** (Alger) (cap.), Alg.
75/E3 **Alginet**, Sp.
132/D4 **Algoa** (bay), SAfr.
144/C1 **Algodón** (riv.), Peru
165/P15 **Algonquin**, Il,US
75/P10 **Algueirão**, Port.
77/H4 **Algund** (Lagundo), It.
92/E3 **Al Ḩadīthah**, Iraq
95/G4 **Al Ḩajar ash Sharqī** (mts.), Oman
95/G5 **Al Ḩallānī yah** (isl.), Oman
74/D4 **Alhama de Granada**, Sp.
74/E4 **Alhama de Murcia**, Sp.
164/B2 **Alhambra**, Ca,US
127/B2 **Al Hammām**, Egypt
75/Q10 **Alhandra**, Port.
93/F4 **Al Hārithah**, Iraq
92/E3 **Al Ḩasakah**, Syria
92/E2 **Al Ḩasakah** (prov.), Syria
74/C4 **Alhaurín el Grande**, Sp.
91/B5 **Al Ḩawāmidī yah**, Egypt
93/F3 **Al Hayy**, Iraq
93/F3 **Al Ḩillah**, Iraq
93/F3 **Al Hindī yah**, Iraq
123/N13 **Al Hoceima**, Mor.
123/N13 **Al Hoceima** (isl.), Sp.
94/E3 **Al Hufūf**, SAr.
92/A2 **Aliağa**, Turk.
81/G2 **Aliákmon** (riv.), Gre.
81/G2 **Aliákmonos** (lake), Gre.
93/F3 **'Alī al Gharbī**, Iraq
93/F3 **'Alī ash Sharqī**, Iraq
162/C3 **Alibates Flint Quarries Nat'l Mon.**, Tx,US
87/J5 **Ali-Bayramly**, Azer.
127/C5 **Al Ibēdiyya**, Sudan
93/M6 **Alibey** (riv.), Turk.
83/J5 **Alibeyköy**, Turk.
75/E3 **Alicante**, Sp.
118/A1 **Alice** (riv.), Austl.
80/E3 **Alice** (pt.), It.
162/D5 **Alice**, Tx,US
117/G2 **Alice Springs**, Austl.
163/F3 **Aliceville**, Al,US
112/C4 **Alicia**, Phil.
80/D3 **Alicudi** (isl.), It.
106/C2 **Aligarh**, India
94/E2 **Alīgudarz**, Iran
124/J8 **Alima** (riv.), Congo
62/E3 **Alingsås**, Swe.
106/B2 **Alī pur**, Pak.
106/E2 **Alī pur Duār**, India
168/G6 **Aliquippa**, Pa,US

91/A4 **Al Iskandarī yah** (gov.), Egypt
93/F3 **Al Iskandarī yah**, Iraq
91/A4 **Al Iskandarī yah** (Alexandria), Egypt
91/C4 **Al Ismā'ī lī yah** (gov.), Egypt
91/C4 **Al Ismā'ī lī yah** (Ismailia), Egypt
146/C2 **Alisos** (riv.), Mex.
125/K2 **Al Jaghbūb**, Libya
123/X18 **Al Jamm**, Tun.
91/D3 **Al Janūb** (gov.), Leb.
91/B4 **Al Jīzah**, Egypt
91/B5 **Al Jīzah** (gov.), Egypt
125/K5 **Al Junaynah**, Sudan
74/A4 **Aljustrel**, Port.
123/W17 **Al Kāf**, Tun.
123/W17 **Al Kāf** (gov.), Tun.
91/E4 **Al Karak**, Jor.
91/E4 **Al Karak** (gov.), Jor.
91/C4 **Al Karnak**, Egypt
69/E2 **Alken**, Belg.
95/G4 **Al Khābūrah**, Oman
91/D4 **Al Khalīl** (Hebron), WBnk.
93/F3 **Al Khāliş**, Iraq
127/B5 **Al Khandaq**, Sudan
91/B4 **Al Khānkah**, Egypt
127/B3 **Al Khārijah**, Egypt
125/M4 **Al Kharţūm Baḩrī** (Khartoum North), Sudan
94/F3 **Al Khobar**, SAr.
124/H1 **Al Khums**, Libya
66/B3 **Alkmaar**, Neth.
124/H3 **Alkoum** (well), Alg.
93/F3 **Al Kūfah**, Iraq
125/K3 **Al Kufrah**, Libya
93/F3 **Al Kūt**, Iraq
93/F4 **Al Kuwait** (Kuwait) (cap.), Kuw.
91/D2 **Al Lādhiqī yah** (prov.), Syria
91/D2 **Al Lādhiqī yah** (Latakia), Syria
106/D2 **Allahābād**, India
157/G3 **Allan**, Sk,Can
157/G3 **Allan** (hills), Sk,Can
161/N9 **Allanburg**, On,Can
104/B5 **Allanmyo**, Burma
157/L3 **Allan Water** (riv.), On,Can
124/H1 **'Allāq** (well), Libya
127/C4 **'Allāqi, Wādī al** (dry riv.), Egypt
54/B1 **Alness**, Sc,UK
54/B1 **Alness** (riv.), Sc,UK
55/L9 **Alnwick**, Eng,UK
121/J6 **Alofi** (cap.), Niue
120/H6 **Alofi** (isl.), Wall.
130/B2 **Aloi**, Ugan.
104/B2 **Along**, India
81/H3 **Alónnisos** (isl.), Gre.
111/F5 **Alor** (isls.), Indo.
74/C4 **Alora**, Sp.
110/B2 **Alor Setar**, Malay.
120/E6 **Alotau**, PNG
117/F3 **Aloysius** (peak), Austl.
79/E6 **Alpe di Poti** (peak), It.
78/D4 **Alpe di Succiso** (peak), It.
66/D5 **Alpen**, Ger.
160/D2 **Alpena**, Mi,US
140/A2 **Alpercatas** (mts.), Braz.
140/A2 **Alpercatas** (riv.), Braz.
77/F4 **Alperschällihorn** (peak), Swi.
66/B4 **Alphen aan de Rijn**, Neth.
74/A3 **Alpiarça**, Port.
78/A2 **Alpignano**, It.
162/C4 **Alpine**, Tx,US
156/F5 **Alpine**, Wy,US
165/D2 **Alpine Wild. Area**, Wa,US
70/B6 **Alpirsbach**, Ger.
84/B4 **Alportel**, Port.
73/G4 **Alps** (mts.), Eur.
99/F3 **Alps-Minami Nat'l Park**, Japan
95/G4 **Al Qābil**, Oman
125/N5 **Al Qaḑrif**, Sudan
93/F4 **Al Qādisī yah** (gov.), Iraq
91/B4 **Al Qāhirah** (gov.), Egypt
91/B4 **Al Qāhirah** (Cairo) (cap.), Egypt
91/B4 **Al Qalyūbī yah** (gov.), Egypt
92/E2 **Al Qāmishlī**, Syria
91/B4 **Al Qanāţir al Khayrī yah**, Egypt
93/F3 **Al Qāsim**, Iraq
93/F4 **Al Qaşr**, Iraq
123/W18 **Al Qaşrayn**, Tun.
123/W18 **Al Qaşrayn** (gov.), Tun.
125/M5 **Al Qaţaynah**, Sudan
124/H3 **Al Qaţrūn**, Libya
123/X18 **Al Qayrawān**, Tun.
123/W18 **Al Qayrawān** (gov.), Tun.
91/D3 **Al Qunayţirah** (prov.), Syria
127/C3 **Al Quşayr**, Egypt
91/D3 **Al Quşayr**, Syria
91/E3 **Al Quţayfah**, Syria
59/E1 **Alrewas**, Eng,UK
62/C4 **Als** (isl.), Den.
76/D2 **Alsace** (hist. reg.), Fr.
73/G2 **Alsace, Reg. d'**, Fr.
64/D5 **Alsace, Ballon d'** (mtn.), Fr.
72/A2 **Alsager**, Eng,UK
156/F3 **Alsask**, Sk,Can

74/D4 **Almanzora** (riv.), Sp.
74/C2 **Almanzor, Pico de** (peak), Sp.
127/B3 **Al Marāghah**, Egypt
124/K1 **Al Marj**, Libya
140/B4 **Almas** (peak), Braz.
137/J6 **Almas** (riv.), Braz.
91/C4 **Al Maţarī yah**, Egypt
93/E2 **Al Mawşil** (Mosul), Iraq
92/E3 **Al Mayādīn**, Syria
75/E3 **Almazora**, Sp.
137/H4 **Almeirim**, Braz.
74/A3 **Almeirim**, Port.
66/C4 **Almelo**, Neth.
140/B5 **Almenara**, Braz.
74/D3 **Almenara** (mtn.), Sp.
74/B2 **Almendra** (res.), Sp.
74/B3 **Almendralejo**, Sp.
66/C4 **Almere**, Neth.
74/D4 **Almería**, Sp.
75/D4 **Almería** (gulf), Sp.
85/M5 **Al'met'yevsk**, Rus.
62/F3 **Älmhult**, Swe.
74/C5 **Almina** (pt.), Sp.
91/B4 **Al Minūfī yah** (gov.), Egypt
127/B2 **Al Minyā**, Egypt
127/B3 **Al Minyā** (gov.), Egypt
93/F3 **Al Miqdādiyah**, Iraq
143/J7 **Almirante Montt** (gulf), Chile
81/H3 **Almirós**, Gre.
81/J5 **Almiroú** (gulf), Gre.
74/C3 **Almodóvar del Campo**, Sp.
74/C4 **Almodóvar del Río**, Sp.
54/C4 **Almond** (riv.), Sc,UK
53/U11 **Almont** (riv.), Fr.
160/E2 **Almonte**, On,Can
74/B4 **Almonte**, Sp.
75/E3 **Almoradí**, Sp.
141/D1 **Almores** (range), Braz.
94/E3 **Al Mubarraz**, SAr.
125/L5 **Al Muglad**, Sudan
123/X18 **Al Muknīn**, Tun.
123/X18 **Al Munastīr** (gov.), Tun.
123/X18 **Al Munastīr**, Tun.
74/D4 **Almuñécar**, Sp.
93/F3 **Al Musayyib**, Iraq
93/F4 **Al Muthanná** (gov.), Iraq
149/H5 **Alto de Tamar** (peak), Col.
137/H7 **Alto Garças**, Braz.
141/B4 **Alto Longá**, Braz.
147/N7 **Alto Lucero**, Mex.
79/E2 **Alto, Monte** (peak), It.
59/F4 **Alton**, Eng,UK
160/B4 **Alton**, Il,US
119/F5 **Altona**, Austl.
157/J3 **Altona**, Mb,Can
160/E3 **Altoona**, Pa,US
140/A3 **Alto Paraíba**, Braz.
144/C3 **Alto Purús** (riv.), Peru
140/B2 **Alto Santo**, Braz.
149/G4 **Altos de Campana Nat'l Park**, Pan.
147/F5 **Altotonga**, Mex.
71/F6 **Altötting**, Ger.
144/C3 **Alto Yurúa** (riv.), Peru
57/F5 **Altrincham**, Eng,UK
70/B4 **Altrip**, Ger.
96/C4 **Altun** (mts.), China
148/D2 **Altun Ha** (ruins), Belz.
158/B2 **Aluras**, Ca,US
159/H4 **Altus**, Ok,US
159/H4 **Altus** (res.), Ok,US
125/M5 **Al Ubayyiḑ**, Sudan
91/A4 **Alucra**, Turk.
125/L5 **Al Uḑayyah**, Sudan
56/E5 **Alun** (riv.), Wal,UK
127/C3 **Al Uqşur** (Luxor), Egypt
86/E3 **Alushta**, Ukr.
125/L3 **Al 'Uwaynāt** (peak), Sudan
159/H3 **Alva**, Ok,US
147/G5 **Alvarado**, Mex.
146/C3 **Alvaro Obregón** (res.), Mex.
62/F1 **Älvdalen**, Swe.
59/E2 **Alvechurch**, Eng,UK
74/A3 **Alverca**, Port.
75/P10 **Alverca do Ribatejo**, Port.
62/F3 **Alvesta**, Swe.
58/D4 **Alveston**, Eng,UK
162/E4 **Alvin**, Tx,US
62/G1 **Älvkarleby**, Swe.
141/A4 **Alvorada**, Braz.
140/A4 **Alvorada do Norte**, Braz.
127/B3 **Al Wādī al Jadīd** (gov.), Egypt
92/B4 **Al Wāḩat al Baḩrtyah** (oasis), Egypt
106/C2 **Alwar**, India
91/B5 **Al Wāsiţah**, Egypt
108/F3 **Alwaye**, India
96/E4 **Alxa Youqi**, China
96/F4 **Alxa Zuoqi**, China
117/G2 **Alyawarra Abor. Land**, Austl.
54/C3 **Alyth**, Sc,UK
63/L4 **Alytus**, Lith.
71/F7 **Alz** (riv.), It.
78/C1 **Alzano Lombardo**, It.
70/C2 **Alzenau in Unterfranken**, Ger.
69/F4 **Alzette** (riv.), Lux.
70/B3 **Alzey**, Ger.

74/D1 **Alsasua**, Sp.
85/M3 **Alsdorf**, Ger.
70/A3 **Alsenz** (riv.), Ger.
63/N6 **Alsfeld**, Ger.
165/O16 **Alsip**, Il,US
67/H1 **Alster** (riv.), Ger.
57/F2 **Alston**, Eng,UK
57/F4 **Alt** (riv.), Eng,UK
61/G1 **Alta**, Nor.
63/S7 **Älta**, Swe.
164/B2 **Altadena**, Ca,US
137/G6 **Alta Floresta**, Braz.
142/D1 **Alta Gracia**, Arg.
102/D1 **Altai** (mts.), Asia
163/H4 **Altamaha** (riv.), Ga,US
137/H4 **Altamira**, Braz.
147/F4 **Altamira**, Mex.
163/H4 **Altamonte Springs**, Fl,US
80/E2 **Altamura**, It.
146/D3 **Altamura** (isl.), Mex.
138/B5 **Altar** (vol.), Ecu.
148/D2 **Altar de los Sacrificios** (ruins), Guat.
96/C3 **Altay**, China
96/C3 **Altay**, Mong.
96/D2 **Altay**, Mong.
88/J4 **Altay Kray**, Rus.
77/E4 **Altdorf**, Swi.
71/E4 **Altdorf bei Nürnberg**, Ger.
75/E3 **Altea**, Sp.
67/E6 **Altena**, Ger.
67/F5 **Altenau** (riv.), Ger.
67/F5 **Altenbeken**, Ger.
64/G3 **Altenburg**, Ger.
70/B2 **Altenstadt**, Ger.
70/B5 **Altensteig**, Ger.
65/G2 **Altentreptow**, Ger.
66/D3 **Alter Rhein** (riv.), Ger.
67/G1 **Altes Land** (reg.), Ger.
70/B5 **Althengstett**, Ger.
57/H4 **Althorpe**, Eng,UK
92/D1 **Altindere Milli Park**, Turk.
91/E1 **Altınözü**, Turk.
136/E7 **Altiplano** (plat.), Bol., Peru
64/F2 **Altmark** (reg.), Ger.
71/E5 **Altmühl** (riv.), Ger.
71/G7 **Altmünster**, Aus.
140/A4 **Alto** (peak), Braz.
80/D1 **Amaro** (peak), It.
100/A4 **Amarume**, Japan
126/C2 **Amasra**, Turk.
92/C1 **Amasya**, Turk.
92/C1 **Amasya** (prov.), Turk.
99/J7 **Amatsukominato**, Japan
167/E1 **Amawalk** (res.), NY,US
70/B5 **Ammer** (riv.), Ger.
151/K2 **Ammerman** (mtn.), Yk,Can
70/E6 **Ammersee** (lake), Ger.
156/F5 **Ammon**, Id,US
109/D3 **Amnat Charoen**, Thai.
69/F5 **Amnéville**, Fr.
104/D4 **Amo** (riv.), China
93/H2 **Amol**, Iran
75/P10 **Amora**, Port.
81/J4 **Amorgós** (isl.), Gre.
163/F3 **Amory**, Ms,US
160/E1 **Amos**, Qu,Can
133/J7 **Ampangalana** (can.), Madg.
133/H9 **Ampanihy**, Madg.
106/D6 **Amparai**, SrL.
141/F2 **Amparo**, Braz.
133/J6 **Ampasindava** (bay), Madg.
144/D4 **Ampato** (peak), Peru
71/G6 **Amper** (riv.), Ger.
59/F2 **Ampthill**, Eng,UK
73/L2 **Amstetten**, Aus.
125/K5 **Am Timan**, Chad
90/F9 **Amudar'ya** (riv.), Asia
130/B2 **Amudat**, Ugan.
151/D5 **Amukta** (passg.), Ak,US
138/B5 **Ambato**, Ecu.
133/H7 **Ambato Boeny**, Madg.
106/C3 **Amravati**, India
106/B3 **Amreli**, India
92/C3 **'Amrīt** (ruins), Syria
108/F3 **Amritsar**, India
64/C1 **Amrun** (riv.), Ger.
66/B4 **Amstel** (riv.), Neth.
66/B4 **Amstelveen**, Neth.
66/B5 **Amsterdam** (cap.), FrAnt.
66/B4 **Amsterdam** (cap.), Neth.
167/N5 **Amsterdam**, NY,US
66/C5 **Amsterdam-Rijnkanaal** (can.), Neth.
57/G1 **Amble**, Eng,UK
166/C3 **Ambler**, Pa,US
57/F3 **Ambleside**, Eng,UK
68/A2 **Ambleteuse**, Fr.
69/F3 **Amblève** (riv.), Belg.
133/H9 **Amboasary**, Madg.
133/H9 **Ambohitra, Tampon** (peak), Madg.
130/C2 **Amboseli Nat'l Park**, Kenya
111/G4 **Ambon**, Indo.
111/G4 **Ambon** (isl.), Indo.
104/A1 **Amdo**, China

71/F6 **Alzkanal** (can.), Ger.
144/D1 **Amacayacú Nat'l Park**, Col.
139/F2 **Amacuro** (riv.), Guy., Ven.
147/K8 **Amacuzac** (riv.), Mex.
94/B4 **Amada** (ruins), Egypt
117/F3 **Amadeus** (lake), Austl.
125/M6 **Amadi**, Sudan
153/J2 **Amadjuak** (lake), NW,Can
74/A3 **Amadora**, Port.
167/F2 **Amagansett Nat'l Wild. Ref.**, NY,US
99/L10 **Amagasaki**, Japan
63/T9 **Amager** (isl.), Den.
98/B4 **Amagi**, Japan
99/F3 **Amagi-san** (mtn.), Japan
138/B5 **Amaguaña**, Ecu.
111/G4 **Amahai**, Indo.
147/L6 **Amajac** (riv.), Mex.
98/A4 **Amakusa** (sea), Japan
62/E2 **Åmål**, Swe.
130/B3 **Amala** (riv.), Kenya
96/G1 **Amalat** (riv.), Rus.
138/C3 **Amalfi**, Col.
80/E2 **Amalfi**, It.
81/G4 **Amaliás**, Gre.
106/C3 **Amalner**, India
144/B2 **Amaluza**, Ecu.
135/E1 **Amambaí**, Braz.
135/E1 **Amambaí** (riv.), Braz.
100/K7 **Amami** (isls.), Japan
100/K6 **Amami-O-Shima** (isl.), Japan
139/G5 **Amaná** (lake), Braz.
80/E3 **Amantea**, It.
121/L6 **Amanu** (atoll), FrPol.
80/B1 **Amiata** (peak), It.
68/B4 **Amiens**, Fr.
91/E1 **Amik** (lake), Turk.
89/U4 **Amila** (riv.), Ak,US
123/H5 **Amirante** (isls.), Sey.
157/H4 **Amisk** (lake), Sk,Can
162/C4 **Amistad** (res.), Mex., US
159/G5 **Amistad Nat'l Rec. Area**, Tx,US
159/K5 **Amite** (riv.), La,US
167/M9 **Amityville**, NY,US
106/C3 **Amla**, India
151/D6 **Amlia** (isl.), Ak,US
56/D5 **Amlwch**, Wal,UK
79/G5 **Ancona** (prov.), It.
138/B5 **Amaná** ...
139/H4 **Amapá** (state), Braz.
139/E3 **Amapá** (terr.), Braz.
139/E3 **Amapá** (state), Ven.
140/A2 **Amarante**, Braz.
74/A2 **Amarante**, Port.
140/A2 **Amarante do Marahão**, Braz.
104/C4 **Amarapura**, Burma
108/C4 **Amaravāti** (riv.), India
159/K5 **Amargosa**, Braz.
158/C3 **Amargosa** (dry riv.), Ca, Nv,US
163/G2 **Amarillo**, Tx,US
91/D4 **'Ammān** (cap.), Jor.
58/C3 **Ammanford**, Wal,UK
61/E2 **Ammarfjället** (peak), Swe.
70/B5 **Ammer** (riv.), Ger.
138/B5 **Ambato**, Ecu.

147/K6 **Amealco**, Mex.
146/D4 **Ameca**, Mex.
147/L7 **Amecameca de Juárez**, Mex.
69/F3 **Amel**, Belg.
66/C2 **Ameland** (isl.), Neth.
66/B5 **Amer** (chan.), Neth.
113/F **American** (highland), Ant.
165/M9 **American** (riv.), Ca,US
165/B3 **American** (lake), Wa,US
141/C2 **Americana**, Braz.
156/E5 **American Falls**, Id,US
156/E5 **American Falls** (res.), Id,US
158/C2 **American Fork**, Ut,US
158/B3 **American, North Fork** (riv.), Ca,US
121/J6 **American Samoa** (terr.), US
158/B3 **American, South Fork** (riv.), Ca,US
163/G3 **Americus**, Ga,US
73/L3 **Ameringkogel** (peak), Aus.
106/C2 **Amersfoort**, Neth.
59/F3 **Amersham**, Eng,UK
113/E **Amery Ice Shelf**, Ant.
157/K5 **Ames**, Ia,US
59/E4 **Amesbury**, Eng,UK
81/H3 **Ámfissa**, Gre.
89/N3 **Amga** (riv.), Rus.
89/N3 **Amga**, Rus.
89/T3 **Amguema** (riv.), Rus.
97/M1 **Amgun'** (riv.), Rus.
161/H2 **Amherst**, NS,Can
168/B1 **Amherst**, Ma,US
168/E5 **Amherst**, Oh,US
165/F7 **Amherstburg**, On,Can
80/B1 **Amiata** (peak), It.
68/B4 **Amiens**, Fr.
91/E1 **Amik** (lake), Turk.
89/U4 **Amila** (riv.), Ak,US
123/H5 **Amirante** (isls.), Sey.
157/H2 **Amisk** (lake), Sk,Can
162/C4 **Amistad** (res.), Mex., US
159/G5 **Amistad Nat'l Rec. Area**, Tx,US
159/K5 **Amite** (riv.), La,US
167/M9 **Amityville**, NY,US
106/C3 **Amla**, India
151/D6 **Amlia** (isl.), Ak,US
56/D5 **Amlwch**, Wal,UK
79/G5 **Ancona** (prov.), It.
109/C2 **Ang Nam Ngum** (lake), Laos
125/L7 **Ango**, Zaire
133/J6 **Angoche**, Moz.
142/B3 **Angol**, Chile
126/C3 **Angola**
160/C3 **Angola**, In,US
148/C2 **Angostura** (res.), Mex.
72/D4 **Angoulême**, Fr.
75/S12 **Angra do Heroísmo**, Azor.,Port.
141/J8 **Angra dos Reis**, Braz.
102/B3 **Angren**, Uzb.
109/C2 **Ang Thong**, Thai.
125/L9 **Angu**, Zaire
151/G3 **Anguilla** (peak), Ak,US
151/G4 **Anguilla** (isl.), UK
137/H8 **Anhandui** (riv.), Braz.
69/D3 **Anholt**, Den.
62/D3 **Anholt** (isl.), Den.
105/F2 **Anhua**, China
100/D4 **Anhui** (prov.), China
100/B3 **Ani**, Japan
151/G4 **Aniakchak** (crater), US
151/G4 **Aniakchak Nat'l Mon. & Prsv.**, Ak,US
68/C3 **Aniche**, Fr.
158/F3 **Animas** (riv.), Co, NM,US
146/B2 **Ánimas, Punta de las** (pt.), Mex.
81/A3 **Anina**, Rom.
97/N2 **Aniva** (bay), Rus.
100/C1 **Aniva, Mys** (cape), Rus.
63/M1 **Anjalamkoski**, Fin.
106/B2 **Anjār**, India
161/N6 **Anjou**, Qu,Can
133/H6 **Anjouan** (isl.), Com.
96/F5 **Ankang**, China
92/C2 **Ankara** (cap.), Turk.
92/C2 **Ankara** (prov.), Turk.
92/A2 **Ankara** (riv.), Turk.
133/H7 **Ankaratra, Massif** (plat.), Madg.
162/C2 **Ankaree** (riv.), Co,US
102/A3 **Ankazoabo**, Madg.
133/H8 **Ankazobe**, Madg.
109/E3 **An Khe**, Viet.
65/G2 **Anklam**, Ger.
105/E3 **Anlong**, China
100/D3 **Anlong Veng**, Camb.
66/D2 **Anloo**, Neth.
100/J7 **Anlu**, China
113/D **Ann** (cape), Ant.
161/G3 **Ann** (cape), Ma,US
160/E4 **Anna** (lake), Va,US
123/V17 **Annaba** (wilaya), Alg.
71/G1 **Annaberg-Buchholz**, Ger.

149/G4 **Anachucuna** (mtn.), Pan.
139/E2 **Anaco**, Ven.
156/E4 **Anaconda**, Mt,US
159/H4 **Anadarko**, Ok,US
89/T3 **Anadyr'**, Rus.
89/U3 **Anadyr'** (gulf), Rus.
89/T3 **Anadyr'** (range), Rus.
90/S3 **Anadyr'** (riv.), Rus.
81/J4 **Anáfi** (isl.), Gre.
92/E3 **'Ānah**, Iraq
164/C3 **Anaheim**, Ca,US
164/G8 **Anaheim Stadium**, Ca,US
156/B2 **Anahim Lake**, BC,Can
162/E4 **Anahuac**, Tx,US
116/B3 **Anai Mudi** (mtn.), India
140/A1 **Anajatuba**, Braz.
106/D4 **Anakāpalle**, India
133/H6 **Analalava**, Madg.
133/J7 **Analamaitso** (plat.), Madg.
149/G1 **Ana María** (gulf), Cuba
110/C3 **Anambas** (isls.), Indo.
129/G5 **Anambra** (state), Nga.
91/C1 **Anamur**, Turk.
91/C1 **Anamur** (riv.), Turk.
98/D4 **Anan**, Japan
146/B2 **Angel de la Guarda** (isl.), Mex.
100/C5 **Anantapur**, India
108/C1 **Anantnag**, India
102/C3 **Anan'yevo**, Kyr.
86/B3 **Anapa**, Rus.
143/K7 **Añapi** (peak), Arg.
137/J7 **Anápolis**, Braz.
164/D2 **Angelus Oaks**, Ca,US
137/H4 **Anapu** (riv.), Braz.
111/J4 **Angemuk** (mtn.), Indo.
61/E2 **Angermanälven** (riv.), Swe.
120/D3 **Anathan** (isl.), NMar.
92/B2 **Anatolia** (reg.), Turk.
65/H2 **Angermünde**, Ger.
139/F4 **Anauá** (riv.), Braz.
140/B2 **Angical do Piauí**, Braz.
161/G2 **Ancaster**, On,Can
140/C2 **Angicos**, Braz.
141/D2 **Anchieta**, Braz.
109/C3 **Angkor** (ruins), Camb.
165/G6 **Anchor** (bay), Mi,US
151/J3 **Anchorage**, Ak,US
151/J3 **Anchorage**, Ak,US
161/G2 **Ancienne-Lorette**, Qu,Can
56/D5 **Anglesey** (isl.), Wal,UK
144/D4 **Ancohuma** (peak), Bol.
72/C5 **Anglet**, Fr.
162/E4 **Angleton**, Tx,US
72/D3 **Anglin** (riv.), Fr.
79/G5 **Ancona**, It.
79/G5 **Ancona** (prov.), It.
138/B4 **Ancón de Sardinas** (bay), Col., Ecu.
143/J7 **Ancud**, Chile
143/B4 **Ancud** (gulf), Chile
97/K2 **Anda**, China
148/C2 **Angostura** (res.), Mex.
133/J7 **Andaingo Gara**, Madg.
61/C3 **Andalsnes**, Nor.
74/C4 **Andalusia** (aut. comm.), Sp.
163/G4 **Andalusia**, Al,US
107/F5 **Andaman** (sea), Asia
107/F5 **Andaman** (isls.), India
107/F5 **Andaman & Nicobar Is.** (terr.), India
133/J7 **Andapa**, Madg.
140/B4 **Andaraí**, Braz.
68/A4 **Andelle** (riv.), Fr.
77/F2 **Andelsbach** (riv.), Ger.
61/F1 **Andenes**, Nor.
69/E3 **Andenne**, Belg.
61/F1 **Anderdalen Nat'l Park**, Nor.
68/D3 **Anderlues**, Belg.
69/G3 **Andernach**, Ger.
151/N2 **Anderson** (riv.), NW,Can
158/B2 **Anderson**, Ca,US
160/C3 **Anderson**, In,US
163/H3 **Anderson**, SC,US
162/E4 **Anderson**, Tx,US
165/B3 **Anderson** (inlet), Wa,US
165/B3 **Anderson** (isl.), Wa,US
163/G3 **Andersonville Nat'l Hist. Site**, Ga,US
134/C4 **Andes** (mts.), SAm.
61/F1 **Andfjorden** (fjord), Nor.
106/C4 **Andhra Pradesh** (state), India
81/H5 **Andikíthira** (isl.), Gre.
92/A2 **Andírin**, Turk.
133/J7 **Andilamena**, Madg.
93/G3 **Andīmeshk**, Iran
139/G3 **Andíparos** (isl.), Gre.
141/B2 **Andira**, Braz.
102/B3 **Andizhan**, Uzb.
74/D1 **Andoain**, Sp.
138/B5 **Andoas Nuevo**, Ecu.
101/E4 **Andong**, SKor.
101/E4 **Andong** (lake), SKor.
75/F1 **Andorra**
75/F1 **Andorra**, Sp.
75/F1 **Andorra la Vella** (cap.), And.
59/E4 **Andover**, Eng,UK
61/E1 **Andøya** (isl.), Nor.
141/B2 **Andradas**, Braz.
141/B2 **Andradina**, Braz.
75/G3 **Andraitx**, Sp.
133/H7 **Andranomavo** (riv.), Madg.
151/C6 **Andreanof** (isls.), Ak,US
141/A6 **Andrelândia**, Braz.
144/C3 **Andres Avelino Cáceres** (dept.), Peru
53/S10 **Andrésy**, Fr.
162/E3 **Andrews**, Tx,US
166/B6 **Andrews A.F.B.**, Md,US

80/E2 **Andria**, It.
133/H8 **Andringitra** (mts.), Madg.
133/J6 **Androntany** (cape), Madg.
150/B1 **Andros**, Bahm.
81/J4 **Andros** (isl.), Gre.
160/G2 **Androscoggin** (riv.), Me, NH,US
74/C3 **Andújar**, Sp.
142/C4 **Anecón Grande** (peak), Arg.
142/E4 **Anegada** (bay), Arg.
150/E3 **Anegada** (isl.), BVI
150/F5 **Anegada** (pt.), Pan.
150/E3 **Anegada** (passg.), West Indies
129/F5 **Aného**, Togo
120/G7 **Aneityum** (isl.), Van.
75/F1 **Aneto, Pico de** (peak), Sp.
107/K2 **Anfu**, China
108/E3 **Angamāli**, India
135/B1 **Angamos** (pt.), Chile
96/E1 **Angara** (riv.), Rus.
96/E1 **Angarsk**, Rus.
67/E5 **Angel** (riv.), Ger.
91/C1 **Angel** (falls), Ven.
146/B2 **Angel de la Guarda** (isl.), Mex.
135/B1 **Angeles**, Phil.
164/B2 **Angeles Nat'l For.**, Ca,US
106/C5 **Anantapur**, India
62/E3 **Ängelholm**, Swe.
141/B2 **Angelina** (riv.), Tx,US
164/E1 **Angelina** (riv.), Tx,US
143/K7 **Angelus** (lake), Mi,US
165/F6 **Angelus** (lake), Mi,US
137/H4 **Anapu** (riv.), Braz.
61/E2 **Angermanälven** (riv.), Swe.
65/H2 **Angermünde**, Ger.
140/B2 **Angical do Piauí**, Braz.
140/C2 **Angicos**, Braz.
140/C2 **Angkor** (ruins), Camb.
56/D5 **Anglesey** (isl.), Wal,UK
72/C5 **Anglet**, Fr.
162/E4 **Angleton**, Tx,US
72/D3 **Anglin** (riv.), Fr.
109/C2 **Ang Nam Ngum** (lake), Laos
125/L7 **Ango**, Zaire
133/J6 **Angoche**, Moz.
142/B3 **Angol**, Chile
126/C3 **Angola**
160/C3 **Angola**, In,US
148/C2 **Angostura** (res.), Mex.
72/D4 **Angoulême**, Fr.
75/S12 **Angra do Heroísmo**, Azor.,Port.
141/J8 **Angra dos Reis**, Braz.
102/B3 **Angren**, Uzb.
109/C2 **Ang Thong**, Thai.
125/L9 **Angu**, Zaire
151/G3 **Anguilla** (peak), Ak,US
151/G4 **Anguilla** (isl.), UK
137/H8 **Anhandui** (riv.), Braz.
69/D3 **Anholt**, Den.
62/D3 **Anholt** (isl.), Den.
105/F2 **Anhua**, China
100/D4 **Anhui** (prov.), China
100/B3 **Ani**, Japan
151/G4 **Aniakchak** (crater), US
151/G4 **Aniakchak Nat'l Mon. & Prsv.**, Ak,US
68/C3 **Aniche**, Fr.
158/F3 **Animas** (riv.), Co, NM,US
146/B2 **Ánimas, Punta de las** (pt.), Mex.
81/A3 **Anina**, Rom.
97/N2 **Aniva** (bay), Rus.
100/C1 **Aniva, Mys** (cape), Rus.
63/M1 **Anjalamkoski**, Fin.
106/B2 **Anjār**, India
161/N6 **Anjou**, Qu,Can
133/H6 **Anjouan** (isl.), Com.
96/F5 **Ankang**, China
92/C2 **Ankara** (cap.), Turk.
92/C2 **Ankara** (prov.), Turk.
92/A2 **Ankara** (riv.), Turk.
133/H7 **Ankaratra, Massif** (plat.), Madg.
162/C2 **Ankaree** (riv.), Co,US
133/J6 **Ankazoabo**, Madg.
133/H8 **Ankazobe**, Madg.
109/E3 **An Khe**, Viet.
65/G2 **Anklam**, Ger.
105/E3 **Anlong**, China
100/D3 **Anlong Veng**, Camb.
66/D2 **Anloo**, Neth.
100/J7 **Anlu**, China
113/D **Ann** (cape), Ant.
161/G3 **Ann** (cape), Ma,US
160/E4 **Anna** (lake), Va,US
123/V17 **Annaba** (wilaya), Alg.
71/G1 **Annaberg-Buchholz**, Ger.
56/B3 **Annaclone**, NI,UK
92/D4 **An Nafūd** (des.), SAr.
125/L5 **An Nahūd**, Sudan
93/F4 **An Najaf**, Iraq
93/F4 **An Najaf** (gov.), Iraq
60/D1 **Annalee** (riv.), Ire.
56/B3 **Annalong**, NI,UK
109/D2 **Annamitique, Chaîne** (mts.), Laos, Viet.
57/E2 **Annan**, Sc,UK

173
Annan – Athen

54/C6 Annan (riv.), Sc,UK
166/A6 Annandale, Va,US
66/B3 Anna Pavlowna, Neth.
142/B5 Anna Pink (bay), Chile
166/B6 Annapolis (cap.), Md,US
106/D2 Annapurna (mtn.), Nepal
94/C3 An Naqb, Ra's, Jor.
165/E7 Ann Arbor, Mi,US
93/F4 An Nāşirīyah, Iraq
54/B6 Annbank Station, Sc,UK
119/C4 Anne (peak), Austl.
116/C3 Annean (lake), Austl.
166/B6 Anne Arundel (co.), Md,US
76/C6 Annecy, Fr.
76/C6 Annecy (lake), Fr.
76/C6 Annecy-le-Vieux, Fr.
76/C5 Annemasse, Fr.
53/U10 Annet-sur-Marne, Fr.
109/E3 An Nhon, Viet.
104/D3 Anning, China
104/D3 Anning (riv.), China
163/G3 Anniston, Al,US
124/F8 Annobón (isl.), EqG.
72/F4 Annonay, Fr.
93/F3 An Nu'manīyah, Iraq
108/F3 Annūr, India
70/A4 Annweiler, Ger.
99/M10 Anō, Japan
75/K7 Anoia (riv.), Sp.
157/K4 Anoka, Mn,US
133/J7 Anosibe an' Ala, Madg.
129/G2 Ânou-Zeggarene (wadi), Niger
109/E4 An Phuoc, Viet.
103/D5 Anqing, China
103/D3 Anqiu, China
107/K2 Anren, China
67/F5 Anröchte, Ger.
69/E2 Ans, Belg.
103/B3 Ansai, China
101/F7 Ansan, SKor.
70/D4 Ansbach, Ger.
138/C3 Anserma, Col.
71/H6 Ansfelden, Aus.
101/B2 Anshan, China
104/E3 Anshun, China
114/D2 Anson (bay), Austl.
162/D3 Anson, Tx,US
101/D4 Ansŏng, SKor.
168/A3 Ansonia, Ct,US
54/D4 Anstruther, Sc,UK
120/E4 Ant (atoll), Micr.
59/H1 Ant (riv.), Eng,UK
91/E1 Antakya (Antioch), Turk.
133/J6 Antalaha, Madg.
91/B1 Antalya, Turk.
91/B1 Antalya (gulf), Turk.
91/A1 Antalya (prov.), Turk.
133/H7 Antananarivo (cap.), Madg.
133/H7 Antananarivo (prov.), Madg.
113/W Antarctic (pen.), Ant.
113/* Antarctica
140/C3 Antas, Braz.
141/B4 Antas (riv.), Braz.
68/D5 Ante (riv.), Fr.
54/A1 An Teallach (mtn.), Sc,UK
131/C4 Antelope Mine, Zim.
74/C4 Antequera, Sp.
159/H3 Anthony, Ks,US
158/F4 Anthony, NM,US
124/D2 Anti-Atlas (mts.), Mor.
73/G5 Antibes, Fr.
161/J1 Anticosti (isl.), Qu,Can
71/G6 Antiesen (riv.), Aus.
72/D2 Antifer, Cap d' (cape), Fr.
160/B2 Antigo, Wi,US
161/J2 Antigonish, NS,Can
150/F3 Antigua (isl.), Anti.
150/F3 Antigua & Barbuda
148/D3 Antigua Guatemala, Guat.
91/D3 Anti-Lebanon (mts.), Leb.
165/L10 Antioch, Ca,US
165/P15 Antioch, Il,US
91/E1 Antioch (Antakya), Turk.
138/C3 Antioquia, Col.
138/C3 Antioquia (dept.), Col.
51/T8 Antipodes (isls.), NZ
138/B5 Antisana (vol.), Ecu.
159/J4 Antlers, Ok,US
135/B1 Antofagasta, Chile
68/C2 Antoing, Belg.
133/J6 Antongil (bay), Madg.
132/C4 Antoniesberg (peak), SAfr.
141/B3 Antonina, Braz.
140/C2 Antonina do Norte, Braz.
147/Q10 Antonio Alzate (lake), Mex.
141/K6 Antônio Carlos, Braz.
159/F3 Antonito, Co,US
147/P7 Antón Lizardo, Mex.
147/G5 Antón Lizardo, Punta (pt.), Mex.
53/S10 Antony, Fr.
56/B2 Antrim, NI,UK
56/B2 Antrim (dist.), NI,UK
56/B1 Antrim (mts.), NI,UK
133/H7 Antsalova, Madg.
133/H7 Antsirabe, Madg.
133/J6 Antsiranana, Madg.
133/J6 Antsiranana (prov.), Madg.
133/H6 Antsohihy, Madg.
142/C3 Antuco (vol.), Chile
112/B4 Antulai, Gunung (mtn.), Malay.
69/E1 Antwerp (prov.), Belg.
68/D1 Antwerp (Antwerpen), Belg.
68/D1 Antwerpen (Antwerp), Belg.
108/H4 Anuradhapura, SrL.
108/H4 Anuradhapura (dist.), SrL.
108/H4 Anuradhapura (ruins), SrL.
151/B6 Anvil (vol.), Ak,US
105/H3 Anxi, China
103/C3 Anyang, China
101/D4 Anyang, SKor.
101/F7 Anyang (riv.), SKor.
96/D4 A'nyêmaqên (mts.), China
103/B4 Anyi, China
105/G3 Anyuan, China
97/M2 Anyuy (riv.), Rus.
76/E6 Anza (riv.), It.
103/C3 Anze, China
68/C2 Anzegem, Belg.
88/J4 Anzhero-Sudzhensk, Rus.
68/C3 Anzin, Fr.
80/C2 Anzio, It.
139/E2 Anzoátegui (state), Ven.
99/L9 Aogaki, Japan
109/B4 Ao Kham (pt.), Thai.
100/B3 Aomori, Japan
100/B3 Aomori (dept.), Japan
81/G2 Aóos (riv.), Gre.
109/B4 Ao Phangnga Nat'l Park, Thai.
109/D3 Aoral (peak), Camb.
73/G4 Aosta, It.
78/A1 Aosta (prov.), It.
78/A1 Aosta, Valle d' (val.), It.
128/C2 Aoudaghost (ruins), Mrta.
125/K5 Aouk (riv.), CAfr., Chad
128/C2 Aoukar (reg.), Mrta.
124/F2 Aoulef, Alg.
99/M10 Aoyama, Japan
124/J3 Aozou, Chad
162/B4 Apache (mts.), Tx,US
163/G4 Apalachicola, Fl,US
147/L7 Apan, Mex.
138/D5 Apaporis (riv.), Braz., Col.
141/B4 Aparados da Serra Nat'l Park, Braz.
141/C2 Aparecida, Braz.
141/B2 Aparecida do Taboado, Braz.
112/C1 Aparri, Phil.
138/B3 Apartado, Col.
121/L6 Apataki, FrPol.
82/D3 Apatin, Yugo.
84/G2 Apatity, Rus.
146/E5 Apatzingán, Mex.
147/K7 Apaxco de Ocampo, Mex.
147/P5 Apaxtla, Mex.
109/D4 Ap Binh Chau, Viet.
66/C4 Apeldoorn, Neth.
66/D4 Apeldoornsch (can.), Neth.
67/E2 Apen, Ger.
52/E4 Apennines (mts.), It.
92/B2 Aphrodisias (ruins), Turk.
110/C3 Api (cape), Indo.
111/F4 Api (cape), Indo.
111/E5 Api (peak), Indo.
102/D5 Api (mtn.), Nepal
121/H6 Apia (cap.), WSam.
137/G6 Apiacás (mts.), Braz.
141/B3 Apiaí, Braz.
147/F5 Apizaco, Mex.
109/D4 Ap Loc Thanh, Viet.
109/E4 Ap Long Hoa, Viet.
109/D4 Ap Luc, Viet.
112/D4 Apo (mtn.), Phil.
147/E3 Apodaca, Mex.
140/C2 Apodi, Braz.
140/C2 Apodi (riv.), Braz.
139/G3 Apoera, Guy.
121/R9 Apolima (str.), WSam.
141/B1 Aporé (riv.), Braz.
148/E3 Aposentillo (pt.), Nic.
160/B2 Apostle (isls.), Wi,US
135/E2 Apóstoles, Arg.
91/D2 Apostolos Andreas (cape), Cyp.
155/K4 Appalachian (mts.), US
70/A5 Appenweier, Ger.
66/D2 Appingedam, Neth.
57/F2 Appleby, Eng,UK
59/E1 Appleby Magna, Eng,UK
161/S9 Appleton, NY,US
160/B2 Appleton, Wi,US
164/C1 Apple Valley, Ca,US
77/G5 Aprica, Passo dell' (pass), It.
80/D2 Apricena, It.
80/C2 Aprilia, It.
86/F3 Apsheronsk, Rus.
119/E1 Apsley Gorge Nat'l Park, Austl.
109/E4 Ap Tan My, Viet.
154/U11 Apua (pt.), Hi,US
78/D4 Apuane (mts.), It.
141/B2 Apucarana, Braz.
139/E3 Apure (riv.), Ven.
138/D3 Apure (state), Ven.
136/D6 Apurímac (riv.), Peru
109/E4 Ap Vinh Hao, Viet.
127/C2 Aqaba (gulf), Asia
92/C4 Aqaba (gulf), Egypt, SAr.
88/H4 Aqmola (cap.), Kaz.
127/D5 'Aqīq, Sudan
102/E4 Aqqikkol (lake), China
93/E2 'Aqrah, Iraq
146/E3 Aquanaval (riv.), Mex.
137/G8 Aquidauana, Braz.
137/G8 Aquidauana (riv.), Braz.
140/C1 Aquiraz, Braz.
72/C4 Aquitaine (reg.), Fr.
96/D4 Ar (riv.), China
60/B5 Ara (riv.), Ire.
99/F2 Ara (riv.), Japan
125/L5 'Arab (riv.), Sudan
163/G3 Arab, Al,US
127/C2 'Arabah, Wādī (dry riv.), Egypt
92/D2 Araban, Turk.
94/D3 Arabian (pen.), Asia
95/H5 Arabian (sea), Asia
127/C3 Arabian (des.), Egypt
91/E3 'Arab, Jabal al (mts.), Syria
127/B2 'Arab, Kalīj al (gulf), Egypt
86/E4 Araç (riv.), Turk.
136/E7 Araca, Bol.
139/F4 Araça (riv.), Braz.
140/C3 Aracaju, Braz.
138/C2 Aracataca, Col.
140/C2 Aracati, Braz.
141/B2 Araçatuba, Braz.
112/B3 Araceli, Phil.
74/B4 Aracena, Sp.
140/C3 Araci, Braz.
140/C2 Aracoiba, Braz.
141/D1 Aracruz, Braz.
141/D1 Araçuaí, Braz.
140/B5 Araçuaí (riv.), Braz.
92/C4 'Arad, Isr.
82/E2 Arad, Rom.
82/E2 Arad (co.), Rom.
125/K4 Arada, Chad
93/H3 Ārādān, Iran
94/D4 'Arafāt, Jabal (mtn.), SAr.
114/E2 Arafura (sea), Austl.
137/H7 Aragarças, Braz.
87/H4 Aragats, Gora (peak), Arm.
60/B5 Araglin (riv.), Ire.
75/E2 Aragon (aut. comm.), Sp.
74/E1 Aragón (riv.), Sp.
139/E2 Aragua (state), Ven.
137/J5 Araguaia (riv.), Braz.
137/H7 Araguaiana, Braz.
137/H5 Araguaia Nat'l Park, Braz.
137/J5 Araguaína, Braz.
141/B1 Araguari, Braz.
137/H3 Araguari (riv.), Braz.
137/J7 Araguari (riv.), Braz.
141/C1 Araguari (Valhas) (riv.), Braz.
137/J5 Araguatins, Braz.
99/F2 Arai, Japan
140/B1 Araioses, Braz.
93/G3 Arāk, Iran
151/D3 Arakamchechan (isl.), Rus.
104/B4 Arakan (mts.), Burma
81/G3 Arákhthos (riv.), Gre.
92/E1 Araklı, Turk.
53/H5 Araks (riv.), Eur., Asia
88/G5 Aral (sea), Uzb., Kaz.
88/G5 Aral'sk, Kaz.
87/H2 Aralsor (lake), Kaz.
93/G3 Ārān, Iran
55/G9 Aran (isl.), Ire.
60/A3 Aran (isls.), Ire.
74/D2 Aranda de Duero, Sp.
146/E4 Arandas, Mex.
82/E3 Arandelovac, Yugo.
74/D2 Aranjuez, Sp.
56/E6 Aran Mawddwy (mtn.), Wal,UK
162/D5 Aransas Pass, Tx,US
108/G3 Arantāngi, India
141/J6 Arantina, Braz.
120/G4 Aranuka (atoll), Kiri.
140/C3 Arapiraca, Braz.
139/H5 Arapiuns (riv.), Braz.
92/D2 Arapkir, Turk.
141/B2 Arapongas, Braz.
141/B4 Araranguá, Braz.
141/B2 Araraquara, Braz.
141/C2 Araras, Braz.
119/B3 Ararat, Austl.
93/F2 Ararat (Ağri) (peak), Turk.
140/A1 Arari, Braz.
140/B2 Araripe (hills), Braz.
140/B2 Araripina, Braz.
92/F2 Aras (riv.), Asia
128/C2 Aratane (well), Mrta.
140/B2 Aratas (res.), Braz.
136/F4 Arauá (riv.), Braz.
138/D3 Arauca, Col.
138/D3 Arauca (inten.), Col.
139/E3 Arauca (riv.), Col., Ven.
141/B3 Araucária, Braz.
138/D2 Araure, Ven.
76/C6 Aravis, Col des (pass), Fr.
120/E5 Arawa, PNG
130/D3 Arawale Nat'l Rsv., Kenya
141/C1 Araxá, Braz.
139/E2 Araya (pen.), Ven.
112/C2 Arayat (mtn.), Phil.
125/N6 Ārba Minch', Eth.
62/F2 Arboga, Swe.
76/C6 Arbois, Mont d' (mtn.), Fr.
77/E5 Arbola, Punta d' (peak), It.
138/B2 Arboletes, Col.
77/F2 Arbon, Swi.
157/H2 Arborfield, Sk,Can
157/J3 Arborg, Mb,Can
54/D3 Arbroath, Sc,UK
72/F5 Arc (riv.), Fr.
73/G4 Arc (riv.), Fr.
72/C4 Arcachon, Fr.
72/C4 Arcachon (lag.), Fr.
72/C4 Arcachon, Pointe d' (pt.), Fr.
164/B2 Arcadia, Ca,US
163/H5 Arcadia, Fl,US
158/A2 Arcata, Ca,US
53/S10 Arc de Triomphe, Fr.
141/G6 Arceburgo, Braz.
84/J2 Archangel (Arkhangel'sk), Rus.
84/H3 Archangel Obl., Rus.
74/E3 Archena, Sp.
118/A1 Archer (riv.), Austl.
118/A1 Archer Bend Nat'l Park, Austl.
162/D3 Archer City, Tx,US
130/C2 Archers Post, Kenya
158/E3 Arches Nat'l Park, Ut,US
74/C4 Archidona, Sp.
54/C2 Archiestown, Sc,UK
78/B1 Arcisate, It.
142/C3 Arco (pass), Arg.
79/D1 Arco, It.
156/E5 Arco, Id,US
141/C2 Arcos, Braz.
74/C4 Arcos de la Frontera, Sp.
140/C3 Arcoverde, Braz.
50/A1 Arctic (ocean)
151/F2 Arctic (coast. pl.), Ak,US
151/J2 Arctic Nat'l Wild. Ref., Ak,US
151/M2 Arctic Red (riv.), NW,Can
83/G5 Arda (riv.), Bul.
78/C3 Arda (riv.), It.
93/G2 Ardabīl, Iran
93/E1 Ardahan, Turk.
93/H3 Ardakān, Iran
62/B1 Årdalstangen, Nor.
57/E6 Arddleen, Wal,UK
72/F4 Ardèche (riv.), Fr.
117/H5 Arden (peak), Austl.
165/M9 Arden-Arcade, Ca,US
69/E4 Ardennes (for.), Eur.
68/D4 Ardennes (dept.), Fr.
69/D4 Ardennes, Canal des (can.), Fr.
60/C3 Arderin (mtn.), Ire.
54/B1 Ardersier, Sc,UK
92/E1 Ardeşen, Turk.
56/C3 Ardglass, NI,UK
74/B3 Ardila (riv.), Sp.
55/H8 Ardivachar (pt.), Sc,UK
54/C3 Ardle (riv.), Sc,UK
159/H4 Ardmore, Ok,US
166/C3 Ardmore, Pa,US
55/H8 Ardnamurchan (pt.), Sc,UK
68/C2 Ardooie, Belg.
54/B5 Ardrossan, Sc,UK
56/C2 Ards (dist.), NI,UK
56/C3 Ards (pen.), NI,UK
61/E3 Åre, Swe.
141/G6 Areado, Braz.
150/E3 Arecibo, PR
140/C2 Areia Branca, Braz.
158/B3 Arena (pt.), Ca,US
146/C3 Arena de la Ventana, Punta (pt.), Mex.
149/E4 Arenal (vol.), CR
137/G6 Arenápolis, Braz.
146/C4 Arena, Punta (pt.), Mex.
74/C2 Arenas de San Pedro, Sp.
143/K8 Arenas, Punta de (pt.), Arg.
62/C2 Arendal, Nor.
66/C6 Arendonk, Belg.
56/E6 Arenig Fawr (mtn.), Wal,UK
75/L6 Arenys de Mar, Sp.
75/L6 Arenys de Munt, Sp.
78/B4 Arenzano, It.
144/D5 Arequipa, Peru
144/C4 Arequipa (dept.), Peru
74/C2 Arévalo, Sp.
79/E6 Arezzo, It.
79/E5 Arezzo (prov.), It.
75/C5 Arga (riv.), Sp.
74/D3 Argamasilla de Alba, Sp.
74/C3 Argamasilla de Calatrava, Sp.
75/N9 Arganda, Sp.
112/C3 Argao, Phil.
77/F2 Argen (riv.), Ger.
73/G5 Argens (riv.), Fr.
78/E3 Argenta, It.
72/C2 Argentan, Fr.
73/G4 Argentera (peak), It.
53/S10 Argenteuil, Fr.
76/D6 Argentière, Aiguille d' (peak), Swi.
135/C4 Argentina
78/A5 Argentina (riv.), It.
143/J7 Argentino (lake), Arg.
75/L6 Argentona, Sp.
83/G3 Argeş (co.), Rom.
83/G3 Argeş (riv.), Rom.
95/J2 Arghandab (riv.), Afg.
60/B6 Argideen (riv.), Ire.
127/B5 Argo, Sudan
81/H4 Argolis (gulf), Gre.
69/E5 Argonne (for.), Fr.
165/Q16 Argonne Nat'l Lab., Il,US
81/H4 Árgos, Gre.
81/G3 Argostólion, Gre.
68/A4 Argueil, Fr.
158/B4 Arguello (pt.), Ca,US
128/A1 Arguin (bay), Mrta.
97/H1 Argun (riv.), China, Rus.
102/E2 Argut (riv.), Rus.
114/D3 Argyle (lake), Austl.
54/A4 Argyll (dist.), Sc,UK
97/J3 Ar Horqin Qi, China
124/C3 Arhreijît (well), Mrta.
62/D3 Århus, Den.
62/D3 Århus (co.), Den.
80/D2 Ariano Irpino, It.
74/C1 Arianza (riv.), Sp.
138/C4 Ariari (riv.), Col.
144/D5 Arica, Chile
116/D5 Arid (cape), Austl.
98/D3 Arida, Japan
164/A1 Arido (mtn.), Ca,US
72/D5 Ariège (riv.), Fr.
83/K5 Arifiye, Turk.
108/B2 Ārifwāla, Pak.
91/E2 Arīḩā, Syria
91/D4 Arīḩā (Jericho), WBnk.
159/G3 Arikaree (riv.), Co,US
150/F5 Arima, Trin.
130/A2 Aringa, Ugan.
140/A4 Arinos, Braz.
137/G6 Arinos (riv.), Braz.
136/F5 Aripuanã, Braz.
136/F5 Aripuanã (riv.), Braz.
136/F5 Ariquemes, Braz.
127/C2 'Arīsh, Wādī al (dry riv.), Egypt
133/H7 Arivonimamo, Madg.
108/G3 Ariyalūr, India
75/F1 Arize (riv.), Fr.
158/D4 Arizona (state), US
62/E2 Årjäng, Swe.
138/C2 Arjona, Col.
74/C4 Arjona, Sp.
162/E3 Arkadelphia, Ar,US
54/A3 Arkaig, Loch (lake), Sc,UK
102/A1 Arkalyk, Kaz.
155/H4 Arkansas (riv.), US
162/E3 Arkansas (state), US
163/F3 Arkansas City, Ar,US
159/H3 Arkansas City, Ks,US
159/H3 Arkansas, Salt Fork (riv.), Ks,US
125/K3 Arkanū (peak), Libya
84/J2 Arkhangel'sk (Archangel), Rus.
60/D4 Arklow, Ire.
65/G1 Arkona, Kap (cape), Ger.
106/C5 Arkonam, India
57/G4 Arksey, Eng,UK
88/H2 Arkticheskiy Institut (isls.), Rus.
74/C1 Arlanza (riv.), Sp.
74/C1 Arlazón (riv.), Sp.
77/G3 Arlbergpass (pass), Aus.
72/F5 Arles, Fr.
76/D3 Arlesheim, Swi.
68/C3 Arleux, Fr.
164/C3 Arlington, Ca,US
163/G4 Arlington, Ga,US
168/C1 Arlington, Ma,US
157/K4 Arlington, Mn,US
162/D3 Arlington, Tx,US
166/A6 Arlington, Va,US
165/Q15 Arlington Heights, Il,US
69/E4 Arlon, Belg.
78/B1 Arluno, It.
129/F4 Arly Nat'l Park, Burk.
129/F4 Arly Res., Ben.
165/G6 Armada, Mi,US
116/K7 Armadale, Austl.
54/C5 Armadale, Sc,UK
56/B3 Armagh, NI,UK
56/B3 Armagh (dist.), NI,UK
72/F3 Armançon (riv.), Fr.
141/B2 Armando Laydner (res.), Braz.
127/C3 Armant, Egypt
87/G3 Armavir, Rus.
73/G5 Arme, Cap d' (cape), Fr.
87/H4 Armenia
138/C3 Armenia, Col.
68/B2 Armentières, Fr.
146/E5 Armería, Mex.
138/C3 Armero, Col.
119/D1 Armidale, Austl.
74/D4 Armilla, Sp.
56/B1 Armoy, NI,UK
142/E2 Armstrong, Arg.
156/D3 Armstrong, BC,Can
57/G4 Armthorpe, Eng,UK
106/C4 Ārmūr, India
166/B5 Army Ordnance Museum, Md,US
153/J3 Arnaud (riv.), Qu,Can
91/C2 Arnauti (cape), Cyp.
93/M6 Arnavutköy, Turk.
59/E3 Arncott, Eng,UK
74/D1 Arnedo, Sp.
68/B2 Arnèke, Fr.
62/D1 Årnes, Nor.
159/H3 Arnett, Ok,US
114/F2 Arnhem (bay), Austl.
114/F2 Arnhem (cape), Austl.
66/C5 Arnhem, Neth.
114/E2 Arnhem Land (reg.), Austl.
106/C5 Arni, India
78/D5 Arno (riv.), It.
120/G4 Arno (atoll), Mrsh.
57/G5 Arnold, Eng,UK
166/B5 Arnold, Md,US
166/C5 Arnold (pt.), NJ,US
168/H6 Arnold, Pa,US
73/K3 Arnoldstein, Aus.
72/E3 Arnon (riv.), Fr.
53/T10 Arnouville-lès-Gonesse, Fr.
160/E2 Arnprior, On,Can
67/F6 Arnsberg, Ger.
57/F3 Arnside, Eng,UK
64/F3 Arnstadt, Ger.
70/C3 Arnstein, Ger.
140/B2 Aroases, Braz.
76/D6 Arolla, Swi.
67/G6 Arolsen, Ger.
72/E3 Aron (riv.), Fr.
75/X16 Arona, Canl.
78/B1 Arona, It.
68/B4 Aronde (riv.), Fr.
120/G5 Arorae (atoll), Kiri.
112/C2 Aroroy, Phil.
77/F4 Aroser Rothern (peak), Swi.
111/H5 Aro Usu (cape), Indo.
53/S11 Arpajon, Fr.
68/B2 Arques, Fr.
106/D2 Arrah, India
125/M5 Ar Rahad, Sudan
140/A4 Arraias, Braz.
137/H6 Arraias (riv.), Braz.
149/G4 Arraiján, Pan.
57/H4 Arram, Eng,UK
93/E3 Ar Ramādī, Iraq
91/E3 Ar Ramthā, Jor.
54/A5 Arran (isl.), Sc,UK
149/E4 Arrancabarba (mtn.), Nic.
92/D3 Ar Raqqah, Syria
92/D2 Ar Raqqah (prov.), Syria
68/B3 Arras, Fr.
91/E2 Ar Rastan, Syria
75/F1 Arrats (riv.), Fr.
142/E5 Arrecifes, Arg.
72/B2 Arrée (mts.), Fr.
63/T9 Arresø (lake), Den.
148/C2 Arriaga, Mex.
93/F4 Ar Rifā'ī, Iraq
141/A5 Arrio Grande, Braz.
94/E4 Ar Riyāḑ (Riyadh) (cap.), SAr.
54/B4 Arrochar, Sc,UK
78/B4 Arroscia (riv.), It.
72/F3 Arroux (riv.), Fr.
60/B1 Arrow, Lough (lake), Ire.
74/B3 Arroyo de la Luz, Sp.
158/B4 Arroyo Grande, Ca,US
93/F4 Ar Rumaythah, Iraq
91/E3 Ar Ruşayfah, Jor.
125/M5 Ar Ruşayriş, Sudan
94/F4 Ar Ruways, SAr.
97/L3 Arsen'yev, Rus.
121/T11 Art (isl.), NCal.
81/G3 Árta, Gre.
81/G3 Árta (gulf), Gre.
147/E3 Arteaga, Mex.
74/A1 Arteijo, Sp.
97/L3 Artem, Rus.
149/F1 Artemisa, Cuba
164/B3 Artesia, Ca,US
159/F4 Artesia, NM,US
77/E3 Arth, Swi.
118/C3 Arthur (pt.), Austl.
116/C5 Arthur (riv.), Austl.
168/G6 Arthur (res.), Pa,US
167/J9 Arthur Kill (str.), NJ, NY,US
115/R11 Arthur's (pass), NZ
135/E3 Artigas, Uru.
68/A2 Artois (reg.), Fr.
68/B2 Artois, Collines de l' (hills), Fr.
141/F7 Artur Nogueira, Braz.
102/C4 Artux, China
92/E1 Artvin, Turk.
92/E1 Artvin (prov.), Turk.
111/H5 Aru (isls.), Indo.
130/A2 Arua, Ugan.
150/D4 Aruba (isl.), Neth.
141/G8 Arujá, Braz.
59/F5 Arun (riv.), Eng,UK
107/F2 Arunachal Pradesh (state), India
59/F5 Arundel, Eng,UK
108/G4 Aruppukkottai, India
111/F3 Arus (cape), Indo.
130/C3 Arusha, Tanz.
130/C4 Arusha (prov.), Tanz.
130/C3 Arusha Chine, Tanz.
130/C3 Arusha Nat'l Park, Tanz.
121/L6 Arutua (atoll), FrPol.
108/H4 Aruvi (riv.), SrL.
125/L7 Aruwimi (riv.), Zaire
96/E2 Arvayheer, Mong.
76/C6 Arve (riv.), Fr.
61/F2 Arvidsjaur, Swe.
62/E2 Arvika, Swe.
158/C4 Arvin, Ca,US
160/B2 Arvon (peak), Mi,US
123/X17 Aryānah (gov.), Tun.
102/A3 Arys', Kaz.
72/B3 Arz (riv.), Fr.
85/J5 Arzamas, Rus.
71/F2 Arzberg, Ger.
67/G4 Arzen, Ger.
123/Q16 Arzew, Alg.
69/F3 Arzfeld, Ger.
79/E1 Arzignano, It.
74/A1 Arzúa, Sp.
69/E1 As, Belg.
71/F2 Aš, Czh.
62/D2 Ås, Nor.
93/G3 Asadābād, Iran
128/D5 Asagny Nat'l Park, IvC.
110/A3 Asahan (riv.), Indo.
99/G3 Asahi, Japan
98/C3 Asahi (riv.), Japan
99/G2 Asahi-Bandai Nat'l Park, Japan
100/C2 Asahi-dake (mtn.), Japan
100/C2 Asahikawa, Japan
99/H7 Asaka, Japan
99/M9 Asake (riv.), Japan
125/P5 Āsalē, Eth.
99/F2 Asama-yama (mtn.), Japan
101/D4 Asan (bay), SKor.
106/E3 Asansol, India
124/J3 Asawanwah (well), Libya
85/P4 Asbest, Rus.
132/C3 Asbestos (mts.), SAfr.
167/D3 Asbury Park, NJ,US
136/F7 Ascención, Bol.
147/J5 Ascención (bay), Mex.
50/J6 Ascension (isl.), StH.
71/G6 Aschach (riv.), Aus.
70/C3 Aschaffenburg, Ger.
67/E5 Ascheberg, Ger.
64/F3 Aschersleben, Ger.
80/A1 Asco (riv.), Fr.
54/A5 Ascog, Sc,UK
80/C1 Ascoli Piceno, It.
80/D2 Ascoli Satriano, It.
144/B2 Ascope, Peru
59/F4 Ascot, Eng,UK
125/P5 Āseb, Erit.
125/N6 Āsela, Eth.
83/G4 Asenovgrad, Bul.
78/C3 Aserei, Monte (peak), It.
96/G2 Asgat, Mong.
59/G4 Ash, Eng,UK
59/E4 Ashampstead, Eng,UK
129/E5 Ashanti (reg.), Gha.
129/E5 Ashanti (uplands), Gha.
57/G5 Ashbourne, Eng,UK
116/C2 Ashburton (riv.), Austl.
115/R11 Ashburton, NZ
58/C5 Ashburton, Eng,UK
59/E1 Ashby (can.), Eng,UK
57/G6 Ashby-de-la-Zouch, Eng,UK
58/D3 Ashchurch, Eng,UK
156/C3 Ashcroft, BC,Can
163/J3 Asheboro, NC,US
157/J3 Ashern, Mb,Can
163/H3 Asheville, NC,US
157/M2 Asheweig (riv.), On,Can
53/M7 Ashford, Eng,UK
59/F1 Ashfordby, Eng,UK
161/Q8 Ashgrove, On,Can
115/S11 Ashhurst, NZ
100/C2 Ashibetsu, Japan
57/G1 Ashington, Eng,UK
99/L10 Ashiya, Japan
98/C4 Ashizuri-misaki (cape), Japan
123/W17 Ashkal (lake), Tun.
93/J2 Ashkhabad (cap.), Trkm.
159/H3 Ashland, Ks,US
160/D4 Ashland, Ky,US
168/C1 Ashland, Ma,US
168/E6 Ashland, Oh,US
168/E6 Ashland (co.), Oh,US
156/C5 Ashland, Or,US
160/B2 Ashland, Wi,US
157/J4 Ashley, ND,US
53/M6 Ashley Green, Eng,UK
114/C2 Ashmore (reef), Austl.
114/C2 Ashmore and Cartier Is. (terr.), Austl.
91/B4 Ashmūn, Egypt
100/C2 Ashoro, Japan
91/E2 Ash Shamāl (gov.), Leb.
93/F4 Ash Shāmīyah, Iraq
95/G3 Ash Shāriqah, UAE
91/B4 Ash Sharqīyah (gov.), Egypt
93/F4 Ash Shaţrah, Iraq
106/C3 Ashta, India
160/D3 Ashtabula, Oh,US
168/G4 Ashtabula (co.), Oh,US
53/N8 Ashtead, Eng,UK
156/F4 Ashton, Id,US
57/F5 Ashton-in-Makerfield, Eng,UK
57/F5 Ashton-under-Lyne, Eng,UK
160/B2 Ashwaubenon, Wi,US
59/F2 Ashwell, Eng,UK
90/* Asia
63/L1 Asikkala, Fin.
123/L13 Asilah, Mor.
80/A2 Asinara (gulf), It.
80/A2 Asinara (isl.), It.
88/J4 Asino, Rus.
94/D5 'Asīr (mts.), SAr., Yemen
127/D5 Asis, Ras (cape), Sudan
92/E2 Aşkale, Turk.
57/E3 Askam in Furness, Eng,UK
62/D2 Asker, Nor.
57/G4 Askern, Eng,UK
62/D2 Askim, Nor.
62/D3 Åskim, Swe.
81/G2 Áskion (peak), Gre.
61/P6 Askja (crater), Ice.
125/N4 Āsmera (cap.), Erit.
62/F3 Asnen (lake), Swe.
53/T9 Asnières-sur-Oise, Fr.
53/S10 Asnières-sur-Seine, Fr.
98/B4 Aso Nat'l Park, Japan
125/M5 Āsosa, Eth.
98/B4 Aso-san (mtn.), Japan
127/D4 Asoteriba, Jabal (peak), Sudan
57/E2 Aspatria, Eng,UK
75/E3 Aspe, Sp.
158/F3 Aspen, Co,US
91/B1 Aspendos (ruins), Turk.
166/A5 Aspen Hill, Md,US
70/C5 Asperg, Ger.
162/C3 Aspermont, Tx,US
167/E1 Aspetuck (riv.), Ct,US
75/F1 Aspin, Col d' (pass), Fr.
115/Q11 Aspiring (peak), NZ
81/H3 Asprópirgos, Gre.
156/G2 Asquith, Sk,Can
128/C2 'Assâba, Massif de l' (reg.), Mrta.
91/B5 Aş Şaff, Egypt
91/D4 Aş Şāfī, Jor.
93/G4 As Sālimīyah, Kuw.
94/E4 As Sālimīyah, SAr.
125/L1 As Sallūm, Egypt
91/D3 As Salţ, Jor.
107/F2 Assam (state), India
93/F4 As Samāwah, Iraq
91/B4 As Sanţah, Egypt
140/C2 Assaré, Braz.
91/D3 Aş Şarīḩ, Jor.
68/D2 Asse, Belg.
131/C5 Assegairivier (riv.), SAfr.
80/A3 Assemini, It.
66/D2 Assen, Neth.
68/C1 Assenede, Belg.
124/J1 As Sidr, Libya
91/B4 As Sinbillāwayn, Egypt
157/G3 Assiniboia, Sk,Can
156/E3 Assiniboine (peak), BC,Can
157/J3 Assiniboine (riv.), Mb,Can
160/F1 Assinika (lake), Qu,Can
141/B2 Assis, Braz.
75/G1 Assou (riv.), Fr.
125/M6 As Sudd (reg.), Sudan
93/F3 As Sulaymānīyah, Iraq
93/F3 As Sulaymānīyah (gov.), Iraq
93/F5 Aş Şummān (mts.), SAr.
91/E3 As Suwaydā', Syria
91/E3 As Suwaydā' (dist.), Syria
93/F3 Aş Şuwayrah, Iraq
91/C4 As Suways (gov.), Egypt
91/C5 As Suways (Suez), Egypt
66/C6 Asten, Neth.
78/B3 Asti, It.
78/B3 Asti (prov.), It.
79/E1 Astico (riv.), It.
141/L6 Astolfo Dutra, Braz.
59/E2 Aston, Eng,UK
58/D2 Aston on Clun, Eng,UK
141/B2 Astorga, Braz.
167/K8 Astoria, NY,US
156/C4 Astoria, Or,US
62/E3 Åstorp, Swe.
87/J3 Astrakhan', Rus.
87/H3 Astrakhan Obl., Rus.
74/B1 Asturias (aut. comm.), Sp.
59/E2 Astwood Bank, Eng,UK
99/L10 Asuka, Japan
99/N9 Asuke, Japan
120/D3 Asuncion (isl.), NMar.
135/E2 Asunción (cap.), Par.
147/F5 Asunción Nochixtlán, Mex.
62/F2 Asunden (lake), Swe.
130/B2 Aswa, Ugan.
130/B2 Aswa (riv.), Ugan.
127/C3 Aswān, Egypt
127/C4 Aswān (gov.), Egypt
127/C4 Aswan High (dam), Egypt
127/B3 Asyūţ, Egypt
127/B3 Asyūţ (gov.), Egypt
127/C2 Asyūţī, Wādī al (dry riv.), Egypt
139/E4 Atabapo (riv.), Col., Ven.
135/C2 Atacama (des.), Chile
135/C1 Atacama, Puna de (plat.), Arg.
138/B4 Atacames, Ecu.
129/F4 Atacora (range), Ben.
121/H5 Atafu (atoll), Tok.
129/F5 Atakpamé, Togo
140/C3 Atalaia, Braz.
99/F3 Atami, Japan
128/B1 Atar, Mrta.
74/D4 Atarfe, Sp.
147/E4 Atarjea, Mex.
106/D2 Atarra, India
96/D3 Atas Bogd (peak), Mong.
158/B4 Atascadero, Ca,US
92/D2 Atatürk (dam), Turk.
92/D2 Atatürk (res.), Turk.
125/M4 Atbara, Sudan
125/M4 Atbara (Atbarah) (riv.), Eth., Sudan
102/A1 Atbasar, Kaz.
159/K5 Atchafalaya (bay), La,US
163/F4 Atchafalaya (riv.), La,US
159/J3 Atchison, Ks,US
129/E5 Atebubu, Gha.
61/G1 Ateelva (riv.), Nor.
147/Q10 Atengo (riv.), Mex.
80/C1 Aterno (riv.), It.
68/C2 Ath, Belg.
156/E2 Athabasca, Ab,Can
152/E3 Athabasca (riv.), Ab,Can
152/F3 Athabasca (lake), Ab, Sk,Can
157/H2 Athapapuskow (lake), Mb,Can
124/K1 Āthār Ţulmaythah (Ptolemaïs) (ruins), Libya
167/J8 Athenia, NJ,US
163/G3 Athens, Al,US
163/H3 Athens, Ga,US
160/D4 Athens, Oh,US
163/G3 Athens, Tn,US
162/E3 Athens, Tx,US

174

Athen – Bambe

81/H4 **Athens** (Athínai) (cap.), Gre.
81/L7 **Athens** (Athínai) (inset) (cap.), Gre.
59/E1 **Atherstone,** Eng,UK
57/F4 **Atherton,** Eng,UK
130/C3 **Athi** (riv.), Kenya
81/H4 **Athínai** (Athens) (cap.), Gre.
81/L7 **Athínai** (Athens) (inset) (cap.), Gre.
130/C3 **Athi River,** Kenya
53/T10 **Athis-Mons,** Fr.
60/C3 **Athlone,** Ire.
54/C3 **Atholl** (forest), Sc,UK
81/J2 **Áthos** (peak), Gre.
124/J5 **Ati,** Chad
130/B2 **Atiak,** Ugan.
141/G8 **Atibaia,** Braz.
141/G7 **Atíbaia** (riv.), Braz.
160/B1 **Atikokan,** On,Can
148/D3 **Atitlán** (lake), Guat.
121/K7 **Atiu** (isl.), Cookls.
151/C5 **Atka** (isl.), Ak,US
87/H2 **Atkarsk,** Rus.
151/M2 **Atkinson** (pt.), NW,Can
163/G3 **Atlanta** (cap.), Ga,US
162/E3 **Atlanta,** Tx,US
50/G3 **Atlantic** (ocean)
157/K5 **Atlantic,** Ia,US
166/D5 **Atlantic** (co.), NJ,US
166/D5 **Atlantic City,** NJ,US
138/C2 **Atlántico** (dept.), Col.
129/F5 **Atlantique** (prov.), Ben.
124/E2 **Atlas** (mts.), Afr.
165/K10 **Atlas** (peak), Ca,US
124/E1 **Atlas Saharien** (mts.), Alg., Mor.
147/M7 **Atlazayanca,** Mex.
151/M4 **Atlin** (lake), BC,Can
147/F5 **Atlixco,** Mex.
163/G4 **Atmore,** Al,US
136/E8 **Atocha,** Bol.
68/D2 **Atomium, The,** Belg.
147/L6 **Atotonilco el Grande,** Mex.
124/B3 **Atoui** (dry riv.), Mrta.
148/B2 **Atoyac** (riv.), Mex.
93/J2 **Atrak** (riv.), Iran
62/E3 **Ätran** (riv.), Swe.
138/B3 **Atrato** (riv.), Col.
99/H7 **Atsugi,** Japan
99/N10 **Atsumi,** Japan
99/N10 **Atsumi** (pen.), Japan
91/D4 **Aţ Ţafīlah,** Jor.
94/D4 **Aţ Ţā'if,** SAr.
91/E3 **At Tall,** Syria
163/G3 **Attalla,** Al,US
91/B4 **At Tall al Kabīr,** Egypt
93/E3 **At Ta'mīn** (gov.), Iraq
153/H3 **Attawapiskat** (riv.), On,Can
71/F6 **Attel** (riv.), Ger.
67/E6 **Attendorn,** Ger.
71/G7 **Attersee** (lake), Aus.
68/C5 **Attichy,** Fr.
108/F4 **Attingal,** India
168/C2 **Attleboro,** Ma,US
59/E2 **Attleborough,** Eng,UK
59/H2 **Attleborough,** Eng,UK
151/A5 **Attu** (isl.), Ak,US
127/C2 **Aţ Ţūr,** Egypt
108/G3 **Āttūr,** India
91/D4 **Aţ Ţūr,** WBnk.
94/D6 **At Turbah,** Yem.
142/D2 **Atuel** (riv.), Arg.
138/B4 **Atuntaqui,** Ecu.
130/B2 **Atura,** Ugan.
62/G2 **Åtvidaberg,** Swe.
158/B3 **Atwater,** Ca,US
159/G3 **Atwood,** Ks,US
168/F6 **Atwood** (lake), Oh,US
150/C2 **Atwood** (Samana) (cay), Bahm.
147/Q10 **Atzcapotzalco,** Mex.
139/E3 **Auari** (riv.), Braz.
69/E4 **Aubange,** Belg.
68/D6 **Aube** (dept.), Fr.
72/F2 **Aube** (riv.), Fr.
72/F4 **Aubenas,** Fr.
76/C4 **Aubert, Mont** (peak), Swi.
53/T10 **Aubervilliers,** Fr.
68/C6 **Aubetin** (riv.), Fr.
68/A5 **Aubette** (riv.), Fr.
72/E4 **Aubin,** Fr.
72/E4 **Aubrac** (mts.), Fr.
163/G3 **Auburn,** Al,US
158/B3 **Auburn,** Ca,US
160/C3 **Auburn,** In,US
168/C1 **Auburn,** Ma,US
161/G2 **Auburn,** Me,US
159/J2 **Auburn,** Ne,US
160/E3 **Auburn,** NY,US
165/C3 **Auburn,** Wa,US
165/F6 **Auburn Hills,** Mi,US
142/C3 **Aucá Mahuida** (peak), Arg.
72/D5 **Auch,** Fr.
68/B3 **Auchel,** Fr.
54/D3 **Auchenblae,** Sc,UK
56/E2 **Auchencairn,** Sc,UK
54/B6 **Auchinleck,** Sc,UK
54/C4 **Auchterarder,** Sc,UK
54/C4 **Auchtermuchty,** Sc,UK
115/R10 **Auckland,** NZ
51/S8 **Auckland** (isls.), NZ
72/E5 **Aude** (riv.), Fr.
68/D2 **Auderghem,** Belg.
76/C3 **Audeux** (riv.), Fr.
72/A3 **Audierne** (bay), Fr.
76/C3 **Audincourt,** Fr.
57/F6 **Audlem,** Eng,UK
57/F5 **Audley,** Eng,UK
125/P6 **Audo** (range), Eth.
69/E5 **Audun-le-Tiche,** Fr.
71/F1 **Aue,** Ger.
67/E2 **Aue** (riv.), Ger.
67/F3 **Aue** (riv.), Ger.
71/F1 **Auerbach,** Ger.
71/E3 **Auerbach in der Oberpfalz,** Ger.
77/G2 **Auerberg** (mtn.), Ger.
77/H5 **Auer** (Ora), It.
71/F2 **Auersberg** (peak), Ger.
70/E3 **Aufess** (riv.), Ger.
56/A3 **Augher,** NI,UK
60/A4 **Aughinish** (isl.), Ire.
56/B3 **Aughnacloy,** NI,UK
132/C3 **Augrabies Falls Nat'l Park,** SAfr.
132/C3 **Augrabiesvalle** (falls), SAfr.
70/D6 **Augsburg,** Ger.
132/A2 **Augub** (peak), Namb.
149/H4 **Augusta** (pt.), Col.
80/D4 **Augusta,** It.
80/D4 **Augusta** (gulf), It.
163/H3 **Augusta,** Ga,US
161/G2 **Augusta** (cap.), Me,US
67/F5 **Augustdorf,** Ger.
65/M2 **Augustów,** Pol.
114/C3 **Augustus** (isl.), Austl.
116/C3 **Augustus** (peak), Austl.
109/B3 **Auk Bok** (isl.), Burma
116/D2 **Auld** (lake), Austl.
54/C1 **Auldearn,** Sc,UK
75/M9 **Aulencia** (riv.), Sp.
77/F2 **Aulendorf,** Ger.
53/T10 **Aulnay-sous-Bois,** Fr.
72/B2 **Aulne** (riv.), Fr.
68/C3 **Aulnoye-Aymeries,** Fr.
77/F4 **Ault, Piz** (peak), Swi.
68/B5 **Aunette** (riv.), Fr.
132/B2 **Auob** (dry riv.), Namb.
132/C2 **Auobrivier** (dry riv.), SAfr.
120/G4 **Aur** (atoll), Mrsh.
70/D3 **Aurach** (riv.), Ger.
106/C4 **Aurangābād,** India
106/D3 **Aurangābād,** India
72/B3 **Auray,** Fr.
72/D5 **Aureilhan,** Fr.
67/E2 **Aurich,** Ger.
141/B2 **Auriflama,** Braz.
72/E4 **Aurillac,** Fr.
140/C2 **Aurora,** Braz.
112/C2 **Aurora,** Phil.
112/C4 **Aurora,** Phil.
159/F3 **Aurora,** Co,US
165/P16 **Aurora,** Il,US
159/J3 **Aurora,** Mo,US
159/H2 **Aurora,** Ne,US
168/F5 **Aurora,** Oh,US
112/C2 **Aurora Mem. Park,** Phil.
118/A1 **Aurukun Abor. Land,** Austl.
79/G1 **Ausa** (riv.), It.
160/C2 **Au Sable** (riv.), Mi,US
65/K3 **Auschwitz** (Oświęcim), Pol.
77/F3 **Ausserrhoden** (demi-canton), Swi.
72/E5 **Aussillon,** Fr.
62/B2 **Aust-Agder** (co.), Nor.
116/C3 **Austin** (lake), Austl.
152/G2 **Austin** (isl.), NW,Can
157/K5 **Austin,** Mn,US
158/C3 **Austin,** Nv,US
162/D4 **Austin** (cap.), Tx,US
168/G5 **Austintown,** Oh,US
114/* **Australia**
119/C3 **Australian Alps** (mts.), Austl.
119/D3 **Australian Cap. Terr.,** Austl.
73/L3 **Austria**
61/P7 **Austurhorn** (pt.), Ice.
68/B3 **Authie** (riv.), Fr.
146/D5 **Autlán,** Mex.
68/B5 **Automne** (riv.), Fr.
72/F3 **Autun,** Fr.
72/E4 **Auvergne** (reg.), Fr.
53/S9 **Auvers-sur-Oise,** Fr.
72/D4 **Auvézère** (riv.), Fr.
72/E3 **Auxerre,** Fr.
76/B3 **Auxonne,** Fr.
160/D2 **Aux Sables** (riv.), On,Can
139/F3 **Auyán-Tepuí** (peak), Ven.
153/K2 **Auyuittuq Nat'l Park,** NW,Can
144/D4 **Auzangate** (peak), Peru
72/E3 **Avallon,** Fr.
161/K2 **Avalon** (pen.), Nf,Can
108/F3 **Avanāshi,** India
141/B2 **Avaré,** Braz.
93/M7 **Avcilar,** Turk.
59/E4 **Avebury,** Eng,UK
59/E4 **Avebury Stone Circle** (ruins), Eng,UK
74/A2 **Aveiro,** Port.
74/A2 **Aveiro** (dist.), Port.
53/P7 **Aveley,** Eng,UK
68/C2 **Avelgem,** Belg.
142/F2 **Avellaneda,** Arg.
80/D2 **Avellino,** It.
68/A4 **Avelon** (riv.), Fr.
158/B3 **Avenal,** Ca,US
167/D2 **Avenel,** NJ,US
68/A46 **Aver** (riv.), Fr.
80/D2 **Aversa,** It.
150/E4 **Aves** (isl.), Ven.
62/G1 **Avesta,** Swe.
72/D4 **Aveyron** (riv.), Fr.
80/C1 **Avezzano,** It.
54/A4 **Avich, Loch** (lake), Sc,UK
54/C2 **Aviemore,** Sc,UK
72/F5 **Avignon,** Fr.
74/C2 **Ávila de los Caballeros,** Sp.
74/C1 **Avilés,** Sp.
68/B3 **Avion,** Fr.
74/B3 **Avis,** Port.
77/H5 **Avisio** (riv.), It.
56/B6 **Avoca,** Ire.
60/D4 **Avoca** (riv.), Ire.
54/B1 **Avoch,** Sc,UK
80/D4 **Avola,** It.
116/C5 **Avon** (riv.), Austl.
72/E2 **Avon,** Fr.
58/D4 **Avon** (co.), Eng,UK
58/C6 **Avon** (riv.), Eng,UK
58/D4 **Avon** (riv.), Eng,UK
59/E2 **Avon** (riv.), Eng,UK
59/E5 **Avon** (riv.), Eng,UK
54/C2 **Avon** (riv.), Sc,UK
54/C5 **Avon** (riv.), Sc,UK
168/B2 **Avon,** Ct,US
168/E5 **Avon,** Oh,US
60/D4 **Avonbeg** (riv.), Ire.
168/E4 **Avon Lake,** Oh,US
157/G3 **Avonlea,** Sk,Can
56/B6 **Avonmore** (riv.), Ire.
58/D4 **Avonmouth,** Eng,UK
116/C4 **Avon Valley Nat'l Park,** Austl.
54/B5 **Avon Water** (riv.), Sc,UK
72/C2 **Avranches,** Fr.
68/B4 **Avre** (riv.), Fr.
72/C3 **Avrillé,** Fr.
99/L10 **Awaji,** Japan
98/D3 **Awaji** (isl.), Japan
91/E3 **A'waj, Nahr al** (riv.), Syria
69/E2 **Awans,** Belg.
125/N6 **Āwasa,** Eth.
125/P6 **Āwash,** Eth.
125/P5 **Āwash Wenz** (riv.), Eth.
132/A2 **Awasibberge** (peak), Namb.
102/D3 **Awat,** China
124/H2 **Awbārī,** Libya
60/B5 **Awbeg** (riv.), Ire.
54/A4 **Awe, Loch** (lake), Sc,UK
125/K2 **Awjilah,** Libya
91/B4 **Awsīm,** Egypt
61/P6 **Axarfjördhur** (bay), Ice.
58/D4 **Axbridge,** Eng,UK
58/D4 **Axe** (riv.), Eng,UK
58/D5 **Axe** (riv.), Eng,UK
66/A6 **Axel,** Neth.
153/S7 **Axel Heiberg** (isl.), NW,Can
129/E5 **Axim,** Gha.
81/H2 **Axios** (riv.), Gre.
165/D2 **Axis** (dam), Wa,US
58/D5 **Axminster,** Eng,UK
147/L8 **Axochiapan,** Mex.
68/D5 **Ay,** Fr.
85/N5 **Ay** (riv.), Rus.
98/D3 **Ayabe,** Japan
142/F3 **Ayacucho,** Arg.
144/C4 **Ayacucho,** Peru
102/D2 **Ayaguz,** Kaz.
102/D2 **Ayaguz** (riv.), Kaz.
102/E4 **Ayakkum** (lake), China
99/M10 **Ayama,** Japan
128/E5 **Ayamé I, Barrage d'** (dam), IvC.
128/E5 **Ayamé II, Barrage d'** (dam), IvC.
74/B4 **Ayamonte,** Sp.
92/C1 **Ayancık,** Turk.
139/G3 **Ayanganna** (peak), Guy.
138/C2 **Ayapel,** Col.
149/H5 **Ayapel, Serranía** (range), Col.
92/C1 **Ayaş,** Turk.
99/H7 **Ayase,** Japan
144/D4 **Ayaviri,** Peru
95/J1 **Āybak,** Afg.
91/G7 **'Aybāl, Jabal** (Har Eval) (mtn.), WBnk.
92/D1 **Aybastı,** Turk.
92/A2 **Aydın,** Turk.
92/B2 **Aydin** (prov.), Turk.
93/N7 **Aydinli,** Turk.
117/F3 **Ayers Rock** (Uluru) (peak), Austl.
104/B5 **Ayeyarwady** (Irrawaddy) (div.), Burma
81/J3 **Áyios Evstrátios** (isl.), Gre.
81/J5 **Áyios Ioánnis, Ákra** (cape), Gre.
81/J5 **Áyios Nikólaos,** Gre.
59/F3 **Aylesbury,** Eng,UK
59/G4 **Aylesford,** Eng,UK
59/H4 **Aylesham,** Eng,UK
152/F2 **Aylmer** (lake), NW,Can
59/H1 **Aylsham,** Eng,UK
92/D2 **'Ayn al 'Arab,** Syria
125/K2 **'Ayn Ath Tha'lab,** Libya
94/D1 **'Ayn, Ra's al,** Syria
125/K3 **'Ayn Zuwayyah** (well), Libya
89/S3 **Ayon** (isl.), Rus.
75/E3 **Ayora,** Sp.
124/D3 **'Ayoûn 'Abd el Mâlek** (well), Mrta.
118/B2 **Ayr,** Austl.
54/B6 **Ayr,** Sc,UK
54/B5 **Ayr** (riv.), Sc,UK
56/D3 **Ayre, Point of** (pt.), Eng,UK
54/B6 **Ayr, Heads of** (pt.), Sc,UK
57/H3 **Ayton,** Eng,UK
54/D5 **Ayton,** Sc,UK
83/H4 **Aytos,** Bul.
72/C3 **Aytré,** Fr.
109/C3 **Ayutthaya** (ruins), Thai.
92/A2 **Ayvalık,** Turk.
69/E3 **Aywaille,** Belg.
108/B1 **Azad Kashmir** (terr.), Pak.
75/F3 **Azahar** (coast), Sp.
99/M9 **Azaj,** Japan
156/C5 **Azalea,** Or,US
106/D2 **Azamgarh,** India
144/D4 **Azángaro,** Peru
144/D4 **Azángaro** (riv.), Peru
124/G2 **Azao** (peak), Alg.
129/E2 **Azaouād** (reg.), Mali
129/G2 **Azaouak, Vallée de l'** (wadi), Mali, Niger
93/F2 **Āzarbāyjān-e Bākhtarī** (gov.), Iran
93/F2 **Āzarbāyjān-e Khāvarī** (gov.), Iran
91/E1 **A'zāz,** Syria
87/H4 **Azerbaijan**
125/N5 **Āzezo,** Eth.
102/E1 **Azhu-Tayga, Gora** (peak), Rus.
92/D2 **'Azīz, Jabal 'Abd al** (mts.), Syria
138/B5 **Azogues,** Ecu.
75/R12 **Azores** (aut. reg.), Port.
75/R12 **Azores** (isls.), Port.
86/F3 **Azov,** Rus.
86/E3 **Azov** (sea), Rus., Ukr.
74/D1 **Azpeitia,** Sp.
158/F3 **Aztec,** NM,US
158/E3 **Aztec Ruins Nat'l Mon.,** NM,US
150/D3 **Azua,** DRep.
74/C3 **Azuaga,** Sp.
138/B5 **Azuay** (prov.), Ecu.
99/M9 **Azuchi,** Japan
149/F5 **Azuero** (pen.), Pan.
142/F3 **Azul,** Arg.
149/E4 **Azul** (mtn.), CR
147/H5 **Azul** (riv.), NAm.
144/B2 **Azul, Cordillera** (mts.), Peru
99/G2 **Azuma-san** (mtn.), Japan
99/F2 **Azumaya-san** (mtn.), Japan
73/G5 **Azur, Côte d'** (coast), Fr.
164/C2 **Azusa,** Ca,US
123/V17 **Azzaba,** Alg.
91/E3 **Az Zabadānī,** Syria
73/K4 **Azzano Decimo,** It.
91/B4 **Az Zaqāzīq,** Egypt
91/E3 **Az Zarqā',** Jor.
124/H1 **Az Zāwiyah,** Libya
93/F4 **Az Zubayr,** Iraq

B

105/E2 **Ba** (riv.), China
121/Y18 **Ba,** Fiji
54/B3 **Bà** (riv.), Sc,UK
109/E3 **Ba** (riv.), Viet.
121/U11 **Baaba** (isl.), NCal.
91/G8 **Ba'al Hazor** (Tall 'Āsūr) (mtn.), WBnk.
77/E3 **Baar,** Swi.
122/G4 **Baarawe,** Som.
66/C4 **Baarn,** Neth.
96/D2 **Baatsagaan,** Mong.
95/J2 **Baba** (mts.), Afg.
83/F4 **Baba** (peak), Bul.
92/B1 **Baba** (pt.), Turk.
86/D4 **Baba Burnu** (pt.), Turk.
83/J3 **Babadag,** Rom.
83/H5 **Babaeski,** Turk.
138/B5 **Babahoyo,** Ecu.
111/G5 **Babar** (isl.), Indo.
130/B4 **Babati,** Tanz.
58/C5 **Babbacombe** (bay), Eng,UK
157/L4 **Babbitt,** Mn,US
158/C3 **Babbitt,** Nv,US
123/G3 **Bab el Mandeb** (str.), Afr., Asia
120/C4 **Babelthuap** (isl.), Palau
70/B3 **Babenhausen,** Ger.
86/A2 **Babia Gora** (peak), Pol.
104/D4 **Babian** (riv.), China
93/F3 **Bābil** (gov.), Iraq
156/B2 **Babine** (lake), BC,Can
152/D3 **Babine** (riv.), BC,Can
93/H2 **Bābol,** Iran
93/H2 **Bābol Sar,** Iran
112/C1 **Babuyan** (chan.), Phil.
112/C1 **Babuyan** (isl.), Phil.
112/C1 **Babuyan** (isls.), Phil.
93/F3 **Babylon** (ruins), Iraq
167/E2 **Babylon,** NY,US
140/A2 **Bacabal,** Braz.
137/H4 **Bacajá** (riv.), Braz.
148/D2 **Bacalar** (lag.), Mex.
111/G4 **Bacan** (isl.), Indo.
112/C1 **Bacarra,** Phil.
83/H2 **Bacău,** Rom.
83/H2 **Bacău** (co.), Rom.
109/D1 **Bac Can,** Viet.
79/F2 **Bacchiglione** (riv.), It.
109/D1 **Bac Giang,** Viet.
152/G2 **Back** (riv.), NW,Can
160/E2 **Back** (lake), On,Can
166/B5 **Back** (riv.), Md,US
82/D3 **Bačka** (reg.), Yugo.
82/D3 **Bačka Palanka,** Yugo.
82/D3 **Bačka Topola,** Yugo.
70/C5 **Backnang,** Ger.
58/D4 **Backwell,** Eng,UK
109/D4 **Bac Lieu,** Viet.
109/D1 **Bac Ninh,** Viet.
112/C2 **Baco** (mtn.), Phil.
112/C3 **Bacolod City,** Phil.
112/E7 **Bacoor,** Phil.
109/D1 **Bac Quang,** Viet.
82/D2 **Bácsalmás,** Hun.
82/D2 **Bács-Kiskun** (co.), Hun.
59/H1 **Bacton,** Eng,UK
57/F4 **Bacup,** Eng,UK
157/H4 **Bad** (riv.), SD,US
71/F5 **Bad Abbach,** Ger.
108/E3 **Badagara,** India
96/E3 **Badain Jaran** (des.), China
74/B3 **Badajoz,** Sp.
75/L7 **Badalona,** Sp.
160/D3 **Bad Axe,** Mi,US
70/B4 **Bad Bergzabern,** Ger.
67/F6 **Bad Berleberg,** Ger.
69/G2 **Bad Breisig,** Ger.
70/C2 **Bad Brückenau,** Ger.
70/B2 **Bad Camberg,** Ger.
64/F1 **Bad Doberan,** Ger.
108/C2 **Baddomalhi,** Pak.
67/G5 **Bad Driburg,** Ger.
70/B4 **Bad Dürkheim,** Ger.
70/B6 **Bad Dürrheim,** Ger.
70/A2 **Bad Ems,** Ger.
73/M2 **Baden,** Aus.
77/E3 **Baden,** Swi.
70/B5 **Baden-Baden,** Ger.
70/B5 **Badener** (peak), Ger.
54/B3 **Badenoch** (dist.), Sc,UK
70/C6 **Baden-Württemberg** (state), Ger.
79/G2 **Baderna,** Cro.
67/F4 **Bad Essen,** Ger.
65/H2 **Bad Freienwalde,** Ger.
67/H5 **Bad Gandersheim,** Ger.
116/B4 **Badgingarra Nat'l Park,** Austl.
73/K3 **Bad Goisern,** Aus.
67/H5 **Bad Harzburg,** Ger.
70/B5 **Bad Herrenalb,** Ger.
64/E3 **Bad Hersfeld,** Ger.
70/B2 **Bad Homburg vor der Höhe,** Ger.
69/G2 **Bad Honnef,** Ger.
77/F5 **Badile, Pizzo** (peak), It.
95/J4 **Badīn,** Pak.
73/K3 **Bad Ischl,** Aus.
70/D2 **Bad Kissingen,** Ger.
70/C3 **Bad König,** Ger.
70/D2 **Bad Königshofen,** Ger.
70/A3 **Bad Kreuznach,** Ger.
76/D2 **Bad Krozingen,** Ger.
157/H4 **Badlands** (uplands), ND,US
157/H5 **Badlands** (hills), SD,US
157/H5 **Badlands Nat'l Park,** SD,US
67/H6 **Bad Langensalza,** Ger.
67/H5 **Bad Lauterberg,** Ger.
70/B5 **Bad Liebenzell,** Ger.
67/F3 **Bad Lippspringe,** Ger.
70/C4 **Bad Mergentheim,** Ger.
67/G4 **Bad Munder am Deister,** Ger.
69/F2 **Bad Münstereifel,** Ger.
70/B2 **Bad Nauheim,** Ger.
67/G4 **Bad Nenndorf,** Ger.
69/G2 **Bad Neuenahr-Ahrweiler,** Ger.
70/D2 **Bad Neustadt an der Saale,** Ger.
67/F4 **Bad Oeynhausen,** Ger.
64/F2 **Bad Oldesloe,** Ger.
103/B5 **Badong,** China
70/C2 **Bad Orb,** Ger.
67/G5 **Bad Pyrmont,** Ger.
77/F3 **Bad Ragaz,** Swi.
95/J3 **Bādrāh,** Pak.
70/C4 **Bad Rappenau,** Ger.
64/G5 **Bad Reichenhall,** Ger.
67/H5 **Bad Sachsa,** Ger.
67/H4 **Bad Salzdetfurth,** Ger.
67/F4 **Bad Salzuflen,** Ger.
64/F3 **Bad Salzungen,** Ger.
67/F5 **Bad Sassendorf,** Ger.
70/C6 **Bad Schussenried,** Ger.
70/B2 **Bad Schwalbach,** Ger.
64/F2 **Bad Schwartau,** Ger.
64/F2 **Bad Segeberg,** Ger.
70/B2 **Bad Söden am Taunus,** Ger.
70/C2 **Bad Soden-Salmünster,** Ger.
67/G6 **Bad Sooden-Allendorf,** Ger.
77/H2 **Bad Tölz,** Ger.
106/D6 **Badulla,** SrL.
70/C6 **Bad Urach,** Ger.
70/B2 **Bad Vilbel,** Ger.
73/M3 **Bad Vöslau,** Aus.
77/F2 **Bad Waldsee,** Ger.
67/G6 **Bad Wildungen,** Ger.
70/C4 **Bad Wimpfen,** Ger.
70/D3 **Bad Windsheim,** Ger.
70/D6 **Bad Wörishofen,** Ger.
77/F2 **Bad Wurzach,** Ger.
67/E2 **Bad Zwischenahn,** Ger.
74/C4 **Baena,** Sp.
141/J6 **Baependi,** Braz.
76/C2 **Baerenkopf** (mtn.), Fr.
69/F2 **Baesweiler,** Ger.
74/D4 **Baeza,** Sp.
129/H5 **Bafang,** Camr.
153/H1 **Baffin** (isl.), NW,Can
153/K1 **Baffin** (bay), Can.,Grld.
162/D5 **Baffin** (bay), Tx,US
124/H7 **Bafia,** Camr.
128/D4 **Bafing** (riv.), Gui., IvC.
128/C3 **Bafing** (riv.), Gui., Mali
129/H5 **Bafoussam,** Camr.
92/C1 **Bafra,** Turk.
92/D1 **Bafra Burnu** (cape), Turk.
128/B2 **Bafrechié** (well), Mrta.
125/L7 **Bafwasende,** Zaire
103/B3 **Bag** (salt lake), China
124/H5 **Baga,** Nga.
112/B4 **Bagahak, Gunung** (peak), Malay.
130/C4 **Bagamoyo,** Tanz.
112/D4 **Baganga,** Phil.
129/G3 **Bagaroua,** Niger
112/E6 **Bagbag** (cr.), Phil.
102/E3 **Bagda** (mts.), China
143/G1 **Bagé,** Braz.
112/C1 **Baggao,** Phil.
58/B4 **Baggy** (pt.), Eng,UK
108/B2 **Bāgh,** Pak.
93/F3 **Baghdad** (gov.), Iraq
94/D2 **Baghdad** (Baghdād) (cap.), Iraq
80/C3 **Bagheria,** It.
95/J1 **Baghlān,** Afg.
92/E2 **Bağırpaşa** (peak), Turk.
58/C3 **Baglan,** Wal,UK
157/K4 **Bagley,** Mn,US
79/F4 **Bagnacavallo,** It.
72/D5 **Bagnères-de-Bigorre,** Fr.
53/S10 **Bagneux,** Fr.
79/E5 **Bagno di Romagna,** It.
53/T10 **Bagnolet,** Fr.
78/D2 **Bagnolo Mella,** It.
72/F4 **Bagnols-sur-Cèze,** Fr.
112/C3 **Bago,** Phil.
128/D3 **Bagoe** (riv.), IvC., Mali
104/B5 **Bago** (Pegu) (div.), Burma
144/B2 **Bagua Grande,** Peru
112/C1 **Baguio,** Phil.
124/J5 **Baguirmi** (reg.), Chad
129/H2 **Bagzane** (peak), Niger
150/B2 **Bahamas**
106/E3 **Baharampur,** India
102/B6 **Bahāwalnagar,** Pak.
95/K3 **Bahāwalpur,** Pak.
92/D2 **Bahçe,** Turk.
130/B4 **Bahi,** Tanz.
140/B4 **Bahia** (state), Braz.
142/E3 **Bahía Blanca,** Arg.
138/A5 **Bahía de Caráquez,** Ecu.
106/D3 **Bahía Honda,** Cuba
148/E2 **Bahía, Islas de la** (isls.), Hon.
125/N5 **Bahir Dar,** Eth.
95/G4 **Bahlah,** Oman
106/D2 **Bahraich,** India
94/F3 **Bahrain**
94/F3 **Bahrain** (gulf), Bahr., SAr.
122/E3 **Baḩr al Arab** (riv.), Sudan
93/E3 **Baḩr al Milḩ** (lake), Iraq
122/D4 **Bahr Aouk** (riv.), CAfr., Chad
127/B2 **Baḩrīyah, Al Wāḩāt al** (oasis), Egypt
103/C2 **Bai** (riv.), China
103/C4 **Bai** (riv.), China
83/F2 **Baia Mare,** Rom.
83/F2 **Baia Sprie,** Rom.
124/J6 **Baïbokoum,** Chad
104/D3 **Baicao** (mts.), China
102/D3 **Baicheng,** China
97/J2 **Baicheng,** China
83/G3 **Băicoi,** Rom.
125/P7 **Baidoa,** Som.
103/D5 **Baidong** (lake), China
161/G1 **Baie-Comeau,** Qu,Can
153/J3 **Baie-du-Poste,** Qu,Can
77/F2 **Baienfurt,** Ger.
70/B5 **Baiersbronn,** Ger.
70/E3 **Baiersdorf,** Ger.
161/G2 **Baie-Saint-Paul,** Qu,Can
161/K1 **Baie Verte,** Nf,Can
103/G7 **Baigou** (riv.), China
103/C3 **Baihua Shan** (mtn.), China
93/E3 **Ba'ījī,** Iraq
89/L4 **Baikal** (Baykal) (lake), Rus.
138/D2 **Bailadores,** Ven.
57/G4 **Baildon,** Eng,UK
74/D3 **Bailén,** Sp.
83/F3 **Băileşti,** Rom.
55/H8 **Bailivanish,** Sc,UK
68/B2 **Bailleul,** Fr.
96/E5 **Bailong** (riv.), China
103/C4 **Bailu** (riv.), China
96/E5 **Baima,** China
57/H5 **Bain** (riv.), Eng,UK
106/E2 **Bainang,** China
163/G4 **Bainbridge,** Ga,US
165/B2 **Bainbridge** (isl.), Wa,US
166/B4 **Bainbridge Nav. Trg. Sta.,** Md,US
102/E5 **Baingoin,** China
97/K2 **Baiquan,** China
102/D4 **Bairab** (lake), China
151/F3 **Baird** (inlet), Ak,US
162/D3 **Baird,** Tx,US
120/G4 **Bairiki** (cap.), Kiri.
97/H3 **Bairin Youqi,** China
119/C3 **Bairnsdale,** Austl.
91/E4 **Bā'ir, Wādī** (riv.), Jor.
112/C3 **Bais,** Phil.
72/D5 **Baïse** (riv.), Fr.
105/F5 **Baisha,** China
105/H3 **Baishi** (peak), China
105/H3 **Baisong** (pass), China
106/D2 **Baitadi,** Nepal
109/D2 **Bai Thuong,** Viet.
75/P10 **Baixa de Banheira,** Port.
140/B4 **Baixa Grande,** Braz.
103/C3 **Baixiang,** China
141/D1 **Baixo Guandu,** Braz.
96/E4 **Baiyin,** China
103/B3 **Baiyu** (mts.), China
105/G3 **Baiyun** (mtn.), China
143/J7 **Baja** (pt.), Chile
82/D2 **Baja,** Hun.
146/B2 **Baja California** (pen.), Mex.
146/B3 **Baja California Sur** (state), Mex.
123/W17 **Bājah,** Tun.
123/W17 **Bājah** (gov.), Tun.
146/B2 **Baja, Punta** (pt.), Mex.
111/F5 **Bajawa,** Indo.
82/D4 **Bajina Bašta,** Yugo.
119/E1 **Bajmba** (peak), Austl.
82/D3 **Bajmok,** Yugo.
150/D3 **Bajos de Haina,** DRep.
102/C2 **Bakanas** (riv.), Kaz.
111/E3 **Bakayan** (peak), Indo.
128/B3 **Bakel,** Sen.
152/G2 **Baker** (lake), NW,Can
143/J6 **Baker** (riv.), Chile
121/H4 **Baker** (isl.), PacUS
158/C4 **Baker,** Ca,US
157/G4 **Baker,** Mt,US
158/D3 **Baker,** Nv,US
156/D4 **Baker,** Or,US
156/C3 **Baker** (peak), Wa,US
158/C4 **Bakersfield,** Ca,US
57/G5 **Bakewell,** Eng,UK
86/E3 **Bakhchisaray,** Ukr.
86/E2 **Bakhmach,** Ukr.
93/F3 **Bākhtarān,** Iran
93/F3 **Bākhtarān** (gov.), Iran
93/H4 **Bakhtegān** (lake), Iran
93/G4 **Bakhtīārī & Chahār Maḩāll** (gov.), Iran
139/G4 **Bakhuis** (mts.), Sur.
61/P6 **Bakkaflói** (bay), Ice.
130/B2 **Bakora Corridor Game Rsv.,** Kenya
126/B1 **Bakoumba,** Gabon
71/G2 **Bakovský Potok** (riv.), Czh.
128/C4 **Bakoye** (riv.), Gui., Mali
87/J4 **Baku** (cap.), Azer.
130/A2 **Baku,** Zaire
113/S **Bakutis** (coast), Ant.
136/E6 **Bala** (mts.), Bol.
92/C2 **Balâ,** Turk.
56/E6 **Bala,** Wal,UK
111/E2 **Balabac** (str.), Malay., Phil.
112/B4 **Balabac,** Phil.
112/B4 **Balabac** (isl.), Phil.
91/E3 **Ba'labakk,** Leb.
121/U12 **Balabio** (isl.), NCal.
93/F3 **Balad,** Iraq
106/D3 **Bālāghāt,** India
80/A1 **Balagne** (range), Fr.
112/E6 **Balagtas,** Phil.
75/F2 **Balaguer,** Sp.
72/C5 **Balaïtous** (mtn.), Fr.
131/D2 **Balaka,** Malw.
85/J4 **Balakhna,** Rus.
87/H1 **Balakovo,** Rus.
112/B4 **Balambangan** (isl.), Malay.
95/H1 **Bālā Morghab,** Afg.
83/G2 **Bălan,** Rom.
147/H5 **Balancán,** Mex.
112/C2 **Balanga,** Phil.
109/E3 **Ba Lang An** (cape), Viet.
106/D3 **Bālāngir,** India
144/B1 **Balao,** Ecu.
112/C1 **Balaoan,** Phil.
85/X9 **Balashikha,** Rus.
87/G2 **Balashov,** Rus.
82/D1 **Balassagyarmat,** Hun.
82/C2 **Balaton** (lake), Hun.
82/C2 **Balatonfüred,** Hun.
139/G5 **Balbina** (res.), Braz.
164/G8 **Balboa,** Ca,US
142/F3 **Balcarce,** Arg.
56/E2 **Balcary** (pt.), Sc,UK
83/J4 **Balchik,** Bul.
115/Q12 **Balclutha,** NZ
59/F4 **Balcombe,** Eng,UK
162/D4 **Balcones Escarpment** (plat.), Tx,US
116/C5 **Bald** (pt.), Austl.
163/H2 **Bald** (peak), Va,US
166/A1 **Bald Eagle Mountain** (ridge), Pa,US
59/F3 **Baldock,** Eng,UK
119/E1 **Bald Rock Nat'l Park,** Austl.
167/L9 **Baldwin,** NY,US
168/H7 **Baldwin,** Pa,US
164/C2 **Baldwin Park,** Ca,US
157/H3 **Baldy** (peak), Mb,Can
148/D2 **Baldy Beacon** (mtn.), Belz.
79/G2 **Bale,** Cro.
75/F3 **Baleares** (Balearic) (isls.), Sp.
75/F3 **Balearic** (Baleares) (isls.), Sp.
141/E1 **Baleia, Ponta da** (pt.), Braz.
153/K3 **Baleine** (riv.), Qu,Can
153/J3 **Baleine, Grande Rivière de la** (riv.), Qu,Can
153/J3 **Baleine, Petite Rivière de la** (riv.), Qu,Can
125/N6 **Bale Mountains Nat'l Park,** Eth.
69/E1 **Balen,** Belg.
112/C2 **Baler,** Phil.
130/B2 **Balesa** (riv.), Kenya
106/E3 **Baleshwar,** India
96/H1 **Baley,** Rus.
54/B4 **Balfron,** Sc,UK
106/B2 **Bali,** India
110/D5 **Bali** (isl.), Indo.
110/D5 **Bali** (sea), Indo.
92/A2 **Balıkesir,** Turk.
92/A2 **Balıkesir** (prov.), Turk.
111/E4 **Balikpapan,** Indo.
112/D3 **Balingasag,** Phil.
70/B6 **Balingen,** Ger.
52/F4 **Balkan** (mts.), Eur.
87/K4 **Balkhan Obl.,** Trkm.
102/C2 **Balkhash,** Kaz.
102/B2 **Balkhash** (lake), Kaz.
60/D2 **Ballagan** (pt.), Ire.
56/C1 **Ballantrae,** Sc,UK
119/B3 **Ballarat,** Austl.
116/D4 **Ballard** (lake), Austl.
106/C4 **Ballarpur,** India
54/C2 **Ballater,** Sc,UK
56/D3 **Ballaugh,** IM,UK
113/L **Balleny** (isls.), Ant.
63/T9 **Ballerup,** Den.
112/C1 **Ballesteros,** Phil.
119/E1 **Ballina,** Austl.
60/A1 **Ballina,** Ire.
55/H9 **Ballinamallard,** NI,UK
60/B3 **Ballinasloe,** Ire.
56/B2 **Ballinderry** (riv.), NI,UK
162/D4 **Ballinger,** Tx,US
54/C4 **Ballingry,** Sc,UK
54/C3 **Ballinluig,** Sc,UK
56/B1 **Ballintoy,** NI,UK
54/B2 **Balloch,** Sc,UK
54/B5 **Balloch,** Sc,UK
76/C2 **Ballon, Col du** (pass), Fr.
76/C2 **Ballon d'Alsace** (mtn.), Fr.
76/C2 **Ballon de Sevance** (mtn.), Fr.
56/C2 **Ballycarry,** NI,UK
56/B1 **Ballycastle,** NI,UK
56/B2 **Ballyclare,** NI,UK
56/C2 **Ballyeaston,** NI,UK
56/A3 **Ballygawley,** NI,UK
56/C3 **Ballygowan,** NI,UK
56/C3 **Ballyhalbert,** NI,UK
60/B5 **Ballyhoura** (mts.), Ire.
56/A1 **Ballykelly,** NI,UK
56/B2 **Ballymena,** NI,UK
56/B2 **Ballymena** (dist.), NI,UK
56/B1 **Ballymoney,** NI,UK
56/B1 **Ballymoney** (dist.), NI,UK
60/C5 **Ballynacourty** (pt.), Ire.
56/C3 **Ballynahinch,** NI,UK
56/C2 **Ballynure,** NI,UK
56/C3 **Ballyquintin** (pt.), NI,UK
60/D5 **Ballyteige** (bay), Ire.
56/C2 **Ballywalter,** NI,UK
143/J7 **Balmaceda** (peak), Chile
82/E2 **Balmazújváros,** Hun.
157/K3 **Balmertown,** On,Can
76/D5 **Balmhorn** (peak), Swi.
131/C2 **Balmoral,** Zam.
54/C2 **Balmoral Castle,** Sc,UK
141/B3 **Balneario Camboriú,** Braz.
143/T12 **Balneario Carras,** Uru.
118/C4 **Balonne** (riv.), Austl.
106/B2 **Bālotra,** India
103/B3 **Balougou,** China
106/D2 **Balrāmpur,** India
83/G3 **Balş,** Rom.
59/E2 **Balsall Common,** Eng,UK
140/A2 **Balsas,** Braz.
140/A3 **Balsas** (riv.), Braz.
146/E5 **Balsas** (riv.), Mex.
147/M6 **Balsas de Agua,** Mex.
63/R6 **Bålsta,** Swe.
55/P12 **Baltasound,** Sc,UK
62/H2 **Baltic** (sea), Eur.
65/K1 **Baltic** (spit), Pol., Rus.
91/B4 **Balţīm,** Egypt
166/B5 **Baltimore,** Md,US
166/B4 **Baltimore** (co.), Md,US
166/B5 **Baltimore Highlands-Lansdown,** Md,US
63/H4 **Baltiysk,** Rus.
67/E1 **Baltrum** (isl.), Ger.
95/H3 **Baluchistan** (reg.), Iran, Pak.
112/C2 **Balud,** Phil.
106/E2 **Bālurghāt,** India
67/E6 **Balve,** Ger.
117/E2 **Balwina Abor. Rsv.,** Austl.
87/J3 **Balykshi,** Kaz.
138/B5 **Balzar,** Ecu.
129/E3 **Bam** (prov.), Burk.
102/F5 **Bam** (lake), China
93/J4 **Bam,** Iran
124/H5 **Bama,** Nga.
160/A1 **Bamaji** (lake), On,Can
128/D3 **Bamako** (cap.), Mali
128/D3 **Bamako** (reg.), Mali
105/E3 **Bama Yaozu Zizhixian,** China
136/C5 **Bambamarca,** Peru
149/E3 **Bambana** (riv.), Nic.
125/K6 **Bambari,** CAfr.
70/D3 **Bamberg,** Ger.

175

Bambe – Bejhi

163/H3 **Bamberg,** SC,US
57/F4 **Bamber Ridge,** Eng,UK
62/C2 **Bamble,** Nor.
141/C2 **Bambuí,** Braz.
129/H5 **Bamenda,** Camr.
95/J2 **Bāmiān,** Afg.
105/G3 **Bamian** (mtn.), China
125/K6 **Bamingui-Bangoran Nat'l Park,** CAfr.
70/B4 **Bammental,** Ger.
58/C5 **Bampton,** Eng,UK
95/H3 **Bampūr** (riv.), Iran
120/F5 **Banaba** (isl.), Kiri.
140/C2 **Banabuiu** (res.), Braz.
130/B3 **Banagi,** Tanz.
112/C2 **Banahao** (mtn.), Phil.
128/D3 **Banamba,** Mali
128/B4 **Banana** (isls.), SLeo.
126/B2 **Banana,** Zaire
141/J7 **Bananal,** Braz.
106/B2 **Banās** (riv.), India
127/C4 **Banās, Ra's** (pt.), Egypt
82/E3 **Banatsko Novo Selo,** Yugo.
112/C1 **Banaue,** Phil.
92/B2 **Banaz,** Turk.
104/B2 **Banbar,** China
56/B3 **Banbridge,** NI,UK
56/B3 **Banbridge** (dist.), NI,UK
59/E2 **Banbury,** Eng,UK
124/B3 **Banc d'Arguin Nat'l Park,** Mrta.
109/C2 **Ban Chiang** (ruins), Thai.
54/D2 **Banchory,** Sc,UK
149/F4 **Banco** (pt.), CR
160/E2 **Bancroft,** On,Can
111/H4 **Banda** (isls.), Indo.
111/G5 **Banda** (sea), Indo.
110/A2 **Banda Aceh,** Indo.
99/G2 **Bandai-Asahi Nat'l Park,** Japan
99/G2 **Bandai-san** (mtn.), Japan
128/D5 **Bandama** (riv.), IvC.
128/D4 **Bandama Blanc** (riv.), IvC.
128/D4 **Bandama Rouge** (riv.), IvC.
95/H3 **Bandar Beheshtī** (Chāh Behār), Iran
93/J5 **Bandar-e 'Abbās,** Iran
93/G2 **Bandar-e Anzalī,** Iran
93/G4 **Bandar-e Būshehr,** Iran
93/G4 **Bandar-e Māhshahr,** Iran
93/H2 **Bandar-e Torkeman,** Iran
112/A4 **Bandar Seri Begawan** (cap.), Bru.
131/D1 **Bandawe,** Malw.
141/D2 **Bandeira** (peak), Braz.
141/G6 **Bandeira do Sul,** Braz.
141/B2 **Bandeirantes,** Braz.
158/F4 **Bandelier Nat'l Mon.,** NM,US
162/D4 **Bandera,** Tx,US
147/N7 **Banderilla,** Mex.
128/E3 **Bandiagara,** Mali
102/B5 **Bandipura,** India
108/F3 **Bandipur Nat'l Park,** India
83/H5 **Bandırma,** Turk.
83/J5 **Bandirma** (gulf), Turk.
60/B6 **Bandon** (riv.), Ire.
107/J5 **Ban Don,** Viet.
126/C1 **Bandundu,** Zaire
110/C5 **Bandung,** Indo.
75/E3 **Bañeres,** Sp.
149/H1 **Banes,** Cuba
54/D1 **Banff,** Sc,UK
156/E3 **Banff Nat'l Park,** Ab, BC,Can
128/D4 **Banfora,** Burk.
108/C2 **Banga,** India
106/C5 **Bangalore,** India
129/H5 **Bangangté,** Camr.
105/J5 **Bangar,** Phil.
125/K7 **Bangassou,** CAfr.
111/E2 **Bangau, Tanjong** (cape), Malay.
111/F4 **Banggai** (isls.), Indo.
102/C5 **Banggong** (lake), China
109/D2 **Banghiang** (riv.), Laos
110/C4 **Bangka** (isl.), Indo.
110/B4 **Bangka** (str.), Indo.
109/C3 **Bangkok** (bight), Thai.
109/C3 **Bangkok** (Krung Thep) (cap.), Thai.
106/E3 **Bangladesh**
109/C5 **Bang Lang** (res.), Thai.
104/C4 **Bangma** (mts.), China
56/C2 **Bangor,** NI,UK
56/D5 **Bangor,** Wal,UK
161/G2 **Bangor,** Me,US
57/F6 **Bangor-is-y-Coed,** Wal,UK
126/D2 **Bangu,** Zaire
112/C1 **Bangued,** Phil.
125/J7 **Bangui** (cap.), CAfr.
112/C1 **Bangui,** Phil.
91/B4 **Banhā,** Egypt
131/D4 **Banhine Nat'l Park,** Moz.
150/D3 **Baní,** DRep.
128/D3 **Bani** (riv.), Mali
128/D3 **Banifing** (riv.), Burk., Mali
95/L2 **Banihāl** (pass), India
127/B2 **Banī Mazār,** Egypt
163/J2 **Banister** (riv.), Va,US
91/D4 **Banī Suhaylah,** Gaza
127/B2 **Banī Suwayf,** Egypt
127/B2 **Banī Suwayf** (gov.), Egypt
91/D2 **Bāniyās,** Syria
82/C3 **Banja Luka,** Bosn.
110/D4 **Banjarmasin,** Indo.
128/A3 **Banjul** (cap.), Gam.
109/B5 **Ban Kantang,** Thai.
107/J4 **Ban Kengkok,** Laos
54/C4 **Bankfoot,** Sc,UK
109/D3 **Ban Khampho,** Laos
54/D2 **Bankhead,** Sc,UK
109/C5 **Ban Khuan Niang,** Thai.
119/B3 **Banks** (cape), Austl.
119/C4 **Banks** (str.), Austl.
152/C3 **Banks** (isl.), BC,Can
152/D1 **Banks** (isl.), NW,Can
115/R11 **Banks** (pen.), NZ
151/H4 **Banks** (pt.), Ak,US
156/D4 **Banks** (lake), Wa,US
120/F6 **Banks** (isls.), Van.
118/H8 **Bankstown,** Austl.
106/E3 **Bānkurā,** India
81/H1 **Bankya,** Bul.
109/D2 **Ban Loboy,** Laos
109/E3 **Ban Mdrack,** Viet.
109/D2 **Ban Mong,** Viet.
109/D2 **Ban Muangsen,** Laos
60/D4 **Bann** (riv.), Ire.
56/B2 **Bann** (riv.), NI,UK
78/A3 **Banna** (riv.), It.
109/D2 **Ban Nape,** Laos
54/C4 **Bannockburn,** Sc,UK
54/C4 **Bannockburn Battlesite** (1314), Sc,UK
60/D5 **Bannow** (bay), Ire.
108/A1 **Bannu,** Pak.
144/B1 **Baños,** Ecu.
82/D3 **Banovići,** Bosn.
109/C4 **Ban Pak Phanang,** Thai.
109/D3 **Ban Phon,** Laos
103/B4 **Banpo** (ruins), China
109/C2 **Ban Sieou,** Laos
65/K4 **Banská Bystrica,** Slvk.
83/F5 **Bansko,** Bul.
53/N8 **Banstead,** Eng,UK
106/B3 **Bānswāra,** India
112/C3 **Bantayan,** Phil.
112/C3 **Bantayan** (isl.), Phil.
110/D5 **Bantenan** (cape), Indo.
109/C2 **Ban Thabok,** Laos
109/B5 **Bantong Group** (isls.), Thai.
60/A6 **Bantry** (bay), Ire.
74/C3 **Bañuelo** (mtn.), Sp.
109/D3 **Ban Xebang-Nouan,** Laos
110/A3 **Banyak** (isls.), Indo.
75/G1 **Banyoles,** Sp.
110/D5 **Banyuwangi,** Indo.
113/J **Banzare** (coast), Ant.
123/W17 **Banzart** (gov.), Tun.
123/W17 **Banzart** (lake), Tun.
123/W17 **Banzart** (Bizerte), Tun.
103/B3 **Baode,** China
103/D3 **Baodi,** China
103/H7 **Baodi,** China
103/C3 **Baoding,** China
103/G7 **Baoding,** China
103/D4 **Baodugu** (mtn.), China
103/C4 **Baofeng,** China
104/E2 **Baoguangsi,** China
109/D1 **Bao Ha,** Viet.
96/F5 **Baoji,** China
107/J2 **Baojing,** China
103/B5 **Baokang,** China
109/D1 **Bao Lac,** Viet.
109/D4 **Bao Loc,** Viet.
149/J2 **Baoruco, Sierra de** (range), DRep.
103/E5 **Baoshan,** China
104/C3 **Baoshan,** China
105/J2 **Baoshan,** China
103/B2 **Baotou,** China
128/D4 **Baoulé** (riv.), IvC., Mali
128/C3 **Baoulé** (riv.), Mali
104/D2 **Baoxing,** China
103/D4 **Baoying,** China
106/D4 **Bāpatla,** India
91/D3 **Bāqa el Gharbiyya,** Isr.
104/B1 **Baqên,** China
109/D4 **Ba Quan** (cape), Viet.
93/F3 **Ba'qūbah,** Iraq
68/D5 **Bar** (riv.), Fr.
82/D4 **Bar,** Yugo.
109/D4 **Ba Ra,** Viet.
125/P7 **Baraawe,** Som.
110/E4 **Barabai,** Indo.
88/H4 **Barabinsk,** Rus.
160/B3 **Baraboo,** Wi,US
74/D1 **Baracaldo,** Sp.
149/H1 **Baracoa,** Cuba
91/E3 **Baradá** (riv.), Syria
142/F2 **Baradero,** Arg.
130/C2 **Baragoi,** Kenya
149/G1 **Baraguá,** Cuba
125/M5 **Bārah,** Sudan
150/D3 **Barahona,** DRep.
104/B3 **Barāk** (riv.), India
108/D1 **Bārā Lācha La** (pass), India
110/D3 **Baram** (cape), Malay.
112/A4 **Baram** (riv.), Malay.
139/G3 **Barama** (riv.), Guy.
106/B4 **Bārāmati,** India
95/K2 **Baramula,** India
106/C2 **Bāran,** India
138/C2 **Baranoa,** Col.
151/L4 **Baranof** (isl.), Ak,US
86/C1 **Baranovichi,** Bela.
82/C3 **Baranya** (co.), Hun.
141/D1 **Barão de Cocais,** Braz.
140/B2 **Barão de Grajaú,** Braz.
83/G2 **Baraolt,** Rom.
69/E3 **Baraque de Fraiture** (hill), Belg.
112/D2 **Baras,** Phil.
111/G5 **Barat Daya** (isls.), Indo.
141/D2 **Barbacena,** Braz.
150/G4 **Barbados**
140/C2 **Barbalha,** Braz.
127/C5 **Barbar,** Sudan
75/F1 **Barbastro,** Sp.
74/C4 **Barbate de Franco,** Sp.
153/T6 **Barbeau** (peak), NW,Can
75/L6 **Barbera del Valles,** Sp.
154/V13 **Barbers** (pt.), Hi,US
154/V13 **Barbers Point Nav. Air Sta.,** Hi,US
133/E2 **Barberton,** SAfr.
168/F5 **Barberton,** Oh,US
72/C4 **Barbezieux-Saint-Hilaire,** Fr.
106/E3 **Barbil,** India
57/F3 **Barbon,** Eng,UK
78/D5 **Barbona, Monte** (peak), It.
138/C3 **Barbosa,** Col.
160/D4 **Barbourville,** Ky,US
150/F3 **Barbuda** (isl.), Anti.
54/A3 **Barcaldine,** Sc,UK
82/F2 **Barcău** (riv.), Rom.
80/D3 **Barcellona Pozzo di Gotto,** It.
75/G2 **Barcelona,** Sp.
139/E2 **Barcelona,** Ven.
75/L7 **Barcelona** (inset), Sp.
74/A2 **Barcelos,** Port.
65/J2 **Barcin,** Pol.
118/A4 **Barcoo** (riv.), Austl.
82/C3 **Barcs,** Hun.
65/L2 **Barczewo,** Pol.
124/J3 **Bardaï,** Chad
91/C4 **Bardawīl, Sabkhat al** (lag.), Egypt
65/L4 **Bardejov,** Slvk.
125/P7 **Bardheere,** Som.
125/L1 **Bardīyah,** Libya
57/H5 **Bardney,** Eng,UK
106/B3 **Bārdoli,** India
56/D6 **Bardsey** (isl.), Wal,UK
160/C4 **Bardstown,** Ky,US
125/R5 **Bareeda,** Som.
78/B2 **Bareggio,** It.
106/C2 **Bareilly,** India
66/B5 **Barendrecht,** Neth.
72/D2 **Barentin,** Fr.
51/L2 **Barents** (sea)
125/N4 **Barentu,** Erit.
166/B3 **Bareville-Leacock-Leola,** Pa,US
72/C2 **Barfleur, Pointe de** (pt.), Fr.
106/D3 **Bargarh,** India
58/C3 **Bargoed,** Wal,UK
67/H1 **Bargteheide,** Ger.
96/F1 **Barguzin** (riv.), Rus.
106/D2 **Barhaj,** India
161/G2 **Bar Harbor,** Me,US
59/G2 **Bar Hill,** Eng,UK
106/C2 **Bāri,** India
80/E2 **Bari,** It.
130/B3 **Bariadi,** Tanz.
130/C3 **Baricho,** Kenya
78/C3 **Barigazzo, Monte** (peak), It.
123/U18 **Barika,** Alg.
130/C5 **Barikiwa,** Tanz.
148/D3 **Barillas,** Guat.
139/G2 **Barima** (riv.), Guy., Ven.
139/F3 **Barima-Waini** (reg.), Guy.
138/D2 **Barinas,** Ven.
138/D2 **Barinas** (state), Ven.
126/C2 **Baringa-Twana,** Zaire
138/D2 **Barinitas,** Ven.
106/E3 **Baripāda,** India
141/B2 **Bariri,** Braz.
127/B3 **Bārīs,** Egypt
106/F3 **Barisāl,** Bang.
110/B4 **Barisan** (mts.), Indo.
110/D4 **Barito** (riv.), Indo.
135/C1 **Baritu Nat'l Park,** Arg.
165/N13 **Bark** (riv.), Wi,US
117/M9 **Barker** (cr.), Austl.
161/S9 **Barker,** NY,US
168/B1 **Barkhamsted** (res.), Ct,US
53/P7 **Barking & Dagenham** (bor.), Eng,UK
156/B3 **Barkley** (sound), BC,Can
160/C4 **Barkley** (lake), Ky,US
114/E3 **Barkly** (tablelands), Austl.
96/C3 **Barkol** (Barkol Kazak Zizhixian), China
57/F6 **Barlaston,** Eng,UK
57/G4 **Barlby,** Eng,UK
69/E6 **Bar-le-Duc,** Fr.
116/C4 **Barlee** (lake), Austl.
116/B2 **Barlee** (range), Austl.
116/B2 **Barlee Range Nature Rsv.,** Austl.
80/E2 **Barletta,** It.
68/B3 **Barlin,** Fr.
65/H2 **Barlinek,** Pol.
135/E2 **Barmejo** (riv.), Arg.
106/B2 **Barmer,** India
58/B1 **Barmouth,** Wal,UK
67/G1 **Barmstedt,** Ger.
108/C2 **Barnāla,** India
57/G2 **Barnard Castle,** Eng,UK
102/D1 **Barnaul,** Rus.
167/D4 **Barnegat** (bay), NJ,US
167/D4 **Barnegat** (inlet), NJ,US
53/N7 **Barnet,** Eng,UK
53/N7 **Barnet** (bor.), Eng,UK
66/C4 **Barneveld,** Neth.
65/G2 **Barnim** (reg.), Ger.
57/F4 **Barnoldswick,** Eng,UK
57/G4 **Barnsley,** Eng,UK
58/B4 **Barnstaple,** Eng,UK
58/B4 **Barnstaple** (Bideford) (bay), Eng,UK
58/E2 **Barnt Green,** Eng,UK
67/G5 **Barntrup,** Ger.
163/H3 **Barnwell,** SC,US
106/B3 **Baroda,** India
78/B1 **Barone, Monte** (peak), It.
95/K1 **Barowghīl** (Khyber) (pass), Afg.
106/F2 **Barpeta,** India
138/D2 **Barquisimeto,** Ven.
56/D1 **Barr,** Sc,UK
140/B3 **Barra,** Braz.
55/H8 **Barra** (isl.), Sc,UK
141/B2 **Barra Bonita,** Braz.
141/B2 **Barra Bonita** (res.), Braz.
140/B4 **Barra da Choça,** Braz.
149/F4 **Barra del Colorado Nat'l Park,** CR
137/G7 **Barra do Bugres,** Braz.
140/A2 **Barra do Corda,** Braz.
137/H7 **Barra do Garças,** Braz.
140/B3 **Barra do Mendes,** Braz.
141/K7 **Barra do Piraí,** Braz.
141/B4 **Barra do Ribeiro,** Braz.
131/D4 **Barra Falsa, Ponta da** (pt.), Moz.
55/H8 **Barra Head** (pt.), Sc,UK
141/J7 **Barra Mansa,** Braz.
144/B3 **Barranca,** Peru
138/C3 **Barrancabermeja,** Col.
146/D3 **Barranca del Cobre Nat'l Park,** Mex.
142/C2 **Barrancas,** Chile
138/C2 **Barranquilla,** Col.
131/D4 **Barra, Ponta da** (pt.), Moz.
149/F4 **Barra Punta Gorda,** Nic.
140/B2 **Barras,** Braz.
141/B3 **Barra Velha,** Braz.
140/A4 **Barreiras,** Braz.
140/B1 **Barreirinhas,** Braz.
74/A3 **Barreiro,** Port.
140/D3 **Barreiros,** Braz.
133/G7 **Barren, Nosy** (isls.), Madg.
141/B2 **Barretos,** Braz.
156/E2 **Barrhead,** Ab,Can
54/B5 **Barrhead,** Sc,UK
56/D1 **Barrhill,** Sc,UK
160/E2 **Barrie,** On,Can
119/B1 **Barrier** (range), Austl.
156/C3 **Barrière,** BC,Can
165/P15 **Barrington,** Il,US
168/C2 **Barrington,** RI,US
165/P15 **Barrington Hills,** Il,US
119/D1 **Barrington Tops** (peak), Austl.
119/D1 **Barrington Tops Nat'l Park,** Austl.
140/B2 **Barro Duro,** Braz.
118/B2 **Barron Gorge Nat'l Park,** Austl.
141/D2 **Barroso,** Braz.
116/B2 **Barrow** (isl.), Austl.
118/B1 **Barrow** (pt.), Austl.
152/G1 **Barrow** (str.), NW,Can
60/D5 **Barrow** (riv.), Ire.
151/G1 **Barrow** (pt.), Ak,US
57/H6 **Barrowby,** Eng,UK
57/F4 **Barrowford,** Eng,UK
57/E3 **Barrow-in-Furness,** Eng,UK
58/C4 **Barry,** Wal,UK
87/L4 **Barsakel'mes** (salt pan), Uzb.
95/L5 **Bārshi,** India
67/G4 **Barsinghausen,** Ger.
63/T8 **Bårslöv,** Swe.
67/E2 **Barssel,** Ger.
158/C4 **Barstow,** Ca,US
146/E2 **Barstow,** Tx,US
72/F2 **Bar-sur-Aube,** Fr.
102/B4 **Bartang** (riv.), Taj.
64/G1 **Barth,** Ger.
83/L5 **Bartın,** Turk.
115/H3 **Bartle Frere** (peak), Austl.
159/J3 **Bartlesville,** Ok,US
165/P16 **Bartlett,** Il,US
149/G1 **Bartolomé Masó,** Cuba
131/D4 **Bartolomeu Dias,** Moz.
59/F3 **Barton in the Clay,** Eng,UK
59/E5 **Barton on Sea,** Eng,UK
59/E1 **Barton under Needwood,** Eng,UK
57/H4 **Barton-upon-Humber,** Eng,UK
65/L1 **Bartoszyce,** Pol.
163/H5 **Bartow,** Fl,US
149/F4 **Barú** (vol.), Pan.
110/B3 **Barumun** (riv.), Indo.
110/A3 **Barus,** Indo.
96/C2 **Baruun Huuray** (reg.), Mong.
96/G2 **Baruun-Urt,** Mong.
106/C3 **Barwāha,** India
106/B3 **Barwāni,** India
119/D1 **Barwon** (riv.), Austl.
65/J3 **Barycz** (riv.), Pol.
87/H1 **Barysh,** Rus.
125/J7 **Basankusu,** Zaire
74/D1 **Basauri,** Sp.
142/F2 **Basavilbaso,** Arg.
112/C3 **Basay,** Phil.
58/D1 **Baschurch,** Eng,UK
76/D2 **Basel,** Swi.
76/D3 **Baselland** (canton), Swi.
80/E2 **Basento** (riv.), It.
132/E3 **Bashee** (riv.), SAfr.
105/J4 **Bashi** (chan.), Phil., Tai.
102/E1 **Bashkaus** (riv.), Rus.
85/M5 **Bashkir Aut. Rep.,** Rus.
112/C4 **Basilan** (isl.), Phil.
112/C4 **Basilan** (peak), Phil.
112/C4 **Basilan** (str.), Phil.
59/G3 **Basildon,** Eng,UK
78/C4 **Basilica di Fieschi,** It.
80/D2 **Basilicata** (reg.), It.
106/C3 **Bāsim,** India
156/F4 **Basin,** Wy,US
59/E4 **Basingstoke,** Eng,UK
53/M8 **Basingstoke** (can.), Eng,UK
91/D2 **Basīt, Ra's al** (pt.), Syria
93/F2 **Başkale,** Turk.
160/F2 **Baskatong** (res.), Qu,Can
92/B2 **Başkomutan Nat'l Park,** Turk.
92/B2 **Başmakçı,** Turk.
106/C3 **Bāsoda,** India
130/B4 **Basodesh,** Tanz.
77/E5 **Basodino, Monte** (peak), It.
125/K7 **Basoko,** Zaire
74/D1 **Basque Provinces** (aut. comm.), Sp.
76/D1 **Bas-Rhin** (dept.), Fr.
119/C3 **Bass** (str.), Austl.
121/L7 **Bass** (isls.), FrPol.
81/G4 **Bassae** (ruins), Gre.
156/E3 **Bassano,** Ab,Can
79/E1 **Bassano del Grappa,** It.
126/H5 **Bassas da India** (isl.), Reun.
104/B5 **Bassein,** Burma
104/B5 **Bassein** (riv.), Burma
106/B4 **Bassein,** India
69/E2 **Bassenge,** Belg.
72/C2 **Basse-Normandie** (reg.), Fr.
56/E2 **Bassenthwaite** (lake), Eng,UK
150/F3 **Basse-Terre,** Guad.
150/F3 **Basse-Terre** (isl.), Guad.
150/F3 **Basseterre** (cap.), StK.
54/D4 **Bass Rock** (isl.), Sc,UK
67/F3 **Bassum,** Ger.
160/B1 **Basswood** (lake), On,Can, Mn,US
62/E3 **Båstad,** Swe.
106/D2 **Bastī,** India
80/A1 **Bastia,** Fr.
80/C1 **Bastia,** It.
69/E3 **Bastogne,** Belg.
141/B2 **Bastos,** Braz.
162/F3 **Bastrop,** La,US
162/D4 **Bastrop,** Tx,US
91/B4 **Basyūn,** Egypt
124/G7 **Bata,** EqG.
112/C2 **Bataan** (mtn.), Phil.
149/F1 **Batabanó** (gulf), Cuba
112/C1 **Batac,** Phil.
89/P3 **Batagay,** Rus.
108/C2 **Batāla,** India
140/B2 **Batalha,** Braz.
74/A3 **Batalha,** Port.
120/B2 **Batan** (isls.), Phil.
104/C2 **Batang,** China
125/J6 **Batangafo,** CAfr.
112/C2 **Batangas,** Phil.
111/H4 **Batanta** (mtn.), Indo.
141/C2 **Batatais,** Braz.
165/P16 **Batavia,** Il,US
160/E3 **Batavia,** NY,US
86/F3 **Bataysk,** Rus.
107/H5 **Batdambang,** Camb.
118/H9 **Bate** (bay), Austl.
124/H8 **Batéké** (plat.), Congo
119/D2 **Batemans Bay,** Austl.
163/H3 **Batesburg,** SC,US
163/F3 **Batesville,** Ar,US
163/F3 **Batesville,** Ms,US
58/D4 **Bath,** Eng,UK
161/G3 **Bath,** Me,US
160/E3 **Bath,** NY,US
54/C5 **Bathgate,** Sc,UK
119/D2 **Bathurst,** Austl.
114/D2 **Bathurst** (isl.), Austl.
161/H2 **Bathurst,** NB,Can
151/N1 **Bathurst** (cape), NW,Can
152/F2 **Bathurst** (inlet), NW,Can
153/R7 **Bathurst** (isl.), NW,Can
125/P5 **Batī,** Eth.
130/C3 **Batian** (peak), Kenya
102/F2 **Batik** (mts.), China
94/E3 **Bāţin, Wādī al** (dry riv.), SAr.
164/C4 **Batiquitos** (lag.), Ca,US
93/H3 **Bāţlāq-e Gāv Khūnī** (marsh), Iran
57/G4 **Batley,** Eng,UK
92/E2 **Batman,** Turk.
123/V18 **Batna,** Alg.
123/T16 **Batna** (wilaya), Alg.
131/B3 **Batoka,** Zam.
163/F4 **Baton Rouge,** (cap.), La,US
124/H7 **Batouri,** Camr.
91/D4 **Baţrā'** (Petra) (ruins), Jor.
161/F2 **Batsican** (riv.), Qu,Can
166/D4 **Batsto** (riv.), NJ,US
166/D4 **Batsto Hist. Vill.,** NJ,US
96/F2 **Batsümber,** Mong.
51/M9 **Batterbee** (cape), Ant.
57/G3 **Battersby,** Eng,UK
53/N7 **Battersea,** Eng,UK
106/D6 **Batticaloa,** SrL.
108/H4 **Batticaloa** (dist.), SrL.
156/F2 **Battle** (riv.), Ab, Sk,Can
59/G5 **Battle,** Eng,UK
156/F3 **Battle** (cr.), Mt,US
160/C3 **Battle Creek,** Mi,US
156/F2 **Battleford,** Sk,Can
158/C2 **Battle Mountain,** Nv,US
168/C2 **Battleship Cove,** Ma,US
54/D3 **Battock** (mtn.), Sc,UK
82/E2 **Battonya,** Hun.
96/E2 **Battsengel,** Mong.
125/N6 **Batu** (peak), Eth.
111/E3 **Batu** (cape), Indo.
110/A4 **Batu** (isls.), Indo.
110/D3 **Batu** (bay), Malay.
110/D3 **Batu** (peak), Malay.
111/F4 **Batudaka** (isl.), Indo.
110/D3 **Batuensambang** (peak), Indo.
110/B3 **Batu Gajah,** Malay.
87/G4 **Batumi,** Geo.
110/B3 **Batu Pahat,** Malay.
110/B3 **Batu Puteh** (peak), Malay.
110/B4 **Baturaja,** Indo.
140/C2 **Baturité,** Braz.
91/F7 **Bat Yam,** Isr.
112/C1 **Bauang,** Phil.
129/H4 **Bauchi** (state), Nga.
157/K3 **Baudette,** Mn,US
138/B3 **Baudó** (mts.), Col.
138/B3 **Baudó** (riv.), Col.
149/G5 **Baudo, Serranía de** (range), Col.
153/L1 **Bauld** (cape), Nf,Can
129/F5 **Bauman** (peak), Togo
70/D2 **Baunach** (riv.), Ger.
67/G6 **Baunatal,** Ger.
112/D3 **Bauñgon,** Phil.
141/B2 **Baurú,** Braz.
65/H3 **Bautzen,** Ger.
71/E5 **Bavaria** (state), Ger.
77/H3 **Bavarian Alps** (mts.), Aus., Ger.
62/G2 **Båven** (lake), Swe.
146/C2 **Bavispe** (riv.), Mex.
110/C4 **Bawang** (cape), Indo.
119/C3 **Baw Baw** (peak), Austl.
119/C3 **Baw Baw Nat'l Park,** Austl.
110/D5 **Bawean** (isl.), Indo.
129/E4 **Bawku,** Gha.
104/C2 **Baxoi,** China
149/G1 **Bayamo,** Cuba
150/E3 **Bayamón,** PR
97/K2 **Bayan,** China
96/F2 **Bayan,** Mong.
96/G2 **Bayandelger,** Mong.
96/D5 **Bayan Har** (mts.), China
96/E2 **Bayanhongor,** Mong.
96/E3 **Bayanleg,** Mong.
102/F2 **Bayannur,** Mong.
149/G4 **Bayano** (res.), Pan.
96/E2 **Bayan-Ovoo,** Mong.
96/D2 **Bayan-Uul,** Mong.
159/G2 **Bayard,** Ne,US
112/C3 **Bayawan,** Phil.
69/G3 **Baybach** (riv.), Ger.
112/D3 **Baybay,** Phil.
92/E1 **Bayburt,** Turk.
92/E1 **Bayburt** (prov.), Turk.
160/D3 **Bay City,** Mi,US
162/E4 **Bay City,** Tx,US
88/G2 **Baydaratskaya** (bay), Rus.
125/P7 **Baydhabo** (Baidoa), Som.
96/D2 **Baydrag** (riv.), Mong.
71/F5 **Bayerischer Wald** (hills), Ger.
71/G5 **Bayerischer Wald Nat'l Park,** Ger.
140/D2 **Bayeux,** Braz.
72/C2 **Bayeux,** Fr.
143/T11 **Baygorria, Artificial de** (res.), Uru.
94/E6 **Bayḩān al Qisāb,** Yem.
92/A2 **Bayındır,** Turk.
96/F1 **Baykal** (lake), Rus.
89/L4 **Baykal** (mts.), Rus.
112/F7 **Bay, Laguna de** (lake), Phil.
163/G4 **Bay Minette,** Al,US
112/C1 **Bayombong,** Phil.
74/A1 **Bayona,** Sp.
163/H4 **Bayonet Point,** Fl,US
72/C5 **Bayonne,** Fr.
167/D2 **Bayonne,** NJ,US
167/E2 **Bayport,** NY,US
95/H1 **Bayram-Ali,** Trkm.
83/H5 **Bayramıç,** Turk.
71/E3 **Bayreuth,** Ger.
167/J9 **Bay Ridge,** NY,US
91/D3 **Bayrūt** (Beirut) (cap.), Leb.
160/E2 **Bays** (lake), On,Can
163/F4 **Bay Saint Louis,** Ms,US
75/E1 **Bayse** (riv.), Fr.
167/K8 **Bayside,** NY,US
58/D1 **Bayston Hill,** Eng,UK
116/K6 **Bayswater,** Austl.
91/D4 **Bayt Laḩm** (Bethlehem), WBnk.
162/E4 **Baytown,** Tx,US
127/C5 **Bayudha** (des.), Sudan
168/F5 **Bay Village,** Oh,US
167/E2 **Bayville,** NY,US
74/D4 **Baza,** Sp.
87/H4 **Bazardyuzyu, Gora** (peak), Rus.
131/D4 **Bazaruto** (isl.), Moz.
129/E4 **Bazèga** (prov.), Burk.
104/E2 **Bazhong,** China
160/F2 **Bazin** (riv.), Qu,Can
167/D4 **Beachwood,** NJ,US
168/F5 **Beachwood,** Oh,US
59/G5 **Beachy Head** (pt.), Eng,UK
58/C2 **Beacon** (hill), Wal,UK
161/N7 **Beaconsfield,** Qu,Can
59/F3 **Beaconsfield,** Eng,UK
58/B5 **Beaford,** Eng,UK
114/E2 **Beagle** (gulf), Austl.
118/A4 **Beal** (mts.), Austl.
133/J6 **Bealanana,** Madg.
156/B3 **Beale** (cape), BC,Can
159/G4 **Beals** (cr.), Tx,US
58/D5 **Beaminster,** Eng,UK
133/H9 **Beampingaratra** (ridge), Madg.
161/R9 **Beamsville,** On,Can
157/K2 **Bear** (lake), Mb,Can
88/C2 **Bear** (isl.), Nor.
151/K2 **Bear** (mtn.), Ak,US
151/K3 **Bear** (mtn.), Ak,US
165/M10 **Bear** (cr.), Ca,US
168/A2 **Bear** (hill), Ct,US
168/A1 **Bear** (mtn.), Ct,US
156/F5 **Bear** (lake), Id, Ut,US
156/F5 **Bear** (riv.), Id, Ut,US
60/A6 **Beara** (pen.), Ire.
113/M **Beardmore** (glac.), Ant.
167/H7 **Bearfort** (mtn.), NJ,US
156/F3 **Bearpaw** (mts.), Mt,US
54/B5 **Bearsden,** Sc,UK
156/F4 **Beartooth** (mts.), Mt, Wy,US
163/F4 **Bear Town,** Ms,US
168/A1 **Beartown Saint For.,** Ma,US
108/D2 **Beās** (riv.), India
74/D1 **Beasain,** Sp.
74/D3 **Beas de Segura,** Sp.
150/D3 **Beata** (cape), DRep.
150/D3 **Beata** (isl.), DRep.
114/F2 **Beatrice** (cape), Austl.
159/H2 **Beatrice,** Ne,US
131/C3 **Beatrice,** Zim.
54/C6 **Beattock,** Sc,UK
158/C3 **Beatty,** Nv,US
72/F5 **Beaucaire,** Fr.
53/S9 **Beauchamp,** Fr.
145/C2 **Beaufort** (sea), Can., US
163/H3 **Beaufort,** SC,US
132/C4 **Beaufort West,** SAfr.
72/D3 **Beaugency,** Fr.
161/N7 **Beauharnois,** Qu,Can
161/N7 **Beauharnois** (co.), Qu,Can
72/F4 **Beaujolais** (mts.), Fr.
59/E5 **Beaulieu,** Eng,UK
54/B2 **Beauly,** Sc,UK
54/B2 **Beauly** (firth), Sc,UK
54/B2 **Beauly** (riv.), Sc,UK
56/D5 **Beaumaris,** Wal,UK
68/B3 **Beaumetz-les-Loges,** Fr.
72/E4 **Beaumont,** Fr.
164/D3 **Beaumont,** Ca,US
162/E4 **Beaumont,** Tx,US
53/S9 **Beaumont-sur-Oise,** Fr.
72/F3 **Beaune,** Fr.
72/C3 **Beaupréau,** Fr.
69/D3 **Beauraing,** Belg.
68/C3 **Beaurevoir,** Fr.
157/J3 **Beauséjour,** Mb,Can
68/B5 **Beauvais,** Fr.
156/G2 **Beauval,** Sk,Can
156/F2 **Beaver** (riv.), Ab, Sk,Can
152/D2 **Beaver** (riv.), Yk,Can
159/G3 **Beaver** (riv.), Co,US
159/G3 **Beaver** (riv.), Ks, Ne,US
160/C2 **Beaver** (isl.), Mi,US
159/G3 **Beaver** (riv.), NM, Ok,US
159/G3 **Beaver,** Ok,US
168/G6 **Beaver** (co.), Pa,US
168/G6 **Beaver** (riv.), Pa,US
158/D3 **Beaver,** Ut,US
151/K3 **Beaver Creek,** Yk,Can
160/B3 **Beaver Dam,** Wi,US
168/G6 **Beaver Falls,** Pa,US
156/E4 **Beaverhead** (riv.), Mt,US
156/D2 **Beaverlodge,** Ab,Can
157/L2 **Beaver Stone** (riv.), On,Can
106/B2 **Beāwar,** India
141/B2 **Bebedouro,** Braz.
140/C2 **Beberibe,** Braz.
57/E5 **Bebington,** Eng,UK
67/G7 **Bebra,** Ger.
59/H2 **Beccles,** Eng,UK
82/E3 **Bečej,** Yugo.
124/E1 **Bechar,** Alg.
151/G4 **Becharof** (lake), Ak,US
151/G4 **Becharof Nat'l Wild. Ref.,** Ak,US
53/N7 **Beckenham,** Eng,UK
69/F5 **Beckingen,** Ger.
57/H5 **Beckingham,** Eng,UK
160/D4 **Beckley,** WV,US
67/F5 **Beckum,** Ger.
83/G2 **Beclean,** Rom.
76/D5 **Becs de Bosson** (peak), Swi.
57/G3 **Bedale,** Eng,UK
66/D7 **Bedburg,** Ger.
66/D5 **Bedburg-Hau,** Ger.
58/C3 **Beddau,** Wal,UK
56/D5 **Beddgelert,** Wal,UK
118/B1 **Bedford** (cape), Austl.
161/F2 **Bedford,** Qu,Can
59/F2 **Bedford,** Eng,UK
160/C4 **Bedford,** In,US
168/F5 **Bedford,** Oh,US
160/E4 **Bedford,** Va,US
168/F5 **Bedford Heights,** Oh,US
59/G2 **Bedford Level** (reg.), Eng,UK
59/F2 **Bedfordshire** (co.), Eng,UK
57/G1 **Bedlington,** Eng,UK
53/M6 **Bedmond,** Eng,UK
124/H4 **Bedouaram** (well), Niger
66/D2 **Bedum,** Neth.
58/C3 **Bedwas,** Wal,UK
59/E2 **Bedworth,** Eng,UK
118/D4 **Beenleigh,** Austl.
58/C5 **Beer,** Eng,UK
70/B3 **Beerfelden,** Ger.
58/C5 **Beer Head** (pt.), Eng,UK
68/C1 **Beernem,** Belg.
91/D4 **Beersheba** (Be'er Sheva'), Isr.
91/D4 **Be'er Sheva'** (Beersheba), Isr.
69/D1 **Beerzel,** Belg.
66/D6 **Beesel,** Neth.
57/G6 **Beeston,** Eng,UK
162/D4 **Beeville,** Tx,US
125/K7 **Befale,** Zaire
67/F5 **Bega** (riv.), Ger.
106/C3 **Begamganj,** India
87/K4 **Begarslan** (peak), Trkm.
82/E3 **Bega Veche** (riv.), Rom.
89/M2 **Begichev** (isl.), Rus.
56/B2 **Beg, Lough** (lake), NI,UK
62/C1 **Begna** (riv.), Nor.
106/E2 **Begusarai,** India
137/H3 **Béhague** (pt.), FrG.
110/B4 **Behala** (str.), Indo.
93/G4 **Behbahān,** Iran
69/F5 **Behren-lès-Forbach,** Fr.
93/H2 **Behshahr,** Iran
105/H2 **Bei** (mtn.), China
102/F3 **Bei** (mts.), China
105/F2 **Bei** (riv.), China
105/G3 **Bei** (riv.), China
97/K2 **Bei'an,** China
96/D4 **Beida** (riv.), China
105/J3 **Beigantang** (isl.), Tai.
78/B4 **Beigua, Monte** (peak), It.
105/F4 **Beihai,** China
103/D3 **Beijing** (cap.), China
103/H6 **Beijing** (prov.), China
103/H7 **Beijing** (inset) (cap.), China
66/D3 **Beilen,** Neth.
105/F4 **Beiliu,** China
71/E4 **Beilngries,** Ger.
96/C5 **Beilu** (riv.), China
105/E4 **Beilun** (pass), China
78/A2 **Beinasco,** It.
54/B3 **Beinn a' Chuallaich** (mtn.), Sc,UK
54/C3 **Beinn a' Ghlò** (mtn.), Sc,UK
54/B2 **Beinn a' Mheadhoin, Loch** (lake), Sc,UK
54/A3 **Beinn Bhàn** (mtn.), Sc,UK
54/B4 **Beinn Bheula** (mtn.), Sc,UK
54/C2 **Beinn Bhrotain** (mtn.), Sc,UK
54/B4 **Beinn Bhuidhe** (mtn.), Sc,UK
54/B2 **Beinn Bhuidhe Mhór** (mtn.), Sc,UK
54/B1 **Beinn Dearg** (mtn.), Sc,UK
54/C3 **Beinn Dearg** (mtn.), Sc,UK
54/B4 **Beinn Dòrain** (mtn.), Sc,UK
54/A1 **Beinn Eighe** (mtn.), Sc,UK
54/B3 **Beinn Heasgarnich** (mtn.), Sc,UK
54/B3 **Beinn Mholach** (mtn.), Sc,UK
54/A4 **Beinn Mhór** (mtn.), Sc,UK
54/B1 **Bein Tharsuinn** (mtn.), Sc,UK
103/E2 **Beipiao,** China
131/D3 **Beira,** Moz.
103/C4 **Beiru** (riv.), China
91/D3 **Beirut** (Bayrūt) (cap.), Leb.
131/C4 **Beitbridge,** Zim.
54/B5 **Beith,** Sc,UK
82/F2 **Beiuş,** Rom.
101/A2 **Beizhen,** China
74/B3 **Beja,** Port.
74/A4 **Beja** (dist.), Port.
123/T15 **Bejaïa,** Alg.
123/T15 **Bejaïa** (wilaya), Alg.
74/C2 **Béjar,** Sp.
95/J3 **Bejhi** (riv.), Pak.

176

Bekaa - Bismu

91/D3 **Bekaa** (Al Biqā') (val.), Leb.
110/C5 **Bekasi,** Indo.
82/E2 **Békés,** Hun.
82/E2 **Békés** (co.), Hun.
82/E2 **Békéscsaba,** Hun.
133/H8 **Bekily,** Madg.
129/E5 **Bekwai,** Gha.
106/B3 **Bela,** India
95/J3 **Bela,** Pak.
130/A2 **Bela,** Zaire
82/E3 **Bela Crkva,** Yugo.
140/B1 **Bela Cruz,** Braz.
166/B4 **Bel Air,** Md,US
117/M8 **Belair Rec. Park,** Austl.
166/B5 **Bel Air South,** Md,US
82/F4 **Bela Palanka,** Yugo.
86/C1 **Belarus**
75/P10 **Belas,** Port.
137/G8 **Bela Vista,** Braz.
131/D5 **Bela Vista,** Moz.
141/B2 **Bela Vista do Paraiso,** Braz.
85/M5 **Belaya** (riv.), Rus.
87/G2 **Belaya Kalitva,** Rus.
86/D2 **Belaya Tserkov',** Ukr.
78/B3 **Belbo** (riv.), It.
65/K3 **Bełchatów,** Pol.
76/D2 **Belchen** (peak), Ger.
153/S7 **Belcher** (chan.), NW,Can
153/H3 **Belcher** (isls.), NW,Can
157/J3 **Belcourt,** ND,US
85/M5 **Belebey,** Rus.
125/Q7 **Beled Weyne,** Som.
140/D2 **Belém,** Braz.
140/C3 **Belém de São Francisco,** Braz.
75/P10 **Belem Tower,** Port.
135/C2 **Belén,** Arg.
91/E1 **Belen,** Turk.
158/F4 **Belen,** NM,US
143/S12 **Belén de Escobar,** Arg.
83/G4 **Belene,** Bul.
74/B1 **Belesar** (res.), Sp.
125/N5 **Beles Wenz** (riv.), Eth.
86/F1 **Belev,** Rus.
56/C2 **Belfast** (cap.), NI,UK
56/C2 **Belfast** (dist.), NI,UK
161/G2 **Belfast,** Me,US
56/C2 **Belfast Lough** (inlet), NI,UK
157/H4 **Belfield,** ND,US
54/E5 **Belford,** Eng,UK
76/C2 **Belfort,** Fr.
76/C2 **Belfort** (dept.), Fr.
106/B4 **Belgaum,** India
64/C3 **Belgium**
86/F2 **Belgorod,** Rus.
86/D3 **Belgorod-Dnestrovskiy,** Ukr.
86/F2 **Belgorod Obl.,** Rus.
156/F4 **Belgrade,** Mt,US
82/E3 **Belgrade** (Beograd) (cap.), Yugo.
60/B1 **Belhavel** (lake), Ire.
82/E4 **Beli Drim** (riv.), Yugo.
82/D3 **Beli Manastir,** Cro.
82/F4 **Beli Timok** (riv.), Yugo.
110/C4 **Belitung** (isl.), Indo.
148/D2 **Belize**
148/D2 **Belize** (riv.), Belz.
148/D2 **Belize City,** Belz.
82/E3 **Beljanica** (peak), Yugo.
89/P2 **Bel'kovskiy** (isl.), Rus.
117/G5 **Bell** (pt.), Austl.
153/H2 **Bell** (pen.), NW,Can
160/E1 **Bell** (riv.), Qu,Can
164/B3 **Bell,** Ca,US
156/B2 **Bella Coola,** BC,Can
56/B2 **Bellaghy,** NI,UK
106/C4 **Bellary,** India
135/E2 **Bella Vista,** Arg.
80/A3 **Bellavista** (cape), It.
165/G7 **Belle** (riv.), On,Can
165/G6 **Belle** (riv.), Mi,US
68/C5 **Belleau,** Fr.
56/B3 **Belleek,** NI,UK
160/D3 **Bellefontaine,** Oh,US
157/G4 **Belle Fourche** (riv.), SD, Wy,US
76/B5 **Bellegarde-sur-Valserine,** Fr.
163/H5 **Belle Glade,** Fl,US
166/A6 **Belle Haven,** Va,US
72/B3 **Belle-Ile** (isl.), Fr.
161/K1 **Belle Isle** (str.), Nf, Qu,Can
118/B2 **Bellenden Ker Nat'l Park,** Austl.
72/E3 **Bellerive-sur-Allier,** Fr.
160/E2 **Belleville,** On,Can
160/B4 **Belleville,** Il,US
159/H3 **Belleville,** Ks,US
165/E7 **Belleville** (lake), Mi,US
167/D2 **Belleville,** NJ,US
168/G7 **Bellevue,** Pa,US
165/C2 **Bellevue,** Wa,US
164/B3 **Bellflower,** Ca,US
164/F8 **Bell Gardens,** Ca,US
57/F1 **Bellingham,** Eng,UK
156/C3 **Bellingham,** Wa,US
163/F4 **Bellingrath Gardens,** Al,US
113/U **Bellingshausen** (sea), Ant.
121/K6 **Bellingshausen** (isl.), FrPol.
67/E2 **Bellingwolde,** Neth.
77/F5 **Bellinzona,** Swi.
166/C4 **Bellmawr,** NJ,US
167/E2 **Bellmore,** NY,US
138/C3 **Bello,** Col.
120/F7 **Bellona** (reefs), NCal.
152/G1 **Bellot** (str.), NW,Can
154/W13 **Bellows A.F.B.,** Hi,US
54/D4 **Bell Rock** (Inchcape) (isl.), Sc,UK
54/B6 **Bellsbank,** Sc,UK
54/B5 **Bellshill,** Sc,UK
73/K3 **Belluno,** It.
79/E1 **Belluno** (prov.), It.
142/E2 **Bell Ville,** Arg.
132/B4 **Bellville,** SAfr.
162/D4 **Bellville,** Tx,US
67/F4 **Belm,** Ger.
165/K11 **Belmont,** Ca,US
168/C1 **Belmont,** Ma,US
140/C4 **Belmonte,** Braz.
148/D2 **Belmopan** (cap.), Belz.
140/B4 **Belo Campo,** Braz.
68/C2 **Beloeil,** Belg.
161/P6 **Beloeil,** Qu,Can
97/K1 **Belogorsk,** Rus.
82/F4 **Belogradchik,** Bul.
141/D1 **Belo Horizonte,** Braz.
159/H3 **Beloit,** Ks,US
160/B3 **Beloit,** Wi,US
140/C3 **Belo Jardim,** Braz.
84/G2 **Belomorsk,** Rus.
126/C1 **Belondo-Kundu,** Zaire
86/F3 **Belorechensk,** Rus.
85/N5 **Beloretsk,** Rus.
82/E4 **Beloševac,** Yugo.
83/H4 **Beloslav,** Bul.
88/J4 **Belovo,** Rus.
84/H3 **Beloye** (lake), Rus.
57/G5 **Belper,** Eng,UK
57/G1 **Belsay,** Eng,UK
156/F4 **Belt,** Mt,US
66/D3 **Belterwijde** (lake), Neth.
59/H1 **Belton,** Eng,UK
162/D4 **Belton,** Tx,US
60/A2 **Beltra** (lake), Ire.
166/B5 **Beltsville,** Md,US
83/H2 **Bel'tsy,** Mol.
166/C2 **Beltzville** (lake), Pa,US
102/E2 **Belukha, Gora** (peak), Rus.
160/B3 **Belvidere,** Il,US
118/B3 **Belyando** (riv.), Austl.
88/G2 **Belyy** (isl.), Rus.
64/G2 **Belzig,** Ger.
65/M3 **Bełżyce,** Pol.
133/H7 **Bemaraha** (plat.), Madg.
133/H7 **Bemarivo** (riv.), Madg.
131/C3 **Bembezi** (riv.), Zim.
74/B1 **Bembibre,** Sp.
59/E5 **Bembridge,** Eng,UK
131/C4 **Bemebesi,** Zim.
157/K4 **Bemidji,** Mn,US
66/C5 **Bemmel,** Neth.
57/H3 **Bempton,** Eng,UK
54/C1 **Ben Aigan** (hill), Sc,UK
54/B3 **Ben Alder** (mtn.), Sc,UK
119/C3 **Benalla,** Austl.
74/C4 **Benalmádena,** Sp.
74/C2 **Benavente,** Sp.
162/D5 **Benavides,** Tx,US
54/C2 **Ben Avon** (mtn.), Sc,UK
56/B1 **Benbane Head** (pt.), NI,UK
55/H8 **Benbecula** (isl.), Sc,UK
117/H4 **Benbonyathe** (peak), Austl.
119/D3 **Ben Boyd Nat'l Park,** Austl.
60/C1 **Benbrack** (mtn.), Ire.
56/B3 **Benburb,** NI,UK
54/C4 **Ben Chonzie** (mtn.), Sc,UK
54/C4 **Ben Cleuch** (mtn.), Sc,UK
54/A4 **Ben Cruachan** (mtn.), Sc,UK
156/C4 **Bend,** Or,US
60/A4 **Ben Dash** (mtn.), Ire.
166/C5 **Ben Davis** (pt.), NJ,US
129/G5 **Bendel** (state), Nga.
151/F2 **Bendeleben** (mtn.), Ak,US
83/J2 **Bendery,** Mol.
119/C3 **Bendigo,** Austl.
62/C4 **Bendorf,** Ger.
91/F7 **Bene Beraq,** Isr.
153/L3 **Benedict** (mtn.), Nf,Can
77/H2 **Benediktenwand** (peak), Ger.
140/B2 **Beneditinos,** Braz.
56/D1 **Beneraid** (hill), Sc,UK
71/H3 **Benešov,** Czh.
80/D2 **Benevento,** It.
59/G3 **Benfleet,** Eng,UK
131/D3 **Benga,** Moz.
106/E4 **Bengal** (bay), Asia
103/D4 **Bengbu,** China
125/K1 **Benghāzī,** Libya
109/D3 **Ben Giang,** Viet.
110/B3 **Bengkalis,** Indo.
110/B3 **Bengkalis** (isl.), Indo.
110/C3 **Bengkayang,** Indo.
110/B4 **Bengkulu,** Indo.
157/G3 **Bengough,** Sk,Can
62/E2 **Bengtsfors,** Swe.
126/B3 **Benguela,** Ang.
131/D4 **Benguerua** (isl.), Moz.
131/C1 **Bengweulu** (lake), Zam.
131/C1 **Bengweulu** (swamp), Zam.
55/J7 **Ben Hope** (mtn.), Sc,UK
136/E6 **Beni** (riv.), Bol.
130/A2 **Beni,** Zaire
124/E1 **Beni Abbes,** Alg.
75/F2 **Benicarló,** Sp.
165/K10 **Benicia,** Ca,US
75/E3 **Benidorm,** Sp.
75/E3 **Benifayó,** Sp.
54/B4 **Ben Ime** (mtn.), Sc,UK
124/D1 **Beni Mellal,** Mor.
129/F4 **Benin**
129/F5 **Benin** (bight), Ben., Nga.
129/G5 **Benin City,** Nga.
124/E1 **Beni Ounif,** Alg.
75/F3 **Benisa,** Sp.
142/B5 **Benjamin** (isl.), Chile
162/D3 **Benjamin,** Tx,US
144/D2 **Benjamin Constant,** Braz.
100/B2 **Benkei-misaki** (cape), Japan
159/G2 **Benkelman,** Ne,US
54/B3 **Ben Lawers** (mtn.), Sc,UK
54/B4 **Ben Ledi** (mtn.), Sc,UK
56/D5 **Benllech,** Wal,UK
54/B4 **Ben Lomond** (mtn.), Sc,UK
119/C4 **Ben Lomond Nat'l Park,** Austl.
54/B4 **Ben Lui** (mtn.), Sc,UK
54/C2 **Ben Macdui** (mtn.), Sc,UK
60/A1 **Benmore** (mtn.), Ire.
54/B4 **Ben More** (mtn.), Sc,UK
55/J7 **Ben More Assynt** (mtn.), Sc,UK
54/D2 **Bennachie** (hill), Sc,UK
56/C1 **Bennane Head** (pt.), Sc,UK
54/A6 **Bennan Head** (pt.), Sc,UK
89/R2 **Bennett** (isl.), Rus.
163/J3 **Bennettsville,** SC,US
54/B3 **Ben Nevis** (mtn.), Sc,UK
161/F3 **Bennington,** Vt,US
132/Q13 **Benoni,** SAfr.
133/J6 **Be, Nosy** (isl.), Madg.
124/H6 **Bénoue Nat'l Park,** Camr.
109/D2 **Ben Quang,** Viet.
54/C2 **Ben Rinnes** (mtn.), Sc,UK
165/Q16 **Bensenville,** Il,US
70/B3 **Bensheim,** Ger.
158/E5 **Benson,** Az,US
157/K4 **Benson,** Mn,US
167/K9 **Bensonhurst,** NY,US
54/A3 **Ben Starav** (mtn.), Sc,UK
54/B2 **Ben Tee** (mtn.), Sc,UK
57/F3 **Bentham,** Eng,UK
67/E4 **Bentheim,** Ger.
104/E5 **Ben Thuy,** Viet.
54/C3 **Ben Tirran** (mtn.), Sc,UK
125/L6 **Bentiu,** Sudan
57/G4 **Bentley,** Eng,UK
141/B4 **Bento Gonçalves,** Braz.
162/E3 **Benton,** Ar,US
160/B4 **Benton,** Il,US
160/B4 **Benton,** Ky,US
110/B3 **Bentong,** Malay.
160/C3 **Benton Harbor,** Mi,US
162/E2 **Bentonville,** Ar,US
109/D4 **Ben Tre,** Viet.
129/G4 **Benue** (riv.), Nga.
129/G5 **Benue** (state), Nga.
54/B4 **Ben Vane** (mtn.), Sc,UK
54/B4 **Ben Vorlich** (mtn.), Sc,UK
54/C3 **Ben Vrackie** (mtn.), Sc,UK
54/B1 **Ben Wyvis** (mtn.), Sc,UK
101/B2 **Benxi,** China
101/C2 **Benxi,** China
82/D3 **Beočin,** Yugo.
82/E3 **Beograd** (Belgrade) (cap.), Yugo.
98/B4 **Beppu,** Japan
98/B4 **Beppu** (bay), Japan
150/F4 **Bequia** (isl.), StV.
140/A1 **Bequimão,** Braz.
124/E1 **Beraber** (well), Alg.
56/A2 **Beragh,** NI,UK
81/F2 **Berat,** Alb.
111/E4 **Beratus** (peak), Indo.
111/H4 **Berau** (bay), Indo.
111/E3 **Berau** (riv.), Indo.
125/Q5 **Berbera,** Som.
124/J7 **Berberati,** CAfr.
139/G3 **Berbice** (riv.), Guy.
68/D1 **Berchem,** Belg.
71/E4 **Berching,** Ger.
73/K3 **Berchtesgaden,** Ger.
73/K3 **Berchtesgaden Nat'l Park,** Ger.
68/A3 **Berck,** Fr.
86/D2 **Berdichev,** Ukr.
88/J4 **Berdsk,** Rus.
86/F3 **Berdyansk,** Ukr.
160/C4 **Berea,** Ky,US
168/F5 **Berea,** Oh,US
86/B2 **Beregovo,** Ukr.
130/B4 **Bereku,** Tanz.
129/E5 **Berekum,** Gha.
127/C4 **Berenice** (ruins), Egypt
58/D5 **Bere Regis,** Eng,UK
161/H2 **Beresford,** NB,Can
157/J5 **Beresford,** SD,US
82/E2 **Berettyo** (riv.), Hun.
82/E2 **Berettyóújfalu,** Hun.
86/D1 **Berezina** (riv.), Bela.
85/N4 **Berezniki,** Rus.
132/B4 **Berg** (riv.), SAfr.
92/A2 **Bergama,** Turk.
77/F6 **Bergamasque Alps** (mts.), It.
78/C1 **Bergamo,** It.
78/C1 **Bergamo** (prov.), It.
67/G3 **Bergen,** Ger.
66/B3 **Bergen,** Neth.
62/A1 **Bergen,** Nor.
167/D1 **Bergen** (co.), NJ,US
67/G3 **Bergen-Belsen,** Ger.
167/E2 **Bergenfield,** NJ,US
66/B6 **Bergen op Zoom,** Neth.
72/D4 **Bergerac,** Fr.
66/C6 **Bergeyk,** Neth.
69/F2 **Bergheim,** Ger.
67/E6 **Bergisch Gladbach,** Ger.
67/E5 **Bergkamen,** Ger.
67/E6 **Bergneustadt,** Ger.
162/D4 **Bergstrom A.F.B.,** Tx,US
66/C2 **Bergum,** Neth.
66/D2 **Bergumermeer** (lake), Neth.
62/G1 **Bergviken** (lake), Swe.
106/D4 **Berhampur,** India
110/C4 **Berikat** (cape), Indo.
89/S4 **Bering** (isl.), Rus.
50/A3 **Bering** (sea)
151/E3 **Bering** (str.), Rus., Ak,US
69/E1 **Beringen,** Belg.
151/E2 **Bering Land Bridge Nat'l Prsv.,** Ak,US
110/B4 **Beritarikap** (cape), Indo.
74/D4 **Berja,** Sp.
66/D4 **Berkel** (riv.), Ger.
66/B5 **Berkel,** Neth.
58/D3 **Berkeley,** Eng,UK
165/K11 **Berkeley,** Ca,US
166/D2 **Berkeley Heights,** NJ,US
53/M6 **Berkhamsted,** Eng,UK
165/F6 **Berkley,** Mi,US
113/W **Berkner** (isl.), Ant.
83/F4 **Berkovitsa,** Bul.
166/C3 **Berks** (co.), Pa,US
59/E4 **Berkshire** (co.), Eng,UK
168/A1 **Berkshire** (co.), Ma,US
168/A1 **Berkshire** (hills), Ma,US
59/E4 **Berkshire Downs** (uplands), Eng,UK
68/C1 **Berlare,** Belg.
66/C5 **Berlicum,** Neth.
65/G2 **Berlin** (cap.), Ger.
168/B2 **Berlin,** Ct,US
161/G2 **Berlin,** NH,US
168/G6 **Berlin** (res.), Oh,US
113/V **Berlioz** (pt.), Ant.
134/C5 **Bermejo** (riv.), Arg.
135/D1 **Bermejo,** Bol.
74/D1 **Bermeo,** Sp.
145/L6 **Bermuda** (isl.), UK
166/A4 **Bermudian** (cr.), Pa,US
76/D3 **Bern** (canton), Swi.
76/D4 **Bern** (cap.), Swi.
144/A2 **Bernal,** Peru
80/E2 **Bernalda,** It.
158/F4 **Bernalillo,** NM,US
152/D1 **Bernard** (riv.), NW,Can
143/J7 **Bernardo O'Higgins Nat'l Park,** Chile
166/D2 **Bernardsville,** NJ,US
72/D2 **Bernay,** Fr.
64/F3 **Bernburg,** Ger.
67/F2 **Berne** (riv.), Ger.
76/D5 **Bernese Alps** (range), Swi.
53/S9 **Bernes-sur-Oise,** Fr.
116/B3 **Bernier** (isl.), Austl.
152/G1 **Bernier** (bay), NW,Can
77/F5 **Bernina** (mts.), It., Swi.
77/G5 **Bernina, Passo del** (pass), Swi.
77/F5 **Bernina, Piz** (peak), Swi.
68/C3 **Bernissart,** Belg.
69/G4 **Bernkastel-Kues,** Ger.
133/H8 **Beroroha,** Madg.
71/H3 **Beroun,** Czh.
71/H3 **Berounka** (riv.), Czh.
82/F5 **Berovo,** Macd.
72/F5 **Berre** (lag.), Fr.
55/K7 **Berriedale,** Sc,UK
58/C1 **Berriew,** Wal,UK
123/S15 **Berrouaghia,** Alg.
150/B1 **Berry** (isls.), Bahm.
72/D3 **Berry** (hist. reg.), Fr.
165/K9 **Berryessa** (lake), Ca,US
165/K9 **Berryessa** (peak), Ca,US
58/C6 **Berry Head** (pt.), Wal,UK
166/A2 **Berry Mountain** (ridge), Pa,US
162/E2 **Berryville,** Ar,US
140/B2 **Bertolínia,** Braz.
124/H7 **Bertoua,** Camr.
143/J7 **Bertrand** (peak), Arg.
69/E4 **Bertrix,** Belg.
79/F3 **Bertuzzi, Valli** (lag.), It.
120/G5 **Beru** (atoll), Kiri.
110/D3 **Beruit** (isl.), Malay.
54/D3 **Bervie Water** (riv.), Sc,UK
119/G5 **Berwick,** Austl.
161/H2 **Berwick,** NB,Can
166/B1 **Berwick,** Pa,US
54/D5 **Berwick-upon-Tweed,** Eng,UK
56/E6 **Berwyn** (mts.), Wal,UK
165/Q16 **Berwyn,** Il,US
166/C3 **Berwyn-Devon,** Pa,US
72/E4 **Bès** (riv.), Fr.
133/H7 **Besalampy,** Madg.
76/C3 **Besançon,** Fr.
111/E4 **Besar** (peak), Indo.
72/E3 **Besbre** (riv.), Fr.
88/F6 **Beshahr,** Iran
82/E3 **Beška,** Yugo.
65/K4 **Beskids** (mts.), Pol.
87/H4 **Beslan,** Rus.
82/F4 **Besna Kobila** (peak), Yugo.
157/G2 **Besnard** (lake), Sk,Can
92/D2 **Besni,** Turk.
78/B1 **Besozzo,** It.
57/G4 **Bessacarr,** Eng,UK
53/S9 **Bessancourt,** Fr.
83/J2 **Bessarabia** (reg.), Mol.
56/B3 **Bessbrook,** NI,UK
163/G3 **Bessemer,** Al,US
160/B2 **Bessemer,** Mi,US
165/D2 **Bessemer** (mtn.), Wa,US
87/K3 **Besshoky, Gora** (peak), Kaz.
66/C6 **Best,** Neth.
67/F6 **Bestwig,** Ger.
74/A1 **Betanzos,** Sp.
123/M14 **Beth** (riv.), Mor.
91/G6 **Beth Alpha Synagogue Nat'l Park,** Isr.
165/L11 **Bethany** (res.), Ca,US
159/J2 **Bethany,** Mo,US
168/A3 **Bethel,** Ct,US
168/G7 **Bethel Park,** Pa,US
56/D5 **Bethesda,** Wal,UK
166/A6 **Bethesda,** Md,US
132/E3 **Bethlehem,** SAfr.
166/C2 **Bethlehem,** Pa,US
91/D4 **Bethlehem** (Bayt Laḩm), WBnk.
76/C2 **Bethoncourt,** Fr.
167/E2 **Bethpage,** NY,US
157/G3 **Bethune,** Sk,Can
68/B2 **Béthune,** Fr.
68/A4 **Béthune** (riv.), Fr.
141/C1 **Betim,** Braz.
133/H8 **Betioky,** Madg.
102/A2 **Betpak-Dala** (des.), Kaz.
69/G6 **Betschdorf,** Fr.
91/D3 **Bet She'an,** Isr.
91/F8 **Bet Shemesh,** Isr.
161/G1 **Betsiamites** (riv.), Qu,Can
133/H7 **Betsiboka** (riv.), Madg.
125/J3 **Bette** (peak), Libya
69/F4 **Bettembourg,** Lux.
106/D2 **Bettiah,** India
106/C3 **Betūl,** India
66/C5 **Betuwe** (reg.), Neth.
56/E5 **Betws-y-Coed,** Wal,UK
69/G2 **Betzdorf,** Ger.
157/H4 **Beulah,** ND,US
165/P14 **Beulah** (lake), Wi,US
66/D3 **Beulakerwijde** (lake), Neth.
59/G4 **Beult** (riv.), Eng,UK
66/C5 **Beuningen,** Neth.
72/D3 **Beuvron** (riv.), Fr.
53/U10 **Beuvronne** (riv.), Fr.
68/B2 **Beuvry,** Fr.
67/H2 **Bevensen,** Ger.
67/E4 **Bever** (riv.), Ger.
68/D1 **Beveren,** Belg.
77/F4 **Beverin, Piz** (peak), Swi.
57/H4 **Beverley,** Eng,UK
164/B2 **Beverly Hills,** Ca,US
165/F6 **Beverly Hills,** Mi,US
67/G5 **Beverungen,** Ger.
66/B4 **Beverwijk,** Neth.
57/F1 **Bewcastle,** Eng,UK
58/D2 **Bewdley,** Eng,UK
59/G4 **Bewl Bridge** (res.), Eng,UK
69/G5 **Bexbach,** Ger.
59/G5 **Bexhill,** Eng,UK
53/P7 **Bexley** (bor.), Eng,UK
83/J5 **Beykoz,** Turk.
93/N6 **Beylerbeyi Palace,** Turk.
69/E2 **Beyne-Heusay,** Belg.
93/M6 **Beyoğlu,** Turk.
83/K5 **Beypazarı,** Turk.
108/E3 **Beypore,** India
108/F3 **Beypore** (riv.), India
92/B2 **Beyşehir,** Turk.
92/B2 **Beyşehir** (lake), Turk.
82/D3 **Bezdan,** Yugo.
71/H1 **Bezděz** (peak), Czh.
71/H4 **Bezdrev** (lake), Czh.
84/H4 **Bezhetsk,** Rus.
72/E5 **Béziers,** Fr.
106/D2 **Bhabua,** India
108/C2 **Bhadaur,** India
106/E3 **Bhadrak,** India
106/C5 **Bhadrāvati,** India
106/A3 **Bhadreswar,** India
106/E2 **Bhāgalpur,** India
108/B2 **Bhāi Pheru,** Pak.
108/A2 **Bhakkar,** Pak.
108/D2 **Bhākra** (dam), India
106/E2 **Bhaktapur,** Nepal
108/B1 **Bhalwāl,** Pak.
104/C3 **Bhamo,** Burma
106/C2 **Bharātpur,** India
104/B3 **Bhareli** (riv.), India
106/B3 **Bharuch,** India
106/D3 **Bhātāpāra,** India
108/C2 **Bhatinda,** India
106/B5 **Bhatkal,** India
106/E3 **Bhātpāra,** India
108/F3 **Bhavāni,** India
108/F3 **Bhavāni** (riv.), India
106/B3 **Bhavnagar,** India
108/B2 **Bhawāna,** Pak.
106/C3 **Bhawāni Mandi,** India
106/D4 **Bhawānipatna,** India
108/B1 **Bhera,** Pak.
106/D3 **Bhilai,** India
106/B2 **Bhīlwāra,** India
106/C4 **Bhīma** (riv.), India
106/D4 **Bhīmavaram,** India
106/D4 **Bhimunipatnam,** India
106/C2 **Bhind,** India
106/B3 **Bhīnmāl,** India
106/B4 **Bhiwandi,** India
106/E2 **Bhojpur,** Nepal
106/C3 **Bhopāl,** India
106/B4 **Bhor,** India
54/A1 **Bhraoin, Loch** (lake), Sc,UK
106/E3 **Bhuban,** India
106/E3 **Bhubaneswar,** India
106/A3 **Bhūj,** India
109/B2 **Bhumibol** (dam), Thai.
106/C3 **Bhusawal,** India
106/E2 **Bhutan**
108/G3 **Bhuvanagiri,** India
102/F5 **Bi** (riv.), China
136/E4 **Biá** (riv.), Braz.
128/E5 **Bia** (riv.), Gui., IvC.
130/A2 **Biaboye,** Zaire
68/B3 **Biache-Saint-Vaast,** Fr.
124/G7 **Biafra** (bight), Afr.
111/J4 **Biak** (isl.), Indo.
65/M2 **Biała Podlaska,** Pol.
65/M3 **Biała Podlaska** (prov.), Pol.
65/L3 **Białobrzegi,** Pol.
65/J2 **Białogard,** Pol.
65/K4 **Białowieski Nat'l Park,** Pol.
65/M2 **Białystok,** Pol.
65/M2 **Białystok** (prov.), Pol.
73/J3 **Bianca** (peak), It.
80/D4 **Biancavilla,** It.
125/L7 **Biaro,** Zaire
72/C5 **Biarritz,** Fr.
127/B2 **Bibā,** Egypt
100/B2 **Bibai,** Japan
70/C6 **Biberach an der Riss,** Ger.
76/D3 **Biberist,** Swi.
104/A3 **Bibiyana** (riv.), Bang., India
138/B5 **Biblián,** Ecu.
70/B3 **Biblis,** Ger.
141/K6 **Bicas,** Braz.
83/H2 **Bicaz,** Rom.
59/E3 **Bicester,** Eng,UK
114/F2 **Bickerton** (isl.), Austl.
116/L7 **Bickley** (brook), Austl.
82/D2 **Bicske,** Hun.
112/B4 **Bidadari, Tanjong** (cape), Malay.
128/D5 **Bidaga** (rapids), IvC.
106/C4 **Bīdar,** India
161/G3 **Biddeford,** Me,US
57/F5 **Biddulph,** Eng,UK
54/A3 **Bidean nam Bian** (mtn.), Sc,UK
58/B4 **Bideford,** Eng,UK
58/B4 **Bideford** (Barnstaple) (bay), Eng,UK
79/F4 **Bidente** (riv.), It.
59/E2 **Bidford on Avon,** Eng,UK
109/E3 **Bi Doup** (peak), Viet.
75/E1 **Bidouze** (riv.), Fr.
126/B4 **Bíe** (plat.), Ang.
70/B3 **Biebesheim am Rhein,** Ger.
65/M2 **Biebzra** (riv.), Pol.
76/D3 **Biel,** Swi.
65/J3 **Bielawa,** Pol.
54/D2 **Bieldside,** Sc,UK
67/F4 **Bielefeld,** Ger.
153/J1 **Bieler** (lake), NW,Can
76/D3 **Bieler** (lake), Swi.
78/B1 **Biella,** It.
65/K4 **Bielsko** (prov.), Pol.
65/K4 **Bielsko-Biała,** Pol.
65/M2 **Bielsk Podlaski,** Pol.
109/D4 **Bien Hoa,** Viet.
76/B5 **Bienne** (riv.), Fr.
109/D1 **Bien Son,** Viet.
153/J3 **Bienville** (lake), Qu,Can
66/B5 **Biesbosch** (reg.), Neth.
66/D5 **Biesme** (riv.), Fr.
76/D5 **Bietschhorn** (peak), Swi.
53/S10 **Bièvre** (riv.), Fr.
53/S10 **Bièvres,** Fr.
80/D2 **Biferno** (riv.), It.
119/B2 **Big** (des.), Austl.
153/J2 **Big** (isl.), NW,Can
152/D1 **Big** (riv.), NW,Can
165/E6 **Big** (lake), Mi,US
83/H5 **Biga,** Turk.
92/B2 **Bigadiç,** Turk.
156/F4 **Big Belt** (mts.), Mt,US
162/C4 **Big Bend Nat'l Park,** Tx,US
159/K4 **Big Black** (riv.), Ms,US
159/H2 **Big Blue** (riv.), Ks, Ne,US
58/C6 **Bigbury** (bay), Eng,UK
151/D2 **Big Diomede** (isl.), Rus.
166/D1 **Big Flat** (brook), NJ,US
157/K4 **Big Fork** (riv.), Mn,US
156/G2 **Biggar,** Sk,Can
54/C5 **Biggar,** Sc,UK
69/G1 **Biggasee** (lake), Ger.
114/D2 **Bigge** (isl.), Austl.
67/E6 **Bigge** (riv.), Ger.
67/E6 **Biggesee** (res.), Ger.
53/P8 **Biggin Hill,** Eng,UK
59/F2 **Biggleswade,** Eng,UK
132/D3 **Big Hole,** SAfr.
156/E4 **Big Hole** (riv.), Mt,US
156/F4 **Bighorn** (lake), Mt, Wy,US
156/G4 **Bighorn** (mts.), Mt, Wy,US
156/G4 **Bighorn** (riv.), Mt, Wy,US
158/E1 **Bighorn** (basin), Wy,US
152/F4 **Bighorn Canyon Nat'l Rec. Area,** Mt,US
150/C1 **Bight, The,** Bahm.
162/C4 **Big Lake,** Tx,US
158/D2 **Big Lost** (riv.), Id,US
165/P14 **Big Muskego** (lake), Wi,US
128/A3 **Bignona,** Sen.
166/C1 **Big Pine** (hill), Pa,US
166/A4 **Big Pipe** (cr.), Md,US
160/C3 **Big Rapids,** Mi,US
156/G2 **Big River,** Sk,Can
165/N16 **Big Rock** (cr.), Il,US
163/H4 **Big Saltilla** (cr.), Ga,US
159/G3 **Big Sandy** (cr.), Co,US
163/F2 **Big Sandy** (riv.), Tn,US
158/E2 **Big Sandy** (riv.), Wy,US
157/J5 **Big Sioux** (riv.), Ia, SD,US
162/C3 **Big Spring,** Tx,US
157/J4 **Big Stone** (lake), Mn, SD,US
160/D4 **Big Stone Gap,** Va,US
156/F4 **Big Timber,** Mt,US
152/H3 **Big Trout** (lake), On,Can
164/B2 **Big Tujunga** (canyon), Ca,US
141/B3 **Biguaçu,** Braz.
158/D2 **Big Wood** (riv.), Id,US
82/B3 **Bihać,** Yugo.
106/E2 **Bihār,** India
106/D3 **Bihār** (state), India
130/A3 **Biharamulo,** Tanz.
130/A3 **Biharamulo Game Rsv.,** Tanz.
82/F2 **Bihor** (co.), Rom.
68/A4 **Bihorel,** Fr.
100/D2 **Bihoro,** Japan
128/A4 **Bijagós** (isls.), GBis.
106/C4 **Bijāpur,** India
93/F3 **Bījār,** Iran
82/D3 **Bijeljina,** Bosn.
82/D4 **Bijelo Polje,** Yugo.
105/H3 **Bijia** (mtn.), China
104/C3 **Bijiang,** China
104/E3 **Bijie,** China
106/C2 **Bijnor,** India
106/B2 **Bīkaner,** India
120/G3 **Bikar** (atoll), Mrsh.
97/L2 **Bikin,** Rus.
97/M2 **Bikin** (riv.), Rus.
120/F3 **Bikini** (atoll), Mrsh.
131/C4 **Bikita,** Zim.
126/C4 **Bikuar Nat'l Park,** Moz.
109/B3 **Bilauktaung** (range), Burma, Thai.
114/G5 **Bilba Morea Claypan** (lake), Austl.
74/D1 **Bilbao,** Sp.
91/B4 **Bilbays,** Egypt
82/D4 **Bileća,** Bosn.
92/B1 **Bilecik,** Turk.
83/K5 **Bilecik** (prov.), Turk.
65/M3 **Biłgoraj,** Pol.
89/S3 **Bilibino,** Rus.
131/D2 **Bilila,** Malw.
109/B2 **Bilin** (riv.), Burma
71/G1 **Bílina,** Czh.
71/G2 **Bílina** (riv.), Czh.
112/D3 **Biliran** (isl.), Phil.
101/B3 **Biliu** (riv.), China
119/C2 **Billabong** (cr.), Austl.
67/H1 **Bille** (riv.), Ger.
67/E5 **Billerbeck,** Ger.
72/C5 **Billère,** Fr.
59/G3 **Billericay,** Eng,UK
117/J5 **Billiat Consv. Park,** Austl.
57/F5 **Billinge,** Eng,UK
57/G2 **Billingham,** Eng,UK
156/F4 **Billings,** Mt,US
59/F4 **Billingshurst,** Eng,UK
90/K10 **Billiton** (isl.), Indo.
158/D4 **Bill Williams** (riv.), Az,US
124/H4 **Bilma,** Niger
118/C4 **Biloela,** Austl.
163/F4 **Biloxi,** Ms,US
117/H3 **Bilpa Morea** (claypan), Austl.
92/B4 **Bilqās Qism Awwal,** Egypt
106/C2 **Bilsi,** India
125/K5 **Biltine,** Chad
69/E2 **Bilzen,** Belg.
111/E5 **Bima,** Indo.
119/D2 **Bimberi** (peak), Austl.
125/J7 **Bimbo,** CAfr.
150/B1 **Bimini** (isls.), Bahm.
71/F6 **Bina** (riv.), Ger.
106/C3 **Bina-Etāwa,** India
123/X17 **Bin 'Arūs** (gov.), Tun.
161/Q9 **Binbrook,** On,Can
57/H5 **Binbrook,** Eng,UK
68/D3 **Binche,** Belg.
104/D3 **Binchuan,** China
96/G2 **Binder,** Mong.
106/D2 **Bindki,** India
112/C3 **Bindoy,** Phil.
126/C2 **Bindu,** Zaire
131/C3 **Bindura,** Zim.
75/F2 **Binéfar,** Sp.
59/F4 **Binfield,** Eng,UK
131/D3 **Binga** (mtn.), Moz.
131/B3 **Binga,** Zim.
70/A3 **Bingen,** Ger.
128/E5 **Bingerville,** IvC.
57/H6 **Bingham,** Eng,UK
160/F3 **Binghamton,** NY,US
57/G4 **Bingley,** Eng,UK
92/E2 **Bingöl,** Turk.
92/E2 **Bingöl** (prov.), Turk.
103/D4 **Binhai,** China
109/D4 **Binh Chanh,** Viet.
109/D4 **Binh Chau,** Viet.
104/B5 **Binhon** (peak), Burma
109/E3 **Binh Son,** Viet.
110/A3 **Binjai,** Indo.
76/D2 **Binningen,** Swi.
111/F5 **Binongko** (isl.), Indo.
110/B2 **Bintang** (peak), Malay.
105/F4 **Binyang,** China
103/D3 **Binzhou,** China
142/B3 **Bío-Bío** (reg.), Chile
142/B3 **Bío-Bío** (riv.), Chile
82/B4 **Biograd,** Cro.
82/D4 **Biogradska Nat'l Park,** Yugo.
124/G7 **Bioko** (isl.), EqG.
106/C4 **Bīr,** India
124/H2 **Birāk,** Libya
124/H2 **Bi'r al Ghuzayyil** (well), Libya
125/K2 **Bi'r al Ḩarash** (well), Libya
149/G1 **Birama** (pt.), Cuba
125/K5 **Birao,** CAfr.
106/E2 **Birātnagar,** Nepal
100/C2 **Biratori,** Japan
152/E3 **Birch** (mts.), Ab,Can
131/D3 **Birchenough Bridge,** Zim.
157/G2 **Birch Hills,** Sk,Can
157/H2 **Birch River,** Mb,Can
113/X **Bird** (isl.), Ant.
115/K4 **Bird Islet** (isl.), Austl.
119/D2 **Birds Rock** (peak), Austl.
92/D2 **Birecik,** Turk.
141/B2 **Birigui,** Braz.
141/G8 **Biritiba-Mirim,** Braz.
95/G2 **Bīrjand,** Iran
70/B3 **Birkenau,** Ger.
120/G4 **Birkenebeu,** Kiri.
57/E5 **Birkenhead,** Eng,UK
54/B5 **Birkenshaw,** Sc,UK
63/T9 **Birkerød,** Den.
77/H3 **Birkkarspitze** (peak), Aus.
83/H2 **Bîrlad,** Rom.
83/H2 **Bîrlad** (riv.), Rom.
102/B3 **Birlik,** Kaz.
59/E2 **Birmingham,** Eng,UK
163/G3 **Birmingham,** Al,US
165/F6 **Birmingham,** Mi,US
54/C3 **Birnam,** Sc,UK
73/K3 **Birnhorn** (peak), Aus.
121/H5 **Birnie** (isl.), Kiri.
129/G3 **Birni Nkonni,** Niger
97/L2 **Birobidzhan,** Rus.
124/E3 **Bîr Ounâne** (well), Mali
60/A2 **Birreencorragh** (mtn.), Ire.
76/D3 **Birs** (riv.), Swi.
76/D3 **Birse** (riv.), Swi.
76/D2 **Birsfelden,** Swi.
85/M5 **Birsk,** Rus.
70/C2 **Birstein,** Ger.
96/C5 **Biru,** China
63/L3 **Biržai,** Lith.
83/F4 **Bis** (lake), Rom.
99/M9 **Bisai,** Japan
130/C2 **Bisa-Nadi Nat'l Rsv.,** Kenya
158/E5 **Bisbee,** Az,US
72/C4 **Biscarrosse,** Fr.
72/C4 **Biscarrosse** (lag.), Fr.
72/B4 **Biscay** (bay), Eur.
150/A1 **Biscayne** (bay), Fl,US
163/H5 **Biscayne Nat'l Park,** Fl,US
80/E2 **Bisceglie,** It.
76/D1 **Bischheim,** Fr.
70/B3 **Bischofsheim,** Ger.
73/K3 **Bischofshofen,** Aus.
69/G6 **Bischwiller,** Fr.
113/V **Biscoe** (isls.), Ant.
79/F5 **Biscubio** (riv.), It.
138/D2 **Biscucuy,** Ven.
94/D4 **Bīshah** (dry riv.), SAr.
102/B3 **Bishkek** (cap.), Kyr.
158/C3 **Bishop,** Ca,US
57/G2 **Bishop Auckland,** Eng,UK
54/B5 **Bishopbriggs,** Sc,UK
58/D2 **Bishops Castle,** Eng,UK
58/D3 **Bishops Cleeve,** Eng,UK
161/L1 **Bishop's Falls,** Nf,Can
59/G3 **Bishop's Stortford,** Eng,UK
59/E5 **Bishops Waltham,** Eng,UK
54/B5 **Bishopton,** Sc,UK
57/H4 **Bishop Wilton,** Eng,UK
70/B6 **Bisingen,** Ger.
124/G1 **Biskra,** Alg.
123/T16 **Biskra** (wilaya), Alg.
65/L2 **Biskupiec,** Pol.
112/D3 **Bislig,** Phil.
161/Q9 **Bismarck,** On,Can
120/D5 **Bismarck** (arch.), PNG
120/D5 **Bismarck** (sea), PNG
157/H4 **Bismarck** (cap.), ND,US
92/E2 **Bismil,** Turk.
149/F3 **Bismuna** (lag.), Nic.

130/A2 Biso, Ugan.
128/B4 Bissau (cap.), GBis.
67/F4 Bissendorf, Ger.
157/K3 Bissett, Mb,Can
83/G2 Bistrița, Rom.
83/G2 Bistrița-Năsăud (co.), Rom.
63/T9 Bistrup, Den.
138/D3 Bita (riv.), Col.
130/A4 Bitale, Tanz.
124/H7 Bitam, Gabon
69/F4 Bitburg, Ger.
69/G5 Bitche, Fr.
124/J5 Bitkin, Chad
92/E2 Bitlis, Turk.
92/E2 Bitlis (prov.), Turk.
82/E5 Bitola, Macd.
82/C5 Bitonto, It.
83/G2 Bitrița (riv.), Rom.
76/D2 Bitschwiller, Fr.
127/C2 Bitter (lakes), Egypt
156/E4 Bitterroot (range), Id, Mt,US
111/G3 Bitung, Indo.
141/B3 Bituruna, Braz.
124/H5 Biu, Nga.
99/M9 Biwa, Japan
98/E3 Biwa (lake), Japan
159/J4 Bixby, Ok,US
91/B4 Biyalā, Egypt
103/C4 Biyang, China
102/E1 Biysk, Rus.
161/N7 Bizard (isl.), Qu,Can
123/W17 Bizerte (Banzart), Tun.
61/M6 Bjargtangar (pt.), Ice.
63/U9 Bjärred, Swe.
82/C3 Bjelovar, Cro.
62/C3 Bjerringbro, Den.
62/D2 Bjørkelangen, Nor.
63/S7 Björknäs, Swe.
62/A1 Bjørnafjorden (fjord), Nor.
153/S7 Bjorne (pen.), NW,Can
62/E3 Bjuv, Swe.
59/E1 Blaby, Eng,UK
65/K3 Blachownia, Pol.
86/D4 Black (sea), Asia, Eur.
160/B1 Black (bay), On,Can
157/L2 Black (riv.), On,Can
151/M3 Black (mtn.), Yk,Can
109/C1 Black (riv.), China
86/D4 Black (sea), Eur.
76/D2 Black (for.), Ger.
132/A2 Black (pt.), Namb.
58/A6 Black (pt.), Eng,UK
58/C3 Black (mtn.), Wal,UK
58/C3 Black (mts.), Wal,UK
159/K3 Black (riv.), Ar, Mo,US
158/D4 Black (mts.), Az,US
158/E4 Black (riv.), Az,US
165/L11 Black (hills), Ca,US
168/B3 Black (pt.), Ct,US
165/G5 Black (riv.), Mi,US
158/F4 Black (range), NM,US
160/F3 Black (riv.), NY,US
168/E5 Black (riv.), Oh,US
166/B2 Black (cr.), Pa,US
157/H5 Black (hills), SD, Wy,US
157/L4 Black (riv.), Wi,US
107/H3 Black (riv.), Viet.
54/D5 Blackadder Water (riv.), Sc,UK
165/P16 Blackberry (cr.), Il,US
59/E3 Black Bourton, Eng,UK
57/F4 Blackburn, Eng,UK
54/C5 Blackburn, Sc,UK
54/B6 Blackcraig (hill), Sc,UK
109/C1 Black (Da) (riv.), Viet.
156/E3 Black Diamond, Ab,Can
59/F4 Blackdown (hill), Eng,UK
58/C5 Blackdown (hills), Eng,UK
118/C3 Blackdown Tableland Nat'l Park, Austl.
156/F4 Black Eagle, Mt,US
168/E5 Black, East Branch (riv.), Oh,US
156/E5 Blackfoot, Id,US
156/F5 Blackfoot (res.), Id,US
54/C4 Blackford, Sc,UK
70/B5 Black Forest (Schwarzwald) (uplands), Ger.
168/E6 Black Fork (riv.), Oh,US
57/G2 Blackhall Rocks, Eng,UK
60/A3 Black Head (pt.), Ire.
56/C2 Black Head (pt.), NI,UK
54/B1 Black Isle (pen.), Sc,UK
158/E3 Black Mesa (upland), Az,US
58/B6 Blackmoor (upland), Eng,UK
53/P6 Blackmore, Eng,UK
118/B1 Black Mountain Nat'l Park, Austl.
57/E4 Blackpool, Eng,UK
132/A2 Black Reef (pt.), Namb.
160/B2 Black River Falls, Wi,US
158/C2 Black Rock (des.), Nv,US
167/G1 Black Rock (pt.), RI,US
57/F4 Blackrod, Eng,UK
160/D4 Blacksburg, Va,US
163/H3 Blackshear (lake), Ga,US
60/D4 Blackstairs (mts.), Ire.
168/C1 Blackstone, Ma,US
168/C2 Blackstone (riv.), RI,US
160/E4 Blackstone, Va,US
119/D1 Black Sugarloaf (peak), Austl.
118/G8 Blacktown, Austl.
161/H2 Blackville, NB,Can
128/E4 Black Volta (riv.), Afr.
163/G3 Black Warrior (riv.), Al,US
118/C3 Blackwater, Austl.
60/C5 Blackwater (riv.), Ire.
60/D2 Blackwater (riv.), Ire.
59/G3 Blackwater (riv.), Eng,UK
56/B3 Blackwater (riv.), NI,UK
54/B3 Blackwater (res.), Sc,UK
159/J3 Blackwater (riv.), Mo,US
159/H3 Blackwell, Ok,US
168/E5 Black, West Branch (riv.), Oh,US
116/B5 Blackwood (riv.), Austl.
58/C3 Blackwood, Wal,UK
166/B6 Bladensburg, Md,US
118/A3 Bladensburg Nat'l Park, Austl.
56/D2 Bladnoch (riv.), Sc,UK
56/E6 Blaenau-Ffestiniog, Wal,UK
58/C3 Blaenavon, Wal,UK
72/D5 Blagnac, Fr.
83/F4 Blagoevgrad, Bul.
97/K1 Blagoveshchensk, Rus.
156/G2 Blaine Lake, Sk,Can
161/N6 Blainville, Qu,Can
159/H2 Blair, Ne,US
166/C1 Blair (hill), Pa,US
54/C3 Blair Atholl, Sc,UK
54/C3 Blairgowrie, Sc,UK
156/E3 Blairmore, Ab,Can
76/A1 Blaise (riv.), Fr.
83/F2 Blaj, Rom.
163/G4 Blakely, Ga,US
73/G4 Blanc (mtn.), Fr.
124/B3 Blanc (cape), Mrta.
142/E3 Blanca (bay), Arg.
136/C5 Blanca (range), Peru
74/E3 Blanca, Sp.
75/E4 Blanca (coast), Sp.
159/F4 Blanca (peak), NM,US
146/B2 Blanca, Punta (pt.), Mex.
117/G5 Blanche (cape), Austl.
116/D2 Blanche (lake), Austl.
117/H4 Blanche (lake), Austl.
76/C6 Blanc, Mont (mtn.), Fr.
68/A2 Blanc Nez (cape), Fr.
143/K6 Blanco (riv.), Arg.
143/K8 Blanco (lake), Chile
142/C1 Blanco (riv.), Chile
149/E4 Blanco (cape), CR
136/B4 Blanco (cape), Peru
156/B5 Blanco (cape), Or,US
159/H5 Blanco (riv.), Tx,US
58/D5 Blandford Forum, Eng,UK
158/E3 Blanding, Ut,US
75/G2 Blanes, Sp.
75/G1 Blanes, Serre de (mtn.), Fr.
65/G4 Blanice (riv.), Czh.
68/C1 Blankenberge, Belg.
69/F3 Blankenheim, Ger.
150/E5 Blanquilla (isl.), Ven.
65/J4 Blansko, Czh.
131/D2 Blantyre, Malw.
54/B5 Blantyre, Sc,UK
72/F3 Blanzy, Fr.
66/C4 Blaricum, Neth.
60/B6 Blarney Castle and Stone, Ire.
77/E4 Blas, Piz (peak), Swi.
71/G4 Blatná, Czh.
70/C6 Blau (riv.), Ger.
70/C6 Blaubeuren, Ger.
76/D2 Blauen (peak), Ger.
70/C6 Blaustein, Ger.
64/E1 Blåvands Huk (pt.), Den.
72/B2 Blavet (riv.), Fr.
114/D2 Blaze (pt.), Austl.
67/H2 Bleckede, Ger.
62/C2 Blefjell (peak), Nor.
69/E2 Blégny, Belg.
68/C2 Bléharies, Belg.
82/B2 Bleiburg, Aus.
67/H6 Bleicherode, Ger.
77/G2 Bleick, Hohe (peak), Ger.
66/B4 Bleiswijk, Neth.
62/F3 Blekinge (co.), Swe.
115/R11 Blenheim, NZ
59/E3 Blenheim Palace, Eng,UK
73/G4 Bléone (riv.), Fr.
68/C4 Blérancourt, Fr.
132/C4 Blesberg (peak), SAfr.
53/N8 Bletchingley, Eng,UK
59/F2 Bletchley, Eng,UK
130/A2 Bleus (mts.), Zaire
59/E3 Blewbury, Eng,UK
123/S15 Blida, Alg.
123/S15 Blida (wilaya), Alg.
57/G5 Blidworth, Eng,UK
71/E2 Blieloch-Stausee (res.), Ger.
69/G5 Blies (riv.), Fr., Ger.
69/G5 Bliesbruck, Fr.
69/G5 Blieskastel, Ger.
121/Y18 Bligh Water (sound), Fiji
112/D4 Blik (mtn.), Phil.
77/E5 Blinnenhorn (peak), Swi.
57/G6 Blithfield (res.), Eng,UK
113/L Blizzard (peak), Ant.
167/G1 Block (isl.), RI,US
167/G1 Block Island (sound), NY, RI,US
167/G1 Block Island C. G. Sta., RI,US
167/G1 Block Island Nat'l Wild. Ref., RI,US
66/B4 Bloemendaal, Neth.
132/D3 Bloemfontein, SAfr.
132/D2 Bloemhofdam (res.), SAfr.
72/D3 Blois, Fr.
66/C3 Blokker, Neth.
67/G5 Blomberg, Ger.
157/J3 Bloodvein (riv.), Mb, On,Can
55/G9 Bloody Foreland (pt.), Ire.
160/B2 Bloomer, Wi,US
168/B2 Bloomfield, Ct,US
167/D2 Bloomfield, NJ,US
158/F3 Bloomfield, NM,US
165/F6 Bloomfield Hills, Mi,US
118/B1 Bloomfield River Abor. Community, Austl.
165/P16 Bloomingdale, Il,US
167/H7 Bloomingdale, NJ,US
164/C2 Bloomington, Ca,US
160/B3 Bloomington, Il,US
160/C4 Bloomington, In,US
157/K4 Bloomington, Mn,US
166/B1 Bloomsburg, Pa,US
110/D5 Blora, Indo.
131/C4 Blouberg (peak), SAfr.
163/G4 Blountstown, Fl,US
113/L Blowaway (peak), Ant.
59/E3 Bloxham, Eng,UK
58/E1 Bloxwich, Eng,UK
71/G2 Blšanka (riv.), Czh.
77/F3 Bludenz, Aus.
104/B4 Blue (mtn.), India
162/D3 Blue (riv.), Ok,US
156/D4 Blue (mts.), Or, Wa,US
157/K5 Blue Earth, Mn,US
160/D4 Bluefield, Va,US
160/D4 Bluefield, WV,US
149/F4 Bluefields, Nic.
149/F4 Bluefields (bay), Nic.
54/C1 Blue Head (pt.), Sc,UK
165/Q16 Blue Island, Il,US
158/C2 Bluejoint (lake), Or,US
131/B2 Blue Lagoon Nat'l Park, Zam.
118/D4 Blue Lake Nat'l Park, Austl.
166/B3 Blue Marsh (lake), Pa,US
158/F3 Blue Mesa (res.), Co,US
149/G2 Blue Mountain (peak), Jam.
166/B3 Blue Mountain (ridge), Pa,US
119/D2 Blue Mountains Nat'l Park, Austl.
114/F2 Blue Mud (bay), Austl.
125/M5 Blue Nile (riv.), Eth., Sudan
152/E1 Bluenose (lake), NW,Can
163/G3 Blue Ridge, Ga,US
163/H2 Blue Ridge (mts.), NC, Va,US
116/C5 Bluff (peak), Austl.
116/B3 Bluff (pt.), Austl.
115/Q12 Bluff, NZ
160/C3 Bluffton, In,US
56/E2 Blumberg, Ger.
141/B3 Blumenau, Braz.
76/D5 Blümlisalp (peak), Swi.
78/D1 Blumone, Cornone di (peak), It.
57/G1 Blyth, Eng,UK
57/G5 Blyth, Eng,UK
59/H2 Blyth (riv.), Eng,UK
54/C5 Blyth Bridge, Sc,UK
57/F6 Blythe (riv.), Eng,UK
158/D4 Blythe, Ca,US
57/F6 Blythe Bridge, Eng,UK
163/F3 Blytheville, Ar,US
109/D4 B'nom M'hai (peak), Viet.
128/C5 Bo, SLeo.
112/C2 Boac, Phil.
148/E3 Boaco, Nic.
141/C2 Boa Esperança, Braz.
140/A2 Boa Esperança (res.), Braz.
103/C4 Bo'ai, China
111/G4 Boano (isl.), Indo.
168/G5 Boardman, Oh,US
153/H2 Boas (riv.), NW,Can
140/C2 Boa Viagem, Braz.
139/F4 Boa Vista, Braz.
122/K10 Boa Vista (isl.), CpV.
163/G3 Boaz, Al,US
105/F4 Bobai, China
123/G6 Bobaomby (cape), Madg.
106/D4 Bobbili, India
70/B3 Bobenheim-Roxheim, Ger.
68/B6 Bobigny, Fr.
70/D6 Böbingen, Ger.
70/C5 Böblingen, Ger.
128/D4 Bobo Dioulasso, Burk.
131/C4 Bobonong, Bots.
82/D4 Bobotov Kuk (peak), Yugo.
82/F4 Bobovdol, Bul.
65/H3 Bóbr (riv.), Pol.
86/G2 Bobrov, Rus.
86/D1 Bobruysk, Bela.
138/D2 Bobures, Ven.
133/H8 Boby (peak), Madg.
136/E5 Boca do Acre, Braz.
141/J7 Bocaina (mts.), Braz.
140/B5 Bocaiúva, Braz.
163/H5 Boca Raton, Fl,US
149/E3 Bocay (riv.), Nic.
131/C4 Bochem, SAfr.
65/L4 Bochnia, Pol.
69/E1 Bocholt, Belg.
66/D5 Bocholt, Ger.
67/E6 Bochum, Ger.
67/H4 Bockenem, Ger.
67/F2 Bockhorn, Ger.
59/G3 Bocking, Eng,UK
138/D2 Boconó, Ven.
69/D3 Bocq (riv.), Belg.
124/J7 Boda, CAfr.
89/M4 Bodaybo, Rus.
54/E2 Boddam, Sc,UK
64/F3 Bode (riv.), Ger.
158/B3 Bodega (bay), Ca,US
66/B4 Bodegraven, Neth.
124/J4 Bodélé (depr.), Chad
61/G2 Boden, Swe.
70/B3 Bodenheim, Ger.
77/F2 Bodensee (Lake Constance) (lake), Ger., Swi.
60/B2 Boderg, Lough (lake), Ire.
106/C4 Bodhan, India
108/F3 Bodināyakkanūr, India
166/B5 Bodkin (pt.), Md,US
58/B6 Bodmin, Eng,UK
58/B5 Bodmin Moor (upland), Eng,UK
61/E2 Bodø, Nor.
140/C2 Bodocó, Braz.
96/C2 Bodonchiyn (riv.), Mong.
82/E1 Bodrog (riv.), Hun.
92/A2 Bodrum, Turk.
109/D4 Bo Duc, Viet.
132/A2 Boegoeberg (peak), Namb.
66/C5 Boekel, Neth.
126/D1 Boende, Zaire
159/K4 Boeuf (riv.), Ar, La,US
130/A2 Boga, Zaire
163/F4 Bogalusa, La,US
119/C1 Bogan (riv.), Austl.
129/E3 Bogandé, Burk.
82/D3 Bogatić, Yugo.
65/H3 Bogatynia, Pol.
92/C1 Boğazkale-Alacahöyük Nat'l Park, Turk.
92/C2 Boğazlıyan, Turk.
102/E5 Bogcang (riv.), China
96/E2 Bogd, Mong.
96/B3 Bogda (mts.), China
102/E3 Bogda Feng (peak), China
71/F5 Bogen, Ger.
63/S7 Bogesundslandet (pen.), Swe.
60/A5 Boggeragh (mts.), Ire.
150/F3 Boggy (peak), Anti.
59/F5 Bognor Regis, Eng,UK
69/D4 Bogny-sur-Meuse, Fr.
112/D3 Bogo, Phil.
119/C3 Bogong (peak), Austl.
119/C3 Bogong Nat'l Park, Austl.
110/C5 Bogor, Indo.
130/A2 Bogoro, Zaire
138/C3 Bogotá (cap.), Col.
167/J8 Bogota, NJ,US
82/E5 Bogovinje, Macd.
106/E3 Bogra, Bang.
57/E1 Bogrie (hill), Sc,UK
128/B2 Bogué, Mrta.
103/D3 Bohai (bay), China
103/E3 Bohai (str.), China
103/D3 Bo Hai (Chihli) (gulf), China
68/C4 Bohain-en-Vermandois, Fr.
71/G3 Bohemia (reg.), Czh.
71/G4 Bohemian Forest (uplands), Ger.
70/B4 Böhl-Iggelheim, Ger.
67/G3 Böhme (riv.), Ger.
67/F4 Bohmte, Ger.
112/C3 Bohol (isl.), Phil.
112/C3 Bohol (str.), Phil.
104/E5 Bo Ho Su, Viet.
102/E3 Bohu, China
80/D2 Boiano, It.
104/B4 Boinu (riv.), Burma, India
140/D4 Boipeda (isl.), Braz.
74/A1 Boiro, Sp.
141/B1 Bois (riv.), Braz.
53/S10 Bois-d'Arcy, Fr.
156/D5 Boise (cap.), Id,US
156/D5 Boise (riv.), Id,US
159/G3 Boise City, Ok,US
68/A5 Bois-Guillaume, Fr.
157/H3 Boissevain, Mb,Can
53/S9 Boissy-l'Aillerie, Fr.
53/T10 Boissy-Saint-Léger, Fr.
67/H2 Boizenburg, Ger.
124/C2 Bojador (cape), WSah.
112/C1 Bojeador (cape), Phil.
130/D2 Boji (plain), Kenya
65/J4 Bojkovice, Czh.
93/J2 Bojnūrd, Iran
106/E3 Bokaro Steel City, India
128/B4 Boké (comm.), Gui.
126/D1 Bokele, Zaire
130/C2 Bokhol (plain), Kenya
62/A2 Boknafjorden (fjord), Nor.
130/C2 Bokol (peak), Kenya
124/J5 Bokoro, Chad
132/E2 Boksburg, SAfr.
163/H5 Bok Tower Gardens, Fl,US
124/H5 Bol, Chad
128/B4 Bolama, GBis.
95/J3 Bolān (pass), Pak.
146/E4 Bolaños, Mex.
74/D3 Bolaños de Calatrava, Sp.
72/D2 Bolbec, Fr.
83/H3 Boldești-Scăeni, Rom.
57/G2 Boldon, Eng,UK
102/D3 Bole, China
129/E4 Bole, Gha.
65/H3 Bolesławiec, Pol.
129/E4 Bolgatanga, Gha.
97/J2 Boli, China
112/B1 Bolinao, Phil.
112/B1 Bolinao (cape), Phil.
165/P16 Bolingbrook, Il,US
142/E3 Bolívar, Arg.
138/B3 Bolívar, Col.
138/C2 Bolívar (dept.), Col.
138/B5 Bolívar (prov.), Ecu.
159/J3 Bolivar, Mo,US
160/B5 Bolivar, Tn,US
139/E3 Bolívar (state), Ven.
139/F3 Bolívar, Cerro (mtn.), Ven.
138/D2 Bolívar, Pico (mtn.), Ven.
136/F7 Bolivia
78/C1 Bollate, It.
69/F4 Bollendorf, Ger.
72/F4 Bollène, Fr.
76/D4 Bolligen, Swi.
57/F5 Bollin (riv.), Eng,UK
57/F5 Bollington, Eng,UK
63/S7 Bollmora, Swe.
62/G1 Bollnäs, Swe.
74/B4 Bollullos Par del Condado, Sp.
62/E3 Bolmen (lake), Swe.
59/F5 Bolney, Eng,UK
126/C1 Bolobo, Zaire
79/E4 Bologna, It.
79/E3 Bologna (prov.), It.
84/G4 Bologoye, Rus.
125/J7 Bolomba, Zaire
97/M2 Bolon' (lake), Rus.
126/C2 Bolongongo, Ang.
109/D3 Bolovens (plat.), Laos
80/B1 Bolsena (lake), It.
87/K2 Bol'shaya Khobda (riv.), Kaz.
87/K1 Bol'shaya Kinel' (riv.), Rus.
85/P2 Bol'shaya Rogovaya (riv.), Rus.
85/N2 Bol'shaya Synya (riv.), Rus.
97/L2 Bol'shaya Ussurka (riv.), Rus.
89/L2 Bol'shevik (isl.), Rus.
85/M2 Bol'shezemel'skaya (tundra), Rus.
88/F2 Bol'shoy Bolvanskiy Nos (pt.), Rus.
87/H2 Bol'shoy Irgiz (riv.), Rus.
89/Q2 Bol'shoy Lyakhovskiy (isl.), Rus.
87/J2 Bol'shoy Uzen' (riv.), Kaz., Rus.
96/D1 Bol'shoy Yenisey (riv.), Rus.
57/G5 Bolsover, Eng,UK
66/C2 Bolsward, Neth.
58/C6 Bolt Head (pt.), Wal,UK
161/Q8 Bolton, On,Can
57/F4 Bolton, Eng,UK
57/G4 Bolton Abbey, Eng,UK
83/K5 Bolu, Turk.
83/K5 Bolu (prov.), Turk.
54/F11 Bolus Head (pt.), Ire.
92/B2 Bolvadin, Turk.
77/H5 Bolzano (Bozen), It.
77/H4 Bolzano-Bozen (prov.), It.
126/B2 Boma, Zaire
119/D2 Bomaderry, Austl.
106/B4 Bombay, India
166/C5 Bombay Hook Nat'l Wild. Ref., De,US
111/H4 Bomberai (pen.), Indo.
130/B2 Bombo, Ugan.
140/C3 Bom Conselho, Braz.
141/C1 Bom Despacho, Braz.
104/B2 Bomi, China
140/A1 Bom Jardim, Braz.
141/J6 Bom Jardim de Minas, Braz.
140/A3 Bom Jesus, Braz.
141/B4 Bom Jesus, Braz.
140/B3 Bom Jesus da Gurguéia (mts.), Braz.
140/B4 Bom Jesus da Lapa, Braz.
141/B1 Bom Jesus de Goiás, Braz.
141/D2 Bom Jesus do Itabapoana, Braz.
141/G8 Bom Jesus dos Perdões, Braz.
67/G3 Bomlitz, Ger.
62/A2 Bømlo (isl.), Nor.
141/B3 Bom Retiro, Braz.
125/L6 Bomu (riv.), Zaire
123/X17 Bon (cape), Tun.
151/K3 Bona (mtn.), Ak,US
150/D4 Bonaire (isl.), NAnt.
148/D2 Bonampak (ruins), Mex.
150/D3 Bonao, DRep.
114/C2 Bonaparte (arch.), Austl.
151/F3 Bonasila (mtn.), Ak,US
161/H1 Bonaventure, Qu,Can
161/H1 Bonaventure (riv.), Qu,Can
161/L1 Bonavista (bay), Nf,Can
161/L1 Bonavista (cape), Nf,Can
54/D6 Bonchester Bridge, Sc,UK
79/E3 Bondeno, It.
118/H8 Bondi, Austl.
125/K7 Bondo, Zaire
112/C2 Bondoc (pen.), Phil.
128/E4 Bondoukou, IvC.
110/D5 Bondowoso, Indo.
111/F4 Bone (gulf), Indo.
67/E5 Bönen, Ger.
111/F5 Bonerate (isls.), Indo.
54/C4 Bo'ness, Sc,UK
102/F5 Bong (lake), China
128/C5 Bong (co.), Libr.
128/C5 Bong (range), Libr.
112/C2 Bongabong, Phil.
125/K7 Bongandanga, Zaire
111/E2 Bongao, Phil.
112/B4 Bonggaw, Phil.
110/E2 Bonggi (isl.), Malay.
112/B4 Bonggi (isl.), Malay.
111/F4 Bongka (riv.), Indo.
133/H7 Bongolava (uplands), Madg.
124/J5 Bongor, Chad
125/K6 Bongos (mts.), CAfr.
109/E3 Bong Son, Viet.
162/D3 Bonham, Tx,US
68/D1 Bonheiden, Belg.
54/B5 Bonhill, Sc,UK
76/D1 Bonhomme, Col du (pass), Fr.
80/A2 Bonifacio (str.), Fr., It.
163/G4 Bonifay, Fl,US
120/D2 Bonin (isls.), Japan
130/D3 Boni Nat'l Rsv., Kenya
164/C5 Bonita, Ca,US
163/H5 Bonita Springs, Fl,US
148/E3 Bonito (peak), Hon.
140/C2 Bonito de Santa Fé, Braz.
69/G2 Bonn, Ger.
53/S11 Bonnelles, Fr.
156/D3 Bonners Ferry, Id,US
156/E4 Bonner-West Riverside, Mt,US
157/K3 Bonnet (lake), Mb,Can
53/T10 Bonneuil-sur-Marne, Fr.
76/C5 Bonneville, Fr.
156/C4 Bonneville (dam), Or, Wa,US
165/C3 Bonney Lake, Wa,US
70/C4 Bönnigheim, Ger.
54/C5 Bonnybridge, Sc,UK
54/C5 Bonnyrigg, Sc,UK
156/F2 Bonnyville, Ab,Can
132/C4 Bontberg (peak), SAfr.
132/C4 Bontebok Nat'l Park, SAfr.
111/E5 Bonthain, Indo.
128/B5 Bonthe, SLeo.
105/J5 Bontoc, Phil.
82/D2 Bonyhád, Hun.
113/J Bonzare (coast), Ant.
68/D1 Boom, Belg.
157/K5 Boone, Ia,US
163/H2 Boone, NC,US
163/F3 Booneville, Ms,US
166/D2 Boonton, NJ,US
96/D2 Bööntsagaan (lake), Mong.
160/C4 Boonville, In,US
116/D4 Boorabbin Nat'l Park, Austl.
125/P6 Boorama, Som.
119/C1 Booroondara (peak), Austl.
68/A5 Boos, Fr.
161/G3 Boothbay Harbor, Me,US
113/D Boothby (cape), Ant.
152/G1 Boothia (gulf), NW,Can
152/G1 Boothia (pen.), NW,Can
57/E5 Bootle, Eng,UK
124/H8 Booué, Gabon
70/D5 Bopfingen, Ger.
69/G3 Boppard, Ger.
119/C1 Boppy (peak), Austl.
140/B3 Boqueirão (mts.), Braz.
142/C4 Boquete (peak), Arg.
146/D3 Boquilla (res.), Mex.
140/B4 Boquira, Braz.
125/N7 Bor (dry riv.), Kenya
85/K4 Bor, Rus.
125/M6 Bor, Sudan
92/C2 Bor, Turk.
82/F3 Bor, Yugo.
121/K6 Bora Bora (isl.), FrPol.
156/E4 Borah (peak), Id,US
62/E3 Borås, Swe.
93/G4 Borāzjān, Iran
136/G4 Borba, Braz.
78/B3 Borbera (riv.), It.
72/D3 Borbonnais (hist. reg.), Fr.
78/B3 Borbore (riv.), It.
140/C2 Borborema (plat.), Braz.
82/E3 Borča, Yugo.
67/F5 Borchen, Ger.
113/M Borchgrevink (coast), Ant.
87/G4 Borçka, Turk.
66/D4 Borculo, Neth.
117/H5 Borda (cape), Austl.
141/G7 Borda da Mata, Braz.
72/C4 Bordeaux, Fr.
153/R7 Borden (isl.), NW,Can
153/H2 Borden (pen.), NW,Can
54/C6 Borders (reg.), Sc,UK
78/A5 Bordighera, It.
123/T15 Bordj Bou Arreridj, Alg.
123/T15 Bordj Bou Arreridj (wilaya), Alg.
75/G4 Bordj el Bahri (cape), Alg.
123/S15 Bordj el Kiffan, Alg.
123/S15 Bordj Manaïel, Alg.
124/G2 Bordj Omar Driss, Alg.
59/F4 Bordon, Eng,UK
53/N7 Borehamwood, Eng,UK
63/L1 Borgå (Porvoo), Fin.
78/A2 Borgaro Torinese, It.
61/E2 Børgefjell Nat'l Park, Nor.
67/G5 Borgentreich, Ger.
66/D3 Borger, Neth.
162/C3 Borger, Tx,US
68/D1 Borgerhout, Belg.
62/G3 Borgholm, Swe.
67/F4 Borgholzhausen, Ger.
67/E4 Borghorst, Ger.
76/D5 Borgne (riv.), Swi.
78/B1 Borgomanero, It.
73/G4 Borgo San Dalmazzo, It.
79/E5 Borgo San Lorenzo, It
78/D2 Borgosatollo, It.
78/B1 Borgosesia, It.
129/F4 Borgou (prov.), Ben.
129/F4 Borgu Game Rsv., Nga.
62/B1 Borgund, Nor.
86/B2 Borislav, Ukr.
87/G2 Borisoglebsk, Rus.
84/F5 Borisov, Bela.
133/H6 Boriziny, Madg.
76/D5 Borken, Ger.
66/D1 Borkum (isl.), Ger.
62/F1 Borlänge, Swe.
78/B3 Bormida (riv.), It.
78/B3 Bormida di Millesimo (riv.), It.
78/B4 Bormida di Spigno (riv.), It.
66/C6 Born, Neth.
64/G3 Borna, Ger.
66/C2 Borndiep (chan.), Neth.
76/C6 Borne (riv.), Fr.
66/D4 Borne, Neth.
68/D1 Bornem, Belg.
110/E3 Borneo (isl.), Asia
69/F2 Bornheim, Ger.
62/F4 Bornholm (co.), Den.
62/F4 Bornholm (isl.), Den.
65/H1 Bornholmsgat (chan.), Swe.
129/H3 Borno (state), Nga.
74/C4 Bornos, Sp.
124/H5 Bornu (plains), Nga.
125/L6 Boro (riv.), Sudan
102/D3 Borohoro (mts.), China, Kaz.
112/D3 Borongan, Phil.
57/G3 Boroughbridge, Eng,UK
84/G4 Borovichi, Rus.
82/D3 Borovo, Cro.
62/D2 Borre, Nor.
86/B3 Borşa, Rom.
97/H1 Borshchovochnyy (mts.), Rus.
82/E1 Borsod-Abaúj-Zemplén (co.), Hun.
66/A6 Borssele, Neth.
102/D3 Bortala (riv.), China
58/B2 Borth, Wal,UK
93/G3 Borūjen, Iran
93/G3 Borūjerd, Iran
96/D3 Bor Ul (mts.), China
96/H1 Borzya, Rus.
80/A2 Bosa, It.
82/C3 Bosanska Dubica, Bosn.
82/C3 Bosanska Gradiška, Bosn.
82/C3 Bosanska Kostajnica, Bosn.
82/C3 Bosanska Krupa, Bosn.
82/D3 Bosanski Brod, Bosn.
82/C3 Bosanski Petrovac, Bosn.
82/D3 Bosanski Šamac, Bosn.
125/Q5 Bosaso (Bender Cassim), Som.
58/B5 Boscastle, Eng,UK
104/E4 Bose, China
59/F5 Bosham, Eng,UK
66/B4 Boskoop, Neth.
65/J4 Boskovice, Czh.
82/D3 Bosna (riv.), Bosn.
82/C3 Bosnia and Hercegovina
99/G3 Bōsō (pen.), Japan
125/J7 Bosobolo, Zaire
83/J5 Bosporus (str.), Turk.
158/F4 Bosque Farms, NM,US
143/K6 Bosques Petrificados Natural Mon., Arg.
124/J6 Bossangoa, CAfr.
162/E3 Bossier City, La,US
102/E3 Bosten (lake), China
57/H6 Boston, Eng,UK
162/E3 Boston (mts.), Ar,US
161/G3 Boston (cap.), Ma,US
162/E3 Boston, Tx,US
168/C1 Boston Common, Ma,US
167/F1 Bostwick (pt.), NY,US
82/D3 Bosut (riv.), Cro.
106/B3 Botād, India
118/H8 Botany (bay), Austl.
163/H3 Boteler (peak), NC,US
133/F2 Botelerpunt (pt.), SAfr.
141/G6 Botelhos, Braz.
81/J1 Botev (peak), Bul.
83/F4 Botevgrad, Bul.
133/E2 Bothaspas (pass), SAfr.
57/E2 Bothel, Eng,UK
165/C2 Bothell, Wa,US
58/D5 Bothenhampton, Eng,UK
84/C3 Bothnia (gulf), Fin., Swe.
63/R7 Botkyrka, Swe.
131/A4 Botletle (riv.), Bots.
86/C3 Botoșani, Rom.
83/H2 Botoșani (co.), Rom.
103/D3 Botou, China
109/D2 Bo Trach, Viet.
69/F3 Botrange (mtn.), Belg.
131/A4 Botswana
80/E3 Botte Donato (peak), It.
57/H4 Bottesford, Eng,UK
57/H6 Bottesford, Eng,UK
78/D1 Botticino, It.
157/H3 Bottineau, ND,US
66/D5 Bottrop, Ger.
141/B2 Botucatu, Braz.
161/L1 Botwood, Nf,Can
128/D4 Bou (riv.), IvC.
128/D5 Bouaflé, IvC.
128/D5 Bouaké, IvC.
124/J6 Bouar, CAfr.
71/F5 Boubín (peak), Czh.
125/J6 Bouca, CAfr.
161/P6 Boucherville, Qu,Can
128/C3 Boucle du Baoulé Nat'l Park, Mali
124/E1 Boudenib, Mor.
129/E2 Boû Djébéha (well), Mali
123/S15 Boufarik, Alg.
53/S9 Bouffémont, Fr.
118/B1 Bougainville (reef), Austl.
143/N7 Bougainville (cape), Falk.
120/E5 Bougainville (isl.), PNG
123/S15 Bougara, Alg.
123/V17 Bougar'oûn (cape), Alg.
128/D4 Bougouni, Mali
128/E4 Bougouriba (prov.), Burk.
72/C3 Bouguenais, Fr.
123/M13 Bouhalla (peak), Mor.
123/V17 Bou Hamdane (riv.), Alg.
123/S15 Bouira, Alg.
123/S15 Bouira (wilaya), Alg.
123/S15 Bou Ismaïl, Alg.
123/R15 Bou Kadir, Alg.
120/B8 Boulder, Austl.
159/F2 Boulder, Co,US
156/E4 Boulder, Mt,US
158/D4 Boulder City, Nv,US
165/P16 Boulder Hill, Il,US
129/E4 Boulgo (prov.), Burk.
129/E3 Boulkiemde (prov.), Burk.
72/C3 Boulogne (riv.), Fr.
53/S10 Boulogne-Billancourt, Fr.
68/A2 Boulogne-sur-Mer, Fr.
57/F4 Boulsworth (hill), Eng,UK
123/S15 Boumerdas, Alg.
123/S15 Boumerdas (wilaya), Alg.
75/F1 Boumort (mtn.), Sp.
151/K3 Boundary, Yk,Can
158/C3 Boundary (peak), Nv,US
166/D2 Bound Brook, NJ,US
128/D4 Boundiali, IvC.
158/E2 Bountiful, Ut,US
51/T8 Bounty (isls.), NZ
164/B1 Bouquet (canyon), Ca,US
164/B1 Bouquet (res.), Ca,US
76/C3 Bourbet, Rochers du (mtn.), Fr.
160/C3 Bourbonnais, Il,US
68/B2 Bourbourg, Fr.
123/L14 Bou Regreg (riv.), Mor.
129/F2 Bouressa (wadi), Mali
76/B5 Bourg-en-Bresse, Fr.
72/E3 Bourges, Fr.
72/F4 Bourg-lès-Valence, Fr.
72/B3 Bourgneuf (bay), Fr.
68/D5 Bourgogne, Fr.
76/B3 Bourgogne (can.), Fr.
72/E3 Bourgogne (reg.), Fr.
72/F4 Bourgoin-Jallieu, Fr.
59/F1 Bourne, Eng,UK
53/M8 Bourne (riv.), Eng,UK
59/F3 Bourne End, Eng,UK
59/E5 Bournemouth, Eng,UK
59/E2 Bournville, Eng,UK

Bourn – Burit

60/A5 **Bourn-Vincent Mem. Nat'l Park**, Ire.
67/E3 **Bourtanger Moor** (reg.), Ger.
59/E3 **Bourton on the Water**, Eng,UK
123/T15 **Bou Sellam** (riv.), Alg.
124/J5 **Bousso**, Chad
128/B2 **Boutilimit**, Mrta.
116/B5 **Bouvard** (cape), Austl.
51/K8 **Bouvet** (isl.), Nor.
68/C5 **Bouzy**, Fr.
67/G5 **Bovenden**, Ger.
139/H4 **Boven Tapanahoni** (riv.), Sur.
66/D3 **Bovenwijde** (lake), Neth.
58/C5 **Bovey Tracey**, Eng,UK
78/D1 **Bovezzo**, It.
53/M6 **Bovingdon**, Eng,UK
93/G4 **Bovīr Aḥmadi and Kohkīlūyeh** (gov.), Iran
79/E2 **Bovolone**, It.
156/E3 **Bow** (riv.), Ab,Can
157/J4 **Bowdle**, SD,US
57/F5 **Bowdon**, Eng,UK
118/C3 **Bowen**, Austl.
66/C5 **Bowen Merwede** (can.), Neth.
57/G3 **Bowes**, Eng,UK
158/E4 **Bowie**, Az,US
166/B6 **Bowie**, Md,US
156/F3 **Bow Island**, Ab,Can
118/B2 **Bowling Green** (cape), Austl.
160/C4 **Bowling Green**, Ky,US
159/K3 **Bowling Green**, Mo,US
160/D3 **Bowling Green**, Oh,US
118/B2 **Bowling Green Bay Nat'l Park**, Austl.
113/G **Bowman** (isl.), Ant.
153/J2 **Bowman** (bay), NW,Can
157/H4 **Bowman**, ND,US
161/S8 **Bowmanville**, Nf,Can
55/H9 **Bowmore**, Sc,UK
57/E2 **Bowness-on-Solway**, Eng,UK
111/F4 **Bowokan** (isls.), Indo.
119/D2 **Bowral**, Austl.
156/C2 **Bowron** (riv.), BC,Can
131/B3 **Bowwood**, Zam.
70/C4 **Boxberg**, Ger.
157/H4 **Box Elder**, SD,US
119/C3 **Box Hill**, Austl.
119/G5 **Box Hill**, Austl.
103/D3 **Boxing**, China
66/C5 **Boxmeer**, Neth.
66/C5 **Boxtel**, Neth.
92/C1 **Boyabat**, Turk.
138/C3 **Boyacá** (dept.), Col.
93/M6 **Boyalik**, Turk.
119/D2 **Boyd-Konangra Nat'l Park**, Austl.
103/C3 **Boye**, China
157/K5 **Boyer** (riv.), Ia,US
156/E2 **Boyle**, Ab,Can
60/D2 **Boyne** (riv.), Ire.
160/C2 **Boyne City**, Mi,US
163/H5 **Boynton Beach**, Fl,US
156/F5 **Boysen** (res.), Wy,US
92/B1 **Boz** (pt.), Turk.
81/J3 **Bozcaada** (isl.), Turk.
92/B2 **Bozdoğan**, Turk.
156/F4 **Bozeman**, Mt,US
77/H5 **Bozen** (Bolzano), It.
92/C2 **Bozkir**, Turk.
124/J6 **Bozoum**, CAfr.
92/D2 **Bozova**, Turk.
92/B2 **Bozüyük**, Turk.
91/C1 **Bozyazı**, Turk.
78/A3 **Bra**, It.
54/C3 **Braan** (riv.), Sc,UK
68/D2 **Brabant** (prov.), Belg.
59/G4 **Brabourne Lees**, Eng,UK
82/C4 **Brač** (isl.), Cro.
80/B1 **Bracciano** (lake), It.
160/E2 **Bracebridge**, On,Can
84/B3 **Bräcke**, Swe.
70/C4 **Brackenheim**, Ger.
162/C4 **Brackettville**, Tx,US
59/E2 **Brackley**, Eng,UK
59/F4 **Bracknell**, Eng,UK
141/B4 **Braço do Norte**, Braz.
82/F2 **Brad**, Rom.
80/D2 **Bradano** (riv.), It.
56/D3 **Bradda Head** (pt.), IM,UK
163/H5 **Bradenton**, Fl,US
57/G4 **Bradford**, Eng,UK
160/E3 **Bradford**, Pa,US
58/D4 **Bradford on Avon**, Eng,UK
59/E5 **Brading**, Eng,UK
58/C5 **Bradninch**, Eng,UK
162/D4 **Brady**, Tx,US
55/P12 **Brae**, Sc,UK
151/L3 **Braeburn**, Yk,Can
54/C2 **Braemar**, Sc,UK
54/C2 **Braemar** (dist.), Sc,UK
54/C2 **Braeriach** (mtn.), Sc,UK
74/A2 **Braga**, Port.
74/A2 **Braga** (dist.), Port.
142/E2 **Bragado**, Arg.
137/J4 **Bragança**, Braz.
74/B2 **Bragança**, Port.
74/B2 **Bragança** (dist.), Port.
141/G7 **Bragança Paulista**, Braz.
107/F2 **Brahmaputra** (riv.), Asia
56/D6 **Braich-y-Pwll** (pt.), Wal,UK
56/B2 **Braid** (riv.), NI,UK
83/H3 **Brăila**, Rom.
83/H3 **Brăila** (co.), Rom.
68/D2 **Braine-l'Alleud**, Belg.
68/D2 **Braine-le-Comte**, Belg.
157/K4 **Brainerd**, Mn,US
59/G3 **Braintree**, Eng,UK
168/D1 **Braintree**, Ma,US
132/C3 **Brak** (riv.), SAfr.
67/F2 **Brake**, Ger.
68/C2 **Brakel**, Belg.
67/G5 **Brakel**, Ger.
128/B2 **Brakna** (reg.), Mrta.
161/Q8 **Bramalea**, On,Can
57/G4 **Bramhope**, Eng,UK
161/Q8 **Brampton**, On,Can
57/F2 **Brampton**, Eng,UK
67/E4 **Bramsche**, Ger.
54/A1 **Bran** (riv.), Sc,UK
139/F5 **Branco** (riv.), Braz.
126/B5 **Brandberg** (peak), Namb.
64/G2 **Brandenburg**, Ger.
64/G2 **Brandenburg** (state), Ger.
54/C1 **Branderburgh**, Sc,UK
54/A4 **Brander, Pass of** (pass), Sc,UK
57/H4 **Brandesburton**, Eng,UK
78/A2 **Brandizzo**, It.
157/J3 **Brandon**, Mb,Can
60/D4 **Brandon** (mtn.), Ire.
59/G2 **Brandon**, Eng,UK
163/H5 **Brandon**, Fl,US
163/F3 **Brandon**, Ms,US
142/F2 **Brandsen**, Arg.
71/H2 **Brandýs nad Labem**, Czh.
166/C4 **Brandywine** (cr.), De, Pa,US
166/C3 **Brandywine, East Branch** (cr.), Pa,US
166/C4 **Brandywine, West Branch** (cr.), Pa,US
65/K1 **Braniewo**, Pol.
59/E5 **Bransgore**, Eng,UK
54/D5 **Branxton**, Eng,UK
77/H5 **Branzoll** (Bronzolo), It.
161/J2 **Bras d'Or** (lake), NS,Can
136/E6 **Brasiléia**, Braz.
140/A4 **Brasília** (cap.), Braz.
140/A5 **Brasília de Minas**, Braz.
140/A4 **Brasília Nat'l Park**, Braz.
141/D1 **Brasil, Planalto do** (plat.), Braz.
83/G3 **Braşov**, Rom.
83/G3 **Braşov** (co.), Rom.
66/B6 **Brasschaat**, Belg.
117/G2 **Brassey** (peak), Austl.
163/H3 **Brasstown Bald** (peak), Ga,US
65/J4 **Bratislava** (cap.), Slvk.
65/J4 **Bratislava** (reg.), Slvk.
89/L4 **Bratsk**, Rus.
161/F3 **Brattleboro**, Vt,US
149/F4 **Braulio Carrillo Nat'l Park**, CR
71/G6 **Braunau am Inn**, Aus.
70/B1 **Braunfels**, Ger.
67/H5 **Braunlage**, Ger.
67/H4 **Braunschweig** (Brunswick), Ger.
58/B4 **Braunton**, Eng,UK
122/J11 **Brava** (isl.), CpV.
75/G2 **Brava** (coast), Sp.
143/T12 **Brava** (pt.), Uru.
62/G2 **Bråviken** (inlet), Swe.
136/F7 **Bravo** (peak), Bol.
144/B2 **Bravo** (peak), Peru
138/C2 **Bravo** (riv.), Ven.
158/D4 **Brawley**, Ca,US
153/J2 **Bray** (isl.), NW,Can
60/D3 **Bray**, Ire.
72/D3 **Braye** (riv.), Fr.
56/B5 **Bray Head** (pt.), Ire.
68/B4 **Bray-sur-Somme**, Fr.
134/D3 **Brazil**
160/C4 **Brazil**, In,US
134/E4 **Brazilian** (plat.), Braz.
139/E4 **Brazo Casiquare** (riv.), Ven.
141/H7 **Brazópolis**, Braz.
162/D4 **Brazos** (riv.), Tx,US
159/H4 **Brazos, Clear Fork** (riv.), Tx,US
159/G4 **Brazos, Double Mtn. Fork** (riv.), Tx,US
143/K7 **Brazo Sur** (riv.), Arg.
126/C1 **Brazzaville** (cap.), Congo
82/D3 **Brčko**, Bosn.
64/J2 **Brda** (riv.), Pol.
71/G3 **Brdy** (mts.), Czh.
164/C3 **Brea**, Ca,US
54/B4 **Breadalbane** (dist.), Sc,UK
58/D3 **Bream**, Eng,UK
54/E6 **Breamish** (riv.), Eng,UK
83/G3 **Breaza**, Rom.
70/B2 **Brechen**, Ger.
54/D3 **Brechin**, Sc,UK
66/B6 **Brecht**, Belg.
157/J4 **Breckenridge**, Mn,US
67/E6 **Breckerfeld**, Ger.
59/G2 **Breckland** (reg.), Eng,UK
143/K8 **Brecknock** (pen.), Chile
168/F5 **Brecksville**, Oh,US
65/J4 **Břeclav**, Czh.
58/C3 **Brecon**, Wal,UK
58/C3 **Brecon Beacons** (mts.), Wal,UK
58/C3 **Brecon Beacons Nat'l Park**, Wal,UK
66/B5 **Breda**, Neth.
68/B1 **Bredene**, Belg.
69/E1 **Bree**, Belg.
132/L10 **Breë** (riv.), SAfr.
77/E1 **Breg** (riv.), Ger.
77/F5 **Bregagno, Monte** (peak), It.
82/F5 **Bregalinca** (riv.), Macd.
77/F2 **Bregenz**, Aus.
77/F3 **Bregenzer Ache** (riv.), Aus.
61/M6 **Breidhafjördhur** (bay), Ice.
76/D1 **Breisach**, Ger.
71/G5 **Breitenauriegel** (peak), Ger.
76/D5 **Breithorn** (peak), Swi.
76/D6 **Breithorn** (peak), Swi., It.
140/B1 **Brejo**, Braz.
140/C2 **Brejo do Cruz**, Braz.
140/B3 **Brejões**, Braz.
140/C2 **Brejo Santo**, Braz.
78/C1 **Brembo** (riv.), It.
67/F2 **Bremen**, Ger.
67/F1 **Bremen** (state), Ger.
67/F2 **Bremen** (state), Ger.
118/E7 **Bremer** (riv.), Austl.
67/F1 **Bremerhaven**, Ger.
165/B2 **Bremerton**, Wa,US
67/G2 **Bremervörde**, Ger.
62/A2 **Bremnes**, Nor.
70/D2 **Brend** (riv.), Ger.
165/E6 **Brendel** (lake), Mi,US
58/C4 **Brendon** (hills), Eng,UK
162/D4 **Brenham**, Tx,US
56/E5 **Brenig, Llyn** (lake), Wal,UK
76/B4 **Brenne** (riv.), Fr.
117/N9 **Brenner** (riv.), Austl.
77/H4 **Brenner** (Brennerpass) (pass), Aus.
77/E4 **Brenno** (riv.), Swi.
53/N7 **Brent** (bor.), Eng,UK
53/N7 **Brent** (res.), Eng,UK
53/N7 **Brent** (riv.), Eng,UK
79/F2 **Brenta** (riv.), It.
77/G5 **Brenta, Cima** (peak), It.
53/P7 **Brentwood**, Eng,UK
165/L11 **Brentwood**, Ca,US
167/E2 **Brentwood**, NY,US
168/H7 **Brentwood**, Pa,US
70/D5 **Brenz** (riv.), Ger.
78/D1 **Brescia**, It.
78/D1 **Brescia** (prov.), It.
68/A4 **Bresle** (riv.), Fr.
73/J3 **Bressanone**, It.
55/P12 **Bressay** (isl.), Sc,UK
72/C3 **Bressuire**, Fr.
65/M2 **Brest**, Bela.
72/A2 **Brest**, Fr.
65/M2 **Brest Obl.**, Bela.
72/B2 **Bretagne** (mts.), Fr.
72/B2 **Bretagne** (reg.), Fr.
133/R15 **Bretagne** (pt.), Reun.
53/S11 **Brétigny-sur-Orge**, Fr.
156/E2 **Breton**, Ab,Can
161/K2 **Breton** (cape), NS,Can
115/R10 **Brett** (cape), NZ
70/C4 **Brettach** (riv.), Ger.
70/B4 **Bretten**, Ger.
70/C3 **Breuberg**, Ger.
53/S11 **Breuillet**, Fr.
66/B4 **Breukelen**, Neth.
137/H4 **Breves**, Braz.
63/S7 **Brevik**, Swe.
153/K2 **Brevoort** (isl.), NW,Can
161/G2 **Brewer**, Me,US
58/D1 **Brewood**, Eng,UK
159/H2 **Brewster**, Ne,US
156/D3 **Brewster**, Wa,US
163/G4 **Brewton**, Al,US
82/B3 **Brežice**, Slov.
83/G3 **Brezoi**, Rom.
125/K6 **Bria**, CAfr.
73/G4 **Briançon**, Fr.
58/C2 **Brianne, Lyn** (res.), Wal,UK
167/D3 **Brick**, NJ,US
53/M6 **Bricket Wood**, Eng,UK
60/B5 **Bride** (riv.), Ire.
56/D3 **Bride**, IM,UK
162/E4 **Bridge City**, Tx,US
58/C4 **Bridgend**, Wal,UK
54/C4 **Bridge of Allan**, Sc,UK
54/D2 **Bridge of Don**, Sc,UK
54/B5 **Bridge of Weir**, Sc,UK
158/C3 **Bridgeport**, Ca,US
168/A3 **Bridgeport**, Ct,US
159/G2 **Bridgeport**, Ne,US
160/D4 **Bridgeport**, WV,US
156/F4 **Bridger**, Mt,US
166/C5 **Bridgeton**, NJ,US
150/G4 **Bridgetown** (cap.), Bar.
119/C4 **Bridgewater**, Austl.
161/H2 **Bridgewater**, NS,Can
168/D2 **Bridgewater**, Ma,US
160/E4 **Bridgewater**, Va,US
58/D1 **Bridgnorth**, Eng,UK
161/G2 **Bridgton**, Me,US
58/D4 **Bridgwater**, Eng,UK
58/C4 **Bridgwater** (bay), Eng,UK
57/H3 **Bridlington**, Eng,UK
57/H3 **Bridlington** (bay), Eng,UK
58/D5 **Bridport**, Eng,UK
53/U10 **Brie** (reg.), Fr.
53/T10 **Brie-Comte-Robert**, Fr.
65/J3 **Brieg Brzeg**, Pol.
66/B5 **Brielle**, Neth.
76/D4 **Brienzersee** (lake), Swi.
163/H3 **Brier** (cr.), Ga,US
57/F4 **Brierfield**, Eng,UK
73/G3 **Brig**, Swi.
77/E1 **Brigach** (riv.), Ger.
167/D5 **Brigantine**, NJ,US
57/H4 **Brigg**, Eng,UK
76/D5 **Brig-Glis**, Swi.
158/D2 **Brigham City**, Ut,US
57/G4 **Brighouse**, Eng,UK
59/E5 **Brighstone**, Eng,UK
59/H3 **Brightlingsea**, Eng,UK
117/M9 **Brighton**, Austl.
118/F6 **Brighton**, Austl.
119/F5 **Brighton**, Austl.
59/F5 **Brighton**, Eng,UK
159/F3 **Brighton**, Co,US
54/C5 **Brightons**, Sc,UK
72/F4 **Brignais**, Fr.
72/G5 **Brignoles**, Fr.
108/G3 **Brihadeshwara Temple**, India
53/S11 **Briis-sous-Forges**, Fr.
79/G3 **Brijuni**, Cro.
128/A3 **Brikama**, Gam.
59/E3 **Brill**, Eng,UK
137/H8 **Brillante** (riv.), Braz.
67/F6 **Brilon**, Ger.
57/G5 **Brimington**, Eng,UK
150/F3 **Brimstone Hill Nat'l Park**, StK.
81/E2 **Brindisi**, It.
58/E3 **Brinkworth**, Eng,UK
74/A1 **Brion**, Sp.
165/K11 **Briones** (res.), Ca,US
118/E6 **Brisbane**, Austl.
118/F6 **Brisbane** (riv.), Austl.
118/E6 **Brisbane For. Park**, Austl.
118/D4 **Brisbane** (inset), Austl.
119/C3 **Brisbane Ranges Nat'l Park**, Austl.
119/D2 **Brisbane Waters Nat'l Park**, Austl.
58/B4 **Bristol** (chan.), UK
58/D4 **Bristol**, Eng,UK
151/F4 **Bristol** (bay), Ak,US
168/B2 **Bristol**, Ct,US
168/C2 **Bristol** (co.), Ma,US
166/D3 **Bristol**, Pa,US
168/C2 **Bristol**, RI,US
168/C2 **Bristol** (co.), RI,US
163/H2 **Bristol**, Tn,US
159/H4 **Bristow**, Ok,US
151/K2 **British** (mts.), Yk,Can, Ak,US
152/D3 **British Columbia** (prov.), Can.
153/S6 **British Empire** (range), NW,Can
90/G10 **British Indian Ocean Terr.**
53/N7 **British Museum**, Eng,UK
150/E3 **British Virgin Islands**
132/P12 **Brits**, SAfr.
72/B2 **Brittany** (reg.), Fr.
157/J4 **Britton**, SD,US
72/D4 **Brive-la-Gaillarde**, Fr.
58/C6 **Brixham**, Eng,UK
59/F2 **Brixworth**, Eng,UK
65/J4 **Brno**, Czh.
63/R6 **Bro**, Swe.
118/C3 **Broad** (sound), Austl.
151/J3 **Broad** (pass), Ak,US
163/H3 **Broad** (riv.), NC, SC,US
160/E1 **Broadback** (riv.), Qu,Can
166/C6 **Broadkill** (riv.), De,US
54/C6 **Broad Law** (mtn.), Sc,UK
119/F5 **Broadmeadows**, Austl.
118/C3 **Broad Sound** (chan.), Austl.
59/H4 **Broadstairs**, Eng,UK
59/E5 **Broadstone**, Eng,UK
157/G4 **Broadus**, Mt,US
168/F5 **Broadview Heights**, Oh,US
119/E1 **Broadwater Nat'l Park**, Austl.
59/E2 **Broadway**, Eng,UK
59/E2 **Broadway** (hill), Eng,UK
58/D5 **Broadwindsor**, Eng,UK
149/F1 **Broa, Ensenada de la** (bay), Cuba
153/R7 **Brock** (isl.), NW,Can
67/H5 **Brocken** (peak), Ger.
59/E5 **Brockenhurst**, Eng,UK
116/C2 **Brockman** (peak), Austl.
168/C1 **Brockton**, Ma,US
160/F2 **Brockville**, On,Can
152/G1 **Brodeur** (pen.), NW,Can
166/C1 **Brodhead** (cr.), Pa,US
54/A5 **Brodick**, Sc,UK
65/K2 **Brodnica**, Pol.
66/B3 **Broek Op Langedijk**, Neth.
119/D2 **Broken** (bay), Austl.
159/J3 **Broken Arrow**, Ok,US
159/H2 **Broken Bow**, Ne,US
159/J4 **Broken Bow**, Ok,US
159/J4 **Broken Bow** (lake), Ok,US
117/J4 **Broken Hill**, Austl.
162/B3 **Brokeoff** (mts.), NM,US
139/H3 **Brokopondo** (dist.), Sur.
53/P7 **Bromley**, Eng,UK
53/P7 **Bromley** (bor.), Eng,UK
131/C3 **Bromley**, Zim.
53/P7 **Bromley Common**, Eng,UK
63/R7 **Bromma**, Swe.
62/F3 **Bromölla**, Swe.
58/D2 **Bromsgrove**, Eng,UK
58/D2 **Bromyard**, Eng,UK
72/F4 **Bron**, Fr.
63/T9 **Brøndby**, Den.
62/C3 **Brønderslev**, Den.
129/E5 **Brong-Ahafo** (reg.), Gha.
78/C2 **Broni**, It.
58/C3 **Bronllys**, Wal,UK
61/E2 **Brønnøysund**, Nor.
161/Q9 **Bronte**, On,Can
80/D4 **Bronte**, It.
167/E2 **Bronx** (co.), NY,US
167/E2 **Bronx** (riv.), NY,US
167/K8 **Bronxville**, NY,US
167/E2 **Bronx Zoo**, NY,US
112/B3 **Brookes Point**, Phil.
168/A3 **Brookfield**, Ct,US
165/Q16 **Brookfield**, Il,US
159/J3 **Brookfield**, Mo,US
165/P13 **Brookfield**, Wi,US
163/F4 **Brookhaven**, Ms,US
167/F2 **Brookhaven**, NY,US
157/J4 **Brookings**, SD,US
168/C1 **Brookline**, Ma,US
168/C2 **Brooklyn**, Ct,US
168/F5 **Brooklyn**, Oh,US
167/K9 **Brooklyn** (Kings) (co.), NY,US
166/B5 **Brooklyn Park**, Md,US
53/N6 **Brookmans Park**, Eng,UK
168/F5 **Brook Park**, Oh,US
156/F3 **Brooks**, Ab,Can
151/E2 **Brooks** (mtn.), Ak,US
151/F2 **Brooks** (range), Ak,US
162/D4 **Brooks A.F.B.**, Tx,US
166/C4 **Brookside**, De,US
163/H4 **Brooksville**, Fl,US
166/C4 **Broomall**, Pa,US
60/C3 **Brosna** (riv.), Ire.
161/P7 **Brossard**, Qu,Can
57/H2 **Brotton**, Eng,UK
57/F2 **Brough**, Eng,UK
161/R8 **Brougham**, On,Can
55/N13 **Brough Head** (pt.), Sc,UK
56/B2 **Broughshane**, NI,UK
59/F2 **Broughton**, Eng,UK
54/C5 **Broughton**, Sc,UK
57/E3 **Broughton in Furness**, Eng,UK
59/G4 **Broughton Street**, Eng,UK
66/A5 **Brouwersdam** (dam), Neth.
117/H5 **Brown** (peak), Austl.
117/G5 **Brown** (pt.), Austl.
58/D2 **Brown Clee** (hill), Eng,UK
162/C3 **Brownfield**, Tx,US
59/E1 **Brownhills**, Eng,UK
156/E3 **Browning**, Mt,US
59/E5 **Brownsea** (isl.), Eng,UK
166/D4 **Browns Mills**, NJ,US
167/K9 **Brownsville**, NY,US
163/F3 **Brownsville**, Tn,US
162/D5 **Brownsville**, Tx,US
58/B5 **Brown Willy** (hill), Eng,UK
162/D4 **Brownwood**, Tx,US
53/N6 **Broxbourne**, Eng,UK
54/C5 **Broxburn**, Sc,UK
76/C4 **Broye** (riv.), Swi.
68/B3 **Bruay-en-Artois**, Fr.
68/C3 **Bruay-sur-l'Escaut**, Fr.
116/C2 **Bruce** (peak), Austl.
160/D2 **Bruce** (pen.), On,Can
76/D1 **Bruche** (riv.), Fr.
70/B2 **Bruchköbel**, Ger.
69/G5 **Bruchmühlbach-Miesau**, Ger.
70/B4 **Bruchsal**, Ger.
67/G5 **Brucht** (riv.), Ger.
73/K3 **Bruck an der Grossglockner-strasse**, Aus.
82/C1 **Bruck an der Leitha**, Aus.
73/L3 **Bruck an der Mur**, Aus.
64/F5 **Bruckmühl**, Ger.
58/D4 **Brue** (riv.), Eng,UK
68/C1 **Bruges** (Brugge), Belg.
68/C1 **Brugge** (Bruges), Belg.
66/D6 **Brüggen**, Ger.
69/F2 **Brühl**, Ger.
132/B2 **Brukkaros** (peak), Namb.
140/B4 **Brumado**, Braz.
69/G6 **Brumath**, Fr.
66/D4 **Brummen**, Neth.
62/D1 **Brumunddal**, Nor.
80/A2 **Bruncu Spina** (peak), It.
59/H1 **Brundall**, Eng,UK
68/D4 **Brune** (riv.), Fr.
158/D2 **Bruneau** (riv.), Id, Nv,US
112/A4 **Brunei**
112/A4 **Brunei** (bay), Bru.
75/M9 **Brunete**, Sp.
73/J3 **Brunico**, It.
76/E4 **Brünigpass** (pass), Swi.
63/R6 **Brunna**, Swe.
77/E4 **Brunnen**, Swi.
53/T10 **Brunoy**, Fr.
67/G1 **Brunsbüttel**, Ger.
69/E2 **Brunssum**, Neth.
119/F5 **Brunswick**, Austl.
143/J8 **Brunswick** (pen.), Chile
163/H4 **Brunswick**, Ga,US
161/G3 **Brunswick**, Me,US
168/F5 **Brunswick**, Oh,US
67/H4 **Brunswick** (Braunschweig), Ger.
149/E3 **Brus** (lag.), Hon.
168/G6 **Brush** (cr.), Pa,US
141/B3 **Brusque**, Braz.
68/D2 **Brussels** (Bruxelles) (cap.), Belg.
58/D4 **Bruton**, Eng,UK
68/D2 **Bruxelles** (Brussels) (cap.), Belg.
53/S11 **Bruyères-le-Châtel**, Fr.
53/S9 **Bruyère-sur-Oise**, Fr.
72/C2 **Bruz**, Fr.
113/U **Bryan** (coast), Ant.
117/H5 **Bryan** (peak), Austl.
160/C3 **Bryan**, Oh,US
162/D4 **Bryan**, Tx,US
86/E1 **Bryansk**, Rus.
86/E1 **Bryansk Obl.**, Rus.
158/D3 **Bryce Canyon Nat'l Park**, Ut,US
57/E5 **Brymbo**, Wal,UK
58/C2 **Bryn Brawd** (mtn.), Wal,UK
62/A2 **Bryne**, Nor.
58/C3 **Brynithel**, Wal,UK
58/C3 **Brynmawr**, Wal,UK
65/J3 **Brzeg Dolny**, Pol.
65/L4 **Brzesko**, Pol.
65/M4 **Brzozów**, Pol.
131/D2 **Bua** (riv.), Malw.
109/C3 **Bua Yai**, Thai.
128/B4 **Buba**, GBis.
130/A3 **Bubanza**, Buru.
128/B4 **Bubaque**, GBis.
93/G4 **Būbiyan** (isl.), Kuw.
130/B4 **Bubu** (riv.), Tanz.
131/C4 **Bubye** (riv.), Zim.
53/S10 **Buc**, Fr.
92/B2 **Bucak**, Turk.
138/C3 **Bucaramanga**, Col.
112/D3 **Bucas Grande** (isl.), Phil.
112/C1 **Bucay**, Phil.
75/P10 **Bucelas**, Port.
153/J1 **Buchan** (gulf), NW,Can
54/D1 **Buchan** (dist.), Sc,UK
128/C5 **Buchanan**, Libr.
159/H5 **Buchanan** (lake), Tx,US
55/L8 **Buchan Ness** (pt.), Sc,UK
161/K1 **Buchans**, Nf,Can
83/H3 **Bucharest** (Bucureşti) (cap.), Rom.
70/C3 **Buchen**, Ger.
130/B3 **Buchenzi**, Tanz.
67/G2 **Buchholz in der Nordheide**, Ger.
70/D6 **Buchloe**, Ger.
54/B4 **Buchlyvie**, Sc,UK
158/B4 **Buchon** (pt.), Ca,US
77/F3 **Buchs**, Swi.
57/F3 **Buckden Pike** (mtn.), Eng,UK
67/G4 **Bückeburg**, Ger.
58/C6 **Buckfastleigh**, Eng,UK
160/D4 **Buckhannon**, WV,US
54/C4 **Buckhaven**, Sc,UK
53/P7 **Buckhurst Hill**, Eng,UK
54/D1 **Buckie**, Sc,UK
160/F2 **Buckingham**, Qu,Can
59/F3 **Buckingham**, Eng,UK
53/N7 **Buckingham Palace**, Eng,UK
59/F3 **Buckinghamshire** (co.), Eng,UK
57/E5 **Buckley**, Wal,UK
58/D2 **Bucknell**, Eng,UK
166/C3 **Bucks** (co.), Pa,US
54/D2 **Bucksburn**, Sc,UK
54/D2 **Buck, The** (mtn.), Sc,UK
161/H2 **Buctouche**, NB,Can
83/H3 **Bucureşti** (Bucharest) (cap.), Rom.
160/D3 **Bucyrus**, Oh,US
130/B2 **Budaka**, Ugan.
82/D2 **Budaörs**, Hun.
82/D2 **Budapest** (cap.), Hun.
106/C2 **Budaun**, India
113/H **Budd** (coast), Ant.
165/B3 **Budd** (inlet), Wa,US
166/D2 **Budd Lake**, NJ,US
54/D4 **Buddon Ness** (pt.), Sc,UK
58/B5 **Bude**, Eng,UK
58/B5 **Bude** (bay), Eng,UK
66/C6 **Budel**, Neth.
64/E1 **Büdelsdorf**, Ger.
70/C2 **Büdingen**, Ger.
125/J7 **Budjala**, Zaire
58/C5 **Budleigh Salterton**, Eng,UK
79/E3 **Budrio**, It.
82/D4 **Budva**, Yugo.
83/J2 **Budzhak** (reg.), Mol., Ukr.
124/G7 **Buea**, Camr.
138/B5 **Buena Fe**, Ecu.
164/C3 **Buena Park**, Ca,US
138/B4 **Buenaventura**, Col.
146/E5 **Buenavista**, Mex.
159/F3 **Buena Vista**, Co,US
160/E4 **Buena Vista**, Va,US
142/B4 **Bueno** (riv.), Chile
141/G7 **Bueno Brandão**, Braz.
141/C1 **Buenópolis**, Braz.
142/F2 **Buenos Aires** (cap.), Arg.
142/C5 **Buenos Aires** (lake), Arg.
142/E3 **Buenos Aires** (prov.), Arg.
143/S12 **Buenos Aires** (inset) (cap.), Arg.
140/C4 **Buerarema**, Braz.
76/C5 **Buet** (mtn.), Fr.
74/A1 **Bueu**, Sp.
119/C3 **Buffalo** (peak), Austl.
156/E2 **Buffalo** (lake), Ab,Can
133/E2 **Buffalo** (riv.), SAfr.
162/E2 **Buffalo** (riv.), Ar,US
157/K4 **Buffalo**, Mn,US
159/J3 **Buffalo**, Mo,US
161/S10 **Buffalo**, NY,US
159/H3 **Buffalo**, Ok,US
166/A2 **Buffalo** (cr.), Pa,US
166/A3 **Buffalo** (cr.), Pa,US
168/H6 **Buffalo** (cr.), Pa,US
157/H4 **Buffalo**, SD,US
163/G3 **Buffalo** (riv.), Tn,US
156/G4 **Buffalo**, Wy,US
165/Q15 **Buffalo Grove**, Il,US
156/F2 **Buffalo Narrows**, Sk,Can
119/B1 **Buffalo Riv. Overflow** (swamp), Austl.
130/C2 **Buffalo Springs Nat'l Rsv.**, Kenya
168/B2 **Buff Cap** (hill), Ct,US
132/B3 **Buffelsrivier** (dry riv.), SAfr.
163/G3 **Buford**, Ga,US
83/G3 **Buftea**, Rom.
86/B1 **Bug** (riv.), Eur.
83/K2 **Bug** (estuary), Ukr.
138/B4 **Buga**, Col.
149/F4 **Bugaba**, Pan.
130/B3 **Bugala** (isl.), Ugan.
72/E5 **Bugarach, Pic de** (peak), Fr.
130/A3 **Bugarama**, Rwa.
130/A3 **Bugaza**, Zaire
59/E2 **Bugbrooke**, Eng,UK
110/D5 **Bugel** (pt.), Indo.
130/A3 **Bugene**, Tanz.
68/D1 **Buggenhout**, Belg.
130/B2 **Bugiri**, Ugan.
82/C3 **Bugojno**, Bosn.
112/B3 **Bugsuk** (isl.), Phil.
85/M5 **Bugul'ma**, Rus.
87/K1 **Buguruslan**, Rus.
96/D4 **Buh** (riv.), China
92/D2 **Buhayrat al Asad** (lake), Syria
92/B4 **Buhayrat al Manzilah** (lake), Egypt
93/E3 **Buḩayrat ath Tharthār** (lake), Iraq
130/B3 **Buhemba**, Tanz.
131/C3 **Buhera**, Zim.
77/E2 **Bühl**, Ger.
156/E5 **Buhl**, Id,US
70/C4 **Bühler** (riv.), Ger.
83/H2 **Buhuşi**, Rom.
129/E4 **Bui** (dam), Gha.
129/E4 **Bui Gorge** (res.), Gha.
58/C2 **Builth Wells**, Wal,UK
142/Q9 **Buin**, Chile
77/G4 **Buin, Piz** (peak), Swi.
140/C3 **Buíque**, Braz.
74/C4 **Bujalance**, Sp.
82/E4 **Bujanovac**, Yugo.
79/G2 **Buje**, Cro.
83/H3 **Bujor**, Rom.
130/A3 **Bujumbura** (cap.), Buru.
65/J2 **Buk**, Pol.
120/E5 **Buka** (isl.), PNG
96/H1 **Bukachacha**, Rus.
102/F4 **Bukadaban Feng** (peak), China
130/B3 **Bukakata**, Ugan.
93/F2 **Būkān**, Iran
130/B3 **Bukasa** (isl.), Ugan.
130/A3 **Bukavu**, Zaire
130/B4 **Bukene**, Tanz.
109/C5 **Buket Bubat** (peak), Malay.
88/G6 **Bukhara**, Uzb.
96/A2 **Bukhtarma** (riv.), Kaz.
130/B3 **Bukima**, Tanz.
110/B4 **Bukittinggi**, Indo.
82/E1 **Bükki Nat'l Park**, Hun.
130/A3 **Bukoba**, Tanz.
130/B3 **Bukonyo**, Tanz.
110/B4 **Buku** (cape), Indo.
112/E6 **Bulacan**, Phil.
112/E6 **Bulacan** (prov.), Phil.
77/E2 **Bülach**, Swi.
112/C2 **Bulalakao**, Phil.
112/C2 **Bulan**, Phil.
92/D1 **Bulancak**, Turk.
106/C2 **Bulandshahr**, India
92/E2 **Bulanık**, Turk.
111/F3 **Bulawa** (peak), Indo.
131/C4 **Bulawayo**, Zim.
92/B2 **Buldan**, Turk.
151/B5 **Buldir** (isl.), Ak,US
96/C2 **Bulgan**, Mong.
96/C2 **Bulgan** (riv.), Mong.
83/G4 **Bulgaria**
80/D2 **Bulgheria** (peak), It.
112/B3 **Buliluyan** (cape), Phil.
118/F7 **Bulimba** (cr.), Austl.
62/D4 **Bülk** (pt.), Ger.
59/E2 **Bulkington**, Eng,UK
156/B2 **Bulkley** (riv.), BC,Can
56/B1 **Bull** (pt.), NI,UK
74/E3 **Bullas**, Sp.
76/D4 **Bulle**, Swi.
119/C3 **Buller** (peak), Austl.
158/D4 **Bullhead City**, Az,US
69/F3 **Büllingen**, Belg.
53/R11 **Bullion**, Fr.
118/A5 **Bulloo** (riv.), Austl.
118/A5 **Bulloo Riv. Overflow** (swamp), Austl.
159/J3 **Bull Shoals** (lake), Ar, Mo,US
68/B3 **Bully-les-Mines**, Fr.
96/D2 **Bulnayn** (mts.), Mong.
142/B3 **Bulnes**, Chile
120/D5 **Bulolo**, PNG
53/Q7 **Bulphan**, Eng,UK
112/D4 **Buluan**, Phil.
111/F5 **Bulukumba**, Indo.
126/D2 **Bulungu**, Zaire
130/B4 **Bulungwa**, Tanz.
125/K7 **Bumba**, Zaire
112/B4 **Bum Bum** (isl.), Malay.
104/C3 **Bumhpa** (peak), Burma
130/C2 **Buna**, Kenya
99/L9 **Bunaga-take** (peak), Japan
112/D3 **Bunawan**, Phil.
130/A3 **Bunazi**, Tanz.
116/B5 **Bunbury**, Austl.
118/D4 **Bundaberg**, Austl.
67/E2 **Bünde**, Ger.
67/F4 **Bünde**, Ger.
106/C2 **Būndi**, India
112/D2 **Bunga** (pt.), Phil.
59/H2 **Bungay**, Eng,UK
130/B2 **Bungoma**, Kenya
110/C3 **Bunguran** (isl.), Indo.
130/A2 **Bunia**, Zaire
63/T9 **Bunkeflo Strand**, Swe.
163/H4 **Bunnell**, Fl,US
66/C4 **Bunnik**, Neth.
75/E3 **Buñol**, Sp.
66/C4 **Bunschoten**, Neth.
59/F3 **Buntingford**, Eng,UK
130/B2 **Bunyala**, Kenya
118/C4 **Bunya Mountains Nat'l Park**, Austl.
92/C2 **Bünyan**, Turk.
118/E6 **Bunya Park**, Austl.
112/B5 **Bunyu** (isl.), Indo.
109/E3 **Buon Me Thuot**, Viet.
109/E3 **Buon Mrong**, Viet.
140/C3 **Buquim**, Braz.
130/C3 **Bura**, Kenya
125/L5 **Buram**, Sudan
102/D5 **Burang**, China
125/M7 **Buranga** (pass), Ugan.
79/F5 **Burano** (riv.), It.
125/Q6 **Burao**, Som.
163/F4 **Buras-Triumph**, La,US
112/D3 **Burauen**, Phil.
94/D3 **Buraydah**, SAr.
69/H2 **Burbach**, Ger.
164/B2 **Burbank**, Ca,US
165/Q16 **Burbank**, Il,US
125/Q6 **Burco** (Burao), Som.
118/B3 **Burdekin** (riv.), Austl.
165/J10 **Burdell** (mtn.), Ca,US
92/B2 **Burdur**, Turk.
92/B2 **Burdur** (lake), Turk.
92/B2 **Burdur** (prov.), Turk.
106/E3 **Burdwān**, India
59/H1 **Bure** (riv.), Eng,UK
67/F5 **Büren**, Ger.
66/C5 **Buren**, Neth.
96/E2 **Bürengiyn** (mts.), Mong.
53/S10 **Bures-sur-Yvette**, Fr.
108/B2 **Būrewāla**, Pak.
97/L1 **Bureya** (mts.), Rus.
97/L1 **Bureya** (riv.), Rus.
59/E3 **Burford**, Eng,UK
64/F2 **Burg**, Ger.
83/H4 **Burgas**, Bul.
83/H4 **Burgas** (bay), Bul.
83/H4 **Burgas** (reg.), Bul.
70/D6 **Burgau**, Ger.
67/H4 **Burgdorf**, Ger.
76/D3 **Burgdorf**, Swi.
73/M3 **Burgenland** (prov.), Aus.
161/K2 **Burgeo**, Nf,Can
132/D3 **Burgersdorp**, SAfr.
116/D4 **Burges** (peak), Austl.
152/C2 **Burgess** (mtn.), NW,Can
151/L2 **Burgess** (mtn.), Yk,Can
59/F5 **Burgess Hill**, Eng,UK
61/E2 **Burgfjället** (peak), Swe.
71/F6 **Burghausen**, Ger.
54/C1 **Burghead**, Sc,UK
54/C1 **Burghead** (bay), Sc,UK
57/J5 **Burgh le Marsh**, Eng,UK
71/F6 **Burgkirchen an der Alz**, Ger.
70/E2 **Burgkunstadt**, Ger.
71/F4 **Burglengenfeld**, Ger.
74/D1 **Burgos**, Sp.
77/H4 **Burgstall** (Postal), It.
67/E4 **Burgsteinfurt**, Ger.
72/F3 **Burgundy** (hist. reg.), Fr.
67/G3 **Burgwedel**, Ger.
96/D4 **Burhan Budai** (mts.), China
92/A2 **Burhaniye**, Turk.
106/C3 **Burhānpur**, India
104/B3 **Burhi Dihing** (riv.), India
112/C2 **Burias** (isl.), Phil.
149/F4 **Burica** (pen.), CR, Pan.
149/F4 **Burica** (pt.), Pan.
165/C3 **Burien**, Wa,US
161/L2 **Burin**, Nf,Can
161/K2 **Burin** (pen.), Nf,Can
109/C3 **Buriram**, Thai.
141/B2 **Buritama**, Braz.
140/B1 **Buriti**, Braz.
141/B1 **Buriti Alegre**, Braz.
140/B2 **Buriti Bravo**, Braz.

179

Burit – Capit

140/B1 Buriti dos Lopes, Braz.
140/A4 Buritis, Braz.
141/C1 Buritizeiro, Braz.
75/E3 Burjasot, Sp.
70/D2 Burkardroth, Ger.
162/D3 Burkburnett, Tx,US
113/S Burke (isl.), Ant.
166/A6 Burke, Va,US
156/B2 Burke Channel (inlet), BC,Can
77/G4 Bürkelkopf (peak), Aus.
129/E3 Burkina Faso
70/C6 Burladingen, Ger.
156/E5 Burley, Id,US
165/K11 Burlingame, Ca,US
161/Q9 Burlington, On,Can
159/G3 Burlington, Co,US
168/B2 Burlington, Ct,US
157/L5 Burlington, Ia,US
159/J3 Burlington, Ks,US
163/J2 Burlington, NC,US
166/D3 Burlington, NJ,US
166/D4 Burlington (co.), NJ,US
161/F2 Burlington, Vt,US
165/P14 Burlington, Wi,US
107/G2 Burma (Myanmar)
83/K3 Burnas (lake), Ukr.
162/D4 Burnet, Tx,US
143/J8 Burney (peak), Chile
158/B2 Burney, Ca,US
59/G3 Burnham on Crouch, Eng,UK
58/D4 Burnham on Sea, Eng,UK
119/C4 Burnie-Somerset, Austl.
57/F4 Burnley, Eng,UK
54/D5 Burnmouth, Sc,UK
156/D5 Burns, Or,US
152/E2 Burnside (riv.), NW,Can
156/B2 Burns Lake, BC,Can
54/C4 Burntisland, Sc,UK
157/J2 Burntwood (riv.), Mb,Can
59/E1 Burntwood, Eng,UK
119/B2 Buronga, Austl.
96/B2 Burqin, China
96/B2 Burqin (riv.), China
115/H6 Burragorang (lake), Austl.
81/G2 Burrel, Alb.
119/D2 Burrendong (res.), Austl.
60/A3 Burren, The (reg.), Ire.
119/D2 Burrewarra (pt.), Austl.
75/E3 Burriana, Sp.
119/D2 Burrinjuck (res.), Austl.
146/E2 Burro, Serranías del (mts.), Mex.
118/A2 Burrowes (pt.), Austl.
56/D2 Burrow Head (pt.), Sc,UK
165/Q16 Burr Ridge, Il,US
118/D4 Burrum River Nat'l Park, Austl.
58/B3 Burry (inlet), Wal,UK
58/B3 Burry Port, Wal,UK
83/J5 Bursa, Turk.
83/J5 Bursa (prov.), Turk.
127/C3 Būr Safājah, Egypt
91/C4 Būr Sa'īd (gov.), Egypt
91/C4 Būr Sa'īd (Port Said), Egypt
67/E6 Burscheid, Ger.
57/F4 Burscough Bridge, Eng,UK
70/B3 Bürstadt, Ger.
127/D5 Būr Sūdān (Port Sudan), Sudan
161/S9 Burt, NY,US
127/C2 Būr Tawfīq, Egypt
59/E5 Burton, Eng,UK
165/E6 Burton, Mi,US
59/F2 Burton Latimer, Eng,UK
59/E1 Burton upon Trent, Eng,UK
111/G4 Buru (isl.), Indo.
91/B4 Burullus, Buḩayrat al (lag.), Egypt
112/C2 Buruncan (pt.), Phil.
130/A2 Burundi
96/F2 Burun Shibertuy (peak), Rus.
130/A3 Bururi, Buru.
140/A2 Buruticupu (riv.), Braz.
151/L3 Burwash Landing, Yk,Can
59/G2 Burwell, Eng,UK
159/H2 Burwell, Ne,US
59/F5 Bury, Eng,UK
89/M4 Buryat Aut. Rep., Rus.
87/J3 Burynshyk (pt.), Kaz.
59/G2 Bury Saint Edmunds, Eng,UK
112/D4 Busa (mtn.), Phil.
78/B3 Busalla, It.
163/H4 Busch Gardens, Fl,US
130/B2 Busembatia, Ugan.
56/B1 Bush (riv.), NI,UK
166/B5 Bush (riv.), Md,US
96/C2 Büs Hayrhan (peak), Mong.
93/G4 Būshehr, Iran
93/G4 Būshehr (gov.), Iran
53/M7 Bushey, Eng,UK
166/C1 Bushkill (falls), Pa,US
166/C1 Bush Kill (riv.), Pa,US
132/B3 Bushmanland (reg.), SAfr.
131/B4 Bushman Pits, Bots.
56/B1 Bushmills, NI,UK
130/B2 Busia, Kenya
125/K7 Businga, Zaire
62/C1 Buskerud (co.), Nor.
65/L3 Busko-Zdrój, Pol.
130/B2 Busoga (prov.), Ugan.
116/B5 Busselton, Austl.
125/L6 Busseri (riv.), Sudan
79/D2 Bussolengo, It.
66/C4 Bussum, Neth.
143/K7 Bustamente (pt.), Arg.
118/C4 Bustard (pt.), Austl.
83/G3 Buşteni, Rom.
78/B1 Busto Arsizio, It.
78/B1 Busto Garolfo, It.
125/K7 Buta, Zaire
130/A3 Butare, Rwa.
120/G4 Butaritari (atoll), Kiri.
156/B3 Bute (inlet), BC,Can
54/A5 Bute (isl.), Sc,UK
54/A5 Bute (sound), Sc,UK
96/E2 Büteeliyn (mts.), Mong.
130/C2 Bute Helu, Kenya
130/A2 Butembo, Zaire
141/B4 Butiá, Braz.
130/A2 Butiaba, Ugan.
167/H8 Butler, NJ,US
168/H6 Butler, Pa,US
168/H6 Butler (co.), Pa,US
111/F5 Buton (isl.), Indo.
53/S9 Butry-sur-Oise, Fr.
76/D4 Bütschelegg (peak), Swi.
156/E4 Butte, Mt,US
70/B3 Büttelborn, Ger.
110/B2 Butterworth, Malay.
112/D3 Butuan City, Phil.
111/F5 Butung (isl.), Indo.
87/G2 Buturlinovka, Rus.
70/B2 Butzbach, Ger.
64/F2 Bützow, Ger.
125/Q7 Buulo Berde, Som.
125/P7 Buur Hakaba, Som.
130/B2 Buvuma (isl.), Ugan.
67/G2 Buxtehude, Ger.
57/G5 Buxton, Eng,UK
84/J4 Buy, Rus.
87/H4 Buynaksk, Rus.
128/D5 Buyo, Barrage de (dam), IvC.
97/H2 Buyr (lake), Mong.
104/D4 Buyuan (riv.), China
93/N7 Büyükada (isl.), Turk.
83/J5 Büyükçekmece, Turk.
93/M6 Büyükçekmece (lake), Turk.
130/C4 Buyuni (pt.), Tanz.
103/E2 Buyun Shan (peak), China
87/J3 Buzachi (pen.), Kaz.
83/H3 Buzău, Rom.
83/H3 Buzău (co.), Rom.
83/H3 Buzău (riv.), Rom.
79/G2 Buzet, Cro.
131/D3 Búzi (riv.), Moz.
82/E3 Buziaş, Rom.
141/H8 Búzios (isl.), Braz.
87/K1 Buzuluk, Rus.
168/C3 Buzzards (bay), Ma,US
60/B5 Bweeng (mtn.), Ire.
83/G4 Byala, Bul.
83/F4 Byala Slatina, Bul.
153/R7 Byam Martin (chan.), NW,Can
153/R7 Byam Martin (isl.), NW,Can
65/J2 Bydgoszcz, Pol.
65/J2 Bydgoszcz (prov.), Pol.
59/E2 Byfield, Eng,UK
53/M8 Byfleet, Eng,UK
116/L7 Byford, Austl.
86/D1 Bykhov, Bela.
56/E5 Bylchau, Wal,UK
153/J1 Bylot (isl.), NW,Can
166/B4 Bynum (run), Md,US
93/F2 Byoyuk-Kirs (peak), Azer.
167/E2 Byram (pt.), Ct,US
167/E1 Byram (riv.), Ct, NY,US
167/L7 Byram (lake), NY,US
113/U Byrd (cape), Ant.
113/L Byrd (glac.), Ant.
143/J6 Byron (isl.), Chile
88/K2 Byrranga (mts.), Rus.
71/F2 Bystice (riv.), Czh.
65/K4 Bystrá (peak), Slvk.
89/N3 Bytantay (riv.), Rus.
65/K3 Bytom, Pol.
65/J1 Bytów, Pol.
93/M6 Büyükçekmece, Turk.

C

109/D2 Ca (riv.), Viet.
126/C3 Caála, Ang.
140/B2 Caatingas (reg.), Braz.
135/E2 Caazapá, Par.
112/D3 Cabadbaran, Phil.
149/G1 Cabaiguán, Cuba
158/F4 Caballo (res.), NM,US
74/C1 Cabañaquinta, Sp.
112/C2 Cabanatuan City, Phil.
58/C2 Caban Coch (res.), Wal,UK
161/G2 Cabano, Qu,Can
112/C1 Cabarroquis, Phil.
112/C3 Cabatuan, Phil.
140/D2 Cabedelo, Braz.
72/E5 Cabestany, Fr.
74/C3 Cabeza del Buey, Sp.
144/B3 Cabeza Lagarto (pt.), Peru
74/C1 Cabezón de la Sal, Sp.
138/D2 Cabimas, Ven.
126/B2 Cabinda, Ang.
140/D3 Cabo, Braz.
124/C2 Cabo Bojador, WSah.
130/C5 Cabo Delgado (prov.), Moz.
141/D2 Cabo Frio, Braz.
160/E2 Cabonga (res.), Qu,Can
118/D4 Caboolture, Austl.
137/H3 Cabo Orange Nat'l Park, Braz.
131/D2 Cabora Bassa (dam), Moz.
131/C2 Cabora Bassa (lake), Moz.
161/J2 Cabot (str.), Nf, NS,Can
141/G6 Cabo Verde, Braz.
74/C4 Cabra, Sp.
140/A5 Cabral (mts.), Braz.
150/D3 Cabral, DRep.
118/G8 Cabramatta, Austl.
80/A3 Cabras, It.
75/G3 Cabrera (isl.), Sp.
156/F3 Cabri, Sk,Can
74/E3 Cabriel (riv.), Sp.
140/C3 Cabrobó, Braz.
138/D2 Cabudare, Ven.
112/C1 Cabugao, Phil.
141/B3 Caçador, Braz.
82/E4 Čačak, Yugo.
141/H8 Caçapava, Braz.
80/A2 Caccia (cape), It.
136/G7 Cáceres, Braz.
138/C3 Cáceres, Col.
74/B3 Cáceres, Sp.
53/S10 Cachan, Fr.
142/Q10 Cachapoal (riv.), Chile
158/B3 Cache (cr.), Ca,US
165/L10 Cache (slough), Ca,US
156/E5 Cache (peak), Id,US
156/C3 Cache Creek, BC,Can
128/A3 Cacheu, GBis.
135/C2 Cachí, Arg.
137/G5 Cachimbo (mts.), Braz.
141/H7 Cachoeira de Minas, Braz.
141/A4 Cachoeira do Sul, Braz.
141/J7 Cachoeira Paulista, Braz.
141/L7 Cachoeiras de Macacu, Braz.
141/B4 Cachoeirinha, Braz.
141/D2 Cachoeiro de Itapemirim, Braz.
141/G6 Caconde, Braz.
141/B1 Caçu, Braz.
126/B3 Cacula, Ang.
140/B4 Caculé, Braz.
75/G1 Cadaques, Sp.
65/K4 Čadca, Slvk.
162/E3 Caddo (mts.), Ar,US
77/F5 Cadelle, Monte (peak), It.
58/C1 Cader Idris (mtn.), Wal,UK
117/G4 Cadibarrawirracanna (lake), Austl.
160/C2 Cadillac, Mi,US
112/C3 Cadiz, Phil.
74/B4 Cádiz, Sp.
74/B4 Cádiz (gulf), Sp.
160/C4 Cadiz, Ky,US
59/E5 Cadnam, Eng,UK
70/D4 Cadolzburg, Ger.
79/D1 Cadria, Monte (peak), It.
72/C2 Caen, Fr.
72/C2 Caen (har.), Fr.
58/D3 Caerleon, Wal,UK
56/D5 Caernafon Castle, Wal,UK
56/D5 Caernarfon, Wal,UK
56/D5 Caernarfon (bay), Wal,UK
58/C3 Caerphilly, Wal,UK
58/C1 Caersws, Wal,UK
91/F6 Caesarea Nat'l Park, Isr.
68/B2 Caëstre, Fr.
140/B4 Caetité, Braz.
140/B3 Cafarnaum, Braz.
135/C2 Cafayate, Arg.
112/C3 Cagayan (isls.), Phil.
112/D3 Cagayan de Oro City, Phil.
112/B4 Cagayan Sulu (isl.), Phil.
80/A3 Cagliari, It.
80/A3 Cagliari (gulf), It.
73/G5 Cagnes-sur-Mer, Fr.
112/C1 Cagoyan (riv.), Phil.
112/C1 Cagua (mtn.), Phil.
138/C4 Caguán (riv.), Col.
150/E3 Caguas, PR
60/A6 Caha (mts.), Ire.
126/B4 Cahama, Ang.
60/A5 Caherbarnagh (mtn.), Ire.
54/F11 Cahirsiveen (Cahirciveen), Ire.
60/D4 Cahore (pt.), Ire.
72/D4 Cahors, Fr.
138/D5 Cahuinari (riv.), Col.
149/F4 Cahuita (pt.), CR
149/F4 Cahuita Nat'l Park, CR
141/B4 Cai (riv.), Braz.
131/D3 Caia, Moz.
131/A1 Caianda, Ang.
137/H7 Caiapó (mts.), Braz.
137/H7 Caiapó (riv.), Braz.
149/G1 Caibarién, Cuba
139/F2 Caicara, Ven.
139/E3 Caicara de Orinoco, Ven.
138/C3 Caicedonia, Col.
140/C2 Caicó, Braz.
150/C2 Caicos (passg.), Bahm., Trks.
150/C2 Caicos (isls.), Trks.
141/G8 Caieiras, Braz.
68/A4 Cailly (riv.), Fr.
112/B2 Caiman (pt.), Phil.
112/F6 Cainta, Phil.
109/D4 Cai Nuoc, Viet.
78/D4 Caio, Monte (peak), It.
113/Y Caird (coast), Ant.
151/G3 Cairn (mtn.), Ak,US
119/B3 Cairn Curran (dam), Austl.
54/B4 Cairndow, Sc,UK
54/C2 Cairn Gorm (mtn.), Sc,UK
54/C2 Cairngorm (mts.), Sc,UK
56/C2 Cairn Pat (hill), Sc,UK
56/C2 Cairnryan, Sc,UK
118/B2 Cairns, Austl.
117/G2 Cairns (peak), Austl.
54/B6 Cairnsmore of Carsphairn (mtn.), Sc,UK
54/B6 Cairn Table (mtn.), Sc,UK
54/C2 Cairn Toul (mtn.), Sc,UK
163/G4 Cairo, Ga,US
160/B4 Cairo, Il,US
91/B4 Cairo (Al Qāhirah) (cap.), Egypt
78/B4 Cairo Montenotte, It.
59/H1 Caister on Sea, Eng,UK
57/H5 Caistor, Eng,UK
161/Q9 Caistor Centre, On,Can
161/Q9 Caistorville, On,Can
126/B3 Caitou, Ang.
126/C4 Caiundo, Ang.
103/C5 Caizi (lake), China
138/B5 Cajabamba, Ecu.
144/B2 Cajabamba, Peru
144/B2 Cajamarca (ruins), Peru
140/A1 Cajari, Braz.
140/C2 Cajazeiras, Braz.
112/C2 Cajidiocan, Phil.
149/E1 Cajón (pt.), Cuba
140/B1 Caju (isl.), Braz.
129/H5 Calabar, Nga.
139/E2 Calabozo, Ven.
80/E3 Calabria (reg.), It.
80/D3 Calabria Nat'l Park, It.
80/E3 Calabria Nat'l Park, It.
74/C4 Calaburras, Punta de (pt.), Sp.
82/F4 Calafat, Rom.
112/C2 Calagua (isls.), Phil.
74/E1 Calahorra, Sp.
68/A2 Calais, Fr.
161/H2 Calais, Me,US
68/A2 Calais, Canal de (can.), Fr.
135/C2 Calalaste (mts.), Arg.
135/C1 Calama, Chile
112/B2 Calamian (isls.), Phil.
82/F3 Călan, Rom.
112/C2 Calapan, Phil.
83/H3 Călăraşi, Rom.
83/H3 Călăraşi (co.), Rom.
138/C3 Calarcá, Col.
74/E3 Calasparra, Sp.
74/E2 Calatayud, Sp.
112/C2 Calauag, Phil.
165/L12 Calaveras (res.), Ca,US
112/C2 Calavite (cape), Phil.
112/C2 Calavite (mtn.), Phil.
112/C1 Calayan, Phil.
112/C1 Calayan (isl.), Phil.
112/D2 Calbayog City, Phil.
112/D3 Calbiga, Phil.
142/B4 Calbuco, Chile
144/D4 Calca, Peru
140/D2 Calcanhar, Ponta do (pt.), Braz.
162/E4 Calcasieu (riv.), La,US
138/A5 Calceta, Ecu.
160/F2 Calcium, NY,US
137/H3 Calçoene, Braz.
106/E3 Calcutta, India
141/G6 Caldas, Braz.
138/C3 Caldas (dept.), Col.
74/A3 Caldas da Rainha, Port.
141/B1 Caldas Novas, Braz.
57/E2 Caldbeck, Eng,UK
67/G6 Calden, Ger.
57/G4 Calder (riv.), Eng,UK
151/M4 Calder (mtn.), Ak,US
54/C5 Caldercruix, Sc,UK
75/L6 Caldes de Montbui, Sp.
57/F2 Caldew (riv.), Eng,UK
58/D3 Caldicot, Wal,UK
156/D5 Caldwell, Id,US
167/H8 Caldwell, NJ,US
162/D4 Caldwell, Tx,US
58/B3 Caldy (isl.), Wal,UK
132/D3 Caledon (riv.), Les., SAfr.
161/Q8 Caledon East, On,Can
161/H2 Caledonia (hills), NB,Can
54/B2 Caledonian (can.), Sc,UK
75/G2 Calella, Sp.
79/E5 Calenzano, It.
142/Q9 Calera de Tango, Chile
149/H1 Caleta (pt.), Cuba
142/D5 Caleta Olivia, Arg.
158/D4 Calexico, Ca,US
55/N13 Calfsound, Sc,UK
57/G3 Calf, The (mtn.), Eng,UK
156/E3 Calgary, Ab,Can
75/S12 Calheta, Azor.,Port.
75/U15 Calheta, Madr.,Port.
163/G3 Calhoun, Ga,US
160/C4 Calhoun, Ky,US
138/B4 Cali, Col.
74/E4 Calida, Costa (coast), Sp.
158/D3 Caliente, Nv,US
158/B3 California (state), US
164/C2 California (aqueduct), Ca,US
160/E4 California, Md,US
159/J3 California, Mo,US
135/D1 Calilegua Nat'l Park, Arg.
83/G3 Călimăneşti, Rom.
108/G3 Calimere (pt.), India
147/H4 Calkiní, Mex.
117/J4 Callabonna (lake), Austl.
54/B4 Callander, Sc,UK
144/B4 Callao, Peru
60/B4 Callaun (mtn.), Ire.
163/G4 Callaway, Fl,US
142/Q9 Calle Larga, Chile
58/B6 Callington, Eng,UK
75/E3 Callosa de Ensarriá, Sp.
75/E3 Callosa de Segura, Sp.
58/D4 Calne, Eng,UK
78/C1 Calolziocorte, It.
68/B3 Calonne-Ricouart, Fr.
112/E6 Caloocan, Phil.
80/D2 Calore (riv.), It.
147/H4 Calotmul, Mex.
118/D4 Caloundra, Austl.
75/F3 Calpe, Sp.
147/L7 Calpulálpan, Mex.
58/B6 Calstock, Eng,UK
80/D4 Caltagirone, It.
80/D4 Caltanissetta, It.
72/F4 Caluire-et-Cuire, Fr.
165/Q16 Calumet (riv.), Il,US
165/Q16 Calumet City, Il,US
165/Q16 Calumet Sag (chan.), Il,US
126/B3 Caluquembe, Ang.
156/A3 Calvert (isl.), BC,Can
57/G5 Calverton, Eng,UK
166/B5 Calverton, Md,US
167/F2 Calverton, NY,US
75/G3 Calviá, Sp.
146/E4 Calvillo, Mex.
79/E4 Calvi, Monte (peak), It.
132/B3 Calvinia, SAfr.
74/C2 Calvitero (mtn.), Sp.
70/B5 Calw, Ger.
59/G2 Cam (riv.), Eng,UK
140/C4 Camaçari, Braz.
126/C3 Camacupa, Ang.
149/G1 Camagüey, Cuba
149/G1 Camagüey (arch.), Cuba
78/D5 Camaiore, It.
149/G1 Camajuaní, Cuba
140/C4 Camamu, Braz.
140/C4 Camamu (bay), Braz.
144/C5 Camaná, Peru
141/G7 Camanducaia, Braz.
141/B4 Camaquã, Braz.
141/A4 Camaquã (riv.), Braz.
75/V15 Câmara de Lobos, Madr.,Port.
73/G5 Camarat (cape), Fr.
74/D1 Camargo, Sp.
164/A2 Camarillo, Ca,US
74/A1 Camariñas, Sp.
149/E3 Camarón (cape), Hon.
142/D5 Camarones (bay), Arg.
74/B4 Camas, Sp.
109/D4 Ca Mau, Viet.
109/D4 Ca Mau (cape), Viet.
148/D3 Camayagua (mts.), Hon.
74/A1 Cambados, Sp.
141/B2 Cambará, Braz.
106/B3 Cambay, India
106/B3 Cambay (gulf), India
141/B2 Cambé, Braz.
59/F4 Camberley Frimley, Eng,UK
53/N7 Camberwell, Eng,UK
109/D3 Cambodia
141/C3 Camboriú, Ponta do (pt.), Braz.
58/A6 Camborne, Eng,UK
68/C3 Cambrai, Fr.
58/C2 Cambrian (mts.), Wal,UK
160/D3 Cambridge, On,Can
115/S10 Cambridge, NZ
59/G2 Cambridge, Eng,UK
168/C1 Cambridge, Ma,US
160/E4 Cambridge, Md,US
157/K4 Cambridge, Mn,US
160/D3 Cambridge, Oh,US
59/G2 Cambridgeshire (co.), Eng,UK
75/F2 Cambrils, Sp.
141/G7 Cambuí, Braz.
141/H6 Cambuquira, Braz.
54/B5 Cambuslang, Sc,UK
149/F5 Cambutal (mtn.), Pan.
119/D2 Camden, Austl.
53/N7 Camden (bor.), Eng,UK
163/G4 Camden, Al,US
162/E3 Camden, Ar,US
161/G2 Camden, Me,US
166/C4 Camden, NJ,US
166/D4 Camden (co.), NJ,US
163/H3 Camden, SC,US
159/J3 Camdenton, Mo,US
126/D3 Cameia Nat'l Park, Ang.
58/B6 Camel (riv.), Eng,UK
166/C1 Camelback (mtn.), Pa,US
58/B5 Camelford, Eng,UK
78/B2 Cameri, It.
153/R7 Cameron (isl.), NW,Can
158/E4 Cameron, Az,US
162/E4 Cameron, La,US
159/J3 Cameron, Mo,US
162/D4 Cameron, Tx,US
129/H5 Cameroon
137/J4 Cametá, Braz.
68/A2 Camiers, Fr.
112/D3 Camiguin (isl.), Phil.
112/C2 Camiling, Phil.
163/G4 Camilla, Ga,US
136/F8 Camiri, Bol.
92/C1 Çamlıdere, Turk.
92/C2 Çamlık Nat'l Park, Turk.
60/C2 Camlin (riv.), Ire.
91/D1 Çamlıyayla, Turk.
131/D4 Camo-Camo, Moz.
140/B1 Camocim, Braz.
107/F6 Camorta (isl.), India
112/D3 Camotes (sea), Phil.
68/A3 Campagne, Fr.
142/F2 Campana, Arg.
143/J7 Campana (isl.), Chile
142/C2 Campanario (peak), Arg.
80/D2 Campanella (cape), It.
141/H6 Campanha, Braz.
80/D2 Campania (reg.), It.
51/T8 Campbell (isl.), NZ
165/L12 Campbell, Ca,US
168/G5 Campbell, Oh,US
156/A2 Campbell Island, BC,Can
156/B3 Campbell River, BC,Can
160/C4 Campbellsville, Ky,US
161/H2 Campbellton, NB,Can
118/G9 Campbelltown, Austl.
161/Q9 Campbellville, On,Can
55/J9 Campbeltown, Sc,UK
161/R9 Campden, On,Can
141/H5 Campeche, Mex.
147/G4 Campeche (bay), Mex.
147/H5 Campeche (state), Mex.
157/H3 Camperville, Mb,Can
141/G6 Campestre, Braz.
109/D1 Cam Pha, Viet.
166/B3 Camp Hill, Pa,US
79/E5 Campi Bisenzio, It.
80/A3 Campidano (range), It.
74/C4 Campillos, Sp.
140/D2 Campina Grande, Braz.
141/F7 Campinas, Braz.
141/B1 Campina Verde, Braz.
138/C4 Campoalegre, Col.
80/D2 Campobasso, It.
141/C2 Campo Belo, Braz.
74/D3 Campo de Criptana, Sp.
78/B1 Campo dei Fiori (peak), It.
138/C2 Campo de la Cruz, Col.
140/B3 Campo Formoso, Braz.
137/H8 Campo Grande, Braz.
135/G2 Campo Largo, Braz.
141/G8 Campo Limpo Paulista, Braz.
140/B2 Campo Maior, Braz.
74/B3 Campo Maior, Port.
78/B4 Campomorone, It.
141/A3 Campo Mourão, Braz.
140/C2 Campo Redondo, Braz.
74/C1 Camporredondo (res.), Sp.
141/D2 Campos, Braz.
140/A4 Campos (reg.), Braz.
141/C1 Campos Altos, Braz.
140/A4 Campos Belos, Braz.
75/G3 Campos del Puerto, Sp.
141/H7 Campos do Jordão, Braz.
141/C2 Campos Gerais, Braz.
141/B3 Campos Novos, Braz.
140/B2 Campos Sales, Braz.
77/E5 Campo Tencia, Pizzo (peak), Swi.
164/C4 Camp Pendleton Marine Corps Base, Ca,US
54/B4 Campsie Fells (hills), Sc,UK
166/B6 Camp Springs, Md,US
162/E4 Campti, La,US
109/E4 Cam Ranh, Viet.
156/E2 Camrose, Ab,Can
109/D1 Cam Thuy, Viet.
83/H5 Çan, Turk.
139/G5 Canaçari (lake), Braz.
152/E2 Canada
142/E2 Cañada de Gómez, Arg.
159/H4 Canadian (riv.), US
162/C3 Canadian, Tx,US
142/C5 Cañadón Grande (mts.), Arg.
138/D2 Canagua, Ven.
139/F3 Canaima Nat'l Park, Ven.
83/H5 Çanakkale, Turk.
83/H5 Çanakkale (prov.), Turk.
121/U12 Canala, NCal.
79/E2 Canalbianco (riv.), It.
142/F3 Canal No. 1 (can.), Arg.
142/F3 Canal No. 11 (can.), Arg.
143/F3 Canal No. 2 (riv.), Arg.
143/F3 Canal No. 5 (riv.), Arg.
142/F3 Canal No. 9 (can.), Arg.
142/E2 Canals, Arg.
75/E3 Canals, Sp.
160/E3 Canandaigua, NY,US
146/C2 Cananea, Mex.
141/C3 Cananéia, Braz.
141/B1 Canápolis, Braz.
144/B1 Cañar, Ecu.
138/B5 Cañar (prov.), Ecu.
165/G7 Canard (riv.), On,Can
149/F1 Canarreos (arch.), Cuba
167/K9 Canarsie, NY,US
75/X16 Canary Is. (aut. comm.), Sp.
149/E4 Cañas, CR
78/D3 Canassa, It.
163/H4 Canaveral (cape), Fl,US
140/C4 Canavieiras, Braz.
119/D2 Canberra (cap.), Austl.
68/A3 Canche (riv.), Fr.
148/E1 Cancún, Mex.
92/A2 Çandarlı (gulf), Turk.
74/C1 Candás, Sp.
140/C4 Candeias, Braz.
147/H5 Candelaria (riv.), Mex.
78/B1 Candelo, It.
161/N7 Candiac, Qu,Can
140/B4 Candiba, Braz.
141/B2 Candido Mota, Braz.
110/D5 Canding (cape), Indo.
92/C2 Çandır, Turk.
157/G2 Candle (lake), Sk,Can
168/A2 Candlewood (res.), Ct,US
167/D3 Candlewood, NJ,US
157/J3 Cando, ND,US
112/C1 Candon, Phil.
78/B1 Canegrate, It.
141/B4 Canela, Braz.
78/B3 Canelli, It.
143/F2 Canelones, Uru.
143/F2 Canelones (dept.), Uru.
144/B4 Canete (riv.), Peru
74/A1 Cangas, Sp.
74/B1 Cangas de Narcea, Sp.
74/C1 Cangas de Onís, Sp.
110/C5 Cangkuang (cape), Indo.
132/C4 Cango Caves, SAfr.
126/D3 Cangombe, Ang.
143/J7 Cangrejo (peak), Arg.
103/D4 Cangshan, China
140/D2 Canguaretama, Braz.
141/A4 Canguçu, Braz.
107/K3 Cangwu, China
104/C4 Cangyuan Vazu Zizhixian (Cangyuan), China
103/D3 Cangzhou, China
109/D1 Canh Cuoc (isl.), Viet.
126/B3 Canhoca, Ang.
118/C4 Cania Gorge Nat'l Park, Austl.
153/K3 Caniapiscau (lake), Qu,Can
153/K3 Caniapiscau (riv.), Qu,Can
80/C4 Canicattì, It.
72/E5 Canigou, Pic de (peak), Fr.
92/C1 Canik (mts.), Turk.
74/D4 Caniles, Sp.
140/C2 Canindé, Braz.
140/B2 Canindé (riv.), Braz.
167/H7 Canistear (res.), NJ,US
92/C1 Çankırı, Turk.
92/C1 Çankırı (prov.), Turk.
112/C3 Canlaon (vol.), Phil.
156/E3 Canmore, Ab,Can
55/H8 Canna (isl.), Sc,UK
108/E3 Cannanore, India
80/E2 Canne (ruins), It.
69/F5 Canner (riv.), Fr.
73/G5 Cannes, Fr.
54/B2 Cannich, Sc,UK
54/B2 Cannich (riv.), Sc,UK
116/C4 Canning (peak), Austl.
116/L7 Canning (res.), Austl.
116/K7 Canning (riv.), Austl.
58/D1 Cannock, Eng,UK
159/G4 Cannon A.F.B., NM,US
157/H4 Cannonball (riv.), ND,US
157/K4 Cannon Falls, Mn,US
141/B4 Canoas, Braz.
141/B3 Canoas (riv.), Braz.
119/D2 Canobolas (peak), Austl.
156/F2 Canoe (lake), Sk,Can
164/E7 Canoga Park, Ca,US
138/D3 Caño Guaritico (riv.), Ven.
141/B3 Canoinhas, Braz.
57/F1 Canonbie, Sc,UK
159/F3 Canon City, Co,US
148/C2 Cañon del Sumidero Nat'l Park, Mex.
147/M8 Cañon de Río Blanco Nat'l Park, Mex.
149/E4 Caño Negro Nat'l Wild. Ref., CR
157/H3 Canora, Sk,Can
150/F4 Canouan (isl.), StV.
140/C3 Cansanção, Braz.
161/J2 Canso (cape), Can.
74/C1 Cantabria (aut. comm.), Sp.
72/E4 Cantal (plat.), Fr.
140/A1 Cantanhede, Braz.
74/A2 Cantanhede, Port.
139/E2 Cantaura, Ven.
118/H8 Canterbury, Austl.
115/R11 Canterbury (bight), NZ
59/H4 Canterbury, Eng,UK
59/H4 Canterbury Cathedral, Eng,UK
109/D4 Can Tho, Viet.
112/D3 Cantilan, Phil.
74/C4 Cantillana, Sp.
140/B3 Canto do Buriti, Braz.
168/B2 Canton, Ct,US
160/B3 Canton, Il,US
168/C1 Canton, Ma,US
165/E7 Canton, Mi,US
163/F3 Canton, Ms,US
160/F2 Canton, NY,US
168/F6 Canton, Oh,US
159/H3 Canton, Ok,US
157/J5 Canton, SD,US
162/E3 Canton, Tx,US
121/H5 Canton (Abariringa) (atoll), Kiri.
105/G4 Canton (Guangzhou), China
78/C1 Cantù, It.
142/F2 Cañuelas, Arg.
119/B3 Canunda Nat'l Park, Austl.
59/G3 Canvey Island, Eng,UK
156/G2 Canwood, Sk,Can
162/C3 Canyon, Tx,US
158/E3 Canyon de Chelly Nat'l Mon., Az,US
158/E3 Canyonlands Nat'l Park, Ut,US
101/C2 Cao (riv.), China
109/D1 Cao Bang, Viet.
105/E3 Caodu (riv.), China
105/J2 Cao'e (riv.), China
54/A3 Caol, Sc,UK
109/D4 Cao Lanh, Viet.
79/F1 Caorle, It.
103/C4 Cao Xian, China
112/B4 Cap (isl.), Phil.
112/C2 Capalonga, Phil.
138/D3 Capanaparo (riv.), Ven.
137/J4 Capanema, Braz.
80/B1 Capanne (peak), It.
78/D5 Capannori, It.
141/B3 Capão Bonito, Braz.
141/D2 Caparaó Nat'l Park, Braz.
74/A3 Caparica, Port.
138/D3 Caparo (riv.), Ven.
161/H1 Cap-Chat, Qu,Can
161/F2 Cap-de-la-Madeleine, Qu,Can
118/B3 Cape (riv.), Austl.
116/D5 Cape Arid Nat'l Park, Austl.
119/D4 Cape Barren (isl.), Austl.
161/J2 Cape Breton (highlands), NS,Can
161/J2 Cape Breton (isl.), NS,Can
161/J2 Cape Breton Highlands Nat'l Park, NS,Can
118/B2 Cape Cleveland Nat'l Park, Austl.
129/E5 Cape Coast, Gha.
161/G3 Cape Cod Nat'l Seashore, Ma,US
163/H5 Cape Coral, Fl,US
163/J3 Cape Fear (riv.), NC,US
159/K3 Cape Girardeau, Mo,US
163/K3 Cape Hatteras Nat'l Seashore, NC,US
151/E2 Cape Krusenstern Nat'l Mon., Ak,US
53/Q8 Capel, Eng,UK
140/C3 Capela, Braz.
56/E5 Capel-Curig, Wal,UK
116/D5 Cape Le Grande Nat'l Park, Austl.
141/D1 Capelinha, Braz.
75/K6 Capellades, Sp.
59/H4 Capel le Ferne, Eng,UK
163/J3 Cape Lookout Nat'l Seashore, NC,US
59/H2 Capel Saint Mary, Eng,UK
166/D5 Cape May (co.), NJ,US
166/D6 Cape May Lighthouse, NJ,US
118/B1 Cape Melville Nat'l Park, Austl.
118/C3 Cape Palmerston Nat'l Park, Austl.
116/B2 Cape Range Nat'l Park, Austl.
166/B5 Cape Saint Claire, Md,US
132/B4 Cape Town (cap.), SAfr.
118/B2 Cape Tribulation Nat'l Park, Austl.
118/B2 Cape Upstart Nat'l Park, Austl.
122/K9 Cape Verde
118/A1 Cape York (pen.), Austl.
149/H2 Cap-Haïtien, Haiti
80/A2 Capicciola (pt.), Fr.
137/J4 Capim (riv.), Braz.
140/D2 Capina, Braz.
141/B1 Capinópolis, Braz.
141/B2 Capirara (res.), Braz.
140/C2 Capistrano, Braz.
162/B3 Capitan (mts.), NM,US
140/B2 Capitão de Campos, Braz.
137/J4 Capitão Poco, Braz.

180

Capit – Chalf

158/E3 Capitol Reef Nat'l Park, Ut,US
140/A4 Capivara (mts.), Braz.
137/H8 Capivara (res.), Braz.
141/J6 Capivari (riv.), Braz.
82/C4 Čapljina, Bosn.
78/D1 Caplone, Monte (peak), It.
131/D2 Capoche (riv.), Moz.
80/D3 Capo d'Orlando, It.
80/A3 Capoterra, It.
112/D2 Capotoan (mtn.), Phil.
80/A1 Capraia (isl.), It.
160/D2 Capreol, On,Can
80/D2 Capri, It.
118/C3 Capricorn (cape), Austl.
118/C3 Capricorn (chan.), Austl.
78/C1 Capriolo, It.
131/A3 Caprivi Strip (reg.), Namb.
162/C3 Cap Rock Escarpment (cliffs), Tx,US
162/C3 Caprock, The (cliffs), NM,US
161/G2 Cap-Rouge, Qu,Can
73/G5 Cap Roux, Pointe du (pt.), Fr.
167/L7 Captain (har.), Ct,US
147/K7 Capulhuac de Mirafuentes, Mex.
159/G3 Capulin Volcano Nat'l Mon., NM,US
138/C4 Caquetá (dept.), Col.
138/D5 Caquetá (riv.), Col.
75/N9 Carabanchel (nrbhd.), Sp.
138/D2 Carabobo (state), Ven.
83/G3 Caracal, Rom.
139/E2 Caracas (cap.), Ven.
140/B3 Caracol, Braz.
58/B5 Caradon (hill), Eng,UK
112/D4 Caraga, Phil.
141/H8 Caraguatatuba, Braz.
141/H8 Caraguatatuba (bay), Braz.
142/B3 Carahue, Chile
137/H5 Carajás (mts.), Braz.
112/C2 Caramoan, Phil.
112/D2 Caramoran, Phil.
136/E7 Caranavi, Bol.
141/D2 Carandaí, Braz.
141/D2 Carangola, Braz.
82/F3 Caransebeş, Rom.
80/D2 Carapelle (riv.), It.
141/G8 Carapicuíba, Braz.
117/H5 Carappee Hill (peak), Austl.
161/H2 Caraquet, NB,Can
82/E3 Caraş-Severin (co.), Rom.
149/F3 Caratasca (lag.), Hon.
78/C1 Carate Brianza, It.
141/D1 Caratinga, Braz.
136/E4 Carauari, Braz.
140/C2 Caraúbas, Braz.
74/E3 Caravaca de la Cruz, Sp.
78/C2 Caravaggio, It.
128/A4 Caravela (isl.), GBis.
140/C5 Caravelas, Braz.
135/F2 Carazinho, Braz.
74/A1 Carballino, Sp.
74/A1 Carballo, Sp.
157/J3 Carberry, Mb,Can
123/U17 Carbon (cape), Alg.
166/C2 Carbon (co.), Pa,US
165/C3 Carbon (riv.), Wa,US
80/A3 Carbonara (cape), It.
80/D4 Carbonara, Pizzo (peak), It.
160/B4 Carbondale, Il,US
160/F3 Carbondale, Pa,US
80/A3 Carbonia, It.
55/H8 Carbost, Sc,UK
75/E3 Carcagente, Sp.
112/C3 Carcar, Phil.
142/E2 Carcaraña, Arg.
72/E5 Carcassonne, Fr.
75/P10 Carcavelos, Port.
74/E3 Carche (mtn.), Sp.
138/B4 Carchi (prov.), Ecu.
152/C2 Carcross, Yt,Can
108/F4 Cardamon (hills), India
75/L6 Cardedeu, Sp.
149/F1 Cárdenas, Cuba
147/F4 Cárdenas, Mex.
148/C2 Cárdenas, Mex.
54/C4 Cardenden, Sc,UK
143/K7 Cardiel (lake), Arg.
58/C4 Cardiff (cap.), Wal,UK
58/B2 Cardigan, Wal,UK
75/F2 Cardona, Sp.
141/B2 Cardoso, Braz.
156/E3 Cardston, Ab,Can
141/H7 Careaçu, Braz.
77/G5 Care Alto, Monte (peak), It.
82/F2 Carei, Rom.
72/C2 Carentan, Fr.
82/F4 Carev vrh (peak), Macd.
116/D4 Carey (lake), Austl.
72/B2 Carhaix-Plouguer, Fr.
142/E3 Carhué, Arg.
141/D2 Cariacica, Braz.
139/F2 Cariaco, Ven.
144/B2 Cariamanga, Ecu.
80/E3 Cariati, It.
145/K8 Caribbean (sea), NAm., SAm.
156/C2 Cariboo (mts.), BC,Can
152/E3 Caribou (mts.), Ab,Can
160/B1 Caribou (lake), On,Can
151/L3 Caribou, Yk,Can
156/F5 Caribou (range), Id,US
161/G2 Caribou, Me,US
112/D3 Carigara, Phil.
78/A3 Carignano, It.
140/B4 Carinhanha, Braz.
140/A4 Carinhanha (riv.), Braz.
80/C3 Carini, It.
73/K3 Carinthia (prov.), Aus.
139/F2 Caripito, Ven.
140/C2 Caririaçu, Braz.
140/B2 Cariri Novos (mts.), Braz.
159/G3 Carizzo (cr.), NM, Tx,US
159/G3 Carizzo (creek), NM, Tx,US
75/E3 Carlet, Sp.
161/H2 Carleton (peak), NB,Can
161/H2 Carleton (riv.), NS,Can
161/H1 Carleton, Qu,Can
160/E2 Carleton Place, On,Can
132/D2 Carletonville, SAfr.
158/C2 Carlin, Nv,US
116/C2 Carlindie Abor. Land, Austl.
118/H8 Carlingford, Austl.
60/D1 Carlingford (mtn.), Ire.
56/B3 Carlingford Lough (inlet), Ire.
160/B4 Carlinville, Il,US
161/Q9 Carlisle, On,Can
57/F2 Carlisle, Eng,UK
166/A3 Carlisle, Pa,US
166/A3 Carlisle Barracks, Pa,US
72/D5 Carlit (peak), Fr.
142/E2 Carlos Casares, Arg.
141/D1 Carlos Chagas, Braz.
149/G1 Carlos M. De Cespedes, Cuba
60/D4 Carlow, Ire.
60/D4 Carlow (co.), Ire.
55/H7 Carloway, Sc,UK
164/C4 Carlsbad, Ca,US
159/F4 Carlsbad, NM,US
159/F4 Carlsbad Caverns Nat'l Park, NM,US
57/G6 Carlton, Eng,UK
157/K4 Carlton, Mn,US
161/Q9 Carluke, On,Can
54/C5 Carluke, Sc,UK
157/H3 Carlyle, Sk,Can
159/K3 Carlyle (lake), Il,US
152/C2 Carmacks, Yk,Can
78/A3 Carmagnola, It.
157/J3 Carman, Mb,Can
58/B3 Carmarthen, Wal,UK
58/B3 Carmarthen (bay), Wal,UK
72/E4 Carmaux, Fr.
91/D3 Carmel (mtn.), Isr.
160/C4 Carmel, In,US
56/D5 Carmel Head (pt.), Wal,UK
91/D3 Carmel, Mount (Har Karmel) (mtn.), Isr.
142/F2 Carmelo, Uru.
146/C3 Carmen (isl.), Mex.
160/B4 Carmi, Il,US
165/M9 Carmichael, Ca,US
141/L6 Carmo, Braz.
141/H6 Carmo da Cachoeira, Braz.
141/H7 Carmo de Minas, Braz.
141/C1 Carmo do Paranaíba, Braz.
141/C2 Carmo do Rio Claro, Braz.
78/B4 Carmo, Monte (peak), It.
74/C4 Carmona, Sp.
56/B1 Carnanmore (mtn.), NI,UK
114/A4 Carnarvon, Austl.
132/C3 Carnarvonleegte (dry riv.), SAfr.
118/B4 Carnarvon Nat'l Park, Austl.
75/P10 Carnaxide, Port.
54/B2 Carn Ban (mtn.), Sc,UK
56/C2 Carncastle, NI,UK
157/H3 Carnduff, Sk,Can
54/B2 Carn Easgann Bàna (mtn.), Sc,UK
56/D5 Carnedd Dafydd (mtn.), Wal,UK
56/E5 Carnedd Llewelyn (mtn.), Wal,UK
116/D3 Carnegie (lake), Austl.
168/G7 Carnegie, Pa,US
54/A2 Càrn Eige (mtn.), Sc,UK
113/S Carney (isl.), Ant.
57/F3 Carnforth, Eng,UK
54/C2 Carn Glas-choire (mtn.), Sc,UK
68/C3 Carnières, Fr.
54/C2 Carn Kitty (hill), Sc,UK
56/B2 Carnlough, NI,UK
54/B3 Carn Mairg (mtn.), Sc,UK
54/C2 Carn Mór (mtn.), Sc,UK
54/C1 Carn na Cailliche (hill), Sc,UK
54/B2 Carn na Saobhaidhe (mtn.), Sc,UK
140/C2 Carnoió, Braz.
117/G5 Carnot (cape), Austl.
124/J7 Carnot, CAfr.
74/A1 Carnota, Sp.
168/G6 Carnot-Moon, Pa,US
54/D4 Carnoustie, Sc,UK
60/D5 Carnsore (pt.), Ire.
152/D2 Carnwath (riv.), NW,Can
54/C5 Carnwath, Sc,UK
160/D3 Caro, Mi,US
140/A2 Carolina, Braz.
150/E3 Carolina, PR
121/K5 Caroline (isl.), Kiri.
120/D4 Caroline (isls.), Micr.
166/C6 Caroline (co.), Md,US
165/P16 Carol Stream, Il,US
139/F3 Caroní (riv.), Ven.
138/D2 Carora, Ven.
76/C5 Carouge, Swi.
86/B2 Carpathian (mts.), Eur.
79/F5 Carpegna, Monte (peak), It.
78/D2 Carpenedolo, It.
114/F2 Carpentaria (gulf), Austl.
165/P15 Carpentersville, Il,US
72/F4 Carpentras, Fr.
79/D3 Carpi, It.
164/A2 Carpinteria, Ca,US
165/B3 Carr (inlet), Wa,US
163/G4 Carrabelle, Fl,US
60/A2 Carra, Lough (lake), Ire.
60/A6 Carran (mtn.), Ire.
60/A5 Carrantuohill (mtn.), Ire.
148/C2 Carranza, Mex.
78/D4 Carrara, It.
54/C2 Carrbridge, Sc,UK
56/D6 Carreg Ddu (pt.), Wal,UK
150/F4 Carriacou (isl.), Gren.
54/B6 Carrick (dist.), Sc,UK
56/C2 Carrickfergus, NI,UK
56/C2 Carrickfergus (dist.), NI,UK
56/A2 Carrickmore, NI,UK
53/S10 Carrières-sous-Poissy, Fr.
56/B3 Carrigatuke (mtn.), NI,UK
60/B6 Carrigtohill, Ire.
157/J4 Carrington, ND,US
74/C1 Carrión (riv.), Sp.
154/E4 Carrizo (mts.), Az,US
162/C2 Carrizo (cr.), NM,US
162/D4 Carrizo Springs, Tx,US
158/E4 Carrizo Wash (dry riv.), Az, NM,US
159/F4 Carrizozo, NM,US
166/A5 Carroll (co.), Md,US
168/F6 Carroll (co.), Oh,US
163/G3 Carrollton, Ga,US
160/C4 Carrollton, Ky,US
159/J3 Carrollton, Mo,US
54/A2 Carron (riv.), Sc,UK
54/A2 Carron, Loch (inlet), Sc,UK
157/H2 Carrot (riv.), Sk,Can
157/H2 Carrot River, Sk,Can
56/C2 Carrowdore, NI,UK
119/G6 Carrum Downs, Austl.
56/C2 Carryduff, NI,UK
92/D1 Çarşamba, Turk.
164/B3 Carson, Ca,US
158/C3 Carson (riv.), Nv,US
158/C3 Carson (sink), Nv,US
158/C3 Carson City (cap.), Nv,US
56/D1 Carsphairn, Sc,UK
156/E3 Carstairs, Ab,Can
54/C5 Carstairs Junction, Sc,UK
162/D3 Carswell A.F.B., Tx,US
142/Q9 Cartagena, Chile
138/C2 Cartagena, Col.
75/E4 Cartagena, Sp.
138/C3 Cartago, Col.
149/F4 Cartago, CR
74/C4 Cártama, Sp.
74/A3 Cartaxo, Port.
74/B4 Cartaya, Sp.
118/A1 Carter (peak), Austl.
54/D6 Carter Bar (hill), Eng,UK
167/D2 Carteret, NJ,US
163/G3 Cartersville, Ga,US
59/E3 Carterton, Eng,UK
80/B4 Carthage (ruins), Tun.
159/J3 Carthage, Mo,US
163/F3 Carthage, Ms,US
163/G2 Carthage, Tn,US
162/E3 Carthage, Tx,US
149/G4 Cartí (mtn.), Pan.
114/C2 Cartier Islet (isl.), Austl.
153/L3 Cartwright, Nf,Can
140/D3 Caruaru, Braz.
136/F1 Carúpano, Ven.
159/K3 Caruthersville, Mo,US
168/D2 Carver, Ma,US
68/B2 Carvin, Fr.
74/A3 Carvoeiro (cape), Port.
165/P15 Cary, Il,US
163/J3 Cary, NC,US
123/L14 Casablanca, Mor.
141/F6 Casa Branca, Braz.
158/E4 Casa Grande, Az,US
158/E4 Casa Grande Nat'l Mon., Az,US
80/D2 Casal di Principe, It.
79/E4 Casalecchio di Reno, It.
78/B2 Casale Monferrato, It.
78/D3 Casalmaggiore, It.
78/C2 Casalpusterlengo, It.
128/A3 Casamance (riv.), Sen.
138/C3 Casanare (inten.), Col.
138/D3 Casanare (riv.), Col.
140/B3 Casa Nova, Braz.
81/F3 Casarano, It.
79/F1 Casarsa della Delizia, It.
146/C2 Casas Grandes (ruins), Mex.
146/C2 Cascada de Bassaseachic Nat'l Park, Mex.
156/C5 Cascade (range), Can., US
156/D4 Cascade (res.), Id,US
165/C3 Cascade-Fairwood, Wa,US
133/R15 Cascades (pt.), Reun.
75/P10 Cascais, Port.
161/H1 Cascapédia (riv.), Qu,Can
140/C2 Cascavel, Braz.
78/D5 Cascina-Navacchio, It.
165/B3 Case (inlet), Wa,US
78/A2 Caselle Torinese, It.
79/E5 Casentino (val.), It.
80/D2 Caserta, It.
113/H Casey, Ant.
113/D Casey (bay), Ant.
123/H3 Caseyr (cape), Som.
131/D3 Cashel, Zim.
60/B3 Cashlaundrumlahan (mtn.), Ire.
156/C4 Cashmere, Wa,US
112/C1 Casiguran, Phil.
112/D2 Casiguran, Phil.
142/E2 Casilda, Arg.
149/F1 Casilda (pt.), Cuba
146/D5 Casimiro Castillo, Mex.
77/G4 Casina, Cima la (Piz Murtaröl) (peak), It.
119/E1 Casino, Austl.
164/A2 Casitas (lake), Ca,US
144/B3 Casma, Peru
75/E2 Caspe, Sp.
157/G5 Casper, Wy,US
88/F6 Caspian (sea), Eur., Asia
165/F6 Cass (lake), Mi,US
75/G2 Cassà de la Selva, Sp.
126/D3 Cassai (riv.), Ang.
126/D3 Cassamba, Ang.
80/E3 Cassano allo Ionio, It.
78/C1 Cassano d'Adda, It.
160/D3 Cass City, Mi,US
141/C2 Cássia, Braz.
152/C3 Cassiar (mts.), BC,Can
141/B1 Cassilândia, Braz.
80/C2 Cassino, It.
159/J3 Cassville, Mo,US
164/B1 Castaic (lake), Ca,US
75/E3 Castalla, Sp.
137/J4 Castanhal, Braz.
148/E3 Castañones (pt.), Nic.
78/C2 Casteggio, It.
80/D4 Castelbuono, It.
79/G6 Castelfidardo, It.
79/D5 Castelfiorentino, It.
79/E3 Castelfranco Emilia, It.
79/E1 Castelfranco Veneto, It.
80/C3 Castellammare (gulf), It.
80/D2 Castellammare di Stabia, It.
78/A2 Castellamonte, It.
78/B1 Castellanza, It.
75/G2 Castellar del Vallès, Sp.
75/K7 Castelldefels, Sp.
75/L7 Castell de Montjuïc, Sp.
78/C2 Castelleone, It.
79/G1 Castello di Miramare, It.
80/D4 Castello Eurialo (ruins), It.
79/E5 Castello, Monte il (peak), It.
75/E3 Castellón de la Plana, Sp.
91/G8 Castel Nat'l Park, Isr.
72/D5 Castelnaudary, Fr.
72/E5 Castelnau-le-Lez, Fr.
74/B3 Castelo Branco, Port.
74/B3 Castelo Branco (dist.), Port.
140/B2 Castelo do Piauí, Braz.
78/C2 Castel San Giovanni, It.
79/E4 Castel San Pietro Terme, It.
72/D4 Castelsarrasin, Fr.
80/C4 Castelvetrano, It.
79/E4 Castenaso, It.
78/D2 Castiglione delle Stiviere, It.
141/B2 Castilho, Braz.
144/A2 Castilla, Peru
74/C2 Castille and León (aut. comm.), Sp.
74/D3 Castille-La Mancha (aut. comm.), Sp.
142/C4 Castillo (peak), Arg.
148/D3 Castillo de San Felipe, Guat.
163/H4 Castillo de San Marcos Nat'l Mon., Fl,US
143/G2 Castillos, Uru.
59/G1 Castle Acre, Eng,UK
158/B3 Castle A.F.B., Ca,US
60/A2 Castlebar, Ire.
55/H8 Castlebay, Sc,UK
58/D4 Castle Cary, Eng,UK
56/B3 Castlecaulfield, NI,UK
58/D4 Castle Combe, Eng,UK
158/E3 Castle Dale, Ut,US
56/B2 Castledawson, NI,UK
57/G6 Castle Donnington, Eng,UK
56/E2 Castle Douglas, Sc,UK
57/G4 Castleford, Eng,UK
156/D3 Castlegar, BC,Can
118/H8 Castle Hill, Austl.
168/C3 Castle Hill C. G. Sta., RI,US
161/L2 Castle Hill Nat'l Hist. Park, Nf,Can
56/D2 Castle Kennedy, Sc,UK
119/C3 Castlemaine, Austl.
118/G8 Castlereagh, Austl.
56/B1 Castlerock, NI,UK
159/F3 Castle Rock, Co,US
157/L5 Castle Rock (lake), Wi,US
168/G7 Castle Shannon, Pa,US
118/C4 Castle Tower Nat'l Park, Austl.
56/D3 Castletown, IM,UK
60/A6 Castletownshend, Ire.
56/C3 Castlewellan, NI,UK
156/F2 Castor, Ab,Can
124/D6 Castos (riv.), Libr.
72/E5 Castres, Fr.
66/B3 Castricum, Neth.
150/F4 Castries (cap.), StL.
141/B3 Castro, Braz.
142/B4 Castro, Chile
140/C4 Castro Alves, Braz.
74/C4 Castro del Río, Sp.
74/B1 Castro de Rey, Sp.
67/E5 Castrop-Rauxel, Ger.
74/D1 Castro-Urdiales, Sp.
165/K11 Castro Valley, Ca,US
80/E3 Castrovillari, It.
74/C3 Castuera, Sp.
150/C1 Cat (isl.), Bahm.
157/K3 Cat (lake), On,Can
148/E3 Catacamas, Hon.
144/A2 Catacaos, Peru
144/B2 Catacocha, Ecu.
120/B3 Cataduanes (isl.), Phil.
141/L6 Cataguases, Braz.
111/F1 Cataiñgan, Phil.
83/K5 Çatalağzı, Turk.
141/C1 Catalão, Braz.
83/J5 Çatalca, Turk.
158/E4 Catalina, Az,US
75/F2 Catalonia (aut. comm.), Sp.
135/C2 Catamarca, Arg.
144/B1 Catamayo, Ecu.
112/C2 Catanauan, Phil.
131/D3 Catandica, Moz.
112/D2 Catanduanes (isl.), Phil.
141/B2 Catanduva, Braz.
80/D4 Catania, It.
80/D4 Catania (gulf), It.
80/E3 Catanzaro, It.
111/F1 Catarman, Indo.
112/D2 Catarman, Phil.
112/D3 Catarman, Phil.
112/D4 Catarman (pt.), Phil.
75/E3 Catarroja, Sp.
117/G5 Catastrophe (cape), Austl.
138/C2 Catatumbo (riv.), Col., Ven.
112/D4 Catatungan (mtn.), Phil.
163/H3 Catawba (riv.), NC, SC,US
105/E4 Cat Ba (isl.), Viet.
112/D3 Catbalogan, Phil.
105/E4 Cat Ba Nat'l Park, Viet.
143/G2 Catedral (peak), Uru.
112/D4 Cateel, Phil.
148/C2 Catemaco (lake), Mex.
140/D3 Catende, Braz.
53/N8 Caterham, Eng,UK
59/F4 Caterham and Warlingham, Eng,UK
127/C2 Catherine, Mount (Jabal Katrīnah) (mtn.), Egypt
149/G4 Cativá, Pan.
54/C3 Cat Law (mtn.), Sc,UK
160/D4 Catlettsburg, Ky,US
112/D3 Catmon, Phil.
115/K4 Cato (isl.), Austl.
147/J4 Catoche, Cabo (cape), Mex.
140/C2 Catolé do Rocha, Braz.
166/B5 Catonsville, Md,US
73/K5 Catria (peak), It.
79/F6 Catria, Monte (peak), It.
139/F4 Catrimani (riv.), Braz.
54/B6 Catrine, Sc,UK
58/D2 Catshill, Eng,UK
160/F3 Catskill (mts.), NY,US
166/B2 Cattawissa (cr.), Pa,US
69/F5 Cattenom, Fr.
57/G3 Catterick, Eng,UK
79/F5 Cattolica, It.
140/C4 Catu, Braz.
112/D2 Catubig, Phil.
112/C1 Cauayan, Phil.
112/C3 Cauayan, Phil.
138/B4 Cauca (dept.), Col.
138/C2 Cauca (riv.), Col.
140/C1 Caucaia, Braz.
138/C3 Caucasia, Col.
86/G4 Caucasus (mts.), Eur.
75/E3 Caudete, Sp.
68/C3 Caudry, Fr.
131/C2 Cauese (mts.), Moz.
54/D6 Cauldcleuch (mtn.), Sc,UK
142/B2 Cauquenes, Chile
139/E3 Caura (riv.), Ven.
131/D3 Cauresi (riv.), Moz.
72/D4 Caussade, Fr.
149/G1 Cauto (riv.), Cuba
108/F3 Cauvery (riv.), India
80/D4 Cava d'Ispica (ruins), It.
74/B2 Cávado (riv.), Port.
72/F5 Cavaillon, Fr.
157/J3 Cavalier, ND,US
124/D6 Cavalla (riv.), IvC., Libr.
128/D5 Cavalla (Cavally) (riv.), IvC., Libr.
80/A1 Cavallo, Capo al (cape), Fr.
128/C5 Cavally (Cavalla) (riv.), IvC., Libr.
60/C2 Cavan (co.), Ire.
79/F2 Cavarzere, It.
158/E4 Cave Creek, Az,US
137/J3 Caviana, Braz.
112/E7 Cavite (prov.), Phil.
83/F2 Cavnic, Rom.
78/B2 Cavour (can.), It.
112/C3 Cawayan, Phil.
54/C1 Cawdor, Sc,UK
119/B2 Cawndilla (lake), Austl.
57/G4 Cawood, Eng,UK
59/H1 Cawston, Eng,UK
141/J6 Caxambu, Braz.
140/B2 Caxias, Braz.
141/B4 Caxias do Sul, Braz.
148/E2 Caxinas (pt.), Hon.
126/B2 Caxito, Ang.
92/B2 Çay, Turk.
93/N6 Çayağzi (riv.), Turk.
138/B4 Cayambe, Ecu.
138/B4 Cayambe (vol.), Ecu.
163/H3 Cayce, SC,US
83/L5 Çaycuma, Turk.
92/E1 Çayeli, Turk.
137/H3 Cayenne (cap.), FrG.
149/F2 Cayman (isls.), UK
149/G2 Cayman Brac (isl.), Cay.
149/F2 Cayman Islands (dpcy.), UK
161/S10 Cayuga (cr.), NY,US
82/B3 Cazin, Bosn.
148/B1 Cazones (riv.), Mex.
74/D4 Cazorla, Sp.
131/D2 Cazula, Moz.
78/D1 Cazzago San Martino, It.
74/C1 Cea (riv.), Sp.
60/D2 Ceanannus Mór (Kells), Ire.
140/C3 Ceará (state), Braz.
140/D2 Ceará-Mirim, Braz.
149/F5 Cébaco (isl.), Pan.
143/G2 Cebollatí (riv.), Uru.
112/C3 Cebu (isl.), Phil.
112/C3 Cebu City, Phil.
80/C2 Ceccano, It.
166/C4 Cecil (co.), Md,US
133/E2 Cecil Macks (pass), Swaz.
116/D3 Cecil Rhodes (peak), Austl.
78/D6 Cecina, It.
79/D6 Cecina (riv.), It.
80/E3 Cecita (lake), It.
157/H2 Cedar (lake), Mb,Can
160/E2 Cedar (lake), On,Can
165/L11 Cedar (mtn.), Ca,US
157/L5 Cedar (riv.), Ia,US
167/D4 Cedar (cr.), NJ,US
165/C3 Cedar (riv.), Wa,US
118/B1 Cedar Bay Nat'l Park, Austl.
159/G3 Cedar Bluff (res.), Ks,US
158/D3 Cedar Breaks Nat'l Mon., Ut,US
158/D3 Cedar City, Ut,US
162/D3 Cedar Creek (res.), Tx,US
157/K5 Cedar Falls, Ia,US
165/D3 Cedar Falls (dam), Wa,US
167/D2 Cedar Grove, NJ,US
163/H4 Cedar Key, Fl,US
157/L5 Cedar Rapids, Ia,US
163/G3 Cedartown, Ga,US
158/B2 Cedarville, Ca,US
74/A1 Cedeira, Sp.
140/C2 Cedro, Braz.
146/B2 Cedros (isl.), Mex.
74/A1 Cee, Sp.
125/Q7 Ceel Dheere, Som.
125/Q5 Ceerigaabo (Erigabo), Som.
80/D3 Cefalù, It.
56/D5 Cefni (riv.), Wal,UK
57/E6 Cefn-mawr, Wal,UK
74/C2 Cega (riv.), Sp.
82/D2 Cegléd, Hun.
74/E3 Cehegín, Sp.
104/E3 Cehong Bouyeizu Zizhixian, China
83/F2 Cehu Silvaniei, Rom.
57/E6 Ceiriog (riv.), Wal,UK
92/C1 Çekerek, Turk.
86/F4 Çekerek (riv.), Turk.
71/H2 Čelákovice, Czh.
74/B1 Celanova, Sp.
148/E1 Celarain, Punta (pt.), Mex.
147/E4 Celaya, Mex.
60/D3 Celbridge, Ire.
111/F3 Celebes (sea), Asia
111/E4 Celebes (Sulawesi) (isl.), Indo.
144/B2 Celendín, Peru
144/B2 Celica, Ecu.
92/D2 Çelikhan, Turk.
160/C3 Celina, Oh,US
82/B2 Celje, Slov.
82/C2 Celldömölk, Hun.
72/E2 Celle (riv.), Fr.
67/H3 Celle, Ger.
58/A4 Celtic (sea), Eur.
58/B2 Cemaes Head (pt.), Wal,UK
110/D3 Cemaru (peak), Indo.
74/E3 Cenajo (res.), Sp.
111/H4 Cenderawasih (bay), Indo.
144/B1 Cenepa (riv.), Peru
107/J2 Cengong, China
78/C3 Ceno (riv.), It.
135/C4 Centenario, Arg.
141/B2 Centenario do Sul, Braz.
158/D4 Centennial (wash), Az,US
156/E4 Centennial (mts.), Id,US
157/H4 Center, ND,US
162/E4 Center, Tx,US
167/E2 Centereach, NY,US
165/F7 Center Line, Mi,US
163/G3 Center Point, Al,US
163/G3 Centerville, Tn,US
162/E4 Centerville, Tx,US
146/E2 Centinela, Picacho del (peak), Mex.
79/E3 Cento, It.
78/C4 Cento Croci, Passo di (pass), It.
142/C4 Central (peak), Arg.
131/B4 Central (dist.), Bots.
140/B3 Central, Braz.
129/E5 Central (reg.), Gha.
91/D3 Central (dist.), Isr.
130/C3 Central (prov.), Kenya
131/D2 Central (reg.), Malw.
112/C1 Central (mts.), Phil.
130/B2 Central (prov.), Ugan.
54/B4 Central (reg.), Sc,UK
131/C2 Central (prov.), Zam.
125/J6 Central African Republic
117/F2 Central Australia Abor. Rsv., Austl.
117/E3 Central Australia (Warburton) Abor. Rsv., Austl.
156/G3 Central Butte, Sk,Can
159/H2 Central City, Ne,US
112/C1 Central, Cordillera (mts.), Phil.
136/C5 Central, Cordillera (range), SAm.
117/F2 Central Desert Abor. Land, Austl.
168/C2 Central Falls, RI,US
160/B4 Centralia, Il,US
156/C4 Centralia, Wa,US
166/A6 Central Intelligence Agency, Va,US
130/C2 Central Island Nat'l Park, Kenya
167/E2 Central Islip, NY,US
131/A4 Central Kalahari Game Rsv., Bots.
95/H3 Central Makrān (range), Pak.
72/E4 Central, Massif (plat.), Fr.
117/G2 Central Mount Stuart (peak), Austl.
117/F2 Central Mount Wedge (peak), Austl.
167/K8 Central Park, New York City, NY,US
137/J7 Central, Planalto (plat.), Braz.
156/C5 Central Point, Or,US
89/L3 Central Siberian (plat.), Rus.
85/N4 Central Ural (mts.), Rus.
72/D3 Centre (reg.), Fr.
123/L14 Centre (reg.), Mor.
166/A2 Centre (co.), Pa,US
123/M13 Centre Nord (reg.), Mor.
123/M14 Centre Sud (reg.), Mor.
163/G3 Centreville, Al,US
104/E3 Cenwanglao (mtn.), China
107/K3 Cenxi, China
72/D4 Céou (riv.), Fr.
82/D3 Čepin, Cro.
111/G4 Ceram (isl.), Indo.
111/G4 Ceram (sea), Indo.
78/B2 Cerano, It.
80/A2 Ceraso (cape), It.
139/E3 Cerbatana (mts.), Ven.
71/F4 Čerchov (peak), Czh.
75/L7 Cerdanyola del Vallès, Sp.
72/D4 Cère (riv.), Fr.
79/E2 Cerea, It.
135/D2 Ceres, Arg.
137/J7 Ceres, Braz.
132/B4 Ceres, SAfr.
138/C2 Cereté, Col.
79/E6 Cerfone (riv.), It.
53/S9 Cergy, Fr.
80/D2 Cerignola, It.
92/C1 Çerkeş, Turk.
83/J5 Çerkezköy, Turk.
92/D2 Çermik, Turk.
71/G5 Černá (peak), Czh.
71/H5 Černá (riv.), Czh.
83/J3 Cernavodă, Rom.
76/D2 Cernay, Fr.
53/R10 Cernay-la-Ville, Fr.
58/D5 Cerne Abbas, Eng,UK
146/C3 Cerralvo (isl.), Mex.
78/D4 Cerreto, Passo del (pass), It.
56/E5 Cerrig-y-Druidion, Wal,UK
81/F2 Cërrik, Alb.
147/E4 Cerritos, Mex.
164/F8 Cerritos, Ca,US
147/F4 Cerro Azul, Mex.
142/C3 Cerro Colorados (res.), Arg.
139/F2 Cerro El Copey Nat'l Park, Ven.
143/G2 Cerro Largo (dept.), Uru.
78/B1 Cerro Maggiore, It.
144/A2 Cerros de Amotape Nat'l Park, Peru
79/E5 Certaldo, It.
78/C2 Certosa di Pavia, It.
78/D5 Certosa di Pisa, It.
80/D2 Cervaro (riv.), It.
80/D2 Cervati (peak), It.
78/D3 Cervellino, Monte (peak), It.
75/F2 Cervera, Sp.
79/F4 Cervia, It.
80/D2 Cervialto (peak), It.
79/G1 Cervignano del Friuli, It.
77/H4 Cervina, Punta (peak), It.
141/F7 Cervo (hills), Braz.
78/B1 Cervo (riv.), It.
74/B1 Cervo, Sp.
78/C1 Cesano Maderno, It.
138/C2 César (riv.), Col.
79/F4 Cesena, It.
79/F4 Cesenatico, It.
79/F1 Cesen, Monte (peak), It.
63/L3 Cēsis, Lat.
71/H5 České Budějovice, Czh.
71/G2 České Středohoří (mts.), Czh.
65/H4 Českomoravská Vysočina (upland), Czh.
71/H2 Český Brod, Czh.
71/H5 Český Krumlov, Czh.
71/F3 Český Les (mts.), Czh.
82/C3 Česma (riv.), Cro.
81/K3 Çeşme, Turk.
149/G1 Céspedes, Cuba
53/T11 Cesson, Fr.
72/C2 Cesson-Sévigné, Fr.
128/C5 Cestos (riv.), Libr.
82/C4 Cetina (riv.), Cro.
82/D4 Cetinje, Yugo.
74/D2 Ceurda del Pozo (res.), Sp.
74/C5 Ceuta, Sp.
77/G5 Cevedale, Monte (peak), It.
72/E5 Cévennes (mts.), Fr.
72/E4 Cévennes Nat'l Park, Fr.
91/D1 Ceyhan, Turk.
91/D1 Ceyhan (riv.), Turk.
92/E2 Ceylânpınar, Turk.
108/H4 Ceylon (isl.), SrL.
72/F4 Cèze (riv.), Fr.
72/C5 Chabarrou (peak), Fr.
116/B2 Chabjuwardoo (bay), Austl.
142/E2 Chacabuco, Arg.
144/D5 Chachani (peak), Peru
144/B2 Chachapoyas, Peru
109/C3 Chachoengsao, Thai.
144/B3 Chaclacayo, Peru
158/F3 Chaco (dry riv.), NM,US
162/B3 Chaco (mesa), NM,US
135/D2 Chaco Austral (plain), Arg.
136/G8 Chaco Boreal (plain), Par.
135/D1 Chaco Central (plain), Arg.
135/E2 Chaco Nat'l Park, Arg.
148/D3 Chacujal (ruins), Guat.
125/J4 Chad
124/H5 Chad (lake), Afr.
109/E4 Cha Da (cape), Viet.
131/D2 Chadiza, Zam.
59/E3 Chadlington, Eng,UK
159/G2 Chadron, Ne,US
83/J2 Chadyr-Lunga, Mol.
123/N13 Chafarinas (isls.), Sp.
101/D2 Chagang-do (prov.), NKor.
102/D5 Chagdo Kangri (peak), China
90/G10 Chagos (arch.), BrIn.
168/F5 Chagrin (riv.), Oh,US
150/F5 Chaguanas, Trin.
144/B1 Chaguarpamba, Ecu.
93/G4 Chahār Maḩāll and Bakhtīārī (gov.), Iran
95/H3 Chāh Behār (Bandar Beheshtī), Iran
109/C3 Chainat, Thai.
135/B5 Chaitén, Chile
109/C3 Chaiyaphum, Thai.
131/C3 Chakari, Zim.
130/C4 Chake Chake, Tanz.
108/B1 Chakwāl, Pak.
76/B4 Chalain (lake), Fr.
108/F3 Chālakudi, India
76/B5 Chalamont, Fr.
76/A5 Chalaronne (riv.), Fr.
148/D3 Chalatenango, ESal.
130/C2 Chalbi (des.), Kenya
97/H2 Chalchyn (riv.), Mong.
147/R10 Chalco, Mex.
147/F5 Chalco de Díaz Covarrubias, Mex.
130/C4 Chale (pt.), Kenya
161/H2 Chaleur (bay), NB, Qu,Can
53/M7 Chalfont Saint Giles, Eng,UK

181

Chalf – Chris

53/M7 Chalfont Saint Peter, Eng,UK
59/E3 Chalgrove, Eng,UK
53/U10 Chalifert (can.), Fr.
130/C4 Chalinze, Tanz.
162/C4 Chalk (mts.), Tx,US
147/F1 Chalk Mountain, Tx,US
72/C3 Challans, Fr.
136/E7 Challapata, Bol.
153/T6 Challenger (mtn.), NW,Can
69/D5 Challerange, Fr.
156/E4 Challis, Id,US
59/G4 Challock, Eng,UK
68/D6 Châlons-sur-Marne, Fr.
76/A4 Chalon-sur-Saône, Fr.
93/G2 Chālūs, Iran
71/F4 Cham, Ger.
71/F4 Cham (riv.), Ger.
77/E3 Cham, Swi.
158/F3 Chama (riv.), Co, NM,US
131/D1 Chama, Zam.
110/B2 Chamah (peak), Malay.
95/J2 Chaman, Pak.
108/D1 Chamba, India
106/C2 Chambal (riv.), India
72/F4 Chambaran (plat.), Fr.
161/G2 Chamberlain (lake), Me,US
157/J5 Chamberlain, SD,US
151/K2 Chamberlin (mtn.), Ak,US
160/E4 Chambersburg, Pa,US
72/F4 Chambéry, Fr.
131/C1 Chambeshi, Zam.
131/C1 Chambeshi (riv.), Zam.
131/C2 Chambishi, Zam.
161/P7 Chambly, Qu,Can
53/S9 Chambly, Fr.
53/S10 Chambourcy, Fr.
93/F3 Chamchamāl, Iraq
149/G4 Chame (pt.), Pan.
72/F4 Chamechaude (mtn.), Fr.
135/C3 Chamical, Arg.
76/C6 Chamonix-Mont-Blanc, Fr.
151/L3 Champagne, Yk,Can
68/C6 Champagne (reg.), Fr.
72/F2 Champagne-Ardennes (reg.), Fr.
53/S9 Champagne-sur-Oise, Fr.
76/B4 Champagnole, Fr.
160/B3 Champaign, Il,US
142/D1 Champaqui (peak), Arg.
69/F6 Champigneulles, Fr.
53/T10 Champigny-sur-Marne, Fr.
160/F2 Champlain (lake), Can., US
147/H5 Champotón, Mex.
147/H5 Champotón (riv.), Mex.
68/B6 Champs-sur-Marne, Fr.
108/F3 Chāmrājnagar, India
135/B2 Chañaral, Chile
74/B4 Chança (riv.), Port.
144/B3 Chancay, Peru
144/B3 Chan Chan (ruins), Peru
142/B2 Chanco, Chile
151/J2 Chandalar (riv.), Ak,US
151/J2 Chandalar, East Fork (riv.), Ak,US
106/C2 Chandausi, India
106/C3 Chanderi, India
108/D2 Chandigarh, India
108/D2 Chandigarh (terr.), India
161/H1 Chandler, Qu,Can
151/H2 Chandler (riv.), Ak,US
162/D3 Chandler, Ok,US
144/D3 Chandless (riv.), Braz., Peru
96/D2 Chandmanī, Mong.
106/C4 Chandrapur, India
138/A5 Chanduy, Ecu.
103/C5 Chang (lake), China
103/L8 Chang (riv.), China
109/C3 Chang (isl.), Thai.
108/F4 Changanācheri, India
131/D4 Changane (riv.), Moz.
131/D3 Changara, Moz.
101/E2 Changbai (peak), China
101/D2 Changbai (mts.), China, NKor.
101/E2 Changbai Chaoxianzu Zizhixian, China
103/F2 Changchun, China
103/D5 Changdang (lake), China
103/E3 Changdao, China
105/F2 Changde, China
103/D4 Changfeng, China
103/C4 Changge, China
98/A2 Changgi-ap (cape), SKor.
101/B3 Changhai, China
105/J3 Changhua, Tai.
101/D5 Changhŭng, SKor.
105/F5 Changjiang, China
105/G2 Changjiang Zhongxiayou (plain), China
101/D2 Changjin (lake), NKor.
101/D2 Changjin (res.), NKor.
103/D3 Changle, China
103/D3 Changli, China
103/E1 Changling, China
104/E2 Changning, China
103/D2 Changping, China
103/H6 Changping, China
103/D3 Changqing, China
101/C3 Changsan-got (cape), NKor.
105/G2 Changsha, China
101/B3 Changshan (arch.), China
103/E5 Changshu, China
103/L8 Changshu, China
104/E3 Changshun, China
101/D5 Changsŏng, SKor.
103/F2 Changtu, China
149/F4 Changuinola, Pan.
101/E5 Ch'angwŏn, SKor.
96/F4 Changwu, China
103/K8 Changxing, China
103/E3 Changxing (isl.), China
103/B5 Changyang, China
103/D5 Chang (Yangtze) (riv.), China
103/D3 Changyi, China
103/C4 Changyuan, China
103/C3 Changzhi, China
103/D5 Changzhou, China
108/G4 Chankanai, SrL.
130/C2 Chanlers (falls), Kenya
109/E2 Chan May Dong (cape), Viet.
72/B4 Channel (isls.), UK
158/C4 Channel (isls.), Ca,US
118/A4 Channel Country (plain), Austl.
72/B2 Channel Islands, UK
158/B4 Channel Islands Nat'l Park, Ca,US
161/K2 Channel-Port aux Basques, Nf,Can
59/H4 Channel Tunnel, UK, Fr.
74/B1 Chantada, Sp.
53/S10 Chanteloup-les-Vignes, Fr.
109/C3 Chanthaburi, Thai.
68/B5 Chantilly, Fr.
152/G2 Chantrey (inlet), NW,Can
159/J3 Chanute, Ks,US
103/D5 Chao (lake), China
103/D2 Chao (riv.), China
97/H4 Chaobai (riv.), China
109/C3 Chao Phraya (riv.), Thai.
97/J2 Chaor (riv.), China
105/H4 Chaoyang, China
105/H4 Chaozhou, China
140/B4 Chapada Diamantina Nat'l Park, Braz.
140/A4 Chapada dos Veadeiros Nat'l Park, Braz.
140/B1 Chapadinha, Braz.
160/F1 Chapais, Qu,Can
146/E4 Chapala, Mex.
146/E4 Chapala (lake), Mex.
138/C4 Chaparral, Col.
87/J1 Chapayevsk, Rus.
141/A3 Chapecó, Braz.
57/G5 Chapel en le Frith, Eng,UK
57/F2 Chapelfell Top (mtn.), Eng,UK
163/J3 Chapel Hill, NC,US
68/D3 Chapelle-Lez-Herlaimont, Belg.
54/D4 Chapel Ness (pt.), Sc,UK
57/J5 Chapel Saint Leonards, Eng,UK
57/G5 Chapeltown, Eng,UK
165/D2 Chaplain (lake), Wa,US
109/D2 Chap Le, Viet.
160/D2 Chapleau, On,Can
156/G3 Chaplin, Sk,Can
159/G2 Chappell, Ne,US
147/Q10 Chapultepec Park, Mex.
89/M4 Chara (riv.), Rus.
138/B3 Charambirá (pt.), Col.
81/L6 Charandra (riv.), Gre.
135/D2 Charata, Arg.
147/E4 Charcas, Mex.
113/U Charcot (isl.), Ant.
58/D5 Chard, Eng,UK
88/G6 Chardzhou, Trkm.
123/N14 Charef, Oued (riv.), Mor.
72/C4 Charente (riv.), Fr.
53/T10 Charenton-le-Pont, Fr.
124/J5 Chari (riv.), Chad
95/J1 Chārīkār, Afg.
59/G4 Charing, Eng,UK
159/J2 Chariton (riv.), Ia, Mo,US
59/E3 Charlbury, Eng,UK
56/B3 Charlemont, NI,UK
68/D3 Charleroi, Belg.
68/D2 Charleroi à Bruxelles, Canal de (can.), Belg.
116/C3 Charles (peak), Austl.
116/D5 Charles (peak), Austl.
153/J2 Charles (isl.), NW,Can
168/C1 Charles (riv.), Ma,US
160/F4 Charles (cape), Va,US
157/K5 Charles City, Ia,US
168/E6 Charles Mill (dam), Oh,US
168/E6 Charles Mill (res.), Oh,US
160/B4 Charleston, Il,US
159/K3 Charleston, Mo,US
163/F3 Charleston, Ms,US
158/D2 Charleston, Nv,US
163/J3 Charleston, SC,US
160/D4 Charleston (cap.), WV,US
168/C3 Charlestown, RI,US
69/D4 Charleville-Mézières, Fr.
160/C2 Charlevoix, Mi,US
156/B2 Charlotte (lake), BC,Can
160/C3 Charlotte, Mi,US
163/H3 Charlotte, NC,US
150/E3 Charlotte Amalie, USVI
160/E4 Charlottesville, Va,US
161/J2 Charlottetown (cap.), PE,Can
153/H3 Charlton (isl.), NW,Can
168/C1 Charlton, Ma,US
58/D3 Charlton Kings, Eng,UK
53/N8 Charlwood, Eng,UK
76/B2 Charmes (res.), Fr.
72/F3 Charolais (mts.), Fr.
53/R9 Chars, Fr.
102/D2 Charsk, Kaz.
118/B3 Charters Towers, Austl.
72/D2 Chartres, Fr.
102/C3 Charyn (riv.), Kaz.
102/D1 Charysh (riv.), Rus.
77/G4 Chaschauna, Piz (peak), Swi.
142/F2 Chascomús, Arg.
156/D3 Chase, BC,Can
72/F4 Chassezac (riv.), Fr.
72/C3 Chassiron, Pointe de (pt.), Fr.
72/C3 Châteaubriant, Fr.
76/D5 Château-d'Oex, Swi.
72/C3 Château-d'Olonne, Fr.
72/D2 Châteaudun, Fr.
161/N7 Châteauguay, Qu,Can
161/N7 Châteauguay (co.), Qu,Can
72/F5 Châteaurenard-Provence, Fr.
72/D3 Château-Renault, Fr.
72/D3 Châteauroux, Fr.
72/C5 Château-Thierry, Fr.
68/D3 Châtelet, Belg.
72/D3 Châtellerault, Fr.
53/S10 Châtenay-Malabry, Fr.
76/D1 Châtenois, Fr.
159/J2 Chatfield, Mn,US
161/H2 Chatham, NB,Can
160/D3 Chatham, On,Can
143/J7 Chatham (isl.), Chile
59/G4 Chatham, Eng,UK
166/D2 Chatham, NJ,US
53/S10 Châtillon, Fr.
72/F3 Châtillon-sur-Seine, Fr.
53/S10 Chatou, Fr.
106/D4 Chatrapur, India
118/H8 Chatswood, Austl.
164/F7 Chatsworth, Ca,US
164/B2 Chatsworth (res.), Ca,US
163/G3 Chatsworth, Ga,US
131/C3 Chatsworth, Zim.
163/G4 Chattahoochee, Fl,US
163/G4 Chattahoochee (riv.), Fl, Ga,US
163/G3 Chattanooga, Tn,US
59/G2 Chatteris, Eng,UK
72/C2 Chaucey (isls.), Fr.
69/E2 Chaudfontaine, Belg.
161/G2 Chaudière (riv.), Qu,Can
109/D4 Chau Doc, Viet.
104/B4 Chauk, Burma
104/C3 Chaukan (pass), India
68/B4 Chaulnes, Fr.
53/U10 Chaumes-en-Brie, Fr.
76/B1 Chaumont, Fr.
68/A5 Chaumont-en-Vexin, Fr.
68/D4 Chaumont-Porcien, Fr.
89/T3 Chaunskaya (bay), Rus.
68/C4 Chauny, Fr.
160/E3 Chautauqua (lake), NY,US
72/D3 Chauvigny, Fr.
108/H4 Chavakachcheri, SrL.
130/B2 Chavakali, Kenya
108/F3 Chavakkad, India
140/B1 Chaval, Braz.
74/B2 Chaves, Port.
144/B3 Chavín de Huantar (ruins), Peru
109/D1 Chay (riv.), Viet.
136/E7 Chayana (riv.), Bol.
85/M4 Chaykovskiy, Rus.
57/G6 Cheadle, Eng,UK
163/G3 Cheaha (peak), Al,US
71/F2 Cheb, Czh.
85/K4 Cheboksary, Rus.
85/K4 Cheboksary (res.), Rus.
160/C2 Cheboygan, Mi,US
123/M13 Chechaouene, Mor.
87/H4 Chechen' (isl.), Rus.
87/H4 Chechen-Ingush Aut. Rep., Rus.
124/D3 Chech, 'Erg (des.), Afr.
101/E4 Chech'ŏn, SKor.
159/J4 Checotah, Ok,US
161/J2 Chedabucto (bay), NS,Can
58/D4 Cheddar, Eng,UK
104/B5 Cheduba (isl.), Burma
104/B5 Cheduba (str.), Burma
161/S10 Cheektowaga, NY,US
160/D1 Cheepash (riv.), On,Can
160/D1 Cheepay (riv.), On,Can
97/L1 Chegdomyn, Rus.
131/C3 Chegutu, Zim.
156/C4 Chehalis, Wa,US
73/G5 Cheiron, Cime du (peak), Fr.
97/K5 Cheju, SKor.
97/K5 Cheju (isl.), SKor.
97/K5 Cheju (str.), SKor.
156/C4 Chelan, Wa,US
156/C4 Chelan (lake), Wa,US
57/F5 Chelford, Eng,UK
123/V17 Chelghoum El Aïd, Alg.
87/L3 Chelkar, Kaz.
53/T10 Chelles, Fr.
65/M3 Chełm, Pol.
65/M3 Chełm (prov.), Pol.
59/G3 Chelmer (riv.), Eng,UK
65/K2 Chełmno, Pol.
59/G3 Chelmsford, Eng,UK
65/K2 Chełmża, Pol.
119/G6 Chelsea, Austl.
53/N7 Chelsea, Eng,UK
168/C1 Chelsea, Ma,US
53/N7 Chelsea & Kensington (bor.), Eng,UK
161/Q8 Cheltenham, On,Can
58/D3 Cheltenham, Eng,UK
85/P5 Chelyabinsk, Rus.
85/P5 Chelyabinsk Obl., Rus.
89/L2 Chelyuskina (cape), Rus.
131/D3 Chemba, Moz.
131/C1 Chembe, Zam.
64/G3 Chemnitz, Ger.
105/F3 Chen (riv.), China
108/A2 Chenāb (riv.), India, Pak.
124/E2 Chenachane (well), Alg.
148/C2 Chenalhó, Mex.
97/H2 Chen Baraq Qi, China
156/D4 Cheney, Wa,US
104/D3 Cheng (lake), China
108/F4 Chengannūr, India
103/C3 Cheng'anpu, China
105/F3 Chengbu Miaozu Zizhixian, China
103/D2 Chengde, China
104/E2 Chengdu, China
105/F2 Chengkou, China
105/F5 Chengmai, China
101/B4 Chengshan (cape), China
103/E3 Chengshan Jiao (cape), China
103/C4 Chengwu, China
53/T10 Chennevières-sur-Marne, Fr.
76/A3 Chenôve, Fr.
107/K2 Chenxi, China
105/G3 Chenzhou, China
83/G5 Chepelare, Bul.
144/B2 Chepén, Peru
121/V12 Chépénéhé, NCal.
135/C3 Chepes, Arg.
142/C2 Chépica, Chile
149/G4 Chepigana, Pan.
130/B2 Cheploske, Kenya
58/D3 Chepstow, Wal,UK
85/M4 Cheptsa (riv.), Rus.
72/D3 Cher (riv.), Fr.
163/J3 Cheraw, SC,US
72/C2 Cherbourg, Fr.
123/S15 Cherchell, Alg.
96/E1 Cheremkhovo, Rus.
84/H4 Cherepovets, Rus.
123/V17 Cherf (riv.), Alg.
123/S16 Chergui (lake), Alg.
123/V18 Cheria, Alg.
86/E2 Cherkassy, Ukr.
86/D2 Cherkassy Obl., Ukr.
87/G3 Cherkessk, Rus.
118/E6 Chermside, Austl.
85/M2 Chernaya (riv.), Rus.
86/D2 Chernigov, Ukr.
86/D2 Chernigov Obl., Ukr.
83/H4 Cherni Lom (riv.), Bul.
83/F4 Cherni Vrŭkh (peak), Bul.
86/C2 Chernovtsy, Ukr.
86/C2 Chernovtsy Obl., Ukr.
85/N4 Chernushka, Rus.
96/H1 Chernyshevsk, Rus.
159/H3 Cherokee, Ok,US
162/E2 Cherokees (lake), Ok,US
107/F2 Cherrapunjee, India
158/D3 Cherry Creek, Nv,US
166/C4 Cherry Hill, NJ,US
89/Q3 Cherskiy (range), Rus.
53/M7 Chertsey, Eng,UK
83/G4 Cherven Bryag, Bul.
86/C2 Chervonograd, Ukr.
59/E3 Cherwell (riv.), Eng,UK
160/C3 Chesaning, Mi,US
160/E4 Chesapeake (bay), Md, Va,US
166/C5 Chesapeake & Delaware (can.), De, Md,US
166/B6 Chesapeake Bay Maritime Museum, Md,US
59/F3 Chesham, Eng,UK
57/F5 Cheshire (co.), Eng,UK
57/F5 Cheshire (plain), Eng,UK
85/K2 Cheshskaya (bay), Rus.
53/N6 Cheshunt, Eng,UK
57/F5 Chester, Eng,UK
158/B2 Chester, Ca,US
166/B5 Chester (riv.), De, Md,US
166/B5 Chester (riv.), Md, De,US
156/F3 Chester, Mt,US
166/C4 Chester, Pa,US
166/C4 Chester (co.), Pa,US
166/C4 Chester (cr.), Pa,US
163/H3 Chester, SC,US
152/G2 Chesterfield (inlet), NW,Can
120/E7 Chesterfield (isls.), NCal.
57/G5 Chesterfield, Eng,UK
133/H7 Chesterfield, Nosy (isl.), Madg.
57/G2 Chester-le-Street, Eng,UK
165/D3 Chester Morse (lake), Wa,US
118/B3 Chesterton (range), Austl.
161/G2 Chesuncook (lake), Me,US
148/D2 Chetumal (bay), Belz., Mex.
147/H5 Chetumal, Mex.
156/C2 Chetwynd, BC,Can
149/H2 Cheval Blanc, Pointe du (pt.), Haiti
76/B3 Chevigny-Saint-Sauveur, Fr.
53/T10 Chevilly-Larue, Fr.
54/D6 Cheviot (hills), Eng, Sc,UK
53/S10 Chevreuse, Fr.
53/T10 Chevry-Cossigny, Fr.
58/D4 Chew (riv.), Eng,UK
156/D3 Chewelah, Wa,US
131/C2 Chewore Game Rsv., Zim.
58/D4 Chew Valley (lake), Eng,UK
159/H4 Cheyenne, Ok,US
157/H4 Cheyenne (riv.), SD, Wy,US
157/G5 Cheyenne (cap.), Wy,US
159/F2 Cheyenne, Dry Fork (riv.), Wy,US
159/G3 Cheyenne Wells, Co,US
106/C3 Chhatarpur, India
106/C3 Chhindwāra, India
109/D3 Chhlong, Camb.
103/D4 Chi (riv.), China
109/C2 Chi (riv.), Thai.
138/C3 Chia, Col.
101/E4 Ch'iak-san Nat'l Park, SKor.
79/E1 Chiampo, It.
109/B2 Chiang Dao (caves), Thai.
104/C5 Chiang Dao Caves, Thai.
109/B2 Chiang Mai, Thai.
109/B2 Chiang Rai, Thai.
80/C1 Chiani (riv.), It.
79/E6 Chianti (mts.), It.
79/E6 Chianti (reg.), It.
147/G5 Chiapas (state), Mex.
78/C4 Chiappa, Punta (pt.), It.
79/G5 Chiaravalle, It.
78/C1 Chiari, It.
77/F6 Chiasso, Swi.
87/G4 Chiatura, Geo.
78/C4 Chiavari, It.
77/F5 Chiavenna, It.
131/C2 Chiawa, Zam.
105/J4 Chiayi, Tai.
99/G3 Chiba, Japan
99/G3 Chiba (pref.), Japan
131/D4 Chibabava, Moz.
131/C4 Chibi, Zim.
160/F1 Chibougamau, Qu,Can
160/F1 Chibougamau (lake), Qu,Can
160/F1 Chibougamau (riv.), Qu,Can
151/D3 Chibukak (pt.), Ak,US
131/D5 Chibuto, Moz.
131/C2 Chibwe, Zam.
165/Q16 Chicago, Il,US
165/Q16 Chicago Heights, Il,US
165/Q16 Chicago, North Branch (riv.), Il,US
165/Q16 Chicago Ridge, Il,US
165/Q16 Chicago Sanitary & Ship (can.), Il,US
144/B2 Chicama, Peru
131/D3 Chicamba Real (dam), Moz.
151/L4 Chichagof (isl.), Ak,US
108/B2 Chīchāwatni, Pak.
103/C2 Chicheng, China
147/H4 Chichén Itzá (ruins), Mex.
116/C2 Chichester (range), Austl.
59/F5 Chichester, Eng,UK
116/C2 Chichester-Millstream Nat'l Park, Austl.
99/F3 Chichibu, Japan
99/F3 Chichibu-Tama Nat'l Park, Japan
148/D3 Chichicastenango, Guat.
148/E3 Chichigalpa, Nic.
120/D2 Chichishima (isls.), Japan
131/D4 Chichocane, Moz.
163/G3 Chickamauga (lake), Tn,US
159/H4 Chickasha, Ok,US
58/D5 Chickerell, Eng,UK
166/B3 Chickies (cr.), Pa,US
74/B4 Chiclana de la Frontera, Sp.
144/B2 Chiclayo, Peru
142/C4 Chico (riv.), Arg.
142/D5 Chico (riv.), Arg.
112/C1 Chico (riv.), Phil.
158/B3 Chico, Ca,US
131/D5 Chicomo, Moz.
146/E4 Chicomostoc (ruins), Mex.
168/B1 Chicopee, Ma,US
126/D4 Chicote, Ang.
161/G1 Chicoutimi, Qu,Can
131/C4 Chicualacuala, Moz.
108/G3 Chidambaram, India
53/P8 Chiddingstone, Eng,UK
131/D5 Chidenguele, Moz.
153/K2 Chidley (cape), Nf,Can
163/H4 Chiefland, Fl,US
109/D1 Chiem Hoa, Viet.
71/F7 Chiemsee (lake), Ger.
80/C1 Chienti (riv.), It.
109/B4 Chieo Lan (res.), Thai.
78/A2 Chieri, It.
69/E5 Chiers (riv.), Fr.
78/D2 Chiese (riv.), It.
80/D1 Chieti, It.
59/E4 Chieveley, Eng,UK
97/H3 Chifeng, China
140/B5 Chifre (mts.), Braz.
99/F3 Chigasaki, Japan
151/G4 Chiginagak (mtn.), Ak,US
147/L7 Chignahuapan, Mex.
161/H2 Chignecto (bay), NB,Can
131/D4 Chigubo, Moz.
53/P7 Chigwell, Eng,UK
99/L10 Chihayaakasaka, Japan
103/D3 Chihli (Bo Hai) (gulf), China
159/H3 Chikaskia (riv.), Ks,US
106/C5 Chikballāpur, India
106/C3 Chikhli, India
106/C5 Chikmagalūr, India
96/G1 Chikoy (riv.), Rus.
98/B4 Chikugo (riv.), Japan
99/F2 Chikuma (riv.), Japan
99/H8 Chikura, Japan
131/D1 Chikwa, Zam.
131/D3 Chikwawa, Malw.
105/J3 Chilaichu (mtn.), Tai.
106/D4 Chilakalūrupet, India
131/C2 Chilanga, Zam.
148/B2 Chilapa, Mex.
106/C6 Chilaw, SrL.
101/E2 Chilbo-san (mtn.), NKor.
147/M7 Chilchotla, Mex.
156/C3 Chilcotin (riv.), BC,Can
163/G3 Childersburg, Al,US
162/C3 Childress, Tx,US
134/B6 Chile
135/C2 Chilecito, Arg.
131/C2 Chilembwe, Zam.
101/D4 Ch'ilgap-san Nat'l Park, SKor.
131/B2 Chililabombwe, Zam.
106/E4 Chilka (lake), India
156/C3 Chilko (lake), BC,Can
151/L4 Chilkoot (pass), BC,Can, Ak,US
142/B3 Chillán, Chile
144/B1 Chillanes, Ecu.
117/F2 Chilla Well Abor. Land, Austl.
160/B3 Chillicothe, Il,US
159/J3 Chillicothe, Mo,US
160/D4 Chillicothe, Oh,US
166/B2 Chillisquaque (cr.), Pa,US
156/C3 Chilliwack, BC,Can
76/C5 Chillon, Swi.
53/S10 Chilly-Mazarin, Fr.
142/B4 Chiloé (isl.), Chile
142/B4 Chiloé Nat'l Park, Chile
156/C5 Chiloquin, Or,US
147/F5 Chilpancingo, Mex.
59/F3 Chiltern (hills), Eng,UK
130/B5 Chilumba, Malw.
131/D2 Chilwa (lake), Malw.
131/D1 Chimaliro (hill), Malw.
148/D3 Chimaltenango, Guat.
131/D3 Chimanimani, Zim.
131/D3 Chimanimani Nat'l Park, Zim.
139/F3 Chimantá-Tepuí (peak), Ven.
68/D3 Chimay, Belg.
88/F5 Chimbay, Uzb.
138/B5 Chimborazo (prov.), Ecu.
138/B5 Chimborazo (vol.), Ecu.
144/B3 Chimbote, Peru
138/C2 Chimichaqua, Col.
102/A3 Chimkent, Kaz.
131/D3 Chimoio, Moz.
131/D3 Chimoio (plat.), Moz.
104/B4 Chin (hills), Burma
104/B4 Chin (state), Burma
101/D5 Chin (isl.), SKor.
90/J6 China
147/F3 China, Mex.
131/B3 Chinamba (hills), Bots.
148/E3 Chinandega, Nic.
162/B4 Chinati (mts.), Tx,US
144/B4 Chincha Alta, Peru
152/E3 Chinchaga (riv.), Ab,Can
138/C3 Chinchiná, Col.
148/E2 Chinchorro, Banco (reef), Mex.
160/F4 Chincoteague, Va,US
126/G4 Chinde, Moz.
96/D4 Chindu, China
104/B4 Chindwin (riv.), Burma
104/E4 Chi Ne, Viet.
138/C3 Chingaza Nat'l Park, Col.
53/P7 Chingford, Eng,UK
106/C5 Chingleput, India
131/B2 Chingola, Zam.
128/B1 Chinguetti, Dhar de (hills), Mrta.
101/E5 Chinhae, SKor.
131/C3 Chinhoyi, Zim.
131/C3 Chinhoyi Caves, Zim.
151/H4 Chiniak (cape), Ak,US
108/B2 Chiniot, Pak.
109/D3 Chinit (riv.), Camb.
101/E5 Chinju, SKor.
125/K6 Chinko (riv.), CAfr.
158/E3 Chinle (dry riv.), Az, Ut,US
108/F3 Chinnalappatti, India
108/F4 Chinnamanūr, India
59/F3 Chinnor, Eng,UK
99/F3 Chino, Japan
164/C2 Chino, Ca,US
164/G8 Chino (hills), Ca,US
156/F3 Chinook, Mt,US
130/B5 Chinsali, Zam.
131/D1 Chintheche, Malw.
138/C2 Chinú, Col.
130/C5 Chinunje, Tanz.
131/D2 Chipata, Zam.
103/D3 Chiping, China
131/D4 Chipinge, Zim.
74/B4 Chipiona, Sp.
163/G4 Chipley, Fl,US
106/B4 Chiplūn, India
130/C4 Chipogolo, Tanz.
131/D2 Chipoka, Malw.
163/G4 Chipola (riv.), Fl,US
131/D2 Chiponde, Malw.
58/D4 Chippenham, Eng,UK
157/K4 Chippewa (riv.), Mn,US
168/F6 Chippewa (cr.), Oh,US
160/B2 Chippewa (riv.), Wi,US
160/B2 Chippewa Falls, Wi,US
168/F5 Chippewa Lake (Chippewa-on-the-Lake), Oh,US
59/E2 Chipping Campden, Eng,UK
59/E3 Chipping Norton, Eng,UK
53/P6 Chipping Ongar, Eng,UK
58/D3 Chipping Sodbury, Eng,UK
53/N8 Chipstead, Eng,UK
161/H2 Chiputneticook (lakes), NB,Can, Me,US
148/D3 Chiquimula, Guat.
148/D3 Chiquimulilla, Guat.
138/C3 Chiquinquirá, Col.
134/C6 Chiquita, Mar (lake), Arg.
134/A3 Chira (riv.), Peru
147/C1 Chiracahua Nat'l Mon., Az,US
131/D2 Chiradzulu, Malw.
106/D4 Chīrāla, India
102/A3 Chirchik, Uzb.
131/D3 Chire (riv.), Moz.
131/C4 Chiredzi, Zim.
124/H3 Chirfa, Niger
158/E4 Chiricahua Nat'l Mon., Az,US
138/C2 Chiriguaná, Col.
151/G4 Chirikof (isl.), Ak,US
149/E4 Chiripa (mtn.), Nic.
100/E1 Chirip Gora (mtn.), Rus.
149/F4 Chiriquí (gulf), Pan.
149/F4 Chiriquí (lag.), Pan.
101/D5 Chiri-san (mtn.), SKor.
101/D5 Chiri-san Nat'l Park, SKor.
57/E6 Chirk, Eng,UK
54/D5 Chirnside, Sc,UK
131/D3 Chiromo, Malw.
83/G4 Chirpan, Bul.
149/F4 Chirripó Grande (mtn.), CR
149/F4 Chirripó Nat'l Park, CR
131/C3 Chirundu, Zim.
99/N10 Chiryu, Japan
131/C2 Chisamba, Zam.
131/B2 Chisasa, Zam.
153/J3 Chisasibi (Fort-George), Qu,Can
59/E3 Chiseldon, Eng,UK
130/B5 Chisenga, Malw.
160/A2 Chisholm, Mn,US
95/K3 Chishtiān Mandi, Pak.
104/E3 Chishui (riv.), China
125/P8 Chisimayu, Som.
130/A5 Chisimba (falls), Zam.
82/E2 Chişineu Criş, Rom.
131/C2 Chisomo, Zam.
85/L5 Chistopol', Rus.
53/M6 Chiswell Green, Eng,UK
53/N7 Chiswick, Eng,UK
99/M10 Chita, Japan
99/M10 Chita (bay), Japan
99/M10 Chita (pen.), Japan
96/G1 Chita, Rus.
126/B4 Chitado, Ang.
130/B5 Chitipa, Malw.
131/D4 Chitobiço, Moz.
131/B3 Chitongo, Zam.
106/B3 Chitorgarh, India
100/B2 Chitose, Japan
106/C5 Chitradurga, India
106/D2 Chitrakut, India
149/F5 Chitré, Pan.
107/F3 Chittagong, Bang.
106/C5 Chittoor, India
108/F3 Chittūr, India
126/D4 Chiume, Ang.
131/C2 Chiundaponde, Zam.
78/A1 Chiusella (riv.), It.
138/D2 Chivacoa, Ven.
78/A2 Chivasso, It.
131/C3 Chivhu, Zim.
142/E2 Chivilcoy, Arg.
130/B5 Chiwanda, Tanz.
148/D3 Chixoy (riv.), Guat., Mex.
131/B3 Chizarira (hills), Zim.
131/B3 Chizarira Nat'l Park, Zim.
131/B2 Chizela, Zam.
123/R15 Chlef, Alg.
123/R15 Chlef (riv.), Alg.
123/R15 Chlef (wilaya), Alg.
71/H5 Chlum (peak), Czh.
54/B3 Chno Dearg (mtn.), Sc,UK
104/C2 Cho (pass), China
101/C3 Ch'o (isl.), NKor.
109/D3 Choam Khsant, Camb.
142/C1 Choapa (riv.), Chile
131/B3 Chobe (dist.), Bots.
131/B3 Chobe (riv.), Bots., Namb.
131/B3 Chobe Nat'l Park, Bots.
65/K4 Choč (peak), Slvk.
65/J4 Choceň, Czh.
101/D4 Choch'iwŏn, SKor.
65/H3 Chocianów, Pol.
138/B3 Chocó (dept.), Col.
158/D4 Chocolate (mts.), Ca,US
144/B2 Chocope, Peru
71/F2 Chodov, Czh.
65/J2 Chodzież, Pol.
99/F3 Chōfu, Japan
99/H7 Chōfū, Japan
120/E5 Choiseul (isl.), Sol.
53/T10 Choisy-le-Roi, Fr.
65/H2 Chojna, Pol.
65/J2 Chojnice, Pol.
65/H3 Chojnów, Pol.
100/B4 Chokai-san (mtn.), Japan
162/D4 Choke Canyon (res.), Tx,US
131/D5 Chokwe, Moz.
96/D5 Chola (mts.), China
72/C3 Cholet, Fr.
101/D5 Chŏlla-Bukto (prov.), SKor.
101/D5 Chŏlla-Namdo (prov.), SKor.
59/E3 Cholsey, Eng,UK
147/L7 Cholula de Rivadabia, Mex.
148/E3 Choluteca, Hon.
148/E3 Choluteca (riv.), Hon., Nic.
131/B3 Choma, Zam.
101/E4 Chŏmch'on, SKor.
106/E2 Chomo Lhāri (mtn.), Bhu.
71/G2 Chomutov, Czh.
71/G2 Chomutovka (riv.), Czh.
99/J7 Chōnan, Japan
101/D4 Ch'ŏnan, SKor.
109/C3 Chon Buri, Thai.
142/B4 Chonchi, Chile
138/A5 Chone, Ecu.
101/D2 Ch'ongch'ŏn (riv.), NKor.
101/E2 Ch'ŏngjin, NKor.
101/E2 Ch'ŏngjin-Si, NKor.
101/E2 Ch'ŏngjin-Si (prov.), NKor.
101/D4 Ch'ŏngju, SKor.
109/C3 Chong Kal, Camb.
103/C2 Chongli, China
103/L8 Chongming (isl.), China
101/G6 Chongmyo Shrine, SKor.
131/B3 Chongo, Zam.
144/B2 Chongoyape, Peru
104/E2 Chongqing, China
105/H3 Chongren, China
101/E4 Ch'ŏngsong, SKor.
131/C2 Chongwe, Zam.
103/C5 Chongyang, China
107/K2 Chongyi, China
105/E4 Chongzuo, China
101/D5 Chŏnju, SKor.
101/G6 Ch'ŏnmasan (mtn.), SKor.
142/A5 Chonos (arch.), Chile
135/A6 Chonos (isls.), Chile
109/D4 Chon Thanh, Viet.
166/C6 Choptank (riv.), Md,US
149/F4 Chorcha (mtn.), Pan.
57/F4 Chorley, Eng,UK
53/M7 Chorleywood, Eng,UK
86/C2 Chortkov, Ukr.
101/D3 Ch'ŏrwŏn, SKor.
65/K3 Chorzów, Pol.
99/G3 Chōshi, Japan
105/J4 Choshui (riv.), Tai.
65/H2 Choszczno, Pol.
144/B2 Chota, Peru
156/E4 Choteau, Mt,US
71/H3 Chotýšanka (riv.), Czh.
132/A2 Chowagasberg (peak), Namb.
163/J2 Chowan (riv.), NC,US
96/G2 Choybalsan, Mong.
115/R11 Christchurch, NZ
59/E5 Christchurch, Eng,UK
59/E5 Christchurch (bay), Eng,UK
151/L4 Christian (sound), Ak,US
149/G2 Christiana, Jam.
132/D2 Christiana, SAfr.
160/D4 Christiansburg, Va,US
166/C4 Christina (riv.), De,US

182

Chris – Coon

156/F2 **Christine** (riv.), Ab,Can
90/K11 **Christmas** (isl.), Austl.
121/K4 **Christmas** (Kiritimati) (atoll), Kiri.
65/H4 **Chrudim**, Czh.
54/B5 **Chryston**, Sc,UK
65/K3 **Chrzanów**, Pol.
105/H2 **Chu** (riv.), China
102/B3 **Chu** (riv.), Kaz.
109/D2 **Chu** (riv.), Viet.
103/E4 **Chuanchang** (riv.), China
103/E5 **Chuansha**, China
156/E5 **Chubbuck**, Id,US
100/A4 **Chūbu** (dist.), Japan
99/F2 **Chūbu** (prov.), Japan
142/C4 **Chubut** (prov.), Arg.
142/D4 **Chubut** (riv.), Arg.
149/G4 **Chucanti** (mtn.), Pan.
98/C3 **Chūgoku** (mts.), Japan
98/C3 **Chūgoku** (prov.), Japan
108/B2 **Chūhar Kāna**, Pak.
110/B3 **Chukai**, Malay.
97/M1 **Chukchagirskoye** (lake), Rus.
89/U3 **Chukchi** (pen.), Rus.
89/S3 **Chukchi Aut. Okr.**, Rus.
151/D3 **Chukotskiy, Mys** (pt.), Rus.
164/C5 **Chula Vista**, Ca,US
144/A2 **Chulucanas**, Peru
88/J4 **Chulym** (riv.), Rus.
102/E1 **Chulyshman** (riv.), Rus.
83/G4 **Chumerna** (peak), Bul.
109/B4 **Chumphon**, Thai.
88/K4 **Chuna** (riv.), Rus.
101/D4 **Ch'unch'ŏn**, SKor.
101/D4 **Ch'ungch'ong-Bukto** (prov.), SKor.
101/D4 **Ch'ungch'ŏng-Namdo** (prov.), SKor.
101/D4 **Ch'ungju**, SKor.
101/D4 **Ch'ungju-ho** (lake), SKor.
101/C2 **Ch'ungman** (riv.), NKor.
101/E5 **Ch'ungmu**, SKor.
101/G6 **Chungnang**, SKor.
130/A5 **Chungu**, Zam.
108/B2 **Chūniān**, Pak.
108/G4 **Chunnakam**, SrL.
89/L3 **Chunya** (riv.), Rus.
130/B5 **Chunya**, Tanz.
135/C1 **Chuquicamata**, Chile
77/F4 **Chur**, Swi.
104/B3 **Churachandpur**, India
57/F4 **Church**, Eng,UK
152/D3 **Churchill** (peak), BC,Can
152/G3 **Churchill**, Mb,Can
152/G3 **Churchill** (cape), Mb,Can
152/G3 **Churchill** (riv.), Mb, Sk,Can
153/K3 **Churchill** (riv.), Nf,Can
156/F1 **Churchill** (lake), Sk,Can
152/G3 **Churchill** (riv.), Mb, Sk,Can
119/G5 **Churchill Nat'l Park**, Austl.
58/D1 **Church Stretton**, Eng,UK
57/G6 **Churnet** (riv.), Eng,UK
106/B2 **Churu**, India
138/D2 **Churuguara**, Ven.
158/E3 **Chuska** (mts.), Az, NM,US
85/N4 **Chusovaya** (riv.), Rus.
85/N4 **Chusovoy**, Rus.
85/K5 **Chuvash Aut. Rep.**, Rus.
101/E4 **Chuwang-san Nat'l Park**, SKor.
104/D3 **Chuxiong**, China
96/B1 **Chuya** (riv.), Rus.
109/E3 **Chu Yang Sin** (peak), Viet.
105/H1 **Chuzhou**, China
99/M9 **Chūzu**, Japan
110/C5 **Ciamis**, Indo.
80/C2 **Ciampino**, It.
110/C5 **Cianjur**, Indo.
165/Q16 **Cicero**, Il,US
140/C3 **Cícero Dantas**, Braz.
80/C2 **Cicero Nat'l Park**, It.
92/C1 **Cide**, Turk.
65/L2 **Ciechanów**, Pol.
65/K2 **Ciechanów** (prov.), Pol.
65/K2 **Ciechocinek**, Pol.
149/G1 **Ciego de Ávila**, Cuba
138/C2 **Ciénaga**, Col.
138/C2 **Ciénaga de Oro**, Col.
149/F1 **Cienfuegos**, Cuba
65/H3 **Cieplice Śląskie Zdrój**, Pol.
65/K4 **Cieszyn**, Pol.
74/E3 **Cieza**, Sp.
92/B2 **Çifteler**, Turk.
149/F1 **Cifuentes**, Cuba
74/D3 **Cigüela** (riv.), Sp.
92/C2 **Cihanbeyli**, Turk.
146/D5 **Cihuatlán**, Mex.
74/C3 **Cijara** (res.), Sp.
110/C5 **Cijulang**, Indo.
110/C5 **Cilacap**, Indo.
93/E1 **Çıldır** (lake), Turk.
58/C2 **Cilfaesty** (hill), Wal,UK
159/G3 **Cimarron**, Ks,US
159/H3 **Cimarron** (riv.), Ks, Ok,US
162/B2 **Cimarron** (range), NM,US
79/D4 **Cimone, Monte** (peak), It.
82/F2 **Cimpeni**, Rom.
83/F2 **Cimpia Turzii**, Rom.
83/G3 **Cimpina**, Rom.
83/G3 **Cimpulung**, Rom.
83/G2 **Cimpulung Moldovenesc**, Rom.
138/D3 **Cinaruco** (riv.), Ven.
75/F1 **Cinca** (riv.), Sp.
82/C4 **Cincar** (peak), Bosn.
160/C4 **Cincinnati**, Oh,US
142/C3 **Cinco Saltos**, Arg.
58/D3 **Cinderford**, Eng,UK
83/F3 **Cindrelu** (peak), Rom.
92/B2 **Çine**, Turk.
69/E3 **Ciney**, Belg.
78/C1 **Cinisello Balsamo**, It.
166/D4 **Cinnaminson**, NJ,US
148/C2 **Cintalapa**, Mex.
80/A1 **Cinto** (mtn.), Fr.
82/C4 **Čiovo** (isl.), Cro.
140/C3 **Cipó**, Braz.
142/D3 **Cipolletti**, Arg.
157/G4 **Circle**, Mt,US
160/D4 **Circleville**, Oh,US
110/C5 **Cirebon**, Indo.
58/E3 **Cirencester**, Eng,UK
78/A2 **Ciriè**, It.
80/E3 **Cirò Marina**, It.
72/C4 **Ciron** (riv.), Fr.
83/G3 **Cisnădie**, Rom.
138/C3 **Cisneros**, Col.
142/B5 **Cisnes** (riv.), Chile
72/D3 **Cisse** (riv.), Fr.
80/C2 **Cisterna di Latina**, It.
148/B2 **Citlaltépetl** (vol.), Mex.
165/M9 **Citrus Heights**, Ca,US
79/E1 **Cittadella**, It.
79/F6 **Città di Castello**, It.
80/E3 **Cittanova**, It.
167/K8 **City** (isl.), NY,US
116/K6 **City Beach**, Austl.
139/F2 **Ciudad Bolívar**, Ven.
147/H5 **Ciudad del Carmen**, Mex.
75/G3 **Ciudadela**, Sp.
139/F2 **Ciudad Guayana**, Ven.
146/E5 **Ciudad Guzmán**, Mex.
147/E5 **Ciudad Hidalgo**, Mex.
146/E3 **Ciudad Lerdo**, Mex.
147/F4 **Ciudad Madero**, Mex.
147/F4 **Ciudad Mante**, Mex.
147/M8 **Ciudad Mendoza**, Mex.
146/C3 **Ciudad Obregón**, Mex.
138/D2 **Ciudad Ojeda**, Ven.
74/D3 **Ciudad Real**, Sp.
74/B2 **Ciudad-Rodrigo**, Sp.
147/M8 **Ciudad Serdán**, Mex.
147/F4 **Ciudad Valles**, Mex.
147/F4 **Ciudad Victoria**, Mex.
92/D1 **Civa** (pt.), Turk.
86/F4 **Civa Burnu** (pt.), Turk.
79/G1 **Cividale del Friuli**, It.
80/C1 **Civita Castellana**, It.
80/B1 **Civitavecchia**, It.
92/B2 **Çivril**, Turk.
103/L9 **Cixi**, China
103/C3 **Ci Xian**, China
92/E2 **Cizre**, Turk.
92/E2 **Cizre** (dam), Turk.
74/E1 **Cizur**, Sp.
54/C4 **Clackmannan**, Sc,UK
59/H3 **Clacton on Sea**, Eng,UK
58/C2 **Claerwen** (res.), Wal,UK
72/D3 **Clain** (riv.), Fr.
152/E3 **Claire** (lake), Ab,Can
158/B2 **Clair Engle** (lake), Ca,US
72/D3 **Claise** (riv.), Fr.
165/A2 **Clallam** (co.), Wa,US
53/S10 **Clamart**, Fr.
59/F5 **Clanfield**, Eng,UK
163/G3 **Clanton**, Al,US
54/A5 **Claonig**, Sc,UK
161/Q9 **Clappison's Corners**, On,Can
142/D4 **Clara** (pt.), Arg.
60/B4 **Clare** (co.), Ire.
54/F10 **Clare** (isl.), Ire.
60/B3 **Clare** (riv.), Ire.
160/C3 **Clare**, Mi,US
164/C2 **Claremont**, Ca,US
161/F3 **Claremont**, NH,US
159/J3 **Claremore**, Ok,US
119/E1 **Clarence** (riv.), Austl.
114/E2 **Clarence** (str.), Austl.
153/T7 **Clarence** (pt.), NW,Can
115/R11 **Clarence**, NZ
161/S9 **Clarence**, NY,US
162/C3 **Clarendon**, Tx,US
156/E3 **Claresholm**, BC,Can
113/J **Clarie** (coast), Ant.
146/B5 **Clarion** (isl.), Mex.
167/H9 **Clark**, NJ,US
166/B3 **Clark** (cr.), Pa,US
157/J4 **Clark**, SD,US
119/D4 **Clarke** (isl.), Austl.
118/B3 **Clarke** (range), Austl.
166/B4 **Clarke** (lake), Pa,US
156/E3 **Clark Fork** (riv.), Id, Mt,US
163/H3 **Clark Hill** (lake), Ga, SC,US
160/D4 **Clarksburg**, WV,US
163/F3 **Clarksdale**, Ms,US
161/G8 **Clarkson**, On,Can
165/F6 **Clarkston**, Mi,US
156/D4 **Clarkston**, Wa,US
162/E3 **Clarksville**, Ar,US
163/G2 **Clarksville**, Tn,US
162/E3 **Clarksville**, Tx,US
141/B1 **Claro** (riv.), Braz.
68/C3 **Clary**, Fr.
56/D1 **Clatteringshaws Loch** (lake), Sc,UK
56/A2 **Claudy**, NI,UK
67/H5 **Clausthal-Zellerfeld**, Ger.
112/D3 **Claver**, Phil.
112/C1 **Claveria**, Phil.
112/D3 **Claveria**, Phil.
165/F6 **Clawson**, Mi,US
159/H3 **Clay Center**, Ks,US
57/G5 **Clay Cross**, Eng,UK
59/H2 **Claydon**, Eng,UK
53/U10 **Claye-Souilly**, Fr.
53/M7 **Claygate**, Eng,UK
56/D3 **Clay Head** (pt.), IM,UK
166/C4 **Claymont**, De,US
165/L11 **Clayton**, Ca,US
163/H3 **Clayton**, Ga,US
166/C4 **Clayton**, NJ,US
159/G3 **Clayton**, NM,US
159/J4 **Clayton**, Ok,US
57/F4 **Clayton-le-Moors**, Eng,UK
143/S11 **Clé** (stream), Arg.
152/E3 **Clear** (hills), Ab,Can
55/G11 **Clear** (cape), Ire.
158/B3 **Clear** (lake), Ca,US
151/J4 **Cleare** (cape), Ak,US
147/E1 **Clear Fork** (riv.), Tx,US
157/J4 **Clear Lake**, SD,US
156/C3 **Clearwater**, BC,Can
163/H5 **Clearwater**, Fl,US
156/D4 **Clearwater** (mts.), Id,US
157/K4 **Clearwater** (riv.), Mn,US
56/E2 **Cleator Moor**, Eng,UK
162/D3 **Cleburne**, Tx,US
57/H4 **Cleethorpes**, Eng,UK
58/D3 **Cleeve** (hill), Eng,UK
117/M8 **Cleland Rec. Area**, Austl.
163/H3 **Clemson**, SC,US
58/D2 **Cleobury Mortimer**, Eng,UK
112/B3 **Cleopatra Needle** (mtn.), Phil.
68/A4 **Clères**, Fr.
69/E3 **Clerf** (riv.), Belg., Lux.
68/B5 **Clermont**, Fr.
58/D4 **Clevedon**, Eng,UK
118/B2 **Cleveland** (cape), Austl.
57/G2 **Cleveland** (co.), Eng,UK
57/^3 **Cleveland** (hills), Eng,UK
163/F3 **Cleveland**, Ms,US
156/E3 **Cleveland** (peak), Mt,US
168/F4 **Cleveland**, Oh,US
163/G3 **Cleveland**, Tn,US
162/E4 **Cleveland**, Tx,US
168/F5 **Cleveland Heights**, Oh,US
141/A3 **Clevelândia**, Braz.
164/C3 **Cleveland Nat'l For.**, Ca,US
60/A2 **Clew** (bay), Ire.
163/H5 **Clewiston**, Fl,US
68/B6 **Clichy**, Fr.
53/T10 **Clichy-sous-Bois**, Fr.
167/K8 **Cliffside Park**, NJ,US
58/D4 **Clifton**, Eng,UK
158/E4 **Clifton**, Az,US
167/D2 **Clifton**, NJ,US
162/D4 **Clifton**, Tx,US
163/J2 **Clifton Forge**, Va,US
58/D2 **Clifton upon Teme**, Eng,UK
68/C5 **Clignon** (riv.), Fr.
163/H3 **Clingmans** (mtn.), Tn,US
156/C3 **Clinton**, BC,Can
157/L5 **Clinton**, Ia,US
160/B3 **Clinton**, Il,US
163/F4 **Clinton**, La,US
168/C1 **Clinton**, Ma,US
165/G6 **Clinton**, Mi,US
165/F6 **Clinton** (riv.), Mi,US
159/J3 **Clinton**, Mo,US
163/F3 **Clinton**, Ms,US
163/J3 **Clinton**, NC,US
166/D1 **Clinton** (res.), NJ,US
159/H4 **Clinton**, Ok,US
166/A1 **Clinton** (co.), Pa,US
163/H3 **Clinton**, SC,US
152/F2 **Clinton-Colden** (lake), NW,Can
152/B2 **Clinton Creek**, Yk,Can
165/G6 **Clinton, Middle Branch** (riv.), Mi,US
165/G6 **Clinton, North Branch** (riv.), Mi,US
166/B6 **Clinton** (Surrattsville), Md,US
54/D5 **Clints Dod** (hill), Sc,UK
160/D3 **Clio**, Mi,US
50/D5 **Clipperton** (isl.), Fr.
59/F2 **Clipston**, Eng,UK
57/F4 **Clitheroe**, Eng,UK
116/B2 **Cloates** (pt.), Austl.
55/H10 **Clogher**, Ire.
60/D2 **Clogherhead**, Ire.
60/D2 **Clogher Head** (pt.), Ire.
56/C3 **Cloghy**, NI,UK
60/B6 **Clonakilty** (bay), Ire.
60/C5 **Clonmel**, Ire.
67/F3 **Cloppenburg**, Ger.
157/K4 **Cloquet**, Mn,US
135/E2 **Closeburn**, Ire.
56/E1 **Closeburn**, Sc,UK
167/K8 **Closter**, NJ,US
156/G4 **Cloud** (peak), Wy,US
162/B3 **Cloudcroft**, NM,US
151/G3 **Cloudy** (mtn.), Ak,US
56/B2 **Cloughmills**, NI,UK
57/H3 **Cloughton**, Eng,UK
58/B4 **Clovelly**, Eng,UK
158/B3 **Cloverdale**, Ca,US
158/C3 **Clovis**, Ca,US
159/G4 **Clovis**, NM,US
54/A3 **Clovullin**, Sc,UK
57/G5 **Clowne**, Eng,UK
54/A2 **Cluanie, Loch** (lake), Sc,UK
83/F2 **Cluj** (co.), Rom.
83/F2 **Cluj-Napoca**, Rom.
58/C2 **Clun**, Eng,UK
58/B3 **Clunderwen**, Wal,UK
76/C5 **Cluses**, Fr.
78/C1 **Clusone**, It.
56/E5 **Clwyd** (co.), Wal,UK
57/E5 **Clwyd** (riv.), Wal,UK
57/E5 **Clwydian** (range), Wal,UK
58/C3 **Clydach**, Wal,UK
161/H2 **Clyde** (riv.), NS,Can
156/E2 **Clyde**, NW,Can
54/B5 **Clyde** (riv.), Sc,UK
54/B5 **Clydebank**, Sc,UK
54/B6 **Clyde, Firth of** (inlet), Sc,UK
54/C5 **Clydesdale** (val.), Sc,UK
55/K10 **Clywd** (riv.), Wal,UK
58/C2 **Clywedog** (riv.), Wal,UK
161/R8 **CN Tower**, On,Can
74/B2 **Côa** (riv.), Port.
158/C4 **Coachella**, Ca,US
56/B2 **Coagh**, NI,UK
146/E3 **Coahuila** (state), Mex.
54/C5 **Coalburn**, Sc,UK
156/E3 **Coaldale**, Ab,Can
159/H4 **Coalgate**, Ok,US
156/E3 **Coalhurst**, Ab,Can
56/B2 **Coalisland**, NI,UK
59/E1 **Coalville**, Eng,UK
158/E2 **Coalville**, Ut,US
140/C4 **Coaraci**, Braz.
136/F4 **Coari**, Braz.
136/F5 **Coari** (riv.), Braz.
152/C2 **Coast** (mts.), BC, Yk,Can
130/C3 **Coast** (prov.), Kenya
154/B4 **Coast** (ranges), Ca,US
163/H4 **Coastal** (plain), US
54/B5 **Coatbridge**, Sc,UK
147/F5 **Coatepec**, Mex.
147/F5 **Coatepec Harinas**, Mex.
166/C4 **Coatesville**, Pa,US
147/K8 **Coatetelco**, Mex.
161/G2 **Coaticook**, Qu,Can
153/H2 **Coats** (isl.), NW,Can
113/Y **Coats Land** (reg.), Ant.
147/G5 **Coatzacoalcos**, Mex.
148/C2 **Coatzacoalcos** (riv.), Mex.
147/L8 **Coatzingo**, Mex.
147/M6 **Coatzintla**, Mex.
147/J4 **Coba** (ruins), Mex.
74/B1 **Coba de Serpe, Sierra de** (mtn.), Sp.
148/D3 **Cobán**, Guat.
119/D3 **Cobberas** (peak), Austl.
168/B1 **Cobble Mountain** (res.), Ma,US
164/B1 **Cobblestone** (mtn.), Ca,US
60/B6 **Cóbh**, Ire.
157/K2 **Cobham** (riv.), Mb, On,Can
53/M8 **Cobham**, Eng,UK
136/E6 **Cobija**, Bol.
114/E2 **Cobourg** (pen.), Austl.
160/E3 **Cobourg**, On,Can
142/B3 **Cobquecura**, Chile
131/D2 **Cóbuè**, Moz.
119/F5 **Coburg**, Austl.
153/T7 **Coburg** (isl.), NW,Can
70/D2 **Coburg**, Ger.
138/B5 **Coca**, Ecu.
138/B5 **Coca** (riv.), Ecu.
140/B1 **Cocal**, Braz.
166/B3 **Cocalico** (cr.), Pa,US
77/G5 **Coca, Pizzo di** (peak), It.
75/E3 **Cocentaina**, Sp.
136/E7 **Cochabamba**, Bol.
139/F2 **Coche** (isl.), Ven.
108/F4 **Cochin**, India
168/C1 **Cochituate**, Ma,US
163/H4 **Cochran**, Ga,US
156/E3 **Cochrane**, Ab,Can
160/D1 **Cochrane**, On,Can
168/B3 **Cockaponset Saint For.**, Ct,US
119/G5 **Cockatoo**, Austl.
116/K7 **Cockburn** (sound), Austl.
143/J8 **Cockburn** (chan.), Chile
54/D5 **Cockburnspath**, Sc,UK
54/D3 **Cock Cairn** (mtn.), Sc,UK
54/D5 **Cockenzie**, Sc,UK
57/E2 **Cockermouth**, Eng,UK
166/B5 **Cockeysville**, Md,US
132/D4 **Cockscomb** (peak), SAfr.
136/A2 **Coco** (isl.), CR
149/G1 **Coco** (cay), Cuba
149/F3 **Coco** (riv.), Hon., Nic.
163/H4 **Cocoa**, Fl,US
158/D4 **Coconino** (plat.), Az,US
119/C2 **Cocoparra Nat'l Park**, Austl.
90/J11 **Cocos** (isls.), Austl.
140/A4 **Côcos**, Braz.
149/G4 **Cocos** (pt.), Pan.
153/K3 **Cod** (isl.), Nf,Can
136/F4 **Codajás**, Braz.
57/G3 **Cod Beck** (riv.), Eng,UK
142/C2 **Codegua**, Chile
139/E2 **Codera** (cape), Ven.
79/F3 **Codigoro**, It.
83/G3 **Codlea**, Rom.
140/B2 **Codó**, Braz.
78/C2 **Codogno**, It.
166/B4 **Codorus** (cr.), Pa,US
79/F1 **Codroipo**, It.
58/D1 **Codsall**, Eng,UK
156/F4 **Cody**, Wy,US
140/B2 **Coelho Neto**, Braz.
67/E5 **Coesfeld**, Ger.
51/M6 **Coetivy** (isl.), Sey.
156/D4 **Coeur d'Alene**, Id,US
156/D4 **Coeur d'Alene** (lake), Id,US
66/D3 **Coevorden**, Neth.
159/J3 **Coffeyville**, Ks,US
117/G5 **Coffin Bay Nat'l Park**, Austl.
119/E1 **Coffs Harbour**, Austl.
147/F5 **Cofre de Perote Nat'l Park**, Mex.
59/G3 **Coggeshall**, Eng,UK
80/A2 **Coghinas** (lake), It.
72/C4 **Cognac**, Fr.
78/B4 **Cogoleto**, It.
166/C5 **Cohansey** (riv.), NJ,US
168/D1 **Cohasset**, Ma,US
116/L7 **Cohunu Nat'l Park**, Austl.
149/F5 **Coiba** (isl.), Pan.
143/K7 **Coig** (riv.), Arg.
142/B5 **Coihaique**, Chile
142/C3 **Coihueco**, Chile
108/F3 **Coimbatore**, India
74/A2 **Coimbra**, Port.
74/A2 **Coimbra** (dist.), Port.
74/C4 **Coín**, Sp.
75/P10 **Coina** (riv.), Port.
72/F4 **Coise** (riv.), Fr.
136/E2 **Cojedes** (riv.), Ven.
138/D2 **Cojedes** (state), Ven.
138/A4 **Cojimíes**, Ecu.
142/C5 **Cojudo Blanco** (peak), Arg.
148/D3 **Cojutepeque**, ESal.
156/F5 **Cokeville**, Wy,US
119/B3 **Colac**, Austl.
159/H2 **Colamus** (riv.), Ne,US
75/P10 **Colares**, Port.
141/D1 **Colatina**, Braz.
113/P **Colbeck** (cape), Ant.
142/C2 **Colbún**, Chile
159/G3 **Colby**, Ks,US
144/D4 **Colca** (riv.), Peru
59/G3 **Colchester**, Eng,UK
168/B2 **Colchester**, Ct,US
156/F2 **Cold** (lake), Ab, Sk,Can
57/F2 **Cold Fell** (mtn.), Eng,UK
54/D5 **Coldingham**, Sc,UK
156/F2 **Cold Lake**, Ab,Can
157/K4 **Cold Spring**, Mn,US
162/E4 **Coldspring**, Tx,US
54/D5 **Coldstream**, Sc,UK
159/H3 **Coldwater**, Ks,US
160/C3 **Coldwater**, Mi,US
59/E3 **Cole** (riv.), Eng,UK
58/D3 **Coleford**, Eng,UK
162/D4 **Coleman**, Tx,US
93/E2 **Çölemerik**, Turk.
56/B1 **Coleraine**, NI,UK
56/B1 **Coleraine** (dist.), NI,UK
108/G3 **Coleroon** (riv.), India
132/D3 **Colesberg**, SAfr.
59/E2 **Coleshill**, Eng,UK
166/A5 **Colesville**, Md,US
156/D4 **Colfax**, Wa,US
153/S6 **Colgate** (cape), NW,Can
142/C5 **Colhué Huapí** (lake), Arg.
109/D2 **Co Lieu**, Viet.
146/E5 **Colima**, Mex.
146/D5 **Colima** (state), Mex.
146/E5 **Colima, de Nevado** (peak), Mex.
142/C2 **Colina**, Chile
140/A2 **Colinas**, Braz.
164/F7 **Coliseum, Los Angles**, Ca,US
63/Q1 **Colkhov** (riv.), Rus.
55/H8 **Coll** (isl.), Sc,UK
74/D2 **Collado-Villalba**, Sp.
78/D3 **Collecchio**, It.
131/C4 **Colleen Bawn**, Zim.
151/J3 **College**, Ak,US
166/B6 **College Park**, Md,US
162/D4 **College Station**, Tx,US
78/A2 **Collegno**, It.
116/C5 **Collie**, Austl.
114/C3 **Collier** (bay), Austl.
116/C3 **Collier** (range), Austl.
57/G2 **Collier Law** (hill), Eng,UK
116/C3 **Collier Range Nat'l Park**, Austl.
163/F3 **Collierville**, Tn,US
58/B6 **Colliford** (res.), Eng,UK
57/G4 **Collingham**, Eng,UK
160/D2 **Collingwood**, On,Can
115/R11 **Collingwood**, NZ
163/F4 **Collins**, Ms,US
159/J3 **Collinsville**, Ok,US
160/E4 **Collinsville**, Va,US
123/V17 **Collo**, Alg.
76/D1 **Colmar**, Fr.
74/D2 **Colmenar Viejo**, Sp.
143/J7 **Colmillo** (cape), Chile
56/D1 **Colmonell**, Sc,UK
59/E3 **Coln** (riv.), Eng,UK
57/F4 **Colne**, Eng,UK
59/G3 **Colne** (riv.), Eng,UK
146/A2 **Colnett, Punta** (pt.), Mex.
53/N6 **Colney Heath**, Eng,UK
109/D1 **Co Loa Citadel**, Viet.
69/F2 **Cologne** (Köln), Ger.
78/C1 **Cologno Monzese**, It.
53/S10 **Colombes**, Fr.
76/A1 **Colombey-les-Deux-Eglises**, Fr.
136/D3 **Colombia**
78/D1 **Colombine, Monte** (peak), It.
141/B3 **Colombo**, Braz.
106/C6 **Colombo** (cap.), SrL.
78/A2 **Colombo, Monte** (peak), It.
72/D5 **Colomiers**, Fr.
142/E2 **Colón**, Arg.
142/F2 **Colón**, Arg.
149/F1 **Colón**, Cuba
149/E3 **Colón** (mts.), Hon.
149/G4 **Colón**, Pan.
144/A1 **Colonche**, Ecu.
120/C4 **Colonia**, Micro.
143/F2 **Colonia** (dept.), Uru.
167/D2 **Colonia**, NJ,US
143/F2 **Colonia Del Sacramento**, Uru.
140/D3 **Colônia Leopoldina**, Braz.
166/B3 **Colonial Park**, Pa,US
55/H8 **Colonsay** (isl.), Sc,UK
143/K7 **Colorado** (peak), Arg.
142/D3 **Colorado** (riv.), Arg.
141/B2 **Colorado**, Braz.
158/D4 **Colorado** (riv.), Mex., US
158/E3 **Colorado** (plat.), US
158/F3 **Colorado** (state), US
162/D4 **Colorado** (riv.), Tx,US
159/F3 **Colorado City**, Co,US
162/C3 **Colorado City**, Tx,US
158/E3 **Colorado Nat'l Mon.**, Co,US
164/C3 **Colorado River** (aqueduct), Ca,US
135/C2 **Colorados, Desagües de los** (marsh), Arg.
159/F3 **Colorado Springs**, Co,US
146/E4 **Colotlán**, Mex.
148/B2 **Colotlipa**, Mex.
136/E7 **Colquiri**, Bol.
148/D2 **Colson** (pt.), Belz.
156/G4 **Colstrip**, Mt,US
56/D1 **Colt** (hill), Sc,UK
142/C2 **Coltauco**, Chile
59/H1 **Coltishall**, Eng,UK
164/C2 **Colton**, Ca,US
134/D4 **Coluene** (riv.), Braz.
144/B1 **Columbe**, Ecu.
152/E3 **Columbia** (mtn.), Ab,Can
156/C2 **Columbia** (mts.), BC,Can
153/T6 **Columbia** (cape), NW,Can
156/C4 **Columbia** (riv.), Can., US
156/D4 **Columbia** (plat.), US
160/C4 **Columbia**, Ky,US
162/E3 **Columbia**, La,US
166/B5 **Columbia**, Md,US
159/J3 **Columbia**, Mo,US
163/F4 **Columbia**, Ms,US
152/E4 **Columbia** (plat.), Or,US
166/B3 **Columbia**, Pa,US
163/H3 **Columbia** (cap.), SC,US
163/G3 **Columbia**, Tn,US
156/E3 **Columbia Falls**, Mt,US
168/G6 **Columbiana** (co.), Oh,US
132/B4 **Columbine** (cape), SAfr.
163/G3 **Columbus**, Ga,US
160/C4 **Columbus**, In,US
163/F3 **Columbus**, Ms,US
156/F4 **Columbus**, Mt,US
159/H2 **Columbus**, Ne,US
158/F5 **Columbus**, NM,US
160/D4 **Columbus** (cap.), Oh,US
162/D4 **Columbus**, Tx,US
163/F3 **Columbus A.F.B.**, Ms,US
158/B3 **Colusa**, Ca,US
152/D2 **Colville** (lake), NW,Can
151/H2 **Colville** (riv.), Ak,US
156/D3 **Colville**, Wa,US
165/B3 **Colvos** (passg.), Wa,US
58/D2 **Colwall**, Eng,UK
58/C4 **Colwinston**, Wal,UK
56/E5 **Colwyn Bay**, Wal,UK
79/F3 **Comacchio**, It.
79/F3 **Comacchio, Valli di** (lag.), It.
107/F2 **Comai**, China
147/G5 **Comalcalco**, Mex.
162/D4 **Comanche**, Tx,US
142/F3 **Comandante Nicanor Otamendi**, Arg.
83/H2 **Comănești**, Rom.
83/G3 **Comarnic**, Rom.
144/B3 **Comas**, Peru
148/E3 **Comayagua**, Hon.
135/B3 **Combarbalá**, Chile
58/B4 **Combe Martin**, Eng,UK
56/C2 **Comber**, NI,UK
104/B5 **Combermere** (bay), Burma
53/T11 **Combs-la-Ville**, Fr.
118/C4 **Comet** (riv.), Austl.
107/F3 **Comilla**, Bang.
68/B2 **Comines**, Belg.
68/C2 **Comines**, Fr.
148/C2 **Comitán**, Mex.
167/E2 **Commack**, NY,US
72/E3 **Commentry**, Fr.
164/B2 **Commerce**, Ca,US
69/E6 **Commercy**, Fr.
139/H3 **Commewijne** (dist.), Sur.
153/H2 **Committee** (bay), NW,Can
102/B4 **Communism** (Kommunizma) (peak), Taj.
78/C1 **Como**, It.
77/F5 **Como** (lake), It.
78/C1 **Como** (prov.), It.
165/P14 **Como** (lake), Wi,US
142/D5 **Comodoro Rivadavia**, Arg.
128/D4 **Comoé** (prov.), Burk.
128/E4 **Comoé Nat'l Park**, IvC.
108/F4 **Comorin** (cape), India
133/G5 **Comoros**
156/B3 **Comox**, BC,Can
68/B5 **Compiègne**, Fr.
146/D4 **Compostela**, Mex.
164/B3 **Compton**, Ca,US
54/C4 **Comrie**, Sc,UK
162/C4 **Comstock**, Tx,US
107/F2 **Cona**, China
104/A2 **Co Nag** (lake), China
128/B4 **Conakry** (cap.), Gui.
128/B4 **Conakry** (comm.), Gui.
138/B5 **Conambo** (riv.), Ecu.
79/F5 **Conca** (riv.), It.
72/B3 **Concarneau**, Fr.
141/E1 **Conceição da Barra**, Braz.
141/B1 **Conceição das Alagoas**, Braz.
137/J5 **Conceição do Araguaia**, Braz.
140/C3 **Conceição do Coité**, Braz.
141/D1 **Conceição do Mato Dentro**, Braz.
141/H6 **Conceição do Rio Verde**, Braz.
141/H7 **Conceição dos Ouros**, Braz.
135/C2 **Concepción**, Arg.
136/E6 **Concepción**, Bol.
136/F7 **Concepción** (lake), Bol.
142/B3 **Concepción**, Chile
146/C3 **Concepción** (bay), Mex.
135/E1 **Concepción**, Par.
136/C6 **Concepción**, Peru
147/E3 **Concepción del Oro**, Mex.
142/F2 **Concepción del Uruguay**, Arg.
146/C3 **Concepción, Punta** (pt.), Mex.
158/B4 **Conception** (pt.), Ca,US
78/D1 **Concesio**, It.
131/C3 **Concession**, Zim.
141/F7 **Conchal**, Braz.
159/F4 **Conchas** (lake), NM,US
53/U10 **Conches**, Fr.
159/G5 **Concho** (riv.), Tx,US
165/K11 **Concord**, Ca,US
163/H3 **Concord**, NC,US
161/G3 **Concord** (cap.), NH,US
135/E3 **Concordia**, Arg.
141/A3 **Concórdia**, Braz.
159/H3 **Concordia**, Ks,US
79/F1 **Concordia Sagittaria**, It.
168/C1 **Concord Museum**, Ma,US
156/C3 **Concrete**, Wa,US
148/D3 **Concuen** (riv.), Guat.
109/D2 **Con Cuong**, Viet.
149/G1 **Condado**, Cuba
115/J5 **Condamine** (riv.), Austl.
140/C3 **Conde**, Braz.
68/C3 **Condé-sur-L'Escaut**, Fr.
72/C2 **Condé-sur-Noireau**, Fr.
140/B4 **Condeúba**, Braz.
118/C4 **Condomine** (riv.), Austl.
156/C4 **Condon**, Or,US
69/D3 **Condroz** (plat.), Belg.
163/G4 **Conecuh** (riv.), Al,US
79/F1 **Conegliano**, It.
162/B2 **Conejos**, Co,US
166/B3 **Conestoga** (riv.), Pa,US
166/B3 **Conewago** (cr.), Pa,US
166/B3 **Conewago** (lake), Pa,US
167/K9 **Coney Island**, NY,US
53/S10 **Conflans-Sainte-Honorine**, Fr.
167/E1 **Congers**, NY,US
105/G4 **Conghua**, China
105/F3 **Congjiang**, China
57/F5 **Congleton**, Eng,UK
126/B1 **Congo**
125/K7 **Congo** (basin), Afr.
126/C1 **Congo** (riv.), Afr.
141/G7 **Congonhal**, Braz.
141/D2 **Congonhas**, Braz.
122/E5 **Congo** (Zaire)
142/C3 **Conguillio Parque Nacional**, Chile
54/B4 **Conic** (hill), Sc,UK
142/C4 **Cónico, Cerro** (peak), Arg.
142/C4 **Cónico, Cerro Nevado** (peak), Chile
74/B4 **Conil de la Frontera**, Sp.
57/H5 **Coningsby**, Eng,UK
57/G5 **Conisbrough**, Eng,UK
57/E3 **Coniston**, Eng,UK
57/E3 **Coniston Water** (lake), Eng,UK
56/C2 **Conlig**, NI,UK
153/J1 **Conn** (lake), NW,Can
60/B2 **Connacht** (prov.), Ire.
57/E5 **Connah's Quay**, Wal,UK
160/D3 **Conneaut**, Oh,US
161/G2 **Connecticut** (riv.), US
161/F3 **Connecticut** (state), US
54/A4 **Connel**, Sc,UK
160/E3 **Connellsville**, Pa,US
60/A2 **Connemara** (dist.), Ire.
55/G10 **Connemara Nat'l Park**, Ire.
112/C1 **Conner**, Phil.
160/C4 **Connersville**, In,US
60/A1 **Conn, Lough** (lake), Ire.
138/B5 **Conocoto**, Ecu.
166/B3 **Conodoguinet** (cr.), Pa,US
143/K7 **Cono Grande** (peak), Arg.
54/B1 **Cononbridge**, Sc,UK
118/D4 **Conondale Nat'l Park**, Austl.
54/B1 **Conon, Falls of** (falls), Sc,UK
168/F6 **Conotton** (cr.), Oh,US
166/B4 **Conowingo** (dam), Md,US
72/E4 **Conques**, Fr.
156/F3 **Conrad**, Mt,US
162/E4 **Conroe**, Tx,US
167/F2 **Conscience Point Nat'l Wild. Ref.**, NY,US
141/D2 **Conselheiro Lafaiete**, Braz.
141/D1 **Conselheiro Pena**, Braz.
57/G2 **Consett**, Eng,UK
166/C3 **Conshohocken**, Pa,US
149/F1 **Consolación del Sur**, Cuba
109/D4 **Con Son** (isl.), Viet.
77/F2 **Constance** (Bodensee) (lake), Ger., Swi.
150/F4 **Constant** (mtn.), Guad.
83/J3 **Constanța**, Rom.
83/J3 **Constanța** (co.), Rom.
75/F2 **Constantí**, Sp.
74/C4 **Constantina**, Sp.
123/V17 **Constantine**, Alg.
123/V17 **Constantine** (gov.), Alg.
151/G4 **Constantine** (cape), Ak,US
150/D3 **Constanza**, DRep.
142/B2 **Constitución**, Chile
143/T11 **Constitución** (res.), Uru.
146/B2 **Constitución de 1857 Nat'l Park**, Mex.
74/D3 **Consuegra**, Sp.
106/E3 **Contai**, India
79/F2 **Contarina**, It.
140/B4 **Contas** (riv.), Braz.
141/C1 **Contegem**, Braz.
68/B4 **Contigny**, Fr.
156/C2 **Continental** (ranges), Ab, BC,Can
148/E1 **Contoy** (isl.), Mex.
165/L11 **Contra Costa** (can.), Ca,US
165/L11 **Contra Costa** (co.), Ca,US
74/E3 **Contreras** (res.), Sp.
151/J3 **Controller** (bay), Ak,US
142/B3 **Contulmo**, Chile
152/E2 **Contwoyto** (lake), NW,Can
68/B4 **Conty**, Fr.
138/C2 **Convención**, Col.
80/E2 **Conversano**, It.
118/C3 **Conway** (cape), Austl.
162/E3 **Conway**, Ar,US
161/G3 **Conway**, NH,US
163/J3 **Conway**, SC,US
118/C3 **Conway Range Nat'l Park**, Austl.
56/E5 **Conway, Vale of** (val.), Wal,UK
56/E5 **Conwy**, Wal,UK
56/D5 **Conwy** (bay), Wal,UK
56/E5 **Conwy** (riv.), Wal,UK
106/E2 **Cooch Behār**, India
118/F7 **Coochiemudlo** (isl.), Austl.
143/K8 **Cook** (bay), Chile
115/R11 **Cook** (str.), NZ
151/H3 **Cook** (inlet), Ak,US
165/Q16 **Cook** (co.), Il,US
116/C5 **Cooke** (peak), Austl.
163/G2 **Cookeville**, Tn,US
113/L **Cook Ice Shelf**, Ant.
121/J6 **Cook Islands** (terr.), NZ
115/R11 **Cook, Mount** (peak), NZ
56/B2 **Cookstown**, NI,UK
56/B2 **Cookstown** (dist.), NI,UK
119/B3 **Coola Coola** (swamp), Austl.
60/D2 **Cooley** (pt.), Ire.
118/D4 **Cooloola Nat'l Park**, Austl.
116/K7 **Cooloongup** (lake), Austl.
119/D3 **Cooma**, Austl.
60/A6 **Coomhola** (riv.), Ire.
165/N15 **Coon** (cr.), Il,US
165/G6 **Coon** (cr.), Mi,US

183
Coona – Dafen

116/D4 **Coonana Abor. Land,** Austl.
106/B5 **Coondapoor,** India
165/G6 **Coon, East Branch** (cr.), Mi,US
116/C2 **Coongan Abor. Land,** Austl.
108/F3 **Coonoor,** India
114/F5 **Cooper** (cr.), Austl.
162/E3 **Cooper,** Tx,US
157/J4 **Cooperstown,** ND,US
116/C3 **Coordewandy** (peak), Austl.
119/A3 **Coorong Nat'l Park,** Austl.
163/G3 **Coosa** (riv.), Al,US
156/B5 **Coos Bay,** Or,US
119/D2 **Cootamundra,** Austl.
138/C3 **Copacabana,** Col.
142/C3 **Copahué** (vol.), Chile
148/D3 **Copán** (ruins), Hon.
74/E4 **Cope** (cape), Sp.
56/C2 **Copeland** (isl.), NI,UK
62/E4 **Copenhagen** (København) (cap.), Den.
81/F2 **Copertino,** It.
119/D1 **Copeton** (dam), Austl.
167/E2 **Copiague,** NY,US
135/B2 **Copiapó,** Chile
79/E3 **Copparo,** It.
139/G3 **Coppename** (riv.), Sur.
67/G4 **Coppenbrügge,** Ger.
162/D4 **Copperas Cove,** Tx,US
131/B2 **Copperbelt** (prov.), Zam.
152/E2 **Coppermine** (riv.), NW,Can
57/F4 **Coppull,** Eng,UK
83/G2 **Copşa Mică,** Rom.
102/E5 **Coqên,** China
57/F1 **Coquet** (riv.), Eng,UK
57/G1 **Coquet Dale** (val.), Eng,UK
135/B2 **Coquimbo,** Chile
142/C1 **Coquimbo** (reg.), Chile
83/G4 **Corabia,** Rom.
140/A5 **Coração de Jesus,** Braz.
118/C1 **Coral** (sea), Austl.
138/C2 **Corales del Rosario Nat'l Park,** Col.
163/H5 **Coral Gables,** Fl,US
115/J2 **Coral Sea Is.** (terr.), Austl.
163/H5 **Coral Springs,** Fl,US
167/F2 **Coram,** NY,US
168/G6 **Coraopolis,** Pa,US
72/E2 **Corbeil-Essonnes,** Fr.
123/T15 **Corbelin** (cape), Alg.
77/F5 **Corbet, Piz** (peak), Swi.
78/B2 **Corbetta,** It.
68/B4 **Corbie,** Fr.
72/E5 **Corbieres** (mts.), Fr.
160/C4 **Corbin,** Ky,US
57/F2 **Corbridge,** Eng,UK
59/F2 **Corby,** Eng,UK
141/K7 **Corcovado** (mon.), Braz.
142/B4 **Corcovado** (gulf), Chile
142/B4 **Corcovado** (vol.), Chile
149/F4 **Corcovado Nat'l Park,** CR
141/D2 **Cordeiro,** Braz.
163/H4 **Cordele,** Ga,US
159/H4 **Cordell** (New Cordell), Ok,US
73/K4 **Cordenons,** It.
112/C1 **Cordillera Central** (mts.), Phil.
138/C4 **Cordillera de los Picachos Nat'l Park,** Col.
141/C1 **Cordisburgo,** Braz.
135/D3 **Córdoba,** Arg.
135/D3 **Córdoba** (mts.), Arg.
142/E2 **Córdoba** (prov.), Arg.
138/C2 **Córdoba** (dept.), Col.
147/F5 **Córdoba,** Mex.
74/C4 **Córdoba,** Sp.
151/J3 **Cordova** (peak), Ak,US
140/B1 **Coreaú,** Braz.
74/E1 **Corella,** Sp.
140/C2 **Coremas,** Braz.
136/G3 **Corentyne** (riv.), Guy.
81/F3 **Corfu** (Kérkira) (isl.), Gre.
74/B3 **Coria,** Sp.
74/B4 **Coria del Río,** Sp.
140/A4 **Coribe,** Braz.
119/D2 **Coricudgy** (peak), Austl.
80/E3 **Corigliano Calabro,** It.
115/J3 **Coringa Islets** (isls.), Austl.
81/H3 **Corinth** (gulf), Gre.
81/H4 **Corinth** (ruins), Gre.
163/F3 **Corinth,** Ms,US
81/H4 **Corinth** (Kórinthos), Gre.
141/C1 **Corinto,** Braz.
148/E3 **Corinto,** Nic.
74/A1 **Coristanco,** Sp.
60/B6 **Cork,** Ire.
60/B6 **Cork** (co.), Ire.
60/B6 **Cork** (har.), Ire.
80/C4 **Corleone,** It.
83/H5 **Çorlu,** Turk.
68/D5 **Cormontreuil,** Fr.
157/H2 **Cormorant,** Mb,Can
157/H2 **Cormorant** (lake), Mb,Can
58/C1 **Corndon** (hill), Wal,UK
141/B2 **Cornélio Procópio,** Braz.
153/K2 **Cornelius Grinnel** (bay), NW,Can
75/L7 **Cornella,** Sp.
119/C3 **Corner** (inlet), Austl.
161/K1 **Corner Brook,** Nf,Can
77/H6 **Cornetto** (peak), It.
168/B3 **Cornfield** (pt.), Ct,US
54/D1 **Cornhill,** Sc,UK
160/E3 **Corning,** NY,US
118/B3 **Cornish** (cr.), Austl.
79/D4 **Corno alle Scale** (peak), It.
78/D1 **Cornone di Blumone** (peak), It.
143/L8 **Cornú** (peak), Arg.
153/S7 **Cornwall** (isl.), NW,Can
160/F2 **Cornwall,** On,Can
161/J2 **Cornwall,** PE,Can
55/J11 **Cornwall** (cape), Eng,UK
58/B6 **Cornwall** (co.), Eng,UK
153/S7 **Cornwallis** (isl.), NW,Can
117/H5 **Corny** (pt.), Austl.
138/D2 **Coro,** Ven.
122/J9 **Coroa** (mtn.), CpV.
140/A2 **Coroatá,** Braz.
136/E7 **Corocoro,** Bol.
141/C1 **Coromandel,** Braz.
106/D5 **Coromandel** (coast), India
115/S10 **Coromandel,** NZ
115/S10 **Coromandel** (pen.), NZ
112/C2 **Coron,** Phil.
112/C3 **Coron** (isl.), Phil.
164/C3 **Corona,** Ca,US
159/F4 **Corona,** NM,US
164/G8 **Corona del Mar,** Ca,US
149/E4 **Coronado** (bay), CR
164/C5 **Coronado,** Ca,US
156/F2 **Coronation,** Ab,Can
152/E2 **Coronation** (gulf), NW,Can
142/E1 **Coronda,** Arg.
142/B3 **Coronel,** Chile
142/E3 **Coronel Dorrego,** Arg.
141/D1 **Coronel Fabriciano,** Braz.
142/D2 **Coronel Moldes,** Arg.
140/B5 **Coronel Murta,** Braz.
135/E2 **Coronel Oviedo,** Par.
142/E3 **Coronel Pringles,** Arg.
142/E3 **Coronel Suárez,** Arg.
141/A3 **Coronel Vivida,** Braz.
139/G3 **Coronie** (dist.), Sur.
144/C4 **Coropuna** (peak), Peru
148/D2 **Corozal,** Belz.
138/C2 **Corozal,** Col.
54/A3 **Corpach,** Sc,UK
162/D5 **Corpus Christi,** Tx,US
74/D3 **Corral de Almaguer,** Sp.
142/E2 **Corral de Bustos,** Arg.
75/Y16 **Corralejo,** Canl.
149/F1 **Corralillo,** Cuba
119/B3 **Corrangamite** (lake), Austl.
149/F4 **Corredor,** CR
79/D3 **Correggio,** It.
140/A3 **Corrente,** Braz.
140/A4 **Corrente** (riv.), Braz.
141/B1 **Corrente** (riv.), Braz.
131/D5 **Correntes, Cabo das** (cape), Moz.
140/A4 **Correntina,** Braz.
60/A3 **Corrib, Lough** (lake), Ire.
54/A5 **Corrie,** Sc,UK
135/E2 **Corrientes,** Arg.
138/B3 **Corrientes** (cape), Col.
149/E1 **Corrientes** (cape), Cuba
144/C1 **Corrientes** (riv.), Ecu., Peru
146/D4 **Corrientes, Cabo** (cape), Mex.
58/C1 **Corris,** Wal,UK
139/G3 **Corriverton,** Guy.
54/C2 **Corryhabbie** (mtn.), Sc,UK
80/A1 **Corse** (cape), Fr.
80/A1 **Corse** (reg.), Fr.
54/B5 **Corse** (hill), Sc,UK
56/D1 **Corserine** (mtn.), Sc,UK
56/C1 **Corsewall** (pt.), Sc,UK
58/D4 **Corsham,** Eng,UK
80/A1 **Corsica** (isl.), Fr.
162/D3 **Corsicana,** Tx,US
78/C2 **Corsico,** It.
166/D5 **Corsons** (inlet), NJ,US
80/A1 **Corte,** Fr.
112/D3 **Cortes,** Phil.
158/E3 **Cortez,** Co,US
73/K3 **Cortina d'Ampezzo,** It.
160/E3 **Cortland,** NY,US
128/B4 **Corubal** (riv.), GBis.
74/A3 **Coruche,** Port.
87/G4 **Çoruh** (riv.), Turk.
92/C1 **Çorum,** Turk.
92/C1 **Çorum** (prov.), Turk.
136/G7 **Corumbá,** Braz.
141/B1 **Corumbá** (riv.), Braz.
140/C5 **Corumbaú** (pt.), Braz.
140/C3 **Coruripe,** Braz.
156/C4 **Corvallis,** Or,US
58/D2 **Corve** (riv.), Eng,UK
75/R12 **Corvo** (isl.), Azor.
80/C1 **Corvo** (peak), It.
57/E6 **Corwen,** Wal,UK
147/G5 **Cosamaloapan,** Mex.
147/P8 **Cosamaloapan de Carpio,** Mex.
147/N7 **Cosautlán de Carvajal,** Mex.
147/M7 **Coscomatepec de Bravo,** Mex.
80/E3 **Cosenza,** It.
160/D3 **Coshocton,** Oh,US
168/E7 **Coshocton** (co.), Oh,US
148/E3 **Cosigüina** (pt.), Nic.
74/D2 **Coslada,** Sp.
116/D3 **Cosmo Newberry Abor. Rsv.,** Austl.
141/F7 **Cosmópolis,** Braz.
72/E3 **Cosne-Cours-sur-Loire,** Fr.
147/N8 **Cosolapa,** Mex.
147/G5 **Cosoleacaque,** Mex.
74/B1 **Cospeito,** Sp.
135/D3 **Cosquín,** Arg.
78/B1 **Cossato,** It.
72/D3 **Cosson** (riv.), Fr.
75/P10 **Costa da Caparica,** Port.
75/C4 **Costa del Sol** (coast), Sp.
164/C3 **Costa Mesa,** Ca,US
149/F4 **Costa Rica**
146/D3 **Costa Rica,** Mex.
78/D1 **Costa Volpino,** It.
59/H1 **Costessey,** Eng,UK
83/G3 **Costeşti,** Rom.
165/M10 **Cosumnes** (riv.), Ca,US
112/D4 **Cotabato City,** Phil.
138/B4 **Cotacachi** (peak), Ecu.
149/H4 **Cotatumbo** (riv.), Col., Ven.
128/D5 **Côte d'Ivoire** (Ivory Coast)
76/A3 **Côte-d'Or** (dept.), Fr.
72/F3 **Côte d'Or** (uplands), Fr.
140/A4 **Cotegipe,** Braz.
72/C2 **Cotentin** (pen.), Fr.
161/N7 **Côte-Saint-Luc,** Qu,Can
58/B3 **Cothi** (riv.), Wal,UK
141/G8 **Cotia,** Braz.
129/F5 **Cotonou,** Ben.
138/B5 **Cotopaxi** (prov.), Ecu.
138/B5 **Cotopaxi** (vol.), Ecu.
138/B5 **Cotopaxi Nat'l Park,** Ecu.
58/D4 **Cotswolds** (hills), Eng,UK
156/C5 **Cottage Grove,** Or,US
65/H3 **Cottbus,** Ger.
59/G2 **Cottenham,** Eng,UK
158/D4 **Cottonwood,** Az,US
162/D2 **Cottonwood** (riv.), Ks,US
159/F5 **Cottonwood** (dry riv.), Tx,US
116/K6 **Cottsloe,** Austl.
150/D3 **Cotuí,** DRep.
162/D4 **Cotulla,** Tx,US
53/U10 **Coubert,** Fr.
72/C4 **Coubre, Pointe de la** (pt.), Fr.
76/C5 **Cou, Col de** (pass), Fr.
68/C5 **Coucy-le-Château-Auffrique,** Fr.
68/B1 **Coudekerque-Branche,** Fr.
72/E5 **Couguille, Pic de** (peak), Fr.
72/D2 **Coulaines,** Fr.
156/D4 **Coulee City,** Wa,US
113/M **Coulman** (isl.), Ant.
68/C6 **Coulommiers,** Fr.
160/E2 **Coulonge** (riv.), Qu,Can
72/D4 **Coulounieix-Chamiers,** Fr.
53/N8 **Coulsdon,** Eng,UK
60/C5 **Coumfea** (mtn.), Ire.
156/D4 **Council,** Id,US
157/K5 **Council Bluffs,** Ia,US
159/H3 **Council Grove,** Ks,US
54/C3 **Coupar Angus,** Sc,UK
53/U10 **Coupvray,** Fr.
139/G3 **Courantyne** (riv.), Sur.
53/S10 **Courbevoie,** Fr.
68/D3 **Courcelles,** Belg.
69/F5 **Courcelles-Chaussy,** Fr.
53/T11 **Courcouronnes,** Fr.
72/E4 **Cournon-d'Auvergne,** Fr.
152/D4 **Courtenay,** BC,Can
161/S8 **Courtice,** On,Can
60/B6 **Courtmacsherry** (bay), Ire.
68/C2 **Courtrai** (Kortrijk), Belg.
53/T10 **Courtry,** Fr.
60/A6 **Cousane Gap** (pass), Ire.
72/C2 **Coutances,** Fr.
156/F3 **Coutts,** Ab,Can
68/D3 **Couvin,** Belg.
75/P10 **Cova da Piedade,** Port.
74/C1 **Covadonga Nat'l Park,** Sp.
83/H3 **Covasna,** Rom.
82/G3 **Covasna** (co.), Rom.
54/B5 **Cove,** Sc,UK
54/D2 **Cove Bay,** Sc,UK
59/E2 **Coventry,** Eng,UK
59/E1 **Coventry** (can.), Eng,UK
168/B2 **Coventry,** Ct,US
93/M7 **Covered Market,** Turk.
74/B2 **Covilhã,** Port.
164/C2 **Covina,** Ca,US
163/H3 **Covington,** Ga,US
160/C4 **Covington,** Ky,US
163/F3 **Covington,** Tn,US
160/E4 **Covington,** Va,US
54/A4 **Cowal** (dist.), Sc,UK
118/H8 **Cowan,** Austl.
116/D4 **Cowan** (lake), Austl.
58/C4 **Cowbridge,** Wal,UK
54/C4 **Cowdenbeath,** Sc,UK
59/E5 **Cowes,** Eng,UK
57/F2 **Cow Green** (res.), Eng,UK
54/C4 **Cowie,** Sc,UK
156/C4 **Cowlitz** (riv.), Wa,US
163/H3 **Cowpens Nat'l Bfld.,** SC,US
119/D2 **Cowra,** Austl.
57/G2 **Coxhoe,** Eng,UK
137/H7 **Coxim,** Braz.
53/T9 **Coye-la-Forêt,** Fr.
147/Q10 **Coyoacán,** Mex.
165/L12 **Coyote** (cr.), Ca,US
147/K7 **Coyotepec,** Mex.
147/E5 **Coyuca,** Mex.
148/A2 **Coyuca de Benítez,** Mex.
147/M6 **Coyutla,** Mex.
159/H2 **Cozad,** Ne,US
148/E1 **Cozumel** (isl.), Mex.
119/C4 **Cradle** (peak), Austl.
119/C4 **Cradle Mountain-Lake Saint Clair Nat'l Park,** Austl.
132/D4 **Cradock,** SAfr.
168/G7 **Crafton,** Pa,US
151/K3 **Crag** (mtn.), Yk,Can
57/F3 **Crag** (hill), Eng,UK
158/F2 **Craig,** Co,US
56/C2 **Craigavad,** NI,UK
56/B3 **Craigavon,** NI,UK
56/B3 **Craigavon** (dist.), NI,UK
54/C2 **Craigellachie,** Sc,UK
119/F5 **Craigieburn,** Austl.
157/G3 **Craik,** Sk,Can
54/D4 **Crail,** Sc,UK
70/D4 **Crailsheim,** Ger.
83/F3 **Craiova,** Rom.
77/E5 **Cramalina, Pizzo** (peak), Swi.
57/G1 **Cramlington,** Eng,UK
56/A1 **Crana** (riv.), Ire.
157/H2 **Cranberry Portage,** Mb,Can
58/D5 **Cranborne Chase** (for.), Eng,UK
119/C3 **Cranbourne,** Austl.
156/E3 **Cranbrook,** BC,Can
59/G4 **Cranbrook,** Eng,UK
162/C4 **Crane,** Tx,US
167/E2 **Crane Neck** (pt.), NY,US
157/J3 **Crane River,** Mb,Can
167/D2 **Cranford,** NJ,US
76/C6 **Cran-Gevrier,** Fr.
59/F4 **Cranleigh,** Eng,UK
168/C2 **Cranston,** RI,US
68/C5 **Craonne,** Fr.
83/F2 **Crasna** (riv.), Rom.
55/L9 **Craster,** Eng,UK
156/C5 **Crater** (lake), Or,US
156/C5 **Crater Lake Nat'l Park,** Or,US
156/E5 **Craters of the Moon Nat'l Mon.,** Id,US
140/B2 **Crateús,** Braz.
80/E3 **Crati** (riv.), It.
140/C2 **Crato,** Braz.
141/C2 **Cravinhos,** Braz.
54/C6 **Crawford,** Sc,UK
168/G4 **Crawford** (co.), Pa,US
160/C3 **Crawfordsville,** In,US
163/G4 **Crawfordville,** Fl,US
59/F4 **Crawley,** Eng,UK
53/P7 **Cray** (riv.), Eng,UK
53/P7 **Crayford,** Eng,UK
156/F4 **Crazy** (mts.), Mt,US
54/B3 **Creag Meagaidh** (mtn.), Sc,UK
166/B1 **Creasy** (Mifflinville), Pa,US
79/E2 **Creazzo,** It.
68/A3 **Crécy-en-Ponthieu,** Fr.
58/D2 **Credenhill,** Eng,UK
161/Q8 **Credit** (riv.), On,Can
58/C5 **Crediton,** Eng,UK
152/F3 **Cree** (lake), Sk,Can
152/F3 **Cree** (riv.), Sk,Can
56/D2 **Cree** (riv.), Sc,UK
146/D3 **Creel,** Mex.
56/D2 **Creetown,** Sc,UK
53/U10 **Crégy-lès-Meaux,** Fr.
157/H2 **Creighton,** Sk,Can
68/B5 **Creil,** Fr.
78/C2 **Crema,** It.
67/H4 **Cremlingen,** Ger.
78/D2 **Cremona,** It.
78/C2 **Cremona** (prov.), It.
68/B5 **Crépy-en-Valois,** Fr.
54/A3 **Creran, Loch** (inlet), Sc,UK
82/B3 **Cres** (isl.), Cro.
158/A2 **Crescent City,** Ca,US
105/F5 **Crescent Group** (isls.), China
142/E2 **Crespo,** Arg.
167/K8 **Cresskill,** NJ,US
72/F4 **Crest,** Fr.
165/P16 **Crest Hill,** Il,US
164/C2 **Crestline,** Ca,US
156/D3 **Creston,** BC,Can
157/K5 **Creston,** Ia,US
163/G4 **Crestview,** Fl,US
57/G5 **Creswell,** Eng,UK
76/B5 **Crêt de la Neige** (mtn.), Fr.
76/B5 **Crêt du Nu** (mtn.), Fr.
81/J5 **Crete** (isl.), Gre.
81/J5 **Crete** (sea), Gre.
159/H2 **Crete,** Ne,US
53/T10 **Créteil,** Fr.
54/B5 **Creuch** (hill), Sc,UK
75/G1 **Creus** (cape), Sp.
72/D3 **Creuse** (riv.), Fr.
71/E3 **Creussen** (riv.), Ger.
69/F5 **Creutzwald-la-Croix,** Fr.
79/E3 **Crevalcore,** It.
75/E3 **Crevillente,** Sp.
57/F5 **Crewe,** Eng,UK
58/D5 **Crewkerne,** Eng,UK
54/B4 **Crianlarich,** Sc,UK
56/D6 **Criccieth,** Wal,UK
141/B4 **Criciúma,** Braz.
58/C3 **Crickhowell,** Wal,UK
59/E3 **Cricklade,** Eng,UK
54/C4 **Crieff,** Sc,UK
68/A3 **Criel-sur-Mer,** Fr.
56/E2 **Criffell** (hill), Eng,UK
86/E3 **Crimean** (pen.), Ukr.
86/E3 **Crimean Obl.,** Ukr.
54/E1 **Crimond,** Sc,UK
124/H7 **Cristal** (mts.), Gabon
140/A5 **Cristalina,** Braz.
141/H7 **Cristina,** Braz.
140/A3 **Cristino Castro,** Braz.
144/J7 **Cristóbal** (pt.), Ecu.
138/C2 **Cristóbal Colón** (peak), Col.
82/F2 **Criştul Alb** (riv.), Rom.
83/G2 **Cristuru Secuiesc,** Rom.
82/E2 **Crişul Negru** (riv.), Rom.
137/H6 **Crixás-Açu** (riv.), Braz.
81/G2 **Crna Reka** (riv.), Macd.
60/A2 **Croaghmoyle** (mtn.), Ire.
119/D3 **Croajingolong Nat'l Park,** Austl.
82/B3 **Croatia**
77/H5 **Croce, Monte** (peak), It.
77/H4 **Croce, Pico di** (peak), It.
161/F2 **Croche** (riv.), Qu,Can
76/C6 **Croche, Aiguille** (peak), Fr.
144/J7 **Crocker** (peak), Ecu.
112/A4 **Crocker** (range), Malay.
56/E1 **Crocketford,** Sc,UK
162/E4 **Crockett,** Tx,US
119/D2 **Crocodile** (pt.), Austl.
166/B5 **Crofton,** Md,US
58/B3 **Crofty,** Wal,UK
60/D4 **Croghan** (mtn.), Ire.
60/A6 **Crohane** (mtn.), Ire.
72/F5 **Croisette** (cape), Fr.
53/T10 **Croissy-Beaubourg,** Fr.
157/L3 **Croix** (lake), Can., US
76/B5 **Croix de la Serra, Col de la** (pass), Fr.
114/E2 **Croker** (isl.), Austl.
54/B1 **Cromarty,** Sc,UK
54/B1 **Cromarty** (firth), Sc,UK
117/F3 **Crombie** (peak), Austl.
54/C2 **Cromdale,** Sc,UK
54/C2 **Cromdale** (hills), Sc,UK
59/H1 **Cromer,** Eng,UK
115/Q12 **Cromwell,** NZ
168/B2 **Cromwell,** Ct,US
109/E3 **Crong A Na** (riv.), Viet.
118/H9 **Cronulla,** Austl.
57/G2 **Crook,** Eng,UK
150/C2 **Crooked** (isl.), Bahm.
150/C2 **Crooked Island** (passg.), Bahm.
157/J4 **Crookston,** Mn,US
57/E5 **Crosby,** Eng,UK
157/H3 **Crosby,** ND,US
162/C3 **Crosbyton,** Tx,US
53/T10 **Crosne,** Fr.
129/H5 **Cross** (riv.), Camr., Nga.
157/J2 **Cross** (lake), Mb,Can
163/H4 **Cross City,** Fl,US
162/F3 **Crossett,** Ar,US
57/F2 **Cross Fell** (mtn.), Eng,UK
156/E3 **Crossfield,** Ab,Can
54/C4 **Crossford,** Sc,UK
56/C3 **Crossgar,** NI,UK
58/C2 **Crossgates,** Wal,UK
54/B6 **Crosshill,** Sc,UK
54/B5 **Crosshouse,** Sc,UK
58/C3 **Crosskeys,** Wal,UK
56/B3 **Crossmaglen,** NI,UK
56/E2 **Crossmichael,** Sc,UK
129/H5 **Cross River** (state), Nga.
167/E1 **Cross River** (res.), NY,US
163/G3 **Crossville,** Tn,US
166/D3 **Crosswicks** (cr.), NJ,US
78/D3 **Crostolo** (riv.), It.
57/F4 **Croston,** Eng,UK
80/E3 **Crotone,** It.
167/E1 **Croton-Harmon** (Croton-on-Hudson), NY,US
167/E1 **Croton-on-Hudson** (Croton-Harmon), NY,US
59/G3 **Crouch** (riv.), Eng,UK
68/C5 **Crouy-sur-Ourq,** Fr.
156/G4 **Crow Agency,** Mt,US
59/G4 **Crowborough,** Eng,UK
119/E1 **Crowdy Bay Nat'l Park,** Austl.
160/E2 **Crowe** (riv.), On,Can
156/F5 **Crowheart,** Wy,US
59/F1 **Crowland,** Eng,UK
57/H4 **Crowle,** Eng,UK
162/E4 **Crowley,** La,US
163/F3 **Crowley's** (ridge), Ar,US
157/K4 **Crow, North Fork** (riv.), Mn,US
160/C3 **Crown Point,** In,US
158/E4 **Crownpoint,** NM,US
153/H1 **Crown Prince Frederik** (isl.), NW,Can
118/D4 **Crows Nest Falls Nat'l Park,** Austl.
59/F4 **Crowthorne,** Eng,UK
53/M7 **Croxley Green,** Eng,UK
119/G5 **Croydon,** Austl.
53/N7 **Croydon,** Eng,UK
53/N7 **Croydon** (bor.), Eng,UK
166/D3 **Croydon,** Pa,US
51/M8 **Crozet** (isls.), FrAnt.
113/M **Crozier** (cape), Ant.
72/A2 **Crozon,** Fr.
54/A4 **Cruach Mhór** (mtn.), Sc,UK
54/A5 **Cruach nan Capull** (mtn.), Sc,UK
149/G1 **Crucero Contramaestre,** Cuba
54/E2 **Cruden Bay,** Sc,UK
54/D3 **Cruick Water** (riv.), Sc,UK
56/B2 **Crumlin,** NI,UK
57/E2 **Crummock Water** (lake), Eng,UK
69/E5 **Crusnes** (riv.), Fr.
149/G2 **Cruz** (cape), Cuba
142/E2 **Cruz Alta,** Arg.
135/F2 **Cruz Alta,** Braz.
75/P10 **Cruz Alta** (mtn.), Port.
140/C4 **Cruz das Almas,** Braz.
135/D3 **Cruz del Eje,** Arg.
141/J7 **Cruzeiro,** Braz.
144/C2 **Cruzeiro do Sul,** Braz.
140/C2 **Cruzeta,** Braz.
141/J6 **Cruzília,** Braz.
82/D3 **Crvenka,** Yugo.
57/E5 **Cryn-y-Brain** (mtn.), Wal,UK
166/C1 **Crystal** (lake), Pa,US
158/C3 **Crystal Bay,** Nv,US
166/C2 **Crystal Cave,** Pa,US
162/D4 **Crystal City,** Tx,US
160/B2 **Crystal Falls,** Mi,US
165/P15 **Crystal Lake,** Il,US
165/K11 **Crystal Springs** (res.), Ca,US
82/E2 **Csongrád,** Hun.
82/E2 **Csongrád** (co.), Hun.
82/C2 **Csorna,** Hun.
82/E2 **Csorvás,** Hun.
82/D2 **Csóványos** (peak), Hun.
93/F3 **Ctesiphon** (ruins), Iraq
126/G3 **Cuamba,** Moz.
126/D4 **Cuando** (riv.), Ang.
126/C4 **Cuangar,** Ang.
126/C2 **Cuango** (riv.), Ang.
126/B2 **Cuanza** (riv.), Ang.
75/E3 **Cuart de Poblet,** Sp.
142/D2 **Cuarto** (riv.), Arg.
146/E3 **Cuatrociénagas,** Mex.
146/D2 **Cuauhtémoc,** Mex.
147/L6 **Cuautepec de Hinojosa,** Mex.
147/Q9 **Cuautitlan,** Mex.
147/Q9 **Cuautitlan** (riv.), Mex.
147/F5 **Cuautla,** Mex.
148/B2 **Cuautla,** Mex.
149/F1 **Cuba**
159/K3 **Cuba,** Mo,US
139/E2 **Cubagua** (isl.), Ven.
126/C4 **Cubango** (riv.), Ang.
141/G8 **Cubatão,** Braz.
140/C2 **Cubati,** Braz.
92/C1 **Çubuk,** Turk.
164/C2 **Cucamonga** (Rancho Cucamonga), Ca,US
164/C2 **Cucamonga Wilderness,** Ca,US
139/E3 **Cuchivero** (riv.), Ven.
148/D3 **Cuchumatanes, Sierra los** (range), Guat.
59/F4 **Cuckfield,** Eng,UK
59/G5 **Cuckmere** (riv.), Eng,UK
109/D1 **Cuc Phuong Nat'l Park,** Viet.
139/E4 **Cucuí,** Braz.
138/C3 **Cúcuta,** Col.
164/F8 **Cudahy,** Ca,US
165/Q14 **Cudahy,** Wi,US
108/G3 **Cuddalore,** India
106/C5 **Cuddapah,** India
57/F5 **Cuddington,** Eng,UK
74/B1 **Cudillero,** Sp.
57/G4 **Cudworth,** Eng,UK
74/C2 **Cuéllar,** Sp.
138/B5 **Cuenca,** Ecu.
74/D2 **Cuenca,** Sp.
74/E2 **Cuenca** (range), Sp.
146/E3 **Cuencamé,** Mex.
147/E5 **Cueramo,** Mex.
147/F5 **Cuernavaca,** Mex.
162/D4 **Cuero,** Tx,US
72/G5 **Cuers,** Fr.
149/H1 **Cueto,** Cuba
138/D2 **Cueva de la Quebroda del Toro Nat'l Park,** Ven.
138/B4 **Cueva de los Guarcharos Nat'l Park,** Col.
74/E4 **Cuevas del Almanzora,** Sp.
53/N6 **Cuffley,** Eng,UK
83/F3 **Cugir,** Rom.
72/D5 **Cugnaux-Vingtcasses,** Fr.
137/G7 **Cuiabá,** Braz.
137/G7 **Cuiabá** (riv.), Braz.
138/D2 **Cuicas,** Ven.
66/C5 **Cuijk,** Neth.
148/D3 **Cuilapa,** Guat.
60/C1 **Cuilcagh** (mtn.), Wal,UK
148/C3 **Cuilco** (riv.), Guat., Mex.
55/H8 **Cuillin** (sound), Sc,UK
126/C2 **Cuilo** (riv.), Ang.
126/C3 **Cuima,** Ang.
76/B4 **Cuisance** (riv.), Fr.
140/C2 **Cuité,** Braz.
147/N8 **Cuitlahuac,** Mex.
126/C4 **Cuito** (riv.), Ang.
126/C4 **Cuito-Cuanavale,** Ang.
139/E5 **Cuiuni** (riv.), Braz.
105/G3 **Cuiwei** (mtn.), China
147/Q10 **Cujimalpa,** Mex.
109/E4 **Cu Lao** (isl.), Viet.
112/C3 **Culasi,** Phil.
56/A1 **Culdaff** (riv.), Ire.
66/C5 **Culemborg,** Neth.
137/H6 **Culene** (riv.), Braz.
119/C1 **Culgoa** (riv.), Austl.
146/D3 **Culiacán,** Mex.
112/B3 **Culion** (isl.), Phil.
112/C3 **Culion Res.,** Phil.
74/D4 **Cúllar Baza,** Sp.
54/D1 **Cullen,** Sc,UK
60/A4 **Cullenagh** (riv.), Ire.
75/E3 **Cullera,** Sp.
74/A1 **Culleredo,** Sp.
60/A2 **Cullin** (lake), Ire.
163/G3 **Cullman,** Al,US
54/B2 **Culloden Battlesite** (1746), Sc,UK
58/C5 **Cullompton,** Eng,UK
56/B2 **Cullybackey,** NI,UK
165/D2 **Culmback** (dam), Wa,US
56/A1 **Culmore,** NI,UK
118/B5 **Culoga** (riv.), Austl.
160/E4 **Culpeper,** Va,US
54/C4 **Culross,** Sc,UK
60/B3 **Cultra, Lough** (lake), Ire.
54/D2 **Cults,** Sc,UK
116/E5 **Culver** (pt.), Austl.
164/B2 **Culver City,** Ca,US
166/D1 **Culvers** (lake), NJ,US
139/E2 **Cumaná,** Ven.
141/B1 **Cumari,** Braz.
138/B4 **Cumbal, Nevado de** (peak), Col.
153/K2 **Cumberland** (pen.), NW,Can
153/K2 **Cumberland** (sound), NW,Can
157/H2 **Cumberland** (delta), Sk,Can
157/H2 **Cumberland** (lake), Sk,Can
163/G3 **Cumberland** (plat.), US
163/H4 **Cumberland** (isl.), Ga,US
163/G2 **Cumberland** (falls), Ky,US
160/C4 **Cumberland** (lake), Ky,US
163/G2 **Cumberland** (riv.), Ky, Tn,US
160/E4 **Cumberland,** Md,US
166/C5 **Cumberland** (co.), NJ,US
166/A3 **Cumberland** (co.), Pa,US
160/D4 **Cumberland Gap Nat'l Hist. Park,** Tn,US
168/C2 **Cumberland Hill,** RI,US
157/H2 **Cumberland House,** Sk,Can
54/C5 **Cumbernauld,** Sc,UK
147/G5 **Cumbres Bastonal, Cerro** (mtn.), Mex.
147/E3 **Cumbres de Monterrey Nat'l Park,** Mex.
57/F2 **Cumbria** (co.), Eng,UK
57/E3 **Cumbrian** (mts.), Eng,UK
106/C4 **Cumbum,** India
54/B6 **Cumnock,** Sc,UK
92/C2 **Çumra,** Turk.
151/M5 **Cumshewa** (pt.), BC,Can
142/B3 **Cunco,** Chile
116/D4 **Cundeelee Abor. Rsv.,** Austl.
138/C3 **Cundinamarca** (dept.), Col.
126/B4 **Cunene** (riv.), Ang.
78/A4 **Cuneo,** It.
78/A3 **Cuneo** (prov.), It.
109/E3 **Cung Son,** Viet.
141/J8 **Cunha,** Braz.
54/B5 **Cunninghame** (dist.), Sc,UK
61/H1 **Čuokkaraš'ša** (peak), Nor.
78/A2 **Cuorgnè,** It.
54/C4 **Cupar,** Sc,UK
165/K12 **Cupertino,** Ca,US
82/E4 **Ćuprija,** Yugo.
139/F3 **Cuquenán** (riv.), Ven.
140/C3 **Curaçá,** Braz.
150/D4 **Curaçao** (isl.), NAnt.
142/C3 **Curacautín,** Chile
142/B3 **Curanilahue,** Chile
138/C5 **Curaray** (riv.), Ecu., Peru
142/Q9 **Curaumilla** (pt.), Chile
82/F2 **Curcubăta** (peak), Rom.
72/E3 **Cure** (riv.), Fr.
133/S15 **Curepipe,** Mrts.
142/B2 **Curepto,** Chile
142/C2 **Curicó,** Chile
140/A3 **Curimatá,** Braz.
141/B3 **Curitiba,** Braz.
141/B3 **Curitibanos,** Braz.
78/B3 **Curone** (riv.), It.
60/D3 **Curragh, The,** Ire.
140/C2 **Currais Novos,** Braz.
159/K3 **Current** (riv.), Ar, Mo,US
54/C5 **Currie,** Sc,UK
158/D2 **Currie,** Nv,US
83/G3 **Curtea de Argeş,** Rom.
82/E2 **Curtici,** Rom.
118/C3 **Curtis** (isl.), Austl.
120/H8 **Curtis** (isl.), NZ
166/B6 **Curtis** (pt.), Md,US
139/H5 **Curuá** (riv.), Braz.
139/H5 **Curuá Una** (riv.), Braz.
144/C2 **Curuçú** (riv.), Braz.
149/E4 **Curú Nat'l Wild. Ref.,** CR
110/B4 **Curup,** Indo.
137/K4 **Cururupu,** Braz.
135/E2 **Curuzú Cuatiá,** Arg.
141/C1 **Curvelo,** Braz.
155/J2 **Curwood** (mtn.), Mi,US
144/D4 **Cusco,** Peru
56/B1 **Cushendall,** NI,UK
56/B3 **Cusher** (riv.), NI,UK
54/D6 **Cushet Law** (mtn.), Eng,UK
159/H4 **Cushing,** Ok,US
78/D4 **Cusna, Monte** (peak), It.
72/E3 **Cusset,** Fr.
163/G3 **Cusseta,** Ga,US
156/G4 **Custer,** Mt,US
157/H5 **Custer,** SD,US
140/C3 **Custódia,** Braz.
58/C5 **Cut** (hill), Eng,UK
156/E3 **Cut Bank,** Mt,US
144/B2 **Cutervo,** Peru
163/G4 **Cuthbert,** Ga,US
156/F2 **Cut Knife,** Sk,Can
142/C3 **Cutral-Có,** Arg.
106/E3 **Cuttack,** India
116/B3 **Cuvier** (cape), Austl.
67/F1 **Cuxhaven,** Ger.
168/F5 **Cuyahoga** (co.), Oh,US
168/F5 **Cuyahoga** (riv.), Oh,US
168/F5 **Cuyahoga Falls,** Oh,US
168/F5 **Cuyahoga Valley Nat'l Rec. Area,** Oh,US
158/C4 **Cuyama** (riv.), Ca,US
112/C3 **Cuyo,** Phil.
112/C3 **Cuyo** (isls.), Phil.
112/C3 **Cuyo East** (chan.), Phil.
112/C3 **Cuyo West** (chan.), Phil.
139/G3 **Cuyuni** (riv.), Guy., Ven.
139/F3 **Cuyuni-Mazaruni** (reg.), Guy.
144/D4 **Cuzco** (ruins), Peru
58/C3 **Cwm,** Wal,UK
58/C3 **Cwmafan,** Wal,UK
58/C3 **Cwmbran,** Wal,UK
157/H5 **C.W. McConaughy** (lake), Ne,US
130/A3 **Cyangugu,** Rwa.
81/J4 **Cyclades** (isls.), Gre.
160/C4 **Cynthiana,** Ky,US
58/B3 **Cynwyl Elfed,** Wal,UK
156/F3 **Cypress** (hills), Ab, Sk,Can
164/B3 **Cypress,** Ca,US
91/C2 **Cyprus**
125/K1 **Cyrenaica** (reg.), Libya
58/B3 **Cywyn** (riv.), Wal,UK
65/J2 **Czaplinek,** Pol.
65/M2 **Czarna Białostocka,** Pol.
65/J2 **Czarnków,** Pol.
65/H4 **Czech Republic**
65/K3 **Częstochowa,** Pol.
65/K3 **Czestochowa** (prov.), Pol.
65/J2 **Człuchów,** Pol.

D

105/J2 **Da** (riv.), China
97/J2 **Da'an,** China
103/B4 **Daba** (mts.), China
130/B5 **Dabaga,** Tanz.
82/D2 **Dabas,** Hun.
92/C5 **Dabbāgh, Jabal** (mtn.), SAr.
138/B3 **Dabeiba,** Col.
106/B3 **Dabhoi,** India
105/G2 **Dabie** (mts.), China
109/D1 **Da** (Black) (riv.), Viet.
165/B2 **Dabob** (bay), Wa,US
125/Q6 **Daborow,** Som.
128/D5 **Dabou,** IvC.
106/C2 **Dabra,** India
65/M2 **Dąbrowa Białostocka,** Pol.
65/K3 **Dąbrowa Górnicza,** Pol.
103/H7 **Dachang Huizu Zizhixian,** China
71/E6 **Dachau,** Ger.
109/D3 **Dac Sut,** Viet.
109/D3 **Dac To,** Viet.
163/H4 **Dade City,** Fl,US
111/H4 **Dadi** (cape), Indo.
106/B4 **Dadra & Nagar Haveli** (terr.), India
104/D2 **Dadu** (riv.), China
95/J3 **Dādu,** Pak.
106/D6 **Daduru** (riv.), SrL.
109/B4 **Daen Noi** (peak), Thai.
112/C2 **Daet,** Phil.
104/E3 **Dafang,** China
103/E4 **Dafeng,** China

185

Digne – Eagle

73/G4 **Digne,** Fr.
72/E3 **Digoin,** Fr.
112/D4 **Digos,** Phil.
106/C3 **Digras,** India
104/B2 **Dihang** (riv.), India
68/D2 **Dijle** (Dyle) (riv.), Belg.
76/A3 **Dijon,** Fr.
125/P5 **Dikhil,** Djib.
91/B4 **Dikirnis,** Egypt
87/H4 **Diklosmta, Gora** (peak), Geo.
68/B1 **Diksmuide,** Belg.
124/H5 **Dikwa,** Nga.
125/N6 **Dīla,** Eth.
68/D2 **Dilbeek,** Belg.
92/A2 **Dilek Yarımadası Nat'l Park,** Turk.
111/G5 **Dili,** Indo.
70/B1 **Dill** (riv.), Ger.
69/H2 **Dillenburg,** Ger.
125/L5 **Dilling,** Sudan
69/F5 **Dillingen,** Ger.
70/D5 **Dillingen an der Donau,** Ger.
154/V12 **Dillingham A.F.B.,** Hi,US
163/J3 **Dillon,** SC,US
126/D3 **Dilolo,** Zaire
69/E1 **Dilsen,** Belg.
104/B3 **Dimāpur,** India
92/D3 **Dimashq** (prov.), Syria
91/E3 **Dimashq** (Damascus) (cap.), Syria
112/C4 **Dimataling,** Phil.
128/D5 **Dimbokro,** IvC.
83/G3 **Dîmboviţa** (co.), Rom.
89/P2 **Dimitriya Lapteva** (str.), Rus.
83/G4 **Dimitrovgrad,** Bul.
87/J1 **Dimitrovgrad,** Rus.
82/F4 **Dimitrovgrad,** Yugo.
124/H6 **Dimlang** (peak), Nga.
91/D4 **Dimona,** Isr.
91/D4 **Dimona, Hare** (mtn.), Isr.
108/B1 **Dina,** Pak.
112/D3 **Dinagat,** Phil.
112/D3 **Dinagat** (isl.), Phil.
106/E2 **Dinājpur,** Bang.
72/B2 **Dinan,** Fr.
108/C1 **Dīnānagar,** India
69/D3 **Dinant,** Belg.
92/B2 **Dinar,** Turk.
72/B2 **Dinard,** Fr.
81/E1 **Dinaric Alps** (range), Bosn., Cro.
58/B2 **Dinas** (pt.), Wal,UK
58/C4 **Dinas Powys,** Wal,UK
125/N5 **Dinder Nat'l Park,** Eth.
108/F3 **Dindigul,** India
108/B1 **Dinga,** Pak.
105/F5 **Ding'an,** China
96/F4 **Dingbian,** China
106/E2 **Dinggyê,** China
54/F10 **Dingle** (bay), Ire.
71/F5 **Dingolfing,** Ger.
112/C1 **Dingras,** Phil.
103/C4 **Dingtao,** China
54/B1 **Dingwall,** Sc,UK
96/E4 **Dingxi,** China
103/C3 **Dingxiang,** China
103/C3 **Dingxing,** China
103/G7 **Dingxing,** China
103/D4 **Dingyuan,** China
109/D1 **Dinh Lap,** Viet.
67/E5 **Dinkel** (riv.), Ger.
70/D4 **Dinkelsbühl,** Ger.
77/G1 **Dinkelscherben,** Ger.
67/F3 **Dinklage,** Ger.
57/G1 **Dinnington,** Eng,UK
131/B4 **Dinokwe,** Bots.
158/E2 **Dinosaur,** Co,US
158/E2 **Dinosaur Nat'l Mon.,** Co, Ut,US
66/D5 **Dinslaken,** Ger.
156/G3 **Dinsmore,** Sk,Can
66/B5 **Dintel Mark** (riv.), Neth.
158/C3 **Dinuba,** Ca,US
66/D5 **Dinxperlo,** Neth.
128/C4 **Dion** (riv.), Gui.
128/A3 **Diourbel,** Sen.
128/A3 **Diourbel** (reg.), Sen.
108/B2 **Dīpālpur,** Pak.
104/B3 **Diphu,** India
104/C2 **Diphu** (pass), India
95/J4 **Diplo,** Pak.
92/E2 **Dipni** (dam), Turk.
112/C3 **Dipolog,** Phil.
118/C3 **Dipperu Nat'l Park,** Austl.
149/H4 **Dique** (can.), Col.
128/E2 **Diré,** Mali
115/G2 **Direction** (cape), Austl.
125/P6 **Dirē Dawa,** Eth.
148/E4 **Diriamba,** Nic.
116/B3 **Dirk Hartog** (isl.), Austl.
124/H4 **Dirkou,** Niger
66/B5 **Dirksland,** Neth.
54/D5 **Dirrington Great Law** (hill), Sc,UK
158/E3 **Dirty Devil** (riv.), Ut,US
116/D2 **Disappointment** (lake), Austl.
121/L6 **Disappointment** (isls.), FrPol.
119/B3 **Discovery** (bay), Austl.
77/F5 **Disgrazi, Monte** (peak), It.
127/C3 **Dishnā,** Egypt
153/L2 **Disko** (isl.), Grld.
57/F5 **Disley,** Eng,UK
164/C3 **Disneyland,** Ca,US
69/E2 **Dison,** Belg.
106/F2 **Dispur,** India
161/G2 **Disraëli,** Qu,Can
59/H2 **Diss,** Eng,UK
67/F4 **Dissen am Teutoburger Wald,** Ger.
56/E2 **Distington,** Eng,UK
166/A6 **District of Columbia** (cap.), US
138/C3 **Distrito Especial** (fed. dist.), Col.
143/S12 **Distrito Federal** (fed. dist.), Arg.
140/A4 **Distrito Federal** (fed. dist.), Braz.
147/F5 **Distrito Federal** (fed. dist.), Mex.
139/E2 **Distrito Federal** (fed. dist.), Ven.
91/B4 **Disūq,** Egypt
59/F5 **Ditchling Beacon** (hill), Eng,UK
80/D4 **Dittaino** (riv.), It.
70/D2 **Dittelbrunn,** Ger.
70/C5 **Ditzingen,** Ger.
95/K4 **Diu** (isl.), India
112/D3 **Diuata** (mts.), Phil.
106/B3 **Diu, Damān and** (terr.), India
82/D4 **Diva** (riv.), Yugo.
72/D3 **Dive** (riv.), Fr.
141/G6 **Divinolândia,** Braz.
141/C2 **Divinópolis,** Braz.
56/B2 **Divis** (mtn.), NI,UK
141/G6 **Divisa Nova,** Braz.
144/C2 **Divisor** (mts.), Braz.
128/D5 **Divo,** IvC.
92/D2 **Divriği,** Turk.
76/D5 **Dix** (lake), Swi.
151/M4 **Dixon** (chan.), Ak,US
165/L10 **Dixon,** Ca,US
160/B3 **Dixon,** Il,US
152/C3 **Dixon Entrance** (chan.), BC,Can
93/E2 **Diyadin,** Turk.
93/F3 **Diyālá** (gov.), Iraq
92/E2 **Diyarbakır,** Turk.
92/E2 **Diyarbakir** (prov.), Turk.
91/B4 **Diyarb Najm,** Egypt
124/H3 **Djado,** Niger
124/H3 **Djado** (plat.), Niger
124/G1 **Djamaa,** Alg.
126/B1 **Djambala,** Congo
130/A2 **Djamu,** Zaire
123/G3 **Djanet,** Alg.
123/S16 **Djelfa,** Alg.
123/S16 **Djelfa** (wilaya), Alg.
125/L6 **Djema,** CAfr.
123/U17 **Djemila** (ruins), Alg.
128/D3 **Djenné,** Mali
129/E3 **Djibo,** Burk.
125/P5 **Djibouti**
125/P5 **Djibouti** (cap.), Djib.
60/D3 **Djouce** (mtn.), Ire.
129/F4 **Djougou,** Ben.
130/A2 **Djugu,** Zaire
52/G3 **Dnepr** (riv.), Eur.
86/E2 **Dneprodzerzhinsk,** Ukr.
86/E2 **Dnepropetrovsk,** Ukr.
86/E2 **Dnepropetrovsk Obl.,** Ukr.
86/D3 **Dnestr** (riv.), Eur.
96/E5 **Do** (riv.), China
129/E3 **Do** (lake), Mali
131/D3 **Doa,** Moz.
124/J6 **Doba,** Chad
167/E1 **Dobbs Ferry,** NY,US
63/K3 **Dobele,** Lat.
63/G4 **Döbeln,** Ger.
111/H4 **Doberai** (pen.), Indo.
82/D3 **Doboj,** Bosn.
71/E2 **Döbra** (hill), Ger.
65/L2 **Dobre Miasto,** Pol.
71/H3 **Dobříš,** Czh.
83/H4 **Dobruja** (reg.), Bul., Rom.
86/D1 **Dobrush,** Bela.
85/N4 **Dobryanka,** Rus.
141/D1 **Doce** (riv.), Braz.
54/B4 **Dochart** (riv.), Sc,UK
59/G1 **Docking,** Eng,UK
163/H4 **Dock Junction,** Ga,US
135/D1 **Doctor Pedro P. Peña,** Par.
82/F2 **Doctor Petru Groza,** Rom.
160/F1 **Doda** (lake), Qu,Can
108/F3 **Doda Betta** (mtn.), India
56/B5 **Dodder** (riv.), Ire.
53/P7 **Doddinghurst,** Eng,UK
159/G3 **Dodge City,** Ks,US
164/F7 **Dodger Stadium, Los Angeles,** Ca,US
160/B3 **Dodgeville,** Wi,US
58/B6 **Dodman** (pt.), Wal,UK
130/B4 **Dodoma,** Tanz.
130/B4 **Dodoma** (prov.), Tanz.
81/G3 **Dodoni** (ruins), Gre.
130/D3 **Dodori Nat'l Rsv.,** Kenya
156/F3 **Dodsland,** Sk,Can
57/G4 **Dodworth,** Eng,UK
66/D4 **Doesburg,** Neth.
66/D5 **Doetinchem,** Neth.
102/E5 **Dogai Coring** (lake), China
92/B2 **Doğanhisar,** Turk.
92/D1 **Doğankent** (riv.), Turk.
92/D2 **Doğanşehir,** Turk.
98/C2 **Dōgo** (isl.), Japan
129/G3 **Dogondoutchi,** Niger
93/F2 **Doğubayazıt,** Turk.
92/D1 **Doğukaradeniz** (mts.), Turk.
94/F3 **Doha** (Ad Dawḩah) (cap.), Qatar
106/B3 **Dohad,** India
109/B2 **Doi Inthanon Nat'l Park,** Thai.
109/B2 **Doi Khun Tan Nat'l Park,** Thai.
106/F1 **Doilungdêqên,** China
74/B1 **Doiras** (res.)
140/B3 **Dois Irmãos** (mts.), Braz.
109/B2 **Doi Suthep-Pui Nat'l Park,** Thai.
62/D1 **Dokka,** Nor.
66/D2 **Dokkum,** Neth.
66/C2 **Dokkumer Ee** (riv.), Neth.
161/F1 **Dolbeau,** Qu,Can
76/B3 **Dôle,** Fr.
76/D6 **Dolent, Mont** (peak), Swi.
58/C1 **Dolgellau,** Wal,UK
80/A3 **Dolianova,** It.
97/N2 **Dolinsk,** Rus.
83/F3 **Dolj** (co.), Rom.
54/C4 **Dollar,** Sc,UK
161/N7 **Dollard-des-Ormeaux,** Qu,Can
67/E2 **Dollard** (Dollart) (bay), Neth.
54/C5 **Dollar Law** (mtn.), Sc,UK
67/E2 **Dollart** (Dollard) (bay), Ger.
64/D5 **Doller** (riv.), Fr.
93/N6 **Dolmançe Palace,** Turk.
70/D1 **Dolmar** (peak), Ger.
82/C5 **Dolmen** (ruins), It.
125/P7 **Dolo,** Eth.
78/D4 **Dolo** (riv.), It.
73/J3 **Dolomite Alps** (Alpi Dolomitiche) (range), It.
73/J3 **Dolomitiche, Alpi** (Dolomite Alps) (range), It.
143/F3 **Dolores,** Arg.
148/D2 **Dolores,** Guat.
112/D2 **Dolores,** Phil.
75/E3 **Dolores,** Sp.
142/F2 **Dolores,** Uru.
158/E3 **Dolores,** Co,US
158/E3 **Dolores** (riv.), Co, Ut,US
147/E4 **Dolores Hidalgo,** Mex.
143/N7 **Dolphin** (cape), Falk.
132/A2 **Dolphin** (pt.), Namb.
152/E1 **Dolphin and Union** (str.), NW,Can
57/F4 **Dolphinholme,** Eng,UK
58/B5 **Dolton,** Eng,UK
165/Q16 **Dolton,** Il,US
109/D2 **Do Luong,** Viet.
111/J4 **Dom** (peak), Indo.
76/D5 **Dom** (peak), Swi.
131/C3 **Doma,** Zim.
131/D2 **Domasi,** Malw.
77/F4 **Domat-Ems,** Swi.
71/F4 **Domažlice,** Czh.
73/G2 **Dombasle-sur-Meurthe,** Fr.
87/G4 **Dombay-Ul'gen, Gora** (peak), Geo.
76/B5 **Dombes** (reg.), Fr.
131/C3 **Domboshawa,** Zim.
82/D2 **Dombóvár,** Hun.
82/E1 **Dombrád,** Hun.
131/D4 **Dom Carlos** (pt.), Moz.
113/J **Dome C** (sta.), Ant.
72/E3 **Domérat,** Fr.
135/C1 **Domeyko** (mts.), Chile
150/F4 **Dominica**
150/F4 **Dominica** (passg.), West Indies
150/D3 **Dominican Republic**
66/C6 **Dommel** (riv.), Belg., Neth.
109/D3 **Dom Noi** (res.), Thai.
85/X9 **Domodedovo,** Rus.
77/E5 **Domodossola,** It.
53/S9 **Domont,** Fr.
135/F3 **Dom Pedrito,** Braz.
140/A2 **Dom Pedro,** Braz.
111/E5 **Dompu,** Indo.
82/D2 **Dömsöd,** Hun.
80/A3 **Domusnovas,** It.
142/C3 **Domuyo** (vol.), Arg.
118/C5 **Domvilk** (peak), Austl.
82/B2 **Domžale,** Slov.
72/C3 **Don** (riv.), Fr.
87/G2 **Don** (ridge), Rus.
87/G3 **Don** (riv.), Rus.
57/G5 **Don** (riv.), Eng,UK
54/D2 **Don** (riv.), Sc,UK
131/D3 **Dona Ana,** Moz.
56/C2 **Donaghadee,** NI,UK
56/B2 **Donaghmore,** NI,UK
163/F4 **Donaldsonville,** La,US
74/B4 **Doñana Nat'l Park,** Sp.
72/E5 **Dona, Pic de la** (peak), Fr.
65/H4 **Donau** (Danube) (riv.), Aus., Ger.
77/E2 **Donaueschingen,** Ger.
70/D5 **Donauwörth,** Ger.
74/C3 **Don Benito,** Sp.
119/G5 **Doncaster,** Austl.
57/G4 **Doncaster,** Eng,UK
126/B2 **Dondo,** Ang.
131/D3 **Dondo,** Moz.
106/D6 **Dondra Head** (pt.), SrL.
55/G9 **Donegal** (bay), Ire.
56/A1 **Donegal** (co.), Ire.
87/G3 **Donets,** (riv.), Rus., Ukr.
86/F3 **Donetsk,** Ukr.
86/F3 **Donetsk Obl.,** Ukr.
104/E2 **Dong** (riv.), China
105/G4 **Dong** (riv.), China
107/J5 **Dong** (riv.), Viet.
129/H5 **Donga** (riv.), Camr., Nga.
101/B2 **Dongbei** (plain), China
104/D3 **Dongchuan,** China
107/J3 **Dong Dang,** Viet.
103/E5 **Dongdongting Shan** (mtn.), China
103/D3 **Dong'e,** China
66/B5 **Dongen,** Neth.
105/F5 **Dongfang,** China
117/J5 **Donggali Consv. Park,** Austl.
101/C3 **Donggou,** China
105/G4 **Dongguan,** China
103/D3 **Dongguang,** China
109/D2 **Dong Ha,** Viet.
103/D4 **Donghai,** China
109/D2 **Donghen,** Laos
109/D2 **Dong Hoi,** Viet.
105/G2 **Dongjing** (riv.), China
103/E2 **Dongliao** (riv.), China
103/C4 **Dongming,** China
105/F4 **Dongnan** (mts.), China
109/D4 **Dong Noi** (riv.), Viet.
130/B4 **Dongobesh,** Tanz.
103/D4 **Dongping,** China
103/D3 **Dongping** (lake), China
105/H4 **Dongshan** (isl.), China
105/H4 **Dongsha** (Pratas) (isl.), China
103/B3 **Dongsheng,** China
103/E4 **Dongtai,** China
103/L9 **Dongtai** (riv.), China
109/D2 **Dong Tau,** Viet.
105/G2 **Dongting** (lake), China
103/D3 **Dongying,** China
103/D5 **Dongzhi,** China
142/Q10 **Donihue,** Chile
57/H6 **Donington,** Eng,UK
152/C2 **Donjek** (riv.), Yk,Can
82/C3 **Donji Vakuf,** Bosn.
70/A3 **Donnersberg** (peak), Ger.
76/D1 **Donon** (mtn.), Fr.
112/C2 **Donsol,** Phil.
104/B5 **Donyan** (riv.), Burma
70/C5 **Donzdorf,** Ger.
116/C2 **Dooleena** (peak), Austl.
54/B6 **Doon** (riv.), Sc,UK
60/A4 **Doonbeg** (riv.), Ire.
151/H2 **Doonerak** (mtn.), Ak,US
54/B6 **Doon, Loch** (lake), Sc,UK
160/C2 **Door** (pen.), Wi,US
66/C4 **Doorn,** Neth.
132/B3 **Doorn** (riv.), SAfr.
78/D1 **Doppo, Monte** (peak), It.
116/D2 **Dora** (lake), Austl.
78/A2 **Dora Baltea** (riv.), It.
75/F2 **Dorada** (coast), Sp.
95/K1 **Do Rāh** (pass), Afg.
102/B4 **Dorāh Ān** (pass), Pak.
73/G4 **Dora Riparia** (riv.), It.
161/H2 **Dorchester,** NB,Can
153/J2 **Dorchester** (cape), NW,Can
58/D5 **Dorchester,** Eng,UK
72/D4 **Dordogne** (riv.), Fr.
66/B5 **Dordrecht,** Neth.
156/G2 **Dore** (lake), Sk,Can
72/E4 **Dore** (mts.), Fr.
72/E4 **Dore** (riv.), Fr.
54/B2 **Dores,** Sc,UK
141/C1 **Dores do Indaiá,** Braz.
71/F6 **Dorfen,** Ger.
71/E6 **Dorfen** (riv.), Ger.
80/A2 **Dorgali,** It.
96/C2 **Dörgön** (lake), Mong.
129/E3 **Dori,** Burk.
161/M7 **Dorion,** Qu,Can
53/N8 **Dorking,** Eng,UK
66/D6 **Dormagen,** Ger.
53/P8 **Dormans Land,** Eng,UK
168/G7 **Dormont,** Pa,US
54/C2 **Dornbach Burn** (riv.), Sc,UK
77/F3 **Dornbirn,** Aus.
166/C2 **Dorney Park/Wildwater Kingdom,** Pa,US
54/B1 **Dornoch,** Sc,UK
55/K8 **Dornoch Firth** (inlet), Sc,UK
70/C6 **Dornstadt,** Ger.
70/B6 **Dornstetten,** Ger.
82/D2 **Dorog,** Hun.
83/H2 **Dorohoi,** Rom.
131/C3 **Dorowa Mining Lease,** Zim.
116/B3 **Dorre** (isl.), Austl.
59/E2 **Dorridge,** Eng,UK
119/E1 **Dorrigo Nat'l Park,** Austl.
58/D1 **Dorrington,** Eng,UK
158/B2 **Dorris,** Ca,US
123/W17 **Dorsale** (mts.), Tun.
70/B2 **Dorsbach** (riv.), Ger.
58/D5 **Dorset** (co.), Eng,UK
66/D5 **Dorsten,** Ger.
67/E5 **Dortmund,** Ger.
67/E4 **Dortmund-Ems** (can.), Ger.
91/E1 **Dörtyol,** Turk.
161/N7 **Dorval,** Qu,Can
67/G3 **Dörverden,** Ger.
142/D5 **Dos Bahias** (cape), Arg.
165/A2 **Dosewallips** (riv.), Wa,US
74/C4 **Dos Hermanas,** Sp.
99/H7 **Dōshi** (riv.), Japan
109/D1 **Do Son,** Viet.
146/B2 **Dos Picachos, Cerro** (mtn.), Mex.
138/C3 **Dos Quebradas,** Col.
64/G2 **Dosse** (riv.), Ger.
129/F3 **Dosso,** Niger
129/F3 **Dosso** (dept.), Niger
87/K3 **Dossor,** Kaz.
163/G4 **Dothan,** Al,US
68/C3 **Douai,** Fr.
124/G7 **Douala,** Camr.
72/A2 **Douarnenez,** Fr.
72/A2 **Douarnenez** (bay), Fr.
118/D4 **Double I.** (pt.), Austl.
76/C3 **Doubs** (dept.), Fr.
76/B4 **Doubs** (riv.), Fr.
116/C5 **Doubtful I.** (bay), Austl.
68/C3 **Douchy-les-Mines,** Fr.
72/C3 **Doué-la-Fontaine,** Fr.
128/E3 **Douentza,** Mali
123/W17 **Dougga** (ruins), Tun.
168/F7 **Doughty** (cr.), Oh,US
56/D3 **Douglas,** IM,UK
54/C5 **Douglas,** Sc,UK
151/H4 **Douglas** (mtn.), Ak,US
158/E5 **Douglas,** Az,US
163/H4 **Douglas,** Ga,US
157/G5 **Douglas,** Wy,US
68/B3 **Doullens,** Fr.
55/N13 **Dounby,** Sc,UK
54/B4 **Doune,** Sc,UK
54/B4 **Doune** (mtn.), Sc,UK
71/G2 **Doupovské Hory** (mts.), Czh.
68/C3 **Dour,** Belg.
137/H8 **Dourados,** Braz.
53/S11 **Dourdan,** Fr.
72/E4 **Dourdou** (riv.), Fr.
74/B2 **Douro** (riv.), Port.
72/F4 **Doux** (riv.), Fr.
72/C4 **Douze** (riv.), Fr.
57/G6 **Dove** (riv.), Eng,UK
57/H3 **Dove** (riv.), Eng,UK
59/H2 **Dove** (riv.), Eng,UK
158/E3 **Dove Creek,** Co,US
116/E5 **Dover** (pt.), Austl.
68/A2 **Dover** (str.), Fr., UK
59/H4 **Dover,** Eng,UK
166/C5 **Dover** (cap.), De,US
161/G3 **Dover,** NH,US
166/D2 **Dover,** NJ,US
168/F6 **Dover,** Oh,US
166/C5 **Dover A.F.B.,** De,US
161/G2 **Dover-Foxcroft,** Me,US
57/G6 **Doveridge,** Eng,UK
93/J2 **Dowghā'ī,** Iran
56/C3 **Down** (dist.), NI,UK
165/P16 **Downers Grove,** Il,US
164/B3 **Downey,** Ca,US
59/G1 **Downham Market,** Eng,UK
158/B3 **Downieville,** Ca,US
166/C3 **Downingtown,** Pa,US
56/C3 **Downpatrick,** NI,UK
59/H4 **Downs, The** (har.), Eng,UK
59/E4 **Downton,** Eng,UK
166/C3 **Doylestown,** Pa,US
98/C3 **Dōzen** (isl.), Japan
160/E2 **Dozois** (res.), Qu,Can
124/D2 **Drâa** (plat.), Alg., Mor.
124/D2 **Drâa** (wadi), Alg., Mor.
72/F4 **Drac** (riv.), Fr.
141/B2 **Dracena,** Braz.
66/D2 **Drachten,** Neth.
83/G3 **Drăgăneşti-Olt,** Rom.
83/G3 **Drăgăşani,** Rom.
139/F2 **Dragon's Mouth** (str.), Trin., Ven.
63/T9 **Dragør,** Den.
73/G5 **Draguignan,** Fr.
143/L8 **Drake** (passage), Arg., Chile
126/E6 **Drakensberg** (range), Afr.
130/A2 **Dramba,** Zaire
62/D2 **Drammen,** Nor.
76/D5 **Drance** (riv.), Swi.
53/T10 **Drancy,** Fr.
76/C5 **Dranse** (riv.), Fr.
56/B2 **Draperstown,** NI,UK
73/L3 **Drau** (riv.), Aus.
82/C3 **Drava** (riv.), Eur.
68/B6 **Draveil,** Fr.
65/H2 **Drawa** (riv.), Pol.
65/H2 **Drawsko Pomorskie,** Pol.
157/J3 **Drayton,** ND,US
156/E2 **Drayton Valley,** Ab,Can
54/B5 **Dreghorn,** Sc,UK
71/G5 **Dreiesselberg** (peak), Ger.
76/D2 **Dreisam** (riv.), Ger.
111/K4 **Drei Zinnen** (peak), PNG
67/E5 **Drensteinfurt,** Ger.
66/D3 **Drenthe** (prov.), Neth.
66/D3 **Drentse Hoofdvaart** (can.), Neth.
65/G3 **Dresden,** Ger.
68/A6 **Dreux,** Fr.
65/H2 **Drezdenko,** Pol.
66/C4 **Driebergen,** Neth.
156/F5 **Driggs,** Id,US
95/J4 **Drigh Road,** Pak.
81/F2 **Drin** (gulf), Alb.
81/F1 **Drin** (riv.), Alb.
82/D3 **Drina** (riv.), Bosn., Yugo.
82/E5 **Drinizi** (riv.), Alb.
62/D2 **Drøbak,** Nor.
82/F3 **Drobeta-Turnu Severin,** Rom.
67/G1 **Drochtersen,** Ger.
60/D2 **Drogheda,** Ire.
86/B2 **Drogobych,** Ukr.
58/D2 **Droitwich,** Eng,UK
69/G6 **Drolingen,** Fr.
67/E6 **Drolshagen,** Ger.
72/F4 **Drôme** (riv.), Fr.
56/A3 **Dromore** (riv.), Ire.
56/B3 **Dromore,** NI,UK
57/G5 **Dronfield,** Eng,UK
54/B6 **Drongan,** Sc,UK
72/D4 **Dronne** (riv.), Fr.
66/C3 **Dronten,** Neth.
72/D4 **Dropt** (riv.), Fr.
63/R7 **Drottningholm Palace,** Swe.
68/A6 **Drouette** (riv.), Fr.
160/C1 **Drowning** (riv.), On,Can
78/A2 **Druento,** It.
56/C3 **Drumaness,** NI,UK
56/C2 **Drumbeg,** NI,UK
156/E3 **Drumheller,** Ab,Can
60/D3 **Drumleck** (pt.), Ire.
118/B4 **Drummond** (peak), Austl.
117/G5 **Drummond** (pt.), Austl.
118/B4 **Drummond** (range), Austl.
161/F2 **Drummondville,** Qu,Can
56/D2 **Drummore,** Sc,UK
54/B2 **Drumnadrochit,** Sc,UK
56/A2 **Drumnakilly,** NI,UK
54/B3 **Drumochter, Pass of** (pass), Sc,UK
66/C5 **Drunen,** Neth.
57/G1 **Druridge** (bay), Eng,UK
63/K4 **Druskininkai,** Lith.
66/C5 **Druten,** Neth.
82/C3 **Drvar,** Bosn.
65/K2 **Drwęca** (riv.), Pol.
165/M10 **Dry** (cr.), Ca,US
151/K3 **Dry Creek,** Yk,Can
160/A1 **Dryden,** On,Can
162/C4 **Dryden,** Tx,US
58/C2 **Drygarn Fawr** (mtn.), Wal,UK
54/B4 **Drymen,** Sc,UK
129/H5 **Dschang,** Camr.
103/B4 **Du** (riv.), China
58/B3 **Duad** (riv.), Wal,UK
150/D3 **Duarte** (peak), DRep.
164/G7 **Duarte,** Ca,US
152/F2 **Dubawnt** (lake), NW,Can
152/F2 **Dubawnt** (riv.), NW,Can
95/G3 **Dubayy,** UAE
119/D2 **Dubbo,** Austl.
130/A2 **Dubele,** Zaire
77/E3 **Dübendorf,** Swi.
60/D3 **Dublin** (bay), Ire.
60/D3 **Dublin** (cap.), Ire.
60/D3 **Dublin** (co.), Ire.
165/L11 **Dublin,** Ca,US
163/H3 **Dublin,** Ga,US
84/H4 **Dubna,** Rus.
65/K4 **Dubnica nad Váhom,** Slvk.
86/C2 **Dubno,** Ukr.
160/E3 **Du Bois,** Pa,US
156/F5 **Dubois,** Wy,US
83/J2 **Dubossary** (res.), Mol.
82/D4 **Dubrovnik,** Cro.
157/L5 **Dubuque,** Ia,US
71/G1 **Duchcov,** Czh.
158/E2 **Duchesne,** Ut,US
158/E2 **Duchesne** (riv.), Ut,US
121/N7 **Ducie** (atoll), Pitc.
165/E6 **Duck** (lake), Mi,US
163/G3 **Duck** (riv.), Tn,US
165/A2 **Duckabush** (riv.), Wa,US
157/G2 **Duck Lake,** Sk,Can
158/D3 **Duckwater,** Nv,US
109/D3 **Duc Lap,** Viet.
109/E3 **Duc Pho,** Viet.
109/D4 **Duc Phong,** Viet.
138/C4 **Duda** (riv.), Col.
57/E3 **Dudden** (riv.), Eng,UK
69/F5 **Dudelange,** Lux.
67/H5 **Duderstadt,** Ger.
88/J3 **Dudinka,** Rus.
58/D2 **Dudley,** Eng,UK
168/C1 **Dudley,** Ma,US
74/C2 **Duero** (Douro) (riv.), Sp.
130/C3 **Dufaja** (riv.), Kenya
113/W **Dufek Massive** (mtn.), Ant.
120/F5 **Duff** (isl.), Sol.
68/D1 **Duffel,** Belg.
57/G6 **Duffield,** Eng,UK
54/C2 **Dufftown,** Sc,UK
78/A1 **Dufour, Punta** (Dufourspitze) (peak), It., Swi.
78/A1 **Dufourspitze** (Punta Dufour) (peak), It., Swi.
82/B3 **Dugi Otok** (isl.), Cro.
158/D2 **Dugway,** Ut,US
54/A2 **Duich, Loch** (inlet), Sc,UK
139/E4 **Duida** (peak), Ven.
139/E4 **Duida Marahuaca Nat'l Park,** Ven.
115/G2 **Duifken** (pt.), Austl.
66/D6 **Duisburg,** Ger.
138/C3 **Duitama,** Col.
66/D5 **Duiven,** Neth.
121/L7 **Duke of Gloucester** (isls.), FrPol.
54/B4 **Duke's** (pass), Sc,UK
168/D3 **Dukes** (co.), Ma,US
65/L4 **Dukielska, Przełęcz** (Dukla) (pass), Pol.
65/L4 **Dukla** (Przełęcz Dukielska) (pass), Pol.
96/D4 **Dulan** China
135/D2 **Dulce** (riv.), Arg.
149/F4 **Dulce** (gulf), CR
158/F3 **Dulce,** NM,US
105/F3 **Duliu** (riv.), China
108/A2 **Dullewāla,** Pak.
67/E5 **Dülmen,** Ger.
54/C2 **Dulnain** (riv.), Sc,UK
104/B3 **Dulong** (pass), China
83/H4 **Dulovo,** Bul.
112/C4 **Dulunguin** (pt.), Phil.
157/K4 **Duluth,** Mn,US
58/C4 **Dulverton,** Eng,UK
91/E3 **Dūmā,** Syria
112/C4 **Dumagasa** (pt.), Phil.
112/C3 **Dumaguete City,** Phil.
112/C4 **Dumalinao,** Phil.
112/C3 **Dumanjug,** Phil.
112/B3 **Dumaran,** Phil.
112/B3 **Dumaran** (isl.), Phil.
119/D1 **Dumaresq** (riv.), Austl.
162/F3 **Dumas,** Ar,US
162/C3 **Dumas,** Tx,US
54/B5 **Dumbarton,** Sc,UK
65/K4 **Ďumbier** (peak), Slvk.
126/C3 **Dumbo,** Ang.
83/G2 **Dumbrăveni,** Rom.
164/B2 **Dume** (pt.), Ca,US
56/E1 **Dumfries,** Sc,UK
54/C6 **Dumfries & Galloway** (reg.), Sc,UK
67/F3 **Dümmer** (lake), Ger.
160/E2 **Dumoine** (lake), Qu,Can
160/E2 **Dumoine** (riv.), Qu,Can
167/E2 **Dumont,** NJ,US
113/K **Dumont d'Urville,** Ant.
91/B4 **Dumyāt** (gov.), Egypt
91/B4 **Dumyāţ** (Damietta), Egypt
65/K5 **Duna** (Danube) (riv.), Hun.
82/D2 **Dunaföldvár,** Hun.
82/D2 **Dunaharaszti,** Hun.
65/K5 **Dunaj** (Danube) (riv.), Slvk.
65/L4 **Dunajec** (riv.), Pol.
65/K5 **Dunakeszi,** Hun.
60/D2 **Dunany** (pt.), Ire.
82/D2 **Dunaújváros,** Hun.
82/D2 **Dunavecse,** Hun.
54/D5 **Dunbar,** Sc,UK
54/C4 **Dunblane,** Sc,UK
158/E4 **Duncan,** Az,US
159/H4 **Duncan,** Ok,US
55/K7 **Duncansby Head** (pt.), Sc,UK
162/D3 **Duncanville,** Tx,US
60/D2 **Dundalk,** Ire.
60/D2 **Dundalk** (bay), Ire.
166/B5 **Dundalk,** Md,US
116/D5 **Dundas** (lake), Austl.
114/E2 **Dundas** (str.), Austl.
153/R7 **Dundas** (pen.), NW,Can
161/Q9 **Dundas,** On,Can
133/E3 **Dundee,** SAfr.
54/D4 **Dundee,** Sc,UK
54/B5 **Dundonald,** Sc,UK
56/C3 **Dundrum,** NI,UK
56/C3 **Dundrum** (bay), NI,UK
156/G3 **Dundurn,** Sk,Can
115/R12 **Dunedin,** NZ
163/H4 **Dunedin,** Fl,US
167/H9 **Dunellen,** NJ,US
54/C4 **Dunfermline,** Sc,UK
56/B2 **Dungannon,** NI,UK
56/B3 **Dungannon** (dist.), NI,UK
106/B3 **Dungarpur,** India
60/C5 **Dungarvan,** Ire.
60/C5 **Dungarvan** (har.), Ire.
71/F5 **Dungau** (reg.), Ger.
143/K8 **Dungeness** (pt.), Arg.
59/G5 **Dungeness** (pt.), Eng,UK
56/B2 **Dungiven,** NI,UK
130/A2 **Dungu,** Zaire
130/A2 **Dungu** (riv.), Zaire
97/K3 **Dunhua,** China
96/C3 **Dunhuang,** China
54/C3 **Dunkeld,** Sc,UK
60/B3 **Dunkellin** (riv.), Ire.
68/B1 **Dunkerque** (Dunkirk), Fr.
58/C4 **Dunkery** (hill), Eng,UK
68/B1 **Dunkirk** (Dunkerque), Fr.
129/E5 **Dunkwa,** Gha.
60/D3 **Dún Laoghaire,** Ire.
56/B2 **Dunloy,** NI,UK
60/A6 **Dunmanus** (bay), Ire.
56/B2 **Dunmurry,** NI,UK
56/A2 **Dunnamanagh,** NI,UK
56/B2 **Dunnamore,** NI,UK
76/D3 **Dünnern** (riv.), Swi.
55/N13 **Dunnet Head** (pt.), Sc,UK
54/C4 **Dunning,** Sc,UK
57/H4 **Dunnington,** Eng,UK
161/Q10 **Dunnville,** On,Can
54/B5 **Dunoon,** Sc,UK
127/B5 **Dunqulah,** Sudan
56/D2 **Dunragit,** Sc,UK
54/C5 **Dun Rig** (mtn.), Sc,UK
54/D5 **Duns,** Sc,UK
56/E1 **Dunscore,** Sc,UK
157/H3 **Dunseith,** ND,US
56/B1 **Dunseverick,** NI,UK
158/B2 **Dunsmuir,** Ca,US
59/F3 **Dunstable,** Eng,UK
69/E5 **Dun-sur-Meuse,** Fr.
54/B5 **Duntocher,** Sc,UK
54/B6 **Dunure,** Sc,UK
97/J1 **Duobukur** (riv.), China
96/H3 **Duolun,** China
165/P16 **Du Page** (co.), Il,US
165/P16 **Du Page** (riv.), Il,US
165/P16 **Du Page, East Branch** (riv.), Il,US
157/H4 **Dupree,** SD,US
116/B2 **Dupuy** (cape), Austl.
141/K7 **Duque de Caxias,** Braz.
143/J7 **Duque de York** (isl.), Chile
168/H7 **Duquesne,** Pa,US
160/B4 **Du Quoin,** Il,US
114/D3 **Durack** (range), Austl.
92/C1 **Durağan,** Turk.
72/F5 **Durance** (riv.), Fr.
146/D3 **Durango,** Mex.
74/D1 **Durango,** Sp.
158/F3 **Durango,** Co,US
159/H4 **Durant,** Ok,US
143/F2 **Durazno,** Uru.
143/F2 **Durazno** (dept.), Uru.
133/E3 **Durban,** SAfr.
132/L10 **Durbanville,** SAfr.
76/C1 **Durbion** (riv.), Fr.
69/E3 **Durbuy,** Belg.
82/C2 **Đurđevac,** Cro.
82/E3 **Durđevo,** Yugo.
69/F2 **Düren,** Ger.
106/D3 **Durg,** India
106/E3 **Durgāpur,** India
161/S8 **Durham** (co.), On,Can
57/G2 **Durham,** Eng,UK
57/F2 **Durham** (co.), Eng,UK
163/J3 **Durham,** NC,US
161/G3 **Durham,** NH,US
59/E5 **Durlston Head** (pt.), Eng,UK
68/D1 **Durme** (riv.), Belg.
82/D4 **Durmitor Nat'l Park,** Yugo.
54/A5 **Duror,** Sc,UK
81/F2 **Durrës,** Alb.
59/E4 **Durrington,** Eng,UK
58/D3 **Dursley,** Eng,UK
92/B2 **Dursunbey,** Turk.
93/M6 **Durusu,** Turk.
93/M6 **Durusu** (lake), Turk.
111/J4 **D'Urville** (cape), Indo.
160/C1 **Dusey** (riv.), On,Can
105/E3 **Dushan,** China
103/D2 **Du Shan** (peak), China
88/G6 **Dushanbe** (cap.), Taj.
105/E3 **Dushui** (riv.), China
66/D6 **Düsseldorf,** Ger.
57/H4 **Dutch** (riv.), Eng,UK
166/B3 **Dutch Wonderland,** Pa,US
67/F4 **Düte** (riv.), Ger.
131/A4 **Dutlwe,** Bots.
132/L10 **Dutoitspiek** (peak), SAfr.
105/E3 **Duyun,** China
83/K5 **Düzce,** Turk.
92/D2 **Düzici,** Turk.
84/H2 **Dvina** (bay), Rus.
85/J3 **Dvina, Northern** (riv.), Rus.
84/F5 **Dvina, Western** (riv.), Bel., Rus.
71/H4 **Dvořiště** (lake), Czh.
106/A3 **Dwārka,** India
156/D4 **Dworshak** (res.), Id,US
56/D6 **Dwyfor** (riv.), Wal,UK
132/C4 **Dwyka** (riv.), SAfr.
86/E1 **Dyat'kovo,** Rus.
153/K2 **Dyer** (cape), NW,Can
143/J7 **Dyer** (cape), Chile
160/C3 **Dyer,** In,US
163/F2 **Dyersburg,** Tn,US
162/D3 **Dyess A.F.B.,** Tx,US
58/B3 **Dyfed** (co.), Wal,UK
56/D6 **Dyffryn,** Wal,UK
58/C1 **Dyfi** (riv.), Wal,UK
65/J4 **Dyje** (riv.), Czh.
87/G4 **Dykh-tau, Gora** (peak), Rus.
68/D2 **Dyle** (Dijle) (riv.), Belg.
71/F5 **Dyleň** (peak), Czh.
65/K2 **Dylewska Gora** (peak), Pol.
59/G4 **Dymchurch,** Eng,UK
87/H4 **Dyul'tydag, Gora** (peak), Rus.
131/D2 **Dzalanyama** (range), Malw., Moz.
133/H6 **Dzaoudzi** (cap.), May.
96/C2 **Dzavhan** (riv.), Mong.
86/F3 **Dzenzik, Mys** (pt.), Ukr.
96/C2 **Dzereg,** Mong.
84/J4 **Dzerzhinsk,** Rus.
102/B3 **Dzhalal-Abad,** Kyr.
102/B3 **Dzhambul,** Kaz.
86/E3 **Dzhankoy,** Ukr.
87/M1 **Dzhetygara,** Kaz.
102/A2 **Dzhezkazgan,** Kaz.
88/G5 **Dzhizak,** Uzb.
89/P4 **Dzhugdzhur** (range), Rus.
65/L2 **Działdowo,** Pol.
147/H4 **Dzibilchaltún** (ruins), Mex.
147/H4 **Dzidzantún,** Mex.
65/J3 **Dzierżoniów,** Pol.
96/B3 **Dzungarian** (basin), China
102/D3 **Dzungarian Gate** (pass), China
96/E2 **Dzüünbayan-Ulaan,** Mong.
102/F2 **Dzüüngovĭ,** Mong.
96/D2 **Dzüünhangay,** Mong.
96/F2 **Dzüünharaa,** Mong.

E

159/G3 **Eads,** Co,US
153/L3 **Eagle** (riv.), Nf,Can
160/A1 **Eagle** (lake), On,Can
156/F3 **Eagle** (riv.), Sk,Can
60/A5 **Eagle** (mtn.), Ire.
158/B2 **Eagle** (lake), Ca,US
158/F3 **Eagle,** Co,US
157/L4 **Eagle** (peak), Mn,US

186

Eagle – Ereğl

168/G5 **Eagle** (cr.), Oh,US
165/P14 **Eagle** (lake), Wi,US
157/H4 **Eagle Butte**, SD,US
162/C4 **Eagle Pass**, Tx,US
57/E1 **Eaglesfield**, Sc,UK
54/B5 **Eaglesham**, Sc,UK
53/M7 **Ealing** (bor.), Eng,UK
57/F4 **Earby**, Eng,UK
160/A1 **Ear Falls**, On,Can
59/G2 **Earith**, Eng,UK
167/D3 **Earle Nav. Weap. Ctr.**, NJ,US
158/C4 **Earlimart**, Ca,US
59/F2 **Earls Barton**, Eng,UK
59/G3 **Earls Colne**, Eng,UK
54/D4 **Earlsferry**, Sc,UK
54/B4 **Earl's Seat** (mtn.), Sc,UK
54/D5 **Earlston**, Sc,UK
59/H2 **Earl Stonham**, Eng,UK
162/D4 **Early**, Tx,US
54/C4 **Earn** (riv.), Sc,UK
54/B4 **Earn, Loch** (lake), Sc,UK
57/G2 **Easington**, Eng,UK
57/G3 **Easingwold**, Eng,UK
163/H3 **Easley**, SC,US
116/D4 **East** (mtn.), Austl.
115/S10 **East** (cape), NZ
151/B6 **East** (cape), Ak,US
168/D1 **East** (pt.), Ma,US
166/C5 **East** (pt.), NJ,US
167/L9 **East** (bay), NY,US
165/C3 **East** (passg.), Wa,US
59/G2 **East Anglia** (reg.), Eng,UK
161/G2 **East Angus**, Qu,Can
53/N7 **East Barnet**, Eng,UK
139/G4 **East Berbice-Corentyne** (reg.), Guy.
139/G3 **East Berbice-Coronie** (reg.), Guy.
59/H3 **East Bergholt**, Eng,UK
157/K4 **East Bethel**, Mn,US
59/G5 **Eastbourne**, Eng,UK
168/D1 **East Bridgewater**, Ma,US
166/D3 **East Brunswick**, NJ,US
150/D2 **East Caicos** (isl.), Trks.
54/C5 **East Calder**, Sc,UK
57/G1 **East Chevington**, Eng,UK
165/R16 **East Chicago**, In,US
105/J3 **East China** (sea), China
53/M8 **East Clandon**, Eng,UK
58/B3 **East Cleddau** (riv.), Wal,UK
168/F4 **East Cleveland**, Oh,US
58/C5 **East Dart** (riv.), Eng,UK
59/G1 **East Dereham**, Eng,UK
165/G7 **East Detroit** (East Pointe), Mi,US
121/Q7 **Easter** (isl.), Chile
132/A2 **Easter** (pt.), Namb.
129/E5 **Eastern** (reg.), Gha.
130/C2 **Eastern** (prov.), Kenya
128/C4 **Eastern** (prov.), SLeo.
108/H4 **Eastern** (prov.), SrL.
127/C5 **Eastern** (reg.), Sudan
130/B2 **Eastern** (prov.), Ugan.
57/H4 **Eastern** (plain), Eng,UK
166/B6 **Eastern** (bay), Md,US
131/C2 **Eastern** (prov.), Zam.
132/D3 **Eastern Cape** (prov.), SAfr.
98/A4 **Eastern Channel** (str.), Japan
108/F4 **Eastern Ghats** (uplands), India
166/B5 **Eastern Neck I. Nat'l Wild. Ref.**, Md,US
88/K4 **Eastern Sayans** (mts.), Rus.
132/E2 **Eastern Transvaal** (prov.), SAfr.
157/J2 **Easterville**, Mb,Can
143/N8 **East Falkland** (isl.), Falk.
68/C2 **East Flanders** (prov.), Belg.
67/E1 **East Frisian** (isls.), Ger.
59/F1 **East Glen** (riv.), Eng,UK
168/C2 **East Greenwich**, RI,US
59/F4 **East Grinstead**, Eng,UK
168/B3 **East Haddam**, Ct,US
168/B1 **Easthampton**, Ma,US
168/B2 **East Hartford**, Ct,US
168/B1 **East Hartland**, Ct,US
168/B3 **East Haven**, Ct,US
156/F4 **East Helena**, Mt,US
165/C2 **East Hill-Meridian**, Wa,US
167/L8 **East Hills**, NY,US
53/M8 **East Horsley**, Eng,UK
160/C2 **East Jordan**, Mi,US
88/J5 **East Kazakhstan Obl.**, Kaz.
54/B5 **East Kilbride**, Sc,UK
101/D3 **East Korea** (Tongjosŏn) (bay), NKor.
162/D3 **Eastland**, Tx,US
160/C3 **East Lansing**, Mi,US
57/G6 **East Leake**, Eng,UK
59/E5 **Eastleigh**, Eng,UK
54/D5 **East Linton**, Sc,UK
168/E5 **East Liverpool**, Oh,US
132/D4 **East London**, SAfr.
168/B1 **East Longmeadow**, Ma,US
164/B2 **East Los Angeles**, Ca,US
168/B3 **East Lyme**, Ct,US
160/F1 **Eastmain** (riv.), Qu,Can
163/H3 **Eastman**, Ga,US
167/E2 **East Meadow**, NY,US
161/G2 **East Millinocket**, Me,US
158/D4 **East Mojave Nat'l Scenic Area**, Ca,US
53/M7 **East Molesey**, Eng,UK
157/K5 **East Nishnabotna** (riv.), Ia,US
167/E2 **East Northport**, NY,US
58/D5 **Easton**, Eng,UK
168/A3 **Easton**, Ct,US
167/E1 **Easton** (res.), Ct,US
168/C1 **Easton**, Ma,US
166/B6 **Easton**, Md,US
166/C2 **Easton**, Pa,US
167/D2 **East Orange**, NJ,US
167/F2 **East Patchogue**, NY,US
163/G3 **East Point**, Ga,US
165/G7 **East Pointe** (East Detroit), Mi,US
161/H2 **Eastport**, Me,US
168/C2 **East Providence**, RI,US
57/H5 **East Retford**, Eng,UK
57/E2 **Eastriggs**, Sc,UK
167/K8 **East River** (str.), NY,US
167/L9 **East Rockaway**, NY,US
167/J8 **East Rutherford**, NJ,US
59/H4 **Eastry**, Eng,UK
160/B4 **East Saint Louis**, Il,US
89/S2 **East Siberian** (sea), Rus.
166/C2 **East Stroudsburg**, Pa,US
59/G5 **East Sussex** (co.), Eng,UK
160/D2 **East Tawas**, Mi,US
58/B4 **East the Water**, Eng,UK
54/C4 **East Wemyss**, Sc,UK
156/C4 **East Wenatchee**, Wa,US
166/D3 **East Windsor**, NJ,US
59/F5 **East Wittering**, Eng,UK
57/G6 **Eastwood**, Eng,UK
161/R8 **East York**, On,Can
59/E2 **Eatington**, Eng,UK
159/F2 **Eaton**, Co,US
156/F3 **Eatonia**, Sk,Can
167/E2 **Eatons Neck** (pt.), NY,US
59/F2 **Eaton Socon**, Eng,UK
167/D3 **Eatontown**, NJ,US
57/H5 **Eau** (riv.), Eng,UK
53/S10 **Eaubonne**, Fr.
153/J3 **Eau Claire** (lake), Qu,Can
160/B2 **Eau Claire**, Wi,US
68/A4 **Eaulne** (riv.), Fr.
120/D4 **Eauripik** (atoll), Micr.
59/E4 **Ebble** (riv.), Eng,UK
58/C3 **Ebbw Vale**, Wal,UK
124/H7 **Ebebiyin**, EqG.
124/G3 **Ebeggi** (well), Alg.
73/K3 **Ebensee**, Aus.
70/B4 **Eberbach**, Ger.
70/E3 **Ebermannstadt**, Ger.
70/D2 **Ebern**, Ger.
70/C5 **Ebersbach an der Fils**, Ger.
71/E6 **Ebersberg**, Ger.
65/G2 **Eberswalde-Finow**, Ger.
100/B2 **Ebetsu**, Japan
107/H2 **Ebian**, China
99/H7 **Ebina**, Japan
102/D3 **Ebinur** (lake), China
128/D3 **Ebo** (lake), Mali
80/D2 **Eboli**, It.
124/H7 **Ebolowa**, Camr.
120/F4 **Ebon** (atoll), Mrsh.
75/F2 **Ebro** (riv.), Sp.
147/F5 **Ecatepec**, Mex.
57/E1 **Ecclefechan**, Sc,UK
57/F5 **Eccles**, Eng,UK
57/F6 **Eccleshall**, Eng,UK
112/C1 **Echague**, Phil.
149/F4 **Echandi** (mtn.), CR
70/C6 **Echaz** (riv.), Ger.
129/H3 **Éché Fadadinga** (wadi), Niger
105/G2 **Echeng**, China
99/M9 **Echigawa**, Japan
71/E6 **Eching**, Ger.
72/F4 **Echirolles**, Fr.
87/H4 **Echmiadzin**, Arm.
166/D1 **Echo** (lake), NJ,US
152/E2 **Echo Bay**, NW,Can
157/L2 **Echoing** (riv.), Mb, On,Can
66/C6 **Echt**, Neth.
119/C3 **Echuca**, Austl.
117/M9 **Echunga** (cr.), Austl.
74/C4 **Écija**, Sp.
64/E1 **Eckernförde**, Ger.
63/H1 **Eckerö** (isl.), Fin.
58/D2 **Eckington**, Eng,UK
153/H1 **Eclipse** (sound), NW,Can
168/G6 **Economy**, Pa,US
141/D1 **Ecoporanga**, Braz.
165/F7 **Ecorse**, Mi,US
165/F7 **Ecorse** (riv.), Mi,US
68/A5 **Écos**, Fr.
53/T9 **Écouen**, Fr.
72/D2 **Ecouves, Signal d'** (peak), Fr.
136/C4 **Ecuador**
76/C4 **Ecublens**, Swi.
125/P5 **Ed**, Eth.
55/N13 **Eday** (isl.), Sc,UK
92/A2 **Edcemit** (gulf), Turk.
54/B1 **Edderton**, Sc,UK
54/C5 **Eddleston**, Sc,UK
119/D4 **Eddystone** (pt.), Austl.
58/B6 **Eddystone** (rocks), Eng,UK
66/C4 **Ede**, Neth.
129/G5 **Ede**, Nga.
124/H7 **Edéa**, Camr.
68/D1 **Edegem**, Belg.
141/B1 **Edéia**, Braz.
82/E1 **Edelény**, Hun.
67/H4 **Edemissen**, Ger.
57/F2 **Eden** (riv.), Eng,UK
54/D4 **Eden** (riv.), Sc,UK
163/J2 **Eden**, NC,US
53/P8 **Edenbridge**, Eng,UK
133/E3 **Edendale**, SAfr.
57/F2 **Edenside** (val.), Eng,UK
67/G6 **Eder** (riv.), Ger.
67/F6 **Eder-Stausee** (res.), Ger.
67/E2 **Edewecht**, Ger.
116/D2 **Edgar** (peak), Austl.
59/E2 **Edgbaston**, Eng,UK
88/C2 **Edge** (isl.), Sval.
151/L4 **Edgecumbe** (cape), Ak,US
153/K2 **Edgell** (isl.), NW,Can
166/B5 **Edgemere**, Md,US
157/G5 **Edgerton**, Wy,US
166/D3 **Edgewater Park**, NJ,US
166/B5 **Edgewood**, Md,US
166/B5 **Edgewood Arsenal** (mil. res.), Md,US
165/C3 **Edgewood-North Hill**, Wa,US
58/D1 **Edgmond**, Eng,UK
53/N7 **Edgware**, Eng,UK
81/H2 **Édhessa**, Gre.
160/D3 **Edinboro**, Pa,US
162/D5 **Edinburg**, Tx,US
54/C5 **Edinburgh** (cap.), Sc,UK
131/D2 **Edingeni**, Malw.
83/H5 **Edirne**, Turk.
83/H5 **Edirne** (prov.), Turk.
166/D2 **Edison**, NJ,US
167/J8 **Edison Nat'l Hist. Site**, NJ,US
163/H3 **Edisto** (riv.), SC,US
163/H3 **Edisto Island**, SC,US
129/F2 **Édjérir** (wadi), Mali
165/C2 **Edmonds**, Wa,US
156/E2 **Edmonton** (cap.), Ab,Can
53/N7 **Edmonton**, Eng,UK
157/K2 **Edmund** (lake), Mb,Can
118/B2 **Edmund Kennedy Nat'l Park**, Austl.
161/G2 **Edmundston**, NB,Can
162/D4 **Edna**, Tx,US
99/H7 **Edo** (riv.), Japan
92/A2 **Edremit**, Turk.
92/A2 **Edremit** (gulf), Turk.
156/D2 **Edson**, Ab,Can
140/D2 **Eduardo Gomes**, Braz.
117/F2 **Edward** (peak), Austl.
130/A3 **Edward** (lake), Ugan., Zaire
118/A1 **Edward River Abor. Community**, Austl.
159/K2 **Edwards** (riv.), Il,US
162/C4 **Edwards** (plat.), Tx,US
158/C4 **Edwards A.F.B.**, Ca,US
160/B4 **Edwardsville**, Il,US
113/P **Edward VII** (pen.), Ant.
113/D **Edward VIII** (bay), Ant.
54/D3 **Edzell**, Sc,UK
147/H5 **Edzná** (ruins), Mex.
68/C1 **Eeklo**, Belg.
158/B3 **Eel** (riv.), Ca,US
66/D2 **Eelde-Paterswolde**, Neth.
66/C4 **Eem** (riv.), Neth.
66/D2 **Eems (Ems)** (riv.), Neth.
66/D2 **Eemshaven** (har.), Neth.
66/D2 **Eemskanaal** (can.), Neth.
66/C6 **Eersel**, Neth.
120/F6 **Efate** (isl.), Van.
157/L5 **Effigy Mounds Nat'l Mon.**, Ia,US
161/R9 **Effingham**, On,Can
53/M8 **Effingham**, Eng,UK
160/B4 **Effingham**, Il,US
83/J3 **Eforie**, Rom.
76/D2 **Efringen-Kirchen**, Ger.
56/E6 **Efyrnwy, Llyn** (lake), Wal,UK
80/C3 **Egadi** (isls.), It.
70/D5 **Egan** (riv.), Ger.
158/D3 **Egan** (range), Nv,US
71/F2 **Eger** (riv.), Ger.
82/E2 **Eger**, Hun.
62/B2 **Egersund**, Nor.
62/D4 **Egeskov**, Den.
77/E3 **Egg**, Swi.
67/F5 **Eggegebirge** (ridge), Ger.
71/F6 **Eggenfelden**, Ger.
70/B4 **Eggenstein-Leopoldshafen**, Ger.
62/F5 **Eggesin**, Ger.
166/C5 **Egg Island** (pt.), NJ,US
57/G3 **Egglescliffe**, Eng,UK
57/G2 **Eggleston**, Eng,UK
53/M7 **Egham**, Eng,UK
69/D2 **Eghezée**, Belg.
96/E1 **Egiyn** (riv.), Mong.
153/R7 **Eglinton** (isl.), NW,Can
56/A1 **Eglinton**, NI,UK
58/C4 **Eglwys Brewis**, Wal,UK
53/S11 **Égly**, Fr.
66/B3 **Egmond aan Zee**, Neth.
115/R10 **Egmont** (cape), NZ
115/R10 **Egmont** (peak), NZ
56/E3 **Egremont**, Eng,UK
92/B2 **Eğridir**, Turk.
92/B2 **Eğridir** (lake), Turk.
140/A4 **Eguas** (riv.), Braz.
127/B3 **Egypt**
70/D3 **Ehebach** (riv.), Ger.
98/C4 **Ehime** (pref.), Japan
77/F1 **Ehingen**, Ger.
76/D1 **Ehn** (riv.), Fr.
70/B1 **Ehringshausen**, Ger.
121/L5 **Eiao** (isl.), FrPol.
74/D1 **Eibar**, Sp.
71/F1 **Eibenstock**, Ger.
66/D4 **Eibergen**, Neth.
69/G6 **Eichel** (riv.), Fr.
70/E6 **Eichenau**, Ger.
71/F5 **Eichendorf**, Ger.
70/C2 **Eichenzell**, Ger.
70/E5 **Eichstätt**, Ger.
62/D1 **Eidsvoll**, Nor.
69/F3 **Eifel** (plat.), Ger.
131/C3 **Eiffel Flats**, Zim.
53/S10 **Eiffel Tower**, Fr.
99/M9 **Eigenji**, Japan
76/D4 **Eiger** (peak), Swi.
55/H8 **Eigg** (isl.), Sc,UK
106/B6 **Eight Degree** (chan.), India, Mald.
113/T **Eights** (coast), Ant.
114/C3 **Eighty Mile** (beach), Austl.
66/B2 **Eijerlandsee Gat** (chan.), Neth.
69/E2 **Eijsden**, Neth.
119/C3 **Eildon** (lake), Austl.
139/G4 **Eilerts de Haan** (mts.), Sur.
54/A3 **Eil, Loch** (inlet), Sc,UK
118/A2 **Einasleigh** (riv.), Austl.
67/G5 **Einbeck**, Ger.
66/C6 **Eindhoven**, Neth.
77/E3 **Einsiedeln**, Swi.
144/D2 **Eirunepé**, Braz.
77/H4 **Eisack (Isarco)** (riv.), It.
69/E4 **Eisch** (riv.), Lux.
67/H7 **Eisenach**, Ger.
70/B3 **Eisenberg**, Ger.
73/L3 **Eisenerz**, Aus.
166/A4 **Eisenhower Nat'l Hist. Site**, Pa,US
65/H2 **Eisenhüttenstadt**, Ger.
73/M3 **Eisenstadt**, Aus.
69/G2 **Eiserfeld**, Ger.
67/F3 **Eiter** (riv.), Ger.
69/G2 **Eitorf**, Ger.
75/E1 **Ejea de los Caballeros**, Sp.
138/D2 **Ejido**, Ven.
103/B3 **Ejin Horo Qi**, China
96/E3 **Ejin Qi**, China
148/B2 **Ejutla**, Mex.
63/K2 **Ekenäs** (Tammisaari), Fin.
66/B6 **Ekeren**, Belg.
63/R7 **Ekerö**, Swe.
63/R7 **Ekerön** (isl.), Swe.
102/C1 **Ekibastuz**, Kaz.
62/F3 **Eksjö**, Swe.
153/H3 **Ekwan** (riv.), On,Can
131/D1 **Ekwendeni**, Malw.
128/C2 **El 'Acâba** (reg.), Mrta.
123/S15 **El Affroun**, Alg.
127/B2 **El Alamein (Al 'Alamayn)**, Egypt
94/B3 **El Amra (Abydos)** (ruins), Egypt
58/C2 **Elan** (riv.), Wal,UK
53/R10 **Élancourt**, Fr.
132/P12 **Elands** (riv.), SAfr.
132/Q12 **Elandsrivier** (riv.), SAfr.
138/A5 **El Anegado**, Ecu.
123/V18 **El Aouinet**, Alg.
74/C4 **El Arahal**, Sp.
128/D2 **El Arhlaf** (well), Mrta.
118/B2 **El Arish**, Austl.
124/F1 **El Asnam**, Alg.
81/H3 **Elassón**, Gre.
74/D1 **El Astillero**, Sp.
91/D5 **Elat**, Isr.
120/D4 **Elato** (atoll), Micr.
92/D2 **Elazığ**, Turk.
92/D2 **Elazığ** (prov.), Turk.
80/B1 **Elba** (isl.), It.
163/G4 **Elba**, Al,US
138/C2 **El Banco**, Col.
74/B1 **El Barco**, Sp.
81/G2 **Elbasan**, Alb.
124/F1 **El Bayadh**, Alg.
70/A1 **Elbbach** (riv.), Ger.
64/E2 **Elbe** (riv.), Ger.
65/H3 **Elbe (Labe)** (riv.), Czh.
130/D2 **El Ben**, Kenya
158/F3 **Elbert** (mtn.), Co,US
163/H3 **Elberton**, Ga,US
67/H2 **Elbe-Seitenkanal** (can.), Ger.
72/D2 **Elbeuf**, Fr.
92/D2 **Elbistan**, Turk.
65/K1 **Elblag**, Pol.
65/K2 **Elblag** (prov.), Pol.
156/G3 **Elbow**, Sk,Can
87/G4 **El'brus, Gora** (peak), Rus.
66/C4 **Elburg**, Neth.
93/G2 **Elburz** (mts.), Iran
148/E3 **El Cajón** (res.), Hon.
164/D5 **El Cajon**, Ca,US
162/D4 **El Campo**, Tx,US
156/E4 **El Capitan** (peak), Mt,US
142/B3 **El Carmen**, Chile
138/C2 **El Carmen de Bolívar**, Col.
75/N8 **El Casar de Talamanca**, Sp.
158/D4 **El Centro**, Ca,US
149/J2 **El Cercado**, DRep.
138/B4 **El Cerrito**, Col.
165/K11 **El Cerrito**, Ca,US
150/F5 **El Cerro del Aripo** (mtn.), Trin.
138/D2 **El Cerrón** (peak), Ven.
138/C2 **El César** (dept.), Col.
75/E3 **Elche**, Sp.
147/F4 **El Chico Nat'l Park**, Mex.
70/D6 **Elchingen**, Ger.
114/F2 **Elcho** (isl.), Austl.
142/C3 **El Chocón** (res.), Arg.
138/C3 **El Cocuy Nat'l Park**, Col.
135/E2 **El Colorado**, Arg.
165/B3 **Eld** (inlet), Wa,US
75/E3 **Elda**, Sp.
130/B2 **Eldama Ravine**, Kenya
64/G2 **Elde** (riv.), Ger.
166/B5 **Eldersburg**, Md,US
128/C1 **El Djouf** (des.), Mali, Mrta.
135/F2 **Eldorado**, Arg.
146/D3 **El Dorado**, Mex.
162/E3 **El Dorado**, Ar,US
162/D2 **El Dorado**, Ks,US
162/C4 **Eldorado**, Tx,US
130/B2 **Eldoret**, Kenya
154/W13 **Eleao** (peak), Hi,US
124/D2 **El Eglab** (plat.), Alg.
82/E2 **Elek**, Hun.
84/H5 **Elektrostal'**, Rus.
83/G4 **Elena**, Bul.
113/W **Elephant** (isl.), Ant.
140/B2 **Elesbão Veloso**, Braz.
75/M8 **El Escorial**, Sp.
93/E2 **Eleşkirt**, Turk.
123/U17 **El Eulma**, Alg.
150/B1 **Eleuthera** (isl.), Bahm.
159/K3 **Eleven Point** (riv.), Ar, Mo,US
81/L6 **Elevsis**, Gre.
74/A1 **El Ferrol**, Sp.
161/Q9 **Elfrida**, On,Can
146/C3 **El Fuerte**, Mex.
54/C1 **Elgin**, Sc,UK
165/P15 **Elgin**, Il,US
157/H4 **Elgin**, ND,US
162/D4 **Elgin**, Tx,US
161/R8 **Elgin Mills**, On,Can
74/D1 **Elgóibar**, Sp.
124/F1 **El Golea**, Alg.
148/D3 **El Golfete** (lake), Guat.
125/N7 **Elgon** (mtn.), Kenya, Ugan.
139/F2 **El Guacharo Nat'l Park**, Ven.
123/T16 **El Ham** (riv.), Alg.
147/F4 **El Higo**, Mex.
126/D2 **Elias Garcia**, Ang.
159/G4 **Elida**, NM,US
54/D4 **Elie**, Sc,UK
63/M1 **Elimäki**, Fin.
162/C4 **El Indio**, Tx,US
59/E5 **Eling**, Eng,UK
87/H3 **Elista**, Rus.
117/M8 **Elizabeth**, Austl.
132/A2 **Elizabeth** (bay), Namb.
168/D3 **Elizabeth** (isls.), Ma,US
167/D2 **Elizabeth**, NJ,US
116/K7 **Elizabethan Village**, Austl.
163/J2 **Elizabeth City**, NC,US
163/H2 **Elizabethton**, Tn,US
160/C4 **Elizabethtown**, Ky,US
166/B3 **Elizabethtown**, Pa,US
124/D1 **El Jadida**, Mor.
65/M2 **Ełk**, Pol.
165/L10 **Elk** (slough), Ca,US
162/B2 **Elk** (mts.), Co,US
166/C5 **Elk** (riv.), Md,US
163/H2 **Elk** (riv.), WV,US
159/H4 **Elk City**, Ok,US
165/M10 **Elk Grove**, Ca,US
165/Q15 **Elk Grove Village**, Il,US
160/C3 **Elkhart**, In,US
159/G3 **Elkhart**, Ks,US
128/C2 **El Khatt** (depr.), Mrta.
124/D3 **El Khatt** (escarp.), Mrta.
157/H3 **Elkhorn**, Mb,Can
159/H2 **Elkhorn** (riv.), Ne,US
83/H4 **Elkhovo**, Bul.
163/H2 **Elkin**, NC,US
160/E4 **Elkins**, WV,US
156/E2 **Elk Island Nat'l Park**, Ab,Can
158/D2 **Elko**, Nv,US
156/F2 **Elk Point**, Ab,Can
160/C2 **Elk Rapids**, Mi,US
166/B5 **Elk Ridge**, Md,US
157/K4 **Elk River**, Mn,US
167/H2 **El Kroub**, Alg.
123/T15 **El Kseur**, Alg.
166/C4 **Elkton**, Md,US
57/G4 **Elland**, Eng,UK
69/F2 **Elle** (riv.), Ger.
153/R7 **Ellef Ringnes** (isl.), NW,Can
130/C2 **Ēl Lēh**, Eth.
57/E2 **Ellen** (riv.), Eng,UK
157/J4 **Ellendale**, ND,US
156/C4 **Ellensburg**, Wa,US
67/H5 **Eller** (riv.), Ger.
69/G4 **Ellerbach** (riv.), Ger.
78/A4 **Ellero** (riv.), It.
119/D3 **Ellery** (peak), Austl.
153/T6 **Ellesmere** (isl.), NW,Can
153/T6 **Ellesmere Island Nat'l Park**, NW,Can
57/F5 **Ellesmere Port**, Eng,UK
142/C2 **El Libertador General Bernardo O'Higgins** (reg.), Chile
152/F2 **Ellice** (riv.), NW,Can
166/B5 **Ellicott City**, Md,US
168/B2 **Ellington**, Ct,US
160/D2 **Elliot Lake**, On,Can
117/H4 **Elliot Price Consv. Park**, Austl.
163/J2 **Elliott** (peak), Va,US
167/J9 **Ellis** (isl.), NY,US
131/B4 **Ellisras**, SAfr.
149/G4 **El Llano**, Pan.
54/D2 **Ellon**, Sc,UK
57/H4 **Ellloughton**, Eng,UK
113/T **Ellsworth** (mts.), Ant.
159/H3 **Ellsworth**, Ks,US
161/G2 **Ellsworth**, Me,US
160/A2 **Ellsworth**, Wi,US
113/U **Ellsworth Land** (reg.), Ant.
70/D5 **Ellwangen**, Ger.
168/G6 **Ellwood City**, Pa,US
161/S10 **Elma**, NY,US
92/C2 **Elmadağ**, Turk.
91/A1 **Elmalı**, Turk.
158/F4 **El Malpais Nat'l Mon.**, NM,US
75/L7 **El Masnou**, Sp.
165/P13 **Elm Grove**, Wi,US
165/Q16 **Elmhurst**, Il,US
123/V17 **El Milia**, Alg.
129/E5 **Elmina**, Gha.
160/E3 **Elmira**, NY,US
164/C1 **El Mirage** (dry lake), Ca,US
144/D5 **El Misti** (vol.), Peru
75/N8 **El Molar**, Sp.
167/E2 **Elmont**, NY,US
75/L6 **El Montcau** (peak), Sp.
164/B2 **El Monte**, Ca,US
167/J9 **Elmora**, NJ,US
142/C1 **El Morrito** (pt.), Chile
158/E4 **El Morro Nat'l Mon.**, NM,US
128/C2 **El Mreyyé** (reg.), Mrta.
67/G1 **Elmshorn**, Ger.
59/G2 **Elmswell**, Eng,UK
165/Q16 **Elmwood Park**, Il,US
167/D2 **Elmwood Park**, NJ,US
124/D3 **El Mzereb** (well), Mali
142/C2 **El Nevado** (peak), Arg.
112/B3 **El Nido**, Phil.
141/H6 **Elói Mendes**, Braz.
72/A2 **Elorn** (riv.), Fr.
144/A1 **El Oro** (prov.), Ecu.
124/G1 **El Oued**, Alg.
118/H8 **Elouera Bushland Rsv.**, Austl.
158/E4 **Eloy**, Az,US
138/B5 **Eloy Alfaro**, Ecu.
147/N8 **El Palmar**, Mex.
142/F1 **El Palmar Nat'l Park**, Arg.
148/E3 **El Paraíso**, Hon.
75/N8 **El Pardo**, Sp.
162/B4 **El Paso**, Tx,US
147/E3 **El Pequeño**, Mex.
139/F2 **El Pilar**, Ven.
106/D6 **Elpitiya**, SrL.
148/A1 **El Potosí Nat'l Park**, Mex.
75/G2 **El Prat de Llobregat**, Sp.
148/D3 **El Progreso**, Guat.
148/E3 **El Progreso**, Hon.
74/B4 **El Puerto de Santa María**, Sp.
159/H4 **El Reno**, Ok,US
164/A2 **El Rio**, Ca,US
149/F4 **El Roble**, Pan.
156/F3 **Elrose**, Sk,Can
151/L3 **Elsa**, Yk,Can
79/E5 **Elsa** (riv.), It.
74/B2 **Elsa** (res.), Sp.
74/C1 **Elsa** (riv.), Sp.
148/D3 **El Salvador**
149/H1 **El Salvador**, Cuba
67/F4 **Else** (riv.), Ger.
164/B3 **El Segundo**, Ca,US
150/D3 **El Seibo**, DRep.
102/F4 **Elsen** (lake), China
70/C3 **Elsenfeld**, Ger.
70/B4 **Elsenz** (riv.), Ger.
67/F2 **Elsfleth**, Ger.
127/B4 **El Shab** (well), Egypt
164/C3 **Elsinore** (lake), Ca,US
139/E2 **El Sombrero**, Ven.
66/C5 **Elst**, Neth.
59/F4 **Elstead**, Eng,UK
147/F4 **El Tajín** (ruins), Mex.
139/F2 **El Tama Nat'l Park**, Ven.
138/B5 **El Tambo**, Ecu.
123/V17 **El Tarf** (gov.), Alg.
74/B1 **El Teleno** (mtn.), Sp.
147/L7 **El Tepotzteco Nat'l Park**, Mex.
53/P7 **Eltham**, Eng,UK
139/E2 **El Tigre**, Ven.
138/D2 **El Tocuyo**, Ven.
87/H2 **El'ton** (lake), Rus.
164/C3 **El Toro**, Ca,US
138/B5 **El Triunfo**, Ecu.
138/D3 **El Tuparro Nat'l Park**, Col.
70/B2 **Eltville am Rhein**, Ger.
106/D4 **Elūrū**, India
74/B3 **Elvas**, Port.
149/F4 **El Venado** (isl.), Nic.
62/D1 **Elverum**, Nor.
138/C3 **El Viejo** (peak), Col.
148/E3 **El Viejo**, Nic.
138/D2 **El Vigía**, Ven.
116/C2 **Elvire** (peak), Austl.
78/B2 **Elvo** (riv.), It.
130/D2 **El Wak**, Kenya
156/F3 **Elwell** (lake), Mt,US
160/C3 **Elwood**, In,US
56/E5 **Elwy** (riv.), Wal,UK
59/G2 **Ely**, Eng,UK
157/L4 **Ely**, Mn,US
158/D3 **Ely**, Nv,US
59/G2 **Ely, Isle of** (reg.), Eng,UK
168/E5 **Elyria**, Oh,US
164/F7 **Elysian Park, Los Angles**, Ca,US
150/E3 **El Yunque** (mtn.), PR
70/B2 **Elz**, Ger.
76/D1 **Elz** (riv.), Ger.
70/B6 **Elzach**, Ger.
69/G3 **Elzbach** (riv.), Ger.
67/G4 **Elze**, Ger.
93/H2 **Emāmshahr**, Iran
62/F3 **Emån** (riv.), Swe.
137/H7 **Emas Nat'l Park**, Braz.
87/L2 **Emba**, Kaz.
87/K3 **Emba** (riv.), Kaz.
135/D1 **Embarcación**, Arg.
163/E2 **Embarras** (riv.), Il,US
100/B1 **Embetsu**, Japan
144/D3 **Embira** (riv.), Braz.
141/C1 **Emborcaçao** (res.), Braz.
130/C3 **Embu**, Kenya
141/G8 **Embu-Guaçu**, Braz.
67/E2 **Emden**, Ger.
104/D2 **Emei**, China
104/D2 **Emei** (peak), China
119/G5 **Emerald**, Austl.
157/J3 **Emerson**, Mb,Can
167/J8 **Emerson**, NJ,US
165/K11 **Emeryville**, Ca,US
92/B2 **Emet**, Turk.
78/D4 **Emilia-Romagna** (reg.), It.
78/A1 **Emilius, Monte** (peak), It.
102/D2 **Emin**, China
102/D2 **Emin** (riv.), China
159/K3 **Eminence**, Mo,US
83/H4 **Emine, Nos** (cape), Bul.
92/B2 **Emirdağ**, Turk.
92/C2 **Emirgazi**, Turk.
130/A3 **Emir Paska** (gulf), Tanz.
133/E2 **Emlembe** (peak), Swaz.
66/D3 **Emlichheim**, Ger.
139/H4 **Emma** (riv.), Sur.
62/F3 **Emmaboda**, Swe.
166/C2 **Emmaus**, Pa,US
76/D4 **Emme** (riv.), Swi.
66/C3 **Emmeloord**, Neth.
66/D3 **Emmen**, Neth.
77/E3 **Emmenbrücke**, Swi.
76/D1 **Emmendingen**, Ger.
76/D3 **Emmental** (val.), Swi.
67/G5 **Emmer** (riv.), Ger.
67/E5 **Emmerbach** (riv.), Ger.
66/D5 **Emmerich**, Ger.
156/D5 **Emmett**, Id,US
59/G1 **Emneth**, Eng,UK
162/E3 **Emory**, Tx,US
76/C5 **Emosson** (lake), Swi.
146/C3 **Empalme**, Mex.
133/E3 **Empangeni**, SAfr.
135/E2 **Empedrado**, Arg.
142/B2 **Empedrado**, Chile
79/D5 **Empoli**, It.
159/H3 **Emporia**, Ks,US
160/E4 **Emporia**, Va,US
67/E4 **Emsbüren**, Ger.
67/E4 **Emsdetten**, Ger.
66/D2 **Ems (Eems)** (riv.), Ger., Neth.
67/E2 **Ems-Jade** (can.), Ger.
67/E3 **Emsland** (reg.), Ger.
67/F3 **Emstek**, Ger.
63/M2 **Emumägi** (hill), Est.
97/J1 **Emur** (riv.), China
99/E3 **Ena**, Japan
130/B3 **Enangiperi**, Kenya
156/G5 **Encampment**, Wy,US
146/B2 **Encantada, Cerro de la** (mtn.), Mex.
146/B3 **Encantado, Cerro** (mtn.), Mex.
146/E4 **Encarnación**, Mex.
135/E2 **Encarnación**, Par.
128/E5 **Enchi**, Gha.
164/C4 **Encinitas**, Ca,US
164/E7 **Encino**, Ca,US
119/A2 **Encounter** (bay), Austl.
141/A4 **Encruzilhada do Sul**, Braz.
130/C3 **Endau** (peak), Kenya
111/F5 **Ende**, Indo.
118/B1 **Endeavour River Nat'l Park**, Austl.
130/B2 **Endebess**, Kenya
121/H5 **Enderbury** (atoll), Kiri.
156/D3 **Enderby**, BC,Can
113/D **Enderby Land** (reg.), Ant.
157/J4 **Enderlin**, ND,US
160/E3 **Endicott**, NY,US
76/D1 **Endingen**, Ger.
144/C3 **Ene** (riv.), Peru
62/D2 **Enebakk**, Nor.
120/F3 **Enewetak** (atoll), Mrsh.
53/N7 **Enfield**, Eng,UK
53/N7 **Enfield** (bor.), Eng,UK
168/B2 **Enfield**, Ct,US
90/M8 **Engaño** (cape), Phil.
100/C1 **Engaru**, Japan
130/C3 **Engaruka** (basin), Tanz.
130/C4 **Engassumet**, Tanz.
87/H2 **Engel's**, Rus.
69/G2 **Engelskirchen**, Ger.
66/D2 **Engelsmanplaat** (isl.), Neth.
77/E2 **Engen**, Ger.
141/D1 **Engenheiro Navarro**, Braz.
141/K7 **Engenheiro Paulo de Froutin**, Braz.
67/F4 **Enger**, Ger.
110/B5 **Enggano** (isl.), Indo.
125/N4 **Enghershatu** (peak), Erit.
68/D2 **Enghien**, Belg.
55/K10 **England**, UK
160/E2 **Englehart**, On,Can
167/E2 **Englewood**, NJ,US
113/V **English** (coast), Ant.
157/K3 **English** (riv.), On,Can
72/B2 **English** (chan.), Eur.
106/E3 **English Bāzār**, India
131/D1 **Engucwini**, Malw.
159/H3 **Enid**, Ok,US
100/B2 **Eniwa**, Japan
70/A4 **Enkenbach-Alsenborn**, Ger.
66/C3 **Enkhuizen**, Neth.
62/G2 **Enköping**, Swe.
80/D4 **Enna**, It.
125/K4 **Ennedi** (plat.), Chad
60/C3 **Ennell, Lough** (lake), Ire.
67/E6 **Ennepe** (riv.), Ger.
67/E6 **Ennepetal**, Ger.
53/S9 **Ennery**, Fr.
67/F5 **Enningerloh**, Ger.
156/F4 **Ennis**, Mt,US
162/D3 **Ennis**, Tx,US
55/H9 **Enniskillen**, NI,UK
71/H6 **Enns**, Aus.
73/L3 **Enns** (riv.), Aus.
118/E6 **Enoggera** (res.), Austl.
168/G6 **Enon** (Enon Valley), Pa,US
163/H3 **Enoree** (riv.), SC,US
105/G4 **Enping**, China
54/B2 **Enrick** (riv.), Sc,UK
66/D4 **Enschede**, Neth.
67/E6 **Ense**, Ger.
103/B5 **Enshi**, China
130/B2 **Entebbe**, Ugan.
71/F3 **Entenbühl** (peak), Ger.
163/G4 **Enterprise**, Al,US
142/F2 **Entre Ríos** (prov.), Arg.
140/C3 **Entre Rios**, Braz.
148/E3 **Entre Ríos, Cordillera** (range), Hon.
74/A3 **Entroncamento**, Port.
129/G5 **Enugu**, Nga.
165/D3 **Enumclaw**, Wa,US
99/N10 **Enushū** (sea), Japan
68/A4 **Envermeu**, Fr.
70/C5 **Enz** (riv.), Ger.
78/D4 **Enza** (riv.), It.
99/F3 **Enzan**, Japan
69/F4 **Enzbach** (riv.), Ger.
66/C4 **Epe**, Neth.
68/C5 **Épernay**, Fr.
166/B3 **Ephrata**, Pa,US
120/F6 **Epi** (isl.), Van.
81/H4 **Epidaurus** (ruins), Gre.
76/C1 **Épinal**, Fr.
53/S10 **Épinay-sur-Orge**, Fr.
53/S10 **Épinay-sur-Seine**, Fr.
81/G3 **Epirus** (reg.), Gre.
69/F5 **Eppelborn**, Ger.
118/H8 **Epping**, Austl.
53/P6 **Epping**, Eng,UK
53/P7 **Epping** (for.), Eng,UK
70/B4 **Eppingen**, Ger.
118/B3 **Epping Forest Nat'l Park**, Austl.
53/N8 **Epsom**, Eng,UK
59/F4 **Epsom and Ewell**, Eng,UK
57/H4 **Epworth**, Eng,UK
124/G7 **Equatorial Guinea**
104/C3 **Er** (lake), China
79/D5 **Era** (riv.), It.
80/E2 **Eraclea** (ruins), It.
80/C4 **Eraclea Minoa** (ruins), It.
53/S9 **Éragny**, Fr.
106/D6 **Eravur**, SrL.
109/B3 **Erawan Nat'l Park**, Thai.
78/C1 **Erba**, It.
92/D1 **Erbaa**, Turk.
70/C3 **Erbach**, Ger.
64/D4 **Erbeskopf** (peak), Ger.
93/E2 **Erçek**, Turk.
93/E2 **Erçek** (lake), Turk.
142/B3 **Ercilla**, Chile
93/E2 **Erciş**, Turk.
92/C2 **Erciyes** (peak), Turk.
68/C3 **Erclin** (riv.), Fr.
82/D2 **Érd**, Hun.
101/E1 **Erdao** (riv.), China
83/H5 **Erdek**, Turk.
83/H5 **Erdek** (gulf), Turk.
91/D1 **Erdemli**, Turk.
96/G3 **Erdene**, Mong.
96/E2 **Erdenedalay**, Mong.
96/E2 **Erdenet**, Mong.
125/K4 **Erdi-Ma** (plat.), Chad
71/E6 **Erding**, Ger.
72/C3 **Erdre** (riv.), Fr.
113/M **Erebus** (vol.), Ant.
141/A3 **Erechim**, Braz.
96/G2 **Ereen Davaanī** (mts.), Mong.
83/K5 **Ereğli**, Turk.

187
Eremo – Fishe

79/E5 **Eremo di Camaldoli**, It.
102/D3 **Erenhaberga** (mts.), China
96/G3 **Erenhot**, China
83/K5 **Erenler**, Turk.
139/H5 **Erepecu** (lake), Braz.
74/C2 **Eresma** (riv.), Sp.
70/C3 **Erfa** (riv.), Ger.
124/E1 **Erfoud**, Mor.
69/F1 **Erft** (riv.), Ger.
69/F2 **Erftstadt**, Ger.
64/F3 **Erfurt**, Ger.
92/D2 **Ergani**, Turk.
124/D3 **'Erg Chech** (des.), Afr.
124/H4 **'Erg du Ténéré** (des.), Niger
83/H5 **Ergene Nehri** (riv.), Turk.
124/D2 **'Erg Iguidi** (des.), Afr.
124/J5 **Erguig** (riv.), Chad
97/H1 **Ergun** (riv.), China, Rus.
97/J1 **Ergun Youqi**, China
97/J1 **Ergun Zuoqi**, China
80/C3 **Erice**, It.
54/B3 **Ericht** (riv.), Sc,UK
54/C3 **Ericht** (riv.), Sc,UK
54/B3 **Ericht, Loch** (lake), Sc,UK
156/D3 **Erickson**, BC,Can
157/J3 **Erickson**, Mb,Can
160/D3 **Erie** (lake), Can., US
161/S9 **Erie** (can.), NY,US
161/S10 **Erie** (co.), NY,US
168/H5 **Erie** (co.), Oh,US
160/D3 **Erie**, Pa,US
168/H4 **Erie Nat'l Wild. Ref.**, Pa,US
125/Q5 **Erigabo**, Som.
157/J3 **Eriksdale**, Mb,Can
120/F4 **Erikub** (atoll), Mrsh.
130/B2 **Erima**, Ugan.
81/G4 **Erímanthos** (peak), Gre.
100/C2 **Erimo**, Japan
100/C3 **Erimo-misaki** (cape), Japan
125/N4 **Eritrea**
66/D6 **Erkelenz**, Ger.
63/H1 **Erken** (isl.), Swe.
60/C4 **Erkina** (riv.), Ire.
65/G2 **Erkner**, Ger.
66/D6 **Erkrath**, Ger.
104/D2 **Erlang** (peak), China
70/E3 **Erlangen**, Ger.
71/G5 **Erlau** (riv.), Ger.
70/B4 **Erlenbach** (riv.), Ger.
76/D4 **Erlenbach**, Swi.
70/C3 **Erlenbach am Main**, Ger.
76/D3 **Erlinsbach**, Swi.
103/F2 **Erlongshan** (res.), China
58/C6 **Erme** (riv.), Eng,UK
66/C4 **Ermelo**, Neth.
133/E2 **Ermelo**, SAfr.
91/C1 **Ermenek**, Turk.
91/C1 **Ermenek** (riv.), Turk.
53/U9 **Ermenonville**, Fr.
53/S10 **Ermont**, Fr.
81/J4 **Ermoúpolis**, Gre.
70/C6 **Erms** (riv.), Ger.
69/H2 **Erndtebrück**, Ger.
72/C2 **Ernée** (riv.), Fr.
55/H9 **Erne, Lower Lough** (lake), NI,UK
60/C1 **Erne, Upper Lough** (lake), NI,UK
108/F3 **Erode**, India
68/D3 **Erquelinnes**, Belg.
124/E1 **Er Rachidīa**, Mor.
123/M13 **Er Rif** (mts.), Mor.
55/G9 **Errigal** (mtn.), Ire.
54/G9 **Erris Head** (pt.), Ire.
78/B4 **Erro** (riv.), It.
54/B3 **Errochty, Loch** (lake), Sc,UK
54/C4 **Errol**, Sc,UK
120/F6 **Erromango** (isl.), Van.
77/F4 **Err, Piz d'** (peak), Swi.
67/H4 **Erse** (riv.), Ger.
76/D1 **Erstein**, Fr.
96/B2 **Ertix** (riv.), China
141/B3 **Erval d'Oeste**, Braz.
160/D4 **Erwin**, Tn,US
67/F5 **Erwitte**, Ger.
104/C3 **Eryuan**, China
81/F2 **Erzen** (riv.), Alb.
71/F2 **Erzgebirge** (Krušné Hory) (mts.), Czh., Ger.
70/B3 **Erzhausen**, Ger.
92/D2 **Erzincan**, Turk.
92/D2 **Erzincan** (prov.), Turk.
92/E2 **Erzurum**, Turk.
92/E1 **Erzurum** (prov.), Turk.
120/D5 **Esa'ala**, PNG
126/D1 **Esambo**, Zaire
100/B3 **Esan-misaki** (cape), Japan
100/B3 **Esashi**, Japan
100/B4 **Esashi**, Japan
100/C1 **Esashi**, Japan
92/D1 **Esbiye**, Turk.
62/C4 **Esbjerg**, Den.
53/U10 **Esbly**, Fr.
63/L1 **Esbo** (Espoo), Fin.
140/D3 **Escada**, Braz.
158/E3 **Escalante** (riv.), Ut,US
163/G4 **Escambia** (riv.), Fl,US
160/C2 **Escanaba**, Mi,US
112/C1 **Escarpada** (pt.), Phil.
68/C3 **Escaudain**, Fr.
68/C3 **Escaut** (riv.), Belg., Fr.
69/E6 **Esch** (riv.), Fr.
77/E1 **Eschach** (riv.), Ger.
77/G2 **Eschach** (riv.), Ger.
76/D1 **Eschau**, Fr.
68/B5 **Esches** (riv.), Fr.
70/A4 **Eschkopf** (mtn.), Ger.
69/E5 **Esch-sur-Alzette**, Lux.
67/H6 **Eschwege**, Ger.
69/F2 **Eschweiler**, Ger.
164/C4 **Escondido**, Ca,US
164/C4 **Escondido** (cr.), Ca,US
146/D4 **Escuinapa**, Mex.
148/D3 **Escuintla**, Guat.
91/G6 **Esdraelon, Plain of** (plain), Isr.
124/H7 **Eséka**, Camr.
92/D2 **Esence** (peak), Turk.
67/E1 **Esens**, Ger.
75/F1 **Esera** (riv.), Sp.
93/G3 **Eşfahān**, Iran
93/H3 **Eşfahān** (gov.), Iran
58/C1 **Esgair Ddu** (mtn.), Wal,UK
57/G2 **Esh**, Eng,UK
55/P12 **Esha Ness** (pt.), Sc,UK
104/D3 **Eshan Yizu Zizhixian**, China
53/M7 **Esher**, Eng,UK
126/D2 **Eshimba**, Zaire
57/G2 **Esh Winning**, Eng,UK
79/G5 **Esina** (riv.), It.
57/E2 **Esk** (riv.), Eng,UK
57/H3 **Esk** (riv.), Eng,UK
55/K9 **Esk** (riv.), Sc,UK
57/E1 **Eskdale** (val.), Sc,UK
92/C2 **Eskil**, Turk.
62/G2 **Eskilstuna**, Swe.
92/D2 **Eskimalatya**, Turk.
151/M2 **Eskimo** (lakes), NW,Can
92/C1 **Eskipazar**, Turk.
92/B2 **Eskişehir**, Turk.
92/B2 **Eskişehir** (prov.), Turk.
74/C1 **Esla** (riv.), Sp.
93/F3 **Eslāmābād**, Iran
67/F6 **Eslohe**, Ger.
62/E4 **Eslöv**, Swe.
92/B2 **Eşme**, Turk.
149/G1 **Esmeralda**, Cuba
138/B4 **Esmeraldas**, Ecu.
138/B4 **Esmeraldas** (prov.), Ecu.
69/E2 **Esneux**, Belg.
138/D1 **Espada** (pt.), Col.
160/D2 **Espanola**, On,Can
144/K7 **Española** (isl.), Ecu.
159/F4 **Española**, NM,US
75/K6 **Esparreguera**, Sp.
67/F4 **Espelkamp**, Ger.
140/D2 **Esperança**, Braz.
116/D5 **Esperance**, Austl.
116/D5 **Esperance** (bay), Austl.
140/B1 **Esperantina**, Braz.
140/A2 **Esperantinópolis**, Braz.
156/B3 **Esperanza** (inlet), BC,Can
150/D3 **Esperanza**, DRep.
146/C3 **Esperanza**, Mex.
147/M8 **Esperanza**, Mex.
74/A3 **Espichel** (cape), Port.
138/C3 **Espinal**, Col.
147/M6 **Espinal**, Mex.
144/D4 **Espinar**, Peru
140/B5 **Espinhaço** (mts.), Braz.
74/A2 **Espinho**, Port.
143/F2 **Espinillo** (pt.), Uru.
140/B4 **Espinosa**, Braz.
141/D1 **Espírito Santo** (state), Braz.
141/G7 **Espírito Santo do Pinhal**, Braz.
148/E2 **Espíritu Santo** (bay), Mex.
146/C3 **Espíritu Santo** (isl.), Mex.
112/D2 **Espiritu Santo** (cape), Phil.
120/F6 **Espiritu Santo** (isl.), Van.
140/C3 **Esplanada**, Braz.
75/L7 **Esplugues**, Sp.
63/L1 **Espoo** (Esbo), Fin.
131/D4 **Espungabera**, Moz.
142/C4 **Esquel**, Arg.
135/E3 **Esquina**, Arg.
63/T8 **Esrum Sø** (lake), Den.
124/D1 **Essaouira**, Mor.
67/G5 **Esse** (riv.), Ger.
66/B6 **Essen**, Belg.
66/E6 **Essen**, Ger.
71/F5 **Essenbach**, Ger.
119/F5 **Essendon**, Austl.
116/D3 **Essendon** (peak), Austl.
139/G3 **Essequibo** (riv.), Guy.
139/G3 **Essequibo Island-West Demerara** (reg.), Guy.
165/G7 **Essex**, On,Can
165/G7 **Essex** (co.), On,Can
53/P6 **Essex** (co.), Eng,UK
166/B5 **Essex**, Md,US
167/D2 **Essex** (co.), NJ,US
70/C5 **Esslingen**, Ger.
53/S11 **Essonne** (dept.), Fr.
53/T11 **Essonne** (riv.), Fr.
76/C1 **Est** (can.), Fr.
146/B1 **Estación Coatiuila**, Mex.
143/L8 **Estados** (isl.), Arg.
93/H4 **Eşţahbān**, Iran
140/C3 **Estância**, Braz.
143/L8 **Estancia La Carmen**, Arg.
143/L8 **Estancia La Sera**, Arg.
147/F4 **Estancia Tamuín**, Mex.
75/F1 **Estats, Pico de** (peak), Sp.
133/E3 **Estcourt**, SAfr.
67/G2 **Este** (riv.), Ger.
79/E2 **Este**, It.
141/B4 **Esteio**, Braz.
148/E3 **Estelí**, Nic.
74/D1 **Estella**, Sp.
164/C3 **Estelle** (mtn.), Ca,US
150/D3 **Este Nat'l Park**, DRep.
74/C4 **Estepa**, Sp.
74/C4 **Estepona**, Sp.
143/G2 **Este, Punta del**, Uru.
157/H3 **Esterhazy**, Sk,Can
124/G7 **Esterias** (cape), Gabon
71/G5 **Esternberg**, Aus.
73/G5 **Estéron** (riv.), Fr.
157/H3 **Estevan**, Sk,Can
68/D3 **Estinnes-Au-Mont**, Belg.
57/G2 **Eston**, Eng,UK
63/L2 **Estonia**
74/A3 **Estoril**, Port.
74/B2 **Estrela, Serra da** (mtn.), Port.
74/A3 **Estrela, Serra da** (range), Port.
146/B2 **Estrella, Punta** (pt.), Mex.
140/B3 **Estrelto** (mts.), Braz.
74/B3 **Estremadura** (aut. comm.), Sp.
74/B3 **Estremoz**, Port.
137/J5 **Estrondo** (mts.), Braz.
82/D2 **Esztergom**, Hun.
120/E4 **Etal** (atoll), Micr.
54/D5 **Etal**, Eng,UK
68/A2 **Étaples**, Fr.
106/C2 **Etāwah**, India
157/H3 **Ethelbert**, Mb,Can
125/N5 **Ethiopia**
125/N6 **Ethiopian** (plat.), Eth.
99/M9 **Eti** (riv.), Japan
53/T11 **Étiolles**, Fr.
54/A4 **Etive, Loch** (inlet), Sc,UK
80/D4 **Etna, Monte** (Mount Etna) (vol.), It.
161/Q8 **Etobicoke**, On,Can
131/B1 **Etoile**, Zaire
151/E3 **Etolin** (str.), Ak,US
100/E1 **Etorofu** (isl.), Rus.
126/C4 **Etosha Nat'l Park**, Namb.
126/C4 **Etosha Pan** (salt pan), Namb.
83/G4 **Etropole**, Bul.
77/G4 **Etsch** (Adige) (riv.), It.
99/F2 **Etsu-Joshin Kogen Nat'l Park**, Japan
91/F7 **Et Taiyiba**, Isr.
69/F4 **Ettelbruck**, Lux.
76/D1 **Ettenheim**, Ger.
66/B5 **Etten-Leur**, Neth.
68/D2 **Etterbeek**, Belg.
166/B3 **Etters** (Goldsboro), Pa,US
91/F7 **Et Tīra**, Isr.
70/B5 **Ettlingen**, Ger.
54/C6 **Ettrick**, Sc,UK
54/C6 **Ettrick Pen** (mtn.), Sc,UK
54/C5 **Ettrick Water** (riv.), Sc,UK
68/A3 **Eu**, Fr.
121/H7 **Eua** (isl.), Tonga
118/B2 **Eubenangee Swamp Nat'l Park**, Austl.
117/F4 **Eucla Motel**, Austl.
168/F4 **Euclid**, Oh,US
140/C3 **Euclides da Cunha**, Braz.
115/H7 **Eucumbene** (lake), Austl.
163/F3 **Eudora**, Ar,US
163/G4 **Eufaula**, Al,US
162/E3 **Eufaula**, Ok,US
159/H4 **Eufaula** (lake), Ok,US
156/C4 **Eugene**, Or,US
146/B3 **Eugenia, Punta** (pt.), Mex.
74/B1 **Eume** (lake), Sp.
118/C3 **Eungella Nat'l Park**, Austl.
162/E4 **Eunice**, La,US
159/G4 **Eunice**, NM,US
69/E2 **Eupen**, Belg.
93/F4 **Euphrates** (riv.), Asia
63/K1 **Eura**, Fin.
72/D2 **Eure** (riv.), Fr.
153/S6 **Eureka**, NW,Can
153/S7 **Eureka** (sound), NW,Can
158/A2 **Eureka**, Ca,US
156/E3 **Eureka**, Mt,US
158/D3 **Eureka**, Nv,US
157/J4 **Eureka**, SD,US
68/B6 **Eurodisney**, Fr.
76/C1 **Euron** (riv.), Fr.
123/M12 **Europa** (pt.), Gib.
126/G5 **Europa** (isl.), Reun.
77/H3 **Europabrücke**, Aus.
52/* **Europe**
66/B5 **Europoort**, Neth.
69/F2 **Euskirchen**, Ger.
163/H4 **Eustis**, Fl,US
64/F1 **Eutin**, Ger.
131/D1 **Eutini**, Malw.
156/B2 **Eutsuk** (lake), BC,Can
57/F4 **Euxton**, Eng,UK
160/E1 **Évain**, Qu,Can
153/H2 **Evans** (str.), NW,Can
160/E1 **Evans** (lake), Qu,Can
159/F2 **Evans**, Co,US
159/F3 **Evans** (mtn.), Co,US
165/Q15 **Evanston**, Il,US
156/F5 **Evanston**, Wy,US
160/C4 **Evansville**, In,US
159/F2 **Evansville**, Wy,US
54/B1 **Evanton**, Sc,UK
156/E5 **Evaporation** (basin), Ut,US
160/C3 **Evart**, Mi,US
132/D2 **Evaton**, SAfr.
93/H5 **Evaz**, Iran
157/K4 **Eveleth**, Mn,US
89/L3 **Evenki Aut. Okr.**, Rus.
59/E3 **Evenlode** (riv.), Eng,UK
119/D3 **Everard** (cape), Austl.
117/G4 **Everard** (lake), Austl.
117/G3 **Everard** (peak), Austl.
58/D4 **Evercreech**, Eng,UK
106/E2 **Everest** (mt.), China, Nep.
168/C1 **Everett**, Ma,US
168/A1 **Everett** (mtn.), Ma,US
165/C2 **Everett**, Wa,US
68/C1 **Evergem**, Belg.
163/H5 **Everglades** (swamp), Fl,US
163/H5 **Everglades Nat'l Park**, Fl,US
163/G4 **Evergreen**, Al,US
165/Q16 **Evergreen Park**, Il,US
59/F3 **Eversholt**, Eng,UK
67/E5 **Everswinkel**, Ger.
59/E2 **Evesham**, Eng,UK
76/C5 **Évian-les-Bains**, Fr.
81/G3 **Évinos** (riv.), Gre.
74/B3 **Évora**, Port.
74/A3 **Évora** (dist.), Port.
68/A5 **Évreux**, Fr.
72/C2 **Évron**, Fr.
81/H4 **Evrótas** (riv.), Gre.
53/T11 **Évry**, Fr.
81/H3 **Évvoia** (gulf), Gre.
81/H3 **Évvoia** (isl.), Gre.
154/V13 **Ewa**, Hi,US
154/V13 **Ewa Beach**, Hi,US
149/G2 **Ewarton**, Jam.
130/B3 **Ewaso Ngiro** (riv.), Kenya
130/C2 **Ewaso Ng'iro** (riv.), Kenya
53/N7 **Ewell**, Eng,UK
97/H2 **Ewenkizu Zizhiqi**, China
166/D3 **Ewing**, NJ,US
159/J3 **Excelsior Springs**, Mo,US
58/C5 **Exe** (riv.), Eng,UK
58/C5 **Exeter**, Eng,UK
161/G3 **Exeter**, NH,US
58/C5 **Exminster**, Eng,UK
58/C4 **Exmoor** (upland), Eng,UK
58/C4 **Exmoor Nat'l Park**, Eng,UK
160/F4 **Exmore**, Va,US
116/B2 **Exmouth** (gulf), Austl.
143/J7 **Exmouth** (pen.), Chile
58/C5 **Exmouth**, Eng,UK
153/L4 **Exploits** (riv.), Nf,Can
141/G7 **Extrema**, Braz.
140/C2 **Exu**, Braz.
150/B1 **Exuma** (sound), Bahm.
70/B6 **Eyach** (riv.), Ger.
57/G5 **Eyam**, Eng,UK
130/B3 **Eyasi** (lake), Tanz.
70/C5 **Eyb** (riv.), Ger.
62/C2 **Eydehamn**, Nor.
59/H2 **Eye**, Eng,UK
59/F1 **Eye** (brook), Eng,UK
54/D5 **Eyemouth**, Sc,UK
91/G8 **Eyn Hemed Nat'l Park**, Isr.
53/P7 **Eynsford**, Eng,UK
117/G5 **Eyre** (pen.), Austl.
117/H4 **Eyre North** (lake), Austl.
117/H4 **Eyre South** (lake), Austl.
93/M6 **Eyüp**, Turk.
93/M6 **Eyüp Mosque**, Turk.
53/T9 **Ézanville**, Fr.
81/K3 **Ezine**, Turk.
124/H3 **Ezzane** (well), Alg.

F

121/L6 **Faaa**, FrPol.
130/D2 **Faafaxdhuun**, Som.
162/B4 **Fabens**, Tx,US
74/B1 **Fabero**, Sp.
62/D4 **Fåborg**, Den.
79/F6 **Fabriano**, It.
138/C3 **Facatativá**, Col.
68/C2 **Faches-Thumesnil**, Fr.
125/K4 **Fada**, Chad
54/A1 **Fada, Lochan** (lake), Sc,UK
129/F3 **Fada-N'Gourma**, Burk.
79/E4 **Faenza**, It.
125/J6 **Fafa** (riv.), CAfr.
74/A2 **Fafe**, Port.
125/P6 **Fafen Shet'** (riv.), Eth.
83/G3 **Făgăraş**, Rom.
62/F2 **Fagersta**, Swe.
79/E4 **Faggiola, Monte** (peak), It.
143/L8 **Fagnano** (lake), Arg.
128/D2 **Faguibine** (lake), Mali
124/F1 **Fahl** (well), Alg.
75/S12 **Faial** (isl.), Azor.,Port.
57/F4 **Failsworth**, Eng,UK
55/P13 **Fair** (isl.), Sc,UK
151/J3 **Fairbanks**, Ak,US
165/J11 **Fairfax**, Ca,US
166/A5 **Fairfax**, Va,US
166/A6 **Fairfax** (co.), Va,US
118/G8 **Fairfield**, Austl.
165/K10 **Fairfield**, Ca,US
167/E1 **Fairfield**, Ct,US
168/A3 **Fairfield** (co.), Ct,US
156/F4 **Fairfield**, Mt,US
167/H8 **Fairfield**, NJ,US
160/C4 **Fairfield**, Oh,US
162/D4 **Fairfield**, Tx,US
59/E3 **Fairford**, Eng,UK
168/D2 **Fairhaven**, Ma,US
161/F3 **Fair Haven**, Vt,US
56/B1 **Fair Head** (pt.), NI,UK
55/P13 **Fair Isle** (isl.), Sc,UK
166/B5 **Fairland**, Md,US
167/D2 **Fair Lawn**, NJ,US
166/D3 **Fairless Hills**, Pa,US
54/B5 **Fairlie**, Sc,UK
59/G5 **Fairlight**, Eng,UK
157/K5 **Fairmont**, Mn,US
160/D4 **Fairmont**, WV,US
165/M9 **Fair Oaks**, Ca,US
162/B2 **Fairplay**, Co,US
156/D1 **Fairview**, Ab,Can
167/K8 **Fairview**, NJ,US
159/H3 **Fairview**, Ok,US
131/D3 **Fairview** (peak), Zim.
168/F5 **Fairview Park**, Oh,US
151/L4 **Fairweather** (cape), Ak,US
151/L4 **Fairweather** (mtn.), BC,Can, Ak,US
165/C3 **Fairwood-Cascade**, Wa,US
108/B2 **Faisalabad**, Pak.
81/J5 **Faistós** (ruins), Gre.
106/D2 **Faizābād**, India
150/E3 **Fajardo**, PR
121/M6 **Fakahina** (isl.), FrPol.
121/H5 **Fakaofo** (atoll), Tok.
121/L6 **Fakarava** (atoll), FrPol.
59/G1 **Fakenham**, Eng,UK
124/G7 **Fako** (peak), Camr.
62/E4 **Fakse Bugt** (bay), Den.
103/E2 **Faku**, China
58/B6 **Fal** (riv.), Eng,UK
104/B4 **Falam**, Burma
123/Q16 **Falcon** (cape), Alg.
162/D5 **Falcon** (res.), Mex., US
138/D2 **Falcón** (state), Ven.
79/G5 **Falconara Marittima**, It.
128/C3 **Falémé** (riv.), Mali, Sen.
121/S9 **Faleolo**, WSam.
162/D5 **Falfurrias**, Tx,US
156/D2 **Falher**, Ab,Can
62/E3 **Falkenberg**, Swe.
59/H2 **Falkenham**, Eng,UK
71/F2 **Falkenstein**, Ger.
54/C5 **Falkirk**, Sc,UK
143/M8 **Falkland** (sound), Falk.
54/C4 **Falkland**, Sc,UK
143/M8 **Falkland Islands** (Islas Malvinas) (dpcy.), UK
62/E2 **Falköping**, Swe.
164/C4 **Fallbrook**, Ca,US
76/D6 **Fallere, Monte** (peak), It.
67/G3 **Fallingbostel**, Ger.
158/C3 **Fallon**, Nv,US
168/C2 **Fall River**, Ma,US
166/A6 **Falls Church**, Va,US
159/J2 **Falls City**, Ne,US
58/A6 **Falmouth**, Eng,UK
58/A6 **Falmouth** (bay), Eng,UK
62/C4 **Falshöft** (pt.), Ger.
149/J2 **Falso, Cabo** (cape), DRep.
149/F3 **Falso, Cabo** (cape), Hon.
146/C4 **Falso, Cabo** (cape), Mex.
143/K8 **Falso Cabo de Hornos** (cape), Chile
62/E4 **Falster** (isl.), Den.
79/E5 **Falterona, Monte** (peak), It.
83/H2 **Fălticeni**, Rom.
62/F1 **Falun**, Swe.
91/C2 **Famagusta**, Cyp.
91/C2 **Famagusta** (bay), Cyp.
91/C2 **Famagusta** (dist.), Cyp.
69/F5 **Fameck**, Fr.
69/E3 **Famenne** (reg.), Belg.
103/D5 **Fanchang**, China
123/G7 **Fandriana**, Madg.
60/D2 **Fane** (riv.), Ire.
121/L6 **Fangatau** (isl.), FrPol.
121/L7 **Fangataufa** (isl.), FrPol.
103/C4 **Fangcheng**, China
109/E1 **Fangcheng**, China
107/J3 **Fangcheng Gezu Zizhixian**, China
105/E2 **Fangdou** (mts.), China
103/B3 **Fangshan**, China
103/B4 **Fang Xian**, China
105/F3 **Fanjing** (peak), China
54/A1 **Fannich, Loch** (lake), Sc,UK
121/K4 **Fanning** (Tabuaeran) (atoll), Kiri.
62/C4 **Fanø** (isl.), Den.
79/G5 **Fano**, It.
103/C3 **Fanshi**, China
109/C1 **Fan Si Pan** (peak), Viet.
167/H9 **Fanwood**, NJ,US
91/B4 **Fāqūs**, Egypt
130/A2 **Faradje**, Zaire
123/G7 **Faradofay**, Madg.
123/G7 **Farafangana**, Madg.
127/A3 **Farāfirah, Wāḩāt al** (oasis), Egypt
88/G6 **Farāh**, Afg.
95/H2 **Farāh** (riv.), Afg.
91/G7 **Fa'rah, Wādī** (dry riv.), WBnk.
158/B3 **Farallon** (isls.), Ca,US
139/E2 **Farallon Centinela** (isl.), Ven.
120/D3 **Farallon de Medinilla** (isl.), NMar.
120/D2 **Farallon de Pajaros** (isl.), NMar.
138/B4 **Farallones de Cali Nat'l Park**, Col.
128/C4 **Faranah** (comm.), Gui.
133/H8 **Faraony** (riv.), Madg.
120/D4 **Faraulep** (atoll), Micr.
68/D3 **Farciennes**, Belg.
59/E5 **Fareham**, Eng,UK
54/D2 **Fare, Hill of** (hill), Sc,UK
63/R7 **Farentuna**, Swe.
115/R11 **Farewell** (cape), NZ
157/J4 **Fargo**, ND,US
157/K4 **Faribault**, Mn,US
106/C2 **Farīdābād**, India
108/C2 **Farīdkot**, India
106/E3 **Farīdpur**, Bang.
59/E3 **Faringdon**, Eng,UK
91/B4 **Fāriskūr**, Egypt
130/B4 **Farkwa**, Tanz.
167/M9 **Farmingdale**, NY,US
168/B2 **Farmington**, Ct,US
161/G2 **Farmington**, Me,US
165/F7 **Farmington**, Mi,US
159/K3 **Farmington**, Mo,US
158/E3 **Farmington**, NM,US
165/F7 **Farmington Hills**, Mi,US
160/E4 **Farmville**, Va,US
59/F4 **Farnborough**, Eng,UK
55/L9 **Farne** (isls.), Eng,UK
59/F4 **Farnham**, Eng,UK
53/P7 **Farningham**, Eng,UK
57/F4 **Farnworth**, Eng,UK
152/C2 **Faro**, Yk,Can
74/B4 **Faro**, Port.
74/A4 **Faro** (dist.), Port.
52/D2 **Faroe** (isls.), Den.
61/F4 **Fårön** (isl.), Swe.
124/H6 **Faro Nat'l Park**, Camr.
116/B2 **Farquhar** (cape), Austl.
123/H5 **Farquhar** (isls.), Sey.
54/B2 **Farrar** (riv.), Sc,UK
168/G5 **Farrell**, Pa,US
167/K9 **Far Rockaway**, NY,US
141/B4 **Farroupilha**, Braz.
106/C2 **Farrukhābād**, India
93/H4 **Fars** (gov.), Iran
81/H3 **Fársala**, Gre.
156/F5 **Farson**, Wy,US
62/B2 **Farsund**, Nor.
94/F5 **Fartak, Ra's** (pt.), Yem.
63/T8 **Farum**, Den.
145/N4 **Farvel** (cape), Grld.
113/T **Farwell** (isl.), Ant.
93/H4 **Fasā**, Iran
80/E2 **Fasano**, It.
91/C1 **Faşıkan** (pass), Turk.
67/H3 **Fassberg**, Ger.
54/D5 **Fast Castle** (pt.), Sc,UK
86/D2 **Fastov**, Ukr.
111/H4 **Fatagar Tuting** (cape), Indo.
108/B1 **Fatahjang**, Pak.
51/T6 **Fataka** (isl.), Sol.
106/B2 **Fatehpur**, India
106/D2 **Fatehpur**, India
128/A3 **Fatick** (reg.), Sen.
74/A3 **Fátima**, Port.
94/C4 **Fāţimah** (dry riv.), SAr.
92/D1 **Fatsa**, Turk.
121/M6 **Fatu Hiva** (isl.), FrPol.
76/C5 **Faucille, Col de la** (pass), Fr.
76/B1 **Faucilles** (mts.), Fr.
56/A2 **Faughan** (riv.), NI,UK
54/C5 **Fauldhouse**, Sc,UK
157/J4 **Faulkton**, SD,US
116/B3 **Faure** (isl.), Austl.
61/E2 **Fauske**, Nor.
79/F6 **Favalto, Monte** (peak), It.
80/C4 **Favara**, It.
76/D1 **Fave** (riv.), Fr.
59/G4 **Faversham**, Eng,UK
59/E5 **Fawley**, Eng,UK
152/H3 **Fawn** (riv.), On,Can
61/M7 **Faxaflói** (bay), Ice.
141/B2 **Faxinal**, Braz.
125/J4 **Faya-Largeau**, Chad
163/G3 **Fayette**, Al,US
159/J3 **Fayette**, Mo,US
163/F4 **Fayette**, Ms,US
162/E2 **Fayetteville**, Ar,US
163/G3 **Fayetteville**, Ga,US
163/J3 **Fayetteville**, NC,US
163/G3 **Fayetteville**, Tn,US
79/G3 **Fažana**, Cro.
129/F4 **Fazao** (mts.), Gha., Togo
129/F4 **Fazao Nat'l Park**, Togo
156/D3 **F.D.R.** (Franklin D. Roosevelt) (lake), Wa,US
60/A5 **Feale** (riv.), Ire.
163/J3 **Fear** (cape), NC,US
55/K8 **Fearn, Hill of** (hill), Sc,UK
166/D3 **Feasterville-Trevose**, Pa,US
158/B3 **Feather** (riv.), Ca,US
57/G4 **Featherstone**, Eng,UK
131/C3 **Featherstone**, Zim.
72/D2 **Fécamp**, Fr.
76/D1 **Fecht** (riv.), Fr.
108/A1 **Fed. Admin. Tribal Areas** (terr.), Pak.
167/K9 **Federal Hall Nat'l Mem.**, NY,US
165/C3 **Federal Way**, Wa,US
70/C6 **Federsee** (lake), Ger.
56/A2 **Feeny**, NI,UK
82/F2 **Fehérgyarmat**, Hun.
64/F1 **Fehmarn** (isl.), Ger.
64/F1 **Fehmarn Belt** (str.), Ger., Den.
103/D4 **Fei** (riv.), China
141/D2 **Feia** (lake), Braz.
103/D3 **Feicheng**, China
103/D5 **Feidong**, China
68/C3 **Feignies**, Fr.
103/D4 **Fei Huang** (riv.), China
140/C4 **Feira de Santana**, Braz.
73/L3 **Feistritz** (riv.), Aus.
103/D5 **Feixi**, China
103/D4 **Fei Xian**, China
82/D2 **Fejér** (co.), Hun.
62/D4 **Fejø** (isl.), Den.
75/G3 **Felanitx**, Sp.
71/H6 **Feldaist** (riv.), Aus.
76/E2 **Feldberg** (peak), Ger.
77/F3 **Feldkirch**, Aus.
73/L3 **Feldkirchen in Kärnten**, Aus.
79/G1 **Feletto Umberto**, It.
131/C3 **Felixburg**, Zim.
141/C1 **Felixlândia**, Braz.
59/H3 **Felixstowe**, Eng,UK
70/C5 **Fellbach**, Ger.
57/G2 **Felling**, Eng,UK
67/G6 **Felsberg**, Ger.
53/M7 **Feltham**, Eng,UK
59/G2 **Feltwell**, Eng,UK
62/D4 **Femø** (isl.), Den.
103/C4 **Fen** (riv.), China
74/A1 **Fene**, Sp.
91/D1 **Fener** (pt.), Turk.
69/G6 **Fénétrange**, Fr.
81/J2 **Fengári** (peak), Gre.
101/C2 **Fengcheng**, China
105/G3 **Fengchuihudie** (peak), China
105/G2 **Fengding** (mtn.), China
103/B5 **Fengjie**, China
103/D5 **Fengle** (riv.), China
103/D5 **Fengnan**, China
103/D2 **Fengning**, China
104/C3 **Fengqing**, China
103/C4 **Fengqiu**, China
103/D3 **Fengrun**, China
105/G3 **Fengshuba** (res.), China
97/J1 **Fengshui** (peak), China
103/H7 **Fengtai**, China
103/D4 **Feng Xian**, China
103/E5 **Fengxian**, China
103/B3 **Fengyang**, China
103/D4 **Fengyang**, China
103/C2 **Fengzhen**, China
151/C5 **Fenimore** (passg.), Ak,US
133/J7 **Fenoarivo Atsinanana**, Madg.
105/H3 **Fenshui** (pass), China
105/H4 **Fenshui Guan** (pass), China
71/G5 **Fensterbach** (riv.), Ger.
59/G2 **Fens, The** (reg.), Eng,UK
165/E6 **Fenton**, Mi,US
165/E6 **Fenton** (lake), Mi,US
103/B3 **Fenxi**, China
86/E3 **Feodosiya**, Ukr.
123/V17 **Fer, Cap de** (cape), Alg.
93/J3 **Ferdows**, Iran
80/C2 **Ferentino**, It.
80/C1 **Ferento** (ruins), It.
102/B3 **Fergana**, Uzb.
60/B4 **Fergus** (riv.), Ire.
157/J4 **Fergus Falls**, Mn,US
152/F2 **Ferguson** (lake), NW,Can
128/D4 **Ferkéssédougou**, IvC.
73/L3 **Ferlach**, Aus.
124/C4 **Ferlo** (reg.), Sen.
128/B3 **Ferlo, Vallée du** (wadi), Sen.
56/A3 **Fermanagh** (dist.), NI,UK
164/B3 **Fermin** (pt.), Ca,US
165/P16 **Fermi Nat'l Accelerator Lab.**, Il,US
80/C1 **Fermo**, It.
147/F4 **Fernández**, Mex.
144/J7 **Fernandina** (isl.), Ecu.
163/H4 **Fernandina Beach**, Fl,US
137/M4 **Fernando de Noronha**, Braz.
134/F3 **Fernando de Noronha** (isl.), Braz.
141/B2 **Fernandópolis**, Braz.
74/C4 **Fernán-Núñez**, Sp.
166/B5 **Ferndale**, Md,US
165/F7 **Ferndale**, Mi,US
59/E5 **Ferndown**, Eng,UK
54/C2 **Ferness**, Sc,UK
76/C5 **Ferney-Voltaire**, Fr.
156/E3 **Fernie**, BC,Can
77/G3 **Fernpass** (pass), Aus.
119/G5 **Ferntree Gully Nat'l Park**, Austl.
108/E3 **Feroke**, India
80/E2 **Ferrandina**, It.
79/E3 **Ferrara**, It.
79/E3 **Ferrara** (prov.), It.
74/A3 **Ferreira do Alentejo**, Port.
144/B2 **Ferreñafe**, Peru
72/C4 **Ferret** (cape), Fr.
162/F4 **Ferriday**, La,US
163/F4 **Ferriday**, La,US
54/D3 **Ferryden**, Sc,UK
57/G2 **Ferryhill**, Eng,UK
58/B3 **Ferryside**, Wal,UK
73/M3 **Fertő** (Neusiedler See) (lake), Aus., Hun.
66/C2 **Ferwerd**, Neth.
123/M13 **Fès**, Mor.
126/C2 **Feshi**, Zaire
54/C2 **Feshie** (riv.), Sc,UK
117/M8 **Festival Centre**, Austl.
163/F2 **Festus**, Mo,US
53/M8 **Fetcham**, Eng,UK
83/H3 **Feteşti**, Rom.
55/P12 **Fethaland** (pt.), Sc,UK
92/B2 **Fethiye**, Turk.
53/R10 **Feucherolles**, Fr.
70/E4 **Feucht**, Ger.
70/D4 **Feuchtwangen**, Ger.
153/J3 **Feuilles** (lake), Qu,Can
153/J3 **Feuilles** (riv.), Qu,Can
72/F4 **Feurs**, Fr.
95/K1 **Feyẕābād**, Afg.
124/H2 **Fezzan** (reg.), Libya
56/E6 **Ffestiniog**, Wal,UK
123/G7 **Fianarantsoa**, Madg.
133/H8 **Fianarantsoa** (prov.), Madg.
124/J6 **Fianga**, Chad
71/F2 **Fichtelberg** (peak), Ger.
71/E2 **Fichtelgebirge** (mts.), Ger.
71/E3 **Fichtelnaab** (riv.), Ger.
132/D3 **Ficksburg**, SAfr.
78/D3 **Fidenza**, It.
128/C4 **Fié** (riv.), Gui., Mali
117/M9 **Field** (riv.), Austl.
83/G3 **Fieni**, Rom.
81/F2 **Fier**, Alb.
76/B6 **Fier** (riv.), Fr.
81/G1 **Fierzë** (lake), Alb.
54/D4 **Fife** (reg.), Sc,UK
54/D4 **Fife Ness** (pt.), Sc,UK
127/C5 **Fifth Cataract** (falls), Sudan
123/Q16 **Figalo** (cape), Alg.
72/E4 **Figeac**, Fr.
117/G2 **Figg** (peak), Austl.
79/E5 **Figline Valdarno**, It.
131/C4 **Figtree**, Zim.
74/A2 **Figueira da Foz**, Port.
75/G1 **Figueres**, Sp.
124/E1 **Figuig**, Mor.
133/G8 **Fiherenana** (riv.), Madg.
120/G6 **Fiji**
131/C4 **Filabusi**, Zim.
135/D1 **Filadelfia**, Par.
113/X **Filchner Ice Shelf**, Ant.
57/H3 **Filey**, Eng,UK
57/H3 **Filey** (bay), Eng,UK
83/F3 **Filiaşi**, Rom.
80/D3 **Filicudi** (isl.), It.
76/C6 **Filière** (riv.), Fr.
129/F3 **Filingué**, Niger
81/J2 **Filippoi** (ruins), Gre.
62/F2 **Filipstad**, Swe.
164/B2 **Fillmore**, Ca,US
158/D3 **Fillmore**, Ut,US
121/S9 **Filo** (peak), WSam.
147/H5 **Filomena Mata**, Mex.
70/C5 **Fils** (riv.), Ger.
58/D3 **Filton**, Eng,UK
113/Z **Fimbul Ice Shelf**, Ant.
124/J8 **Fimi** (riv.), Zaire
79/E3 **Finale Emilia**, It.
78/B4 **Finale Ligure**, It.
128/C3 **Fina Rsv.**, Mali
53/N7 **Finchley**, Eng,UK
54/C1 **Findhorn**, Sc,UK
54/C1 **Findhorn** (riv.), Sc,UK
160/D3 **Findlay**, Oh,US
54/D1 **Findochty**, Sc,UK
119/D4 **Fingal**, Austl.
153/K2 **Finger** (lake), On,Can
160/E3 **Finger** (lakes), NY,US
131/C2 **Fingoè**, Moz.
72/E4 **Finiels, Sommet de** (peak), Fr.
91/B1 **Finike**, Turk.
74/A1 **Finisterre** (cape), Sp.
117/G3 **Finke** (riv.), Austl.
117/G3 **Finke Gorge Nat'l Park**, Austl.
73/K3 **Finkenstein**, Aus.
61/H2 **Finland**
63/L2 **Finland** (gulf), Eur.
152/D3 **Finlay** (riv.), BC,Can
162/B4 **Finlay** (mts.), Tx,US
55/H9 **Finn** (riv.), Ire.
67/E6 **Finnentrop**, Ger.
165/C2 **Finn Hill-Inglewood**, Wa,US
118/B1 **Finnigan** (peak), Austl.
117/G5 **Finnis** (cape), Austl.
61/G1 **Finnmark** (co.), Nor.
78/C1 **Fino Mornasco**, It.
62/F2 **Finspång**, Swe.
76/E4 **Finsteraarhorn** (peak), Swi.
55/N13 **Finstown**, Sc,UK
56/A3 **Fintona**, NI,UK
54/A1 **Fionn Loch** (lake), Sc,UK
80/B1 **Fiora** (riv.), It.
79/D3 **Fiorano**, It.
78/C3 **Fiorenzuola d'Arda**, It.
165/C2 **Fircrest-Silver Lake**, Wa,US
167/E2 **Fire Island Nat'l Seash.**, NY,US
79/E5 **Firenze** (prov.), It.
79/E5 **Firenze** (Florence), It.
142/E2 **Firmat**, Arg.
72/F4 **Firminy**, Fr.
106/C2 **Fīrozābād**, India
108/C2 **Fīrozpur**, India
127/C3 **First Cataract** (falls), Egypt
93/H4 **Fīrūzābād**, Iran
73/L3 **Fischbacher** (mts.), Aus.
131/C2 **Fisenge**, Zam.
132/B2 **Fish** (riv.), Namb.
132/C3 **Fish** (riv.), SAfr.
57/G2 **Fishburn**, Eng,UK
113/E **Fisher** (glac.), Ant.

Fishe – Galil

157/J3 **Fisher** (bay), Mb,Can
153/H2 **Fisher** (str.), NW,Can
157/J3 **Fisher Branch,** Mb,Can
118/F6 **Fisherman** (isl.), Austl.
167/G1 **Fishers** (isl.), NY,US
58/B3 **Fishguard,** Wal,UK
166/A1 **Fishing** (cr.), Pa,US
166/B1 **Fishing** (cr.), Pa,US
86/F4 **Fisht, Gora** (peak), Rus.
57/J6 **Fishtoft,** Eng,UK
63/S7 **Fisksätra,** Swe.
55/P13 **Fitful Head** (pt.), Sc,UK
121/S8 **Fito** (peak), WSam.
63/R7 **Fittja,** Swe.
151/L2 **Fitton** (mtn.), Yk,Can
163/H4 **Fitzgerald,** Ga,US
116/C5 **Fitzgerald River Nat'l Park,** Austl.
156/B3 **Fitz Hugo** (sound), BC,Can
143/J7 **Fitzroy** (peak), Arg.
118/C3 **Fitzroy** (riv.), Austl.
153/R7 **Fitzwilliam** (str.), NW,Can
80/C2 **Fiumicino,** It.
56/A3 **Fivemiletown,** NI,UK
54/A2 **Five Sisters** (mtn.), Sc,UK
130/A4 **Fizi,** Zaire
62/A1 **Fjell,** Nor.
59/F3 **Flackwell Heath,** Eng,UK
159/G3 **Flagler,** Co,US
163/H4 **Flagler Beach,** Fl,US
158/E4 **Flagstaff,** Az,US
160/B2 **Flambeau** (riv.), Wi,US
161/Q9 **Flamborough,** On,Can
57/H3 **Flamborough,** Eng,UK
57/H3 **Flamborough Head** (pt.), Eng,UK
64/G2 **Fläming** (hills), Ger.
156/F5 **Flaming Gorge** (res.), Ut, Wy,US
156/F5 **Flaming Gorge Nat'l Rec. Area,** Ut, Wy,US
157/K2 **Flanagan** (riv.), On,Can
68/B2 **Flanders** (reg.), Belg., Fr.
157/J4 **Flandreau,** SD,US
167/K9 **Flatbush,** NY,US
151/L3 **Flat Creek,** Yk,Can
156/E4 **Flathead** (lake), Mt,US
156/E4 **Flathead** (riv.), Mt,US
156/E4 **Flathead, South Fork** (riv.), Mt,US
58/C4 **Flat Holm** (isl.), Eng,UK
159/K3 **Flat River,** Mo,US
165/F7 **Flat Rock,** Mi,US
118/B1 **Flattery** (cape), Austl.
156/B3 **Flattery** (cape), Wa,US
138/B5 **Flavio Alfaro,** Ecu.
77/F3 **Flawil,** Swi.
59/F4 **Fleet,** Eng,UK
57/E4 **Fleetwood,** Eng,UK
62/B2 **Flekkefjord,** Nor.
119/F5 **Flemington Racecourse,** Austl.
62/G2 **Flen,** Swe.
64/E1 **Flensburg,** Ger.
69/E2 **Fleron,** Belg.
72/C2 **Flers,** Fr.
60/A5 **Flesk** (riv.), Ire.
76/D5 **Fletschhorn** (peak), Swi.
68/D3 **Fleurus,** Belg.
72/D3 **Fleury-les-Aubrais,** Fr.
66/C4 **Flevoland** (prov.), Neth.
77/G3 **Flexenpass** (pass), Aus.
70/C2 **Flieden,** Ger.
70/C2 **Flieden** (riv.), Ger.
56/E2 **Flimby,** Eng,UK
116/B5 **Flinders** (bay), Austl.
117/G5 **Flinders** (isl.), Austl.
119/D3 **Flinders** (isl.), Austl.
117/H5 **Flinders** (range), Austl.
118/C2 **Flinders** (reefs), Austl.
118/A2 **Flinders** (riv.), Austl.
117/H5 **Flinders Chase Nat'l Park,** Austl.
117/H4 **Flinders Ranges Nat'l Park,** Austl.
157/L3 **Flindt** (riv.), On,Can
157/H2 **Flin Flon,** Mb,Can
153/J2 **Flint** (lake), NW,Can
121/K6 **Flint** (isl.), Kiri.
57/E5 **Flint,** Wal,UK
163/G4 **Flint** (riv.), Ga,US
159/H3 **Flint** (hills), Ks,US
165/E5 **Flint,** Mi,US
62/D4 **Flintbek,** Ger.
164/B2 **Flintridge-La Cañada,** Ca,US
165/F6 **Flint, South Branch** (riv.), Mi,US
62/E1 **Flisa,** Nor.
59/F3 **Flitwick,** Eng,UK
147/Q10 **Floating Gardens,** Mex.
62/E3 **Floda,** Swe.
54/D5 **Flodden,** Eng,UK
67/F1 **Flögelner See** (lake), Ger.
65/G3 **Flöha** (riv.), Ger.
116/C2 **Flora** (peak), Austl.
112/C1 **Flora,** Phil.
160/B4 **Flora,** Il,US
167/E2 **Floral Park,** NY,US
69/F5 **Florange,** Fr.
140/C2 **Florânia,** Braz.
69/D3 **Floreffe,** Belg.
163/G3 **Florence,** Al,US
158/E4 **Florence,** Az,US
159/F3 **Florence,** Co,US
163/J3 **Florence,** SC,US
79/E5 **Florence** (Firenze), It.
164/F8 **Florence-Graham,** Ca,US
138/C4 **Florencia,** Col.
68/D3 **Florennes,** Belg.
142/E3 **Flores** (riv.), Arg.
156/B3 **Flores** (isl.), BC,Can
148/D2 **Flores,** Guat.
111/F5 **Flores** (isl.), Indo.
111/E5 **Flores** (sea), Indo.
75/R12 **Flores** (isl.), Azor.,Port.
143/F2 **Flores** (dept.), Uru.
140/B2 **Flores do Piauí,** Braz.
140/C3 **Floresta,** Braz.
162/D4 **Floresville,** Tx,US
166/D2 **Florham Park,** NJ,US
140/B2 **Floriano,** Braz.
141/B3 **Florianópolis,** Braz.
138/B4 **Florida,** Col.
149/G1 **Florida,** Cuba
155/K7 **Florida** (str.), Cuba, US
143/F2 **Florida,** Uru.
143/F2 **Florida** (dept.), Uru.
163/H4 **Florida** (state), US
163/H5 **Florida** (bay), Fl,US
138/C3 **Floridablanca,** Col.
163/H5 **Florida Keys** (isls.), Fl,US
80/D4 **Floridia,** It.
165/M10 **Florin,** Ca,US
81/G2 **Flórina,** Gre.
159/K3 **Florissant,** Mo,US
61/C3 **Florø,** Nor.
70/B2 **Flörsheim am Main,** Ger.
70/B2 **Florstadt,** Ger.
162/C3 **Floydada,** Tx,US
77/G4 **Fluchthorn** (peak), Aus.
77/F4 **Flüelapass** (pass), Swi.
66/C3 **Fluessen** (lake), Neth.
80/A3 **Flumendosa** (riv.), It.
160/D3 **Flushing,** Mi,US
167/K8 **Flushing,** NY,US
66/A6 **Flushing** (Vlissingen), Neth.
120/D5 **Fly** (riv.), PNG
113/T **Flying Fish** (cape), Ant.
61/P6 **Fnjóská** (riv.), Ice.
157/H3 **Foam Lake,** Sk,Can
82/D4 **Foča,** Bosn.
54/C1 **Fochabers,** Sc,UK
83/H3 **Focşani,** Rom.
107/K3 **Fogang,** China
80/D2 **Foggia,** It.
79/F5 **Foglia** (riv.), It.
63/J2 **Föglö** (isl.), Fin.
122/J10 **Fogo** (isl.), CpV.
73/L3 **Fohnsdorf,** Aus.
64/E1 **Föhr** (isl.), Ger.
72/D5 **Foix,** Fr.
62/B1 **Folarskardnuten** (peak), Nor.
61/D2 **Folda** (fjord), Nor.
81/J4 **Folégandros** (isl.), Gre.
153/J2 **Foley** (isl.), NW,Can
80/C1 **Foligno,** It.
59/H4 **Folkestone,** Eng,UK
163/H4 **Folkston,** Ga,US
80/B1 **Follonica** (gulf), It.
152/F3 **Fond du Lac** (riv.), Sk,Can
160/B3 **Fond du Lac,** Wi,US
80/C2 **Fondi,** It.
61/D3 **Fongen** (peak), Nor.
74/B1 **Fonsagrada,** Sp.
138/C2 **Fonseca,** Col.
148/E3 **Fonseca** (gulf), NAm.
72/F4 **Fontaine,** Fr.
72/E2 **Fontainebleau,** Fr.
76/A3 **Fontaine-lès-Dijon,** Fr.
68/D3 **Fontaine-L'Evêque,** Belg.
164/C2 **Fontana,** Ca,US
72/C3 **Fontenay-le-Comte,** Fr.
53/S10 **Fontenay-le-Fleury,** Fr.
53/S11 **Fontenay-les-Briis,** Fr.
53/T10 **Fontenay-sous-Bois,** Fr.
53/U10 **Fontenay-Trésigny,** Fr.
156/F5 **Fontenelle** (res.), Wy,US
73/G4 **Font Sancte, Pic de la** (peak), Fr.
61/P6 **Fontur** (pt.), Ice.
119/F5 **Footscray,** Austl.
96/F5 **Foping,** China
151/H3 **Foraker** (mtn.), Ak,US
69/F5 **Forbach,** Fr.
70/B5 **Forbach,** Ger.
119/D2 **Forbes,** Austl.
74/A1 **Forcarey,** Sp.
70/E3 **Forchheim,** Ger.
76/D5 **Forclaz, Col de la** (pass), Swi.
54/D5 **Ford,** Eng,UK
165/E7 **Ford** (lake), Mi,US
167/K8 **Fordham,** NY,US
59/E5 **Fordingbridge,** Eng,UK
167/D2 **Fords,** NJ,US
162/E3 **Fordyce,** Ar,US
58/C4 **Foreland** (pt.), Eng,UK
59/E5 **Foreland, The** (pt.), Eng,UK
156/F3 **Foremost,** Ab,Can
59/H4 **Foreness** (pt.), Eng,UK
163/F3 **Forest,** Ms,US
167/K9 **Forest Hills,** NY,US
119/D4 **Forestier** (cape), Austl.
161/G1 **Forestville,** Qu,Can
166/B6 **Forestville,** Md,US
72/E4 **Forez** (mts.), Fr.
54/D3 **Forfar,** Sc,UK
53/S11 **Forges-les-Bains,** Fr.
77/G2 **Forggensee** (lake), Ger.
161/H1 **Forillon Nat'l Park,** Qu,Can
56/B3 **Forkill,** NI,UK
79/F4 **Forlì,** It.
79/F4 **Forlì** (prov.), It.
79/F4 **Forlimpopoli,** It.
54/D2 **Formartine** (dist.), Sc,UK
57/E4 **Formby,** Eng,UK
57/E4 **Formby** (pt.), Eng,UK
75/F3 **Formentera** (isl.), Sp.
75/G3 **Formentor, Cabo de** (cape), Sp.
80/C2 **Formia,** It.
141/C2 **Formiga,** Braz.
79/D3 **Formigine,** It.
135/E2 **Formosa,** Arg.
140/A4 **Formosa,** Braz.
137/G6 **Formosa** (mts.), Braz.
128/A4 **Formosa** (isl.), GBis.
132/C4 **Formosa** (peak), SAfr.
140/A3 **Formosa do Rio Prêto,** Braz.
140/A4 **Formoso** (riv.), Braz.
79/E5 **Fornacelle,** It.
62/D3 **Fornæs** (cape), Den.
54/C1 **Forres,** Sc,UK
163/F3 **Forrest City,** Ar,US
62/E2 **Forshaga,** Swe.
63/K1 **Forssa,** Fin.
118/A3 **Forsyth** (range), Austl.
163/H3 **Forsyth,** Ga,US
156/G4 **Forsyth,** Mt,US
167/D5 **Forsythe Nat'l Wild. Ref.,** NJ,US
95/K3 **Fort Abbās,** Pak.
140/C1 **Fortaleza,** Braz.
140/A2 **Fortaleza dos Nogueiras,** Braz.
143/G2 **Fortaleza Santa Teresa,** Uru.
54/B2 **Fort Augustus,** Sc,UK
132/D4 **Fort Beaufort,** SAfr.
161/H2 **Fort Beauséjour Nat'l Hist. Park,** NB,Can
166/A6 **Fort Belvoir** (mil. res.), Va,US
156/F4 **Fort Benton,** Mt,US
158/B3 **Fort Bragg,** Ca,US
161/F2 **Fort Chambly Nat'l Hist. Park,** Qu,Can
159/H4 **Fort Cobb** (res.), Ok,US
159/F2 **Fort Collins,** Co,US
162/C4 **Fort Davis,** Tx,US
69/E5 **Fort de Douaumont,** Fr.
150/F4 **Fort-de-France,** Mart.
150/F4 **Fort Desaix,** Mart.
69/E5 **Fort de Vaux,** Fr.
166/D3 **Fort Dix** (mil. res.), NJ,US
157/K5 **Fort Dodge,** Ia,US
126/D3 **Forte Cameia,** Ang.
78/D5 **Forte dei Marmi,** It.
161/S10 **Fort Erie,** On,Can
116/C2 **Fortescue** (riv.), Austl.
160/A1 **Fort Frances,** On,Can
163/F4 **Fort Gaines,** Al,US
161/R9 **Fort George,** On,Can
153/J3 **Fort-George** (Chisasibi), Qu,Can
159/J4 **Fort Gibson,** Ok,US
162/E2 **Fort Gibson** (lake), Ok,US
124/C3 **Fort-Gouraud,** Mrta.
60/D5 **Forth** (mtn.), Ire.
54/C5 **Forth,** Sc,UK
54/C4 **Forth** (riv.), Sc,UK
167/D2 **Fort Hamilton** (mil. res.), NY,US
167/D3 **Fort Hancock** (mil. res.), NJ,US
54/B4 **Forth, Carse of** (plain), Sc,UK
54/D4 **Forth, Firth of** (inlet), Sc,UK
147/N8 **Fortín de las Flores,** Mex.
166/B3 **Fort Indiantown Gap** (mil. res.), Pa,US
161/G2 **Fort Kent,** Me,US
163/H5 **Fort Lauderdale,** Fl,US
167/E2 **Fort Lee,** NJ,US
165/B3 **Fort Lewis** (mil. res.), Wa,US
159/F2 **Fort Lupton,** Co,US
156/E3 **Fort Macleod,** Ab,Can
157/L5 **Fort Madison,** Ia,US
165/F7 **Fort Malden Nat'l Hist. Park,** On,Can
163/H4 **Fort Matanzas Nat'l Mon.,** Fl,US
166/B5 **Fort McHenry Nat'l Mon. & Hist. Site,** Md,US
152/E3 **Fort McMurray,** Ab,Can
166/B5 **Fort Meade** (mil. res.), Md,US
160/C2 **Fort Michilimackinac,** Mi,US
167/D3 **Fort Monmouth** (mil. res.), NJ,US
159/G2 **Fort Morgan,** Co,US
163/J3 **Fort Moultrie,** SC,US
163/H5 **Fort Myers,** Fl,US
152/D3 **Fort Nelson** (riv.), BC,Can
57/F4 **Forton,** Eng,UK
80/D2 **Fortore** (riv.), It.
163/G3 **Fort Payne,** Al,US
157/G4 **Fort Peck** (dam), Mt,US
156/G4 **Fort Peck** (lake), Mt,US
163/H5 **Fort Pierce,** Fl,US
157/H4 **Fort Pierre,** SD,US
130/A2 **Fort Portal,** Ugan.
157/H3 **Fort Qu'Appelle,** Sk,Can
163/K3 **Fort Raleigh Nat'l Hist. Site,** NC,US
157/J5 **Fort Randall** (dam), SD,US
161/J2 **Fortress of Louisbourg Nat'l Hist. Park,** NS,Can
131/C4 **Fort Rixon,** Zim.
54/B1 **Fortrose,** Sc,UK
156/B2 **Fort Saint James,** BC,Can
152/D3 **Fort Saint John,** BC,Can
156/E2 **Fort Saskatchewan,** Ab,Can
159/J3 **Fort Scott,** Ks,US
87/J3 **Fort-Shevchenko,** Kaz.
162/E3 **Fort Smith,** Ar,US
162/C4 **Fort Stockton,** Tx,US
159/F4 **Fort Sumner,** NM,US
167/E2 **Fort Tilden** (mil. res.), NY,US
157/J4 **Fort Totten,** ND,US
140/A2 **Fortuna,** Braz.
161/L2 **Fortune,** Nf,Can
161/L2 **Fortune** (bay), Nf,Can
150/C2 **Fortune** (Long Cay) (cay), Bahm.
58/D5 **Fortuneswell,** Eng,UK
159/F4 **Fort Union Nat'l Mon.,** NM,US
167/D2 **Fort Wadsworth** (mil. res.), NY,US
163/G4 **Fort Walton Beach,** Fl,US
166/A6 **Fort Washington Park,** Md,US
160/C3 **Fort Wayne,** In,US
160/F2 **Fort Wellington Nat'l Hist. Park,** On,Can
54/A3 **Fort William,** Sc,UK
162/D3 **Fort Worth,** Tx,US
157/H4 **Fort Yates,** ND,US
118/B2 **Forty Mile Scrub Nat'l Park,** Austl.
93/H5 **Forūr** (isl.), Iran
105/G4 **Foshan,** China
153/S7 **Fosheim** (pen.), NW,Can
57/G3 **Foss** (riv.), Eng,UK
78/A3 **Fossano,** It.
53/T9 **Fosses,** Fr.
69/D3 **Fosses-la-Ville,** Belg.
156/C4 **Fossil,** Or,US
156/F5 **Fossil Butte Nat'l Mon.,** Wy,US
79/F5 **Fossombrone,** It.
160/D3 **Fostoria,** Oh,US
72/C2 **Fougères,** Fr.
125/N3 **Foul** (bay), Egypt, Sudan
108/H4 **Foul** (pt.), SrL.
55/N12 **Foula** (isl.), Sc,UK
59/G3 **Foulness** (isl.), Eng,UK
59/G3 **Foulness** (pt.), Eng,UK
57/H4 **Foulness** (riv.), Eng,UK
59/H1 **Foulsham,** Eng,UK
129/H5 **Foumban,** Camr.
159/F3 **Fountain,** Co,US
57/G3 **Fountains Abbey,** Eng,UK
164/C3 **Fountain Valley,** Ca,US
162/E3 **Fourche La Fave** (riv.), Ar,US
59/E4 **Four Marks,** Eng,UK
68/D4 **Fourmies,** Fr.
151/D5 **Four Mountains** (isls.), Ak,US
133/R15 **Fournaise, Piton de la** (peak), Reun.
127/C5 **Fourth Cataract** (falls), Sudan
128/B4 **Fouta Djallon** (reg.), Gha.
115/Q12 **Foveaux** (str.), NZ
58/B6 **Fowey,** Eng,UK
58/B6 **Fowey** (riv.), Eng,UK
119/B1 **Fowlers Gap,** Austl.
93/G2 **Fowman,** Iran
151/M3 **Fox** (mtn.), Yk,Can
151/E5 **Fox** (isls.), Ak,US
165/P15 **Fox** (lake), Il,US
160/B3 **Fox** (riv.), Il, Wi,US
165/B3 **Fox** (isl.), Wa,US
156/D2 **Fox Creek,** Ab,Can
153/H2 **Foxe** (chan.), NW,Can
153/J2 **Foxe** (pen.), NW,Can
153/J2 **Foxe Basin** (sound), NW,Can
62/D2 **Foxen** (lake), Swe.
115/R11 **Fox Glacier,** NZ
165/P15 **Fox Lake,** Il,US
59/G2 **Foxton,** Eng,UK
156/F3 **Fox Valley,** Sk,Can
54/B2 **Foyers,** Sc,UK
56/A2 **Foyle** (riv.), NI,UK
56/A1 **Foyle, Lough** (inlet), Ire., NI,UK
74/B1 **Foz,** Sp.
126/B4 **Foz do Cunene,** Ang.
135/F2 **Foz do Iguaçu,** Braz.
75/F2 **Fraga,** Sp.
149/G1 **Fragosa** (cay), Cuba
141/B3 **Fraiburgo,** Braz.
136/E7 **Frailes** (range), Bol.
68/C3 **Frameries,** Belg.
168/C1 **Framingham,** Ma,US
59/H2 **Framlingham,** Eng,UK
141/C2 **Franca,** Braz.
81/E2 **Francavilla Fontana,** It.
72/D3 **France**
53/T9 **France, Pays de** (plain), Fr.
72/E5 **France, Roc de** (mtn.), Fr.
152/C2 **Frances** (lake), Yk,Can
149/F1 **Frances** (cape), Cuba
126/B1 **Franceville,** Gabon
76/C3 **Franche-Comté** (hist. reg.), Fr.
73/G3 **Franche-Comté** (reg.), Fr.
157/J5 **Francis Case** (lake), SD,US
147/H5 **Francisco Escárcega,** Mex.
146/E3 **Francisco I. Madero,** Mex.
131/B4 **Francistown,** Bots.
141/G8 **Franco da Rocha,** Braz.
156/B2 **Francois** (lake), BC,Can
53/S10 **Franconville,** Fr.
66/C2 **Franeker,** Neth.
67/F6 **Frankenberg-Eder,** Ger.
70/D4 **Frankenhöhe** (mts.), Ger.
160/D3 **Frankenmuth,** Mi,US
70/B3 **Frankenthal,** Ger.
71/E2 **Franken Wald** (for.), Ger.
160/C3 **Frankfort,** In,US
160/C4 **Frankfort** (cap.), Ky,US
65/H2 **Frankfurt,** Ger.
70/B2 **Frankfurt am Main,** Ger.
116/D5 **Frank Hann Nat'l Park,** Austl.
70/E3 **Fränkische Alb** (mts.), Ger.
70/D4 **Fränkische Rezat** (riv.), Ger.
70/C2 **Fränkische Saale** (riv.), Ger.
70/E2 **Fränkische Schweiz** (reg.), Ger.
119/C3 **Frankland** (cape), Austl.
113/M **Franklin** (isl.), Ant.
151/N1 **Franklin** (bay), NW,Can
152/D2 **Franklin** (mts.), NW,Can
151/G1 **Franklin** (pt.), Ak,US
160/C4 **Franklin,** In,US
160/C4 **Franklin,** Ky,US
168/C1 **Franklin,** Ma,US
163/H3 **Franklin,** NC,US
168/H5 **Franklin,** Pa,US
163/G3 **Franklin,** Tn,US
162/D4 **Franklin,** Tx,US
160/E4 **Franklin,** Va,US
165/P14 **Franklin,** Wi,US
160/E4 **Franklin,** WV,US
156/D3 **Franklin D. Roosevelt** (lake), Wa,US
167/D1 **Franklin Lakes,** NJ,US
119/C4 **Franklin-Lower Gordon Wild Rivers Nat'l Park,** Austl.
166/D1 **Franklin Mineral Museum,** NJ,US
165/Q16 **Franklin Park,** Il,US
168/G6 **Franklin Park,** Pa,US
167/E2 **Franklin Square,** NY,US
135/F2 **Fransisco Beltrão,** Braz.
141/G8 **Fransisco Morato,** Braz.
140/B5 **Fransisco Sá,** Braz.
88/F2 **Franz Josef Land** (arch.), Rus.
118/D4 **Fraser** (isl.), Austl.
116/C3 **Fraser** (peak), Austl.
156/B2 **Fraser** (lake), BC,Can
156/C3 **Fraser** (riv.), BC,Can
165/G6 **Fraser,** Mi,US
54/D1 **Fraserburgh,** Sc,UK
156/B2 **Fraser Lake,** BC,Can
119/C3 **Fraser Nat'l Park,** Austl.
79/E2 **Frassine** (riv.), It.
79/F5 **Frati, Monte dei** (peak), It.
77/E2 **Frauenfeld,** Swi.
142/F2 **Fray Bentos,** Uru.
158/C4 **Frazier Park,** Ca,US
69/F2 **Frechen,** Ger.
114/A5 **Frecinet** (estuary), Austl.
132/E3 **Fred** (mtn.), SAfr.
63/T9 **Fredensborg,** Den.
62/C4 **Fredericia,** Den.
115/J4 **Frederick** (reef), Austl.
160/E4 **Frederick,** Md,US
166/A5 **Frederick** (co.), Md,US
159/H4 **Frederick,** Ok,US
162/D4 **Fredericksburg,** Tx,US
160/E4 **Fredericksburg,** Va,US
161/H2 **Fredericton** (cap.), NB,Can
63/T9 **Frederiksberg,** Den.
63/T9 **Frederiksborg** (co.), Den.
62/E4 **Frederiksborg Castle,** Den.
62/D3 **Frederikshavn,** Den.
63/T9 **Frederikssund,** Den.
139/G4 **Frederik Willem IV** (falls), Sur.
158/D3 **Fredonia,** Az,US
159/J3 **Fredonia,** Ks,US
160/E3 **Fredonia,** NY,US
62/D2 **Fredrikstad,** Nor.
159/H3 **Freedom,** Ok,US
167/D3 **Freehold,** NJ,US
117/G2 **Freeling** (peak), Austl.
117/H4 **Freeling Heights** (peak), Austl.
150/B1 **Freeport,** Bahm.
160/B3 **Freeport,** Il,US
167/E2 **Freeport,** NY,US
162/E4 **Freeport,** Tx,US
162/D5 **Freer,** Tx,US
128/B4 **Freetown** (cap.), SLeo.
168/C2 **Freetown-Fall River Saint For.,** Ma,US
72/B2 **Fréhel** (cape), Fr.
64/G3 **Freib** (riv.), Ger.
65/G3 **Freiberg,** Ger.
64/G3 **Freiberger Mulde** (riv.), Ger.
76/D2 **Freiburg,** Ger.
77/E3 **Freienbach,** Swi.
141/D1 **Frei Inocêncio,** Braz.
71/F7 **Freilassing,** Ger.
142/B3 **Freire,** Chile
69/G4 **Freisen,** Ger.
71/E6 **Freising,** Ger.
71/H6 **Freistadt,** Aus.
65/G3 **Freital,** Ger.
73/G5 **Fréjus,** Fr.
116/K7 **Fremantle,** Austl.
58/B4 **Fremington,** Eng,UK
165/L11 **Fremont,** Ca,US
160/C3 **Fremont,** Mi,US
159/H2 **Fremont,** Ne,US
160/D3 **Fremont,** Oh,US
158/E3 **Fremont** (riv.), Ut,US
156/F5 **Fremont** (peak), Wy,US
160/D2 **French** (riv.), On,Can
166/C3 **French** (cr.), Pa,US
168/H5 **French** (cr.), Pa,US
166/C3 **French Creek Saint Park,** Pa,US
121/J2 **French Frigate** (shoals), Hi,US
134/D2 **French Guiana** (dpcy.), Fr.
156/G3 **Frenchman** (riv.), Can., US
159/G2 **Frenchman** (cr.), Ne,US
161/R8 **Frenchman's** (bay), On,Can
119/C4 **Frenchmans Cap** (peak), Austl.
121/M6 **French Polynesia** (terr.), Fr.
123/R16 **Frenda,** Alg.
53/S9 **Frépillon,** Fr.
137/H5 **Fresco** (riv.), Braz.
59/E5 **Freshwater,** Eng,UK
142/B4 **Fresia,** Chile
53/S10 **Fresnes,** Fr.
146/E4 **Fresnillo,** Mex.
158/C3 **Fresno,** Ca,US
63/R6 **Frestaby,** Swe.
54/C3 **Freuchie, Loch** (lake), Sc,UK
69/G2 **Freudenberg,** Ger.
70/B6 **Freudenstadt,** Ger.
116/B3 **Freycinet** (har.), Austl.
119/D4 **Freycinet Nat'l Park,** Austl.
69/F5 **Freyming-Merlebach,** Fr.
71/E4 **Freystadt,** Ger.
71/G5 **Freyung,** Ger.
126/B4 **Fria** (cape), Namb.
135/C2 **Frías,** Arg.
76/D4 **Fribourg,** Swi.
76/D4 **Fribourg** (canton), Swi.
70/B2 **Friedberg,** Ger.
70/D6 **Friedberg,** Ger.
67/E2 **Friedeburg,** Ger.
70/B2 **Friedrichsdorf,** Ger.
77/F2 **Friedrichshafen,** Ger.
69/G5 **Friedrichsthal,** Ger.
67/G7 **Frielendorf,** Ger.
70/A6 **Friesenheim,** Ger.
66/C2 **Friesland** (prov.), Neth.
67/E2 **Friesoythe,** Ger.
59/F4 **Frimley,** Eng,UK
59/H3 **Frinton,** Eng,UK
50/G7 **Frio** (cape), Braz.
159/H5 **Frio** (riv.), Tx,US
54/D3 **Friockheim,** Sc,UK
168/A1 **Frissel** (mtn.), Ct,US
67/G6 **Fritzlar,** Ger.
73/K3 **Friuli-Venezia Giulia** (reg.), It.
56/E2 **Frizington,** Eng,UK
153/K2 **Frobisher** (bay), NW,Can
156/F1 **Frobisher** (lake), Sk,Can
57/F5 **Frodsham,** Eng,UK
61/D3 **Frohavet** (bay), Nor.
68/D3 **Froidchapelle,** Belg.
87/G2 **Frolovo,** Rus.
117/J4 **Frome** (lake), Austl.
117/H4 **Frome** (riv.), Austl.
58/D4 **Frome,** Eng,UK
58/D2 **Frome** (riv.), Eng,UK
58/D5 **Frome** (riv.), Eng,UK
159/F2 **Front** (range), Co,US
140/B2 **Fronteiras,** Braz.
147/E3 **Frontera,** Mex.
147/G5 **Frontera,** Mex.
72/E5 **Frontignan,** Fr.
160/E4 **Front Royal,** Va,US
80/C2 **Frosinone,** It.
61/E3 **Frösö,** Swe.
113/J **Frost** (glac.), Ant.
69/F6 **Frouard,** Fr.
60/B6 **Frower** (pt.), Ire.
61/D3 **Frøya** (isl.), Nor.
153/H2 **Frozen** (str.), NW,Can
161/Q9 **Fruitland,** On,Can
82/D3 **Fruška Gora Nat'l Park,** Yugo.
141/B2 **Frutal,** Braz.
142/B4 **Frutillar,** Chile
65/K4 **Frýdek-Místek,** Czh.
103/C5 **Fu** (riv.), China
105/H3 **Fu'an,** China
79/D5 **Fucecchio,** It.
103/D3 **Fucheng,** China
64/E3 **Fuchskaute** (peak), Ger.
69/H2 **Fuchskauten** (peak), Ger.
98/C3 **Fuchū,** Japan
103/D5 **Fuchun** (riv.), China
111/H4 **Fudi** (mtn.), Indo.
105/J3 **Fuding,** China
74/C4 **Fuengirola,** Sp.
74/D2 **Fuenlabrada,** Sp.
75/N8 **Fuente,** Sp.
75/E4 **Fuente-Álamo,** Sp.
74/B3 **Fuente del Maestre,** Sp.
74/C3 **Fuente Obejuna,** Sp.
74/E1 **Fuenterrabía,** Sp.
74/C4 **Fuentes de Andalucía,** Sp.
146/C3 **Fuerte** (riv.), Mex.
136/G8 **Fuerte Olimpo,** Par.
112/C1 **Fuga** (isl.), Phil.
107/G2 **Fugong,** China
103/C4 **Fugou,** China
96/B2 **Fuhai,** China
64/F3 **Fuhne** (riv.), Ger.
67/H4 **Fuhse** (riv.), Ger.
99/F3 **Fuji,** Japan
99/F3 **Fuji** (riv.), Japan
105/H3 **Fujian** (prov.), China
99/F3 **Fujieda,** Japan
99/F3 **Fuji-Hakone-Izu Nat'l Park,** Japan
99/L10 **Fujiidera,** Japan
99/H7 **Fujimi,** Japan
99/H7 **Fujino,** Japan
99/F3 **Fujinomiya,** Japan
99/F2 **Fujioka,** Japan
99/F3 **Fujisawa,** Japan
99/J7 **Fujishiro,** Japan
99/M9 **Fujiwara,** Japan
99/F3 **Fujiyama** (mtn.), Japan
99/F3 **Fujiyoshida,** Japan
100/C2 **Fukagawa,** Japan
102/E3 **Fukang,** China
98/D3 **Fukuchiyama,** Japan
98/A4 **Fukue,** Japan
98/A4 **Fukue** (isl.), Japan
98/E2 **Fukui,** Japan
98/E3 **Fukui** (pref.), Japan
98/B4 **Fukuoka,** Japan
98/B4 **Fukuoka** (pref.), Japan
99/E3 **Fukuroi,** Japan
113/C **Fukushima** (peak), Ant.
100/B3 **Fukushima,** Japan
99/G2 **Fukushima,** Japan
99/F2 **Fukushima** (pref.), Japan
98/C3 **Fukuyama,** Japan
95/J2 **Fūlādī** (mtn.), Afg.
59/G2 **Fulbourn,** Eng,UK
70/C1 **Fulda,** Ger.
70/C2 **Fulda** (riv.), Ger.
57/G4 **Fulford,** Eng,UK
105/E2 **Fuling,** China
164/C3 **Fullerton,** Ca,US
166/C2 **Fullerton** (Whitehall), Pa,US
161/Q9 **Fulton,** On,Can
160/B4 **Fulton,** Ky,US
159/K3 **Fulton,** Mo,US
160/E3 **Fulton,** NY,US
62/E1 **Fulufjället** (peak), Swe.
57/F4 **Fulwood,** Eng,UK
79/F5 **Fumaiolo, Monte** (peak), It.
72/D4 **Fumel,** Fr.
104/D3 **Fumin,** China
99/H7 **Funabashi,** Japan
120/G5 **Funafuti** (atoll), Tuv.
120/G5 **Funafuti** (cap.), Tuv.
103/C4 **Funan,** China
138/C2 **Fundación,** Col.
161/H2 **Fundy** (bay), NB, NS,Can
161/H2 **Fundy Nat'l Park,** NB,Can
131/D4 **Funhalouro,** Moz.
103/D4 **Funing,** China
104/E4 **Funing,** China
60/B5 **Funshion** (riv.), Ire.
77/G4 **Fuorn** (Ofenpass) (pass), Swi.
103/C3 **Fuping,** China
107/J2 **Fuquan,** China
101/C2 **Fur** (riv.), China
76/B6 **Furan** (riv.), Fr.
131/D2 **Furancungo,** Moz.
100/C2 **Furano,** Japan
63/T9 **Furesø** (lake), Den.
84/J4 **Furmanov,** Rus.
54/A4 **Furnace,** Sc,UK
141/B6 **Furnas** (res.), Braz.
119/C4 **Furneaux Group** (isls.), Austl.
67/E3 **Fürstenau,** Ger.
82/C2 **Fürstenfeld,** Aus.
70/E6 **Fürstenfeldbruck,** Ger.
65/H2 **Fürstenwalde,** Ger.
70/D4 **Fürth,** Ger.
71/F4 **Furth im Wald,** Ger.
70/B6 **Furtwangen im Schwarzwald,** Ger.
100/B4 **Furukawa,** Japan
153/H2 **Fury and Hecla** (str.), NW,Can
138/C3 **Fusagasugá,** Col.
103/B4 **Fushan,** China
103/E3 **Fushan,** China
101/B2 **Fushun,** China
99/M9 **Fuso,** Japan
101/D1 **Fusong,** China
99/H7 **Fussa,** Japan
77/G2 **Füssen,** Ger.
109/D1 **Fusui,** China
99/M10 **Futami,** Japan
82/D3 **Futog,** Yugo.
142/B4 **Futrono,** Chile
99/F3 **Futtsu,** Japan
120/H6 **Futuna** (isl.), Wall.
91/B4 **Fuwah,** Egypt
103/B3 **Fu Xian,** China
104/D3 **Fuxian** (lake), China
101/A1 **Fuxin,** China
101/A1 **Fuxin Monggolzu Zizhixian,** China
103/C4 **Fuyang,** China
105/F3 **Fuyi** (riv.), China
97/J2 **Fuyu,** China
104/E3 **Fuyuan,** China
96/B2 **Fuyun,** China
65/L5 **Füzesabony,** Hun.
105/H3 **Fuzhou,** China
53/P6 **Fyfield,** Eng,UK
62/D4 **Fyn** (co.), Den.
61/D5 **Fyn** (isl.), Den.
54/A4 **Fyne, Loch** (inlet), Sc,UK
63/R6 **Fysingen** (lake), Swe.
54/D2 **Fyvie,** Sc,UK

G

125/Q6 **Gaalkacyo** (Galcaio), Som.
66/D5 **Gaanderen,** Neth.
66/C2 **Gaast,** Neth.
72/C5 **Gabas** (riv.), Fr.
158/C3 **Gabbs,** Nv,US
126/B3 **Gabela,** Ang.
124/H1 **Gabes** (gulf), Tun.
124/H7 **Gabon**
131/B5 **Gaborone** (cap.), Bots.
60/A6 **Gabriel** (mtn.), Ire.
83/G4 **Gabrovo,** Bul.
82/D4 **Gacko,** Bosn.
106/C4 **Gadag-Betgeri,** India
163/G3 **Gadsden,** Al,US
63/T9 **Gadstrup,** Den.
131/C3 **Gadzema,** Zim.
83/G3 **Găeşti,** Rom.
80/C2 **Gaeta,** It.
80/C2 **Gaeta** (gulf), It.
163/H3 **Gaffney,** SC,US
84/G5 **Gagarin,** Rus.
70/B5 **Gaggenau,** Ger.
128/D5 **Gagnoa,** IvC.
161/G1 **Gagnon,** Qu,Can
53/T10 **Gagny,** Fr.
86/G4 **Gagra,** Geo.
77/G3 **Gaichtpass** (pass), Aus.
82/A2 **Gail** (riv.), Aus.
70/C5 **Gaildorf,** Ger.
72/D5 **Gaillac,** Fr.
168/B3 **Gaillard** (lake), Ct,US
73/K3 **Gailtaler Alps** (mts.), Aus.
142/D4 **Gaiman,** Arg.
71/E5 **Gaimersheim,** Ger.
163/H4 **Gainesville,** Fl,US
163/H3 **Gainesville,** Ga,US
159/J3 **Gainesville,** Mo,US
162/D3 **Gainesville,** Tx,US
57/G2 **Gainford,** Eng,UK
57/H5 **Gainsborough,** Eng,UK
117/G4 **Gairdner** (lake), Austl.
131/C3 **Gairezi** (riv.), Zim.
54/C2 **Gairn** (riv.), Sc,UK
166/A5 **Gaithersburg,** Md,US
101/B2 **Gai Xian,** China
63/L3 **Gaizina Kalns** (peak), Lat.
132/C2 **Gakarosa** (peak), SAfr.
130/C3 **Galana** (riv.), Kenya
74/D2 **Galapagar,** Sp.
144/J6 **Galápagos** (isls.), Ecu.
144/J7 **Galápagos** (prov.), Ecu.
144/J7 **Galápagos Nat'l Park,** Ecu.
54/D5 **Galashiels,** Sc,UK
83/J3 **Galaţi,** Rom.
83/H3 **Galaţi** (co.), Rom.
81/F2 **Galatina,** It.
81/F2 **Galatone,** It.
160/D4 **Galax,** Va,US
81/H3 **Galaxídhiou,** Gre.
111/G3 **Galela,** Indo.
160/B3 **Galena,** Il,US
142/B3 **Galera** (pt.), Chile
138/A4 **Galera** (pt.), Ecu.
150/F5 **Galera** (pt.), Trin.
160/B3 **Galesburg,** Il,US
60/A5 **Galey** (riv.), Ire.
56/B2 **Galgorm,** NI,UK
84/H4 **Galich,** Rus.
65/L3 **Galicia** (reg.), Pol., Ukr.
74/A1 **Galicia** (aut. comm.), Sp.
82/E5 **Galičica Nat'l Park,** Macd.
168/C3 **Galilee,** RI,US
91/D3 **Galilee, Sea of** (Tiberias) (lake), Isr.
141/D1 **Galiléia,** Braz.

189

Galin – Gokwe

77/F3 **Galinakopf** (peak), Aus.
160/D3 **Galion,** Oh,US
55/H7 **Gallan Head** (pt.), Sc,UK
78/B1 **Gallarate,** It.
163/G2 **Gallatin,** Tn,US
106/D6 **Galle,** SrL.
143/K7 **Gallegos** (riv.), Arg.
60/B6 **Galley Head** (pt.), Ire.
78/B2 **Galliate,** It.
138/D1 **Gallinas** (pt.), Col.
162/B3 **Gallinas** (mts.), NM,US
81/E2 **Gallipoli,** It.
83/H5 **Gallipoli** (pen.), Turk.
83/H5 **Gallipoli** (Gelibolu), Turk.
160/D4 **Gallipolis,** Oh,US
61/G2 **Gällivare,** Swe.
80/C3 **Gallo** (cape), It.
77/G4 **Gallo** (lake), It.
56/D2 **Galloway, Mull of** (pt.), Sc,UK
158/E4 **Gallup,** NM,US
53/R10 **Gally** (riv.), Fr.
118/H8 **Galston,** Austl.
54/B5 **Galston,** Sc,UK
96/D2 **Galt,** Mong.
165/M10 **Galt,** Ca,US
60/B5 **Galty** (mts.), Ire.
60/B5 **Galtymore** (mtn.), Ire.
96/E2 **Galuut,** Mong.
142/B3 **Galvarino,** Chile
162/E4 **Galveston,** Tx,US
162/E4 **Galveston** (bay), Tx,US
162/E4 **Galveston** (isl.), Tx,US
142/E2 **Gálvez,** Arg.
60/A3 **Galway,** Ire.
60/A3 **Galway** (bay), Ire.
60/B3 **Galway** (co.), Ire.
109/D1 **Gam** (riv.), Viet.
132/C2 **Gamagara** (dry riv.), SAfr.
99/E3 **Gamagōri,** Japan
112/D2 **Gamay,** Phil.
106/E2 **Gamba,** China
129/E4 **Gambaga Scarp** (escarp.), Gha., Togo
106/A2 **Gambat,** Pak.
125/M6 **Gambēla,** Eth.
125/M6 **Gambela Nat'l Park,** Eth.
79/F4 **Gambettola,** It.
128/B3 **Gambia**
128/A3 **Gambia** (Gambie) (riv.), Afr.
128/B3 **Gambie** (Gambia) (riv.), Afr.
121/M7 **Gambier** (isls.), FrPol.
161/L1 **Gambo,** Nf,Can
126/C1 **Gamboma,** Congo
132/C4 **Gamka** (riv.), SAfr.
132/B3 **Gamkab** (dry riv.), Namb.
59/F2 **Gamlingay,** Eng,UK
84/D2 **Gammelstad,** Swe.
70/C6 **Gammertingen,** Ger.
117/H4 **Gammon Ranges Nat'l Park,** Austl.
99/M9 **Gamo,** Japan
65/G5 **Gamsfeld** (peak), Aus.
130/C1 **Gamud** (peak), Eth.
105/G2 **Gan** (riv.), China
160/E2 **Gananoque,** On,Can
93/G4 **Ganāveh,** Iran
126/B3 **Ganda,** Ang.
126/D2 **Gandajika,** Zaire
112/D2 **Gandara,** Phil.
161/L1 **Gander,** Nf,Can
161/L1 **Gander** (lake), Nf,Can
67/F2 **Ganderkesee,** Ger.
106/B3 **Gāndhīhām,** India
106/B3 **Gandhinagar,** India
106/B3 **Gāndhi Sāgar** (res.), India
75/E3 **Gandía,** Sp.
130/A3 **Gandjo,** Zaire
149/F4 **Gandoca-Manzanillo Nat'l Wild. Ref.,** CR
140/C4 **Gandu,** Braz.
124/C4 **Ganeb** (well), Mrta.
106/C2 **Gangāpur,** India
106/E2 **Gangārāmpur,** India
96/E4 **Gangca,** China
102/D5 **Gangdisê** (mts.), China
69/F2 **Gangelt,** Ger.
106/E3 **Ganges** (riv.), India
80/D4 **Gangi,** It.
71/F6 **Gangkofen,** Ger.
106/E2 **Gangtok,** India
91/G7 **Gan Hashlosha Nat'l Park,** Isr.
63/T9 **Ganløse,** Den.
107/H2 **Ganluo,** China
97/J2 **Gannan,** China
156/F5 **Gannett** (peak), Wy,US
103/B3 **Ganquan,** China
102/F4 **Gansu** (prov.), China
76/D4 **Gantrisch** (peak), Swi.
112/B3 **Gantung** (mtn.), Phil.
124/H6 **Ganye,** Nga.
103/D4 **Ganyu,** China
105/G3 **Ganzhou,** China
129/E3 **Ganzourgou** (prov.), Burk.
105/G3 **Gao** (mtn.), China
129/E2 **Gao,** Mali
129/E2 **Gao** (reg.), Mali
105/G2 **Gao'an,** China
103/C3 **Gaocheng,** China
103/D5 **Gaochun,** China
96/E4 **Gaolan,** China
105/G4 **Gaolan** (isl.), China
104/C3 **Gaoligong** (mts.), China
103/D3 **Gaomi,** China
103/C4 **Gaoping,** China
103/D3 **Gaoqing,** China
54/A3 **Gaor Bheinn** (Gulvain) (mtn.), Sc,UK
96/D4 **Gaotai,** China
103/D3 **Gaotang,** China
128/E4 **Gaoua,** Burk.
103/C3 **Gaoyang,** China
103/C3 **Gaoyi,** China
103/D4 **Gaoyou,** China
103/D4 **Gaoyou** (lake), China
105/F4 **Gaozhou,** China
73/G4 **Gap,** Fr.
60/C5 **Gap, The** (pass), Ire.
102/C5 **Gar,** China
96/D5 **Gar** (riv.), China
149/G4 **Garachiné** (pt.), Pan.
106/E3 **Garai** (riv.), Bang.
60/B2 **Gara, Lough** (lake), Ire.
130/A2 **Garamba Nat'l Park,** Zaire
140/C3 **Garanhuns,** Braz.
130/C2 **Garba Tula,** Kenya
64/E2 **Garbsen,** Ger.
141/B2 **Garça,** Braz.
140/B3 **Garças** (riv.), Braz.
53/S10 **Garches,** Fr.
71/F6 **Garching an der Alz,** Ger.
74/C3 **Garcia de Sota** (res.), Sp.
72/F5 **Gard** (riv.), Fr.
78/D1 **Garda** (lake), It.
123/V17 **Garde, Cap de** (cape), Alg.
64/F2 **Gardelegen,** Ger.
116/K7 **Garden** (isl.), Austl.
164/B3 **Gardena,** Ca,US
163/H3 **Garden City,** Ga,US
159/G3 **Garden City,** Ks,US
165/F7 **Garden City,** Mi,US
167/E2 **Garden City,** NY,US
156/A2 **Gardener Canal** (inlet), BC,Can
164/C3 **Garden Grove,** Ca,US
167/D3 **Garden State Arts Ctr.,** NJ,US
54/D1 **Gardenstown,** Sc,UK
95/J2 **Gardēz,** Afg.
161/G2 **Gardiner,** Me,US
156/F4 **Gardiner,** Mt,US
167/F1 **Gardiners** (bay), NY,US
167/F1 **Gardiners** (isl.), NY,US
168/B2 **Gardner** (lake), Ct,US
121/H5 **Gardner** (Nikumaroro) (atoll), Kiri.
78/D1 **Gardone val Trompia,** It.
54/B4 **Gare Loch** (inlet), Sc,UK
54/B4 **Garelochhead,** Sc,UK
124/G2 **Garet el Djenoun** (peak), Alg.
156/E4 **Garfield** (peak), Mt,US
167/D2 **Garfield,** NJ,US
168/F5 **Garfield Heights,** Oh,US
57/G4 **Garforth,** Eng,UK
72/D4 **Gargan** (mtn.), Fr.
53/T10 **Garges-lès-Gonesse,** Fr.
57/F4 **Gargrave,** Eng,UK
106/C3 **Garhākotā,** India
108/A2 **Garh Mahārāja,** Pak.
141/B4 **Garibaldi,** Braz.
54/D2 **Garioch** (dist.), Sc,UK
130/C3 **Garissa,** Kenya
162/D3 **Garland,** Tx,US
78/B2 **Garlasco,** It.
56/D2 **Garlieston,** Sc,UK
77/H3 **Garmisch-Partenkirchen,** Ger.
54/C1 **Garmouth,** Sc,UK
168/A1 **Garnet** (hill), Ma,US
131/C2 **Garneton,** Zam.
159/J3 **Garnett,** Ks,US
119/B2 **Garnpung** (lake), Austl.
63/S6 **Garnsviken** (lake), Swe.
72/D4 **Garonne** (riv.), Fr.
141/B4 **Garopaba,** Braz.
129/E2 **Garou** (lake), Mali
124/H6 **Garoua,** Camr.
124/H6 **Garoua Boulaï,** Camr.
75/K7 **Garraf** (range), Sp.
56/D6 **Garreg,** Wal,UK
67/F3 **Garrel,** Ger.
157/H4 **Garrison,** ND,US
157/H4 **Garrison** (dam), ND,US
56/C1 **Garron** (pt.), NI,UK
153/H2 **Garry** (bay), NW,Can
152/F2 **Garry** (lake), NW,Can
54/A2 **Garry** (riv.), Sc,UK
54/B3 **Garry** (riv.), Sc,UK
54/B2 **Garry, Loch** (lake), Sc,UK
130/D3 **Garsen,** Kenya
57/F4 **Garstang,** Eng,UK
71/H6 **Garsten,** Aus.
67/H6 **Garte** (riv.), Ger.
72/D3 **Gartempe** (riv.), Fr.
58/C2 **Garth,** Wal,UK
54/B4 **Gartmore,** Sc,UK
70/B5 **Gärtringen,** Ger.
110/C5 **Garut,** Indo.
56/B2 **Garvagh,** NI,UK
65/L3 **Garwolin,** Pol.
165/R16 **Gary,** In,US
104/D2 **Garzê,** China
138/C4 **Garzón,** Col.
102/F4 **Gas** (lake), China
61/P6 **Gæsafjöll** (peak), Ice.
112/C2 **Gasan,** Phil.
160/C3 **Gas City,** In,US
159/J3 **Gasconade** (riv.), Mo,US
72/C5 **Gascony** (reg.), Fr.
116/C3 **Gascoyne** (peak), Austl.
116/C3 **Gascoyne** (riv.), Austl.
141/B3 **Gaspar,** Braz.
110/C4 **Gaspar** (riv.), Indo.
161/H1 **Gaspé,** Qu,Can
161/H1 **Gaspé** (pen.), Qu,Can
161/H1 **Gaspé, Cap de** (cape), Qu,Can
161/S9 **Gasport,** NY,US
100/B4 **Gas-san** (mtn.), Japan
78/A2 **Gassino Torinese,** It.
163/J2 **Gaston** (lake), NC, Va,US
163/H3 **Gastonia,** NC,US
91/C2 **Gata** (cape), Cyp.
74/B2 **Gata** (range), Sp.
74/D4 **Gata, Cabo de** (cape), Sp.
63/P2 **Gatchina,** Rus.
56/D2 **Gatehouse-of-Fleet,** Sc,UK
152/F1 **Gateshead** (isl.), NW,Can
57/G2 **Gateshead,** Eng,UK
151/H2 **Gates of the Arctic Nat'l Pk. & Prsv.,** Ak,US
162/D4 **Gatesville,** Tx,US
167/E3 **Gateway Nat'l Rec. Area,** NJ, NY,US
131/C4 **Gaths Mine,** Zim.
72/C3 **Gâtine** (hills), Fr.
160/F2 **Gatineau,** Qu,Can
160/F2 **Gatineau** (riv.), Qu,Can
78/B1 **Gattianara,** It.
149/G4 **Gatun** (dam), Pan.
149/G4 **Gatún** (lake), Pan.
69/H4 **Gau-Bickelheim,** Ger.
107/F2 **Gauhāti,** India
63/L3 **Gauja** (riv.), Lat.
57/G2 **Gaunless** (riv.), Eng,UK
54/B3 **Gaur** (riv.), Sc,UK
106/E2 **Gauripur,** India
106/E2 **Gauri Sankar** (mtn.), Nepal
62/C2 **Gausta** (peak), Nor.
71/E6 **Gauting,** Ger.
63/L3 **Gauya Nat'l Park,** Lat.
75/G2 **Gavà,** Sp.
81/J5 **Gávdhos** (isl.), Gre.
74/E1 **Gave de Pau** (riv.), Fr.
68/C2 **Gavere,** Belg.
78/B1 **Gavirate,** It.
62/G1 **Gävle,** Swe.
62/G1 **Gävleborg** (co.), Swe.
117/H5 **Gawler,** Austl.
117/G5 **Gawler** (ranges), Austl.
96/D3 **Gaxun** (lake), China
87/L2 **Gay,** Rus.
160/D4 **Gay** (peak), WV,US
97/K3 **Gaya** (riv.), China
106/E3 **Gayā,** India
129/F4 **Gaya,** Niger
130/A3 **Gayaza,** Ugan.
168/D3 **Gay Head** (pt.), Ma,US
160/C2 **Gaylord,** Mi,US
86/D2 **Gaysin,** Ukr.
131/D4 **Gaza** (prov.), Moz.
91/D4 **Gaza** (Ghazzah), Gaza
91/C4 **Gaza Strip**
91/E1 **Gaziantep,** Turk.
91/E1 **Gaziantep** (prov.), Turk.
97/H1 **Gazimur** (riv.), Rus.
91/C1 **Gazipaşa,** Turk.
76/D1 **Gazon de Faing** (peak), Fr.
125/K7 **Gbadolite,** Zaire
128/C5 **Gbarnga,** Libr.
65/K1 **Gdańsk,** Pol.
65/K1 **Gdańsk** (prov.), Pol.
65/K1 **Gdańsk** (gulf), Pol., Rus.
65/K1 **Gdynia,** Pol.
103/D5 **Ge** (lake), China
54/A3 **Geal Charn** (mtn.), Sc,UK
54/C2 **Geal Charn** (mtn.), Sc,UK
168/F5 **Geauga** (co.), Oh,US
70/D1 **Gebaberg** (peak), Ger.
111/G3 **Gebe** (isl.), Indo.
127/D4 **Gebeit Mine,** Sudan
83/J5 **Gebze,** Turk.
110/C5 **Gede** (peak), Indo.
130/D3 **Gede,** Kenya
91/F8 **Gedera,** Isr.
70/C2 **Gedern,** Ger.
130/D3 **Gedi Ruins Nat'l Mon.,** Kenya
92/B2 **Gediz,** Turk.
92/A2 **Gediz** (riv.), Turk.
62/D4 **Gedser** (cape), Den.
69/E1 **Geel,** Belg.
119/C3 **Geelong,** Austl.
116/B4 **Geelvink** (chan.), Austl.
67/E3 **Geeste,** Ger.
67/F2 **Geeste** (riv.), Ger.
67/H2 **Geesthacht,** Ger.
102/D5 **Gê'gyai,** China
67/G4 **Gehrden,** Ger.
58/C2 **Geifas** (mtn.), Wal,UK
77/G3 **Geige, Hohe** (peak), Aus.
152/F3 **Geikie** (riv.), Sk,Can
69/F2 **Geilenkirchen,** Ger.
99/M10 **Geinō,** Japan
71/E5 **Geisenfeld,** Ger.
70/A3 **Geisenheim,** Ger.
70/B6 **Geislingen,** Ger.
70/C5 **Geislingen an der Steige,** Ger.
130/B3 **Geita,** Tanz.
104/D4 **Gejiu,** China
125/L6 **Gel** (riv.), Sudan
80/D4 **Gela,** It.
80/D4 **Gela** (gulf), It.
125/Q6 **Geladī,** Eth.
130/C3 **Gelai** (peak), Tanz.
77/E5 **Gelato** (mtn.), It.
66/C4 **Gelderland** (prov.), Neth.
66/C5 **Geldermalsen,** Neth.
66/D5 **Geldern,** Ger.
66/C6 **Geldrop,** Neth.
69/E2 **Geleen,** Neth.
92/B2 **Gelendost,** Turk.
86/F3 **Gelendzhik,** Rus.
83/H5 **Gelibolu** (Gallipoli), Turk.
86/C4 **Gelibolu Yarımadas Nat'l Park,** Turk.
93/E2 **Gelincik** (peak), Turk.
58/C3 **Gelligaer,** Wal,UK
70/C2 **Gelnhausen,** Ger.
66/E5 **Gelsenkirchen,** Ger.
69/D2 **Gembloux,** Belg.
125/J7 **Gemena,** Zaire
66/C5 **Gemert,** Neth.
83/J5 **Gemlik,** Turk.
83/J5 **Gemlik** (gulf), Turk.
73/K3 **Gemona del Friuli,** It.
132/C2 **Gemsbok-Kalahari Nat'l Park,** SAfr.
132/C2 **Gemsbok Nat'l Park,** Bots.
151/G3 **Gemuk** (mtn.), Ak,US
70/C2 **Gemünden am Main,** Ger.
97/J1 **Gen** (riv.), China
125/N6 **Genalē Wenz** (riv.), Eth.
68/D2 **Genappe,** Belg.
80/A3 **Genargentu** (mts.), It.
92/E2 **Genç,** Turk.
66/D5 **Gendringen,** Neth.
66/C5 **Gendt,** Neth.
66/D3 **Genemuiden,** Neth.
142/D3 **General Acha,** Arg.
142/D2 **General Alvear,** Arg.
142/F2 **General Belgrano,** Arg.
142/E2 **General Cabrera,** Arg.
142/B5 **General Carrera** (lake), Chile
167/K8 **General Grant Nat'l Mem.,** NY,US
147/F5 **General Juan Álvarez,** Mex.
148/B2 **General Juan Álvarez Nat'l Park,** Mex.
143/F3 **General Juan Madariaga,** Arg.
143/S12 **General Las Heras,** Arg.
135/C1 **General Martín Miguel de Güemes,** Arg.
142/E2 **General Pico,** Arg.
135/D2 **General Pinedo,** Arg.
142/D3 **General Roca,** Arg.
143/S12 **General San Martín,** Arg.
112/D4 **General Santos,** Phil.
83/J4 **General-Toshevo,** Bul.
112/E7 **General Trias,** Phil.
142/E2 **General Viamonte,** Arg.
142/E2 **General Villegas,** Arg.
77/F6 **Generoso, Monte** (peak), Swi.
165/E6 **Genesee** (co.), Mi,US
160/E3 **Genesee** (riv.), NY,US
157/L5 **Geneseo,** Il,US
160/E3 **Geneseo,** NY,US
163/G4 **Geneva,** Al,US
165/P16 **Geneva,** Il,US
159/H2 **Geneva,** Ne,US
160/E3 **Geneva,** NY,US
165/P14 **Geneva** (lake), Wi,US
76/C5 **Geneva** (Genève), Swi.
76/C5 **Geneva** (Léman) (lake), Fr., Swi.
76/C5 **Genève** (canton), Swi.
76/C5 **Genève** (Geneva), Swi.
105/E3 **Gengding** (mtn.), China
70/B6 **Gengenbach,** Ger.
104/C4 **Gengma Daizu Vazu Zizhixian,** China
86/E3 **Genichesk,** Ukr.
74/C4 **Genil** (riv.), Sp.
69/E2 **Genk,** Belg.
70/D6 **Gennach** (riv.), Ger.
66/C5 **Gennep,** Neth.
53/S10 **Gennevilliers,** Fr.
78/B4 **Genoa** (Genova), It.
78/B4 **Genova** (gulf), It.
78/C4 **Genova** (prov.), It.
78/B4 **Genova** (Genoa), It.
144/K6 **Genovesa** (isl.), Ecu.
68/C1 **Gent-Brugge** (can.), Belg.
110/C5 **Genteng** (cape), Indo.
68/C1 **Gent** (Ghent), Belg.
63/T9 **Gentofte,** Den.
116/B5 **Geographe** (bay), Austl.
116/B3 **Geographe** (chan.), Austl.
116/D2 **George** (lake), Austl.
119/D2 **George** (lake), Austl.
118/C3 **George** (pt.), Austl.
153/K3 **George** (riv.), Qu,Can
132/C4 **George,** SAfr.
130/A3 **George** (lake), Ugan.
163/H4 **George** (lake), Fl,US
88/E1 **George Land** (isl.), Rus.
118/G9 **Georges** (riv.), Austl.
161/Q8 **Georgetown,** On,Can
149/F2 **George Town,** Cay.
139/G3 **Georgetown** (cap.), Guy.
163/H4 **Georgetown,** Ga,US
160/C4 **Georgetown,** Ky,US
163/J3 **Georgetown,** SC,US
162/D4 **Georgetown,** Tx,US
113/L **George V** (coast), Ant.
113/V **George VI** (sound), Ant.
162/D4 **George West,** Tx,US
87/G4 **Georgia**
156/B3 **Georgia** (str.), Can., US
163/G3 **Georgia** (state), US
160/D2 **Georgian** (bay), On,Can
160/D2 **Georgian Bay Islands Nat'l Park,** On,Can
117/H2 **Georgina** (riv.), Austl.
83/H4 **Georgi Traykov,** Bul.
67/F4 **Georgsmarienhütte,** Ger.
64/G3 **Gera,** Ger.
68/C2 **Geraardsbergen,** Belg.
140/A3 **Geral** (mts.), Braz.
140/A4 **Geral de Goiás** (Espigão Mestre) (range), Braz.
115/R11 **Geraldine,** NZ
116/B4 **Geraldton,** Austl.
160/C1 **Geraldton,** On,Can
76/C1 **Gérardmer,** Fr.
72/F4 **Gerbier de Jonc** (mtn.), Fr.
67/H3 **Gerdau** (riv.), Ger.
151/H3 **Gerdine** (mtn.), Ak,US
83/L5 **Gerede,** Turk.
95/H2 **Gereshk,** Afg.
77/H2 **Geretsried,** Ger.
158/C2 **Gerlach,** Nv,US
65/L4 **Gerlachovský Štít** (peak), Slvk.
166/A5 **Germantown,** Md,US
163/F3 **Germantown,** Tn,US
64/E3 **Germany**
71/E6 **Germering,** Ger.
70/B4 **Germersheim,** Ger.
132/E2 **Germiston,** SAfr.
70/B5 **Gernsbach,** Ger.
69/F3 **Gerolstein,** Ger.
70/D3 **Gerolzhofen,** Ger.
75/G2 **Gerona** (Girona), Sp.
75/E1 **Ger, Pic du** (peak), Fr.
68/D3 **Gerpinnes,** Belg.
53/M7 **Gerrards Cross,** Eng,UK
72/D5 **Gers** (riv.), Fr.
69/G5 **Gersheim,** Ger.
70/B3 **Gerspenz** (riv.), Ger.
70/E5 **Gerstetten,** Ger.
70/D6 **Gersthofen,** Ger.
102/D5 **Gêrzê,** China
92/C1 **Gerze,** Turk.
66/E5 **Gescher,** Ger.
67/F5 **Geseke,** Ger.
125/P6 **Gestro Wenz** (riv.), Eth.
74/D2 **Getafe,** Sp.
103/B5 **Getai,** China
69/E2 **Gete** (riv.), Belg.
166/A4 **Gettysburg,** Pa,US
157/J4 **Gettysburg,** SD,US
166/A4 **Gettysburg Nat'l Mil. Park,** Pa,US
141/A3 **Getúlio Vargas,** Braz.
113/S **Getz Ice Shelf,** Ant.
69/E2 **Geul** (riv.), Belg., Neth.
110/A3 **Geureudong** (peak), Indo.
93/E2 **Gevaş,** Turk.
67/E6 **Gevelsberg,** Ger.
82/F5 **Gevgelija,** Macd.
125/P5 **Gewanē,** Eth.
70/C3 **Geyersberg** (peak), Ger.
133/H6 **Geyser** (reef), Madg.
83/K5 **Geyve,** Turk.
102/B4 **Gez** (riv.), China
124/G1 **Ghadāmis,** Libya
127/C3 **Ghadir, Bi'r** (well), Egypt
108/D2 **Ghaggar** (riv.), India
129/E4 **Ghana**
126/D5 **Ghanzi,** Bots.
131/A4 **Ghanzi** (dist.), Bots.
127/B5 **Gharb Binna,** Sudan
124/F1 **Ghardaïa,** Alg.
124/H1 **Gharyān,** Libya
124/H3 **Ghāt,** Libya
124/J5 **Ghazal** (riv.), Chad
123/P13 **Ghazaouet,** Alg.
106/C2 **Ghaziābād,** India
95/J2 **Ghaznī,** Afg.
91/D4 **Ghazzah** (Gaza), Gaza
78/D2 **Ghedi,** It.
96/G2 **Ghengis Khan Wall** (ruins), Mong.
68/C1 **Ghent** (Gent), Belg.
83/H2 **Gheorghe Gheorghiu-Dej,** Rom.
83/G2 **Gheorgheni,** Rom.
83/F2 **Gherla,** Rom.
142/C5 **Ghio** (lake), Arg.
106/A2 **Ghotki,** Pak.
95/H2 **Ghūrīān,** Afg.
109/D4 **Gia Nghia,** Viet.
132/E3 **Giant's Castle** (peak), SAfr.
56/B1 **Giant's Causeway,** NI,UK
80/D4 **Giarre,** It.
109/E3 **Gia Vuc,** Viet.
156/E2 **Gibbons,** Ab,Can
76/D4 **Gibloux, Mont** (peak), Swi.
74/B4 **Gibraleón,** Sp.
74/B4 **Gibraltar** (str.), Afr., Eur.
161/R8 **Gibraltar** (pt.), On,Can
74/C4 **Gibraltar** (dpcy.), UK
55/M10 **Gibraltar** (pt.), UK
164/A1 **Gibraltar** (res.), Ca,US
165/F7 **Gibraltar,** Mi,US
119/E1 **Gibraltar Range Nat'l Park,** Austl.
116/E2 **Gibson** (des.), Austl.
116/E3 **Gibson Desert Nature Rsv.,** Austl.
108/C2 **Giddarbāha,** India
162/D4 **Giddings,** Tx,US
91/C4 **Gidi** (Mamarr al Jady) (pass), Egypt
125/N6 **Gidollē,** Eth.
72/E3 **Gien,** Fr.
70/D5 **Giengen an der Brenz,** Ger.
72/F4 **Gier** (riv.), Fr.
76/E4 **Giessbachfälle** (falls), Swi.
76/D1 **Giessen** (riv.), Fr.
70/B1 **Giessen,** Ger.
66/B5 **Giessendam,** Neth.
68/B6 **Gif,** Fr.
153/H1 **Gifford** (riv.), NW,Can
54/D5 **Gifford,** Sc,UK
163/H5 **Gifford,** Fl,US
76/C5 **Giffre** (riv.), Fr.
67/H4 **Gifhorn,** Ger.
53/S10 **Gif-sur-Yvette,** Fr.
99/E3 **Gifu,** Japan
99/E3 **Gifu** (pref.), Japan
146/C3 **Giganta, Sierra de la** (mts.), Mex.
148/E4 **Gigante** (pt.), Nic.
57/F3 **Giggleswick,** Eng,UK
80/B1 **Giglio** (isl.), It.
74/C1 **Gijón,** Sp.
130/A3 **Gikongoro,** Rwa.
158/D4 **Gila** (riv.), Az, NM,US
158/D4 **Gila Bend,** Az,US
158/E4 **Gila Cliff Dwellings Nat'l Mon.,** NM,US
93/G2 **Gīlān** (gov.), Iran
57/H4 **Gilberdyke Newport,** Eng,UK
118/A2 **Gilbert** (riv.), Austl.
120/G5 **Gilbert** (isls.), Kiri.
160/A2 **Gilbert,** Mn,US
140/A3 **Gilbués,** Braz.
70/E6 **Gilching,** Ger.
142/C2 **Gil de Vilches Nat'l Park,** Chile
58/C3 **Gilfach Goch,** Wal,UK
56/B3 **Gilford,** NI,UK
167/D4 **Gilford Park,** NJ,US
130/C3 **Gilgil,** Kenya
95/K1 **Gilgit** (riv.), Pak.
63/T8 **Gilleleje,** Den.
117/H5 **Gilles** (lake), Austl.
157/G4 **Gillette,** Wy,US
76/C3 **Gilley,** Fr.
156/B3 **Gillies Bay,** BC,Can
58/D4 **Gillingham,** Eng,UK
59/G4 **Gillingham,** Eng,UK
60/B1 **Gill, Lough** (lake), Ire.
162/E3 **Gilmer,** Tx,US
95/K1 **Gilqit** (riv.), Pak.
97/K1 **Gilyuy** (riv.), Rus.
66/B5 **Gilze,** Neth.
125/N6 **Gīmbī,** Eth.
150/F4 **Gimie** (mtn.), StL.
157/J3 **Gimli,** Mb,Can
75/F1 **Gimone** (riv.), Fr.
99/M9 **Ginan,** Japan
69/E2 **Gingelom,** Belg.
130/C1 **Gingero,** Eth.
112/D3 **Gingoog,** Phil.
80/E2 **Ginosa,** It.
100/J7 **Ginowan,** Japan
74/B1 **Ginzo de Limia,** Sp.
125/Q7 **Giohar,** Som.
80/D3 **Gioia** (gulf), It.
80/E2 **Gioia del Colle,** It.
80/D3 **Gioia Tauro,** It.
81/J3 **Gioūra** (isl.), Gre.
77/G4 **Gioveretto** (peak), It.
79/E5 **Giovi, Monte** (peak), It.
59/G2 **Gipping** (riv.), Eng,UK
168/G5 **Girard,** Oh,US
138/C3 **Girardot,** Col.
126/B4 **Giraul,** Ang.
122/D6 **Giraul de Cima,** Ang.
54/D2 **Girdle Head** (pt.), Sc,UK
55/K8 **Girdle Ness** (pt.), Sc,UK
92/D1 **Giresun,** Turk.
92/D1 **Giresun** (prov.), Turk.
106/E3 **Gīrīdīh,** India
80/E3 **Girifalco,** It.
53/N7 **Girling** (res.), Eng,UK
138/C3 **Girón,** Col.
138/B5 **Girón,** Ecu.
75/G2 **Girona** (Gerona), Sp.
72/C4 **Gironde** (riv.), Fr.
119/D1 **Girraween Nat'l Park,** Austl.
59/G2 **Girton,** Eng,UK
56/D1 **Girvan,** Sc,UK
56/D1 **Girvan, Water of** (riv.), Sc,UK
115/S10 **Gisborne,** NZ
130/A3 **Gisenyi,** Rwa.
62/E3 **Gislaved,** Swe.
68/A5 **Gisors,** Fr.
68/B1 **Gistel,** Belg.
130/A3 **Gitarama,** Rwa.
130/A3 **Gitega,** Buru.
84/B2 **Gittsfjället** (peak), Swe.
77/F5 **Giubiasco,** Swi.
80/C1 **Giulianova,** It.
83/G4 **Giurgiu,** Rom.
83/G3 **Giurgiu** (co.), Rom.
78/C1 **Giussano,** It.
91/F7 **Giv'atayim,** Isr.
69/D3 **Givet,** Fr.
72/F4 **Givors,** Fr.
76/C5 **Givrine, Col de la** (pass), Swi.
69/D6 **Givry-en-Argonne,** Fr.
131/C4 **Giyani,** SAfr.
125/N6 **Giyon,** Eth.
91/B5 **Giza, Pyramids of** (Ahrāmāt al Jīzah), Egypt
89/R3 **Gizhiga** (bay), Rus.
65/L1 **Giżycko,** Pol.
81/G2 **Gjirokastër,** Alb.
62/D1 **Gjøvik,** Nor.
81/F2 **Gjuhëzës, Kep i** (cape), Alb.
161/K2 **Glace Bay,** NS,Can
156/D3 **Glacier,** BC,Can
156/C3 **Glacier** (peak), Wa,US
151/L4 **Glacier Bay Nat'l Park & Prsv.,** Ak,US
156/D3 **Glacier Nat'l Park,** Can., US
66/D5 **Gladbeck,** Ger.
63/T9 **Gladsakse,** Den.
118/C3 **Gladstone,** Austl.
160/C3 **Gladwin,** Mi,US
62/D2 **Glafsfjorden** (lake), Swe.
57/H3 **Glaisdale,** Eng,UK
52/E2 **Glåma** (riv.), Nor.
54/D3 **Glamis,** Sc,UK
69/G4 **Glan** (riv.), Ger.
112/D4 **Glan,** Phil.
58/C3 **Glanamman,** Wal,UK
60/A5 **Glanaruddery** (mts.), Ire.
68/D4 **Gland** (riv.), Fr.
77/E3 **Glärnisch** (range), Swi.
77/F4 **Glarus** (canton), Swi.
77/E4 **Glarus Alps** (range), Swi.
58/C2 **Glasbury,** Wal,UK
54/B5 **Glasgow,** Sc,UK
160/C4 **Glasgow,** Ky,US
156/G3 **Glasgow,** Mt,US
56/D6 **Glaslyn** (riv.), Wal,UK
54/C3 **Glas Maol** (mtn.), Sc,UK
56/D3 **Glass** (riv.), IM,UK
54/B2 **Glass** (riv.), Sc,UK
162/D2 **Glass** (mts.), Ok,US
162/C4 **Glass** (mts.), Tx,US
166/C4 **Glassboro,** NJ,US
54/B1 **Glass, Loch** (lake), Sc,UK
166/B6 **Glassmanor-Oxon Hill,** Md,US
58/D4 **Glastonbury,** Eng,UK
168/B2 **Glastonbury,** Ct,US
70/B6 **Glatt** (riv.), Ger.
77/E2 **Glatt** (riv.), Swi.
85/M4 **Glazov,** Rus.
70/C5 **Glems** (riv.), Ger.
59/G2 **Glemsford,** Eng,UK
57/H6 **Glen** (riv.), Eng,UK
119/C3 **Glenaladale Nat'l Park,** Austl.
160/E4 **Glen Allen,** Va,US
56/C2 **Glenarm,** NI,UK
56/C2 **Glenarm** (riv.), NI,UK
56/B2 **Glenavy,** NI,UK
119/D2 **Glenbawn** (dam), Austl.
157/J3 **Glenboro,** Mb,Can
118/G8 **Glenbrook,** Austl.
166/B5 **Glen Burnie,** Md,US
158/E3 **Glen Canyon** (dam), Az,US
158/E3 **Glen Canyon Nat'l Rec. Area,** Az, Ut,US
56/E1 **Glencaple,** Sc,UK
131/C3 **Glenclova,** Zim.
133/E3 **Glencoe,** SAfr.
54/A3 **Glencoe,** Sc,UK
54/B3 **Glen Coe** (pass), Sc,UK
165/Q15 **Glencoe,** Il,US
167/E2 **Glen Cove,** NY,US
158/D4 **Glendale,** Az,US
164/B2 **Glendale,** Ca,US
156/C5 **Glendale,** Or,US
131/C3 **Glendale,** Zim.
165/P16 **Glendale Heights,** Il,US
157/G4 **Glendive,** Mt,US
159/F2 **Glendo** (res.), Wy,US
164/C2 **Glendora,** Ca,US
56/B1 **Glendun** (riv.), NI,UK
166/A6 **Glen Echo,** Md,US
117/M8 **Glenelg,** Austl.
119/B3 **Glenelg** (riv.), Austl.
55/J8 **Glenelg,** Sc.,UK
56/A2 **Glenelly** (riv.), NI,UK
116/C3 **Glengarry** (range), Austl.
56/D2 **Glenluce,** Sc,UK
167/D1 **Glenmere** (lake), NY,US
54/B2 **Glen Mòr** (val.), Sc,UK
166/C4 **Glenolden,** Pa,US
151/M4 **Glenora,** BC,Can
118/H8 **Glenorie,** Austl.
159/H4 **Glenpool,** Ok,US
167/J8 **Glen Ridge,** NJ,US
167/D2 **Glen Rock,** NJ,US
162/D3 **Glen Rose,** Tx,US
54/C4 **Glenrothes,** Sc,UK
160/F3 **Glens Falls,** NY,US
56/B2 **Glenshane** (pass), NI,UK
166/C3 **Glenside,** Pa,US
56/D1 **Glentrool,** Sc,UK
157/H4 **Glen Ullin,** ND,US
55/H9 **Glenveagh Nat'l Park,** Ire.
165/Q15 **Glenview,** Il,US
165/Q15 **Glenview Nav. Air Sta.,** Il,US
161/Q8 **Glen Williams,** On,Can
158/F3 **Glenwood Springs,** Co,US
54/A2 **Gleouraich** (mtn.), Sc,UK
81/L7 **Glifáhda,** Gre.
67/H1 **Glinde,** Ger.
61/D3 **Glittertinden** (peak), Nor.
65/K3 **Gliwice,** Pol.
158/E4 **Globe,** Az,US
77/G4 **Glockturm** (peak), Aus.
65/H5 **Gloggnitz,** Aus.
65/J3 **Głogów,** Pol.
65/J3 **Głogówek,** Pol.
70/E6 **Glonn** (riv.), Ger.
149/G1 **Gloria** (bay), Cuba
133/H5 **Glorieuses, Iles** (isls.), Reun.
118/E6 **Glorious** (mtn.), Austl.
151/D3 **Glory of Russia** (cape), Ak,US
57/G5 **Glossop,** Eng,UK
63/T9 **Glostrup,** Den.
160/F2 **Gloucester,** On,Can
58/D3 **Gloucester,** Eng,UK
166/C4 **Gloucester** (co.), NJ,US
166/C4 **Gloucester City,** NJ,US
58/D3 **Gloucestershire** (co.), Eng,UK
58/D3 **Gloucester, Vale of** (val.), Eng,UK
148/E2 **Glovers** (reef), Belz.
161/L1 **Glovertown,** Nf,Can
65/K3 **Głowno,** Pol.
65/J3 **Głubczyce,** Pol.
65/J3 **Głuchołazy,** Pol.
64/E1 **Glücksburg,** Ger.
67/G1 **Glückstadt,** Ger.
86/E2 **Glukhov,** Ukr.
63/T9 **Glumslöv,** Swe.
60/D2 **Glyde** (riv.), Ire.
58/C3 **Glyncorrwg,** Wal,UK
56/C2 **Glynn,** NI,UK
58/C3 **Glyn Neath,** Wal,UK
65/H4 **Gmünd,** Aus.
129/E3 **Gnagna** (prov.), Burk.
67/G2 **Gnarrenburg,** Ger.
63/H5 **Gniew,** Pol.
65/J2 **Gniezno,** Pol.
82/E4 **Gnjilane,** Yugo.
58/D1 **Gnosall,** Eng,UK
98/C3 **Gō** (riv.), Japan
106/B4 **Goa** (state), India
106/F2 **Goālpāra,** India
54/A5 **Goat Fell** (mtn.), Sc,UK
57/H3 **Goathland,** Eng,UK
125/N6 **Goba,** Eth.
131/D5 **Goba,** Moz.
126/C5 **Gobabeb,** Namb.
126/C5 **Gobabis,** Namb.
96/E3 **Gobi** (des.), China, Mong.
71/G6 **Göblberg** (peak), Aus.
98/D4 **Gobō,** Japan
57/E6 **Gobowen,** Eng,UK
66/D5 **Goch,** Ger.
70/D2 **Gochsheim,** Ger.
109/D4 **Go Cong,** Viet.
59/F4 **Godalming,** Eng,UK
109/D4 **Go Dau Ha,** Viet.
106/D4 **Godāvari** (riv.), India
125/P6 **Godē,** Eth.
82/F3 **Godeanu** (peak), Rom.
160/D3 **Goderich,** On,Can
106/B3 **Godhra,** India
59/F2 **Godmanchester,** Eng,UK
111/F4 **Godo** (mtn.), Indo.
99/M9 **Gōdo,** Japan
82/D2 **Gödöllő,** Hun.
58/A6 **Godolphin Cross,** Eng,UK
142/C2 **Godoy Cruz,** Arg.
157/K2 **Gods** (lake), Mb,Can
157/K2 **Gods** (riv.), Mb,Can
153/H2 **Gods Mercy** (bay), NW,Can
53/N8 **Godstone,** Eng,UK
145/M3 **Godthåb** (Nuuk), Grld.
102/C4 **Godwin Austen** (K2) (peak), China, Pak.
160/E1 **Goéland** (lake), Qu,Can
66/A5 **Goerce,** Neth.
66/A6 **Goes,** Neth.
160/B2 **Gogebic** (range), Mi,US
63/M1 **Gogland** (isl.), Rus.
106/D2 **Gogra** (riv.), India
67/G3 **Gohbach** (riv.), Ger.
140/D2 **Goiana,** Braz.
141/B1 **Goiandira,** Braz.
137/J7 **Goiânia,** Braz.
140/D2 **Goianinha,** Braz.
137/H7 **Goiás,** Braz.
140/A4 **Goiás** (state), Braz.
141/B1 **Goiás** (state), Braz.
141/B1 **Goiatuba,** Braz.
54/B4 **Goil, Loch** (inlet), Sc,UK
66/C5 **Goirle,** Neth.
98/D3 **Gojō,** Japan
100/B4 **Gojōme,** Japan
108/B2 **Gojra,** Pak.
86/E4 **Gok** (riv.), Turk.
98/B4 **Gokase** (riv.), Japan
99/M9 **Gokashō,** Japan
83/G5 **Gökçeada** (isl.), Turk.
91/C1 **Göksu** (riv.), Turk.
92/D2 **Göksun,** Turk.
131/C3 **Gokwe,** Zim.

190

Golan – Gross

91/D3 **Golan Heights** (reg.), Syria
92/C2 **Gölbaşı**, Turk.
92/D2 **Gölbaşı**, Turk.
76/C1 **Golbey**, Fr.
57/F5 **Golborne**, Eng,UK
83/J5 **Gölcük**, Turk.
165/B2 **Gold** (mtn.), Wa,US
77/F3 **Goldach**, Swi.
65/M1 **Gołdap**, Pol.
70/C3 **Goldbach**, Ger.
156/B5 **Gold Beach**, Or,US
118/D4 **Gold Coast**, Austl.
129/E5 **Gold Coast** (reg.), Gha.
156/D3 **Golden**, BC,Can
60/B5 **Golden**, Ire.
159/F3 **Golden**, Co,US
156/C4 **Goldendale**, Wa,US
64/F3 **Goldene Aue** (reg.), Ger.
165/J11 **Golden Gate** (chan.), Ca,US
132/E3 **Golden Gate Highlands Nat'l Park**, SAfr.
165/J11 **Golden Gate Nat'l Rec. Area**, Ca,US
156/B3 **Golden Hinde** (peak), BC,Can
67/F3 **Goldenstedt**, Ger.
108/C2 **Golden Temple**, India
60/B4 **Golden Vale** (plain), Ire.
131/C3 **Golden Valley**, Zim.
158/C3 **Goldfield**, Nv,US
156/B2 **Gold River**, BC,Can
163/J3 **Goldsboro**, NC,US
162/D4 **Goldthwaite**, Tx,US
92/E1 **Göle**, Turk.
65/H2 **Goleniów**, Pol.
149/F4 **Golfito Nat'l Wild. Ref.**, CR
91/A1 **Gölhisar**, Turk.
162/D4 **Goliad**, Tx,US
92/D1 **Gölköy**, Turk.
70/D3 **Gollach** (riv.), Ger.
92/A2 **Gölmarmara**, Turk.
96/C4 **Golmud**, China
131/D2 **Golomoti Station**, Malw.
100/D2 **Golovnina Gora** (mtn.), Rus.
100/D2 **Golovnino**, Rus.
93/G3 **Golpāyegān**, Iran
83/K5 **Gölpazarı**, Turk.
65/K2 **Golub-Dobrzyń**, Pol.
83/H4 **Golyama Kamchiya** (riv.), Bul.
83/G5 **Golyama Syutkya** (peak), Bul.
83/G5 **Golyam Perelik** (peak), Bul.
130/A3 **Goma**, Zaire
112/B4 **Gomantong Caves**, Malay.
70/C6 **Gomaringen**, Ger.
130/A2 **Gombari**, Zaire
130/A4 **Gombe** (riv.), Tanz.
130/A4 **Gombe Nat'l Park**, Tanz.
86/D1 **Gomel'**, Bela.
86/C2 **Gomel' Obl.**, Bela.
53/S10 **Gometz-le-Châtel**, Fr.
146/E3 **Gómez Palacio**, Mex.
64/F2 **Gommern**, Ger.
77/F3 **Goms**, Swi.
76/E5 **Goms** (val.), Swi.
59/F4 **Gomshall**, Eng,UK
93/J3 **Gonābād**, Iran
149/H2 **Gonaïves**, Haiti
131/C4 **Gonarezhou Nat'l Park**, Zim.
149/H2 **Gonâve** (gulf), Haiti
149/H2 **Gonâve** (isl.), Haiti
93/H2 **Gonbad-e Qābūs**, Iran
140/A2 **Gonçalves Dias**, Braz.
106/D2 **Gondā**, India
106/B3 **Gondal**, India
125/N5 **Gonder**, Eth.
106/D3 **Gondia**, India
74/A2 **Gondomar**, Port.
74/A1 **Gondomar**, Sp.
83/H5 **Gönen**, Turk.
53/T10 **Gonesse**, Fr.
105/F3 **Gong'an**, China
107/F2 **Gongbo'gyamda**, China
104/D2 **Gongga** (peak), China
106/F2 **Gonggar**, China
96/E4 **Gonghe**, China
102/D3 **Gongliu**, China
129/H4 **Gongola** (riv.), Nga.
129/H4 **Gongola** (state), Nga.
119/C1 **Gongolgon**, Austl.
107/G2 **Gongshan Drungzu Nuzu Zizhixian**, China
104/D3 **Gongwang** (mts.), China
103/C4 **Gong Xian**, China
103/F2 **Gongzhuling**, China
130/C4 **Gonja**, Tanz.
104/C2 **Gonjo**, China
100/B3 **Gonohe**, Japan
82/C2 **Gönyű**, Hun.
112/C1 **Gonzaga**, Phil.
162/D4 **Gonzales**, Tx,US
147/F4 **González**, Mex.
113/J **Goodenough** (cape), Ant.
162/C4 **Goodfellow A.F.B.**, Tx,US
131/B5 **Goodhope**, Bots.
132/B4 **Good Hope, Cape of** (cape), SAfr.
156/E5 **Gooding**, Id,US
159/G3 **Goodland**, Ks,US
118/E7 **Goodna**, Austl.
58/B3 **Goodwick**, Wal,UK
132/B4 **Goodwood**, SAfr.
66/C4 **Gooimeer** (lake), Neth.
57/H4 **Goole**, Eng,UK
116/D4 **Goongarrie Nat'l Park**, Austl.
66/D4 **Goor**, Neth.
157/H2 **Goose** (lake), Mb,Can
154/B3 **Goose** (lake), Ca, Or,US
166/C5 **Goose** (pt.), De,US
153/K3 **Goose Bay-Happy Valley**, Nf,Can
57/F5 **Goostrey**, Eng,UK
108/F3 **Gopichettipālaiyam**, India
70/C5 **Göppingen**, Ger.
109/D4 **Go Quao**, Viet.
65/J3 **Góra**, Pol.
65/L3 **Góra Kalwaria**, Pol.
106/D2 **Gorakhpur**, India
82/D4 **Goražde**, Bosn.
149/F1 **Gorda** (pt.), Cuba
149/F3 **Gorda** (pt.), Nic.
149/F4 **Gorda** (pt.), Nic.
158/A2 **Gorda** (pt.), Ca,US
92/B2 **Gördes**, Turk.
119/C4 **Gordon** (lake), Austl.
54/D5 **Gordon**, Sc,UK
124/J6 **Goré**, Chad
125/N6 **Gorē**, Eth.
115/Q12 **Gore**, NZ
59/G1 **Gore** (pt.), Eng,UK
151/H4 **Gore** (pt.), Ak,US
54/C5 **Gorebridge**, Sc,UK
92/D1 **Görele**, Turk.
72/B2 **Gorey**, Chl,UK
93/H2 **Gorgān**, Iran
93/H2 **Gorgān** (riv.), Iran
69/F4 **Gorge du Loup**, Lux.
128/B3 **Gorgol** (reg.), Mrta.
128/B2 **Gorgol** (riv.), Mrta.
78/C6 **Gorgona** (isl.), It.
78/C1 **Gorgonzola**, It.
87/H4 **Gori**, Geo.
66/B5 **Gorinchem**, Neth.
59/E3 **Goring**, Eng,UK
59/F5 **Goring by Sea**, Eng,UK
79/G1 **Gorizia**, It.
79/G1 **Gorizia** (prov.), It.
83/F3 **Gorj** (co.), Rom.
86/D1 **Gorki**, Bela.
84/J4 **Gor'kiy** (res.), Rus.
85/K4 **Gor'kiy** (Nizhniy Novgorod), Rus.
65/L4 **Gorlice**, Pol.
65/H3 **Görlitz**, Ger.
58/C2 **Gorllwyn** (mtn.), Wal,UK
86/F2 **Gorlovka**, Ukr.
60/D2 **Gormanston**, Ire.
161/R8 **Gormley**, On,Can
83/G4 **Gorna Oryakhovitsa**, Bul.
76/D6 **Gorner** (glac.), It., Swi.
82/E3 **Gornji Milanovac**, Yugo.
82/C4 **Gornji Vakuf**, Bosn.
88/J4 **Gorno-Altay Aut. Obl.**, Rus.
102/E1 **Gorno-Altaysk**, Rus.
88/H6 **Gorno-Badakhstan Aut. Obl.**, Taj.
85/J4 **Gorodets**, Rus.
120/D5 **Goroka**, PNG
131/C3 **Goromonzi**, Zim.
111/H4 **Gorong** (isl.), Indo.
131/D3 **Gorongosa, Serra da** (peak), Moz.
131/D3 **Gorongoza**, Moz.
131/D3 **Gorongoza Nat'l Park**, Moz.
111/F3 **Gorontalo**, Indo.
79/F3 **Goro, Po di** (riv.), It.
58/B3 **Gorseinon**, Wal,UK
66/D4 **Gorssel**, Neth.
56/A2 **Gortin**, NI,UK
86/C2 **Goryn'** (riv.), Bela., Ukr.
65/H2 **Gorzów** (prov.), Pol.
65/H2 **Gorzów Wielkopolski**, Pol.
98/D3 **Gōse**, Japan
99/F2 **Gosen**, Japan
57/G2 **Gosforth**, Eng,UK
100/B3 **Goshogawara**, Japan
67/H5 **Goslar**, Ger.
82/B3 **Gospić**, Cro.
59/E5 **Gosport**, Eng,UK
77/F3 **Gossau**, Swi.
77/H4 **Gossenass** (Colle Isarco), It.
82/E5 **Gostivar**, Macd.
65/J3 **Gostyń**, Pol.
65/K2 **Gostynin**, Pol.
62/G2 **Göta** (can.), Swe.
62/E3 **Götaland** (reg.), Swe.
62/D3 **Göteborg**, Swe.
62/D2 **Göteborg och Bohus** (co.), Swe.
124/H6 **Gotel** (mts.), Camr., Nga.
99/F3 **Gotemba**, Japan
67/H7 **Gotha**, Ger.
159/G2 **Gothenburg**, Ne,US
62/G3 **Gotland** (co.), Swe.
62/G3 **Gotland** (isl.), Swe.
98/A4 **Gotō** (isls.), Japan
83/F5 **Gotse Delchev**, Bul.
63/H2 **Gotska Sandön** (isl.), Swe.
63/H2 **Gotska Sandön Nat'l Park**, Swe.
98/C3 **Gōtsu**, Japan
67/G5 **Göttingen**, Ger.
77/E2 **Gottmadingen**, Ger.
66/B4 **Gouda**, Neth.
50/J8 **Gough** (isl.), StH.
160/F1 **Gouin** (res.), Qu,Can
160/C2 **Goulais** (riv.), On,Can
119/D2 **Goulburn**, Austl.
114/E2 **Goulburn** (isls.), Austl.
119/D2 **Goulburn** (riv.), Austl.
113/P **Gould** (coast), Ant.
116/C3 **Gould** (peak), Austl.
162/F3 **Gould**, Ar,US
105/F4 **Goulou** (mts.), China
104/E3 **Goulou** (peak), China
128/E2 **Goundam**, Mali
129/H3 **Gouré**, Niger
132/C4 **Gourits** (riv.), SAfr.
129/F3 **Gourma** (prov.), Burk.
129/F3 **Gourma** (reg.), Burk.
129/E2 **Gourma-Rharous**, Mali
68/A5 **Gournay-en-Bray**, Fr.
125/J4 **Gouro**, Chad
54/B5 **Gourock**, Sc,UK
53/T9 **Goussainville**, Fr.
141/D1 **Gouvêa**, Braz.
68/B5 **Gouvieux**, Fr.
86/C2 **Goverla** (peak), Ukr.
140/A2 **Governador Archer**, Braz.
140/C2 **Governador Dix-Sept Rosado**, Braz.
141/D1 **Governador Valadares**, Braz.
112/D4 **Governor Generoso**, Phil.
167/J9 **Governors** (isl.), NY,US
96/D3 **Govĭ Altayn** (mts.), Mong.
108/D2 **Govind Sāgar** (res.), India
95/H3 **Gowd-e-Zereh** (lake), Afg.
58/B3 **Gower** (pen.), Wal,UK
60/C2 **Gowna, Lough** (lake), Ire.
54/C4 **Gowrie, Carse of** (plain), Sc,UK
57/H4 **Goxhill**, Eng,UK
135/E2 **Goya**, Arg.
57/F5 **Goyt** (riv.), Eng,UK
99/M9 **Gozaisho-yama** (peak), Japan
102/D4 **Gozha** (lake), China
80/D4 **Gozo** (isl.), Malta
132/D4 **Graaff-Reinet**, SAfr.
66/D4 **Graafschap** (reg.), Neth.
132/B2 **Graberberg** (peak), Namb.
64/F2 **Grabow**, Ger.
140/A2 **Graça Aranha**, Braz.
82/B3 **Gračac**, Cro.
82/D3 **Gračanica**, Bosn.
163/G4 **Graceville**, Fl,US
149/F3 **Gracias a Dios** (cape), Nic.
75/S12 **Graciosa** (isl.), Azor.,Port.
82/D3 **Gradačac**, Bosn.
137/H5 **Gradaús**, Braz.
79/G1 **Gradisca d'Isonzo**, It.
79/G1 **Grado**, It.
74/B1 **Grado**, Sp.
71/E6 **Gräfelfing**, Ger.
71/E3 **Grafenwöhr**, Ger.
59/F2 **Grafham Water** (lake), Eng,UK
71/E6 **Grafing bei München**, Ger.
62/C1 **Gråfjell** (peak), Nor.
119/E1 **Grafton**, Austl.
118/B2 **Grafton** (passg.), Austl.
168/C1 **Grafton**, Ma,US
157/J3 **Grafton**, ND,US
160/D4 **Grafton**, WV,US
152/C3 **Graham** (isl.), BC,Can
153/S7 **Graham** (isl.), NW,Can
162/D3 **Graham**, Tx,US
165/C3 **Graham**, Wa,US
88/G1 **Graham Bell** (isl.), Rus.
164/F8 **Graham-Florence**, Ca,US
113/V **Graham Land** (reg.), Ant.
132/D4 **Grahamstown**, SAfr.
59/G4 **Grain**, Eng,UK
128/C5 **Grain Coast** (reg.), Libr.
140/A2 **Grajaú**, Braz.
137/J4 **Grajaú** (riv.), Braz.
65/M2 **Grajewo**, Pol.
72/D4 **Gramat** (plat.), Fr.
54/B3 **Grampian** (mts.), Sc,UK
54/D2 **Grampian** (reg.), Sc,UK
119/B3 **Grampians Nat'l Park**, Austl.
66/D3 **Gramsbergen**, Neth.
62/D1 **Gran**, Nor.
138/C4 **Granada**, Col.
148/E4 **Granada**, Nic.
74/D4 **Granada**, Sp.
143/K7 **Gran Altiplanicie Central** (plat.), Arg.
143/K7 **Gran Bajo de San Julián** (val.), Arg.
142/C5 **Gran Bajo Oriental** (val.), Arg.
162/D3 **Granbury**, Tx,US
159/F2 **Granby**, Co,US
168/B2 **Granby**, Ct,US
134/C5 **Gran Chaco** (plain), SAm.
144/B3 **Gran Chavin** (dept.), Peru
161/H2 **Grand** (lake), NB,Can
161/K1 **Grand** (lake), Nf,Can
161/Q9 **Grand** (riv.), On,Can
153/J3 **Grand** (riv.), Qu,Can
103/D4 **Grand** (can.), China
56/B5 **Grand** (can.), Ire.
130/C3 **Grand** (falls), Kenya
158/D3 **Grand** (canyon), Az,US
159/J3 **Grand** (riv.), Ia, Mo,US
159/J5 **Grand** (lake), La,US
160/C2 **Grand** (isl.), Mi,US
162/E2 **Grand** (riv.), Mo,US
161/S9 **Grand** (isl.), NY,US
168/G5 **Grand** (riv.), Oh,US
157/H4 **Grand** (riv.), SD,US
76/D2 **Grand Alsace** (can.), Fr.
150/B1 **Grand Bahama** (isl.), Bahm.
161/L2 **Grand Bank**, Nf,Can
128/C5 **Grand Bassa** (co.), Libr.
128/E5 **Grand-Bassam**, IvC.
161/H2 **Grand Bay**, NB,Can
165/E6 **Grand Blanc**, Mi,US
158/D3 **Grand Canyon Nat'l Park**, Az,US
128/C5 **Grand Cape Mount** (co.), Libr.
149/F2 **Grand Cayman** (isl.), Cay.
156/F2 **Grand Centre**, Ab,Can
76/C2 **Grand-Charmont**, Fr.
76/B6 **Grand Colombier** (mtn.), Fr.
76/D6 **Grand Combin** (peak), Swi.
156/D4 **Grand Coulee**, Wa,US
156/D4 **Grand Coulee** (dam), Wa,US
76/C2 **Grand Drumont** (mtn.), Fr.
143/K7 **Grande** (bay), Arg.
143/K8 **Grande** (riv.), Arg.
136/F7 **Grande** (riv.), Bol.
141/K8 **Grande** (isl.), Braz.
139/H5 **Grande** (lake), Braz.
139/F4 **Grande** (mts.), Braz.
141/J7 **Grande** (riv.), Braz.
147/Q9 **Grande** (riv.), Mex.
149/G4 **Grande** (pt.), Pan.
143/T11 **Grande** (stream), Uru.
156/D2 **Grande Cache**, Ab,Can
133/G5 **Grande Comore** (isl.), Com.
80/C1 **Grande, Corno** (peak), It.
137/H4 **Grande de Gurupá**, Braz.
139/F5 **Grande de Manacapurú** (lake), Braz.
149/E3 **Grande de Matagalpa** (riv.), Nic.
76/D5 **Grande Dixence, Barrage de la** (dam), Swi.
139/G5 **Grande do Curuaí** (lake), Braz.
80/C4 **Grande, Monte** (peak), It.
156/D2 **Grande Prairie**, Ab,Can
124/H4 **Grand 'Erg de Bilma** (des.), Niger
124/E1 **Grand Erg Occidental** (des.), Alg.
124/G1 **Grand Erg Oriental** (des.), Alg.
162/C4 **Grande, Rio** (riv.), Mex., US
150/C3 **Grande Rivière du Nord**, Haiti
76/D6 **Grandes Jorasses** (peak), It.
68/B1 **Grande-Synthe**, Fr.
150/F3 **Grande-Terre** (isl.), Guad.
161/H2 **Grand Falls**, NB,Can
161/L1 **Grand Falls**, Nf,Can
156/D3 **Grand Forks**, BC,Can
157/J4 **Grand Forks**, ND,US
68/B2 **Grand-Fort-Philippe**, Fr.
160/C3 **Grand Haven**, Mi,US
159/H2 **Grand Island**, Ne,US
163/F4 **Grand Isle**, La,US
128/D5 **Grand Jide** (co.), Libr.
158/E3 **Grand Junction**, Co,US
159/J3 **Grand Lake O'The Cherokees** (lake), Ok,US
161/H2 **Grand Manan** (isl.), NB,Can
157/L4 **Grand Marais**, Mn,US
68/C6 **Grand Marin** (riv.), Fr.
161/F2 **Grand-Mère**, Qu,Can
161/K2 **Grand Miquelon** (isl.), StP.
76/C5 **Grand Mont Ruan** (mtn.), Fr.
76/D5 **Grand Muveran** (peak), Swi.
74/A3 **Grândola**, Port.
157/L4 **Grand Portage Nat'l Mon.**, Mn,US
69/D5 **Grandpré**, Fr.
161/H2 **Grand Pré Nat'l Hist. Park**, NS,Can
157/J2 **Grand Rapids**, Mb,Can
160/C3 **Grand Rapids**, Mi,US
157/K4 **Grand Rapids**, Mn,US
72/F5 **Grand Rhône** (riv.), Fr.
76/C4 **Grand Taureau** (mtn.), Fr.
156/F5 **Grand Teton** (peak), Wy,US
156/F5 **Grand Teton Nat'l Park**, Wy,US
53/M6 **Grand Union** (can.), Eng,UK
157/H3 **Grandview**, Mb,Can
156/D4 **Grandview**, Wa,US
142/C2 **Graneros**, Chile
62/E1 **Granfjället** (peak), Swe.
117/M8 **Grange**, Austl.
60/B2 **Grange** (riv.), Ire.
57/F3 **Grange**, Eng,UK
76/C5 **Grange, Mont de** (mtn.), Fr.
54/C4 **Grangemouth**, Sc,UK
151/L3 **Granger** (mtn.), Yk,Can
156/D4 **Grangeville**, Id,US
156/B2 **Granisle**, BC,Can
156/F4 **Granite** (peak), Mt,US
160/B4 **Granite City**, Il,US
140/B1 **Granja**, Braz.
142/D5 **Gran Laguna Salada** (lake), Arg.
75/G2 **Granollers**, Sp.
78/A1 **Gran Paradiso Nat'l Park**, It.
149/H2 **Gran Piedra** (hill), Cuba
73/J3 **Gran Pilastro** (peak), It.
139/F3 **Gran Sabana, La** (plain), Ven.
75/Y16 **Gran Tarajal**, Canl.,Sp.
57/H6 **Grantham**, Eng,UK
54/C2 **Grantown-on-Spey**, Sc,UK
158/F4 **Grants**, NM,US
160/A2 **Grantsburg**, Wi,US
156/C5 **Grants Pass**, Or,US
144/B2 **Gran Vilaya** (ruins), Peru
157/H1 **Granville** (lake), Mb,Can
72/C2 **Granville**, Fr.
140/B5 **Grão Mogol**, Braz.
165/B3 **Grapeview-Allyn**, Wa,US
67/F2 **Grasberg**, Ger.
70/B3 **Grasellenbach**, Ger.
57/E3 **Grasmere**, Eng,UK
62/H1 **Grasø** (isl.), Swe.
165/P15 **Grass** (lake), Il,US
73/G5 **Grasse**, Fr.
161/Q9 **Grassie**, On,Can
57/G3 **Grassington**, Eng,UK
156/G3 **Grasslands Nat'l Park**, Sk,Can
63/T8 **Græsted**, Den.
82/B2 **Gratkorn**, Aus.
144/A2 **Grau** (dept.), Peru
77/F4 **Graubünden** (canton), Swi.
72/E5 **Graulhet**, Fr.
140/D3 **Gravatá**, Braz.
66/C5 **Grave**, Neth.
156/G3 **Gravelbourg**, Sk,Can
68/B2 **Gravelines**, Fr.
78/B1 **Gravellona Toce**, It.
131/C4 **Gravelotte**, SAfr.
160/E2 **Gravenhurst**, On,Can
53/Q7 **Gravesend**, Eng,UK
68/A5 **Gravigny**, Fr.
80/E2 **Gravina di Puglia**, It.
149/H2 **Gravois, Pointe à** (pt.), Haiti
76/B3 **Gray**, Fr.
160/C2 **Grayling**, Mi,US
53/P7 **Grays**, Eng,UK
156/F5 **Grays** (lake), Id,US
156/B4 **Grays** (har.), Wa,US
165/P15 **Grayslake**, Il,US
157/H3 **Grayson**, Sk,Can
73/L3 **Graz**, Aus.
119/C4 **Great** (lake), Austl.
157/G3 **Great** (plains), Can., US
60/B6 **Great** (isl.), Ire.
50/E3 **Great** (lakes), NAm.
158/C2 **Great** (basin), US
167/D4 **Great** (bay), NJ,US
167/J8 **Great** (falls), NJ,US
150/B1 **Great Abaco** (isl.), Bahm.
65/L5 **Great Alföld** (plain), Hun.
116/E5 **Great Australian** (bight), Austl.
150/B1 **Great Bahama** (bank), Bahm.
59/F2 **Great Barford**, Eng,UK
118/B1 **Great Barrier** (reef), Austl.
115/S10 **Great Barrier** (isl.), NZ
118/B2 **Great Barrier Reef Marine Park**, Austl.
59/G2 **Great Barton**, Eng,UK
158/D3 **Great Basin Nat'l Park**, Nv,US
152/D2 **Great Bear** (lake), NW,Can
159/H3 **Great Bend**, Ks,US
91/C4 **Great Bitter** (lake), Egypt
53/M8 **Great Bookham**, Eng,UK
132/C3 **Great Brak** (riv.), SAfr.
55/L9 **Great Britain** (isl.), UK
166/D5 **Great Cedar** (swamp), NJ,US
51/P5 **Great Coco** (isl.), Burma
59/G2 **Great Cornard**, Eng,UK
54/B5 **Great Cumbrae** (isl.), Sc,UK
156/F5 **Great Divide** (basin), Wy,US
115/H7 **Great Dividing** (range), Austl.
57/H4 **Great Driffield**, Eng,UK
59/G3 **Great Dunmow**, Eng,UK
166/D5 **Great Egg** (har.), NJ,US
166/D4 **Great Egg Harbor** (riv.), NJ,US
129/F5 **Greater Accra** (reg.), Gha.
87/L3 **Greater Barsuki** (des.), Kaz.
53/P7 **Greater London** (co.), Eng,UK
57/F5 **Greater Manchester** (co.), Eng,UK
110/C4 **Greater Sunda** (isls.), Indo.
150/C2 **Great Exuma** (isl.), Bahm.
156/F4 **Great Falls**, Mt,US
132/D4 **Great Fish** (pt.), SAfr.
132/D4 **Great Fish** (riv.), SAfr.
59/F2 **Great Gransden**, Eng,UK
150/B1 **Great Guana** (cay), Bahm.
57/G2 **Greatham**, Eng,UK
57/F4 **Great Harwood**, Eng,UK
106/D2 **Great Himalaya** (range), Asia
150/C2 **Great Inagua** (isl.), Bahm.
106/A2 **Great Indian** (des.), India, Pak.
132/C3 **Great Karoo** (reg.), SAfr.
132/D4 **Great Kei** (riv.), SAfr.
165/Q15 **Great Lakes Nav. Trng. Ctr.**, Il,US
58/D2 **Great Malvern**, Eng,UK
59/E3 **Great Milton**, Eng,UK
58/B5 **Great Mis Tor** (hill), Eng,UK
167/E2 **Great Neck**, NY,US
107/F6 **Great Nicobar** (isl.), India
59/G1 **Great Ouse** (riv.), Eng,UK
119/C4 **Great Oyster** (bay), Austl.
167/F2 **Great Peconic** (bay), NY,US
163/J3 **Great Pee Dee** (riv.), SC,US
167/H8 **Great Piece** (meadows), NJ,US
130/B4 **Great Rift** (val.), Afr.
130/B4 **Great Ruaha** (riv.), Tanz.
76/D6 **Great Saint Bernard** (pass), Swi., It.
150/B1 **Great Sale** (cay), Bahm.
158/D2 **Great Salt** (lake), Ut,US
158/D2 **Great Salt Lake** (des.), Ut,US
159/F3 **Great Sand Dunes Nat'l Mon.**, Co,US
127/A3 **Great Sand Sea** (des.), Egypt, Libya
116/D2 **Great Sandy** (des.), Austl.
158/B2 **Great Sandy** (des.), Or,US
118/D4 **Great Sandy Nat'l Park**, Austl.
128/B4 **Great Scarcies** (riv.), Gui., SLeo.
59/G2 **Great Shelford**, Eng,UK
57/F3 **Great Shunner Fell** (mtn.), Eng,UK
152/E2 **Great Slave** (lake), NW,Can
163/H3 **Great Smoky Mts. Nat'l Park**, NC, Tn,US
167/E2 **Great South** (bay), NY,US
59/G4 **Great Stour** (riv.), Eng,UK
166/D2 **Great Swamp Nat'l Wild. Ref.**, NJ,US
109/B3 **Great Tenasserim** (riv.), Burma
58/B5 **Great Torrington**, Eng,UK
117/F3 **Great Victoria** (des.), Austl.
117/E4 **Great Victoria Desert Nature Rsv.**, Austl.
103/B3 **Great Wall** (ruins), China
53/P7 **Great Warley**, Eng,UK
119/C4 **Great Western Tiers** (mts.), Austl.
132/B4 **Great Winterhoek** (peak), SAfr.
58/D2 **Great Witley**, Eng,UK
59/H1 **Great Yarmouth**, Eng,UK
93/E2 **Great Zab** (riv.), Iraq
131/C4 **Great Zimbabwe** (ruins), Zim.
129/H2 **Grébon** (peak), Niger
91/D2 **Greco** (cape), Cyp.
80/D2 **Greco** (peak), It.
71/E4 **Greding**, Ger.
74/C2 **Gredos** (range), Sp.
81/G3 **Greece**
159/F2 **Greeley**, Co,US
153/S6 **Greely** (fjord), NW,Can
119/D3 **Green** (cape), Austl.
160/C4 **Green** (riv.), Ky,US
157/M4 **Green** (bay), Mi, Wi,US
158/E3 **Green** (riv.), Ut, Wy,US
161/G3 **Green** (mts.), Vt,US
165/D3 **Green** (riv.), Wa,US
160/B2 **Green Bay**, Wi,US
166/B5 **Greenbelt**, Md,US
166/B6 **Greenbelt Park**, Md,US
160/C4 **Greencastle**, In,US
163/H4 **Green Cove Springs**, Fl,US
165/Q14 **Greendale**, Wi,US
163/H2 **Greeneville**, Tn,US
160/C4 **Greenfield**, In,US
161/F3 **Greenfield**, Ma,US
165/P14 **Greenfield**, Wi,US
161/P7 **Greenfield Park**, Qu,Can
166/B5 **Green Haven**, Md,US
56/C2 **Greenisland**, NI,UK
145/R2 **Greenland** (sea)
145/N2 **Greenland** (Kalaallit Nunaat) (dpcy.), Den.
166/C3 **Green Lane** (res.), Pa,US
54/D5 **Greenlaw**, Sc,UK
54/C6 **Green Lowther** (mtn.), Sc,UK
54/B5 **Greenock**, Sc,UK
60/D5 **Greenore** (pt.), Ire.
116/B4 **Greenough** (riv.), Austl.
151/K2 **Greenough** (mtn.), Ak,US
167/H8 **Green Pond** (lake), NJ,US
161/R8 **Green River**, On,Can
158/E3 **Green River**, Ut,US
156/F5 **Green River**, Wy,US
163/G3 **Greensboro**, Al,US
163/J2 **Greensboro**, NC,US
160/C4 **Greensburg**, In,US
160/E3 **Greensburg**, Pa,US
161/Q9 **Greensville**, On,Can
158/E5 **Green Valley**, Az,US
166/A5 **Green Valley**, Md,US
128/C5 **Greenville**, Libr.
163/G4 **Greenville**, Al,US
158/B2 **Greenville**, Ca,US
160/C4 **Greenville**, Ky,US
160/C3 **Greenville**, Mi,US
163/F3 **Greenville**, Ms,US
163/J3 **Greenville**, NC,US
160/C3 **Greenville**, Oh,US
168/G5 **Greenville**, Pa,US
168/C2 **Greenville**, RI,US
163/H3 **Greenville**, SC,US
162/D3 **Greenville**, Tx,US
165/D3 **Greenwater** (riv.), Wa,US
53/P7 **Greenwich** (bor.), Eng,UK
167/E1 **Greenwich**, Ct,US
167/L8 **Greenwich** (pt.), Ct,US
53/P7 **Greenwich Observatory**, Eng,UK
167/K9 **Greenwich Village**, NY,US
161/R8 **Greenwood**, On,Can
163/F3 **Greenwood**, Ms,US
167/D1 **Greenwood** (lake), NJ, NY,US
163/H3 **Greenwood**, SC,US
163/H3 **Greenwood** (lake), SC,US
159/J4 **Greers Ferry** (lake), Ar,US
60/D4 **Greese** (riv.), Ire.
66/D6 **Grefrath**, Ger.
144/D2 **Gregório** (riv.), Braz.
116/C3 **Gregory** (lake), Austl.
117/E2 **Gregory** (lake), Austl.
117/H4 **Gregory** (lake), Austl.
118/A2 **Gregory** (range), Austl.
157/J5 **Gregory**, SD,US
116/E2 **Gregory Lake Abor. Land**, Austl.
65/G1 **Greifswald**, Ger.
65/G1 **Greifswalder Bodden** (bay), Ger.
82/B2 **Greimberg** (peak), Aus.
64/G3 **Greiz**, Ger.
85/N4 **Gremyachinsk**, Rus.
62/D3 **Grenå**, Den.
150/F5 **Grenada**
163/F3 **Grenada**, Ms,US
76/D3 **Grenchen**, Swi.
157/H3 **Grenfell**, Sk,Can
72/F4 **Grenoble**, Fr.
114/G2 **Grenville** (cape), Austl.
76/D2 **Grenzach-Wyhlen**, Ger.
61/E2 **Gressåmoen Nat'l Park**, Nor.
57/E2 **Greta** (riv.), Eng,UK
57/F3 **Greta** (riv.), Eng,UK
157/J3 **Gretna**, Mb,Can
57/E2 **Gretna**, Sc,UK
163/F4 **Gretna**, La,US
59/F1 **Gretton**, Eng,UK
53/U10 **Gretz-Armainvilliers**, Fr.
63/T9 **Greve**, Den.
79/E5 **Greve** (riv.), It.
66/B5 **Grevelingendam** (dam), Neth.
67/E4 **Greven**, Ger.
81/G2 **Grevená**, Gre.
66/D6 **Grevenbroich**, Ger.
69/F4 **Grevenmacher** (dist.), Lux.
64/F2 **Grevesmühlen**, Ger.
66/A5 **Grevlingen** (chan.), Neth.
114/F2 **Grey** (cape), Austl.
118/A5 **Grey** (range), Austl.
161/K2 **Grey** (riv.), Nf,Can
56/C2 **Grey** (pt.), NI,UK
56/C2 **Grey Abbey**, NI,UK
156/F4 **Greybull**, Wy,US
151/L3 **Grey Hunter** (peak), Yk,Can
115/R11 **Greymouth**, NZ
118/B2 **Grey Peaks Nat'l Park**, Austl.
57/F2 **Greystoke**, Eng,UK
60/D3 **Greystones**, Ire.
133/E3 **Greytown**, SAfr.
69/D2 **Grez-Doiceau**, Belg.
58/B6 **Gribbin** (pt.), Eng,UK
77/E5 **Gridone** (Monte Limidario) (peak), It.
77/E3 **Griefensee** (lake), Swi.
66/C2 **Griend** (isl.), Neth.
70/B3 **Griesheim**, Ger.
77/H3 **Griesskogel** (peak), Aus.
163/G3 **Griffin**, Ga,US
119/C2 **Griffith**, Austl.
165/R16 **Griffith**, In,US
164/F7 **Griffith Park, Los Angeles**, Ca,US
78/C1 **Grigna** (peak), It.
68/B6 **Grigny**, Fr.
148/C2 **Grijalva** (riv.), Mex.
119/C4 **Grim** (cape), Austl.
68/D2 **Grimbergen**, Belg.
58/D2 **Grimley**, Eng,UK
64/G1 **Grimmen**, Ger.
161/Q9 **Grimsby**, On,Can
57/H4 **Grimsby**, Eng,UK
77/E4 **Grimselpass** (pass), Swi.
61/N6 **Grimsey** (isl.), Ice.
62/C2 **Grimstad**, Nor.
62/C4 **Grindsted**, Den.
153/S7 **Grinnel** (pen.), NW,Can
82/B2 **Grintavec** (peak), Slov.
132/E3 **Griqualand East** (reg.), SAfr.
132/C2 **Griqualand West** (reg.), SAfr.
68/A2 **Gris Nez** (cape), Fr.
53/U10 **Grisy-Suisnes**, Fr.
165/K10 **Grizzly** (bay), Ca,US
82/C3 **Grmeč** (mtn.), Bosn.
140/B1 **Groaíras**, Braz.
69/D1 **Grobbendonk**, Belg.
71/E6 **Gröbenzell**, Ger.
65/J3 **Grodków**, Pol.
63/K5 **Grodno**, Bela.
63/L5 **Grodno Obl.**, Bela.
65/J2 **Grodzisk Wielkopolski**, Pol.
66/D4 **Groenlo**, Neth.
162/D4 **Groesbeck**, Tx,US
66/C5 **Groesbeek**, Neth.
72/B3 **Groix** (isl.), Fr.
65/L3 **Grójec**, Pol.
64/F1 **Grömitz**, Ger.
66/E4 **Gronau**, Ger.
66/D2 **Groningen**, Neth.
66/D2 **Groningen** (prov.), Neth.
77/H5 **Gronlait** (peak), It.
132/C4 **Groot** (riv.), SAfr.
132/Q13 **Grootdraaidam** (res.), SAfr.
114/F2 **Groote Eylandt** (isl.), Austl.
66/D2 **Grootegast**, Neth.
126/C4 **Grootfontein**, Namb.
131/B4 **Grootgeluk**, SAfr.
131/C4 **Groot-Letabarivier** (riv.), SAfr.
132/D2 **Groot-Marico** (riv.), SAfr.
132/C3 **Grootvloer** (salt pan), SAfr.
150/F4 **Gros Islet**, StL.
161/K1 **Gros Morne** (peak), Nf,Can
161/K1 **Gros Morne Nat'l Park**, Nf,Can
72/F3 **Grosne** (riv.), Fr.
67/G6 **Grossalmerode**, Ger.
70/C5 **Grossbottwar**, Ger.
67/E3 **Grosse Aa** (riv.), Ger.
165/F7 **Grosse Ile**, Mi,US
165/F7 **Grosse Ile** (isl.), Mi,US
71/F5 **Grosse Laber** (riv.), Ger.
70/C6 **Grosse Lauter** (riv.), Ger.
71/G6 **Grosse Mühl** (riv.), Aus.
132/A2 **Grosse Münzenberg** (peak), Namb.
69/G2 **Grosse Nister** (riv.), Ger.
67/G3 **Grossenkneten**, Ger.
70/C1 **Grossenlüder**, Ger.
165/G7 **Grosse Pointe**, Mi,US
165/G7 **Grosse Pointe Farms**, Mi,US
165/G7 **Grosse Pointe Park**, Mi,US
165/G7 **Grosse Pointe Shores**, Mi,US
165/G7 **Grosse Pointe Woods**, Mi,US
76/D5 **Grosser Aletsch** (glac.), Swi.
71/G4 **Grosser Arber** (peak), Ger.
67/G3 **Grosser Aue** (riv.), Ger.
64/F3 **Grosser Beer-Berg** (peak), Ger.
73/L3 **Grosser Bösenstein** (peak), Aus.
77/G3 **Grosser Daumen** (peak), Ger.
70/B2 **Grosser Feldberg** (peak), Ger.
70/D2 **Grosser Gleichberg** (peak), Ger.
70/B6 **Grosser Heuberg** (mts.), Ger.

191
Gross – Harli

67/F1 **Grosser Knechtsand** (isl.), Ger.
71/H6 **Grosse Rodl** (riv.), Aus.
65/H4 **Grosser Peilstein** (peak), Aus.
73/L3 **Grosser Priel** (peak), Aus.
65/H5 **Grosser Pyhrgas** (peak), Aus.
71/G5 **Grosser Rachel** (peak), Ger.
67/E2 **Grosses Meer** (lake), Ger.
82/A2 **Grosses Wiesbachhorn** (peak), Aus.
80/B1 **Grosseto,** It.
70/B3 **Grossgerau,** Ger.
73/K3 **Grossglockner** (peak), Aus.
67/H1 **Grosshansdorf,** Ger.
73/H5 **Grosso** (cape), Fr.
140/C2 **Grossos,** Braz.
69/F5 **Grossrosseln,** Ger.
70/B3 **Gross Unstadt,** Ger.
70/B3 **Gross-Zimmern,** Ger.
69/E2 **Grote Gete** (riv.), Belg.
69/D1 **Grote Nete** (riv.), Belg.
168/B3 **Groton,** Ct,US
157/J4 **Groton,** SD,US
79/G1 **Grotta Gigante,** It.
80/E2 **Grottaglie,** It.
69/E3 **Grotte de Han,** Belg.
75/E1 **Grottes de Bétharram,** Fr.
123/L14 **Grou** (riv.), Mor.
156/D2 **Grouard Mission,** Ab,Can
160/D1 **Groundhog** (riv.), On,Can
66/C2 **Grouw,** Neth.
59/E3 **Grove,** Eng,UK
166/B5 **Grove** (pt.), Md,US
159/J3 **Grove,** Ok,US
168/G5 **Grove City,** Pa,US
158/B4 **Grover City,** Ca,US
162/E4 **Groves,** Tx,US
166/A6 **Groveton,** Va,US
87/H4 **Groznyy,** Rus.
83/H4 **Grudovo,** Bul.
65/K2 **Grudziądz,** Pol.
78/A2 **Grugliasco,** It.
130/B3 **Grumeti** (riv.), Tanz.
62/E2 **Grums,** Swe.
70/C2 **Gründau,** Ger.
57/E2 **Grune** (pt.), Eng,UK
70/B3 **Grünstadt,** Ger.
71/E6 **Grünwald,** Ger.
76/D4 **Gruyère** (lake), Swi.
86/F1 **Gryazi,** Rus.
65/H2 **Gryfice,** Pol.
65/H2 **Gryfino,** Pol.
105/H3 **Gu** (mtn.), China
142/B4 **Guabun** (pt.), Chile
149/G1 **Guacanayabo** (gulf), Cuba
138/E2 **Guacara,** Ven.
139/E2 **Guacharo Nat'l Park,** Ven.
141/D2 **Guaçuí,** Braz.
146/E4 **Guadalajara,** Mex.
74/D2 **Guadalajara,** Sp.
120/E6 **Guadalcanal** (isl.), Sol.
74/E4 **Guadalentín** (riv.), Sp.
74/D3 **Guadalimlar** (riv.), Sp.
75/N8 **Guadalix** (riv.), Sp.
75/E2 **Guadalope** (riv.), Sp.
74/D4 **Guadalquivir** (riv.), Sp.
140/B2 **Guadalupe,** Braz.
146/E4 **Guadalupe,** Mex.
147/Q9 **Guadalupe** (res.), Mex.
149/G4 **Guadalupe,** Pan.
144/B2 **Guadalupe,** Peru
144/C4 **Guadalupe,** Peru
74/C3 **Guadalupe** (range), Sp.
162/B3 **Guadalupe** (mts.), NM, Tx,US
162/B4 **Guadalupe** (peak), Tx,US
162/D4 **Guadalupe** (riv.), Tx,US
162/B4 **Guadalupe Mts. Nat'l Park,** Tx,US
146/D3 **Guadalupe Victoria,** Mex.
147/M7 **Guadalupe Victoria,** Mex.
75/M8 **Guadarrama** (pass), Sp.
74/C2 **Guadarrama** (range), Sp.
74/C3 **Guadarrama** (riv.), Sp.
150/F3 **Guadeloupe** (dept.), Fr.
150/F3 **Guadeloupe** (passg.), NAm.
150/F3 **Guadeloupe Nat'l Park,** Guad.
147/Q9 **Guadelupe, Basilica of,** Mex.
74/B4 **Guadiana** (riv.), Sp., Port.
74/D4 **Guadiana Menor** (riv.), Sp.
74/D4 **Guadix,** Sp.
142/B4 **Guafo** (chan.), Chile
142/B4 **Guafo** (isl.), Chile
138/B5 **Guagua Pichincha** (peak), Ecu.
141/B4 **Guaíba,** Braz.
141/B4 **Guaiba** (riv.), Braz.
149/G1 **Guaicanamar,** Cuba
149/G1 **Guáimaro,** Cuba
138/D4 **Guainía** (comm.), Col.
138/D4 **Guainía** (riv.), Col., Ven.
139/F3 **Guaiquinima** (peak), Ven.
141/B2 **Guaíra,** Braz.
142/B4 **Guaiteca** (isl.), Chile
136/E6 **Guajará-Mirim,** Braz.
138/D1 **Guajira** (pen.), Col., Ven.
138/B5 **Gualaceo,** Ecu.
158/B3 **Gualala,** Ca,US
148/D3 **Gualán,** Guat.
80/C1 **Gualdo Tadino,** It.
142/F2 **Gualeguay,** Arg.
142/F2 **Gualeguay** (riv.), Arg.
142/F2 **Gualeguaychú,** Arg.
142/D4 **Gualicho** (val.), Arg.
120/D3 **Guam** (isl.), PacUS
142/B5 **Guamblin** (isl.), Chile
144/B1 **Guamote,** Ecu.
146/D3 **Guamuchil,** Mex.
103/D3 **Gu'an,** China
103/H7 **Gu'an,** China
149/F1 **Guanabacoa,** Cuba
141/K7 **Guanabara** (bay), Braz.
149/E1 **Guanahacabibes** (gulf), Cuba
149/E1 **Guanahacabibes** (pen.), Cuba
148/E2 **Guanaja** (isl.), Hon.
149/F1 **Guanajay,** Cuba
147/E4 **Guanajuato,** Mex.
147/E4 **Guanajuato** (state), Mex.
139/F3 **Guanajuña,** Ven.
140/B4 **Guanambi,** Braz.
138/D2 **Guanare,** Ven.
138/D2 **Guanare** (riv.), Ven.
139/E3 **Guanay** (peak), Ven.
103/C3 **Guancen Shan** (mtn.), China
103/B3 **Guandi Shan** (mtn.), China
103/B5 **Guandu,** China
149/E1 **Guane,** Cuba
105/H3 **Guangchang,** China
103/D5 **Guangde,** China
105/G3 **Guangdong** (prov.), China
103/C3 **Guangling,** China
101/B3 **Guanglu** (isl.), China
104/D3 **Guangmao** (mtn.), China
103/D5 **Guangming Ding** (peak), China
104/E3 **Guangnan,** China
103/C3 **Guangping,** China
105/H3 **Guangping,** China
103/D3 **Guangrao,** China
103/C4 **Guangshan,** China
105/F4 **Guangxi Zhuangzu Zizhiqu** (aut. reg.), China
104/E1 **Guangyuan,** China
105/H3 **Guangze,** China
105/G4 **Guangzhou** (Canton), China
141/D1 **Guanhães,** Braz.
139/F2 **Guanipa** (riv.), Ven.
105/F2 **Guanmian** (mts.), China
103/D4 **Guannan,** China
149/H1 **Guantánamo,** Cuba
149/H2 **Guantánamo Bay U.S. Nav. Base,** Cuba
103/C3 **Guantao,** China
103/G6 **Guanting** (res.), China
138/B5 **Guanujo,** Ecu.
103/C3 **Guan Xian,** China
104/D2 **Guan Xian,** China
103/D4 **Guanyun,** China
138/B3 **Guapa,** Col.
141/B4 **Guaporé,** Braz.
136/F6 **Guaporé** (riv.), Braz.
140/A4 **Guara** (riv.), Braz.
75/E1 **Guara** (peak), Sp.
140/D2 **Guarabira,** Braz.
141/B2 **Guaraci,** Braz.
140/B2 **Guaraciaba do Norte,** Braz.
137/J5 **Guaraí,** Braz.
141/B3 **Guaramirim,** Braz.
138/B5 **Guaranda,** Ecu.
141/K6 **Guarani,** Braz.
141/D2 **Guarapari,** Braz.
141/B3 **Guarapuava,** Braz.
141/K6 **Guarará,** Braz.
141/B2 **Guararapes,** Braz.
141/G8 **Guararema,** Braz.
140/C5 **Guaratinga,** Braz.
141/H7 **Guaratinguetá,** Braz.
141/B3 **Guaratuba,** Braz.
74/B2 **Guarda,** Port.
74/B2 **Guarda** (dist.), Port.
77/H4 **Guardia Alta** (peak), It.
74/B3 **Guareña,** Sp.
149/H1 **Guarico** (pt.), Cuba
139/E2 **Guárico** (res.), Ven.
139/E2 **Guárico** (riv.), Ven.
139/E2 **Guárico** (state), Ven.
141/G9 **Guarujá,** Braz.
141/G8 **Guarulhos,** Braz.
146/C3 **Guasave,** Mex.
138/D3 **Guasdualito,** Ven.
78/D3 **Guastalla,** It.
148/D3 **Guatemala**
148/D3 **Guatemala** (cap.), Guat.
138/C3 **Guateque,** Col.
138/C4 **Guaviare** (comm.), Col.
138/D4 **Guaviare** (riv.), Col.
141/G6 **Guaxupé,** Braz.
138/C4 **Guayabero** (riv.), Col.
149/G1 **Guayabo** (cay), Cuba
147/F4 **Guayalejo** (riv.), Mex.
150/E3 **Guayama,** PR
148/E3 **Guayape** (riv.), Hon.
138/B5 **Guayaquil,** Ecu.
144/A1 **Guayaquil** (gulf), Ecu.
136/E6 **Guayaramerín,** Bol.
138/C4 **Guayas** (riv.), Col.
138/B5 **Guayas,** Ecu.
138/A5 **Guayas** (prov.), Ecu.
146/C3 **Guaymas,** Mex.
85/N4 **Gubakha,** Rus.
79/F6 **Gubbio,** It.
65/H3 **Guben,** Ger.
65/H3 **Gubin,** Pol.
86/F2 **Gubkin,** Rus.
103/B4 **Gucheng,** China
103/C3 **Gucheng,** China
105/F1 **Gucheng,** China
96/E2 **Guchin-Us,** Mong.
108/F3 **Gūdalūr,** India
108/F4 **Gūdalūr,** India
75/E2 **Gúdar** (range), Sp.
62/D3 **Gudenå** (riv.), Den.
67/G6 **Gudensberg,** Ger.
87/H4 **Gudermes,** Rus.
106/D4 **Gudivāda,** India
105/G4 **Gudou** (peak), China
106/C5 **Gūdūr,** India
76/D2 **Guebwiller,** Fr.
74/D1 **Guecho,** Sp.
128/B1 **Guelb Azefal** (mts.), Mrta.
123/V17 **Guelma,** Alg.
123/V17 **Guelma** (wilaya), Alg.
160/D3 **Guelph,** On,Can
124/C2 **Guelta Zemmur,** WSah.
69/F5 **Guénange,** Fr.
72/B3 **Guérande,** Fr.
72/D3 **Guéret,** Fr.
74/D1 **Guernica y Luno,** Sp.
72/B2 **Guernsey** (isl.), Chl,UK
147/E5 **Guerrero** (state), Mex.
72/F3 **Gueugnon,** Fr.
129/H3 **Guézaoua,** Niger
125/N6 **Gugē** (peak), Eth.
120/D3 **Guguan** (isl.), NMar.
105/F4 **Gui** (riv.), China
75/X16 **Guía de Isora,** Sp.
136/F2 **Guiana Highlands** (mts.), SAm.
103/D5 **Guichi,** China
148/C2 **Guichicovi,** Mex.
124/H6 **Guidder,** Camr.
128/B3 **Guidimaka** (reg.), Mrta.
107/J2 **Guiding,** China
107/K2 **Guidong,** China
80/C2 **Guidonia,** It.
128/D5 **Guiglo,** IvC.
53/U11 **Guignes,** Fr.
68/C5 **Guignicourt,** Fr.
138/E2 **Güigüe,** Ven.
112/E6 **Guiguinto,** Phil.
112/C3 **Guihulñgan,** Phil.
131/D5 **Guija,** Moz.
53/M8 **Guildford,** Eng,UK
72/F4 **Guilherand,** Fr.
105/F3 **Guilin,** China
153/J3 **Guillaume-Delisle** (lake), Qu,Can
74/B4 **Guillena,** Sp.
58/C1 **Guilsfield,** Wal,UK
140/A1 **Guimarães,** Braz.
74/A2 **Guimarães,** Port.
112/C3 **Guimaras** (isl.), Phil.
112/C2 **Guimba,** Phil.
103/D4 **Guimeng Ding** (mtn.), China
96/E4 **Guinan,** China
54/A1 **Guinard** (riv.), Sc,UK
112/D3 **Guindulman,** Phil.
128/C4 **Guinea**
124/F7 **Guinea** (gulf), Afr.
128/B3 **Guinea-Bissau**
72/B2 **Guingamp,** Fr.
112/C2 **Guintinguintin** (mtn.), Phil.
148/E4 **Guiones** (pt.), CR
72/A2 **Guipavas,** Fr.
137/H7 **Guiratinga,** Braz.
139/F2 **Güiria,** Ven.
57/G2 **Guisborough,** Eng,UK
68/C4 **Guise,** Fr.
57/G4 **Guiseley,** Eng,UK
74/B1 **Guitiriz,** Sp.
112/D3 **Guiuan,** Phil.
105/F4 **Gui Xian,** China
104/E3 **Guiyang,** China
105/G3 **Guiyang,** China
138/B4 **Güiza** (riv.), Col.
104/E3 **Guizhou** (prov.), China
72/C4 **Gujan-Mestras,** Fr.
106/B3 **Gujarāt** (state), India
108/B1 **Gūjar Khān,** Pak.
108/C1 **Gujrānwāla,** Pak.
108/C1 **Gujrāt,** Pak.
86/F2 **Gukovo,** Rus.
96/E4 **Gulang,** China
106/C4 **Gulbarga,** India
69/G3 **Guldenbach** (riv.), Ger.
163/F4 **Gulf Islands Nat'l Seashore,** US
163/F4 **Gulfport,** Ms,US
163/G4 **Gulf Shores,** Al,US
88/G5 **Gulistan,** Uzb.
97/J2 **Guliya** (peak), China
56/B2 **Gulladuff,** NI,UK
54/D4 **Gullane,** Sc,UK
54/D4 **Gullane Head** (pt.), Sc,UK
156/F3 **Gull Lake,** Sk,Can
92/B2 **Güllükdağı** (Termessos) Nat'l Park, Turk.
91/C1 **Gülnar,** Turk.
69/E2 **Gulpen,** Neth.
92/C2 **Gülşehir,** Turk.
130/B2 **Gulu,** Ugan.
83/G4 **Gŭlŭbovo,** Bul.
54/A3 **Gulvain** (Gaor Bheinn) (mtn.), Sc.,UK
108/A2 **Gumal** (riv.), Pak.
126/D4 **Gumare,** Bots.
130/B5 **Gumbiro,** Tanz.
99/F2 **Gumma** (pref.), Japan
67/E6 **Gummersbach,** Ger.
86/E4 **Gümüşhacıköy,** Turk.
92/D1 **Gümüşhane,** Turk.
92/D1 **Gümüşhane** (prov.), Turk.
125/N5 **Guna** (peak), Eth.
106/C3 **Guna,** India
70/A6 **Gundelfingen,** Ger.
70/D5 **Gundelfingen an der Donau,** Ger.
70/C4 **Gundelsheim,** Ger.
108/F3 **Gundlupet,** India
92/B2 **Güney,** Turk.
92/D2 **Güneydogu Toroslar** (mts.), Turk.
157/J2 **Gunisao** (lake), Mb,Can
157/J2 **Gunisao** (riv.), Mb,Can
119/D1 **Gunnedah,** Austl.
158/F3 **Gunnison,** Co,US
158/F3 **Gunnison** (riv.), Co,US
158/E3 **Gunnison,** Ut,US
166/B5 **Gunpowder** (riv.), Md,US
102/B4 **Gunt** (riv.), Taj.
163/G3 **Guntersville,** Al,US
163/G3 **Guntersville** (dam), Al,US
163/G3 **Guntersville** (lake), Al,US
106/D4 **Guntūr,** India
112/A5 **Gunung Mulu Nat'l Park,** Malay.
70/D6 **Günz** (riv.), Ger.
70/D6 **Günzburg,** Ger.
70/D4 **Gunzenhausen,** Ger.
103/C4 **Guo** (riv.), China
103/D4 **Guoyang,** China
125/N6 **Guragē** (peak), Eth.
83/G2 **Gura Humorului,** Rom.
135/F2 **Gural** (mts.), Braz.
96/B2 **Gurbantünggut** (des.), China
108/C1 **Gurdāspur,** India
92/D1 **Gürgentepe,** Turk.
140/B3 **Gurguéia** (riv.), Braz.
139/F3 **Guri** (res.), Ven.
73/L3 **Gurk** (riv.), Aus.
73/K3 **Gurkthaler** (mts.), Aus.
165/Q15 **Gurnee,** Il,US
131/D3 **Guro,** Moz.
92/E2 **Güroymak,** Turk.
93/M7 **Gürpinar,** Turk.
83/J5 **Gürsu,** Turk.
92/D2 **Gürün,** Turk.
137/J6 **Gurupi,** Braz.
137/J4 **Gurupi** (mts.), Braz.
140/A1 **Gurupi** (riv.), Braz.
106/B3 **Guru Sikhar** (mtn.), India
131/C3 **Guruve,** Zim.
96/G2 **Gurvandzagal,** Mong.
87/J3 **Gur'yev,** Kaz.
87/J3 **Gur'yev Obl.,** Kaz.
103/C4 **Gushi,** China
100/J7 **Gushikawa,** Japan
84/J5 **Gus'-Khrustal'nyy,** Rus.
80/A3 **Guspini,** It.
63/S7 **Gustausberg,** Swe.
147/Q10 **Gustavo A. Marrero,** Mex.
64/G2 **Güstrow,** Ger.
67/F5 **Gütersloh,** Ger.
159/H4 **Guthrie,** Ok,US
159/G4 **Guthrie,** Tx,US
147/F4 **Gutiérrez Zamora,** Mex.
167/J8 **Guttenberg,** NJ,US
61/E3 **Gutulia Nat'l Park,** Nor.
103/B3 **Guxian,** China
139/G3 **Guyana**
53/S10 **Guyancourt,** Fr.
163/H2 **Guyandotte** (riv.), WV,US
103/B2 **Guyang,** China
72/C4 **Guyenne** (reg.), Fr.
119/E1 **Guy Fawkes Riv. Nat'l Park,** Austl.
59/G1 **Guyhirn,** Eng,UK
159/G3 **Guymon,** Ok,US
96/F4 **Guyuan,** China
96/H3 **Guyuan,** China
107/J2 **Guzhang,** China
103/D4 **Guzhen,** China
146/D2 **Guzman** (lake), Mex.
131/B3 **Gwaai,** Zim.
95/H3 **Gwādar,** Pak.
131/B3 **Gwai** (riv.), Zim.
106/C2 **Gwalior,** India
131/C4 **Gwanda,** Zim.
59/F1 **Gwash** (riv.), Eng,UK
58/C2 **Gwaunceste** (mtn.), Wal,UK
159/J3 **G. W. Carver Nat'l Mon.,** Mo,US
65/J2 **Gwda** (riv.), Pol.
58/A6 **Gweek,** Eng,UK
131/B3 **Gwembe,** Zam.
58/D3 **Gwent** (co.), Wal,UK
57/E5 **Gwersyllt,** Wal,UK
131/C3 **Gweru,** Zim.
119/D1 **Gwydir** (riv.), Austl.
56/D5 **Gwynedd** (co.), Wal,UK
107/F2 **Gyaca,** China
87/H4 **Gyandzhe,** Azer.
106/E2 **Gyangzê,** China
97/D5 **Gyaring** (lake), China
129/F5 **Gyasikan,** Gha.
88/H2 **Gyda** (pen.), Rus.
62/D4 **Gyldenløveshøj** (peak), Den.
118/D4 **Gympie,** Austl.
104/B5 **Gyobingauk,** Burma
82/E2 **Gyoma,** Hun.
82/D2 **Gyöngyös,** Hun.
82/C2 **Győr,** Hun.
82/C2 **Győr-Sopron** (co.), Hun.
82/E2 **Gyula,** Hun.

H

68/D2 **Haacht,** Belg.
66/D4 **Haaksbergen,** Neth.
68/D2 **Haaltert,** Belg.
66/E6 **Haan,** Ger.
121/H6 **Ha'apai Group** (isls.), Tonga
61/H2 **Haapavesi,** Fin.
63/K2 **Haapsalu,** Est.
71/E6 **Haar,** Ger.
70/A4 **Haardt** (mts.), Ger.
66/B4 **Haarlem,** Neth.
115/Q11 **Haast,** NZ
117/F2 **Haasts Bluff Abor. Land,** Austl.
95/J3 **Hab** (riv.), Pak.
96/B2 **Habahe,** China
71/F2 **Habartov,** Czh.
130/C2 **Habaswein,** Kenya
69/E4 **Habay,** Belg.
93/E3 **Habbānīyah,** Iraq
77/H3 **Habicht** (peak), Aus.
107/F3 **Habiganj,** Bang.
99/L10 **Habikino,** Japan
100/D2 **Habomai** (isls.), Rus.
100/B1 **Haboro,** Japan
139/F3 **Hacha** (falls), Ven.
67/F3 **Hache** (riv.), Ger.
97/N5 **Hachijō** (isl.), Japan
100/B3 **Hachimantai-Towada Nat'l Park,** Japan
100/A3 **Hachimori,** Japan
100/B3 **Hachinohe,** Japan
99/F3 **Hachiōji,** Japan
92/C2 **Hacıbektaş,** Turk.
164/C3 **Hacienda Heights,** Ca,US
92/C2 **Hacılar,** Turk.
117/H4 **Hack** (peak), Austl.
167/D2 **Hackensack,** NJ,US
167/J8 **Hackensack** (riv.), NJ, NY,US
166/D2 **Hackettstown,** NJ,US
53/N7 **Hackney** (bor.), Eng,UK
109/D1 **Ha Coi,** Viet.
108/B1 **Hadāli,** Pak.
70/B2 **Hadamar,** Ger.
99/F3 **Hadano,** Japan
127/D4 **Hadarba, Ras** (cape), Sudan
125/J4 **Haddad** (wadi), Chad
168/B3 **Haddam,** Ct,US
59/F3 **Haddenham,** Eng,UK
54/D5 **Haddington,** Sc,UK
166/C4 **Haddonfield,** NJ,US
166/C4 **Haddon** (Westmont), NJ,US
95/G4 **Ḩadd, Ra's al** (pt.), Oman
129/H3 **Hadejia** (riv.), Nga.
67/F1 **Hadelner** (can.), Ger.
91/D3 **Hadera,** Isr.
62/C4 **Haderslev,** Den.
94/G5 **Hadhramaut** (region), Yem.
91/C1 **Hadım,** Turk.
123/S15 **Hadjout,** Alg.
82/E2 **Hadjú-Bihar** (co.), Hun.
152/F1 **Hadley** (bay), NW,Can
53/Q8 **Hadlow,** Eng,UK
57/F1 **Hadrian's Wall** (ruins), Eng,UK
61/E1 **Hadselfjorden** (fjord), Nor.
101/C3 **Haeju,** NKor.
101/C4 **Haeju** (bay), NKor.
154/S9 **Haena** (pt.), Hi,US
131/C4 **Haenertsburg,** SAfr.
92/D2 **Hafik,** Turk.
108/B1 **Hāfizābād,** Pak.
61/N7 **Hafnarfjördhur,** Ice.
94/E3 **Ḩafr al Bāţin,** SAr.
93/G4 **Haft Gel,** Iran
123/H3 **Hafun, Ras** (pt.), Som.
151/F4 **Hagemeister** (isl.), Ak,US
67/E6 **Hagen,** Ger.
67/E4 **Hagen am Teutoburger Wald,** Ger.
64/F2 **Hagenow,** Ger.
159/F4 **Hagerman,** NM,US
160/E4 **Hagerstown,** Md,US
62/E1 **Hagfors,** Swe.
98/B3 **Hagi,** Japan
109/D1 **Ha Giang,** Viet.
58/D2 **Hagley,** Eng,UK
69/F5 **Hagondange,** Fr.
60/A4 **Hags Head** (pt.), Ire.
157/G2 **Hague,** Sk,Can
72/C2 **Hague, Cap de la** (cape), Fr.
69/G6 **Haguenau,** Fr.
66/B4 **Hague, The** ('s-Gravenhage) (cap.), Neth.
120/D2 **Hahashima** (isl.), Jap.
67/H6 **Hahle** (riv.), Ger.
117/M9 **Hahndorf,** Austl.
69/G3 **Hahnenbach** (riv.), Ger.
103/D3 **Hai** (riv.), China
103/E4 **Hai'an,** China
99/L10 **Haibara,** Japan
101/B2 **Haicheng,** China
71/E3 **Haidenaab** (riv.), Ger.
109/D1 **Hai Duong,** Viet.
91/D3 **Haifa** (dist.), Isr.
91/D3 **Haifa** (Hefa), Isr.
105/G4 **Haifeng,** China
69/H2 **Haiger,** Ger.
70/B6 **Haigerloch,** Ger.
109/D1 **Hai Hau,** Viet.
105/F4 **Haikou,** China
97/H2 **Hailar,** China
97/J2 **Hailar** (riv.), China
160/E2 **Haileybury,** On,Can
105/F4 **Hailing** (isl.), China
59/G5 **Hailsham,** Eng,UK
97/K2 **Hailun,** China
103/E5 **Haimen,** China
105/F5 **Hainan** (isl.), China
105/F5 **Hainan** (prov.), China
105/F4 **Hainan** (str.), China
68/B2 **Hainaut** (prov.), Belg.
70/C1 **Hainburg,** Ger.
163/H4 **Haines City,** Fl,US
151/L3 **Haines Junction,** Yk,Can
67/H6 **Hainich** (mts.), Ger.
103/L9 **Haining,** China
109/D1 **Haiphong** (Hai Phong), Viet.
105/H3 **Haitan** (isl.), China
149/H2 **Haiti**
109/E2 **Hai Van** (pass), Viet.
107/K3 **Haixia** (str.), China
103/D3 **Haixing,** China
103/E3 **Haiyang,** China
101/B3 **Haiyang** (isl.), China
96/F4 **Haiyuan,** China
103/D4 **Haizhou** (bay), China
71/F2 **Háj** (peak), Czh.
65/L5 **Hajdú-Bihar** (co.), Hun.
82/E2 **Hajdúboszormény,** Hun.
82/E2 **Hajdúdorog,** Hun.
82/E2 **Hajdúhadház,** Hun.
82/E2 **Hajdúnánás,** Hun.
82/E2 **Hajdúszoboszló,** Hun.
99/F1 **Hajiki-zaki** (pt.), Japan
65/M2 **Hajnówka,** Pol.
107/F2 **Hājo,** India
121/L5 **Hakahau,** Fr.Pol.
117/G3 **Hakee** (peak), Austl.
93/E2 **Hakkâri** (prov.), Turk.
98/D3 **Hakken-san** (mtn.), Japan
100/B3 **Hakkōda-san** (mtn.), Japan
100/B3 **Hakodate,** Japan
99/H7 **Hakone,** Japan
99/H8 **Hakone-Fuji-Izu Nat'l Park,** Japan
99/E2 **Hakui,** Japan
99/M10 **Hakusan,** Japan
99/E2 **Haku-san** (mtn.), Japan
99/E2 **Hakusan Nat'l Park,** Japan
95/J3 **Hāla,** Pak.
92/D3 **Ḩalab** (prov.), Syria
91/E1 **Ḩalab** (Aleppo), Syria
93/F3 **Ḩalabjah,** Iraq
147/M6 **Halachó,** Mex.
127/D4 **Ḩalā'ib,** Sudan
112/C2 **Halcon** (mtn.), Phil.
62/D2 **Halden,** Nor.
64/F2 **Haldensleben,** Ger.
161/Q10 **Haldimand,** On,Can
96/G2 **Haldzan,** Mong.
116/C3 **Hale** (peak), Austl.
130/C4 **Hale,** Tanz.
57/F5 **Hale,** Eng,UK
154/T10 **Haleakala Nat'l Park,** Hi,US
167/J8 **Haledon,** NJ,US
69/E2 **Halen,** Belg.
165/P14 **Hales Corners,** Wi,US
58/D2 **Halesowen,** Eng,UK
59/H2 **Halesworth,** Eng,UK
163/G3 **Haleyville,** Al,US
128/E5 **Half Assini,** Gha.
166/A3 **Half Falls** (mtn.), Pa,US
165/K12 **Half Moon Bay,** Ca,US
91/D4 **Ḩalḩūl,** WBnk.
160/E2 **Haliburton** (hills), On,Can
118/B2 **Halifax** (bay), Austl.
161/J2 **Halifax** (cap.), NS,Can
57/G4 **Halifax,** Eng,UK
168/D2 **Halifax,** Ma,US
63/K1 **Halikko,** Fin.
93/J4 **Halīl** (riv.), Iran
63/T9 **Häljarp,** Swe.
151/H1 **Halkett** (cape), Ak,US
153/K2 **Hall** (pen.), NW,Can
120/E4 **Hall** (isls.), Micr.
151/D3 **Hall** (isl.), Ak,US
55/K7 **Halladale** (riv.), Sc,UK
166/B3 **Hallam** (Hellam), Pa,US
62/E3 **Halland** (co.), Swe.
97/K5 **Halla-san** (mtn.), SKor.
68/D2 **Halle,** Belg.
67/F4 **Halle,** Ger.
61/E4 **Hällefors,** Swe.
73/K3 **Hallein,** Aus.
68/A4 **Hallencourt,** Fr.
64/F3 **Halle-Neustadt,** Ger.
71/E5 **Hallertau** (reg.), Ger.
113/M **Hallett** (cape), Ant.
162/D4 **Hallettsville,** Tx,US
62/C1 **Hallingdalselvi** (riv.), Nor.
157/J3 **Hallock,** Mn,US
62/F2 **Hallsberg,** Swe.
63/R7 **Hallsfjärden** (lake), Swe.
70/D3 **Hallstadt,** Ger.
62/G2 **Hallstahammar,** Swe.
64/B4 **Hallu** (riv.), Fr.
68/B3 **Hallue** (riv.), Fr.
68/C2 **Halluin,** Fr.
76/E3 **Hallwilersee** (lake), Swi.
101/E5 **Hallyŏ Haesang Nat'l Park,** SKor.
111/G3 **Halmahera** (isl.), Indo.
111/G4 **Halmahera** (sea), Indo.
62/E3 **Halmstad,** Swe.
123/X17 **Ḩalq al Wādī,** Tun.
62/E3 **Hälsingborg,** Swe.
59/G3 **Halstead,** Eng,UK
66/B5 **Halsteren,** Neth.
96/C4 **Haltang** (riv.), China
57/H4 **Haltemprice,** Eng,UK
67/E5 **Haltern,** Ger.
161/Q8 **Halton** (co.), On,Can
161/Q8 **Halton Hills,** On,Can
57/F2 **Haltwhistle,** Eng,UK
67/E6 **Halver,** Ger.
67/E3 **Halverder Aa** (riv.), Ger.
68/C4 **Ham,** Fr.
98/C3 **Hamada,** Japan
93/G3 **Hamadān,** Iran
93/G3 **Hamadān** (gov.), Iran
91/E2 **Ḩamāh,** Syria
92/D3 **Ḩamāh** (prov.), Syria
99/M10 **Hamajima,** Japan
99/E3 **Hamakita,** Japan
99/E3 **Hamamatsu,** Japan
100/D2 **Hamanaka,** Japan
62/D1 **Hamar,** Nor.
127/C3 **Ḩamāţah, Jabal** (mtn.), Egypt
100/C1 **Hamatombetsu,** Japan
106/D6 **Hambantota,** SrL.
59/E5 **Hamble,** Eng,UK
57/G3 **Hambleton** (hills), Eng,UK
67/G3 **Hambühren,** Ger.
67/G1 **Hamburg,** Ger.
67/H1 **Hamburg** (state), Ger.
162/F3 **Hamburg,** Ar,US
160/E3 **Hamburg,** NY,US
168/B3 **Hamden,** Ct,US
63/K1 **Häme** (prov.), Fin.
63/K1 **Hämeenkyrö,** Fin.
63/L1 **Hämeenlinna,** Fin.
116/B3 **Hamelin,** Austl.
116/B3 **Hamelin Pool** (bay), Austl.
67/G4 **Hameln,** Ger.
116/C2 **Hamersley** (range), Austl.
116/C2 **Hamersley Range Nat'l Park,** Austl.
59/H3 **Hamford Water** (inlet), Eng,UK
101/E2 **Hamgyŏng** (mts.), NKor.
101/D2 **Hamgyŏng-Namdo** (prov.), NKor.
101/D3 **Hamhŭng,** NKor.
101/D3 **Hamhŭng-Si** (prov.), NKor.
96/C3 **Hami,** China
112/D4 **Hamiguitan** (mtn.), Phil.
119/B3 **Hamilton,** Austl.
153/L3 **Hamilton** (inlet), Nf,Can
161/Q9 **Hamilton,** On,Can
161/Q9 **Hamilton** (har.), On,Can
115/S10 **Hamilton,** NZ
54/B5 **Hamilton,** Sc,UK
163/G3 **Hamilton,** Al,US
165/L12 **Hamilton** (mtn.), Ca,US
156/E4 **Hamilton,** Mt,US
160/C4 **Hamilton,** Oh,US
162/D4 **Hamilton,** Tx,US
167/K8 **Hamilton Grange Mem.,** NY,US
166/D3 **Hamilton Square-Mercerville,** NJ,US
63/M1 **Hamina,** Fin.
108/D2 **Hamīrpur,** India
67/E5 **Hamm,** Ger.
123/V17 **Hamma-Bouziane,** Alg.
123/X17 **Hammāmāt** (gulf), Tun.
123/Q16 **Hamman, Oued el** (riv.), Alg.
62/E2 **Hammarön** (isl.), Swe.
68/D1 **Hamme,** Belg.
67/F2 **Hamme** (riv.), Ger.
70/C2 **Hammelburg,** Ger.
166/B3 **Hammer** (cr.), Pa,US
61/G1 **Hammerfest,** Nor.
62/F4 **Hammershus,** Den.
53/N7 **Hammersmith & Fulham** (bor.), Eng,UK
66/D5 **Hamminkeln,** Ger.
168/B3 **Hammonasset** (pt.), Ct,US
165/R16 **Hammond,** In,US
163/F4 **Hammond,** La,US
53/N6 **Hammond Street,** Eng,UK
166/D4 **Hammonton,** NJ,US
55/P12 **Hamnavoe,** Sc,UK
69/E1 **Hamont-Achel,** Belg.
168/B1 **Hampden** (co.), Ma,US
59/E4 **Hampshire** (co.), Eng,UK
168/B1 **Hampshire** (co.), Ma,US
59/E4 **Hampshire Downs** (hills), Eng,UK
53/N7 **Hampstead,** Eng,UK
160/E4 **Hampton,** Va,US
167/F2 **Hampton Bays,** NY,US
53/M7 **Hampton Court,** Eng,UK
166/B5 **Hampton Nat'l Hist. Site,** Md,US
119/G6 **Hampton Park,** Austl.
124/H1 **Ḩamrā** (upland), Libya
165/F7 **Hamtramck,** Mi,US
99/H7 **Hamura,** Japan
101/E2 **Hamyŏng-Bukto** (prov.), NKor.
103/C5 **Han** (riv.), China
101/D4 **Han** (riv.), SKor.
100/B4 **Hanamaki,** Japan
154/U11 **Hanamalo** (pt.), Hi,US
97/M5 **Hanamatsu,** Japan
130/B4 **Hanang** (peak), Tanz.
70/B2 **Hanau,** Ger.
103/C5 **Hanchuan,** China
160/B2 **Hancock,** Mi,US
168/G6 **Hancock** (co.), WV,US
168/A1 **Hancock Shaker Village,** Ma,US
99/M10 **Handa,** Japan
103/C3 **Handan,** China
63/S7 **Handen,** Swe.
130/C4 **Handeni,** Tanz.
59/E1 **Handsworth,** Eng,UK
158/C3 **Hanford,** Ca,US
96/D2 **Hangayn** (mts.), Mong.
103/B3 **Hanggin Qi,** China
58/C5 **Hangingstone** (hill), Eng,UK
132/L11 **Hangklip** (cape), SAfr.
63/K2 **Hangö** (Hanko), Fin.
108/A1 **Hangu,** Pak.
103/L9 **Hangzhou,** China
96/C2 **Hanhöhiy** (mts.), Mong.
92/E2 **Hani,** Turk.
157/J4 **Hankinson,** ND,US
63/K2 **Hanko** (Hangö), Fin.
157/G3 **Hanley,** Sk,Can
156/F3 **Hanna,** Ab,Can
156/G5 **Hanna,** Wy,US
99/L10 **Hannan,** Japan
159/K3 **Hannibal,** Mo,US
99/H7 **Hannō,** Japan
67/G4 **Hannover,** Ger.
69/E2 **Hannut,** Belg.
62/F4 **Hanöbukten** (bay), Swe.
109/D1 **Hanoi** (Ha Noi) (cap.), Viet.
160/D2 **Hanover,** On,Can
143/J7 **Hanover** (isl.), Chile
168/D1 **Hanover,** Ma,US
161/F3 **Hanover,** NH,US
166/B4 **Hanover,** Pa,US
165/P16 **Hanover Park,** Il,US
164/B2 **Hansen** (dam), Ca,US
164/F7 **Hansen Dam Rec. Area,** Ca,US
103/D5 **Hanshan,** China
106/C2 **Hānsi,** India
168/D1 **Hanson,** Ma,US
102/D3 **Hantengri Feng** (peak), China
153/J2 **Hantzsch** (riv.), NW,Can
106/B2 **Hanumāngarh,** India
96/E2 **Hanuy** (riv.), Mong.
104/D2 **Hanyuan,** China
96/F5 **Hanzhong,** China
121/L6 **Hao** (atoll), FrPol.
61/H2 **Haparanda,** Swe.
117/M9 **Happy Valley** (res.), Austl.
153/K3 **Happy Valley-Goose Bay,** Nf,Can
96/D4 **Har** (lake), China
96/C2 **Har** (lake), Mong.
96/F2 **Haraa** (riv.), Mong.
99/G2 **Haramachi,** Japan
108/B2 **Harappa** (ruins), Pak.
131/C3 **Harare** (cap.), Zim.
96/F2 **Har-Ayrag,** Mong.
128/C5 **Harbel,** Libr.
97/K2 **Harbin,** China
91/E1 **Harbiye,** Turk.
161/L2 **Harbour Breton,** Nf,Can
59/E2 **Harbury,** Eng,UK
77/F3 **Hard,** Aus.
106/C3 **Hardā,** India
62/B1 **Hardangervidda Nat'l Park,** Nor.
132/B2 **Hardap** (dam), Namb.
67/H3 **Hardau** (riv.), Ger.
67/G5 **Hardegsen,** Ger.
66/D3 **Hardenberg,** Neth.
66/C4 **Harderwijk,** Neth.
70/C3 **Hardheim,** Ger.
156/G4 **Hardin,** Mt,US
95/L3 **Hardwār,** India
143/K8 **Hardy** (pen.), Chile
161/L1 **Hare** (bay), Nf,Can
68/C2 **Harelbeke,** Belg.
67/E3 **Haren,** Ger.
66/D2 **Haren,** Neth.
125/P6 **Hārer,** Eth.
91/G7 **Har Eval** (Jabal 'Aybāl) (mtn.), WBnk.
166/B4 **Harford** (co.), Md,US
125/P6 **Hargeysa,** Som.
83/G2 **Harghita** (co.), Rom.
83/G2 **Harghita** (peak), Rom.
63/K2 **Hari** (str.), Est.
110/B4 **Hari** (riv.), Indo.
106/C5 **Harihar,** India
98/D3 **Harima** (sound), Japan
66/B5 **Haringvliet** (chan.), Neth.
66/B5 **Haringvlietdam** (dam), Neth.
108/F4 **Haripād,** India
95/H2 **Harīrūd** (riv.), Afg.
63/K1 **Harjavalta,** Fin.
160/D4 **Harlan,** Ky,US
56/D6 **Harlech,** Wal,UK
167/K8 **Harlem,** NY,US
59/H2 **Harleston,** Eng,UK
66/C2 **Harlingen,** Neth.
162/D5 **Harlingen,** Tx,US

192

Harli – Hogar

59/F3 **Harlington,** Eng,UK
53/P6 **Harlow,** Eng,UK
156/F4 **Harlowton,** Mt,US
66/B4 **Harmelen,** Neth.
68/B3 **Harnes,** Fr.
156/D5 **Harney** (lake), Or,US
156/D5 **Harney** (val.), Or,US
157/H5 **Harney** (peak), SD,US
108/A1 **Harnoli,** Pak.
61/F3 **Härnösand,** Swe.
74/D1 **Haro,** Sp.
146/C3 **Haro, Cabo** (pt.), Mex.
59/F3 **Harpenden,** Eng,UK
151/L3 **Harper** (mtn.), Yk,Can
128/D5 **Harper,** Libr.
151/K3 **Harper** (mtn.), Ak,US
162/D2 **Harper,** Ks,US
160/E4 **Harpers Ferry Nat'l Hist. Park,** WV,US
165/G7 **Harper Woods,** Mi,US
97/H3 **Harqin Qi,** China
103/D2 **Harqin Zuoyi Monggolzu Zizhixian,** China
160/E1 **Harricana** (riv.), Qu,Can
163/G3 **Harriman,** Tn,US
167/D1 **Harriman Saint Park,** NY,US
117/G4 **Harris** (lake), Austl.
117/F3 **Harris** (peak), Austl.
55/H8 **Harris** (reg.), Sc,UK
160/B4 **Harrisburg,** Il,US
159/G2 **Harrisburg,** Ne,US
166/B3 **Harrisburg** (cap.), Pa,US
64/E1 **Harrislee,** Ger.
132/E3 **Harrismith,** SAfr.
156/C3 **Harrison** (lake), BC,Can
153/L3 **Harrison** (cape), Nf,Can
151/H1 **Harrison** (bay), Ak,US
162/E2 **Harrison,** Ar,US
159/G2 **Harrison,** Ne,US
167/J9 **Harrison,** NJ,US
167/E2 **Harrison,** NY,US
168/F7 **Harrison** (co.), Oh,US
160/E4 **Harrisonburg,** Va,US
160/C4 **Harrodsburg,** Ky,US
57/G4 **Harrogate,** Eng,UK
53/N7 **Harrow,** Eng,UK
53/M7 **Harrow** (bor.), Eng,UK
159/J3 **Harry S Truman** (res.), Mo,US
67/G2 **Harsefeld,** Ger.
67/F5 **Harsewinkel,** Ger.
61/F1 **Harstad,** Nor.
152/C2 **Hart** (riv.), Yk,Can
167/K8 **Hart** (isl.), NY,US
158/C2 **Hart** (lake), Or,US
132/C3 **Hartbeesrivier** (dry riv.), SAfr.
62/B1 **Hårteigen** (peak), Nor.
66/B5 **Hartelkanaal** (can.), Neth.
54/C6 **Hart Fell** (mtn.), Sc,UK
168/B2 **Hartford** (cap.), Ct,US
168/B2 **Hartford** (co.), Ct,US
160/C3 **Hartford City,** In,US
54/C5 **Harthill,** Sc,UK
159/H2 **Hartington,** Ne,US
58/B5 **Hartland,** Eng,UK
58/B4 **Hartland** (pt.), Eng,UK
58/D2 **Hartlebury,** Eng,UK
57/G2 **Hartlepool,** Eng,UK
53/P7 **Hartley,** Eng,UK
157/H3 **Hartney,** Mb,Can
132/D3 **Harts** (riv.), SAfr.
167/E1 **Hartsdale,** NY,US
163/G3 **Hartselle,** Al,US
59/E1 **Hartshill,** Eng,UK
165/B3 **Hartstene** (isl.), Wa,US
163/H3 **Hartwell,** Ga,US
163/H3 **Hartwell** (lake), Ga, SC,US
119/C4 **Hartz Mtn. Nat'l Park,** Austl.
69/G6 **Hartzviller,** Fr.
95/K3 **Hārūnābād,** Pak.
111/E3 **Harun, Bukit** (peak), Indo.
102/F2 **Har Us** (lake), Mong.
96/D2 **Har-Us** (riv.), Mong.
95/H2 **Hārūt** (riv.), Afg.
165/Q16 **Harvey,** Il,US
157/J4 **Harvey,** ND,US
166/B1 **Harveys** (lake), Pa,US
59/H3 **Harwich,** Eng,UK
57/G5 **Harworth,** Eng,UK
106/C2 **Haryana** (state), India
67/H5 **Harz** (mts.), Ger.
92/C2 **Hasan** (peak), Turk.
167/D2 **Hasbrouck Heights,** NJ,US
67/E3 **Hase** (riv.), Ger.
70/D1 **Hasel** (riv.), Ger.
67/E3 **Haselünne,** Ger.
76/D3 **Hasenmalt** (mtn.), Swi.
99/M9 **Hashima,** Japan
98/D3 **Hashimoto,** Japan
124/D2 **Hasi el Farsía** (well), WSah.
95/K3 **Hāsilpur,** Pak.
162/D3 **Haskell,** Tx,US
70/B6 **Haslach im Kinzigtal,** Ger.
59/F4 **Haslemere,** Eng,UK
165/F6 **Hasler** (cr.), Mi,US
57/F4 **Haslingden,** Eng,UK
57/F5 **Haslington,** Eng,UK
91/E1 **Hassa,** Turk.
106/C5 **Hassan,** India
70/D2 **Hassberge** (hills), Ger.
153/S7 **Hassel** (sound), NW,Can
69/E2 **Hasselt,** Belg.
66/D3 **Hasselt,** Neth.
70/D2 **Hassfurt,** Ger.
123/S16 **Hassi Bahbah,** Alg.
124/G1 **Hassi Messaoud,** Alg.
62/E3 **Hässleholm,** Swe.
70/B4 **Hassloch,** Ger.
115/S10 **Hastings,** NZ
55/M11 **Hastings,** UK
59/G5 **Hastings,** Eng,UK
160/C3 **Hastings,** Mi,US
157/K4 **Hastings,** Mn,US
159/H2 **Hastings,** Ne,US
59/G5 **Hastings Battlesite,** Eng,UK
167/E1 **Hastings-on-Hudson,** NY,US
99/H7 **Hasuda,** Japan
123/W18 **Ḥaţab** (riv.), Tun.
99/M9 **Hatashō,** Japan
91/E1 **Hatay** (prov.), Turk.
166/C3 **Hatboro,** Pa,US
158/F4 **Hatch,** NM,US
109/B5 **Hat Chao Mai Nat'l Park,** Thai.
143/J7 **Hatcher** (peak), Arg.
82/F3 **Haţeg,** Rom.
53/N6 **Hatfield,** Eng,UK
119/E1 **Hat Head Nat'l Park,** Austl.
57/G5 **Hathersage,** Eng,UK
106/C2 **Hāthras,** India
94/C4 **Ḥāţibah, Ra's** (pt.), SAr.
109/D4 **Ha Tien,** Viet.
109/D2 **Ha Tinh,** Viet.
109/B5 **Hat Nai Yang Nat'l Park,** Thai.
99/H7 **Hatogaya,** Japan
150/D3 **Hato Mayor,** DRep.
99/H7 **Hatoyama,** Japan
106/C3 **Hatta,** India
119/B2 **Hattah-Kulkyne Nat'l Park,** Austl.
66/D4 **Hattem,** Neth.
67/F2 **Hatten,** Ger.
163/K3 **Hatteras** (cape), NC,US
70/B2 **Hattersheim am Mein,** Ger.
163/F4 **Hattiesburg,** Ms,US
67/E6 **Hattingen,** Ger.
57/G6 **Hatton,** Eng,UK
54/E2 **Hatton,** Sc,UK
63/L1 **Hattula,** Fin.
82/D2 **Hatvan,** Hun.
109/C5 **Hat Yai,** Thai.
67/F6 **Hatzfeld,** Ger.
109/E3 **Hau Bon,** Viet.
68/B2 **Haubourdin,** Fr.
125/Q6 **Haud** (reg.), Eth., Som.
62/A2 **Haugesund,** Nor.
109/D4 **Hau Giang** (riv.), Viet.
61/H2 **Haukipudas,** Fin.
70/C1 **Haune** (riv.), Ger.
71/F7 **Haunsberg** (peak), Aus.
167/E2 **Hauppauge,** NY,US
115/S10 **Hauraki** (gulf), NZ
62/A1 **Haus,** Nor.
63/L1 **Hausjärvi,** Fin.
75/E1 **Hauskoa** (mtn.), Fr.
77/F4 **Hausstock** (peak), Swi.
124/D1 **Haut Atlas** (mts.), Mor.
76/B1 **Haute-Marne** (dept.), Fr.
72/D2 **Haute-Normandie** (reg.), Fr.
161/G1 **Hauterive,** Qu,Can
76/B2 **Haute-Saône** (dept.), Fr.
76/C5 **Haute-Savoie** (dept.), Fr.
69/E3 **Hautes Fagnes** (uplands), Belg.
68/C3 **Hautmont,** Fr.
76/B1 **Hautmont, Côte de** (hill), Fr.
76/D2 **Haut-Rhin** (dept.), Fr.
53/S10 **Hauts-de-Seine** (dept.), Fr.
130/A2 **Haut-Zaire** (reg.), Zaire
149/F1 **Havana** (La Habana) (cap.), Cuba
121/V13 **Havannah** (chan.), NCal.
59/F5 **Havant,** Eng,UK
158/D4 **Havasu** (lake), Az, Ca,US
65/G2 **Havel** (riv.), Ger.
64/G2 **Havelland** (reg.), Ger.
163/J3 **Havelock,** NC,US
115/S10 **Havelock North,** NZ
59/G3 **Havengore** (isl.), Eng,UK
58/B3 **Haverfordwest,** Wal,UK
59/G2 **Haverhill,** Eng,UK
161/G3 **Haverhill,** Ma,US
53/P7 **Havering** (bor.), Eng,UK
167/E1 **Haverstraw,** NY,US
65/K4 **Havířov,** Czh.
67/E5 **Havixbeck,** Ger.
65/H4 **Havlíčkuv Brod,** Czh.
156/F3 **Havre,** Mt,US
166/B4 **Havre de Grace,** Md,US
161/J1 **Havre-Saint-Pierre,** Qu,Can
83/H5 **Havsa,** Turk.
92/C1 **Havza,** Turk.
154/S10 **Hawaii** (state), US
154/U11 **Hawaii** (isl.), Hi,US
121/H2 **Hawaiian** (isls.), Hi,US
164/F8 **Hawaiian Gardens,** Ca,US
154/U11 **Hawaii Volcanoes Nat'l Park,** Hi,US
93/G4 **Ḥawallī,** Kuw.
57/E5 **Hawarden,** Wal,UK
157/J5 **Hawarden,** Ia,US
115/R10 **Hawera,** NZ
57/F3 **Hawes,** Eng,UK
57/F2 **Haweswater** (res.), Eng,UK
54/D6 **Hawick,** Sc,UK
119/E2 **Hawke** (cape), Austl.
115/S10 **Hawke** (bay), NZ
118/G8 **Hawkesbury** (riv.), Austl.
156/A2 **Hawkesbury** (isl.), BC,Can
160/F2 **Hawkesbury,** On,Can
150/C1 **Hawks Nest** (pt.), Bahm.
93/F4 **Hawr al Ḥammār** (lake), Iraq
91/B4 **Ḥawsh 'Īsá,** Egypt
164/B3 **Hawthorne,** Ca,US
167/J8 **Hawthorne,** NJ,US
158/C3 **Hawthorne,** Nv,US
57/G3 **Haxby,** Eng,UK
118/C3 **Hay** (pt.), Austl.
117/H3 **Hay** (riv.), Austl.
152/E3 **Hay** (riv.), Ab, NW,Can
100/B4 **Hayachine-san** (mtn.), Japan
99/H7 **Hayama,** Japan
69/F5 **Hayange,** Fr.
57/F5 **Haydock,** Eng,UK
57/F2 **Haydon Bridge,** Eng,UK
152/G3 **Hayes** (riv.), Mb,Can
152/G2 **Hayes** (riv.), NW,Can
153/T7 **Hayes** (pen.), Grld.
53/M7 **Hayes,** Eng,UK
151/J3 **Hayes** (mtn.), Ak,US
58/A6 **Hayle,** Eng,UK
58/A6 **Hayle** (riv.), Eng,UK
59/F5 **Hayling** (isl.), Eng,UK
92/C2 **Haymana,** Turk.
162/E3 **Haynesville,** La,US
58/C2 **Hay on Wye,** Wal,UK
83/H5 **Hayrabolu,** Turk.
159/H3 **Hays,** Ks,US
159/H3 **Haysville,** Ks,US
165/K11 **Hayward,** Ca,US
160/B2 **Hayward,** Wi,US
59/F5 **Haywards Heath,** Eng,UK
93/J4 **Hazār** (mtn.), Iran
160/D4 **Hazard,** Ky,US
106/E3 **Hazāribag,** India
68/B2 **Hazebrouck,** Fr.
57/F5 **Hazel Grove,** Eng,UK
165/F7 **Hazel Park,** Mi,US
153/R7 **Hazen** (str.), NW,Can
151/E3 **Hazen** (bay), Ak,US
66/B4 **Hazerswoude-Dorp,** Neth.
163/F4 **Hazlehurst,** Ms,US
59/F3 **Hazlemere,** Eng,UK
167/D3 **Hazlet,** NJ,US
156/B2 **Hazleton** (mts.), BC,Can
166/C2 **Hazleton,** Pa,US
117/F2 **Hazlett** (lake), Austl.
99/N10 **Hazu,** Japan
105/G3 **He** (riv.), China
59/G1 **Heacham,** Eng,UK
59/G4 **Headcorn,** Eng,UK
57/G4 **Headingley,** Eng,UK
131/D3 **Headlands,** Zim.
158/B3 **Healdsburg,** Ca,US
119/G5 **Healesville,** Austl.
57/G6 **Heanor,** Eng,UK
131/C4 **Heany Junction,** Zim.
51/P8 **Heard** (isl.), Austl.
162/D4 **Hearne,** Tx,US
113/V **Hearst** (isl.), Ant.
160/D1 **Hearst,** On,Can
157/H4 **Heart** (riv.), ND,US
54/D5 **Heart Law** (hill), Sc,UK
161/J1 **Heath** (pt.), Qu,Can
118/G9 **Heathcote Nat'l Park,** Austl.
59/G5 **Heathfield,** Eng,UK
162/D5 **Hebbronville,** Tx,US
57/F4 **Hebden Bridge,** Eng,UK
103/G6 **Hebei** (prov.), China
162/E3 **Heber Springs,** Ar,US
103/C4 **Hebi,** China
52/C3 **Hebrides** (isls.), Sc,UK
55/H8 **Hebrides** (sea), Sc,UK
55/H8 **Hebrides, Inner** (isls.), Sc,UK
55/G8 **Hebrides, Outer** (isls.), Sc,UK
168/B2 **Hebron,** Ct,US
159/H2 **Hebron,** Ne,US
91/D4 **Hebron** (Al Khalīl), WBnk.
151/M5 **Hecate** (str.), BC,Can
105/F3 **Hechi,** China
70/B6 **Hechingen,** Ger.
69/E1 **Hechtel,** Belg.
104/E2 **Hechuan,** China
57/H6 **Heckington,** Eng,UK
157/J4 **Hecla,** SD,US
153/R7 **Hecla and Griper** (bay), NW,Can
156/D3 **Hector** (peak), Ab,Can
62/C2 **Heddal,** Nor.
62/F1 **Hedemora,** Swe.
105/F4 **Hedi** (res.), China
62/D1 **Hedmark** (co.), Nor.
100/K7 **Hedo-misaki** (cape), Japan
57/H4 **Hedon,** Eng,UK
67/E4 **Heek,** Ger.
66/B3 **Heemskerk,** Neth.
66/B4 **Heemstede,** Neth.
66/D4 **Heerde,** Neth.
66/C3 **Heerenveen,** Neth.
66/B3 **Heerhugowaard,** Neth.
69/E2 **Heerlen,** Neth.
69/E2 **Heers,** Belg.
66/C5 **Heesch,** Neth.
66/C6 **Heeze,** Neth.
91/D3 **Ḥefa** (Haifa), Isr.
103/D5 **Hefei,** China
103/B5 **Hefeng Tujiazu Zizhixian,** China
97/L2 **Hegang,** China
77/E2 **Hegau** (reg.), Ger.
99/L10 **Heguri,** Japan
96/D4 **Hei** (riv.), China
100/B4 **Hei** (riv.), Japan
103/B3 **Heicha Shan** (mtn.), China
64/E1 **Heide,** Ger.
119/G5 **Heidelberg,** Austl.
70/B4 **Heidelberg,** Ger.
133/E2 **Heidelberg,** SAfr.
163/F4 **Heidelberg,** Ms,US
66/D5 **Heiden,** Ger.
70/D5 **Heidenheim,** Ger.
97/K1 **Heihe,** China
64/F1 **Heikendorf,** Ger.
132/D2 **Heilbron,** SAfr.
70/C4 **Heilbronn,** Ger.
70/D4 **Heilbronn,** Ger.
64/F1 **Heiligenhafen,** Ger.
66/D6 **Heiligenhaus,** Ger.
67/H6 **Heiligenstadt,** Ger.
97/L2 **Heilong** (Amur) (riv.), China
66/B3 **Heiloo,** Neth.
70/D4 **Heilsbronn,** Ger.
61/N7 **Heimaey** (isl.), Ice.
154/V12 **Heimano** (stream), Hi,US
66/D4 **Heino,** Neth.
63/M1 **Heinola,** Fin.
66/D6 **Heinsberg,** Ger.
101/B2 **Heishan,** China
103/C3 **Heituo Shan** (mtn.), China
99/M9 **Heiwa,** Japan
103/D3 **Hejian,** China
103/B4 **Hejin,** China
102/E3 **Hejing,** China
92/D2 **Hekimhan,** Turk.
99/M10 **Hekinan,** Japan
61/N7 **Hekla** (vol.), Ice.
107/H3 **Hekou,** China
96/F4 **Helan** (mts.), China
70/D2 **Heldburg,** Ger.
66/D6 **Helden,** Neth.
116/L6 **Helena** (brook), Austl.
163/F3 **Helena,** Ar,US
156/E4 **Helena** (cap.), Mt,US
54/B4 **Helensburgh,** Sc,UK
62/F3 **Helgasjön** (lake), Swe.
64/D1 **Helgoland** (isl.), Ger.
64/D1 **Helgoländer Bucht** (bay), Ger.
141/H7 **Heliodora,** Braz.
63/T8 **Hellebæk,** Den.
93/G4 **Ḥelleh** (riv.), Iran
66/D4 **Hellendoorn,** Neth.
69/F3 **Hellenthal,** Ger.
66/B5 **Hellevoetsluis,** Neth.
74/E3 **Hellín,** Sp.
156/D4 **Hells** (canyon), Id, Or,US
156/D4 **Hells Canyon Nat'l Rec. Area,** Id, Or,US
130/C3 **Hell's Gate Nat'l Park,** Kenya
95/H2 **Helmand** (riv.), Afg.
71/E2 **Helmbrechts,** Ger.
64/F3 **Helme** (riv.), Ger.
151/K2 **Helmet** (mtn.), Ak,US
66/C6 **Helmond,** Neth.
57/G3 **Helmsley,** Eng,UK
64/F2 **Helmstedt,** Ger.
97/K3 **Helong,** China
158/E3 **Helper,** Ut,US
71/G6 **Helpfau-Uttendorf,** Aus.
57/F5 **Helsby,** Eng,UK
76/E5 **Helsenhorn** (peak), Swi.
63/T8 **Helsinge,** Den.
63/L1 **Helsingfors** (Helsinki) (cap.), Fin.
63/T8 **Helsingør,** Den.
63/L1 **Helsinki** (Helsingfors) (cap.), Fin.
58/A6 **Helston,** Eng,UK
61/G3 **Helvetinjärven Nat'l Park,** Fin.
60/C5 **Helvick** (pt.), Ire.
68/C2 **Hem,** Fr.
68/B2 **Hem** (riv.), Fr.
71/E4 **Hemau,** Ger.
53/M6 **Hemel Hempstead,** Eng,UK
67/E6 **Hemer,** Ger.
164/D3 **Hemet,** Ca,US
67/G4 **Hemmingen,** Ger.
67/G1 **Hemmoor,** Ger.
162/E4 **Hemphill,** Tx,US
167/E2 **Hempstead,** NY,US
167/L8 **Hempstead** (har.), NY,US
59/H1 **Hemsby,** Eng,UK
57/G4 **Hemsworth,** Eng,UK
103/B4 **Henan** (prov.), China
74/D2 **Henares** (riv.), Sp.
100/A3 **Henashi-zaki** (pt.), Japan
72/C5 **Hendaye,** Fr.
83/K5 **Hendek,** Turk.
142/E3 **Henderson,** Arg.
121/N7 **Henderson** (isl.), Pitc.
160/C4 **Henderson,** Ky,US
163/J2 **Henderson,** NC,US
158/D3 **Henderson,** Nv,US
163/F3 **Henderson,** Tn,US
162/E3 **Henderson,** Tx,US
165/B3 **Henderson** (bay), Wa,US
163/H3 **Hendersonville,** NC,US
163/G2 **Hendersonville,** Tn,US
53/N7 **Hendon,** Eng,UK
66/B5 **Hendrik-Ido-Ambacht,** Neth.
139/G3 **Hendrik Top** (peak), Sur.
132/D3 **Hendrik Verwoerdam** (res.), SAfr.
59/F5 **Henfield,** Eng,UK
103/L8 **Heng** (isl.), China
105/G3 **Heng** (peak), China
104/D3 **Heng** (riv.), China
107/K2 **Hengdong,** China
104/C2 **Hengduan** (mts.), China
66/D4 **Hengelo,** Neth.
71/G5 **Hengersberg,** Ger.
103/B4 **Hengku,** China
103/B3 **Hengshan,** China
103/C3 **Heng Shan** (mtn.), China
103/C3 **Hengshui,** China
105/F4 **Heng Xian,** China
105/G3 **Hengyang,** China
68/B3 **Hénin-Beaumont,** Fr.
117/M8 **Henley Beach,** Austl.
59/F3 **Henley-on-Thames,** Eng,UK
166/C6 **Henlopen** (cape), De,US
59/E2 **Henly-in-Arden,** Eng,UK
72/B3 **Hennebont,** Fr.
69/G2 **Hennef,** Ger.
69/E2 **Henri-Chapelle,** Belg.
162/D3 **Henrietta,** Tx,US
153/H3 **Henrietta Maria** (cape), On,Can
139/E2 **Henri Pittier Nat'l Park,** Ven.
151/M5 **Henry** (cape), BC,Can
158/E3 **Henry** (mts.), Ut,US
159/J4 **Henryetta,** Ok,US
165/F7 **Henry Ford Museum & Greenfield Vill.,** Mi,US
68/C3 **Hensies,** Belg.
96/F2 **Hentiyn** (mts.), Mong.
104/B5 **Henzada,** Burma
70/B3 **Heppenheim an der Bergstrasse,** Ger.
105/F4 **Hepu,** China
104/D3 **Heqing,** China
103/B3 **Hequ,** China
61/N6 **Heradhsvötn** (riv.), Ice.
95/H2 **Herāt,** Afg.
75/G1 **Hérault** (riv.), Fr.
118/B2 **Herbert** (riv.), Austl.
156/G3 **Herbert,** Sk,Can
118/B2 **Herbert Riv.** (falls), Austl.
118/B2 **Herbert Riv. Falls Nat'l Park,** Austl.
53/S10 **Herblay,** Fr.
76/D1 **Herbolzheim,** Ger.
70/D5 **Herbrechtingen,** Ger.
82/D4 **Hercegnovi,** Yugo.
165/K10 **Hercules,** Ca,US
67/E6 **Herdecke,** Ger.
69/G2 **Herdorf,** Ger.
149/E4 **Heredia,** CR
58/D2 **Hereford,** Eng,UK
166/D5 **Hereford** (inlet), NJ,US
162/C3 **Hereford,** Tx,US
58/D2 **Hereford & Worcester** (co.), Eng,UK
121/L6 **Hereheretue** (isl.), FrPol.
83/J5 **Hereke,** Turk.
74/C3 **Herencia,** Sp.
69/D1 **Herentals,** Belg.
67/F4 **Herford,** Ger.
76/C2 **Héricourt,** Fr.
159/H3 **Herington,** Ks,US
77/F3 **Herisau,** Swi.
69/E2 **Herk** (riv.), Belg.
69/E2 **Herk-de-Stad,** Belg.
96/G2 **Herlen** (riv.), Mong.
63/T9 **Herlev,** Den.
55/P12 **Herma Ness** (pt.), Sc,UK
163/F2 **Hermann,** Mo,US
67/H3 **Hermannsburg,** Ger.
117/G2 **Hermannsburg Abor. Land,** Austl.
68/B5 **Hermes,** Fr.
156/D4 **Hermiston,** Or,US
168/G5 **Hermitage,** Pa,US
91/D3 **Hermon** (mtn.), Leb., Syria
164/B3 **Hermosa Beach,** Ca,US
146/C2 **Hermosillo,** Mex.
142/E2 **Hernando,** Arg.
163/F3 **Hernando,** Ms,US
74/E1 **Hernani,** Sp.
68/D2 **Herne,** Belg.
67/E5 **Herne,** Ger.
59/H4 **Herne Bay,** Eng,UK
62/C3 **Herning,** Den.
91/G8 **Herodian** (ruins), WBnk.
91/G8 **Herodion Nat'l Park,** WBnk.
146/B2 **Heroica Caborca,** Mex.
70/E3 **Heroldsberg,** Ger.
70/D1 **Herpf** (riv.), Ger.
70/B5 **Herrenberg,** Ger.
147/J5 **Herrero** (pt.), Mex.
70/D4 **Herrieden,** Ger.
77/H2 **Herrsching am Ammersee,** Ger.
72/D5 **Hers** (riv.), Fr.
71/E3 **Hersbruck,** Ger.
67/E6 **Herscheid,** Ger.
151/L2 **Herschel,** Yk,Can
69/D1 **Herselt,** Belg.
166/B3 **Hershey,** Pa,US
69/E2 **Herstal,** Belg.
59/G5 **Herstmonceux,** Eng,UK
67/E5 **Herten,** Ger.
59/F3 **Hertford,** Eng,UK
53/N6 **Hertfordshire** (co.), Eng,UK
69/E2 **Herve,** Belg.
118/D4 **Hervey** (bay), Austl.
118/D4 **Hervey Bay,** Austl.
70/B4 **Herxheim bei Landau,** Ger.
67/H5 **Herzberg am Harz,** Ger.
67/F5 **Herzebrock-Clarholz,** Ger.
68/C2 **Herzele,** Belg.
91/F7 **Herzliyya,** Isr.
70/D3 **Herzogenaurach,** Ger.
82/B1 **Herzogenburg,** Aus.
69/F2 **Herzogenrath,** Ger.
69/D3 **Hesbaye** (plat.), Belg.
105/F4 **Heshan,** China
96/F4 **Heshui,** China
103/C3 **Heshun,** China
69/F4 **Hesperange,** Lux.
164/C2 **Hesperia,** Ca,US
151/M3 **Hess** (riv.), Yk,Can
67/G6 **Hesse** (state), Ger.
67/F5 **Hessel** (riv.), Ger.
67/G6 **Hessisch Lichtenau,** Ger.
67/G4 **Hessisch Oldendorf,** Ger.
57/H4 **Hessle,** Eng,UK
57/E5 **Heswall,** Eng,UK
165/L11 **Hetch Hetchy** (aqueduct), Ca,US
157/H4 **Hettinger,** ND,US
57/G2 **Hetton-le-Hole,** Eng,UK
70/C5 **Heubach,** Ger.
67/E5 **Heubach** (riv.), Ger.
70/B1 **Heuchelheim,** Ger.
65/H5 **Heukuppe** (peak), Aus.
69/E1 **Heusden-Zolder,** Belg.
70/B2 **Heusenstamm,** Ger.
69/F5 **Heusweiler,** Ger.
72/D2 **Hève, Cap de la** (cape), Fr.
82/E2 **Heves,** Hun.
65/L5 **Heves** (co.), Hun.
167/L9 **Hewlett,** NY,US
167/E2 **Hewlett** (pt.), NY,US
77/G3 **Hexenkopf** (peak), Aus.
57/F2 **Hexham,** Eng,UK
103/D5 **He Xian,** China
97/H3 **Hexigten,** China
97/H3 **Hexigten Qi,** China
132/L10 **Hex River** (mts.), SAfr.
132/L10 **Hex River** (pass), SAfr.
93/N7 **Heybeli** (isl.), Turk.
57/F3 **Heysham,** Eng,UK
66/C6 **Heythuysen,** Neth.
57/F4 **Heywood,** Eng,UK
103/C4 **Heze,** China
104/E3 **Hezhang,** China
163/H5 **Hialeah,** Fl,US
159/J3 **Hiawatha,** Ks,US
157/K4 **Hibbing,** Mn,US
119/C4 **Hibbs** (pt.), Austl.
149/F1 **Hicacos** (pt.), Cuba
154/W13 **Hickam A.F.B.,** Hi,US
151/M4 **Hickman** (mtn.), BC,Can
160/B4 **Hickman,** Ky,US
165/Q16 **Hickory** (cr.), Il,US
163/H3 **Hickory,** NC,US
166/C1 **Hickory Run Saint Park,** Pa,US
167/E2 **Hicksville,** NY,US
99/E3 **Hida** (riv.), Japan
100/C2 **Hidaka,** Japan
99/H7 **Hidaka,** Japan
100/C2 **Hidaka** (mts.), Japan
98/D4 **Hidaka** (riv.), Japan
147/E3 **Hidalgo,** Mex.
148/B1 **Hidalgo** (state), Mex.
67/F4 **Hiddenhausen,** Ger.
140/B2 **Hidrolândia,** Braz.
92/B2 **Hierapolis** (ruins), Turk.
67/E2 **Hieve** (lake), Ger.
99/H7 **Higashikurume,** Japan
99/H7 **Higashimurayama,** Japan
99/G1 **Higashine,** Japan
99/L10 **Higashi-Ōsaka,** Japan
99/K10 **Higashiura,** Japan
99/H7 **Higashiyamato,** Japan
99/L10 **Higashiyoshino,** Japan
156/C5 **High** (des.), Or,US
166/C1 **High** (hill), Pa,US
59/F2 **Higham Ferrers,** Eng,UK
58/D4 **Highbridge,** Eng,UK
162/E4 **High Island,** Tx,US
54/B2 **Highland** (reg.), Sc,UK
164/C2 **Highland,** Ca,US
150/A1 **Highland** (pt.), Fl,US
165/R16 **Highland,** In,US
165/Q15 **Highland Park,** Il,US
165/F7 **Highland Park,** Mi,US
166/D3 **Highland Park,** NJ,US
58/D2 **Highley,** Eng,UK
157/J4 **Highmore,** SD,US
112/C2 **High Park** (mtn.), Phil.
163/H3 **High Point,** NC,US
166/D1 **High Point** (peak), NJ,US
166/D2 **High Point Saint Park,** NJ,US
156/D2 **High Prairie,** Ab,Can
157/H2 **Highrock** (lake), Mb,Can
57/F3 **High Street** (mtn.), Eng,UK
57/E4 **Hightown,** Eng,UK
58/B5 **High Willhays** (hill), Eng,UK
59/E3 **Highworth,** Eng,UK
59/F3 **High Wycombe,** Eng,UK
150/D3 **Higüey,** DRep.
91/B4 **Hihyā,** Egypt
61/J3 **Hiidenportin Nat'l Park,** Fin.
63/K2 **Hiiumaa** (isl.), Est.
94/C3 **Hijāz, Jabal al** (mts.), SAr.
98/B4 **Hiji,** Japan
142/Q9 **Hijuelas de Conchali,** Chile
99/L9 **Hikami,** Japan
98/E3 **Hikone,** Japan
121/L6 **Hikueru** (atoll), FrPol.
115/S10 **Hikurangi** (peak), NZ
69/H2 **Hilchenbach,** Ger.
70/D2 **Hildburghausen,** Ger.
66/D6 **Hilden,** Ger.
67/G4 **Hildesheim,** Ger.
166/B3 **Hill** (isl.), Pa,US
150/G4 **Hillaby** (mtn.), Bar.
113/L **Hillary** (coast), Ant.
159/H3 **Hill City,** Ks,US
167/D1 **Hillcrest,** NY,US
67/F4 **Hille,** Ger.
66/B4 **Hillegom,** Neth.
62/E4 **Hillerød,** Den.
56/B2 **Hillhall,** NI,UK
53/M7 **Hillingdon** (bor.), Eng,UK
54/C1 **Hill of Fearn,** Sc,UK
157/J4 **Hillsboro,** ND,US
158/F4 **Hillsboro,** NM,US
160/D4 **Hillsboro,** Oh,US
156/C4 **Hillsboro,** Or,US
162/D3 **Hillsboro,** Tx,US
118/C3 **Hillsborough** (chan.), Austl.
56/B3 **Hillsborough,** NI,UK
165/K11 **Hillsborough,** Ca,US
166/D3 **Hillsborough,** NJ,US
160/C3 **Hillsdale,** Mi,US
167/D1 **Hillsdale,** NJ,US
54/D3 **Hillside,** Sc,UK
167/D2 **Hillside,** NJ,US
55/P12 **Hillswick,** Sc,UK
56/B3 **Hilltown,** NI,UK
154/U11 **Hilo,** Hi,US
112/D3 **Hilonghilong** (mtn.), Phil.
70/E4 **Hilpoltstein,** Ger.
57/E3 **Hilpsford** (pt.), Eng,UK
163/H3 **Hilton Head** (isl.), SC,US
163/H3 **Hilton Head Island,** SC,US
66/C6 **Hilvarenbeek,** Neth.
66/C4 **Hilversum,** Neth.
77/E2 **Hilzingen,** Ger.
108/D2 **Himachal Pradesh** (state), India
106/D2 **Himalaya, Great** (range), Asia
112/C3 **Himamaylan,** Phil.
98/D3 **Himeji,** Japan
98/D3 **Himeji Castle,** Japan
99/E2 **Himi,** Japan
125/N5 **Himora,** Eth.
91/E2 **Ḥimş,** Syria
92/D3 **Ḥimş** (prov.), Syria
112/D3 **Hinatuan,** Phil.
149/H2 **Hinche,** Haiti
115/H3 **Hinchinbrook** (isl.), Austl.
151/J3 **Hinchinbrook** (chan.), Ak,US
118/B2 **Hinchinbrook I. Nat'l Park,** Austl.
59/E1 **Hinckley,** Eng,UK
117/G5 **Hincks Consv. Park,** Austl.
57/H2 **Hinderwell,** Eng,UK
57/F4 **Hindley,** Eng,UK
119/B2 **Hindmarsh** (lake), Austl.
95/J1 **Hindu Kush** (mts.), Afg., Pak.
106/C5 **Hindupur,** India
163/H4 **Hinesville,** Ga,US
106/C3 **Hinganghāt,** India
95/J3 **Hingol** (riv.), Pak.
106/C4 **Hingoli,** India
95/J3 **Hingorja,** Pak.
92/E2 **Hınıs,** Turk.
99/H7 **Hino,** Japan
99/M9 **Hino** (riv.), Japan
99/H7 **Hinode,** Japan
99/H7 **Hinohara,** Japan
74/C3 **Hinojosa del Duque,** Sp.
98/C3 **Hino-misaki** (cape), Japan
165/Q16 **Hinsdale,** Il,US
57/F6 **Hinstock,** Eng,UK
67/E2 **Hinte,** Ger.
77/F4 **Hinterrhein** (riv.), Swi.
77/F3 **Hinterrugg** (peak), Swi.
156/D2 **Hinton,** Ab,Can
160/D4 **Hinton,** WV,US
112/D3 **Hinunangan,** Phil.
77/E3 **Hinwil,** Swi.
66/B3 **Hippolytushoef,** Neth.
57/G3 **Hipswell,** Eng,UK
99/L9 **Hira** (mts.), Japan
98/A4 **Hirado,** Japan
98/D3 **Hirakata,** Japan
106/D3 **Hirakud** (res.), India
130/C3 **Hiraman** (riv.), Kenya
100/B3 **Hiranai,** Japan
100/H8 **Hirara,** Japan
98/C3 **Hirata,** Japan
99/H7 **Hiratsuka,** Japan
92/C2 **Hirfanlı** (dam), Turk.
83/H2 **Hîrlău,** Rom.
100/C2 **Hiro'o,** Japan
100/B3 **Hirosaki,** Japan
98/C3 **Hiroshima,** Japan
98/C3 **Hiroshima** (pref.), Japan
70/E3 **Hirschaid,** Ger.
71/E3 **Hirschau,** Ger.
68/D4 **Hirson,** Fr.
83/H3 **Hîrşova,** Rom.
62/C3 **Hirtshals,** Den.
58/C3 **Hirwaun,** Wal,UK
98/E3 **Hisai,** Japan
106/C2 **Hisār,** India
96/E2 **Hishig-Öndör,** Mong.
150/C2 **Hispaniola** (isl.), DRep., Haiti
93/E3 **Hīt,** Iraq
99/G2 **Hitachi,** Japan
99/G2 **Hitachi-ōta,** Japan
59/F3 **Hitchin,** Eng,UK
98/B4 **Hitoyoshi,** Japan
61/C3 **Hitra** (isl.), Nor.
63/T8 **Hittarp,** Swe.
121/M5 **Hiva Oa** (isl.), FrPol.
99/L9 **Hiyoshi,** Japan
62/F2 **Hjälmaren** (lake), Swe.
84/B2 **Hjartfjellet** (peak), Nor.
63/U9 **Hjärup,** Swe.
62/F2 **Hjo,** Swe.
62/C3 **Hjørring,** Den.
109/B1 **Hka** (riv.), Burma
104/C2 **Hkakabo** (peak), Burma
65/J4 **Hlohovec,** Slvk.
118/G8 **Hmas-Nirimba,** Austl.
104/C5 **Hmawbi,** Burma
129/F5 **Ho,** Gha.
109/D1 **Hoa Bin,** Viet.
109/E4 **Hoa Da,** Viet.
109/C1 **Hoang Lien** (mts.), Viet.
153/K2 **Hoare** (bay), NW,Can
99/G2 **Hobara,** Japan
119/C4 **Hobart,** Austl.
159/H4 **Hobart,** Ok,US
113/Q **Hobbs** (coast), Ant.
159/G4 **Hobbs,** NM,US
68/D1 **Hoboken,** Belg.
167/D2 **Hoboken,** NJ,US
102/E2 **Hoboksar Monggol Zizhixian** (Hoboksar), China
62/C3 **Hobro,** Den.
125/Q6 **Hobyo,** Som.
82/A2 **Hochalmspitze** (peak), Aus.
70/C3 **Höchberg,** Ger.
77/F3 **Hochfinsler** (peak), Swi.
77/G3 **Hochgrat** (peak), Ger.
70/B2 **Hochheim am Main,** Ger.
109/D4 **Ho Chi Minh City** (Saigon), Viet.
104/E4 **Ho Chi Minh Mausoleum,** Viet.
73/K3 **Hochkönig** (peak), Aus.
101/D2 **Hŏch'ŏn** (riv.), NKor.
73/L3 **Hochschwab** (peak), Aus.
69/G3 **Hochsimmer** (peak), Ger.
70/D3 **Höchstadt an der Aisch,** Ger.
70/B3 **Höchst im Odenwald,** Ger.
77/G3 **Hochvogel** (peak), Aus.
77/F4 **Hochwang** (peak), Swi.
70/B4 **Hockenheim,** Ger.
59/G3 **Hockley,** Eng,UK
57/F4 **Hodder** (riv.), Eng,UK
53/N6 **Hoddesdon,** Eng,UK
164/C4 **Hodges** (lake), Ca,US
156/G3 **Hodgeville,** Sk,Can
128/C2 **Hodh** (reg.), Mrta.
91/F7 **Hod HaSharon,** Isr.
128/D2 **Hodh ech Chargui** (reg.), Mrta.
128/C2 **Hodh el Gharbi** (reg.), Mrta.
82/E2 **Hódmezovásárhely,** Hun.
123/T16 **Hodna, Chott el** (salt lake), Alg.
57/F6 **Hodnet,** Eng,UK
65/J4 **Hodonín,** Czh.
69/E2 **Hoegnel** (riv.), Belg.
66/B5 **Hoekse Waard** (polder), Neth.
69/G6 **Hoenheim,** Fr.
69/E2 **Hoensbroek,** Neth.
69/E2 **Hoeselt,** Belg.
66/C4 **Hoevelaken,** Neth.
66/B5 **Hoeven,** Neth.
130/B2 **Hoeys Bridge,** Kenya
71/E2 **Hof,** Ger.
165/P15 **Hoffman Estates,** Il,US
67/G6 **Hofgeismar,** Ger.
103/B3 **Hofong Qagan** (salt lake), China
62/G1 **Hofors,** Swe.
61/P6 **Hofsá** (riv.), Ice.
61/N7 **Hofsjökull** (glac.), Ice.
98/B3 **Hōfu,** Japan
117/H2 **Hogarth** (peak), Austl.

66/C4 Hoge Veluwe Nat'l Park, Neth.
130/C4 Hogoro, Tanz.
67/G6 Hohegrass (peak), Ger.
71/E6 Hohenbrunn, Ger.
77/F3 Hohenems, Aus.
67/H4 Hohenhameln, Ger.
70/C4 Hohenloher Ebene (plain), Ger.
71/E1 Hohenwarte-Stausee (res.), Ger.
73/K3 Hoher Dachstein (peak), Aus.
73/K3 Hohe Tauern (mts.), Aus.
73/K3 Hohe Tauern Nat'l Park, Aus.
76/D4 Hohgant (peak), Swi.
103/B2 Hohhot, China
76/D1 Hohneck (mtn.), Fr.
69/G3 Höhr-Grenzhausen, Ger.
102/F4 Hoh Sai (lake), China
102/F4 Hoh Xil (lake), China
102/E4 Hoh Xil (mts.), China
109/E3 Hoi An, Viet.
130/A2 Hoima, Ugan.
162/D2 Hoisington, Ks,US
109/D1 Hoi Xuan, Viet.
98/C4 Hōjō, Japan
115/R11 Hokitika, NZ
100/C2 Hokkaidō (dept.), Japan
100/B2 Hokkaidō (isl.), Japan
62/C2 Hokksund, Nor.
99/G2 Hokota, Japan
99/K10 Hokudan, Japan
99/M9 Hokusei, Japan
130/D3 Hola, Kenya
62/D4 Holbaek, Den.
57/J6 Holbeach, Eng,UK
59/H3 Holbrook, Eng,UK
158/E4 Holbrook, Az,US
168/C1 Holbrook, Ma,US
168/C1 Holden, Ma,US
159/H4 Holdenville, Ok,US
57/H4 Holderness (pen.), Eng,UK
159/H2 Holdrege, Ne,US
149/G1 Holguín, Cuba
151/G3 Holitna (riv.), Ak,US
166/B6 Holland (pt.), Md,US
160/C3 Holland, Mi,US
163/F3 Hollandale, Ms,US
66/B4 Hollandse IJssel (riv.), Neth.
55/N13 Hollandstoun, Sc,UK
59/H2 Hollesley, Eng,UK
159/H4 Hollis, Ok,US
116/B2 Hollister (peak), Austl.
158/B3 Hollister, Ca,US
168/C1 Holliston, Ma,US
69/E2 Hollogne-aux-Pierres, Belg.
63/L1 Hollola, Fin.
159/F4 Holloman A.F.B., NM,US
62/E4 Höllviksnäs, Swe.
163/F3 Holly Springs, Ms,US
164/F7 Hollywood, Ca,US
163/H5 Hollywood, Fl,US
164/F7 Hollywood Bowl, Los Angeles, Ca,US
61/F3 Holm, Swe.
152/E1 Holman, NW,Can
167/D3 Holmdel, NJ,US
118/C2 Holmes (reefs), Austl.
168/F6 Holmes (co.), Oh,US
156/F4 Holmes (peak), Wy,US
57/F5 Holmes Chapel, Eng,UK
53/N8 Holmesdale (val.), Eng,UK
62/D2 Holmestrand, Nor.
57/H4 Holme upon Spalding Moor, Eng,UK
57/G4 Holmfirth, Eng,UK
54/B6 Holmhead, Sc,UK
113/C Holm-Lützow (bay), Ant.
61/F3 Holmsjön (lake), Swe.
91/D3 Ḥolon, Isr.
62/C3 Holstebro, Den.
163/H2 Holston (riv.), Tn,US
58/B5 Holsworthy, Eng,UK
59/H1 Holt, Eng,UK
66/D4 Holten, Neth.
159/J3 Holton, Ks,US
167/E2 Holtsville, NY,US
56/D5 Holy (isl.), Wal,UK
56/D5 Holyhead, Wal,UK
56/D5 Holyhead (mtn.), Wal,UK
54/E5 Holy (Lindisfarne) (isl.), Eng,UK
159/G2 Holyoke, Co,US
168/B1 Holyoke, Ma,US
57/E5 Holywell, Wal,UK
56/C2 Holywood, NI,UK
64/F5 Holzkirchen, Ger.
67/G5 Holzminden, Ger.
67/E6 Holzwickede, Ger.
132/B3 Hom (dry riv.), Namb.
130/B3 Homa Bay, Kenya
66/D6 Homberg, Ger.
67/G6 Homberg, Ger.
129/E3 Hombori Tondo (peak), Mali
69/F5 Hombourg-Haut, Fr.
69/G5 Homburg, Ger.
153/K2 Home (bay), NW,Can
69/E5 Homécourt, Fr.
162/E3 Homer, La,US
163/H5 Homestead, Fl,US
163/H5 Homestead A.F.B., Fl,US
163/G3 Homewood, Al,US
165/Q16 Homewood, Il,US
163/F4 Homochitto (riv.), Ms,US
131/D4 Homoíne, Moz.
112/D3 Homonhon (isl.), Phil.
106/B5 Honāvar, India
100/C2 Honbetsu, Japan
109/D4 Hon Chong, Viet.
138/C3 Honda, Col.
58/C3 Honddu (riv.), Wal,UK
148/D2 Hondo (riv.), Belz., Mex.
98/B4 Hondo, Japan
165/L12 Hondo (arroyo), Ca,US
159/F4 Hondo (dry riv.), NM,US
162/D4 Hondo, Tx,US
147/Q9 Hondo de Tepotzotlán (riv.), Mex.
66/D3 Hondsrug (reg.), Neth.
148/E3 Honduras
148/D2 Honduras (gulf), NAm.
147/L6 Honey, Mex.
158/B2 Honey (lake), Ca,US
165/P14 Honey (cr.), Wi,US
59/E2 Honeybourne, Eng,UK
105/G2 Hong (lake), China
103/C4 Hong (riv.), China
103/C5 Hong'an, China
101/D4 Hongch'ŏn, SKor.
107/J2 Hongdu (riv.), China
109/D1 Hong Gai, Viet.
103/C5 Honghu, China
105/F3 Hongjiang, China
105/G4 Hong Kong (dpcy.), UK
103/B3 Hongliu (riv.), China
105/H2 Hongmiao (mtn.), China
109/C1 Hong (Red) (riv.), Viet.
76/D5 Hongrin (lake), Swi.
105/H3 Hongshan (mtn.), China
105/E4 Hongshui (riv.), China
101/D4 Hongsŏng, SKor.
103/C3 Hongtao Shan (mtn.), China
103/B3 Hongtong, China
161/H1 Honguedo (passg.), Qu,Can
104/D2 Hongya, China
103/B5 Hongyan, China
96/E5 Hongyuan, China
103/D4 Hongze, China
103/D4 Hongze (lake), China
120/E5 Honiara (cap.), Sol.
58/C5 Honiton, Eng,UK
100/B4 Honjō, Japan
154/T10 Honolulu (cap.), Hi,US
154/V13 Honolulu (co.), Hi,US
109/D4 Hon Quan, Viet.
97/M5 Honshu (isl.), Japan
116/C5 Hood (pt.), Austl.
165/J10 Hood (mtn.), Ca,US
156/C4 Hood (mtn.), Or,US
156/C4 Hood Canal (inlet), Wa,US
66/B4 Hoofddorp, Neth.
66/C6 Hoogeloon, Neth.
66/B6 Hoogerheide, Neth.
66/D3 Hoogeveen, Neth.
66/D3 Hoogeveense Vaart (can.), Neth.
66/D2 Hoogezand, Neth.
106/E3 Hooghly-Chinsura, India
68/C2 Hooglede, Belg.
66/B6 Hoogstraten, Belg.
118/C3 Hook (isl.), Austl.
59/F4 Hook, Eng,UK
60/D5 Hook Head (pt.), Ire.
160/C3 Hoopeston, Il,US
66/C3 Hoorn, Neth.
66/C3 Hoornse Hop (bay), Neth.
158/D3 Hoover (dam), Az,US
92/E1 Hopa, Turk.
166/D2 Hopatcong, NJ,US
166/D2 Hopatcong (lake), NJ,US
116/D5 Hope (lake), Austl.
156/C3 Hope, BC,Can
57/E5 Hope, Wal,UK
162/E3 Hope, Ar,US
54/C1 Hopeman, Sc,UK
153/K2 Hopes Advance (cape), Qu,Can
58/C6 Hope's Nose (pt.), Eng,UK
58/D2 Hope under Dinmore, Eng,UK
118/B1 Hope Vale Abor. Community, Austl.
118/B1 Hope Vale Abor. Land, Austl.
160/E4 Hopewell, Va,US
166/C3 Hopewell Furnace Nat'l Hist. Site, Pa,US
117/F3 Hopkins (lake), Austl.
119/B3 Hopkins (riv.), Austl.
160/C4 Hopkinsville, Ky,US
168/C3 Hopkinton, RI,US
67/F6 Hoppecke (riv.), Ger.
164/B2 Hopper Mountain Nat'l Wild. Ref., Ca,US
67/E4 Hopsten, Ger.
156/C4 Hoquiam, Wa,US
151/J2 Horace (mtn.), Ak,US
99/L9 Hōrai-san (peak), Japan
92/E1 Horasan, Turk.
71/G4 Horažďovice, Czh.
70/B6 Horb am Neckar, Ger.
91/D3 Ḥorbat Qesari (ruins), Isr.
57/G4 Horbury, Eng,UK
62/A1 Hordaland (co.), Nor.
57/G2 Horden, Eng,UK
83/G3 Horezu, Rom.
77/E3 Horgen, Swi.
96/F3 Hörh (peak), Mong.
51/S6 Horiara (cap.), Sol.
103/B2 Horinger, China
53/N8 Horley, Eng,UK
113/R Horlick Ice Stream, Ant.
150/E3 Hormigüeros, PR
93/H5 Hormozgān (gov.), Iran
93/H5 Hormuz (str.), Iran, Oman
73/L2 Horn, Aus.
61/M6 Horn (pt.), Ice.
65/L4 Hornád (riv.), Slvk.
61/E2 Hornavan (lake), Swe.
67/F5 Horn-Bad Meinberg, Ger.
63/T8 Hornbæk, Den.
161/Q8 Hornby, On,Can
57/H5 Horncastle, Eng,UK
53/P7 Hornchurch, Eng,UK
160/E3 Hornell, NY,US
160/C1 Hornepayne, On,Can
143/L8 Horn (Hornos) (cape), Chile
70/B5 Hornisgrinde (peak), Ger.
71/F2 Horní Slavkov, Czh.
143/L8 Hornos (Horn) (cape), Chile
143/L8 Hornos Nat'l Park, Cabo de, Chile
68/A4 Hornoy-le-Bourg, Fr.
118/H8 Hornsby, Austl.
57/H4 Hornsea, Eng,UK
62/C4 Hörnum (cape), Ger.
64/E1 Hornum Odde (cape), Ger.
100/C2 Horoshiri-dake (mtn.), Japan
103/E1 Horqin Youyi Zhongqi, China
103/E2 Horqin Zuoyi Houqi, China
103/E1 Horqin Zuoyi Zhongqi, China
58/B6 Horrabridge, Eng,UK
159/F2 Horse (cr.), Ne, Wy,US
160/C4 Horse Cave, Ky,US
156/C2 Horsefly (lake), BC,Can
62/C4 Horsens, Den.
59/H3 Horsey (isl.), Eng,UK
57/G4 Horsforth, Eng,UK
119/B3 Horsham, Austl.
59/F4 Horsham, Eng,UK
166/C3 Horsham, Pa,US
62/G1 Horslandet (pen.), Swe.
66/D6 Horst, Neth.
67/E4 Hörstel, Ger.
67/E4 Horstmar, Ger.
75/S12 Horta, Azor.,Port.
75/N9 Hortaleza, Sp.
62/D2 Horten, Nor.
82/E2 Hortobágyi Nat'l Park, Hun.
151/N2 Horton (riv.), NW,Can
167/F1 Horton (pt.), NY,US
53/P7 Horton Kirby, Eng,UK
71/H4 Horusický Rybník (lake), Czh.
91/D4 Ḥorvot 'Avedat (ruins), Isr.
91/D4 Ḥorvot Meẓada (Masada) (ruins), Isr.
77/E3 Horw, Swi.
57/F4 Horwich, Eng,UK
160/D2 Horwood (lake), On,Can
70/C2 Hösbach, Ger.
106/C3 Hoshangābād, India
108/C2 Hoshiārpur, India
106/C4 Hospet, India
143/K8 Hoste (isl.), Chile
55/P12 Hoswick, Sc,UK
99/E2 Hotaka, Japan
99/E2 Hotaka-dake (mtn.), Japan
102/C4 Hotan, China
102/D4 Hotan (riv.), China
157/H5 Hot Springs, SD,US
162/E3 Hot Springs Nat'l Park, Ar,US
162/E3 Hot Springs Village, Ar,US
152/E2 Hottah (lake), NW,Can
132/A2 Hottentot (bay), Namb.
132/A2 Hottentots (pt.), Namb.
105/E2 Hou (riv.), China
68/B3 Houdain, Fr.
128/D4 Houet (prov.), Burk.
160/B2 Houghton, Mi,US
160/C2 Houghton Lake, Mi,US
57/G2 Houghton-le-Spring, Eng,UK
53/S10 Houilles, Fr.
161/H2 Houlton, Me,US
103/B4 Houma, China
163/F4 Houma, La,US
53/M7 Hounslow (bor.), Eng,UK
68/B2 Houplines, Fr.
68/A3 Hourdel, Pointe du (pt.), Fr.
54/A2 Hourn, Loch (inlet), Sc,UK
168/A3 Housatonic (riv.), Ct, Ma,US
168/A2 Housatonic Saint For., Ct,US
158/D3 House (range), Ut,US
57/F1 Housesteads Roman Fort, Eng,UK
156/B2 Houston, BC,Can
159/K3 Houston, Mo,US
163/F3 Houston, Ms,US
162/E4 Houston, Tx,US
66/C4 Houten, Neth.
68/B2 Houthulst, Belg.
116/B4 Houtman Abrolhos (isls.), Austl.
66/C3 Houtribdijk (dam), Neth.
63/J1 Houtskär (isl.), Fin.
62/D1 Hov, Nor.
96/C2 Hovd, Mong.
63/T9 Hove (riv.), Den.
59/F5 Hove, Eng,UK
67/F5 Hövelhof, Ger.
158/E3 Hovenweep Nat'l Mon., Co,US
59/H1 Hoveton, Eng,UK
62/E1 Hovfjället (peak), Swe.
57/H3 Hovingham, Eng,UK
96/E1 Hövsgöl (lake), Mong.
151/K2 Howard (hill), Ak,US
151/G2 Howard (pass), Ak,US
166/B5 Howard (co.), Md,US
167/K9 Howard Beach, NY,US
165/D3 Howard Hanson (dam), Wa,US
165/D3 Howard Hanson (res.), Wa,US
57/H4 Howden, Eng,UK
119/D3 Howe (cape), Austl.
160/D3 Howell, Mi,US
167/D3 Howell, NJ,US
133/E3 Howick, SAfr.
121/H4 Howland (isl.), PacUS
55/H8 Howmore, Sc,UK
106/E3 Howrah, India
64/E3 Höxter, Ger.
102/E3 Hoxud, China
55/N13 Hoy (isl.), Sc,UK
65/H3 Hoyerswerda, Ger.
57/E5 Hoylake, Eng,UK
57/G5 Hoyland Nether, Eng,UK
75/N8 Hoyo-de-Manzanares, Sp.
69/E3 Hoyoux (riv.), Belg.
96/E2 Hoyt Tamir (riv.), Mong.
99/M9 Hozumi, Japan
71/G3 Hracholusky, Údolní nádrž (res.), Czh.
65/H3 Hradec Králové, Czh.
71/G2 Hradiště (peak), Czh.
82/D4 Hrasnica, Bosn.
82/B2 Hrastnik, Slov.
79/G1 Hrastovlje, Slov.
61/M6 Hrolleifsborg (peak), Ice.
65/K4 Hron (riv.), Slvk.
82/D1 Hron (riv.), Slvk.
65/J3 Hronov, Czh.
65/M3 Hrubieszów, Pol.
65/J3 Hrubý Jeseník (mts.), Czh.
61/P6 Hrútafjöll (peak), Ice.
105/J4 Hsiukulan (mtn.), Tai.
105/J3 Hsüeh (peak), Tai.
96/G5 Hua (peak), China
96/F4 Huachi, China
144/B3 Huacho, Peru
97/L2 Huachuan, China
96/G3 Huade, China
97/K3 Huadian, China
105/J2 Huading (mtn.), China
109/B3 Hua Hin, Thai.
121/K6 Huahine (isl.), FrPol.
103/C4 Huai (riv.), China
103/D4 Huai'an, China
96/H5 Huaibei, China
103/C4 Huaibin, China
105/F3 Huaihua, China
105/G4 Huaiji, China
103/C2 Huailai, China
103/D4 Huainan, China
103/D5 Huaining, China
103/C2 Huairen, China
103/D2 Huairou, China
103/C4 Huaiyang, China
103/D4 Huaiyin, China
103/D4 Huaiyuan, China
147/F5 Huajuapan de León, Mex.
142/C2 Hualañé, Chile
144/B2 Huallaga (riv.), Peru
144/B2 Huamachuco, Peru
147/F5 Huamantla, Mex.
126/C3 Huambo, Ang.
148/C2 Huamelula, Mex.
105/G2 Huan (riv.), China
97/L2 Huanan, China
144/C4 Huancavelica, Peru
144/C3 Huancayo, Peru
136/E8 Huanchaca (peak), Bol.
109/C2 Huang (riv.), Laos, Thai.
103/C4 Huangchuan, China
103/C5 Huanggang, China
105/H3 Huanggang (peak), China
103/D3 Huanghua, China
105/H3 Huangjinkenggang (mtn.), China
103/B4 Huangling, China
103/B4 Huanglong, China
103/B4 Huanglongtan, China
103/B4 Huangmao (peak), China
103/C5 Huangmei, China
103/C5 Huangpi, China
107/J2 Huangping, China
103/C2 Huangqi (lake), China
103/D5 Huangshan, China
103/C5 Huangshi, China
103/C5 Huangtang (lake), China
103/B4 Huangtu (plat.), China
107/H4 Huang (Yellow) (riv.), China
103/B4 Huangyunpu, China
96/E4 Huangzhong, China
107/J3 Huanjiang, China
101/C2 Huanren, China
144/C4 Huanta, Peru
103/D3 Huantai, China
144/B3 Huánuco, Peru
136/E7 Huanuni, Bol.
96/F4 Huan Xian, China
149/E3 Huapi (mts.), Nic.
147/F5 Huaquechula, Mex.
144/A1 Huaquillas, Ecu.
144/B3 Huaral, Peru
144/B3 Huaráz, Peru
144/B3 Huarmey, Peru
144/B3 Huascarán (peak), Peru
144/B3 Huascarán Nat'l Park, Peru
103/B4 Hua Shan (peak), China
105/G3 Huashi (mts.), China
146/C3 Huatabampo, Mex.
136/E6 Huatunas (lake), Bol.
148/B2 Huatusco, Mex.
147/F4 Huauchinango, Mex.
144/B3 Huaura, Peru
147/F5 Huautla, Mex.
103/C4 Hua Xian, China
104/E2 Huaying, China
144/B3 Huayllay, Peru
107/K3 Huazhou, China
151/L3 Hubbard (mtn.), Ak,US, Yk,Can
168/G5 Hubbard, Oh,US
159/H4 Hubbard Creek (res.), Tx,US
103/C5 Hubei (prov.), China
103/B4 Hubei Kou (pass), China
106/C4 Hubli-Dhārwār, India
66/D6 Hückelhoven, Ger.
67/E6 Hückeswagen, Ger.
57/G5 Hucknall Torkard, Eng,UK
68/A2 Hucqueliers, Fr.
57/G4 Huddersfield, Eng,UK
63/R7 Huddinge, Swe.
67/F2 Hude, Ger.
62/G1 Hudiksvall, Swe.
113/L Hudson (cape), Ant.
153/H2 Hudson (bay), Can.
153/J2 Hudson (str.), NW, Qu,Can
161/M7 Hudson, Qu,Can
168/C1 Hudson, Ma,US
167/J9 Hudson (co.), NJ,US
160/F3 Hudson (riv.), NJ, NY,US
160/F3 Hudson, NY,US
157/H2 Hudson Bay, Sk,Can
152/D3 Hudson's Hope, BC,Can
109/D2 Hue, Viet.
82/F2 Huedin, Rom.
148/D3 Huehuetenango, Guat.
147/L6 Huehuetla, Mex.
147/L8 Huehuetlán el Chico, Mex.
147/L7 Huejotzingo, Mex.
147/F4 Huejutla, Mex.
74/B4 Huelva, Sp.
74/B3 Huelva (prov.), Sp.
142/B4 Huequi (vol.), Chile
74/E4 Huércal-Overa, Sp.
159/F3 Huerfano (riv.), Co,US
75/E1 Huesca, Sp.
74/D4 Huéscar, Sp.
142/F3 Huesos (riv.), Arg.
147/E5 Huetamo, Mex.
148/C2 Hueyapan de Ocampo, Mex.
77/E2 Hüfingen, Ger.
106/E3 Hugli (riv.), India
159/G3 Hugo, Co,US
159/J4 Hugo, Ok,US
159/G3 Hugoton, Ks,US
103/C3 Huguan, China
96/H2 Hui (riv.), China
132/B2 Huib-Hoch (plat.), Namb.
147/K6 Huichapan, Mex.
126/B4 Huila (plat.), Ang.
138/C4 Huila (dept.), Col.
138/C4 Huila, Nevado del (peak), Col.
107/H2 Huili, China
147/G5 Huimanguillo, Mex.
103/D3 Huimin, China
97/K3 Huinan, China
142/D2 Huinca Renancó, Arg.
96/F4 Huining, China
101/D2 Hŭisaek-pong (mtn.), NKor.
103/E5 Hui Shan (mtn.), China
107/J2 Huishui, China
72/D2 Huisne (riv.), Fr.
66/C5 Huissen, Neth.
107/J2 Huitong, China
63/K1 Huittinen, Fin.
147/M7 Huitzilan, Mex.
147/F5 Huitzuco, Mex.
103/C4 Hui Xian, China
148/C3 Huixtla, Mex.
104/D3 Huize, China
66/C4 Huizen, Neth.
105/G4 Huizhou, China
108/B2 Hujra, Pak.
101/C5 Hŭksan (arch.), SKor.
97/K2 Hulan, China
96/K2 Hulan (riv.), China
96/F2 Huld, Mong.
157/G4 Hulett, Wy,US
160/F2 Hull, Qu,Can
57/H4 Hull, Eng,UK
57/H4 Hull (riv.), Eng,UK
168/D1 Hull, Ma,US
67/F4 Hüllhorst, Ger.
121/H5 Hull (Orona) (atoll), Kiri.
66/B6 Hulst, Neth.
103/B3 Hulu (riv.), China
96/H2 Hulun (lake), China
97/K1 Huma, China
97/K1 Huma (riv.), China
135/C1 Humahuaca, Arg.
136/F5 Humaitá, Braz.
126/B4 Humbe, Ang.
161/K2 Humber (riv.), Nf,Can
161/R8 Humber (bay), On,Can
161/Q8 Humber (riv.), On,Can
57/H4 Humber (riv.), Eng,UK
57/H4 Humberside (co.), Eng,UK
57/H4 Humberston, Eng,UK
140/B1 Humberto de Campos, Braz.
162/E4 Humble, Tx,US
146/E1 Humble City, NM,US
157/G2 Humboldt, Sk,Can
149/G5 Humboldt (bay), Col.
120/F7 Humboldt (peak), NCal.
158/C2 Humboldt (range), Nv,US
158/D2 Humboldt (riv.), Nv,US
163/F3 Humboldt, Tn,US
119/C2 Hume (lake), Austl.
65/L4 Humenné, Slvk.
63/T9 Humlebæk, Den.
151/K2 Humphrey (pt.), Ak,US
158/E4 Humphreys (peak), Az,US
57/F1 Humshaugh, Eng,UK
101/C2 Hun (riv.), China
124/J2 Hūn, Libya
61/N6 Húnaflói (bay), Ice.
105/F2 Hunan (prov.), China
97/L3 Hunchun, China
82/F3 Hunedoara, Rom.
82/F2 Hunedoara (co.), Rom.
64/E3 Hünfeld, Ger.
82/D2 Hungary
70/B2 Hungen, Ger.
59/E4 Hungerford, Eng,UK
96/C2 Hüngüy (riv.), Mong.
109/D1 Hung Yen, Viet.
101/D2 Hunjiang, China
57/H3 Hunmanby, Eng,UK
69/G1 Hunspatch, Fr.
69/G4 Hunsrück (mts.), Ger.
59/G1 Hunstanton, Eng,UK
67/F2 Hunte (riv.), Ger.
119/C4 Hunter (isl.), Austl.
119/D2 Hunter (riv.), Austl.
156/A3 Hunter (isl.), BC,Can
151/H3 Hunter (mtn.), Ak,US
166/D2 Hunterdon (co.), NJ,US
160/C4 Huntingburg, In,US
59/F2 Huntingdon, Eng,UK
57/G4 Huntington, Eng,UK
160/C3 Huntington, In,US
167/E2 Huntington, NY,US
167/M8 Huntington (bay), NY,US
166/B1 Huntington (cr.), Pa,US
160/D4 Huntington, WV,US
164/C3 Huntington Beach, Ca,US
164/B3 Huntington Park, Ca,US
167/M8 Huntington Station, NY,US
165/F7 Huntington Woods, Mi,US
115/S10 Huntly, NZ
54/D2 Huntly, Sc,UK
151/M4 Hunts Inlet, BC,Can
160/E2 Huntsville, On,Can
163/G3 Huntsville, Al,US
166/B1 Huntsville (res.), Pa,US
162/E4 Huntsville, Tx,US
147/H4 Hunucmá, Mex.
66/D5 Hünxe, Ger.
103/C3 Hunyuan, China
105/H2 Huo (mtn.), China
102/D3 Huocheng, China
103/C4 Huojia, China
97/H2 Huolin Gol, China
109/D2 Huong Hoa, Viet.
109/D2 Huong Khe, Viet.
109/D2 Huong Son, Viet.
107/J4 Huong Thuy, Viet.
103/D4 Huoqiu, China
103/D5 Huoshan, China
103/B3 Huo Shan (mtn.), China
103/B3 Huo Xian, China
125/R5 Hurdiyo, Som.
53/S11 Hurepoix (reg.), Fr.
103/E2 Hure Qi, China
158/E4 Hurley, NM,US
54/B5 Hurlford, Sc,UK
160/D2 Huron (lake), Can., US
165/G6 Huron (pt.), Mi,US
165/F7 Huron (riv.), Mi,US
168/E5 Huron, Oh,US
168/E5 Huron (co.), Oh,US
168/E5 Huron (riv.), Oh,US
157/J4 Huron, SD,US
160/D4 Hurricane, WV,US
59/F5 Hurstpierpoint, Eng,UK
68/D4 Hurtaut (riv.), Fr.
69/F2 Hürth, Ger.
57/G3 Hurworth, Eng,UK
106/D3 Husainābād, India
59/E2 Husbands Bosworth, Eng,UK
83/J2 Huşi, Rom.
64/E1 Husum, Ger.
159/H3 Hutchinson, Ks,US
157/K4 Hutchinson, Mn,US
104/D3 Hutiaoxia, China
57/J5 Huttoft, Eng,UK
118/C4 Hutton (peak), Austl.
53/Q7 Hutton, Eng,UK
57/H4 Hutton Cranswick, Eng,UK
57/G3 Hutton Rudby, Eng,UK
161/Q8 Huttonville, On,Can
96/B3 Hutubi, China
103/C3 Hutuo (riv.), China
103/B4 Hu Xian, China
69/E2 Huy, Belg.
57/F5 Huyton-with-Roby, Eng,UK
103/E5 Huzhou, China
61/P7 Hvannadalshnúkur (peak), Ice.
82/C4 Hvar (isl.), Cro.
63/T9 Hvidovre, Den.
61/N7 Hvítá (riv.), Ice.
131/B3 Hwange, Zim.
131/B3 Hwange (Wankie) Nat'l Park, Zim.
101/D3 Hwanghae-Bukto (prov.), NKor.
101/C3 Hwanghae-Namdo (prov.), NKor.
101/D3 Hwangju (riv.), NKor.
142/B5 Hyades (peak), Chile
96/C2 Hyargas, Mong.
96/C2 Hyargas (lake), Mong.
166/B6 Hyattsville, Md,US
57/F5 Hyde, Eng,UK
53/N7 Hyde Park, Eng,UK
106/C4 Hyderābād, India
95/J3 Hyderābād, Pak.
73/G5 Hyères, Fr.
73/G5 Hyères (isls.), Fr.
152/D2 Hyland (riv.), Yk,Can
160/D4 Hylton (hill), Ky,US
98/D3 Hyōgo (pref.), Japan
101/G6 Hyŏndŭngsan (mtn.), SKor.
98/D3 Hyō-no-sen (mtn.), Japan
158/E2 Hyrum, Ut,US
59/E5 Hythe, Eng,UK
59/H4 Hythe, Eng,UK
98/B4 Hyūga, Japan
63/L1 Hyvinkää, Fin.

I

141/B2 Iacanga, Braz.
140/A4 Iaciara, Braz.
144/D3 Iaco (riv.), Braz., Peru
140/B4 Iaçu, Braz.
82/A2 Iâf di Montasio (peak), It.
83/H3 Ialomiţa (riv.), Rom.
141/D1 Iapu, Braz.
83/H2 Iaşi, Rom.
83/H2 Iaşi (co.), Rom.
112/B2 Iba, Phil.
129/F5 Ibadan, Nga.
138/C3 Ibagué, Col.
141/B2 Ibaiti, Braz.
112/C3 Ibajay, Phil.
130/A3 Ibanda, Ugan.
149/E3 Ibans (lag.), Hon.
158/D2 Ibapah, Ut,US
82/E4 Ibar (riv.), Yugo.
98/C3 Ibara, Japan
99/L10 Ibaraki, Japan
99/F2 Ibaraki (pref.), Japan
138/B4 Ibarra, Ecu.
135/E2 Ibarreta, Arg.
125/L6 Ibba (riv.), Sudan
67/E4 Ibbenbüren, Ger.
129/F2 Ibdekhene (wadi), Mali
135/E2 Ibera, Esteros de (marshes), Arg.
74/D2 Ibérico, Sistema (range), Sp.
161/P7 Iberville, Qu,Can
98/E3 Ibi (riv.), Japan
75/E3 Ibi, Sp.
141/C1 Ibiá, Braz.
140/B2 Ibiapaba (mts.), Braz.
140/B1 Ibiapina, Braz.
140/C4 Ibicaraí, Braz.
140/C3 Ibimirim, Braz.
140/B5 Ibirapuã, Braz.
141/B2 Ibitinga, Braz.
141/F8 Ibiúna, Braz.
75/F3 Ibiza, Sp.
75/F3 Ibiza (isl.), Sp.
98/D3 Ibo (riv.), Japan
126/H3 Ibo, Moz.
140/B4 Ibotirama, Braz.
124/H8 Iboundji (peak), Gabon
65/L4 Ibrány, Hun.
91/B5 Ibshawāy, Egypt
59/E1 Ibstock, Eng,UK
111/G3 Ibu (mtn.), Indo.
99/M9 Ibuki, Japan
99/M9 Ibuki-yama (peak), Japan
138/D5 Içá (riv.), Braz.
144/C4 Ica, Peru
139/E4 Içana, Braz.
138/D4 Içana (riv.), Braz., Col.
91/C1 İçel (prov.), Turk.
61/N7 Iceland
141/B2 Icém, Braz.
106/B4 Ichalkaranji, India
106/D4 Ichchāpuram, India
70/D6 Ichenhausen, Ger.
99/J7 Ichihara, Japan
99/L9 Ichijima, Japan
99/H7 Ichikawa, Japan
100/B3 Ichinohe, Japan
98/E3 Ichinomiya, Japan
100/B4 Ichinoseki, Japan
99/M10 Ichishi, Japan
67/E6 Ichtegem, Belg.
140/C2 Icó, Braz.
151/K4 Icy (bay), Ak,US
151/F1 Icy (cape), Ak,US
151/L4 Icy (str.), Ak,US
159/J4 Idabel, Ok,US
156/E5 Idaho (state), US
156/E5 Idaho Falls, Id,US
108/F3 Idāppādi, India
106/B3 Idar, India
69/G4 Idarkopf (peak), Ger.
69/G4 Idar-Oberstein, Ger.
99/L10 Ide, Japan
124/G3 Ideles, Alg.
96/D2 Ider (riv.), Mong.
127/C3 Idfū, Egypt
81/J5 Ídhi (peak), Gre.
79/E3 Idice (riv.), It.
92/E2 Idil, Turk.
130/A3 Idjwe (isl.), Zaire
91/B4 Idkū, Egypt
57/H5 Idle (riv.), Eng,UK
91/E2 Idlib, Syria
91/E2 Idlib (prov.), Syria
82/B3 Idrija, Slov.
123/M13 Idriss I (dam), Mor.
123/M13 Idriss I (res.), Mor.
78/D1 Idro (lake), It.
70/B2 Idstein, Ger.
100/J7 Ie (isl.), Japan
68/B2 Ieper, Belg.
81/J5 Ierápetra, Gre.
130/C5 Ifakara, Tanz.
120/D4 Ifalik (isl.), Micr.
133/H8 Ifanadiana, Madg.
129/G5 Ife, Nga.
77/G3 Ifen, Hoher (peak), Ger., Aus.
99/M10 Iga, Japan
99/M10 Iga (riv.), Japan
130/B4 Igalula, Tanz.
130/B2 Iganga, Ugan.
140/B4 Igaporã, Braz.
138/C5 Igara Paraná (riv.), Col.
141/C2 Igarapava, Braz.
137/J4 Igarapé-Miri, Braz.
140/D2 Igarassu, Braz.
141/G8 Igaratá, Braz.
88/J3 Igarka, Rus.
106/B4 Igatpuri, India
130/B5 Igawa, Tanz.
93/F2 Iğdır, Turk.
53/P8 Ightham, Eng,UK
151/H2 Igikpak (mtn.), Ak,US
80/A3 Iglesias, It.
160/B1 Ignace, On,Can
147/P8 Ignacio de la Llave, Mex.
83/J5 İğneada (cape), Turk.
76/A2 Ignon (riv.), Fr.
53/S10 Igny, Fr.
130/B3 Igombe, Tanz.
130/B4 Igombe (riv.), Tanz.
144/C1 Igora Paraná (riv.), Col.
85/M4 Igra, Rus.
141/B3 Iguaçu (riv.), Braz.
135/F2 Iguaçu Nat'l Park, Braz.
140/B4 Iguaí, Braz.
148/B2 Iguala, Mex.
75/F2 Igualada, Sp.
147/F5 Iguala de la Independencia, Mex.
135/E2 Iguape (riv.), Braz.
141/C3 Iguape, Braz.
141/C3 Iguape (riv.), Braz.
140/C2 Iguatu, Braz.
134/D5 Iguazú (falls), Braz.
135/F2 Iguazu Nat'l Park, Arg.
130/B4 Igugunu, Tanz.
124/D2 Iguidi, 'Erg (des.), Afr.
100/J7 Iheya (isl.), Japan
133/H8 Ihosy, Madg.
133/G8 Ihotry (lake), Madg.
88/C3 Ii (riv.), Fin.
99/E3 Iida, Japan
99/F2 Iide-san (mtn.), Japan
84/E2 Iijoki (riv.), Fin.
99/M10 Iinan, Japan
61/H3 Iisalmi, Fin.
99/M10 Iitaka, Japan
63/M1 Iitti, Fin.
99/F2 Iiyama, Japan
98/B4 Iizuka, Japan
130/D3 Ijara, Kenya
124/C3 Ijill (peak), Mrta.
66/C4 IJmeer (bay), Neth.
66/B4 IJmuiden, Neth.
128/B2 Ijnaoun (well), Mrta.
61/H2 Ijoki (riv.), Fin.
66/C4 IJssel (riv.), Neth.
66/C3 IJsselmeer (lake), Neth.
66/C2 IJsselmeer (Afsluitdijk) (dam), Neth.
66/C3 IJsselmuiden, Neth.
66/C4 IJsselstein, Neth.
135/F2 Ijuí, Braz.
98/B5 Ijūin, Japan
68/B2 Ijzer (riv.), Belg.
85/M5 Ik (riv.), Rus.
133/H7 Ikahavo (plat.), Madg.
130/A4 Ikamba, Tanz.
81/J4 Ikaría (isl.), Gre.
130/B4 Ikasi, Tanz.
62/C3 Ikast, Den.
98/C3 Ikeda, Japan
126/D1 Ikela, Zaire
99/M10 Ikenokoya-yama (peak), Japan
83/F4 Ikhtiman, Bul.
98/A4 Iki (chan.), Japan
98/A4 Iki (isl.), Japan
92/C2 Ikizce, Turk.
99/L10 Ikoma, Japan
130/B3 Ikoma, Tanz.
133/H7 Ikopa (riv.), Madg.
130/B4 Ikungi, Tanz.
130/B4 Ikungu, Tanz.
144/D5 Ilabaya, Peru
130/A4 Ilagala, Tanz.
112/C1 Ilagan, Phil.
108/G4 Ilaiyānkudi, India
93/F3 Īlām, Iran

Īlām – Jamāl

93/F3 Īlām (gov.), Iran
106/E2 Ilam, Nepal
130/B4 Ilangali, Tanz.
144/D5 Ilave, Peru
65/K2 Iława, Pol.
125/M4 'Ilay, Sudan
79/E5 Il Castello, Monte (peak), It.
58/D4 Ilchester, Eng,UK
156/G2 Ile-à-la-Crosse, Sk,Can
157/G2 Ile-a-la-Crosse (lake), Sk,Can
126/D1 Ilebo, Zaire
72/E2 Ile-de-France (reg.), Fr.
161/N6 Ile-de-Montréal (co.), Qu,Can
161/N6 Ile-Jésus (co.), Qu,Can
87/K2 Ilek (riv.), Kaz., Rus.
60/A6 Ilen (riv.), Ire.
161/N7 Ile-Perrot, Qu,Can
128/E5 Iles Ehotilés Nat'l Park, IvC.
129/G5 Ilesha, Nga.
76/D4 Ilfis (riv.), Swi.
53/P7 Ilford, Eng,UK
118/B3 Ilfracombe, Austl.
58/B4 Ilfracombe, Eng,UK
86/E4 Ilgaz, Turk.
92/C1 Ilğazdağı Nat'l Park, Turk.
92/B2 Ilgın, Turk.
141/H8 Ilhabela, Braz.
141/J8 Ilha Grande (bay), Braz.
141/B1 Ilha Solteira (res.), Braz.
74/A2 Ílhavo, Port.
140/C4 Ilhéus, Braz.
102/C3 Ili (riv.), China, Kaz.
151/G4 Iliamna (lake), Ak,US
151/H3 Iliamna (vol.), Ak,US
92/E2 Ilıca, Turk.
112/C3 Iligan (bay), Phil.
112/D3 Iligan City, Phil.
138/B5 Iliniza (peak), Ecu.
92/E2 Ilisu (res.), Turk.
83/H6 Ilium (Troy) (ruins), Turk.
57/G6 Ilkeston, Eng,UK
57/G4 Ilkley, Eng,UK
77/F3 Ill (riv.), Aus.
76/D1 Ill (riv.), Fr.
142/C1 Illapel, Chile
79/E1 Illasi (riv.), It.
117/G3 Illbillee (peak), Austl.
129/G3 Illéla, Niger
70/D6 Iller (riv.), Ger.
70/D6 Illertissen, Ger.
74/D2 Illescas, Sp.
136/E7 Illimani (peak), Bol.
69/G5 Illingen, Ger.
160/B4 Illinois (state), US
160/B3 Illinois (riv.), Il,US
124/G2 Illizi, Alg.
76/D1 Illkirch-Graffenstaden, Fr.
77/E3 Illnau, Swi.
58/A6 Illogan, Eng,UK
74/D4 Illora, Sp.
76/D2 Illzach, Fr.
71/E5 Ilm (riv.), Ger.
61/G3 Ilmajoki, Fin.
67/G5 Ilme (riv.), Ger.
84/F4 Il'men' (lake), Rus.
64/F3 Ilmenau, Ger.
67/H2 Ilmenau (riv.), Ger.
58/D5 Ilminster, Eng,UK
144/D5 Ilo, Peru
112/C3 Iloilo City, Phil.
130/B4 Ilongero, Tanz.
129/G4 Ilorin, Nga.
87/H2 Ilovlya (riv.), Rus.
67/H4 Ilse (riv.), Ger.
67/H4 Ilsede, Ger.
67/H5 Ilsenburg, Ger.
70/C4 Ilsfeld, Ger.
83/H5 Ilyas (pt.), Turk.
85/N3 Ilych (riv.), Rus.
71/G5 Ilz (riv.), Ger.
98/C3 Imabari, Japan
99/F2 Imaichi, Japan
133/H8 Imaloto (riv.), Madg.
92/C2 İmamoğlu, Turk.
84/F2 Imandra (lake), Rus.
98/A4 Imari, Japan
63/N1 Imatra, Fin.
98/E3 Imazu, Japan
99/J7 Imba, Japan
138/B4 Imbabura (prov.), Ecu.
141/B4 Imbituba, Braz.
141/B3 Imbituva, Braz.
125/P6 Īmī, Eth.
87/J5 Imishli, Azer.
81/L7 Imittós (mtn.), Gre.
101/C5 Imja (isl.), SKor.
101/D3 Imjin (riv.), NKor., SKor.
158/C2 Imlay, Nv,US
67/G6 Immenhausen, Ger.
77/G2 Immenstadt im Allgäu, Ger.
57/H4 Immingham, Eng,UK
163/H5 Immokalee, Fl,US
151/J2 Imnavait (mtn.), Ak,US
129/G5 Imo (state), Nga.
79/E4 Imola, It.
140/A2 Imperatriz, Braz.
78/B5 Imperia, It.
78/A5 Imperia (prov.), It.
157/G3 Imperial, Sk,Can
144/B4 Imperial, Peru
159/G2 Imperial, Ne,US
164/C5 Imperial Beach, Ca,US
99/H7 Imperial Palace, Japan
78/A5 Impero (riv.), It.
124/J7 Impfondo, Congo
104/B3 Imphāl, India
83/J5 İmrali (isl.), Turk.
92/D2 İmranlı, Turk.
77/G3 Imst, Aus.
112/E7 Imus, Phil.
112/E7 Imus (riv.), Phil.
131/A3 Imusho, Zam.
99/E3 Ina, Japan
99/L10 Ina (riv.), Japan
65/H2 Ina (riv.), Pol.
112/D3 Inabanga, Phil.
99/M9 Inabe, Japan
113/E Inaccessability, Pole of, Ant.
99/L10 Inagawa, Japan
99/H7 Inagi, Japan
140/C3 Inajá, Braz.
144/D4 Inambari (riv.), Peru
124/G2 I-n-Amenas, Alg.
99/K10 Inami, Japan
123/M13 Inaouene (riv.), Mor.
61/H1 Inari (lake), Fin.
83/G2 Inău (peak), Rom.
99/G2 Inawashiro (lake), Japan
99/M9 Inazawa, Japan
144/D4 Inca (dept.), Peru
75/G3 Inca, Sp.
91/C1 Incekum (pt.), Turk.
129/F2 I-n-Chaouâg (wadi), Mali
54/D4 Inchcape (Bell Rock) (isl.), Sc,UK
54/B5 Inchinnan, Sc,UK
128/B2 Inchiri (reg.), Mrta.
54/C4 Inchkeith (isl.), Sc,UK
55/J7 Inchnadamph, Sc,UK
101/D4 Inch'ŏn, SKor.
101/D4 Inch'ŏn-Jikhalsi, SKor.
131/D3 Inchope, Moz.
92/A2 İncirliova, Turk.
131/D5 Incomati (riv.), Moz.
141/G7 Inconfidentes, Braz.
124/E3 I-n-Dagouber (well), Mali
141/C1 Indaiá (riv.), Braz.
141/C2 Indaiatuba, Braz.
112/C4 Indanan, Phil.
104/B3 Indawgyi (lake), Burma
69/F2 Inde (riv.), Ger.
69/F2 Inden, Ger.
158/C3 Independence, Ca,US
159/J3 Independence, Ks,US
159/J3 Independence, Mo,US
158/C2 Independence (mts.), Nv,US
166/C4 Independence Nat'l Hist. Park, Pa,US
140/B2 Independência, Braz.
87/J2 Inder (lake), Kaz.
106/C3 India
51/N6 Indian (ocean)
160/C3 Indiana (state), US
160/E3 Indiana, Pa,US
165/R16 Indiana Dunes Nat'l Lakesh., In,US
160/C4 Indianapolis (cap.), In,US
166/B3 Indian Echo Caverns, Pa,US
157/H3 Indian Head, Sk,Can
163/F3 Indianola, Ms,US
163/H5 Indiantown, Fl,US
141/B1 Indiaporã, Braz.
89/Q3 Indigirka (riv.), Rus.
82/E3 Inđija, Yugo.
158/C4 Indio, Ca,US
109/C1 Indochina (reg.), Asia
111/E4 Indonesia
118/E6 Indooroopilly, Austl.
106/C3 Indore, India
110/B4 Indragiri (riv.), Indo.
110/C5 Indramayu (cape), Indo.
106/D4 Indrāvati (riv.), India
72/D3 Indre (riv.), Fr.
72/D3 Indrois (riv.), Fr.
78/B1 Induno Olona, It.
90/F7 Indus (riv.), Asia
95/J4 Indus, Mouths of the, Pak.
92/C1 İnebolu, Turk.
129/E1 I-n-Echaï (well), Mali
92/B1 İnegöl, Turk.
82/E2 Ineu, Rom.
124/D1 Inezgane, Mor.
132/C4 Infanta (cape), SAfr.
146/E5 Infiernillo (res.), Mex.
74/C1 Infiesto, Sp.
140/D2 Ingá, Braz.
138/B5 Ingapirca, Ecu.
138/B5 Ingapirca (ruins), Ecu.
63/S7 Ingarö, Swe.
63/S7 Ingarö (isl.), Swe.
53/Q7 Ingatestone, Eng,UK
68/C2 Ingelmunster, Belg.
118/G8 Ingleburn, Austl.
70/B2 Ingleheim, Ger.
57/G2 Ingleton, Eng,UK
161/Q8 Inglewood, On,Can
164/B3 Inglewood, Ca,US
165/C2 Inglewood-Finn Hill, Wa,US
163/H4 Inglis, Fl,US
96/G1 Ingoda (riv.), Rus.
57/J5 Ingoldmells, Eng,UK
71/E5 Ingolstadt, Ger.
53/Q7 Ingrave, Eng,UK
113/E Ingrid Christianson (coast), Ant.
129/G2 I-n-Guezzâm, Alg.
86/E3 Ingulets (riv.), Ukr.
87/G4 Inguri (riv.), Geo.
131/D4 Inhambane, Moz.
131/D4 Inhambane (prov.), Moz.
140/C3 Inhambupe, Braz.
131/D3 Inhaminga, Moz.
131/D5 Inharrime, Moz.
131/D4 Inhassoro, Moz.
140/B2 Inhuma, Braz.
137/J7 Inhumas, Braz.
139/H4 Inini (riv.), FrG.
138/D4 Inírida (riv.), Col.
54/F10 Inishbofin (isl.), Ire.
60/A6 Inishcarra (res.), Ire.
56/A1 Inishowen (pen.), Ire.
56/B1 Inishowen Head (pt.), Ire.
165/F7 Inkster, Mi,US
98/C3 Inland (sea), Japan
104/C4 Inle (lake), Burma
129/E2 I-n-Milach (well), Mali
73/K2 Inn (riv.), Eur.
71/H6 Innbach (riv.), Aus.
54/B5 Innellan, Sc,UK
148/D2 Inner (chan.), Belz.
55/J8 Inner (sound), Sc,UK
54/C4 Innerdouny (hill), Sc,UK
55/H8 Inner Hebrides (isls.), Sc,UK
77/F3 Innerhoden (demi-canton), Swi.
54/C5 Innerleithen, Sc,UK
96/G3 Inner Mongolia (reg.), China
67/H4 Innerste (riv.), Ger.
117/H5 Innes Nat'l Park, Austl.
73/K3 Innichen (San Candido), It.
118/B2 Innisfail, Austl.
156/E2 Innisfail, Ab,Can
151/G3 Innoko (riv.), Ak,US
151/G3 Innoko Nat'l Wild. Ref., Ak,US
77/H3 Innsbruck, Aus.
71/G6 Innviertel (reg.), Aus.
60/C2 Inny (riv.), Ire.
58/B5 Inny (riv.), Eng,UK
98/C4 Ino, Japan
141/B1 Inocência, Braz.
126/C1 Inongo, Zaire
65/K4 Inovec (peak), Slvk.
65/K2 Inowrocław, Pol.
129/E1 I-n-Sâkâne, Erg (des.), Mali
124/F2 I-n-Salah, Alg.
54/D2 Insch, Sc,UK
116/B3 Inscription (cape), Austl.
104/C5 Insein, Burma
156/A2 Inside (passg.), BC,Can
131/C3 Insiza, Zim.
85/P2 Inta, Rus.
129/F2 I-n-Tassik (well), Mali
156/B2 Interior (plat.), BC,Can
157/K3 International Falls, Mn,US
157/H3 International Peace Garden, Can., US
109/B2 Inthanon (peak), Thai.
83/H3 Întorsura Buzăului, Rom.
99/G3 Inubō-zaki (pt.), Japan
153/J3 Inukjuak, Qu,Can
143/K8 Inútil (bay), Chile
99/E3 Inuyama, Japan
54/C1 Inver (bay), Sc,UK
54/A4 Inveraray, Sc,UK
54/D3 Inverbervie, Sc,UK
115/Q12 Invercargill, NZ
119/D1 Inverell, Austl.
54/B2 Invergarry, Sc,UK
54/B1 Invergordon, Sc,UK
54/C4 Invergowrie, Sc,UK
55/J8 Inverie, Sc,UK
54/D3 Inverkeilor, Sc,UK
54/C4 Inverkeithing, Sc,UK
157/H3 Invermay, Sk,Can
161/J2 Inverness, NS,Can
54/B2 Inverness, Sc,UK
163/G3 Inverness, Al,US
163/H4 Inverness, Fl,US
78/B1 Inveruno, It.
54/D2 Inverurie, Sc,UK
117/H5 Investigator (str.), Austl.
167/L9 Inwood, NY,US
131/D3 Inyanga, Zim.
131/D3 Inyangani (peak), Zim.
131/C3 Inyati, Zim.
151/D2 Inymney, Gora (mtn.), Rus.
158/C3 Inyo (mts.), Ca,US
130/B4 Inyonga, Tanz.
87/H1 Inza, Rus.
78/C1 Inzago, It.
99/J7 Inzai, Japan
81/G3 Ioánnina, Gre.
159/J3 Iola, Ks,US
95/H1 Iolotan', Trkm.
55/H8 Iona (isl.), Sc,UK
126/B4 Iona Nat'l Park, Ang.
160/C3 Ionia, Mi,US
81/F3 Ionian (sea), Eur.
81/F3 Ionian (isls.), Gre.
81/J4 Íos (isl.), Gre.
128/A2 Iouîk (cape), Mrta.
157/K5 Iowa (state), US
157/L5 Iowa (riv.), Ia,US
157/L5 Iowa City, Ia,US
157/K5 Iowa Falls, Ia,US
141/B1 Ipameri, Braz.
142/B5 Ipan (isl.), Chile
141/D1 Ipanema, Braz.
141/D1 Ipatinga, Braz.
65/K4 Ipel' (Ipoly) (riv.), Hun., Slvk.
138/B4 Ipiales, Col.
140/C4 Ipiaú, Braz.
140/C4 Ipirá, Braz.
141/B3 Ipiranga, Braz.
110/B3 Ipoh, Malay.
130/B4 Ipole, Tanz.
65/K4 Ipoly (Ipel') (riv.), Hun., Slvk.
137/H7 Iporá, Braz.
81/K2 Ipsala, Turk.
118/E7 Ipswich, Austl.
59/H2 Ipswich, Eng,UK
157/J4 Ipswich, SD,US
140/B2 Ipu, Braz.
141/B2 Ipuã, Braz.
140/B2 Ipubi, Braz.
140/B2 Ipueiras, Braz.
141/G7 Ipuiúna, Braz.
130/A4 Ipumba (hill), Tanz.
140/B3 Ipupiara, Braz.
136/D8 Iquique, Chile
144/C1 Iquitos, Peru
99/M10 Irago (chan.), Japan
99/E3 Irago-misaki (cape), Japan
81/J4 Iráklia (isl.), Gre.
81/J5 Iráklion, Gre.
140/B4 Iramaia, Braz.
130/B3 Iramba, Tanz.
94/F2 Iran
110/D3 Iran (mts.), Indo., Malay.
95/H3 Irānshahr, Iran
147/E4 Irapuato, Mex.
92/E3 Iraq
140/C4 Irará, Braz.
141/B3 Irati, Braz.
111/H4 Irau (mtn.), Indo.
140/C1 Iraucuba, Braz.
91/D3 Irbid, Jor.
91/E3 Irbid (gov.), Jor.
93/F2 Irbīl, Iraq
93/E3 Irbīl (gov.), Iraq
140/B3 Irecê, Braz.
55/G10 Ireland
60/D3 Ireland's Eye (isl.), Ire.
85/N5 Iremel', Gora (peak), Rus.
141/A3 Iretama, Braz.
58/C2 Irfon (riv.), Wal,UK
129/G2 Irhazer Oua-n-Agadez (wadi), Niger
101/D5 Iri, SKor.
111/H4 Irian Jaya (reg.), Indo.
139/G4 Iricoumé (mts.), Braz.
128/D2 Irigui (reg.), Mali, Mrta.
87/L2 Iriklinskiy (res.), Rus.
130/B4 Iringa, Tanz.
130/B5 Iringa (prov.), Tanz.
108/F3 Irinjālakuda, India
100/G8 Iriomote (isl.), Japan
137/H4 Iriri (riv.), Braz.
56/C4 Irish (sea), Ire., UK
96/E1 Irkut (riv.), Rus.
96/E1 Irkutsk, Rus.
57/F5 Irlam, Eng,UK
167/J9 Ironbound, NJ,US
58/D1 Iron Bridge, Eng,UK
82/F3 Iron Gate (gorge), Rom.
160/B2 Iron Mountain, Mi,US
160/B2 Iron River, Mi,US
160/D4 Ironton, Oh,US
160/B2 Ironwood, Mi,US
160/D1 Iroquois Falls, On,Can
99/F3 Irō-zaki (pt.), Japan
86/E1 Irput' (riv.), Bela., Rus.
104/B5 Irrawaddy (riv.), Burma
104/B5 Irrawaddy (Ayeyarwady) (div.), Burma
104/B5 Irrawaddy, Mouths of the, Burma
69/F4 Irrel, Ger.
69/F3 Irsen (riv.), Ger.
57/E3 Irt (riv.), Eng,UK
57/F1 Irthing (riv.), Eng,UK
59/F2 Irthlingborough, Eng,UK
88/G4 Irtysh (riv.), Kaz., Rus.
99/H7 Iruma, Japan
130/A2 Irumu, Zaire
74/E1 Irún, Sp.
54/B5 Irvine, Sc,UK
54/B5 Irvine (bay), Sc,UK
54/B5 Irvine (riv.), Sc,UK
164/C3 Irvine, Ca,US
162/D3 Irving, Tx,US
167/D2 Irvington, NJ,US
167/E1 Irvington, NY,US
118/C3 Isaac (riv.), Austl.
144/J7 Isabela (isl.), Ecu.
112/C4 Isabela, Phil.
150/E3 Isabela, PR
148/E3 Isabelia, Cordillera (range), Nic.
153/K2 Isabella (bay), NW,Can
153/R7 Isachsen (cape), NW,Can
61/M6 Ísafjardhardjúp (fjord), Ice.
98/B4 Isahaya, Japan
133/H8 Isalo Nat'l Park, Madg.
133/H8 Isalo Ruiniform, Massif (plat.), Madg.
133/E3 Isandhlwana Battlesite, SAfr.
131/C1 Isangano Nat'l Park, Zam.
130/A3 Isango-Isoro, Zaire
64/G4 Isar (riv.), Aus., Ger.
73/J3 Isarco (Eisack) (riv.), It.
80/C2 Ischia, It.
67/H3 Ise (riv.), Ger.
99/E3 Ise, Japan
99/M10 Ise (bay), Japan
59/F2 Ise (riv.), Eng,UK
99/F3 Isehara, Japan
167/D2 Iselin, NJ,US
71/F6 Isen (riv.), Ger.
130/B5 Isenyela, Tanz.
78/D1 Iseo (lake), It.
130/B4 Iseramagazi, Tanz.
72/F4 Isère (riv.), Fr.
67/E6 Iserlohn, Ger.
80/D2 Isernia, It.
99/F2 Isesaki, Japan
99/E3 Ise-Shima Nat'l Park, Japan
85/Q4 Iset' (riv.), Rus.
129/F5 Iseyin, Nga.
99/L10 Ishi (riv.), Japan
99/F2 Ishibashi, Japan
99/M9 Ishibe, Japan
100/B4 Ishidoriya, Japan
100/H8 Ishigaki, Japan
100/G8 Ishigaki (isl.), Japan
99/F2 Ishige, Japan
100/B2 Ishikari, Japan
100/B2 Ishikari (bay), Japan
100/C2 Ishikari (mts.), Japan
99/G2 Ishikawa, Japan
99/E2 Ishikawa (pref.), Japan
99/N10 Ishiki, Japan
88/H4 Ishim (riv.), Kaz., Rus.
85/R4 Ishim, Rus.
87/L1 Ishimbay, Rus.
99/G1 Ishinomaki, Japan
99/G2 Ishioka, Japan
98/C4 Ishizuchi-san (mtn.), Japan
63/T9 Ishøj, Den.
160/C2 Ishpeming, Mi,US
136/E7 Isiboro Securé Nat'l Park, Bol.
143/G1 Isidoro, Uru.
88/H4 Isil'kul', Rus.
130/C2 Isiolo, Kenya
125/L7 Isiro, Zaire
127/C4 Is, Jabal (peak), Sudan
91/E1 İskenderun, Turk.
91/D1 İskenderun (gulf), Turk.
92/C1 İskilip, Turk.
81/H1 Iskŭr (res.), Bul.
81/H1 Iskŭr (riv.), Bul.
147/G5 Isla, Mex.
54/C2 Isla (riv.), Sc,UK
54/C3 Isla (riv.), Sc,UK
147/H5 Isla Aguada, Mex.
150/D3 Isla Cabritos Nat'l Park, DRep.
74/B4 Isla Cristina, Sp.
142/Q9 Isla de Maipo, Chile
138/C2 Isla de Salamanca Nat'l Park, Col.
118/C4 Isla Gorge Nat'l Park, Austl.
91/E1 İslâhiye, Turk.
146/D4 Isla Isabela Nat'l Park, Mex.
108/B1 Islāmābād (cap.), Pak.
108/B1 Islāmābād Cap. Terr. (terr.), Pak.
142/B5 Isla Magdalena Nat'l Park, Chile
106/E2 Islāmpur, India
117/H4 Island (lag.), Austl.
157/K2 Island (lake), Mb,Can
165/C2 Island (co.), Wa,US
167/D4 Island Beach Saint Park, NJ,US
157/K2 Island Lake, Mb,Can
161/K1 Islands (bay), Nf,Can
55/J9 Islay (isl.), Sc,UK
72/D4 Isle (riv.), Fr.
59/G2 Isleham, Eng,UK
56/D3 Isle of Man, UK
56/D2 Isle of Whithorn, Sc,UK
160/B1 Isle Royale (isl.), Mi,US
160/B2 Isle Royale Nat'l Park, Mi,US
53/N7 Islington (bor.), Eng,UK
167/E2 Islip, NY,US
91/C4 Ismailia (Al Ismā'īlīyah), Egypt
85/X9 Ismailovo Park, Rus.
71/E6 Ismaning, Ger.
127/C3 Isnā, Egypt
77/G2 Isny, Ger.
99/M10 Isobe, Japan
63/L1 Isojärven Nat'l Park, Fin.
63/J1 Isojärvi (lake), Fin.
130/B5 Isoka, Zam.
79/E2 Isola Della Scala, It.
80/C2 Isola del Liri, It.
80/E3 Isola di Capo Rizzuto, It.
79/G1 Isonzo (riv.), It.
92/B2 Isparta, Turk.
92/B2 Isparta (prov.), Turk.
72/C5 Ispéguy, Col d' (pass), Fr.
83/H4 Isperikh, Bul.
92/E1 İspir, Turk.
91/C3 Israel
139/G3 Issano, Guy.
165/C2 Issaquah, Wa,US
165/C2 Issaquah (cr.), Wa,US
66/D5 Issel (riv.), Ger.
66/D5 Isselburg, Ger.
128/D5 Issia, IvC.
72/E4 Issoire, Fr.
72/E3 Issoudun, Fr.
66/D5 Issum, Ger.
130/B4 Issuna, Tanz.
102/C3 Issyk-Kul' (lake), Kyr.
68/B6 Issy-les-Moulineaux, Fr.
82/E1 Istállós-kő (peak), Hun.
92/B1 İstanbul, Turk.
83/J5 İstanbul (prov.), Turk.
93/M6 İstanbul (inset), Turk.
79/G2 Istarske Toplice, Cro.
83/H5 Istranca (mts.), Turk.
72/F5 Istres, Fr.
82/A3 Istria (pen.), Cro.
112/D4 Isulan, Phil.
140/C3 Itabaiana, Braz.
140/D2 Itabaiana, Braz.
140/C3 Itabaianinha, Braz.
141/D2 Itabapoana (riv.), Braz.
140/B4 Itaberaba, Braz.
141/D1 Itabira, Braz.
141/D2 Itabirito, Braz.
141/L7 Itaboraí, Braz.
140/C4 Itabuna, Braz.
137/H5 Itacaiunas (riv.), Braz.
140/A4 Itacarambi, Braz.
139/G5 Itacoatiara, Braz.
144/D2 Itacuaí (riv.), Braz.
140/C3 Itacuruba, Braz.
140/B4 Itaetê, Braz.
101/G6 It'aewŏn, SKor.
130/B4 Itaga, Tanz.
140/C4 Itagibá, Braz.
141/K7 Itaguaí, Braz.
141/C2 Itaguara, Braz.
138/C3 Itagüí, Col.
141/B2 Itaí, Braz.
140/C3 Itaíba, Braz.
140/C2 Itaiçaba, Braz.
140/B2 Itainópolis, Braz.
141/B3 Itaiópolis, Braz.
135/F1 Itaipu (res.), Braz., Par.
135/F2 Itaipú (dam), Par.
137/G4 Itaituba, Braz.
141/B1 Itajá, Braz.
141/B3 Itajaí, Braz.
141/B3 Itajaí (riv.), Braz.
141/H7 Itajubá, Braz.
140/C4 Itajuípe, Braz.
99/G3 Itako, Japan
52/E4 Italy
140/C5 Itamaraju, Braz.
141/D1 Itamarandiba, Braz.
141/D1 Itambacuri, Braz.
140/B4 Itambé, Braz.
141/D1 Itambé (peak), Braz.
99/L10 Itami, Japan
141/J7 Itamonte, Braz.
104/B3 Itanagar, India
141/G9 Itanhaém, Braz.
141/C2 Itanhandu, Braz.
140/B5 Itanhém, Braz.
141/D1 Itanhém (riv.), Braz.
141/D1 Itanhomi, Braz.
140/B5 Itaobim, Braz.
141/D2 Itaocara, Braz.
140/C1 Itapagé, Braz.
140/C4 Itaparica (isl.), Braz.
140/C4 Itapebi, Braz.
141/C2 Itapecerica, Braz.
140/A1 Itapecuru-Mirim, Braz.
141/D2 Itapemirim, Braz.
141/D2 Itaperuna, Braz.
140/B4 Itapetinga, Braz.
141/B2 Itapetininga, Braz.
141/B2 Itapeva, Braz.
141/G8 Itapevi, Braz.
140/C3 Itapicuri (riv.), Braz.
140/A1 Itapicuru (riv.), Braz.
140/C1 Itapipoca, Braz.
141/G7 Itapira, Braz.
140/C4 Itapitanga, Braz.
141/B2 Itaporanga, Braz.
141/G8 Itaquaquecetuba, Braz.
140/B4 Itarantim, Braz.
141/B3 Itararé, Braz.
141/F9 Itariri, Braz.
106/C3 Itārsi, India
140/B4 Itaruçu, Braz.
141/C2 Itatiaia Nat'l Park, Braz.
141/G8 Itatiba, Braz.
141/C2 Itatinga (res.), Braz.
140/B2 Itaueira, Braz.
140/B3 Itaueira (riv.), Braz.
141/C2 Itaúna, Braz.
100/B3 Itayanagi, Japan
105/J4 Itbayat (isl.), Phil.
59/E4 Itchen (riv.), Eng,UK
125/K7 Itembiri (riv.), Zaire
136/F6 Iténez (riv.), Bol.
126/E4 Itezhi-Tezhi (dam), Zam.
160/E3 Ithaca, NY,US
81/G3 Ithaca (Itháki) (isl.), Gre.
81/G3 Itháki (Ithaca) (isl.), Gre.
67/G5 Ith Hils (ridge), Ger.
58/C2 Ithon (riv.), Wal,UK
130/B4 Itigi, Tanz.
140/B5 Itinga, Braz.
99/F3 Itō, Japan
130/B4 Itobo, Tanz.
99/E2 Itoigawa, Japan
100/J7 Itoman, Japan
72/D2 Iton (riv.), Fr.
140/B4 Itororó, Braz.
77/F5 I Tre Signori, Pizzo de (peak), It.
99/H7 Itsukaichi, Japan
67/F6 Itter (riv.), Ger.
80/A2 Ittiri, It.
141/C2 Itu, Braz.
140/C4 Ituberá, Braz.
144/D2 Ituí (riv.), Braz.
141/B1 Ituiutaba, Braz.
141/B1 Itumbiara, Braz.
141/B1 Itumbiara (res.), Braz.
141/J6 Itumirim, Braz.
157/H3 Ituna, Sk,Can
130/B5 Itungi Port, Tanz.
137/J5 Itupiranga, Braz.
141/B3 Ituporanga, Braz.
141/B1 Iturama, Braz.
141/J6 Itutinga (res.), Braz.
141/C2 Ituverava, Braz.
136/E5 Ituxi (riv.), Braz.
143/F2 Ituzaingó, Uru.
91/B4 Ityāy al Bārūd, Egypt
70/E2 Itz (riv.), Ger.
64/E2 Itzehoe, Ger.
151/C2 Iul'tin, Gora (mtn.), Rus.
141/D2 Iuna, Braz.
141/B3 Ivaí (riv.), Braz.
141/B3 Ivaiporã, Braz.
61/H1 Ivalo, Fin.
61/H1 Ivalojoki (riv.), Fin.
73/M2 Ivančice, Czh.
82/D4 Ivangrad, Yugo.
160/D1 Ivanhoe (riv.), On,Can
82/E4 Ivanjica, Yugo.
86/C2 Ivano-Frankovsk, Ukr.
86/C2 Ivano-Frankovsk Obl., Ukr.
84/J4 Ivanovo, Rus.
85/J4 Ivanovo Obl., Rus.
81/J2 Ivaylovgrad (res.), Bul.
85/P3 Ivdel, Rus.
53/M7 Iver, Eng,UK
54/G11 Iveragh (pen.), Ire.
53/M7 Iver Heath, Eng,UK
124/H7 Ivindo (riv.), Gabon
133/H8 Ivohibe, Madg.
133/J7 Ivondro (riv.), Madg.
128/D5 Ivory Coast (reg.), IvC.
128/D5 Ivory Coast (Côte d'Ivoire)
62/F3 Ivösjön (lake), Swe.
78/A2 Ivrea, It.
68/B6 Ivry-sur-Seine, Fr.
58/C6 Ivybridge, Eng,UK
99/F2 Iwai, Japan
100/B4 Iwaizumi, Japan
99/G2 Iwaki, Japan
100/B3 Iwaki-san (mtn.), Japan
98/C3 Iwakuni, Japan
99/M9 Iwakura, Japan
98/D3 Iwami, Japan
100/B2 Iwamizawa, Japan
100/B2 Iwanai, Japan
99/G1 Iwanuma, Japan
99/E3 Iwata, Japan
100/B4 Iwate, Japan
100/B4 Iwate (dept.), Japan
100/B4 Iwate-san (mtn.), Japan
99/H7 Iwatsuki, Japan
129/G5 Iwo, Nga.
120/D2 Iwo Jima (isl.), Japan
148/D3 Ixcán (riv.), Guat., Mex.
64/C3 Ixelles, Belg.
147/F4 Ixmiquilpan, Mex.
147/L7 Ixtacihuatl-Popotzteco Nat'l Park, Mex.
147/Q10 Ixtapalapa, Mex.
147/K8 Ixtapan de la Sal, Mex.
146/D4 Ixtlán del Río, Mex.
59/G2 Ixworth, Eng,UK
96/D1 Iya (riv.), Rus.
98/C4 Iyo, Japan
98/C4 Iyo (sea), Japan
148/D3 Izabal (lake), Guat.
147/H4 Izamal, Mex.
87/H4 Izberbash, Rus.
68/C2 Izegem, Belg.
151/F4 Izembek Nat'l Wild. Ref., Ak,US
85/M4 Izhevsk, Rus.
85/M2 Izhma (riv.), Rus.
151/E5 Izigan (cape), Ak,US
95/G4 Izkī, Oman
83/J3 Izmail, Ukr.
92/A2 İzmir, Turk.
92/A2 İzmir (prov.), Turk.
83/J5 İzmit, Turk.
83/J5 İzmit (gulf), Turk.
74/C4 Iznájar, Sp.
83/J5 İznik, Turk.
83/H5 İznik (lake), Turk.
79/G1 Izola, Slov.
148/E3 Izopo (pt.), Hon.
91/E3 Izra', Syria
82/D2 Izsák, Hun.
97/M5 Izu (isls.), Japan
99/F3 Izu (pen.), Japan
147/F5 Izúcar de Matamoros, Mex.
99/H8 Izu-Fuji-Hakone Nat'l Park, Japan
98/A3 Izuhara, Japan
98/B4 Izumi, Japan
98/D3 Izumi, Japan
99/L10 Izumi-ōtsu, Japan
98/D3 Izumi-Sano, Japan
98/C3 Izumo, Japan
86/F2 Izyum, Ukr.

J

63/M1 Jääsjarvi (lake), Fin.
127/B5 Jabal Abyad (plat.), Sudan
149/F5 Jabalí (pt.), Pan.
91/D2 Jabal Lubnān (gov.), Leb.
74/D3 Jabalón (riv.), Sp.
106/C3 Jabalpur, India
91/D4 Jabālyah, Gaza
68/C1 Jabbeke, Belg.
92/D3 Jabbūl, Sabkhat al (lake), Syria
127/C4 Jabjabah, Wādī (dry riv.), Egypt, Sudan
91/D2 Jablah, Syria
81/G2 Jablanica (mts.), Alb.
65/H3 Jablonec nad Nisou, Czh.
140/D3 Jaboatão, Braz.
141/B2 Jaboticabal, Braz.
82/E3 Jabuka, Yugo.
110/B4 Jabung (cape), Indo.
75/E1 Jaca, Sp.
140/B3 Jacaré (riv.), Braz.
141/C2 Jacareí, Braz.
125/Q5 Jaceel (riv.), Som.
140/B5 Jacinto, Braz.
161/G2 Jackman, Me,US
158/D2 Jackpot, Nv,US
162/D3 Jacksboro, Tx,US
166/A2 Jacks Mountain (ridge), Pa,US
163/G4 Jackson, Al,US
158/B3 Jackson, Ca,US
160/C3 Jackson, Mi,US
157/K5 Jackson, Mn,US
159/K3 Jackson, Mo,US
163/F3 Jackson (cap.), Ms,US
156/D5 Jackson (mts.), Nv,US
160/D4 Jackson, Oh,US
163/F3 Jackson, Tn,US
156/F5 Jackson, Wy,US
156/F4 Jackson (lake), Wy,US
167/K9 Jackson Heights, NY,US
163/G3 Jacksonville, Al,US
162/E3 Jacksonville, Ar,US
163/H4 Jacksonville, Fl,US
160/B4 Jacksonville, Il,US
163/J3 Jacksonville, NC,US
162/E4 Jacksonville, Tx,US
163/H4 Jacksonville Beach, Fl,US
149/H2 Jacmel, Haiti
146/E3 Jaco, Mex.
95/J3 Jacobābād, Pak.
140/B3 Jacobina, Braz.
146/E5 Jacona de Plancarte, Mex.
161/H1 Jacques-Cartier (mtn.), Qu,Can
161/G2 Jacques-Cartier (riv.), Qu,Can
135/F2 Jacuí (riv.), Braz.
140/C3 Jacuipe (riv.), Braz.
141/C3 Jacupiranga, Braz.
138/D2 Jacúra, Ven.
95/H3 Jaddi (pt.), Pak.
64/E2 Jade (bay), Ger.
67/F2 Jade (riv.), Ger.
67/F2 Jadebusen (bay), Ger.
144/B2 Jaén, Peru
112/C2 Jaen, Phil.
74/D4 Jaén, Sp.
119/A3 Jaffa (cape), Austl.
108/H4 Jaffna, SrL.
108/H4 Jaffna (dist.), SrL.
108/D2 Jagādhri, India
106/D4 Jagdalpur, India
106/D2 Jagdīspur, India
112/D3 Jagna, Phil.
108/C2 Jagraon, India
70/C4 Jagst (riv.), Ger.
106/C4 Jagtiāl, India
140/C4 Jaguaquara, Braz.
143/G2 Jaguarão, Braz.
143/G2 Jaguarão (riv.), Braz.
140/B3 Jaguarari, Braz.
140/C2 Jaguaretama, Braz.
141/G7 Jaguari (riv.), Braz.
141/B3 Jaguariaíva, Braz.
140/C2 Jaguaribe, Braz.
140/C2 Jaguaribe (riv.), Braz.
141/G7 Jaguariúna, Braz.
140/C2 Jaguaruana, Braz.
119/D3 Jagungal (peak), Austl.
93/H4 Jahrom, Iran
139/H4 Jai (cr.), Sur.
140/B2 Jaicós, Braz.
111/G3 Jailolo, Indo.
96/E4 Jainca, China
106/C2 Jaipur, India
106/B2 Jaisalmer, India
82/C3 Jajce, Bosn.
106/E3 Jājpur, India
110/C5 Jakarta (cap.), Indo.
61/G3 Jakobstad, Fin.
162/B3 Jal, NM,US
147/M7 Jalacingo, Mex.
97/J2 Jalaid Qi, China
95/K2 Jalālābād, Afg.
108/C2 Jalālābād, India
148/D3 Jalapa, Guat.
147/N7 Jalapa Enríquez, Mex.
61/G3 Jalasjärvi, Fin.
141/B2 Jales, Braz.
106/C3 Jālgaon, India
93/F4 Jalīb ash Shuyūkh, Kuw.
124/H6 Jalingo, Nga.
146/D4 Jalisco (state), Mex.
80/A4 Jālitah, Jazīrat (isl.), Tun.
76/C6 Jallouvre, Pic de (peak), Fr.
106/C4 Jālna, India
74/E2 Jalón (riv.), Sp.
106/B2 Jālor, India
146/E4 Jalpa, Mex.
106/E2 Jalpaiguri, India
148/C2 Jaltepec (riv.), Mex.
147/G5 Jáltipan, Mex.
125/K2 Jālū, Libya
120/F4 Jaluit (atoll), Mrsh.
93/F3 Jalūlā', Iraq
125/P7 Jamaame, Som.
129/H4 Jamaare (riv.), Nga.
149/G2 Jamaica
149/H2 Jamaica (chan.), Haiti, Jam.
167/K9 Jamaica, NY,US
167/E3 Jamaica (bay), NY,US
106/E3 Jamālpur, Bang.
106/E2 Jamālpur, India

195
Jaman – Kalug

150/D4 Jamanota (peak), Aru.
137/G5 Jamanxim (riv.), Braz.
147/N7 Jamapa, Mex.
136/F5 Jamari (riv.), Braz.
110/B4 Jambi, Indo.
112/B4 Jambongan (isl.), Malay.
110/A2 Jambuair (cape), Indo.
155/K1 James (lake), On,Can
153/H3 James (bay), On, Qu,Can
142/B5 James (pt.), Chile
157/J4 James (riv.), ND, SD,US
160/E4 James (riv.), Va,US
154/V12 James Campbell Nat'l Wild. Ref., Hi,US
167/F2 Jamesport, NY,US
152/G1 James Ross (str.), NW,Can
157/J4 Jamestown, ND,US
160/E3 Jamestown, NY,US
163/G2 Jamestown, Tn,US
148/B2 Jamiltepec, Mex.
62/C3 Jammerbugt (bay), Den.
102/B5 Jammu, India
102/C5 Jammu and Kashmīr (state), India
106/B3 Jāmnagar, India
95/K3 Jāmpur, Pak.
61/H3 Jämsä, Fin.
106/E3 Jamshedpur, India
61/E3 Jämtland (co.), Swe.
106/E3 Jamūi, India
157/H2 Jan (lake), Sk,Can
63/L1 Janakkala, Fin.
140/B4 Janaúba, Braz.
137/J3 Janaucu (isl.), Braz.
141/B2 Jandaia do Sul, Braz.
74/C4 Jándula (riv.), Sp.
116/L6 Jane (brook), Austl.
160/B3 Janesville, Wi,US
131/D5 Jangamo, Moz.
106/C4 Jangaon, India
106/E3 Jangipur, India
65/K2 Janikowo, Pol.
91/D3 Janīn, WBnk.
82/D3 Janja, Bosn.
52/D1 Jan Mayen (isl.), Nor.
146/C2 Janos, Mex.
82/D2 Jánoshalma, Hun.
65/M3 Janów Lubelski, Pol.
140/A4 Januária, Braz.
91/C5 Janūb Sīnā' (gov.), Egypt
106/C3 Jaora, India
97/M4 Japan
97/L4 Japan (sea), Asia
99/E3 Japanese Alps (range), Japan
99/E2 Japanese Alps Nat'l Park, Japan
139/E5 Japurá (riv.), Braz.
150/D3 Jarabacoa, DRep.
74/C2 Jaraíz de la Vera, Sp.
108/B2 Jarānwāla, Pak.
91/D3 Jarash, Jor.
124/H1 Jarbah (isl.), Tun.
140/C2 Jardim, Braz.
140/C2 Jardim do Seridó, Braz.
135/E2 Jardín América, Arg.
149/G1 Jardines de la Reina (arch.), Cuba
141/C2 Jardinópolis, Braz.
63/R7 Jarfalla, Swe.
137/H3 Jari (riv.), Braz.
106/E3 Jaridih, India
124/H1 Jarjīs, Tun.
62/G2 Järna, Swe.
69/E5 Jarny, Fr.
112/D3 Jaro, Phil.
65/J3 Jarocin, Pol.
65/H3 Jaroměř, Czh.
65/M3 Jarosław, Pol.
57/G2 Jarrow, Eng,UK
109/C2 Jars (plain), Laos
103/E1 Jarud Qi, China
63/L1 Järvenpää, Fin.
69/F6 Jarville-la-Malgrange, Fr.
121/J5 Jarvis (isl.), PacUS
65/L4 Jasło, Pol.
156/D2 Jasper, Ab,Can
163/G3 Jasper, Al,US
163/H4 Jasper, Fl,US
163/G3 Jasper, Ga,US
160/C4 Jasper, In,US
162/E4 Jasper, Tx,US
156/D2 Jasper Nat'l Park, Ab, BC,Can
106/C2 Jaspur, India
70/C2 Jassa (riv.), Ger.
65/J2 Jastrowie, Pol.
65/K4 Jastrzębie Zdroj, Pol.
82/E2 Jászapáti, Hun.
82/D2 Jászárokszállás, Hun.
82/D2 Jászberény, Hun.
82/E2 Jászladány, Hun.
82/E2 Jász-Nagykun-Szolnok (co.), Hun.
141/B1 Jataí, Braz.
139/G5 Jatapu (riv.), Braz.
148/D2 Jataté (riv.), Mex.
140/C2 Jati, Braz.
149/G1 Jatibonico, Cuba
75/E3 Játiva, Sp.
141/B2 Jaú, Braz.
139/F5 Jaú (riv.), Braz.
139/E5 Jauaperi (riv.), Braz.
139/F5 Jauaperi (riv.), Braz.
139/H5 Jauaru (mts.), Braz.
139/F3 Jaua Sarisarinama Nat'l Park, Ven.
108/B1 Jauharābād, Pak.
144/C3 Jauja, Peru
76/D4 Jaunpass (pass), Swi.
110/C5 Java (isl.), Indo.
110/D5 Java (sea), Indo.
144/C2 Javari (riv.), Braz.
75/F3 Jávea, Sp.
143/J6 Javier (isl.), Chile
82/D1 Javorie (peak), Slvk.
71/G2 Javornice (riv.), Czh.
71/G4 Javorník (peak), Czh.
71/H3 Javorová Skála (peak), Czh.
125/Q7 Jawhar (Giohar), Som.
65/J3 Jawor, Pol.
111/J4 Jaya (peak), Indo.
144/B2 Jayanca, Peru
111/K4 Jayapura, Indo.
162/C3 Jayton, Tx,US
59/H3 Jaywick, Eng,UK
94/D5 Jazā'ir Farasān (isls.), SAr.
54/D6 Jedburgh, Sc,UK
65/L3 Jędrzejów, Pol.
54/D6 Jed Water (riv.), Sc,UK
64/F2 Jeetze (riv.), Ger.
168/G7 Jefferson (co.), Oh,US
156/C4 Jefferson (peak), Or,US
162/E3 Jefferson, Tx,US
165/B2 Jefferson (co.), Wa,US
165/N14 Jefferson (co.), Wi,US
159/J3 Jefferson City (cap.), Mo,US
160/C4 Jeffersonville, In,US
156/G5 Jeffrey City, Wy,US
71/G2 Jehličná (mtn.), Czh.
142/B5 Jeinemeni (peak), Chile
63/L3 Jēkabpils, Lat.
65/J3 Jelcz-Laskowice, Pol.
65/H3 Jelenia Góra, Pol.
65/H3 Jelenia Góra (prov.), Pol.
106/E2 Jelep (pass), China
63/K3 Jelgava, Lat.
68/C3 Jemappes, Belg.
110/D5 Jember, Indo.
130/C4 Jembiani, Tanz.
158/F4 Jemez Pueblo, NM,US
96/B2 Jeminay, China
111/E4 Jempang (riv.), Indo.
127/C3 Jemsa, Egypt
64/F3 Jena, Ger.
162/E4 Jena, La,US
111/E5 Jeneponto, Indo.
162/E4 Jennings, La,US
152/F2 Jenny Lind (isl.), NW,Can
153/H2 Jens Muck (isl.), NW,Can
140/B4 Jequié, Braz.
140/A5 Jequitaí, Braz.
140/B5 Jequitinhonha, Braz.
140/C5 Jequitinhonha (riv.), Braz.
123/N13 Jerada, Mor.
149/H2 Jérémie, Haiti
140/C3 Jeremoabo, Braz.
146/E4 Jerez, Mex.
74/B4 Jerez de la Frontera, Sp.
74/B3 Jerez de los Caballeros, Sp.
167/E2 Jericho, NY,US
91/D4 Jericho (Arīḩā), WBnk.
168/C2 Jerimoth (hill), RI,US
156/E5 Jerome, Id,US
168/E6 Jerome Fork (riv.), Oh,US
72/B2 Jersey (isl.), Chl,UK
167/D2 Jersey City, NJ,US
167/H8 Jersey City (res.), NJ,US
160/B4 Jerseyville, Il,US
94/B2 Jerusalem (cap.), Isr.
91/F8 Jerusalem (dist.), Isr.
91/G8 Jerusalem Walls Nat'l Park, Isr.
91/D4 Jerusalem (Yerushalayim) (cap.), Isr.
156/C3 Jervis (inlet), BC,Can
67/G6 Jesberg, Ger.
82/B2 Jesenice, Slov.
71/F2 Jesenice, Údolní nádrž (res.), Czh.
79/G5 Jesi, It.
62/D1 Jessheim, Nor.
106/E3 Jessore, Bang.
141/H7 Jesuânia, Braz.
163/H4 Jesup, Ga,US
161/N6 Jésus (isl.), Qu,Can
135/D3 Jesús María, Arg.
149/G1 Jesús Menéndez, Cuba
128/A4 Jeta (isl.), GBis.
159/H3 Jetmore, Ks,US
106/B3 Jetpur, India
68/D3 Jeumont, Fr.
67/E1 Jever, Ger.
157/G5 Jewel Cave Nat'l Mon., SD,US
106/D4 Jeypore, India
81/F1 Jezerce (peak), Alb.
71/G4 Jezerní Stěna (peak), Czh.
65/K2 Jeziorák (lake), Pol.
106/E3 Jhā Jhā, India
106/C3 Jhālawār, India
108/B2 Jhang Sadar, Pak.
106/C2 Jhānsi, India
106/D3 Jhārsuguda, India
108/B1 Jhawārian, Pak.
108/B1 Jhelum (riv.), India, Pak.
108/B1 Jhelum, Pak.
108/B2 Jhumra, Pak.
104/B1 Ji (riv.), China
103/L8 Jiading, China
106/E3 Jiāganj, India
107/K2 Jiahe, China
96/F5 Jialing (riv.), China
103/C4 Jialu (riv.), China
97/L2 Jiamusi, China
105/F4 Jian (riv.), China
105/H3 Jian (riv.), China
104/E2 Jiancheng, China
109/E1 Jiang (riv.), China
107/J2 Jiang'an, China
104/C3 Jiangao (mtn.), China
104/D4 Jiangcheng Hanizu Yizu Zizhixian (Jiangcheng), China
104/D3 Jiangchuan, China
103/D4 Jiangdu, China
105/F3 Jianghua Yaozu Zizhixian, China
104/E2 Jiangjin, China
103/C5 Jiangling, China
105/G4 Jiangmen, China
103/D5 Jiangning, China
103/D4 Jiangsu (prov.), China
105/G3 Jiangxi (prov.), China
103/B4 Jiang Xian, China
103/E5 Jiangyin, China
105/F3 Jiangyong, China
104/E2 Jiangyou, China
107/J2 Jianhe, China
103/D4 Jianhu, China
103/C5 Jianli, China
105/H3 Jian'ou, China
97/H3 Jianping, China
103/B5 Jianshi, China
104/D4 Jianshui, China
105/H3 Jianyang, China
103/C3 Jiaocheng, China
97/K3 Jiaohe, China
105/J2 Jiaojiang, China
103/C3 Jiaokou, China
97/J3 Jiaolai (riv.), China
103/D4 Jiaonan, China
103/D4 Jiaozuo, China
103/D4 Jiashan, China
103/L9 Jiashan, China
102/C4 Jiashi, China
103/B3 Jia Xian, China
103/D4 Jiaxiang, China
103/L9 Jiaxing, China
97/L2 Jiayin, China
103/C5 Jiayu, China
96/D4 Jiayuguan, China
83/F2 Jibou, Rom.
95/G4 Jibsh, Ra's (pt.), Oman
147/N8 Jicaro, Mex.
149/F5 Jicarón (isl.), Pan.
65/H3 Jičín, Czh.
147/F5 Jico, Mex.
97/L2 Jidong, China
103/C4 Jieshou, China
103/B3 Jiexiu, China
105/H4 Jieyang, China
116/D2 Jigalong Abor. Land, Austl.
149/G1 Jiguaní, Cuba
96/E5 Jigzhi, China
65/H4 Jihlava, Czh.
71/H4 Jihočeský (reg.), Czh.
65/J4 Jihomoravský (reg.), Czh.
123/U17 Jijel, Alg.
123/U17 Jijel (gov.), Alg.
83/H2 Jijia (riv.), Rom.
125/P6 Jijiga, Eth.
75/E3 Jijona, Sp.
127/A4 Jilf al Kabīr, Ḩadabat al (upland), Egypt
141/B2 Jilhá (res.), Braz.
65/J4 Jilhava (riv.), Czh.
102/E2 Jili (lake), China
125/P7 Jilib, Som.
97/K3 Jilin, China
101/D1 Jilin (prov.), China
97/J1 Jilin (riv.), China
75/E2 Jiloca (riv.), Sp.
125/N6 Jīma, Eth.
131/A1 Jimbe, Ang.
82/E3 Jimbolia, Rom.
74/C4 Jimena de la Frontera, Sp.
146/D3 Jiménez, Mex.
103/E3 Jimo, China
96/B3 Jimsar, China
105/G2 Jin (riv.), China
105/H3 Jin (riv.), China
103/D3 Jinan, China
96/E4 Jinchang, China
103/C3 Jinci Temple, China
106/C2 Jīnd, India
119/D3 Jindabyne (dam), Austl.
65/H4 Jindřichuv Hradec, Czh.
105/E2 Jinfo (mtn.), China
103/B4 Jing (riv.), China
103/B3 Jingbian, China
103/D5 Jingde, China
105/H2 Jingdezhen, China
107/H3 Jingdong, China
105/G3 Jinggangshan, China
103/D3 Jinghai, China
102/D3 Jinghe, China
104/D4 Jinghong, China
103/E4 Jingjiang, China
103/B3 Jingle, China
103/C5 Jingmen, China
96/F4 Jingning, China
104/D3 Jingping (mts.), China
103/C5 Jingshan, China
104/E4 Jingxi, China
103/D5 Jing Xian, China
105/F3 Jing Xian, China
101/D1 Jingyu, China
96/E4 Jingyuan, China
103/D4 Jinhu, China
105/H2 Jinhua, China
103/C2 Jining, China
103/D4 Jining, China
130/B2 Jinja, Ugan.
107/H2 Jinkouhe, China
105/H3 Jinmen (isl.), China
148/E3 Jinotega, Nic.
148/E4 Jinotepe, Nic.
104/D4 Jinping, China
105/F3 Jinping, China
103/B4 Jinqian (riv.), China
103/E5 Jinshan, China
104/D3 Jinsha (Yangtze) (riv.), China
107/K2 Jinshi, China
103/D5 Jintan, China
112/C2 Jintotolo (chan.), Phil.
106/C4 Jintūr, India
103/E2 Jinxi, China
105/H3 Jinxi, China
103/D4 Jinxiang, China
107/K3 Jinxiu Yaozu Zizhixian, China
105/J2 Jinyun, China
103/C5 Jinzhai, China
103/E2 Jinzhou, China
101/A3 Jinzhou (bay), China
136/F6 Ji-Paraná, Braz.
136/F5 Jiparaná (riv.), Braz.
138/A5 Jipijapa, Ecu.
146/E5 Jiquilpan de Juárez, Mex.
147/Q9 Jiquipilco, Mex.
127/B3 Jirgā, Egypt
71/G2 Jiřkov, Czh.
103/B4 Jishan, China
105/F2 Jishou, China
91/E2 Jisr ash Shughūr, Syria
83/F4 Jiu (riv.), Rom.
104/D2 Jiuding (mtn.), China
105/G2 Jiugong (mtn.), China
105/H2 Jiuhua (mtn.), China
103/C5 Jiujiang, China
105/G2 Jiuling (mts.), China
104/D2 Jiulong, China
97/K3 Jiutai, China
105/E3 Jiuwan (mts.), China
105/H2 Jixi, China
103/C4 Ji Xian, China
103/D2 Ji Xian, China
97/L2 Jixian, China
103/D3 Jiyang, China
103/C4 Jiyuan, China
91/B5 Jizah, Ahrāmāt al (Pyramids of Giza) (ruins), Egypt
103/C3 Jize, China
71/H2 Jizera (riv.), Czh.
98/C3 Jizō-zaki (pt.), Japan
104/D3 Jizu (mtn.), China
94/F5 Jiz', Wādī al (dry riv.), Yem.
141/B3 Joaçaba, Braz.
147/N8 Joachín, Mex.
140/B5 Joaíma, Braz.
140/D2 João Câmara, Braz.
140/A2 João Lisboa, Braz.
141/D1 João Monlevade, Braz.
140/D2 João Pessoa, Braz.
141/C1 João Pinheiro, Braz.
135/D2 Joaquín V. González, Arg.
149/G1 Jobabo, Cuba
70/B4 Jockgrim, Ger.
74/D4 Jódar, Sp.
106/B2 Jodhpur, India
69/D2 Jodoigne, Belg.
61/J3 Joensuu, Fin.
99/F2 Jōetsu, Japan
69/F5 Joeuf, Fr.
132/E2 Johannesburg, SAfr.
158/C4 Johannesburg, Ca,US
71/F2 Johanngeorgenstadt, Ger.
156/D4 John Day, Or,US
156/C4 John Day (riv.), Or,US
156/C4 John Day Fossil Beds Nat'l Mon., Or,US
156/D4 John Day, Middle Fork (riv.), Or,US
156/D4 John Day, North Fork (riv.), Or,US
116/C4 John Forrest Nat'l Park, Austl.
160/E4 John H. Kerr (dam), Va,US
162/C2 John Martin (res.), Co,US
55/K7 John O'Groats, Sc,UK
54/D3 Johnshaven, Sc,UK
161/S9 Johnson (cr.), NY,US
163/H2 Johnson City, Tn,US
162/D4 Johnson City, Tx,US
159/G3 Johnson (Johnson City), Ks,US
151/M3 Johnsons Crossing, Yk,Can
116/D5 Johnston (lake), Austl.
121/J3 Johnston (atoll), PacUS
58/B3 Johnston, Wal,UK
130/A5 Johnston (falls), Zam.
54/B5 Johnstone, Sc,UK
160/E3 Johnstown, Pa,US
110/B3 Johor Baharu, Malay.
72/E3 Joigny, Fr.
141/B3 Joinvile, Braz.
113/W Joinville (isl.), Ant.
147/F5 Jojutla, Mex.
147/K8 Jojutla de Juárez, Mex.
125/M6 Jokau, Sudan
61/F2 Jokkmokk, Swe.
61/P6 Jökulsargljufur Nat'l Park, Ice.
165/P16 Joliet, Il,US
160/F2 Joliette, Qu,Can
162/D4 Jollyville, Tx,US
112/C4 Jolo, Phil.
112/C4 Jolo (isl.), Phil.
112/C2 Jomalig (isl.), Phil.
110/D5 Jombang, Indo.
104/C2 Jomda, China
130/B3 Jomu, Tanz.
77/E3 Jona, Swi.
147/L8 Jonacatepec
63/L4 Jonava, Lith.
153/S7 Jones (sound), NW,Can
167/L9 Jones (inlet), NY,US
166/A2 Jones (mtn.), Pa,US
167/L9 Jones Beach Saint Park, NY,US
163/F3 Jonesboro, Ar,US
162/E3 Jonesboro, La,US
56/B3 Jonesborough, NI,UK
62/F3 Jönköping, Swe.
62/F3 Jönköping (co.), Swe.
161/G1 Jonquière, Qu,Can
116/K6 Joondalup (lake), Austl.
159/J3 Joplin, Mo,US
166/B5 Joppa (Joppatowne), Md,US
92/D4 Jordan
161/R9 Jordan, On,Can
91/D4 Jordan (riv.), Jor., WBnk.
156/G4 Jordan, Mt,US
166/C2 Jordan (cr.), Pa,US
158/E2 Jordan (riv.), Ut,US
140/B4 Jordânia, Braz.
161/R9 Jordan Station, On,Can
156/D5 Jordan Valley, Or,US
63/S7 Jordbro, Swe.
143/J7 Jorge (cape), Chile
104/B3 Jorhāt, India
67/G1 Jork, Ger.
162/B3 Jornada del Muerto (val.), NM,US
62/B2 Jørpeland, Nor.
129/H4 Jos (plat.), Nga.
112/D4 Jose Abad Santos, Phil.
141/B2 José Bonifacio, Braz.
147/N7 José Cardel, Mex.
140/B2 José de Freitas, Braz.
135/B5 José de San Martín, Arg.
112/C2 Jose Pañganiban, Phil.
114/D2 Joseph Bonaparte (gulf), Austl.
99/F2 Joshin-Etsu Kogen Nat'l Park, Japan
168/B3 Joshua (pt.), Ct,US
158/D4 Joshua Tree Nat'l Mon., Ca,US
62/C1 Jotunheimen Nat'l Park, Nor.
72/C2 Jouanne (riv.), Fr.
68/C6 Jouarre, Fr.
72/D3 Joué-lès-Tours, Fr.
118/B2 Jourama Falls Nat'l Park, Austl.
162/D4 Jourdanton, Tx,US
66/C3 Joure, Neth.
63/N1 Joutseno, Fin.
76/C4 Joux (lake), Fr.
53/S10 Jouy-en-Josas, Fr.
53/S9 Jouy-le-Moutier, Fr.
149/F1 Jovellanos, Cuba
93/J2 Joveyn (riv.), Iran
107/F2 Jowai, India
151/M3 Joy (mtn.), Yk,Can
60/A2 Joyce's Country (dist.), Ire.
99/L10 Jōyō, Japan
100/B2 Jozankei Spa, Japan
164/E7 J. Paul Getty Museum, Ca,US
128/A2 Jreïda, Mrta.
105/F2 Ju (riv.), China
146/E3 Juan Aldama, Mex.
103/C4 Juancheng, China
156/B3 Juan de Fuca (str.), Can., US
133/G7 Juan de Nova (isl.), Reun.
134/A6 Juan Fernández (isls.), Chile
139/F2 Juangriego, Ven.
144/B2 Juanjuí, Peru
143/T12 Juan L. Lacaze, Uru.
142/F3 Juárez, Arg.
141/J8 Juatinga (pt.), Braz.
140/B3 Juazeiro, Braz.
140/C2 Juazeiro do Norte, Braz.
125/M7 Juba, Sudan
125/P7 Jubba (riv.), Eth., Som.
144/B1 Jubones (riv.), Ecu.
75/Y17 Juby (cape), Mor.
74/D3 Júcar (riv.), Sp.
140/C2 Jucás, Braz.
66/D6 Jüchen, Ger.
146/E4 Juchipila, Mex.
147/N7 Juchique de Ferrer, Mex.
148/C2 Juchitán, Mex.
140/B5 Jucurucu (riv.), Braz.
140/C2 Jucurutu, Braz.
91/G8 Judaea (reg.), WBnk.
149/E4 Judas (pt.), CR
73/L3 Judenburg, Aus.
156/F4 Judith (riv.), Mt,US
127/B3 Juhaynah, Egypt
105/F3 Juicai (mtn.), China
149/E3 Juigalpa, Nic.
53/U9 Juilly, Fr.
105/H2 Juilong (mtn.), China
72/E2 Juine (riv.), Fr.
66/D1 Juist (isl.), Ger.
141/K6 Juiz de Fora, Braz.
159/G2 Julesburg, Co,US
144/D4 Juliaca, Peru
73/K3 Julian Alps (mts.), It., Slov.
139/G4 Juliana Top (peak), Sur.
69/F2 Jülich, Ger.
77/F5 Julierpass (pass)
108/C2 Jullundur, India
103/C3 Julu, China
103/C3 Juma (riv.), China
74/E3 Jumilla, Sp.
131/C3 Jumbo, Zim.
123/W17 Jūmīn (riv.), Tun.
63/L2 Juminda (pt.), Est.
106/D2 Jumla, Nepal
67/E2 Jümme (riv.), Ger.
100/B4 Jūmonji, Japan
105/G2 Jun (mtn.), China
106/B3 Junāgadh, India
103/D4 Junan, China
142/C2 Juncal (peak), Arg., Chile
162/D4 Junction, Tx,US
158/D3 Junction, Ut,US
159/H3 Junction City, Ks,US
156/C4 Junction City, Or,US
141/G8 Jundiaí, Braz.
103/H6 Jundu (mts.), China
123/W17 Jundūbah, Tun.
123/W17 Jundūbah (gov.), Tun.
151/M4 Juneau (cap.), Ak,US
103/B3 Jungar Qi, China
76/D4 Jungfrau (peak), Swi.
76/D4 Jungfraujoch, Swi.
63/S7 Jungfrufjärden (bay), Swe.
166/A2 Juniata (co.), Pa,US
166/A2 Juniata (riv.), Pa,US
142/E2 Junín, Arg.
138/A5 Junín, Ecu.
144/C3 Junín, Peru
135/B4 Junín de los Andes, Arg.
68/D5 Juniville, Fr.
103/C3 Junji Guan (pass), China
104/E2 Junlian, China
163/H5 Juno Beach, Fl,US
141/B2 Junqueirópolis, Braz.
141/E1 Juparanã (lake), Braz.
161/J1 Jupiter (riv.), Qu,Can
163/H5 Jupiter, Fl,US
165/A2 Jupiter (mtn.), Wa,US
141/C3 Juquiá, Braz.
141/F8 Juquitiba, Braz.
125/L6 Jur (riv.), Sudan
76/C4 Jura (mts.), Eur.
76/B4 Jura (dept.), Fr.
76/D3 Jura (canton), Swi.
55/H9 Jura (isl.), Sc,UK
55/J9 Jura (sound), Sc,UK
72/C5 Jurançon, Fr.
68/C2 Jurbise, Belg.
56/D3 Jurby Head (pt.), IM,UK
63/K3 Jūrmala, Lat.
139/E5 Juruá (riv.), Braz.
136/G6 Juruena (riv.), Braz.
137/G4 Juruti, Braz.
99/M9 Jushiyama, Japan
142/D2 Justo Daract, Arg.
136/E5 Jutaí, Braz.
139/E5 Jutaí (riv.), Braz.
148/D3 Jutiapa, Guat.
148/E3 Juticalpa, Hon.
61/D4 Jutland (pen.), Den.
61/H3 Juva, Fin.
149/K7 Juventud (isl.), Cuba
53/T10 Juvisy-sur-Orge, Fr.
103/D4 Ju Xian, China
103/D4 Juye, China
103/C5 Juzhang (riv.), China
82/E4 Južna Morava (riv.), Yugo.
131/B5 Jwaneng, Bots.
63/T9 Jyllinge, Den.
61/H3 Jyväskylä, Fin.

K

102/C4 K2 (Godwin Austen) (mtn.), China, Pak.
124/F5 Ka (riv.), Nga.
101/C3 Ka (isl.), NKor.
130/B2 Kaabong, Ugan.
132/C3 Kaap (plat.), SAfr.
63/K1 Kaarina, Fin.
66/D6 Kaarst, Ger.
82/E4 Kaba, Hun.
111/F5 Kabaena (isl.), Indo.
147/H4 Kabah (ruins), Mex.
130/A3 Kabale, Ugan.
130/A2 Kabalega (falls), Ugan.
130/A2 Kabalega Nat'l Park, Ugan.
126/E2 Kabalo, Zaire
126/E2 Kabamba (lake), Zaire
112/C3 Kabankalan, Phil.
87/G4 Kabardin-Balkar Aut. Rep., Rus.
130/A3 Kabare, Zaire
108/F3 Kabbani (riv.), India
130/B2 Kaberamaido, Ugan.
160/C1 Kabinakagami (lake), On,Can
126/D2 Kabinda, Zaire
123/V17 Kabir (riv.), Alg.
92/F3 Kabīr Kūh (mts.), Syria
108/A2 Kabīrwāla, Pak.
80/A5 Kabīyah (lag.), Tun.
95/J2 Kābol (Kābul) (cap.), Afg.
131/B2 Kabompo, Zam.
131/A2 Kabompo (riv.), Zam.
126/E2 Kabongo, Zaire
95/J2 Kabul (riv.), Afg.
95/J2 Kābul (Kābol) (cap.), Afg.
131/C2 Kabunda, Zaire
112/D5 Kaburuang (isl.), Indo.
131/C2 Kabwe, Zam.
82/E4 Kačanik, Yugo.
131/C2 Kachalola, Zam.
151/H4 Kachemak (bay), Ak,US
131/B3 Kachikau, Bots.
104/C3 Kachin (state), Burma
92/E1 Kaçkar (peak), Turk.
108/F4 Kadaianallur, India
130/B2 Kadam (peak), Ugan.
109/B3 Kadan (isl.), Burma
71/G2 Kadaň, Czh.
120/G6 Kadavu (isl.), Fiji
124/J7 Kadéï (riv.), CAfr., Congo
83/H5 Kadıköy, Turk.
93/N7 Kadıköy, Turk.
131/B1 Kadilo, Zaire
92/C2 Kadınhanı, Turk.
129/E3 Kadiogo (prov.), Burk.
106/C5 Kadiri, India
92/D2 Kadirli, Turk.
157/H5 Kadoka, SD,US
99/L10 Kadoma, Japan
131/C3 Kadoma, Zim.
129/G4 Kaduna, Nga.
129/G4 Kaduna (riv.), Nga.
129/G4 Kaduna (state), Nga.
125/L5 Kāduqlī, Sudan
128/B2 Kaédi, Mrta.
124/H5 Kaélé, Camr.
154/V12 Kaena (pt.), Hi,US
109/C2 Kaeng Khlo, Thai.
109/B3 Kaeng Krachan Nat'l Park, Thai.
101/D3 Kaesŏng, NKor.
101/D4 Kaesŏng-Si, NKor.
87/H5 Kafan, Arm.
95/J2 Kafar Jar Ghar (mts.), Afg.
132/D4 Kaffraria (reg.), SAfr.
128/B3 Kaffrine, Sen.
125/K6 Kafia Kingi, Sudan
81/J3 Kafirévs, Akra (cape), Gre.
91/B4 Kafr ad Dawwār, Egypt
91/B4 Kafr ash Shaykh, Egypt
91/B4 Kafr ash Shaykh (gov.), Egypt
91/B4 Kafr az Zayyāt, Egypt
91/G7 Kafr Qari', Isr.
91/F7 Kafr Qāsim, Isr.
130/A2 Kafu (riv.), Ugan.
131/B1 Kafubu (riv.), Zaire
131/C2 Kafue, Zam.
131/C2 Kafue (dam), Zam.
131/C2 Kafue (riv.), Zam.
131/B2 Kafue Flats (swamp), Zam.
131/B2 Kafue Nat'l Park, Zam.
131/D1 Kafukule, Malw.
130/A5 Kafulwe, Zam.
98/E2 Kaga, Japan
124/J6 Kaga Bandoro, CAfr.
88/G6 Kagan, Uzb.
98/D3 Kagawa (pref.), Japan
130/A3 Kagera (riv.), Rwa., Tanz.
130/A4 Kagera, Tanz.
63/U8 Kågeröd, Swe.
83/J5 Kağıthane, Turk.
93/M6 Kağıthane (riv.), Turk.
93/E1 Kağızman, Turk.
98/B5 Kagoshima, Japan
98/B5 Kagoshima (bay), Japan
98/B5 Kagoshima (pref.), Japan
83/J3 Kagul, Mol.
130/B3 Kahama, Tanz.
154/W12 Kahana, Hi,US
110/D4 Kahayan (riv.), Indo.
130/C3 Kahe, Tanz.
126/C2 Kahemba, Zaire
130/C5 Kahindi, Tanz.
154/T10 Kahiu (pt.), Hi,US
96/D1 Kahmsara (riv.), Rus.
108/C2 Kāhna, Pak.
159/K2 Kahoka, Mo,US
154/T10 Kahoolawe (isl.), Hi,US
61/G1 Kahperusvaara (peak), Fin.
92/D2 Kahramanmaraş, Turk.
92/D2 Kahraman Maraş (prov.), Turk.
95/K3 Kahror Pakka, Pak.
92/D2 Kâhta, Turk.
154/T10 Kahuku (pt.), Hi,US
154/T10 Kahului, Hi,US
126/E1 Kahuzi-Biega Nat'l Park, Zaire
111/H5 Kai (isls.), Indo.
115/R11 Kaiapoi, NZ
158/D3 Kaibab (plat.), Az,US
99/L9 Kaibara, Japan
111/H5 Kai Besar (isl.), Indo.
102/E3 Kaidu (riv.), China
139/G3 Kaieteur (falls), Guy.
139/G3 Kaieteur Nat'l Park, Guy.
96/G5 Kaifeng, China
98/D4 Kaifu, Japan
103/C5 Kaijiang, China
111/H5 Kai Kecil (isl.), Indo.
115/R10 Kaikohe, NZ
115/R11 Kaikoura, NZ
105/E3 Kaili, China
103/E2 Kailu, China
154/U11 Kailua, Hi,US
132/B2 Kainab (dry riv.), Namb.
82/B2 Kainach (riv.), Aus.
98/D3 Kainan, Japan
131/B2 Kaindu, Zam.
129/G4 Kainji (dam), Nga.
129/G4 Kainji (lake), Nga.
115/R10 Kaipara (har.), NZ
99/H7 Kaisei, Japan
76/D4 Kaiseregg (peak), Swi.
69/G5 Kaiserslautern, Ger.
76/D1 Kaiserstuhl (peak), Ger.
115/R10 Kaitaia, NZ
117/G2 Kaitej Abor. Land, Austl.
102/C6 Kaithal, India
130/B3 Kaiti, Tanz.
154/T10 Kaiwi (chan.), Hi,US
107/J2 Kaiyang, China
103/F2 Kaiyuan, China
104/D4 Kaiyuan, China
99/M9 Kaizu, Japan
99/L10 Kaizuka, Japan
52/F2 Kajaani, Fin.
130/C3 Kajiado, Kenya
101/E5 Kaji-san (mtn.), SKor.
130/A2 Kajo-Kaji, Sudan
125/M5 Kākā, Sudan
61/G3 Kakaanpää, Fin.
130/B2 Kakamega, Kenya
99/E3 Kakamigahara, Japan
82/D3 Kakanj, Bosn.
151/M4 Kaketsa (mtn.), BC,Can
86/E3 Kakhovka, Ukr.
86/E3 Kakhovka (res.), Ukr.
131/C2 Kakielo, Zaire
106/D4 Kākināda, India
130/B2 Kakiri, Ugan.
99/L9 Kako (riv.), Japan
131/A2 Kakonga, Zam.
130/A3 Kakonko, Tanz.
128/B4 Kakrima (riv.), Gui.
99/G2 Kakuda, Japan
130/B2 Kakuma, Kenya
131/C2 Kakumbi, Zam.
100/B4 Kakunodate, Japan
130/A3 Kakuto, Ugan.
130/C3 Kakya, Kenya
108/H4 Kala (riv.), SrL.
123/X18 Kalaa-Kebia, Tun.
145/N2 Kalaallit Nunaat (Greenland) (dpcy.), Den.
108/A1 Kālābāgh, Pak.
126/D3 Kalabo, Zam.
87/G2 Kalach, Rus.
88/H4 Kalachinsk, Rus.
87/G2 Kalach-na-Donu, Rus.
107/F3 Kaladan (riv.), Burma
154/U11 Ka Lae (cape), Hi,US
126/D5 Kalahari (des.), Afr.
132/C2 Kalahari-Gemsbok Nat'l Park, SAfr.
81/L7 Kalamáki, Gre.
124/H5 Kalamaloué Nat'l Park, Camr.
131/B4 Kalamare, Bots.
81/H2 Kalamariá, Gre.
81/H4 Kalamáta, Gre.
160/C3 Kalamazoo, Mi,US
130/B4 Kalangali, Tanz.
109/C2 Kalasin, Thai.
95/J3 Kalāt, Pak.
116/B3 Kalbarri Nat'l Park, Austl.
123/X18 Kalbīyah (lake), Tun.
61/N7 Kaldakvísl (riv.), Ice.
92/C1 Kalecik, Turk.
67/H5 Kalefeld, Ger.
130/A3 Kalehe, Zaire
130/A4 Kalemie, Zaire
131/B1 Kalene Hill, Zam.
93/J2 Kāl-e Shūr (riv.), Iran
65/K3 Kalety, Pol.
131/B2 Kaleya, Zam.
116/D4 Kalgoorlie-Boulder, Austl.
63/R7 Kalhall, Swe.
83/J4 Kaliakra, Nos (pt.), Bul.
110/C5 Kalianda, Indo.
112/C3 Kalibo, Phil.
126/E1 Kalima, Zaire
110/D4 Kalimantan (reg.), Indo.
63/J4 Kaliningrad, Rus.
63/H4 Kaliningrad (lag.), Rus.
63/J4 Kaliningrad Obl., Rus.
87/H2 Kalininsk, Rus.
86/D1 Kalinkovichi, Bela.
130/B2 Kaliro, Ugan.
130/A3 Kalisizo, Ugan.
156/E3 Kalispell, Mt,US
65/K3 Kalisz, Pol.
65/J3 Kalisz (prov.), Pol.
130/A4 Kaliua, Tanz.
61/G2 Kalix, Swe.
61/G2 Kalixälv (riv.), Swe.
106/E2 Kāliyāganj, India
160/C2 Kalkaska, Mi,US
108/G3 Kallakkurichchi, India
108/F4 Kallidaikurichchi, India
62/F3 Kallinge, Swe.
81/J5 Kallithea, Gre.
61/E3 Kallsjön (lake), Swe.
62/G3 Kalmar, Swe.
62/G3 Kalmar (co.), Swe.
62/G3 Kalmarsund (sound), Swe.
70/B4 Kalmit (mtn.), Ger.
66/B6 Kalmthout, Belg.
87/H3 Kalmyk Aut. Rep., Rus.
82/D2 Kalocsa, Hun.
154/T10 Kalohi (chan.), Hi,US
106/B3 Kālol, India
131/B3 Kalomo, Zam.
130/B2 Kalongo, Ugan.
106/C2 Kālpi, India
102/C3 Kalpin, China
64/E2 Kaltenkirchen, Ger.
77/H5 Kaltern (Caldaro), It.
106/D6 Kalu (riv.), SrL.
84/H5 Kaluga, Rus.
84/G5 Kaluga Obl., Rus.

197

Khach – Kōnan

87/J4 Khachmas, Azer.
104/B5 Khadaungnge (peak), Burma
94/E3 Khafjī, Ra's al, SAr.
106/D2 Khairābād, India
95/J3 Khairpur, Pak.
131/A5 Khakhea, Bots.
81/H3 Khalándrion, Gre.
81/H2 Khalkhidhikhi (pen.), Gre.
81/H3 Khalkís, Gre.
96/E1 Khamar-Daban (mts.), Rus.
106/D3 Khamaria, India
95/J4 Khambaliya, India
106/C3 Khāmgaon, India
94/D5 Khamīs Mushayţ, SAr.
106/D4 Khammam, India
95/J1 Khānābād, Afg.
93/F3 Khānaqīn, Iraq
106/C3 Khandwa, India
124/F1 Khanem (well), Alg.
108/A2 Khānewāl, Pak.
108/B2 Khāngāh Dogrān, Pak.
81/J5 Khaniá, Gre.
97/L3 Khanka (lake), Rus.
96/E1 Khankh, Mong.
108/D2 Khanna, India
95/K3 Khānpur, Pak.
88/G3 Khanty-Mansiysk, Rus.
88/G3 Khanty-Mansiysk Aut. Okr., Rus.
91/D4 Khān Yūnus, Gaza
109/C3 Khao Chamao-Khao Wong Nat'l Park, Thai.
109/C3 Khao Khitchakut Nat'l Park, Thai.
109/B3 Khao Laem (res.), Thai.
109/B3 Khao Sam Roi Yot Nat'l Park, Thai.
109/C3 Khao Yai Nat'l Park, Thai.
106/E3 Kharagpur, India
108/A1 Kharak, Pak.
95/J3 Khārān, Pak.
108/D2 Kharar, India
106/C3 Khargon, India
108/B1 Khāriān, Pak.
127/B3 Khārijah, Al Wāḥāt al (oasis), Egypt
127/C3 Kharīt, Wādī al (dry riv.), Egypt
93/G4 Khārk (isl.), Iran
86/F2 Khar'kov, Ukr.
86/F2 Khar'kov Obl., Ukr.
83/G5 Kharmanli, Bul.
84/J4 Kharovsk, Rus.
123/M13 Kharrour (riv.), Mor.
125/M4 Khartoum (cap.), Sudan
125/M4 Khartoum North, Sudan
125/M4 Kharṭūm (Khartoum) (cap.), Sudan
130/B3 Kharumwa, Tanz.
87/H4 Khasavyurt, Rus.
95/H2 Khāsh (riv.), Afg.
95/H3 Khāsh, Iran
87/G4 Khashuri, Geo.
83/G5 Khaskovo, Bul.
83/G5 Khaskovo (reg.), Bul.
89/L2 Khatanga (gulf), Rus.
89/L2 Khatanga (riv.), Rus.
91/C4 Khatmia (pass), Egypt
95/G3 Khaymah, Ra's al, UAE
93/F3 Khazzān Darbandīkhān (res.), Iraq
93/F3 Khazzān Dūkān (res.), Iraq
125/M4 Khazzān Jabal Al Awliyā (dam), Sudan
123/S15 Khemis el Khechna, Alg.
123/S15 Khemis Miliana, Alg.
123/V18 Khenchela, Alg.
124/D1 Khenifra, Mor.
93/G4 Khersān (riv.), Iran
86/E3 Kherson, Ukr.
86/E3 Kherson Obl., Ukr.
86/G1 Khilok, Rus.
96/F1 Khilok (riv.), Rus.
81/K3 Khíos, Gre.
81/J3 Khíos (isl.), Gre.
83/G4 Khisarya, Bul.
88/G5 Khiva, Uzb.
86/C2 Khmel'nitskiy, Ukr.
95/J2 Khojak (pass), Pak.
109/C3 Khok Samrong, Thai.
95/J1 Kholm, Afg.
97/N2 Kholmsk, Rus.
131/D2 Kholombidzo (falls), Malw.
93/G3 Khomeynīshahr, Iran
109/C2 Khon Kaen, Thai.
87/G2 Khopër (riv.), Rus.
97/M2 Khor (riv.), Rus.
93/J3 Khorāsān (gov.), Iran
126/C5 Khorixas, Namb.
130/D2 Khorof Harar, Kenya
102/B4 Khorog, Taj.
93/G3 Khorramābād, Iran
93/G4 Khorramshahr, Iran
109/C2 Kho Sawai (plat.), Thai.
151/G3 Khotol (mtn.), Ak,US
124/D1 Khouribga, Mor.
107/F3 Khowai, India
95/J2 Khowst, Afg.
81/J2 Khrisoúpolis, Gre.
87/L2 Khromtau, Kaz.
81/J5 Khrysi (isl.), Gre.
109/C2 Khuan Ubon Ratana (res.), Thai.
108/C2 Khudiān, Pak.
131/B4 Khudumelapye, Bots.
102/A3 Khudzhand, Taj.
106/E3 Khulna, Bang.
95/L1 Khūnjerāb (pass), Pak.
106/C3 Khurai, India
106/E3 Khurda, India
106/C2 Khurja, India
108/B1 Khushāb, Pak.
86/B2 Khust, Ukr.
95/J3 Khuzdār, Pak.
93/G4 Khūzestān (gov.), Iran
93/G4 Khūzestan, Jolgeh-ye (plain), Iran
97/L3 Khvalynka, Rus.
93/G3 Khvonsār, Iran
93/F2 Khvoy, Iran
102/B5 Khyber (pass), Afg., Pak.
119/D2 Kiama, Austl.
112/D4 Kiamba, Phil.
162/E3 Kiamichi (mts.), Ok,US
112/C1 Kiangan, Phil.
130/A2 Kibali (riv.), Zaire
130/A4 Kibanga, Zaire
130/B3 Kibara, Tanz.
130/B5 Kibau, Tanz.
112/D4 Kibawe, Phil.
130/C4 Kibaya, Tanz.
57/G2 Kibblesworth, Eng,UK
130/C4 Kiberege, Tanz.
61/J1 Kibergneset (pt.), Nor.
130/C4 Kibindu, Tanz.
130/C4 Kibiti, Tanz.
130/A2 Kiboga, Ugan.
130/C3 Kiboko, Kenya
130/A3 Kibondo, Tanz.
130/C3 Kibongoto, Tanz.
130/B3 Kibungo, Rwa.
130/A3 Kibuye, Rwa.
130/A4 Kibwesa, Tanz.
130/C3 Kibwezi, Kenya
82/E5 Kičevo, Macd.
60/A6 Kid (mtn.), Ire.
111/G2 Kidapawan, Phil.
58/D2 Kidderminster, Eng,UK
125/M7 Kidepo Valley Nat'l Park, Ugan.
130/C4 Kidete, Tanz.
130/C4 Kidodi, Tanz.
57/F5 Kidsgrove, Eng,UK
130/C4 Kidugallo, Tanz.
58/B3 Kidwelly, Wal,UK
64/F1 Kiel (bay), Den., Ger.
64/F1 Kiel, Ger.
65/L3 Kielce, Pol.
65/L3 Kielce (prov.), Pol.
57/F1 Kielder, Eng,UK
57/F1 Kielder (res.), Eng,UK
131/B1 Kiembe, Zaire
109/D1 Kien An, Viet.
109/D4 Kien Duc, Viet.
109/D4 Kien Thanh, Viet.
67/E6 Kierspe, Ger.
86/D2 Kiev (Kiyev) (cap.), Ukr.
86/D2 Kiev Obl., Ukr.
128/C2 Kiffa, Mrta.
81/L6 Kifisiá, Gre.
93/F3 Kifrī, Iraq
130/A3 Kigali (cap.), Rwa.
130/B4 Kiganga, Tanz.
130/A4 Kigoma, Tanz.
130/A4 Kigoma (prov.), Tanz.
154/T10 Kihei, Hi,US
63/L2 Kihnu (isl.), Est.
63/J1 Kihti (str.), Fin.
130/C5 Kihundo, Tanz.
130/C4 Kihurio, Tanz.
98/D4 Kii (chan.), Japan
98/D4 Kii (mts.), Japan
102/D3 Kiines (riv.), China
130/C4 Kijungu, Tanz.
100/L6 Kikai (isl.), Japan
130/A3 Kikarara, Ugan.
154/R9 Kikepa (pt.), Hi,US
151/H2 Kikiktat (mtn.), Ak,US
82/E3 Kikinda, Yugo.
130/B4 Kikombo, Tanz.
100/B3 Kikonai, Japan
126/C2 Kikwit, Zaire
62/E2 Kil, Swe.
130/C3 Kilaguni, Kenya
108/G4 Kilakarai, India
130/B3 Kilalo, Tanz.
148/E3 Kilambe (mtn.), Nic.
54/B5 Kilbarchan, Sc,UK
54/B5 Kilbirnie, Sc,UK
54/A6 Kilbrannan (sound), Sc,UK
161/Q9 Kilbride, On,Can
55/H8 Kilchoan, Sc,UK
60/A3 Kilcolgan (pt.), Ire.
54/B5 Kilcreggan, Sc,UK
60/B3 Kilcrow (riv.), Ire.
60/D3 Kildare (co.), Ire.
84/G1 Kil'den (isl.), Rus.
130/B2 Kildepo Valley Nat'l Park, Ugan.
131/C3 Kildonan, Zim.
130/A2 Kilembe, Ugan.
162/E3 Kilgore, Tx,US
130/B3 Kilgoris, Kenya
57/H3 Kilham, Eng,UK
153/R7 Kilian (isl.), NW,Can
130/C3 Kilifi, Kenya
108/F4 Kilikollūr, India
130/C3 Kilimanjaro (mtn.), Tanz.
130/C3 Kilimanjaro Nat'l Park, Tanz.
130/B4 Kilimatinde, Tanz.
83/K5 Kilimli, Turk.
130/C4 Kilindoni, Tanz.
108/H4 Kilinochchi (dist.), SrL.
91/E1 Kilis, Turk.
86/D3 Kiliya, Ukr.
56/B3 Kilkeel, NI,UK
60/C4 Kilkenny, Ire.
60/C4 Kilkenny (co.), Ire.
81/H2 Kilkís, Gre.
60/A1 Killala (bay), Ire.
156/F2 Killam, Ab,Can
57/G5 Killamarsh, Eng,UK
118/H8 Killara, Austl.
157/J3 Killarney, Mb,Can
60/A5 Killarney, Ire.
168/F6 Killbuck (cr.), Oh,US
157/H4 Killdeer, ND,US
54/B4 Killearn, Sc,UK
162/D4 Killeen, Tx,US
54/C3 Killiecrankie (pass), Sc,UK
54/B4 Killin, Sc,UK
56/C3 Killinchy, NI,UK
153/K2 Killinek (isl.), NW,Can
81/H4 Killíni (peak), Gre.
56/C3 Killough, NI,UK
167/K8 Kill Van Kull (str.), NJ, NY,US
56/A2 Killyclogher, NI,UK
56/C3 Killyleagh, NI,UK
60/D3 Kilmacanoge, Ire.
54/B5 Kilmacolm, Sc,UK
54/B5 Kilmarnock, Sc,UK
58/B5 Kilmar Tor (hill), Eng,UK
54/B5 Kilmaurs, Sc,UK
60/D4 Kilmichael (pt.), Ire.
55/J8 Kilninver, Sc,UK
130/C5 Kilombero (riv.), Tanz.
130/A2 Kilomines, Zaire
130/C4 Kilosa, Tanz.
56/B1 Kilraghts, NI,UK
56/B2 Kilrea, NI,UK
54/D4 Kilrenny, Sc,UK
54/B5 Kilsyth, Sc,UK
130/A5 Kilwa (isl.), Zam.
130/C5 Kilwa Kivinje, Tanz.
130/C5 Kilwa Masoko, Tanz.
56/C2 Kilwaughter, NI,UK
54/B5 Kilwinning, Sc,UK
130/B3 Kimali, Tanz.
130/C4 Kimamba, Tanz.
157/H5 Kimball, Ne,US
157/J5 Kimball, SD,US
120/E5 Kimbe, PNG
118/B2 Kimberley (cape), Austl.
114/D3 Kimberley (plat.), Austl.
156/E3 Kimberley, BC,Can
132/D3 Kimberley, SAfr.
101/E2 Kimch'aek, NKor.
101/E4 Kimch'ŏn, SKor.
101/E5 Kimhae, SKor.
63/K1 Kimito (isl.), Fin.
99/F3 Kimitsu, Japan
101/D5 Kimje, SKor.
101/G7 Kimnyangjang-ni, SKor.
81/J4 Kímolos (isl.), Gre.
130/B2 Kimoset, Kenya
86/F1 Kimovsk, Rus.
126/D2 Kimpanga, Zaire
84/H4 Kimry, Rus.
111/E2 Kinabalu, Gunung (peak), Malay.
112/B4 Kinabalu Nat'l Park, Malay.
111/E2 Kinabatangan (riv.), Malay.
130/C4 Kinango, Kenya
156/D2 Kinbasket (lake), BC,Can
55/K7 Kinbrace, Sc,UK
156/G3 Kincaid, Sk,Can
160/D2 Kincardine, On,Can
54/C4 Kincardine, Sc,UK
119/B2 Kinchega Nat'l Park, Austl.
54/C2 Kincraig, Sc,UK
126/D2 Kindambi, Zaire
73/L3 Kindberg, Aus.
57/G5 Kinder Scout (mtn.), Eng,UK
128/B4 Kindia, Gui.
128/B4 Kindia (comm.), Gui.
126/E1 Kindu, Zaire
87/J1 Kinel', Rus.
84/J4 Kineshma, Rus.
59/E2 Kineton, Eng,UK
119/C3 King (isl.), Austl.
116/C5 King (lake), Austl.
118/B4 King (peak), Austl.
114/C3 King (sound), Austl.
156/B2 King (isl.), BC,Can
151/N4 King (mtn.), BC,Can
151/K3 King (peak), Yk,Can
146/E2 King (mtn.), Tx,US
165/D2 King (co.), Wa,US
118/C4 Kingaroy, Austl.
153/R7 King Christian (isl.), NW,Can
145/P3 King Christian IX Land (reg.), Grld.
145/Q2 King Christian X Land (reg.), Grld.
161/Q8 King City, On,Can
158/B3 King City, Ca,US
159/H4 Kingfisher, Ok,US
145/N3 King Frederik VI Coast (reg.), Grld.
145/Q2 King Frederik VIII Land (reg.), Grld.
121/L6 King George (isl.), FrPol.
160/E4 King George, Va,US
53/N7 King George's (res.), Eng,UK
54/C4 Kinghorn, Sc,UK
119/C3 Kinglake Nat'l Park, Austl.
114/D3 King Leopold (ranges), Austl.
121/J4 Kingman (reef), PacUS
158/D4 Kingman, Az,US
159/H3 Kingman, Ks,US
166/C3 King of Prussia, Pa,US
158/C3 Kings (riv.), Ca,US
158/E2 Kings (peak), Ut,US
58/C6 Kingsbridge, Eng,UK
167/K9 Kings (Brooklyn) (co.), NY,US
158/C3 Kings Canyon Nat'l Park, Ca,US
59/E4 Kingsclere, Eng,UK
59/F1 King's Cliffe, Eng,UK
58/D2 Kingsland, Eng,UK
53/M6 Kings Langley, Eng,UK
59/G1 King's Lynn, Eng,UK
116/K6 Kings Park, Austl.
163/H2 Kingsport, Tn,US
54/C4 King's Seat (hill), Sc,UK
59/E2 Kings Sutton, Eng,UK
58/C5 Kingsteignton, Eng,UK
119/C4 Kingston, Austl.
160/E2 Kingston, On,Can
149/G2 Kingston (cap.), Jam.
120/F7 Kingston, Norfl.
168/D2 Kingston, Ma,US
160/F3 Kingston, NY,US
166/C1 Kingston, Pa,US
168/C3 Kingston, RI,US
119/A3 Kingston South East, Austl.
59/F4 Kingston upon Thames, Eng,UK
53/N7 Kingston upon Thames (bor.), Eng,UK
150/F4 Kingstown (cap.), StV.
163/J3 Kingstree, SC,US
127/C3 Kings, Valley of the, Egypt
162/D5 Kingsville, Tx,US
58/D2 Kingswinford, Eng,UK
58/D4 Kingswood, Eng,UK
91/D3 King Ţalāl (dam), Jor.
56/C2 Kington, Eng,UK
54/B2 Kingussie, Sc,UK
152/G2 King William (isl.), NW,Can
132/D4 King William's Town, SAfr.
131/C1 Kiniama, Zaire
92/A2 Kınık, Turk.
151/L4 Kinkaid (mtn.), Ak,US
126/B1 Kinkala, Congo
98/D3 Kinki (prov.), Japan
128/B4 Kinkon, Chutes de (falls), Gui.
54/A1 Kinlochewe, Sc,UK
54/B3 Kinlochleven, Sc,UK
54/B3 Kinloch Rannoch, Sc,UK
54/C1 Kinloss, Sc,UK
56/E5 Kinmel, Wal,UK
62/E3 Kinna, Swe.
54/D1 Kinnairds Head (pt.), Sc,UK
166/D2 Kinnelon, NJ,US
167/H8 Kinnelon (lake), NJ,US
91/F8 Kinneret-Negev Conduit, Isr.
108/H4 Kinniya, SrL.
98/D3 Kino (riv.), Japan
160/D1 Kinoje (riv.), On,Can
69/E1 Kinrooi, Belg.
54/C4 Kinross, Sc,UK
71/F4 Kinsach (riv.), Ger.
161/R8 Kinsale, On,Can
60/B6 Kinsale (har.), Ire.
126/C1 Kinshasa (cap.), Zaire
159/H3 Kinsley, Ks,US
163/J3 Kinston, NC,US
129/E4 Kintampo, Gha.
130/B4 Kintinku, Tanz.
54/D2 Kintore, Sc,UK
55/J9 Kintyre (pen.), Sc,UK
56/C1 Kintyre, Mull of (pt.), Sc,UK
99/F2 Kinu (riv.), Japan
130/B4 Kinyangiri, Tanz.
125/M7 Kinyeti (peak), Sudan
70/B6 Kinzig (riv.), Ger.
70/C2 Kinzig (riv.), Ger.
130/B4 Kiomboi, Tanz.
81/G4 Kiparissía (gulf), Gre.
160/E2 Kipawa (lake), Qu,Can
130/A4 Kipili, Tanz.
131/C2 Kipilingu, Zaire
130/D3 Kipini, Kenya
130/B2 Kipkarren (riv.), Kenya
157/H3 Kipling, Sk,Can
54/B4 Kippen, Sc,UK
60/D3 Kippure (mtn.), Ire.
131/B1 Kipushi, Zaire
99/N10 Kira, Japan
81/H3 Kira Panayía (isl.), Gre.
71/F1 Kirchberg, Ger.
70/B3 Kirchheimbolanden, Ger.
70/C5 Kirchheim unter Teck, Ger.
67/F6 Kirchhundem, Ger.
67/F4 Kirchlengern, Ger.
67/G3 Kirchlinteln, Ger.
77/H2 Kirchsee (lake), Ger.
71/E6 Kirchseeon, Ger.
70/A7 Kirchzarten, Ger.
56/C3 Kircubbin, NI,UK
56/D2 Kircudbright (bay), Sc,UK
89/L4 Kirensk, Rus.
102/B3 Kirgizskiy (mts.), Kyr.
88/F5 Kirgiz Steppe (grsld.), Kaz., Rus.
120/H5 Kiribati
91/E1 Kırıkhan, Turk.
92/C2 Kırıkkale, Turk.
92/C2 Kirikkale (prov.), Turk.
96/C3 Kirikkuduk, China
63/Q2 Kirishi, Rus.
98/B5 Kirishima-Yaku Nat'l Park, Japan
98/B5 Kirishima-yama (mtn.), Japan
121/K4 Kiritimati (Christmas) (atoll), Kiri.
92/A2 Kırkağaç, Turk.
57/G4 Kirkburton, Eng,UK
57/F5 Kirkby, Eng,UK
57/G5 Kirkby in Ashfield, Eng,UK
57/F3 Kirkby Lonsdale, Eng,UK
57/H3 Kirkbymoorside, Eng,UK
57/F3 Kirkby Stephen, Eng,UK
54/C4 Kirkcaldy, Sc,UK
56/C2 Kirkcolm, Sc,UK
54/C6 Kirkconnel, Sc,UK
56/D2 Kirkcowan, Sc,UK
56/D2 Kirkcudbright, Sc,UK
106/B4 Kirkee, India
62/E1 Kirkenær, Nor.
61/J1 Kirkenes, Nor.
57/F4 Kirkham, Eng,UK
54/B2 Kirkhill, Sc,UK
56/D2 Kirkinner, Sc,UK
54/B5 Kirkintilloch, Sc,UK
63/L1 Kirkkonummi (Kyrkslätt), Fin.
161/N7 Kirkland, Qu,Can
54/C6 Kirkland (hill), Sc,UK
165/C2 Kirkland, Wa,US
160/D1 Kirkland Lake, On,Can
92/A2 Kırklar (peak), Turk.
83/H5 Kırklareli, Turk.
83/H5 Kırklareli (prov.), Turk.
54/C5 Kirkliston, Sc,UK
56/D3 Kirkmichael, IM,UK
54/C5 Kirkmuirhill, Sc,UK
83/L2 Kirkovgrad Obl., Ukr.
113/M Kirkpatrick (mtn.), Ant.
159/J2 Kirksville, Mo,US
54/C3 Kirkton of Glenisla, Sc,UK
93/F3 Kirkūk, Iraq
55/N13 Kirkwall, Sc,UK
69/G4 Kirn, Ger.
130/C4 Kirongwe, Tanz.
130/B5 Kiropa, Tanz.
86/E1 Kirov, Rus.
87/H4 Kirovakan, Arm.
85/L4 Kirovo-Chepetsk, Rus.
86/E2 Kirovograd, Ukr.
86/D2 Kirovograd Obl., Ukr.
54/D3 Kirriemuir, Sc,UK
87/G1 Kirsanov, Rus.
92/C2 Kırşehir, Turk.
92/C2 Kirsehir (prov.), Turk.
57/H6 Kirton, Eng,UK
57/H5 Kirton in Lindsey, Eng,UK
61/G2 Kiruna, Swe.
168/F4 Kirwan (res.), Oh,US
99/F2 Kiryū, Japan
100/A4 Kisakata, Japan
125/L7 Kisangani, Zaire
130/C4 Kisarawe, Tanz.
99/F3 Kisarazu, Japan
65/K5 Kisbér, Hun.
88/J4 Kiselevsk, Rus.
130/B3 Kisesa, Tanz.
130/B3 Kisessa, Tanz.
93/H5 Kīsh (isl.), Iran
130/A3 Kishanda, Tanz.
106/E2 Kishanganj, India
106/B2 Kishangarh, India
83/J2 Kishinëv (cap.), Mol.
100/D2 Kishiro-Shitsugen Nat'l Park, Japan
98/D3 Kishiwada, Japan
106/F3 Kishorganj, Bang.
108/C1 Kishtwar, India
165/N15 Kishwaukee (riv.), Il,US
130/B4 Kisigo (riv.), Tanz.
130/B3 Kisii, Kenya
130/C4 Kisiju, Tanz.
130/C4 Kisiwani, Tanz.
151/B6 Kiska (isl.), Ak,US
151/B5 Kiska (vol.), Ak,US
156/C2 Kiskatinaw (riv.), BC,Can
157/J2 Kiskitto (lake), Mb,Can
82/D2 Kiskőrös, Hun.
82/D2 Kiskunfélegyháza, Hun.
82/D2 Kiskunhalas, Hun.
82/D2 Kiskunmajsa, Hun.
82/D2 Kiskunsági Nat'l Park, Hun.
87/G4 Kislovodsk, Rus.
125/P8 Kismaayo (Chisimayu), Som.
99/E3 Kiso (riv.), Japan
99/M9 Kisogawa, Japan
99/M9 Kisozaki, Japan
163/H4 Kissimmee, Fl,US
163/H4 Kissimmee (lake), Fl,US
70/D6 Kissing, Ger.
157/H2 Kississing (lake), Mb,Can
77/F2 Kisslegg, Ger.
82/E2 Kisújszállás, Hun.
130/B3 Kisumu, Kenya
82/F1 Kisvárda, Hun.
130/C5 Kiswere, Tanz.
99/G2 Kita (inlet), Japan
128/C3 Kita, Mali
99/M9 Kitagata, Japan
99/G2 Kita-Ibaraki, Japan
100/B4 Kitakami, Japan
100/B4 Kitakami (mts.), Japan
99/F2 Kitakata, Japan
98/B4 Kitakyūshū, Japan
130/B2 Kitale, Kenya
100/C2 Kitami, Japan
100/C1 Kitami (mts.), Japan
99/H6 Kitamoto, Japan
130/C5 Kitangari, Tanz.
130/B4 Kitangiri (lake), Tanz.
160/D3 Kitchener, On,Can
61/J3 Kitee, Fin.
130/A4 Kitendwe, Zaire
130/B2 Kitgum, Ugan.
81/H4 Kithira (isl.), Gre.
81/J4 Kithnos (isl.), Gre.
156/A2 Kitimat, BC,Can
156/A2 Kitimat Arm (inlet), BC,Can
165/B3 Kitsap (co.), Wa,US
165/B2 Kitsap Lake-Erlands Point, Wa,US
166/C1 Kittatinny (mts.), NJ, Pa,US
161/G3 Kittery, Me,US
130/C3 Kitui, Kenya
130/C3 Kitumbeine (peak), Tanz.
130/C5 Kitumbini, Tanz.
130/B4 Kitunda, Tanz.
130/D5 Kitunguli, Tanz.
131/C2 Kitwe, Zam.
73/K3 Kitzbühel, Aus.
70/D3 Kitzingen, Ger.
130/D3 Kiunga, Kenya
130/D3 Kiunga Marine Nat'l Rsv., Kenya
61/H3 Kiuruvesi, Fin.
130/C4 Kiuyu (pt.), Tanz.
61/H2 Kivalo (mts.), Fin.
63/M1 Kivijärvi (lake), Fin.
63/M2 Kiviõli, Est.
130/A3 Kivu (lake), Rwa., Zaire
130/A3 Kivu (reg.), Zaire
130/B5 Kiwira, Tanz.
86/D2 Kiyev (res.), Ukr.
86/D2 Kiyev (Kiev) (cap.), Ukr.
99/H7 Kiyokawa, Japan
99/H7 Kiyose, Japan
99/M9 Kiyosu, Japan
126/C2 Kizamba, Zaire
85/N4 Kizel, Rus.
102/B4 Kizil (riv.), China
92/C1 Kızılcahamam, Turk.
92/B2 Kızıldag Nat'l Park, Turk.
92/B2 Kızılhisar, Turk.
92/C1 Kızılırmak (riv.), Turk.
92/E2 Kızıltepe, Turk.
130/C5 Kizimbani, Tanz.
130/C4 Kizimkazi, Tanz.
87/H4 Kizlyar, Rus.
99/L10 Kizu, Japan
98/E3 Kizu (riv.), Japan
100/B3 Kizukuri, Japan
87/L5 Kizyl-Arvat, Trkm.
84/C1 Kjerkestinden (peak), Nor.
61/E2 Kjølen (Kölen) (mts.), Nor., Swe.
71/G3 Klabava (riv.), Czh.
82/D3 Kladanj, Bosn.
71/H2 Kladno, Czh.
82/F3 Kladovo, Yugo.
73/L3 Klagenfurt, Aus.
63/J4 Klaipėda, Lith.
156/C5 Klamath (mts.), Ca, Or,US
156/C5 Klamath (riv.), Ca, Or,US
156/C5 Klamath Falls, Or,US
88/B3 Klar (riv.), Swe.
61/E3 Klarälven (riv.), Swe.
71/G4 Klatovy, Czh.
77/H4 Klausen (Chiusa), It.
77/E4 Klausenpass (pass), Swi.
151/L3 Klaza (mtn.), Yk,Can
66/E3 Klazienaveen, Neth.
69/G5 Kleinblittersdorf, Ger.
161/Q8 Kleinburg, On,Can
65/G3 Kleine Elster (riv.), Ger.
76/E4 Kleine Emme (riv.), Swi.
69/E2 Kleine Gete (riv.), Belg.
71/F5 Kleine Laber (riv.), Ger.
66/B6 Kleine Nete (riv.), Belg.
131/C4 Klein-Letabarivier (riv.), SAfr.
132/Q12 Kleinolifants (riv.), SAfr.
62/A1 Kleppestø, Nor.
132/D2 Klerksdorp, SAfr.
71/H5 Klet' (peak), Czh.
66/D5 Kleve, Ger.
70/C3 Klingenberg am Main, Ger.
71/F2 Klingenthal, Ger.
71/F2 Klínovec (peak), Czh.
86/E1 Klintsy, Rus.
132/E2 Klip (riv.), SAfr.
62/E3 Klippan, Swe.
82/C3 Ključ, Bosn.
65/K2 Kľodawa, Pol.
65/J3 Kłodzko, Pol.
77/E3 Klöntalersee (lake), Swi.
67/F3 Klosterbach (riv.), Ger.
73/M2 Klosterneuburg, Aus.
73/L3 Klosterwappen (peak), Aus.
77/E3 Kloten, Swi.
64/F2 Klötze, Ger.
151/L3 Kluane, Yk,Can
151/K3 Kluane Nat'l Park, Yk,Can
65/K3 Kluczbork, Pol.
151/L3 Klukshu, Yk,Can
66/B5 Klundert, Neth.
67/E3 Klüstenkanal (can.), Ger.
84/J4 Klyaz'ma (riv.), Rus.
89/S4 Klyuchevskaya (peak), Rus.
57/G3 Knaresborough, Eng,UK
59/F3 Knebworth, Eng,UK
157/K2 Knee (lake), Mb,Can
83/G4 Knezha, Bul.
156/B3 Knight (inlet), BC,Can
58/C2 Knighton, Wal,UK
82/C3 Knin, Cro.
73/L3 Knittelfeld, Aus.
70/B4 Knittlingen, Ger.
71/H5 Knížecí Stolec (peak), Czh.
71/F3 Knížecí Strom (peak), Czh.
82/F4 Knjaževac, Yugo.
116/C5 Knob (cape), Austl.
112/C2 Knob (peak), Phil.
116/B4 Knobby (pt.), Austl.
54/D1 Knoch (hill), Sc,UK
60/C6 Knockadoon Head (pt.), Ire.
60/B1 Knockalongy (mtn.), Ire.
60/C5 Knockanaffrin (mtn.), Ire.
60/A6 Knockboy (mtn.), Ire.
56/B2 Knockcloghrim, NI,UK
60/A6 Knockeirke (mtn.), Ire.
56/B1 Knocklayd (mtn.), NI,UK
60/C5 Knockmealdown (mtn.), Ire.
60/B5 Knockmealdown (mts.), Ire.
60/B5 Knockshanahullion (mtn.), Ire.
68/C1 Knokke-Heist, Belg.
132/A2 Knoll (pt.), Namb.
62/D3 Knøsen (peak), Den.
62/E4 Knösen (pt.), Swe.
81/J5 Knosós (Knossos) (ruins), Gre.
57/F4 Knott End, Eng,UK
57/G4 Knottingley, Eng,UK
164/G8 Knott's Berry Farm, Ca,US
113/G Knox (coast), Ant.
119/G5 Knox, Austl.
151/M4 Knox (cape), BC,Can
168/E7 Knox (co.), Oh,US
168/E6 Knox (lake), Oh,US
163/H3 Knoxville, Tn,US
57/F5 Knutsford, Eng,UK
132/C4 Knysna, SAfr.
97/M2 Ko (peak), Rus.
130/C4 Koani, Tanz.
98/B5 Kobayashi, Japan
98/D3 Kōbe, Japan
63/T9 København (co.), Den.
62/E4 København (Copenhagen) (cap.), Den.
63/T9 København (Copenhagen) (inset) (cap.), Den.
111/G4 Kobipato (peak), Indo.
69/G3 Koblenz, Ger.
65/N2 Kobrin, Bela.
151/G2 Kobuk (riv.), Ak,US
151/G2 Kobuk Valley Nat'l Park, Ak,US
99/F3 Kobushi-ga-take (mtn.), Japan
71/H3 Kocába (riv.), Czh.
83/J5 Kocaeli (prov.), Turk.
92/D2 Koçalı, Turk.
82/F5 Kočani, Macd.
82/B3 Kočevje, Slov.
153/J2 Koch (isl.), NW,Can
101/D5 Koch'ang, SKor.
77/H2 Kochelsee (lake), Ger.
70/C4 Kocher (riv.), Ger.
98/C4 Kōchi, Japan
98/C4 Kōchi (pref.), Japan
151/H4 Kodiak, Ak,US
151/H4 Kodiak (isl.), Ak,US
151/H4 Kodiak Nat'l Wild. Ref., Ak,US
106/B3 Kodinār, India
125/M6 Kodok, Sudan
100/B3 Kodomari, Japan
83/H2 Kodry (hills), Mol.
68/B1 Koekelare, Belg.
106/D3 Koel (riv.), India
69/F5 Koenigsmacker, Fr.
139/G4 Koetari (riv.), Guy., Sur.
158/D4 Kofa (mts.), Az,US
111/G4 Kofiau (isl.), Indo.
129/E5 Koforidua, Gha.
99/F3 Kōfu, Japan
102/D3 Koga, China
99/F2 Koga, Japan
130/B4 Koga, Tanz.
99/H7 Koganei, Japan
62/E4 Køge, Den.
62/E4 Køge Bugt (bay), Den.
128/B4 Kogon (riv.), Gui.
101/D5 Kŏgum (isl.), SKor.
108/A1 Kohāt, Pak.
104/B3 Kohīma, India
93/G4 Kohkīlūyeh and Bovīr Aḥmadī (gov.), Iran
71/H5 Kohout (peak), Czh.
63/M2 Kohtla-Järve, Est.
101/D5 Kohŭng, SKor.
147/H5 Kohunlich (ruins), Mex.
132/A2 Koichab (dry riv.), Namb.
151/K3 Koidern, Yk,Can
99/H7 Koito (riv.), Japan
130/C3 Koito, Kenya
63/M3 Koiva (riv.), Est.
101/E5 Kōje (isl.), SKor.
65/L4 Kojšovská Hol'a (peak), Slvk.
109/B1 Kok (riv.), Burma
99/M10 Kōka, Japan
99/J7 Kokai (riv.), Japan
102/B3 Kokand, Uzb.
63/J2 Kökar (isl.), Fin.
102/A1 Kokchetav, Kaz.
63/J1 Kokemäenjoki (riv.), Fin.
61/G3 Kokkola, Fin.
128/C3 Kokofata, Mali
154/W13 Koko Head (crater), Hi,US
130/A2 Kokola, Zaire
160/C3 Kokomo, In,US
131/A5 Kokong, Bots.
106/F2 Kokrajhar, India
102/C3 Kokshaal-Tau (mts.), Kyr.
68/B1 Koksijde, Belg.
153/K3 Koksoak (riv.), Qu,Can
132/E3 Kokstad, SAfr.
98/B5 Kokubu, Japan
84/H1 Kola (pen.), Rus.
84/G1 Kola (riv.), Rus.
108/F4 Kolachel, India
111/F4 Kolaka, Indo.
106/C5 Kolār, India
82/D4 Kolašin, Yugo.
64/G5 Kolbermoor, Ger.
130/D3 Kolbio, Kenya
65/L3 Kolbuszowa, Pol.
128/B3 Kolda, Sen.
128/B3 Kolda (reg.), Sen.
62/C4 Kolding, Den.
61/E2 Kölen (Kjølen) (mts.), Nor., Swe.
120/C5 Kolepom (isl.), Indo.
63/N2 Kolgompya (cape), Rus.
85/K1 Kolguyev (isl.), Rus.
106/B4 Kolhāpur, India
128/B3 Koliba (riv.), Gui.
65/H3 Kolín, Czh.
63/K3 Kolkasrags (pt.), Lat.
71/F5 Kollbach (riv.), Ger.
66/D2 Kollum, Neth.
66/D7 Köln (Cologne), Ger.
65/L2 Kolno, Pol.
86/A1 Koło, Pol.
130/B4 Kolo, Tanz.
65/H1 Kołobrzeg, Pol.
128/C3 Kolokani, Mali
86/F1 Kolomna, Rus.
86/C2 Kolomyya, Ukr.
106/C6 Kolonnawa, SrL.
128/D3 Kolossa (riv.), Mali
88/J4 Kolpashevo, Rus.
63/P2 Kolpino, Rus.
82/E3 Kolubara (riv.), Yugo
65/K3 Koluszki, Pol.
102/A1 Koluton (riv.), Kaz.
85/N2 Kolva (riv.), Rus.
131/B1 Kolwezi, Zaire
89/R2 Kolyma (lowland), Rus.
89/R3 Kolyma (range), Rus.
89/R3 Kolyma (riv.), Rus.
82/F4 Kom (peak), Bul.
99/H7 Koma (riv.), Japan
82/E2 Komádi, Hun.
129/H4 Komadugu Gana (riv.), Nga.
129/H3 Komadugu Yobé (riv.), Nga.
99/H7 Komae, Japan
99/E3 Komagane, Japan
99/M9 Komaki, Japan
130/A2 Komanda, Zaire
89/S4 Komandorskiye (isls.), Rus.
65/K5 Komárno, Slvk.
82/D2 Komárom, Hun.
82/D2 Komárom-Esztergom (co.), Hun.
132/R12 Komatirivier (riv.), SAfr.
98/E2 Komatsu, Japan
98/D4 Komatsushima, Japan
130/B3 Kome (isl.), Tanz.
130/B3 Kome (isl.), Ugan.
79/G1 Komen, Slov.
85/L2 Komi Aut. Rep., Rus.
85/M3 Komi-Permyak Aut. Okr., Rus.
82/D2 Komló, Hun.
86/F2 Kommunarsk, Ukr.
102/B4 Kommunizma (Communism) (peak), Taj.
111/E5 Komodo (isl.), Indo.
111/E5 Komodo I. Nat'l Park, Indo.
128/E5 Komoé (riv.), IvC.
98/E3 Komono, Japan
81/J2 Komotiní, Gre.
132/D3 Kompasberg (peak), SAfr.
83/J2 Komrat, Mol.
89/L1 Komsomolets (isl.), Rus.
85/P2 Komsomol'skiy, Rus.
97/M1 Komsomol'sk-na-Amure, Rus.
81/K3 Kömür (pt.), Turk.
102/A2 Kon (riv.), Kaz.
84/H4 Konakovo, Rus.
99/M10 Kōnan, Japan
99/M9 Kōnan, Japan

120/F4 **Lae** (atoll), Mrsh.
120/D5 **Lae**, PNG
62/D3 **Laesø** (isl.), Den.
148/E3 **La Esperanza, Sierra** (range), Hon.
74/B1 **La Estaca de Bares, Punta de** (cape), Sp.
74/A1 **La Estrada**, Sp.
135/D3 **La Falda**, Arg.
165/K11 **Lafayette**, Ca,US
163/G3 **La Fayette**, Ga,US
160/C3 **Lafayette**, In,US
162/E4 **Lafayette**, La,US
72/D2 **La Ferté-Bernard**, Fr.
72/C2 **La Ferté-Macé**, Fr.
68/C6 **La Ferté-sous-Jouarre**, Fr.
160/E1 **Laflamme** (riv.), Qu,Can
72/C3 **La Flèche**, Fr.
73/L3 **Lafnitz** (riv.), Aus.
161/M6 **Lafontaine**, Qu,Can
73/G4 **La Font Sancte, Pic de** (peak), Fr.
138/C2 **La Fría**, Ven.
107/F6 **Lāfūl**, India
130/C2 **Laga Balal** (riv.), Kenya
130/C2 **Laga Mado Gali** (riv.), Kenya
130/C2 **Laga Merille** (riv.), Kenya
62/E3 **Lagan** (riv.), Swe.
56/B3 **Lagan** (riv.), NI,UK
53/S10 **La Garenne-Colombes**, Fr.
79/D2 **Lagarina** (val.), It.
162/B2 **La Garita** (mts.), Co,US
75/L6 **La Garriga**, Sp.
140/C3 **Lagarto**, Braz.
130/D2 **Laga Sure** (riv.), Kenya
112/C1 **Lagawe**, Phil.
130/A2 **Lagbo**, Zaire
124/H6 **Lagdo** (riv.), Camr.
124/H6 **Lagdo, Barrage de** (dam), Camr.
67/F5 **Lage**, Ger.
62/C1 **Lågen** (riv.), Nor.
62/D1 **Lågen** (riv.), Nor.
141/B3 **Lages**, Braz.
66/C4 **Lage Vaart** (can.), Neth.
54/B2 **Laggan**, Sc,UK
54/B3 **Laggan, Loch** (lake), Sc,UK
130/C2 **Lagh Bogal** (riv.), Kenya
130/C2 **Lagh Bor** (riv.), Kenya
130/D2 **Lagh Kutula** (riv.), Kenya
124/F1 **Laghouat**, Alg.
60/C5 **Laghtnafrankee** (mtn.), Ire.
53/U9 **Lagny-le-Sec**, Fr.
53/U10 **Lagny-sur-Marne**, Fr.
141/C2 **Lagoa da Prata**, Braz.
141/C1 **Lagoa Formosa**, Braz.
141/B4 **Lagoa Vermelha**, Braz.
140/A2 **Lago da Pedra**, Braz.
148/D3 **Lago de Atitlán Nat'l Park**, Guat.
77/E5 **Lago Gelato, Pizzo di** (peak), It.
142/C4 **Lago Puelo Nat'l Park**, Arg.
129/F5 **Lagos**, Nga.
129/F5 **Lagos** (state), Nga.
74/A4 **Lagos**, Port.
146/E4 **Lagos de Moreno**, Mex.
145/K4 **La Grande** (riv.), Can.
156/D4 **La Grande**, Or,US
73/G4 **La Grande Ruine** (mtn.), Fr.
163/G3 **La Grange**, Ga,US
160/C4 **La Grange**, Ky,US
162/D4 **La Grange**, Tx,US
139/F3 **La Gran Sabana** (plain), Ven.
149/J4 **La Grita**, Ven.
138/C2 **La Guajira** (dept.), Col.
74/A2 **La Guardia**, Sp.
142/D3 **La Guerra** (peak), Arg.
141/B4 **Laguna**, Braz.
165/M10 **Laguna** (cr.), Ca,US
164/C3 **Laguna Beach**, Ca,US
142/C3 **Laguna Blanca Nat'l Park**, Arg.
74/C2 **Laguna de Duero**, Sp.
139/E2 **Laguna de la Restinga Nat'l Park**, Ven.
142/C3 **Laguna del Laja Nat'l Park**, Chile
164/C3 **Laguna Hills**, Ca,US
143/J6 **Laguna San Rafael Nat'l Park**, Chile
148/B2 **Lagunas de Chacahua Nat'l Park**, Mex.
146/D4 **Lagunillas**, Mex.
138/D2 **Lagunillas**, Ven.
149/E3 **Laguntara** (lag.), Hon.
149/F1 **La Habana** (Havana) (cap.), Cuba
164/C3 **La Habra**, Ca,US
110/B4 **Lahat**, Indo.
161/H2 **La Have** (riv.), NS,Can
135/B2 **La Higuera**, Chile
93/G2 **Lāhījān**, Iran
64/E3 **Lahn** (riv.), Ger.
69/G3 **Lahnstein**, Ger.
62/E3 **Laholm**, Swe.
62/E3 **Laholmsbukten** (bay), Swe.
108/C2 **Lahore**, Pak.
70/A6 **Lahr**, Ger.
63/L1 **Lahti**, Fin.
124/J6 **Laï**, Chad
103/D4 **Lai'an**, China
79/D6 **Laiatico**, It.
107/J3 **Laibin**, China
109/C1 **Lai Chau**, Viet.
70/C6 **Laichingen**, Ger.
54/B3 **Laidon, Loch** (lake), Sc,UK
103/B5 **Laifeng**, China
72/D2 **L'Aigle**, Fr.
61/G3 **Laihia**, Fin.
78/C1 **Lainate**, It.
61/G2 **Lainioälven** (riv.), Swe.
130/C2 **Laisamis**, Kenya
103/C3 **Laishui**, China
63/J1 **Laitila**, Fin.
77/H5 **Laives** (Leifers), It.
103/D3 **Laiwu**, China
103/E3 **Laixi**, China
103/E3 **Laiyang**, China
103/C3 **Laiyuan**, China
103/D3 **Laizhou** (bay), China
142/C3 **Laja** (lake), Chile
140/B3 **Laje**, Braz.
141/B4 **Lajeado**, Braz.
140/C3 **Lajedo**, Braz.
75/S12 **Lajes do Pico**, Azor.,Port.
141/D2 **Lajinha**, Braz.
82/D2 **Lajosmizse**, Hun.
138/B5 **La Joya de los Sachas**, Ecu.
159/G3 **La Junta**, Co,US
130/A3 **L'Akagera Nat'l Park**, Rwa.
165/J9 **Lake** (co.), Ca,US
165/P15 **Lake** (co.), Il,US
165/R16 **Lake** (co.), In,US
168/F4 **Lake** (co.), Oh,US
168/E5 **Lake** (plains), Oh,US
117/F3 **Lake Amadeus Abor. Land**, Austl.
157/J5 **Lake Andes**, SD,US
164/C2 **Lake Arrowhead**, Ca,US
148/D3 **Lake Atitlán Nat'l Park**, Guat.
130/C2 **Lake Bogoria Nat'l Rsv.**, Kenya
162/E4 **Lake Charles**, La,US
158/F3 **Lake City**, Co,US
163/H4 **Lake City**, Fl,US
157/K4 **Lake City**, Mn,US
151/H3 **Lake Clark Nat'l Park & Prsv.**, Ak,US
57/E2 **Lake District Nat'l Park**, Eng,UK
164/C3 **Lake Elsinore**, Ca,US
117/H4 **Lake Eyre Nat'l Park**, Austl.
118/B1 **Lakefield Nat'l Park**, Austl.
165/Q15 **Lake Forest**, Il,US
168/E6 **Lake Fork** (riv.), Oh,US
162/E3 **Lake Fork** (res.), Tx,US
158/D4 **Lake Havasu City**, Az,US
167/D3 **Lakehurst Nav. Air Eng. Ctr.**, NJ,US
162/E4 **Lake Jackson**, Tx,US
163/H4 **Lakeland**, Fl,US
156/D3 **Lake Louise**, Ab,Can
117/F2 **Lake Mackay Abor. Land**, Austl.
131/D2 **Lake Malawi Nat'l Park**, Malw.
130/B3 **Lake Manyara Nat'l Park**, Tanz.
130/A3 **Lake Mburo Nat'l Park**, Ugan.
158/D4 **Lake Mead Nat'l Rec. Area**, Az, Nv,US
81/G2 **Lake Mikri Prespa Nat'l Park**, Gre.
166/D1 **Lake Mohawk**, NJ,US
130/C3 **Lake Nakuru Nat'l Park**, Kenya
59/G2 **Lakenheath**, Eng,UK
159/J3 **Lake of the Ozarks** (lake), Mo,US
157/K3 **Lake of the Woods** (lake), Can., US
165/F6 **Lake Orion**, Mi,US
164/C3 **Lake Perris Saint Rec. Area**, Ca,US
158/B3 **Lakeport**, Ca,US
162/F3 **Lake Providence**, La,US
163/F3 **Lake Providence**, La,US
167/E2 **Lake Ronkonkoma**, NY,US
119/C4 **Lake Saint Clair-Cradle Mountain Nat'l Park**, Austl.
61/H1 **Lakesfjorden** (fjord), Nor.
166/B5 **Lake Shore**, Md,US
164/D5 **Lakeside**, Ca,US
160/E4 **Lakeside**, Va,US
165/R16 **Lake Station**, In,US
156/C5 **Lakeview**, Or,US
168/D2 **Lakeville**, Ma,US
165/F6 **Lakeville** (lake), Mi,US
163/H5 **Lake Wales**, Fl,US
164/B3 **Lakewood**, Ca,US
159/F3 **Lakewood**, Co,US
165/Q16 **Lakewood**, Il,US
167/D3 **Lakewood**, NJ,US
168/F5 **Lakewood**, Oh,US
156/C3 **Lakewood**, Wa,US
163/H5 **Lake Worth**, Fl,US
165/P15 **Lake Zurich**, Il,US
63/L2 **Lakhemaasskiy Nat'l Park**, Est.
106/D2 **Lakhīmpur**, India
61/N7 **Laki** (vol.), Ice.
108/A1 **Lakki**, Pak.
81/H4 **Lakonía** (gulf), Gre.
106/B5 **Lakshadweep** (isls.), India
106/B6 **Lakshadweep** (terr.), India
112/C4 **Lala**, Phil.
130/B3 **Lalago**, Tanz.
108/B1 **Lāla Mūsa**, Pak.
133/H8 **Lalana** (riv.), Madg.
110/B4 **Lalang** (riv.), Indo.
106/E3 **Lālgola**, India
108/B2 **Lāliān**, Pak.
125/N5 **Lalībela**, Eth.
138/A5 **La Libertad**, Ecu.
148/D2 **La Libertad**, Guat.
142/C2 **La Ligua**, Chile
97/K3 **Lalin** (riv.), China
74/A1 **Lalín**, Sp.
74/C4 **La Línea de la Concepción**, Sp.
106/C3 **Lalitpur**, India
75/L6 **La Llagosta**, Sp.
116/C2 **Lalla Rookh Abor. Land**, Austl.
156/F1 **La Loche**, Sk,Can
68/D3 **La Louvière**, Belg.
74/C4 **La Luisiana**, Sp.
74/B4 **La Luz, Costa de** (coast), Sp.
56/D1 **Lamachan** (mtn.), Sc,UK
80/A2 **La Maddalena**, It.
62/D3 **La Madeleine**, Fr.
129/F4 **Lama-Kara**, Togo
161/G2 **La Malbaie**, Qu,Can
148/D2 **Lamanai** (ruins), Belz.
110/D4 **Lamandau** (riv.), Indo.
159/G3 **Lamar**, Co,US
152/E2 **La Martre** (lake), NW,Can
72/B2 **Lamballe**, Fr.
135/E2 **Lambaré**, Par.
126/B1 **Lambaréné**, Gabon
141/H6 **Lambari**, Braz.
60/D3 **Lambay** (isl.), Ire.
144/B2 **Lambayeque**, Peru
56/B3 **Lambeg**, NI,UK
128/C3 **Lambé Koba** (riv.), Mali
113/E **Lambert** (glac.), Ant.
160/D3 **Lambertville**, Mi,US
53/N7 **Lambeth** (bor.), Eng,UK
59/E3 **Lambourn**, Eng,UK
78/C2 **Lambro** (riv.), It.
165/H6 **Lambton** (co.), On,Can
74/B2 **Lamego**, Port.
138/C4 **La Mensura** (peak), Col.
161/H2 **Lamèque** (isl.), NB,Can
144/C3 **La Merced**, Peru
72/F3 **La Mère Boitier, Signal de** (mtn.), Fr.
164/C5 **La Mesa**, Ca,US
162/C3 **Lamesa**, Tx,US
81/H3 **Lamía**, Gre.
166/D2 **Lamington** (riv.), NJ,US
118/D5 **Lamington Nat'l Park**, Austl.
164/B3 **La Mirada**, Ca,US
112/C4 **Lamitan**, Phil.
54/A5 **Lamlash**, Sc,UK
54/D5 **Lammermuir** (hills), Sc,UK
160/B3 **La Moine** (riv.), Il,US
112/C2 **Lamon** (bay), Phil.
73/J4 **Lamone** (riv.), It.
158/C4 **Lamont**, Ca,US
144/C3 **La Montaña** (reg.), Peru
75/K7 **La Morella** (peak), Sp.
53/T9 **Lamorlaye**, Fr.
120/D4 **Lamotrek** (isl.), Micr.
157/J4 **La Moure**, ND,US
142/Q9 **Lampa**, Chile
112/B2 **Lampang**, Thai.
109/C2 **Lam Pao** (res.), Thai.
162/D4 **Lampasas**, Tx,US
162/D4 **Lampasas** (riv.), Tx,US
80/C5 **Lampedusa** (isl.), It.
70/B3 **Lampertheim**, Ger.
58/B2 **Lampeter**, Wal,UK
58/B3 **Lamphey**, Wal,UK
109/B2 **Lamphun**, Thai.
157/H3 **Lampman**, Sk,Can
130/D3 **Lamu**, Kenya
130/D3 **Lamu** (isl.), Kenya
149/F4 **La Muerte, Cerro** (mtn.), CR
130/B2 **Lamwa** (peak), Ugan.
105/J4 **Lan** (isl.), Tai.
154/T10 **Lanai** (isl.), Hi,US
154/T10 **Lanaihale** (peak), Hi,US
69/E2 **Lanaken**, Belg.
112/D4 **Lanao** (lake), Phil.
75/F3 **La Nao, Cabo de** (cape), Sp.
148/C2 **Lana, Rio de la** (riv.), Mex.
54/C5 **Lanark**, Sc,UK
109/B4 **Lanbi** (isl.), Burma
96/D5 **Lancang** (riv.), China
107/G3 **Lancang Lahuzu Zizhixian** (Lancang), China
57/F4 **Lancashire** (co.), Eng,UK
57/F4 **Lancashire** (plain), Eng,UK
153/H1 **Lancaster** (sound), NW,Can
57/F3 **Lancaster**, Eng,UK
158/C4 **Lancaster**, Ca,US
168/C1 **Lancaster**, Ma,US
161/S10 **Lancaster**, NY,US
160/D4 **Lancaster**, Oh,US
166/B3 **Lancaster**, Pa,US
166/B4 **Lancaster** (co.), Pa,US
163/H3 **Lancaster**, SC,US
160/B3 **Lancaster**, Wi,US
57/G2 **Lanchester**, Eng,UK
80/D1 **Lanciano**, It.
65/M3 **Łańcut**, Pol.
76/C5 **Lancy**, Swi.
71/F5 **Landau an der Isar**, Ger.
70/B4 **Landau in der Pfalz**, Ger.
77/G3 **Landeck**, Aus.
69/E2 **Landen**, Belg.
70/B4 **Landenburg**, Ger.
117/G2 **Lander** (riv.), Austl.
156/F5 **Lander**, Wy,US
72/A2 **Landerneau**, Fr.
72/C4 **Landes** (reg.), Fr.
72/B3 **Landes de Lanvaux** (reg.), Fr.
156/F2 **Landis**, Sk,Can
166/B3 **Landis Valley Museum**, Pa,US
166/B3 **Landisville-Salunga**, Pa,US
72/A2 **Landivisiau**, Fr.
67/G1 **Land Kehdingen** (reg.), Ger.
140/B2 **Landri Sales**, Braz.
70/D6 **Landsberg**, Ger.
118/B3 **Landsborough** (cr.), Austl.
58/A6 **Land's End** (pt.), Eng,UK
71/F5 **Landshut**, Ger.
62/E4 **Landskrona**, Swe.
66/B4 **Landsmeer**, Neth.
69/G5 **Landstuhl**, Ger.
57/F2 **Lanercost**, Eng,UK
72/B3 **Lanester**, Fr.
163/G3 **Lanett**, Al,US
105/J2 **Lang** (mtn.), China
54/D3 **Lang Craig** (pt.), Sc,UK
157/J3 **Langdon**, ND,US
132/G3 **Langeberg** (mts.), SAfr.
132/L10 **Langeberg** (mts.), SAfr.
62/D4 **Langeland** (isl.), Den.
67/H5 **Langelsheim**, Ger.
67/F1 **Langen**, Ger.
77/F2 **Langenargen**, Ger.
70/D6 **Langenau**, Ger.
67/E6 **Langenberg**, Ger.
157/H3 **Langenburg**, Sk,Can
66/D6 **Langenfeld**, Ger.
67/G4 **Langenhagen**, Ger.
65/H4 **Langenlois**, Aus.
70/C2 **Langenselbold**, Ger.
76/D3 **Langenthal**, Swi.
70/D4 **Langenzenn**, Ger.
67/E1 **Langeoog** (isl.), Ger.
76/D3 **Langeten** (riv.), Swi.
103/D3 **Langfang**, China
156/G2 **Langham**, Sk,Can
59/F1 **Langham**, Eng,UK
57/F1 **Langholm**, Sc,UK
61/N7 **Langjökull** (glac.), Ice.
110/A2 **Langkawi** (isl.), Malay.
109/B4 **Lang Kha Tuk** (peak), Thai.
53/M7 **Langley**, Eng,UK
76/D4 **Langnau im Emmental**, Swi.
59/G5 **Langney** (pt.), UK
61/E1 **Langøya** (isl.), Nor.
102/C5 **Langqên** (riv.), China
76/B2 **Langres**, Fr.
76/B2 **Langres, Plateau de** (plat.), Fr.
110/A3 **Langsa**, Indo.
109/D1 **Lang Son**, Viet.
161/R8 **Langstaff**, On,Can
162/C4 **Langtry**, Tx,US
75/G1 **Languedoc** (hist. reg.), Fr.
72/E5 **Languedoc-Roussillon** (reg.), Fr.
67/G3 **Langwedel**, Ger.
77/G1 **Langweid am Lech**, Ger.
103/D5 **Langxi**, China
103/C3 **Langya Shan** (mtn.), China
166/B6 **Lanham-Seabrook**, Md,US
157/G3 **Lanigan**, Sk,Can
154/W12 **Lanikai** (pt.), Hi,US
142/C3 **Lanin** (vol.), Chile
142/C3 **Lanin Nat'l Park**, Arg.
72/D5 **Lannemezan**, Fr.
72/D5 **Lannemezan** (plat.), Fr.
58/A6 **Lanner**, Eng,UK
72/B2 **Lannion**, Fr.
72/B2 **Lannion** (bay), Fr.
53/S11 **La Norville**, Fr.
109/B2 **Lan Sang Nat'l Park**, Thai.
166/C3 **Lansdale**, Pa,US
166/C4 **Lansdowne**, Pa,US
166/B5 **Lansdowne-Baltimore Highlands**, Md,US
160/B2 **L'Anse**, Mi,US
161/L1 **L'Anse aux Meadows Nat'l Hist. Park**, Nf,Can
105/G3 **Lanshan**, China
151/M3 **Lansing**, Yk,Can
165/Q16 **Lansing**, Il,US
160/C3 **Lansing** (cap.), Mi,US
109/B5 **Lanta** (isl.), Thai.
76/C2 **Lanterne** (riv.), Fr.
143/S12 **Lanús**, Arg.
80/A3 **Lanusei**, It.
112/D3 **Lanuza**, Phil.
105/H2 **Lanxi**, China
96/E4 **Lanzhou**, China
101/D2 **Lao** (mts.), China
105/G2 **Lao** (riv.), China
112/C1 **Laoag**, Phil.
109/C1 **Lao Cai**, Viet.
105/G2 **Laodao** (riv.), China
97/H3 **Laoha** (riv.), China
103/B4 **Laohekou**, China
60/C4 **Laois** (Leix) (co.), Ire.
103/B4 **Laojun Shan** (mtn.), China
68/C4 **Laon**, Fr.
139/E2 **La Orchila** (isl.), Ven.
144/C3 **La Oroya**, Peru
109/C2 **Laos**
103/E3 **Laoshan**, China
103/E3 **Lao Shan** (peak), China
103/E3 **Laotie Shan** (mtn.), China
103/F2 **Laotuding Shan** (peak), China
123/M13 **Laou** (riv.), Mor.
75/G1 **Laouzas, Barrage de** (dam), Fr.
141/B3 **Lapa**, Braz.
129/G4 **Lapai**, Nga.
146/D3 **La Palma**, Mex.
142/D3 **La Pampa** (prov.), Arg.
136/E7 **La Paz** (cap.), Bol.
144/D4 **La Paz** (dept.), Bol.
148/E3 **La Paz**, Hon.
146/C3 **La Paz**, Mex.
146/C3 **La Paz** (bay), Mex.
112/D3 **La Paz**, Phil.
143/F2 **La Paz**, Uru.
143/T12 **La Paz**, Uru.
160/F2 **La Pêche**, Qu,Can
84/F3 **Lapeenranta**, Fin.
165/F5 **Lapeer**, Mi,US
165/F6 **Lapeer** (co.), Mi,US
149/F4 **La Peña**, Pan.
100/B1 **La Pérouse** (str.), Japan, Rus.
76/D1 **La Petite-Raon**, Fr.
61/H3 **Lapinlahti**, Fin.
61/F1 **Lapland** (reg.), Eur.
143/F2 **La Plata**, Arg.
138/C4 **La Plata**, Col.
162/B2 **La Plata** (peak), Co,US
160/E4 **La Plata**, Md,US
143/T12 **La Plata, Rio de** (est.), Arg.,Urg.
68/D3 **La Plate Taile, Barrage de** (dam), Belg.
161/G2 **La Pocatière**, Qu,Can
74/C1 **La Pola de Gordón**, Sp.
160/C3 **La Porte**, In,US
97/N1 **Lapotina** (mtn.), Rus.
82/E3 **Lapovo**, Yugo.
146/B3 **La Poza**, Mex.
63/N1 **Lappeenranta**, Fin.
71/F4 **Lappersdorf**, Ger.
61/H2 **Lappi** (prov.), Fin.
161/N7 **La Prairie**, Qu,Can
161/N7 **La Prarie** (co.), Qu,Can
162/D4 **La Pryor**, Tx,US
89/N2 **Laptev** (sea), Rus.
61/G3 **Lapua**, Fin.
75/G3 **La Puebla**, Sp.
74/C4 **La Puebla de Cazalla**, Sp.
74/B4 **La Puebla del Río**, Sp.
74/C3 **La Puebla de Montalbán**, Sp.
164/C2 **La Puente**, Ca,US
138/A5 **La Puntilla** (pt.), Ecu.
65/M2 **Łapy**, Pol.
127/B4 **Laqiyat al Arba'īn**, Sudan
136/E8 **La Quiaca**, Arg.
80/C1 **L'Aquila**, It.
93/H5 **Lār**, Iran
138/D2 **Lara** (state), Ven.
74/A1 **Laracha**, Sp.
123/L13 **Larache**, Mor.
93/J5 **Lārak** (isl.), Iran
74/C4 **La Rambla**, Sp.
159/F2 **Laramie** (riv.), Co, Wy,US
157/G5 **Laramie**, Wy,US
156/G5 **Laramie** (mts.), Wy,US
157/G5 **Laramie** (peak), Wy,US
141/A3 **Laranjeiras do Sul**, Braz.
111/H5 **Larat** (isl.), Indo.
75/G1 **La Raviège, Barrage de** (dam), Fr.
123/S15 **Larba**, Alg.
167/K8 **Larchmont**, NY,US
72/B2 **L'Arcouest, Pointe de** (pt.), Fr.
156/A2 **Laredo** (sound), BC,Can
144/B3 **Laredo**, Peru
74/D1 **Laredo**, Sp.
162/D5 **Laredo**, Tx,US
66/C4 **Laren**, Neth.
149/F1 **Largo** (cay), Cuba
54/D4 **Largo** (bay), Sc,UK
163/H5 **Largo**, Fl,US
166/B6 **Largo**, Md,US
54/B5 **Largs**, Sc,UK
76/D2 **Largue** (riv.), Fr.
74/E1 **La Rhune** (mtn.), Fr.
111/F4 **Lariang** (riv.), Indo.
74/C4 **La Rinconada**, Sp.
135/C2 **La Rioja**, Arg.
74/D1 **La Rioja** (aut. comm.), Sp.
81/H3 **Lárisa**, Gre.
59/G2 **Lark** (riv.), Eng,UK
95/J3 **Lārkāna**, Pak.
54/C5 **Larkhall**, Sc,UK
59/E4 **Larkhill**, Eng,UK
165/J11 **Larkspur**, Ca,US
72/B3 **Larmor-Plage**, Fr.
91/C2 **Larnaca**, Cyp.
91/C2 **Larnaca** (dist.), Cyp.
56/C2 **Larne**, NI,UK
56/C2 **Larne** (dist.), NI,UK
159/H3 **Larned**, Ks,US
56/C2 **Larne Lough** (inlet), NI,UK
156/F1 **La Roche** (lake), Sk,Can
72/C3 **La Rochelle**, Fr.
76/C5 **La Roche-sur-Foron**, Fr.
72/C3 **La Roche-sur-Yon**, Fr.
74/D3 **La Roda**, Sp.
150/D3 **La Romana**, DRep.
157/G2 **La Ronge**, Sk,Can
157/G2 **La Ronge** (lake), Sk,Can
130/A2 **Laropi**, Ugan.
163/F4 **Larose**, La,US
148/E3 **Larreynaga**, Nic.
166/A1 **Larrys** (cr.), Pa,US
152/G1 **Larsen** (sound), NW,Can
113/V **Larsen Ice Shelf**, Ant.
64/A3 **L'Artois, Collines de** (hills), Fr.
74/B1 **La Rúa**, Sp.
62/D2 **Larvik**, Nor.
161/N7 **La Salle**, Qu,Can
160/B3 **La Salle**, Il,US
159/G3 **Las Animas**, Co,US
160/E1 **La Sarre**, Qu,Can
73/G5 **La Sauvette** (mtn.), Fr.
139/E1 **Las Aves** (isls.), Ven.
139/E3 **Las Bonitas**, Ven.
135/D2 **Las Breñas**, Arg.
74/C4 **Las Cabezas de San Juan**, Sp.
142/C2 **Las Cabras**, Chile
147/E4 **las Campanas Nat'l Park, Cerro de**, Mex.
143/G2 **Lascano**, Uru.
147/G5 **Las Choapas**, Mex.
161/L1 **La Scie**, Nf,Can
158/F4 **Las Cruces**, NM,US
135/B2 **La Serena**, Chile
75/F1 **La Seu d'Urgell**, Sp.
72/F5 **La Seyne-sur-Mer**, Fr.
142/F3 **Las Flores**, Arg.
138/C4 **Las Hermosas Nat'l Park**, Col.
104/C4 **Lashio**, Burma
95/H2 **Lashkar Gāh**, Afg.
149/G1 **La Sierpe**, Cuba
80/E3 **La Sila** (mts.), It.
143/J8 **La Silueta** (peak), Chile
142/C3 **Las Lajas** (peak), Arg.
144/A2 **Las Lomas**, Peru
135/D1 **Las Lomitas**, Arg.
148/D2 **Las Margaritas**, Mex.
149/J2 **Las Matas de Farfán**, DRep.
139/E2 **Las Mercedes**, Ven.
112/D2 **Las Navas**, Phil.
68/D2 **Lasne-Chapelle-Saint-Lambert**, Belg.
74/D3 **La Solana**, Sp.
111/F4 **Lasolo** (riv.), Indo.
68/B4 **La Somme, Canal de** (can.), Fr.
142/C2 **Las Palmas de Cocalán Nat'l Park**, Chile
74/D3 **Las Pedroñeras**, Sp.
78/C4 **La Spezia**, It.
78/C4 **La Spezia** (prov.), It.
143/F2 **Las Piedras**, Uru.
112/E6 **Las Piñas**, Phil.
142/E2 **Las Rosas**, Arg.
75/N9 **Las Rozas**, Sp.
158/B2 **Lassen** (peak), Ca,US
158/B2 **Lassen Volcanic Nat'l Park**, Ca,US
113/V **Lassiter** (coast), Ant.
161/N6 **L'Assomption** (co.), Qu,Can
161/P6 **L'Assomption** (riv.), Qu,Can
54/C5 **Lasswade**, Sc,UK
74/D3 **Las Tablas de Daimiel Nat'l Park**, Sp.
135/D2 **Las Termas**, Arg.
157/G3 **Last Mountain** (lake), Sk,Can
82/C4 **Lastovo** (isl.), Cro.
82/C4 **Lastovski** (chan.), Cro.
79/E5 **Lastra a Signa**, It.
149/G1 **Las Tunas**, Cuba
146/D4 **Las Varas**, Mex.
142/E1 **Las Varillas**, Arg.
159/F4 **Las Vegas**, NM,US
158/D3 **Las Vegas**, Nv,US
161/K1 **La Tabatière**, Qu,Can
138/B5 **Latacunga**, Ecu.
113/U **Latady** (isl.), Ant.
91/D2 **Latakia** (Al Lādhiqīyah), Syria
129/F4 **L'Atakora** (prov.), Ben.
77/H5 **Latemar** (peak), It.
80/E2 **Laterza**, It.
72/C4 **La Teste-de-Buch**, Fr.
76/C6 **La Tête à l'Ane** (peak), Fr.
72/C3 **Lathan** (riv.), Fr.
165/M11 **Lathrop**, Ca,US
148/E3 **La Tigra Nat'l Park**, Hon.
53/M7 **Latimer**, Eng,UK
80/C2 **Latina**, It.
79/G1 **Latisana**, It.
65/L4 **Latorica** (riv.), Slvk.
139/E2 **La Tortuga** (isl.), Ven.
114/B3 **Latouche Treville** (cape), Austl.
76/C5 **La Tour-de-Peilz**, Swi.
112/C1 **La Trinidad**, Phil.
119/C3 **Latrobe** (peak), Austl.
119/C3 **Latrobe** (riv.), Austl.
138/B5 **La Troncal**, Ecu.
77/G4 **Latsch** (Laces), It.
72/E5 **Lattes**, Fr.
161/F2 **La Tuque**, Qu,Can
106/C4 **Lātūr**, India
63/L3 **Latvia**
70/B1 **Laubach**, Ger.
144/D5 **Lauca Nat'l Park**, Chile
73/G3 **Lauch** (riv.), Fr.
77/F1 **Lauchert** (riv.), Ger.
70/C3 **Lauda-Königshofen**, Ger.
54/D5 **Lauder**, Sc,UK
165/N14 **Lauderdale** (lakes), Wi,US
67/H2 **Lauenburg**, Ger.
70/D2 **Lauer** (riv.), Ger.
70/E3 **Lauf**, Ger.
70/C4 **Lauffen am Neckar**, Ger.
58/B3 **Laugharne**, Wal,UK
117/G2 **Laughlen** (peak), Austl.
162/C4 **Laughlin A.F.B.**, Tx,US
120/H6 **Lau Group** (isls.), Fiji
61/G3 **Lauhanvuoren Nat'l Park**, Fin.
70/D5 **Lauingen**, Ger.
61/H3 **Laukaa**, Fin.
119/C4 **Launceston**, Austl.
58/B5 **Launceston**, Eng,UK
60/A5 **Laune** (riv.), Ire.
53/U9 **Launette** (riv.), Fr.
142/B4 **La Unión**, Chile
148/E3 **La Unión**, ESal.
144/A2 **La Unión**, Peru
75/E4 **La Unión**, Sp.
70/C6 **Laupheim**, Ger.
77/E5 **Laurasca, Cima della** (peak), It.
166/B5 **Laurel**, Md,US
163/F4 **Laurel**, Ms,US
156/F4 **Laurel**, Mt,US
56/B3 **Laurelvale**, NI,UK
167/D3 **Laurence Harbor**, NJ,US
54/D3 **Laurencekirk**, Sc,UK
163/H3 **Laurens**, SC,US
160/C1 **Laurentian** (plat.), Can.
56/D2 **Laurieston**, Sc,UK
163/J3 **Laurinburg**, NC,US
160/B2 **Laurium**, Mi,US
76/C4 **Lausanne**, Swi.
111/E4 **Laut** (isl.), Indo.
142/B3 **Lautaro**, Chile
69/G5 **Lauter** (riv.), Fr., Ger.
70/C5 **Lauter** (riv.), Ger.
71/E4 **Lauterach** (riv.), Ger.
64/E3 **Lauterbach**, Ger.
70/E2 **Lauterbach** (riv.), Ger.
120/G6 **Lautoka**, Fiji
62/D2 **Lauve**, Nor.
66/D2 **Lauwers** (chan.), Neth.
66/D2 **Lauwersmeer** (lake), Neth.
158/B2 **Lava Beds Nat'l Mon.**, Ca,US
78/C4 **Lavagna**, It.
78/C4 **Lavagna** (riv.), It.
161/N6 **Laval**, Qu,Can
72/C2 **Laval**, Fr.
143/G2 **Lavalleja** (dept.), Uru.
76/B2 **La Vallinot**, Fr.
93/H5 **Lāvān** (isl.), Iran
73/B3 **Lavant** (riv.), Aus.
142/B3 **Lavapié** (pt.), Chile
77/F1 **Lavaur**, Fr.
150/D3 **La Vega**, DRep.
138/C1 **La Vela, Cabo de** (pt.), Col.
72/D5 **Lavelanet**, Fr.
80/D2 **Lavello**, It.
146/C3 **La Ventana**, Mex.
79/E5 **La Verna**, It.
164/C2 **La Verne**, Ca,US
53/R10 **La Verrière**, Fr.
139/E2 **La Victoria**, Ven.
79/E4 **Lavino** (riv.), It.
141/C2 **Lavras**, Braz.
140/C2 **Lavras da Mangabeira**, Braz.
81/J4 **Lávrion**, Gre.
131/C2 **Lavushi Manda Nat'l Park**, Zam.
139/H4 **Lawa** (riv.), FrG., Sur.
95/K1 **Lawarai** (pass), Pak.
110/D3 **Lawit** (mtn.), Indo.
164/B3 **Lawndale**, Ca,US
159/J3 **Lawrence**, Ks,US
161/G3 **Lawrence**, Ma,US
167/E2 **Lawrence**, NY,US
168/G5 **Lawrence** (co.), Pa,US
160/C4 **Lawrenceburg**, In,US
163/G2 **Lawrenceburg**, Ky,US
163/G3 **Lawrenceburg**, Tn,US
56/B3 **Lawrencetown**, NI,UK
163/H3 **Lawrenceville**, Ga,US
166/D3 **Lawrenceville**, NJ,US
159/H4 **Lawton**, Ok,US
110/D5 **Lawu** (peak), Indo.
92/C4 **Lawz, Jabal al** (mtn.), SAr.
62/F2 **Laxa**, Swe.
56/D3 **Laxey**, IM,UK
69/F6 **Laxou**, Fr.
72/C3 **Lay** (riv.), Fr.
85/N2 **Laya** (riv.), Rus.
111/E4 **Layar** (cape), Indo.
121/H2 **Laycan** (isl.), Hi,US
94/E4 **Laylá**, SAr.
72/C3 **Layon** (riv.), Fr.
158/E2 **Layton**, Ut,US
82/E3 **Lazarevac**, Yugo.
112/C3 **Lazi**, Phil.
80/C1 **Lazio** (reg.), It.
57/F2 **Lazonby**, Eng,UK
78/C3 **Lazzaro, Monte** (peak), It.
59/F3 **Lea** (riv.), Eng,UK
109/C3 **Leach**, Camb.
59/E3 **Leach** (riv.), Eng,UK
157/H4 **Lead**, SD,US
57/H5 **Leadenham**, Eng,UK
156/F3 **Leader**, Sk,Can
54/D5 **Leader Water** (riv.), Sc,UK
58/D2 **Leadon** (riv.), Eng,UK
162/B2 **Leadville**, Co,US
163/F4 **Leaf** (riv.), Ms,US
119/B2 **Leaghur** (lake), Austl.
159/J5 **League City**, Tx,US
162/D4 **Leakey**, Tx,US
59/E2 **Leam** (riv.), Eng,UK
165/G7 **Leamington**, On,Can
105/H2 **Le'an** (riv.), China
116/B4 **Leander** (pt.), Austl.
60/A5 **Leane** (lake), Ire.
59/F4 **Leatherhead**, Eng,UK
68/D3 **L'Eau d'Heure** (riv.), Belg.
68/D3 **L'Eau d'Heure, Barrage de** (dam), Belg.
159/J3 **Leavenworth**, Ks,US
156/C4 **Leavenworth**, Wa,US
69/F5 **Lebach**, Ger.
112/D4 **Lebak**, Phil.
82/E4 **Lebane**, Yugo.
91/D3 **Lebanon**
91/D3 **Lebanon** (mts.), Leb.
168/B2 **Lebanon**, Ct,US
160/C3 **Lebanon**, In,US
160/C4 **Lebanon**, Ky,US
159/J3 **Lebanon**, Mo,US
161/F3 **Lebanon**, NH,US
156/C4 **Lebanon**, Or,US
166/B3 **Lebanon**, Pa,US
166/B3 **Lebanon** (co.), Pa,US
163/G2 **Lebanon**, Tn,US
160/D4 **Lebanon**, Va,US
166/C5 **Lebanon-Rising Sun**, De,US
68/D2 **Lebbeke**, Belg.
86/E2 **Lebedin**, Ukr.
160/E1 **Lebel-sur-Quévillon**, Qu,Can
123/M13 **Lebene** (riv.), Mor.
72/D3 **Le Blanc**, Fr.
53/T10 **Le Blanc-Mesnil**, Fr.
131/C5 **Lebombo** (mts.), Moz., SAfr.
65/J1 **Lębork**, Pol.
74/B4 **Lebrija**, Sp.
135/B4 **Lebu**, Chile
74/A2 **Leça da Palmeira**, Port.
73/G5 **Le Cannet**, Fr.
68/C3 **Le Cateau**, Fr.
81/F2 **Lecce**, It.
78/C1 **Lecci** (lake), It.
78/C1 **Lecco**, It.
77/G1 **Lech** (riv.), Aus., Ger.
107/K2 **Lechang**, China
76/D3 **Le Chasseral** (peak), Swi.
76/C4 **Le Chasseron** (peak), Swi.
149/G1 **Leche** (lag.), Cuba
53/S10 **Le Chesnay**, Fr.
76/C5 **Le Cheval Blanc** (mtn.), Fr.
59/E3 **Lechlade**, Eng,UK
77/G3 **Lechtaler Alps** (mts.), Aus.
64/E1 **Leck**, Ger.
60/A3 **Leckavrea** (mtn.), Ire.
73/J5 **Le Cornate** (peak), It.
75/G1 **Le Crès**, Fr.
72/F3 **Le Creusot**, Fr.
65/M3 **Łęczna**, Pol.
67/E2 **Leda** (riv.), Ger.
110/B3 **Ledang** (peak), Malay.
58/D2 **Ledbury**, Eng,UK
68/C2 **Lede**, Belg.
68/C2 **Ledegem**, Belg.
105/F5 **Ledong**, China
79/D1 **Ledro** (lake), It.
152/E2 **Leduc**, Ab,Can
77/F5 **Ledu, Pizzo** (peak), It.
60/B6 **Lee** (riv.), Ire.
166/B1 **Lee** (mtn.), Pa,US
157/K4 **Leech** (lake), Mn,US
57/G4 **Leeds**, Eng,UK
57/G4 **Leeds and Liverpool** (can.), Eng,UK
66/D2 **Leek**, Neth.
57/F5 **Leek**, Eng,UK
53/N7 **Lee** (Lea) (riv.), UK
67/E2 **Leer**, Ger.
66/C5 **Leerdam**, Neth.
66/C4 **Leersum**, Neth.
163/H4 **Leesburg**, Fl,US
160/E4 **Leesburg**, Va,US
162/E4 **Leesville**, La,US
168/F7 **Leesville** (dam), Oh,US
168/F7 **Leesville** (res.), Oh,US
119/C2 **Leeton**, Austl.
132/L10 **Leeu** (riv.), SAfr.
66/C2 **Leeuwarden**, Neth.
116/B5 **Leeuwin** (cape), Austl.
116/B5 **Leeuwin-Naturaliste Nat'l Park**, Austl.
158/C3 **Lee Vining**, Ca,US

200

Leewa – Lizar

150/F3 **Leeward Islands** (isls.), West Indies
72/B2 **Leff** (riv.), Fr.
129/H5 **Lefo** (peak), Camr.
116/D4 **Lefroy** (lake), Austl.
74/D2 **Leganés**, Sp.
112/C2 **Legazpi**, Phil.
74/D1 **Legazpia**, Sp.
119/C4 **Legges Tor** (peak), Austl.
65/L2 **Legionowo**, Pol.
79/E2 **Legnago**, It.
78/B1 **Legnano**, It.
65/J3 **Legnica**, Pol.
65/H3 **Legnica** (prov.), Pol.
77/F5 **Legnone, Monte** (peak), It.
76/C5 **Le Grammont** (peak), Swi.
76/D2 **Le Grand Ballon** (mtn.), Fr.
116/D5 **Le Grande** (cape), Austl.
102/C5 **Leh**, India
72/D2 **Le Havre**, Fr.
166/C2 **Lehigh** (co.), Pa,US
166/C2 **Lehigh** (riv.), Pa,US
163/H5 **Lehigh Acres**, Fl,US
67/G4 **Lehrte**, Ger.
105/G3 **Lei** (riv.), China
108/A2 **Leiah**, Pak.
73/L3 **Leibnitz**, Aus.
107/H2 **Leibo**, China
59/E1 **Leicester**, Eng,UK
168/C1 **Leicester**, Ma,US
59/E1 **Leicestershire** (co.), Eng,UK
117/H2 **Leichhardt** (dam), Austl.
118/B3 **Leichhardt** (mts.), Austl.
114/F3 **Leichhardt** (riv.), Austl.
66/E6 **Leichlingen**, Ger.
66/B4 **Leiden**, Neth.
66/B4 **Leiderdorp**, Neth.
66/B4 **Leidschendam**, Neth.
66/A7 **Leie** (riv.), Belg.
77/H5 **Leifers** (Laives), It.
53/N8 **Leigh**, Eng,UK
53/P8 **Leigh**, Eng,UK
59/F3 **Leighton Buzzard**, Eng,UK
105/F3 **Leigong** (mtn.), China
70/C5 **Lein** (riv.), Ger.
67/G5 **Leine** (riv.), Ger.
67/H6 **Leinefelde**, Ger.
70/C5 **Leinfelden-Echterdingen**, Ger.
60/D4 **Leinster** (mtn.), Ire.
60/C3 **Leinster** (prov.), Ire.
58/D2 **Leintwardine**, Eng,UK
166/C5 **Leipsic** (riv.), De,US
64/G3 **Leipzig**, Ger.
68/C2 **Leir** (riv.), Belg.
62/C1 **Leira**, Nor.
74/A3 **Leiria**, Port.
74/A3 **Leiria** (dist.), Port.
117/F2 **Leisler** (peak), Austl.
59/H2 **Leiston cum Sizewell**, Eng,UK
160/C4 **Leitchfield**, Ky,US
59/F4 **Leith** (hill), Eng,UK
54/C5 **Leith**, Sc,UK
82/C2 **Leitha** (riv.), Aus.
60/C2 **Leitrim** (co.), Ire.
60/C4 **Leix (Laois)** (co.), Ire.
60/D3 **Leixlip**, Ire.
105/G3 **Leiyang**, China
103/B4 **Leiyuanzhen**, China
105/F4 **Leizhou** (pen.), China
66/B5 **Lek** (riv.), Neth.
66/B5 **Lekkerkerk**, Neth.
129/G5 **Lekki** (lag.), Nga.
62/F1 **Leksands-Noret**, Swe.
84/F3 **Leksozero** (lake), Rus.
111/G3 **Lelai** (cape), Indo.
163/F3 **Leland**, Ms,US
62/E2 **Lelång** (lake), Swe.
103/D3 **Leling**, China
76/C3 **Le Locle**, Swi.
120/F4 **Lelu**, Micro.
73/G5 **Le Luc**, Fr.
66/C3 **Lelystad**, Neth.
143/L8 **Le Maire** (str.), Arg.
77/E5 **Lema, Monte** (peak), It., Swi.
76/C5 **Léman** (Geneva) (lake), Fr., Swi.
72/D3 **Le Mans**, Fr.
157/J5 **Le Mars**, Ia,US
69/G5 **Lembach**, Fr.
70/B6 **Lemberg** (peak), Ger.
110/A3 **Lembu** (peak), Indo.
141/C2 **Leme**, Braz.
53/T11 **Le Mée-sur-Seine**, Fr.
61/H1 **Lemenjoen Nat'l Park**, Fin.
53/S10 **Le Mesnil-le-Roi**, Fr.
53/R10 **Le Mesnil-Saint-Denis**, Fr.
67/F4 **Lemgo**, Ger.
63/H2 **Lemland** (isl.), Fin.
66/C3 **Lemmer**, Neth.
157/H4 **Lemmon**, SD,US
76/C5 **Le Môle** (mtn.), Fr.
164/C5 **Lemon Grove**, Ca,US
76/C4 **Le Morond** (mtn.), Fr.
72/E4 **Le Moure de la Gardille** (mtn.), Fr.
148/D3 **Lempa** (riv.), NAm.
63/K1 **Lempäälä**, Fin.
72/E4 **Lempdes**, Fr.
104/B4 **Lemro** (riv.), Burma
80/E2 **Le Murge** (upland), It.
85/P2 **Lemva** (riv.), Rus.
62/C3 **Lemvig**, Den.
67/F2 **Lemwerder**, Ger.
62/D1 **Lena**, Nor.
89/N3 **Lena** (riv.), Rus.
166/D5 **Lenape** (lake), NJ,US
140/B1 **Lençóis Maranhenses Nat'l Park**, Braz.
141/B2 **Lençóis Paulista**, Braz.
79/E2 **Lendinara**, It.
60/C2 **Lene, Lough** (lake), Ire.
67/H4 **Lengede**, Ger.
71/F1 **Lengenfeld**, Ger.
67/E4 **Lengerich**, Ger.
77/H2 **Lenggries**, Ger.
105/F3 **Lengshuijiang**, China
105/F3 **Lengshuitan**, China
135/B3 **Lengua de Vaca** (pt.), Chile
131/D3 **Lengwe Nat'l Park**, Malw.
130/C1 **Lenia**, Eth.
102/B4 **Lenina, Pik** (peak), Kyr.
84/F4 **Leningrad** (Saint Petersburg), Rus.
85/V7 **Leningrad** (Saint Petersburg) (inset), Rus.
113/L **Leningradskaya**, Ant.
102/D1 **Leninogorsk**, Kaz.
85/M5 **Leninogorsk**, Rus.
88/J4 **Leninsk-Kuznetskiy**, Rus.
82/E2 **Leninváros**, Hun.
53/H5 **Lenkoran'**, Azer.
67/E6 **Lenne** (riv.), Ger.
67/F6 **Lennestadt**, Ger.
70/C5 **Lenningen**, Ger.
143/L8 **Lennox** (isl.), Chile
54/B5 **Lennox** (hills), Sc,UK
164/F8 **Lennox**, Ca,US
54/B5 **Lennoxtown**, Sc,UK
78/D2 **Leno**, It.
163/H3 **Lenoir**, NC,US
163/G3 **Lenoir City**, Tn,US
76/C4 **Le Noirmont** (mtn.), Fr.
76/C5 **Le Noirmont** (peak), Swi.
68/B3 **Lens**, Fr.
89/M3 **Lensk**, Rus.
61/F1 **Lenvik**, Nor.
54/B4 **Leny, Pass of** (pass), Sc,UK
76/E3 **Lenzburg**, Swi.
129/E4 **Léo**, Burk.
73/L3 **Leoben**, Aus.
68/B2 **Leoberghe**, Fr.
79/E1 **Leogra** (riv.), It.
157/J4 **Leola**, SD,US
166/B3 **Leola-Leacock-Bareville**, Pa,US
58/D2 **Leominster**, Eng,UK
72/C4 **Leon** (lag.), Fr.
147/E4 **León**, Mex.
148/E3 **León**, Nic.
74/C1 **León**, Sp.
162/D3 **Leon** (riv.), Tx,US
165/F6 **Leonard**, Mi,US
70/C5 **Leonberg**, Ger.
71/H6 **Leonding**, Aus.
77/E5 **Leone, Monte** (peak), It.
142/E2 **Leones**, Arg.
80/D4 **Leonforte**, It.
167/K8 **Leonia**, NJ,US
147/F2 **Leon Valley**, Tx,US
113/F **Leopold and Astrid** (coast), Ant.
141/L6 **Leopoldina**, Braz.
68/C1 **Leopoldkanaal** (can.), Belg.
69/E1 **Leopoldsburg**, Belg.
67/F4 **Leopoldshöhe**, Ger.
159/G3 **Leoti**, Ks,US
156/G2 **Leoville**, Sk,Can
72/D4 **Le Passage**, Fr.
74/B4 **Lepe**, Sp.
53/S10 **Le Pecq**, Fr.
82/F3 **Lepenski Vir**, Yugo.
76/D2 **Le Petit Ballon** (mtn.), Fr.
131/B4 **Lephepe**, Bots.
105/H2 **Leping**, China
53/U9 **Le Plessis-Belleville**, Fr.
53/T10 **Le Plessis-Trévise**, Fr.
77/E5 **Lepontine Alps** (mts.), It., Swi.
133/R15 **Le Port**, Reun.
68/A2 **Le Portel**, Fr.
61/H3 **Leppävirta**, Fin.
102/C2 **Lepsy** (riv.), Kaz.
75/F1 **Le Puech** (mtn.), Fr.
72/E4 **Le Puy**, Fr.
128/D4 **Léraba** (riv.), Burk., IvC.
53/T10 **Le Raincy**, Fr.
78/A2 **Lera, Monte** (peak), It.
80/D4 **Lercara Friddi**, It.
147/P8 **Lerdo de Tejada**, Mex.
78/C4 **Lerici**, It.
75/F2 **Lérida** (Lleida), Sp.
147/K7 **Lerma** (riv.), Mex.
132/D3 **Le Rouxdam, P. K.** (res.), SAfr.
62/E3 **Lerum**, Swe.
55/P12 **Lerwick**, Sc,UK
68/A5 **Les Andelys**, Fr.
149/H2 **Les Cayes**, Haiti
161/M7 **Les Cèdres**, Qu,Can
53/R10 **Les Clayes-sous-Bois**, Fr.
76/D5 **Les Diablerets** (range), Swi.
76/D5 **Le Sépey**, Swi.
104/D2 **Leshan**, China
72/C3 **Les Herbiers**, Fr.
53/T10 **Lésigny**, Fr.
78/C3 **Lesima, Monte** (peak), It.
82/E4 **Leskovac**, Yugo.
54/C4 **Leslie**, Sc,UK
53/T10 **Les Lilas**, Fr.
54/C5 **Lesmahagow**, Sc,UK
53/S10 **Les Molières**, Fr.
68/A6 **Les Mureaux**, Fr.
72/A2 **Lesneven**, Fr.
133/D3 **Lesotho**
97/L2 **Lesozavodsk**, Rus.
75/G1 **L'Espinouse, Sommet de** (peak), Fr.
72/C3 **Les Sables-d'Olonne**, Fr.
69/E4 **Lesse** (riv.), Belg.
62/F3 **Lessebo**, Swe.
150/E3 **Lesser Antilles** (isls.), NAm.
87/G4 **Lesser Kavkaz** (mts.), Eur.
156/D2 **Lesser Slave** (lake), Ab,Can
111/E5 **Lesser Sunda** (isls.), Indo.
68/C2 **Lessines**, Belg.
69/E5 **L'Est, Canal de** (can.), Fr.
76/C4 **Le Suchet** (peak), Swi.
68/B6 **Les Ulis**, Fr.
110/D3 **Lesung** (peak), Indo.
81/J3 **Lésvos** (isl.), Gre.
56/C2 **Leswalt**, Sc,UK
65/J3 **Leszno**, Pol.
65/J3 **Leszno** (prov.), Pol.
131/C4 **Letaba**, SAfr.
133/R15 **Le Tampon**, Reun.
53/S10 **L'Étang-la-Ville**, Fr.
59/F3 **Letchworth**, Eng,UK
54/D3 **Letham**, Sc,UK
156/E3 **Lethbridge**, Ab,Can
67/F2 **Lethe** (riv.), Ger.
111/G5 **Leti** (isls.), Indo.
144/D2 **Leticia**, Col.
103/D3 **Leting**, China
131/B4 **Letlhakane**, Bots.
131/B5 **Letlhakeng**, Bots.
104/B5 **Letpadan**, Burma
68/A3 **Le Tréport**, Fr.
109/B4 **Letsôk-Aw** (isl.), Burma
55/H9 **Letterkenny**, Ire.
54/D4 **Leuchars**, Sc,UK
55/H7 **Leurbost**, Sc,UK
66/C4 **Leusden-Zuid**, Neth.
110/A3 **Leuser** (peak), Indo.
70/D4 **Leutershausen**, Ger.
77/G2 **Leutkirch im Allgäu**, Ger.
69/D2 **Leuven** (Louvain), Belg.
68/C2 **Leuze-en-Hainaut**, Belg.
81/H3 **Levádhia**, Gre.
53/S10 **Levallois-Perret**, Fr.
61/D3 **Levanger**, Nor.
78/C4 **Levante** (coast), It.
142/B5 **Level** (isl.), Chile
162/C3 **Levelland**, Tx,US
133/F2 **Leven** (pt.), SAfr.
57/H4 **Leven**, Eng,UK
57/F3 **Leven** (riv.), Eng,UK
57/G3 **Leven** (riv.), Eng,UK
54/D4 **Leven**, Sc,UK
54/C4 **Leven** (riv.), Sc,UK
54/A3 **Leven, Loch** (inlet), Sc,UK
54/C4 **Leven, Loch** (lake), Sc,UK
77/E5 **Leventina** (Prato), It.
114/C3 **Leveque** (cape), Austl.
66/D6 **Leverkusen**, Ger.
53/S10 **Le Vésinet**, Fr.
65/K4 **Levice**, Slvk.
115/S11 **Levin**, NZ
161/G2 **Lévis**, Qu,Can
53/R10 **Lévis-Saint-Nom**, Fr.
167/E2 **Levittown**, NY,US
166/D3 **Levittown**, Pa,US
81/G3 **Levkás**, Gre.
81/G3 **Levkás** (isl.), Gre.
65/L4 **Levoča**, Slvk.
83/G4 **Levski**, Bul.
59/G5 **Lewes**, Eng,UK
161/K1 **Lewis** (hills), Nf,Can
115/R11 **Lewis** (pass), NZ
55/H7 **Lewis** (isl.), Sc,UK
156/E3 **Lewis** (range), Mt,US
156/C4 **Lewis** (riv.), Wa,US
157/J5 **Lewis & Clark** (lake), Ne, SD,US
163/G3 **Lewisburg**, Tn,US
160/D4 **Lewisburg**, WV,US
55/H7 **Lewis, Butt of** (promontory), Sc,UK
59/F4 **Lewisham** (bor.), Eng,UK
161/L1 **Lewisporte**, Nf,Can
163/G3 **Lewis Smith** (lake), Al,US
156/D4 **Lewiston**, Id,US
161/G2 **Lewiston**, Me,US
161/R9 **Lewiston**, NY,US
156/F4 **Lewistown**, Mt,US
160/E3 **Lewistown**, Pa,US
111/F5 **Lewotobi** (peak), Indo.
160/C4 **Lexington**, Ky,US
168/C1 **Lexington**, Ma,US
163/H3 **Lexington**, NC,US
159/H2 **Lexington**, Ne,US
163/H3 **Lexington**, SC,US
163/F3 **Lexington**, Tn,US
163/H2 **Lexington**, Va,US
160/E4 **Lexington Park**, Md,US
57/G3 **Leyburn**, Eng,UK
104/E3 **Leye**, China
57/F4 **Leyland**, Eng,UK
112/D3 **Leyte**, Phil.
112/D3 **Leyte** (gulf), Phil.
112/D3 **Leyte** (isl.), Phil.
53/N7 **Leyton**, Eng,UK
72/F4 **Lez** (riv.), Fr.
65/M3 **Leżajsk**, Pol.
81/F2 **Lezhë**, Alb.
104/E2 **Lezhi**, China
72/E5 **Lézignan-Corbières**, Fr.
86/E2 **L'gov**, Rus.
54/C1 **Lhanbyrd**, Sc,UK
104/B2 **Lhari**, China
106/F2 **Lhasa**, China
106/E2 **Lhazê**, China
104/C2 **Lhorong**, China
75/G2 **L'Hospitalet**, Sp.
106/F2 **Lhozhag**, China
107/G2 **Lhünzê**, China
103/B5 **Li** (riv.), China
103/C4 **Li** (riv.), China
105/F3 **Li** (riv.), China
104/E3 **Lian** (riv.), China
105/G3 **Lian** (riv.), China
105/H3 **Liancheng**, China
68/B5 **Liancourt**, Fr.
98/B2 **Liancourt** (rocks), Japan, SKor.
103/C2 **Liangcheng**, China
110/D3 **Liangpran** (peak), Indo.
103/D4 **Liang Shan** (mtn.), China
104/D3 **Liangwan** (mts.), Laos
103/B3 **Liangzhen**, China
103/C5 **Liangzi** (lake), China
107/K2 **Lianhua**, China
105/G4 **Lianhua** (mts.), China
105/H3 **Lianjiang**, China
105/G3 **Liannan Yaozu Zizhixian**, China
103/D4 **Lianshui**, China
105/G3 **Lian Xian**, China
105/G2 **Lianyun** (peak), China
103/D4 **Lianyungang**, China
101/A2 **Liao** (riv.), China
103/C3 **Liaocheng**, China
101/A2 **Liaodong** (gulf), China
101/B3 **Liaodong** (pen.), China
101/B2 **Liaoning** (prov.), China
101/B2 **Liaoyang**, China
103/F2 **Liaoyuan**, China
101/B2 **Liaozhong**, China
95/K3 **Liāquatpur**, Pak.
152/D2 **Liard** (riv.), Can.
112/C3 **Libacao**, Phil.
156/E3 **Libby**, Mt,US
125/J7 **Libenge**, Zaire
159/G3 **Liberal**, Ks,US
68/C3 **Libercourt**, Fr.
141/J7 **Liberdade**, Braz.
137/H6 **Liberdade** (riv.), Braz.
65/H3 **Liberec**, Czh.
128/C5 **Liberia**
149/E4 **Liberia**, CR
143/F2 **Libertad**, Uru.
135/D1 **Libertador General San Martín**, Arg.
163/G2 **Liberty**, Ky,US
166/B5 **Liberty** (res.), Md,US
162/E2 **Liberty**, Mo,US
163/F4 **Liberty**, Ms,US
162/E4 **Liberty**, Tx,US
165/Q15 **Libertyville**, Il,US
112/C2 **Libmanan**, Phil.
105/E3 **Libo**, China
111/G4 **Libobo** (cape), Indo.
71/G2 **Liboc** (riv.), Czh.
112/C2 **Libon**, Phil.
147/M7 **Libres**, Mex.
124/G7 **Libreville** (cap.), Gabon
125/J2 **Libya**
125/K2 **Libyan** (des.), Afr.
125/K1 **Libyan** (plat.), Libya
142/C2 **Licantén**, Chile
80/C4 **Licata**, It.
92/E2 **Lice**, Turk.
70/B1 **Lich**, Ger.
103/C3 **Licheng**, China
59/E1 **Lichfield**, Eng,UK
131/D2 **Lichinga**, Moz.
131/D2 **Lichinga** (plat.), Moz.
67/F5 **Lichtenau**, Ger.
70/E2 **Lichtenfels**, Ger.
66/D5 **Lichtenvoorde**, Neth.
68/C1 **Lichtervelde**, Belg.
105/F2 **Lichuan**, China
105/H3 **Lichuan**, China
140/B4 **Licinio de Almeida**, Braz.
160/C4 **Licking** (riv.), Ky,US
165/L12 **Lick Observatory**, Ca,US
80/D2 **Licosa** (cape), It.
63/L5 **Lida**, Bela.
57/F1 **Liddell Water** (riv.), Sc,UK
153/R7 **Liddon** (gulf), NW,Can
62/H2 **Lidingö**, Swe.
62/E2 **Lidköping**, Swe.
59/F2 **Lidlington**, Eng,UK
79/F2 **Lido**, It.
79/F1 **Lido di Iesolo**, It.
80/C2 **Lido di Ostia**, It.
65/K2 **Lidzbark**, Pol.
65/L1 **Lidzbark Warmiński**, Pol.
132/E2 **Liebenbergsvlei** (riv.), SAfr.
117/F2 **Liebig** (peak), Austl.
146/B3 **Liebre** (bay), Mex.
77/F3 **Liechtenstein**
68/D2 **Liedekerke**, Belg.
69/E2 **Liège**, Belg.
69/E3 **Liège** (prov.), Belg.
61/J3 **Lieksa**, Fin.
66/C5 **Lienden**, Neth.
67/E4 **Lienen**, Ger.
73/K3 **Lienz**, Aus.
63/J3 **Liepāja**, Lat.
68/D1 **Lier**, Belg.
72/E1 **Lies** (riv.), Belg.
69/F3 **Lieser** (riv.), Ger.
63/K1 **Liesjärven Nat'l Park**, Fin.
76/D3 **Liestal**, Swi.
63/K1 **Lieto**, Fin.
68/B3 **Liévin**, Fr.
160/F2 **Lièvre** (riv.), Qu,Can
76/B2 **Liez** (lake), Fr.
73/L3 **Liezen**, Aus.
60/D3 **Liffey** (riv.), Ire.
121/V12 **Lifou** (isl.), NCal.
58/B5 **Lifton**, Eng,UK
130/B5 **Liganga**, Tanz.
111/F1 **Ligao**, Phil.
77/F5 **Ligoncio, Pizzo** (peak), It.
78/B3 **Ligure, Appenino** (mts.), It.
78/C4 **Liguria** (reg.), It.
73/H5 **Ligurian** (sea), Eur.
115/J3 **Lihou** (reef), Austl.
107/H2 **Lijiang** (Lijiang Naxizu Zizhixian), China
103/D3 **Lijin**, China
105/H2 **Liju** (mtn.), China
131/B1 **Likasi**, Zaire
156/C2 **Likely**, BC,Can
131/D2 **Likoma** (isl.), Malw.
124/J8 **Likouala** (riv.), Congo
80/A1 **L'Ile-Rousse**, Fr.
53/T10 **L'Ile-Saint-Denis**, Fr.
67/F2 **Lilienthal**, Ger.
107/K2 **Liling**, China
69/D1 **Lille**, Belg.
68/C2 **Lille**, Fr.
62/C4 **Lille Bælt** (chan.), Den.
62/D1 **Lillehammer**, Nor.
63/T9 **Lillerød**, Den.
68/B2 **Lillers**, Fr.
62/C2 **Lillesand**, Nor.
62/D2 **Lillestrøm**, Nor.
113/L **Lillie Marleen Hütte**, Ant.
54/D5 **Lilliesleaf**, Sc,UK
156/C3 **Lillooet**, BC,Can
156/C3 **Lillooet** (riv.), BC,Can
131/D2 **Lilongwe** (cap.), Malw.
112/C3 **Liloy**, Phil.
119/G5 **Lilydale**, Austl.
82/D4 **Lim** (riv.), Yugo.
144/B4 **Lima** (cap.), Peru
144/B3 **Lima** (dept.), Peru
74/A2 **Lima** (riv.), Port.
157/L4 **Lima** (peak), Mn,US
160/C3 **Lima**, Oh,US
142/Q9 **Limache**, Chile
77/E5 **Limadario, Monte** (Gridone) (peak), It.
141/K6 **Lima Duarte**, Braz.
65/L4 **Limanowa**, Pol.
91/C2 **Limassol**, Cyp.
91/C2 **Limassol** (dist.), Cyp.
56/B1 **Limavady**, NI,UK
56/A2 **Limavady** (dist.), NI,UK
142/C4 **Limay** (riv.), Arg.
68/A6 **Limay**, Fr.
112/A4 **Limbang** (riv.), Malay.
80/A2 **Limbara** (peak), It.
106/B3 **Limbdi**, India
149/H2 **Limbé**, Haiti
131/D2 **Limbe**, Malw.
78/C1 **Limbiate**, It.
69/E2 **Limburg** (prov.), Belg.
69/E1 **Limburg** (prov.), Neth.
70/B2 **Limburg an der Lahn**, Ger.
70/B4 **Limburgerhof**, Ger.
161/G8 **Limehouse**, On,Can
53/T10 **Limeil-Brévannes**, Fr.
141/C2 **Limeira**, Braz.
54/C4 **Limekilns**, Sc,UK
60/B4 **Limerick**, Ire.
60/B5 **Limerick** (co.), Ire.
62/C3 **Limfjorden** (chan.), Den.
74/B2 **Limia** (riv.), Sp.
114/F2 **Limmen** (bight), Austl.
81/J3 **Límnos** (isl.), Gre.
140/D2 **Limoeiro**, Braz.
140/C2 **Limoeiro do Norte**, Braz.
72/D4 **Limoges**, Fr.
72/D4 **Limogne** (plat.), Fr.
149/F4 **Limón**, CR
159/G3 **Limon**, Co,US
53/S11 **Limours**, Fr.
72/D4 **Limousin** (mts.), Fr.
72/D4 **Limousin** (reg.), Fr.
72/E5 **Limoux**, Fr.
126/F5 **Limpopo** (riv.), Afr.
53/P8 **Limpsfield**, Eng,UK
105/F5 **Limu** (mtn.), China
131/A2 **Limulunga**, Zam.
130/C3 **Limuru**, Kenya
112/C4 **Linao** (pt.), Phil.
112/B3 **Linapacan** (isl.), Phil.
77/G4 **Linard, Piz** (peak), Swi.
142/C2 **Linares**, Chile
147/F3 **Linares**, Mex.
74/D3 **Linares**, Sp.
104/D4 **Lincang**, China
103/C3 **Lincheng**, China
105/H3 **Linchuan**, China
142/E2 **Lincoln**, Arg.
161/R9 **Lincoln**, On,Can
145/L1 **Lincoln** (sea), Can., Grld.
57/H5 **Lincoln**, Eng,UK
160/B3 **Lincoln**, Il,US
168/C1 **Lincoln**, Ma,US
161/G2 **Lincoln**, Me,US
159/H2 **Lincoln** (cap.), Ne,US
156/B4 **Lincoln Beach**, Or,US
156/B4 **Lincoln City**, Or,US
57/H5 **Lincoln Heath** (woodl.), Eng,UK
117/G5 **Lincoln Nat'l Park**, Austl.
167/F7 **Lincoln Park**, Mi,US
167/D2 **Lincoln Park**, NJ,US
57/H5 **Lincolnshire** (co.), Eng,UK
57/H5 **Lincolnshire Wolds** (hills), Eng,UK
163/H3 **Lincolnton**, NC,US
167/D3 **Lincroft**, NJ,US
80/A2 **L'Incudine, Mont** (mtn.), Fr.
77/F2 **Lindau**, Ger.
66/D3 **Linde** (riv.), Neth.
118/C3 **Lindeman** (isl.), Austl.
70/B1 **Linden**, Ger.
139/G3 **Linden**, Guy.
163/G3 **Linden**, Al,US
167/D2 **Linden**, NJ,US
77/F2 **Lindenberg im Allgäu**, Ger.
165/P15 **Lindenhurst**, Il,US
167/E2 **Lindenhurst**, NY,US
166/D4 **Lindenwold**, NJ,US
62/F2 **Lindesberg**, Swe.
62/B3 **Lindesnes** (cape), Nor.
130/C5 **Lindi**, Tanz.
130/C5 **Lindi** (prov.), Tanz.
97/J2 **Lindian**, China
54/E5 **Lindisfarne** (Holy) (isl.), Eng,UK
67/E6 **Lindlar**, Ger.
119/D3 **Lind Nat'l Park**, Austl.
62/E3 **Lindome**, Swe.
116/F3 **Lindsay** (mtn.), Austl.
117/C5 **Lindsay** (mtn.), Austl.
160/E2 **Lindsay**, On,Can
158/C3 **Lindsay**, Ca,US
162/D2 **Lindsborg**, Ks,US
121/K4 **Line** (isls.), Kiri.
166/B2 **Line Mountain** (ridge), Pa,US
103/B3 **Linfen**, China
54/A2 **Ling** (riv.), Sc,UK
166/A5 **Linganore** (cr.), Md,US
105/F5 **Lingao**, China
112/C1 **Lingayen**, Phil.
112/C1 **Lingayen** (gulf), Phil.
103/B4 **Lingbao**, China
103/D4 **Lingbi**, China
103/C4 **Lingchuan**, China
66/C5 **Linge** (riv.), Neth.
67/E3 **Lingen**, Ger.
53/N8 **Lingfield**, Eng,UK
110/B3 **Lingga** (isls.), Indo.
69/G6 **Lingolsheim**, Fr.
103/C3 **Lingqiu**, China
103/C3 **Lingshan**, China
105/F4 **Lingshan**, China
103/B3 **Lingshi**, China
105/F5 **Lingshui**, China
128/B3 **Linguère**, Sen.
103/D3 **Ling Xian**, China
103/E5 **Lingyang Shan** (mtn.), China
103/L8 **Lingyen Shan** (mtn.), China
103/C3 **Lingyin Si**, China
103/D2 **Lingyuan**, China
107/J3 **Lingyun**, China
105/J2 **Linhai**, China
141/D1 **Linhares**, Braz.
103/A2 **Linhe**, China
62/F2 **Linköping**, Swe.
54/C5 **Linlithgow**, Sc,UK
103/C3 **Linliu Shan** (mtn.), China
77/E3 **Linmat** (riv.), Swi.
61/J3 **Linnansaaren Nat'l Park**, Fin.
58/A3 **Linney Head** (pt.), Wal,UK
54/A3 **Linnhe, Loch** (inlet), Sc,UK
69/F2 **Linnich**, Ger.
80/C5 **Linosa** (isl.), It.
103/C3 **Linqing**, China
103/D3 **Linqu**, China
103/C4 **Linquan**, China
103/C4 **Linru**, China
141/B2 **Lins**, Braz.
103/D4 **Linshu**, China
149/G2 **Linstead**, Jam.
133/H9 **Linta** (riv.), Madg.
77/E4 **Linth** (riv.), Swi.
59/G2 **Linton**, Eng,UK
160/C4 **Linton**, In,US
157/H4 **Linton**, ND,US
57/H5 **Linwood**, Eng,UK
107/K2 **Linwu**, China
103/C3 **Linxi**, China
103/C3 **Lin Xian**, China
131/A3 **Linyanti** (swamp), Bots., Namb.
103/B4 **Linyi**, China
103/D3 **Linyi**, China
103/D4 **Linyi**, China
103/C4 **Linying**, China
71/H6 **Linz**, Aus.
96/E4 **Linze**, China
103/C3 **Linzhang**, China
72/E5 **Lions** (gulf), Fr.
131/C3 **Lions Den**, Zim.
80/D3 **Lipari** (isl.), It.
80/D3 **Lipari** (isls.), It.
61/J3 **Liperi**, Fin.
86/F1 **Lipetsk**, Rus.
86/F1 **Lipetsk Obl.**, Rus.
136/E8 **Lípez** (range), Bol.
136/E8 **Lípez** (riv.), Bol.
59/F4 **Liphook**, Eng,UK
105/F3 **Liping**, China
82/E4 **Lipljan**, Yugo.
65/K2 **Lipno**, Pol.
71/H5 **Lipno, Údolní nádrž** (res.), Czh.
131/D1 **Lipoche**, Moz.
82/E2 **Lipova**, Rom.
66/E5 **Lippe** (riv.), Ger.
67/F5 **Lippetal**, Ger.
67/F5 **Lippstadt**, Ger.
65/K4 **Liptovský Mikuláš**, Slvk.
119/C3 **Liptrap** (cape), Austl.
105/F3 **Lipu**, China
102/D5 **Lipu La** (pass), India
102/D5 **Lipu Lekh Shankou** (pass), China
130/B2 **Lira**, Ugan.
126/C1 **Liranga**, Congo
131/D2 **Lirangwe**, Malw.
80/C2 **Liri** (riv.), It.
75/E3 **Liria**, Sp.
77/F5 **Liro** (riv.), It.
125/K7 **Lisala**, Zaire
74/A3 **Lisboa** (dist.), Port.
74/A3 **Lisboa** (Lisbon) (cap.), Port.
161/G2 **Lisbon**, Me,US
157/J4 **Lisbon**, ND,US
74/A3 **Lisbon** (Lisboa) (cap.), Port.
75/P10 **Lisbon** (Lisboa) (inset) (cap.), Port.
56/B2 **Lisburn**, NI,UK
56/B3 **Lisburn** (dist.), NI,UK
151/E2 **Lisburne** (cape), Ak,US
103/B4 **Li Shan** (mtn.), China
104/D3 **Lishe** (riv.), China
103/F2 **Lishu**, China
105/H2 **Lishui**, China
121/H2 **Lisianski** (isl.), Hi,US
86/F2 **Lisichansk**, Ukr.
72/D2 **Lisieux**, Fr.
58/B6 **Liskeard**, Eng,UK
165/P16 **Lisle**, Il,US
68/B5 **L'Isle-Adam**, Fr.
72/F5 **L'Isle-sur-la-Sorgue**, Fr.
119/E1 **Lismore**, Austl.
56/B3 **Lisnacree**, NI,UK
56/B3 **Lisnaskea**, NI,UK
59/F4 **Liss**, Eng,UK
66/B4 **Lisse**, Neth.
53/T11 **Lisses**, Fr.
67/E6 **Lister** (riv.), Ger.
160/D3 **Listowel**, On,Can
104/D2 **Litang**, China
104/D2 **Litang** (riv.), China
91/D3 **Līṭānī** (riv.), Leb.
71/G3 **Litavka** (riv.), Czh.
168/A2 **Litchfield**, Ct,US
168/A2 **Litchfield** (co.), Ct,US
160/B4 **Litchfield**, Il,US
157/K4 **Litchfield**, Mn,US
131/C2 **Liteta**, Zam.
66/C5 **Lith**, Neth.
57/F5 **Litherland**, Eng,UK
119/D2 **Lithgow**, Austl.
63/K4 **Lithuania**
166/B3 **Lititz**, Pa,US
71/H1 **Litoměřice**, Czh.
130/C5 **Litoo**, Tanz.
63/M4 **Litovskiy Nat'l Park**, Lith.
118/D4 **Littabella Nat'l Park**, Austl.
77/E3 **Littau**, Swi.
163/H4 **Little** (riv.), Ga,US
159/J4 **Little** (riv.), La,US
163/J3 **Little** (riv.), NC,US
159/J4 **Little** (riv.), Ok,US
162/D4 **Little** (riv.), Tx,US
160/D1 **Little Abitibi** (riv.), On,Can
65/J5 **Little Alföld** (plain), Hun.
107/F5 **Little Andaman** (isl.), India
168/G6 **Little Beaver, Middle Fork** (cr.), Oh,US
168/G6 **Little Beaver, North Fork** (cr.), Oh,US
168/G6 **Little Beaver, West Fork** (cr.), Oh,US
156/F4 **Little Belt** (mts.), Mt,US
53/N6 **Little Berkhamstead**, Eng,UK
156/G4 **Little Bighorn Nat'l Mon.**, Mt,US
91/C4 **Little Bitter** (lake), Egypt
159/H2 **Little Blue** (riv.), Ks, Ne,US
57/F4 **Littleborough**, Eng,UK
165/Q16 **Little Calumet** (riv.), Il,US
149/F2 **Little Cayman** (isl.), Cay.
53/M7 **Little Chalfont**, Eng,UK
158/E4 **Little Colorado** (riv.), Az,US
54/B5 **Little Cumbrae** (isl.), Sc,UK
160/D2 **Little Current**, On,Can
160/C1 **Little Current** (riv.), On,Can
58/C5 **Little Dart** (riv.), Eng,UK
119/B3 **Little Desert Nat'l Park**, Austl.
151/E2 **Little Diomede** (isl.), Ak,US
167/D4 **Little Egg** (har.), NJ,US
157/K4 **Little Falls**, Mn,US
167/J8 **Little Falls**, NJ,US
162/C3 **Littlefield**, Tx,US
166/B1 **Little Fishing** (cr.), Pa,US
157/K4 **Little Fork** (riv.), Mn,US
59/F5 **Littlehampton**, Eng,UK
150/C2 **Little Inagua** (isl.), Bahm.
132/C4 **Little Karoo** (reg.), SAfr.
166/C2 **Little Lehigh** (riv.), Pa,US
55/H8 **Little Minch** (sound), Sc,UK
161/K2 **Little Miquelon** (isl.), StP.
159/J4 **Little Missouri** (riv.), Ar,US
157/H4 **Little Missouri** (riv.), ND, SD,US
166/B1 **Little Muncy** (cr.), Pa,US
167/K8 **Little Neck** (bay), NY,US
107/F6 **Little Nicobar** (isl.), India
59/G2 **Little Ouse** (riv.), Eng,UK
117/M8 **Little Para** (res.), Austl.
117/M8 **Little Para** (riv.), Austl.
166/B5 **Little Patuxent** (riv.), Md,US
167/F2 **Little Peconic** (bay), NY,US
59/G2 **Littleport**, Eng,UK
159/J4 **Little Red** (riv.), Ar,US
162/E3 **Little Rock** (cap.), Ar,US
165/N16 **Little Rock** (cr.), Il,US
148/D2 **Little Rocky** (pt.), Belz.
151/L3 **Little Salmon**, Yk,Can
128/B4 **Little Scarcies** (riv.), Gui., SLeo.
166/C2 **Little Schuylkill** (riv.), Pa,US
168/G5 **Little Shenango** (riv.), Pa,US
157/K5 **Little Sioux** (riv.), Ia,US
151/B5 **Little Sitkin** (isl.), Ak,US
156/D2 **Little Smoky** (riv.), Ab,Can
158/E2 **Little Snake** (riv.), Co, Wy,US
59/G4 **Little Stour** (riv.), Eng,UK
59/F2 **Little Stukeley**, Eng,UK
166/B3 **Little Swatara** (cr.), Pa,US
161/G2 **Littleton**, NH,US
160/B4 **Little Wabash** (riv.), Il,US
159/G2 **Little White** (riv.), SD,US
156/E5 **Little Wood** (riv.), Id,US
93/E3 **Little Zab** (riv.), Iraq
71/G1 **Litvínov**, Czh.
101/C1 **Liu** (riv.), China
96/F5 **Liuba**, China
107/J3 **Liucheng**, China
101/C1 **Liuhe**, China
105/J2 **Liuheng** (isl.), China
130/B5 **Liuli**, Tanz.
103/B3 **Liulin**, China
126/D3 **Liuwa Pan Nat'l Park**, Zam.
105/G4 **Liuxi** (riv.), China
107/K2 **Liuyang**, China
105/G2 **Liuyang** (riv.), China
105/F3 **Liuzhou**, China
79/G2 **Livade**, Cro.
79/F1 **Livenza** (riv.), It.
163/H4 **Live Oak**, Fl,US
69/F6 **Liverdun**, Fr.
165/L11 **Livermore**, Ca,US
162/B4 **Livermore** (peak), Tx,US
118/G8 **Liverpool**, Austl.
161/H2 **Liverpool**, NS,Can
151/M2 **Liverpool** (bay), NW,Can
153/J1 **Liverpool** (cape), NW,Can
57/F5 **Liverpool**, Eng,UK
57/E5 **Liverpool** (bay), Eng,UK
57/H2 **Liverton**, Eng,UK
148/D3 **Livingston**, Guat.
54/C5 **Livingston**, Sc,UK
165/E6 **Livingston** (co.), Mi,US
156/F4 **Livingston**, Mt,US
167/D2 **Livingston**, NJ,US
162/E4 **Livingston**, Tx,US
159/J5 **Livingston** (lake), Tx,US
156/E3 **Livingstone** (range), Ab,Can
131/B3 **Livingstone**, Zam.
126/B1 **Livingstone, Chutes de** (Livingstone) (falls), Congo
131/C2 **Livingstone Mem.**, Zam.
131/D1 **Livingstonia**, Malw.
82/C4 **Livno**, Bosn.
86/F1 **Livny**, Rus.
61/H2 **Livojoki** (riv.), Fin.
165/F7 **Livonia**, Mi,US
78/D5 **Livorno**, It.
78/D6 **Livorno** (prov.), It.
140/B4 **Livramento do Brumado**, Braz.
72/F4 **Livron-sur-Drôme**, Fr.
68/B6 **Livry-Gargan**, Fr.
130/C5 **Liwale**, Tanz.
131/D2 **Liwonde**, Malw.
131/D2 **Liwonde Nat'l Park**, Malw.
105/F2 **Li Xian**, China
103/D4 **Lixin**, China
103/D5 **Liyang**, China
58/A7 **Lizard**, Eng,UK
58/A7 **Lizard** (pt.), Eng,UK

140/A5 **Luziânia**, Braz.
140/B1 **Luzilândia**, Braz.
130/B2 **Luzinga**, Ugan.
71/H4 **Lužnice** (riv.), Czh.
120/B2 **Luzon** (str.)
112/C1 **Luzon** (isl.), Phil.
86/C2 **L'viv**, Ukr.
86/B2 **L'viv Obl.**, Ukr.
130/B2 **Lwala** (peak), Ugan.
130/A5 **Lwena Mission**, Zam.
109/C1 **Lwi** (riv.), Burma
130/A3 **Lyantonde**, Ugan.
85/P3 **Lyapin** (riv.), Rus.
83/G4 **Lyaskovets**, Bul.
61/F2 **Lycksele**, Swe.
166/A1 **Lycoming** (co.), Pa,US
59/G5 **Lydd**, Eng,UK
113/Y **Lyddan** (isl.), Ant.
133/E2 **Lydenburg**, SAfr.
58/D3 **Lydney**, Eng,UK
117/F2 **Lyell Brown** (peak),
Austl.
156/F5 **Lyman**, Wy,US
58/C5 **Lyme** (bay), Eng,UK
58/D5 **Lyme Regis**, Eng,UK
59/E5 **Lymington**, Eng,UK
57/F5 **Lymm**, Eng,UK
65/L1 **Lyna** (riv.), Pol.
55/N13 **Lynas** (pt.), Wal,UK
167/E2 **Lynbrook**, NY,US
160/E4 **Lynchburg**, Va,US
163/H3 **Lynches** (riv.), SC,US
118/A2 **Lynd** (riv.), Austl.
59/E5 **Lyndhurst**, Eng,UK
167/D2 **Lyndhurst**, NJ,US
168/F4 **Lyndhurst**, Oh,US
168/H6 **Lyndora**, Pa,US
57/F1 **Lyne** (riv.), Eng,UK
55/N13 **Lyness**, Sc,UK
63/T9 **Lyngby-Tårbæk**, Den.
62/B2 **Lyngdal**, Nor.
63/T9 **Lynge**, Den.
61/G1 **Lyngen** (fjord), Nor.
161/G3 **Lynn**, Ma,US
163/G4 **Lynn Haven**, Fl,US
165/C2 **Lynnwood**, Wa,US
58/C4 **Lynton**, Eng,UK
164/B3 **Lynwood**, Ca,US
152/F2 **Lynx** (lake), NW,Can
72/F4 **Lyon**, Fr.
54/B3 **Lyon** (riv.), Sc,UK
54/B3 **Lyon, Loch** (lake),
Sc,UK
116/C2 **Lyons** (riv.), Austl.
159/H3 **Lyons**, Ks,US
58/C4 **Lype** (hill), Eng,UK
120/E5 **Lyra** (reef), PNG
68/B2 **Lys** (riv.), Fr.
78/A1 **Lys** (riv.), It.
65/K4 **Lysá** (peak), Czh.
62/D2 **Lysaker**, Nor.
71/H2 **Lysá nad Labem**, Czh.
84/E5 **Lysaya, Gora** (hill),
Bela.
62/D2 **Lysekil**, Swe.
65/L3 **Łysica** (peak), Pol.
71/F2 **Lysina** (peak), Czh.
68/C2 **Lys-lez-Lannoy**, Fr.
76/D3 **Lyss**, Swi.
62/D3 **Lystrup**, Den.
85/N4 **Lys'va**, Rus.
58/D5 **Lytchett Matravers**,
Eng,UK
57/E4 **Lytham Saint Anne's**,
Eng,UK
85/X9 **Lytkarino**, Rus.
164/C2 **Lytle** (cr.), Ca,US
156/C3 **Lytton**, BC,Can
86/F1 **Lyubertsy**, Rus.
83/H5 **Lyubimets**, Bul.
86/E2 **Lyubotin**, Ukr.
86/E1 **Lyudinovo**, Rus.
58/C3 **Lywyd** (riv.), Wal,UK

M

109/C1 **Ma** (riv.), Laos, Viet.
91/D3 **Ma'alot**, Isr.
91/D4 **Ma'ān**, Jor.
91/E5 **Ma'ān** (gov.), Jor.
84/F2 **Maanselkä** (mts.),
Fin.
103/D5 **Ma'anshan**, China
66/C6 **Maarheeze**, Neth.
91/E2 **Ma'arrat an Nu'mān**,
Syria
66/C4 **Maarssen**, Neth.
64/C3 **Maas** (riv.), Eur.
66/C6 **Maasbracht**, Neth.
66/D6 **Maasbree**, Neth.
69/E1 **Maaseik**, Belg.
112/D3 **Maasin**, Phil.
69/E2 **Maasmechelen**, Belg.
66/B5 **Maassluis**, Neth.
131/C4 **Maasstroom**, SAfr.
69/E2 **Maastricht**, Neth.
131/D4 **Maave**, Moz.
91/G6 **Ma'ayan Harod Nat'l**
Park, Isr.
131/A3 **Mababe** (depr.), Bots.
112/D3 **Mabaho** (mtn.), Phil.
112/C2 **Mabalacat**, Phil.
131/D4 **Mabalane**, Moz.
100/B3 **Mabechi** (riv.), Japan
107/H2 **Mabian**, China
112/C3 **Mabinay**, Phil.
112/D3 **Mabini**, Phil.
57/J5 **Mablethorpe**, Eng,UK
131/B5 **Mabote**, Moz.
132/C2 **Mabuasehube Game**
Rsv., Bots.
130/B3 **Mabuki**, Tanz.
131/B5 **Mabuli**, Bots.
142/B5 **Macá** (peak), Chile
141/D2 **Macaé**, Braz.
140/D2 **Macaíba**, Braz.
131/D2 **Macaloge**, Moz.
137/H3 **Macapá**, Braz.

144/B2 **Macará**, Ecu.
140/B4 **Macarani**, Braz.
138/B5 **Macas**, Ecu.
140/C2 **Macau**, Braz.
105/G4 **Macau** (cap.), Macau
105/G4 **Macau** (dpcy.), Port.
140/B4 **Macaúbas**, Braz.
120/H7 **Macauley** (isl.), NZ
138/C4 **Macaya** (riv.), Col.
149/H2 **Macaya, Pic de**
(peak), Haiti
163/H4 **Macclenny**, Fl,US
57/F5 **Macclesfield**, Eng,UK
57/F5 **Macclesfield** (can.),
Eng,UK
147/G5 **Macuspana**, Mex.
132/D3 **Macdhui** (peak), SAfr.
163/H5 **MacDill A.F.B.**, Fl,US
117/F2 **MacDonald** (lake),
Austl.
117/G2 **Macdonnell** (ranges),
Austl.
54/C1 **Macduff**, Sc,UK
81/G2 **Macedonia**
81/G2 **Macedonia** (reg.),
Gre., Macd.
168/K5 **Macedonia**, Oh,US
140/D3 **Maceió**, Braz.
140/C2 **Maceió** (pt.), Braz.
80/C1 **Macerata**, It.
79/G6 **Macerata** (prov.), It.
113/E **Macey** (peak), Ant.
117/H5 **Macfarlane** (lake),
Austl.
60/A4 **Macgillycuddy's**
Reeks (mts.), Ire.
140/B5 **Machacalis**, Braz.
136/E7 **Machacamarca**, Bol.
132/D3 **Machache** (peak),
Les.
138/B5 **Machachi**, Ecu.
141/H6 **Machado**, Braz.
149/H4 **Machado, Ciénaga de**
(lake), Col.
131/D4 **Machaíla**, Moz.
130/C3 **Machakos**, Kenya
144/B1 **Machala**, Ecu.
138/A5 **Machalilla Nat'l**
Park, Ecu.
131/D4 **Machanga**, Moz.
148/D2 **Machaquilá** (riv.),
Guat.
56/D2 **Machars, The** (pen.),
Sc,UK
117/H3 **Machattie** (lake),
Austl.
131/D4 **Machaze**, Moz.
138/C2 **Machedo** (lake), Col.
131/C3 **Macheke**, Zim.
131/C4 **Machemma** (ruins),
SAfr.
58/C3 **Machen**, Wal,UK
103/C5 **Macheng**, China
161/H2 **Machias**, Me,US
74/D1 **Machichaco** (cape),
Sp.
75/V15 **Machico**, Madr.,Port.
99/H7 **Machida**, Japan
131/B3 **Machili** (riv.), Zam.
106/D4 **Machilipatnam**, India
96/D5 **Machiques**, Ven.
159/F4 **Macho** (dry riv.),
NM,US
131/B3 **Machobani**, Zam.
71/H1 **Machovo Jezero**
(res.), Czh.
144/C4 **Machu Picchu**
(ruins), Peru
136/F6 **Machupo** (riv.), Bol.
58/C1 **Machynlleth**, Wal,UK
131/D5 **Macia**, Moz.
83/J3 **Măcin**, Rom.
128/D3 **Macina** (reg.), Mali
119/D1 **Macintyre** (riv.),
Austl.
158/E3 **Mack**, Co,US
118/C3 **Mackay**, Austl.
117/F2 **Mackay** (lake), Austl.
113/E **MacKenzie** (bay), Ant.
147/E5 **Madre del Sur,**
Sierra (mts.), Mex.
146/C2 **Madre Occidental,**
Sierra (mts.), Mex.
72/E5 **Madrès** (mtn.), Fr.
148/C3 **Madre, Sierra** (mts.),
Mex.
112/C1 **Madre, Sierra** (mts.),
Phil.
138/C4 **Madrid**, Col.
74/C2 **Madrid** (aut. comm.),
Sp.
74/D2 **Madrid** (cap.), Sp.
74/D3 **Madridejos**, Sp.
75/N9 **Madrid** (inset) (cap.),
Sp.
77/F4 **Madrisahorn** (peak),
Swi.
106/D4 **Madugula**, India
130/B3 **Madukani**, Tanz.
108/T3 **Madukkkarai**, India
110/D5 **Madura** (isl.), Indo.
106/B4 **Madurai**, India
99/F2 **Maebashi**, Japan
109/C2 **Mae Charim**, Thai.
109/B2 **Mae Ping Nat'l Park**,
Thai.
58/C3 **Maesteg**, Wal,UK
149/G2 **Maestra, Sierra**
(range), Cuba
109/B2 **Mae Tho** (peak),
Thai.
120/F6 **Maewo** (isl.), Van.
109/B2 **Mae Ya** (mtn.), Thai.
130/C5 **Mafia** (chan.), Tanz.
130/C5 **Mafia** (isl.), Tanz.
132/D2 **Mafikeng**, SAfr.
87/M4 **Mafou** (riv.), Gui.
141/B3 **Mafra**, Braz.
74/A3 **Mafra**, Port.
131/C3 **Mafungabusi** (plat.),
Zim.
89/R4 **Magadan**, Rus.
130/C3 **Magadi**, Kenya

119/C1 **Macquarie** (riv.),
Austl.
119/C4 **Macquarie** (riv.),
Austl.
115/G8 **Macquarie Harbour**
(bay), Austl.
113/D **Mac-Robertson Land**
(reg.), Ant.
136/F5 **Macuim** (riv.), Braz.
138/D1 **Macuira Nat'l Park**,
Col.
144/B1 **Macuma** (riv.), Ecu.
117/H3 **Macumba** (riv.),
Austl.
146/C3 **Macuzari** (res.), Mex.
156/C5 **Mad** (riv.), Ca,US
91/D4 **Ma'dabā**, Jor.
133/H8 **Madagascar**
124/H3 **Madana**, Niger
83/G5 **Madan**, Bul.
106/C5 **Madanapalle**, India
120/D5 **Madang**, PNG
124/H1 **Madani'yīn**, Tun.
129/G3 **Madaoua**, Niger
106/F3 **Mādārī pur**, Bang.
160/E2 **Madawaska** (riv.),
On,Can
161/G2 **Madawaska**, Me,US
149/G4 **Madden** (dam), Pan.
136/F5 **Madeira** (riv.), Braz.
75/V15 **Madeira** (isl.), Madr.,
Port.
75/U14 **Madeira** (aut. reg.),
Port.
77/G3 **Mädelegabel** (peak),
Ger., Aus.
157/L4 **Madelin** (isl.), Wi,US
92/D2 **Maden**, Turk.
146/C2 **Madera**, Mex.
154/V3 **Madera** (vol.), Nic.
146/E2 **Madera** (mtn.), Tx,US
106/E2 **Madhipura**, India
106/C4 **Madhya Pradesh**
(state), India
130/B3 **Madiany**, Kenya
130/B5 **Madibura**, Tanz.
136/E6 **Madidi** (riv.), Bol.
159/H4 **Madill**, Ok,US
126/B1 **Madingo-Kayes**,
Congo
130/B2 **Madi Opei**, Ugan.
163/G3 **Madison**, Al,US
163/H4 **Madison**, Fl,US
160/C4 **Madison**, In,US
163/F3 **Madison**, Ms,US
156/F4 **Madison** (riv.), Mt,US
159/H2 **Madison**, Ne,US
166/D2 **Madison**, NJ,US
157/J4 **Madison**, SD,US
160/B3 **Madison** (cap.),
Wi,US
160/D4 **Madison**, WV,US
165/F6 **Madison Heights**,
Mi,US
160/C4 **Madisonville**, Ky,US
162/E4 **Madisonville**, Tx,US
130/C2 **Mado Gashi**, Kenya
96/D5 **Madoi**, China
76/C1 **Madon** (riv.), Fr.
80/C4 **Madonie Nebrodi**
(mts.), It.
77/G5 **Madonna di**
Campiglio, It.
95/G5 **Madrakah, Ra's al**
(pt.), Oman
130/B6 **Madras**, India
156/C4 **Madras**, Or,US
147/F3 **Madre** (lag.), Mex.
112/C1 **Madre** (mts.), Phil.
58/D3 **Madre**, Wal,UK
161/J6 **Madre de Deus de**
Minas, Braz.
134/C4 **Madre de Dios** (riv.),
Bol., Peru
143/J7 **Madre de Dios** (isl.),
Chile

132/P12 **Magalies Berg**
(range), SAfr.
112/C2 **Magallanes**, Phil.
143/K8 **Magallanes**
(Magellan) (str.), Arg.,
Chile
143/K8 **Magallanes y**
Antártica Chilena
(reg.), Chile
138/C2 **Magangué**, Col.
112/D4 **Maganoy**, Phil.
129/H3 **Magaria**, Niger
159/J4 **Magazine** (peak),
Ar,US
97/K1 **Magdagachi**, Rus.
161/J2 **Magdalen** (isls.),
Qu,Can
143/T12 **Magdalena**, Arg.
136/F6 **Magdalena**, Bol.
138/C2 **Magdalena** (dept.),
Col.
138/C3 **Magdalena** (riv.), Col.
146/C2 **Magdalena**, Mex.
111/E3 **Magdalena, Gunung**
(peak), Malay.
64/F2 **Magdeburg**, Ger.
64/F2 **Magdeburger Börde**
(plain), Ger.
58/D5 **Maiden Newton**,
Eng,UK
54/B6 **Maidens**, Sc,UK
165/F4 **Maidstone**, On,Can
156/F2 **Maidstone**, Sk,Can
59/G4 **Maidstone**, Eng,UK
124/H5 **Maiduguri**, Nga.
130/A2 **Maie**, Zaire
68/B4 **Maignelay-**
Montigny, Fr.
59/E5 **Maigue** (riv.), Ire.
106/D3 **Maihar**, India
89/J4 **Maihara**, Japan
106/B5 **Malabar** (coast),
India
108/E3 **Malabar Coast** (reg.),
India
95/K3 **Maisi**, Pak.
131/B4 **Main** (riv.), Ger.
124/G7 **Maiko** (cap.), EqG.
112/E6 **Malabon**, Phil.
141/D1 **Malacacheta**, Braz.
112/F6 **Malacanang Palace**,
Phil.
109/B5 **Malacca** (str.),
Malay., Thai.
70/E4 **Malacky**, Slvk.
65/J4 **Malad City**, Id,US
74/C4 **Málaga**, Sp.
164/F8 **Malaga** (cove), Ca,US
61/C3 **Måløy**, Nor.
57/F5 **Malpas**, Eng,UK
136/B3 **Malpelo** (isl.), Col.
74/A1 **Malpica**, Sp.
71/H5 **Malsch** (riv.), Aus.
70/B5 **Malsch**, Ger.
71/H5 **Malše** (riv.), Czh.
77/G4 **Mals** (Malles) It.
57/F5 **Manchester**, Eng,UK
168/B2 **Manchester**, Ct,US
160/C4 **Manchester**, Ky,US
161/G3 **Manchester**, NH,US
163/G2 **Manchester**, Tn,US
101/B2 **Manchuria** (reg.),
China
93/H4 **Mand** (riv.), Iran
130/B4 **Manda**, Tanz.
130/B5 **Manda**, Tanz.
141/B2 **Mandaguari**, Braz.
62/B2 **Mandal**, Nor.
111/K4 **Mandala** (peak), Indo.
104/C4 **Mandalay**, Burma
109/A1 **Mandalay** (div.),
Burma
104/C4 **Mandalay Palace**,
Burma
89/L5 **Mandalgovĭ**, Mong.
93/F3 **Mandalī**, Iraq
112/E6 **Mandaluyong**, Phil.
157/H4 **Mandan**, ND,US
125/J6 **Manda Nat'l Park**,
Chad
103/D4 **Mandang Shan** (mtn.),
China
111/F5 **Mandasavu** (peak),
Indo.
112/C3 **Mandaue**, Phil.
123/G3 **Mandeb, Bâb el** (str.),
Afr., Asia
78/C4 **Mandello del Lario**,
It.
125/P7 **Mandera**, Kenya
130/C4 **Mandera**, Tanz.
70/F3 **Manderscheid**, Ger.
76/C3 **Mandeure**, Fr.
149/G2 **Mandeville**, Jam.
108/D2 **Mandi**, India
130/A2 **Mandié**, Moz.
131/D1 **Mandimba**, Moz.
124/J6 **Mambéré** (riv.), CAfr.
92/D2 **Mambij**, Syria
131/B3 **Mambova**, Zam.
130/C3 **Mambrui**, Kenya
112/C2 **Mamburao**, Phil.
69/F4 **Mamer**, Lux.
72/D2 **Mamers**, Fr.
68/B2 **Mametz**, Fr.
81/L6 **Mándra**, Gre.
133/H9 **Mandrare** (riv.),
Madg.
133/J6 **Mandritsara**, India
133/J8 **Mandsaur**, India
116/B5 **Mandurah**, Austl.
81/E2 **Manduria**, It.
106/A3 **Māndvi**, India
108/D3 **Mandya**, India
106/D2 **Mane** (pass), Nepal
59/G2 **Manea**, Eng,UK
106/D3 **Manendragarh**, India
129/H5 **Manéngouba, Massif**
du (peak), Camr.
72/B3 **Manerbio**, It.
92/B5 **Manfalût**, Egypt
80/E2 **Manfredonia** (gulf), It.
103/B4 **Mang** (riv.), China
140/B4 **Manga**, Braz.

203
Manga – Mays

140/A3 **Mangabeiras** (hills), Braz.
126/C1 **Mangai,** Zaire
121/K7 **Mangaia** (isl.), Cookls.
107/F2 **Mangaldai,** India
112/C1 **Mangaldan,** Phil.
83/J4 **Mangalia,** Rom.
130/C4 **Mangalisa** (peak), Tanz.
106/B5 **Mangalore,** India
141/J7 **Mangaratiba,** Braz.
121/M7 **Mangareva** (isl.), FrPol.
105/E3 **Mangchang,** China
60/A6 **Mangerton** (mtn.), Ire.
104/B4 **Mangin** (range), Burma
87/K4 **Mangistauz Obl.,** Kaz.
111/E3 **Mangkalihat** (cape), Indo.
108/B1 **Mangla,** Pak.
108/B1 **Mangla** (dam), Pak.
108/B1 **Mangla** (res.), Pak.
144/A1 **Manglaralto,** Ecu.
138/B4 **Manglares** (pt.), Col.
116/K7 **Mangles** (bay), Austl.
129/F4 **Mango,** Togo
131/D2 **Mangoche,** Malw.
133/H8 **Mangoky** (riv.), Madg.
111/G4 **Mangole** (isl.), Indo.
133/J7 **Mangoro** (riv.), Madg.
58/D4 **Mangotsfield,** Eng,UK
106/B3 **Māngrol,** India
143/G2 **Mangueira** (lake), Braz.
159/H4 **Mangum,** Ok,US
130/A2 **Manguredjipa,** Zaire
131/C4 **Mangwe,** Zim.
87/J3 **Mangyshlak** (pen.), Kaz.
87/K4 **Mangyshlak** (plat.), Kaz.
96/C2 **Manhan,** Mong.
167/L8 **Manhasset,** NY,US
167/L8 **Manhasset** (bay), NY,US
159/H3 **Manhattan,** Ks,US
156/F4 **Manhattan,** Mt,US
167/J9 **Manhattan** (isl.), NY,US
164/B3 **Manhattan Beach,** Ca,US
131/D5 **Manhiça,** Moz.
141/D2 **Manhuaçu,** Braz.
141/D2 **Manhumirim,** Braz.
81/H4 **Máni** (pen.), Gre.
133/H7 **Mania** (riv.), Madg.
131/D2 **Maniamba,** Moz.
131/D3 **Manica,** Moz.
131/D3 **Manica** (prov.), Moz.
131/C3 **Manicaland** (prov.), Zim.
136/F5 **Manicoré,** Braz.
136/F5 **Manicoré** (riv.), Braz.
157/J3 **Manicouagan,** Mb,Can
161/G1 **Manicouagan** (res.), Qu,Can
161/G1 **Manicouagan** (riv.), Qu,Can
161/H1 **Manicouagan, Petit Lac** (lake), Qu,Can
118/C3 **Manifold** (cape), Austl.
121/L6 **Manihi** (isl.), FrPol.
121/J6 **Manihiki** (atoll), Cookls.
112/C2 **Manila** (cap.), Phil.
158/E2 **Manila,** Ut,US
112/E6 **Manila** (inset) (cap.), Phil.
133/J7 **Maningory** (riv.), Madg.
111/G4 **Manipa** (str.), Indo.
104/B3 **Manipur** (state), India
92/A2 **Manisa,** Turk.
92/B2 **Manisa** (prov.), Turk.
56/D3 **Man, Isle of** (isl.), UK
160/C2 **Manistee,** Mi,US
160/C2 **Manistee** (riv.), Mi,US
152/G3 **Manitoba** (prov.), Can.
157/J3 **Manitoba** (lake), Mb,Can
161/H1 **Manitou** (riv.), Qu,Can
160/D2 **Manitoulin** (isl.), On,Can
162/B2 **Manitou Springs,** Co,US
160/C1 **Manitouwadge,** On,Can
160/C2 **Manitowoc,** Wi,US
160/F2 **Maniwaki,** Qu,Can
138/C3 **Manizales,** Col.
131/D5 **Manjacaze,** Moz.
108/F3 **Manjeri,** India
106/C4 **Manjlegaon,** India
95/L5 **Mānjra** (riv.), India
157/K4 **Mankato,** Mn,US
131/C5 **Mankayane,** Swaz.
128/D4 **Mankono,** IvC.
108/H4 **Mankulam,** SrL.
96/F3 **Manlay,** Mong.
74/D2 **Manlleu,** Sp.
118/H8 **Manly,** Austl.
106/B3 **Manmād,** India
105/J5 **Manmanoc** (mtn.), Phil.
109/B4 **Man Mia** (peak), Thai.
108/G4 **Mannar** (gulf), India, SrL.
108/G4 **Mannar,** SrL.
108/H4 **Mannar** (dist.), SrL.
108/G4 **Mannar** (isl.), SrL.
108/G3 **Mannārgudi,** India
77/E3 **Männedorf,** Swi.
132/C4 **Mannetjiesberg** (peak), SAfr.
70/B4 **Mannheim,** Ger.
153/Q7 **Manning** (cape), NW,Can
163/H3 **Manning,** SC,US
166/C4 **Mannington Meadow** (lake), NJ,US
59/H3 **Manningtree,** Eng,UK
76/D4 **Männlifluh** (peak), Swi.
80/A2 **Mannu** (riv.), It.
80/A3 **Mannu** (riv.), It.
128/C5 **Mano** (riv.), Libr., SLeo.
126/E2 **Manono,** Zaire
167/F2 **Manorville,** NY,US
72/F5 **Manosque,** Fr.
161/G1 **Manouane** (lake), Qu,Can
161/G1 **Manouane** (riv.), Qu,Can
121/H5 **Manra** (Sydney) (atoll), Kiri.
75/F2 **Manresa,** Sp.
131/C1 **Mansa,** Zam.
128/B3 **Mansa Konko,** Gam.
112/C2 **Mansalay,** Phil.
153/H2 **Mansel** (isl.), NW,Can
57/G5 **Mansfield,** Eng,UK
162/E3 **Mansfield,** La,US
168/C1 **Mansfield,** Ma,US
168/E6 **Mansfield,** Oh,US
168/B2 **Mansfield Hollow** (dam), Ct,US
57/G5 **Mansfield Woodhouse,** Eng,UK
138/A5 **Manta,** Ecu.
112/B3 **Mantalingajan** (mtn.), Phil.
130/B3 **Mantare,** Tanz.
144/C3 **Mantaro** (riv.), Peru
158/B3 **Manteca,** Ca,US
141/D1 **Mantena,** Braz.
68/A6 **Mantes-la-Jolie,** Fr.
68/A6 **Mantes-la-Ville,** Fr.
106/C4 **Manthani,** India
158/E3 **Manti,** Ut,US
141/C2 **Mantiquiera** (range), Braz.
103/C3 **Mantou Shan** (mtn.), China
79/D2 **Mantova,** It.
78/D2 **Mantova** (prov.), It.
63/L1 **Mäntsälä,** Fin.
149/E1 **Mantua,** Cuba
85/K4 **Manturovo,** Rus.
63/M1 **Mäntyharju,** Fin.
144/D3 **Manú** (riv.), Peru
121/J6 **Manua** (isls.), ASam.
121/K6 **Manuae** (atoll), Cookls.
154/W13 **Manuawili,** Hi,US
137/J6 **Manuel Alves** (riv.), Braz.
110/C5 **Manuk** (riv.), Indo.
112/C3 **Manukan,** Phil.
115/R10 **Manukau,** NZ
166/D5 **Manumuskin** (riv.), NJ,US
144/C3 **Manú Nat'l Park,** Peru
136/E6 **Manuripe** (riv.), Bol.
120/D5 **Manus** (isl.), PNG
166/D2 **Manville,** NJ,US
162/E4 **Many,** La,US
131/C3 **Manyame** (riv.), Zim.
130/B3 **Manyara** (lake), Tanz.
87/G3 **Manych** (riv.), Rus.
87/G3 **Manych-Gudilo** (lake), Rus.
158/E3 **Many Farms,** Az,US
130/B4 **Manyoni,** Tanz.
74/D3 **Manzanares,** Sp.
75/N8 **Manzanares** (riv.), Sp.
149/G1 **Manzanillo,** Cuba
146/D5 **Manzanillo,** Mex.
149/F4 **Manzanillo-Gandoca Nat'l Wild. Ref.,** CR
162/B3 **Manzano** (mts.), NM,US
130/A4 **Manzanza,** Zaire
97/H2 **Manzhouli,** China
76/A5 **Manziat,** Fr.
127/C2 **Manzilah, Buḩayat al** (lake), Egypt
123/W17 **Manzil bū Ruqaybah,** Tun.
123/X17 **Manzil Tamīn,** Tun.
133/E2 **Manzini,** Swaz.
124/J5 **Mao,** Chad
150/D3 **Mao,** DRep.
111/J4 **Maoke** (mts.), Indo.
105/F4 **Maoming,** China
104/D3 **Maotou** (peak), China
131/C4 **Mapai,** Moz.
102/D5 **Mapam** (lake), China
146/D3 **Mapimí** (depr.), Mex.
161/Q8 **Maple,** On,Can
157/K5 **Maple** (riv.), Ia,US
157/J4 **Maple** (riv.), ND,US
156/F3 **Maple Creek,** Sk,Can
168/F5 **Maple Heights,** Oh,US
166/D4 **Maple Shade,** NJ,US
167/D2 **Maplewood,** NJ,US
101/F6 **Map'o,** SKor.
114/G2 **Mapoon Mission Sta.,** Austl.
139/G5 **Mapuera** (riv.), Braz.
106/B4 **Mapusa,** India
131/D5 **Maputo** (cap.), Moz.
131/D5 **Maputo** (prov.), Moz.
131/D5 **Maputo** (riv.), Moz.
127/D5 **Maqdam, Ras** (cape), Sudan
95/J2 **Maqor,** Afg.
102/D5 **Maquan** (riv.), China
126/C2 **Maquela do Zombo,** Ang.
159/K2 **Maquoteka** (riv.), Ia,US
141/B3 **Mar** (range), Braz.
104/D1 **Mar** (riv.), China
54/D2 **Mar** (dist.), Sc,UK
130/B3 **Mara** (prov.), Tanz.
130/B3 **Mara** (riv.), Tanz.
137/J5 **Marabá,** Braz.
137/J3 **Maracá** (isl.), Braz.
138/D2 **Maracaibo,** Ven.
138/D2 **Maracaibo** (lake), Ven.
137/H7 **Maracaju** (mts.), Braz.
140/B4 **Maracás,** Braz.
140/B4 **Maracás** (hills), Braz.
139/E2 **Maracay,** Ven.
74/D4 **Maracena,** Sp.
124/J2 **Marādah,** Libya
129/G3 **Maradi,** Niger
129/G3 **Maradi** (dept.), Niger
93/F2 **Marāgheh,** Iran
139/E4 **Marahuaca** (peak), Ven.
112/C1 **Maraira** (pt.), Phil.
159/J3 **Marais des Cygnes** (riv.), Ks, Mo,US
137/J4 **Marajó,** Braz.
137/J4 **Marajó** (bay), Braz.
134/D3 **Marajó** (isl.), Braz.
130/C2 **Maralal,** Kenya
117/F4 **Maralinga-Tjarutja Abor. Land,** Austl.
112/D4 **Maramag,** Phil.
141/K8 **Marambaia** (isl.), Braz.
163/F2 **Maramec** (riv.), Mo,US
83/F2 **Maramureş** (co.), Rom.
158/E4 **Marana,** Az,US
93/F2 **Marand,** Iran
140/C1 **Maranguape,** Braz.
140/A4 **Maranhão** (riv.), Braz.
140/A2 **Maranhão** (state), Braz.
79/G1 **Marano** (lag.), It.
118/C4 **Maranoa** (riv.), Austl.
136/C4 **Marañón** (riv.), Peru
79/E1 **Marano Vicentino,** It.
128/D5 **Maraoue Nat'l Park,** IvC.
110/B4 **Marapi** (peak), Indo.
110/C4 **Maras** (peak), Indo.
83/H3 **Mărăşeşti,** Rom.
160/C1 **Marathon,** On,Can
163/H5 **Marathon,** Fl,US
162/C4 **Marathon,** Tx,US
141/A4 **Marau,** Braz.
159/G5 **Maravillas** (cr.), Tx,US
112/D3 **Marawi,** Phil.
127/B5 **Marawī,** Sudan
58/A6 **Marazion,** Eng,UK
70/C5 **Marbach am Neckar,** Ger.
74/C4 **Marbella,** Sp.
156/F5 **Marbleton,** Wy,US
64/E3 **Marburg,** Ger.
166/B4 **Marburg** (lake), Pa,US
82/C2 **Marcali,** Hun.
126/B4 **Marca, Ponta da** (pt.), Ang.
59/G1 **March,** Eng,UK
164/C3 **March A.F.B.,** Ca,US
72/D3 **Marche** (mts.), Fr.
79/F5 **Marche** (reg.), It.
69/E3 **Marche-en-Famenne,** Belg.
144/J6 **Marchena** (isl.), Ecu.
74/C4 **Marchena,** Sp.
135/D3 **Mar Chiquita** (lake), Arg.
71/H6 **Marchtrenk,** Aus.
76/B3 **Marcilly-sur-Tille,** Fr.
68/A2 **Marck,** Fr.
140/B1 **Marco,** Braz.
163/H5 **Marco,** Fl,US
144/C4 **Marcona,** Peru
156/E3 **Marconi** (peak), BC,Can
142/E2 **Marcos Juárez,** Arg.
68/C2 **Marcq-en-Baroeul,** Fr.
151/J3 **Marcus Baker** (mtn.), Ak,US
160/F2 **Marcy** (peak), NY,US
95/K2 **Mardān,** Pak.
143/F3 **Mar del Plata,** Arg.
59/G4 **Marden,** Eng,UK
92/E2 **Mardin,** Turk.
92/E2 **Mardin** (prov.), Turk.
121/W12 **Maré** (isl.), NCal.
79/F5 **Marecchia** (riv.), It.
118/B2 **Mareeba,** Austl.
54/A1 **Maree, Loch** (lake), Sc,UK
57/H5 **Mareham le Fen,** Eng,UK
59/G5 **Maresfield,** Eng,UK
162/B4 **Marfa,** Tx,US
108/B1 **Margalla Hills Nat'l Park,** Pak.
58/C3 **Margam,** Wal,UK
86/E3 **Marganets,** Ukr.
106/B4 **Margao,** India
116/C2 **Margaret** (peak), Austl.
164/C4 **Margarita** (peak), Ca,US
139/F2 **Margarita** (isl.), Ven.
59/H4 **Margate,** Eng,UK
166/D5 **Margate City,** NJ,US
72/E4 **Margeride** (mts.), Fr.
130/A2 **Margherita** (peak), Ugan.
82/F2 **Marghita,** Rom.
102/B3 **Margilan,** Uzb.
102/E5 **Margog Caka** (lake), China
112/C4 **Margosatubig,** Phil.
69/E2 **Margraten,** Neth.
113/V **Marguerite** (bay), Ant.
119/D4 **Maria** (peak), Austl.
121/K7 **Maria** (isl.), FrPol.
112/C2 **Maria Aurora,** Phil.
146/D4 **María Cleófas** (isl.), Mex.
141/H7 **Maria da Fé,** Braz.
119/D4 **Maria Island Nat'l Park,** Austl.
130/C3 **Mariakani,** Kenya
146/D4 **María Madre** (isl.), Mex.
146/D4 **María Magdalena** (isl.), Mex.
149/F1 **Marianao,** Cuba
163/F3 **Marianna,** Ar,US
163/G4 **Marianna,** Fl,US
78/C1 **Mariano Comense,** It.
71/F3 **Mariánské Lázně** (Marienbad), Czh.
156/F3 **Marias** (riv.), Mt,US
149/F5 **Mariato** (pt.), Pan.
82/B2 **Maribor,** Slov.
141/L7 **Maricá,** Braz.
139/E5 **Marié** (riv.), Braz.
113/S **Marie Byrd Land** (reg.), Ant.
150/F4 **Marie-Galante** (isl.), Guad.
63/H1 **Mariehamn,** Fin.
63/U9 **Marieholm,** Swe.
149/F1 **Mariel,** Cuba
71/F3 **Marienbad** (Mariánské Lázně), Czh.
67/E6 **Marienheide,** Ger.
62/E2 **Mariestad,** Swe.
163/G3 **Marietta,** Ga,US
160/D4 **Marietta,** Oh,US
130/B2 **Marigat,** Kenya
72/F5 **Marignane,** Fr.
112/D3 **Marihatag,** Phil.
112/F6 **Marikina,** Phil.
112/F6 **Marikina** (riv.), Phil.
112/E6 **Marilao,** Phil.
141/B2 **Marília,** Braz.
74/A1 **Marín,** Sp.
165/J10 **Marin** (co.), Ca,US
164/B3 **Marina del Rey,** Ca,US
164/F8 **Marina del Rey** (har.), Ca,US
112/C2 **Marinduque** (isl.), Phil.
117/M8 **Marineland,** Austl.
130/D3 **Marine Nat'l Rsv.,** Kenya
53/R9 **Marines,** Fr.
160/C2 **Marinette,** Wi,US
165/K10 **Marine World** (Africa USA), Ca,US
141/B2 **Maringá,** Braz.
131/D3 **Marínguè,** Moz.
74/A3 **Marinha Grande,** Port.
115/J3 **Marion** (reef), Austl.
163/G3 **Marion,** Al,US
160/B4 **Marion,** Il,US
160/C3 **Marion,** In,US
160/B4 **Marion,** Ky,US
160/C2 **Marion,** Mi,US
160/D3 **Marion,** Oh,US
163/H3 **Marion** (lake), SC,US
160/D4 **Marion,** Va,US
158/C3 **Mariposa,** Ca,US
136/F8 **Mariscal Estigarribia,** Par.
83/H5 **Maritsa** (riv.), Bul., Turk.
86/F3 **Mariupol',** Ukr.
85/K4 **Mariy Aut. Rep.,** Rus.
91/D3 **Marj 'Uyūn,** Leb.
66/B6 **Mark** (riv.), Belg.
96/B2 **Markakol** (lake), Kaz.
104/C2 **Markam,** China
125/P7 **Marka** (Merca), Som.
62/E3 **Markaryd,** Swe.
93/G3 **Markazī** (gov.), Iran
77/F2 **Markdorf,** Ger.
66/C4 **Marken** (isl.), Neth.
66/C4 **Markerwaard** (polder), Neth.
59/E1 **Market Bosworth,** Eng,UK
59/F1 **Market Deeping,** Eng,UK
57/F6 **Market Drayton,** Eng,UK
59/F2 **Market Harborough,** Eng,UK
56/B3 **Markethill,** NI,UK
57/H5 **Market Rasen,** Eng,UK
57/H4 **Market Weighton,** Eng,UK
70/C5 **Markgroningen,** Ger.
153/J2 **Markham** (bay), NW,Can
161/R8 **Markham,** On,Can
65/L2 **Marki,** Pol.
54/C4 **Markinch,** Sc,UK
102/C4 **Markit,** China
158/C3 **Markleeville,** Ca,US
71/F2 **Markneukirchen,** Ger.
81/L7 **Markópoulon,** Gre.
87/H2 **Marks,** Rus.
162/E4 **Marksville,** La,US
70/C3 **Marktheidenfeld,** Ger.
71/E6 **Markt Indersdorf,** Ger.
77/G2 **Marktoberdorf,** Ger.
71/F3 **Marktredwitz,** Ger.
71/E6 **Markt Schwaben,** Ger.
159/J3 **Mark Twain** (lake), Mo,US
67/E5 **Marl,** Ger.
167/D3 **Marlboro,** NJ,US
59/E4 **Marlborough,** Eng,UK
168/C1 **Marlborough,** Ma,US
68/B3 **Marles-les-Mines,** Fr.
77/H4 **Marling** (Marlengo), It.
59/F3 **Marlow,** Eng,UK
166/D4 **Marlton,** NJ,US
68/C3 **Marly,** Fr.
53/T9 **Marly-la-Ville,** Fr.
53/S10 **Marly-le-Roi,** Fr.
69/F5 **Marly-sur-Seille,** Fr.
72/D4 **Marmande,** Fr.
83/H5 **Marmara** (isl.), Turk.
53/F4 **Marmara** (sea), Turk.
92/B2 **Marmaris,** Turk.
136/F5 **Marmelos** (riv.), Braz.
116/D4 **Marmion** (lake), Austl.
160/A1 **Marmion** (lake), On,Can
73/J3 **Marmolada** (peak), It.
74/C3 **Marmolejo,** Sp.
77/F5 **Marmontana, Monte** (peak), It.
68/C6 **Marne** (dept.), Fr.
72/E2 **Marne** (riv.), Fr.
76/B3 **Marne à la Saône** (can.), Fr.
69/D6 **Marne au Rhin, Canal de la** (can.), Fr.
58/D5 **Marnhull,** Eng,UK
124/J6 **Maro,** Chad
121/H2 **Maro** (reef), Hi,US
133/J6 **Maroantsetra,** Madg.
121/L6 **Marokau** (atoll), FrPol.
123/G7 **Marolambo,** Madg.
53/S11 **Marolles-en-Hurepoix,** Fr.
133/J6 **Maromokotro** (peak), Madg.
131/C3 **Marondera,** Zim.
139/H3 **Maroni** (riv.), FrG., Sur.
118/D4 **Maroochydore-Mooloolaba,** Austl.
79/E1 **Marostica,** It.
124/H5 **Maroua,** Camr.
139/H4 **Marouni** (riv.), FrG.
133/H7 **Marovoay,** Madg.
139/H3 **Marowijne** (dist.), Sur.
69/G5 **Marpingen,** Ger.
57/F5 **Marple,** Eng,UK
96/D5 **Marqên Gangri** (peak), China
120/D8 **Marquarie** (riv.), Austl.
121/M5 **Marquesas** (isls.), FrPol.
160/C2 **Marquette,** Mi,US
131/D5 **Marracuene,** Moz.
125/K5 **Marrah** (mts.), Sudan
125/K5 **Marrah** (peak), Sudan
124/D1 **Marrakech,** Mor.
131/D3 **Marromeu,** Moz.
126/G3 **Marrupa,** Moz.
124/J1 **Marsá al Burayqah,** Libya
130/C2 **Marsabit,** Kenya
80/C4 **Marsala,** It.
125/L1 **Marsá Matrūh,** Egypt
53/U10 **Marsange** (riv.), Fr.
67/F6 **Marsberg,** Ger.
80/C1 **Marsciano,** It.
57/G4 **Marsden,** Eng,UK
66/B3 **Marsdiep** (chan.), Neth.
72/F5 **Marseille,** Fr.
162/E4 **Marsh** (isl.), La,US
165/F7 **Marsh** (cr.), Mi,US
166/A4 **Marsh** (cr.), Pa,US
117/H2 **Marshall** (riv.), Austl.
156/F2 **Marshall,** Sk,Can
157/K4 **Marshall,** Mn,US
159/J3 **Marshall,** Mo,US
162/E3 **Marshall,** Tx,US
120/G3 **Marshall Islands**
157/K5 **Marshalltown,** Ia,US
159/J3 **Marshfield,** Mo,US
160/B2 **Marshfield,** Wi,US
59/E3 **Marsh Gibbon,** Eng,UK
166/C6 **Marshyhope** (cr.), De, Md,US
57/G2 **Marske-by-the-Sea,** Eng,UK
78/A1 **Mars, Monte** (peak), It.
62/G2 **Märsta,** Swe.
109/B2 **Martaban** (gulf), Burma
156/G2 **Martensville,** Sk,Can
168/D3 **Martha's Vineyard** (isl.), Ma,US
76/D5 **Martigny,** Swi.
72/F5 **Martigues,** Fr.
113/S **Martin** (pen.), Ant.
65/K4 **Martin,** Slvk.
163/G3 **Martin** (lake), Al,US
157/H5 **Martin,** SD,US
163/F2 **Martin,** Tn,US
80/E2 **Martina Franca,** It.
78/C1 **Martinengo,** It.
147/F4 **Martínez,** Mex.
165/K10 **Martinez,** Ca,US
163/H3 **Martinez,** Ga,US
147/M6 **Martínez de la Torre,** Mex.
141/C1 **Martinho Campos,** Braz.
150/F4 **Martinique** (isl.), Fr.
150/F4 **Martinique** (passg.), West Indies
140/B1 **Martinópole,** Braz.
141/B2 **Martinópolis,** Braz.
140/C2 **Martins,** Braz.
160/E4 **Martinsburg,** WV,US
160/C4 **Martinsville,** In,US
160/E4 **Martinsville,** Va,US
137/N8 **Martin Vaz,** Braz.
50/H7 **Martin Vaz** (isls.), Braz.
58/D2 **Martley,** Eng,UK
58/D5 **Martock,** Eng,UK
75/F2 **Martorell,** Sp.
74/D4 **Martos,** Sp.
160/F1 **Martre** (riv.), Qu,Can
157/J5 **Marty,** SD,US
98/C3 **Marugame,** Japan
99/F2 **Maruko,** Japan
66/D2 **Marum,** Neth.
130/C5 **Marumba,** Tanz.
98/E2 **Maruoka,** Japan
121/M7 **Marutea** (atoll), FrPol.
99/H7 **Maruyama,** Japan
93/H4 **Marv Dasht,** Iran
118/D4 **Mary** (riv.), Austl.
95/H1 **Mary,** Trkm.
116/B2 **Mary Anne** (passg.), Austl.
118/D4 **Maryborough,** Austl.
119/B3 **Maryborough,** Austl.
163/G4 **Mary Esther,** Fl,US
157/H3 **Maryfield,** Sk,Can
54/D3 **Marykirk,** Sc,UK
128/C5 **Maryland** (co.), Libr.
160/E4 **Maryland** (state), US
166/B5 **Maryland City,** Md,US
131/C3 **Maryland Junction,** Zim.
56/E2 **Maryport,** Eng,UK
161/L2 **Marystown,** Nf,Can
159/H3 **Marysville,** Ks,US
165/H6 **Marysville,** Mi,US
165/C1 **Marysville,** Wa,US
159/J2 **Maryville,** Mo,US
163/H3 **Maryville,** Tn,US
80/D2 **Marzano** (peak), It.
138/B3 **Marzo** (pt.), Col.
147/F3 **Marzo, 18 de,** Mex.
124/H2 **Marzūq,** Libya
124/H3 **Marzūq, Şhrā** (des.), Libya
130/C2 **Masabit Nat'l Rsv.,** Kenya
91/D4 **Masada** (Ḥorvot Meẕada) (ruins), Isr.
130/B3 **Masai Mara Nat'l Reserve,** Kenya
130/C4 **Masai Steppe** (grsld.), Tanz.
130/A3 **Masaka,** Ugan.
123/X18 **Masākin,** Tun.
75/E3 **Masamagrell,** Sp.
111/F4 **Masamba,** Indo.
101/E5 **Masan,** SKor.
130/A4 **Masangwe** (hill), Tanz.
101/F7 **Masan-ni,** SKor.
130/C5 **Masasi,** Tanz.
148/E4 **Masaya,** Nic.
112/C2 **Masbate,** Phil.
112/C2 **Masbate** (isl.), Phil.
123/R16 **Mascara,** Alg.
123/R16 **Mascara** (wilaya), Alg.
133/S15 **Mascarene** (isls.), Mrts., Reun.
161/N6 **Mascouche,** Qu,Can
130/A3 **Masereka,** Zaire
132/D3 **Maseru** (cap.), Les.
131/C4 **Mashaba,** Zim.
90/E6 **Mashad,** Iran
57/G3 **Masham,** Eng,UK
107/J3 **Mashan,** China
95/G1 **Mashhad,** Iran
100/B2 **Mashike,** Japan
95/H3 **Māshkel, Hāmūn-i-** (lake), Pak.
95/H3 **Māshkīd** (riv.), Iran
131/C3 **Mashonaland Central** (prov.), Zim.
131/C3 **Mashonaland East** (prov.), Zim.
131/C3 **Mashonaland West** (prov.), Zim.
91/B4 **Mashtūl as Sūq,** Egypt
100/D2 **Mashū** (lake), Japan
87/L1 **Masim** (peak), Rus.
130/A2 **Masindi,** Ugan.
130/B2 **Masindi Port,** Ugan.
112/B2 **Masinloc,** Phil.
95/G5 **Masira** (gulf), Oman
95/G4 **Maşīrah** (isl.), Oman
130/A3 **Masisi,** Zaire
93/G4 **Masjed-e Soleymān,** Iran
148/D2 **Maskall,** Belz.
60/A2 **Mask, Lough** (lake), Ire.
63/R7 **Måsnaren** (lake), Swe.
133/J6 **Masoala** (cape), Madg.
133/J6 **Masoala** (pen.), Madg.
160/C3 **Mason,** Mi,US
162/D4 **Mason,** Tx,US
165/A3 **Mason** (co.), Wa,US
165/A3 **Mason** (lake), Wa,US
157/K5 **Mason City,** Ia,US
75/X17 **Maspalomas,** Canl.,Sp.
75/K6 **Masquefa,** Sp.
78/D4 **Massa,** It.
78/D4 **Massa-Carrara** (prov.), It.
161/F3 **Massachusetts** (state), US
161/G3 **Massachusetts** (bay), Ma,US
78/D5 **Massaciuccoli** (lake), It.
80/E2 **Massafra,** It.
79/E4 **Massa Lombarda,** It.
131/D4 **Massangena,** Moz.
140/B1 **Massapê,** Braz.
167/E2 **Massapequa,** NY,US
167/M9 **Massapequa Park,** NY,US
78/D5 **Massarosa,** It.
160/F2 **Massena,** NY,US
153/S7 **Massey** (sound), NW,Can
126/D3 **Massibi,** Ang.
72/E4 **Massif Central** (plat.), Fr.
168/F6 **Massillon,** Oh,US
131/D4 **Massinga,** Moz.
131/D4 **Massingir,** Moz.
113/G **Masson** (isl.), Ant.
53/S10 **Massy,** Fr.
115/S11 **Masterton,** NZ
66/B5 **Mastgat** (chan.), Neth.
167/F2 **Mastic,** NY,US
167/F2 **Mastic Beach,** NY,US
71/H3 **Mastnik** (riv.), Czh.
95/J3 **Mastung,** Pak.
98/B3 **Masuda,** Japan
130/C5 **Masuguru,** Tanz.
110/B4 **Masurai** (peak), Indo.
131/C4 **Masvingo,** Zim.
131/C4 **Masvingo** (prov.), Zim.
130/B3 **Maswa Game Rsv.,** Tanz.
91/E2 **Maşyāf,** Syria
81/F2 **Mat** (riv.), Alb.
131/B3 **Matabeleland North** (prov.), Zim.
131/C4 **Matabeleland South** (prov.), Zim.
126/B2 **Matadi,** Zaire
162/C3 **Matador,** Tx,US
148/E3 **Matagalpa,** Nic.
149/E3 **Matagalpa, Rio Grande de** (riv.), Nic.
160/E1 **Matagami** (lake), Qu,Can
162/D4 **Matagorda** (bay), Tx,US
162/D4 **Matagorda** (isl.), Tx,US
106/D6 **Matale,** SrL.
128/B3 **Matam,** Sen.
147/F3 **Matamoros,** Mex.
125/K3 **Ma'ṭan as Sarra** (well), Libya
131/C1 **Matanda,** Zam.
130/C5 **Matandu** (riv.), Tanz.
161/H1 **Matane,** Qu,Can
161/H1 **Matane** (riv.), Qu,Can
149/F1 **Matanzas,** Cuba
141/B2 **Matão,** Braz.
146/C2 **Matape** (riv.), Mex.
161/H1 **Matapedia** (riv.), Qu,Can
139/F2 **Mata, Punta de,** Ven.
142/C2 **Mataquito** (riv.), Chile
94/C6 **Matara** (ruins), Egypt
106/D6 **Matara,** SrL.
111/E5 **Mataram,** Indo.
75/G2 **Mataró,** Sp.
121/L7 **Mataura,** FrPol.
120/H6 **Mata Utu** (cap.), Wall.
167/D3 **Matawan,** NJ,US
147/E4 **Matehuala,** Mex.
131/C4 **Mateke** (hills), Zim.
80/E2 **Matera,** It.
82/F2 **Mátészalka,** Hun.
131/B3 **Matetsi,** Zim.
130/B2 **Matheniko Game Rsv.,** Kenya
130/C2 **Mathew's** (peak), Kenya
164/C3 **Mathews** (lake), Ca,US
162/D4 **Mathis,** Tx,US
106/C2 **Mathurā,** India
112/D4 **Mati,** Phil.
141/K6 **Matias Barbosa,** Braz.
148/C2 **Matías Romero,** Mex.
149/E3 **Matíguas,** Nic.
164/A2 **Matilija** (dam), Ca,US
130/B5 **Matimbuka,** Tanz.
141/B3 **Matinhos,** Braz.
167/E2 **Matinicock** (pt.), NY,US
123/W17 **Mātir,** Tun.
138/D3 **Matiyuri** (riv.), Ven.
57/G5 **Matlock,** Eng,UK
131/C4 **Matobo** (Matopos) Nat'l Park, Zim.
136/G7 **Mato Grosso,** Braz.
137/J7 **Mato Grosso** (plat.), Braz.
141/A1 **Mato Grosso do Sul** (state), Braz.
131/D5 **Matolo-Rio,** Moz.
130/C4 **Matombo,** Tanz.
131/C4 **Matopos,** Zim.
131/C4 **Matopos** (Matobo) Nat'l Park, Zim.
74/A2 **Matosinhos,** Port.
140/B4 **Mato Verde,** Braz.
95/G4 **Maţraḩ,** Oman
140/D3 **Matriz de Camaragibe,** Braz.
132/B4 **Matroosberg** (peak), SAfr.
127/A2 **Maţrūḩ,** Egypt
127/B2 **Maţrūḩ** (gov.), Egypt
63/K2 **Matsalu** (str.), Est.
133/H8 **Matsiatra** (riv.), Madg.
99/L10 **Matsubara,** Japan
99/H7 **Matsubushi,** Japan
99/H7 **Matsuda,** Japan
99/H7 **Matsudo,** Japan
98/C3 **Matsue,** Japan
100/B3 **Matsumae,** Japan
99/E2 **Matsumoto,** Japan
98/E3 **Matsusaka,** Japan
99/G1 **Matsushima,** Japan
98/E2 **Matsutō,** Japan
98/C4 **Matsuyama,** Japan
160/D1 **Mattagami** (riv.), On,Can
108/F4 **Mattancherry Palace,** India
160/E2 **Mattawa,** On,Can
76/D6 **Matterhorn** (peak), It., Swi.
76/D5 **Mattertal** (val.), Swi.
165/Q16 **Matteson,** Il,US
151/H2 **Matthews** (mtn.), Ak,US
71/G6 **Mattig** (riv.), Aus.
76/E5 **Mattmarksee** (lake), Swi.
98/E2 **Mattō,** Japan
56/B4 **Mattock** (riv.), Ire.
160/B4 **Mattoon,** Il,US
131/D3 **Matundwe** (range), Malw., Moz.
139/F2 **Maturín,** Ven.
131/C3 **Matusadona Nat'l Park,** Zim.
112/D4 **Matutum** (mtn.), Phil.
139/G3 **Maú** (riv.), Braz., Guy.
130/B3 **Mau** (peak), Kenya
141/C2 **Mauá,** Braz.
68/C3 **Maubeuge,** Fr.
104/B5 **Ma-ubin,** Burma
54/B5 **Mauchline,** Sc,UK
116/B2 **Maud** (pt.), Austl.
54/D1 **Maud,** Sc,UK
106/D2 **Maudaha,** India
131/D5 **Mau-é-Ele,** Moz.
136/G4 **Maués,** Braz.
136/G4 **Maués Açu** (riv.), Braz.
120/D3 **Maug** (isls.), NMar.
56/D3 **Maughold,** IM,UK
56/D3 **Maughold Head** (pt.), IM,UK
72/F5 **Mauguio,** Fr.
60/B4 **Mauherslieve** (mtn.), Ire.
154/T10 **Maui** (isl.), Hi,US
121/K7 **Mauke** (isl.), Cookls.
70/B5 **Maulbronn,** Ger.
68/A6 **Mauldre** (riv.), Fr.
142/B2 **Maule** (reg.), Chile
142/C1 **Maule** (riv.), Chile
72/C3 **Mauléon,** Fr.
142/B4 **Maullín,** Chile
160/C3 **Maumee** (riv.), In, Oh,US
60/A2 **Maumtrasna** (mtn.), Ire.
131/A3 **Maun,** Bots.
154/U11 **Mauna Kea** (vol.), Hi,US
154/U11 **Mauna Loa** (vol.), Hi,US
131/B4 **Maunatlala,** Bots.
121/K6 **Maupiti** (isl.), FrPol.
77/E3 **Maur,** Swi.
106/C2 **Mau Rānīpur,** India
53/S10 **Maurecourt,** Fr.
68/A6 **Maurepas,** Fr.
117/F4 **Maurice** (lake), Austl.
166/C5 **Maurice** (riv.), NJ,US
161/F2 **Mauricie Nat'l Park,** Qu,Can
141/B1 **Maurilândia,** Braz.
128/B2 **Mauritania**
140/C2 **Mauriti,** Braz.
123/H6 **Mauritius**
130/C4 **Maurui,** Tanz.
160/B3 **Mauston,** Wi,US
76/D6 **Mauvoisin, Barrage de** (dam), Swi.
108/F4 **Māvelikara,** India
82/E5 **Mavrovo Nat'l Park,** Macd.
131/C3 **Mavuradonha** (mts.), Zim.
109/B4 **Maw Daung** (pass), Thai.
113/E **Mawson,** Ant.
113/D **Mawson** (coast), Ant.
147/H4 **Maxcanú,** Mex.
69/F6 **Maxéville,** Fr.
71/F4 **Maxhütte-Haidhof,** Ger.
131/D4 **Maxixe,** Moz.
54/D4 **May** (isl.), Sc,UK
160/F4 **May** (cape), NJ,US
148/D2 **Maya** (mts.), Belz., Guat.
110/C4 **Maya** (isl.), Indo.
89/P4 **Maya** (riv.), Rus.
150/C2 **Mayaguana** (isl.), Bahm.
150/C2 **Mayaguana** (passg.), Bahm.
150/E3 **Mayagüez,** PR
95/K1 **Mayakovskogo** (peak), Taj.
102/B4 **Mayakovskogo, Pik** (peak), Taj.
107/J2 **Mayang,** China
149/H1 **Mayarí,** Cuba
99/L10 **Maya-san** (peak), Japan
54/B6 **Maybole,** Sc,UK
125/N5 **Maych'ew,** Eth.
112/D3 **Maydolong,** Phil.
69/G3 **Mayen,** Ger.
72/C2 **Mayenne,** Fr.
72/C3 **Mayenne** (riv.), Fr.
156/E2 **Mayerthorpe,** Ab,Can
54/C5 **Mayfield,** Sc,UK
160/B4 **Mayfield,** Ky,US
168/F4 **Mayfield Heights,** Oh,US
86/G3 **Maykop,** Rus.
59/G3 **Mayland,** Eng,UK
104/C4 **Maymyo,** Burma
168/C1 **Maynard,** Ma,US
142/C5 **Mayo** (riv.), Arg.
151/L3 **Mayo,** Yk,Can
60/A2 **Mayo,** Ire.
60/A2 **Mayo** (co.), Ire.
146/C3 **Mayo** (riv.), Mex.
112/C2 **Mayon** (vol.), Phil.
74/D1 **Mayor** (cape), Sp.
122/G6 **Mayotte** (isl.), Fr.
133/H6 **Mayotte** (terr.), Fr.
112/C1 **Mayoyao,** Phil.
149/G2 **May Pen,** Jam.
93/F4 **Maysān** (gov.), Iraq

Maysv – Millp

160/D4 **Maysville**, Ky,US
131/C1 **Mayuka**, Zam.
108/G3 **Mayuram**, India
157/J4 **Mayville**, ND,US
164/F8 **Maywood**, Ca,US
165/Q16 **Maywood**, Il,US
167/J8 **Maywood**, NJ,US
131/B2 **Mazabuka**, Zam.
137/H4 **Mazagão**, Braz.
72/E5 **Mazamet**, Fr.
93/H2 **Māzandarān** (gov.), Iran
80/C4 **Mazara** (val.), It.
80/C4 **Mazara del Vallo**, It.
95/J1 **Mazār-e Sharīf**, Afg.
74/A1 **Mazaricos**, Sp.
74/E4 **Mazarrón**, Sp.
139/G3 **Mazaruni** (riv.), Guy.
146/C2 **Mazatán**, Mex.
148/D3 **Mazatenango**, Guat.
146/D4 **Mazatlán**, Mex.
63/K3 **Mažeikiai**, Lith.
118/B3 **Mazeppa Nat'l Park**, Austl.
56/B3 **Mazetown**, NI,UK
92/D2 **Mazıkıran** (pass), Turk.
68/B3 **Mazingarbe**, Fr.
126/D2 **Mazingu**, Zaire
131/D3 **Mazoe** (riv.), Moz.
131/C3 **Mazoe**, Zim.
96/D3 **Mazong** (peak), China
131/C3 **Mazowe** (riv.), Zim.
131/C4 **Mazunga**, Zim.
65/L2 **Mazury** (reg.), Pol.
131/B3 **Mbabala**, Zam.
130/A5 **Mbabala** (isl.), Zam.
133/E2 **Mbabane** (cap.), Swaz.
124/H6 **Mbabo** (peak), Camr.
124/J7 **Mbaïki**, CAfr.
125/H6 **Mbakaou** (lake), Camr.
130/A5 **Mbala**, Zam.
131/C4 **Mbalabala**, Zim.
124/H7 **Mbalam**, Camr.
130/C3 **Mbalambala**, Kenya
130/B2 **Mbale**, Ugan.
124/H7 **Mbalmayo**, Camr.
129/H5 **Mbam** (riv.), Camr.
131/D3 **Mbamba Bay**, Tanz.
129/H5 **Mbam, Massif du** (peak), Camr.
125/J7 **Mbandaka**, Zaire
130/C5 **Mbaranganda** (riv.), Tanz.
130/C5 **Mbarangandu**, Tanz.
130/A3 **Mbarara**, Ugan.
125/J7 **Mbata**, CAfr.
121/Y18 **Mbengga** (isl.), Fiji
131/C4 **Mberengwa**, Zim.
130/A5 **Mbereshi Mission**, Zam.
130/B5 **Mbeya**, Tanz.
130/B5 **Mbeya** (peak), Tanz.
130/B4 **Mbeya** (prov.), Tanz.
130/B5 **Mbeya** (range), Tanz.
131/D1 **Mbeya**, Zam.
126/B1 **M'Bigou**, Gabon
124/G7 **Mbini**, EqG.
124/H7 **Mbini** (riv.), EqG.
130/A4 **Mbirira**, Tanz.
130/A3 **Mbirizi**, Ugan.
131/C4 **Mbizi**, Zim.
130/B4 **Mbogo**, Tanz.
130/A3 **Mboko**, Zaire
131/C2 **Mboloma**, Zam.
125/L6 **Mbomou** (riv.), CAfr.
128/B3 **Mboune, Vallée du** (wadi), Sen.
128/A3 **M'Bour**, Sen.
126/D2 **Mbuji-Mayi**, Zaire
130/B3 **Mbulu**, Tanz.
130/C3 **Mbuvu**, Kenya
131/D2 **Mbuzi**, Zam.
130/C5 **Mbwemburu** (riv.), Tanz.
130/B4 **Mbwikwe**, Tanz.
159/J4 **McAlester**, Ok,US
162/D5 **McAllen**, Tx,US
156/C2 **McBride**, BC,Can
156/D4 **McCall**, Id,US
162/C4 **McCamey**, Tx,US
165/C3 **McChord A.F.B.**, Wa,US
165/M9 **McClellan A.F.B.**, Ca,US
157/H4 **McClusky**, ND,US
163/F4 **McComb**, Ms,US
159/G2 **McConaughy** (lake), Ne,US
159/H3 **McConnell A.F.B.**, Ks,US
159/G2 **McCook**, Ne,US
163/H3 **McCormick**, SC,US
157/J3 **McCreary**, Mb,Can
158/C2 **McDermitt**, Nv,US
51/N8 **McDonald** (isls.), Austl.
151/F3 **McDonald** (mtn.), Ak,US
117/H5 **McDonnell** (peak), Austl.
151/L2 **McDougall** (pass), NW, Yk,Can
162/F3 **McGehee**, Ar,US
163/F3 **McGehee**, Ar,US
156/C2 **McGregor** (riv.), BC,Can
165/G7 **McGregor**, On,Can
166/D3 **McGuire A.F.B.**, NJ,US
165/P15 **McHenry**, Il,US
165/N15 **McHenry** (co.), Il,US
130/C5 **Mchinga**, Tanz.
131/D2 **Mchinji**, Malw.
121/H5 **McKean** (atoll), Kiri.
153/K2 **McKeand** (riv.), NW,Can
168/H7 **McKeesport**, Pa,US
168/G7 **McKees Rocks**, Pa,US
163/F2 **McKenzie**, Tn,US
151/H3 **McKinley** (mtn.), Ak,US
151/J3 **McKinley Park**, Ak,US
156/B5 **McKinleyville**, Ca,US
162/D3 **McKinney**, Tx,US
117/G2 **McLaren Creek Abor. Land**, Austl.
157/H4 **McLaughlin**, SD,US
166/A6 **McLean**, Va,US
156/D2 **McLennan**, Ab,Can
114/A4 **McLeod** (lake), Austl.
156/D2 **McLeod** (riv.), Ab,Can
152/E2 **McLeod** (bay), NW,Can
156/C2 **McLeod Lake**, BC,Can
152/F1 **M'Clintock** (chan.), NW,Can
153/Q7 **M'Clure** (str.), NW,Can
156/C4 **McMinnville**, Or,US
163/G3 **McMinnville**, Tn,US
113/M **McMurdo**, Ant.
165/B3 **McNeil** (isl.), Wa,US
131/D2 **Mcocha**, Malw.
159/H3 **McPherson**, Ks,US
130/B4 **Mdabulo**, Tanz.
130/B4 **Mdaburo**, Tanz.
130/B5 **Mdandu**, Tanz.
96/E5 **Mê** (riv.), China
158/D3 **Mead** (lake), Az, Nv,US
151/G2 **Meade** (riv.), Ak,US
156/F2 **Meadow Lake**, Sk,Can
167/J8 **Meadowlands Sports Complex**, NJ,US
161/Q8 **Meadowvale**, On,Can
158/D3 **Meadow Valley** (riv.), Nv,US
163/F4 **Meadville**, Ms,US
160/D3 **Meadville**, Pa,US
100/C2 **Me-akan-dake** (mtn.), Japan
60/A6 **Mealagh** (riv.), Ire.
54/B3 **Meall a' Bhuiridh** (mtn.), Sc,UK
54/B3 **Meall Buidhe** (mtn.), Sc,UK
54/C3 **Meall Dearg** (mtn.), Sc,UK
54/B2 **Meall Dubh** (mtn.), Sc,UK
54/C4 **Meall nam Fuaran** (mtn.), Sc,UK
54/C3 **Meall Tairneachan** (mtn.), Sc,UK
168/G5 **Meander Creek** (res.), Oh,US
140/A1 **Mearim** (riv.), Braz.
54/D3 **Mearns, Howe of the** (dist.), Sc,UK
59/E1 **Measham**, Eng,UK
151/F2 **Meat** (mtn.), Ak,US
60/D2 **Meath** (co.), Ire.
157/G2 **Meath Park**, Sk,Can
53/U10 **Meaux**, Fr.
147/M6 **Mecapalapa**, Mex.
94/C4 **Mecca** (Makkah), SAr.
166/A3 **Mechanicsburg**, Pa,US
166/B3 **Mechanicsburg Nav. Supply Dep.**, Pa,US
68/D1 **Mechelen** (Malines), Belg.
92/C1 **Mecitözü**, Turk.
77/F2 **Meckenbeuren**, Ger.
69/G2 **Meckenheim**, Ger.
62/D4 **Mecklenburg** (bay), Ger.
64/F1 **Mecklenburger Bucht** (bay), Ger.
64/F2 **Mecklenburg-Western Pomerania** (state), Ger.
131/D2 **Mecuia** (peak), Moz.
78/C1 **Meda**, It.
106/C4 **Medak**, India
110/A3 **Medan**, Indo.
143/L7 **Medanosa** (pt.), Arg.
138/D2 **Médanos de Coro Nat'l Park**, Ven.
59/F1 **Medbourne**, Eng,UK
123/S15 **Médéa**, Alg.
123/S15 **Médéa** (wilaya), Alg.
75/G4 **Medea** (wilaya), Alg.
67/F6 **Medebach**, Ger.
140/B5 **Medeiros Neto**, Braz.
138/C3 **Medellín**, Col.
78/B2 **Mede Lomellina**, It.
77/E4 **Medel, Piz** (peak), Swi.
66/C3 **Medemblik**, Neth.
57/G5 **Meden** (riv.), Eng,UK
92/C2 **Medetsiz** (peak), Turk.
168/C1 **Medford**, Ma,US
167/F2 **Medford**, NY,US
156/C5 **Medford**, Or,US
160/B2 **Medford**, Wi,US
83/J3 **Medgidia**, Rom.
83/G2 **Mediaş**, Rom.
156/D4 **Medical Lake**, Wa,US
158/F2 **Medicine Bow** (range), Co, Wy,US
157/G5 **Medicine Bow**, Wy,US
156/F3 **Medicine Hat**, Ab,Can
140/B5 **Medina**, Braz.
59/E5 **Medina** (riv.), Eng,UK
157/J4 **Medina**, ND,US
168/F5 **Medina**, Oh,US
168/F5 **Medina** (co.), Oh,US
159/H5 **Medina**, Tx,US
94/C4 **Medina** (Al Madīnah), SAr.
74/C2 **Medina del Campo**, Sp.
74/C4 **Medina-Sidonia**, Sp.
51/K4 **Mediterranean** (sea)
156/F2 **Medley**, Ab,Can
87/L2 **Mednogorsk**, Rus.
87/H2 **Medveditsa, Gora** (riv.), Rus.
89/S2 **Medvezh'i** (isls.), Rus.
84/G3 **Medvezh'yegorsk**, Rus.
53/P8 **Medway** (riv.), Eng,UK
168/C1 **Medway**, Ma,US
158/F2 **Meeker**, Co,US
67/G3 **Meerbach** (riv.), Ger.
66/D6 **Meerbusch**, Ger.
69/E1 **Meerhout**, Belg.
69/E2 **Meerssen**, Neth.
106/C2 **Meerut**, India
59/E1 **Meese** (riv.), Eng,UK
156/F4 **Meeteetse**, Wy,US
125/N7 **Mēga**, Eth.
125/P6 **Megalo**, Eth.
161/G2 **Megantic** (peak), Qu,Can
81/H3 **Mégara**, Gre.
107/F2 **Meghalaya** (state), India
91/G6 **Megiddo** (ruins), Isr.
160/E1 **Mégiscane** (lake), Qu,Can
160/E1 **Mégiscane** (riv.), Qu,Can
91/A1 **Megista** (isl.), Gre.
131/C4 **Meguzalala**, Moz.
69/E2 **Mehaigne** (riv.), Belg.
116/C2 **Meharry** (mtn.), Austl.
123/R16 **Mehdia**, Alg.
67/G1 **Mehe** (riv.), Ger.
106/C3 **Mehkar**, India
93/H5 **Mehrān** (riv.), Iran
93/H4 **Mehriz**, Iran
106/B3 **Mehsāna**, India
105/G4 **Mei** (riv.), China
130/B4 **Meia Meia**, Tanz.
141/B1 **Meia Ponte** (riv.), Braz.
124/H6 **Meiganga**, Camr.
153/R6 **Meighen** (isl.), NW,Can
54/C3 **Meigle**, Sc,UK
107/H2 **Meigu**, China
97/K3 **Meihekou**, China
54/B4 **Meikle Bin** (mtn.), Sc,UK
54/D5 **Meikle Says Law** (mtn.), Sc,UK
104/B4 **Meiktila**, Burma
77/E3 **Meilen**, Swi.
67/H4 **Meine**, Ger.
67/E6 **Meinerzhagen**, Ger.
70/D1 **Meiningen**, Ger.
103/D5 **Meishan**, China
104/D2 **Meishan**, China
103/C5 **Meishan** (res.), China
65/G3 **Meissen**, Ger.
67/G6 **Meissner** (peak), Ger.
70/D5 **Meitingen**, Ger.
99/M10 **Meiwa**, Japan
105/H3 **Meizhou**, China
79/E2 **Mejaniga**, It.
124/H7 **Mekambo**, Gabon
125/N5 **Mek'elē**, Eth.
123/M14 **Meknès**, Mor.
109/D4 **Mekong** (riv.), Asia
111/F4 **Mekongga** (peak), Indo.
104/D4 **Mekong** (Lancang) (riv.), China
109/D4 **Mekong, Mouths of the**, Viet.
110/B3 **Melaka**, Malay.
120/E5 **Melanesia** (reg.)
108/F4 **Melappālaiyam**, India
110/D4 **Melawi** (riv.), Indo.
59/G2 **Melbourn**, Eng,UK
119/C3 **Melbourne**, Austl.
152/F2 **Melbourne** (isl.), NW,Can
57/G6 **Melbourne**, Eng,UK
163/H4 **Melbourne**, Fl,US
119/F5 **Melbourne** (inset), Austl.
142/B5 **Melchor** (isl.), Chile
148/D2 **Melchor de Mencos**, Guat.
58/D5 **Melcombe Regis**, Eng,UK
79/F4 **Meldola**, It.
64/E1 **Meldorf**, Ger.
78/B5 **Mele, Capo** (cape), It.
78/C2 **Melegnano**, It.
82/E3 **Melenci**, Yugo.
84/J5 **Melenki**, Rus.
87/K1 **Meleuz**, Rus.
153/J3 **Mélèzes** (riv.), Qu,Can
77/E5 **Melezza** (riv.), It.
124/J5 **Melfi**, Chad
80/D2 **Melfi**, It.
157/G2 **Melfort**, Sk,Can
61/D3 **Melhus**, Nor.
58/D2 **Melibocus** (peak), Ger.
130/C3 **Melili** (peak), Kenya
123/N13 **Melilla**, Sp.
142/B5 **Melimoyu** (peak), Chile
142/Q9 **Melipilla**, Chile
81/F3 **Melissano**, It.
157/H3 **Melita**, Mb,Can
80/D4 **Melito di Porto Salvo**, It.
86/E3 **Melitopol'**, Ukr.
73/G2 **Melk**, Aus.
125/P7 **Melka Meri**, Eth.
58/D4 **Melksham**, Eng,UK
78/D2 **Mella** (riv.), It.
62/E2 **Mellan Fryken** (lake), Swe.
68/C2 **Melle**, Belg.
67/F4 **Melle**, Ger.
123/W17 **Mellègue** (riv.), Alg.
62/E2 **Mellerud**, Swe.
74/B1 **Mellid**, Sp.
57/F3 **Melling**, Eng,UK
115/K3 **Mellish** (reef), Austl.
143/J7 **Mellizo Sur** (peak), Chile
70/D2 **Mellrichstadt**, Ger.
67/F1 **Mellum** (isl.), Ger.
71/H2 **Mělník**, Czh.
143/G2 **Melo**, Uru.
54/D5 **Melrose**, Sc,UK
54/D5 **Melrose Abbey**, Sc,UK
165/Q16 **Melrose Park**, Il,US
77/F3 **Mels**, Swi.
67/G6 **Melsungen**, Ger.
57/G4 **Meltham**, Eng,UK
119/C3 **Melton**, Austl.
57/H6 **Melton Mowbray**, Eng,UK
53/T11 **Melun**, Fr.
108/G3 **Melūr**, India
116/K7 **Melville**, Austl.
114/F2 **Melville** (bay), Austl.
118/B1 **Melville** (cape), Austl.
114/E2 **Melville** (isl.), Austl.
153/L3 **Melville** (lake), Nf,Can
153/R7 **Melville** (isl.), NW,Can
153/H2 **Melville** (pen.), NW,Can
157/H3 **Melville**, Sk,Can
112/B4 **Melville** (cape), Phil.
167/E2 **Melville**, NY,US
165/F7 **Melvindale**, Mi,US
82/D2 **Mélykút**, Hun.
78/C2 **Melzo**, It.
102/D5 **Mêmar** (lake), China
66/D1 **Memmert** (isl.), Ger.
77/G2 **Memmingen**, Ger.
109/D4 **Memot**, Camb.
91/B5 **Memphis** (ruins), Egypt
165/G6 **Memphis**, Mi,US
159/J2 **Memphis**, Mo,US
163/F3 **Memphis**, Tn,US
162/C3 **Memphis**, Tx,US
162/E3 **Mena**, Ar,US
56/D5 **Menai** (str.), Wal,UK
56/D5 **Menai Bridge**, Wal,UK
66/C2 **Menaldum**, Neth.
133/H9 **Menarandra** (riv.), Madg.
162/D4 **Menard**, Tx,US
160/B2 **Menasha**, Wi,US
133/H7 **Menavava** (riv.), Madg.
110/D4 **Mendawai** (riv.), Indo.
72/E4 **Mende**, Fr.
67/E6 **Menden**, Ger.
151/E4 **Mendenhall** (cape), Ak,US
141/K7 **Mendes**, Braz.
125/N6 **Mendī**, Eth.
69/G3 **Mendig**, Ger.
58/D4 **Mendip** (hills), Eng,UK
158/B3 **Mendocino**, Ca,US
154/B3 **Mendocino** (cape), Ca,US
165/M11 **Mendota-Delta** (can.), Ca,US
142/C2 **Mendoza**, Arg.
142/C2 **Mendoza** (prov.), Arg.
133/H9 **Mendrare** (riv.), Madg.
77/E6 **Mendrisio**, Swi.
82/F3 **Mehedinţi** (co.), Rom.
78/C3 **Menegosa, Monte** (peak), It.
138/D2 **Mene Grande**, Ven.
92/A2 **Menemen**, Turk.
68/C2 **Menen**, Belg.
130/C3 **Menengai Crater**, Kenya
96/H2 **Menengiyn** (plain), Mong.
80/C4 **Menfi**, It.
103/D4 **Mengcheng**, China
70/C6 **Mengen**, Ger.
110/C4 **Menggala**, Indo.
109/C1 **Menghai**, China
74/D4 **Mengibar**, Sp.
109/C1 **Mengla**, China
104/C4 **Menglian Daizu Lahuzu Vazu Zizhixian**, China
103/D4 **Menglianggu** (mtn.), China
105/F3 **Mengshan**, China
103/C4 **Meng Xian**, China
103/D4 **Mengyin**, China
104/D4 **Mengzi**, China
119/B2 **Menindee** (dam), Austl.
119/B2 **Menindee** (lake), Austl.
142/B5 **Menlolat** (peak), Chile
165/K12 **Menlo Park**, Ca,US
53/T11 **Mennecy**, Fr.
160/C2 **Menominee**, Mi,US
160/B3 **Menomonee Falls**, Wi,US
160/B2 **Menomonie**, Wi,US
126/C3 **Menongue**, Ang.
75/H3 **Menorca** (Minorca) (isl.), Sp.
110/A4 **Mentawai** (isls.), Indo.
110/A4 **Mentawai** (str.), Indo.
162/C4 **Mentone**, Tx,US
160/D3 **Mentor**, Oh,US
76/C4 **Mentue** (riv.), Swi.
53/R9 **Menucourt**, Fr.
111/E3 **Menyapa** (peak), Indo.
96/E4 **Menyuan**, China
123/W17 **Menzel Bourguiba**, Tun.
151/M3 **Menzie** (mtn.), Yk,Can
59/E5 **Meon** (riv.), Eng,UK
53/Q7 **Meopham**, Eng,UK
111/H4 **Meos Waar** (isl.), Indo.
126/B2 **Mepala**, Ang.
87/G4 **Mepistskaro** (peak), Geo.
66/D3 **Meppel**, Neth.
67/E3 **Meppen**, Ger.
75/E2 **Mequinenzo** (res.), Sp.
77/F5 **Mera** (riv.), It., Swi.
159/K3 **Meramec** (riv.), Mo,US
77/H4 **Merano**, It.
110/D4 **Meratus** (mts.), Indo.
120/D5 **Merauke**, Indo.
125/P7 **Merca**, Som.
73/G4 **Mercantour Nat'l Park**, Fr.
158/B3 **Merced**, Ca,US
158/C3 **Merced** (riv.), Ca,US
142/C1 **Mercedario** (peak), Arg.
142/D2 **Mercedes**, Arg.
142/F2 **Mercedes**, Arg.
143/F2 **Mercedes**, Uru.
166/D3 **Mercer** (co.), NJ,US
168/G5 **Mercer** (co.), Pa,US
165/C2 **Mercer** (isl.), Wa,US
165/C2 **Mercer Island**, Wa,US
166/D3 **Mercerville-Hamilton Square**, NJ,US
68/D2 **Merchtem**, Belg.
161/N7 **Mercier**, Qu,Can
156/D2 **Mercoal**, Ab,Can
158/D3 **Mercury**, Nv,US
153/K2 **Mercy** (cape), Yk,Can
72/E5 **Merdellou** (mtn.), Fr.
58/D4 **Mere**, Eng,UK
143/M8 **Meredith** (cape), Falk.
162/C3 **Meredith** (lake), Tx,US
86/F2 **Merefa**, Ukr.
68/C2 **Merelbeke**, Belg.
109/D3 **Mereuch**, Camb.
53/Q8 **Mereworth**, Eng,UK
97/J2 **Mergel** (riv.), China
109/B3 **Mergui**, Burma
109/B4 **Mergui** (arch.), Burma
68/B3 **Méricourt**, Fr.
147/H4 **Mérida**, Mex.
74/B3 **Mérida**, Sp.
138/D2 **Mérida**, Ven.
138/D3 **Mérida** (mts.), Ven.
138/D2 **Mérida** (state), Ven.
168/B2 **Meriden**, Ct,US
163/F3 **Meridian**, Ms,US
162/D4 **Meridian**, Tx,US
165/C2 **Meridian-East Hill**, Wa,US
72/C4 **Mérignac**, Fr.
70/D6 **Mering**, Ger.
68/D1 **Merksem**, Belg.
66/B6 **Merksplas**, Belg.
143/S12 **Merlo**, Arg.
125/M4 **Meroe** (ruins), Sudan
91/D3 **Meron, Har** (mtn.), Isr.
119/F5 **Merri** (cr.), Austl.
55/J9 **Merrick** (mtn.), UK
167/E2 **Merrick**, NY,US
160/B2 **Merrill**, Wi,US
166/C2 **Merrill Creek** (res.), NJ,US
161/G3 **Merrimack**, NH,US
58/D5 **Merriott**, Eng,UK
156/C3 **Merritt**, BC,Can
163/H4 **Merritt Island**, Fl,US
54/D5 **Merse** (dist.), Sc,UK
57/F5 **Mersey** (riv.), Eng,UK
57/F5 **Merseyside** (co.), Eng,UK
91/D1 **Mersin**, Turk.
110/B3 **Mersing**, Malay.
53/N8 **Merstham**, Eng,UK
69/F5 **Mertert**, Lux.
58/C3 **Merthyr Tydfil**, Wal,UK
53/N7 **Merton** (bor.), Eng,UK
113/K **Mertz** (glac.), Ant.
162/C4 **Mertzon**, Tx,US
68/B5 **Méru**, Fr.
130/C2 **Meru**, Kenya
130/C3 **Meru** (peak), Tanz.
130/C2 **Meru Nat'l Park**, Kenya
68/B2 **Merville**, Fr.
66/C5 **Merwedekanaal** (can.), Neth.
53/S9 **Méry-sur-Oise**, Fr.
69/F2 **Merzenich**, Ger.
92/C1 **Merzifon**, Turk.
69/F5 **Merzig**, Ger.
143/K7 **Mesa** (peak), Arg.
151/G3 **Mesa** (mtn.), Ak,US
158/E4 **Mesa**, Az,US
157/K4 **Mesabi** (range), Mn,US
81/E2 **Mesagne**, It.
81/J5 **Mesarás** (gulf), Gre.
158/E3 **Mesa Verde Nat'l Park**, Co,US
162/C3 **Mescalero** (ridge), NM,US
67/F6 **Meschede**, Ger.
79/F5 **Mescolino, Monte** (peak), It.
78/C4 **Mesco, Punta di** (pt.), It.
160/F1 **Mesgouez** (lake), Qu,Can
168/B2 **Meshomasic Saint For.**, Ct,US
81/G3 **Mesolóngion**, Gre.
142/F2 **Mesopotamia** (reg.), Arg.
93/E3 **Mesopotamia** (reg.), Iraq
80/E3 **Mesoraca**, It.
162/D3 **Mesquite**, Tx,US
124/E1 **Mesrouh** (peak), Mor.
124/F1 **Messaad**, Alg.
143/J7 **Messier** (chan.), Chile
80/D3 **Messina**, It.
80/D4 **Messina** (str.), It.
131/C4 **Messina**, SAfr.
131/D2 **Messinge** (riv.), Moz.
81/H4 **Messíni**, Gre.
81/H4 **Messini** (gulf), Gre.
70/C7 **Messkirch**, Ger.
70/B6 **Messstetten**, Ger.
53/U10 **Messy**, Fr.
83/F5 **Mesta** (riv.), Bul.
79/F2 **Mestre**, It.
130/C4 **Mesumba** (peak), Tanz.
128/C5 **Mesurado** (cape), Libr.
138/C4 **Meta** (dept.), Col.
138/D3 **Meta** (riv.), Col., Ven.
161/G1 **Métabetchouan**, Qu,Can
161/G1 **Métabetchouane** (riv.), Qu,Can
153/K2 **Meta Incognita** (pen.), NW,Can
163/F4 **Metairie**, La,US
79/D6 **Metallifere** (mts.), It.
135/D2 **Metán**, Arg.
131/D2 **Metangula**, Moz.
80/E2 **Metaponto** (ruins), It.
79/F5 **Metauro** (riv.), It.
81/G3 **Metéora**, Gre.
57/H5 **Metheringham**, Eng,UK
54/C4 **Methil**, Sc,UK
54/D2 **Methlick**, Sc,UK
81/G4 **Methóni**, Gre.
54/C4 **Methven**, Sc,UK
138/C4 **Metica** (riv.), Col.
82/C4 **Metković**, Cro.
160/B4 **Metropolis**, Il,US
161/R8 **Metro Toronto Zoo**, On,Can
69/D3 **Mettet**, Belg.
67/E4 **Mettingen**, Ger.
69/F5 **Mettlach**, Ger.
66/D6 **Mettmann**, Ger.
108/F3 **Mettupālaiyam**, India
108/F3 **Mettūr**, India
125/N6 **Metu**, Eth.
167/D2 **Metuchen**, NJ,US
69/F5 **Metz**, Fr.
70/C5 **Metzingen**, Ger.
53/S10 **Meudon**, Fr.
68/C2 **Meulebeke**, Belg.
76/C1 **Meurthe** (riv.), Fr.
69/E6 **Meurthe-et-Moselle** (dept.), Fr.
69/E3 **Meuse** (riv.), Belg., Fr.
68/E6 **Meuse** (dept.), Fr.
72/F2 **Meuse** (uplands), Fr.
69/E5 **Meuse, Cotes de** (uplands), Fr.
76/A3 **Meuzin** (riv.), Fr.
91/G8 **Mevasseret Ẕiyyon**, Isr.
57/G5 **Mexborough**, Eng,UK
162/D4 **Mexia**, Tx,US
137/J3 **Mexiana**, Braz.
145/G7 **México**
147/E5 **México** (state), Mex.
154/H6 **Mexico** (gulf), NAm
159/K3 **Mexico**, Mo,US
147/K7 **Mexico City** (cap.), Mex.
147/Q10 **Mexico City** (inset) (cap.), Mex.
93/H3 **Meybod**, Iran
112/F6 **Meycauayan**, Phil.
93/H4 **Meydān-e Gel** (lake), Iran
132/Q13 **Meyerton**, SAfr.
95/H1 **Meymaneh**, Afg.
76/C5 **Meyrin**, Swi.
76/C6 **Meythet**, Fr.
91/D4 **Meẕada, Ḥorvot** (Masada) (ruins), Isr.
83/F4 **Mezdra**, Bul.
84/J2 **Mezen'** (bay), Rus.
53/H2 **Mezen'** (riv.), Rus.
63/P4 **Mezha** (riv.), Rus.
88/J4 **Mezhdurechensk**, Rus.
88/E2 **Mezhdusharskiy** (isl.), Rus.
82/E2 **Mezoberény**, Hun.
82/E2 **Mezokovácsháza**, Hun.
82/E2 **Mezőkövesd**, Hun.
82/E2 **Mezőtúr**, Hun.
77/G5 **Mezzana, Cima** (peak), It.
130/B3 **Mfangano** (isl.), Ugan.
130/B5 **Mfrika**, Tanz.
130/C4 **Mgambo**, Tanz.
130/C4 **Mgera**, Tanz.
130/C5 **Mgeta**, Tanz.
130/B4 **Mgori**, Tanz.
54/B2 **Mhòr, Loch** (lake), Sc,UK
106/C3 **Mhow**, India
130/B3 **Mhunze**, Tanz.
103/D3 **Mi** (riv.), China
148/B2 **Miahuatlán**, Mex.
74/C3 **Miajadas**, Sp.
158/E4 **Miami**, Az,US
163/H5 **Miami**, Fl,US
159/J3 **Miami**, Ok,US
163/H5 **Miami Beach**, Fl,US
108/B2 **Miān Channūn**, Pak.
103/B4 **Mianchi**, China
93/F2 **Mīāndoāb**, Iran
133/H7 **Miandrivazo**, Madg.
93/F2 **Mīāneh**, Iran
108/B1 **Miāni**, Pak.
104/D2 **Mianmian** (mts.), China
104/D2 **Mianning**, China
167/E1 **Mianus** (riv.), Ct,US
108/A1 **Miānwāli**, Pak.
104/E2 **Mianyang**, China
104/E2 **Mianzhu**, China
103/E3 **Miaodao** (isls.), China
105/F3 **Miao'er** (peak), China
103/H6 **Miaofeng Shan** (mtn.), China
85/P5 **Miass**, Rus.
85/Q5 **Miass** (riv.), Rus.
65/J2 **Miastko**, Pol.
127/C5 **Miberika**, Sudan
156/D2 **Mica Creek**, BC,Can
65/L4 **Michalovce**, Slvk.
151/K2 **Michelson** (mtn.), Ak,US
70/C3 **Michelstadt**, Ger.
150/D3 **Miches**, DRep.
160/C3 **Michigan** (lake), Can., US
160/C2 **Michigan** (state), US
160/C3 **Michigan City**, In,US
160/C2 **Michipicoten** (isl.), On,Can
147/E5 **Michoacán** (state), Mex.
87/G1 **Michurinsk**, Rus.
57/F2 **Mickle Fell** (mtn.), Eng,UK
57/F2 **Mickleton**, Eng,UK
149/E3 **Mico** (riv.), Nic.
150/F4 **Micoud**, StL.
120/E3 **Micronesia** (reg.)
120/D4 **Micronesia, Fed. States of**
129/G2 **Midal** (well), Niger
157/H3 **Midale**, Sk,Can
66/A6 **Middelburg**, Neth.
132/D3 **Middelburg**, SAfr.
133/E2 **Middelburg**, SAfr.
64/E1 **Middelfart**, Den.
66/B5 **Middelharnis**, Neth.
68/B1 **Middelkerke**, Belg.
165/M11 **Middle** (riv.), Ca,US
167/L9 **Middle** (bay), NY,US
166/A2 **Middle** (cr.), Pa,US
158/C2 **Middle Alkali** (lake), Ca,US
107/F5 **Middle Andaman** (isl.), India
168/D2 **Middleboro**, Ma,US
168/F5 **Middleburg Heights**, Oh,US
168/A2 **Middlebury**, Ct,US
161/F2 **Middlebury**, Vt,US
150/D2 **Middle Caicos** (isl.), Trks.
162/C4 **Middle Concho** (riv.), Tx,US
57/G3 **Middleham**, Eng,UK
159/G2 **Middle Loup** (riv.), Ne,US
159/J2 **Middle Raccoon** (riv.), Ia,US
166/B5 **Middle River**, Md,US
165/F7 **Middle Rouge** (riv.), Mi,US
160/D4 **Middlesboro**, Ky,US
57/G2 **Middlesbrough**, Eng,UK
59/F4 **Middlesex** (reg.), Eng,UK
168/B2 **Middlesex** (co.), Ct,US
168/C1 **Middlesex** (co.), Ma,US
166/D2 **Middlesex**, NJ,US
166/D3 **Middlesex** (co.), NJ,US
156/C4 **Middle Sister** (peak), Or,US
57/F4 **Middleton**, Eng,UK
59/E2 **Middleton Cheney**, Eng,UK
57/F2 **Middleton-in-Teesdale**, Eng,UK
56/B3 **Middletown**, NI,UK
168/B2 **Middletown**, Ct,US
167/D3 **Middletown**, NJ,US
166/B3 **Middletown**, Pa,US
168/C2 **Middletown**, RI,US
57/F5 **Middlewich**, Eng,UK
58/C3 **Mid Glamorgan** (co.), Wal,UK
59/F5 **Midhurst**, Eng,UK
72/D5 **Midi** (can.), Fr.
72/D4 **Midi-Pyrénées** (reg.), Fr.
116/L6 **Midland**, Austl.
160/E2 **Midland**, On,Can
160/C3 **Midland**, Mi,US
162/C4 **Midland**, Tx,US
167/J8 **Midland Park**, NJ,US
131/C3 **Midlands** (prov.), Zim.
165/Q16 **Midlothian**, Il,US
114/G6 **Midona** (lake), Austl.
72/C5 **Midou** (riv.), Fr.
112/D4 **Midsayap**, Phil.
58/D4 **Midsomer Norton**, Eng,UK
107/H2 **Midu**, China
120/H2 **Midway** (isls.), PacUS
119/C4 **Midway Point-Sorell**, Austl.
159/H4 **Midwest City**, Ok,US
92/C5 **Midyan** (reg.), SAr.
92/E2 **Midyat**, Turk.
55/P12 **Mid Yell**, Sc,UK
86/B4 **Midzhur** (peak), Bul.
82/F4 **Midžor** (peak), Yugo.
98/B4 **Mie**, Japan
98/E3 **Mie** (pref.), Japan
65/H2 **Międzychód**, Pol.
65/M3 **Międzyrzec Podlaski**, Pol.
65/H2 **Międzyrzecz**, Pol.
65/L3 **Mielec**, Pol.
124/J7 **Miéle I**, Congo
83/G2 **Miercurea Ciuc**, Rom.
74/C1 **Mieres**, Sp.
73/J3 **Miesbach**, Ger.
125/P6 **Mī'ēso**, Eth.
72/E3 **Migennes**, Fr.
130/B3 **Migori**, Kenya
130/B3 **Migori** (riv.), Kenya
147/N8 **Miguel Aleman** (res.), Mex.
140/B2 **Miguel Alves**, Braz.
146/E3 **Miguel Auza**, Mex.
140/B3 **Miguel Calmon**, Braz.
147/Q10 **Miguel Hidalgo**, Mex.
146/C3 **Miguel Hidalgo** (res.), Mex.
141/B2 **Miguelópolis**, Braz.
141/K7 **Miguel Pereira**, Braz.
74/D3 **Miguelturra**, Sp.
98/D3 **Mihama**, Japan
98/C3 **Mihara**, Japan
99/G2 **Miharu**, Japan
108/H4 **Mihintale** (ruins), SrL.
95/J3 **Mihrābpur**, Pak.
75/E2 **Mijares** (riv.), Sp.
74/C4 **Mijas**, Sp.
66/B4 **Mijdrecht**, Neth.
100/B2 **Mikasa**, Japan
99/N10 **Mikawa** (bay), Japan
99/N9 **Mikawa-Mino** (mts.), Japan
130/C4 **Mikese**, Tanz.
83/F4 **Mikhaylovgrad**, Bul.
82/F4 **Mikhaylovgrad** (reg.), Bul.
87/G2 **Mikhaylovka**, Rus.
99/K10 **Miki**, Japan
130/D5 **Mikindani**, Tanz.
61/H3 **Mikkeli**, Fin.
63/L1 **Mikkeli** (prov.), Fin.
81/J4 **Míkonos** (isl.), Gre.
81/G2 **Mikri Prespa** (lake), Gre.
99/M10 **Mikuma**, Japan
130/C4 **Mikumi**, Tanz.
130/C4 **Mikumi Nat'l Park**, Tanz.
98/E2 **Mikuni**, Japan
99/F2 **Mikuni-tōge** (pass), Japan
123/V17 **Mila**, Alg.
123/U17 **Mila** (gov.), Alg.
140/C2 **Milagres**, Braz.
138/B5 **Milagro**, Ecu.
52/D4 **Milan**, It.
131/D3 **Milange**, Moz.
78/C2 **Milan** (Milano), It.
78/C2 **Milano** (prov.), It.
78/C2 **Milano** (Milan), It.
92/A2 **Milas**, Turk.
80/D3 **Milazzo**, It.
58/D5 **Milborne Port**, Eng,UK
59/G2 **Mildenhall**, Eng,UK
119/B2 **Mildura**, Austl.
104/D3 **Mile**, China
130/A5 **Milepa**, Tanz.
162/C4 **Miles**, Tx,US
157/G4 **Miles City**, Mt,US
71/G1 **Milešovka** (peak), Czh.
157/G3 **Milestone**, Sk,Can
80/D2 **Miletto** (peak), It.
71/H4 **Milevsko**, Czh.
59/F4 **Milford**, Eng,UK
56/B3 **Milford**, NI,UK
168/A3 **Milford**, Ct,US
166/C6 **Milford**, De,US
162/D2 **Milford** (lake), Ks,US
168/C1 **Milford**, Ma,US
158/D3 **Milford**, Ut,US
58/A3 **Milford Haven**, Wal,UK
58/A3 **Milford Haven** (inlet), Wal,UK
59/E5 **Milford on Sea**, Eng,UK
120/G4 **Mili** (atoll), Mrsh.
123/S15 **Miliana**, Alg.
65/J3 **Milicz**, Pol.
154/V13 **Mililani Town**, Hi,US
156/F3 **Milk** (riv.), Can., US
59/E4 **Milk** (hill), Eng,UK
156/E3 **Milk River**, Ab,Can
113/G **Mill** (isl.), Ant.
153/J2 **Mill** (isl.), NW,Can
165/G5 **Mill** (cr.), Mi,US
168/F7 **Mill** (cr.), Oh,US
168/G5 **Mill** (cr.), Oh,US
72/E4 **Millau**, Fr.
165/K11 **Millbrae**, Ca,US
117/M8 **Millbrook** (res.), Austl.
58/B6 **Millbrook**, Eng,UK
167/H9 **Millburn**, NJ,US
168/C1 **Millbury**, Ma,US
163/H3 **Milledgeville**, Ga,US
161/N6 **Mille Iles** (riv.), Qu,Can
160/B1 **Mille Lacs** (lake), On,Can
157/K4 **Mille Lacs** (lake), Mn,US
157/J4 **Miller**, SD,US
87/G2 **Millerovo**, Rus.
163/G3 **Millers Ferry** (dam), Al,US
166/B4 **Millersville**, Pa,US
56/C1 **Milleur** (pt.), Sc,UK
72/D4 **Millevaches** (plat.), Fr.
161/Q9 **Millgrove**, On,Can
161/R8 **Milliken**, On,Can
161/G2 **Millinocket**, Me,US
168/C1 **Millis**, Ma,US
56/C2 **Millisle**, NI,UK
57/E3 **Millom**, Eng,UK
54/B5 **Millport**, Sc,UK

205

Mills – Mopei

157/G5 Mills, Wy,US
167/F1 Millstone (pt.), Ct,US
166/D3 Millstone (riv.), NJ,US
116/C2 Millstream-Chichester Nat'l Park, Austl.
57/F3 Millthrop, Eng,UK
167/H10 Milltown, NJ,US
165/J11 Mill Valley, Ca,US
166/C5 Millville, NJ,US
162/E3 Millwood (lake), Ar,US
120/E5 Milne (bay), PNG
54/B5 Milngavie, Sc,UK
57/F4 Milnrow, Eng,UK
128/C4 Milo (riv.), Gui.
161/G2 Milo, Me,US
81/J4 Mílos (isl.), Gre.
147/Q10 Milpa Alta, Mex.
165/L12 Milpitas, Ca,US
70/C1 Milseburg (peak), Ger.
70/C3 Miltenberg, Ger.
161/Q8 Milton, On,Can
115/Q12 Milton, NZ
57/F2 Milton, Eng,UK
59/G4 Milton, Eng,UK
163/G4 Milton, Fl,US
168/C1 Milton, Ma,US
161/G3 Milton, NH,US
168/F5 Milton (res.), Oh,US
166/B1 Milton, Pa,US
156/D4 Milton-Freewater, Or,US
161/Q8 Milton Heights, On,Can
59/F2 Milton Keynes, Eng,UK
54/D3 Milton Ness (pt.), Sc,UK
54/B5 Milton of Campsie, Sc,UK
55/G10 Miltown Malbay, Ire.
105/G2 Miluo (riv.), China
58/C4 Milverton, Eng,UK
165/Q13 Milwaukee, Wi,US
165/Q14 Milwaukee (co.), Wi,US
70/D2 Milz (riv.), Ger.
98/B4 Mimi (riv.), Japan
72/C4 Mimizan, Fr.
100/B3 Mimmaya, Japan
104/D2 Min (riv.), China
105/H3 Min (riv.), China
123/R16 Mīna (riv.), Alg.
158/C3 Mina, Nv,US
111/F3 Minahasa (pen.), Indo.
99/M10 Minakuchi, Japan
98/B4 Minamata, Japan
99/F3 Minami-Alps Nat'l Park, Japan
99/M10 Minamichita, Japan
120/D2 Minamiiō (isl.), Japan
100/B3 Minamikayabe, Japan
120/E2 Minami-Tori-Shima (isl.), Japan
99/L10 Minamiyamashiro, Japan
149/G1 Minas, Cuba
138/B5 Minas (peak), Ecu.
143/G2 Minas, Uru.
149/F1 Minas de Matahambre, Cuba
74/B4 Minas de Riotinto, Sp.
141/H6 Minas Gerais (state), Braz.
140/B5 Minas Novas, Braz.
147/G5 Minatitlán, Mex.
104/B4 Minbu, Burma
142/C1 Mincha, Chile
108/B2 Minchinābād, Pak.
58/D3 Minchinhampton, Eng,UK
142/B4 Minchinmávida (vol.), Chile
55/H8 Minch, The (sound), Sc,UK
79/D2 Mincino (riv.), It.
112/C4 Mindanao (isl.), Phil.
112/C3 Mindanao (sea), Phil.
70/D6 Mindel (riv.), Ger.
70/D6 Mindelheim, Ger.
122/J10 Mindelo, CpV.
67/F4 Minden, Ger.
162/E3 Minden, La,US
159/H2 Minden, Ne,US
112/C2 Mindoro (isl.), Phil.
112/C2 Mindoro (str.), Phil.
60/C5 Mine Head (pt.), Ire.
58/C4 Minehead, Eng,UK
137/H7 Mineiros, Braz.
167/E2 Mineola, NY,US
147/L6 Mineral del Monte, Mex.
87/G3 Mineral'nye Vody, Rus.
162/D3 Mineral Wells, Tx,US
73/H5 Minerbio (pt.), Fr.
102/D4 Minfeng, China
103/C3 Ming (riv.), China
131/B1 Minga, Zaire
161/J1 Mingan (riv.), Qu,Can
95/K2 Mingāora, Pak.
87/H4 Mingechaur, Azer.
87/H4 Mingechaur (res.), Azer.
104/B4 Mingin, Burma
130/C5 Mingoyo, Tanz.
104/D2 Mingshan, China
97/K2 Mingshui, China
109/A1 Mingun, Ancient City of (ruins), Burma
96/E4 Minhe, China
74/B1 Minho (riv.), Sp.
116/D4 Minigwal (lake), Austl.
157/L3 Miniss (lake), On,Can
157/H2 Minitonas, Mb,Can
96/E4 Minle, China
157/K4 Minneapolis, Mn,US
157/J3 Minnedosa, Mb,Can
157/K4 Minnesota (state), US
157/K4 Minnesota (riv.), Mn,US
56/D2 Minnigaff, Sc,UK
160/B1 Minnis (lake), On,Can
160/A1 Minnitaki (lake), On,Can
99/E3 Mino, Japan
99/F3 Minobu, Japan
99/N9 Mino-Mikawa (mts.), Japan
99/L10 Mino'o, Japan
99/L10 Mino'o (riv.), Japan
75/G3 Minorca (Menorca) (isl.), Sp.
157/H3 Minot, ND,US
96/E4 Minqin, China
105/H3 Minqing, China
103/C4 Minquan, China
67/F1 Minsener Oog (isl.), Ger.
86/C1 Minsk (cap.), Bela.
65/L2 Mińsk Mazowiecki, Pol.
86/C1 Minsk Obl., Bela.
59/G4 Minster, Eng,UK
102/B4 Mintaka (pass), China
54/E1 Mintlaw, Sc,UK
161/H2 Minto, NB,Can
152/E1 Minto (inlet), NW,Can
151/L3 Minto, Yk,Can
80/C2 Minturno, It.
91/B4 Minūf, Egypt
88/K4 Minusinsk, Rus.
96/E5 Min Xian, China
91/B4 Minyā al Qamḩ, Egypt
102/E3 Miquan, China
161/K2 Miquelon, StP.
138/B4 Mira (riv.), Col., Ecu.
74/A2 Mira, Port.
74/A4 Mira (riv.), Port.
161/M6 Mirabel, Qu,Can
140/A5 Mirabela, Braz.
141/D2 Miracema, Braz.
137/J5 Miracema do Norte, Braz.
140/A2 Mirador, Braz.
142/C4 Mirador (pass), Chile
106/B4 Miraj, India
164/C2 Mira Loma, Ca,US
142/F3 Miramar, Arg.
164/C5 Miramar Nav. Air Sta., Ca,US
81/J5 Mirambéllou (gulf), Gre.
164/A2 Mira Monte, Ca,US
137/G8 Miranda (riv.), Braz.
139/E2 Miranda (state), Ven.
74/D1 Miranda de Ebro, Sp.
79/E3 Mirandola, It.
141/B2 Mirandópolis, Braz.
79/F2 Mirano, It.
141/B2 Mirante do Paranapanema, Braz.
141/B2 Mirassol, Braz.
79/F2 Mira Taglio, It.
149/E4 Miravalles (vol.), CR
74/B1 Miravalles (mtn.), Sp.
76/C1 Mirecourt, Fr.
57/G4 Mirfield, Eng,UK
86/E2 Mirgorod, Ukr.
143/G2 Mirim (lake), Braz., Uru.
140/A1 Mirinzal, Braz.
138/D5 Miritiparaná (riv.), Col.
95/H3 Mirjāveh, Iran
79/G2 Mirna (riv.), Cro.
113/G Mirnyy, Ant.
89/M3 Mirnyy, Rus.
157/H2 Mirond (lake), Sk,Can
166/D4 Mirror (lake), NH,US
81/H4 Mirtóön (sea), Gre.
101/E5 Miryang, SKor.
106/D2 Mirzāpur, India
79/G5 Misa (riv.), It.
125/M7 Misa, Zaire
127/A4 Misâha, Bîr (well), Egypt
98/D3 Misaki, Japan
147/F5 Misantla, Mex.
130/C4 Misasa, Tanz.
100/B3 Misawa, Japan
97/L2 Mishan, China
168/D2 Mishaum (pt.), Ma,US
160/C3 Mishawaka, In,US
151/F2 Misheguk (mtn.), Ak,US
99/F3 Mishima, Japan
80/C3 Misilmeri, It.
146/B2 Misión de San Fernando, Mex.
135/F2 Misiones (mts.), Arg.
149/F3 Miskitos (cay), Nic.
82/E1 Miskolc, Hun.
99/M10 Misono, Japan
111/H4 Misool (isl.), Indo.
157/L4 Misquah (hills), Mn,US
124/J1 Mişrātah, Libya
125/L1 Mişrātah (pt.), Libya
140/C2 Missão Velha, Braz.
160/D1 Missinaibi (lake), On,Can
160/D1 Missinaibi (riv.), On,Can
164/C5 Mission (bay), Ca,US
162/D5 Mission, Tx,US
164/C4 Mission Ind. Res., Ca,US
164/C3 Mission Viejo, Ca,US
157/M2 Missisa (lake), On,Can
160/E1 Missisicabi (riv.), On,Can
161/Q8 Mississauga, On,Can
116/D5 Mississippi (pt.), Austl.
155/J6 Mississippi (delta), US
155/H5 Mississippi (riv.), US
163/F3 Mississippi (state), US
120/C5 Missol (isl.), Indo.
156/E4 Missoula, Mt,US
155/G3 Missouri (riv.), US
159/J3 Missouri (state), US
162/E4 Missouri City, Tx,US
157/H3 Missouri, Coteau du (upland), Can., US
130/B3 Missungwi, Tanz.
118/B3 Mistake (cr.), Austl.
161/L2 Mistaken (pt.), Can.
161/F1 Mistassibi (riv.), Qu,Can
161/G1 Mistassibi Nord Est (riv.), Qu,Can
160/F1 Mistassini, Qu,Can
160/F1 Mistassini (lake), Qu,Can
161/F1 Mistassini (riv.), Qu,Can
65/J4 Mistelbach an der Zaya, Aus.
59/H3 Mistley, Eng,UK
81/H4 Mistrás (ruins), Gre.
80/D4 Mistretta, It.
151/M4 Misty Fjords Nat'l Mon., Ak,US
99/M10 Misugi, Japan
131/C2 Miswa, Zam.
99/H7 Mitaka, Japan
99/N9 Mitake, Japan
146/D4 Mita, Punta de (pt.), Mex.
117/M9 Mitcham, Austl.
58/D3 Mitcheldean, Eng,UK
118/A1 Mitchell (riv.), Austl.
163/H3 Mitchell (mtn.), NC,US
159/G2 Mitchell, Ne,US
157/J5 Mitchell, SD,US
118/A1 Mitchell & Alice Rivers Nat'l Park, Austl.
91/B4 Mīt Ghamr, Egypt
106/B2 Mithankot, Pak.
95/J4 Mithi, Pak.
121/K6 Mitiaro (isl.), CookIs.
81/K3 Mitilíni, Gre.
148/B2 Mitla (ruins), Mex.
91/C4 Mitla (Mamarr Mitlah) (pass), Egypt
99/G2 Mito, Japan
124/G7 Mitra (peak), EqG.
143/L8 Mitre (pen.), Arg.
53/T10 Mitry-Mory, Fr.
133/H7 Mitsinjo, Madg.
133/J6 Mitsio, Nosy (isl.), Madg.
125/N4 Mits'iwa, Erit.
99/M10 Mitsue, Japan
99/F2 Mitsukaidō, Japan
99/F2 Mitsuke, Japan
77/F3 Mittagspitze (peak), Aus.
67/F4 Mittelland (can.), Ger.
67/E3 Mittelradde (riv.), Ger.
77/H3 Mittenwald, Ger.
71/F3 Mitterteich, Ger.
71/E6 Mittlere-Isar (can.), Ger.
64/G3 Mittweida, Ger.
130/A4 Mitumba (mts.), Zaire
126/E2 Mitwaba, Zaire
99/H7 Miura, Japan
99/H7 Miura (pen.), Japan
148/D3 Mixco Viejo (ruins), Guat.
103/C4 Mi Xian, China
147/F4 Mixquiahuala, Mex.
148/B2 Mixteco (riv.), Mex.
99/M10 Miya (riv.), Japan
99/M10 Miyagawa, Japan
99/G1 Miyagi (pref.), Japan
100/B4 Miyako, Japan
100/B8 Miyako (isls.), Japan
98/B5 Miyakonojō, Japan
99/L9 Miyama, Japan
98/B5 Miyanojō, Japan
99/H6 Miyashiro, Japan
98/B5 Miyazaki, Japan
98/B4 Miyazaki (pref.), Japan
98/D3 Miyazu, Japan
107/H2 Miyi, China
98/C3 Miyoshi, Japan
97/H1 Miyun, China
103/D2 Miyun (res.), China
56/B6 Mizen Head (pt.), Ire.
83/H3 Mizil, Rom.
104/B4 Mizoram (state), India
99/E3 Mizunami, Japan
100/B4 Mizusawa, Japan
62/F2 Mjölby, Swe.
62/D2 Mjøndalen, Nor.
62/E3 Mjörn (lake), Swe.
62/D1 Mjøsa (lake), Nor.
130/B4 Mkalama, Tanz.
130/C4 Mkata, Tanz.
130/C4 Mkata (plain), Tanz.
130/C4 Mkoani, Tanz.
130/C4 Mkokotoni, Tanz.
130/C4 Mkomazi Game Rsv., Tanz.
130/A4 Mkombo (riv.), Tanz.
130/C4 Mkondoa (riv.), Tanz.
124/D1 Mkorn (peak), Mor.
130/C4 Mkumbi (pt.), Tanz.
130/C4 Mkushi, Zam.
131/C2 Mkushi (riv.), Zam.
133/F2 Mkuze (riv.), SAfr.
71/H2 Mladá Boleslav, Czh.
82/E3 Mladenovac, Yugo.
130/B4 Mlala (hills), Tanz.
65/L2 Mława, Pol.
82/C4 Mljet (isl.), Cro.
82/C4 Mljet Nat'l Park, Cro.
131/D2 Mlolo, Zam.
131/B4 Mmadinare, Bots.
131/B4 Mmamabula, Bots.
131/B5 Mmathethe, Bots.
130/D3 Mnazini, Kenya
71/H3 Mníšek, Czh.
130/B5 Mnyera (riv.), Tanz.
61/E2 Mo, Nor.
111/G5 Moa (isl.), Indo.
149/H1 Moa, Cuba
128/C5 Moa (riv.), Libr., SLeo.
130/C4 Moa, Tanz.
158/E3 Moab, Ut,US
120/H6 Moala Group (isls.), Fiji
119/C3 Moama, Austl.
131/D5 Moamba, Moz.
74/A1 Moaña, Sp.
126/B1 Moanda, Gabon
93/G3 Mobārakeh, Iran
125/K7 Mobaye, CAfr.
159/J3 Moberly, Mo,US
156/C2 Moberly Lake, BC,Can
163/F4 Mobile, Al,US
157/H4 Mobridge, SD,US
150/D3 Moca, DRep.
91/C1 Moca (peak), Turk.
138/B5 Mocache, Ecu.
137/J4 Mocajuba, Braz.
126/H4 Moçambique, Moz.
126/B4 Moçâmedes, Ang.
104/E4 Moc Chau, Viet.
144/B3 Moche (ruins), Peru
139/E2 Mochima Nat'l Park, Ven.
109/D4 Moc Hoa, Viet.
131/B5 Mochudi, Bots.
130/D5 Mocímboa da Praia, Moz.
62/E3 Möckeln (lake), Swe.
70/C4 Möckmühl, Ger.
138/B4 Mocoa, Col.
141/G6 Mococa, Braz.
126/G4 Mocuba, Moz.
106/B3 Modāsa, India
58/C6 Modbury, Eng,UK
132/D3 Modderrivier (riv.), SAfr.
79/D3 Modena, It.
79/D4 Modena (prov.), It.
73/G2 Moder (riv.), Fr., Ger.
158/B3 Modesto, Ca,US
80/D4 Modica, It.
124/H4 Modjigo (reg.), Niger
65/J4 Mödling, Aus.
82/D3 Modriča, Bosn.
109/E3 Mo Duc, Viet.
80/E2 Modugno, It.
119/C3 Moe, Austl.
132/A2 Moeb (bay), Namb.
72/B3 Moëlan-sur-Mer, Fr.
57/E5 Moel Fammau (mtn.), Wal,UK
57/E6 Moel Fferna (mtn.), Wal,UK
58/C1 Moelfre (mtn.), UK
58/C2 Moel Hywel (mtn.), Wal,UK
57/E6 Moel Sych (mtn.), Wal,UK
58/C2 Moel y Llyn (mtn.), UK
120/E4 Moen, Micr.
158/E3 Moenkopi (dry riv.), Az,US
121/K7 Moerai, FrPol.
66/D6 Moers, Ger.
68/C1 Moervaart (can.), Belg.
77/F5 Moesa (riv.), Swi.
54/C6 Moffat, Sc,UK
165/K12 Moffett Field Nav. Air Sta., Ca,US
108/C2 Moga, India
125/Q7 Mogadishu (cap.), Som.
100/B4 Mogami, Japan
99/G2 Mogami (riv.), Japan
131/B4 Mogapinyana, Bots.
75/L6 Mogent (riv.), Sp.
141/G8 Mogi das Cruzes, Braz.
141/G7 Mogi-Guaçu, Braz.
86/D1 Mogilëv, Bela.
86/D1 Mogilëv Obl., Bela.
86/C2 Mogilev-Podol'skiy, Ukr.
65/J2 Mogilno, Pol.
141/F7 Mogi-Mirim, Braz.
79/F1 Mogliano Veneto, It.
97/H1 Mogocha, Rus.
104/C4 Mogok, Burma
131/B4 Mogolrivier (riv.), SAfr.
143/F3 Mogotes (pt.), Arg.
130/B3 Mogotio, Kenya
148/E3 Mogotón (peak), Nic.
74/B4 Moguer, Sp.
82/D3 Mohács, Hun.
157/H3 Mohall, ND,US
123/N13 Mohamed V (dam), Mor.
123/N13 Mohamed V (res.), Mor.
123/R16 Mohammadia, Alg.
123/L14 Mohammedia, Mor.
166/D1 Mohawk (lake), NJ,US
160/F3 Mohawk (riv.), NY,US
168/F6 Mohawk (lake), Oh,US
133/G6 Mohéli (isl.), Com.
126/D4 Mohembo, Bots.
60/A4 Moher, Cliffs of, Ire.
151/E3 Mohican (cape), Ak,US
168/E7 Mohican (riv.), Oh,US
168/E6 Mohican State Pk., Oh,US
76/D2 Möhlin, Swi.
67/F6 Möhne (riv.), Ger.
67/F6 Möhnestausee (res.), Ger.
130/C5 Mohoro, Tanz.
83/H2 Moineşti, Rom.
102/A3 Moinkum (des.), Kaz.
129/E5 Moinsi (hills), Gha.
160/E2 Moira (riv.), On,Can
72/F4 Moirans, Fr.
153/K3 Moisie (riv.), Qu,Can
72/D4 Moissac, Fr.
75/Q10 Moita, Port.
158/C4 Mojave (des.), Ca,US
158/C4 Mojave (dry riv.), Ca,US
104/D4 Mojiang Hanizu Zizhixian, China
141/G7 Moji-Guaçu (riv.), Braz.
157/L3 Mojikit (lake), On,Can
136/E6 Mojos (plain), Bol.
137/J4 Moju (riv.), Braz.
99/F2 Mōka, Japan
154/W13 Mokapu (pt.), Hi,US
165/M11 Mokelumne (aqueduct), Ca,US
158/B3 Mokelumne (riv.), Ca,US
165/Q16 Mokena, Il,US
120/F4 Mokil (atoll), Micr.
109/B3 Mokochu (peak), Thai.
104/B3 Mokokchūng, India
124/H5 Mokolo, Camr.
101/D5 Mokp'o, SKor.
82/E3 Mokrin, Yugo.
87/G1 Moksha (riv.), Rus.
69/E1 Mol, Belg.
82/E3 Mol, Yugo.
80/E2 Mola di Bari, It.
148/E1 Molas (pt.), Mex.
82/B3 Molat (isl.), Cro.
74/E3 Molatón (mtn.), Sp.
57/E5 Mold, Wal,UK
83/H2 Moldavia (reg.), Rom.
83/G2 Moldavian Carpathians (range), Rom.
61/C3 Molde, Nor.
86/C3 Moldova
83/H2 Moldova (riv.), Rom.
82/E3 Moldova Nouă, Rom.
83/G3 Moldoveanu (peak), Rom.
53/M7 Mole (riv.), Eng,UK
149/H2 Môle, Cap du (cape), Haiti
129/E4 Mole Game Rsv., Gha.
131/B5 Molepolole, Bots.
80/E2 Molfetta, It.
103/F2 Molihong Shan (peak), China
142/C2 Molina, Chile
74/E3 Molina de Segura, Sp.
160/B3 Moline, Il,US
79/E3 Molinella, It.
147/L7 Molino de Flores Nat'l Park, Mex.
130/A5 Moliro, Zaire
80/D2 Molise (reg.), It.
73/K3 Möll (riv.), Aus.
61/D5 Møllebjerg (peak), Den.
144/C5 Mollendo, Peru
76/C4 Mollendruz, Col du (pass), Swi.
75/F2 Mollerussa, Sp.
142/C2 Molles (pt.), Chile
75/L6 Mollet del Vallès, Sp.
75/L7 Mollins de Rei, Sp.
64/F2 Mölln, Ger.
62/E3 Mölndal, Swe.
62/E3 Mölnlycke, Swe.
130/B3 Molo, Kenya
63/M4 Molodechno, Bela.
113/D Molodezhnaya, Ant.
84/H4 Mologa (riv.), Rus.
154/T10 Molokai (isl.), Hi,US
85/L4 Moloma (riv.), Rus.
132/C2 Molopo (dry riv.), Bots.
132/C2 Moloporivier (dry riv.), SAfr.
124/J7 Moloundou, Camr.
76/D1 Molsheim, Fr.
157/J2 Molson (lake), Mb,Can
111/H5 Molu (isl.), Indo.
111/G4 Molucca (sea), Indo.
111/G3 Moluccas (isls.), Indo.
77/G5 Molveno (lake), It.
140/C2 Mombaça, Braz.
130/C4 Mombasa, Kenya
100/C1 Mombetsu, Japan
100/C2 Mombetsu, Japan
130/C4 Mombo, Tanz.
70/C2 Mömbris, Ger.
83/G5 Momchilgrad, Bul.
111/H4 Momfafa (cape), Indo.
100/B3 Momoishi, Japan
138/C2 Mompós, Col.
104/B4 Mon (riv.), Burma
104/C5 Mon (state), Burma
62/E4 Møn (isl.), Den.
150/D3 Mona (passg.), NAm.
150/E3 Mona (isl.), PR
168/G6 Monaca, Pa,US
73/G5 Monaco
73/G5 Monaco (cap.), Mona.
54/B2 Monadhliath (mts.), Sc,UK
139/F2 Monagas (state), Ven.
60/D1 Monaghan, Ire.
60/D1 Monaghan (co.), Ire.
149/F5 Monagrillo, Pan.
149/F4 Monagrillo (ruins), Pan.
162/C4 Monahans, Tx,US
54/A2 Monar, Loch (lake), Sc,UK
156/D3 Monashee (mts.), BC,Can
118/H8 Mona Vale, Austl.
75/E3 Moncada, Sp.
78/A3 Moncalieri, It.
74/D2 Moncayo (range), Sp.
76/E4 Mönch (peak), Swi.
84/G2 Monchegorsk, Rus.
66/D6 Mönchengladbach, Ger.
74/A4 Monchique, Port.
74/A4 Monchique (range), Port.
163/H3 Moncks Corner, SC,US
161/H2 Moncton, NB,Can
74/A2 Mondego (cape), Port.
74/A2 Mondego (riv.), Port.
130/B4 Mondo, Tanz.
74/B1 Mondoñedo, Sp.
69/F5 Mondorf-les-Bains, Lux.
78/A4 Mondovi, It.
74/D1 Mondragón, Sp.
80/C2 Mondragone, It.
71/G7 Mondsee (lake), Aus.
130/C3 Monduli, Tanz.
74/B3 Monesterio, Sp.
159/J3 Monett, Mo,US
56/C2 Money Head (pt.), Sc,UK
56/B2 Moneymore, NI,UK
56/C2 Moneyreagh, NI,UK
79/G1 Monfalcone, It.
78/B3 Monferrato (reg.), It.
74/B1 Monforte, Sp.
130/C5 Monga, Tanz.
141/G9 Mongaguá, Braz.
109/D1 Mong Cai, Viet.
116/C4 Mongers (lake), Austl.
106/E2 Monghyr, India
125/J5 Mongo, Chad
128/C4 Mongo (riv.), Gui., SLeo.
96/D2 Mongolia
125/K5 Mongororo, Chad
126/B1 Mongoungou, Gabon
131/A2 Mongu, Zam.
66/D6 Monheim, Ger.
102/F2 Mönh Hayrhan Uul (peak), Mong.
96/E1 Mönh Sarĭdag (peak), Mong.
56/E1 Moniaive, Sc,UK
130/A2 Monietu, Zaire
54/D4 Monifieth, Sc,UK
75/K6 Monistrol de Montserrat, Sp.
158/C3 Monitor (range), Nv,US
112/D4 Monkayo, Phil.
131/D2 Monkey Bay, Malw.
116/B3 Monkey Mia, Austl.
65/M2 Mońki, Pol.
126/D1 Monkoto, Zaire
166/B5 Monks (isl.), Md,US
58/D3 Monmouth, Eng,UK
160/B3 Monmouth, Il,US
167/D3 Monmouth (co.), NJ,US
156/C4 Monmouth, Or,US
58/D2 Monmow (riv.), UK
66/C4 Monnickendam, Neth.
129/F5 Mono (prov.), Ben.
129/F5 Mono (riv.), Ben., Togo
149/F4 Mono (pt.), Nic.
164/A1 Mono (cr.), Ca,US
158/C3 Mono (lake), Ca,US
166/A4 Monocacy (riv.), Md, Pa,US
82/E2 Monopoli, It.
82/D2 Monor, Hun.
161/G8 Mono Road, On,Can
75/E3 Monóvar, Sp.
80/C3 Monreale, It.
168/A3 Monroe, Ct,US
163/H3 Monroe, Ga,US
162/E3 Monroe, La,US
160/D3 Monroe, Mi,US
165/E7 Monroe (co.), Mi,US
163/H3 Monroe, NC,US
167/D1 Monroe, NY,US
166/C1 Monroe (co.), Pa,US
158/D3 Monroe, Ut,US
160/B3 Monroe, Wi,US
163/G4 Monroeville, Al,US
168/H7 Monroeville, Pa,US
128/C5 Monrovia (cap.), Libr.
164/C2 Monrovia, Ca,US
68/C3 Mons, Belg.
69/F2 Monschau, Ger.
144/B2 Monsefú, Peru
79/E2 Monselice, It.
140/B2 Monsenhor Hipólito, Braz.
140/B2 Monsenhor Tabosa, Braz.
167/D1 Monsey, NY,US
168/B1 Monson, Ma,US
66/B4 Monster, Neth.
62/G3 Mönsteras, Swe.
79/D5 Monsummano Terme, It.
70/A2 Montabaur, Ger.
77/F3 Montafon (val.), Aus.
79/E2 Montagnana, It.
133/J6 Montagne d'Ambre Nat'l Park, Madg.
53/U9 Montagny-Sainte-Félicité, Fr.
161/J2 Montague, PE,Can
151/L3 Montague, Yk,Can
151/J4 Montague (isl.), Ak,US
151/J4 Montague (str.), Ak,US
162/D3 Montague, Tx,US
80/E2 Montalbano Jonico, It.
156/F4 Montana (state), US
144/C3 Montaña, La (reg.), Peru
141/D1 Montanha, Braz.
72/E3 Montargis, Fr.
68/B5 Montataire, Fr.
72/D4 Montauban, Fr.
75/F1 Montaud, Pic de (peak), Fr.
167/G1 Montauk (pt.), NY,US
126/E6 Mont aux Sources (peak), Les.
72/F3 Montbard, Fr.
76/C2 Montbéliard, Fr.
75/L7 Montcada i Reixac, Sp.
72/F3 Montceau-les-Mines, Fr.
164/C2 Montclair, Ca,US
167/J8 Montclair, NJ,US
72/C5 Mont-de-Marsan, Fr.
68/B4 Montdidier, Fr.
148/B2 Monte Albán (ruins), Mex.
139/H5 Monte Alegre, Braz.
140/D2 Monte Alegre, Braz.
141/B1 Monte Alegre de Minas, Braz.
140/A3 Monte Alegre do Piauí, Braz.
141/B2 Monte Alto, Braz.
140/B4 Monte Azul, Braz.
116/B2 Montebello (isls.), Austl.
164/B2 Montebello, Ca,US
79/F1 Montebelluna, It.
135/F2 Montecarlo, Arg.
141/C1 Monte Carmelo, Braz.
138/D2 Monte Carmelo, Ven.
135/E3 Monte Caseros, Arg.
79/D5 Montecatini Terme, It.
150/D3 Monte Cristi, DRep.
80/B1 Montecristo (isl.), It.
148/D3 Montecristo Nat'l Park, ESal.
148/E3 Monte el Chile (mtn.), Hon.
79/F5 Montefeltro (reg.), It.
74/C4 Montefrío, Sp.
149/G2 Montego Bay, Jam.
79/E2 Montegrotto Terme, It.
140/C2 Monteiro, Braz.
75/P10 Montelavar, Port.
72/F4 Montélimar, Fr.
74/C4 Montellano, Sp.
158/D2 Montello, Nv,US
79/E5 Montelupo Fiorentino, It.
142/D5 Montemayor (plat.), Arg.
147/F3 Montemorelos, Mex.
74/A3 Montemor-o-Novo, Port.
74/A2 Montemuro (mtn.), Port.
141/B4 Montenegro, Braz.
82/D4 Montenegro (rep.), Yugo.
80/D2 Montenero di Bisaccia, It.
64/B5 Montenoison, Butte de (mtn.), Fr.
140/C5 Monte Pascoal Nat'l Park, Braz.
150/D3 Monte Plata, DRep.
72/E2 Montereau-faut-Yonne, Fr.
158/B3 Monterey, Ca,US
158/B3 Monterey (bay), Ca,US
164/B2 Monterey Park, Ca,US
138/C2 Montería, Col.
136/F7 Montero, Bol.
135/C2 Monteros, Arg.
76/D6 Monte Rosa (mtn.), It., Swi.
77/G4 Monterosso (peak), It.
80/C1 Monterotondo, It.
147/E3 Monterrey, Mex.
143/K7 Montes (pt.), Arg.
140/A2 Montes Altos, Braz.
80/D2 Monte Sant'Angelo, It.
80/E2 Montescaglioso, It.
140/B5 Montes Claros, Braz.
80/D1 Montesilvano Marina, It.
53/S10 Montesson, Fr.
72/F4 Monteux, Fr.
79/E5 Montevarchi, It.
143/F2 Montevideo (cap.), Uru.
143/T12 Montevideo (dept.), Uru.
157/K4 Montevideo, Mn,US
53/U10 Montévrain, Fr.
165/L10 Montezuma (slough), Ca,US
69/E5 Montfaucon, Fr.
53/T10 Montfermeil, Fr.
66/B4 Montfoort, Neth.
53/T10 Montgeron, Fr.
58/C1 Montgomery, Wal,UK
163/G3 Montgomery (cap.), Al,US
166/A5 Montgomery (co.), Md,US
166/C3 Montgomery (co.), Pa,US
168/G6 Montgomery (dam), Pa,US
160/D4 Montgomery, WV,US
166/A5 Montgomery Village, Md,US
166/C3 Montgomeryville, Pa,US
72/E5 Montgrand (mtn.), Fr.
76/C5 Monthey, Swi.
53/U9 Monthyon, Fr.
162/F3 Monticello, Ar,US
165/K9 Monticello (dam), Ca,US
163/H4 Monticello, Fl,US
160/C3 Monticello, In,US
160/C4 Monticello, Ky,US
159/K2 Monticello, Mo,US
158/E3 Monticello, Ut,US
160/E4 Monticello, Va,US
78/D2 Montichiari, It.
68/B3 Montigny-en-Gohelle, Fr.
53/S10 Montigny-le-Bretonneux, Fr.
53/S10 Montigny-lès-Cormeilles, Fr.
69/F5 Montigny-lès-Metz, Fr.
68/D3 Montigny-le-Tilleul, Belg.
74/A3 Montijo, Port.
74/B3 Montijo, Sp.
74/C4 Montilla, Sp.
72/D2 Montivilliers, Fr.
161/G1 Mont-Joli, Qu,Can
160/F2 Mont-Laurier, Qu,Can
53/S11 Montlhéry, Fr.
72/E3 Montluçon, Fr.
161/G2 Montmagny, Qu,Can
53/S10 Montmorency, Fr.
72/D3 Montmorillon, Fr.
79/F4 Montone (riv.), It.
74/C3 Montoro, Sp.
166/B1 Montour (co.), Pa,US
166/B2 Montour (ridge), Pa,US
128/D5 Mont Peko Nat'l Park, IvC.
149/G2 Montpelier, Jam.
156/F5 Montpelier, Id,US
161/F2 Montpelier (cap.), Vt,US
72/E5 Montpellier, Fr.
160/C2 Montreal (riv.), On,Can
161/N7 Montréal, Qu,Can
157/G2 Montreal (lake), Sk,Can
157/G2 Montreal Lake, Sk,Can
161/N6 Montréal-Nord, Qu,Can
68/A3 Montreuil, Fr.
76/C5 Montreux, Swi.
54/D3 Montrose, Sc,UK
158/F3 Montrose, Co,US
54/D3 Montrose Basin (lag.), Sc,UK
164/B2 Montrose-La Crescenta, Ca,US
53/S10 Montrouge, Fr.
161/N6 Mont-Royal, Qu,Can
53/U10 Montry, Fr.
161/P6 Mont-Saint-Hilaire, Qu,Can
69/E4 Mont-Saint-Martin, Fr.
160/F2 Mont-Saint-Michel, Qu,Can
72/C2 Mont-Saint-Michel, Fr.
72/C2 Mont-Saint-Michel (bay), Fr.
128/D4 Mont Sangbé Nat'l Park, IvC.
75/L6 Montseny Nat'l Park, Sp.
128/C5 Montserrado (co.), Libr.
75/F2 Montserrat (mtn.), Sp.
150/F3 Montserrat (isl.), UK
53/S9 Montsoult, Fr.
167/J7 Montvale, NJ,US
166/D2 Montville, NJ,US
159/G4 Monument Draw (cr.), NM, Tx,US
104/B4 Monywa, Burma
78/C1 Monza, It.
131/B3 Monze, Zam.
75/F2 Monzón, Sp.
131/B4 Mookane, Bots.
132/P13 Mool (riv.), SAfr.
118/D4 Mooloolaba-Maroochydore, Austl.
119/G5 Moorabbin, Austl.
157/G4 Moorcroft, Wy,US
116/C4 Moore (lake), Austl.
161/R8 Moore (pt.), On,Can
159/H4 Moore, Ok,US
121/K6 Moorea (isl.), FrPol.
163/H5 Moore Haven, Fl,US
116/B4 Moore River Nat'l Park, Austl.
150/B1 Moore's (isl.), Bahm.
166/D4 Moorestown, NJ,US
163/H3 Mooresville, NC,US
54/C5 Moorfoot (hills), Sc,UK
157/J4 Moorhead, Mn,US
164/B2 Moorpark, Ca,US
68/C2 Moorslede, Belg.
71/E6 Moosburg, Ger.
160/D1 Moose (riv.), On,Can
157/H3 Moose (mtn.), Sk,Can
160/D1 Moose Factory, On,Can
161/G2 Moosehead (lake), Me,US
151/H3 Mooseheart (mtn.), Ak,US
157/G3 Moose Jaw, Sk,Can
157/H3 Moosomin, Sk,Can
160/D1 Moosonee, On,Can
131/D3 Mopeia, Moz.

131/B4 **Mopipi,** Bots.
128/D3 **Mopti,** Mali
128/E3 **Mopti** (reg.), Mali
144/D5 **Moquegua,** Peru
144/D4 **Moquegua-Tacna-Puno** (reg.), Peru
82/D2 **Mór,** Hun.
124/H5 **Mora,** Camr.
74/D3 **Mora,** Sp.
62/F1 **Mora,** Swe.
159/F4 **Mora,** NM,US
159/F4 **Mora** (riv.), NM,US
81/F1 **Morača** (riv.), Yugo.
106/C2 **Morādābād,** India
140/C2 **Morada Nova,** Braz.
141/C1 **Morada Nova de Mina,** Braz.
142/C2 **Morado Nat'l Park,** Chile
133/H7 **Morafenobe,** Madg.
65/K2 **Morąg,** Pol.
165/K11 **Moraga,** Ca,US
168/H6 **Moraine Saint Pk.,** Pa,US
53/R10 **Morainvilliers,** Fr.
142/B5 **Moraleda** (chan.), Chile
74/B2 **Moraleja,** Sp.
148/D3 **Morales,** Guat.
133/J7 **Moramanga,** Madg.
158/E2 **Moran,** Wy,US
118/C3 **Moranbah,** Austl.
121/M7 **Morane** (isl.), FrPol.
53/T10 **Morangis,** Fr.
149/G2 **Morant Bay,** Jam.
55/J8 **Morar, Loch** (lake), Sc,UK
76/D4 **Morat** (lake), Swi.
74/E3 **Moratalla,** Sp.
65/J4 **Morava** (riv.), Czh.
81/G1 **Morava** (riv.), Yugo.
65/J4 **Moravia** (reg.), Czh.
65/J4 **Moravská Třebová,** Czh.
65/H4 **Moravské Budějovice,** Czh.
136/G2 **Morawhanna,** Guy.
54/C1 **Moray** (firth), Sc,UK
69/G4 **Morbach,** Ger.
68/B2 **Morbecque,** Fr.
77/F5 **Morbegno,** It.
62/G3 **Mörbylanga,** Swe.
76/C5 **Morclan, Pic de** (mtn.), Fr.
76/C5 **Morclan, Pic de** (peak), Fr.
157/J3 **Morden,** Mb,Can
53/N7 **Morden,** Eng,UK
119/G6 **Mordialloc,** Austl.
87/G1 **Mordvian Aut. Rep.,** Rus.
157/H4 **Moreau** (riv.), SD,US
54/D5 **Morebattle,** Sc,UK
57/F3 **Morecambe,** Eng,UK
57/E3 **Morecambe** (bay), Eng,UK
119/D1 **Moree,** Austl.
160/D4 **Morehead,** Ky,US
163/J3 **Morehead City,** NC,US
147/E5 **Morelia,** Mex.
148/B2 **Morelos** (state), Mex.
131/A3 **Moremi Wild. Rsv.,** Bots.
106/C2 **Morena,** India
74/C3 **Morena** (range), Sp.
83/G3 **Moreni,** Rom.
164/C3 **Moreno Valley,** Ca,US
61/C3 **Møre og Romsdal** (co.), Nor.
152/C3 **Moresby** (isl.), BC,Can
118/F6 **Moreton** (bay), Austl.
118/D4 **Moreton** (cape), Austl.
118/D4 **Moreton** (isl.), Austl.
53/P6 **Moreton,** Eng,UK
58/C5 **Moretonhampstead,** Eng,UK
118/D4 **Moreton I. Nat'l Park,** Austl.
59/E3 **Moreton in Marsh,** Eng,UK
85/N2 **Moreyu** (riv.), Rus.
76/C4 **Morez,** Fr.
167/F1 **Morgan** (pt.), Ct,US
163/F4 **Morgan City,** La,US
160/C4 **Morganfield,** Ky,US
80/D4 **Morgantina** (ruins), It.
163/H3 **Morganton,** NC,US
160/C4 **Morgantown,** Ky,US
160/E4 **Morgantown,** WV,US
72/E3 **Morge** (riv.), Fr.
76/C4 **Morges,** Swi.
95/H1 **Morghāb** (riv.), Afg.
76/C5 **Morgins, Pas de** (pass), Fr., Swi.
142/B3 **Morguilla** (pt.), Chile
96/C3 **Mori,** China
79/D1 **Mori,** It.
100/B2 **Mori,** Japan
117/M8 **Morialta Consv. Park,** Austl.
159/F4 **Moriarty,** NM,US
156/B2 **Morice** (lake), BC,Can
54/B1 **Morie, Loch** (lake), Sc,UK
99/L10 **Moriguchi,** Japan
102/F3 **Mori Kazak Zizhixian** (Mori), China
97/J2 **Morin Dawa,** China
67/G5 **Moringen,** Ger.
156/E2 **Morinville,** Ab,Can
100/B4 **Morioka,** Japan
54/B2 **Moriston** (riv.), Sc,UK
99/H7 **Moriya,** Japan
98/D3 **Moriyama,** Japan
72/B2 **Morlaix,** Fr.
68/D3 **Morlanwelz,** Belg.
70/B3 **Mörlenbach,** Ger.
57/G4 **Morley,** Eng,UK
54/D1 **Mormond** (hill), Sc,UK
106/B4 **Mormugao,** India
118/F6 **Morningside,** Austl.
60/B5 **Morningstar** (riv.), Ire.
114/F3 **Mornington** (isl.), Austl.
143/J7 **Mornington** (isl.), Chile
95/J3 **Moro,** Pak.
123/M13 **Morocco**
144/B3 **Morococha,** Peru
130/C4 **Morogoro,** Tanz.
130/C4 **Morogoro** (prov.), Tanz.
119/C3 **Moroka-Wonnangatta Nat'l Park,** Austl.
147/E4 **Moroleón,** Mex.
133/G8 **Morombe,** Madg.
142/F2 **Morón,** Arg.
149/G1 **Morón,** Cuba
96/E2 **Mörön,** Mong.
138/D2 **Morón,** Ven.
144/B1 **Morona** (riv.), Ecu., Peru
138/B5 **Morona-Santiago** (prov.), Ecu.
133/H8 **Morondara** (riv.), Madg.
133/H8 **Morondava,** Madg.
74/C4 **Morón de la Frontera,** Sp.
133/G5 **Moroni** (cap.), Com.
111/G3 **Morotai** (isl.), Indo.
111/G3 **Morotai** (str.), Indo.
130/B2 **Moroto,** Ugan.
130/B2 **Moroto** (peak), Ugan.
99/H7 **Moroyama,** Japan
87/G2 **Morozovsk,** Rus.
140/B3 **Morpará,** Braz.
57/G1 **Morpeth,** Eng,UK
91/C2 **Morphou,** Cyp.
91/C2 **Morphou** (bay), Cyp.
66/C3 **Morra** (lake), Neth.
159/G2 **Morrill,** Ne,US
140/B1 **Morrinhos,** Braz.
141/B1 **Morrinhos,** Braz.
117/F3 **Morris** (peak), Austl.
157/J3 **Morris,** Mb,Can
164/C2 **Morris** (res.), Ca,US
160/B3 **Morris,** Il,US
157/K4 **Morris,** Mn,US
166/D2 **Morris** (co.), NJ,US
145/P1 **Morris Jesup** (cape), Grld.
58/C3 **Morriston,** Wal,UK
166/D2 **Morristown,** NJ,US
163/H2 **Morristown,** Tn,US
166/D2 **Morristown Nat'l Mil. Park,** NJ,US
166/D3 **Morrisville,** Pa,US
118/A2 **Morr Morr Abor. Land,** Austl.
158/B4 **Morro Bay,** Ca,US
138/D2 **Morrocoy Nat'l Park,** Ven.
126/C3 **Morro de Môco** (peak), Ang.
149/F5 **Morro de Puercos** (pt.), Pan.
141/B3 **Morro do Capão Doce** (hill), Braz.
140/B3 **Morro do Chapéu,** Braz.
144/B2 **Morropón,** Peru
147/F5 **Morro, Punta del** (pt.), Mex.
140/A1 **Morros,** Braz.
149/G4 **Morrosquillo** (gulf), Col.
131/D3 **Morrumbala,** Moz.
131/D4 **Morrumbene,** Moz.
62/C3 **Mørs** (isl.), Den.
53/T11 **Morsang-sur-Orge,** Fr.
69/G2 **Morsbach,** Ger.
87/G1 **Morshansk,** Rus.
87/J3 **Morskoy** (isl.), Kaz.
76/C1 **Mortagne** (riv.), Fr.
78/B2 **Mortara,** It.
76/B3 **Morte** (riv.), Fr.
58/B4 **Morte** (pt.), UK
76/C3 **Morteau,** Fr.
137/H6 **Mortes** (riv.), Braz.
59/E4 **Mortimer,** Eng,UK
58/D2 **Mortimers Cross,** Eng,UK
160/B3 **Morton,** Il,US
165/Q15 **Morton Grove,** Il,US
119/D2 **Morton Nat'l Park,** Austl.
167/F1 **Morton Nat'l Wild. Ref.,** NY,US
68/D1 **Mortsel,** Belg.
141/G7 **Morungaba,** Braz.
72/E3 **Morvan** (plat.), Fr.
54/C2 **Morven** (mtn.), Sc,UK
106/B3 **Morvi,** India
119/C3 **Morwell,** Austl.
74/A1 **Mos,** Sp.
70/C4 **Mosbach,** Ger.
75/P10 **Moscavide,** Port.
84/G5 **Moscow** (upland), Rus.
156/D4 **Moscow,** Id,US
84/H5 **Moscow** (Moskva) (cap.), Rus.
85/X9 **Moscow** (Moskva) (inset) (cap.), Rus.
84/H5 **Moscow Obl.,** Rus.
113/H **Moscow Univ. Ice Shelf,** Ant.
69/F4 **Mosel** (riv.), Ger.
131/B5 **Moselebe** (dry riv.), Bots.
68/F5 **Moselle** (dept.), Fr.
69/F5 **Moselle** (riv.), Fr.
76/C2 **Moselotte** (riv.), Fr.
156/D4 **Moses Lake,** Wa,US
131/B4 **Mosetse,** Bots.
115/R12 **Mosgiel,** NZ
132/C2 **Moshaweng** (dry riv.), SAfr.
63/M2 **Moshchnyy** (isl.), Rus.
130/C3 **Moshi,** Tanz.
131/B5 **Moshupa,** Bots.
65/J2 **Mosina,** Pol.
131/B3 **Mosi-oa-Tunya Nat'l Park,** Zam.
131/B3 **Mosi-oa-Tunya** (Victoria) (falls), Zam.
61/E2 **Mosjøen,** Nor.
84/G5 **Moskva** (riv.), Rus.
84/H5 **Moskva** (Moscow) (cap.), Rus.
85/X9 **Moskva** (Moscow) (inset) (cap.), Rus.
131/B5 **Mosomane,** Bots.
82/C2 **Mosonmagyaróvár,** Hun.
159/G4 **Mosquero,** NM,US
149/E3 **Mosquitia** (reg.), Hon.
149/G4 **Mosquito** (pt.), Pan.
168/G5 **Mosquito Creek** (res.), Oh,US
149/F4 **Mosquitos** (gulf), Pan.
149/E4 **Mosquitos, Costa de** (reg.), Nic.
62/D2 **Moss,** Nor.
76/D5 **Mosses, Col des** (pass), Swi.
128/E4 **Mossi Highlands** (upland), Burk.
70/C6 **Mössingen,** Ger.
57/F4 **Mossley,** Eng,UK
56/C2 **Mossley,** NI,UK
140/C2 **Mossoró,** Braz.
163/F4 **Moss Point,** Ms,US
56/B1 **Moss-side,** NI,UK
71/G1 **Most,** Czh.
123/R16 **Mostaganem,** Alg.
123/R15 **Mostaganem** (wilaya), Alg.
82/C4 **Mostar,** Bosn.
141/B4 **Mostardas,** Braz.
74/D2 **Móstoles,** Sp.
57/E5 **Mostyn,** Wal,UK
93/E2 **Mosul** (Al Mawşil), Iraq
62/B2 **Møsvatnet** (lake), Nor.
148/D3 **Motagua** (riv.), Guat.
62/F2 **Motala,** Swe.
148/D2 **Mother** (pt.), Belz.
54/C5 **Motherwell,** Sc,UK
101/B2 **Motian** (mtn.), China
103/E2 **Motian Ling** (mtn.), China
106/D2 **Motīhāri,** India
131/B4 **Motloutse,** Bots.
131/B4 **Motloutse** (riv.), Bots.
130/A2 **Moto,** Zaire
100/J7 **Motobu,** Japan
131/A5 **Motokwe,** Bots.
99/G2 **Motomiya,** Japan
99/J7 **Motono,** Japan
61/K1 **Motovskiy** (gulf), Rus.
79/G2 **Motovun,** Cro.
100/B4 **Motoyoshi,** Japan
74/D4 **Motril,** Sp.
100/A2 **Motsuta-misaki** (cape), Japan
157/H4 **Mott,** ND,US
78/B1 **Mottarone** (peak), It.
115/R11 **Motueka,** NZ
147/H4 **Motul de Felipe Carrillo Puerto,** Mex.
88/K4 **Motygino,** Rus.
149/J1 **Mouchoir** (passg.), Trks.
128/B2 **Mougris** (well), Mrta.
128/E3 **Mouhoun** (prov.), Burk.
126/B1 **Mouila,** Gabon
124/H4 **Moul** (well), Niger
119/C2 **Moulamein** (riv.), Austl.
57/F5 **Mouldsworth,** Eng,UK
72/E3 **Moulins,** Fr.
104/C5 **Moulmein,** Burma
123/N13 **Moulouya** (riv.), Mor.
59/G2 **Moulton,** Eng,UK
163/H4 **Moultrie,** Ga,US
163/H3 **Moultrie** (lake), SC,US
159/J3 **Mound City,** Ks,US
124/J6 **Moundou,** Chad
160/D4 **Moundsville,** WV,US
109/C3 **Moung Roessei,** Camb.
109/D3 **Mounlapamok,** Laos
75/E1 **Moun Né** (mtn.), Fr.
118/B3 **Mount Aberdeen Nat'l Park,** Austl.
106/B3 **Mount Abu,** India
152/D2 **Mountain** (riv.), NW,Can
166/A3 **Mountain** (cr.), Pa,US
58/C3 **Mountain Ash,** Wal,UK
163/G3 **Mountain Brook,** Al,US
159/J3 **Mountain Grove,** Mo,US
162/E2 **Mountain Home,** Ar,US
156/E5 **Mountain Home,** Id,US
167/H9 **Mountainside,** NJ,US
162/E3 **Mountain View,** Ar,US
165/K12 **Mountain View,** Ca,US
132/D4 **Mountain Zebra Nat'l Park,** SAfr.
163/H2 **Mount Airy,** NC,US
117/G2 **Mount Allan Abor. Land,** Austl.
112/D4 **Mount Apo Nat'l Park,** Phil.
112/C2 **Mount Arayat Nat'l Park,** Phil.
165/D3 **Mount Baker-Snoqualmie Nat'l For.,** Wa,US
117/M9 **Mount Barker,** Austl.
117/G2 **Mount Barkly Abor. Land,** Austl.
118/C5 **Mount Barney Nat'l Park,** Austl.
117/M9 **Mount Bold** (res.), Austl.
119/C3 **Mount Buffalo Nat'l Park,** Austl.
160/C4 **Mount Carmel,** Il,US
166/B2 **Mount Carmel,** Pa,US
125/M2 **Mount Catherine** (peak), Egypt
165/G6 **Mount Clemens,** Mi,US
118/E6 **Mount Coot'tha,** Austl.
126/F4 **Mount Darwin,** Zim.
165/L11 **Mount Diablo Saint Park,** Ca,US
119/B3 **Mount Eccles Nat'l Park,** Austl.
130/B2 **Mount Elgon Nat'l Park,** Kenya
118/B2 **Mount Elliot Nat'l Park,** Austl.
119/B3 **Mount Emu** (cr.), Austl.
119/C4 **Mount Field Nat'l Park,** Austl.
119/B3 **Mount Gambier,** Austl.
120/D5 **Mount Hagen,** PNG
166/D4 **Mount Holly,** NJ,US
161/Q9 **Mount Hope,** On,Can
119/D3 **Mount Imlay Nat'l Park,** Austl.
117/H2 **Mount Isa,** Austl.
166/B3 **Mount Joy,** Pa,US
119/D1 **Mount Kaputar Nat'l Park,** Austl.
130/C3 **Mount Kenya Nat'l Park,** Kenya
167/E1 **Mount Kisco,** NY,US
165/C2 **Mountlake Terrace,** Wa,US
166/D4 **Mount Laurel,** NJ,US
168/G7 **Mount Lebanon,** Pa,US
117/M9 **Mount Lofty** (ranges), Austl.
115/S10 **Mount Maunganui,** NZ
118/D4 **Mount Mistake Nat'l Park,** Austl.
160/D3 **Mount Morris,** Mi,US
118/E6 **Mount Nebo,** Austl.
53/Q7 **Mountnessing,** Eng,UK
163/J3 **Mount Olive,** NC,US
81/H3 **Mount Parnes Nat'l Park,** Gre.
161/L2 **Mount Pearl,** Nf,Can
157/L5 **Mount Pleasant,** Ia,US
160/C3 **Mount Pleasant,** Mi,US
162/E3 **Mount Pleasant,** Tx,US
158/E3 **Mount Pleasant,** Ut,US
165/Q15 **Mount Prospect,** Il,US
166/B6 **Mount Rainier,** Md,US
156/C4 **Mount Rainier Nat'l Park,** Wa,US
117/H5 **Mount Remarkable Nat'l Park,** Austl.
156/D3 **Mount Revelstoke Nat'l Park,** BC,Can
119/B3 **Mount Richmond Nat'l Park,** Austl.
159/G2 **Mount Rushmore Nat'l Mem.,** SD,US
58/A6 **Mount's** (bay), Eng,UK
131/D4 **Mount Selinda,** Zim.
118/B2 **Mount Spec Nat'l Park,** Austl.
160/D4 **Mount Sterling,** Ky,US
160/B4 **Mount Vernon,** Il,US
160/C4 **Mount Vernon,** In,US
167/E2 **Mount Vernon,** NY,US
168/E7 **Mount Vernon,** Oh,US
166/A6 **Mount Vernon,** Va,US
156/C3 **Mount Vernon,** Wa,US
118/C4 **Mount Walsh Nat'l Park,** Austl.
119/E1 **Mount Warning Nat'l Park,** Austl.
116/C2 **Mount Welcome Abor. Land,** Austl.
119/D4 **Mount William Nat'l Park,** Austl.
74/B3 **Moura,** Port.
72/C5 **Mourenx,** Fr.
56/B3 **Mourne** (dist.), NI,UK
56/B3 **Mourne** (mts.), NI,UK
68/C2 **Mouscron,** Belg.
124/J5 **Moussoro,** Chad
53/T9 **Moussy-le-Neuf,** Fr.
76/D3 **Moutier,** Swi.
68/C2 **Mouvaux,** Fr.
76/B1 **Mouzon** (riv.), Fr.
140/C3 **Moxotó** (riv.), Braz.
60/B1 **Moy** (riv.), Ire.
56/B3 **Moy,** NI,UK
130/C2 **Moyalē,** Eth.
101/B4 **Moye** (isl.), China
124/D1 **Moyen Atlas** (mts.), Mor.
69/F5 **Moyeuvre-Grande,** Fr.
56/B2 **Moygashel,** NI,UK
56/B1 **Moyle** (dist.), NI,UK
111/E5 **Moyo** (isl.), Indo.
130/A2 **Moyo,** Ugan.
144/B2 **Moyobamba,** Peru
130/A3 **Moyowosi** (riv.), Tanz.
102/C4 **Moyu,** China
148/D3 **Moyuta,** Guat.
131/D3 **Mozambique**
126/G5 **Mozambique** (chan.), Afr.
84/H5 **Mozhaysk,** Rus.
85/M4 **Mozhga,** Rus.
86/D1 **Mozyr',** Bela.
130/A5 **Mpalapata,** Zam.
130/A4 **Mpanda,** Tanz.
126/C4 **Mpangu,** Namb.
131/B4 **Mphoengs,** Zim.
130/B2 **Mpigi,** Ugan.
131/C1 **Mpika,** Zam.
130/A5 **Mporokoso,** Zam.
129/E5 **Mpraeso,** Gha.
130/A5 **Mpulungu,** Zam.
130/C4 **Mpwapwa,** Tanz.
65/L2 **Mrągowo,** Pol.
82/C3 **Mrkonjić Grad,** Bosn.
130/C4 **Msanga,** Tanz.
123/T16 **M'Sila,** Alg.
123/T16 **M'Sila** (riv.), Alg.
123/T16 **M'Sila** (wilaya), Alg.
131/C2 **Msoro,** Zam.
123/N13 **Msoun** (riv.), Mor.
84/G4 **Msta** (riv.), Rus.
130/A5 **Msumbu Nat'l Park,** Zam.
130/C5 **Mswega,** Tanz.
65/L4 **Mszana Dolna,** Pol.
130/A4 **Mtakuja,** Tanz.
130/C5 **Mtalika,** Tanz.
131/D3 **Mtarazi Falls Nat'l Park,** Zim.
130/C3 **Mtito Andei,** Kenya
130/C4 **Mtondoni,** Tanz.
130/B5 **Mtorwi** (peak), Tanz.
86/F1 **Mtsensk,** Rus.
130/D5 **Mtwara,** Tanz.
130/C5 **Mtwara** (prov.), Tanz.
104/B4 **Mu** (riv.), Burma
126/G4 **Mualama,** Moz.
109/D2 **Muang Gnommarat,** Laos
109/C2 **Muang Kenthao,** Laos
109/D3 **Muang Khong,** Laos
109/D3 **Muang Khongxedon,** Laos
109/D3 **Muang Lakhonpheng,** Laos
109/D1 **Muang Soy,** Laos
109/C2 **Muang Thathom,** Laos
109/D2 **Muang Xamteu,** Laos
109/D2 **Muang Xepon,** Laos
110/B3 **Muar,** Malay.
110/B4 **Muarabungo,** Indo.
95/J4 **Muāri** (pt.), Pak.
131/C3 **Mubayira,** Zim.
130/A2 **Mubende,** Ugan.
124/H5 **Mubi,** Nga.
139/F4 **Mucajaí** (riv.), Braz.
69/G2 **Much,** Ger.
131/C2 **Muchinga** (mts.), Zam.
131/C2 **Muchinga Escarpment** (cliff), Zam.
58/D1 **Much Wenlock,** Eng,UK
55/H8 **Muck** (isl.), Sc,UK
56/B2 **Muckamore Abbey,** NI,UK
165/C3 **Muckleshoot Ind. Res.,** Wa,US
60/D1 **Muckno** (lake), Ire.
126/H3 **Mucojo,** Moz.
148/E3 **Mucupina** (mtn.), Hon.
92/C2 **Mucur,** Turk.
141/D1 **Mucuri** (riv.), Braz.
126/D3 **Mucussueje,** Ang.
97/K3 **Mudanjiang,** China
83/J5 **Mudanya,** Turk.
70/C3 **Mudbach** (riv.), Ger.
97/K2 **Muddan** (riv.), China
61/F2 **Muddas Nat'l Park,** Swe.
166/B4 **Muddy** (cr.), Pa,US
158/E3 **Muddy** (riv.), Ut,US
159/H4 **Muddy Boggy** (cr.), Ok,US
168/E6 **Muddy Fork** (riv.), Oh,US
166/B4 **Muddy Run** (res.), Pa,US
69/G2 **Mudersbach,** Ger.
119/D2 **Mudgee,** Austl.
156/G1 **Mudjatik** (riv.), Sk,Can
165/D3 **Mud Mountain** (dam), Wa,US
165/D3 **Mud Mountain** (lake), Wa,US
109/B2 **Mudon,** Burma
108/F3 **Mudumalai Wild. Sanct.,** India
143/J8 **Muela** (peak), Chile
91/G7 **Mufjir, Nahr** (dry riv.), WBnk.
105/G2 **Mufu** (peak), China
131/C2 **Mufulira,** Zam.
131/C2 **Mufulwe** (hills), Zam.
130/B3 **Mugango,** Tanz.
74/A1 **Mugardos,** Sp.
79/G1 **Muggia,** It.
74/A1 **Mugia,** Sp.
92/B2 **Muğla,** Turk.
91/A1 **Muğla** (prov.), Turk.
87/L2 **Mugodzharskoye** (mts.), Kaz.
130/A4 **Mugombazi,** Tanz.
130/A4 **Muhala,** Zaire
127/D4 **Muḩammad Qawl,** Sudan
127/C3 **Muḩammad, Ra's** (pt.), Egypt
130/A3 **Muhavura** (vol.), Rwa.
130/C4 **Muheza,** Tanz.
131/B1 **Muhila** (mts.), Zaire
70/B5 **Mühlacker,** Ger.
70/A2 **Mühlbach** (riv.), Ger.
71/F6 **Mühldorf,** Ger.
67/H6 **Mühlhausen,** Ger.
70/B2 **Mühlheim am Main,** Ger.
71/G6 **Mühlviertel** (reg.), Aus.
61/H2 **Muhos,** Fin.
94/C2 **Mūḩ, Sabkhat al** (lake), Syria
92/D3 **Mūḩ, Sabkhat al** (riv.), Syria
63/K2 **Muhu** (isl.), Est.
130/A3 **Muhutwe,** Tanz.
66/C4 **Muiden,** Neth.
54/B5 **Muirkirk,** Sc,UK
54/B1 **Muir of Ord,** Sc,UK
166/B2 **Muir-Orwin-Reinerton,** Pa,US
165/J11 **Muir Woods Nat'l Mon.,** Ca,US
101/D5 **Muju,** SKor.
86/B2 **Mukachevo,** Ukr.
100/B2 **Mukawa,** Japan
100/C2 **Mu-kawa** (riv.), Japan
127/D4 **Mukawwar** (isl.), Sudan
108/C2 **Mukeriān,** India
157/M2 **Muketei** (riv.), On,Can
91/E3 **Mukhayyam al Yarmūk,** Syria
165/C2 **Mukilteo,** Wa,US
99/L10 **Mukō,** Japan
130/A3 **Muko,** Ugan.
130/B2 **Mukono,** Ugan.
120/D2 **Mukoshima** (isls.), Japan
109/B4 **Mu Ko Similan Nat'l Park,** Thai.
109/B4 **Mu Ko Surin Nat'l Park,** Thai.
108/C2 **Muktsar,** India
131/C2 **Mukuku,** Zam.
130/A5 **Mukunsa,** Zam.
130/A5 **Mukwakwa,** Zam.
131/C1 **Mukwikile,** Zam.
74/E3 **Mula,** Sp.
97/K2 **Mulan,** China
131/D3 **Mulanje,** Malw.
151/G4 **Mulchatna** (riv.), Ak,US
142/B3 **Mulchén,** Chile
64/G3 **Mulde** (riv.), Ger.
113/D **Mule** (pt.), Ant.
74/D4 **Mulhacén, Cerro de** (mtn.), Sp.
64/F3 **Mülhausen,** Ger.
66/D6 **Mülheim an der Ruhr,** Ger.
76/D2 **Mulhouse,** Fr.
130/B5 **Mulilansolo Mission,** Zam.
103/D3 **Muling** (pass), China
97/L2 **Muling** (riv.), China
121/R9 **Mulinu'u** (cape), WSam.
104/D3 **Muli Zangzu Zizhixian,** China
60/B4 **Mulkear** (riv.), Ire.
95/L2 **Mulkila** (mtn.), India
55/J8 **Mull** (isl.), Sc,UK
54/A1 **Mullach Coire Mhic Fhearchair** (mtn.), Sc,UK
60/A6 **Mullaghanish** (mtn.), Ire.
60/A5 **Mullaghareirk** (mts.), Ire.
60/D3 **Mullaghcleevaun** (mtn.), Ire.
56/B2 **Mullaghmore** (mtn.), NI,UK
108/H4 **Mullaittivu** (dist.), SrL.
54/A2 **Mullardoch, Loch** (lake), Sc,UK
159/G2 **Mullen,** Ne,US
110/D4 **Muller** (mts.), Indo.
76/D2 **Müllheim,** Ger.
166/D5 **Mullica** (riv.), NJ,US
60/C2 **Mullingar,** Ire.
163/J3 **Mullins,** SC,US
58/A6 **Mullion,** Eng,UK
131/B3 **Mulobezi,** Zam.
126/C4 **Mulondo,** Ang.
108/A2 **Multān,** Pak.
60/B4 **Multeen** (riv.), Ire.
156/C3 **Multnomah** (falls), Or,US
110/D3 **Mulu, Gunung** (peak), Malay.
131/C2 **Mulungushi,** Zam.
131/B1 **Mulungwishi,** Zaire
127/B5 **Mulwad,** Sudan
131/C2 **Mumbotuta** (falls), Zaire, Zam.
126/C3 **Mumbué,** Ang.
131/B2 **Mumbwa,** Zam.
131/B1 **Mumena,** Zaire
70/B3 **Mümling** (riv.), Ger.
109/B5 **Mum Nauk** (pt.), Thai.
130/C3 **Mumoni** (peak), Kenya
109/C3 **Mun** (riv.), Thai.
111/F4 **Muna** (isl.), Indo.
63/M3 **Munamägi** (hill), Est.
71/E2 **Münchberg,** Ger.
71/E6 **München** (Munich), Ger.
76/D2 **Münchenstein,** Swi.
138/B4 **Munchique** (peak), Col.
138/B4 **Munchique Nat'l Park,** Col.
160/C3 **Muncie,** In,US
166/B1 **Muncy** (cr.), Pa,US
108/F4 **Mundakāyam,** India
165/P15 **Mundelein,** Il,US
129/H5 **Mundemba,** Camr.
64/E3 **Munden,** Ger.
67/G6 **Münden,** Ger.
59/H1 **Mundesley,** Eng,UK
59/G2 **Mundford,** Eng,UK
116/K7 **Mundijong,** Austl.
140/B3 **Mundo Novo,** Braz.
106/C3 **Mungaolī,** India
119/B2 **Mungo Nat'l Park,** Austl.
102/F1 **Mungun-Tayga, Gora** (peak), Rus.
71/E6 **Munich** (München), Ger.
160/C2 **Munising,** Mi,US
89/L4 **Munku-Sardyk** (peak), Rus.
96/D1 **Munku-Sasan** (peak), Rus.
70/D2 **Münnerstadt,** Ger.
143/J8 **Muñoz Gamero** (pen.), Chile
101/D4 **Munsan,** SKor.
70/C6 **Münsingen,** Ger.
76/D4 **Münsingen,** Swi.
63/R7 **Munsön** (isl.), Swe.
168/F6 **Munson** (hill), Oh,US
67/E5 **Münster,** Ger.
67/H3 **Munster,** Ger.
70/B3 **Münster,** Ger.
60/B5 **Munster** (prov.), Ire.
60/C4 **Munster** (riv.), Ire.
165/Q16 **Munster,** In,US
67/E4 **Münsterland** (reg.), Ger.
83/F2 **Muntele Mare** (peak), Rom.
112/F7 **Muntinglupa,** Phil.
110/C4 **Muntok,** Indo.
76/D3 **Müntschemier,** Swi.
92/D2 **Munzur Vadisi Nat'l Park,** Turk.
109/D1 **Muong Khuong,** Viet.
61/G1 **Muonioälv** (riv.), Swe.
61/G1 **Muoniojoki** (riv.), Fin.
126/C4 **Mupa Nat'l Park,** Moz.
101/A4 **Muping,** China
125/Q7 **Muqdisho** (Mogadishu) (cap.), Som.
73/L3 **Mur** (riv.), Aus.
82/C2 **Mura** (riv.), Slvk.
93/E2 **Muradiye,** Turk.
99/F1 **Murakami,** Japan
143/J7 **Murallón** (peak), Chile
130/A3 **Muramvya,** Buru.
130/C3 **Murang'a,** Kenya
92/B2 **Murat** (peak), Turk.
86/D5 **Murat Daği** (peak), Turk.
92/E2 **Muratlı,** Turk.
100/B4 **Murayama,** Japan
116/C3 **Murchison** (peak), Austl.
116/B3 **Murchison** (riv.), Austl.
115/R11 **Murchison,** NZ
75/E4 **Murcia,** Sp.
74/E4 **Murcia** (aut. comm.), Sp.
166/C6 **Murderkill** (riv.), De,US
161/H1 **Murdochville,** Qu,Can
118/B1 **Murdock** (pt.), Austl.
83/G2 **Mureş** (co.), Rom.
83/G2 **Mureş** (riv.), Rom.
72/D5 **Muret,** Fr.
131/C3 **Murewa,** Zim.
162/E3 **Murfreesboro,** Ar,US
163/G3 **Murfreesboro,** Tn,US
70/B5 **Murg** (riv.), Ger.
95/H1 **Murgab** (riv.), Trkm.
110/D5 **Muria** (peak), Indo.
141/D2 **Muriaé,** Braz.
95/G3 **Mūrīān, Hāmūn-e Jaz** (lake), Iran
76/D4 **Muri bei Bern,** Swi.
140/D3 **Murici,** Braz.
64/G2 **Müritz See** (lake), Ger.
130/C3 **Murka,** Kenya
125/N6 **Murle,** Eth.
84/G1 **Murmansk,** Rus.
84/G2 **Murmansk Obl.,** Rus.
77/H2 **Murnau,** Ger.
99/M10 **Muro,** Japan
75/G3 **Muro,** Sp.
84/J5 **Murom,** Rus.
130/A3 **Murongo,** Tanz.
100/B2 **Muroran,** Japan
74/A1 **Muros,** Sp.
98/D4 **Muroto,** Japan
98/D4 **Muroto-zaki** (pt.), Japan
65/J2 **Murowana Goślina,** Pol.
163/G3 **Murphy,** NC,US
160/B4 **Murphysboro,** Il,US
70/C5 **Murr** (riv.), Ger.
148/E3 **Murra,** Nic.
119/D2 **Murramarang Nat'l Park,** Austl.
119/A2 **Murray** (riv.), Austl.
120/D5 **Murray** (lake), PNG
160/B4 **Murray,** Ky,US
163/H3 **Murray** (lake), SC,US
117/H5 **Murray Bridge,** Austl.
119/C2 **Murrumbidgee** (riv.), Austl.
168/H7 **Murrysville,** Pa,US
82/C2 **Murska Sobota,** Slov.
77/G4 **Murtaröl, Piz** (Cima la Casina) (peak), Swi.
57/G2 **Murton,** Eng,UK
112/A5 **Murud, Gunung** (peak), Malay.
115/S10 **Murupara,** NZ
121/M7 **Mururoa** (isl.), FrPol.
106/D3 **Murwāra,** India
119/E1 **Murwillumbah,** Austl.
65/H5 **Mürz** (riv.), Aus.
73/L3 **Mürzzuschlag,** Aus.
92/E2 **Muş,** Turk.
92/E2 **Muş** (prov.), Turk.
83/F4 **Musala** (peak), Bul.
93/H5 **Musandam** (pen.), Oman
130/A3 **Musasa,** Tanz.
99/H7 **Musashino,** Japan
95/G4 **Muscat** (Musqaţ) (cap.), Oman
166/C2 **Musconetcong** (riv.), NJ,US
167/E1 **Muscoot** (res.), NY,US
164/C2 **Muscoy,** Ca,US
130/A4 **Muse,** Tanz.
126/E5 **Musekwapoort** (pass), SAfr.
75/N9 **Museo del Prado,** Sp.
165/C2 **Museum of Flight,** Wa,US
117/F3 **Musgrave** (ranges), Austl.
161/L1 **Musgrave Harbour,** Nf,Can
106/E3 **Mushābani,** India
91/G8 **Mushāsh, Wādī** (dry riv.), WBnk.
60/B5 **Musheramore** (mtn.), Ire.
126/C1 **Mushie,** Zaire
110/B4 **Musi** (riv.), Indo.
138/B3 **Musinga** (peak), Col.
165/P14 **Muskego,** Wi,US
160/C3 **Muskegon,** Mi,US
160/C3 **Muskegon** (riv.), Mi,US
160/D4 **Muskingum** (riv.), Oh,US
159/J4 **Muskogee,** Ok,US
160/E2 **Muskoka** (lake), On,Can
131/C2 **Musofu,** Zam.
130/B3 **Musoma,** Tanz.
79/G5 **Musone** (riv.), It.
95/G4 **Musqaţ** (Muscat) (cap.), Oman
161/J1 **Musquaro** (riv.), Qu,Can
120/D5 **Mussau** (isl.), PNG
54/C5 **Musselburgh,** Sc,UK
156/F4 **Musselshell** (riv.), Mt,US
80/C4 **Mussomeli,** It.
108/B2 **Mustafābād,** Pak.
92/B1 **Mustafakemalpaşa,** Turk.
106/D2 **Mustāng,** Nepal
159/H4 **Mustang,** Ok,US
71/G4 **Můstek** (peak), Czh.
142/C5 **Musters** (lake), Arg.
101/E2 **Musu-dan** (pt.), NKor.
149/E3 **Musún** (mtn.), Nic.
119/D2 **Muswellbrook,** Austl.
127/B3 **Mūt,** Egypt
91/C1 **Mut,** Turk.
131/D3 **Mutambara,** Zim.
140/C4 **Mutá, Ponta do** (pt.), Braz.
131/D3 **Mutare,** Zim.
131/C2 **Mutenge,** Zam.
131/C3 **Mutepatepa,** Zim.
54/C4 **Muthill,** Sc,UK
111/F5 **Mutis** (peak), Indo.
131/D3 **Mutoko,** Zim.
133/H6 **Mutsamudu,** Com.
100/B3 **Mutsu,** Japan
100/B3 **Mutsu** (bay), Japan
77/G3 **Muttekopf** (peak), Aus.
76/D2 **Muttenz,** Swi.
70/B4 **Mutterstadt,** Ger.
77/G4 **Muttler** (peak), Swi.
108/G3 **Muttupet,** India
141/D1 **Mutum,** Braz.
108/H4 **Mutur,** SrL.
130/A2 **Mutwanga,** Zaire
108/F4 **Mūvattupula,** India
130/B4 **Muwale,** Tanz.
130/A3 **Muyinga,** Buru.
87/L4 **Muynak,** Uzb.
131/B1 **Muyuya,** Zaire
108/A2 **Muzaffargarh,** Pak.
106/C2 **Muzaffarnagar,** India
106/E2 **Muzaffarpur,** India
141/G6 **Muzambinho,** Braz.
102/D3 **Muzat** (riv.), China
131/B3 **Muzoka,** Zam.
146/E3 **Múzquiz,** Mex.
102/D4 **Muztag** (peak), China
102/E4 **Muztag** (peak), China
102/C4 **Muztagata** (peak), China
130/C4 **Mvomero,** Tanz.
131/C3 **Mvuma,** Zim.
126/C2 **Mwadi-Kalumbu,** Zaire
131/B1 **Mwadingusha,** Zaire
130/B3 **Mwadui,** Tanz.
131/C3 **Mwami,** Zim.
130/D3 **Mwana** (cape), Kenya
131/D2 **Mwanza,** Malw.
130/B3 **Mwanza,** Tanz.
130/B3 **Mwanza** (prov.), Tanz.
131/D2 **Mwase Lundaz,** Zam.
130/C5 **Mwaya,** Tanz.
55/G10 **Mweelrea** (mtn.), Ire.
130/C3 **Mweiga,** Kenya
126/D1 **Mweka,** Zaire
130/A5 **Mwenda,** Zam.
126/D2 **Mwene-Ditu,** Zaire
131/C4 **Mwenezi,** Zim.
131/C4 **Mwenezi** (riv.), Zim.
130/A5 **Mwense,** Zam.
130/B5 **Mwenzo Mission,** Zam.

130/C4 Mwera, Tanz.
130/A5 Mweru (lake), Zaire, Zam.
130/A5 Mweru-Wantipa (lake), Zam.
130/A5 Mweru-Wantipa Nat'l Park, Zam.
130/A4 Mwesi, Tanz.
130/A4 Mwesi (peak), Tanz.
130/A5 Mwimba, Tanz.
131/B1 Mwinilunga, Zam.
130/B4 Mwitikira, Tanz.
131/B2 Mwombezhi (riv.), Zam.
119/E2 Myall Lakes Nat'l Park, Austl.
104/B5 Myanaung, Burma
96/C2 Myangad, Mong.
107/G2 Myanmar (Burma)
104/B5 Myaungmya, Burma
104/B4 Myingyan, Burma
104/B4 Myintha, Burma
104/C4 Myitinge (riv.), Burma
104/C3 Myitkyina, Burma
104/B4 Myittha (riv.), Burma
65/J4 Myjava, Slvk.
58/C2 Mynydd Eppynt (mts.), Wal,UK
58/B2 Mynydd Pencarreg (mtn.), Wal,UK
104/B4 Myohaung, Burma
99/F2 Myōkō-san (mtn.), Japan
163/J3 Myrtle Beach, SC,US
163/J3 Myrtle Beach A.F.B., SC,US
156/C5 Myrtle Creek, Or,US
62/D2 Mysen, Nor.
65/K4 Myślenice, Pol.
65/H2 Myślibórz, Pol.
71/H5 Myslivna (peak), Czh.
109/E3 My Son (ruins), Viet.
106/C5 Mysore, India
165/B1 Mystery Bay Rec. Area, Wa,US
166/D4 Mystic Island, NJ,US
168/C3 Mystic Seaport, Ct,US
65/K3 Myszków, Pol.
109/D4 My Tho, Viet.
84/H5 Mytishchi, Rus.
71/G3 Mže (riv.), Czh.
131/D1 Mzimba, Malw.
131/D1 Mzuzu, Malw.

N

109/C1 Na (riv.), Viet.
71/E4 Naab (riv.), Ger.
66/B5 Naaldwijk, Neth.
63/K1 Naantali, Fin.
66/C4 Naarden, Neth.
71/H6 Naarn (riv.), Aus.
60/D3 Naas, Ire.
132/B3 Nababeep, SAfr.
106/E3 Nabadwīp, India
98/E3 Nabari, Japan
99/M10 Nabari (riv.), Japan
116/D3 Nabberu (lake), Austl.
71/F4 Nabburg, Ger.
130/C4 Naberera, Tanz.
85/M5 Naberezhnye Chelny, Rus.
108/D2 Nābha, India
94/D5 Nabī Shu'ayb, Jabal an (mtn.), Yem.
161/J1 Nabisipi (riv.), Qu,Can
144/B1 Nabón, Ecu.
112/C2 Nabua, Phil.
123/X17 Nābul, Tun.
123/X17 Nābul (gov.), Tun.
91/D3 Nābulus, WBnk.
112/D4 Nabunturan, Phil.
126/H3 Nacala, Moz.
148/E3 Nacaome, Hon.
98/D4 Nachi-Katsuura, Japan
130/C5 Nachingwea, Tanz.
65/J3 Náchod, Czh.
67/E6 Nachrodt-Wiblingwerde, Ger.
142/B3 Nacimiento, Chile
63/S7 Nacka, Swe.
162/E4 Nacogdoches, Tx,US
58/D4 Nadder (riv.), Eng,UK
120/G6 Nadi, Fiji
106/B3 Nadiād, India
82/E2 Nădlac, Rom.
123/N13 Nador, Mor.
101/D5 Naejang-san Nat'l Park, SKor.
57/H3 Nafferton, Eng,UK
95/J3 Nag, Pak.
104/B3 Naga (hills), India
112/C2 Naga City, Phil.
98/C4 Nagahama, Japan
98/E3 Nagahama, Japan
99/G1 Nagai, Japan
107/F2 Nāgāland (state), India
99/F2 Nagano, Japan
99/E3 Nagano (pref.), Japan
100/B2 Naganuma, Japan
99/F2 Nagaoka, Japan
98/D3 Nagaokakyō, Japan
108/G3 Nagappattinam, India
99/J7 Nagara, Japan
99/E3 Nagara (riv.), Japan
99/H7 Nagareyama, Japan
106/B4 Nagar Haveli, Dadrak (terr.), India
106/C4 Nāgārjuna Sāgar (res.), India
106/F2 Nagarzê, China
151/M5 Nagas (pt.), BC,Can
98/A4 Nagasaki, Japan
98/A4 Nagasaki (pref.), Japan
98/A4 Nagasaki Peace Park, Japan
99/M9 Nagashima, Japan
98/B3 Nagato, Japan
106/B2 Nāgaur, India
106/C3 Nāgda, India
108/F4 Nāgercoil, India
60/B5 Nagles (mts.), Ire.
100/J7 Nago, Japan
70/B5 Nagold, Ger.
130/B2 Nagongera, Ugan.
102/F2 Nagoonnuur, Mong.
87/H5 Nagorno-Karabakh Aut. Obl., Azer.
99/E3 Nagoya, Japan
99/M9 Nagoya Castle, Japan
106/C3 Nāgpur, India
104/B2 Nagqu, China
96/C5 Nagqu (riv.), China
63/J1 Nagu, Fin.
150/D3 Nagua, DRep.
99/H7 Naguri, Japan
82/C2 Nagyatád, Hun.
82/E1 Nagyhalász, Hun.
82/E2 Nagykálló, Hun.
82/C2 Nagykanizsa, Hun.
82/D2 Nagykáta, Hun.
82/D2 Nagykőrös, Hun.
82/E1 Nagy-Milic (peak), Hun.
100/J7 Naha, Japan
108/D2 Nāhan, India
152/D2 Nahanni Nat'l Park, NW,Can
91/D3 Nahariyya, Isr.
120/D2 Nahashima (isls.), Japan
93/G3 Nahāvand, Iran
69/G4 Nahe (riv.), Ger.
129/E4 Nahouri (prov.), Burk.
142/B3 Nahuelbuta Nat'l Park, Chile
142/C4 Nahuel Huapí (lake), Arg.
142/C4 Nahuel Huapí Nat'l Park, Arg.
146/D3 Naica, Mex.
96/C4 Naij Gol (riv.), China
98/C3 Naikai-Seto Nat'l Park, Japan
71/E2 Naila, Ger.
58/D4 Nailsea, Eng,UK
58/D3 Nailsworth, Eng,UK
103/E2 Naiman Qi, China
106/D3 Nainpur, India
54/C1 Nairn, Sc,UK
54/B2 Nairn (riv.), Sc,UK
117/M9 Nairne, Austl.
117/M9 Nairne (cr.), Austl.
130/C3 Nairobi (cap.), Kenya
130/C3 Nairobi Nat'l Park, Kenya
130/C3 Naivasha, Kenya
93/G3 Najafābād, Iran
92/E5 Najd (des.), SAr.
74/D1 Nájera, Sp.
106/C2 Najībābād, India
99/K9 Naka, Japan
98/D4 Naka (riv.), Japan
99/G2 Naka (riv.), Japan
99/H7 Nakai, Japan
99/F1 Nakajō, Japan
154/T10 Nakalele (pt.), Hi,US
99/G2 Nakaminato, Japan
98/C4 Nakamura, Japan
99/F2 Nakano, Japan
98/C3 Nakano (lake), Japan
100/B3 Nakasato, Japan
100/D2 Nakashibetsu, Japan
130/B2 Nakasongola, Ugan.
98/B5 Nakatane, Japan
98/B4 Nakatsu, Japan
99/E3 Nakatsugawa, Japan
125/N4 Nak'fa, Erit.
87/H5 Nakhichevan', Azer.
87/H5 Nakhichevan Aut. Rep., Azer.
97/L3 Nakhodka, Rus.
109/C3 Nakhon Nayok, Thai.
109/C3 Nakhon Pathom, Thai.
109/D2 Nakhon Phanom, Thai.
109/C3 Nakhon Ratchasima, Thai.
109/C3 Nakhon Sawan, Thai.
109/B4 Nakhon Si Thammarat, Thai.
63/J1 Nakkila, Fin.
65/J2 Nakło nad Notecią, Pol.
108/C2 Nakodar, India
130/B5 Nakonde, Zam.
101/E3 Naksan-sa, SKor.
62/D4 Nakskov, Den.
101/E5 Naktong (riv.), SKor.
130/C3 Nakuru, Kenya
151/D3 Nakusp, BC,Can
95/J3 Nāl (riv.), Pak.
96/F2 Nalayh, Mong.
131/D5 Nalázi, Moz.
69/F5 Nalbach, Ger.
107/F2 Nalbāri, India
119/D3 Nalbaugh Nat'l Park, Austl.
87/G4 Nal'chik, Rus.
109/C2 Nale, Laos
106/C4 Nalgonda, India
83/K5 Nallıhan, Turk.
74/B1 Nalón (riv.), Sp.
124/H1 Nālūt, Libya
104/A2 Nam (lake), China
101/D3 Nam (riv.), NKor.
101/D5 Nam (riv.), SKor.
131/D2 Namadzi, Malw.
93/G3 Namak (lake), Iran
108/G3 Nāmakkal, India
95/G2 Namakzār-e Shadād (salt dep.), Iran
130/C3 Namanga, Kenya
103/B3 Namangan, Uzb.
101/G7 Namansansong Prov. Park, SKor.
130/A4 Namanyere, Tanz.
130/C5 Namaputa, Tanz.
132/B3 Namaqualand (reg.), SAfr.
111/J4 Namaripi (cape), Indo.
130/B2 Namasagali, Ugan.
130/C5 Namasakata, Tanz.
130/C5 Nambanje, Tanz.
69/G4 Namborn, Ger.
118/D4 Nambour, Austl.
116/B4 Nambung Nat'l Park, Austl.
109/D4 Nam Can, Viet.
109/C1 Nam Cum, Viet.
101/E2 Namdae (riv.), NKor.
109/D1 Nam Dinh, Viet.
63/S7 Nämdöfjärden (sound), Swe.
160/B2 Namekagon (riv.), Wi,US
129/E3 Namemtenga (prov.), Burk.
99/E2 Namerikawa, Japan
126/G4 Nametil, Moz.
101/D5 Namhae (isl.), SKor.
126/B5 Namib (des.), Namb.
132/B2 Namibia
132/A2 Namib-Naukluft Park, Namb.
99/G2 Namie, Japan
100/B3 Namioka, Japan
131/D2 Namitete, Malw.
106/D2 Namja (pass), Nepal
104/B2 Namjagbarwa (peak), China
106/E2 Namling, China
77/G3 Namloser Wetterspitze (peak), Aus.
109/C2 Nam Nao Nat'l Park, Thai.
109/B4 Namnoi (peak), Burma
119/D1 Namoi (riv.), Austl.
120/E4 Namonuito (atoll), Micr.
120/F4 Namorik (atoll), Mrsh.
156/D5 Nampa, Id,US
101/C3 Namp'o, NKor.
126/G4 Nampula, Moz.
102/D6 Namsê Shankou (pass), China
61/D2 Namsos, Nor.
109/B2 Nam Tok Mae Surin Nat'l Park, Thai.
120/F4 Namu (atoll), Mrsh.
109/C2 Nam Un (res.), Thai.
69/D3 Namur, Belg.
69/D3 Namur (prov.), Belg.
131/B2 Namwala, Zam.
101/D5 Namwŏn, SKor.
65/J3 Namysłów, Pol.
105/G3 Nan (mts.), China
104/E1 Nan (riv.), China
105/F1 Nan (riv.), China
109/C2 Nan, Thai.
109/C2 Nan (riv.), Thai.
147/L7 Nanacamilpa, Mex.
100/B3 Nanae, Japan
156/C3 Nanaimo, BC,Can
154/V13 Nanakuli, Hi,US
105/H4 Nan'ao (isl.), China
99/E2 Nanao, Japan
144/C1 Nanay (riv.), Peru
142/C2 Nancagua, Chile
97/K2 Nancha, China
105/G2 Nanchang, China
104/E2 Nanchong, China
105/E2 Nanchuan, China
69/F6 Nancy, Fr.
148/E4 Nandaime, Nic.
107/J3 Nandan, China
106/C4 Nānded, India
131/C4 Nandi Mill, Zim.
104/C4 Nanding (riv.), China
105/F5 Nandu (riv.), China
106/B3 Nandurbār, India
53/T11 Nandy, Fr.
106/C4 Nandyāl, India
105/H3 Nanfeng, China
105/J4 Nang (isl.), China
95/K1 Nanga Parbat (mtn.), Pak.
110/D4 Nangapinoh, Indo.
101/D2 Nangnim (mts.), NKor.
103/C3 Nangong, China
112/C3 Nangtud (mtn.), Phil.
130/C5 Nangua, Tanz.
104/B2 Nang Xian, China
103/E5 Nanhui, China
104/D3 Nanjian Yizu Zizhixian, China
103/D4 Nanjing, China
104/C4 Nanka (riv.), Burma, China
108/B2 Nankāna Sāhib, Pak.
98/C4 Nankoku, Japan
104/D4 Nanlan (riv.), Burma, China
103/C3 Nanle, China
103/D4 Nanling, China
105/F4 Nanliu (riv.), China
97/K3 Nanlou (peak), China
62/D1 Nannestad, Nor.
105/F4 Nanning, China
99/M9 Nannō, Japan
60/D2 Nanny (riv.), Ire.
104/E3 Nanpan (riv.), China
106/D2 Nānpāra, India
103/D3 Nanpi, China
105/H3 Nanping, China
99/M10 Nansei, Japan
100/J7 Nansei-Shotō (Ryukyu) (isls.), Japan
153/S6 Nansen (sound), NW,Can
130/B3 Nansio, Tanz.
99/F2 Nantai-san (mtn.), Japan
53/S10 Nanterre, Fr.
72/C3 Nantes, Fr.
53/U9 Nanteuil-le-Haudouin, Fr.
160/D3 Nanticoke, On,Can
166/B1 Nanticoke, Pa,US
54/A4 Nant, Loch (lake), Sc,UK
156/E3 Nanton, Ab,Can
103/E4 Nantong, China
161/G3 Nantucket (isl.), MA,US
57/F5 Nantwich, Eng,UK
58/C3 Nantyglo, Wal,UK
167/D1 Nanuet, NY,US
121/Z18 Nanuku (chan.), Fiji
120/G5 Nanumanga (atoll), Tuv.
120/G5 Nanumea (isl.), Tuv.
141/D1 Nanuque, Braz.
103/C4 Nanwon (res.), China
103/B4 Nanwutai (mtn.), China
104/E2 Nanxi, China
130/C5 Nanyamba, Tanz.
103/D4 Nanyang, China
103/D4 Nanyang (lake), China
130/C2 Nanyuki, Kenya
103/B5 Nanzhang, China
103/C4 Nanzhao, China
153/J3 Naococane (lake), Qu,Can
106/A3 Naokot, Pak.
97/L2 Naoli (riv.), China
147/N7 Naolinco de Victoria, Mex.
128/D5 Naoua (falls), IvC.
81/H2 Náousa, Gre.
105/F4 Naozhou (isl.), China
165/K10 Napa, Ca,US
165/K10 Napa (riv.), Ca,US
165/K10 Napa (val.), Ca,US
130/B2 Napak (peak), Ugan.
160/E2 Napanee, On,Can
127/B5 Napata (ruins), Sudan
165/P16 Naperville, Il,US
76/D4 Napf (peak), Swi.
115/S10 Napier, NZ
132/L11 Napier, SAfr.
161/N7 Napierville (co.), Qu,Can
163/H5 Naples, Fl,US
80/D2 Naples (Napoli), It.
107/J3 Napo, China
138/B5 Napo (prov.), Ecu.
138/C5 Napo (riv.), Ecu., Peru
157/J4 Napoleon, ND,US
80/D2 Napoli (gulf), It.
80/D2 Napoli (Naples), It.
118/A4 Nappa Merrie, Austl.
59/E2 Napton on the Hill, Eng,UK
121/L6 Napuka (isl.), FrPol.
98/D3 Nara, Japan
98/D3 Nara (pref.), Japan
128/D3 Nara, Mali
95/J4 Nāra (riv.), Pak.
102/D5 Nara Logna (pass), Nepal
138/B5 Naranjal, Ecu.
144/B1 Naranjito, Ecu.
147/E3 Naranjo, Mex.
106/D4 Narasannapeta, India
99/J7 Narashino, Japan
109/C5 Narathiwat, Thai.
106/F3 Nārāyanganj, Bang.
106/C4 Nārāyanpet, India
58/B3 Narberth, Wal,UK
72/E5 Narbonne, Fr.
74/B1 Narcea (riv.), Sp.
81/F2 Nardò, It.
58/B6 Nare (pt.), UK
118/G9 Narellan, Austl.
153/T7 Nares (str.), NW,Can
65/L2 Narew (riv.), Pol.
149/G4 Narganá, Pan.
133/H6 Narinda (bay), Madg.
138/B4 Nariño (dept.), Col.
143/K8 Nariz (peak), Chile
106/D2 Narkatiāganj, India
106/C3 Narmada (riv.), India
87/G4 Narman, Turk.
80/C1 Narni, It.
53/K2 Narodnaya (peak), Rus.
130/B3 Narok, Kenya
130/B3 Naro Moru, Kenya
74/A1 Narón, Sp.
108/C1 Nārowāl, Pak.
61/G3 Närpes, Fin.
112/B3 Narra, Phil.
119/D1 Narrabri, Austl.
168/C2 Narragansett (bay), RI,US
167/J9 Narrows, The (str.), NJ,US
106/C3 Narsimhapur, India
106/C3 Narsingarh, India
130/C5 Narungombe, Tanz.
98/D3 Naruto, Japan
63/N2 Narva, Est.
63/M2 Narva (bay), Est., Rus.
63/M2 Narva (res.), Est., Rus.
63/M2 Narva (riv.), Est., Rus.
112/C1 Narvacan, Phil.
61/F1 Narvik, Nor.
85/M2 Nar'yan-Mar, Rus.
102/C3 Naryn, Kyr.
102/B3 Naryn (riv.), Kyr.
91/E2 Naşarī'yah, Jabal an (mts.), Syria
83/G2 Năsăud, Rom.
160/F4 NASA Wallops Space Ctr., Va,US
54/A1 Na Sealga, Loch (lake), Sc,UK
59/F3 Nash, Eng,UK
58/C4 Nash (pt.), Wal,UK
161/G3 Nashua, NH,US
162/E3 Nashville, Ar,US
163/G2 Nashville (cap.), Tn,US
82/D3 Našice, Cro.
65/L2 Nasielsk, Pol.
63/K1 Nasijärvi (lake), Fin.
106/B4 Nāsik, India
125/M6 Nāşir, Sudan
106/B2 Nasīrābād, India
95/J3 Nasīrābād, Pak.
112/C3 Naso (pt.), Phil.
121/Z17 Nasorolevu (peak), Fiji
151/N4 Nass (riv.), BC,Can
70/D2 Nassach (riv.), Ger.
150/B1 Nassau (cap.), Bahm.
143/L8 Nassau (bay), Chile
121/J6 Nassau (isl.), Cookls.
167/E2 Nassau (co.), NY,US
127/C4 Nasser (res.), Egypt
62/F3 Nässjö, Swe.
153/J3 Nastapoka (isls.), NW,Can
63/K1 Nastola, Fin.
62/D4 Næstved, Den.
99/F2 Nasu-dake (mtn.), Japan
112/C2 Nasugbu, Phil.
104/C5 Nat (peak), Burma
131/B4 Nata, Bots.
138/C4 Natagaima, Col.
160/C1 Natagani (riv.), On,Can
140/D2 Natal, Braz.
108/G3 Nataraja Temple, India
99/L9 Natashō, Japan
161/J1 Natashquan (riv.), Qu,Can
168/B2 Natchaug Saint For., Ct,US
163/F4 Natchez, Ms,US
162/E4 Natchitoches, La,US
76/D5 Naters, Swi.
121/Z17 Natewa (bay), Fiji
168/B2 Nathan Hale Saint Mon., Ct,US
106/B3 Nāthdwāra, India
131/D2 Nathenje, Malw.
168/C1 Natick, Ma,US
147/E3 Natillas, Mex.
156/B2 Nation (riv.), BC,Can
81/L6 National Archaeological Museum, Gre.
164/C5 National City, Ca,US
59/E2 National Exhibition Centre, Eng,UK
166/B5 Nat'l Agriculture Research Ctr., Md,US
166/B5 Nat'l Aquarium, Md,US
166/A5 Nat'l Institutes of Health, Md,US
166/B5 Nat'l Security Agency, Md,US
130/B3 Natron (lake), Tanz.
108/G3 Nattam, India
107/G4 Nattaung (peak), Burma
110/C3 Natuna (isls.), Indo.
158/E3 Natural Bridges Nat'l Mon., Ut,US
116/B5 Naturaliste (cape), Austl.
119/D4 Naturaliste (cape), Austl.
116/B3 Naturaliste (chan.), Austl.
116/B5 Naturaliste-Leeuwin Nat'l Park, Austl.
77/G4 Naturno (Naturns), It.
77/G4 Naturns (Naturno), It.
147/K7 Naucalpan de Juárez, Mex.
132/E3 Naudesnek (pass), SAfr.
168/A3 Naugatuck, Ct,US
168/A2 Naugatuck (riv.), Ct,US
147/M7 Nauhcampatépetl (vol.), Mex.
70/B3 Nauheim, Ger.
112/C2 Naujan, Phil.
63/K3 Naujoji-Akmenė, Lith.
132/A2 Naukluft-Namib Game Rsv., Namb.
120/F5 Nauru
147/N6 Nautla, Mex.
75/N8 Navacarrada (pass), Sp.
78/A4 Nava, Colle di (pass), It.
158/E3 Navajo Nat'l Mon., Az,US
112/D3 Naval, Phil.
75/M9 Navalcarnero, Sp.
74/C3 Navalmoral de la Mata, Sp.
56/B4 Navan, Ire.
89/T3 Navarin (cape), Rus.
143/L8 Navarino (isl.), Chile
74/D1 Navarre (aut. comm.), Sp.
142/F2 Navarro, Arg.
149/H2 Navassa (isl.), USVI
58/A6 Navax (pt.), UK
78/D1 Nave, It.
74/B1 Navia, Sp.
74/B1 Navia (riv.), Sp.
142/C2 Navidad, Chile
137/H8 Naviraí, Braz.
83/J3 Năvodari, Rom.
88/G5 Navoi, Uzb.
146/C3 Navojoa, Mex.
146/D3 Navolato, Mex.
112/E6 Navotas, Phil.
81/G3 Návpaktos, Gre.
81/H4 Návplion, Gre.
106/B3 Navsāri, India
153/H1 Navy Board (inlet), NW,Can
106/E3 Nawābganj, Bang.
106/D2 Nawābganj, India
95/J3 Nawābshāh, Pak.
108/A1 Nawān Jandānwāla, Pak.
108/D2 Nawāshahr, India
95/G5 Nawş, Ra's (pt.), Oman
107/J2 Naxi, China
81/J4 Náxos (isl.), Gre.
146/D4 Nayarit (state), Mex.
59/G3 Nayland, Eng,UK
107/J2 Nayong, China
100/C1 Nayoro, Japan
96/B2 Nayramadlīn (peak), Mong.
102/E2 Nayramadlīn Orgil (peak), Mong.
131/D2 Nayuci, Malw.
102/B4 Nayzatash, Pereval (pass), Taj.
140/C4 Nazaré, Braz.
74/A3 Nazaré, Port.
140/B2 Nazaré do Piauí, Braz.
141/G8 Nazaré Paulista, Braz.
68/C2 Nazareth, Belg.
91/D3 Nazareth (Nazerat), Isr.
146/D3 Nazas (riv.), Mex.
144/C4 Nazca, Peru
144/C4 Nazca Lines, Peru
100/K6 Naze, Japan
91/D3 Nazerat (Nazareth), Isr.
59/H3 Naze, The (pt.), Eng,UK
92/B2 Nazilli, Turk.
125/N6 Nazrēt, Eth.
88/H4 Nazyvayevsk, Rus.
131/B2 Nchanga, Zam.
130/A5 Nchelenge, Zam.
131/D2 Ncheu, Malw.
131/D2 Nchisi, Malw.
131/C2 Ndabala, Zam.
130/B4 Ndala, Tanz.
126/B2 Ndalatando, Ang.
125/K6 Ndele, CAfr.
120/F6 Ndende (isl.), Sol.
131/D1 Ndengu, Tanz.
124/J5 N'Djamena (cap.), Chad
124/H8 N'Djolé, Gabon
131/C2 Ndola, Zam.
130/C3 Ndolo Corner, Kenya
129/H5 Ndop, Camr.
128/B2 Ndrhamcha, Sebkha de (dry lake), Mrta.
130/B4 Nduguti, Tanz.
130/B4 Nduli, Tanz.
130/C5 Ndumbwe, Tanz.
130/C4 Ndungu, Tanz.
72/C4 Né (riv.), Fr.
81/J5 Néa Alikarnassós, Gre.
56/B2 Neagh, Lough (lake), NI,UK
81/H3 Néa Ionía, Gre.
117/F3 Neale (lake), Austl.
83/H2 Neamţ (co.), Rom.
151/A6 Near (isls.), Ak,US
58/C3 Neath, Wal,UK
58/C3 Neath (riv.), Wal,UK
56/D3 Neb (riv.), IM,UK
130/A2 Nebbi, Ugan.
77/G3 Nebel-Horn (peak), Ger.
87/K5 Nebit-Dag, Trkm.
139/E4 Neblina, Pico da (peak), Braz.
118/E6 Nebo (mtn.), Austl.
159/G2 Nebraska (state), US
159/J2 Nebraska City, Ne,US
80/C4 Nebrodi, Madonie (mts.), It.
156/B2 Nechako (riv.), BC,Can
162/E4 Neches (riv.), Tx,US
125/N6 Nechisar Nat'l Park, Eth.
71/G2 Nechranice, Údolní nádrž (res.), Czh.
70/B4 Neckar (riv.), Ger.
70/B4 Neckargemünd, Ger.
70/C4 Neckarsulm, Ger.
121/J2 Necker (isl.), Hi,US
142/F3 Necochea, Arg.
138/B2 Necoclí, Col.
80/C1 Necropoli (ruins), It.
74/A1 Neda, Sp.
66/C6 Nederweert, Neth.
116/K6 Nedlands, Austl.
108/F4 Nedumangād, India
66/D4 Neede, Neth.
168/C1 Needham, Ma,US
59/H2 Needham Market, Eng,UK
59/F2 Needingworth, Eng,UK
158/D4 Needles, Ca,US
59/E5 Needles, The (seastacks), UK
160/B2 Neenah, Wi,US
157/J3 Neepawa, Mb,Can
116/K6 Neerabup Nat'l Park, Austl.
69/E1 Neerpelt, Belg.
71/E2 Neetze (riv.), Ger.
69/F2 Neffelbach (riv.), Ger.
85/M4 Neftekamsk, Rus.
90/C7 Nefud (des.), SAr.
56/D6 Nefyn, Wal,UK
131/C2 Nega Nega, Zam.
160/C2 Negaunee, Mi,US
125/N6 Negēlē, Eth.
91/D4 Negev (reg.), Isr.
91/F8 Negev-Kinneret Conduit, Isr.
83/G3 Negoiu (peak), Rom.
130/C5 Negomano, Moz.
106/C6 Negombo, SrL.
82/F3 Negotin, Yugo.
82/F5 Negotino, Macd.
148/D2 Negra (pt.), Belz.
140/A3 Negra (mts.), Braz.
144/A2 Negra (pt.), Peru
107/F4 Negrais (cape), Burma
74/A1 Negreira, Sp.
83/H2 Negreşti, Rom.
149/G2 Negril, Jam.
144/A2 Negritos, Peru
142/C3 Negro (peak), Arg.
142/D3 Negro (riv.), Arg.
136/F7 Negro (riv.), Bol.
137/G7 Negro (riv.), Braz.
136/F4 Negro (riv.), Braz., Ven.
143/T11 Negro (stream), Uru.
143/F2 Negro (riv.), Uru., Braz.
112/C3 Negros (isl.), Phil.
95/G2 Nehbandān, Iran
150/D3 Neiba, DRep.
149/J2 Neiba, Sierra de (range), DRep.
133/R15 Neiges, Piton des (peak), Reun.
103/C4 Neihuang, China
104/E2 Neijiang, China
54/B5 Neilston, Sc,UK
103/B2 Nei Monggol (aut. reg.), China
96/G3 Nei Monggol (plat.), China
103/C3 Neiqiu, China
138/C4 Neiva, Col.
103/B4 Neixiang, China
152/G3 Nejanilini (lake), Mb,Can
148/C2 Nejapa, Mex.
71/F2 Nejdek, Czh.
125/N6 Nejo, Eth.
125/N6 Nek'emtē, Eth.
84/G4 Nelidovo, Rus.
159/H2 Neligh, Ne,US
108/G3 Nellikkuppam, India
106/C5 Nellore, India
119/B3 Nelson (cape), Austl.
156/D3 Nelson, BC,Can
152/G3 Nelson (riv.), Mb,Can
143/J7 Nelson (str.), Chile
115/R11 Nelson, NZ
57/F4 Nelson, Eng,UK
58/C3 Nelson, Wal,UK
151/F3 Nelson (isl.), Ak,US
119/E2 Nelson Bay, Austl.
133/E2 Nelspruit, SAfr.
128/D2 Néma, Mrta.
128/D2 Néma, Dhar (hills), Mrta.
63/K4 Neman (Nemunas) (riv.), Eur.
78/C1 Nembro, It.
83/H2 Nemira (peak), Rom.
97/J2 Nemor (riv.), China
72/E2 Nemours, Fr.
63/K4 Nemunas (Neman) (riv.), Eur.
100/D2 Nemuro, Japan
100/D2 Nemuro (pen.), Japan
100/D2 Nemuro (str.), Japan, Rus.
97/J2 Nen (riv.), China
59/G1 Nene (riv.), Eng,UK
85/M2 Nenets Aut. Okr., Rus.
97/K2 Nenjiang, China
159/J3 Neosho (riv.), Ks, Mo,US
159/J3 Neosho, Mo,US
75/F1 Néouville, Pic de (peak), Fr.
147/Q10 Neo Volcanica, Cordillera (range), Mex.
106/D2 Nepal
106/D2 Nepālganj, Nepal
106/C3 Nepanagar, India
118/G8 Nepean (riv.), Austl.
160/F2 Nepean, Can.
144/B3 Nepeña, Peru
165/F5 Nepessina (lake), Mi,US
158/E3 Nephi, Ut,US
60/A1 Nephin (mtn.), Ire.
60/A1 Nephin Beg (mtn.), Ire.
60/A2 Nephin Beg (range), Ire.
161/H2 Nepisiguit (riv.), NB,Can
71/H2 Neratovice, Czh.
96/H1 Nercha (riv.), Rus.
84/J4 Nerekhta, Rus.
70/D5 Neresheim, Ger.
82/D4 Neretva (riv.), Bosn., Cro.
63/L4 Neris (riv.), Lith.
74/D4 Nerja, Sp.
144/A2 Ñermete (pt.), Peru
79/F5 Nerone, Monte (peak), It.
70/D6 Nersingen, Ger.
74/B4 Nerva, Sp.
78/A5 Nèrvia (riv.), It.
78/B1 Nerviano, It.
166/C1 Nescopeck (cr.), Pa,US
86/C4 Nesebŭr, Bul.
166/C3 Neshaminy (cr.), Pa,US
168/G5 Neshannock (cr.), Pa,US
53/S9 Nesles-la-Vallée, Fr.
54/B2 Ness (riv.), Sc,UK
159/H3 Ness City, Ks,US
67/H6 Nesse (riv.), Ger.
151/M4 Nesselrode (mtn.), Ak,US
54/B2 Ness, Loch (lake), Sc,UK
57/E5 Neston, Eng,UK
81/J2 Néstos (riv.), Gre.
91/F8 Nes Ziyyona, Isr.
91/D3 Netanya, Isr.
67/G5 Nethe (riv.), Ger.
58/D3 Netherend, Eng,UK
66/B5 Netherlands
150/D5 Netherlands Antilles (isls.), Neth.
54/C2 Nethy Bridge, Sc,UK
59/E5 Netley, Eng,UK
80/E3 Neto (riv.), It.
69/H2 Netphen, Ger.
66/D6 Nette (riv.), Ger.
67/H5 Nette (riv.), Ger.
69/G3 Nettebach (riv.), Ger.
69/F3 Nettersheim, Ger.
66/D6 Nettetal, Ger.
153/J2 Nettilling (lake), NW,Can
57/H5 Nettleham, Eng,UK
80/C2 Nettuno, It.
147/L7 Netzahualcóyotl, Mex.
71/E6 Neubiberg, Ger.
65/G2 Neubrandenburg, Ger.
70/E5 Neuburg an der Donau, Ger.
76/C4 Neuchâtel, Swi.
76/C4 Neuchâtel (canton), Swi.
76/C4 Neuchâtel (lake), Swi.
70/B5 Neuenbürg, Ger.
76/D2 Neuenburg am Rhein, Ger.
70/D4 Neuendettelsau, Ger.
65/G2 Neuenhagen, Ger.
66/D4 Neuenhaus, Ger.
67/E4 Neuenkirchen, Ger.
67/F3 Neuenkirchen, Ger.
67/E6 Neuenrade, Ger.
70/C4 Neuenstadt am Kocher, Ger.
71/E6 Neufahrn bei Freising, Ger.
69/E4 Neufchâteau, Belg.
76/B1 Neufchâteau, Fr.
70/E1 Neuhaus am Rennweg, Ger.
77/E2 Neuhausen am Rheinfall, Swi.
70/C2 Neuhof, Ger.
70/B4 Neuhofen, Ger.
68/B5 Neuilly-en-Thelle, Fr.
68/C5 Neuilly-Saint-Front, Fr.
53/T10 Neuilly-sur-Marne, Fr.
53/S10 Neuilly-sur-Seine, Fr.
70/B2 Neu-Isenburg, Ger.
77/H5 Neumarkt (Egna), It.
71/E4 Neumarkt in der Oberpfalz, Ger.
64/E1 Neumünster, Ger.
82/C2 Neunkirchen, Aus.
69/G5 Neunkirchen, Ger.
69/H2 Neunkirchen, Ger.
69/G2 Neunkirchen-Seelscheid, Ger.
142/C3 Neuquén, Arg.
142/C3 Neuquén (prov.), Arg.
142/C3 Neuquén (riv.), Arg.
64/G2 Neuruppin, Ger.
70/D6 Neusäss, Ger.
163/J3 Neuse (riv.), NC,US
66/D6 Neuss, Ger.
67/G4 Neustadt am Rübenberge, Ger.
70/D3 Neustadt an der Aisch, Ger.
71/E5 Neustadt an der Donau, Ger.
70/B4 Neustadt an der Weinstrasse, Ger.
70/E2 Neustadt bei Coburg, Ger.
64/F1 Neustadt in Holstein, Ger.
64/G2 Neustrelitz, Ger.
71/F5 Neutraubling, Ger.
70/D6 Neu-Ulm, Ger.
72/G2 Neuves-Maisons, Fr.
76/A6 Neuville-sur-Saône, Fr.
67/F1 Neuwerk (isl.), Ger.
69/G3 Neuwied, Ger.
63/P2 Neva (riv.), Rus.
74/D4 Nevada (mts.), Sp.
158/C3 Nevada (state), US
159/J3 Nevada, Mo,US
142/C4 Nevado Cónico (peak), Chile
135/C1 Nevado de Chañi (peak), Arg.
135/C2 Nevado del Candado (peak), Arg.
136/C3 Nevado del Huila (peak), Col.
138/C4 Nevado del Huila Nat'l Park, Col.
147/K7 Nevado de Toluca Nat'l Park, Mex.
142/C2 Nevado, Sierra del (mts.), Arg.
63/N3 Nevel', Rus.
68/C1 Nevele, Belg.
97/N2 Nevel'sk, Rus.
72/E3 Nevers, Fr.
82/D4 Nevesinje, Bosn.
87/G3 Nevinnomyssk, Rus.
150/F3 Nevis (isl.), StK.
150/F3 Nevis (peak), StK.
79/F5 Nevola (riv.), It.
92/C2 Nevşehir, Turk.
92/C2 Nevsehir (prov.), Turk.
139/G4 New (riv.), Guy.
59/E5 New (for.), Eng,UK
160/D4 New (riv.), WV,US
56/E2 New Abbey, Sc,UK
135/C5 Newala, Tanz.
160/C4 New Albany, In,US
163/F3 New Albany, Ms,US

New A – North

209
North – Olima

57/H5 North Hykeham, Eng,UK
85/Q5 North Kazakhstan Obl., Rus.
130/C3 North Kitui Nat'l Rsv., Kenya
101/D2 North Korea
104/B3 North Lakhimpur, India
158/D3 North Las Vegas, Nv,US
167/M9 North Lindenhurst, NY,US
162/E3 North Little Rock, Ar,US
164/F8 North Long Beach, Ca,US
159/G2 North Loup (riv.), Ne,US
131/D1 North Luangwa Nat'l Park, Zam.
153/R7 North Magnetic Pole, NAm
55/H8 North Minch (The Minch) (sound), Sc,UK
157/J2 North Moose (lake), Mb,Can
166/B1 North Mtn. (ridge), Pa,US
163/J3 North Myrtle Beach, SC,US
61/H1 North (Nordkapp) (cape), Nor.
168/F5 North Olmsted, Oh,US
87/G4 North Ossetian Aut. Rep., Rus.
120/F3 North Pacific (ocean)
161/R9 North Pelham, On,Can
58/C4 North Petherton, Eng,UK
118/E6 North Pine (riv.), Austl.
166/D2 North Plainfield, NJ,US
159/G2 North Platte (riv.), US
159/G2 North Platte, Ne,US
163/G3 Northport, Al,US
167/E2 Northport (Old Northport), NY,US
166/A5 North Potomac, Md,US
168/C2 North Providence, RI,US
157/K5 North Raccoon (riv.), Ia,US
64/E3 North Rhine-Westphalia (state), Ger.
164/E7 Northridge, Ca,US
168/E5 North Ridgeville, Oh,US
158/D3 North Rim, Az,US
55/N13 North Ronaldsay (isl.), Sc,UK
168/F5 North Royalton, Oh,US
156/F2 North Saskatchewan (riv.), Ab, Sk,Can
57/G2 North Shields, Eng,UK
88/K2 North Siberian (plain), Rus.
159/J2 North Skunk (riv.), Ia,US
57/J5 North Somercotes, Eng,UK
118/D4 North Stradbroke (isl.), Austl.
115/R10 North Taranaki (bight), NZ
167/E1 North Tarrytown, NY,US
57/H5 North Thoresby, Eng,UK
59/E4 North Tidworth, Eng,UK
55/H7 North Tolsta, Sc,UK
161/S9 North Tonawanda, NY,US
57/F1 North Tyne (riv.), Eng,UK
55/H8 North Uist (isl.), Sc,UK
161/J2 Northumberland (str.), Can.
57/F1 Northumberland (co.), Eng,UK
166/B2 Northumberland (co.), Pa,US
57/F1 Northumberland Nat'l Park, Eng,UK
158/B2 North Umpqua (riv.), Or,US
152/D4 North Vancouver, BC,Can
165/F7 Northville, Mi,US
59/H1 North Walsham, Eng,UK
53/P6 North Weald Bassett, Eng,UK
116/B2 North West (cape), Austl.
132/D2 North-West (prov.), SAfr.
149/G2 Northwest (pt.), Jam.
108/H4 North Western (prov.), SrL.
131/B2 North-Western (prov.), Zam.
102/B4 Northwest Frontier (prov.), Pak.
161/L1 North West Gander (riv.), Nf,Can
54/A2 North West Highlands (mts.), Sc,UK
150/B1 North West Providence (chan.), Bahm.
152/E2 Northwest Territories (terr.), Can.
57/H5 North Wheatley, Eng,UK
57/F5 Northwich, Eng,UK
162/D3 North Wichita (riv.), Tx,US
57/G5 North Wingfield, Eng,UK
157/J4 Northwood, ND,US
161/R8 North York, On,Can
57/H3 North York Moors Nat'l Park, Eng,UK
57/G3 North Yorkshire (co.), Eng,UK
151/F3 Norton (bay), Ak,US
151/E3 Norton (sound), Ak,US
159/H3 Norton, Ks,US
168/F5 Norton, Oh,US
160/D4 Norton, Va,US
131/C3 Norton, Zim.
57/F6 Norton Bridge, Eng,UK
160/C3 Norton Shores, Mi,US
64/E1 Nortorf, Ger.
161/Q8 Norval, On,Can
113/Z Norvegia (cape), Ant.
69/F2 Nörvenich, Ger.
164/B3 Norwalk, Ca,US
167/E1 Norwalk, Ct,US
167/M7 Norwalk (riv.), Ct,US
160/D3 Norwalk, Oh,US
61/B3 Norway
157/J2 Norway House, Mb,Can
153/S7 Norwegian (bay), NW,Can
52/C2 Norwegian (sea), Eur.
168/D1 Norwell, Ma,US
59/H1 Norwich, Eng,UK
168/B2 Norwich, Ct,US
160/F3 Norwich, NY,US
168/C1 Norwood, Ma,US
100/D2 Nosappu-misaki (cape), Japan
99/L10 Nose, Japan
100/B1 Noshappu-misaki (cape), Japan
95/K1 Noshaq (mtn.), Pak.
100/B3 Noshiro, Japan
83/H4 Nos Maslen Nos (pt.), Bul.
110/E2 Nosong (cape), Malay.
112/A4 Nosong, Tanjong (cape), Malay.
132/C2 Nosop (dry riv.), Bots.
86/D2 Nosovka, Ukr.
95/G3 Nosratābād, Iran
140/C3 Nossa Senhora da Glória, Braz.
140/C3 Nossa Senhora das Dores, Braz.
55/K7 Noss Head (pt.), Sc,UK
132/B2 Nossob (dry riv.), Namb.
132/C2 Nossobrivier (dry riv.), SAfr.
143/J7 Notch (cape), Chile
65/J2 Notec (riv.), Pol.
80/D4 Noto, It.
80/D4 Noto (gulf), It.
80/D4 Noto (val.), It.
99/E2 Noto (pen.), Japan
80/D4 Noto Antica (ruins), It.
62/C2 Notodden, Nor.
99/M9 Notogawa, Japan
100/C1 Notoro (lake), Japan
161/L1 Notre Dame (bay), Nf,Can
161/G1 Notre Dame (mts.), Qu,Can
53/T10 Notre Dame, Fr.
161/N7 Notre-Dame-de-l'Ile-Perrot, Qu,Can
117/G5 Nott (peak), Austl.
160/E1 Nottaway (riv.), Qu,Can
62/D2 Nøtterøy, Nor.
153/H2 Nottingham (isl.), NW,Can
57/G6 Nottingham, Eng,UK
57/H5 Nottinghamshire (co.), Eng,UK
67/E5 Nottuln, Ger.
122/A2 Nouadhibou, Mrta.
128/B2 Nouakchott (cap.), Mrta.
75/F1 Noue (riv.), Fr.
121/V13 Nouméa (cap.), NCal.
132/D3 Noupoort, SAfr.
68/A3 Nouvion, Fr.
69/D4 Nouzonville, Fr.
137/H8 Nova Andradina, Braz.
83/F3 Novaci, Rom.
140/D2 Nova Cruz, Braz.
65/K4 Nová Dubnica, Slvk.
141/L7 Nova Friburgo, Braz.
79/G1 Nova Gorica, Slov.
82/C3 Nova Gradiška, Cro.
141/K7 Nova Iguaçu, Braz.
112/F6 Novaliches (res.), Phil.
131/D3 Nova Lusitânia, Moz.
131/D4 Nova Mambone, Moz.
140/C2 Nova Olinda, Braz.
136/G4 Nova Olinda do Norte, Braz.
82/E3 Nova Pazova, Yugo.
141/B4 Nova Prata, Braz.
78/B2 Novara, It.
78/B1 Novara (prov.), It.
140/B2 Nova Russas, Braz.
161/J2 Nova Scotia (prov.), Can.
131/D4 Nova Sofala, Moz.
140/C3 Nova Soure, Braz.
165/J10 Novato, Ca,US
82/D4 Nova Varoš, Yugo.
141/D1 Nova Venécia, Braz.
137/H6 Nova Xavantina, Braz.
86/E3 Novaya Kakhovka, Ukr.
89/R2 Novaya Sibir' (isl.), Rus.
88/E2 Novaya Zemlya (isl.), Rus.
83/H4 Nova Zagora, Bul.
75/E3 Novelda, Sp.
79/D3 Novellara, It.
65/J4 Nové Mesto nad Váhom, Slvk.
79/E2 Noventa Vicentina, It.
65/K5 Nové Zámky, Slvk.
84/F4 Novgorod, Rus.
63/P2 Novgorod Obl., Rus.
165/F7 Novi, Mi,US
82/E3 Novi Bečej, Yugo.
79/G2 Novigrad, Cro.
83/F4 Novi Iskŭr, Bul.
78/B3 Novi Ligure, It.
83/H4 Novi Pazar, Bul.
82/E4 Novi Pazar, Yugo.
82/D3 Novi Sad, Yugo.
141/K6 Novo (riv.), Braz.
87/G2 Novoanninskiy, Rus.
136/F5 Novo Aripuanã, Braz.
85/K4 Novocheboksarsk, Rus.
86/G3 Novocherkassk, Rus.
86/C2 Novograd-Volynskiy, Ukr.
63/L5 Novogrudok, Bela.
141/B4 Novo Hamburgo, Braz.
141/B2 Novo Horizonte, Braz.
71/H5 Novohradské Hory (mts.), Czh.
88/G5 Novokazalinsk, Kaz.
87/J1 Novokuybyshevsk, Rus.
88/J4 Novokuznetsk, Rus.
63/P1 Novoladozhskiy (can.), Rus.
113/A Novolazarevskaya, Ant.
82/B3 Novo Mesto, Slov.
82/E3 Novo Miloševo, Yugo.
86/F1 Novomoskovsk, Rus.
86/E3 Novomoskovsk, Ukr.
140/B2 Novo Oriente, Braz.
63/N4 Novopolotsk, Bela.
86/F3 Novorossiysk, Rus.
86/F3 Novoshakhtinsk, Rus.
88/J4 Novosibirsk, Rus.
87/L2 Novotroitsk, Rus.
86/D2 Novoukrainka, Ukr.
86/C2 Novovolynsk, Ukr.
85/L4 Novovyatsk, Rus.
86/D1 Novozybkov, Rus.
82/C3 Novska, Cro.
65/K4 Nový Jičín, Czh.
87/K4 Novyy Uzen', Kaz.
65/L3 Nowa Dęba, Pol.
65/J3 Nowa Ruda, Pol.
65/M3 Nowa Sarzyna, Pol.
65/H3 Nowa Sól, Pol.
159/J3 Nowata, Ok,US
65/K2 Nowe, Pol.
65/K2 Nowe Miasto Lubawskie, Pol.
60/A6 Nowen (mtn.), Ire.
106/C2 Nowgong, India
107/F2 Nowgong, India
151/H3 Nowitna (riv.), Ak,US
151/H3 Nowitna Nat'l Wild. Ref., Ak,US
65/H2 Nowogard, Pol.
158/F1 Nowood (riv.), Wy,US
95/K2 Nowshera, Pak.
65/K1 Nowy Dwór Gdański, Pol.
65/L4 Nowy Sącz, Pol.
65/L4 Nowy Sącz (prov.), Pol.
65/L4 Nowy Targ, Pol.
65/J2 Nowy Tomyśl, Pol.
74/A1 Noya, Sp.
68/B5 Noye (riv.), Fr.
108/F3 Noyil (riv.), India
68/C4 Noyon, Fr.
131/D3 Nsanje, Malw.
129/E5 Nsawam, Gha.
130/G5 Nsumba Nat'l Park, Zam.
130/A2 Ntoroko, Ugan.
130/A3 Ntungamo, Ugan.
130/A2 Ntusi, Ugan.
131/B4 Ntwetwe Pan (salt pan), Bots.
104/C3 Nu (mts.), China
96/D5 Nu (riv.), China
125/M5 Nūbah (mts.), Sudan
104/B2 Nubgang (pass), China
127/C4 Nubian (des.), Sudan
158/E3 Nucla, Co,US
162/D4 Nueces (riv.), Tx,US
152/G2 Nueltin (lake), NW,Can
66/C6 Nuenen, Neth.
103/E2 Nü'er (riv.), China
148/D2 Nueva Coahuila Nat'l Cap. Park, Mex.
148/D3 Nueva Concepción, Guat.
139/E2 Nueva Esparta (state), Ven.
149/F1 Nueva Gerona, Cuba
143/F2 Nueva Helvecia, Uru.
142/B3 Nueva Imperial, Chile
136/C3 Nueva Loja, Ecu.
138/B4 Nueva Loja (Lago Agrio), Ecu.
148/D3 Nueva Ocotepéque, Hon.
143/S11 Nueva Palmira, Uru.
147/N8 Nueva Patria, Mex.
142/E2 Nueve de Julio, Arg.
149/G1 Nuevitas, Cuba
142/D4 Nuevo (gulf), Arg.
146/D2 Nuevo Casas Grandes, Mex.
147/F3 Nuevo León (state), Mex.
143/S11 Nuevo Palmira, Uru.
77/E5 Nufenenpass (pass), Swi.
120/E5 Nuguria (isls.), PNG
121/J2 Nuhau (isl.), Hi,US
67/F6 Nuhne (riv.), Ger.
120/G5 Nui (atoll), Tuv.
99/N10 Nukata, Japan
151/F4 Nuklunek (mtn.), Ak,US
121/H7 Nuku'alofa (cap.), Tonga
120/G5 Nukufetau (atoll), Tuv.
121/L5 Nuku Hiva (isl.), FrPol.
120/H5 Nukulaelae (isl.), Tuv.
120/F5 Nukumanu (atoll), PNG
121/H5 Nukunonu (atoll), Tok.
120/E4 Nukuoro (isl.), Micr.
88/F5 Nukus, Uzb.
121/M6 Nukutavake (isl.), FrPol.
75/E3 Nules, Sp.
116/E5 Nullarbor (plain), Austl.
117/F4 Nullarbor Nat'l Park, Austl.
124/H6 Numan, Nga.
66/B5 Numansdorp, Neth.
99/F2 Numata, Japan
99/F3 Numazu, Japan
130/A3 Numbi, Zaire
69/G2 Nümbrecht, Ger.
111/H4 Numfoor (isl.), Indo.
119/G5 Nunawading, Austl.
59/E1 Nuneaton, Eng,UK
119/D3 Nungatta Nat'l Park, Austl.
130/B3 Nungwe, Tanz.
151/E4 Nunivak (isl.), Ak,US
66/C4 Nunspeet, Neth.
57/G2 Nunthorpe, Eng,UK
97/J1 Nuomin (riv.), China
128/C5 Nuon (riv.), IvC., Libr.
80/A2 Nuoro, It.
138/B3 Nuquí, Col.
91/E1 Nur (mts.), Turk.
102/B2 Nura (riv.), Kaz.
69/F3 Nürburgring, Ger.
78/C3 Nure (riv.), It.
92/D2 Nurhak, Turk.
127/B5 Nuri (ruins), Sudan
63/L1 Nurmijärvi, Fin.
70/E4 Nürnberg, Ger.
119/C1 Nurri (peak), Austl.
70/C5 Nürtingen, Ger.
104/C2 Nu (Salween) (riv.), China
92/D2 Nusaybin, Turk.
151/G4 Nushagak (riv.), Ak,US
95/J3 Nushki, Pak.
54/C5 Nutberry (hill), Sc,UK
69/E2 Nuth, Neth.
167/D2 Nutley, NJ,US
145/M3 Nuuk (Godthåb), Grld.
121/X15 Nuupere (pt.), FrPol.
127/C2 Nuwaybi', Egypt
132/L10 Nuy (riv.), SAfr.
131/D3 Nuza (peak), Zim.
131/B3 Nxai Pan (salt pan), Bots.
131/B3 Nxai Pan Nat'l Park, Bots.
130/A3 Nyabisindu, Rwa.
167/E1 Nyack, NY,US
130/B4 Nyahua, Tanz.
130/C2 Nyahururu Falls, Kenya
104/B2 Nyainqêntanglha (mts.), China
102/F5 Nyainqêntanglha Feng (peak), China
104/B1 Nyainrong, China
130/B3 Nyakabindi, Tanz.
130/A3 Nyakanyasi, Tanz.
131/D1 Nyaki Nat'l Park, Malw.
131/A2 Nyakulenga, Zam.
125/K5 Nyala, Sudan
106/E2 Nyalam, China
130/B3 Nyalikungu, Tanz.
131/C3 Nyamandhlovu, Zim.
131/D3 Nyamapande, Zim.
130/B3 Nyambiti, Tanz.
125/L6 Nyamlell, Sudan
130/C5 Nyamtumbo, Tanz.
84/J3 Nyandoma, Rus.
131/D3 Nyanga (peak), Zim.
131/D3 Nyanyadzi, Zim.
130/B3 Nyanza (prov.), Kenya
130/A4 Nyanza-Lac, Buru.
130/C4 Nyanzwa, Tanz.
130/A3 Nyaruonga, Tanz.
131/D2 Nyasa (Malawi) (lake), Afr.
131/D3 Nyazura, Zim.
64/F1 Nyborg, Den.
62/F3 Nybro, Swe.
106/F2 Nyêmo, China
130/C3 Nyeri, Kenya
104/D1 Nyikog (riv.), China
102/E5 Nyima, China
131/C2 Nyimba, Zam.
65/L5 Nyíradony, Hun.
82/F2 Nyírbátor, Hun.
82/E2 Nyíregyháza, Hun.
130/C2 Nyiru (peak), Kenya
62/C3 Nykøbing, Den.
62/D4 Nykøbing, Den.
62/G2 Nyköping, Swe.
63/R7 Nykvarn, Swe.
131/C5 Nylrivier (riv.), SAfr.
132/E2 Nylstroom, SAfr.
62/G2 Nynäshamn, Swe.
76/C5 Nyon, Swi.
71/G3 Nýřany, Czh.
71/G4 Nýrsko, Údolní nádrž (res.), Czh.
65/J3 Nysa, Pol.
156/D5 Nyssa, Or,US
100/A4 Nyūdo-zaki (pt.), Japan
84/F2 Nyuk (lake), Rus.
126/E2 Nyunzu, Zaire
99/E2 Nyūzen, Japan
130/B4 Nzega, Tanz.
128/C5 Nzérékoré, Gui.
128/C4 Nzérékoré (comm.), Gui.
128/D5 Nzi (riv.), IvC.

O

100/A3 Ō (isl.), Japan
59/E1 Oadby, Eng,UK
157/H4 Oahe (lake), ND, SD,US
157/H4 Oahe (dam), SD,US
154/V13 Oahu (isl.), Hi,US
157/J3 Oakbank, Mb,Can
165/Q14 Oak Creek, Wi,US
157/J4 Oakes, ND,US
165/Q16 Oak Forest, Il,US
59/F1 Oakham, Eng,UK
160/D4 Oak Hill, WV,US
158/C3 Oakhurst, Ca,US
165/K11 Oakland, Ca,US
165/F6 Oakland (co.), Mi,US
165/F6 Oakland (lake), Mi,US
167/D1 Oakland, NJ,US
165/A3 Oakland (bay), Wa,US
165/Q16 Oak Lawn, Il,US
59/E3 Oakley, Eng,UK
59/F2 Oakley, Eng,UK
165/L11 Oakley, Ca,US
159/G3 Oakley, Ks,US
168/H6 Oakmont, Pa,US
116/D2 Oakover (riv.), Austl.
165/Q16 Oak Park, Il,US
165/F7 Oak Park, Mi,US
156/C5 Oakridge, Or,US
160/C4 Oak Ridge, Tn,US
161/R8 Oak Ridges, On,Can
58/D3 Oaksey, Eng,UK
164/B1 Oaks, The, Ca,US
161/Q9 Oakville, On,Can
168/A2 Oakville, Ct,US
115/R12 Oamaru, NZ
55/H9 Oa, Mull of (pt.), Sc,UK
164/B2 Oat (mtn.), Ca,US
148/B2 Oaxaca, Mex.
148/B2 Oaxaca (state), Mex.
88/H3 Ob' (gulf), Rus.
88/G3 Ob' (riv.), Rus.
120/F6 Oba (isl.), Van.
160/D2 Obabika (lake), On,Can
98/D3 Obama, Japan
129/H5 Oban (hills), Camr., Nga.
115/Q12 Oban, NZ
55/J8 Oban, Sc,UK
100/B4 Obanazawa, Japan
99/N9 Obara, Japan
160/D1 Obasatika (riv.), On,Can
99/M10 Obata, Japan
135/E2 Oberá, Arg.
77/E4 Oberalppass (pass), Swi.
77/E4 Oberalpstock (peak), Swi.
70/D4 Oberasbach, Ger.
70/B4 Oberderdingen, Ger.
71/F6 Oberhaching, Ger.
66/D6 Oberhausen, Ger.
70/B5 Oberkirch, Ger.
70/D5 Oberkochen, Ger.
65/H3 Oberlausitz (reg.), Ger.
159/G3 Oberlin, Ks,US
168/E5 Oberlin, Oh,US
76/D1 Obernai, Fr.
70/C3 Obernburg am Main, Ger.
70/B6 Oberndorf am Neckar, Ger.
67/G4 Obernkirchen, Ger.
71/F3 Oberpfälzer Wald (for.), Ger.
70/B3 Ober Ramstadt, Ger.
77/F3 Oberriet, Swi.
71/E6 Oberschleissheim, Ger.
77/E3 Obersiggenthal, Swi.
77/G2 Oberstaufen, Ger.
77/G3 Oberstdorf, Ger.
69/G4 Oberthal, Ger.
70/B2 Obertshausen, Ger.
70/B2 Oberursel, Ger.
73/L3 Oberwölz, Aus.
111/G4 Obi (isl.), Indo.
111/G4 Obi (isls.), Indo.
111/G4 Obi (str.), Indo.
139/H5 Óbidos, Braz.
100/C2 Obihiro, Japan
82/E4 Obilić, Yugo.
100/B1 Obira, Japan
99/J7 Obitsu (riv.), Japan
109/B2 Ob Luang Gorge, Thai.
97/L2 Obluch'ye, Rus.
84/H5 Obninsk, Rus.
125/L6 Obo, CAfr.
125/P5 Obock, Djib.
65/J2 Oborniki, Pol.
65/J3 Oborniki Śląskie, Pol.
65/J2 Obra (riv.), Pol.
82/E3 Obrenovac, Yugo.
71/G7 Obtrumer See (lake), Aus.
99/M10 Ōbu, Japan
129/E5 Obuasi, Gha.
77/E4 Obwalden (demi-canton), Swi.
163/H4 Ocala, Fl,US
138/C2 Ocaña, Col.
72/C5 Occabe, Sommet d' (peak), Fr.
136/E7 Occidental, Cordillera (range), SAm.
151/L4 Ocean (cape), Ak,US
166/D4 Ocean (co.), NJ,US
160/F4 Ocean City, Md,US
166/D5 Ocean City, NJ,US
156/B2 Ocean Falls, BC,Can
120/* Oceania
164/C4 Oceanside, Ca,US
167/E2 Oceanside, NY,US
109/D4 Oc-Eo, Ancient City of (ruins), Viet.
87/G4 Ochamchira, Geo.
100/D2 Ochiishi-misaki (cape), Japan
54/C4 Ochil (hills), Sc,UK
149/G2 Ocho Rios, Jam.
70/D3 Ochsenfurt, Ger.
70/C6 Ochsenhausen, Ger.
77/F3 Ochsenkopf (peak), Aus.
67/E4 Ochtrup, Ger.
67/F2 Ochtum (riv.), Ger.
59/E3 Ock (riv.), Eng,UK
62/G1 Ockelbo, Swe.
163/H4 Ocmulgee (riv.), Ga,US
83/F2 Ocna Mureş, Rom.
144/C4 Ocoña (riv.), Peru
163/H3 Oconee (lake), Ga,US
163/H3 Oconee (riv.), Ga,US
150/D3 Ocos (bay), DRep.
148/E3 Ocotal, Nic.
166/B4 Octararo (cr.), Pa,US
72/C2 Octeville, Fr.
168/A1 October Mtn. Saint For., Ma,US
89/L1 October Revolution (isl.), Rus.
139/E2 Ocumare del Tuy, Ven.
129/E5 Oda, Gha.
98/C3 Oda, Japan
94/C4 Oda (peak), Sudan
61/P7 Ódáðahraun (lava flow), Ice.
101/E4 Odaesan Nat'l Park, SKor.
99/M10 Ōdai, Japan
98/E3 Ōdaigahara-san (mtn.), Japan
127/D4 Oda, Jabal (peak), Sudan
63/T8 Ödåkra, Swe.
100/B3 Ōdate, Japan
99/F3 Odawara, Japan
62/B1 Odda, Nor.
62/D4 Odder, Den.
125/P7 Oddur, Som.
67/F6 Odeborn (riv.), Ger.
74/A4 Odemira, Port.
92/A2 Ödemiş, Turk.
132/D2 Odendaalsrus, SAfr.
62/D4 Odense, Den.
67/E6 Odenthal, Ger.
166/B5 Odenton, Md,US
65/H2 Oderhaff (lag.), Ger., Pol.
65/H2 Oder (Odra) (riv.), Ger., Pol.
79/F1 Oderzo, It.
86/D3 Odessa, Ukr.
162/C4 Odessa, Tx,US
156/D4 Odessa, Wa,US
166/C5 Odessa, Hist. Homes of, De,US
83/J2 Odessa Obl., Ukr.
72/B2 Odet (riv.), Fr.
128/D4 Odienné, IvC.
84/H5 Odintsovo, Rus.
112/C2 Odioñgan, Phil.
75/P10 Odivelas, Port.
83/H3 Odobeşti, Rom.
72/C2 Odon (riv.), Fr.
109/D4 Odongk, Camb.
66/D3 Odoorn, Neth.
83/G2 Odorheiu Secuiesc, Rom.
65/H2 Odra (Oder) (riv.), Ger., Pol.
82/D3 Odžaci, Yugo.
124/J7 Odzala Nat'l Park, Congo
131/D3 Odzi, Zim.
131/D3 Odzi (riv.), Zim.
99/L9 Ōe, Japan
66/B4 Oegstgeest, Neth.
140/B2 Oeiras, Braz.
67/F5 Oelde, Ger.
71/F2 Oelsnitz, Ger.
121/M7 Oeno (atoll), Pitc.,UK
67/E5 Oer-Erkenschwick, Ger.
70/D2 Oerlenbach, Ger.
69/E4 Oesling (mts.), Lux.
66/B6 Oesterdam (dam), Neth.
70/B3 Oestrich-Winkel, Ger.
81/H3 Oeta Nat'l Park, Gre.
92/E1 Of, Turk.
80/D2 Ofanto (riv.), It.
91/D4 Ofaqim, Isr.
77/E5 Ofenhorn (Punta d'Arbola) (peak), Swi.
77/G4 Ofenpass (Fuorn) (pass), Swi.
60/C3 Offaly (co.), Ire.
70/B2 Offenbach, Ger.
70/A6 Offenburg, Ger.
70/B4 Offersheim, Ger.
73/G3 Oftringen, Swi.
100/B4 Ōfunato, Japan
100/A4 Oga, Japan
100/A4 Oga (pen.), Japan
100/B4 Ogachi, Japan
125/P6 Ogadēn (reg.), Eth.
98/E3 Ōgaki, Japan
159/G2 Ogallala, Ne,US
120/D2 Ogasawara, Japan
100/A3 Ōgata, Japan
100/B4 Ogatsu, Japan
100/B3 Ogawara (lake), Japan
129/G4 Ogbomosho, Nga.
158/E2 Ogden, Ut,US
160/F2 Ogdensburg, NY,US
163/H3 Ogeechee (riv.), Ga,US
78/C1 Oggiono, It.
160/D2 Ogidaki (mtn.), On,Can
151/L3 Ogilvie (mts.), Yk,Can
152/C2 Ogilvie (riv.), Yk,Can
78/D2 Oglio (riv.), It.
58/C4 Ogmore by Sea, Wal,UK
76/B3 Ognon (riv.), Fr.
111/F3 Ogoamas (peak), Indo.
157/M3 Ogoki (lake), On,Can
157/L3 Ogoki (res.), On,Can
157/M3 Ogoki (riv.), On,Can
124/G8 Ogooué (riv.), Gabon
99/H7 Ogose, Japan
83/F4 Ogosta (riv.), Bul.
63/L3 Ogre, Lat.
99/M9 Oguchi, Japan
82/B3 Ogulin, Cro.
129/F5 Ogun (riv.), Nga.
129/F5 Ogun (state), Nga.
87/K5 Ogurchinskiy (isl.), Trkm.
124/G2 Ohanet, Alg.
118/G8 O'Hares (cr.), Austl.
100/B3 Ōhata, Japan
67/E2 Ohe (riv.), Ger.
143/J7 O'Higgins (lake), Chile
160/B4 Ohio (riv.), US
160/D3 Ohio (state), US
70/C1 Ohm (riv.), Ger.
57/F1 Oh Me Edge (hill), Eng,UK
163/H3 Ohoopee (riv.), Ga,US
71/H2 Ohře (riv.), Czh.
64/F2 Ohre (riv.), Ger.
82/E5 Ohrid (lake), Alb., Macd.
82/E5 Ohrid, Macd.
104/C2 Oi (riv.), China
99/H7 Ōi, Japan
99/F3 Ōi (riv.), Japan
137/H3 Oiapoque, Braz.
137/H3 Oiapoque (riv.), Braz.
54/B2 Oich, Loch (lake), Sc,UK
75/P10 Oieras, Port.
68/B3 Oignies, Fr.
76/B5 Oignin (riv.), Fr.
168/H4 Oil (cr.), Pa,US
168/H5 Oil City, Pa,US
168/H4 Oil Creek Saint Pk., Pa,US
66/C5 Oirschot, Neth.
68/B5 Oise (dept.), Fr.
68/B5 Oise (riv.), Fr.
68/C5 Oise à l'Aisne, Canal de (can.), Fr.
68/A4 Oisemont, Fr.
99/H7 Ōiso, Japan
66/C5 Oisterwijk, Neth.
68/C3 Oisy-le-Verger, Fr.
98/B4 Ōita, Japan
98/B4 Ōita (pref.), Japan
98/B4 Ōita (riv.), Japan
164/A2 Ojai, Ca,US
65/K3 Ojcowski Nat'l Park, Pol.
99/L10 Ōji, Japan
99/F2 Ojiya, Japan
146/E4 Ojocaliente, Mex.
146/B3 Ojo de Liebre (lag.), Mex.
149/G2 Ojo del Toro (peak), Cuba
135/C2 Ojos del Salado (peak), Arg., Chile
85/J4 Oka (riv.), Rus.
161/M6 Oka Ind. Res., Qu,Can
153/K3 Okak (isl.), Nf,Can
156/C3 Okanagan (lake), BC,Can
156/D3 Okanagan Falls, BC,Can
126/B1 Okanda Nat'l Park, Gabon
156/D3 Okanogan, Wa,US
156/D3 Okanogan (riv.), Wa,US
108/B2 Okāra, Pak.
126/C4 Okaukuejo, Namb.
131/A3 Okavango Delta (reg.), Bots.
98/B4 Ōkawa, Japan
99/F2 Okaya, Japan
98/C3 Okayama, Japan
98/C3 Okayama (pref.), Japan
99/E3 Okazaki, Japan
163/H5 Okeechobee, Fl,US
163/H5 Okeechobee (lake), Fl,US
99/H7 Okegawa, Japan
58/C5 Okehampton, Eng,UK
58/B5 Okement (riv.), Eng,UK
67/H4 Oker (riv.), Ger.
89/Q4 Okha, Rus.
81/J3 Ókhi (peak), Gre.
89/Q4 Okhotsk (sea), Japan, Rus.
98/C2 Oki (isls.), Japan
98/C2 Oki-Daisen Nat'l Park, Japan
100/K7 Okinawa (isl.), Japan
100/J7 Okinawa (isls.), Japan
100/J8 Okinawa (pref.), Japan
100/K7 Okinoerabu (isl.), Japan
120/C2 Okino-Tori-Shima (Parece Vela) (isl.), Japan
107/G4 Okkan, Burma
159/H4 Oklahoma (state), US
159/H4 Oklahoma City (cap.), Ok,US
163/H4 Oklawaha (riv.), Fl,US
159/J4 Okmulgee, Ok,US
157/K5 Okoboji (lakes), Ia,US
130/B2 Okok (riv.), Ugan.
163/F3 Okolona, Ms,US
100/C1 Okoppe, Japan
156/E3 Okotoks, Ab,Can
122/E6 Okovango (riv.), Afr.
127/C4 Oko, Wādī (dry riv.), Sudan
61/E2 Oksskolten (peak), Nor.
87/J1 Oktyabr'sk, Rus.
85/M5 Oktyabr'skiy, Rus.
98/B4 Ōkuchi, Japan
84/G4 Okulovka, Rus.
100/A2 Okushiri, Japan
100/A2 Okushiri (isl.), Japan
99/H7 Okutama, Japan
126/D5 Okwa (riv.), Bots.
158/C3 Olancha, Ca,US
148/E3 Olanchito, Hon.
62/G3 Öland (isl.), Swe.
62/G3 Ölands norra udde (pt.), Swe.
62/G3 Ölands södra udde (pt.), Swe.
73/G4 Olan, Pic d' (peak), Fr.
80/D2 Olanto (riv.), It.
158/F3 Olathe, Co,US
159/J3 Olathe, Ks,US
142/E3 Olavarría, Arg.
65/J3 Oława, Pol.
67/F5 Ölbach (riv.), Ger.
80/A2 Olbia, It.
77/H1 Olching, Ger.
161/S9 Olcott, NY,US
165/L11 Old (riv.), Ca,US
149/G1 Old Bahama (chan.), Bahm., Cuba
165/D3 Old Baldy (mtn.), Wa,US
59/G2 Old Bedford (can.), Eng,UK
167/D3 Old Bridge, NJ,US
91/G8 Old City, Isr.
151/L2 Old Crow, Yk,Can
130/B3 Oldeani, Tanz.
130/B3 Oldeani (peak), Tanz.
66/C4 Oldebroek, Neth.
67/F2 Oldenburg, Ger.
70/B3 Oldenwald (for.), Ger.
66/D4 Oldenzaal, Neth.
156/F4 Old Faithful (geyser), Wy,US
167/E2 Old Field (pt.), NY,US
161/R9 Old Fort Niagara, NY,US
57/F4 Oldham, Eng,UK
168/B3 Old Lyme, Ct,US
156/E3 Oldman (riv.), Ab,Can
56/E3 Old Man of Coolston, The (mtn.), Eng,UK
55/N13 Old Man of Hoy, Sc,UK
166/C4 Oldmans (cr.), NJ,US
54/D2 Oldmeldrum, Sc,UK
59/F2 Old Nene (riv.), Eng,UK
167/E2 Old Northport (Northport), NY,US
130/C3 Ol-Doinyo Sabuk Nat'l Park, Kenya
67/F1 Oldoog (isl.), Ger.
66/B4 Old Rhine (riv.), Neth.
168/B1 Old Sturbridge Village, Ma,US
161/G2 Old Town, Me,US
130/B3 Olduvai Gorge, Tanz.
53/M7 Old Windsor, Eng,UK
157/G3 Old Wives (lake), Sk,Can
160/E3 Olean, NY,US
65/M1 Olecko, Pol.
78/B1 Oleggio, It.
74/A1 Oleiros, Sp.
89/N4 Olekma (riv.), Rus.
165/B2 Olele (pt.), Wa,US
139/H4 Olemari (riv.), Sur.
84/G1 Olenegorsk, Rus.
89/N2 Olenek (bay), Rus.
89/N2 Olenëk (riv.), Rus.
102/B1 Olenty (riv.), Kaz.
72/C4 Oléron (isl.), Fr.
75/K6 Olesa de Montserrat, Sp.
65/J3 Oleśnica, Pol.
65/K3 Olesno, Pol.
67/E5 Olfen, Ger.
117/F3 Olga (peak), Austl.
78/C1 Olginate, It.
96/B2 Ölgiy, Mong.
74/B4 Olhão, Port.
140/C3 Olho d'Água dos Flores, Braz.
73/L4 Olib (isl.), Cro.
80/A2 Oliena, It.
132/B2 Olifants (dry riv.), Namb.
132/B3 Olifants (riv.), SAfr.
132/E2 Olifantsrivier (riv.), SAfr.
120/D4 Olimarao (atoll), Micr.

210

Ólimb – Pakan

81/H2 Ólimbos (Mount Olympus) (peak), Gre.
141/B2 Olímpia, Braz.
92/B2 Olimpos Beydağları Nat'l Park, Turk.
140/D3 Olinda, Braz.
140/C3 Olindina, Braz.
142/E2 Oliva, Arg.
75/E3 Oliva, Sp.
74/B3 Oliva de la Frontera, Sp.
74/A3 Olivais, Port.
141/C2 Oliveira, Braz.
74/B3 Olivenza, Sp.
156/D3 Oliver, BC,Can
72/D3 Olivet, Fr.
136/E8 Ollagüe (vol.), Bol.
53/S11 Ollainville, Fr.
75/E3 Ollería, Sp.
108/F3 Ollūr, India
130/B3 Olmesutye, Kenya
144/B2 Olmos, Peru
168/F5 Olmsted Falls, Oh,US
142/Q9 Olmué, Chile
59/F2 Olney, Eng,UK
160/B4 Olney, Il,US
166/A5 Olney, Md,US
62/F3 Olofström, Swe.
130/C3 Oloitokitok, Kenya
161/J1 Olomane (riv.), Qu,Can
65/J4 Olomouc, Czh.
112/C2 Olongapo, Phil.
72/C3 Olonne-sur-Mer, Fr.
130/C3 Olorgasailie Nat'l Mon., Kenya
72/C5 Oloron-Sainte-Marie, Fr.
75/G1 Olot, Sp.
89/S3 Oloy (range), Rus.
67/E6 Olpe, Ger.
67/F6 Olsberg, Ger.
66/D4 Olst, Neth.
65/L2 Olsztyn, Pol.
65/L2 Olsztyn (prov.), Pol.
65/L2 Olsztynek, Pol.
83/G3 Olt (co.), Rom.
83/G4 Olt (riv.), Rom.
142/C4 Olte (mts.), Arg.
76/D3 Olten, Swi.
83/H3 Oltenița, Rom.
130/C3 Oltepesi, Kenya
83/F3 Olteț (riv.), Rom.
92/E1 Oltu, Turk.
92/E1 Oltu (riv.), Turk.
105/J4 Oluan Pi (cape), Tai.
112/C4 Olutanga (isl.), Phil.
74/C4 Olvera, Sp.
81/G4 Olympia (ruins), Gre.
165/B3 Olympia (cap.), Wa,US
81/G4 Olympia (Olimbía) (ruins), Gre.
156/B4 Olympic (mts.), Wa,US
165/A1 Olympic Game Farm, Wa,US
165/A2 Olympic Nat'l For., Wa,US
156/B4 Olympic Nat'l Park, Wa,US
91/C2 Olympus (mtn.), Cyp.
156/C4 Olympus (peak), Wa,US
81/H2 Olympus, Mount (Ólimbos) (peak), Gre.
81/H2 Olympus Nat'l Park, Gre.
89/S3 Olyutorskiy (bay), Rus.
100/B3 Ōma, Japan
85/K2 Oma (riv.), Rus.
99/E2 Ōmachi, Japan
99/F3 Omae-zaki (pt.), Japan
100/B4 Ōmagari, Japan
56/A2 Omagh, NI,UK
56/A2 Omagh (dist.), NI,UK
159/J2 Omaha, Ne,US
156/D3 Omak, Wa,US
108/G3 Omalūr, India
95/G4 Oman
95/G4 Oman (gulf), Asia
126/C5 Omaruru, Namb.
126/C4 Omatako (riv.), Namb.
100/B3 Ōma-zaki (pt.), Japan
111/F5 Ombai (str.), Indo.
58/D2 Ombersley, Eng,UK
126/B4 Ombombo, Namb.
126/A1 Omboué, Gabon
80/B1 Ombrone (riv.), It.
125/M4 Omdurman, Sudan
99/H7 Ōme, Japan
78/B1 Omegna, It.
92/E2 Ömerli, Turk.
92/B1 Ömerli (dam), Turk.
93/N7 Ömerli (res.), Turk.
148/E4 Ometepe (isl.), Nic.
148/B2 Ometepec, Mex.
99/M9 Ōmi, Japan
99/M9 Ōmihachiman, Japan
80/E1 Omiš, Cro.
148/B2 Omitlán (riv.), Mex.
99/G2 Ōmiya, Japan
152/C3 Ommancy (cape), Ak,US
151/M4 Ommaney (cape), Ak,US
66/D3 Ommen, Neth.
96/F2 Ömnödelger, Mong.
96/C2 Ömnögovĭ, Mong.
80/A2 Omodeo (lake), It.
90/Q3 Omolon (riv.), Rus.
125/N6 Omo Nat'l Park, Eth.
100/B4 Omono (riv.), Japan
125/N6 Omo Wenz (riv.), Eth.
88/H4 Omsk, Rus.
100/C1 Ōmu, Japan
130/A2 Omugo, Ugan.
83/G3 Omul (peak), Rom.
98/A4 Ōmura, Japan
83/H4 Omurtag, Bul.
98/B4 Ōmuta, Japan
85/M4 Omutninsk, Rus.
99/G1 Onagawa, Japan
159/J5 Onalaska, Tx,US
74/D1 Oñate, Sp.
160/C2 Onaway, Mi,US
142/E1 Oncativo, Arg.
56/D3 Onchan, IM,UK
126/B4 Oncocúa, Ang.
75/E3 Onda, Sp.
126/C4 Ondangua, Namb.
65/L4 Ondava (riv.), Slvk.
126/C4 Ondjiva, Ang.
129/G5 Ondo (state), Nga.
96/G2 Öndörhaan, Mong.
96/C2 Öndorhangay, Mong.
84/H3 Onega, Rus.
84/H2 Onega (bay), Rus.
84/G3 Onega (lake), Rus.
84/H2 Onega (pen.), Rus.
84/H3 Onega (riv.), Rus.
156/C3 One Hundred Mile House, BC,Can
160/F3 Oneida, NY,US
159/H2 O'Neill, Ne,US
160/F3 Oneonta, NY,US
76/C5 Onex, Swi.
96/E2 Ongiyn (riv.), Mong.
130/C3 Ongobit, Kenya
106/D4 Ongole, India
157/H4 Onida, SD,US
75/E3 Onil, Sp.
133/G8 Onilahy (riv.), Madg.
129/G5 Onitsha, Nga.
133/H7 Onive (riv.), Madg.
117/M8 Onkaparinga (riv.), Austl.
68/C3 Onnaing, Fr.
58/D2 Onny (riv.), Eng,UK
98/D3 Ono, Japan
98/E3 Ōno, Japan
98/B4 Onoda, Japan
98/C3 Onomichi, Japan
96/G1 Onon (riv.), Mong., Rus.
120/G5 Onotoa (atoll), Kiri.
99/E3 Ontake-san (mtn.), Japan
152/H3 Ontario (prov.), Can.
160/E3 Ontario (lake), Can., US
164/C2 Ontario, Ca,US
156/D4 Ontario, Or,US
166/C3 Ontelaunee (lake), Pa,US
75/E3 Onteniente, Sp.
160/B2 Ontonagon, Mi,US
120/F5 Ontong Java (isl.), Sol.
101/D4 Onyang, SKor.
162/E2 Oologan (lake), Ok,US
66/A6 Oostburg, Neth.
66/C4 Oostelijk Flevoland (polder), Neth.
68/B1 Oostende, Belg.
66/B5 Oosterhout, Neth.
66/A5 Oosterschelde (chan.), Neth.
64/B3 Oosterschelde (estuary), Neth.
66/A5 Oosterscheldedam (dam), Neth.
68/C2 Oosterzele, Belg.
68/C1 Oostkamp, Belg.
66/C4 Oostvaarderplassen (lake), Neth.
66/B4 Oostzaan, Neth.
108/F3 Ootacamund, India
157/B2 Ootsa (lake), BC,Can
154/V12 Opaeula (stream), Hi,US
126/D1 Opala, Zaire
65/J2 Opalenica, Pol.
82/B3 Opatija, Cro.
65/L3 Opatów, Pol.
65/J4 Opava, Czh.
163/G3 Opelika, Al,US
162/E4 Opelousas, La,US
160/E2 Opeongo (lake), On,Can
78/C2 Opera, It.
69/E1 Opglabbeek, Belg.
116/C2 Ophthalmia (range), Austl.
66/C5 Oploo, Neth.
66/B3 Opmeer, Neth.
65/L3 Opoczno, Pol.
65/J3 Opole, Pol.
65/J3 Opole (prov.), Pol.
65/L3 Opole Lubelskie, Pol.
163/G4 Opp, Al,US
61/D3 Oppdal, Nor.
62/C1 Oppland (co.), Nor.
156/D4 Opportunity, Wa,US
68/D2 Opwijk, Belg.
146/D3 Ora (riv.), Mex.
82/E2 Oradea, Rom.
167/J8 Oradell, NJ,US
167/J8 Oradell (res.), NJ,US
82/E4 Orahovac, Yugo.
106/C2 Orai, India
76/B4 Orain (riv.), Fr.
123/Q16 Oran, Alg.
123/Q16 Oran (wilaya), Alg.
101/E2 Orang (riv.), NKor.
132/B3 Orange (riv.), Afr.
119/D2 Orange, Austl.
72/F4 Orange, Fr.
139/H4 Orange (mts.), Sur.
164/C3 Orange, Ca,US
164/C3 Orange (co.), Ca,US
168/A3 Orange, Ct,US
167/D2 Orange, NJ,US
166/D1 Orange (co.), NY,US
162/E4 Orange, Tx,US
160/E4 Orange, Va,US
163/H3 Orangeburg, SC,US
132/D3 Orange Free State (prov.), SAfr.
163/H4 Orange Park, Fl,US
160/D3 Orangeville, On,Can
148/D2 Orange Walk, Belz.
128/A4 Orango (isl.), GBis.
65/G2 Oranienburg, Ger.
66/D3 Oranjekanaal (can.), Neth.
150/D4 Oranjestad, Aru.
123/Q16 Oran, Sebkha d' (lake), Alg.
131/B4 Orapa, Bots.
91/F7 Or 'Aqiva, Isr.
112/D2 Oras, Phil.
83/F3 Orăştie, Rom.
82/E3 Oravița, Rom.
72/E5 Orb (riv.), Fr.
78/B3 Orba (riv.), It.
78/A2 Orbassano, It.
76/C4 Orbe (riv.), Swi.
74/C1 Órbigo (riv.), Sp.
165/F6 Orchard (lake), Mi,US
162/B2 Orchard City, Co,US
156/E4 Orchard Homes, Mt,US
165/F6 Orchard Lake Village, Mi,US
54/B4 Orchy (riv.), Sc,UK
78/A2 Orco (riv.), It.
72/F3 Or, Côte d' (uplands), Fr.
159/H2 Ord, Ne,US
74/A1 Ordenes, Sp.
75/F1 Ordesa y Monte Perdido Nat'l Park, Sp.
103/B3 Ordos (des.), China
92/D1 Ordu, Turk.
92/D1 Ordu (prov.), Turk.
159/G3 Ordway, Co,US
62/F2 Örebro, Swe.
62/F2 Örebro (co.), Swe.
156/C4 Oregon (state), US
158/B2 Oregon Caves Nat'l Mon., Or,US
156/C4 Oregon City, Or,US
86/F1 Orël, Rus.
86/E2 Orel' (riv.), Ukr.
86/E1 Orel Obl., Rus.
158/E2 Orem, Ut,US
87/K2 Orenburg, Rus.
87/K1 Orenburg Obl., Rus.
74/B1 Orense, Sp.
81/K2 Orestiás, Gre.
62/E4 Øresund (sound), Den., Swe.
59/H2 Orford, Eng,UK
59/H2 Orford Ness (pt.), UK
158/D4 Organ Pipe Cactus Nat'l Mon., Az,US
141/L7 Órgãos (mts.), Braz.
53/S11 Orge (riv.), Fr.
53/R10 Orgeval, Fr.
83/J2 Orgeyev, Mol.
86/D5 Orhaneli, Turk.
83/J5 Orhangazi, Turk.
96/F2 Orhon (riv.), Mong.
72/C5 Orhy, Pic d' (peak), Fr.
60/D2 Oriel (mtn.), Ire.
167/F1 Orient (pt.), NY,US
135/C6 Oriental (val.), Arg.
147/M7 Oriental, Mex.
136/D6 Oriental, Cordillera (range), SAm.
75/E3 Orihuela, Sp.
160/E2 Orillia, On,Can
63/L1 Orimattila, Fin.
165/K11 Orinda, Ca,US
139/F2 Orinoco (riv.), Col., Ven.
139/F2 Orinoco (delta), Ven.
112/C2 Orion, Phil.
165/F6 Orion (lake), Mi,US
106/D3 Orissa (state), India
80/A3 Oristano, It.
80/A3 Oristano (gulf), It.
63/L1 Orivesi, Fin.
139/H5 Oriximiná, Braz.
147/F5 Orizaba, Mex.
147/K6 Orizabita, Mex.
82/D4 Orjen (peak), Yugo.
67/F6 Orke (riv.), Ger.
55/N13 Orkney (isls.), Sc,UK
162/C4 Orla, Tx,US
141/C2 Orlândia, Braz.
163/H4 Orlando, Fl,US
80/D3 Orlando, Capo d' (cape), It.
165/Q16 Orland Park, Il,US
63/R7 Orlången (lake), Swe.
72/D2 Orléanais (hist. reg.), Fr.
72/D3 Orléans, Fr.
158/B2 Orleans, Ca,US
71/H3 Orlík, Údolní nádrž (res.), Czh.
65/K4 Orlová, Czh.
53/T10 Orly, Fr.
54/D5 Ormiston, Sc,UK
112/D3 Ormoc City, Phil.
163/H4 Ormond Beach, Fl,US
76/C4 Or, Mont d' (mtn.), Fr.
57/F4 Ormskirk, Eng,UK
72/F2 Ornain (riv.), Fr.
69/F5 Orne (riv.), Fr.
61/E2 Ørnes, Nor.
65/L1 Orneta, Pol.
61/F3 Örnsköldsvik, Swe.
77/F5 Orobie, Alpi (range), It.
140/C3 Orocó, Braz.
128/D4 Orodara, Burk.
75/E1 Oroel (peak), Sp.
156/D4 Orofino, Id,US
121/L6 Orohena (peak), FrPol.
79/E1 Orolo (riv.), It.
120/E4 Oroluk (atoll), Micr.
161/H2 Oromocto, NB,Can
80/A1 Oro, Monte d' (mtn.), Fr.
121/H5 Orona (Hull) (atoll), Kiri.
161/G2 Orono, Me,US
91/E2 Orontes (riv.), Asia
130/B2 Oropoi, Kenya
97/J1 Oroqen Zizhiqi, China
112/C3 Oroquieta, Phil.
140/C2 Orós, Braz.
140/C2 Orós (res.), Braz.
80/A2 Orosei (gulf), It.
82/E2 Orosháza, Hun.
82/D2 Oroszlány, Hun.
158/C2 Orovada, Nv,US
158/E4 Oro Valley, Az,US
158/B3 Oroville, Ca,US
156/D3 Oroville, Wa,US
53/P7 Orpington, Eng,UK
57/F4 Orrell, Eng,UK
54/B2 Orrin (res.), Sc,UK
54/B2 Orrin (riv.), Sc,UK
168/F6 Orrville, Oh,US
53/T9 Orry-la-Ville, Fr.
62/F1 Orsa, Swe.
53/S10 Orsay, Fr.
53/Q7 Orsett, Eng,UK
84/F5 Orsha, Bela.
87/L2 Orsk, Rus.
82/F3 Orșova, Rom.
61/C3 Ørsta, Nor.
78/B1 Orta (lake), It.
92/B2 Ortaca, Turk.
92/C1 Ortaköy, Turk.
80/D2 Orta Nova, It.
74/B1 Ortegal (cape), Sp.
70/C2 Ortenberg, Ger.
72/C5 Orthez, Fr.
77/H5 Ortigara, Monte (peak), It.
74/B1 Ortigueira, Sp.
77/G4 Ortles (peak), It.
77/G5 Ortles (mts.), It., Swi.
136/E6 Ortón (riv.), Bol.
97/H2 Orton (riv.), China
80/D1 Ortona, It.
165/F6 Ortonville, Mi,US
157/J4 Ortonville, Mn,US
70/B3 Ortze (riv.), Ger.
93/F2 Orūmīyeh, Iran
136/E7 Oruro, Bol.
62/D2 Orust (isl.), Swe.
80/C1 Orvieto, It.
113/V Orville (coast), Ant.
59/H2 Orwell (riv.), Eng,UK
166/B2 Orwin-Reinerton-Muir, Pa,US
96/H2 Orxon (riv.), China
83/F4 Oryakhovo, Bul.
91/F7 Or Yehuda, Isr.
78/C2 Orzinuovi, It.
62/A1 Os, Nor.
149/F4 Osa (pen.), CR
85/M4 Osa, Rus.
159/J3 Osage (riv.), Mo,US
159/J3 Osage Beach, Mo,US
98/D3 Ōsaka, Japan
99/L10 Ōsaka (bay), Japan
98/D3 Ōsaka (pref.), Japan
99/L10 Ōsaka Castle, Japan
98/L10 Ōsaka (inset), Japan
101/D4 Osan, SKor.
141/G8 Osasco, Braz.
151/E3 Osborn (mtn.), Ak,US
159/H3 Osborne, Ks,US
62/E3 Osby, Swe.
163/F3 Osceola, Ar,US
64/F2 Oschersleben, Ger.
162/B3 Oscura (mts.), NM,US
102/B3 Osh, Kyr.
126/C4 Oshakati, Namb.
100/B2 Oshamambe, Japan
161/S8 Oshawa, On,Can
100/B4 Oshika (pen.), Japan
100/A2 Oshima (pen.), Japan
126/C4 Oshivelo, Namb.
157/H5 Oshkosh, Ne,US
160/B2 Oshkosh, Wi,US
129/G5 Oshogbo, Nga.
126/C1 Oshwe, Zaire
82/D3 Osijek, Cro.
79/G6 Osimo, It.
78/C1 Osio Sotto, It.
86/D1 Osipovichi, Bela.
157/K5 Oskaloosa, Ia,US
62/G3 Oskarshamn, Swe.
86/F2 Oskol (riv.), Rus., Ukr.
62/D2 Oslo (cap.), Nor.
62/D2 Oslofjord (fjord), Nor.
106/C4 Osmānābād, India
92/C1 Osmancık, Turk.
83/K5 Osmaneli, Turk.
91/E1 Osmaniye, Turk.
67/F4 Osnabrück, Ger.
53/S9 Osny, Fr.
165/M11 Oso (mtn.), Ca,US
130/A3 Oso (riv.), Zaire
141/B4 Osório, Braz.
142/B4 Osorno, Chile
156/D3 Osoyoos, BC,Can
78/D1 Ospitaletto, It.
118/B1 Osprey (reef), Austl.
66/C5 Oss, Neth.
119/C4 Ossa (peak), Austl.
81/H3 Ossa (mtn.), Gre.
74/B3 Ossa (range), Port.
129/G5 Osse (riv.), Nga.
57/G4 Ossett, Eng,UK
167/E1 Ossining, NY,US
84/G4 Ostashkov, Rus.
67/E4 Ostbevern, Ger.
67/G1 Oste (riv.), Ger.
68/B1 Ostend (Oostende), Belg.
64/F2 Osterburg, Ger.
67/F4 Ostercappeln, Ger.
62/E1 Österdalälven (riv.), Swe.
66/D1 Osterems (chan.), Neth.
62/F2 Östergötland (co.), Swe.
71/G5 Osterhofen, Ger.
67/F2 Osterholz-Scharmbeck, Ger.
67/H5 Osterode, Ger.
64/F3 Osterode am Harz, Ger.
61/E3 Östersund, Swe.
70/C5 Ostfildern, Ger.
62/D2 Østfold (co.), Nor.
67/E2 Ostfriesland (reg.), Ger.
62/H1 Östhammar, Swe.
76/D1 Ostheim, Fr.
70/B3 Osthofen, Ger.
80/C2 Ostia Antica (ruins), It.
79/E2 Ostiglia, It.
148/E4 Ostional Nat'l Wild. Ref., CR
77/F2 Ostrach (riv.), Ger.
62/E2 Östra Silen (lake), Swe.
65/K4 Ostrava, Czh.
67/E2 Ostrhauderfehn, Ger.
68/C3 Ostricourt, Fr.
70/B4 Östringen, Ger.
82/D4 Oštri Rt (cape), Yugo.
65/K2 Ostróda, Pol.
86/F2 Ostrogozhsk, Rus.
65/L2 Ostrołęka, Pol.
65/L2 Ostrołęka (prov.), Pol.
71/F2 Ostrov, Czh.
63/N3 Ostrov, Rus.
65/L3 Ostrowiec Świętokrzyski, Pol.
65/L2 Ostrów Mazowiecka, Pol.
65/J3 Ostrów Wielkopolski, Pol.
65/J3 Ostrzeszów, Pol.
62/E4 Ostseebad Binz, Ger.
67/H1 Oststeinbek, Ger.
80/E2 Ostuni, It.
81/G2 Osum (riv.), Alb.
83/G4 Osŭm (riv.), Bul.
98/B5 Ōsumi (isls.), Japan
98/B5 Ōsumi (pen.), Japan
98/B5 Ōsumi (str.), Japan
74/C4 Osuna, Sp.
141/B2 Osvaldo Cruz, Braz.
57/G3 Oswaldkirk, Eng,UK
57/F4 Oswaldtwistle, Eng,UK
166/D4 Oswego (riv.), NJ,US
160/E3 Oswego, NY,US
57/E6 Oswestry, Eng,UK
65/K3 Oświęcim (Auschwitz), Pol.
98/F2 Ōta, Japan
98/C3 Ōta (riv.), Japan
98/C3 Ōtake, Japan
99/G3 Ōtaki, Japan
99/G2 Ōtakine-yama (mtn.), Japan
100/B2 Otaru, Japan
71/H4 Otava (riv.), Czh.
138/B4 Otavalo, Ecu.
126/C4 Otavi, Namb.
99/G2 Ōtawara, Japan
83/F3 Oțelu Roșu, Rom.
121/L6 Otepa, FrPol.
146/C3 Oteros (riv.), Mex.
96/D2 Otgon, Mong.
96/D2 Otgon Tenger (peak), Mong.
156/D4 Othello, Wa,US
53/U9 Othis, Fr.
81/F3 Othonoí (isl.), Gre.
129/F4 Oti (riv.), Gui.
115/R11 Otira, NZ
168/A1 Otis (res.), Ma,US
126/C5 Otjikango, Namb.
126/C5 Otjinene, Namb.
126/C5 Otjiwarongo, Namb.
126/B4 Otjokavare, Namb.
57/G4 Otley, Eng,UK
100/C2 Otofuke, Japan
103/A3 Otog Qi, China
96/F4 Otog Qianqi, China
157/L3 Otoskwin (riv.), On,Can
99/N10 Otowa, Japan
62/B2 Otra (riv.), Nor.
87/J1 Otradnyy, Rus.
81/F2 Otranto (str.), Alb., It.
81/F2 Otranto, It.
65/J4 Otrokovice, Czh.
98/D3 Ōtsu, Japan
100/B4 Ōtsuchi, Japan
61/D3 Otta, Nor.
160/F2 Ottawa (cap.), Can.
153/H3 Ottawa (isls.), NW,Can
160/E2 Ottawa (riv.), On, Qu,Can
160/B3 Ottawa, Il,US
159/J3 Ottawa, Ks,US
160/C3 Ottawa, Oh,US
58/C5 Otter (riv.), Eng,UK
168/G5 Otter (cr.), Pa,US
57/F1 Otterburn, Eng,UK
67/F1 Otterndorf, Ger.
67/G2 Ottersberg, Ger.
53/M7 Ottershaw, Eng,UK
58/C5 Ottery Saint Mary, Eng,UK
68/D2 Ottignies-Louvain-La-Neuve, Belg.
77/G2 Ottobeuren, Ger.
71/E6 Ottobrunn, Ger.
157/K5 Ottumwa, Ia,US
69/G5 Ottweiler, Ger.
147/L7 Otumba de Gómez Farías, Mex.
119/B3 Otway (cape), Austl.
143/J8 Otway (bay), Chile
143/K8 Otway (sound), Chile
119/B3 Otway Nat'l Park, Austl.
65/L2 Otwock, Pol.
77/G4 Ötztal Alps (mts.), Aus., It.
77/G3 Ötztaler Ache (riv.), Aus.
100/B4 Ou (mts.), Japan
109/C1 Ou (riv.), Laos
162/E3 Ouachita (riv.), Ar, La,US
159/J4 Ouachita (mts.), Ar, Ok,US
124/C3 Ouadane, Mrta.
125/K6 Ouadda, CAfr.
125/J5 Ouaddaï (reg.), Chad
129/E3 Ouagadougou (cap.), Burk.
125/K6 Ouaka (riv.), CAfr.
128/D2 Oualâta, Dhar (hills), Mrta.
125/K6 Ouanda Djalle, CAfr.
72/E3 Ouanne (riv.), Fr.
124/C3 Ouarane (reg.), Mrta.
124/G1 Ouargla, Alg.
124/D1 Ouarzazate, Mor.
161/F1 Ouasiemsca (riv.), Qu,Can
123/S16 Ouassel, Nahr (riv.), Alg.
125/J6 Oubangui (riv.), CAfr.
129/E3 Oubritenga (prov.), Burk.
76/B3 Ouche (riv.), Fr.
99/L10 Ōuda, Japan
129/E3 Oudalan (prov.), Burk.
66/B5 Oud-Beijerland, Neth.
66/A5 Ouddorp, Neth.
66/D5 Oude IJssel (riv.), Neth.
68/C2 Oudenaarde, Belg.
66/B5 Oudenbosch, Neth.
68/B1 Oudenburg, Belg.
66/E2 Oude Pekela, Neth.
66/D2 Oude Westereems (chan.), Neth.
72/C3 Oudon (riv.), Fr.
132/C4 Oudtshoorn, SAfr.
66/B6 Oud-Turnhout, Belg.
128/E2 Oued el Hadjar (well), Mali
123/R16 Oued Rhiou, Alg.
124/D1 Oued Zem, Mor.
129/F5 Ouémé (prov.), Ben.
129/F4 Ouémé (riv.), Ben.
121/V13 Ouen (isl.), NCal.
123/W18 Ouenza, Alg.
123/M13 Ouerrha (riv.), Mor.
72/A2 Ouessant (isl.), Fr.
124/J7 Ouesso, Congo
129/H5 Ouest (prov.), Camr.
149/H1 Ouest (pt.), Haiti
149/H2 Ouest (pt.), Haiti
123/M13 Ouezzane, Mor.
60/C2 Oughter, Lough (lake), Ire.
125/J6 Ouham (riv.), CAfr., Chad
68/C5 Ouichy-le-Château, Fr.
123/P13 Oujda, Mor.
61/J2 Oulangan Nat'l Park, Fin.
117/H5 Oulnina (peak), Austl.
61/H2 Oulu, Fin.
61/H2 Oulu (prov.), Fin.
61/H2 Oulujärvi (lake), Fin.
123/V18 Oum El Bouaghi, Alg.
123/V18 Oum El Bouaghi (gov.), Alg.
75/J5 Oum El Bouaghi (wilaya), Alg.
124/D1 Oum er Rhia (riv.), Mor.
125/J5 Oum Hadjer, Chad
84/E2 Ounasjoki (riv.), Fin.
59/F2 Oundle, Eng,UK
125/K4 OuniangaKebir, Chad
69/E2 Oupeye, Belg.
69/E4 Our (riv.), Belg.
69/F4 Our (riv.), Eur.
76/A2 Ource (riv.), Fr.
68/C5 Ourcq (riv.), Fr.
61/H1 Øure Anarjokka Nat'l Park, Nor.
61/F1 Øure Dividal Nat'l Park, Nor.
125/J3 Ouri, Chad
140/B2 Ouricuri, Braz.
141/B2 Ourinhos, Braz.
129/H3 Ourofané, Niger
141/G7 Ouro Fino, Braz.
131/D5 Ouro, Ponta do (pt.), Moz.
141/D2 Ouro Preto, Braz.
69/E3 Ourthe (riv.), Belg.
69/E3 Ourthe Occidentale (riv.), Belg.
69/E3 Ourthe Oriental (riv.), Belg.
57/H4 Ouse (riv.), Eng,UK
59/G5 Ouse (riv.), Eng,UK
72/B3 Oust (riv.), Fr.
75/Q11 Outão, Port.
160/E2 Outaouais (riv.), Qu,Can
161/G1 Outardes (riv.), Qu,Can
161/G1 Outardes Quatre (res.), Qu,Can
128/D2 Outeid Arkas (well), Mali
55/G8 Outer Hebrides (isls.), Sc,UK
74/A1 Outes, Sp.
126/C5 Outjo, Namb.
156/G3 Outlook, Sk,Can
68/A2 Outreau, Fr.
161/N6 Outremont, Qu,Can
121/V12 Ouvéa (atoll), NCal.
121/V12 Ouvéa (lag.), NCal.
78/B3 Ovada, It.
121/Y18 Ovalau (isl.), Fiji
135/B3 Ovalle, Chile
139/E3 Ovana (peak), Ven.
74/A2 Ovar, Port.
69/G2 Overath, Ger.
66/B5 Overflakkee (isl.), Neth.
68/D2 Overijse, Belg.
66/D3 Overijssel (prov.), Neth.
66/D4 Overijssels (can.), Neth.
159/J3 Overland Park, Ks,US
166/B5 Overlea, Md,US
142/C5 Overo (peak), Arg.
69/E1 Overpelt, Belg.
59/E1 Overseal, Eng,UK
59/H1 Overstrand, Eng,UK
59/E4 Overton, Eng,UK
57/F6 Overton, Wal,UK
158/D3 Overton, Nv,US
61/G2 Övertorneå, Swe.
74/C1 Oviedo, Sp.
62/E1 Övre Fryken (lake), Swe.
61/J1 Øvre Pasvik Nat'l Park, Nor.
126/C1 Owando, Congo
100/B3 Ōwani, Japan
99/N9 Owariasahi, Japan
98/E3 Owase, Japan
166/D1 Owassa (lake), NJ,US
159/J3 Owasso, Ok,US
157/K4 Owatonna, Mn,US
160/E3 Owego, NY,US
60/C3 Owel, Lough (lake), Ire.
115/R11 Owen (peak), NZ
130/B2 Owen Falls (dam), Ugan.
60/A1 Oweniny (riv.), Ire.
56/A2 Owenkillew (riv.), NI,UK
158/C3 Owens (riv.), Ca,US
160/C4 Owensboro, Ky,US
160/D2 Owen Sound, On,Can
158/C2 Owhyee (mts.), Id,US
166/B5 Owings Mills, Md,US
156/F4 Owl Creek (mts.), Wy,US
160/C3 Owosso, Mi,US
156/D5 Owyhee (riv.), Id, Or,US
158/C2 Owyhee, Nv,US
158/C2 Owyhee (lake), Or,US
156/D5 Owyhee, South Fork (riv.), Id, Nv,US
94/E1 Owzan (riv.), Iran
157/H3 Oxbow, Sk,Can
165/F6 Oxbow (lake), Mi,US
62/G2 Oxelösund, Swe.
157/K2 Oxford (lake), Mb,Can
59/E3 Oxford, Eng,UK
59/E3 Oxford (can.), Eng,UK
168/A3 Oxford, Ct,US
165/F6 Oxford, Mi,US
163/F3 Oxford, Ms,US
160/C4 Oxford, Oh,US
59/E3 Oxfordshire (co.), Eng,UK
53/M7 Oxhey, Eng,UK
147/H4 Oxkutzcab, Mex.
118/E7 Oxley (cr.), Austl.
164/A2 Oxnard, Ca,US
166/A6 Oxon Hill Farm, Md,US
166/B6 Oxon Hill-Glassmanor, Md,US
53/M8 Oxshott, Eng,UK
60/B1 Ox (Slieve Gamph) (mts.), Ire.
53/N8 Oxted, Eng,UK
54/D5 Oxton, Sc,UK
99/E2 Oyabe, Japan
99/F2 Oyama, Japan
99/M10 Ōyamada, Japan
99/L10 Oyamazaki, Japan
137/H3 Oyapock (riv.), FrG.
124/H7 Oyem, Gabon
156/F3 Oyen, Ab,Can
55/J7 Oykell (riv.), Sc,UK
129/F5 Oyo, Nga.
129/F4 Oyo (state), Nga.
99/L10 Ōyodo, Japan
98/B5 Ōyodo (riv.), Japan
144/B3 Oyón, Peru
76/B5 Oyonnax, Fr.
167/E2 Oyster Bay, NY,US
167/L8 Oyster Bay (har.), NY,US
167/E2 Oyster Bay Nat'l Wild. Ref., NY,US
67/G2 Oyten, Ger.
130/B3 Oyugis, Kenya
112/C3 Ozamiz City, Phil.
72/D2 Ozanne (riv.), Fr.
159/J3 Ozark (plat.), US
163/G4 Ozark, Al,US
162/E3 Ozark, Ar,US
162/E3 Ozark (mts.), Ar, Mo,US
159/J3 Ozarks, Lake of the (lake), Mo,US
82/E1 Ózd, Hun.
89/S4 Ozernoy (cape), Rus.
156/B3 Ozette (lake), Wa,US
157/L3 Ozhiski (lake), On,Can
80/A2 Ozieri, It.
65/K3 Ozimek, Pol.
53/U10 Ozoir-la-Ferrière, Fr.
162/C4 Ozona, Tx,US
167/K9 Ozone Park, NY,US
65/K3 Ozorków, Pol.
53/U11 Ozouer-le-Voulgis, Fr.
98/C4 Ōzu, Japan
147/L7 Ozumba de Alzate, Mex.

P

70/E5 Paar (riv.), Ger.
132/B4 Paarl, SAfr.
63/T8 Påarp, Swe.
65/K3 Pabianice, Pol.
106/E3 Pābna, Bang.
136/F6 Pacaás Novos (mts.), Braz.
136/F6 Pacaás Novos Nat'l Park, Braz.
137/H4 Pacajá (riv.), Braz.
140/C2 Pacajus, Braz.
139/F4 Pacaraimã (mts.), Braz., Ven.
144/B2 Pacasmayo, Peru
140/C1 Pacatuba, Braz.
144/C2 Pacaya Samiria Nat'l Rsv., Peru
80/C4 Paceco, It.
144/B4 Pachacamac (ruins), Peru
144/C4 Pachamarca (riv.), Peru
168/C2 Pachaug (pond), Ct,US
168/C2 Pachaug Saint For., Ct,US
80/D4 Pachino, It.
144/C3 Pachitea (riv.), Peru
106/C3 Pachmarhī, India
148/B1 Pachuca, Mex.
147/F4 Pachuca de Soto, Mex.
130/A2 Pachwa, Ugan.
50/B4 Pacific (ocean)
156/B3 Pacific (ranges), BC,Can
144/J8 Pacific (ocean), Ecu.
165/K11 Pacifica, Ca,US
164/B2 Pacifico (mtn.), Ca,US
164/E7 Pacific Palisades, Ca,US
152/D4 Pacific Rim Nat'l Park, BC,Can
110/D5 Pacinan (cape), Indo.
110/D5 Pacitan, Indo.
75/P10 Paço de Arcos, Port.
112/D4 Padada, Phil.
110/B4 Padang, Indo.
110/B4 Padangpanjang, Indo.
110/A3 Padangsidempuan, Indo.
112/A4 Padas (riv.), Malay.
53/N7 Paddington, Eng,UK
59/G4 Paddock Wood, Eng,UK
67/F5 Paderborn, Ger.
130/B2 Padibe, Ugan.
95/J3 Pad Īdan, Pak.
57/F4 Padiham, Eng,UK
136/F7 Padilla, Bol.
82/E3 Padina, Yugo.
61/E2 Padjelanta Nat'l Park, Swe.
108/F4 Padmanābhapuram, India
79/E2 Padova (prov.), It.
79/E2 Padova (Padua), It.
126/B2 Padrão, Ponta do (pt.), Ang.
162/D5 Padre (isl.), Tx,US
162/D5 Padre Island Nat'l Seashore, Tx,US
74/A1 Padrón, Sp.
132/D4 Padrone (cape), SAfr.
58/B5 Padstow, Eng,UK
79/E2 Padua (Padova), It.
160/B4 Paducah, Ky,US
162/C3 Paducah, Tx,US
101/E4 Paektŏk-san (mtn.), SKor.
101/E2 Paektu-San (mtn.), NKor.
101/C4 Paengnyŏng (isl.), SKor.
79/F1 Paese, It.
131/C4 Pafúri, Moz.
82/B3 Pag, Cro.
82/B3 Pag (isl.), Cro.
112/C4 Pagadian, Phil.
110/B4 Pagai Selatan (isl.), Indo.
110/A4 Pagai Utara (isl.), Indo.
120/D3 Pagan (isl.), NMar.
158/E3 Page, Az,US
130/B2 Pager (riv.), Ugan.
112/A4 Pagon, Bukit (mtn.), Malay.
121/H6 Pago Pago (cap.), ASam.
158/F3 Pagosa Springs, Co,US
160/C1 Pagwachuan (riv.), On,Can
110/B3 Pahang (riv.), Malay.
149/F3 Pāhara (lag.), Nic.
158/D3 Pahrump, Nv,US
147/L6 Pahuatlán de Valle, Mex.
158/C3 Pahute Mesa (upland), Nv,US
103/C5 Pai (lake), China
81/L7 Paiania, Gre.
58/C6 Paignton, Eng,UK
144/B2 Paiján, Peru
63/L1 Päijänne (lake), Fin.
154/T10 Pailolo (chan.), Hi,US
63/K1 Paimio, Fin.
142/C2 Paine, Chile
143/J7 Paine (peak), Chile
160/D3 Painesville, Oh,US
58/C2 Painscastle, Wal,UK
157/J2 Paint (lake), Mb,Can
158/E4 Painted (des.), Az,US
162/D4 Paint Rock, Tx,US
160/D4 Paintsville, Ky,US
54/B5 Paisley, Sc,UK
144/A2 Paita, Peru
106/C4 Paithan, India
61/G2 Pajala, Swe.
138/A5 Paján, Ecu.
65/K3 Pajęczno, Pol.
140/C3 Pajeú (riv.), Braz.
149/F4 Pajonal Abajo, Pan.
110/B3 Pakanbaru, Indo.

211
Pakar – Peram

139/F3 Pakaraima (mts.), Guy.
119/G6 Pakenham, Austl.
143/J7 Pakenham (cape), Chile
81/J5 Pákhnes (peak), Gre.
85/X9 Pakhra (riv.), Rus.
95/H3 Pakistan
82/B3 Paklenica Nat'l Park, Cro.
104/B4 Pakokku, Burma
156/F3 Pakowki (lake), Ab,Can
108/B2 Pākpattan, Pak.
107/H6 Pak Phanang, Thai.
82/C3 Pakrac, Cro.
82/D2 Paks, Hun.
130/A2 Pakwach, Ugan.
109/D3 Pakxe, Laos
124/H6 Pala, Chad
75/N9 Palacio Real, Sp.
75/G2 Palafrugell, Sp.
80/D4 Palagonia, It.
80/E1 Palagruža (isls.), Cro.
108/F4 Palai, India
164/C4 Pala Ind. Res., Ca,US
81/F3 Palaiokastritsa, Gre.
53/S10 Palaiseau, Fr.
106/D4 Pālakolla, India
131/C4 Palalarivier (riv.), SAfr.
75/G2 Palamós, Sp.
112/C1 Palanan, Phil.
112/C1 Palanan (mtn.), Phil.
112/C1 Palanan (pt.), Phil.
112/C2 Palanas, Phil.
110/D4 Palangkaraya, Indo.
106/B3 Pālanpur, India
154/T10 Palaoa (pt.), Hi,US
131/B4 Palapye, Bots.
106/C5 Palar (riv.), India
74/B1 Palas de Rey, Sp.
165/P15 Palatine, Il,US
163/H4 Palatka, Fl,US
120/C4 Palau
112/B3 Palawan (chan.), Phil.
112/B3 Palawan (isl.), Phil.
112/C2 Palayan, Phil.
108/F4 Pālayankottai, India
80/D4 Palazzolo Acreide, It.
124/G8 Palé, EqG.
111/F3 Paleleh, Indo.
110/B4 Palembang, Indo.
142/B4 Palena (riv.), Chile
74/C1 Palencia, Sp.
147/H5 Palenque Nat'l Park, Mex.
161/Q9 Palermo, On,Can
80/C3 Palermo, It.
162/E4 Palestine, Tx,US
162/E3 Palestine (lake), Tx,US
95/K5 Pālghar, India
108/F3 Pālghāt, India
101/D5 P'algong-san (mtn.), SKor.
101/E4 P'algong-san (mtn.), SKor.
116/B2 Palgrave (peak), Austl.
140/C2 Palhano, Braz.
141/B3 Palhoça, Braz.
106/B2 Pāli, India
143/K8 Pali Aike Nat'l Park, Chile
82/D2 Palić, Yugo.
154/V13 Palikea (peak), Hi,US
81/H3 Palioúrion, Ákra (cape), Gre.
167/K8 Palisades (bluff), NJ,US
167/D1 Palisades Intst. Park, NJ, NY,US
167/E2 Palisades Park, NJ,US
106/B3 Pālitāna, India
82/C3 Paljenik (peak), Bosn.
108/G4 Palk (str.), India, SrL.
108/G4 Palk (bay), SrL.
77/G4 Palla Bianca (Weisskugel) (mtn.), It.
61/H1 Pallas-Ounastunturin Nat'l Park, Fin.
61/H1 Pallastunturi (peak), Fin.
130/B2 Pallisa, Ugan.
115/S11 Palliser (cape), NZ
115/H3 Palm (isls.), Austl.
140/A4 Palma (riv.), Braz.
130/D5 Palma, Moz.
75/G3 Palma, Sp.
140/C2 Palmácia, Braz.
74/C4 Palma del Río, Sp.
80/C4 Palma di Montechiaro, It.
149/H4 Palmar (riv.), Ven.
140/D3 Palmares, Braz.
141/B3 Palmas, Braz.
128/D5 Palmas (cape), Libr.
149/H1 Palma Soriano, Cuba
163/H4 Palm Bay, Fl,US
118/H8 Palm Beach, Austl.
164/B1 Palmdale, Ca,US
141/B3 Palmeira, Braz.
140/C3 Palmeira dos Índios, Braz.
140/B4 Palmeiras, Braz.
140/A3 Palmeiras (riv.), Braz.
126/B2 Palmeirinhas, Ponta das (pt.), Ang.
75/Q10 Palmela, Port.
113/V Palmer (arch.), Ant.
168/B1 Palmer, Ma,US
113/V Palmer Land (reg.), Ant.
118/C3 Palmerston (cape), Austl.
121/J6 Palmerston (atoll), CookIs.
115/R12 Palmerston, NZ
118/B2 Palmerston Nat'l Park, Austl.
115/S11 Palmerston North, NZ
163/H5 Palmetto, Fl,US
163/H4 Palm Harbor, Fl,US
80/D3 Palmi, It.
118/B2 Palm I. Abor. Settlement, Austl.
142/C2 Palmilla, Chile
149/F1 Palmillas (pt.), Cuba
138/B4 Palmira, Col.
141/B2 Palmital, Braz.
158/C4 Palm Springs, Ca,US
121/J4 Palmyra (isl.), PacUS
92/D3 Palmyra (ruins), Syria
166/B3 Palmyra, Pa,US
106/E3 Palmyras (pt.), India
56/E2 Palnackie, Sc,UK
108/F3 Palni, India
108/F3 Palni (hills), India
112/D3 Palo, Phil.
165/K12 Palo Alto, Ca,US
159/G3 Palo Duro (cr.), Ok, Tx,US
139/H4 Palomeu (riv.), Sur.
73/J4 Palon (peak), It.
79/E1 Palon, Cima (peak), It.
162/D3 Palo Pinto, Tx,US
75/E4 Palos, Cabo de (cape), Sp.
165/Q16 Palos Hills, Il,US
164/F8 Palos Verdes (hills), Ca,US
164/F8 Palos Verdes (pt.), Ca,US
164/B3 Palos Verdes Estates, Ca,US
149/E4 Palo Verde Nat'l Park, CR
106/D2 Pālpa, Nepal
135/C1 Palpalá, Arg.
111/G4 Palpetu (cape), Indo.
92/D2 Palu, Turk.
112/C2 Paluan, Phil.
110/C3 Pamangkat, Indo.
72/D5 Pamiers, Fr.
102/B4 Pamir (riv.), Afg., Taj.
102/B4 Pamir (reg.), China, Taj.
163/J3 Pamlico (riv.), NC,US
163/J3 Pamlico (sound), NC,US
162/C3 Pampa, Tx,US
142/E2 Pampa Humida (plain), Arg.
142/E3 Pampas (plain), Arg.
144/C4 Pampas (riv.), Peru
142/D3 Pampa Seca (plain), Arg.
138/C3 Pamplona, Col.
74/E1 Pamplona, Sp.
83/K5 Pamukova, Turk.
112/D4 Panabo, Phil.
158/D3 Panaca, Nv,US
106/C6 Panadura, SrL.
83/G4 Panagyurishte, Bul.
110/B5 Panaitan (isl.), Indo.
106/B4 Panāji, India
149/F4 Panama
149/G4 Panamá (bay), Pan.
149/F4 Panama (can.), Pan.
149/G4 Panamá (cap.), Pan.
149/G4 Panama (gulf), Pan.
149/G4 Panama (isth.), Pan.
163/G4 Panama City, Fl,US
158/C3 Panamint (range), Ca,US
112/D3 Panaon (isl.), Phil.
79/E3 Panaro (riv.), It.
112/C3 Panay (gulf), Phil.
112/C3 Panay (isl.), Phil.
158/C3 Pancake (range), Nv,US
82/E3 Pančevo, Yugo.
82/E4 Pančičev vrh (peak), Yugo.
83/H3 Panciu, Rom.
131/D5 Panda, Moz.
131/B1 Panda, Zaire
108/E3 Pandalayini, India
131/B3 Pandamatenga, Bots.
112/C3 Pandan, Phil.
112/D2 Pandan, Phil.
135/B2 Pan de Azúcar Nat'l Park, Chile
106/C4 Pandharpur, India
117/H3 Pandie Pandie, Austl.
143/G2 Pando, Uru.
107/F2 Pandu, India
63/L4 Panevėžys, Lith.
102/D3 Panfilov, Kaz.
104/C4 Pang (riv.), Burma
121/H7 Pangai, Tonga
81/J2 Pangaíon (peak), Gre.
130/C4 Pangani, Tanz.
130/C4 Pangani (riv.), Tanz.
59/E4 Pangbourne, Eng,UK
110/A3 Pangkalanberandan, Indo.
111/F4 Pangkalaseang (cape), Indo.
110/C4 Pangkalpinang, Indo.
104/C3 Pangsau (pass), India
158/D3 Panguitch, Ut,US
112/C4 Pangutaran, Phil.
112/C4 Pangutaran (isl.), Phil.
112/B4 Pangutaran (isls.), Phil.
162/C3 Panhandle, Tx,US
111/J4 Paniai (lake), Indo.
154/R10 Paniau (peak), Hi,US
120/F7 Panié (peak), NCal.
106/C2 Pānīpat, India
112/C3 Panitan, Phil.
95/K1 Panj (Pyandzh) (riv.), Afg., Taj.
106/D3 Panna, India
118/F7 Pannikin (isl.), Austl.
141/B2 Panorama, Braz.
108/G3 Panruti, India
97/K3 Panshi, China
57/E6 Pant, Eng,UK
59/G3 Pant (riv.), Eng,UK
137/G7 Pantanal (marsh), Braz.
137/G7 Pantanal Matogrossense Nat'l Park, Braz.
80/B4 Pantelleria (isl.), It.
53/T10 Pantin, Fr.
74/B1 Pantón, Sp.
112/D4 Pantukan, Phil.
147/F4 Pánuco, Mex.
147/F4 Pánuco (riv.), Mex.
104/D3 Panzhihua, China
148/D3 Panzós, Guat.
140/C3 Pão de Açúcar, Braz.
80/E3 Paola, It.
159/J3 Paola, Ks,US
158/F3 Paonia, Co,US
124/J6 Paoua, CAfr.
109/C3 Paoy Pet, Camb.
82/C2 Pápa, Hun.
148/E4 Papagayo (gulf), CR
108/G3 Papanāsam, India
141/B3 Papanduva, Braz.
147/F4 Papantla, Mex.
147/M6 Papantla de Olarte, Mex.
121/X15 Papara, FrPol.
55/N13 Papa Westray (isl.), Sc,UK
121/L6 Papeete, FrPol.
121/X15 Papeete (cap.), FrPol.
67/E2 Papenburg, Ger.
66/B5 Papendrecht, Neth.
121/X15 Papenoo, FrPol.
121/X15 Papetoai, FrPol.
91/C2 Paphos, Cyp.
91/C2 Paphos (dist.), Cyp.
159/H2 Papillion, Ne,US
81/G2 Papingut, Maj'e (peak), Alb.
111/H4 Papisoi (cape), Indo.
60/A5 Paps, The (mtn.), Ire.
120/D5 Papua (gulf), PNG
120/D5 Papua New Guinea
141/C1 Pará (riv.), Braz.
139/G5 Pará (state), Braz.
140/A1 Pará (state), Braz.
139/H3 Para (dist.), Sur.
139/E3 Pará (falls), Ven.
112/C2 Paracale, Phil.
141/K7 Paracambi, Braz.
144/B4 Paracas (pen.), Peru
144/B4 Paracas Nat'l Rsv., Peru
140/A5 Paracatu, Braz.
140/A5 Paracatu (riv.), Braz.
105/F5 Paracel (isls.), China
90/N7 Parace Vela (Okino-Tori-Shima) (isl.), Japan
82/E4 Paraćin, Yugo.
75/N8 Paracuellos, Sp.
140/C1 Paracuru, Braz.
141/C1 Pará de Minas, Braz.
139/G4 Para de Oeste (riv.), Braz.
106/E3 Paradip, India
156/F2 Paradise Hill, Sk,Can
140/A1 Paragominas, Braz.
163/F2 Paragould, Ar,US
136/F6 Paraguá (riv.), Bol.
139/F3 Paragua (riv.), Ven.
141/H6 Paraguaçu, Braz.
140/B4 Paraguaçu (riv.), Braz.
141/B2 Paraguaçu Paulista, Braz.
137/G6 Paraguai (riv.), Braz.
138/D1 Paraguaná (pen.), Ven.
135/E2 Paraguarí, Par.
134/D5 Paraguay
140/C2 Paraíba (state), Braz.
141/D2 Paraíba do Sul (riv.), Braz.
140/A2 Paraibano, Braz.
141/H8 Paraibuna (riv.), Braz.
141/K6 Paraibuna (riv.), Braz.
140/A3 Paraim (riv.), Braz.
63/K1 Parainen (Pargas), Fin.
149/F4 Paraíso, CR
147/G5 Paraíso, Mex.
137/J6 Paraíso do Norte de Goiás, Braz.
141/G7 Paraisópolis, Braz.
129/F4 Parakou, Ben.
108/G4 Paramagudi, India
139/H3 Paramaribo (cap.), Sur.
139/H3 Paramaribo (dist.), Sur.
140/B2 Parambu, Braz.
138/C3 Paramillo (peak), Col.
138/B3 Paramillo Nat'l Park, Col.
140/B4 Paramirim, Braz.
140/B4 Paramirim (riv.), Braz.
164/B3 Paramount, Ca,US
167/D2 Paramus, NJ,US
89/R4 Paramushir (isl.), Rus.
141/B3 Paraná (state), Braz.
134/D5 Paraná (riv.), SAm.
141/B3 Paranaguá, Braz.
141/B3 Paranaguá (bay), Braz.
141/B1 Paranaíba, Braz.
134/E3 Paranaíba (riv.), Braz.
141/B1 Paranaiba (riv.), Braz.
143/S11 Paraná Ibicuy (riv.), Arg.
141/B2 Paranapanema (riv.), Braz.
141/B3 Paranapiacaba (range), Braz.
112/E6 Parañaque, Phil.
134/D4 Paranatinga (riv.), Braz.
139/G5 Paraná Urariá (riv.), Braz.
137/H8 Paranavai, Braz.
112/C4 Parang, Phil.
108/H4 Parangi (riv.), SrL.
141/C1 Paraopeba, Braz.
137/J8 Parapanema (riv.), Braz.
115/S11 Paraparaumu, NZ
136/F7 Parapetí (riv.), Bol.
141/J8 Parati, Braz.
140/B4 Paratinga, Braz.
141/H8 Paratinga (riv.), Braz.
53/T10 Paray-Vieille-Poste, Fr.
106/C4 Parbhani, India
64/F2 Parchim, Ger.
65/M3 Parczew, Pol.
91/D3 Pardes Hanna, Isr.
91/F7 Pardes Hanna-Karkur, Isr.
106/B3 Pārdi, India
141/G6 Pardo (riv.), Braz.
65/H3 Pardubice, Czh.
110/D5 Pare, Indo.
130/C3 Pare (mts.), Tanz.
136/F6 Parecis (mts.), Braz.
75/P10 Parede, Port.
142/C2 Paredones, Chile
160/E1 Parent (lake), Qu,Can
111/E4 Parepare, Indo.
75/L6 Parets del Vallès, Sp.
81/G3 Párga, Gre.
63/K1 Pargas (Parainen), Fin.
139/F2 Paria (gulf), Trin., Ven.
158/E3 Paria (riv.), Az, Ut,US
136/F1 Paria (pen.), Ven.
139/E2 Pariaguán, Ven.
110/B4 Pariaman, Indo.
139/F4 Parima (riv.), Braz.
139/E4 Parima (mts.), Braz., Ven.
144/D5 Parinacota (peak), Bol.
144/A2 Pariñas (pt.), Peru
139/G5 Parintins, Braz.
68/B6 Paris (cap.), Fr.
162/E3 Paris, Ar,US
160/B4 Paris, Tn,US
162/E3 Paris, Tx,US
53/T10 Paris (inset) (cap.), Fr.
149/F4 Parita (bay), Pan.
158/F2 Park (range), Co,US
167/K8 Parkchester, NY,US
158/D4 Parker, Az,US
159/F3 Parker, Co,US
160/D4 Parkersburg, WV,US
119/D2 Parkes, Austl.
59/H3 Parkeston, Eng,UK
160/B2 Park Falls, Wi,US
56/B2 Parkgate, NI,UK
58/A5 Park Head (pt.), UK
59/E5 Parkhurst, Eng,UK
165/C3 Parkland, Wa,US
157/K4 Park Rapids, Mn,US
165/Q15 Park Ridge, Il,US
167/D1 Park Ridge, NJ,US
157/J3 Park River, ND,US
166/B5 Parkville, Md,US
166/B4 Parkville, Pa,US
165/L9 Parkway-Sacramento, Ca,US
74/D2 Parla, Sp.
106/D4 Parlakhemundi, India
106/C4 Parli, India
78/D3 Parma, It.
78/D3 Parma (prov.), It.
78/D3 Parma (riv.), It.
168/F5 Parma, Oh,US
168/F5 Parma Heights, Oh,US
53/S9 Parmain, Fr.
140/A3 Parnaguá, Braz.
140/B1 Parnaíba, Braz.
140/B1 Parnaíba (riv.), Braz.
140/C3 Parnamirim, Braz.
140/B2 Parnarama, Braz.
81/H3 Parnassós (peak), Gre.
81/H3 Parnassos Nat'l Park, Gre.
81/H3 Párnis (peak), Gre.
81/H4 Párnon (mts.), Gre.
63/L2 Pärnu, Est.
63/L2 Pärnu (bay), Est.
101/D3 P'aro-ho (lake), SKor.
115/G5 Paroo (riv.), Austl.
81/J4 Páros (isl.), Gre.
132/B4 Parow, SAfr.
158/D3 Parowan, Ut,US
143/C3 Parral, Chile
118/H8 Parramatta, Austl.
146/E3 Parras de la Fuente, Mex.
58/D4 Parrett (riv.), Eng,UK
163/H5 Parris Island Marine Base, SC,US
149/E4 Parrita, CR
131/B4 Parr's Halt, Bots.
153/H2 Parry (bay), NW,Can
152/F1 Parry (chan.), NW,Can
153/R7 Parry (isls.), NW,Can
160/D2 Parry Sound, On,Can
77/G3 Parseierspitze (peak), Aus.
157/H4 Parshall, ND,US
166/D2 Parsippany, NJ,US
156/C2 Parsnip (riv.), BC,Can
159/J3 Parsons, Ks,US
84/C2 Pårtefjället (peak), Swe.
72/C3 Parthenay, Fr.
62/E3 Partille, Swe.
80/C3 Partinico, It.
97/L3 Partizansk, Rus.
160/D1 Partridge (riv.), On,Can
60/A2 Partry (mts.), Ire.
106/C4 Partūr, India
139/H2 Paru (riv.), Braz.
137/G3 Paru de Oeste (riv.), Braz.
108/F3 Parūr, India
106/D4 Pārvatīpuram, India
57/G5 Parwich, Eng,UK
132/D2 Parys, SAfr.
161/K1 Pasadena, Nf,Can
164/B2 Pasadena, Ca,US
166/B5 Pasadena, Md,US
162/E4 Pasadena, Tx,US
138/A5 Pasado (cape), Ecu.
144/B1 Pasaje, Ecu.
109/C3 Pa Sak (riv.), Thai.
110/B3 Pasaman (peak), Indo.
112/C2 Pasay City, Phil.
163/F4 Pascagoula, Ms,US
83/H2 Paşcani, Rom.
71/H6 Pasching, Aus.
156/D4 Pasco, Wa,US
144/B3 Pasco, Cerro de, Peru
143/J7 Pascua (riv.), Chile
144/B1 Pascuales, Ecu.
68/A3 Pas-de-Calais (dept.), Fr.
68/B3 Pas-en-Artois, Fr.
112/C2 Pasig, Phil.
104/B2 Pāsighāt, India
92/E2 Pasinler, Turk.
148/D2 Pasión, Río de la (riv.), Guat.
65/K1 Pasłęk, Pol.
65/L2 Pasłęka (riv.), Pol.
116/D5 Pasley (cape), Austl.
82/B4 Pašman (isl.), Cro.
95/H3 Pasni, Pak.
147/N8 Paso del Macho, Mex.
135/E2 Paso de Los Libres, Arg.
142/C2 Paso del Planchón (peak), Chile
158/B4 Paso Robles (El Paso de Robles), Ca,US
108/C1 Pasrūr, Pak.
151/M3 Pass (peak), Yk,Can
140/B2 Passagem Franca, Braz.
167/D2 Passaic, NJ,US
166/D1 Passaic (co.), NJ,US
167/D2 Passaic (riv.), NJ,US
141/J7 Passa Quatro, Braz.
71/G5 Passau, Ger.
68/C2 Passendale, Belg.
80/D4 Passero (pt.), It.
112/C3 Passi, Phil.
135/F2 Passo Fundo, Braz.
141/A3 Passo Fundo (res.), Braz.
129/E3 Passoré (prov.), Burk.
141/C2 Passos, Braz.
76/D3 Passwang (peak), Swi.
73/G4 Passy, Fr.
138/B5 Pastaza (prov.), Ecu.
136/C4 Pastaza (riv.), Ecu., Peru
63/J5 Pastek (riv.), Pol.
138/B4 Pasto, Col.
151/F3 Pastol (bay), Ak,US
140/A2 Pastos Bons, Braz.
112/C1 Pasuquin, Phil.
110/D5 Pasuruan, Indo.
82/D2 Pásztó, Hun.
112/C3 Patag Nat'l Park, Phil.
142/D4 Patagonia (reg.), Arg.
110/B4 Patah (peak), Indo.
106/B3 Pātan, India
166/B5 Patapsco (riv.), Md,US
166/B4 Patapsco, North Branch (riv.), Md,US
167/E2 Patchogue, NY,US
58/D3 Patchway, Eng,UK
130/D3 Pate (isl.), Kenya
57/G3 Pateley Bridge, Eng,UK
75/E3 Paterna, Sp.
80/D4 Paternò, It.
167/D2 Paterson, NJ,US
108/C1 Pathānkot, India
156/G5 Pathfinder (res.), Wy,US
110/D5 Pati, Indo.
138/B4 Patía (riv.), Col.
108/D2 Patiāla, India
112/C4 Patikul, Phil.
106/E2 Patna, India
54/B6 Patna, Sc,UK
112/C2 Patnanongan (isl.), Phil.
112/C3 Patnongon, Phil.
93/E2 Patnos, Turk.
141/A3 Pato Branco, Braz.
163/G2 Patoka (riv.), In,US
81/F2 Patos, Alb.
140/C2 Patos, Braz.
141/B4 Patos (lake), Braz.
141/C1 Patos de Minas, Braz.
81/G3 Pátrai, Gre.
81/G3 Patrai (gulf), Gre.
117/F2 Patricia (peak), Austl.
143/J7 Patricio Lynch (isl.), Chile
57/H4 Patrington, Eng,UK
141/C1 Patrocínio, Braz.
163/G4 Patsaliga (cr.), Al,US
77/H3 Patscherkofel (peak), Aus.
109/C5 Pattani, Thai.
109/C3 Pattaya, Thai.
67/G4 Pattensen, Ger.
108/C2 Patti, India
80/D3 Patti, It.
58/D1 Pattingham, Eng,UK
108/B2 Pattoki, Pak.
108/G3 Pattukkottai, India
151/N4 Pattullo (mtn.), BC,Can
140/C2 Patu, Braz.
148/E3 Patuca (mts.), Hon.
149/E3 Patuca (pt.), Hon.
149/E3 Patuca (riv.), Hon.
166/B6 Patuxent (riv.), Md,US
166/B5 Patuxent Nat. Wild. Ref., Md,US
166/A5 Patuxent River Saint Park, Md,US
147/E5 Pátzcuaro, Mex.
72/C5 Pau, Fr.
140/C4 Pau Brasil, Braz.
140/C2 Pau dos Ferros, Braz.
136/E5 Pauini (riv.), Braz.
104/B5 Pauksa (peak), Burma
149/E3 Paulaya (riv.), Hon.
141/F7 Paulínia, Braz.
166/D1 Paulins Kill (riv.), NJ,US
140/B3 Paulistana, Braz.
78/C2 Paullo, It.
140/C3 Paulo Afonso, Braz.
140/C3 Paulo Afonso Nat'l Park, Braz.
140/A2 Paulo Ramos, Braz.
166/C4 Paulsboro, NJ,US
159/H4 Pauls Valley, Ok,US
58/D4 Paulton, Eng,UK
104/B5 Paungde, Burma
102/C5 Pauri, India
141/D1 Pavão, Braz.
78/C2 Pavia, It.
78/C2 Pavia (prov.), It.
83/G4 Pavlikeni, Bul.
102/C1 Pavlodar, Kaz.
151/F4 Pavlof (vol.), Ak,US
86/E2 Pavlograd, Ukr.
84/J5 Pavlovo, Rus.
79/D4 Pavullo nel Frignano, It.
110/D4 Pawan (riv.), Indo.
159/H3 Pawhuska, Ok,US
104/C4 Pawn (riv.), Burma
159/H3 Pawnee (riv.), Ks,US
160/C3 Paw Paw, Mi,US
168/C2 Pawtucket, RI,US
166/B5 Pawtuxent (riv.), Md,US
81/F3 Paxoí (isl.), Gre.
81/G3 Paxoí (Yáios), Gre.
110/B4 Payakumbuh, Indo.
142/C3 Payén, Altiplanicie del (plat.), Arg.
76/C4 Payerne, Swi.
156/D4 Payette, Id,US
156/D5 Payette (riv.), Id,US
85/P1 Pay-Khoy (mts.), Rus.
153/J2 Payne (lake), Qu,Can
116/C4 Paynes Find, Austl.
143/F2 Paysandú, Uru.
143/F1 Paysandú (dept.), Uru.
53/T9 Pays de France (plain), Fr.
72/C3 Pays de la Loire (reg.), Fr.
158/E4 Payson, Az,US
158/E2 Payson, Ut,US
142/C3 Payún (peak), Arg.
148/D3 Paz (riv.), ESal., Guat.
92/D1 Pazar, Turk.
92/D2 Pazarcık, Turk.
83/G4 Pazardzhik, Bul.
86/D5 Pazaryeri, Turk.
141/A2 Peabiru, Braz.
152/E3 Peace (riv.), Ab, BC,Can
163/H5 Peace (riv.), Fl,US
98/C3 Peace Mem. Park, Japan
156/D1 Peace River, Ab,Can
156/D3 Peachland, BC,Can
163/G3 Peachtree City, Ga,US
116/D5 Peak Charles Nat'l Park, Austl.
57/G5 Peak District Nat'l Park, Eng,UK
60/A6 Peakeen (mtn.), Ire.
154/W13 Pearl (har.), Hi,US
163/F4 Pearl (riv.), La, Ms,US
163/F3 Pearl, Ms,US
121/H2 Pearl and Hermes (reef), Hi,US
154/W13 Pearl City, Hi,US
105/G4 Pearl River (estuary), China, HK
167/D1 Pearl River, NY,US
162/D4 Pearsall, Tx,US
153/R7 Peary (chan.), NW,Can
159/H4 Pease (riv.), Tx,US
126/G4 Pebane, Moz.
144/D1 Pebas, Peru
59/E2 Pebworth, Eng,UK
82/E4 Peć, Yugo.
164/C4 Pechanga Ind. Res., Ca,US
75/G1 Pech de Guillaument (mtn.), Fr.
85/N2 Pechora, Rus.
85/M1 Pechora (bay), Rus.
85/M2 Pechora (riv.), Rus.
166/C1 Pecks (pond), Pa,US
167/F2 Peconic (riv.), NY,US
159/F5 Pecos (riv.), NM, Tx,US
162/C4 Pecos, Tx,US
159/F4 Pecos Nat'l Mon., NM,US
68/C3 Pecquencourt, Fr.
82/D2 Pécs, Hun.
119/C4 Pedder (lake), Austl.
149/E4 Pedernal (pt.), Nic.
150/D3 Pedernales, DRep.
141/B2 Pederneiras, Braz.
164/C3 Pedley, Ca,US
140/B5 Pedra Azul, Braz.
141/H7 Pedralva, Braz.
141/G7 Pedreira, Braz.
140/B2 Pedreiras, Braz.
106/D6 Pedro (pt.), SrL.
140/C2 Pedro Avelino, Braz.
149/F1 Pedro Betancourt, Cuba
138/A5 Pedro Carbo, Ecu.
136/E3 Pedro II, Braz.
139/E4 Pedro II (isl.), Braz.
135/E1 Pedro Juan Caballero, Par.
141/C1 Pedro Leopoldo, Braz.
141/A4 Pedro Osório, Braz.
140/B2 Pedro Segundo, Braz.
54/C5 Peebles, Sc,UK
116/B2 Peedamulla Abor. Land, Austl.
167/E1 Peekskill, NY,US
116/B5 Peel (inlet), Austl.
118/F6 Peel (isl.), Austl.
152/G1 Peel (sound), NW,Can
161/Q8 Peel (co.), On,Can
151/L2 Peel (riv.), Yk,Can
56/D3 Peel, IM,UK
57/F1 Peel Fell (mtn.), Eng,UK
62/E5 Peene (riv.), Ger.
69/E1 Peer, Belg.
115/R11 Pegasus (bay), NZ
71/E3 Pegnitz, Ger.
71/E3 Pegnitz (riv.), Ger.
75/E3 Pego, Sp.
57/G1 Pegswood, Eng,UK
104/C5 Pegu, Burma
104/B4 Pegu (mts.), Burma
104/C5 Pegu (riv.), Burma
104/B5 Pegu (Bago) (div.), Burma
59/H4 Pegwell (bay), Eng,UK
142/E2 Pehuajó, Arg.
142/C2 Pehuenche (pass), Chile
103/B3 Peijiachuankou, China
105/J4 Peinanchu (mtn.), Tai.
67/H4 Peine, Ger.
63/M2 Peipus (lake), Est., Rus.
77/H2 Peissenburg, Ger.
105/J4 Peitawu (peak), Tai.
77/G2 Peiting, Ger.
141/K6 Peixe (riv.), Braz.
103/D4 Pei Xian, China
141/C2 Peixoto (res.), Braz.
110/C5 Pekalongan, Indo.
110/B3 Pekan Nanas, Malay.
160/B3 Pekin, Il,US
142/C5 Pelada (plain), Arg.
80/C5 Pelagie (isls.), It.
82/F3 Peleaga, Vîrful (peak), Rom.
161/D3 Pelee (isl.), On,Can
160/D3 Pelee (pt.), On,Can
150/F4 Pelée (mtn.), Mart.
161/R9 Pelham, On,Can
163/G3 Pelham, Al,US
167/K8 Pelham, NY,US
167/K8 Pelham Bay Park, NY,US
65/H4 Pelhřimov, Czh.
156/E2 Pelican (mts.), Ab,Can
157/H2 Pelican (lake), Sk,Can
157/H2 Pelican Narrows, Sk,Can
128/A4 Pelindã, Ponta de (pt.), GBis.
82/E5 Pelister (peak), Macd.
82/E5 Pelister Nat'l Park, Macd.
82/C4 Pelješac (pen.), Cro.
152/H2 Pelly (bay), NW,Can
151/M3 Pelly (riv.), Yk,Can
151/L3 Pelly Crossing, Yk,Can
81/G3 Pelopónnisos (reg.), Gre.
80/D3 Peloritani (mts.), It.
141/A4 Pelotas, Braz.
141/B3 Pelotas (riv.), Braz.
65/K2 Pelplin, Pol.
111/F4 Pemali (cape), Indo.
111/F5 Pemali (cape), Indo.
110/A3 Pematangsiantar, Indo.
126/H3 Pemba, Moz.
123/G5 Pemba (isl.), Tanz.
130/C4 Pemba (prov.), Tanz.
131/B3 Pemba, Zam.
156/C3 Pemberton, BC,Can
156/E2 Pembina (riv.), Ab,Can
157/J3 Pembina (riv.), Can., US
157/J3 Pembina, ND,US
160/E2 Pembroke, On,Can
58/B3 Pembroke, Wal,UK
168/D1 Pembroke, Ma,US
58/B3 Pembroke Dock, Wal,UK
55/J11 Pembrokeshire Coast Nat'l Park, Wal,UK
53/P8 Pembury, Eng,UK
142/B3 Pemuco, Chile
149/F4 Peña Blanca (mtn.), Pan.
74/A2 Penafiel, Port.
142/Q9 Peñaflor, Chile
74/D2 Peñalara (mtn.), Sp.
140/A1 Penalva, Braz.
142/B2 Penápolis, Braz.
74/C2 Peñaranda de Bracamonte, Sp.
75/E2 Peñarroya (mtn.), Sp.
74/C3 Peñarroya-Pueblonuevo, Sp.
58/C4 Penarth, Wal,UK
143/L8 Peñas (cape), Arg.
143/J6 Penas (gulf), Chile
74/C1 Peñas (cape), Sp.
159/F4 Peñasco (dry riv.), NM,US
142/B3 Penco, Chile
81/L6 Pendelikón (mtn.), Gre.
140/C2 Pendências, Braz.
93/N7 Pendik, Turk.
129/F4 Pendjari (riv.), Ben., Burk.
129/F4 Pendjari Nat'l Park, Ben.
57/F4 Pendle (hill), Eng,UK
156/D4 Pendleton, Or,US
156/D4 Pend Oreille (lake), Id,US
156/D3 Pend Oreille (riv.), Id, Wa,US
74/A2 Peneda-Gerês Nat'l Park, Port.
140/C3 Penedo, Braz.
58/C1 Penegoes, Wal,UK
160/E2 Penetanguishene, On,Can
106/C4 Penganga (riv.), India
53/N7 Penge, Eng,UK
105/H4 Penghu (isl.), Tai.
103/E3 Penglai, China
104/D2 Peng Xian, China
141/B3 Penha, Braz.
131/D3 Penhalonga, Zim.
156/E2 Penhold, Ab,Can
74/C4 Penibético, Sistema (range), Sp.
78/C3 Penice, Monte (peak), It.
74/A3 Peniche, Port.
54/C5 Penicuik, Sc,UK
139/F2 Península de Paria Nat'l Park, Ven.
140/A3 Penitente (mts.), Braz.
147/E4 Pénjamo, Mex.
58/D1 Penkridge, Eng,UK
56/E5 Penmaenmawr, Wal,UK
72/A3 Penmarch, Fr.
72/A3 Penmarc'h, Pointe de (pt.), Fr.
80/D1 Penna, Punta della (cape), It.
82/C5 Penne (pt.), It.
106/C5 Penner (riv.), India
166/C2 Penn Forest (res.), Pa,US
168/H7 Penn Hills, Pa,US
76/D6 Pennine Alps (mts.), It., Swi.
57/F2 Pennine Chain (range), Eng,UK
166/A2 Penns (cr.), Pa,US
166/C4 Pennsauken, NJ,US
166/A2 Penns Creek (mtn.), Pa,US
166/C4 Pennsville, NJ,US
160/E3 Pennsylvania (state), US
153/S7 Penny (str.), NW,Can
160/E3 Penn Yan, NY,US
166/C3 Pennypack (cr.), Pa,US
160/G2 Penobscot (riv.), Me,US
149/F4 Penonomé, Pan.
56/E1 Penpont, Sc,UK
56/D5 Penrhyn Mawr (pt.), Wal,UK
56/D6 Penrhyn Mawr (pt.), Wal,UK
121/K5 Penrhyn (Tongareva) (atoll), CookIs.
118/G8 Penrith, Austl.
57/F2 Penrith, Eng,UK
58/A6 Penryn, Eng,UK
113/X Pensacola (mts.), Ant.
163/G4 Pensacola, Fl,US
157/G3 Pense, Sk,Can
53/P8 Penshurst, Eng,UK
58/B5 Pensilva, Eng,UK
166/A6 Pentagon, Va,US
120/F6 Pentecost (isl.), Van.
140/C1 Pentecoste, Braz.
83/H3 Penteleu (peak), Rom.
156/D3 Penticton, BC,Can
58/B5 Pentire (pt.), UK
54/C5 Pentland (hills), Sc,UK
55/N13 Pentland Firth (inlet), Sc,UK
58/C3 Pentrych, Wal,UK
142/C2 Peñuelas Nat'l Park, Chile
58/A6 Penwith (pen.), Eng,UK
57/E6 Pen-y-Cae, Wal,UK
57/F3 Pen-y-Ghent (mtn.), Eng,UK
56/E5 Pen-y-Gogarth (pt.), Wal,UK
58/C2 Pen y Gurnos (mtn.), Wal,UK
87/H1 Penza, Rus.
58/A6 Penzance, Eng,UK
87/G1 Penza Obl., Rus.
77/H2 Penzberg, Ger.
89/S3 Penzhina (bay), Rus.
89/S3 Penzhina (riv.), Rus.
160/B3 Peoria, Il,US
149/F1 Pepe (cape), Cuba
154/U11 Pepeekeo (pt.), Hi,US
69/E2 Pepinster, Belg.
168/F5 Pepper Pike, Oh,US
167/D2 Pequannock, NJ,US
166/B4 Pequea (cr.), Pa,US
166/D2 Pequest (riv.), NJ,US
115/G2 Pera (head), Austl.
110/B4 Perabumulih, Indo.
75/M9 Perales (riv.), Sp.
108/G3 Perambalūr, India

212

Percé – Polon

161/H1 **Percé,** Qu,Can
76/C6 **Percée, Pointe** (peak), Fr.
72/D2 **Perche** (hills), Fr.
65/J4 **Perchtoldsdorf,** Aus.
116/E2 **Percival** (lakes), Austl.
118/C3 **Percy** (isls.), Austl.
140/A3 **Perdida** (riv.), Braz.
75/F1 **Perdido** (mtn.), Sp.
138/C3 **Pereira,** Col.
141/B2 **Pereira Barreto,** Braz.
140/C2 **Pereiro,** Braz.
142/E2 **Pergamino,** Arg.
92/A2 **Pergamum** (ruins), Turk.
77/H5 **Pergine Valsugana,** It.
79/F5 **Pergola,** It.
161/G1 **Péribonca** (lake), Qu,Can
161/G1 **Péribonca** (riv.), Qu,Can
149/F1 **Perico,** Cuba
72/D4 **Périgueux,** Fr.
138/C2 **Perijá** (mts.), Col., Ven.
94/D6 **Perim** (isl.), Yem.
81/J3 **Peristéra** (isl.), Gre.
81/L6 **Peristéri,** Gre.
143/K6 **Perito Moreno Nat'l Park,** Arg.
108/F3 **Periyakulam,** India
108/F3 **Periyar** (riv.), India
108/F4 **Periyar Wild. Sanct.,** India
166/C3 **Perkasie,** Pa,US
166/C3 **Perkiomen** (cr.), Pa,US
69/F5 **Perl,** Ger.
149/F3 **Perlas** (lag.), Nic.
149/F3 **Perlas** (pt.), Nic.
149/G4 **Perlas** (arch.), Pan.
64/F2 **Perleberg,** Ger.
85/N4 **Perm',** Rus.
85/M4 **Perm' Obl.,** Rus.
140/C3 **Pernambuco** (state), Braz.
72/F4 **Pernes-les-Fontaines,** Fr.
82/F4 **Pernik,** Bul.
63/K1 **Perniö,** Fin.
116/B3 **Peron** (pen.), Austl.
68/B4 **Péronne,** Fr.
147/F5 **Perote,** Mex.
85/X9 **Perovo,** Rus.
72/E5 **Perpignan,** Fr.
164/C3 **Perris,** Ca,US
164/C3 **Perris** (res.), Ca,US
149/G1 **Perros** (bay), Cuba
72/B2 **Perros-Guirec,** Fr.
161/N7 **Perrot** (isl.), Qu,Can
152/F2 **Perry** (riv.), NW,Can
163/H4 **Perry,** Fl,US
163/H3 **Perry,** Ga,US
159/H3 **Perry,** Ok,US
166/A3 **Perry** (co.), Pa,US
166/B5 **Perry Hall,** Md,US
168/F6 **Perry Heights,** Oh,US
162/C2 **Perryton,** Tx,US
159/K3 **Perryville,** Mo,US
53/S9 **Persan,** Fr.
94/F3 **Persepolis** (ruins), Iran
63/R7 **Pershagen,** Swe.
58/D2 **Pershore,** Eng,UK
94/E3 **Persian** (gulf), Asia
116/B4 **Perth,** Austl.
160/E2 **Perth,** On,Can
54/C4 **Perth,** Sc,UK
167/D2 **Perth Amboy,** NJ,US
116/K6 **Perth** (inset), Austl.
116/K6 **Perth Zoo,** Austl.
72/F5 **Pertuis,** Fr.
72/C3 **Pertuis Breton** (inlet), Fr.
80/A2 **Pertusato** (cape), Fr.
144/C3 **Peru**
160/B3 **Peru,** Il,US
160/C3 **Peru,** In,US
82/D4 **Perućačko** (lake), Bosn.
80/C1 **Perugia,** It.
141/G9 **Peruíbe,** Braz.
108/F3 **Perumpāvūr,** India
68/C2 **Péruwelz,** Belg.
85/J5 **Pervomaysk,** Rus.
86/D2 **Pervomaysk,** Ukr.
85/N4 **Pervoural'sk,** Rus.
79/E5 **Pesa** (riv.), It.
110/B4 **Pesagi** (peak), Indo.
79/F5 **Pesaro,** It.
79/F5 **Pesaro e Urbino** (prov.), It.
105/H4 **Pescadore** (chan.), Tai.
80/D1 **Pescara,** It.
87/J4 **Peschanyy, Mys** (cape), Kaz.
79/D5 **Pescia,** It.
85/L2 **Pesha** (riv.), Rus.
95/K2 **Peshāwar,** Pak.
83/G4 **Peshtera,** Bul.
160/B2 **Peshtigo** (riv.), Wi,US
140/C3 **Pesqueira,** Braz.
72/C4 **Pessac,** Fr.
72/D5 **Pessons, Pic dels** (peak), And.
82/D2 **Pest** (co.), Hun.
84/G4 **Pestovo,** Rus.
91/D3 **Petaḥ Tiqwa,** Isr.
163/F4 **Petal,** Ms,US
81/J4 **Petalión** (gulf), Gre.
165/J10 **Petaluma,** Ca,US
165/J10 **Petaluma** (riv.), Ca,US
69/E4 **Pétange,** Lux.
139/E2 **Petare,** Ven.
146/D3 **Petatlán** (riv.), Mex.
131/C2 **Petauke,** Zam.
160/E2 **Petawana** (riv.), On,Can
160/E2 **Petawawa,** On,Can
148/D2 **Peten Itzá** (lake), Guat.
157/L4 **Petenwell** (lake), Wi,US
160/E2 **Peterborough,** On,Can
59/F1 **Peterborough,** Eng,UK
54/D2 **Peterculter,** Sc,UK
54/E2 **Peterhead,** Sc,UK
113/T **Peter I** (isl.), Ant.
50/E9 **Peter I** (isl.), Nor.
57/G2 **Peterlee,** Eng,UK
117/F3 **Petermann Abor. Land,** Austl.
142/C2 **Peteroa** (vol.), Arg.
156/F1 **Peter Pond** (lake), Sk,Can
166/B3 **Peters** (mtn.), Pa,US
70/C1 **Petersberg,** Ger.
160/E4 **Petersburg,** Va,US
59/F5 **Petersfield,** Eng,UK
67/F4 **Petershagen,** Ger.
159/F3 **Peterson A.F.B.,** Co,US
80/E3 **Petilia Policastro,** It.
149/H2 **Pétionville,** Haiti
161/H2 **Petitcodiac,** NB,Can
149/H2 **Petite Rivière de l'Artibonite,** Haiti
69/F5 **Petite-Rosselle,** Fr.
149/H2 **Petit Goâve,** Haiti
68/C6 **Petit Marin** (riv.), Fr.
161/K1 **Petit Mécatina** (riv.), Qu,Can
68/C6 **Petit Morin** (riv.), Fr.
53/S9 **Petit Rosne** (riv.), Fr.
61/J3 **Petkeljärven Nat'l Park,** Fin.
106/B3 **Petlād,** India
147/H4 **Peto,** Mex.
142/C2 **Petorca,** Chile
160/C2 **Petoskey,** Mi,US
89/M2 **Petra** (isls.), Rus.
91/D4 **Petra** (Baṭrā') (ruins), Jor.
75/E3 **Petrel,** Sp.
80/C2 **Petrella** (peak), It.
83/F5 **Petrich,** Bul.
158/E4 **Petrified Forest Nat'l Park,** Az,US
83/F3 **Petrila,** Rom.
63/N2 **Petrodvorets,** Rus.
83/F4 **Petrokhanski Prokhod** (pass), Bul.
140/C3 **Petrolândia,** Braz.
140/B3 **Petrolina,** Braz.
88/G4 **Petropavlovsk,** Kaz.
89/R4 **Petropavlovsk-Kamchatskiy,** Rus.
141/K7 **Petrópolis,** Braz.
83/F3 **Petroşani,** Rom.
82/D3 **Petrovaradin,** Yugo.
87/H1 **Petrovsk,** Rus.
96/F1 **Petrovsk-Zabaykal'skiy,** Rus.
84/G3 **Petrozavodsk,** Rus.
63/P1 **Petrozavodsk Obl.,** Rus.
57/F2 **Petterill** (riv.), Eng,UK
59/F5 **Petworth,** Eng,UK
82/A2 **Petzeck** (peak), Aus.
151/G4 **Peulik** (mtn.), Ak,US
142/C2 **Peumo,** Chile
59/G5 **Pevensey,** Eng,UK
165/P13 **Pewaukee** (lake), Wi,US
59/E4 **Pewsey,** Eng,UK
85/K2 **Peza** (riv.), Rus.
72/E5 **Pézenas,** Fr.
77/G1 **Pfaffenhofen an der Roth,** Ger.
77/E3 **Pfäffikon,** Swi.
71/F4 **Pfahl** (ridge), Ger.
69/G5 **Pfälzer Wald** (for.), Ger.
71/F6 **Pfarrkirchen,** Ger.
71/E5 **Pfettrach** (riv.), Ger.
67/G6 **Pfieffe** (riv.), Ger.
70/B5 **Pfinztal,** Ger.
70/B5 **Pforzheim,** Ger.
71/F3 **Pfreimd** (riv.), Ger.
70/B3 **Pfrimm** (riv.), Ger.
77/G2 **Pfronten,** Ger.
77/G4 **Pfroslkopf** (peak), Aus.
77/F2 **Pfullendorf,** Ger.
70/B3 **Pfungstadt,** Ger.
108/C2 **Phagwāra,** India
109/C1 **Phak** (riv.), Laos
131/C4 **Phalaborwa,** SAfr.
108/B1 **Phālia,** Pak.
106/B2 **Phalodi,** India
131/D2 **Phalombe,** Malw.
109/C3 **Phanat Nikhom,** Thai.
109/B4 **Phangan** (isl.), Thai.
109/C3 **Phang Hoei** (range), Thai.
109/C3 **Phanom Dongrak** (mts.), Camb., Thai.
109/E4 **Phan Rang,** Viet.
109/E4 **Phan Thiet,** Viet.
162/D5 **Pharr,** Tx,US
104/E4 **Phat Diem,** Viet.
109/C5 **Phatthalung,** Thai.
109/C2 **Phaya Fo** (peak), Thai.
109/B2 **Phayao,** Thai.
163/G3 **Phenix City,** Al,US
132/C2 **Phepane** (dry riv.), SAfr.
109/B3 **Phet Buri,** Thai.
109/C2 **Phetchabun,** Thai.
109/C2 **Phichit,** Thai.
163/F3 **Philadelphia,** Ms,US
166/C4 **Philadelphia,** Pa,US
94/B4 **Philae** (ruins), Egypt
157/H4 **Philip,** SD,US
68/D3 **Philippeville,** Belg.
160/D1 **Philippi,** WV,US
120/B3 **Philippine** (sea), Asia
112/* **Philippines**
70/B4 **Philippsburg,** Ger.
156/E4 **Philipsburg,** Mt,US
66/B5 **Philipsdam** (dam), Neth.
108/C2 **Phillaur,** India
159/H3 **Phillipsburg,** Ks,US
166/C2 **Phillipsburg,** NJ,US
109/C3 **Phimai** (ruins), Thai.
109/C2 **Phitsanulok,** Thai.
109/D4 **Phnom Penh** (Phnum Penh) (cap.), Camb.
109/D3 **Phnum Tbeng Meanchey,** Camb.
109/C5 **Pho** (pt.), Thai.
121/H5 **Phoenix** (isls.), Kiri.
158/D4 **Phoenix** (cap.), Az,US
163/H2 **Phoenix** (peak), NC,US
60/D3 **Phoenix Park,** Ire.
121/H5 **Phoenix** (Rawaki) (atoll), Kiri.
166/C3 **Phoenixville,** Pa,US
109/C1 **Phongsali,** Laos
109/C2 **Phou Bia** (peak), Laos
109/D2 **Phou Huatt** (peak), Viet.
109/C1 **Phou Loi** (peak), Laos
109/D2 **Phou Xai Lai Leng** (peak), Laos
109/C2 **Phrae,** Thai.
109/C3 **Phra Nakhon Si Ayutthaya,** Thai.
109/B4 **Phra Thong** (isl.), Thai.
109/C4 **Phsar Ream,** Camb.
109/D2 **Phuc Loi,** Viet.
104/E4 **Phuc Yen,** Viet.
109/C2 **Phu Hin Rong Kla Nat'l Park,** Thai.
109/E4 **Phu Hoi,** Viet.
109/B5 **Phuket,** Thai.
109/B5 **Phuket** (isl.), Thai.
109/C2 **Phu Kradung Nat'l Park,** Thai.
106/D3 **Phulabāni,** India
108/B1 **Phularwan,** Pak.
109/D2 **Phu Loc,** Viet.
109/D1 **Phu Luong,** Viet.
109/D1 **Phu Luong** (peak), Viet.
109/D1 **Phu Ly,** Viet.
109/D4 **Phumi Banam,** Camb.
109/D3 **Phumi Chhlong,** Camb.
109/D4 **Phumi Chhuk,** Camb.
109/C4 **Phumi Choan,** Camb.
109/D3 **Phumi Kampong Putrea Chas,** Camb.
109/D3 **Phumi Kampong Trabek,** Camb.
109/C3 **Phumi Kouk Kduoch,** Camb.
109/C4 **Phumi Krek,** Camb.
109/D3 **Phumi Labang Siek,** Camb.
109/D3 **Phumi Mlu Prey,** Camb.
109/D3 **Phumi O Pou,** Camb.
109/C3 **Phumi Phang,** Camb.
109/D3 **Phumi Phsar,** Camb.
109/D3 **Phumi Phsa Romeas,** Camb.
109/D3 **Phumi Prek Kak,** Camb.
109/D3 **Phumi Prek Preah,** Camb.
109/C3 **Phumi Samraong,** Camb.
109/D3 **Phumi Spoe Tbong,** Camb.
109/D3 **Phumi Sre Ta Chan,** Camb.
109/C3 **Phumi Ta Krei,** Camb.
109/C3 **Phumi Thma Pok,** Camb.
109/C3 **Phumi Toek Sok,** Camb.
109/C4 **Phumi Veal Renh,** Camb.
109/E3 **Phu My,** Viet.
109/E3 **Phu Nhon,** Viet.
109/D2 **Phu Phan Nat'l Park,** Thai.
109/C4 **Phu Quoc,** Viet.
109/C4 **Phu Quoc** (isl.), Viet.
109/D4 **Phu Rieng Sron,** Viet.
109/C2 **Phu Rua Nat'l Park,** Thai.
109/D1 **Phu Tho,** Viet.
109/D2 **Phu Vang,** Viet.
103/D4 **Pi** (riv.), China
140/C3 **Piaçabuçu,** Braz.
78/C2 **Piacenza,** It.
78/C3 **Piacenza** (prov.), It.
140/C2 **Piancó,** Braz.
79/F6 **Pian di Serra** (peak), It.
78/A2 **Pianezza,** It.
79/E4 **Pianoro,** It.
80/A1 **Pianosa** (isl.), It.
65/L2 **Piaseczno,** Pol.
83/H2 **Piatra Neamţ,** Rom.
140/B3 **Piauí** (riv.), Braz.
140/B2 **Piauí** (state), Braz.
79/F1 **Piave** (riv.), It.
80/D4 **Piazza Armerina,** It.
77/G5 **Piazzi, Cima de'** (peak), It.
125/M6 **Pibor Post,** Sudan
160/C1 **Pic** (riv.), On,Can
136/E8 **Pica,** Chile
72/E2 **Picardie** (reg.), Fr.
68/B4 **Picardy** (reg.), Fr.
166/D2 **Picatinny Arsenal** (mil. res.), NJ,US
163/F4 **Picayune,** Ms,US
80/E2 **Piccolo** (lag.), It.
135/D1 **Pichanal,** Arg.
142/C2 **Pichidegua,** Chile
142/C2 **Pichilemu,** Chile
138/B5 **Pichincha,** Ecu.
138/B4 **Pichincha** (prov.), Ecu.
161/R8 **Pickering,** On,Can
57/H3 **Pickering,** Eng,UK
57/H3 **Pickering, Vale of** (val.), Eng,UK
157/L3 **Pickle Lake,** On,Can
75/S12 **Pico** (isl.), Azor.,Port.
139/E4 **Pico da Neblina Nat'l Park,** Braz.
147/M7 **Pico de Orizaba Nat'l Park,** Mex.
164/B3 **Pico Rivera,** Ca,US
140/B2 **Picos,** Braz.
142/D5 **Pico Truncado,** Arg.
68/B4 **Picquigny,** Fr.
117/G5 **Picraman** (lake), Austl.
144/B2 **Picsi,** Peru
160/E3 **Picton,** On,Can
161/J2 **Pictou,** NS,Can
58/D5 **Piddle** (riv.), Eng,UK
106/D6 **Pidurutagala** (peak), SrL.
141/J6 **Piedade do Rio Grande,** Braz.
138/C3 **Piedecuesta,** Col.
78/B2 **Piedmont** (reg.), It.
165/K11 **Piedmont,** Ca,US
143/F2 **Piedras** (pt.), Arg.
144/D3 **Piedras** (riv.), Peru
147/N8 **Piedras Negras,** Mex.
65/K3 **Piekary Śląskie,** Pol.
132/B4 **Piekenierskloof** (pass), SAfr.
61/H3 **Pieksämäki,** Fin.
61/J3 **Pielinen** (lake), Fin.
65/L4 **Pieniński Nat'l Park,** Pol.
75/K6 **Piera,** Sp.
159/H2 **Pierce,** Ne,US
165/C3 **Pierce** (co.), Wa,US
156/F2 **Pierceland,** Sk,Can
55/N13 **Pierowall,** Sc,UK
157/H4 **Pierre** (cap.), SD,US
53/T10 **Pierrefitte-sur-Seine,** Fr.
161/N7 **Pierrefonds,** Qu,Can
68/C5 **Pierrefonds,** Fr.
72/F4 **Pierrelatte,** Fr.
53/S9 **Pierrelaye,** Fr.
133/E3 **Pietermaritzburg,** SAfr.
131/C4 **Pietersburg,** SAfr.
78/B4 **Pietra Ligure,** It.
78/A5 **Pietravecchia, Monte** (peak), It.
133/E2 **Piet Retief,** SAfr.
83/G2 **Pietrosul** (peak), Rom.
86/C3 **Pietrosul, Vîrful** (peak), Rom.
78/C2 **Pieve Emanuele,** It.
156/E2 **Pigeon** (lake), Ab,Can
157/L3 **Pigeon** (riv.), Can., US
160/B4 **Piggott,** Ar,US
149/F1 **Pigs** (bay), Cuba
142/E3 **Pigüé,** Arg.
66/B4 **Pijnacker,** Neth.
148/E3 **Pijol** (peak), Hon.
166/C1 **Pike** (co.), Pa,US
120/D4 **Pikelot** (isl.), Micr.
159/F3 **Pikes** (peak), Co,US
166/B1 **Pikes Creek** (res.), Pa,US
166/B5 **Pikesville,** Md,US
160/D4 **Pikeville,** Ky,US
112/D4 **Pikit,** Phil.
65/J2 **Piła,** Pol.
65/J2 **Piła** (prov.), Pol.
131/B5 **Pilane,** Bots.
132/P12 **Pilanesberg** (range), SAfr.
140/B3 **Pilão Arcado,** Braz.
142/E1 **Pilar,** Arg.
140/D3 **Pilar,** Braz.
135/E2 **Pilar,** Par.
111/F1 **Pilar,** Phil.
76/E4 **Pilatus** (peak), Swi.
136/F8 **Pilaya** (riv.), Bol.
165/D1 **Pilchuck** (riv.), Wa,US
134/C5 **Pilcomayo** (riv.), SAm.
53/P7 **Pilgrims Hatch,** Eng,UK
112/C2 **Pili,** Phil.
86/B2 **Pilica** (riv.), Pol.
81/H3 **Pílion** (peak), Gre.
82/D2 **Pilis,** Hun.
82/D2 **Pilis** (peak), Hun.
65/K5 **Pilisvörösvár,** Hun.
106/C2 **Pilkhua,** India
119/C4 **Pillar** (cape), Austl.
57/E2 **Pillar** (mtn.), Eng,UK
165/K12 **Pillar** (pt.), Ca,US
76/D5 **Pillon, Col du** (pass), Swi.
140/A5 **Pilões** (mts.), Braz.
163/G2 **Pilot** (peak), Tn,US
71/G3 **Pilsen** (Plzeň), Czh.
77/H1 **Pilsensee** (lake), Ger.
158/E4 **Pima,** Az,US
106/B4 **Pimpri-Chinchwad,** India
149/G5 **Piña** (pt.), Pan.
146/B2 **Pinacote, Cerro** (mtn.), Mex.
143/J7 **Pinaculo** (peak), Arg.
112/C2 **Pinamalayan,** Phil.
109/B5 **Pinang** (cape), Malay.
110/A2 **Pinang** (isl.), Malay.
92/D2 **Pınarbaşı,** Turk.
149/F1 **Pinar del Río,** Cuba
83/H5 **Pınarhisar,** Turk.
144/B1 **Piñas,** Ecu.
112/C2 **Pinatubo, Mount** (vol.), Phil.
157/K3 **Pinawa,** Mb,Can
57/H6 **Pinchbeck,** Eng,UK
156/E3 **Pincher Creek,** Ab,Can
160/D3 **Pinconning,** Mi,US
82/E2 **Pincota,** Rom.
161/N7 **Pincourt,** Qu,Can
65/L3 **Pińczów,** Pol.
141/H7 **Pindamonhangaba,** Braz.
140/A2 **Pindaré** (riv.), Braz.
140/A1 **Pindaré-Mirim,** Braz.
108/B1 **Pind Dādan Khān,** Pak.
108/B1 **Pindi Gheb,** Pak.
140/B3 **Pindobaçu,** Braz.
81/G3 **Pindos Nat'l Park,** Gre.
81/G2 **Pindus** (mts.), Gre.
106/B3 **Pindwāra,** India
165/G6 **Pine** (riv.), Mi,US
163/F4 **Pine** (hills), Ms,US
157/G4 **Pine** (hills), Mt,US
166/A1 **Pine** (cr.), Pa,US
166/D4 **Pine Barrens** (reg.), NJ,US
162/E3 **Pine Bluff,** Ar,US
157/G5 **Pine Bluffs,** Wy,US
167/H7 **Pinecliff** (lake), NJ,US
167/E1 **Pine Creek** (pt.), Ct,US
75/G2 **Pineda de Mar,** Sp.
156/F5 **Pinedale,** Wy,US
157/J3 **Pine Falls,** Mb,Can
84/J2 **Pinega** (riv.), Rus.
166/D4 **Pine Hill,** NJ,US
157/L2 **Pineimuta** (riv.), On,Can
113/T **Pine Island** (bay), Ant.
160/A2 **Pine Island,** Mn,US
132/L10 **Pinelands,** SAfr.
157/H5 **Pine Ridge,** SD,US
73/G4 **Pinerolo,** It.
167/D2 **Pines** (lake), NJ,US
165/G6 **Pine, South Branch** (riv.), Mi,US
133/E3 **Pinetown,** SAfr.
109/B2 **Ping** (riv.), Thai.
104/D4 **Pingbian Miaozu Zizhixian,** China
105/E2 **Pingchang,** China
103/C3 **Pingding,** China
103/C4 **Pingdingshan,** China
103/D3 **Pingdu,** China
120/F4 **Pingelap** (atoll), Micr.
103/D2 **Pinggu,** China
107/J3 **Pingguo,** China
103/L9 **Pinghu,** China
105/G2 **Pingjing Guan** (pass), China
105/F3 **Pingle,** China
103/B4 **Pinglu,** China
103/C3 **Pinglu,** China
107/K3 **Pingnan,** China
103/D2 **Pingquan,** China
103/C3 **Pingshan,** China
103/C3 **Pingshun,** China
107/J2 **Pingtang,** China
105/J4 **Pingtung,** Tai.
103/C3 **Pingxiang,** China
104/E4 **Pingxiang,** China
105/G3 **Pingxiang,** China
103/C3 **Pingxing Guan** (pass), China
97/J4 **Pingyang,** China
103/C3 **Pingyao,** China
103/D4 **Pingyi,** China
103/D3 **Pingyin,** China
103/C4 **Pingyu,** China
103/D3 **Pingyuan,** China
141/G7 **Pinhal,** Braz.
75/Q10 **Pinhal Novo,** Port.
138/B4 **Pinhão,** Braz.
140/A1 **Pinheiro,** Braz.
141/D1 **Pinheiros,** Braz.
81/G3 **Piniós** (riv.), Gre.
81/G4 **Piniós** (riv.), Gre.
116/K6 **Pinjar** (lake), Austl.
117/G5 **Pinkawillinie Consv. Park,** Austl.
66/C2 **Pinkegat** (chan.), Neth.
158/B3 **Pinnacles Nat'l Mon.,** Ca,US
67/G1 **Pinnau** (riv.), Ger.
67/G1 **Pinneberg,** Ger.
142/C3 **Pino Hachado** (pass), Arg.
165/K10 **Pinole,** Ca,US
158/C4 **Pinos** (peak), Ca,US
149/F1 **Pinos** (Juventad) (isl.), Cuba
74/D4 **Pinos-Puente,** Sp.
148/B2 **Pinotepa Nacional,** Mex.
114/E4 **Pinrang,** Indo.
121/V13 **Pins** (isl.), NCal.
120/F7 **Pins, Ile des** (isl.), NCal.
86/C1 **Pinsk,** Bela.
144/J6 **Pinta** (isl.), Ecu.
142/C3 **Pinto,** Chile
75/N9 **Pinto,** Sp.
112/D3 **Pintuyan,** Phil.
158/D3 **Pioche,** Nv,US
140/B2 **Pio IX,** Braz.
80/B1 **Piombino,** It.
116/L7 **Pioneer World,** Austl.
88/J2 **Pioner** (isl.), Rus.
65/L3 **Pionki,** Pol.
139/F5 **Piorini** (riv.), Braz.
78/A3 **Piossasco,** It.
78/B3 **Piota** (riv.), It.
65/K3 **Piotrków** (prov.), Pol.
65/K3 **Piotrków Trybunalski,** Pol.
79/F2 **Piove di Sacco,** It.
79/E1 **Piovene-Rocchette,** It.
140/A1 **Pio XII,** Braz.
106/B2 **Pīpār,** India
158/D3 **Pipe Spring Nat'l Mon.,** Az,US
157/H3 **Pipestone** (cr.), Mb, Sk,Can
157/L2 **Pipestone** (riv.), On,Can
157/J4 **Pipestone,** Mn,US
157/J4 **Pipestone Nat'l Mon.,** Mn,US
108/A1 **Piplān,** Pak.
161/G1 **Pipmuacan** (res.), Qu,Can
116/C2 **Pippingara Abor. Land,** Austl.
160/C3 **Piqua,** Oh,US
141/H7 **Piquete,** Braz.
141/A3 **Piquiri** (riv.), Braz.
141/B1 **Piracanjuba,** Braz.
141/C2 **Piracicaba,** Braz.
140/B1 **Piracuruca,** Braz.
101/C2 **Pirae-bong** (mtn.), NKor.
141/K7 **Piraí,** Braz.
141/B3 **Piraí do Sul,** Braz.
81/H4 **Piraiévs,** Gre.
141/B2 **Piraju,** Braz.
141/B2 **Pirajuí,** Braz.
143/J7 **Pirámide** (peak), Chile
79/G1 **Piran,** Slov.
135/E2 **Pirané,** Arg.
141/D2 **Piranga** (riv.), Braz.
140/C2 **Piranhas** (riv.), Braz.
140/C2 **Piranji** (riv.), Braz.
140/A1 **Pirapemas,** Braz.
141/C1 **Pirapora,** Braz.
141/B2 **Pirapòzinho,** Braz.
141/C2 **Pirássununga,** Braz.
142/C1 **Pircas** (peak), Arg.
141/B1 **Pires do Rio,** Braz.
81/G4 **Pírgos,** Gre.
83/F5 **Pirin** (mtn.), Bul.
83/F5 **Pirin** (mts.), Bul.
81/H2 **Pirin** (peak), Bul.
83/F5 **Pirin Nat'l Park,** Bul.
140/B2 **Piripiri,** Braz.
140/B3 **Piritaba,** Braz.
138/D2 **Píritu,** Ven.
63/K1 **Pirkkala,** Fin.
108/B2 **Pīr Mahal,** Pak.
69/G5 **Pirmasens,** Ger.
65/G3 **Pirna,** Ger.
82/F4 **Pirot,** Yugo.
108/C1 **Pir Panjal** (range), India
149/G5 **Pirre** (mtn.), Pan.
164/B1 **Piru** (cr.), Ca,US
164/B2 **Piru** (lake), Ca,US
86/E2 **Piryatin,** Ukr.
78/D5 **Pisa,** It.
79/D6 **Pisa** (prov.), It.
78/D4 **Pisanino, Monte** (peak), It.
111/E2 **Pisau, Tanjong** (cape), Malay.
138/C3 **Pisba Nat'l Park,** Col.
166/D2 **Piscataway,** NJ,US
144/B4 **Pisco,** Peru
144/C4 **Pisco** (riv.), Peru
71/H4 **Písek,** Czh.
71/H3 **Písek** (peak), Czh.
102/C4 **Pishan,** China
95/J2 **Pishīn,** Pak.
77/G4 **Pisoc, Piz** (peak), Swi.
135/C2 **Pissis** (peak), Arg.
68/B4 **Pissy,** Fr.
165/P15 **Pistakee** (lake), Il,US
80/E2 **Pisticci,** It.
79/D5 **Pistoia,** It.
79/D5 **Pistoia** (prov.), It.
74/C1 **Pisuerga** (riv.), Sp.
65/L2 **Pisz,** Pol.
158/B2 **Pit** (riv.), Ca,US
138/B4 **Pitalito,** Col.
141/B3 **Pitanga,** Braz.
121/N7 **Pitcairn** (isl.), Pitc.
121/N7 **Pitcairn Islands** (terr.), UK
61/G2 **Piteå,** Swe.
61/F2 **Piteälv** (riv.), Swe.
83/G3 **Piteşti,** Rom.
72/E2 **Pithiviers,** Fr.
117/F3 **Pitjantjatjara Abor. Lands,** Austl.
54/C3 **Pitlochry,** Sc,UK
166/C4 **Pitman,** NJ,US
54/D2 **Pitmedden,** Sc,UK
112/C2 **Pitogo,** Phil.
142/B3 **Pitrufquén,** Chile
131/B5 **Pitsane,** Bots.
118/H8 **Pitt** (lake), Austl.
54/D4 **Pittenweem,** Sc,UK
149/F4 **Pittier** (mtn.), CR
165/L10 **Pittsburg,** Ca,US
159/J3 **Pittsburg,** Ks,US
162/E3 **Pittsburg,** Tx,US
168/H7 **Pittsburgh,** Pa,US
168/A1 **Pittsfield,** Ma,US
161/G2 **Pittsfield,** Me,US
166/C1 **Pittston,** Pa,US
77/G3 **Pitzbach** (riv.), Aus.
141/C2 **Piũí,** Braz.
144/A2 **Piura,** Peru
106/D2 **Piuthān,** Nepal
81/F1 **Piva** (riv.), Yugo.
138/C2 **Pivijay,** Col.
82/D4 **Pivsko** (lake), Yugo.
104/D2 **Pi Xian,** China
85/K4 **Pizhma** (riv.), Rus.
77/F4 **Pizol** (peak), Swi.
80/E3 **Pizzo,** It.
80/C1 **Pizzuto** (peak), It.
132/D3 **P. K. Le Rouxdam** (res.), SAfr.
148/D2 **Placentia** (pt.), Belz.
161/L2 **Placentia** (bay), Nf,Can
164/C3 **Placentia,** Ca,US
148/E2 **Placer,** Mex.
112/D3 **Placer,** Phil.
165/M9 **Placer** (co.), Ca,US
149/G1 **Placetas,** Cuba
53/T9 **Plailly,** Fr.
109/C3 **Plai Mat** (riv.), Thai.
76/C1 **Plaine** (riv.), Fr.
166/D2 **Plainfield,** NJ,US
162/C3 **Plains,** Tx,US
166/D3 **Plainsboro,** NJ,US
160/A2 **Plainview,** Mn,US
167/E2 **Plainview,** NY,US
162/C3 **Plainview,** Tx,US
168/B2 **Plainville,** Ct,US
159/H3 **Plainville,** Ks,US
168/C1 **Plainville,** Ma,US
53/R10 **Plaisir,** Fr.
111/E5 **Plampang,** Indo.
150/C2 **Plana** (cays), Bahm.
140/A4 **Planaltina,** Braz.
141/D1 **Planalto do Brasil** (plat.), Braz.
138/C2 **Planeta Rica,** Col.
162/D3 **Plano,** Tx,US
163/H5 **Plantation,** Fl,US
163/H4 **Plant City,** Fl,US
163/F4 **Plaquemine,** La,US
74/B2 **Plasencia,** Sp.
135/E4 **Plata** (estuary), Arg.
80/C4 **Platani** (riv.), It.
143/F2 **Plata, Río de la** (estuary), Arg.
129/H4 **Plateau** (state), Nga.
68/D3 **Plate Taile, Barrage de la** (dam), Belg.
138/C2 **Plato,** Col.
159/J2 **Platte** (riv.), Mo,US
159/H2 **Platte** (riv.), Ne,US
157/J5 **Platte,** SD,US
160/B3 **Platteville,** Wi,US
71/F5 **Plattling,** Ger.
160/F2 **Plattsburgh,** NY,US
71/F2 **Plauen,** Ger.
82/D4 **Plav,** Yugo.
77/G4 **Plavna Dadaint, Piz** (peak), Swi.
148/E3 **Playa de los Muertos** (ruins), Hon.
146/C2 **Playa Noriega** (lake), Mex.
138/A5 **Playas,** Ecu.
158/E5 **Playas** (lake), NM,US
109/E3 **Play Cu** (Pleiku), Viet.
157/J2 **Playgreen** (lake), Mb,Can
165/K11 **Pleasant Hill,** Ca,US
168/E6 **Pleasant Hill** (dam), Oh,US
168/E6 **Pleasant Hill** (res.), Oh,US
168/H7 **Pleasant Hills,** Pa,US
165/L11 **Pleasanton,** Ca,US
162/D4 **Pleasanton,** Tx,US
165/Q14 **Pleasant Prairie,** Wi,US
166/D5 **Pleasantville,** NJ,US
167/E1 **Pleasantville,** NY,US
71/G5 **Plechý** (Plöckenstein) (peak), Czh., Ger.
109/E3 **Pleiku** (Play Cu), Viet.
70/D4 **Pleinfeld,** Ger.
64/G3 **Pleisse** (riv.), Ger.
119/G5 **Plenty** (riv.), Austl.
115/S10 **Plenty** (bay), NZ
157/G3 **Plentywood,** Mt,US
72/B2 **Plérin,** Fr.
71/F2 **Plesná** (riv.), Czh.
65/J3 **Pleszew,** Pol.
161/G1 **Plétipi** (lake), Qu,Can
67/E6 **Plettenberg,** Ger.
83/G4 **Pleven,** Bul.
82/B3 **Plitvice Lakes Nat'l Park,** Cro.
73/L4 **Plitvička Jezera Nat'l Park,** Cro.
82/D4 **Pljevlja,** Yugo.
82/B4 **Ploča, Rt** (pt.), Yugo.
65/K2 **Płock,** Pol.
65/K2 **Płock** (prov.), Pol.
71/G5 **Plöckenstein** (Plechý) (peak), Ger.
82/C4 **Pločno** (peak), Bosn.
72/B3 **Ploemeur,** Fr.
83/H3 **Ploieşti,** Rom.
76/C2 **Plombières-les-Bains,** Fr.
64/F1 **Plön,** Ger.
156/G2 **Plonge** (lake), Sk,Can
65/L2 **Płońsk,** Pol.
65/H3 **Ploučnice** (riv.), Czh.
72/B2 **Ploufragan,** Fr.
72/A2 **Plougastel-Daoulas,** Fr.
83/G4 **Plovdiv,** Bul.
83/G5 **Plovdiv** (reg.), Bul.
160/B2 **Plover,** Wi,US
167/F1 **Plum** (isl.), NY,US
168/H7 **Plum,** Pa,US
56/A2 **Plumbridge,** NI,UK
116/E4 **Plumridge Lakes Nature Rsv.,** Austl.
131/B4 **Plumtree,** Zim.
63/J4 **Plungė,** Lith.
150/F3 **Plymouth** (cap.), Monts.
58/B6 **Plymouth,** Eng,UK
58/B6 **Plymouth** (sound), Eng,UK
160/C3 **Plymouth,** In,US
168/D2 **Plymouth,** Ma,US
168/D2 **Plymouth** (co.), Ma,US
161/G3 **Plymouth,** NH,US
166/C1 **Plymouth,** Pa,US
160/C3 **Plymouth,** Wi,US
168/D2 **Plymouth Rock,** Ma,US
58/C2 **Plynlimon** (mtn.), UK
71/G3 **Plzeň** (Pilsen), Czh.
65/J2 **Pniewy,** Pol.
129/E4 **Pô,** Burk.
79/E3 **Po** (riv.), It.
78/C2 **Po** (val.), It.
141/G8 **Poá,** Braz.
139/E2 **Poa** (riv.), Ven.
102/D3 **Pobedy, Pik** (peak), Kyr.
65/J2 **Pobiedziska,** Pol.
163/F2 **Pocahontas,** Ar,US
140/A2 **Poção de Pedra,** Braz.
156/E5 **Pocatello,** Id,US
86/E1 **Pochep,** Rus.
148/B3 **Pochutla,** Mex.
71/G6 **Pöcking,** Ger.
120/E6 **Pocklington** (reef), PNG
57/H4 **Pocklington,** Eng,UK
140/B4 **Poções,** Braz.
141/H6 **Poço Fundo,** Braz.
159/J4 **Pocola,** Ok,US
137/G7 **Poconé,** Braz.
166/C1 **Pocono** (cr.), Pa,US
166/C1 **Pocono** (lake), Pa,US
166/C1 **Pocono** (mts.), Pa,US
141/G6 **Poços de Caldas,** Braz.
149/F4 **Pocrí,** Pan.
65/K3 **Poddębice,** Pol.
79/F3 **Po di Goro** (riv.), It.
79/F2 **Po di Venezia** (riv.), It.
79/E3 **Po di Volano** (riv.), It.
65/M3 **Podlasie** (reg.), Pol.
84/H5 **Podol'sk,** Rus.
128/B2 **Podor,** Sen.
84/G3 **Podporozh'ye,** Rus.
82/C3 **Podravska Slatina,** Cro.
82/E4 **Podujevo,** Yugo.
79/E6 **Poggibonsi,** It.
81/G2 **Pogradec,** Alb.
151/F5 **Pogromni** (vol.), Ak,US
154/U11 **Pohakuloa** (mil. res.), Hi,US
101/E4 **P'ohang,** SKor.
166/C2 **Pohatcong** (cr.), NJ,US
161/G2 **Pohénégamook,** Qu,Can
61/G3 **Pohjanmaa** (reg.), Fin.
120/E4 **Pohnpei** (isl.), Micr.
166/C2 **Pohopoco** (cr.), Pa,US
166/C2 **Pohopoco Mtn.** (ridge), Pa,US
71/E6 **Poing,** Ger.
113/H **Poinsett** (cape), Ant.
152/E2 **Point** (lake), NW,Can
163/F4 **Point au Fer** (isl.), La,US
150/F3 **Pointe-à-Pitre,** Guad.
161/N7 **Pointe-Claire,** Qu,Can
161/F2 **Pointe-du-Lac,** Qu,Can
126/B1 **Pointe-Noire,** Congo
75/G4 **Pointe Pescade, Cap de la** (cape), Alg.
150/F5 **Point Fortin,** Trin.
168/C3 **Point Judith Coast Guard Sta.,** RI,US
119/E1 **Point Lookout** (peak), Austl.
164/A2 **Point Mugo Nav. Air Sta.,** Ca,US
164/A2 **Point Mugo State Park,** Ca,US
108/H4 **Point Pedro,** SrL.
160/D3 **Point Pelee Nat'l Park,** On,Can
167/D3 **Point Pleasant,** NJ,US
160/C4 **Point Pleasant,** Oh,US
160/D4 **Point Pleasant,** WV,US
168/G7 **Point Saint Park,** Pa,US
116/E4 **Point Salvation Abor. Rsv.,** Austl.
116/C1 **Poissonnier** (pt.), Austl.
53/S10 **Poissy,** Fr.
72/D3 **Poitiers,** Fr.
72/C3 **Poitou** (hist. reg.), Fr.
72/C3 **Poitou-Charentes** (reg.), Fr.
63/K1 **Pojo,** Fin.
61/J3 **Pojois-Karjala** (prov.), Fin.
140/C4 **Pojuca,** Braz.
106/B2 **Pokaran,** India
106/D2 **Pokhara,** Nepal
87/K1 **Pokhvistnevo,** Rus.
109/E4 **Po Klong Garai Cham Towers,** Viet.
125/L7 **Poko,** Zaire
71/H2 **Polabská Nížina** (reg.), Czh.
74/C1 **Pola de Laviana,** Sp.
74/C1 **Pola de Lena,** Sp.
74/C1 **Pola de Siero,** Sp.
86/A2 **Pol'ana** (peak), Slvk.
65/K2 **Poland**
65/L3 **Połaniec,** Pol.
85/P2 **Polar Urals** (mts.), Rus.
92/C2 **Polatlı,** Turk.
65/J2 **Połczyn-Zdrój,** Pol.
95/J1 **Pol-e-Khomri,** Afg.
113/E **Pole of Inaccessibility,** Ant.
79/E2 **Polesine** (reg.), It.
59/E1 **Polesworth,** Eng,UK
82/E2 **Polgár,** Hun.
101/D5 **Pŏlgyo,** SKor.
81/J4 **Poliaigos** (isl.), Gre.
80/D3 **Policastro** (gulf), It.
65/H2 **Police,** Pol.
80/E2 **Policoro,** It.
81/H2 **Políkhni,** Gre.
112/C2 **Polillo** (isl.), Phil.
112/C2 **Polillo** (isls.), Phil.
112/C2 **Polillo** (str.), Phil.
80/E3 **Polistena,** It.
65/J3 **Polkowice,** Pol.
108/F3 **Pollāchi,** India
75/G3 **Pollensa,** Sp.
148/D3 **Polochic** (riv.), Guat.
112/D4 **Polomolok,** Phil.
143/G2 **Polonia** (cape), Uru.
108/H5 **Polonnaruwa,** SrL.

213

Polon – Pusan

108/H4 Polonnaruwa (dist.), SrL.
86/C2 Polonnoye, Ukr.
63/N4 Polotsk, Bela.
58/B6 Polperro, Eng,UK
83/G4 Polski Trŭmbesh, Bul.
156/E4 Polson, Mt,US
86/E2 Poltava, Ukr.
86/E2 Poltava Obl., Ukr.
71/H5 Poluška (peak), Czh.
84/F3 Polvijärvi, Fin.
84/G1 Polyarnyy, Rus.
121/J3 Polynesia (reg.)
141/D2 Pomba (riv.), Braz.
140/C2 Pombal, Braz.
74/A3 Pombal, Port.
65/H2 Pomerania (reg.), Pol.
65/H1 Pomeranian (bay), Ger., Pol.
141/B3 Pomerode, Braz.
139/G3 Pomeroon-Supernaam (reg.), Guy.
56/B2 Pomeroy, NI,UK
156/D4 Pomeroy, Wa,US
120/E5 Pomio, PNG
164/C2 Pomona, Ca,US
83/H4 Pomorie, Bul.
91/C2 Pomos (pt.), Cyp.
79/F3 Po, Mouths of the, It.
163/H5 Pompano Beach, Fl,US
80/D2 Pompei (ruins), It.
141/C1 Pompeu, Braz.
167/H8 Pompton (lakes), NJ,US
167/H8 Pompton (riv.), NJ,US
167/D1 Pompton Lakes, NJ,US
129/E4 Pô Nat'l Park, Burk.
159/H3 Ponca City, Ok,US
150/E3 Ponce, PR
160/E1 Poncheville (lake), Qu,Can
76/B5 Poncin, Fr.
153/J1 Pond (inlet), NW,Can
168/A3 Pond (pt.), Ct,US
108/G3 Pondicherry, India
108/G3 Pondicherry (terr.), India
78/B5 Ponente (coast), It.
74/B1 Ponferrada, Sp.
133/E2 Pongolo (riv.), SAfr.
130/C4 Pongwe, Tanz.
128/E4 Poni (prov.), Burk.
65/M3 Poniatowa, Pol.
108/G3 Ponnaiyar (riv.), India
108/E3 Ponnani, India
156/E2 Ponoka, Ab,Can
84/H2 Ponoy (riv.), Rus.
78/D5 Ponsacco, It.
68/D3 Pont-à-Celles, Belg.
140/C5 Ponta da Baleia (pt.), Braz.
75/S12 Ponta da Pico (mtn.), Azor.,Port.
75/T13 Ponta Delgada, Azor.,Port.
75/U15 Ponta do Sol, Madr.,Port.
141/B3 Ponta Grossa, Braz.
141/B1 Pontalina, Braz.
69/F6 Pont-à-Mousson, Fr.
137/G8 Ponta Porã, Braz.
58/C3 Pontardawe, Wal,UK
58/B3 Pontardulais, Wal,UK
76/C4 Pontarlier, Fr.
79/E5 Pontassieve, It.
53/T10 Pontault-Combault, Fr.
160/E1 Pontax (riv.), Qu,Can
53/U10 Pontcarré, Fr.
163/F4 Pontchartrain (lake), La,US
72/B3 Pontchâteau, Fr.
72/E4 Pont-du-Château, Fr.
80/C2 Pontecorvo, It.
78/D5 Pontedera, It.
74/A3 Ponte de Sor, Port.
57/G4 Pontefract, Eng,UK
57/G1 Ponteland, Eng,UK
141/D2 Ponte Nova, Braz.
58/C2 Ponterwyd, Wal,UK
79/E2 Ponte San Nicolò, It.
58/D1 Pontesbury, Eng,UK
136/G7 Pontes e Lacerda, Braz.
112/C3 Pontevedra, Phil.
74/A1 Pontevedra, Sp.
160/B3 Pontiac, Il,US
165/F6 Pontiac, Mi,US
165/F6 Pontiac (lake), Mi,US
110/C4 Pontianak, Indo.
72/B2 Pontivy, Fr.
53/S9 Pontoise, Fr.
163/F3 Pontotoc, Ms,US
58/C2 Pontrhydfendigaid, Wal,UK
58/D3 Pontrilas, Eng,UK
68/B5 Pont-Sainte-Maxence, Fr.
72/F4 Pont-Saint-Esprit, Fr.
58/B3 Pontyates, Wal,UK
58/C3 Pontyclun, Wal,UK
58/C3 Pont y Cymmer, Wal,UK
58/C3 Pontypool, Wal,UK
58/C3 Pontypridd, Wal,UK
80/C2 Ponziane (isls.), It.
58/E5 Poole, Eng,UK
59/E5 Poole (bay), Eng,UK
55/J8 Poolewe, Sc,UK
106/B4 Poona, India
116/C3 Poondarrie (peak), Austl.
117/F3 Poondinna (peak), Austl.
136/E7 Poopó (lake), Bol.
63/K2 Põõsapää Neem (pt.), Est.
167/F2 Poosepatuck Ind. Res., NY,US
104/B4 Popa (peak), Burma
138/B4 Popayán, Col.
68/B2 Poperinge, Belg.
146/C2 Popigochic (riv.), Mex.
119/B2 Popilta (lake), Austl.
119/B2 Popio (lake), Austl.
157/K2 Poplar (riv.), Mb, On,Can
166/B6 Poplar (isl.), Md,US
157/G3 Poplar, Mt,US
157/G3 Poplar (riv.), Mt,US
159/K3 Poplar Bluff, Mo,US
163/F4 Poplarville, Ms,US
124/J6 Popokabaka, Zaire
120/D5 Popondetta, PNG
83/H4 Popovo, Bul.
71/E4 Poppberg (peak), Ger.
65/L4 Poprad, Slvk.
65/L4 Poprad (riv.), Slvk.
140/B2 Poranga, Braz.
137/J6 Porangatu, Braz.
106/A3 Porbandar, India
138/C3 Porce (riv.), Col.
79/F1 Porcia, It.
74/C4 Porcuna, Sp.
151/K2 Porcupine (riv.), Yk,Can, Ak,US
118/B3 Porcupine Gorge Nat'l Park, Austl.
157/H2 Porcupine Plain, Sk,Can
79/F1 Pordenone, It.
79/F1 Pordenone (prov.), It.
79/G2 Poreč, Cro.
63/J1 Pori, Fin.
115/R11 Porirua, NZ
84/E4 Porkhov, Rus.
139/F2 Porlamar, Ven.
58/C4 Porlock, Eng,UK
118/A1 Pormpuraaw Abor. Land, Austl.
97/N2 Poronaysk, Rus.
116/C5 Porongurup Nat'l Park, Austl.
113/J Porpoise (bay), Ant.
76/D3 Porrentruy, Swi.
74/A1 Porriño, Sp.
61/H1 Porsangen (fjord), Nor.
62/C2 Porsgrunn, Nor.
92/B2 Porsuk (riv.), Turk.
136/F7 Portachuelo, Bol.
117/M8 Port Adelaide, Austl.
56/B3 Portadown, NI,UK
56/C3 Portaferry, NI,UK
160/C3 Portage, Mi,US
168/F5 Portage (co.), Oh,US
168/F6 Portage (lakes), Oh,US
160/B3 Portage, Wi,US
168/F5 Portage Lakes, Oh,US
157/J3 Portage la Prairie, Mb,Can
156/B3 Port Alberni, BC,Can
74/B3 Portalegre, Port.
74/B3 Portalegre (dist.), Port.
159/G4 Portales, NM,US
132/D4 Port Alfred, SAfr.
156/B3 Port Alice, BC,Can
156/C3 Port Angeles, Wa,US
149/G2 Port Antonio, Jam.
54/A3 Port Appin, Sc,UK
162/E4 Port Arthur, Tx,US
55/H9 Port Askaig, Sc,UK
161/K1 Port au Choix, Nf,Can
161/K1 Port au Choix Nat'l Hist. Park, Nf,Can
117/H5 Port Augusta, Austl.
149/H2 Port-au-Prince (cap.), Haiti
56/C3 Portavogie, NI,UK
67/F4 Porta Westfalica, Ger.
54/A5 Port Bannatyne, Sc,UK
107/F5 Port Blair, India
162/E4 Port Bolivar, Tx,US
128/E5 Port-Bouët, IvC.
153/K2 Port Burwell, Qu,Can
161/H1 Port-Cartier, Qu,Can
163/H5 Port Charlotte, Fl,US
167/E2 Port Chester, NY,US
160/D3 Port Clinton, Oh,US
161/R10 Port Colborne, On,Can
161/Q8 Port Credit, On,Can
161/S8 Port Darlington, On,Can
119/C4 Port Davey (har.), Austl.
149/H2 Port-de-Paix, Haiti
110/B3 Port Dickson, Malay.
165/B1 Port Discovery (bay), Wa,US
151/M4 Port Edward, BC,Can
140/B4 Porteirinha, Braz.
137/H4 Portel, Braz.
160/D2 Port Elgin, Can.
132/D4 Port Elizabeth, SAfr.
55/H9 Port Ellen, Sc,UK
56/D3 Port Erin, IM,UK
166/C1 Porters (lake), Pa,US
132/L10 Porterville, SAfr.
158/C3 Porterville, Ca,US
72/F4 Portes-lès-Valence, Fr.
149/J3 Portete (bay), Col.
124/B3 Port-Étienne, Mrta.
72/D5 Portet-sur-Garonne, Fr.
58/B3 Port Eynon, Wal,UK
58/B3 Port Eynon (pt.), Wal,UK
165/B2 Port Gamble Ind. Res., Wa,US
126/A1 Port-Gentil, Gabon
54/B5 Port Glasgow, Sc,UK
56/B2 Portglenone, NI,UK
54/C1 Portgordon, Sc,UK
58/C3 Porth, Wal,UK
129/G5 Port Harcourt, Nga.
156/B3 Port Hardy, BC,Can
161/J2 Port Hawkesbury, NS,Can
58/C4 Porthcawl, Wal,UK
116/C2 Port Hedland, Austl.
58/A6 Porthleven, Eng,UK
56/D6 Porthmadog, Wal,UK
164/A2 Port Hueneme, Ca,US
165/H6 Port Huron, Mi,US
74/A4 Portimão, Port.
58/B5 Port Isaac, Eng,UK
58/B5 Port Isaac (bay), Eng,UK
58/D4 Portishead, Eng,UK
167/E2 Port Jefferson, NY,US
166/D1 Port Jervis, NY,US
54/D1 Portknockie, Sc,UK
119/B3 Portland, Austl.
119/C4 Portland (cape), Austl.
149/G2 Portland (pt.), Jam.
58/D6 Portland (pt.), Eng,UK
151/N4 Portland (inlet), BC,Can, Ak,US
160/C3 Portland, In,US
161/G3 Portland, Me,US
156/C4 Portland, Or,US
162/G2 Portland, Tn,US
55/K11 Portland, Bill of (pt.), Eng,UK
58/D5 Portland, Isle of (pen.), Eng,UK
162/D4 Port Lavaca, Tx,US
54/D2 Portlethen, Sc,UK
117/G5 Port Lincoln, Austl.
133/S15 Port Louis (cap.), Mrts.
119/E1 Port Macquarie, Austl.
165/B2 Port Madison Ind. Res., Wa,US
54/C1 Portmahomack, Sc,UK
149/G2 Port Maria, Jam.
60/D3 Portmarnock, Ire.
156/B3 Port McNeill, BC,Can
161/H1 Port-Menier, Qu,Can
149/G2 Portmore, Jam.
120/D5 Port Moresby (cap.), PNG
161/G1 Portneuf (riv.), Qu,Can
140/B1 Pôrto, Braz.
80/A1 Porto (gulf), Fr.
74/A2 Porto, Port.
74/A2 Porto (dist.), Port.
141/B4 Pôrto Alegre, Braz.
126/B3 Porto Amboim, Ang.
141/B3 Pôrto Belo, Braz.
149/G4 Portobelo Nat'l Park, Pan.
140/D3 Pôrto Calvo, Braz.
79/G6 Portocivitanova, It.
140/C3 Pôrto da Fôlha, Braz.
80/C4 Porto Empedocle, It.
80/B1 Portoferraio, It.
141/C2 Pôrto Ferreira, Braz.
55/H7 Port of Ness, Sc,UK
140/A2 Porto Franco, Braz.
150/F5 Port-of-Spain (cap.), Trin.
79/F1 Portogruaro, It.
79/E3 Portomaggiore, It.
137/J6 Porto Nacional, Braz.
129/F5 Porto-Novo (cap.), Ben.
108/G3 Portonovo, India
163/H4 Port Orange, Fl,US
79/G6 Porto Recanati, It.
79/G1 Portorož, Slov.
80/C1 Porto San Giorgio, It.
80/B1 Porto Santo Stefano, It.
140/C5 Porto Seguro, Braz.
80/A2 Porto Torres, It.
141/B3 Pôrto União, Braz.
136/F5 Pôrto Velho, Braz.
138/A5 Portoviejo, Ecu.
56/C2 Portpatrick, Sc,UK
119/C3 Port Phillip (bay), Austl.
117/H5 Port Pirie, Austl.
55/H8 Portree, Sc,UK
167/J9 Port Richmond, NY,US
56/B1 Portrush, NI,UK
127/C2 Port Said (Būr Sa'īd), Egypt
163/G4 Port Saint Joe, Fl,US
72/F5 Port-Saint-Louis-du-Rhône, Fr.
163/H5 Port Saint Lucie, Fl,US
56/D3 Port Saint Mary, IM,UK
59/E5 Portsea (isl.), Eng,UK
54/D5 Port Seton, Sc,UK
151/M4 Port Simpson, BC,Can
59/F5 Portslade by Sea, Eng,UK
59/E5 Portsmouth, Eng,UK
161/G3 Portsmouth, NH,US
160/D4 Portsmouth, Oh,US
168/C2 Portsmouth, RI,US
160/E4 Portsmouth, Va,US
54/D1 Portsoy, Sc,UK
119/E2 Port Stephens (bay), Austl.
56/B1 Portstewart, NI,UK
127/D5 Port Sudan (Būr Sūdān), Sudan
58/C3 Port Talbot, Wal,UK
156/C3 Port Townsend, Wa,US
74/A3 Portugal
74/D1 Portugalete, Sp.
138/D2 Portuguesa (riv.), Ven.
138/D2 Portuguesa (state), Ven.
164/F8 Portuguese Bend, Ca,US
167/E2 Port Washington, NY,US
160/C3 Port Washington, Wi,US
56/D2 Port William, Sc,UK
63/L1 Porvoo (Borgå), Fin.
135/E2 Posadas, Arg.
74/C4 Posadas, Sp.
82/C3 Posavina (val.), Bosn., Cro.
111/F4 Poso (lake), Indo.
101/D5 Posŏng, SKor.
101/D5 Posŏng (bay), SKor.
101/D5 Posŏng (riv.), SKor.
138/A5 Posorja, Ecu.
140/A4 Posse, Braz.
165/C2 Possession (pt.), Wa,US
165/C2 Possession (sound), Wa,US
162/C3 Post, Tx,US
63/M4 Postavy, Bela.
124/F3 Poste Maurice Cortier (ruins), Alg.
124/F3 Poste Weygand (ruins), Alg.
156/D4 Post Falls, Id,US
132/C3 Postmasburg, SAfr.
82/B3 Postojna, Slov.
139/G3 Potaro-Siparuni (reg.), Guy.
132/D2 Potchefstroom, SAfr.
159/J4 Poteau, Ok,US
80/D2 Potenza, It.
80/C1 Potenza (riv.), It.
131/C5 Potgietersrus, SAfr.
156/D4 Potholes (res.), Wa,US
140/B2 Poti (riv.), Braz.
87/G4 Poti, Geo.
79/E6 Poti, Alpe di (peak), It.
140/C4 Potiraguá, Braz.
166/A5 Potomac, Md,US
160/E4 Potomac (riv.), Md, Va,US
136/E7 Potosí, Bol.
159/K3 Potosi, Mo,US
135/C2 Potrerillos, Chile
64/G2 Potsdam, Ger.
160/F2 Potsdam, NY,US
53/N6 Potters Bar, Eng,UK
59/F2 Potterspury, Eng,UK
59/F2 Potton, Eng,UK
166/C3 Pottstown, Pa,US
166/B2 Pottsville, Pa,US
106/D6 Pottuvil, SrL.
160/F3 Poughkeepsie, NY,US
60/D3 Poulaphouca (res.), Ire.
57/G5 Poulter (riv.), Eng,UK
57/F4 Poulton-le-Fylde, Eng,UK
73/G4 Pourri (mtn.), Fr.
141/H7 Pouso Alegre, Braz.
109/C3 Pouthisat, Camb.
109/C3 Pouthisat (riv.), Camb.
65/K4 Považská Bystrica, Slvk.
74/A2 Póvoa de Varzim, Port.
87/G2 Povorino, Rus.
97/L3 Povorotnyy, Mys (cape), Rus.
153/J2 Povungnituk (riv.), Qu,Can
164/C5 Poway, Ca,US
157/G4 Powder (riv.), Mt, Wy,US
150/B1 Powell (pt.), Bahm.
158/E3 Powell (lake), Az, Ut,US
166/B3 Powell (cr.), Pa,US
156/F4 Powell, Wy,US
156/B3 Powell River, BC,Can
161/R9 Power (res.), NY,US
60/B6 Power Head (pt.), Ire.
165/P14 Powers (lake), Wi,US
58/C2 Powys (co.), Wal,UK
58/C1 Powys, Vale (vall.), Wal,UK
137/H7 Poxoréo, Braz.
105/G2 Poyang (lake), China
57/F5 Poynton, Eng,UK
74/A1 Poyo, Sp.
92/C2 Pozantı, Turk.
82/E3 Požarevac, Yugo.
147/F4 Poza Rica, Mex.
82/E4 Požega, Yugo.
65/J2 Poznań, Pol.
65/J2 Poznań (prov.), Pol.
74/D4 Pozo Alcón, Sp.
74/C3 Pozoblanco, Sp.
75/N9 Pozuelo de Alarcón, Sp.
139/E2 Pozuelos, Ven.
80/D4 Pozzallo, It.
80/C1 Pozzoni (peak), It.
65/K2 Prabuty, Pol.
109/B4 Pracham Hiang (pt.), Thai.
71/H4 Prachatice, Czh.
109/C3 Prachin Buri, Thai.
109/C3 Prachin Buri (riv.), Thai.
109/B4 Prachuap Khiri Khan, Thai.
77/G4 Prad am Stilfserjoch (Prato allo Stelvio), It.
65/J3 Praděd (peak), Czh.
138/B4 Pradera, Col.
140/C5 Prado, Braz.
164/C3 Prado (dam), Ca,US
164/C3 Prado Flood Control Basin, Ca,US
77/E4 Pragelpass (pass), Swi.
71/H2 Prague (Praha) (cap.), Czh.
71/G3 Praha (peak), Czh.
71/H2 Praha (reg.), Czh.
71/H2 Praha (Prague) (cap.), Czh.
83/G3 Prahova (co.), Rom.
122/K11 Praia (cap.), CpV.
75/S12 Praia de Vitória, Azor.,Port.
141/G9 Praia Grande, Braz.
159/G4 Prairie Dog Town Fork (riv.), Ok, Tx,US
160/B3 Prairie du Chien, Wi,US
161/N6 Prairies (riv.), Qu,Can
157/J4 Prairies, Coteau des (upland), US
162/E4 Prairie View, Tx,US
71/G6 Pram (riv.), Aus.
109/B3 Pran Buri (res.), Thai.
106/D4 Prānhita (riv.), India
110/A3 Prapat, Indo.
109/D3 Prasat Preah Vihear, Camb.
65/K3 Praszka, Pol.
140/C2 Prata, Braz.
141/B1 Prata, Braz.
140/A5 Prata (riv.), Braz.
141/B1 Prata (riv.), Braz.
105/H4 Pratas (reef), China
105/H4 Pratas (Dongsha) (isl.), China
77/F4 Prätigau (val.), Swi.
79/E5 Prato, It.
80/C1 Pratola Peligna, It.
79/E5 Pratomagno (mts.), It.
143/J7 Pratt (isl.), Chile
159/H3 Pratt, Ks,US
76/D2 Pratteln, Swi.
163/G3 Prattville, Al,US
74/B1 Pravia, Sp.
55/K11 Prawle (pt.), Eng,UK
111/E5 Praya, Indo.
83/G3 Predeal, Rom.
157/H3 Preeceville, Sk,Can
57/F6 Prees, Eng,UK
57/F4 Preesall, Eng,UK
64/F1 Preetz, Ger.
65/L1 Pregolya (riv.), Rus.
160/E1 Preissac (lake), On,Can
109/D4 Prek Pouthi, Camb.
75/L7 Premiá de Mar, Sp.
65/G2 Prenzlau, Ger.
65/J4 Přerov, Czh.
73/J3 Presanella (peak), It.
77/G5 Presanella, Cima (peak), It.
57/F5 Prescot, Eng,UK
160/F2 Prescott, On,Can
158/D4 Prescott, Az,US
82/E4 Preševo, Yugo.
135/D2 Presidencia Roque Sáenz Peña, Arg.
140/A2 Presidente Dutra, Braz.
141/A2 Presidente Epitácio, Braz.
141/C1 Presidente Olegário, Braz.
141/B2 Presidente Prudente, Braz.
142/B5 Presidente Ríos (lake), Chile
141/B2 Presidente Venceslau, Braz.
146/D4 Presidio (riv.), Mex.
162/B4 Presidio, Tx,US
83/H4 Preslav, Bul.
53/U10 Presles-en-Brie, Fr.
77/G6 Presolana, Pizzo della (peak), It.
65/L4 Prešov, Slvk.
81/G2 Prespa (lake), Eur.
161/G2 Presque Isle, Me,US
57/E5 Prestatyn, Wal,UK
129/E5 Prestea, Gha.
58/D2 Presteigne, Wal,UK
71/G3 Přeštice, Czh.
119/G5 Preston, Austl.
116/C2 Preston (cape), Austl.
57/F4 Preston, Eng,UK
58/D5 Preston, Eng,UK
54/D5 Preston, Sc,UK
156/F5 Preston, Id,US
54/D5 Prestonpans, Sc,UK
160/D4 Prestonsburg, Ky,US
57/F4 Prestwich, Eng,UK
54/B6 Prestwick, Sc,UK
59/F3 Prestwood, Eng,UK
140/A3 Prêto (riv.), Braz.
140/A5 Prêto (riv.), Braz.
132/E2 Pretoria (cap.), SAfr.
132/Q12 Pretoria-Witwatersrand-Vereeniging (prov.), SAfr.
166/B4 Pretty Boy (res.), Md,US
67/F4 Preussisch Oldendorf, Ger.
81/G3 Préveza, Gre.
151/D4 Pribilof (isls.), Ak,US
82/D4 Priboj, Yugo.
71/H3 Příbram, Czh.
158/E3 Price, Ut,US
158/E3 Price (riv.), Ut,US
163/F4 Prichard, Al,US
74/C4 Priego de Córdoba, Sp.
132/C3 Prieska, SAfr.
156/D3 Priest (lake), Id,US
156/D3 Priest River, Id,US
74/C1 Prieta (mtn.), Sp.
65/K4 Prievidza, Slvk.
64/F2 Prignitz (reg.), Ger.
82/C3 Prijedor, Bosn.
82/D4 Prijepolje, Yugo.
87/H3 Prikaspian (plain), Kaz., Rus.
87/H3 Prikumsk, Rus.
81/G2 Prilep, Maced.
76/C4 Prilly, Swi.
86/E2 Priluki, Ukr.
80/C2 Prima Porta, It.
166/C6 Prime Hook Nat'l Wild. Ref., De,US
140/B1 Primeira Cruz, Braz.
143/J7 Primero (cape), Chile
59/E1 Primethorpe, Eng,UK
89/P5 Primorsk Kray, Rus.
86/F3 Primorsko-Akhtarsk, Rus.
156/F2 Primrose (lake), Ab, Sk,Can
156/F2 Primrose (lake), Ab, Sk,Can
69/F5 Prims (riv.), Ger.
152/E1 Prince Albert (pen.), NW,Can
152/E1 Prince Albert (sound), NW,Can
157/G2 Prince Albert, Sk,Can
157/G2 Prince Albert Nat'l Park, Sk,Can
152/D1 Prince Alfred (cape), NW,Can
153/J2 Prince Charles (isl.), NW,Can
51/L8 Prince Edward (isls.), SAfr.
161/J2 Prince Edward Island (prov.), Can.
161/J2 Prince Edward Island Nat'l Park, PE,Can
156/C2 Prince George, BC,Can
166/B6 Prince Georges (co.), Md,US
153/R7 Prince Gustav Adolf (sea), NW,Can
113/C Prince Harold (coast), Ant.
152/G1 Prince Leopold (isl.), NW,Can
66/C2 Princenhof (lake), Neth.
114/G2 Prince of Wales (isl.), Austl.
152/G1 Prince of Wales (isl.), NW,Can
152/E1 Prince of Wales (str.), NW,Can
151/M4 Prince of Wales (isl.), Ak,US
113/C Prince Olav (coast), Ant.
153/R7 Prince Patrick (isl.), NW,Can
152/G1 Prince Regent (inlet), NW,Can
151/M4 Prince Rupert, BC,Can
140/C2 Princesa Isabel, Braz.
59/F3 Princes Risborough, Eng,UK
113/A Princess Astrid (coast), Ant.
118/A1 Princess Charlotte (bay), Austl.
153/S6 Princess Margaret (range), NW,Can
113/Z Princess Martha (coast), Ant.
113/B Princess Ragnhild (coast), Ant.
156/A2 Princess Royal (isl.), BC,Can
156/C3 Princeton, BC,Can
160/B3 Princeton, Il,US
160/C4 Princeton, In,US
160/C4 Princeton, Ky,US
157/K4 Princeton, Mn,US
166/D3 Princeton, NJ,US
160/D4 Princeton, WV,US
151/J3 Prince William (sound), Ak,US
124/G7 Príncipe (isl.), SaoT.
151/K3 Prindle (vol.), Ak,US
156/C4 Prineville, Or,US
66/B5 Prinsenbeek, Neth.
66/C2 Prinses Margriet (can.), Neth.
149/F3 Prinzapolka, Nic.
149/E3 Prinzapolka (riv.), Nic.
80/D4 Priolo di Gargallo, It.
74/A1 Prior (cape), Sp.
63/P1 Priozersk, Rus.
86/C2 Pripet (marshes), Bela., Ukr.
82/E4 Priština, Yugo.
64/G2 Pritzwalk, Ger.
72/F4 Privas, Fr.
87/H2 Privolzhskiy, Rus.
87/K1 Priyutovo, Rus.
82/E4 Prizren, Yugo.
82/C3 Prnjavor, Bosn.
110/D5 Probolinggo, Indo.
162/D3 Proctor (lake), Tx,US
106/C5 Proddatūr, India
147/M7 Profesor Rafael Ramírez, Mex.
69/D3 Profondeville, Belg.
168/F6 Pro Football Hall of Fame, Oh,US
148/D1 Progreso, Mex.
149/F4 Progreso, Pan.
143/T12 Progreso, Uru.
147/K6 Progreso de Obregon, Mex.
97/K2 Progress, Rus.
79/E3 Progresso, It.
87/H4 Prokhladnyy, Rus.
102/E1 Prokop'yevsk, Rus.
82/E4 Prokuplje, Yugo.
104/B5 Prome, Burma
166/C1 Promised Land (lake), Pa,US
141/B2 Promissão, Braz.
141/B2 Promissão (res.), Braz.
140/C3 Propriá, Braz.
65/J2 Prosna (riv.), Pol.
117/M8 Prospect, Austl.
168/B2 Prospect, Ct,US
151/L3 Prospector (mtn.), Yk,Can
112/D3 Prosperidad, Phil.
65/J4 Prostějov, Czh.
65/L3 Prószowice, Pol.
83/H4 Provadiya, Bul.
73/G5 Provence (mts.), Fr.
72/F5 Provence (reg.), Fr.
73/G4 Provence-Alpes-Côte d'Azur (reg.), Fr.
168/C2 Providence (cap.), RI,US
168/C2 Providence (co.), RI,US
136/F6 Providência (mts.), Braz.
149/F3 Providencia (isl.), Col.
150/C2 Providenciales (isl.), Trks.
72/E2 Provins, Fr.
158/E2 Provo, Ut,US
75/T13 Provoação, Azor.,Port.
156/F2 Provost, Ab,Can
82/C4 Prozor, Bosn.
141/B3 Prudentópolis, Braz.
57/G2 Prudhoe, Eng,UK
151/J1 Prudhoe (bay), Ak,US
65/J3 Prudnik, Pol.
69/F3 Prüm (riv.), Ger.
65/K1 Pruszcz Gdański, Pol.
65/L2 Pruszków, Pol.
83/J2 Prut (riv.), Eur.
113/F Prydz (bay), Ant.
162/E2 Pryor (cr.), Ok,US
65/L2 Przasnysz, Pol.
65/H3 Przemków, Pol.
65/M4 Przemyśl, Pol.
65/M4 Przemyśl (prov.), Pol.
65/M3 Przeworsk, Pol.
102/C3 Przheval'sk, Kyr.
84/C5 Przylądek Rozewie (cape), Pol.
65/L3 Przysucha, Pol.
81/J3 Psará (isl.), Gre.
84/F4 Pskov (lake), Est., Rus.
84/F4 Pskov, Rus.
63/N3 Pskov Obl., Rus.
71/H2 Pšovka (riv.), Czh.
65/K4 Pszczyna, Pol.
63/M5 Ptich' (riv.), Bela.
81/G2 Ptolemaïs, Gre.
82/B2 Ptuj, Slov.
109/C2 Pua, Thai.
104/E3 Pu'an, China
105/F4 Pubei, China
144/C3 Pucallpa, Peru
144/B1 Pucará, Ecu.
165/G7 Puce, On,Can
103/B4 Pucheng, China
71/E6 Puchheim, Ger.
101/D4 Puch'on, SKor.
142/Q9 Puchuncaví, Chile
83/G3 Pucioasa, Rom.
65/K1 Puck, Pol.
59/G3 Puckeridge, Eng,UK
142/C3 Pucón, Chile
148/D2 Pucté, Mex.
61/H2 Pudasjärvi, Fin.
58/D5 Puddletown, Eng,UK
57/G4 Pudsey, Eng,UK
104/D3 Pudu (riv.), China
108/G3 Pudukkottai, India
147/F5 Puebla, Mex.
147/F5 Puebla (state), Mex.
74/A1 Puebla del Caramiñal, Sp.
147/L7 Puebla de Zaragoza, Mex.
138/C2 Pueblito, Col.
147/L8 Pueblo (state), Mex.
159/F3 Pueblo, Co,US
148/E3 Pueblo Nuevo, Nic.
148/D3 Pueblo Nuevo Tiquisate, Guat.
164/G8 Puente (hills), Ca,US
142/C2 Puente Alto, Chile
74/A1 Puenteareas, Sp.
74/A1 Puente Caldelas, Sp.
74/A1 Puente-Ceso, Sp.
147/K8 Puente de Ixtla, Mex.
142/C2 Puente del Inca, Arg.
74/A1 Puentedeume, Sp.
74/C4 Puente-Genil, Sp.
144/B3 Puente Piedra, Peru
74/B1 Puentes de García Rodríguez, Sp.
154/R10 Pueo (pt.), Hi,US
104/D4 Pu'er, China
158/E4 Puerco (riv.), Az, NM,US
158/F4 Puerco (riv.), NM,US
142/B5 Puerto Aisén, Chile
149/F4 Puerto Armuelles, Pan.
138/B4 Puerto Asís, Col.
139/E3 Puerto Ayacucho, Ven.
148/D3 Puerto Barrios, Guat.
138/C3 Puerto Berrío, Col.
138/D2 Puerto Cabello, Ven.
138/D2 Puerto Cumarebo, Ven.
146/B2 Puerto de La Libertad, Mex.
74/A1 Puerto del Son, Sp.
135/F2 Puerto Iguazú, Arg.
139/E2 Puerto La Cruz, Ven.
74/C3 Puertollano, Sp.
74/E4 Puerto Lumbreras, Sp.
142/D4 Puerto Madryn, Arg.
144/D4 Puerto Maldonado, Peru
142/B4 Puerto Montt, Chile
143/J7 Puerto Natales, Chile
149/G1 Puerto Padre, Cuba
146/B2 Puerto Peñasco, Mex.
150/D3 Puerto Plata, DRep.
112/B3 Puerto Princesa, Phil.
142/B4 Puerto Quellón, Chile
74/B4 Puerto Real, Sp.
150/E3 Puerto Rico (commonwealth), US
50/F5 Puerto Rico (isl.), US
136/G7 Puerto Suárez, Bol.
144/B3 Puerto Supe, Peru
138/B4 Puerto Tejada, Col.
146/D4 Puerto Vallarta, Mex.
142/B4 Puerto Varas, Chile
142/C5 Pueyrredón (lake), Arg.
56/D5 Puffin (isl.), Wal,UK
87/J1 Pugachev, Rus.
130/B4 Puge, Tanz.
165/C2 Puget (sound), Wa,US
80/E2 Puglia (reg.), It.
72/E5 Puigmal (mtn.), Fr.
75/G1 Puigsacalm (mtn.), Sp.
104/D2 Pujiang, China
138/B5 Pujilí, Ecu.
101/D2 Pujŏn (lake), NKor.
110/C5 Pujut (cape), Indo.
101/F6 Puk'ansan (mtn.), SKor.
101/D4 Puk'an-san Nat'l Park, SKor.
121/J6 Pukapuka (isl.), Cookls.
121/M6 Puka Puka (atoll), FrPol.
121/M6 Pukarua (isl.), FrPol.
160/C1 Pukaskwa Nat'l Park, On,Can
101/E2 Pukdae (riv.), NKor.
101/D4 Pukhan (riv.), NKor., SKor.
101/E2 Pukp'ot'ae-san (mtn.), NKor.
79/G3 Pula, Cro.
136/E8 Pulacayo, Bol.
101/A3 Pulandian (bay), China
111/F1 Pulanduta (pt.), Phil.
112/D3 Pulangi (riv.), Phil.
120/D4 Pulap (atoll), Micr.
163/G3 Pulaski, Tn,US
160/D4 Pulaski, Va,US
65/L3 Puľawy, Pol.
59/F5 Pulborough, Eng,UK
101/E5 Pulguk-sa, SKor.
66/D7 Pulheim, Ger.
111/G3 Pulisan (cape), Indo.
108/F4 Puliyangudi, India
77/H1 Pullach im Isartal, Ger.
156/D4 Pullman, Wa,US
76/C5 Pully, Swi.
112/C1 Pulog (mtn.), Phil.
65/G3 Pulsnitz (riv.), Ger.
65/L2 Pułtusk, Pol.
120/D4 Puluwat (atoll), Micr.
130/B4 Puma, Tanz.
58/C2 Pumpsaint, Wal,UK
107/F2 Pumu (pass), China
144/A1 Puná (isl.), Ecu.
121/X15 Punaauia, FrPol.
108/F4 Punalūr, India
136/E7 Punata, Bol.
108/C1 Pūnch, India
108/C1 Punch (riv.), India
131/C4 Punda Marie-Ruskamp, SAfr.
110/B3 Punggai (cape), Malay.
131/D3 Púnguè (riv.), Moz.
131/D3 Pungwe (falls), Zim.
126/E1 Punia, Zaire
108/C2 Punjab (state), India
108/B2 Punjab (plains), Pak.
108/B2 Punjab (prov.), Pak.
108/G4 Punkudutivu (isl.), SrL.
144/D4 Puno, Peru
143/K8 Punta Arenas, Chile
138/D2 Punta Cardón, Ven.
77/E5 Punta d'Arbola (Ofenhorn) (peak), It.
149/F4 Punta Gorda (bay), Nic.
163/H5 Punta Gorda, Fl,US
149/E4 Puntarenas, CR
74/B4 Punta Umbría, Sp.
154/S10 Puolo (pt.), Hi,US
144/D4 Pupuya (peak), Bol.
103/C5 Puqi, China
144/C4 Puquio, Peru
88/H3 Pur (riv.), Rus.
138/B4 Puracé (vol.), Col.
138/B4 Puracé Nat'l Park, Col.
58/D5 Purbeck, Isle of (pen.), Eng,UK
159/H4 Purcell, Ok,US
138/D5 Puré (riv.), Col.
142/B3 Purén, Chile
159/G3 Purgatoire (riv.), Co,US
106/D3 Purī, India
138/C4 Purificación, Col.
63/L2 Purikari (pt.), Est.
53/N8 Purley, Eng,UK
66/B3 Purmerend, Neth.
106/C4 Pūrna, India
106/C3 Pūrna (riv.), India
135/B5 Purranque, Chile
147/E4 Puruándiro de Calderón, Mex.
138/D5 Puruê (riv.), Braz.
139/F3 Puruni (riv.), Guy.
134/C3 Purus (riv.), Braz.
136/F4 Purús (riv.), Braz.
83/G4 Pŭrvomay, Bul.
110/C5 Purwokerto, Indo.
106/C4 Pusad, India
101/E5 Pusan, SKor.
101/E5 Pusan-Jikhalsi (prov.), SKor.

214

Pusat – Rema

110/A2 Pusat Gayo (mts.), Indo.
63/P2 Pushkin, Rus.
82/E2 Püspökladány, Hun.
130/A5 Puta, Zam.
142/C2 Putaendo, Chile
165/L9 Putah (cr.), Ca,US
110/D4 Puting (cape), Indo.
148/B2 Putla, Mex.
168/C2 Putnam, Ct,US
138/C4 Putomayo (inten.), Col.
142/B4 Putomayo (riv.), Col.
88/K3 Putorana (mts.), Rus.
142/C4 Putrachoique (peak), Arg.
108/G4 Puttalam, SrL.
108/G4 Puttalam (dist.), SrL.
68/D1 Putte, Belg.
66/C4 Putten, Neth.
66/B5 Putten (isl.), Neth.
71/E3 Puttlach (riv.), Ger.
69/F5 Püttlingen, Ger.
128/C5 Putu (range), Libr.
136/D4 Putumayo (riv.), SAm.
110/D3 Putussibau, Indo.
154/T10 Puu Kukui (peak), Hi,US
63/M1 Puula (lake), Fin.
154/V12 Puu o Mahuka Heiau Saint Mon., Hi,US
68/D1 Puurs, Belg.
103/B3 Pu Xian, China
165/C3 Puyallup, Wa,US
165/C3 Puyallup (riv.), Wa,US
165/C3 Puyallup Ind. Res., Wa,US
103/C4 Puyang, China
72/E4 Puy de Barbier (peak), Fr.
72/E4 Puy de Sancy (peak), Fr.
142/B4 Puyehué (lake), Chile
142/B4 Puyehué (vol.), Chile
142/B4 Puyehué Nat'l Park, Chile
72/D5 Puymorens, Col de (pass), Fr.
138/B5 Puyo, Ecu.
75/E3 Puzal, Sp.
130/C4 Pwani (prov.), Tanz.
130/A5 Pweto, Zaire
56/D6 Pwllheli, Wal,UK
104/B5 Pyamalaw (riv.), Burma
95/K1 Pyandzh (Panj) (riv.), Afg., Taj.
84/F2 Pyaozero (lake), Rus.
107/G4 Pyapon, Burma
88/J2 Pyasina (riv.), Rus.
87/G3 Pyatigorsk, Rus.
72/F4 Pyfara (mtn.), Fr.
61/H3 Pyhä-Häkin Nat'l Park, Fin.
61/H3 Pyhäjärvi, Fin.
63/K1 Pyhäjärvi (lake), Fin.
63/M1 Pyhäjärvi (lake), Fin.
61/H2 Pyhätunturi (peak), Fin.
63/M1 Pyhtää, Fin.
104/C5 Pyinmana, Burma
58/C3 Pyle, Wal,UK
168/G4 Pymatuning (res.), Oh,US
101/C2 P'yongan-Bukto (prov.), NKor.
101/C3 P'yŏngan-Namdo (prov.), NKor.
101/D4 Pyŏngt'aek, SKor.
101/C3 P'yŏngyang (cap.), NKor.
101/C3 P'yŏngyang-Si, NKor.
101/D5 Pyŏnsanbando Nat'l Park, SKor.
151/M4 Pyramid (mtn.), BC,Can
164/B1 Pyramid (lake), Ca,US
158/C3 Pyramid (lake), Nv,US
75/E1 Pyrenees (range), Eur.
72/C5 Pyrénées Occidentales Nat'l Park, Fr.
65/H2 Pyrzyce, Pol.
85/O4 Pyshma (riv.), Rus.
104/C5 Pyu, Burma

Q

91/E4 Qā'al Jafr (salt pan), Jor.
91/D3 Qabātiyah, WBnk.
124/H1 Qābis, Tun.
108/A2 Qādirpur Rān, Pak.
93/H2 Qā'emshahr, Iran
81/G1 Qafa e Malit (pass), Alb.
124/G1 Qafşah, Tun.
97/J2 Qagan (lake), China
103/C2 Qahar Youyi Qianqi, China
96/C4 Qaidam (basin), China
91/F7 Qalansuwa, Isr.
93/F2 Qal'at Dizah, Iraq
93/F4 Qal'at Sukkar, Iraq
91/B4 Qallīn, Egypt
91/D3 Qalqīlyah, WBnk.
91/B4 Qalyūb, Egypt
94/F5 Qamar, Ghubbat al (bay), Yem.
90/J6 Qamdo, China
124/K1 Qamīnis, Libya
91/G7 Qanah, Wādī (dry riv.), WBnk.
95/J2 Qandahār, Afg.
93/F2 Qarāmqū (riv.), Iran
123/W17 Qar'at al Ashkal (lake), Tun.
125/Q6 Qardho, Som.
93/G3 Qareh Chāy (riv.), Iran
93/F2 Qareh Sū (riv.), Iran
102/F4 Qarqan (riv.), China
81/G2 Qarrit, Qaf'e (pass), Alb.
80/B4 Qarţājannah (ruins), Tun.
127/B2 Qārūn, Birkat (lake), Egypt
93/F3 Qaşr-e-Shīrīn, Iran
127/A3 Qaşr Farāfirah, Egypt
91/E3 Qaţanā, Syria
94/F3 Qatar
127/A2 Qattara (depr.), Egypt
91/E2 Qaţţīnah (lake), Syria
106/A2 Qāzi Ahmad, Pak.
93/G2 Qazvīn, Iran
81/F2 Qendrevica (peak), Alb.
93/H5 Qeshm (isl.), Iran
94/E1 Qezel (riv.), Iran
93/F2 Qezel Owzan (riv.), Iran
107/J2 Qi (riv.), China
103/D4 Qian (can.), China
101/B2 Qian (mts.), China
101/B2 Qian (peak), China
103/D5 Qian (riv.), China
105/F2 Qian (riv.), China
97/J3 Qian'an, China
105/G2 Qianjiang, China
103/D5 Qianqiu Guan (pass), China
103/E2 Qian Shan (peak), China
97/H3 Qianxi, China
104/D3 Qiaojia, China
97/J5 Qidong, China
102/E4 Qiemo, China
103/B5 Qifeng Guan (pass), China
103/D3 Qihe, China
108/C1 Qila Dīdār Singh, Pak.
96/D4 Qilian (mts.), China
96/D4 Qilian (peak), China
91/G8 Qilţ, Wādī (dry riv.), WBnk.
102/F4 Qimantag (mts.), China
103/D5 Qimen, China
103/B4 Qin (mts.), China
103/C4 Qin (riv.), China
127/C3 Qinā, Egypt
127/C3 Qinā (gov.), Egypt
127/C3 Qinā, Wādī (dry riv.), Egypt
105/F2 Qing (riv.), China
97/K2 Qing'an, China
103/E3 Qingdao, China
103/C4 Qingfeng, China
97/K2 Qinggang, China
96/D4 Qinghai (lake), China
96/D4 Qinghai (mts.), China
104/B1 Qinghai (prov.), China
103/C3 Qinghe, China
105/G2 Qingjiang, China
103/D2 Qinglong, China
103/E5 Qingpu, China
104/D2 Qingshen, China
105/F3 Qingshui (riv.), China
103/B3 Qingshuihe, China
104/C3 Qingshuilang (mts.), China
103/D5 Qingyang, China
105/G4 Qingyuan (mts.), China
103/D3 Qingyun, China
97/H4 Qingzhou, China
103/D3 Qinhuangdao, China
103/C4 Qinshui, China
103/C4 Qinyang, China
103/C3 Qinyuan, China
105/F4 Qinzhou, China
107/K4 Qionghai, China
104/D2 Qionglai, China
104/D2 Qionglai (mts.), China
107/K4 Qiongshan, China
109/E2 Qiongzhong, China
97/J2 Qipan (pass), China
91/E2 Qiqihar, China
96/B3 Qiquanhu, China
102/D4 Qira, China
91/D3 Qiryat Ata, Isr.
91/D3 Qiryat Bialik, Isr.
91/D4 Qiryat Gat, Isr.
91/F8 Qiryat Mal'akhi, Isr.
91/D3 Qiryat Shemona, Isr.
91/D3 Qiryat Yam, Isr.
96/B3 Qitai, China
97/L2 Qitaihe, China
105/G3 Qitian (mtn.), China
103/E3 Qixia, China
103/C4 Qi Xian, China
104/E3 Qixing (pass), China
97/L2 Qixing (riv.), China
93/G3 Qom, Iran
93/G3 Qom (riv.), Iran
106/E2 Qomolangma (Everest) (peak), China
95/J1 Qondūz (riv.), Afg.
107/F2 Qonggyai, China
105/E2 Qu (riv.), China
105/H2 Qu (riv.), China
168/B1 Quabbin (res.), Ma,US
59/F3 Quainton, Eng,UK
67/E3 Quakenbrück, Ger.
166/C3 Quakertown, Pa,US
96/H5 Quan (riv.), China
162/D3 Quanah, Tx,US
103/B4 Quanbao Shan (mtn.), China
109/E3 Quang Ngai, Viet.
109/E3 Quang Trach, Viet.
109/D2 Quang Tri, Viet.
103/E3 Quanjiao, China
58/C4 Quantocks (hills), Eng,UK
105/F3 Quanzhou, China
105/H3 Quanzhou, China
157/G3 Qu'Appelle (riv.), Mb, Sk,Can
157/H3 Qu'Appelle, Sk,Can
157/G3 Qu'Appelle (dam), Sk,Can
153/K2 Quaqtaq, Qu,Can
68/C3 Quaregnon, Belg.
110/E4 Quarles (mts.), Indo.
79/D5 Quarrata, It.
80/A3 Quartu Sant'Elena, It.
164/B1 Quartz Hill, Ca,US
77/G4 Quattervals (peak), Swi.
123/W17 Qubāllāt, Tun.
93/J2 Qūchān, Iran
119/D2 Queanbeyan, Austl.
153/J3 Québec (prov.), Can.
161/G2 Québec (cap.), Qu,Can
141/J7 Quebra-Cangalha (mts.), Braz.
147/M8 Quecholac, Mex.
142/B4 Quedal (pt.), Chile
58/D3 Quedgeley, Eng,UK
166/C5 Queen Annes (co.), Md,US
152/C3 Queen Charlotte (isls.), BC,Can
152/C3 Queen Charlotte (sound), BC,Can
156/B3 Queen Charlotte (str.), BC,Can
162/E3 Queen City, Tx,US
153/R7 Queen Elizabeth (isls.), NW,Can
113/G Queen Mary (coast), Ant.
53/M7 Queen Mary (res.), Eng,UK
164/F8 Queen Mary, Ca,US
113/P Queen Maud (mts.), Ant.
152/F2 Queen Maud (gulf), NW,Can
113/Z Queen Maud Land (reg.), Ant.
114/D2 Queens (chan.), Austl.
153/S7 Queens (chan.), NW,Can
167/E2 Queens (co.), NY,US
56/E1 Queensberry (mtn.), Sc,UK
57/G4 Queensbury, Eng,UK
57/E5 Queensferry, Wal,UK
118/B3 Queensland (state), Austl.
161/R9 Queenston, On,Can
115/Q12 Queenstown, NZ
132/D3 Queenstown, SAfr.
116/D4 Queen Victoria Spring Nature Rsv., Austl.
71/A4 Queich (riv.), Ger.
142/B4 Queilén, Chile
137/H4 Queimada, Braz.
140/C3 Queimadas, Braz.
126/G4 Quelimane, Moz.
74/A3 Queluz, Port.
149/H1 Quemado, Punta del (pt.), Cuba
59/E3 Quenington, Eng,UK
142/F3 Quequén, Arg.
142/F3 Quequén Grande (riv.), Arg.
144/A2 Querecotillo, Peru
147/E4 Querétaro, Mex.
147/F4 Querétaro (state), Mex.
149/E4 Quesada, CR
74/D4 Quesada, Sp.
103/C4 Queshan, China
156/C2 Quesnel, BC,Can
156/C2 Quesnel (lake), BC,Can
109/E3 Que Son, Viet.
159/F3 Questa, NM,US
76/B3 Quetigny, Fr.
95/J2 Quetta, Pak.
142/B5 Queulat Nat'l Park, Chile
136/C4 Quevedo, Ecu.
138/B5 Quevedo (riv.), Ecu.
148/D3 Quezaltenango, Guat.
112/B3 Quezon, Phil.
112/D4 Quezon, Phil.
112/C2 Quezon City, Phil.
112/C2 Quezon Nat'l Park, Phil.
103/D4 Qufu, China
126/B3 Quibala, Ang.
138/B3 Quibdó, Col.
72/B3 Quiberon (bay), Fr.
138/D2 Quíbor, Ven.
126/B2 Quiçama Nat'l Park, Ang.
67/G1 Quickborn, Ger.
69/G5 Quierschied, Ger.
76/B3 Quigney, Fr.
158/D4 Quijotoa, Az,US
142/B4 Quilán (cape), Chile
142/Q9 Quilicura, Chile
157/G2 Quill (lakes), Sk,Can
144/C4 Quillabamba, Peru
136/E7 Quillacollo, Bol.
142/B4 Quillagua (pt.), Chile
142/C3 Quilleco, Chile
142/C2 Quillota, Chile
108/F4 Quilon, India
142/C2 Quilpué, Chile
135/D2 Quimilí, Arg.
72/A3 Quimper, Fr.
163/G4 Quincy, Fl,US
160/B4 Quincy, Il,US
168/C1 Quincy, Ma,US
156/D4 Quincy, Wa,US
53/T10 Quincy-sous-Sénart, Fr.
138/C3 Quindío (dept.), Col.
168/C2 Quinebaug (riv.), Ct,US
109/E3 Qui Nhon, Viet.
158/C2 Quinn (riv.), Nv,US
168/B3 Quinnipac (riv.), Ct,US
168/C1 Quinsigamond (res.), Ma,US
74/D3 Quintanar de la Orden, Sp.
148/D2 Quintana Roo (state), Mex.
142/Q9 Quintero, Chile
142/D2 Quinto (riv.), Arg.
130/D5 Quionga, Moz.
140/C3 Quipapá, Braz.
142/B3 Quirihue, Chile
130/D5 Quirimba (arch.), Moz.
141/B1 Quirinópolis, Braz.
139/F2 Quiriquire, Ven.
144/B3 Quiruvilca, Peru
161/H2 Quispamsis, NB,Can
131/D5 Quissico, Moz.
135/D2 Quitilipi, Arg.
163/H4 Quitman, Ga,US
163/F3 Quitman, Ms,US
162/E3 Quitman, Tx,US
138/B5 Quito (cap.), Ecu.
140/C2 Quixadá, Braz.
140/C2 Quixeramobim, Braz.
105/G3 Qujiang, China
104/D3 Qujing, China
96/C4 Qumar (riv.), China
152/G2 Quoich (riv.), NW,Can
54/A2 Quoich, Loch (lake), Sc,UK
56/C3 Quoile (riv.), NI,UK
132/B4 Quoin (pt.), SAfr.
91/E2 Qurnat as Sawdā' (mtn.), Leb.
127/C3 Qūş, Egypt
107/F2 Qusum, China
103/B4 Quwo, China
96/F4 Quwu (mts.), China
103/C3 Quyang, China
109/C1 Quynh Nhai, Viet.
103/C3 Quzhou, China
105/H2 Quzhou, China
82/D5 Qyteti Stalin, Alb.

R

73/L3 Raab (riv.), Aus.
61/H2 Raahe, Fin.
66/D4 Raalte, Neth.
66/B5 Raamsdonk, Neth.
63/T9 Råån (riv.), Swe.
91/F7 Ra'anana, Isr.
153/S7 Raanes (pen.), NW,Can
130/D3 Raas Jumbo, Som.
82/B3 Rab, Cro.
82/B3 Rab (isl.), Cro.
82/C2 Rába (riv.), Hun.
80/D5 Rabat, Malta
123/L13 Rabat (cap.), Mor.
120/E5 Rabaul, PNG
79/E4 Rabbi (riv.), It.
118/B3 RAbbot (peak), Austl.
148/D3 Rabinal, Guat.
77/F4 Rabiusa (riv.), Swi.
65/K4 Rabka, Pol.
106/C4 Rabkavi, India
161/S8 Raby (pt.), On,Can
78/A3 Racconigi, It.
163/F4 Raccoon (pt.), La,US
168/G6 Raccoon (cr.), Pa,US
168/G6 Raccoon Creek Saint Pk., Pa,US
153/L4 Race (cape), Nf,Can
109/D4 Rach Gia, Viet.
109/D4 Rach Gia (bay), Viet.
65/K3 Racibórz, Pol.
165/Q14 Racine, Wi,US
165/P14 Racine (co.), Wi,US
76/C3 Racine, Mont (peak), Swi.
82/D2 Ráckeve, Hun.
83/G2 Rădăuţi, Rom.
71/G3 Radbuza (riv.), Czh.
57/F4 Radcliffe, Eng,UK
57/G6 Radcliffe on Trent, Eng,UK
71/G3 Radeč (peak), Czh.
82/A2 Radenthein, Aus.
67/E6 Radevormwald, Ger.
160/D4 Radford, Va,US
106/B3 Radhanpur, India
156/G2 Radisson, Sk,Can
53/N6 Radlett, Eng,UK
83/G4 Radnevo, Bul.
77/E2 Radolfzell, Ger.
65/L3 Radom, Pol.
65/L3 Radom (prov.), Pol.
82/F4 Radomir, Bul.
65/K3 Radomsko, Pol.
82/F5 Radoviš, Macd.
62/A1 Radøy (isl.), Nor.
58/D4 Radstock, Eng,UK
63/K4 Radviliškis, Lith.
58/C3 Radyr, Wal,UK
65/K2 Radziejów, Pol.
65/L2 Radzymin, Pol.
65/M3 Radzyń Podlaski, Pol.
153/H3 Rae (isth.), NW,Can
152/E2 Rae (riv.), NW,Can
106/D2 Rāe Bareli, India
163/J3 Raeford, NC,US
69/F2 Raeren, Belg.
66/D5 Raesfeld, Ger.
116/D4 Raeside (lake), Austl.
101/A2 Raeyang (riv.), China
135/D3 Rafaela, Arg.
91/D4 Rafaḩ, Gaza
125/K7 Rafai, CAfr.
93/J4 Rafsanjān, Iran
156/E5 Raft (riv.), Id, Ut,US
125/L6 Raga, Sudan
112/D4 Ragang (mtn.), Phil.
112/C2 Ragay (gulf), Phil.
116/D5 Ragged (peak), Austl.
143/J8 Ragged (pt.), Chile
56/A1 Raghtin More (mtn.), Ire.
58/D3 Raglan, Wal,UK
61/E2 Rago Nat'l Park, Nor.
53/P8 Ragstone (range), Eng,UK
80/D4 Ragusa, It.
67/F4 Rahden, Ger.
95/K3 Rahīmyār Khān, Pak.
130/C2 Rahole Nat'l Rsv., Kenya
167/D2 Rahway, NJ,US
121/K6 Raiatea (isl.), FrPol.
106/C4 Raichūr, India
106/D3 Raigarh, India
164/C3 Railroad Canyon (res.), Ca,US
158/E3 Rainbow Bridge Nat'l Mon., Ut,US
57/F4 Rainford, Eng,UK
53/P7 Rainham, Eng,UK
156/C4 Rainier (peak), Wa,US
163/G3 Rainsville, Al,US
57/G5 Rainworth, Eng,UK
157/K3 Rainy (lake), Can., US
157/K3 Rainy (riv.), Can., US
160/A1 Rainy River, On,Can
106/D3 Raipur, India
64/F1 Raisdorf, Ger.
165/E8 Raisin (riv.), Mi,US
61/G3 Raisio, Fin.
68/C3 Raismes, Fr.
121/L7 Raivavae (isl.), FrPol.
108/C2 Raiwind, Pak.
110/A3 Raja (pt.), Indo.
106/D4 Rajahmundry, India
106/C5 Rājampet, India
110/D3 Rajang (riv.), Malay.
95/K3 Rājanpur, Pak.
108/F4 Rājapālaiyam, India
106/B4 Rājāpur, India
106/B2 Rājasthān (state), India
106/C3 Rājgarh, India
95/L3 Rājgarh, India
106/B3 Rājkot, India
106/D3 Rāj-Nāndagaon, India
108/D2 Rājpura, India
106/E3 Rājshāhi, Bang.
106/B3 Rājula, India
121/J5 Rakahanga (atoll), CookIs.
95/K1 Rakaposhi (mtn.), Pak.
104/B5 Rakhine (state), Burma
95/H3 Rakhshān (riv.), Pak.
62/D2 Rakkestad, Nor.
131/B4 Rakops, Bots.
71/G2 Rakovnicky Potok (riv.), Czh.
71/G2 Rakovník, Czh.
83/G4 Rakovski, Bul.
63/M2 Rakvere, Est.
130/B3 Rakwaro, Kenya
71/H2 Rakytka (riv.), Czh.
163/J3 Raleigh (cap.), NC,US
120/F4 Ralik Chain (arch.), Mrsh.
156/F3 Ralston, Ab,Can
140/A4 Ramalho (mts.), Braz.
91/D4 Rām Allāh, WBnk.
108/G4 Rāmanāthapuram, India
108/G4 Ramanathaswamy Temple, India
167/H7 Ramapo (mts.), NJ,US
167/J7 Ramapo (riv.), NJ, NY,US
106/B4 Ramas (cape), India
91/D3 Ramat Gan, Isr.
91/F7 Ramat HaSharon, Isr.
131/B5 Ramatlabama, Bots.
76/C1 Rambervillers, Fr.
121/Z17 Rambi (isl.), Fiji
68/A6 Rambouillet, Fr.
58/B6 Rame (pt.), UK
106/E2 Rāmechhāp, Nepal
108/G4 Rāmeshwaram, India
60/C6 Ram Head (pt.), Ire.
93/G4 Rāmhormoz, Iran
91/D4 Ramla, Isr.
63/T8 Ramløse, Den.
91/D5 Ramm, Jabal (mtn.), Jor.
131/B4 Ramokgwebana, Bots.
91/D4 Ramon, Har (mtn.), Isr.
60/C2 Ramor, Lough (lake), Ire.
147/E3 Ramos Arizpe, Mex.
131/B5 Ramotswa, Bots.
104/B5 Ramree (isl.), Burma
94/F1 Ramsar (Sakht Sar), Iran
57/F4 Ramsbottom, Eng,UK
59/E4 Ramsbury, Eng,UK
160/D2 Ramsey (lake), On,Can
59/F2 Ramsey, Eng,UK
56/D3 Ramsey, IM,UK
56/D3 Ramsey (bay), IM,UK
58/A3 Ramsey (isl.), Wal,UK
167/J7 Ramsey, NJ,US
59/H4 Ramsgate, Eng,UK
69/G5 Ramstein-Miesenbach, Ger.
120/D5 Ramu (riv.), PNG
106/E3 Rānāghāt, India
142/C2 Rancagua, Chile
72/B2 Rance (riv.), Fr.
72/E5 Rance (riv.), Fr.
141/B2 Rancharia, Braz.
138/C2 Ranchería (riv.), Col.
158/G4 Ranchester, Wy,US
106/E3 Rānchī, India
165/M9 Rancho Cordova, Ca,US
164/C2 Rancho Cucamonga (Cucamonga), Ca,US
164/B3 Rancho Palos Verdes, Ca,US
142/B4 Ranco (lake), Chile
125/P5 Randa, Djib.
62/A2 Randaberg, Nor.
166/B5 Randallstown, Md,US
56/B2 Randalstown, NI,UK
80/D4 Randazzo, It.
132/P13 Randburg, SAfr.
77/E2 Randen, Hoher (peak), Ger.
62/D3 Randers, Den.
168/C1 Randolph, Ma,US
166/D2 Randolph, NJ,US
162/D4 Randolph A.F.B., Tx,US
65/H2 Randow (riv.), Ger.
62/D1 Randsfjorden (lake), Nor.
118/H8 Randwick, Austl.
109/C2 Rang (peak), Thai.
104/B4 Rāngāmāti, Bang.
108/G3 Ranganathaswamy Temple, India
111/E4 Rangasa (cape), Indo.
158/E2 Ranger, Co,US
162/D3 Ranger, Tx,US
115/R11 Rangiora, NZ
121/L6 Rangiroa (atoll), FrPol.
104/C5 Rangoon (div.), Burma
104/C5 Rangoon (Yangon) (cap.), Burma
106/E2 Rangpur, Bang.
106/C5 Rānībennur, India
117/H2 Ranken (riv.), Austl.
162/C4 Rankin, Tx,US
77/F3 Rankweil, Aus.
106/A3 Rann of Kutch (swamp), India,Pak.
54/B3 Rannoch, Loch (lake), Sc,UK
109/B4 Ranong, Thai.
69/G3 Ransbach-Baumbach, Ger.
161/S9 Ransomville, NY,US
68/D1 Ranst, Belg.
111/F4 Rantekombola (peak), Indo.
160/B3 Rantoul, Il,US
109/D2 Rao Co (peak), Laos
76/C1 Raon-L'Étape, Fr.
120/H7 Raoul (isl.), NZ
103/B3 Raoyang, China
121/L7 Rapa (isl.), FrPol.
78/C4 Rapallo, It.
142/Q10 Rapel (lake), Chile
142/B5 Raper (cape), Chile
157/H4 Rapid City, SD,US
160/E4 Rappahannock (riv.), Va,US
106/D2 Rapti (riv.), India
167/D3 Raritan (bay), NY, NJ,US
166/D2 Raritan (riv.), NY, NJ,US
166/D2 Raritan, North Branch (riv.), NJ,US
166/D2 Raritan, South Branch (riv.), NJ,US
121/L6 Raroia (atoll), FrPol.
121/J7 Rarotonga (isl.), CookIs.
142/E4 Rasa (pt.), Arg.
92/E2 Ra's al 'Ayn, Syria
125/J7 Ra's al Unūf, Libya
123/Q16 Râs el Ma, Alg.
123/T16 Râs el Oued, Alg.
127/C2 Ras Gharib, Egypt
56/B2 Rasharkin, NI,UK
91/D3 Rāshayyā, Leb.
91/B4 Rashīd (Rosetta), Egypt
93/G2 Rasht, Iran
108/G3 Rāsipuram, India
82/E4 Raška, Yugo.
152/G2 Rasmussen (basin), NW,Can
75/P10 Raso (cape), Port.
116/E4 Rason (lake), Austl.
87/G1 Rasskazovo, Rus.
70/B5 Rastatt, Ger.
67/F2 Rastede, Ger.
151/B6 Rat (isls.), Ak,US
110/B5 Rata (cape), Indo.
106/B2 Ratangarh, India
109/B3 Rat Buri, Thai.
106/C2 Rāth, India
157/K5 Rathbun (lake), Ia,US
64/G2 Rathenow, Ger.
56/B3 Rathfriland, NI,UK
56/B1 Rathlin (isl.), NI,UK
56/B1 Rathlin (sound), NI,UK
120/F4 Ratik Chain (arch.), Mrsh.
66/D6 Ratingen, Ger.
106/C3 Ratlām, India
106/B4 Ratnāgiri, India
106/D6 Ratnapura, SrL.
159/F3 Raton, NM,US
159/H3 Rattle Snake (cr.), Ks,US
54/C3 Rattray, Sc,UK
62/F1 Rättvik, Swe.
64/F2 Ratzeburg, Ger.
110/B3 Raub, Malay.
142/F3 Rauch, Arg.
61/P6 Raudhinúpur (pt.), Ice.
62/D1 Raufoss, Nor.
70/D3 Rauhe Ebrach (riv.), Ger.
71/E3 Rauher Kulm (hill), Ger.
141/D2 Raul Soares, Braz.
63/J1 Rauma, Fin.
59/F2 Raunds, Eng,UK
115/S10 Raupehu (vol.), NZ
106/D3 Raurkela, India
100/D1 Rausu, Japan
80/C4 Ravanusa, It.
66/C6 Ravels, Belg.
57/E3 Ravenglass, Eng,UK
79/F4 Ravenna, It.
79/F4 Ravenna (prov.), It.
168/F5 Ravenna, Oh,US
168/F5 Ravenna Arsenal (mil. res.), Oh,US
77/F2 Ravensburg, Ger.
57/G5 Ravenshead, Eng,UK
160/D4 Ravenswood, WV,US
60/D5 Raven, The (pt.), Ire.
108/B2 Rāvi (riv.), India, Pak.
82/B2 Ravne na Koroškem, Slov.
121/H5 Rawaki (Phoenix) (atoll), Kiri.
108/B1 Rāwalpindi, Pak.
65/L3 Rawa Mazowiecka, Pol.
65/J3 Rawicz, Pol.
156/G5 Rawlins, Wy,US
117/E3 Rawlinson (peak), Austl.
57/G5 Rawmarsh, Eng,UK
142/D4 Rawson, Arg.
57/F4 Rawtenstall, Eng,UK
161/K2 Ray (cape), Nf,Can
110/D4 Raya (peak), Indo.
106/C5 Rāyadrug, India
106/D4 Rāyagada, India
97/K2 Raychikhinsk, Rus.
59/G3 Rayleigh, Eng,UK
156/E3 Raymond, Ab,Can
162/D5 Raymondville, Tx,US
157/G3 Raymore, Sk,Can
168/C2 Raynham, Ma,US
109/C3 Rayong, Thai.
147/E5 Rayón Nat'l Park, Mex.
87/H4 Razdan, Arm.
83/J3 Razelm (lake), Rom.
83/H4 Razgrad, Bul.
81/K1 Razgrad (reg.), Bul.
83/F5 Razlog, Bul.
72/A2 Raz, Pointe du (pt.), Fr.
72/C3 Ré (isl.), Fr.
58/D2 Rea (riv.), Eng,UK
59/F4 Reading, Eng,UK
166/C3 Reading, Pa,US
144/C3 Real, Cordillera (range), Bol., Peru
60/B3 Rea, Lough (lake), Ire.
109/C3 Reang Kesei, Camb.
121/M6 Reao (atoll), FrPol.
116/D4 Rebecca (lake), Austl.
141/B3 Rebouças, Braz.
100/B1 Rebun, Japan
100/B1 Rebun (isl.), Japan
79/G6 Recanati, It.
78/C4 Recco, It.
116/E5 Recherche (arch.), Austl.
69/F6 Réchicourt-le-Château, Fr.
86/D1 Rechitsa, Bela.
140/D3 Recife, Braz.
132/D4 Recife (cape), SAfr.
67/E4 Recke, Ger.
67/E5 Recklinghausen, Ger.
64/G2 Recknitz (riv.), Ger.
109/B2 Reclining Buddha (Shwethalyaung) (ruins), Burma
135/E2 Reconquista, Arg.
94/C4 Red (sea), Afr., Asia
104/D4 Red (riv.), China, Viet.
56/B1 Red (bay), NI,UK
159/J5 Red (riv.), US
162/D2 Red (hills), Ks,US
65/K1 Reda, Pol.
167/D3 Red Bank, NJ,US
158/B2 Red Bluff, Ca,US
159/G4 Red Bluff (lake), NM, Tx,US
59/F3 Redbourn, Eng,UK
53/P7 Redbridge (bor.), Eng,UK
57/G2 Redcar, Eng,UK
156/F3 Redcliff, Ab,Can
131/C3 Redcliff, Zim.
118/F6 Redcliffe, Austl.
116/D4 Redcliffe (peak), Austl.
159/H2 Red Cloud, Ne,US
156/E2 Red Deer, Ab,Can
156/F3 Red Deer (riv.), Ab,Can
157/H2 Red Deer (lake), Mb,Can
157/H2 Red Deer (riv.), Mb, Sk,Can
158/B2 Redding, Ca,US
168/A3 Redding, Ct,US
59/E2 Redditch, Eng,UK
57/F1 Rede (riv.), Eng,UK
140/A3 Redenção do Gurguéia, Braz.
157/J4 Redfield, SD,US
165/F7 Redford, Mi,US
53/N8 Redhill, Eng,UK
154/T10 Red Hill (peak), Hi,US
77/G5 Re di Castello, Monte (peak), It.
161/K1 Red Indian (lake), Nf,Can
69/G6 Réding, Fr.
157/K3 Red Lake, On,Can
157/K3 Red Lake (riv.), Mn,US
166/A5 Redland, Md,US
118/F7 Redland Bay, Austl.
164/C2 Redlands, Ca,US
166/B4 Red Lion, Pa,US
156/F4 Red Lodge, Mt,US
156/C4 Redmond, Or,US
165/C2 Redmond, Wa,US
70/D4 Rednitz (riv.), Ger.
159/G4 Red, North Fork (riv.), Ok, Tx,US
72/B3 Redon, Fr.
74/A1 Redondela, Sp.
139/F4 Redondo (peak), Braz.
74/B3 Redondo, Port.
164/B3 Redondo Beach, Ca,US
151/H3 Redoubt (vol.), Ak,US
157/J3 Red (Red R. of the North) (riv.), Mb,Can
157/J3 Red River of the North (riv.), US
157/K5 Red Rock (lake), Ia,US
117/E5 Red Rocks (pt.), Austl.
58/A6 Redruth, Eng,UK
159/G4 Red, Salt Fork (riv.), Ok, Tx,US
127/D4 Red Sea (hills), Sudan
152/D2 Redstone (riv.), NW,Can
157/K2 Red Sucker (lake), Mb,Can
157/H3 Redvers, Sk,Can
129/E4 Red Volta (riv.), Burk., Gui.
156/E2 Redwater, Ab,Can
158/B2 Redway, Ca,US
159/G2 Red Willow (cr.), Ne,US
160/A2 Red Wing, Mn,US
165/K12 Redwood City, Ca,US
157/K4 Redwood Falls, Mn,US
158/A2 Redwood Nat'l Park, Ca,US
160/C3 Reed City, Mi,US
59/H1 Reedham, Eng,UK
158/C3 Reedley, Ca,US
166/D5 Reeds (bay), NJ,US
160/B3 Reedsburg, Wi,US
156/B5 Reedsport, Or,US
119/B3 Reedy (cr.), Austl.
147/J5 Reef (pt.), Belz.
120/F6 Reef (isls.), Sol.
115/R11 Reefton, NZ
60/B2 Ree, Lough (lake), Ire.
59/H1 Reepham, Eng,UK
66/D5 Rees, Ger.
158/C3 Reese (riv.), Nv,US
162/C3 Reese A.F.B., Tx,US
66/D3 Reest (riv.), Neth.
57/G3 Reeth, Eng,UK
66/B4 Reeuwijk, Neth.
92/D2 Refahiye, Turk.
162/D4 Refugio, Tx,US
65/H2 Rega (riv.), Pol.
71/G5 Regen, Ger.
71/F4 Regen (riv.), Ger.
141/E1 Regência, Pontal de (pt.), Braz.
140/B2 Regeneração, Braz.
71/F4 Regensburg, Ger.
77/E3 Regensdorf, Swi.
71/F4 Regenstauf, Ger.
118/H8 Regents Park, Austl.
53/N7 Regent's Park, Eng,UK
124/F2 Reggane, Alg.
66/D4 Regge (riv.), Neth.
80/D3 Reggio di Calabria, It.
78/D3 Reggio nell'Emilia, It.
78/D3 Reggio nell'Emilia (prov.), It.
83/G2 Reghin, Rom.
157/G3 Regina (cap.), Sk,Can
137/H3 Régina, FrG.
158/F3 Regina, NM,US
157/G3 Regina Beach, Sk,Can
141/C3 Registro, Braz.
70/D3 Regnitz (riv.), Ger.
74/B3 Reguengosde Monsaraz, Port.
71/F2 Rehau, Ger.
67/G4 Rehburg-Loccum, Ger.
69/F5 Rehlingen-Siersburg, Ger.
126/C5 Rehoboth, Namb.
168/C2 Rehoboth, Ma,US
91/F8 Reḥovot, Isr.
70/D3 Reiche Ebrach (riv.), Ger.
70/B2 Reichelsheim, Ger.
70/B3 Reichelsheim, Ger.
71/F1 Reichenbach, Ger.
69/G2 Reichshof, Ger.
156/F3 Reid (lake), Sk,Can
163/J2 Reidsville, NC,US
53/N8 Reigate, Eng,UK
68/D5 Reims, Fr.
68/D5 Reims, Cathédrale de, Fr.
143/J7 Reina Adelaida (arch.), Chile
76/D3 Reinach, Swi.
67/H1 Reinbek, Ger.
157/J2 Reindeer (isl.), Mb,Can
157/H1 Reindeer (lake), Mb, Sk,Can
157/H1 Reindeer (riv.), Sk,Can
70/B3 Reinheim, Ger.
74/C1 Reinosa, Sp.
61/G1 Reisduoddarhal'di (peak), Nor.
70/B1 Reiskirchen, Ger.
71/F5 Reissingerbach (riv.), Ger.
166/B5 Reisterstown, Md,US
66/D2 Reitdiep (riv.), Neth.
75/H4 Rejaïa (wilaya), Alg.
156/F5 Reliance, Wy,US
123/R16 Relizane, Alg.
123/R16 Relizane (wilaya), Alg.
67/G1 Rellingen, Ger.
69/G2 Remagen, Ger.
140/B3 Remanso, Braz.
53/S11 Remarde (riv.), Fr.

162/D4 **Round Rock,** Tx,US
156/F4 **Roundup,** Mt,US
166/D2 **Round Valley** (res.), NJ,US
58/E4 **Roundway** (hill), Eng,UK
55/N13 **Rousay** (isl.), Sc,UK
118/G8 **Rouse Hill,** Austl.
72/F4 **Roussillon,** Fr.
69/E5 **Rouvres-en-Woërve,** Fr.
160/E1 **Rouyn-Noranda,** Qu,Can
61/H2 **Rovaniemi,** Fin.
78/D1 **Rovato,** It.
79/E1 **Rovereto,** It.
109/D3 **Rovieng Tbong,** Camb.
79/E2 **Rovigo,** It.
79/E2 **Rovigo** (prov.), It.
79/G2 **Rovinj,** Cro.
86/C2 **Rovno,** Ukr.
86/C2 **Rovno Obl.,** Ukr.
130/B5 **Rovuma** (riv.), Moz.
114/B3 **Rowley** (shoals), Austl.
153/J2 **Rowley** (isl.), NW,Can
128/B4 **Roxa** (isl.), GBis.
112/B3 **Roxas,** Phil.
112/C1 **Roxas,** Phil.
111/F1 **Roxas City,** Indo.
163/J2 **Roxboro,** NC,US
62/F2 **Roxen** (lake), Swe.
128/A3 **Roxo** (cape), Sen.
159/F4 **Roy,** NM,US
158/D2 **Roy,** Ut,US
73/G4 **Roya** (riv.), Fr.
60/D3 **Royal** (can.), Ire.
161/Q9 **Royal Botanical Garden,** On,Can
152/H4 **Royale** (isl.), Mi,US
59/E2 **Royal Leamington Spa,** Eng,UK
59/G4 **Royal Military** (can.), Eng,UK
132/E3 **Royal Natal Nat'l Park,** SAfr.
118/H9 **Royal Nat'l Park,** Austl.
165/F6 **Royal Oak,** Mi,US
101/D4 **Royal Paekje Tombs,** SKor.
109/D2 **Royal Tombs,** Viet.
59/G4 **Royal Tunbridge Wells,** Eng,UK
72/C4 **Royan,** Fr.
68/B4 **Roye,** Fr.
62/D2 **Røyken,** Nor.
59/F2 **Royston,** Eng,UK
57/F4 **Royton,** Eng,UK
82/E4 **Rožaje,** Yugo.
71/H4 **Rožmberk** (lake), Czh.
65/L4 **Rožňava,** Slvk.
68/D4 **Rozoy-sur-Serre,** Fr.
65/M3 **Roztoczański Nat'l Park,** Pol.
71/H2 **Roztoky,** Czh.
78/C2 **Rozzano,** It.
162/E3 **R.S. Kerr** (lake), Ok,US
87/G1 **Rtishchevo,** Rus.
57/E6 **Ruabon,** Wal,UK
126/B4 **Ruacana** (falls), Ang.
126/B4 **Ruacana,** Namb.
130/B4 **Ruaha Nat'l Park,** Tanz.
94/E5 **Rub' al Khali** (des.), SAr.
130/C4 **Rubeha** (mts.), Tanz.
53/U11 **Rubelles,** Fr.
100/C2 **Rubeshibe,** Japan
86/F2 **Rubezhnoye,** Ukr.
75/G2 **Rubí,** Sp.
164/C3 **Rubidoux,** Ca,US
79/D3 **Rubiera,** It.
140/B5 **Rubim,** Braz.
130/A3 **Rubondo Nat'l Park,** Tanz.
71/G4 **Řubřina** (riv.), Czh.
102/D1 **Rubtsovsk,** Rus.
130/B4 **Rubuga,** Tanz.
158/D2 **Ruby** (lake), Nv,US
158/D2 **Ruby** (mts.), Nv,US
158/D2 **Ruby Valley,** Nv,US
66/B5 **Rucphen,** Neth.
116/D2 **Rudall River Nat'l Park,** Austl.
65/K2 **Ruda Woda** (lake), Pol.
57/G6 **Ruddington,** Eng,UK
65/G2 **Rüdersdorf,** Ger.
70/A3 **Rüdesheim,** Ger.
130/B5 **Rudewa,** Tanz.
130/C4 **Rudi,** Tanz.
65/M3 **Rudnik,** Pol.
87/M1 **Rudnyy,** Kaz.
88/F1 **Rudolf** (isl.), Rus.
64/F3 **Rudolstadt,** Ger.
103/E4 **Rudong,** China
93/G2 **Rūdsar,** Iran
57/H3 **Rudston,** Eng,UK
56/B1 **Rue** (pt.), NI,UK
53/S10 **Rueil-Malmaison,** Fr.
54/A4 **Ruell** (riv.), Sc,UK
72/D4 **Ruelle-sur-Touvre,** Fr.
82/F4 **Ruen** (Rujen) (peak), Bul., Mac.
131/D3 **Ruenya** (riv.), Zim.
77/H3 **Ruetzbach** (riv.), Aus.
125/M5 **Rufā'ah,** Sudan
81/F3 **Ruffano,** It.
130/C4 **Rufiji** (riv.), Tanz.
142/E2 **Rufino,** Arg.
131/C2 **Rufunsa,** Zam.
103/E4 **Rugao,** China
59/E2 **Rugby,** Eng,UK
157/J3 **Rugby,** ND,US
58/E1 **Rugeley,** Eng,UK
65/G1 **Rügen** (isl.), Ger.
63/K3 **Ruhnu saar** (isl.), Est.
66/D6 **Ruhr** (riv.), Ger.
67/D6 **Ruhrgebiet** (reg.), Ger.
103/B4 **Ruicheng,** China
159/F4 **Ruidoso,** NM,US
66/D3 **Ruinen,** Neth.
130/C5 **Ruipa,** Tanz.
53/M7 **Ruislip,** Eng,UK
146/D4 **Ruiz,** Mex.
138/C3 **Ruiz, Nevado del** (peak), Col.
82/F4 **Rujen** (Ruen) (peak), Bul., Macd.
125/J8 **Ruki** (riv.), Zaire
130/B5 **Rukwa** (lake), Tanz.
130/A4 **Rukwa** (prov.), Tanz.
70/B4 **Rülzheim,** Ger.
77/H3 **Rum,** Aus.
150/C2 **Rum** (cay), Bahm.
82/D3 **Ruma,** Yugo.
130/B2 **Ruma Nat'l Park,** Kenya
125/L6 **Rumbek,** Sudan
93/N6 **Rumeli Hisar,** Turk.
161/G2 **Rumford,** Me,US
65/K1 **Rumia,** Pol.
76/B6 **Rumilly,** Fr.
58/C4 **Rumney,** Wal,UK
100/B2 **Rumoi,** Japan
131/D1 **Rumphi,** Malw.
167/E3 **Rumson,** NJ,US
68/D1 **Rumst,** Belg.
130/C2 **Rumuruti,** Kenya
56/B1 **Runabay Head** (pt.), NI,UK
103/C4 **Runan,** China
57/F5 **Runcorn,** Eng,UK
130/B3 **Runere,** Tanz.
63/T9 **Rungsted,** Den.
125/L7 **Rungu,** Zaire
130/A4 **Rungwa,** Tanz.
130/B4 **Rungwa,** Tanz.
130/B4 **Rungwa** (riv.), Tanz.
130/B4 **Rungwa Game Rsv.,** Tanz.
130/B5 **Rungwe** (peak), Tanz.
70/B2 **Runkel,** Ger.
62/F1 **Runn** (lake), Swe.
166/C4 **Runnemede,** NJ,US
159/G4 **Running Water Draw** (cr.), NM, Tx,US
126/C4 **Runtu,** Namb.
96/D3 **Ruo** (riv.), China
63/N1 **Ruokolahti,** Fin.
102/E4 **Ruoqiang,** China
108/D2 **Rūpar,** India
110/B3 **Rupat** (isl.), Indo.
83/G2 **Rupea,** Rom.
68/D1 **Rupel** (riv.), Belg.
160/E1 **Rupert** (riv.), Qu,Can
156/E5 **Rupert,** Id,US
153/J3 **Rupert House** (Waskaganish), Qu,Can
69/G2 **Ruppichteroth,** Ger.
69/F1 **Rur** (riv.), Ger.
136/E6 **Rurrenabaque,** Bol.
121/K7 **Rurutu** (isl.), FrPol.
131/D3 **Rusape,** Zim.
165/G7 **Ruscom** (riv.), On,Can
59/E4 **Rushall,** Eng,UK
103/E3 **Rushan,** China
157/K4 **Rush City,** Mn,US
59/F2 **Rushden,** Eng,UK
160/C4 **Rushville,** In,US
159/G2 **Rushville,** Ne,US
162/E4 **Rusk,** Tx,US
57/H5 **Ruskington,** Eng,UK
140/C2 **Russas,** Braz.
118/F7 **Russell** (isl.), Austl.
157/H3 **Russell,** Mb,Can
157/H1 **Russell** (lake), Mb,Can
152/F1 **Russell** (isl.), NW,Can
163/H3 **Russell** (lake), Ga, SC,US
159/H3 **Russell,** Ks,US
163/G3 **Russellville,** Al,US
162/E3 **Russellville,** Ar,US
160/C4 **Russellville,** Ky,US
70/B3 **Rüsselsheim,** Ger.
87/G2 **Russia**
158/B3 **Russian** (riv.), Ca,US
87/H4 **Rustavi,** Geo.
132/D2 **Rustenburg,** SAfr.
162/E3 **Ruston,** La,US
130/A3 **Rutana,** Buru.
74/C4 **Rute,** Sp.
111/F5 **Ruteng,** Indo.
131/C4 **Rutenga,** Zim.
158/D3 **Ruth,** Nv,US
67/F6 **Rüthen,** Ger.
167/D2 **Rutherford,** NJ,US
54/B5 **Rutherglen,** Sc,UK
57/E5 **Ruthin,** Wal,UK
77/E3 **Rüti,** Swi.
161/F3 **Rutland,** Vt,US
59/F1 **Rutland Water** (res.), Eng,UK
77/E4 **Rütli,** Swi.
102/C5 **Rutog,** China
130/A3 **Rutshuru,** Zaire
130/A3 **Rutshuru** (riv.), Zaire
66/D4 **Ruurlo,** Neth.
80/E2 **Ruvo di Puglia,** It.
130/C4 **Ruvu,** Tanz.
130/C4 **Ruvu** (riv.), Tanz.
130/A3 **Ruvubu** (riv.), Buru.
130/C5 **Ruvuma** (prov.), Tanz.
130/B5 **Ruvuma** (riv.), Tanz.
131/C3 **Ruwa,** Zim.
92/D3 **Ruwaq, Jabal ar** (mts.), Syria
130/A2 **Ruwenzori** (range), Ugan.
131/C3 **Ruya** (riv.), Zim.
103/C4 **Ruyang,** China
140/B4 **Ruy Barbosa,** Braz.
130/A3 **Ruyigi,** Buru.
87/H1 **Ruzayevka,** Rus.
130/A3 **Ruzizi** (riv.), Buru., Zaire
65/K4 **Ružomberok,** Slvk.
130/A2 **Rwanda**
130/A2 **Rwenjaza,** Ugan.
130/A3 **Rwenzori Nat'l Park,** Ugan.
56/C2 **Ryan, Loch** (inlet), Sc,UK
118/A1 **Ryan, Mount** (peak), Austl.
119/D2 **Ryan, Mount** (peak), Austl.
86/F1 **Ryazan',** Rus.
84/J5 **Ryazan' Obl.,** Rus.
86/G1 **Ryazhsk,** Rus.
84/G1 **Rybachiy** (pen.), Rus.
102/C3 **Rybach'ye,** Kyr.
84/H4 **Rybinsk,** Rus.
84/H4 **Rybinsk** (res.), Rus.
65/K3 **Rybnik,** Pol.
83/J2 **Rybnitsa,** Mol.
156/D2 **Rycroft,** Ab,Can
118/H8 **Ryde,** Austl.
59/E5 **Ryde,** Eng,UK
63/T9 **Rydebäck,** Swe.
59/G5 **Rye,** Eng,UK
59/G5 **Rye** (bay), Eng,UK
57/H3 **Rye** (riv.), Eng,UK
167/L8 **Rye,** NY,US
158/C2 **Rye Patch** (res.), Nv,US
62/D2 **Rygge,** Nor.
65/L3 **Ryki,** Pol.
63/J1 **Rymättyla** (isl.), Fin.
87/J2 **Ryn-Peski** (des.), Kaz.
99/F1 **Ryōtsu,** Japan
99/M9 **Ryōzen-yama** (peak), Japan
65/K2 **Rypin,** Pol.
86/B2 **Rysy** (peak), Slvk.
57/G2 **Ryton,** Eng,UK
59/E2 **Ryton on Dunsmore,** Eng,UK
62/F4 **Rytterknægten** (peak), Den.
99/G3 **Ryūgasaki,** Japan
100/H8 **Ryukyu** (Nansei-Shotō) (isls.), Japan
99/M9 **Ryūō,** Japan
65/M3 **Rzeszów,** Pol.
65/L3 **Rzeszów** (prov.), Pol.
84/G4 **Rzhev,** Rus.

S

63/K1 **Sääksjärvi** (lake), Fin.
70/B4 **Saalbach** (riv.), Ger.
67/G4 **Saale** (riv.), Ger.
76/D1 **Saales, Col de** (pass), Fr.
64/F3 **Saalfeld,** Ger.
73/K3 **Saalfelden am Steinernen Meer,** Aus.
76/D4 **Saane** (riv.), Swi.
156/C3 **Saanich,** BC,Can
130/C2 **Saanta** (peak), Kenya
69/F5 **Saar** (riv.), Ger.
69/F5 **Saarbrücken,** Ger.
63/K2 **Saaremaa** (isl.), Est.
69/F5 **Saarland** (state), Ger.
69/F5 **Saarlouis,** Ger.
76/D5 **Saastal** (vall.), Swi.
109/D3 **Sab** (riv.), Camb.
150/F3 **Saba** (isl.), NAnt.
82/D3 **Šabac,** Yugo.
75/G2 **Sabadell,** Sp.
98/E3 **Sabae,** Japan
111/E2 **Sabah** (state), Malay.
149/F1 **Sabana** (arch.), Cuba
138/C2 **Sabanalarga,** Col.
150/D3 **Sabaneta,** DRep.
110/A2 **Sabang,** Indo.
149/G4 **Sabanita,** Pan.
125/M6 **Sabat** (riv.), Eth., Sudan
95/H2 **Şāberi, Hāmūn-e** (lake), Afg.
124/H2 **Sabhā,** Libya
127/B3 **Sabie,** Egypt
133/F2 **Sabie** (riv.), Moz.
127/B3 **Sabie,** SAfr.
133/E2 **Sabierivier** (riv.), SAfr.
149/G1 **Sabinal** (cay), Cuba
75/E1 **Sabiñánigo,** Sp.
162/E4 **Sabine** (lake), La, Tx,US
162/E4 **Sabine** (riv.), La, Tx,US
159/J5 **Sabine Pass** (waterway), US
159/J5 **Sabine Pass** (waterway), La, Tx,US
80/C1 **Sabini** (mts.), It.
141/D1 **Sabinópolis,** Braz.
94/F4 **Sabkhat Maṭṭī** (salt marsh), UAE
112/C2 **Sablayan,** Phil.
161/J3 **Sable** (isl.), Can.
161/H3 **Sable** (cape), NS,Can
163/H5 **Sable** (cape), Fl,US
72/C3 **Sablé-sur-Sarthe,** Fr.
75/H1 **Sablon, Pointe du** (pt.), Fr.
140/C2 **Saboeiro,** Braz.
74/B2 **Sabor** (riv.), Port.
111/H4 **Sabra** (cape), Indo.
113/J **Sabrina** (coast), Ant.
93/J2 **Sabzevār,** Iran
156/D4 **Sacajawea** (peak), Or,US
158/E4 **Sacaton,** Az,US
74/A3 **Sacavém,** Port.
78/A4 **Saccarello, Monte** (Mont Saccarel), Fr.
78/A4 **Saccarel, Mont** (Monte Saccarello) (mtn.), Fr.
80/C2 **Sacco** (riv.), It.
83/G3 **Săcele,** Rom.
157/L2 **Sachigo** (lake), On,Can
157/L2 **Sachigo** (riv.), On,Can
168/C3 **Sachuest Point Nat'l Wild. Ref.,** RI,US
79/F1 **Sacile,** It.
76/D2 **Säckingen,** Ger.
161/H2 **Sackville,** NB,Can
53/S10 **Saclay,** Fr.
161/G3 **Saco,** Me,US
141/C1 **Sacramento,** Braz.
144/C2 **Sacramento** (plain), Peru
165/M9 **Sacramento** (cap.), Ca,US
165/M10 **Sacramento** (co.), Ca,US
158/B2 **Sacramento** (riv.), Ca,US
158/B3 **Sacramento** (val.), Ca,US
159/F4 **Sacramento** (mts.), NM,US
165/L10 **Sacramento River Deep Water Ship** (can.), Ca,US
74/D4 **Sacratif** (cape), Sp.
154/W12 **Sacred** (falls), Hi,US
57/G2 **Sacriston,** Eng,UK
80/E2 **Sacro** (peak), It.
78/B1 **Sacro Monte,** It.
147/L7 **Sacromonte Nat'l Park,** Mex.
74/A1 **Sada,** Sp.
130/C4 **Sadani,** Tanz.
156/C2 **Saddle** (hills), Ab, BC,Can
167/J8 **Saddle** (riv.), NJ,US
167/J8 **Saddle Brook,** NJ,US
54/A2 **Saddle, The** (mtn.), Sc,UK
57/G4 **Saddleworth,** Eng,UK
109/D4 **Sa Dec,** Viet.
108/D2 **Sādhaura,** India
95/K3 **Sādiqābād,** Pak.
104/B3 **Sadiya,** India
99/F2 **Sado** (isl.), Japan
74/A3 **Sado** (riv.), Port.
98/B4 **Sadowara,** Japan
106/B2 **Sādri,** India
112/D3 **Sadripante** (mtn.), Phil.
127/C3 **Safājah, Bi'r** (well), Egypt
124/H1 **Safāqis,** Tun.
123/X18 **Safāqis** (gov.), Tun.
108/A1 **Safed Koh** (range), Pak.
94/E3 **Saffānīyah, Ra's as** (pt.), SAr.
62/E2 **Säffle,** Swe.
158/E4 **Safford,** Az,US
59/G2 **Saffron Walden,** Eng,UK
124/D1 **Safi,** Mor.
95/H2 **Safid** (mts.), Afg.
95/J1 **Safīd** (riv.), Afg.
95/K1 **Safid Khers** (mts.), Afg., Taj.
91/E2 **Şāfītā,** Syria
84/G5 **Šafonovo,** Rus.
92/C1 **Safranbolu,** Turk.
106/E2 **Saga,** China
98/B4 **Saga,** Japan
98/A4 **Saga** (pref.), Japan
99/G1 **Sagae,** Japan
104/B4 **Sagaing,** Burma
104/B3 **Sagaing** (div.), Burma
99/H7 **Sagami** (bay), Japan
99/H7 **Sagami** (riv.), Japan
99/F3 **Sagami** (sea), Japan
99/F3 **Sagamihara,** Japan
99/H7 **Sagamiko,** Japan
167/E2 **Sagamore Hill Nat'l Hist. Site,** NY,US
130/C3 **Sagana,** Kenya
106/C3 **Sāgar,** India
151/J2 **Sagavanirktok** (riv.), Ak,US
112/C3 **Sagay,** Phil.
112/D3 **Sagay,** Phil.
160/D3 **Saginaw,** Mi,US
160/D3 **Saginaw** (bay), Mi,US
153/K3 **Saglek** (bay), Nf,Can
80/A1 **Sagone** (gulf), Fr.
74/A4 **Sagres,** Port.
102/E2 **Sagsay** (riv.), Mong.
67/E2 **Sagter Ems** (riv.), Ger.
149/H1 **Sagua de Tánamo,** Cuba
149/F1 **Sagua la Grande,** Cuba
158/E4 **Saguaro Nat'l Mon.,** Az,US
161/G1 **Saguenay** (riv.), Qu,Can
124/C2 **Saguia el Hamra** (wadi), Mor., WSah.
75/E3 **Sagunto,** Sp.
53/R9 **Sagy,** Fr.
106/E2 **Sa'gya,** China
87/K2 **Sagyz** (riv.), Kaz.
91/E4 **Saḩāb,** Jor.
127/B5 **Sahaba,** Sudan
138/C2 **Sahagún,** Col.
93/F2 **Sahand** (mtn.), Iran
124/G3 **Sahara** (des.), Afr.
95/L3 **Sahāranpur,** India
106/E2 **Saharsa,** India
123/T15 **Sahel** (riv.), Alg.
106/E2 **Sāhibganj,** India
108/B2 **Sāhīwāl,** Pak.
124/H2 **Şaḩrā Awbārī** (des.), Libya
125/K2 **Sahra' Rabyānah** (des.), Libya
146/E4 **Sahuayo de Díaz,** Mex.
106/D2 **Sai** (riv.), India
99/E2 **Sai** (riv.), Japan
123/R16 **Saïda,** Alg.
123/R16 **Saïda** (wilaya), Alg.
106/D2 **Saidpur,** India
98/C2 **Saigō,** Japan
109/D4 **Saigon** (Ho Chi Minh City), Viet.
98/C4 **Saijō,** Japan
98/A4 **Saikai Nat'l Park,** Japan
98/B4 **Saiki,** Japan
106/C4 **Sailu,** India
63/M1 **Saimaa** (lake), Fin.
68/C4 **Sains-Richaumont,** Fr.
54/D5 **Saint Abbs,** Sc,UK
54/D5 **Saint Abb's Head** (pt.), Sc,UK
72/E5 **Saint-Affrique,** Fr.
58/A6 **Saint Agnes,** Eng,UK
58/A6 **Saint Agnes** (pt.), Eng,UK
161/L2 **Saint Alban's,** Nf,Can
53/N6 **Saint Albans,** Eng,UK
53/M6 **Saint Albans** (val.), Eng,UK
161/F2 **Saint Albans,** Vt,US
160/D4 **Saint Albans,** WV,US
156/E2 **Saint Albert,** Ab,Can
58/D5 **Saint Aldhelm's Head** (pt.), Eng,UK
68/C3 **Saint-Amand-les-Eaux,** Fr.
72/E3 **Saint-Amand-Montrond,** Fr.
161/G1 **Saint-Ambroise,** Qu,Can
68/C2 **Saint-André,** Fr.
133/R15 **Saint-André,** Reun.
72/F2 **Saint-André-les-Vergers,** Fr.
54/D4 **Saint Andrews,** Sc,UK
54/D4 **Saint Andrews** (bay), Sc,UK
128/B5 **Saint Ann** (cape), SLeo.
72/B2 **Saint Anne,** Chl,UK
161/Q9 **Saint Anns,** On,Can
58/A3 **Saint Ann's** (pt.), UK
161/L1 **Saint Anthony,** Nf,Can
156/F5 **Saint Anthony,** Id,US
161/N6 **Saint-Antoine,** Qu,Can
68/D6 **Saint-Armand-sur-Fion,** Fr.
53/R11 **Saint-Arnoult-en-Yvelines,** Fr.
56/E5 **Saint Asaph,** Wal,UK
58/C4 **Saint Athan,** Wal,UK
72/B2 **Saint Aubin,** Chl,UK
161/N6 **Saint-Augustin,** Qu,Can
163/H4 **Saint Augustine,** Fl,US
163/H4 **Saint Augustine Beach,** Fl,US
58/B6 **Saint Austell,** Eng,UK
58/B6 **Saint Austell** (bay), Eng,UK
72/B3 **Saint-Avé,** Fr.
69/F5 **Saint-Avold,** Fr.
150/F3 **Saint Barthélemy** (isl.), Fr.
72/D5 **Saint-Barthélemy, Pic de** (peak), Fr.
56/E3 **Saint Bees,** Eng,UK
56/E2 **Saint Bees Head** (pt.), Eng,UK
161/M6 **Saint-Benoît,** Qu,Can
133/R15 **Saint-Benoît,** Reun.
161/P7 **Saint-Blaise,** Qu,Can
132/C4 **Saint Blaize** (cape), SAfr.
54/D5 **Saint Boswells,** Sc,UK
58/D3 **Saint Briavels,** Eng,UK
53/T10 **Saint-Brice-sous-Forêt,** Fr.
58/A3 **Saint Brides** (bay), Wal,UK
72/B2 **Saint-Brieuc,** Fr.
72/B2 **Saint-Brieuc** (bay), Fr.
161/P6 **Saint-Bruno** (co.), Qu,Can
161/P6 **Saint-Bruno-de-Montarville,** Qu,Can
161/M6 **Saint-Canut,** Qu,Can
161/R9 **Saint Catharines,** On,Can
150/F4 **Saint Catherine** (mtn.), Gren.
59/E5 **Saint Catherine's** (hill), Eng,UK
59/E5 **Saint Catherine's** (pt.), Eng,UK
72/F4 **Saint-Chamond,** Fr.
165/P16 **Saint Charles,** Il,US
160/E4 **Saint Charles,** Md,US
159/K3 **Saint Charles,** Mo,US
53/S11 **Saint-Chéron,** Fr.
150/D4 **Saint Christoffel** (peak), NAnt.
165/G7 **Saint Clair** (lake), On,Can, Mi,US
165/H6 **Saint Clair** (riv.), On,Can, Mi,US
165/G6 **Saint Clair** (co.), Mi,US
165/G7 **Saint Clair** (lake), On,Can, Mi,US
165/H6 **Saint Clair** (riv.), On,Can, Mi,US
165/G6 **Saint Clair Shores,** Mi,US
76/B5 **Saint-Claude,** Fr.
58/B3 **Saint Clears,** Wal,UK
53/S10 **Saint-Cloud,** Fr.
157/K4 **Saint Cloud,** Mn,US
58/B6 **Saint Columb Major,** Eng,UK
54/E1 **Saint Combs,** Sc,UK
161/N7 **Saint-Constant,** Qu,Can
116/B3 **Saint Cricq** (cape), Austl.
157/K4 **Saint Croix** (riv.), Mn, Wi,US
160/A2 **Saint Croix** (riv.), Mn, Wi,US
150/E3 **Saint Croix** (isl.), USVI
151/M3 **Saint Cyr** (mtn.), Yk,Can
53/S10 **Saint-Cyr-l'École,** Fr.
53/S11 **Saint-Cyr-sous-Dourdan,** Fr.
54/D3 **Saint Cyrus,** Sc,UK
58/A3 **Saint David's,** Wal,UK
58/A3 **Saint David's Head** (pt.), Wal,UK
53/T10 **Saint-Denis,** Fr.
133/R15 **Saint-Denis,** Reun.
76/A5 **Saint-Didier-sur-Saône,** Fr.
76/C1 **Saint-Dié,** Fr.
72/F2 **Saint-Dizier,** Fr.
72/E3 **Saint-Doulchard,** Fr.
160/F2 **Sainte-Agathe-des-Monts,** Qu,Can
161/H1 **Sainte-Anne-des-Monts,** Qu,Can
161/N6 **Sainte-Anne-des-Plaines,** Qu,Can
161/G2 **Sainte-Foy,** Qu,Can
159/K3 **Sainte Genevieve,** Mo,US
53/T11 **Sainte-Geneviève-des-Bois,** Fr.
161/P6 **Sainte-Julie-de-Verchères,** Qu,Can
161/J2 **Saint Eleanors,** PE,Can
151/K3 **Saint Elias** (mts.), Can., US
151/K4 **Saint Elias** (cape), Ak,US
151/K3 **Saint Elias** (mtn.), Ak,US
151/K3 **Saint Elias** (mts.), Yk,Can, Ak,US
151/K3 **Saint Elias-Wrangell Nat'l Park and Prsv.,** Ak,US
161/H1 **Sainte-Marguerite** (riv.), Qu,Can
161/G2 **Sainte-Marie,** Qu,Can
76/D1 **Sainte-Marie-aux-Mines,** Fr.
133/J7 **Sainte Marie, Nosy** (isl.), Madg.
73/G5 **Sainte-Maxime,** Fr.
68/C5 **Saint-Erme-Outre-et-Ramecourt,** Fr.
157/J3 **Sainte Rose du Lac,** Mb,Can
72/C4 **Saintes,** Fr.
161/M6 **Sainte-Scholastique,** Qu,Can
72/E5 **Saint-Estève,** Fr.
161/N6 **Sainte-Thérèse,** Qu,Can
161/N6 **Sainte-Thérèse-Ouest,** Qu,Can
72/F4 **Saint-Étienne,** Fr.
72/D2 **Saint-Étienne-du-Rouvray,** Fr.
161/N6 **Saint-Eustache,** Qu,Can
150/F3 **Saint Eustatius** (isl.), NAnt.
53/T11 **Saint-Fargeau-Ponthierry,** Fr.
161/F1 **Saint-Félicien,** Qu,Can
76/B6 **Saint-Felix,** Fr.
54/E1 **Saint Fergus,** Sc,UK
56/C3 **Saintfield,** NI,UK
72/E2 **Saint-Florentin,** Fr.
72/E3 **Saint-Florent-sur-Cher,** Fr.
125/K6 **Saint-Floris Nat'l Park,** CAfr.
72/E4 **Saint-Flour,** Fr.
132/D4 **Saint Francis** (cape), SAfr.
159/K4 **Saint Francis** (riv.), Ar, Mo,US
159/G3 **Saint Francis,** Ks,US
165/Q14 **Saint Francis,** Wi,US
163/F4 **Saint Francisville,** La,US
163/F2 **Saint Francois** (mts.), Mo,US
72/D5 **Saint-Gaudens,** Fr.
161/K1 **Saint George** (cape), Can.
161/H2 **Saint George,** Nb,Can
161/K1 **Saint George** (cape), Nf,Can
151/E4 **Saint George** (isl.), Ak,US
158/A2 **Saint George** (pt.), Ca,US
167/J9 **Saint George,** NY,US
163/H3 **Saint George,** SC,US
158/D3 **Saint George,** Ut,US
161/K1 **Saint George's,** Nf,Can
161/K1 **Saint George's** (bay), Nf,Can
161/J2 **Saint Georges** (bay), NS,Can
161/G2 **Saint-Georges,** Qu,Can
150/F4 **Saint George's** (cap.), Gren.
56/C6 **Saint George's** (chan.), Ire., UK
53/S10 **Saint-Germain-en-Laye,** Fr.
53/T11 **Saint-Germain-lès-Corbeil,** Fr.
53/U10 **Saint-Germain-sur-Morin,** Fr.
68/A5 **Saint-Germer-de-Fly,** Fr.
68/C3 **Saint-Ghislain,** Belg.
72/F5 **Saint-Gilles,** Fr.
72/C3 **Saint-Gilles-Croix-de-Vie,** Fr.
72/D5 **Saint-Girons,** Fr.
77/E4 **Saint Gotthard** (pass), Swi.
58/B3 **Saint Govan's Head** (pt.), Wal,UK
53/S10 **Saint-Gratien,** Fr.
118/F6 **Saint Helena** (isl.), Austl.
132/B4 **Saint Helena** (bay), SAfr.
122/B6 **Saint Helena** (isl.), UK
165/J9 **Saint Helena** (mtn.), Ca,US
119/D4 **Saint Helens** (pt.), Austl.
57/F5 **Saint Helens,** Eng,UK
156/C4 **Saint Helens,** Or,US
156/C4 **Saint Helens, Mount** (vol.), Wa,US
72/B2 **Saint Helier,** Chl,UK
72/C3 **Saint-Herblain,** Fr.
161/M6 **Saint-Hermas,** Qu,Can
106/E3 **Sainthia,** India
161/G1 **Saint-Honoré,** Qu,Can
161/P7 **Saint-Hubert,** Qu,Can
161/F2 **Saint-Hyacinthe,** Qu,Can
160/C1 **Saint Ignace** (isl.), On,Can
160/C2 **Saint Ignace,** Mi,US
118/H8 **Saint Ives,** Austl.
58/A6 **Saint Ives,** Eng,UK
59/F2 **Saint Ives,** Eng,UK
58/A6 **Saint Ives** (bay), Eng,UK
161/P7 **Saint-Jacques-le-Mineur,** Qu,Can
152/C3 **Saint James** (cape), BC,Can
157/K5 **Saint James,** Mn,US
167/E2 **Saint James,** NY,US
161/P7 **Saint-Jean** (co.), Qu,Can
161/G1 **Saint-Jean** (lake), Qu,Can
161/H1 **Saint-Jean** (riv.), Qu,Can
72/C4 **Saint-Jean-d'Angély,** Fr.
72/D3 **Saint-Jean-de-la-Ruelle,** Fr.
72/C5 **Saint-Jean-de-Luz,** Fr.
155/M2 **Saint-Jean, Lac** (lake), Qu,Can
161/G2 **Saint-Jean-Port-Joli,** Qu,Can
161/F2 **Saint-Jean-sur-Richelieu,** Qu,Can
161/N6 **Saint-Jérôme,** Qu,Can
156/D4 **Saint Joe** (riv.), Id,US
154/C2 **Saint Joe** (riv.), Id, Wa,US
161/H2 **Saint John,** NB,Can
161/H2 **Saint John** (riv.), NB,Can
161/G2 **Saint John** (riv.), Can., US
72/B2 **Saint John,** Chl,UK
161/G2 **Saint John** (riv.), NB,Can, Me,US
150/E3 **Saint John** (isl.), USVI
150/F3 **Saint John's** (cap.), Anti.
161/L2 **Saint John's** (cap.), Nf,Can
56/C3 **Saint John's** (pt.), IM,UK
158/E4 **Saint Johns,** Az,US
155/K6 **Saint Johns** (riv.), Fl,US
161/F2 **Saint Johnsbury,** Vt,US
166/C5 **Saint Jones** (riv.), De,US
160/B1 **Saint Joseph** (lake), On,Can
133/R15 **Saint-Joseph,** Reun.
160/C2 **Saint Joseph** (isl.), Mi,US
160/C3 **Saint Joseph** (riv.), Mi,US
159/J3 **Saint Joseph,** Mo,US
72/E5 **Saint-Juéry,** Fr.
76/C5 **Saint-Julien-en-Genevois,** Fr.
72/D4 **Saint-Junien,** Fr.
58/A6 **Saint Just,** Eng,UK
58/A6 **Saint Just in Roseland,** Eng,UK
119/F5 **Saint Kilda,** Austl.
55/G8 **Saint Kilda** (isl.), Sc,UK
150/F3 **Saint Kitts** (isl.), StK.
150/F3 **Saint Kitts and Nevis**
161/P6 **Saint-Lambert,** Qu,Can
157/J3 **Saint Laurent,** Mb,Can
161/N6 **Saint-Laurent,** Qu,Can
68/B3 **Saint-Laurent-Blangy,** Fr.
139/H3 **Saint-Laurent du Maroni,** FrG.
161/J1 **Saint Lawrence** (gulf), Can.
161/L2 **Saint Lawrence,** Nf,Can
161/P6 **Saint Lawrence** (riv.), Can., US
151/D3 **Saint Lawrence** (isl.), Ak,US
160/E2 **Saint Lawrence Islands Nat'l Park,** Can.
161/M7 **Saint-Lazare,** Qu,Can
119/G5 **Saint Leonard** (mtn.), Austl.
161/N6 **Saint-Léonard,** Qu,Can
133/R15 **Saint-Leu,** Reun.
53/S9 **Saint-Leu-la-Forêt,** Fr.
72/C2 **Saint-Lô,** Fr.
161/N7 **Saint Louis** (lake), Qu,Can
157/G2 **Saint Louis,** Sk,Can
76/D2 **Saint-Louis,** Fr.
133/R15 **Saint-Louis,** Reun.
128/A2 **Saint-Louis,** Sen.
128/B3 **Saint-Louis** (reg.), Sen.
156/A2 **Saint Louis** (riv.), Mn,US
159/K3 **Saint Louis,** Mo,US
161/H2 **Saint-Louis-de-Kent,** NB,Can
149/H2 **Saint-Louis du Nord,** Haiti
161/P7 **Saint-Luc,** Qu,Can
150/F4 **Saint Lucia**
150/F4 **Saint Lucia** (passg.), Mart., StL.
133/F3 **Saint Lucia** (cape), SAfr.
133/F3 **Saint Lucia, Lake** (lag.), SAfr.
55/P12 **Saint Magnus** (bay), Sc,UK
72/C3 **Saint-Maixent-L'École,** Fr.
157/J3 **Saint Malo,** Mb,Can
72/B2 **Saint-Malo,** Fr.
72/B2 **Saint-Malo** (gulf), Fr.
53/T10 **Saint-Mandé,** Fr.
72/F5 **Saint-Mandrier-sur-Mer,** Fr.
149/H2 **Saint-Marc,** Haiti
149/H2 **Saint-Marc, Pointe de** (pt.), Haiti
53/U9 **Saint-Mard,** Fr.
59/H4 **Saint Margaret's at Cliffe,** Eng,UK
55/N13 **Saint Margaret's Hope,** Sc,UK
156/D4 **Saint Maries,** Id,US
157/J3 **Saint Martin** (lake), Mb,Can
150/F3 **Saint Martin** (isl.), Fr.
76/A5 **Saint-Martin-Belle-Roche,** Fr.
68/A2 **Saint-Martin-Boulogne,** Fr.
68/C6 **Saint-Martin-d'Ablois,** Fr.
72/F4 **Saint-Martin-d'Hères,** Fr.
53/T9 **Saint-Martin-du-Tertre,** Fr.
104/A4 **Saint Martins** (isl.), Bang.
150/F3 **Saint Martin** (Sint Maarten) (isl.), Fr.
117/H4 **Saint Mary** (peak), Austl.
128/A3 **Saint Mary** (cape), Gam.
118/G8 **Saint Marys,** Austl.
160/D3 **Saint Mary's,** Nf,Can
161/J2 **Saint Marys** (riv.), NS,Can
55/N13 **Saint Mary's,** Sc,UK
151/F3 **Saint Marys,** Ak,US
163/H4 **Saint Marys,** Ga,US
160/E3 **Saint Marys,** Pa,US
131/B2 **Saint Mary's,** Zam.
161/N7 **Saint-Mathieu,** Qu,Can
151/D3 **Saint Matthew** (isl.), Ak,US
163/H3 **Saint Matthews,** SC,US
120/E5 **Saint Matthias** (isls.), PNG
53/T10 **Saint-Maur-des-Fossés,** Fr.
160/F1 **Saint-Maurice** (riv.), Qu,Can
76/C5 **Saint-Maurice,** Swi.
76/B6 **Saint-Maurice-de-Gourdans,** Fr.
58/A6 **Saint Mawes,** Eng,UK
69/F6 **Saint-Max,** Fr.
58/C3 **Saint Mellons,** Wal,UK
68/D6 **Saint-Memmie,** Fr.
53/S11 **Saint-Michel-sur-Orge,** Fr.
54/D4 **Saint Monance,** Sc,UK
72/B3 **Saint-Nazaire,** Fr.
59/F2 **Saint Neots,** Eng,UK
69/E2 **Saint-Nicolas,** Belg.
53/S10 **Saint-Nom-la-Bretèche,** Fr.
68/B2 **Saint-Omer,** Fr.
68/A4 **Saint-Omer-en-Chaussée,** Fr.
53/S9 **Saint-Ouen-l'Aumône,** Fr.
161/G2 **Saint-Pamphile,** Qu,Can
161/G2 **Saint-Pascal,** Qu,Can
53/U9 **Saint-Pathus,** Fr.
50/H5 **Saint Paul** (isls.), Braz.
156/F2 **Saint Paul,** Ab,Can
51/N7 **Saint Paul** (isl.), FrAnt.
129/F5 **Saint Paul** (cape), Gha.
128/C5 **Saint Paul** (riv.), Gui., Libr.
133/R15 **Saint-Paul,** Reun.

217

Saint – San M

151/E4 Saint Paul (isl.), Ak,US
159/J3 Saint Paul, Ks,US
157/K4 Saint Paul (cap.), Mn,US
72/C5 Saint-Paul-lès-Dax, Fr.
118/B1 Saint Pauls (peak), Austl.
167/E2 Saint Paul's Church Nat'l Hist. Site, NY,US
72/F4 Saint-Paul-Trois-Châteaux, Fr.
117/G5 Saint Peter (isl.), Austl.
157/K4 Saint Peter, Mn,US
137/M3 Saint Peter and Saint Paul (rocks), Braz.
72/B2 Saint Peter Port, Chl,UK
59/H4 Saint Peter's, Eng,UK
163/H5 Saint Petersburg, Fl,US
84/F4 Saint Petersburg (Leningrad), Rus.
85/V7 Saint Petersburg (Leningrad) (inset), Rus.
84/G3 Saint Petersburg Obl., Rus.
161/P7 Saint-Philippe-de-La Prairie, Qu,Can
133/R15 Saint-Pierre, Reun.
161/K2 Saint Pierre (isl.), StP.
161/K2 Saint Pierre (isl.), StP,Fr
161/K2 Saint Pierre & Miquelon (dpcy.), Fr
72/D3 Saint-Pierre-des-Corps, Fr.
72/C5 Saint-Pierre-du-Mont, Fr.
53/T11 Saint-Pierre-du-Perray, Fr.
157/J3 Saint Pierre-Jolys, Mb,Can
76/C4 Saint-Point (lake), Fr.
72/B2 Saint-Pol-de-Léon, Fr.
68/B1 Saint-Pol-sur-Mer, Fr.
72/E5 Saint-Pons (mtn.), Fr.
53/S9 Saint-Prix, Fr.
68/C4 Saint-Quentin, Fr.
68/C4 Saint Quentin, Canal de (can.), Fr.
73/G5 Saint-Raphaël, Fr.
72/F5 Saint-Rémy-de-Provence, Fr.
53/S10 Saint-Rémy-lès-Chevreuse, Fr.
68/A3 Saint-Riquier, Fr.
72/B2 Saint Sampson's, Chl,UK
68/C3 Saint-Saulve, Fr.
163/H4 Saint Simons (isl.), Ga,US
163/H4 Saint Simons Island, Ga,US
53/U9 Saint-Soupplets, Fr.
161/H2 Saint Stephen, NB,Can
58/B6 Saint Stephen in Brannel, Eng,UK
160/D3 Saint Thomas, On,Can
150/E3 Saint Thomas (isl.), USVI
161/N7 Saint-Urbain-Premier, Qu,Can
72/F3 Saint-Vallier, Fr.
68/B2 Saint-Venant, Fr.
117/H5 Saint Vincent (gulf), Austl.
119/C4 Saint Vincent (pt.), Austl.
150/F4 Saint Vincent (passg.), StL., StV.
150/F4 Saint Vincent (isl.), StV.
150/F4 Saint Vincent and the Grenadines
69/F3 Saint Vith, Belg.
53/T11 Saint-Vrain, Fr.
156/F2 Saint Walburg, Sk,Can
53/T9 Saint-Witz, Fr.
106/D2 Sāipal (mtn.), Nepal
120/D3 Saipan (isl.), NMar.
99/F2 Saitama (pref.), Japan
98/B4 Saito, Japan
130/B2 Saiwa Swamp Nat'l Park, Kenya
109/B3 Sai Yok Nat'l Park, Thai.
144/D5 Sajama Nat'l Park, Bol.
82/E1 Sajószentpéter, Hun.
132/C3 Sak (riv.), SAfr.
99/H7 Sakado, Japan
99/J7 Sakae, Japan
99/M9 Sakahogi, Japan
98/E2 Sakai, Japan
99/F2 Sakai, Japan
99/H7 Sakai (riv.), Japan
98/C3 Sakaide, Japan
98/C3 Sakaiminato, Japan
157/H3 Sakakawea (lake), ND,US
153/J3 Sakami (lake), Qu,Can
131/C2 Sakania, Zaire
83/K5 Sakarya (prov.), Turk.
86/D4 Sakarya (riv.), Turk.
92/B2 Sakarya (str.), Turk.
100/A4 Sakata, Japan
98/C4 Sakawa, Japan
133/H7 Sakay (riv.), Madg.
130/A3 Sake, Zaire
133/H7 Sakeny (riv.), Madg.
89/Q4 Sakhalin (gulf), Rus.
89/Q4 Sakhalin (isl.), Rus.
100/C1 Sakhalin Obl., Rus.
94/F1 Sakht Sar (Ramsar), Iran
86/E3 Saki, Ukr.
100/G8 Sakishima (isls.), Japan
87/L1 Sakmara (riv.), Rus.
109/D2 Sakon Nakhon, Thai.
168/C3 Sakonnet (pt.), RI,US
95/J3 Sakrand, Pak.
99/F2 Saku, Japan
99/J7 Sakura, Japan
99/L10 Sakurai, Japan
122/K10 Sal (isl.), CpV.
148/E3 Sal (pt.), Hon.
87/G3 Sal (riv.), Rus.
65/J4 Šal'a, Slvk.
62/G2 Sala, Swe.
80/D2 Sala Consilina, It.
146/A1 Salada (dry lake), Mex.
135/E2 Saladas, Arg.
142/F2 Saladillo, Arg.
143/S12 Saladillo (riv.), Arg.
142/D3 Salado (riv.), Arg.
142/F2 Salado (riv.), Arg.
149/G1 Salado (riv.), Cuba
158/F4 Salado (dry riv.), NM,US
134/C5 Salado del Norte (riv.), Arg.
129/E4 Salaga, Gha.
93/E3 Şalāḩ ad Dīn (gov.), Iraq
111/G4 Salahatu (mtn.), Indo.
82/F2 Sălaj (co.), Rom.
124/J5 Salal, Chad
127/D4 Şalālah, Sudan
148/D3 Salamá, Guat.
142/D5 Salamanca (plain), Arg.
142/C1 Salamanca, Chile
147/E4 Salamanca, Mex.
74/C2 Salamanca, Sp.
160/E3 Salamanca, NY,US
125/J6 Salamat (riv.), Chad
138/C3 Salamina, Col.
81/H3 Salamís, Gre.
81/L7 Salamís (isl.), Gre.
91/E2 Salamīyah, Syria
109/C1 Sala Mok, Laos
74/B1 Salas, Sp.
75/G1 Salat (riv.), Fr.
87/K1 Salavat, Rus.
120/B5 Salayar (isl.), Indo.
50/D7 Sala y Gomez (isls.), Chile
72/E3 Salbris, Fr.
144/C4 Salcantay (peak), Peru
150/D3 Salcedo, DRep.
112/D3 Salcedo, Phil.
58/C6 Salcombe, Eng,UK
132/K10 Saldanhabaai (bay), SAfr.
63/K3 Saldus, Lat.
119/C3 Sale, Austl.
123/L13 Salé, Mor.
57/F5 Sale, Eng,UK
111/G3 Salebabu (isl.), Indo.
88/G3 Salekhard, Rus.
77/F2 Salem, Ger.
108/G3 Salem, India
63/R7 Salem, Swe.
160/C4 Salem, In,US
159/K3 Salem, Mo,US
161/G3 Salem, NH,US
166/C4 Salem, NJ,US
166/C4 Salem (co.), NJ,US
166/C4 Salem (cr.), NJ,US
168/G6 Salem, Oh,US
156/C4 Salem (cap.), Or,US
160/D4 Salem, Va,US
80/C4 Salemi, It.
80/F2 Salentina (pen.), It.
80/D2 Salerno, It.
80/D2 Salerno (gulf), It.
59/G3 Sales (pt.), UK
57/F5 Salford, Eng,UK
82/D1 Salgótarján, Hun.
140/C3 Salgueiro, Braz.
159/F3 Salida, Co,US
92/B2 Salihli, Turk.
131/D2 Salima, Malw.
127/B4 Salīmah (oasis), Sudan
74/B1 Salime (res.), Sp.
130/C5 Salims, Tanz.
150/C2 Salina (pt.), Bahm.
80/D3 Salina (isl.), It.
159/H3 Salina, Ks,US
158/E3 Salina, Ut,US
148/C2 Salina Cruz, Mex.
140/B5 Salinas, Braz.
138/A5 Salinas, Ecu.
147/E4 Salinas, Mex.
158/B3 Salinas, Ca,US
158/B3 Salinas (riv.), Ca,US
75/G3 Salinas, Cabo de (cape), Sp.
159/F4 Salinas Nat'l Mon., NM,US
144/D4 Salinas y Aguada Blanca Nat'l Rsv., Peru
80/D2 Saline (marsh), It.
54/C4 Saline, Sc,UK
159/J4 Saline (riv.), Ar,US
159/G3 Saline (riv.), Ks,US
165/E7 Saline (riv.), Mi,US
137/J4 Salinópolis, Braz.
117/M8 Salisbury, Austl.
153/J2 Salisbury (isl.), NW,Can
59/E4 Salisbury, Eng,UK
58/D4 Salisbury (plain), Eng,UK
160/F4 Salisbury, Md,US
163/H3 Salisbury, NC,US
140/B3 Salitre (riv.), Braz.
138/B5 Salitre, Ecu.
61/J2 Salla, Fin.
76/C6 Sallanches, Fr.
66/D4 Salland (reg.), Neth.
128/B4 Sallatouk (pt.), Gui.
68/B3 Sallaumines, Fr.
75/F2 Sallent, Sp.
159/J4 Sallisaw, Ok,US
127/D5 Sallūm, Sudan
106/D2 Sallyāna, Nepal
60/D3 Sally Gap (pass), Ire.
69/F3 Salm (riv.), Ger.
93/F2 Salmās, Iran
156/D4 Salmon (riv.), Id,US
156/D3 Salmon Arm, BC,Can
158/D2 Salmon Falls (riv.), Id, Nv,US
156/E4 Salmon River (mts.), Id,US
156/E4 Salmon, South Fork (riv.), Id,US
63/K1 Salo, Fin.
78/D1 Salò, It.
76/B2 Salon (riv.), Fr.
72/F5 Salon-de-Provence, Fr.
125/K8 Salonga Nat'l Park, Zaire
81/H3 Salonika (Thermaic) (gulf), Gre.
81/H2 Salonika (Thessaloníki), Gre.
82/E2 Salonta, Rom.
74/B3 Salor (riv.), Sp.
128/B3 Saloum, Vallée du (wadi), Sen.
63/M1 Salpausselkä (mts.), Fin.
75/G1 Salses, Fr.
87/G3 Sal'sk, Rus.
80/C4 Salso (riv.), It.
78/C3 Salsomaggiore Terme, It.
108/B1 Salt (range), Pak.
132/C3 Salt (riv.), SAfr.
149/J1 Salt (cay), Trks.
158/E4 Salt (riv.), Az,US
165/Q16 Salt (cr.), Il,US
146/D2 Salt (cr.), Tx,US
135/C1 Salta, Arg.
58/B6 Saltash, Eng,UK
57/H2 Saltburn, Eng,UK
54/B5 Saltcoats, Sc,UK
60/D5 Saltee (isls.), Ire.
61/E2 Saltfjorden (fjord), Nor.
58/D4 Saltford, Eng,UK
63/T9 Saltholm (isl.), Den.
163/H4 Saltilla (riv.), Ga,US
147/E3 Saltillo, Mex.
158/E2 Salt Lake City (cap.), Ut,US
168/B3 Salt Meadow Nat'l Wild. Ref., Ct,US
159/J2 Salt, North Fork (riv.), Mo,US
142/E2 Salto, Arg.
141/C2 Salto, Braz.
80/C1 Salto (riv.), It.
135/E3 Salto, Uru.
143/F1 Salto (dept.), Uru.
140/C5 Salto da Divisa, Braz.
135/F1 Salto del Guairá, Par.
158/C4 Salton Sea (lake), Ca,US
141/A3 Salto Santiago (res.), Braz.
63/S7 Saltsjöbaden, Swe.
163/H3 Saluda (riv.), SC,US
112/C3 Salug, Phil.
106/D4 Sālūr, India
77/H5 Salurn (Salorno), It.
137/H2 Salut (isls.), FrG.
78/A3 Saluzzo, It.
143/J7 Salvación (bay), Chile
140/C4 Salvador, Braz.
74/A3 Salvaterra de Magos, Port.
74/A1 Salvatierra de Miño, Sp.
90/J8 Salween (riv.), Asia
87/J5 Sal'yany, Azer.
160/D4 Salyersville, Ky,US
65/H5 Salza (riv.), Aus.
71/F6 Salzach (riv.), Aus., Ger.
67/E4 Salzbergen, Ger.
73/K3 Salzburg, Aus.
73/K3 Salzburg (prov.), Aus.
67/H4 Salzgitter, Ger.
67/G4 Salzhemmendorf, Ger.
67/F5 Salzkotten, Ger.
64/F2 Salzwedel, Ger.
74/C1 Sama, Sp.
110/C4 Samak (cape), Indo.
112/C4 Samales (isls.), Phil.
106/D4 Sāmalkot, India
127/B2 Samālūt, Egypt
150/D3 Samaná, DRep.
150/D3 Samaná (cape), DRep.
108/D2 Samāna, India
149/H1 Samana (Atwood) (cay), Bahm.
91/D1 Samandağı, Turk.
93/N7 Samandira, Turk.
100/C2 Samani, Japan
91/B4 Samannūd, Egypt
112/D3 Samar (isl.), Phil.
112/D2 Samar (sea), Phil.
87/J1 Samara, Rus.
87/K1 Samara (riv.), Rus.
87/J1 Samara Obl., Rus.
78/B1 Samarate, It.
97/M2 Samarga (riv.), Rus.
91/G7 Samaria (reg.), WBnk.
91/G7 Samaria Nat'l Park, WBnk.
81/H5 Samarias Gorge Nat'l Park, Gre.
111/E4 Samarinda, Indo.
88/G6 Samarkand, Uzb.
93/E3 Sāmarrā', Iraq
95/K3 Samasata, Pak.
140/A2 Sambaíba, Braz.
106/D3 Sambalpur, India
126/C2 Samba Lucala, Ang.
133/H7 Sambao (riv.), Madg.
110/D4 Sambar (cape), Indo.
110/C3 Sambas, Indo.
133/J6 Sambava, Madg.
86/B2 Sambor, Ukr.
143/F2 Samborombón (bay), Arg.
143/T12 Samborombón (riv.), Arg.
109/D3 Sambor Prei Kuk (ruins), Camb.
68/C3 Sambre (riv.), Belg.,Fr.
68/C4 Sambre à l'Oise, Canal de (can.), Fr.
130/C3 Samburu, Kenya
130/C2 Samburu Nat'l Rsv., Kenya
101/E4 Samch'ŏk, SKor.
101/E5 Samch'ŏnp'o, SKor.
130/C4 Same, Tanz.
131/C1 Samfya Mission, Zam.
144/C2 Samiria (riv.), Peru
109/C4 Samit (cape), Camb.
109/C3 Samkos (peak), Camb.
165/C2 Sammamish (lake), Wa,US
101/E5 Samnangjin, SKor.
82/B3 Samobor, Cro.
78/D4 Samoggia (riv.), It.
83/F4 Samokov, Bul.
75/Q10 Samora (riv.), Port.
75/Q10 Samora Correia, Port.
81/J2 Samothráki (isl.), Gre.
142/D2 Sampacho, Arg.
110/D4 Sampit, Indo.
110/D4 Sampit (riv.), Indo.
162/E4 Sam Rayburn (res.), Tx,US
109/C1 Sam Sao (mts.), Laos, Viet.
62/D4 Samsø (isl.), Den.
62/D4 Samsø Bælt (chan.), Den.
118/E6 Samson (mtn.), Austl.
109/D2 Sam Son, Viet.
118/E6 Samsonvale (lake), Austl.
92/D1 Samsun, Turk.
92/C1 Samsun (prov.), Turk.
109/B4 Samui (isl.), Thai.
99/H7 Samukawa, Japan
108/B2 Samundri, Pak.
87/J4 Samur (riv.), Azer., Rus.
109/C3 Samut Prakan, Thai.
109/C3 Samut Sakhon, Thai.
109/C3 Samut Songkhram, Thai.
109/D3 San (riv.), Camb.
97/H5 San (riv.), China
128/D3 San, Mali
65/M3 San (riv.), Pol.
82/C3 Sana (riv.), Bosn.
144/B2 Saña, Peru
94/D5 Sanaa (Sana) (cap.), Yem.
74/A1 San Adrián, Cabo de (cape), Sp.
122/D4 Sanaga (riv.), Afr.
112/D4 San Agustin (cape), Phil.
138/B4 San Agustín Archaeological Park, Col.
75/N8 San Agustin de Guadalix, Sp.
151/F5 Sanak (isl.), Ak,US
111/G4 Sanama (isl.), Indo.
134/B5 San Ambrosio (isl.), Chile
93/F3 Sanandaj, Iran
165/K11 San Andreas (lake), Ca,US
149/F3 San Andrés (isl.), Col.
148/B1 San Andrés (lag.), Mex.
112/D2 San Andres, Phil.
158/F4 San Andres (mts.), NM,US
143/S12 San Andrés de Giles, Arg.
74/C1 San Andrés del Rabanedo, Sp.
147/G5 San Andrés Tuxtla, Mex.
141/B3 Sananduva, Braz.
162/C4 San Angelo, Tx,US
165/J11 San Anselmo, Ca,US
149/H4 San Antero, Col.
143/F3 San Antonio (cape), Arg.
142/C2 San Antonio, Chile
138/B4 San Antonio, Ecu.
112/C2 San Antonio, Phil.
164/C2 San Antonio (mtn.), Ca,US
158/F4 San Antonio, NM,US
162/D4 San Antonio, Tx,US
162/D4 San Antonio (riv.), Tx,US
75/F3 San Antonio Abad, Sp.
149/E1 San Antonio, Cabo de (cape), Cuba
147/M8 San Antonio Cañada, Mex.
142/F2 San Antonio de Areco, Arg.
139/F2 San Antonio del Golfo, Ven.
138/C3 San Antonio del Táchira, Ven.
142/D4 San Antonio Oeste, Arg.
146/B2 San Antonio, Punta (pt.), Mex.
162/E4 San Augustine, Tx,US
108/D2 Sanaur, India
106/C3 Sanāwad, India
80/D2 San Bartolomeo in Galdo, It.
79/E5 San Benedetto (mts.), It.
80/C1 San Benedetto del Tronto, It.
146/C5 San Benedicto (isl.), Mex.
147/R10 San Bernardino (riv.), Mex.
112/D2 San Bernardino (str.), Phil.
164/C2 San Bernardino, Ca,US
164/C2 San Bernardino (co.), Ca,US
164/C2 San Bernardino (mts.), Ca,US
147/L7 San Bernardino Contla, Mex.
164/C2 San Bernardino Nat'l For., Ca,US
142/C2 San Bernardo, Chile
138/C2 San Bernardo (pt.), Col.
146/C3 San Blas, Mex.
163/G4 San Blas (cape), Fl,US
162/E3 San Bois (mts.), Ok,US
79/E2 San Bonifacio, It.
136/E6 San Borja, Bol.
161/S9 Sanborn, NY,US
165/K11 San Bruno, Ca,US
164/A2 San Buenaventura (Ventura), Ca,US
142/C3 San Carlos, Chile
112/C2 San Carlos, Phil.
143/G2 San Carlos, Uru.
158/E4 San Carlos (lake), Az,US
165/K11 San Carlos, Ca,US
138/D2 San Carlos, Ven.
142/C4 San Carlos de Bariloche, Arg.
138/D2 San Carlos del Zulia, Ven.
79/E5 San Casciano in Val di Pesa, It.
81/F2 San Cataldo, It.
104/E3 Sancha (riv.), China
146/E4 Sánchez Román, Mex.
142/C2 San Clemente, Chile
74/D3 San Clemente, Sp.
164/C4 San Clemente, Ca,US
158/C4 San Clemente (isl.), Ca,US
78/C2 San Colombano al Lambro, It.
135/D3 San Cristóbal, Arg.
149/F1 San Cristóbal, Cuba
150/D3 San Cristóbal, DRep.
144/K7 San Cristóbal (isl.), Ecu.
148/E3 San Cristobal (vol.), Nic.
120/F6 San Cristobal (isl.), Sol.
146/B1 San Cristobal (cr.), Az,US
138/C3 San Cristóbal, Ven.
148/C2 San Cristóbal de las Casas, Mex.
149/G1 Sancti Spíritus, Cuba
156/F2 Sand (riv.), Ab,Can
132/D3 Sand (riv.), SAfr.
58/D4 Sand (pt.), Eng,UK
159/G2 Sand (hills), Ne,US
98/D3 Sanda, Japan
56/C1 Sanda (isl.), Sc,UK
109/D3 Sandan, Camb.
83/F5 Sandanski, Bul.
55/N13 Sanday (isl.), Sc,UK
57/F5 Sandbach, Eng,UK
67/F2 Sande, Ger.
62/D2 Sandefjord, Nor.
113/Q Sanders (coast), Ant.
162/C4 Sanderson, Tx,US
163/H3 Sandersville, Ga,US
118/F6 Sandgate, Austl.
56/D2 Sandhead, Sc,UK
161/Q8 Sandhill, On,Can
59/F4 Sandhurst, Eng,UK
143/L8 San Diego (cape), Arg.
164/C5 San Diego, Ca,US
164/C4 San Diego (aqueduct), Ca,US
164/C5 San Diego (bay), Ca,US
164/C4 San Diego (co.), Ca,US
164/C5 San Diego (riv.), Ca,US
162/D5 San Diego, Tx,US
164/C4 San Diego Wild Animal Park, Ca,US
164/C5 San Diego Zoo, Ca,US
164/C5 San Dieguito (riv.), Ca,US
92/B2 Sandıklı, Turk.
164/C2 San Dimas, Ca,US
80/D4 San Dimitri, Ras (pt.), Malta
111/E3 Sandkan, Malay.
62/A2 Sandnes, Nor.
61/E2 Sandnessjøen, Nor.
126/D2 Sandoa, Zaire
65/L3 Sandomierz, Pol.
138/B4 Sandoná, Col.
79/F1 San Donà di Piave, It.
128/B3 Sandougou (riv.), Gam., Sen.
117/G2 Sandover (riv.), Austl.
59/E5 Sandown, Eng,UK
156/D3 Sandpoint, Id,US
119/F5 Sandringham, Austl.
59/G1 Sandringham, Eng,UK
131/C4 Sandrivier (riv.), SAfr.
167/L8 Sands (pt.), NY,US
105/E3 Sandu Shuizu Zizhixian, China
160/D3 Sandusky, Mi,US
160/D3 Sandusky, Oh,US
62/D2 Sandvika, Nor.
62/G1 Sandviken, Swe.
118/B2 Sandwich (cape), Austl.
59/H4 Sandwich, Eng,UK
118/D4 Sandy (cape), Austl.
157/K2 Sandy (lake), On,Can
59/F2 Sandy, Eng,UK
168/F6 Sandy (cr.), Oh,US
168/H5 Sandy (cr.), Pa,US
168/C3 Sandy (pt.), RI,US
158/E2 Sandy, Ut,US
157/H2 Sandy Bay, Sk,Can
167/D3 Sandy Hook (bay), NJ,US
167/J10 Sandy Hook (pen.), NJ,US
167/D3 Sandy Hook Lighthouse, NJ,US
163/G3 Sandy Springs, Ga,US
69/E4 Sanem, Lux.
80/C2 San Felice Circeo, It.
142/C2 San Felipe, Chile
147/E4 San Felipe, Mex.
138/D2 San Felipe, Ven.
144/A2 San Felipe de Vichayal, Peru
134/A5 San Félix (isl.), Chile
143/S12 San Fernando, Arg.
142/C2 San Fernando, Chile
147/F3 San Fernando, Mex.
112/C1 San Fernando, Phil.
112/C2 San Fernando, Phil.
74/B4 San Fernando, Sp.
150/F5 San Fernando, Trin.
164/B2 San Fernando, Ca,US
164/B2 San Fernando (val.), Ca,US
139/E3 San Fernando de Apure, Ven.
75/N9 San Fernando-de-Henares, Sp.
61/E3 Sånfjällets Nat'l Park, Swe.
151/K3 Sanford (mtn.), Ak,US
163/H4 Sanford, Fl,US
161/G3 Sanford, Me,US
163/J3 Sanford, NC,US
135/D3 San Francisco, Arg.
112/D3 San Francisco, Phil.
158/E4 San Francisco (riv.), Az, NM,US
165/K11 San Francisco, Ca,US
165/K11 San Francisco (bay), Ca,US
165/K11 San Francisco (co.), Ca,US
138/D2 San Francisco, Ven.
165/K11 San Francisco Bay Nat'l Wild. Ref., Ca,US
138/A4 San Francisco, Cabo de (cape), Ecu.
150/D3 San Francisco de Macorís, DRep.
142/C2 San Francisco de Mostazal, Chile
138/B4 San Gabriel, Ecu.
164/B2 San Gabriel, Ca,US
164/B2 San Gabriel (mts.), Ca,US
164/C2 San Gabriel (res.), Ca,US
164/C2 San Gabriel (riv.), Ca,US
147/M8 San Gabriel Chilac, Mex.
146/B2 San Gabriel, Punta (pt.), Mex.
164/C2 San Gabriel, West Fork (riv.), Ca,US
164/C2 San Gabriel Wilderness, Ca,US
106/B4 Sangamner, India
160/B3 Sangamon (riv.), Il,US
95/H2 Sangān (mtn.), Afg.
138/B5 Sangay (vol.), Ecu.
138/B5 Sangay Nat'l Park, Ecu.
130/A3 Sange, Zaire
74/A1 Sangenjo, Sp.
149/G1 San Germán, Cuba
103/C2 Sanggan (riv.), China
110/D3 Sanggau, Indo.
101/B4 Sanggou (bay), China
124/J7 Sangha (riv.), CAfr., Congo
95/J3 Sanghar, Pak.
112/D5 Sangihe (isl.), Indo.
120/B4 Sangihe (isls.), Indo.
138/C3 San Gil, Col.
80/E2 San Giorgio Ionico, It.
80/C4 San Giovanni Gemini, It.
80/E3 San Giovanni in Fiore, It.
79/E3 San Giovanni in Persiceto, It.
79/E2 San Giovanni Lupatoto, It.
79/E5 San Giovanni Valdarno, It.
96/D2 Sangiyn Dalay (lake), Mong.
101/E4 Sangju, SKor.
111/E3 Sangkulirang, Indo.
108/B2 Sāngla, Pak.
112/E6 Sangley Point Nav. Air Sta., Phil.
106/B4 Sāngli, India
124/H7 Sangmélima, Camr.
99/L10 Sangō, Japan
158/C4 San Gorgonio (peak), Ca,US
104/B3 Sangpang (mts.), Burma
159/F3 Sangre de Cristo (mts.), Co, NM,US
150/F5 Sangre Grande, Trin.
107/F2 Sangri, China
80/D2 Sangro (riv.), It.
108/C2 Sangrūr, India
136/G6 Sangue (riv.), Braz.
129/E4 Sanguie (prov.), Burk.
78/C2 San Guiliano Milanese, It.
103/D3 Sanhe, China
146/B3 San Hipólito, Punta (pt.), Mex.
132/E3 Sani (pass), SAfr.
148/D2 San Ignacio, Belz.
136/E6 San Ignacio, Bol.
136/F7 San Ignacio, Bol.
142/B3 San Ignacio, Chile
146/B2 San Ignacio (riv.), Mex.
112/C1 San Ildefonso (cape), Phil.
98/D3 San'in Kaigin Nat'l Park, Japan
149/F4 San Isidro, CR
148/D2 San Isidro, Mex.
148/E3 San Isidro, Nic.
138/C2 San Jacinto, Col.
112/C2 San Jacinto, Phil.
164/C3 San Jacinto (riv.), Ca,US
142/C2 San Javier, Chile
75/E4 San Javier, Sp.
131/B2 Sanje, Zam.
99/F2 Sanjō, Japan
136/F6 San Joaquín, Bol.
144/K7 San Joaquín (peak), Ecu.
148/C2 San Joaquín, Mex.
165/M11 San Joaquin (co.), Ca,US
164/G8 San Joaquin (hills), Ca,US
165/L10 San Joaquin (riv.), Ca,US
158/B3 San Joaquin (val.), Ca,US
142/E1 San Jorge, Arg.
142/D5 San Jorge (cape), Arg.
142/D5 San Jorge (gulf), Arg.
138/C3 San Jorge (riv.), Col.
146/B2 San Jorge (bay), Mex.
148/E4 San Jorge, Nic.
75/F2 San Jorge (gulf), Sp.
142/D4 San José (gulf), Arg.
149/E4 San José (cap.), CR
148/D3 San José, Guat.
146/C3 San José (isl.), Mex.
144/B2 San José, Peru
112/C2 San Jose, Phil.
75/F3 San José, Sp.
143/F2 San José (dept.), Uru.
143/T11 San José (riv.), Uru.
165/L12 San Jose, Ca,US
164/G7 San Jose (hills), Ca,US
112/C3 San Jose de Buenavista, Phil.
136/F7 San José de Chiquitos, Bol.
139/E2 San José de Guanipa, Ven.
139/E2 San José de Guaribe, Ven.
135/C3 San José de Jáchal, Arg.
112/F6 San Jose del Monte, Phil.
144/C4 San José de Los Molinos, Peru
142/Q9 San José de Maipo, Chile
143/F2 San José de Mayo, Uru.
147/E4 San José Iturbide, Mex.
142/C1 San Juan, Arg.
143/M8 San Juan (cape), Arg.
142/C1 San Juan (prov.), Arg.
135/C3 San Juan (riv.), Arg.
138/B3 San Juan (riv.), Col.
149/E4 San Juan (riv.), CR, Nic.
150/D3 San Juan, DRep.
148/D3 San Juan (pt.), ESal.
112/C2 San Juan, Phil.
112/F6 San Juan (riv.), Phil.
150/E3 San Juan (cap.), PR
164/C3 San Juan (cr.), Ca,US
158/F3 San Juan (mts.), Co,US
158/E3 San Juan (riv.), Co, Ut,US
162/A2 San Juan (basin), NM,US
135/E2 San Juan Bautista, Par.
164/C3 San Juan Capistrano, Ca,US
75/E3 San Juan de Alicante, Sp.
74/B4 San Juan de Aznalfarache, Sp.
146/D5 San Juan de Lima, Punta (pt.), Mex.
112/F6 San Juan del Monte, Phil.
139/E2 San Juan de los Morros, Ven.
146/B3 San Juanico, Punta (pt.), Mex.
147/M8 San Juan Ixcaquixtla, Mex.
147/M7 San Juan Ixtenco, Mex.
147/R9 San Juan Teotihuacan, Mex.
143/K7 San Julián, Gran Bajo de (val.), Arg.
135/D3 San Justo, Arg.
128/C4 Sankanbiriwa (peak), SLeo.
108/F4 Sankaranāyinarkovil, India
128/C4 Sankoroni (riv.), Gui., Mali
73/L3 Sankt Andrä, Aus.
69/G2 Sankt Augustin, Ger.
77/F3 Sankt Gallen, Swi.
77/F3 Sankt Gallen (canton), Swi.
70/B6 Sankt Georgen im Schwarzwald, Ger.
77/G5 Sankt Gertraud (Santa Gertrude), It.
69/G5 Sankt Ingbert, Ger.
77/H4 Sankt Jakob (San Giacomo), It.
73/K3 Sankt Johann im Pongau, Aus.
73/K3 Sankt Johann in Tirol, Aus.
77/H4 Sankt Leonhard in Passeier (San Leonardo in Passiria), It.
77/H4 Sankt Martin in Passeier (San Martino in Passiria), It.
77/H5 Sankt Michael (San Michele), It.
76/D5 Sankt Niklaus, Swi.
73/L2 Sankt Pölten, Aus.
73/L3 Sankt Veit an der Glan, Aus.
69/G5 Sankt Wendel, Ger.
146/B3 San Lázaro, Cabo (cape), Mex.
79/E4 San Lazzaro, It.
165/K11 San Leandro, Ca,US
165/K11 San Leandro (res.), Ca,US
136/E6 San Lorenzo, Bol.
143/J6 San Lorenzo (peak), Chile
138/B4 San Lorenzo, Ecu.
136/B4 San Lorenzo (cape), Ecu.
148/E3 San Lorenzo, Hon.
80/A3 San Lorenzo (cape), It.
146/D3 San Lorenzo (riv.), Mex.
148/E3 San Lorenzo, Nic.
165/K11 San Lorenzo, Ca,US
74/C2 San Lorenzo de El Escorial, Sp.
74/B4 Sanlúcar de Barrameda, Sp.
148/E3 San Lucas, Nic.
146/C4 San Lucas, Cabo (cape), Mex.
142/D2 San Luis, Arg.
142/D2 San Luis (mts.), Arg.
142/D2 San Luis (prov.), Arg.
149/H1 San Luis, Cuba
148/D2 San Luis, Guat.
162/B2 San Luis (val.), Co,US
147/E4 San Luis de la Paz, Mex.
158/B4 San Luis Obispo, Ca,US
147/E4 San Luis Potosí, Mex.
147/E4 San Luis Potosí (state), Mex.
164/C4 San Luis Rey (riv.), Ca,US
158/E4 San Manuel, Az,US
138/C2 San Marcos, Col.
148/D3 San Marcos, Guat.
164/C4 San Marcos, Ca,US
162/D4 San Marcos, Tx,US
79/G5 San Maria di Porto Novo, It.
112/C1 San Mariano, Phil.
79/F5 San Marino
79/F5 San Marino (cap.), SMar.
164/F7 San Marino, Ca,US
142/C2 San Martín, Arg.
143/J7 San Martín (lake), Arg.
136/F6 San Martín (riv.), Bol.
138/C4 San Martín, Col.
147/L7 San Martín de las Pirámides, Mex.
142/C4 San Martín de los Andes, Arg.
144/B2 San Martín-La Libertad (dept.), Peru
79/E2 San Martino Buon Albergo, It.
79/E1 San Martino di Lupari, It.
147/L7 San Martín Texmelucan, Mex.
129/E3 Sanmatenga (prov.), Burk.
112/F6 San Mateo, Phil.
165/K11 San Mateo, Ca,US
165/K12 San Mateo (co.), Ca,US
164/C4 San Mateo (cr.), Ca,US
162/B3 San Mateo (mts.), NM,US
147/K7 San Mateo Atenco, Mex.
142/D4 San Matías (gulf), Arg.
136/G7 San Matías, Bol.
147/L7 San Matías Tlalancaleca, Mex.
78/A2 San Mauro Torinese, It.

Sanm – Sawm

103/B4 Sanmenxia, China
77/H5 San Michele (Sankt Michael), It.
136/F6 San Miguel (riv.), Bol.
138/B4 San Miguel (riv.), Col., Ecu.
148/D3 San Miguel, ESal.
149/G4 San Miguel (gulf), Pan.
112/C2 San Miguel (bay), Phil.
147/E4 San Miguel de Allende, Mex.
142/F2 San Miguel del Monte, Arg.
138/B4 San Miguel de los Bancos, Ecu.
135/C2 San Miguel de Tucumán, Arg.
147/L6 San Miguel Regla, Mex.
147/K8 San Miguel Totomaloya, Mex.
147/K7 San Miguel Zinacantepec, Mex.
105/H3 Sanming, China
79/D5 San Miniato, It.
99/L9 Sannan, Japan
125/M5 Sannār, Sudan
80/D2 Sannicandro Garganico, It.
158/C4 San Nicolas (isl.), Ca,US
142/E2 San Nicolás de los Arroyos, Arg.
147/M7 San Nicolás Terrenate, Mex.
147/E4 San Nicolás Tolentino, Mex.
89/P2 Sannikova (str.), Rus.
100/B3 Sannohe, Japan
53/S10 Sannois, Fr.
99/F2 Sano, Japan
65/M4 Sanok, Pol.
138/C2 San Onofre, Col.
164/C4 San Onofre (mtn.), Ca,US
142/B4 San Pablo, Chile
165/K11 San Pablo, Ca,US
165/K10 San Pablo (bay), Ca,US
165/K11 San Pablo (res.), Ca,US
165/K10 San Pablo Bay Nat'l Wild. Ref., Ca,US
112/C2 San Pablo City, Phil.
112/C2 San Pascual, Phil.
142/F2 San Pedro, Arg.
142/C2 San Pedro, Chile
135/C1 San Pedro (vol.), Chile
149/G1 San Pedro (riv.), Cuba
148/D2 San Pedro (riv.), Guat., Mex.
128/D5 San Pédro, IvC.
146/D3 San Pedro (riv.), Mex.
135/E1 San Pedro, Par.
74/B3 San Pedro (range), Sp.
158/E4 San Pedro (riv.), Az,US
164/F8 San Pedro, Ca,US
164/B3 San Pedro (bay), Ca,US
164/B3 San Pedro (chan.), Ca,US
148/D3 San Pedro Carchá, Guat.
144/C3 San Pedro de Cajas, Peru
146/E3 San Pedro de las Colinas, Mex.
144/B2 San Pedro de Lloc, Peru
75/E4 San Pedro del Pinatar, Sp.
150/D3 San Pedro de Macorís, DRep.
146/B2 San Pedro Martir (mts.), Mex.
148/D3 San Pedro Sula, Hon.
80/A3 San Pietro (isl.), It.
54/C6 Sanquhar, Sc,UK
138/B4 Sanquianga Nat'l Park, Col.
146/B2 San Quintín, Cabo (cape), Mex.
142/C2 San Rafael, Arg.
147/H4 San Rafael, Mex.
165/J11 San Rafael, Ca,US
164/F7 San Rafael (hills), Ca,US
158/E3 San Rafael (riv.), Ut,US
149/J4 San Rafael, Ven.
138/D2 San Rafael del Moján, Ven.
149/E4 San Ramón, CR
144/C3 San Ramón, Peru
149/G2 San Ramón, Uru.
165/L11 San Ramon, Ca,US
135/D1 San Ramón de la Nueva Orán, Arg.
78/A5 San Remo, It.
150/D4 San Román (cape), Ven.
74/C4 San Roque, Sp.
142/B3 San Rosendo, Chile
162/D4 San Saba, Tx,US
159/H5 San Saba (riv.), Tx,US
150/C1 San Salvador (isl.), Bahm.
144/J7 San Salvador (isl.), Ecu.
148/D3 San Salvador (cap.), ESal.
143/S11 San Salvador (riv.), Uru.
135/C1 San Salvador de Jujuy, Arg.
147/M7 San Salvador el Seco, Mex.
147/M8 San Salvador Huixcolotla, Mex.
80/D1 San Salvo, It.
74/E1 San Sebastián, Sp.
74/D2 San Sebastián de los Reyes, Sp.
148/E3 San Sebastían de Yali, Nic.
78/D1 San Sebastiano, It.
79/F5 Sansepolcro, It.
80/D2 San Severo, It.
105/F3 Sansui, China
96/F2 Sant, Mong.
144/B3 Santa, Peru
144/B3 Santa (riv.), Peru
136/E6 Santa Ana, Bol.
136/E7 Santa Ana, Bol.
138/A5 Santa Ana, Ecu.
148/D3 Santa Ana, ESal.
148/D3 Santa Ana (vol.), ESal.
146/C2 Santa Ana, Mex.
164/C3 Santa Ana, Ca,US
164/C3 Santa Ana (mts.), Ca,US
164/C3 Santa Ana (riv.), Ca,US
147/L7 Santa Ana Chiautempan, Mex.
138/D2 Santa Ana, Falcón, Ven.
138/D2 Santa Ana, Trujillo, Ven.
141/D1 Santa Bárbara, Braz.
142/B3 Santa Bárbara, Chile
138/C3 Santa Bárbara, Col.
148/D3 Santa Bárbara, Hon.
112/C2 Santa Barbara, Phil.
164/A2 Santa Barbara, Ca,US
164/A2 Santa Barbara (chan.), Ca,US
164/A1 Santa Barbara (co.), Ca,US
138/D3 Santa Bárbara, Ven.
141/C2 Santa Bárbara d'Oeste, Braz.
112/C3 Santa Catalina, Phil.
164/C4 Santa Catalina (gulf), Ca,US
164/B4 Santa Catalina (isl.), Ca,US
141/B3 Santa Catarina (isl.), Braz.
141/B3 Santa Catarina (state), Braz.
141/B3 Santa Cecília, Braz.
147/Q9 Santa Cecilia Pyramid, Mex.
149/G1 Santa Clara, Cuba
74/A4 Santa Clara (res.), Port.
165/L12 Santa Clara, Ca,US
165/L12 Santa Clara (co.), Ca,US
164/B2 Santa Clara (riv.), Ca,US
75/G2 Santa Coloma de Farners, Sp.
75/L7 Santa Coloma de Gramanet, Sp.
74/A1 Santa Comba, Sp.
79/D5 Santa Croce sull'Arno, It.
143/K7 Santa Cruz (prov.), Arg.
143/K7 Santa Cruz (riv.), Arg.
136/F7 Santa Cruz, Bol.
142/C2 Santa Cruz, Braz.
142/C2 Santa Cruz, Chile
148/E4 Santa Cruz, CR
144/J7 Santa Cruz (isl.), Ecu.
112/B2 Santa Cruz, Phil.
112/C1 Santa Cruz, Phil.
112/C2 Santa Cruz, Phil.
112/D4 Santa Cruz, Phil.
120/F6 Santa Cruz (isls.), Sol.
158/E5 Santa Cruz (dry riv.), Az,US
158/B3 Santa Cruz, Ca,US
164/A2 Santa Cruz (isl.), Ca,US
75/S12 Santa Cruz da Graciosa, Azor.,Port.
75/R12 Santa Cruz das Flores, Azor.,Port.
140/C4 Santa Cruz da Vitória, Braz.
148/D3 Santa Cruz del Quiché, Guat.
75/X16 Santa Cruz de Tenerife, Canl
149/G1 Santa Cruz del Sur, Cuba
140/C2 Santa Cruz do Capibaribe, Braz.
140/B2 Santa Cruz do Piauí, Braz.
141/B2 Santa Cruz do Rio Pardo, Braz.
135/F2 Santa Cruz do Sul, Braz.
148/D3 Santa Cruz, Sierra de (range), Guat.
148/B2 Santa Cruz Zenzontepec, Mex.
75/L7 Sant Adrià de Besòs, Sp.
142/D5 Santa Elena (peak), Arg.
148/E4 Santa Elena (bay), CR
148/E4 Santa Elena (cape), CR
138/A5 Santa Elena, Ecu.
146/E3 Santa Elena, Mex.
74/A1 Santa Eugenia de Ribeira, Sp.
75/F3 Santa Eulalia del Río, Sp.
142/E1 Santa Fé, Arg.
142/E2 Santa Fé (prov.), Arg.
74/D4 Santa Fé, Sp.
163/H4 Santa Fe (riv.), Fl,US
159/F4 Santa Fe (cap.), NM,US
141/B2 Santa Fe do Sul, Braz.
164/B2 Santa Felicia (dam), Ca,US
164/F8 Santa Fe Springs, Ca,US
80/D3 Sant'Agata di Militello, It.
77/G5 Santa Gertrude (Sankt Gertraud), It.
77/H5 Santa Giustina (lake), It.
140/A1 Santa Helena, Braz.
141/B1 Santa Helena de Goiás, Braz.
140/A1 Santa Inês, Braz.
140/C4 Santa Inês, Braz.
143/J8 Santa Inés (isl.), Chile
147/L7 Santa Inés Zacatelco, Mex.
141/G8 Santa Isabel, Braz.
144/B1 Santa Isabel, Ecu.
148/D2 Santa Isabel (riv.), Guat.
120/E5 Santa Isabel (isl.), Sol.
124/G7 Santa Isabel, Pico de (peak), EqG.
141/C1 Santa Juliana, Braz.
138/B5 Santa Lucía, Ecu.
143/F2 Santa Lucía, Uru.
143/G2 Santa Lucía (riv.), Uru.
140/C3 Santa Luz, Braz.
140/A1 Santa Luzia, Braz.
140/C2 Santa Luzia, Braz.
141/D1 Santa Luzia, Braz.
122/J10 Santa Luzia (isl.), CpV.
142/E2 Santa Magdalena, Arg.
146/B3 Santa Magdalena (isl.), Mex.
146/B3 Santa Margarita (isl.), Mex.
164/C4 Santa Margarita (riv.), Ca,US
78/C4 Santa Margherita Ligure, It.
135/F2 Santa Maria, Braz.
140/A4 Santa Maria (hills), Braz.
142/C2 Santa María, Chile
142/B3 Santa María (isl.), Chile
144/J7 Santa María (isl.), Ecu.
147/L7 Santa Mariá, Mex.
146/C3 Santa María (bay), Mex.
146/D2 Santa María (riv.), Mex.
148/A1 Santa María (riv.), Mex.
112/C1 Santa Maria, Phil.
112/D4 Santa Maria, Phil.
75/T13 Santa Maria (isl.), Azor.,Port.
158/B4 Santa Maria, Ca,US
131/D5 Santa Maria, Cabo de (cape), Moz.
74/B4 Santa Maria, Cabo de (cape), Port.
80/D2 Santa Maria Capua Vetere, It.
140/C3 Santa Maria da Boa Vista, Braz.
140/A4 Santa Maria da Vitória, Braz.
81/F3 Santa Maria di Leuca (cape), It.
141/D1 Santa Maria do Suaçi, Braz.
148/B3 Santa María Huatulco, Mex.
138/C2 Santa Marta, Col.
141/B4 Santa Marta Grande, Cabo de (cape), Braz.
138/C2 Santa Marta, Nevada de (mts.), Col.
164/B2 Santa Monica, Ca,US
164/B3 Santa Monica (bay), Ca,US
164/B2 Santa Monica (mts.), Ca,US
164/B2 Santa Monica Mts. Nat'l Rec. Area, Ca,US
140/A4 Santana, Braz.
140/B1 Santana (isl.), Braz.
75/P11 Santana, Port.
75/V15 Santana, Madr.,Port.
140/B1 Santana do Acaraú, Braz.
140/C2 Santana do Cariri, Braz.
140/C3 Santana do Ipanema, Braz.
135/E3 Santana do Livramento, Braz.
138/B4 Santander, Col.
138/C3 Santander (dept.), Col.
112/C3 Santander, Phil.
74/D1 Santander, Sp.
78/C2 Sant'Angelo Lodigiano, It.
80/A3 Sant'Antioco, It.
80/A3 Sant'Antioco (isl.), It.
79/D2 Sant'Antonio, It.
164/A2 Santa Paula, Ca,US
164/A2 Santa Paula (peak), Ca,US
75/E3 Santa Pola, Sp.
75/E3 Santa Pola, Cabo de (cape), Sp.
79/F4 Sant'Apollinare in Classe, It.
140/B2 Santa Quitéria, Braz.
140/B1 Santa Quitéria do Maranhão, Braz.
79/F4 Santarcángelo, It.
139/H5 Santarém, Braz.
74/A3 Santarém, Port.
74/A3 Santarém (dist.), Port.
140/A2 Santa Rita, Braz.
140/D2 Santa Rita, Braz.
138/D2 Santa Rita, Ven.
140/A3 Santa Rita de Cássia, Braz.
141/H7 Santa Rita do Sapucaí, Braz.
142/D3 Santa Rosa, Arg.
142/D4 Santa Rosa (val.), Arg.
135/F2 Santa Rosa, Braz.
144/B1 Santa Rosa, Ecu.
147/F4 Santa Rosa, Mex.
158/B3 Santa Rosa, Ca,US
158/B4 Santa Rosa (isl.), Ca,US
159/F4 Santa Rosa, NM,US
158/C2 Santa Rosa (range), Nv,US
142/D2 Santa Rosa de Calamuchita, Arg.
148/D3 Santa Rosa de Copán, Hon.
138/C3 Santa Rosa de Osos, Col.
141/C2 Santa Rosa de Viterbo, Braz.
146/B3 Santa Rosalía, Mex.
138/D2 Santa Rosalía, Ven.
146/B2 Santa Rosalia, Punta (pt.), Mex.
148/E4 Santa Rosa Nat'l Park, CR
164/B2 Santa Susana (mts.), Ca,US
137/J6 Santa Teresa (riv.), Braz.
117/G2 Santa Teresa Abor. Land, Austl.
143/G2 Santa Teresa Nat'l Park, Uru.
137/H6 Santa Teresinha, Braz.
143/F3 Santa Teresita, Arg.
141/B1 Santa Vitória, Braz.
143/G2 Santa Vitória do Palmar, Braz.
164/A2 Santa Ynez (mts.), Ca,US
164/A1 Santa Ynez (riv.), Ca,US
75/L7 Sant Boi de Llobregat, Sp.
75/F2 Sant Carles de la Ràpita, Sp.
75/G2 Sant Celoni, Sp.
75/G2 Sant Cugat del Vallès, Sp.
164/D5 Santee, Ca,US
163/H3 Santee (dam), SC,US
163/J3 Santee (riv.), SC,US
146/E5 San Telmo, Punta (pt.), Mex.
78/A3 Santena, It.
79/E4 Santerno (riv.), It.
80/D3 Sant'Eufemia (gulf), It.
75/L7 Sant Feliu, Sp.
75/G2 Sant Feliu de Guíxols, Sp.
75/G2 Sant Feliu de Llobregat, Sp.
75/F1 Sant Gervàs (peak), Sp.
78/B2 Santhia, It.
135/F2 Santiago, Braz.
142/C2 Santiago (cap.), Chile
143/J7 Santiago (cape), Chile
150/D3 Santiago, DRep.
144/B1 Santiago (riv.), Ecu., Peru
147/E3 Santiago, Mex.
162/B5 Santiago (riv.), Mex.
149/F4 Santiago, Pan.
149/F4 Santiago (mtn.), Pan.
112/C1 Santiago, Phil.
164/C3 Santiago (peak), Ca,US
164/C3 Santiago (res.), Ca,US
162/C4 Santiago (mts.), Tx,US
144/B2 Santiago de Cao, Peru
74/A1 Santiago de Compostela, Sp.
149/H1 Santiago de Cuba, Cuba
135/D2 Santiago del Estero, Arg.
146/D4 Santiago Ixcuintla, Mex.
148/B2 Santiago Jocotepec, Mex.
147/M8 Santiago Miahuatlán, Mex.
146/D3 Santiago Papasquiaro, Mex.
142/Q9 Santiago, Región Metropolitana de (reg.), Chile
147/G5 Santiago Tuxtla, Mex.
78/D3 Sant'Ilario d'Enza, It.
77/F3 Säntis (peak), Swi.
75/K6 Sant Jeroni (mtn.), Sp.
75/K6 Sant Llorenc del Munt Nat'l Park, Sp.
99/K9 Santō, Japan
140/C4 Santo Amaro, Braz.
141/G8 Santo Amaro (isl.), Braz.
140/C3 Santo Amaro das Brotas, Braz.
141/B2 Santo Anastácio, Braz.
141/G8 Santo André, Braz.
135/F2 Santo Ângelo, Braz.
122/J9 Santo Antão (isl.), CpV.
124/G7 Santo António, SaoT.
140/C4 Santo Antônio de Jesus, Braz.
141/D2 Santo Antônio de Pádua, Braz.
140/B5 Santo Antônio do Jacinto, Braz.
140/A2 Santo Antônio dos Lopes, Braz.
149/F1 Santo Domingo, Cuba
150/D3 Santo Domingo (cap.), DRep.
138/B5 Santo Domingo de los Colorados, Ecu.
146/B3 Santo Domingo, Punta (pt.), Mex.
140/C4 Santo Estêvão, Braz.
135/E3 Santo Grande (res.), Uru.
75/E3 Santomera, Sp.
74/D1 Santoña, Sp.
140/B4 Santo Onofre (riv.), Braz.
81/J4 Santorini (Thíra), Gre.
141/G8 Santos, Braz.
141/K6 Santos Dumont, Braz.
144/J7 Santo Tomás (vol.), Ecu.
112/C1 Santo Tomas (mtn.), Phil.
146/A2 Santo Tomás, Punta (pt.), Mex.
142/E1 Santo Tomé, Arg.
75/K7 Sant Pere de Ribes, Sp.
75/K7 Sant Sadurní d'Anoia, Sp.
78/B2 Santuario di Crea, It.
78/A1 Santuario di Oropa, It.
74/D1 Santurce-Antiguo, Sp.
75/K6 Sant Vincenç de Castellet, Sp.
75/L7 Sant Vincenç dels Hort, Sp.
142/B5 San Valentín (peak), Chile
142/C2 San Vicente, Chile
148/D3 San Vicente, ESal.
164/D5 San Vicente (res.), Ca,US
74/B3 San Vicente de Alcántara, Sp.
144/B4 San Vicente de Cañete, Peru
75/E3 San Vicente del Raspeig, Sp.
79/G6 San Vicino, Monte (peak), It.
80/B1 San Vincenzo, It.
80/C3 San Vito (cape), It.
79/F1 San Vito al Tagliamento, It.
105/F5 Sanya, China
131/C3 Sanyati (riv.), Zim.
140/B2 São Benedito, Braz.
140/B1 São Benedito do Rio Prêto, Braz.
140/A1 São Bento, Braz.
141/H7 São Bento do Sapucaí, Braz.
140/C3 São Bento do Una, Braz.
141/G8 São Bernardo do Campo, Braz.
135/E2 São Borja, Braz.
141/C2 São Carlos, Braz.
140/C3 São Cristóvão, Braz.
140/A4 São Desidério, Braz.
140/A4 São Desidério (riv.), Braz.
140/A4 São Domingos, Braz.
140/A4 São Domingos (riv.), Braz.
141/B1 São Domingos (riv.), Braz.
140/A2 São Domingos do Maranhão, Braz.
137/H5 São Félix do Xingu, Braz.
141/D2 São Fidélis, Braz.
140/A4 São Francisco, Braz.
135/G2 São Francisco (isl.), Braz.
140/B3 São Francisco (mts.), Braz.
137/L5 São Francisco (riv.), Braz.
141/B3 São Francisco do Sul, Braz.
141/B4 São Fransisco de Paula, Braz.
135/F3 São Gabriel, Braz.
141/D1 São Gabriel da Palha, Braz.
141/K7 São Gonçalo, Braz.
141/C1 São Gonçalo do Abaeté, Braz.
141/H6 São Gonçalo do Sapucaí, Braz.
141/C1 São Gotardo, Braz.
130/B5 Sao Hill, Tanz.
141/C2 São Joachim da Barra, Braz.
137/K4 São João, Braz.
136/F5 São João (mts.), Braz.
140/A1 São João Batista, Braz.
141/B3 São João Batista, Braz.
141/D2 São João da Barra, Braz.
141/G6 São João da Boa Vista, Braz.
74/A2 São João da Madeira, Port.
140/A4 São João da Ponte, Braz.
75/P10 São João das Lampas, Port.
141/C2 São João del Rei, Braz.
141/K7 São João de Meriti, Braz.
140/B4 São João do Paraíso, Braz.
140/B3 São João do Piauí, Braz.
140/B2 São João dos Patos, Braz.
141/D1 São João Evangelista, Braz.
141/K6 São João Nepomuceno, Braz.
141/B4 São Joaquim, Braz.
141/B4 São Joaquim Nat'l Park, Braz.
75/S12 São Jorge (isl.), Azor.,Port.
141/B3 São José, Braz.
140/D2 São José de Mipibu, Braz.
140/C2 São José de Piranhas, Braz.
140/A1 São José de Ribamar, Braz.
140/C2 São José do Belmonte, Braz.
140/D2 São José do Campestre, Braz.
140/C2 São José do Egito, Braz.
141/A5 São José do Norte, Braz.
141/G6 São José do Rio Pardo, Braz.
141/B2 São José do Rio Preto, Braz.
141/H8 São José dos Campos, Braz.
141/B3 São José dos Pinhais, Braz.
141/B4 São Leopoldo, Braz.
141/H7 São Lourenço, Braz.
137/G7 São Lourenço (riv.), Braz.
75/Q10 São Lourenço, Port.
141/B4 São Lourenço do Sul, Braz.
126/C3 São Lucas, Ang.
140/A1 São Luís, Braz.
140/D3 São Luís do Quitunde, Braz.
141/B2 São Manoel, Braz.
140/A1 São Marcos (bay), Braz.
140/A5 São Marcos (riv.), Braz.
141/E1 São Mateus, Braz.
141/D1 São Mateus (riv.), Braz.
140/A2 São Mateus do Maranhão, Braz.
141/B3 São Mateus do Sul, Braz.
140/C2 São Miguel, Braz.
75/T13 São Miguel (isl.), Azor.,Port.
141/C2 São Miguel Arcanjo, Braz.
140/C3 São Miguel dos Campos, Braz.
140/B2 São Miguel do Tapuio, Braz.
150/D3 Saona (isl.), DRep.
76/C3 Saône, Fr.
76/A4 Saône (riv.), Fr.
76/B4 Saône-et-Loire (dept.), Fr.
122/J10 São Nicolau (isl.), CpV.
141/G8 São Paulo, Braz.
141/H8 São Paulo (state), Braz.
136/E4 São Paulo de Olivença, Braz.
140/D2 São Paulo do Potengi, Braz.
141/D2 São Pedro da Aldeia, Braz.
140/B2 São Pedro do Piauí, Braz.
140/C2 São Rafael, Braz.
140/A2 São Raimundo das Mangabeiras, Braz.
140/B3 São Raimundo Nonato, Braz.
99/M9 Saori, Japan
140/A5 São Romão, Braz.
134/F3 São Roque (cape), Braz.
140/D2 São Roque, Cabo de (cape), Braz.
75/S12 São Roque do Pico, Azor.,Port.
141/H8 São Sebastião, Braz.
141/H8 São Sebastião (isl.), Braz.
131/D4 São Sebastião (pt.), Moz.
141/C2 São Sebastião do Paraíso, Braz.
141/B1 São Simão (res.), Braz.
74/A4 São Teotónio, Port.
141/C2 São Tiago, Braz.
122/K10 São Tiago (isl.), CpV.
134/E5 São Tomé (cape), Braz.
124/G7 São Tomé (cap.), SaoT.
124/G7 São Tomé (isl.), SaoT.
124/F7 São Tomé and Príncipe
141/D2 São Tomé, Cabo de (cape), Braz.
124/E1 Saoura (dry riv.), Alg.
141/G8 São Vicente, Braz.
122/J10 São Vicente (isl.), CpV.
74/A4 São Vicente, Cabo de (cape), Port.
83/K5 Sapanca, Turk.
81/H1 Sapareva Banya, Bul.
140/D2 Sapé, Braz.
163/H4 Sapelo (isl.), Ga,US
81/G4 Sapiéndza (isl.), Gre.
76/D1 Sapin Sec, Roche du (mtn.), Fr.
149/G5 Sapo, Serraniía de (range), Pan.
66/D2 Sappemeer, Neth.
100/B2 Sapporo, Japan
80/D2 Sapri, It.
141/H7 Sapucaí (riv.), Braz.
93/F2 Saqqez, Iran
138/B5 Saquisilí, Ecu.
82/E4 Šar (mts.), Yugo.
112/C3 Sara, Phil.
93/F2 Sarāb, Iran
109/C3 Sara Buri, Thai.
75/E2 Saragossa (Zaragoza), Sp.
144/B1 Saraguro, Ecu.
108/B1 Sarāi Ālamgīr, Pak.
82/D4 Sarajevo (cap.), Bosn.
163/F4 Saraland, Al,US
139/H3 Saramacca (dist.), Sur.
104/B3 Saramati (mtn.), India
110/D4 Saran (peak), Indo.
102/B2 Saran', Kaz.
160/F2 Saranac Lake, NY,US
130/B4 Saranda, Tanz.
81/L6 Sarandapótamos (riv.), Gre.
81/G3 Sarandë, Alb.
143/G2 Sarandí Del Yi, Uru.
112/D4 Sarangani (isls.), Phil.
106/C3 Sārangpur, India
87/H1 Saransk, Rus.
85/M4 Sarapul, Rus.
138/D3 Sarare (riv.), Ven.
163/H5 Sarasota, Fl,US
165/K12 Saratoga, Ca,US
156/G5 Saratoga, Wy,US
160/F3 Saratoga Springs, NY,US
87/H2 Saratov, Rus.
87/J1 Saratov (res.), Rus.
87/H2 Saratov Obl., Rus.
95/H3 Sarāvān, Iran
110/D3 Sarawak (state), Malay.
92/A1 Saray, Turk.
92/B2 Sarayköy, Turk.
92/C2 Sarayönü, Turk.
82/D2 Sárbogárd, Hun.
77/G5 Sarca (riv.), It.
53/T10 Sarcelles, Fr.
106/B2 Sardārshahar, India
80/A2 Sardegna (reg.), It.
73/G5 Sardinaux, Cap de (cape), Fr.
80/A2 Sardinia (isl.), It.
159/K4 Sardis (lake), Ms,US
159/J4 Sardis (lake), Ok,US
61/F2 Sareks Nat'l Park, Swe.
61/F2 Sarektjåkko (peak), Swe.
111/E4 Sarempaka (peak), Indo.
78/D1 Sarezzo, It.
108/B1 Sargodha, Pak.
125/J6 Sarh, Chad
93/H2 Sārī, Iran
111/J4 Saribi (cape), Indo.
120/D3 Sarigan (isl.), NMar.
92/B2 Sarıgöl, Turk.
92/E1 Sarıkamış, Turk.
92/C2 Sarıkaya, Turk.
92/C2 Sarikaya (prov.), Turk.
76/D4 Sarine (riv.), Swi.
125/K2 Sarīr Kalanshiyū (des.), Libya
125/J3 Sarīr Tibastī (des.), Libya
162/D5 Sarita, Tx,US
82/E2 Sarkad, Hun.
87/L4 Sarkamyshskoye (lake), Trkm., Uzb.
88/H5 Sarkand, Kaz.
92/B2 Şarkîkaraağaç, Turk.
92/D2 Şarkışla, Turk.
83/H5 Şarköy, Turk.
72/D4 Sarlat-La-Canéda, Fr.
143/K8 Sarmiento (peak), Chile
76/E4 Sarnen, Swi.
165/H6 Sarnia, On,Can
86/C2 Sarny, Ukr.
100/C1 Saroma (lake), Japan
81/H4 Saronic (gulf), Gre.
81/L7 Saronikós (gulf), Gre.
78/C1 Saronno, It.
83/H5 Saros (gulf), Turk.
82/E1 Sárospatak, Hun.
62/D2 Sarpsborg, Nor.
69/F6 Sarre (riv.), Fr.
69/G6 Sarrebourg, Fr.
69/G5 Sarreguemines, Fr.
74/B1 Sarria, Sp.
67/G4 Sarstedt, Ger.
148/D3 Sarstún (riv.), Belz., Guat.
89/P3 Sartang (riv.), Rus.
72/C3 Sarthe (riv.), Fr.
53/S10 Sartrouville, Fr.
92/A2 Saruhanlı, Turk.
82/D2 Sárvitz (riv.), Hun.
82/D2 Sárvíz (riv.), Hun.
102/C2 Sary Ishikotrau (des.), Kaz.
102/B2 Saryshagan, Kaz.
102/A2 Sarysu (riv.), Kaz.
78/C4 Sarzana, It.
157/K3 Sasaginnigak (lake), Mb,Can
106/D3 Sasarām, India
99/L9 Sasayama, Japan
99/L9 Sasayama (riv.), Japan
98/A4 Sasebo, Japan
152/F3 Saskatchewan (prov.), Can.
156/F3 Saskatchewan (riv.), Can.
156/G2 Saskatoon, Sk*,Can
149/E3 Saslaya (mtn.), Nic.
149/E3 Saslaya Nat'l Park, Nic.
87/G1 Sasovo, Rus.
166/B5 Sassafras (riv.), Md,US
128/D5 Sassandra, IvC.
128/D5 Sassandra (riv.), IvC.
80/A2 Sassari, It.
67/F5 Sassenberg, Ger.
66/B4 Sassenheim, Neth.
65/G1 Sassnitz, Ger.
79/D3 Sassuolo, It.
66/A6 Sas Van Gent, Neth.
102/D2 Sasykkol (lake), Kaz.
98/B5 Sata-misaki (cape), Japan
106/B4 Sātāra, India
120/E4 Satawan (atoll), Micr.
62/F1 Säter, Swe.
144/C3 Satipo, Peru
57/G2 Satley, Eng,UK
106/D3 Satna, India
82/E1 Sátoraljaújhely, Hun.
102/A2 Satpayev, Kaz.
106/C3 Satpura (range), India
108/F4 Sāttānkulam, India
108/F4 Sāttūr, India
82/F2 Satu Mare, Rom.
82/F2 Satu Mare (co.), Rom.
109/C5 Satun, Thai.
121/R9 Satupaitea, WSam.
108/F3 Satyamangalam, India
142/E3 Sauce Grande (riv.), Arg.
140/B3 Saúde, Braz.
94/D4 Saudi Arabia
64/D4 Sauer (riv.), Ger.
67/F5 Sauer (riv.), Ger.
69/F4 Sauer (riv.), Ger., Lux.
69/G1 Sauerland (reg.), Ger.
136/G6 Sauêruiná (riv.), Braz.
167/E1 Saugatuck (riv.), Ct,US
157/K4 Sauk (riv.), Mn,US
157/K4 Sauk Centre, Mn,US
157/K4 Sauk Rapids, Mn,US
137/H3 Saül, FrG.
72/D3 Sauldre (riv.), Fr.
70/C6 Saulgau, Ger.
160/C2 Sault Sainte Marie, On,Can
160/C2 Sault Sainte Marie, Mi,US
69/E6 Saulx (riv.), Fr.
118/D3 Saumarez (reefs), Austl.
72/C3 Saumur, Fr.
116/E3 Saunders (peak), Austl.
58/B3 Saundersfoot, Wal,UK
126/D2 Saurimo, Ang.
165/K11 Sausalito, Ca,US
53/S9 Sausseron (riv.), Fr.
82/C3 Sava (riv.), Eur.
80/E2 Sava, It.
164/D5 Savage (dam), Ca,US
121/H6 Savai'i (isl.), WSam.
161/G1 Savane (riv.), Qu,Can
116/L6 Savannah (brook), Austl.
163/H3 Savannah, Ga,US
163/H3 Savannah (riv.), Ga, SC,US
163/F3 Savannah, Tn,US
107/H4 Savannakhet, Laos
109/D2 Savannakhet, Laos
149/G2 Savanna la Mar, Jam.
160/B1 Savant (lake), On,Can
106/B4 Sāvantvādi, India
92/A2 Savaştepe, Turk.
126/C4 Savate, Ang.
131/D4 Save (riv.), Moz., Zim.
93/G3 Sāveh, Iran
79/E4 Savena (riv.), It.
83/H2 Săveni, Rom.
69/G6 Saverne, Fr.
78/A3 Savigliano, It.
79/F4 Savignano sul Rubicone, It.
53/T11 Savigny-le-Temple, Fr.
53/T10 Savigny-sur-Orge, Fr.
168/B2 Saville (dam), Ct,US
79/F5 Savio (riv.), It.
156/C3 Savona, BC,Can
78/B4 Savona, It.
78/B4 Savona (prov.), It.
61/J3 Savonlinna, Fin.
76/C6 Savoy Alps (mts.), Fr.
62/F3 Sävsjö, Swe.
111/F5 Savu (sea), Indo.
79/G2 Savudrija, Cro.
110/B4 Sawahlunto, Indo.
127/D5 Sawākin, Sudan
109/B2 Sawankhalok, Thai.
99/G3 Sawara, Japan
99/F2 Sawasaki-bana (pt.), Japan
158/F3 Sawatch (range), Co,US
59/G3 Sawbridgeworth, Eng,UK
124/J2 Sawdā (mts.), Libya
94/D5 Sawdā', Jabal (mtn.), SAr.
125/L5 Sawdirī, Sudan
111/H4 Saweba (cape), Indo.
56/A2 Sawel (mtn.), NI,UK
127/B3 Sawhāj, Egypt
127/B3 Sawhāj (gov.), Egypt
107/F6 Sāwi, India
131/C3 Sawmills, Zim.

94/G5 Sawqirah, Ghubbat (bay), Oman
95/G5 Şawqirah, Ra's (pt.), Oman
59/G2 Sawston, Eng,UK
119/E1 Sawtell, Austl.
156/E4 Sawtooth (range), Id,US
111/F6 Sawu (isls.), Indo.
75/E3 Sax, Sp.
63/T9 Saxån (riv.), Swe.
63/S7 Saxarfjärden (sound), Swe.
57/H5 Saxilby, Eng,UK
59/H2 Saxmundham, Eng,UK
65/G3 Saxony (state), Ger.
64/F3 Saxony-Anhalt (state), Ger.
99/F3 Sayama, Japan
92/C3 Şaydā, Leb.
147/H4 Sayil (ruins), Mex.
69/G2 Saynbach (riv.), Ger.
96/G3 Saynshand, Mong.
102/D3 Sayram (lake), China
167/D3 Sayreville, NJ,US
167/E2 Sayville, NY,US
81/F2 Sazan (isl.), Alb.
71/H3 Sázava (riv.), Czh.
93/M6 Sazli Dere (riv.), Turk.
57/E3 Scafell Pikes (mtn.), Eng,UK
55/H8 Scalasaig, Sc,UK
57/H3 Scalby, Eng,UK
54/C5 Scald Law (mtn.), Sc,UK
80/D3 Scalea, It.
79/D4 Scale, Corno alle (peak), It.
77/F5 Scalino, Pizzo (peak), It.
55/P12 Scalloway, Sc,UK
79/D3 Scandiano, It.
79/E5 Scandicci, It.
55/N13 Scapa Flow (chan.), Sc,UK
116/K6 Scarborough, Austl.
161/R8 Scarborough, On,Can
57/H3 Scarborough, Eng,UK
68/B3 Scarpe (riv.), Fr.
167/E1 Scarsdale, NY,US
56/E1 Scar Water (riv.), Sc,UK
60/A4 Scattery (isl.), Ire.
53/S10 Sceaux, Fr.
68/D2 Schaerbeek, Belg.
77/E2 Schaffhausen, Swi.
77/E2 Schaffhausen (canton), Swi.
66/B3 Schagen, Neth.
66/C5 Schaijk, Neth.
67/E6 Schalksmühle, Ger.
119/C3 Schanck (cape), Austl.
77/H2 Scharfreiter (peak), Aus.
67/F1 Scharhorn (isl.), Ger.
77/H3 Scharnitz (pass), Ger.
165/P15 Schaumburg, Il,US
66/D2 Scheemda, Neth.
67/G2 Scheessel, Ger.
68/C2 Schelde (Scheldt) (riv.), Belg.
68/C2 Scheldt (Schelde) (riv.), Belg.
70/C6 Schelklingen, Ger.
158/D3 Schell Creek (range), Nv,US
67/H4 Schellerten, Ger.
160/F3 Schenectady, NY,US
67/G1 Schenefeld, Ger.
165/R16 Schererville, In,US
66/D5 Schermbeck, Ger.
66/C3 Scherpenzeel, Neth.
77/F3 Schesaplana (peak), Aus.
70/E3 Schesslitz, Ger.
66/B5 Schiedam, Neth.
67/G5 Schieder-Schwalenberg, Ger.
54/B3 Schiehallion (mtn.), Sc,UK
71/F5 Schierling, Ger.
66/D2 Schiermonnikoog (isl.), Neth.
69/G5 Schiffweiler, Ger.
66/C5 Schijndel, Neth.
68/D1 Schilde, Belg.
66/D2 Schildmeer (lake), Neth.
67/F1 Schillighörn (cape), Ger.
69/G6 Schiltigheim, Fr.
69/E2 Schinnen, Neth.
79/E1 Schio, It.
66/D4 Schipbeek (riv.), Neth.
81/G2 Schkumbin (riv.), Alb.
77/G4 Schlanders (Silandro), It.
67/F5 Schlangen, Ger.
69/F2 Schleiden, Ger.
64/E1 Schleswig, Ger.
67/H1 Schleswig-Holstein (state), Ger.
64/E1 Schleswig-Holsteinisches Wattenmeer Nat'l Park, Ger.
70/D2 Schleuse (riv.), Ger.
77/E3 Schlieren, Swi.
71/F5 Schloss Herrenchiemsee, Ger.
67/F5 Schloss Holte-Stukenbrock, Ger.
67/G4 Schloss Wilhelmstein, Ger.
76/D1 Schlucht, Col de la (pass), Fr.
70/C2 Schlüchtern, Ger.
77/G4 Schluderns (Sluderno), It.
64/F3 Schmalkalden, Ger.
67/F6 Schmallenberg, Ger.
70/C6 Schmeich (riv.), Ger.
77/F1 Schmeie (riv.), Ger.
69/F5 Schmelz, Ger.
70/B2 Schmitten, Ger.
70/D6 Schmutter (riv.), Ger.
71/E3 Schnaittach, Ger.
71/F1 Schneeberg, Ger.
71/E2 Schneeberg (peak), Ger.
69/F3 Schneifel (plat.), Ger.
64/D4 Schneifel (upland), Ger.
67/G2 Schneverdingen, Ger.
154/V12 Schofield Barracks, Hi,US
143/L7 Scholl, Cerro (mtn.), Arg.
70/B5 Schömberg, Ger.
70/C5 Schönaich, Ger.
76/D2 Schönau, Ger.
70/C2 Schondra (riv.), Ger.
64/F2 Schönebeck, Ger.
77/G2 Schongau, Ger.
71/F2 Schönheide, Ger.
64/F2 Schöningen, Ger.
71/F2 Schonwald, Ger.
66/D3 Schoonebeek, Neth.
66/B5 Schoonhoven, Neth.
66/B3 Schoorl, Neth.
70/A3 Schopfheim, Ger.
71/G7 Schörfling am Attersee, Aus.
70/C5 Schorndorf, Ger.
67/E1 Schortens, Ger.
68/D1 Schoten, Belg.
70/C2 Schotten, Ger.
119/D4 Schouten (isl.), Austl.
120/C5 Schouten (isls.), Indo.
66/A5 Schouwen (isl.), Neth.
72/D5 Schrader (peak), Fr.
124/H3 ŞChrā Marzūq (des.), Libya
70/B6 Schramberg, Ger.
77/H3 Schrankogel (peak), Aus.
76/E4 Schreckhorn (peak), Swi.
160/C1 Schreiber, On,Can
70/B4 Schriesheim, Ger.
70/E5 Schrobenhausen, Ger.
132/B2 Schroffenstein (peak), Namb.
162/D4 Schulenburg, Tx,US
67/H4 Schunter (riv.), Ger.
77/F2 Schussen (riv.), Ger.
77/F1 Schussenried, Ger.
70/A6 Schutter (riv.), Ger.
70/E5 Schutter (riv.), Ger.
70/A6 Schutterwald, Ger.
67/E4 Schüttorf, Ger.
166/B2 Schuylkill (co.), Pa,US
166/C3 Schuylkill (riv.), Pa,US
70/E4 Schwabach, Ger.
70/D5 Schwäbische Alb (range), Ger.
70/C5 Schwäbisch Gmünd, Ger.
70/C4 Schwäbisch Hall, Ger.
70/D6 Schwabmünchen, Ger.
70/C4 Schwaigern, Ger.
69/F5 Schwalbach, Ger.
70/B2 Schwalbach am Taunus, Ger.
67/G6 Schwalm (riv.), Ger.
66/D6 Schwalmtal, Ger.
71/F4 Schwandorf im Bayern, Ger.
110/D4 Schwaner (mts.), Indo.
67/F2 Schwanewede, Ger.
65/G3 Schwartz Elster (riv.), Ger.
132/B2 Schwartzerberg (peak), Namb.
70/E4 Schwarzach (riv.), Ger.
71/F4 Schwarzach (riv.), Ger.
71/E4 Schwarze Laber (riv.), Ger.
67/H2 Schwarzenbek, Ger.
71/E2 Schwarzenbruck, Ger.
69/F3 Schwarzer Mann (peak), Ger.
71/F4 Schwarzer Regen (riv.), Ger.
77/H3 Schwarzhorn (peak), Aus.
70/B6 Schwarzwald (Black Forest) (for.), Ger.
73/J3 Schwaz, Aus.
65/J4 Schwechat, Aus.
65/H2 Schwedt, Ger.
70/D2 Schweinfurt, Ger.
67/E6 Schwelm, Ger.
64/F2 Schwerin, Ger.
64/F2 Schweriner (lake), Ger.
67/E6 Schwerte, Ger.
70/B4 Schwetzingen, Ger.
67/G1 Schwinge (riv.), Ger.
67/G5 Schwülme (riv.), Ger.
77/E3 Schwyz, Swi.
77/E3 Schwyz (canton), Swi.
80/C4 Sciacca, It.
80/D4 Scicli, It.
55/H11 Scilly (isls.), Eng,UK
160/D4 Scioto (riv.), Oh,US
168/D1 Scituate, Ma,US
168/C2 Scituate (res.), RI,US
157/G3 Scobey, Mt,US
59/G1 Scolt (pt.), UK
80/D4 Scordia, It.
57/G3 Scotch Corner, Eng,UK
166/D2 Scotch Plains, NJ,US
113/W Scotia (sea), Ant.
55/J8 Scotland, UK
113/M Scott, Ant.
113/L Scott (coast), Ant.
117/M9 Scott (cr.), Austl.
114/C2 Scott (reef), Austl.
152/D3 Scott (cape), BC,Can
153/R7 Scott (cape), NW,Can
152/F2 Scott (lake), NW,Can
159/G3 Scott City, Ks,US
116/B5 Scott Nat'l Park, Austl.
117/M9 Scotts (cr.), Austl.
159/G2 Scottsbluff, Ne,US
159/F2 Scotts Bluff Nat'l Mon., Ne,US
163/G3 Scottsboro, Al,US
160/C4 Scottsburg, In,US
158/E4 Scottsdale, Az,US
119/C4 Scotts Peak (dam), Austl.
160/C4 Scottsville, Ky,US
160/C3 Scottville, Mi,US
55/K7 Scrabster, Sc,UK
166/C1 Scranton, Pa,US
164/C5 Scripps Aquarium/Museum, Ca,US
78/B3 Scrivia (riv.), It.
57/H4 Scunthorpe, Eng,UK
165/N14 Scuppernong (riv.), Wi,US
55/K8 Scurdie Ness (pt.), Sc,UK
82/D4 Scutari (lake), Alb., Yugo.
155/K5 Sea (isls.), Ga,US
140/B4 Seabra, Braz.
59/G5 Seaford, UK
167/M9 Seaford, NY,US
56/C3 Seaforde, NI,UK
57/G2 Seaham, Eng,UK
153/H2 Seahorse (pt.), NW,Can
152/G3 Seal (riv.), Mb,Can
142/B5 Seal (pt.), Chile
132/C4 Seal (cape), SAfr.
53/P8 Seal, Eng,UK
164/B3 Seal Beach, Ca,US
164/F8 Seal Beach Nat'l Wild. Ref., Ca,US
57/H3 Seamer, Eng,UK
141/A3 Seara, Braz.
158/D4 Searchlight, Nv,US
162/F3 Searcy, Ar,US
57/E3 Seascale, Eng,UK
156/C4 Seaside, Or,US
165/C3 SeaTac, Wa,US
58/C5 Seaton, Eng,UK
58/B6 Seaton (riv.), Eng,UK
57/G2 Seaton Carew, Eng,UK
57/G1 Seaton Valley, Eng,UK
165/C2 Seattle, Wa,US
165/C2 Seattle Art Museum, Wa,US
165/C2 Seattle Ctr., Wa,US
167/E2 Seatuck Nat'l Wild. Ref., NY,US
168/F5 Sea World, Oh,US
148/E3 Sébaco, Nic.
123/T15 Sebaou (riv.), Alg.
163/H5 Sebastian, Fl,US
146/B2 Sebastián Vizcaíno (bay), Mex.
119/B3 Sebastopol, Austl.
112/B4 Sebatik (isl.), Malay., Indo.
110/D4 Sebayan (peak), Indo.
123/Q16 Sebdou, Alg.
83/F3 Sebeş, Rom.
131/B4 Sebina, Bots.
92/D1 Şebinkarahisar, Turk.
82/D2 Sebiş, Rom.
65/H3 Sebnitz, Ger.
112/C4 Seboto (pt.), Phil.
123/M13 Sebou (riv.), Mor.
163/H5 Sebring, Fl,US
112/B5 Sebuku (bay), Indo.
111/E4 Sebuku (isl.), Indo.
167/J8 Secaucus, NJ,US
79/D3 Secchia (riv.), It.
144/A2 Sechura, Peru
144/A2 Sechura (bay), Peru
144/A2 Sechura (des.), Peru
68/C2 Seclin, Fr.
143/L7 Seco (riv.), Arg.
127/B4 Second Cataract (falls), Sudan
166/B3 Second Mtn. (ridge), Pa,US
164/C4 Second San Diego (aqueduct), Ca,US
167/H8 Second Watchung (mtn.), NJ,US
106/C4 Secunderābād, India
136/E7 Securé (riv.), Bol.
159/J3 Sedalia, Mo,US
68/D4 Sedan, Fr.
109/B3 Sedaung (mtn.), Burma
57/F3 Sedbergh, Eng,UK
127/B4 Seddenga Temple (ruins), Sudan
91/D4 Sederot, Isr.
57/G2 Sedgefield, Eng,UK
151/L2 Sedgwick (mtn.), Yk,Can
128/B3 Sedhiou, Sen.
71/H3 Sedlčany, Czh.
71/H1 Sedlo (peak), Czh.
158/E4 Sedona, Az,US
123/V17 Sedrata, Alg.
65/L3 Sędziszów, Pol.
72/C2 Sée (riv.), Fr.
60/A6 Seefin (mtn.), Ire.
60/C5 Seefin (mtn.), Ire.
70/B3 Seeheim-Jugenheim, Ger.
71/G7 Seekirchen am Wallersee, Aus.
168/C2 Seekonk, Ma,US
132/D3 Seekooi (riv.), SAfr.
67/H5 Seesen, Ger.
67/G2 Seeve (riv.), Ger.
71/G7 Seewalchen am Attersee, Aus.
92/C2 Şefaatlı, Turk.
131/B4 Sefare, Bots.
93/G2 Sefīd Rūd (riv.), Iran
123/M14 Sefrou, Mor.
112/B5 Segama (riv.), Malay.
110/B3 Segamat, Malay.
83/F3 Segarcea, Rom.
80/C4 Segesta (ruins), It.
84/G3 Segezha, Rus.
75/E3 Segorbe, Sp.
128/D3 Ségou, Mali
128/D3 Ségou (reg.), Mali
138/C3 Segovia, Col.
74/C2 Segovia, Sp.
84/G3 Segozero (lake), Rus.
78/C2 Segrate, It.
72/C3 Segré, Fr.
75/F2 Segre (riv.), Sp.
151/D5 Seguam (isl.), Ak,US
151/D5 Seguam (passg.), Ak,US
124/H3 Séguédine, Niger
128/D5 Séguéla, IvC.
162/D4 Seguin, Tx,US
74/D3 Segura (riv.), Sp.
126/D5 Sehithwa, Bots.
106/C3 Sehore, India
95/J3 Sehwān, Pak.
99/L10 Seika, Japan
100/B3 Seikan (tunnel), Japan
76/B4 Seille (riv.), Fr.
69/F6 Seille (riv.), Fr.
159/H3 Seiling, Ok,US
61/G3 Seinäjoki, Fin.
157/L3 Seine (riv.), On,Can
72/C2 Seine (bay), Fr.
72/D2 Seine (riv.), Fr.
53/U10 Seine-et-Marne (dept.), Fr.
53/T10 Seine-Saint-Denis (dept.), Fr.
61/G3 Seitsemisen Nat'l Park, Fin.
99/M10 Seiwa, Japan
75/P10 Seixal, Port.
62/D4 Sejerø (isl.), Den.
130/B3 Seke, Tanz.
130/B4 Sekenke, Tanz.
99/E3 Seki, Japan
91/A1 Seki (riv.), Turk.
99/M9 Sekigahara, Japan
99/H6 Sekiyado, Japan
131/A5 Sekoma, Bots.
129/E5 Sekondi, Gha.
156/C4 Selah, Wa,US
80/A3 Selargius, It.
111/H5 Selaru (isl.), Indo.
110/D4 Selatan (cape), Indo.
151/F2 Selawik (lake), Ak,US
151/G2 Selawik Nat'l Wild. Ref., Ak,US
111/F5 Selayar (isl.), Indo.
71/F2 Selb, Ger.
71/E2 Selbitz (riv.), Ger.
57/G4 Selby, Eng,UK
157/H4 Selby, SD,US
92/A2 Selçuk, Turk.
167/E2 Selden, NY,US
80/D2 Sele (riv.), It.
131/B4 Selebi-Phikwe, Bots.
130/B5 Seleli (hill), Tanz.
97/L1 Selemdzha (riv.), Rus.
92/B2 Selendi, Turk.
96/F1 Selenga (riv.), Rus.
96/E2 Selenge, Mong.
96/E2 Selenge (riv.), Mong.
76/D1 Sélestat, Fr.
102/B1 Selety (riv.), Kaz.
102/B1 Seletyteniz (lake), Kaz.
84/G4 Seliger (lake), Rus.
158/D4 Seligman, Az,US
131/B4 Selika, Bots.
80/C4 Selinunte (ruins), It.
156/D3 Selkirk (mts.), BC,Can
157/J3 Selkirk, Mb,Can
54/D5 Selkirk, Sc,UK
158/E5 Sells, Az,US
58/E2 Selly Oak, Eng,UK
67/E5 Selm, Ger.
163/G3 Selma, Al,US
163/F3 Selmer, Tn,US
151/M3 Selous (mtn.), Yk,Can
131/C3 Selous, Zim.
130/C5 Selous Game Rsv., Tanz.
59/F5 Selsey, Eng,UK
59/F5 Selsey Bill (pt.), Eng,UK
72/C2 Sélune (riv.), Fr.
136/E5 Selvas (for.), Braz.
117/H2 Selwyn (range), Austl.
70/B3 Selz (riv.), Ger.
124/C2 Semara, WSah.
110/D5 Semarang, Indo.
112/B4 Sembakung (riv.), Indo.
71/H2 Sembera (riv.), Czh.
93/F2 Şemdinli, Turk.
85/K4 Semenov, Rus.
110/D5 Semeru (peak), Indo.
151/G4 Semidi (isls.), Ak,US
86/F2 Semiluki, Rus.
156/F5 Seminoe (res.), Wy,US
163/G4 Seminole (lake), Ga,US
162/C3 Seminole, Tx,US
102/D1 Semipalatinsk, Kaz.
112/C2 Semirara (isl.), Phil.
151/B5 Semisopochnoi (isl.), Ak,US
110/D4 Semitau, Indo.
93/H3 Semnān, Iran
93/H3 Semnān (gov.), Iran
72/C3 Semnon (riv.), Fr.
69/E4 Semois (riv.), Belg.
76/C2 Semouse (riv.), Fr.
76/B1 Semoutiers, Fr.
69/D4 Semoy (riv.), Fr.
76/E3 Sempacher See (lake), Swi.
84/B2 Semskefjellet (peak), Nor.
109/D3 Sen (riv.), Camb.
109/C3 Sena, Thai.
140/C2 Senador Pompeu, Braz.
131/A3 Senanga, Zam.
163/F3 Senatobia, Ms,US
59/E2 Sence (riv.), Eng,UK
98/B5 Sendai, Japan
99/G1 Sendai (bay), Japan
98/B5 Sendai (riv.), Japan
98/D3 Sendai (riv.), Japan
67/E5 Senden, Ger.
70/D6 Senden, Ger.
67/E5 Sendenhorst, Ger.
65/J4 Senec, Slvk.
68/D2 Seneffe, Belg.
128/B3 Senegal
128/B2 Sénégal (riv.), Afr.
132/D3 Senekal, SAfr.
160/C2 Seney Nat'l Wild. Ref., Mi,US
65/H3 Senftenberg, Ger.
130/A5 Senga Hill Mission, Zam.
141/B3 Sengés, Braz.
102/D5 Sênggê (riv.), China
142/C5 Senguerr (riv.), Arg.
131/C3 Sengwe (riv.), Zim.
140/B3 Senhor do Bonfim, Braz.
65/J4 Senica, Slvk.
79/G5 Senigallia, It.
79/E4 Senio (riv.), It.
92/B2 Senirkent, Turk.
80/E2 Senise, It.
82/B3 Senj, Cro.
61/F1 Senja (isl.), Nor.
100/G8 Senkaku-Shotō (isls.), Jap.
68/B5 Senlis, Fr.
99/L10 Sennan, Japan
125/M5 Sennar (dam), Sudan
68/D2 Senne (riv.), Belg.
160/E1 Senneterre, Qu,Can
58/C3 Sennybridge, Wal,UK
129/F3 Séno (prov.), Burk.
72/E2 Sens, Fr.
148/D3 Sensuntepeque, ESal.
82/E3 Senta, Yugo.
126/E2 Sentery, Zaire
156/C2 Sentinel (peak), BC,Can
120/E4 Senyavin (isls.), Micr.
106/C3 Seoni, India
106/C3 Seonī Mālwā, India
89/N6 Seoul (cap.), SKor.
101/G7 Seoul Grand Park, SKor.
101/F6 Seoul (inset) (cap.), SKor.
101/D4 Seoul-Jikhalsi, SKor.
101/D4 Seoul (Sŏul) (cap.), SKor.
141/K8 Sepetiba (bay), Braz.
120/D5 Sepik (riv.), PNG
65/J2 Sępólno Krajeńskie, Pol.
83/G4 Septemvri, Bul.
161/H1 Sept-Îles, Qu,Can
164/F7 Sepulveda (dam), Ca,US
165/A1 Sequim (bay), Wa,US
158/C3 Sequoia Nat'l Park, Ca,US
78/C1 Serada, Monte (peak), It.
69/E2 Seraing, Belg.
76/B6 Séran (riv.), Fr.
110/C5 Serang, Indo.
110/C3 Serasan (str.), Indo., Malay.
82/E4 Serbia (rep.), Yugo.
78/D5 Serchio (riv.), It.
87/H1 Serdobsk, Rus.
151/D2 Serdtse-Kamen, Mys (pt.), Rus.
92/C2 Şereflikoçhisar, Turk.
78/C1 Seregno, It.
72/F3 Serein (riv.), Fr.
110/B3 Seremban, Malay.
130/B3 Serengeti (plain), Tanz.
130/B3 Serengeti Nat'l Park, Tanz.
131/C2 Serenje, Zam.
130/B2 Serere, Ugan.
85/K5 Sergach, Rus.
88/J2 Sergeya Kirova (isls.), Rus.
140/C3 Sergipe (state), Braz.
84/H4 Sergiyev Posad, Rus.
112/A4 Seria, Bru.
78/C1 Seriate, It.
81/J4 Sérifos (isl.), Gre.
91/B1 Serik, Turk.
137/H5 Seringa (mts.), Braz.
78/C2 Serio (riv.), It.
111/G5 Sermata (isl.), Indo.
77/G5 Serottini, Monte (peak), It.
88/G4 Serov, Rus.
131/B4 Serowe, Bots.
74/B4 Serpa, Port.
80/A3 Serpeddi (peak), It.
119/C4 Serpentine (dam), Austl.
117/F4 Serpentine (lakes), Austl.
139/F2 Serpent's Mouth (str.), Trin., Ven.
128/C3 Serpent, Vallée du (wadi), Mali
84/H5 Serpukhov, Rus.
141/D2 Serra, Braz.
141/J8 Serra da Bocaina Nat'l Park, Braz.
141/C2 Serra da Canastra Nat'l Park, Braz.
140/B3 Serra de Capivara Nat'l Park, Braz.
141/D1 Serra do Cipo Nat'l Park, Braz.
141/K7 Serra dos Órgãos Nat'l Park, Braz.
81/H2 Sérrai, Gre.
80/E3 Serralta di San Vito (peak), It.
80/A3 Serramanna, It.
78/D5 Serra, Monte (peak), It.
136/E3 Serranía de la Neblina Nat'l Park, Ven.
149/G3 Serranilla Bank (reef), Col.
141/B1 Serranópolis, Braz.
123/W17 Serrat (cape), Tun.
140/C2 Serra Talhada, Braz.
68/C4 Serre (riv.), Fr.
140/C3 Serrinha, Braz.
74/A3 Sertã, Port.
140/C3 Sertânia, Braz.
141/C2 Sertãozinho, Braz.
91/C1 Sertavul (pass), Turk.
96/C4 Serteng (mts.), China
131/B4 Serule, Bots.
131/B4 Serurumi (dry riv.), Bots.
110/D4 Seruyan (riv.), Indo.
112/B5 Sesayap (riv.), Indo.
130/B3 Sese (isls.), Ugan.
127/B4 Sesebi (ruins), Sudan
131/B3 Sesheke, Zam.
78/B2 Sesia (riv.), It.
74/A3 Sesimbra, Port.
63/N1 Seskar (isl.), Rus.
164/A1 Sespe (cr.), Ca,US
164/B1 Sespe Condor Sanct., Ca,US
74/D1 Sestao, Sp.
78/B1 Sesto Calende, It.
79/E5 Sesto Fiorentino, It.
78/C1 Sesto San Giovanni, It.
78/C4 Sestri Levante, It.
63/N1 Sestroretsk, Rus.
80/A3 Sestu, It.
77/G4 Sesvenna, Piz (peak), It.
82/C3 Sesvete, Cro.
100/A2 Setana, Japan
72/E5 Sète, Fr.
140/B2 Sete Cidades Nat'l Park, Braz.
141/C1 Sete Lagoas, Braz.
95/J3 Sethārja, Pak.
123/U17 Sétif, Alg.
123/U17 Sétif (wilaya), Alg.
99/E3 Seto, Japan
98/C3 Seto-Naikai Nat'l Park, Japan
100/K6 Setouchi, Japan
78/B4 Settepani, Monte (peak), It.
78/A2 Settimo Torinese, It.
157/J2 Setting (lake), Mb,Can
57/F3 Settle, Eng,UK
150/B1 Settlement (pt.), Bahm.
99/L10 Settsu, Japan
74/A3 Setúbal, Port.
75/Q11 Setúbal (bay), Port.
74/A3 Setúbal (dist.), Port.
72/C4 Seudre (riv.), Fr.
72/C4 Seugne (riv.), Fr.
160/A1 Seul (lake), On,Can
87/H4 Sevan (lake), Arm.
93/F1 Sevan Nat'l Park, Arm.
86/E3 Sevastopol', Ukr.
57/H3 Seven (riv.), Eng,UK
60/B6 Seven Heads (pt.), Ire.
168/F5 Seven Hills, Oh,US
55/F10 Seven Hogs, The (isls.), Ire.
53/P8 Sevenoaks, Eng,UK
157/L2 Severn (riv.), On,Can
58/D3 Severn (riv.), Eng,UK
166/B5 Severn, Md,US
166/B5 Severn (riv.), Md,US
166/B5 Severna Park, Md,US
85/P3 Severnaya Sos'va (riv.), Rus.
90/K2 Severnaya Zemlya (arch.), Rus.
58/C4 Severn, Mouth of the (estuary), Eng,UK
85/Q2 Severnyy, Rus.
65/G3 Severočeský (reg.), Czh.
86/F2 Severodonetsk, Ukr.
84/H2 Severodvinsk, Rus.
89/R4 Severo-Kuril'sk, Rus.
65/J4 Severomoravský (reg.), Czh.
84/G1 Severomorsk, Rus.
85/N3 Severoural'sk, Rus.
78/C1 Seveso, It.
158/D3 Sevier (des.), Ut,US
158/D3 Sevier (riv.), Ut,US
163/H3 Sevierville, Tn,US
138/C3 Sevilla, Col.
119/G5 Seville, Austl.
74/C4 Seville, Sp.
83/G4 Sevlievo, Bul.
53/T10 Sevran, Fr.
53/S10 Sèvres, Fr.
128/C5 Sewa (riv.), SLeo.
151/E2 Seward (pen.), Ak,US
159/H2 Seward, Ne,US
151/M5 Sewell Inlet, BC,Can
156/D2 Sexsmith, Ab,Can
123/V17 Seybouse (riv.), Alg.
123/H5 Seychelles
92/B2 Seydişehir, Turk.
91/D1 Seyhan (dam), Turk.
91/D1 Seyhan (riv.), Turk.
119/C3 Seymour, Austl.
162/D3 Seymour, Tx,US
76/C6 Seynod, Fr.
93/N6 Şeytan (riv.), Turk.
74/A3 Sezimbra, Port.
80/C2 Sezze, It.
83/G3 Sfîntu Gheorghe, Rom.
123/Q16 Sfizef, Alg.
66/C4 's-Graveland, Neth.
66/B5 's-Gravendeel, Neth.
66/B4 's-Gravenhage (The Hague) (cap.), Neth.
54/A2 Sgurr a' Chaorachain (mtn.), Sc,UK
54/B2 Sgurr a' choire Ghlais (mtn.), Sc,UK
54/B1 Sgurr a' Mhuilinn (mtn.), Sc,UK
54/A1 Sgurr Mór (mtn.), Sc,UK
54/A2 Sgurr na Ciche (mtn.), Sc,UK
54/A2 Sgurr na Lapaich (mtn.), Sc,UK
103/C4 Sha (riv.), China
105/H3 Sha (riv.), China
103/B4 Shaanxi (prov.), China
130/A4 Shaba (reg.), Zaire
130/C2 Shaba Nat'l Rsv., Kenya
125/P7 Shabeelle, Webi (riv.), Som.
126/E1 Shabunda, Zaire
102/C4 Shache, China
113/M Shackleton (coast), Ant.
113/G Shackleton Ice Shelf, Ant.
166/A2 Shade Mtn. (ridge), Pa,US
85/P4 Shadrinsk, Rus.
162/B4 Shafter, Tx,US
58/D4 Shaftesbury, Eng,UK
102/C2 Shagan (riv.), Kaz.
108/D2 Shāhābād, India
95/J3 Shāhdādkot, Pak.
95/J3 Shāhdādpur, Pak.
106/D3 Shahdol, India
125/K1 Shaḩḩāt, Libya
106/C2 Shāhjahānpur, India
108/B2 Shāh Kot, Pak.
108/B1 Shāhpur, Pak.
95/K3 Shāhpura, India
106/A2 Shāhpur Chākar, Pak.
127/C3 Shā'ib al Banāt, Jabal (mtn.), Egypt
106/C3 Shājāpur, India
108/C1 Shakargarh, Pak.
126/D4 Shakawe, Bots.
168/F5 Shaker Heights, Oh,US
88/H5 Shakhtinsk, Kaz.
86/G3 Shakhty, Rus.
84/K4 Shakhun'ya, Rus.
100/B2 Shakotan (pen.), Japan
87/H4 Shalbuzdag, Gora (peak), Rus.
58/C5 Shaldon, Eng,UK
117/M8 Shallow Reach (inlet), Austl.
104/C2 Shaluli (mts.), China
130/B4 Shama (riv.), Tanz.
91/C4 Shamal Sīnā' (gov.), Egypt
157/M2 Shamattawa (riv.), On,Can
106/C3 Shāmgarh, India
106/C1 Shāmli, India
92/E5 Shammar, Jabal (mts.), SAr.
166/B2 Shamokin, Pa,US
166/B2 Shamokin (cr.), Pa,US
151/L3 Shamrock (mtn.), Yk,Can
162/C3 Shamrock, Tx,US
131/C3 Shamva, Zim.
104/C4 Shan (plat.), Burma
104/C4 Shan (state), Burma
105/H3 Shan (pass), China
123/W18 Sha'nabī, Jabal ash (peak), Tun.
125/M4 Shandī, Sudan
103/D3 Shandong (pen.), China
101/A4 Shandong (prov.), China
131/C3 Shangani, Zim.
131/C3 Shangani (riv.), Zim.
103/C4 Shangcai, China
103/C5 Shangcheng, China
105/G4 Shangchuan (isl.), China
105/G3 Shangdu, China
103/E5 Shanghai, China
103/E5 Shanghai (mun.), China
103/L8 Shanghai (inset), China
103/D3 Shanghe, China
103/B3 Shanglin, China
103/C4 Shangqiu, China
105/H2 Shangrao, China
103/C4 Shangshui, China
109/E1 Shangsi, China
103/C2 Shangyi, China
105/G3 Shangyou (riv.), China
59/E5 Shanklin, Eng,UK
105/F3 Shanmatang (mtn.), China
60/A3 Shannawona (mtn.), Ire.
104/C3 Shan-ngaw (range), Burma
60/B4 Shannon (riv.), Ire.
96/C3 Shanshan, China
89/P4 Shantar (isls.), Rus.
105/H4 Shantou, China
130/B3 Shanwa, Tanz.
103/B3 Shanxi (prov.), China
103/C3 Shanyin, China
105/F3 Shaodong, China
105/G3 Shaoguan, China
105/J2 Shaoxing, China
105/F3 Shaoyang, China
57/F2 Shap, Eng,UK
113/L Shapeless (peak), Ant.
85/M2 Shapkina (riv.), Rus.
93/F2 Shaqlāwah, Iraq
95/G5 Sharbatāt, Ra's ash (pt.), Oman
100/D2 Shari, Japan
116/B3 Shark (bay), Austl.
150/A1 Shark (pt.), Fl,US
167/E3 Shark River (inlet), NJ,US
127/C3 Sharm ash Shaykh, Egypt
59/F2 Sharnbrook, Eng,UK
168/G5 Sharon, Pa,US
157/K2 Sharpe (lake), Mb,Can
157/J4 Sharpe (lake), SD,US
108/C2 Sharqpur, Pak.
85/K4 Shar'ya, Rus.
131/B4 Shashe, Bots.
131/C4 Shashe (riv.), Bots., Zim.
125/N6 Shashemenē, Eth.
103/C5 Shashi, China
158/B2 Shasta (dam), Ca,US
158/B2 Shasta (lake), Ca,US
158/B2 Shasta (peak), Ca,US
86/B2 Shatskiy Nat'l Park, Ukr.
93/F4 Shatt al Arab (riv.), Iran, Iraq
124/G1 Shaţţ al Jarīd (dry lake), Tun.
159/H3 Shattuck, Ok,US
156/F3 Shaunavon, Sk,Can
59/E4 Shaw, Eng,UK
163/H3 Shaw A.F.B., SC,US
160/B2 Shawano, Wi,US
161/M6 Shawbridge, Qu,Can
58/D1 Shawbury, Eng,UK
161/F2 Shawinigan, Qu,Can
159/H4 Shawnee, Ok,US
93/E2 Shaykhān, Iraq
92/C3 Shaykh, Jabal ash (mtn.), Leb.
86/C1 Shchara (riv.), Bela.
86/F1 Shchekino, Rus.
85/X9 Shchelkovo, Rus.
86/G2 Shchigry, Rus.
102/B1 Shchuchinsk, Kaz.
167/K8 Shea Stadium, New York City, NY,US
125/P6 Shebelē Wenz (riv.), Eth.
95/J1 Sheberghān, Afg.
160/C3 Sheboygan, Wi,US
161/H2 Shediac, NB,Can
54/C3 Shee (riv.), Sc,UK
60/C2 Sheelin, Lough (lake), Ire.
151/F2 Sheep (mtn.), Ak,US
167/K9 Sheepshead Bay, NY,US
66/D5 's-Heerenberg, Neth.
57/G5 Sheffield, Eng,UK
163/G3 Sheffield, Al,US
167/M7 Sheffield (isl.), Ct,US
168/E5 Sheffield Lake, Oh,US
59/F2 Shefford, Eng,UK
125/P6 Shēh Husēn, Eth.
143/K7 Shehuen (riv.), Arg.
60/A6 Shehy (mts.), Ire.
103/B3 Shejaping, China
160/C1 Shekak (riv.), On,Can
108/B2 Shekhūpura, Pak.
87/H4 Sheki, Azer.
89/T2 Shelagskiy (cape), Rus.
161/H3 Shelburne, NS,Can
163/F3 Shelby, Ms,US
156/F3 Shelby, Mt,US
163/H3 Shelby, NC,US
163/F2 Shelbyville (lake), Il,US
160/C4 Shelbyville, In,US
163/G3 Shelbyville, Tn,US
89/R3 Shelekhov (gulf), Rus.
151/H4 Shelikof (str.), Ak,US
157/G2 Shellbrook, Sk,Can
166/B3 Shelley (isl.), Pa,US
160/B2 Shell Lake, Wi,US
59/G4 Shell Ness (pt.), UK
157/K5 Shell Rock (riv.), Ia,US
167/F1 Shelter (isl.), NY,US
167/F1 Shelter Island (sound), NY,US
168/A3 Shelton, Ct,US
165/A3 Shelton, Wa,US
87/J4 Shemakha, Azer.
151/A5 Shemya (isl.), Ak,US
157/K5 Shenandoah, Ia,US
166/B2 Shenandoah, Pa,US
160/E4 Shenandoah Nat'l Park, Va,US
168/G5 Shenango (riv.), Pa,US
168/G5 Shenango River (res.), Oh, Pa,US
103/C3 Shenchi, China

123/V17 **Smendou** (riv.), Alg.
66/D3 **Smilde**, Neth.
113/V **Smith** (pen.), Ant.
156/B3 **Smith** (inlet), BC,Can
153/J2 **Smith** (isl.), NW,Can
156/F4 **Smith** (riv.), Mt,US
156/B2 **Smithers**, BC,Can
163/J3 **Smithfield**, NC,US
158/E2 **Smithfield**, Ut,US
160/E4 **Smith Mtn.** (lake), Va,US
160/E2 **Smiths Falls**, On,Can
167/E2 **Smithtown**, NY,US
167/E2 **Smithtown** (bay), NY,US
161/Q9 **Smithville**, On,Can
159/J4 **Smithville**, Ok,US
166/D5 **Smithville, Hist. Homes of**, NJ,US
119/E1 **Smoky** (cape), Austl.
156/D2 **Smoky** (riv.), Ab,Can
159/H3 **Smoky** (hills), Ks,US
159/G3 **Smoky Hill** (riv.), Ks,US
156/E2 **Smoky Lake**, Ab,Can
61/C3 **Smøla** (isl.), Nor.
84/G5 **Smolensk**, Rus.
84/F5 **Smolensk Obl.**, Rus.
81/G2 **Smólikas** (peak), Gre.
83/G5 **Smolyan**, Bul.
160/D1 **Smooth Rock Falls**, On,Can
71/G5 **Smrčina** (peak), Czh.
71/H4 **Smutná** (riv.), Czh.
113/U **Smyley** (isl.), Ant.
166/C5 **Smyrna** (riv.), De,US
163/G3 **Smyrna**, Ga,US
56/D3 **Snaefell** (mtn.), IM,UK
151/M2 **Snake** (riv.), Yk,Can
156/D4 **Snake** (riv.), US
159/G2 **Snake** (riv.), Ne,US
156/E5 **Snake River** (plain), Id,US
115/Q12 **Snares** (isls.), NZ
66/C2 **Sneek**, Neth.
66/C2 **Sneekermeer** (lake), Neth.
132/D3 **Sneeuberg** (mts.), SAfr.
132/B4 **Sneeuberg** (peak), SAfr.
132/L11 **Sneeuwkop** (peak), SAfr.
161/Q8 **Snelgrove**, On,Can
59/G1 **Snettisham**, Eng,UK
65/H3 **Sněžka** (peak), Czh.
82/B3 **Snežnik** (peak), Yugo.
65/L2 **Śniardwy** (lake), Pol.
59/G4 **Snodland**, Eng,UK
61/D3 **Snøhetta** (peak), Nor.
165/C2 **Snohomish**, Wa,US
165/D2 **Snohomish** (co.), Wa,US
165/C2 **Snohomish** (riv.), Wa,US
165/D2 **Snoqualmie** (falls), Wa,US
165/D2 **Snoqualmie** (riv.), Wa,US
165/D3 **Snoqualmie, Middle Fork** (riv.), Wa,US
165/D3 **Snoqualmie-Mount Baker Nat'l For.**, Wa,US
165/D2 **Snoqualmie, North Fork** (riv.), Wa,US
165/D3 **Snoqualmie, South Fork** (riv.), Wa,US
61/E2 **Snøtind** (peak), Nor.
56/D5 **Snowdon** (mtn.), Wal,UK
56/D5 **Snowdonia Nat'l Park**, Wal,UK
158/E4 **Snowflake**, Az,US
157/H2 **Snow Lake**, Mb,Can
119/D3 **Snowy** (riv.), Austl.
151/K2 **Snowy** (peak), Ak,US
119/D3 **Snowy River Nat'l Park**, Austl.
166/A2 **Snyder** (co.), Pa,US
162/C3 **Snyder**, Tx,US
138/C3 **Soacha**, Col.
133/H7 **Soalala**, Madg.
78/A2 **Soana** (riv.), It.
133/J7 **Soanierana-Ivongo**, Madg.
57/G6 **Soar** (riv.), Eng,UK
101/D5 **Sobaek** (mts.), SKor.
149/G4 **Soberania Nat'l Park**, Pan.
71/H4 **Soběslav**, Czh.
111/K4 **Sobger** (riv.), Indo.
95/J3 **Sobhādero**, Pak.
140/B3 **Sobradinho** (res.), Braz.
140/B1 **Sobral**, Braz.
77/G5 **Sobretta, Monte** (peak), It.
99/M9 **Sobue**, Japan
79/G1 **Soča** (riv.), Slov.
144/D5 **Socabaya**, Peru
65/L2 **Sochaczew**, Pol.
86/F4 **Sochi**, Rus.
121/K6 **Society** (isls.), FrPol.
141/G7 **Socorro**, Braz.
138/C3 **Socorro**, Col.
146/C5 **Socorro** (isl.), Mex.
158/F4 **Socorro**, NM,US
162/B4 **Socorro**, Tx,US
90/E8 **Socotra** (isl.), Yem.
109/D4 **Soc Trang**, Viet.
74/D3 **Socuéllamos**, Sp.
61/H2 **Sodankylä**, Fin.
156/F5 **Soda Springs**, Id,US
99/H7 **Sodegaura**, Japan
62/G1 **Söderhamn**, Swe.
62/G2 **Söderköping**, Swe.
62/G2 **Södermanland** (co.), Swe.
62/G2 **Södertälje**, Swe.
63/R7 **Södertorn** (pen.), Swe.
125/N6 **Sodo**, Eth.
63/R7 **Södra Björkfjärden** (bay), Swe.
63/S7 **Södra Ljusterö** (isl.), Swe.
131/C4 **Soekmekaar**, SAfr.
67/F5 **Soest**, Ger.
66/C4 **Soest**, Neth.
67/E3 **Soeste** (riv.), Ger.
131/D3 **Sofala** (prov.), Moz.
133/J6 **Sofia** (riv.), Madg.
83/F4 **Sofia (Sofiya)** (cap.), Bul.
82/F4 **Sofiya** (reg.), Bul.
83/F4 **Sofiya (Sofia)** (cap.), Bul.
130/C4 **Soga**, Tanz.
138/C3 **Sogamoso**, Col.
138/C3 **Sogamoso** (riv.), Col.
62/A1 **Sognafjorden** (fjord), Nor.
62/B2 **Søgne**, Nor.
62/A1 **Sogn og Fjordane** (co.), Nor.
112/D3 **Sogod**, Phil.
124/J4 **Sogollé** (well), Chad
92/C1 **Soğuksu Nat'l Park**, Turk.
92/B2 **Söğüt**, Turk.
130/B2 **Sogwass** (peak), Ugan.
97/K5 **Sŏgwip'o**, SKor.
59/G2 **Soham**, Eng,UK
68/D2 **Soignies**, Belg.
53/U11 **Soignolles-en-Brie**, Fr.
68/C5 **Soissons**, Fr.
53/T11 **Soisy-sur-Seine**, Fr.
98/C3 **Sōja**, Japan
106/B2 **Sojat**, India
101/C3 **Sŏjosŏn** (bay), NKor.
87/J1 **Sok** (riv.), Rus.
109/C3 **Sok** (pt.), Thai.
99/H7 **Sōka**, Japan
101/E3 **Sokch'o**, SKor.
92/A2 **Söke**, Turk.
96/F1 **Sokhor** (peak), Rus.
82/E4 **Sokobanja**, Yugo.
129/F4 **Sokodé**, Togo
71/G4 **Sokol** (peak), Czh.
84/J4 **Sokol**, Rus.
65/M2 **Sokółka**, Pol.
71/F2 **Sokolov**, Czh.
65/M2 **Sokołów Podlaski**, Pol.
129/G4 **Sokoto** (plains), Nga.
129/G4 **Sokoto** (riv.), Nga.
129/G3 **Sokoto** (state), Nga.
62/A2 **Sola**, Nor.
112/C1 **Solana**, Phil.
164/C5 **Solana Beach**, Ca,US
140/D2 **Solânea**, Braz.
138/B3 **Solano** (pt.), Col.
112/C1 **Solano**, Phil.
165/L10 **Solano** (co.), Ca,US
77/H3 **Solbad Hall in Tirol**, Aus.
74/C4 **Sol, Costa del** (coast), Sp.
75/P10 **Sol, Costa do** (reg.), Port.
159/J2 **Soldier** (riv.), Ia,US
138/C2 **Soledad**, Col.
164/B2 **Soledad** (canyon), Ca,US
139/F2 **Soledad**, Ven.
147/N7 **Soledad de Doblado**, Mex.
141/A4 **Soledade**, Braz.
59/E5 **Solent** (chan.), Eng,UK
79/E2 **Solesino**, It.
69/E4 **Soleuvre** (mtn.), Lux.
92/E2 **Solhan**, Turk.
86/C1 **Soligorsk**, Bela.
59/E2 **Solihull**, Eng,UK
85/N4 **Solikamsk**, Rus.
87/K2 **Sol'-Iletsk**, Rus.
139/E5 **Solimões** (Amazon) (riv.), Braz.
67/E6 **Solingen**, Ger.
61/F3 **Sollefteå**, Swe.
62/G2 **Sollentuna**, Swe.
75/G3 **Sóller**, Sp.
63/T9 **Søllerød**, Den.
67/G5 **Solling** (mts.), Ger.
70/B2 **Solmsbach** (riv.), Ger.
61/D3 **Søln** (peak), Nor.
63/S7 **Solna**, Swe.
76/B5 **Solnan** (riv.), Fr.
110/D5 **Solo** (riv.), Indo.
110/B4 **Solok**, Indo.
148/D3 **Sololá**, Guat.
120/E5 **Solomon** (sea), PNG, Sol.
162/D2 **Solomon** (riv.), Ks,US
120/E6 **Solomon Islands**
159/G3 **Solomon, North Fork** (riv.), Ks,US
168/F5 **Solon**, Oh,US
87/L4 **Solonchak Goklenkui** (salt marsh), Trkm.
76/D3 **Solothurn**, Swi.
76/D3 **Solothurn** (canton), Swi.
84/G2 **Solovetskiy** (isls.), Rus.
75/F2 **Solsona**, Sp.
82/D2 **Solt**, Hun.
82/B4 **Šolta** (isl.), Cro.
67/G3 **Soltau**, Ger.
70/D2 **Soltvadkert**, Hun.
82/E5 **Solunska** (peak), Macd.
58/A3 **Solva** (riv.), Wal,UK
158/B4 **Solvang**, Ca,US
62/F3 **Sölvesborg**, Swe.
56/E2 **Solway Firth** (inlet), Eng, Sc,UK
131/B2 **Solwezi**, Zam.
99/G2 **Sōma**, Japan
92/A2 **Soma**, Turk.
131/C3 **Somabhula**, Zim.
68/C3 **Somain**, Fr.
123/G4 **Somalia**
161/F1 **Somaqua** (riv.), Qu,Can
82/D3 **Sombor**, Cro.
146/E4 **Sombrerete**, Mex.
141/B4 **Sombrio**, Braz.
57/G5 **Somercotes**, Eng,UK
66/C6 **Someren**, Neth.
63/K1 **Somero**, Fin.
156/E3 **Somers**, Mt,US
152/G1 **Somerset** (isl.), NW,Can
58/D4 **Somerset** (co.), Eng,UK
160/C4 **Somerset**, Ky,US
168/C2 **Somerset**, Ma,US
166/D3 **Somerset**, NJ,US
166/D2 **Somerset** (co.), NJ,US
161/S9 **Somerset**, NY,US
119/C4 **Somerset-Burnie**, Austl.
132/D4 **Somerset East**, SAfr.
132/B4 **Somerset West**, SAfr.
59/F2 **Somersham**, Eng,UK
166/D5 **Somers Point**, NJ,US
161/G3 **Somersworth**, NH,US
58/D4 **Somerton**, Eng,UK
158/D4 **Somerton**, Az,US
168/C1 **Somerville**, Ma,US
166/D2 **Somerville**, NJ,US
159/H5 **Somerville** (lake), Tx,US
83/F2 **Someş** (riv.), Rom.
83/G2 **Someşul Mare** (riv.), Rom.
101/D5 **Sŏmjin** (riv.), SKor.
78/B1 **Somma Lombardo**, It.
123/T15 **Sommam** (riv.), Alg.
72/D1 **Somme** (bay), Fr.
68/B4 **Somme** (dept.), Fr.
68/A3 **Somme** (riv.), Fr.
68/D6 **Somme** (riv.), Fr.
68/B4 **Somme, Canal de La** (can.), Fr.
62/F3 **Sommen** (lake), Swe.
68/D5 **Somme-Soude** (riv.), Fr.
82/C2 **Somogy** (co.), Hun.
59/F5 **Somptin**, Eng,UK
62/C4 **Sønderborg**, Den.
132/L11 **Sonderend** (riv.), SAfr.
62/C4 **Sønderjylland** (co.), Den.
77/F5 **Sondrio**, It.
77/F5 **Sondrio** (prov.), It.
106/C2 **Sonepat**, India
106/D3 **Sonepur**, India
109/E3 **Song Cau**, Viet.
109/D4 **Song Dinh**, Viet.
130/B5 **Songea**, Tanz.
103/F1 **Songhua** (riv.), China
103/E5 **Songjiang**, China
103/L8 **Songjiang**, China
102/B3 **Song-Kel'** (lake), Kyr.
109/C5 **Songkhla**, Thai.
109/C2 **Songkhram** (riv.), Thai.
97/J2 **Songling**, China
109/C1 **Song Ma**, Viet.
104/D3 **Songming**, China
101/D4 **Sŏngnam**, SKor.
131/D2 **Songo**, Moz.
126/B2 **Songololo**, Zaire
103/C4 **Song Shan** (peak), China
101/D4 **Songt'an**, SKor.
105/F2 **Songtao Miaozu Zizhixian**, China
105/H3 **Songxi**, China
103/C4 **Song Xian**, China
103/B5 **Songzi**, China
105/G2 **Songzi Guan** (pass), China
105/G2 **Songzi Hudu** (riv.), China
109/E3 **Son Ha**, Viet.
99/M10 **Soni**, Japan
96/G3 **Sonid Youqi**, China
96/G3 **Sonid Zuoqi**, China
109/C1 **Son La**, Viet.
95/J3 **Sonmiāni** (bay), Pak.
70/E2 **Sonneberg**, Ger.
59/F4 **Sonning**, Eng,UK
77/H3 **Sonnjoch** (peak), Aus.
64/G5 **Sonntagshorn** (peak), Ger.
140/A3 **Sono** (riv.), Braz.
140/A5 **Sono** (riv.), Braz.
98/D3 **Sonobe**, Japan
165/K10 **Sonoma**, Ca,US
165/J10 **Sonoma** (co.), Ca,US
165/J10 **Sonoma** (cr.), Ca,US
165/J10 **Sonoma** (mts.), Ca,US
146/C2 **Sonora** (riv.), Mex.
158/B3 **Sonora**, Ca,US
162/C4 **Sonora**, Tx,US
93/F3 **Sonqor**, Iran
66/D5 **Sonsbeck**, Ger.
74/D3 **Sonseca**, Sp.
138/C3 **Sonsón**, Col.
148/D3 **Sonsonate**, ESal.
120/C4 **Sonsorol** (isls.), Palau
82/D3 **Sonta**, Yugo.
109/D1 **Son Tay**, Viet.
77/G2 **Sonthofen**, Ger.
67/G6 **Sontra**, Ger.
111/G3 **Sopi** (cape), Indo.
109/C1 **Sopka**, Laos
95/K2 **Sopore**, India
83/G4 **Sopot**, Bul.
65/K1 **Sopot**, Pol.
82/C2 **Sopron**, Hun.
58/D3 **Sôr** (riv.), Wal,UK
80/C2 **Sora**, It.
101/E3 **Sŏrak-san** (mtn.), SKor.
101/E3 **Sŏraksan Nat'l Park**, SKor.
161/F2 **Sorel**, Qu,Can
91/F8 **Soreq, Nabel** (dry riv.), Isr.
78/C2 **Soresina**, It.
72/F5 **Sorgues**, Fr.
92/C2 **Sorgun**, Turk.
74/D2 **Soria**, Sp.
143/F2 **Soriano** (dept.), Uru.
110/A3 **Sorikmerapi** (peak), Indo.
87/K3 **Sor Karatuley** (salt pan), Kaz.
87/K3 **Sor Kaydak** (salt marsh), Kaz.
87/K3 **Sor Mertvyy Kultuk** (salt marsh), Kaz.
68/D4 **Sormonne** (riv.), Fr.
62/D4 **Sorø**, Den.
141/C2 **Sorocaba**, Braz.
87/K1 **Sorochinsk**, Rus.
83/J1 **Soroki**, Mol.
120/D4 **Sorol** (atoll), Micr.
111/H4 **Sorong**, Indo.
139/G3 **Sororieng** (mtn.), Guy.
130/B2 **Soroti**, Ugan.
61/G1 **Sørøya** (isl.), Nor.
61/G1 **Sørøysundet** (chan.), Nor.
67/E6 **Sorpestausee** (res.), Ger.
74/A3 **Sorraia** (riv.), Port.
80/D2 **Sorrento**, It.
126/B5 **Sorris-Sorris**, Namb.
80/A2 **Sorso**, It.
112/D2 **Sorsogon**, Phil.
84/F3 **Sortavala**, Rus.
63/K3 **Sörve** (pt.), Est.
101/D4 **Sŏsan**, SKor.
101/C4 **Sŏsan Haean Nat'l Park**, SKor.
67/H5 **Söse** (riv.), Ger.
86/F1 **Sosna** (riv.), Rus.
142/C2 **Sosneado** (peak), Arg.
85/M3 **Sosnogorsk**, Rus.
85/L4 **Sosnovka**, Rus.
65/K3 **Sosnowiec**, Pol.
130/B3 **Sotik**, Kenya
79/F2 **Sottomarina**, It.
68/D6 **Soude** (riv.), Fr.
150/F3 **Soufrière** (peak), Guad.
150/F4 **Soufrière** (peak), StV.
123/V17 **Souk Ahras**, Alg.
123/V17 **Souk Ahras** (gov.), Alg.
161/M7 **Soulanges** (co.), Qu,Can
101/D4 **Sŏul (Seoul)** (cap.), SKor.
69/G1 **Soultz-sous-Forets**, Fr.
129/E3 **Soum** (prov.), Burk.
69/E2 **Soumagne**, Belg.
132/E3 **Sources, Mont aux** (peak), Les.
137/J4 **Soure**, Braz.
74/A2 **Soure**, Port.
123/S15 **Sour El Ghozlane**, Alg.
157/H3 **Souris**, Mb,Can
161/J2 **Souris**, PE,Can
157/H3 **Souris** (riv.), Can., US
128/E3 **Sourou** (prov.), Burk.
124/D2 **Sous** (wadi), Mor.
140/C2 **Sousa**, Braz.
74/B3 **Sousel**, Port.
132/C3 **Sout** (dry riv.), SAfr.
132/M11 **Sout** (riv.), SAfr.
118/G8 **South** (cr.), Austl.
161/H2 **South** (mts.), NS,Can
153/H2 **South** (bay), NW,Can
60/A3 **South** (sound), Ire.
115/Q12 **South** (cape), NZ
115/Q11 **South** (isl.), NZ
126/D6 **South Africa**
53/M7 **Southall**, Eng,UK
59/E2 **Southam**, Eng,UK
167/H10 **South Amboy**, NJ,US
153/H2 **Southampton** (cape), NW,Can
145/J3 **Southampton** (isl.), NW,Can
153/H2 **Southampton** (isl.), NW,Can
160/D2 **Southampton**, On,Can
59/E5 **Southampton**, Eng,UK
59/E5 **Southampton Water** (inlet), Eng,UK
107/F5 **South Andaman** (isl.), India
163/J2 **South Anna** (riv.), Va,US
50/J6 **South Atlantic** (ocean)
163/H3 **South Augusta**, Ga,US
153/K3 **South Aulatsivik** (isl.), Nf,Can
117/F4 **South Australia** (state), Austl.
163/F3 **Southaven**, Ms,US
56/D3 **South Barrule** (mtn.), IM,UK
160/C3 **South Bend**, In,US
53/P8 **Southborough**, Eng,UK
168/C1 **Southborough**, Ma,US
160/E4 **South Boston**, Va,US
59/F5 **Southbourne**, Eng,UK
58/C6 **South Brent**, Eng,UK
168/B1 **Southbridge**, Ma,US
130/A3 **South Buganda** (prov.), Ugan.
161/F2 **South Burlington**, Vt,US
168/A3 **Southbury**, Ct,US
149/J1 **South Caicos** (isl.), Trks.
163/H3 **South Carolina** (state), US
90/L8 **South China** (sea), Asia
157/H4 **South Dakota** (state), US
58/D5 **South Dorset Downs** (uplands), Eng,UK
59/F5 **South Downs** (hills), Eng,UK
51/S8 **South East** (cape), Austl.
119/C3 **South East** (pt.), Austl.
150/C2 **Southeast** (pt.), Bahm.
131/B5 **South-East** (dist.), Bots.
149/G2 **Southeast** (pt.), Jam.
151/E3 **Southeast** (cape), Ak,US
165/P16 **South Elgin**, Il,US
57/G4 **South Elmsall**, Eng,UK
56/C1 **Southend**, Sc,UK
59/G3 **Southend-on-Sea**, Eng,UK
116/K7 **Southern** (riv.), Austl.
131/B5 **Southern** (dist.), Bots.
91/D4 **Southern** (dist.), Isr.
131/D2 **Southern** (reg.), Malw.
128/B5 **Southern** (prov.), SLeo.
130/A3 **Southern** (prov.), Ugan.
131/B3 **Southern** (prov.), Zam.
115/Q11 **Southern Alps** (range), NZ
121/J6 **Southern Cook** (isls.), CookIs.
152/G3 **Southern Indian** (lake), Mb,Can
163/J3 **Southern Pines**, NC,US
54/C5 **Southern Uplands** (mts.), Sc,UK
85/N5 **Southern Ural** (mts.), Rus.
59/G1 **Southery**, Eng,UK
119/C4 **South Esk** (riv.), Austl.
54/C5 **South Esk** (riv.), Sc,UK
54/D3 **South Esk** (riv.), Sc,UK
116/E2 **Southesk Tablelands** (plat.), Austl.
168/F4 **South Euclid**, Oh,US
165/F7 **Southfield**, Mi,US
59/H4 **South Foreland** (pt.), Eng,UK
158/F3 **South Fork**, Co,US
163/F2 **South Fulton**, Tn,US
53/N7 **Southgate**, Eng,UK
164/B3 **South Gate**, Ca,US
165/F7 **Southgate**, Mi,US
113/X **South Georgia** (isl.), UK
58/C4 **South Glamorgan** (co.), Wal,UK
168/B1 **South Hadley**, Ma,US
58/C6 **South Hams** (plain), Eng,UK
59/F5 **South Hayling**, Eng,UK
160/E4 **South Hill**, Va,US
66/B5 **South Holland** (prov.), Neth.
165/Q16 **South Holland**, Il,US
53/N8 **South Holmwood**, Eng,UK
130/C2 **South Horr**, Kenya
168/B2 **Southington**, Ct,US
130/C2 **South Island Nat'l Park**, Kenya
130/C3 **South Kinangop**, Kenya
57/G4 **South Kirkby**, Eng,UK
130/C3 **South Kitui Nat'l Rsv.**, Kenya
101/D4 **South Korea**
158/C3 **South Lake Tahoe**, Ca,US
159/H2 **South Loup** (riv.), Ne,US
131/C2 **South Luangwa Nat'l Park**, Zam.
113/K **South Magnetic Pole**, Ant.
165/Q14 **South Milwaukee**, Wi,US
59/G3 **Southminster**, Eng,UK
58/C4 **South Molton**, Eng,UK
157/J2 **South Moose** (lake), Mb,Can
151/M5 **South Moresby Nat'l Park Rsv.**, BC,Can
166/A3 **South Mtn.** (ridge), Pa,US
57/G5 **South Normanton**, Eng,UK
53/P7 **South Ockenden**, Eng,UK
167/H9 **South Orange**, NJ,US
113/W **South Orkney** (isls.), UK
87/G4 **South Ossetian Aut. Obl.**, Geo.
53/M7 **South Oxhey**, Eng,UK
167/M9 **South Oyster** (bay), NY,US
120/G7 **South Pacific** (ocean)
117/M8 **South Para** (res.), Austl.
117/M8 **South Para** (riv.), Austl.
164/F7 **South Pasadena**, Ca,US
116/K6 **South Perth**, Austl.
58/D5 **South Petherton**, Eng,UK
118/E6 **South Pine** (riv.), Austl.
166/D2 **South Plainfield**, NJ,US
159/G2 **South Platte** (riv.), Co, Ne,US
113/W **South Polar** (plat.), Ant.
113/A **South Pole**, Ant.
57/E4 **Southport**, Eng,UK
163/J3 **Southport**, NC,US
165/C3 **South Prairie** (cr.), Wa,US
54/C5 **South Queensferry**, Sc,UK
166/D3 **South River**, NJ,US
55/N13 **South Ronaldsay** (isl.), Sc,UK
131/D1 **South Rukuru** (riv.), Malw.
113/Y **South Sandwich** (isls.), UK
165/K11 **South San Francisco**, Ca,US
156/F3 **South Saskatchewan** (riv.), Ab, Sk,Can
113/W **South Shetland** (isls.), UK
57/G2 **South Shields**, Eng,UK
159/H2 **South Sioux City**, Ne,US
159/J2 **South Skunk** (riv.), Ia,US
106/E3 **South Suburban**, India
115/R10 **South Taranaki** (bight), NZ
130/B2 **South Turkana Nat'l Rsv.**, Kenya
57/F2 **South Tyne** (riv.), Eng,UK
112/C4 **South Ubian**, Phil.
55/H8 **South Uist** (isl.), Sc,UK
158/B2 **South Umpqua** (riv.), Or,US
53/N7 **Southwark** (bor.), Eng,UK
57/H5 **Southwell**, Eng,UK
119/C4 **South West** (cape), Austl.
150/B1 **Southwest** (pt.), Bahm.
150/C2 **Southwest** (pt.), Bahm.
119/C4 **South West Nat'l Park**, Austl.
164/F8 **South Whittier**, Ca,US
168/B1 **Southwick**, Ma,US
166/B1 **South Williamsport**, Pa,US
59/H2 **Southwold**, Eng,UK
59/G3 **South Woodham Ferrers**, Eng,UK
118/C4 **Southwood Nat'l Park**, Austl.
57/G5 **South Yorkshire** (co.), Eng,UK
131/C4 **Soutpansberg** (mts.), SAfr.
83/G2 **Sovata**, Rom.
80/E3 **Soverato Marina**, It.
63/J4 **Sovetsk**, Rus.
97/N2 **Sovetskaya Gavan'**, Rus.
131/B4 **Sowa Pan** (salt pan), Bots.
57/G4 **Sowerby Bridge**, Eng,UK
132/D2 **Soweto**, SAfr.
100/B1 **Sōya-misaki** (cape), Japan
84/J2 **Soyana** (riv.), Rus.
101/D4 **Soyang** (lake), SKor.
72/D4 **Soyaux**, Fr.
113/E **Soyuz**, Ant.
86/D1 **Sozh** (riv.), Eur.
69/E3 **Spa**, Belg.
113/U **Spaatz** (isl.), Ant.
163/H4 **Spaceport USA**, Fl,US
165/D2 **Spada** (lake), Wa,US
74/C2 **Spain**
57/H6 **Spalding**, Eng,UK
165/C3 **Spanaway**, Wa,US
60/A4 **Spanish** (pt.), Ire.
55/J9 **Spanish Head** (pt.), IM,UK
149/G2 **Spanish Town**, Jam.
77/E4 **Spannort** (peak), Swi.
158/C3 **Sparks**, Nv,US
163/H2 **Sparta**, NC,US
166/D1 **Sparta**, NJ,US
163/G3 **Sparta**, Tn,US
160/B3 **Sparta**, Wi,US
163/H3 **Spartanburg**, SC,US
81/H4 **Spárta (Spárti)**, Gre.
123/M13 **Spartel** (cape), Mor.
81/H4 **Spárti (Sparta)**, Gre.
80/A3 **Spartivento** (cape), It.
80/E4 **Spartivento** (cape), It.
156/E3 **Sparwood**, BC,Can
97/L3 **Spassk-Dal'niy**, Rus.
81/H5 **Spátha, Ákra** (cape), Gre.
54/B3 **Spean** (riv.), Sc,UK
54/B3 **Spean Bridge**, Sc,UK
157/H4 **Spearfish**, SD,US
77/F3 **Speer** (peak), Swi.
130/B3 **Speke** (gulf), Tanz.
57/F5 **Speke**, Eng,UK
117/H5 **Spencer** (cape), Austl.
117/H5 **Spencer** (gulf), Austl.
151/E2 **Spencer** (pt.), Ak,US
157/K5 **Spencer**, Ia,US
168/C1 **Spencer**, Ma,US
67/F4 **Spenge**, Ger.
57/G2 **Spennymoor**, Eng,UK
81/H3 **Sperkhiós** (riv.), Gre.
56/A2 **Sperrin** (mts.), NI,UK
70/C3 **Spessart** (range), Ger.
54/C1 **Spey** (bay), Sc,UK
54/C1 **Spey** (riv.), Sc,UK
70/B4 **Speyer**, Ger.
70/B4 **Speyerbach** (riv.), Ger.
161/Q8 **Speyside**, On,Can
80/E3 **Spezzano Albanese**, It.
71/F2 **Špičák** (peak), Czh.
153/H2 **Spicer** (isl.), NW,Can
67/E1 **Spiekeroog** (isl.), Ger.
76/D4 **Spiez**, Swi.
66/B5 **Spijkenisse**, Neth.
151/K2 **Spike** (mtn.), Ak,US
82/A2 **Spilimbergo**, It.
57/J5 **Spilsby**, Eng,UK
80/A2 **Spina, Bruncu** (peak), It.
95/J2 **Spin Būldak**, Afg.
69/E5 **Spincourt**, Fr.
78/B3 **Spinetta Marengo**, It.
156/D2 **Spirit River**, Ab,Can
156/G2 **Spiritwood**, Sk,Can
65/L4 **Spišská Nová Ves**, Slvk.
59/E5 **Spithead** (chan.), Eng,UK
108/D1 **Spiti** (riv.), India
88/B2 **Spitsbergen** (isl.), Sval.
73/K3 **Spittal an der Drau**, Aus.
157/K2 **Split** (lake), Mb,Can
82/C4 **Split**, Cro.
167/H8 **Splitrock** (res.), NJ,US
77/F4 **Splügenpass** (pass), It.
156/D4 **Spokane** (riv.), Id, Wa,US
156/D4 **Spokane**, Wa,US
77/G5 **Spöl** (riv.), It.
80/C1 **Spoleto**, It.
160/B3 **Spoon** (riv.), Il,US
160/B2 **Spooner**, Wi,US
166/D3 **Spotswood**, NJ,US
157/K3 **Sprague**, Mb,Can
66/C5 **Sprang-Capelle**, Neth.
110/D2 **Spratly** (isls.)
65/H2 **Spree** (riv.), Ger.
79/F1 **Spresiano**, It.
69/E3 **Sprimont**, Belg.
163/G4 **Spring** (cr.), Ga,US
162/E4 **Spring**, Tx,US
131/C5 **Springbokvlakte** (val.), SAfr.
161/K1 **Springdale**, Nf,Can
162/E2 **Springdale**, Ar,US
67/G4 **Springe**, Ger.
159/F3 **Springer**, NM,US
158/E4 **Springerville**, Az,US
159/G3 **Springfield**, Co,US
160/B4 **Springfield** (cap.), Il,US
168/B1 **Springfield**, Ma,US
159/J3 **Springfield**, Mo,US
167/H9 **Springfield**, NJ,US
160/D4 **Springfield**, Oh,US
156/C4 **Springfield**, Or,US
163/G2 **Springfield**, Tn,US
166/A6 **Springfield**, Va,US
161/F3 **Springfield**, Vt,US
161/H2 **Springhill**, NS,Can
162/E3 **Springhill**, La,US
132/E2 **Springs**, SAfr.
157/H3 **Springside**, Sk,Can
119/G5 **Springvale**
164/D5 **Spring Valley**, Ca,US
157/K5 **Spring Valley**, Mn,US
167/D1 **Spring Valley**, NY,US
67/E6 **Sprockhövel**, Ger.
59/H1 **Sprowston**, Eng,UK
160/E4 **Spruce** (peak), WV,US
166/C2 **Spruce Run** (res.), NJ,US
66/B5 **Spui** (riv.), Neth.
57/J4 **Spurn Head** (pt.), Eng,UK
156/C3 **Squamish**, BC,Can
165/B3 **Squaxin I. Ind. Res.**, Wa,US
168/D3 **Squibnocket** (pt.), Ma,US
80/E3 **Squillace** (gulf), It.
81/F2 **Squinzano**, It.
117/E3 **Squires** (peak), Austl.
82/D3 **Srbobran**, Yugo.
109/C4 **Sre Ambel**, Camb.
82/D3 **Srebrenica**, Bosn.
83/G4 **Sredna** (mts.), Bul.
83/G4 **Srednogorie**, Bul.
109/D3 **Sre Khtum**, Camb.
65/J2 **Śrem**, Pol.
82/E3 **Sremčica**, Yugo.
82/D3 **Sremska Mitrovica**, Yugo.
109/C3 **Sreng** (riv.), Camb.
109/D3 **Sre Noy**, Camb.
109/D3 **Srepok** (riv.), Camb.
97/H1 **Sretensk**, Rus.
95/K3 **Sri Dungargarh**, India
95/K3 **Sri Gangānagar**, India
106/D4 **Srikākulam**, India
104/B5 **Sri Kshetra** (ruins), Burma
106/D6 **Sri Lanka**
95/K2 **Srīnagar**, India
108/G3 **Srīrangam**, India
108/F4 **Srīvaikuntam**, India
106/B4 **Srīvardhan**, India
108/F4 **Srīvilliputtūr**, India
65/J3 **Środa Śląska**, Pol.
65/J2 **Środa Wielkopolska**, Pol.
118/A2 **Staaten** (riv.), Austl.
118/A2 **Staaten River Nat'l Park**, Austl.
61/H1 **Stabbursdalen Nat'l Park**, Nor.
62/D4 **Staberhuk** (pt.), Ger.
66/B6 **Stabroek**, Belg.
67/G1 **Stade**, Ger.
68/C2 **Staden**, Belg.
66/D3 **Stadskanaal**, Neth.
70/D6 **Stadtbergen**, Ger.
67/G4 **Stadthagen**, Ger.
66/D5 **Stadtlohn**, Ger.
77/E3 **Stäfa**, Swi.
62/E4 **Staffanstorp**, Swe.
70/E2 **Staffelberg** (peak), Ger.
76/E3 **Staffelegg** (pass), Swi.
77/H2 **Staffelsee** (lake), Ger.
78/C3 **Staffora** (riv.), It.
57/F6 **Stafford**, Eng,UK
168/B2 **Stafford**, Ct,US
58/D2 **Stafford & Worcester** (can.), Eng,UK
57/F5 **Staffordshire** (co.), Eng,UK
80/B4 **Stagnone** (isls.), It.
57/G2 **Staindrop**, Eng,UK
53/M7 **Staines**, Eng,UK
53/T10 **Stains**, Fr.
54/B5 **Stake, Hill of** (hill), Sc,UK
165/M12 **Stakes** (mtn.), Ca,US
86/F2 **Stakhanov**, Ukr.
58/D5 **Stalbridge**, Eng,UK
59/H1 **Stalham**, Eng,UK
153/S6 **Stallworthy** (cape), NW,Can
65/M3 **Stalowa Wola**, Pol.
57/F5 **Stalybridge**, Eng,UK
83/G4 **Stamboliyski**, Bul.
59/F1 **Stamford**, Eng,UK
167/E1 **Stamford**, Ct,US
57/H4 **Stamford Bridge**, Eng,UK
61/E1 **Stamsund**, Nor.
60/D2 **Stamullin**, Ire.
132/E2 **Standerton**, SAfr.
57/F4 **Standish-with-Langtree**, Eng,UK
59/G4 **Stanford le Hope**, Eng,UK
53/P6 **Stanford Rivers**, Eng,UK
62/D1 **Stange**, Nor.
133/E3 **Stanger**, SAfr.
57/F2 **Stanhope**, Eng,UK
165/M12 **Stanislaus** (co.), Ca,US
158/B3 **Stanislaus** (riv.), Ca,US
83/F4 **Stanke Dimitrov**, Bul.
117/F2 **Stanley** (peak), Austl.
161/H2 **Stanley**, NB,Can
108/F3 **Stanley** (res.), India
57/G2 **Stanley**, Eng,UK
143/N7 **Stanley**, (cap.),Falk.
54/C4 **Stanley**, Sc,UK
157/H3 **Stanley**, ND,US
125/L8 **Stanley** (falls), Zaire
82/E4 **Stanovo**, Yugo.
89/N4 **Stanovoy** (range), Rus.
53/P8 **Stansted**, Eng,UK
59/G3 **Stansted Mountfitchet**, Eng,UK
59/G2 **Stanton**, Eng,UK
164/C3 **Stanton**, Ca,US
160/D4 **Stanton**, Ky,US
162/C3 **Stanton**, Tx,US
53/M7 **Stanwell**, Eng,UK
66/D3 **Staphorst**, Neth.
59/E4 **Stapleford**, Eng,UK
53/P7 **Stapleford Abbotts**, Eng,UK
59/G4 **Staplehurst**, Eng,UK
65/L3 **Starachowice**, Pol.
82/E3 **Stara Pazova**, Yugo.
82/F3 **Stara Planina** (mts.), Yugo.
84/F4 **Staraya Russa**, Rus.
83/G4 **Stara Zagora**, Bul.
121/K5 **Starbuck** (isl.), Kiri.
118/B1 **Starcke Nat'l Park**, Austl.
65/H2 **Stargard Szczeciński**, Pol.
168/F6 **Stark** (co.), Oh,US
163/H4 **Starke**, Fl,US
163/F3 **Starkville**, Ms,US
77/H2 **Starnbergersee** (lake), Ger.
86/F3 **Staroderevyan-kovskaya**, Rus.
86/E1 **Starodub**, Rus.
65/K2 **Starogard Gdański**, Pol.
86/F3 **Staroshcher-binovskaya**, Rus.
58/C6 **Start** (bay), Eng,UK
58/C6 **Start** (pt.), Eng,UK
55/N13 **Start** (pt.), Sc,UK
65/L3 **Staszów**, Pol.
160/E3 **State College**, Pa,US
166/C6 **State Fairgnds.**, De,US
167/D2 **Staten** (isl.), NY,US
163/H3 **Statesboro**, Ga,US
163/H3 **Statesville**, NC,US
167/J9 **Statue of Liberty Nat'l Mon.**, NY,US
64/E3 **Staufenberg**, Ger.
76/D2 **Staufen im Breisgau**, Ger.
58/D3 **Staunton**, Eng,UK
160/E4 **Staunton**, Va,US
58/D2 **Staunton on Wye**, Eng,UK
77/G4 **Stausee Gepatsch** (lake), Aus.

222

Staus – Tachi

71/E1 Stausee-Hohenwarte (res.), Ger.
62/A2 Stavanger, Nor.
57/F3 Staveley, Eng,UK
57/G5 Staveley, Eng,UK
87/G3 Stavropol', Rus.
87/G3 Stavropol' Kray, Rus.
119/B3 Stawell, Austl.
156/C4 Stayton, Or,US
165/L10 Steamboat (slough), Ca,US
158/F2 Steamboat Springs, Co,US
67/H3 Stederau (riv.), Ger.
119/F5 Steele (cr.), Austl.
157/J4 Steele, ND,US
54/C4 Steele's Knowe (hill), Sc,UK
168/G5 Steel Museum, Youngstown, Oh,US
133/E2 Steelpoortrivier (riv.), SAfr.
66/B5 Steenbergen, Neth.
158/C2 Steens (mtn.), Or,US
153/J1 Steensby (inlet), NW,Can
66/D3 Steenwijk, Neth.
116/B3 Steep (pt.), Austl.
157/G1 Steephill (lake), Sk,Can
58/C4 Steep Holm (isl.), Eng,UK
57/J5 Steeping (riv.), Eng,UK
151/J2 Steese Nat'l Rec. Area, Ak,US
152/F1 Stefansson (isl.), NW,Can
142/C5 Steffen (peak), Chile
76/D4 Steffisburg, Swi.
82/A2 Steiermark (prov.), Aus.
70/D3 Steigerwald (for.), Ger.
131/C4 Steilloopbrug, SAfr.
64/F4 Stein, Ger.
69/E2 Stein, Neth.
77/E2 Steina (riv.), Ger.
70/E2 Steinach (riv.), Ger.
157/J3 Steinbach, Mb,Can
70/E4 Stein bei Nürnberg, Ger.
76/D2 Steinen, Ger.
67/F3 Steinfeld, Ger.
67/F5 Steinhagen, Ger.
77/E3 Steinhausen, Swi.
67/G5 Steinheim, Ger.
70/D5 Steinheim am Albuch, Ger.
70/C5 Steinheim an der Murr, Ger.
67/G4 Steinhuder Meer (lake), Ger.
61/D2 Steinkjer, Nor.
68/D1 Stekene, Belg.
77/F5 Stella, Pizzo (peak), It.
161/J2 Stellarton, NS,Can
67/H2 Stelle, Ger.
132/B4 Stellenbosch, SAfr.
73/H5 Stello (mtn.), Fr.
77/G5 Stelvio Nat'l Park, It.
77/G4 Stelvio, Passo di (pass), It.
64/F2 Stendal, Ger.
83/G4 Steneto Nat'l Park, Bul.
63/R7 Stenhamra, Swe.
54/C4 Stenhousemuir, Sc,UK
63/T9 Stenløse, Den.
62/D2 Stenungsund, Swe.
87/H5 Stepanakert, Azer.
119/B1 Stephens Creek, Austl.
161/K1 Stephenville, Nf,Can
162/D3 Stephenville, Tx,US
159/G2 Sterling, Co,US
168/C1 Sterling, Ma,US
162/C4 Sterling City, Tx,US
165/F6 Sterling Heights, Mi,US
87/K1 Sterlitamak, Rus.
71/H5 Sternstein (peak), Aus.
77/H4 Sterzing (Vipiteno), It.
71/H2 Štěti, Czh.
156/E2 Stettler, Ab,Can
168/G7 Steubenville, Oh,US
59/F3 Stevenage, Eng,UK
117/G3 Stevenson (cr.), Austl.
157/J2 Stevenson (lake), Mb,Can
151/H4 Stevenson (str.), Ak,US
168/A3 Stevenson (dam), Ct,US
160/B2 Stevens Point, Wi,US
54/B5 Stevenston, Sc,UK
156/E4 Stevensville, Mt,US
66/C3 Stevinsluizen (dam), Neth.
114/E2 Stewart (cape), Austl.
151/L3 Stewart (riv.), Yk,Can
115/Q12 Stewart (isl.), NZ
151/L3 Stewart Crossing, Yk,Can
54/B5 Stewarton, Sc,UK
151/L3 Stewart River, Yk,Can
56/B2 Stewartstown, NI,UK
157/K5 Stewartville, Mn,US
59/F5 Steyning, Eng,UK
71/H6 Steyr, Aus.
71/H6 Steyr (riv.), Aus.
165/D2 Stickney (mtn.), Wa,US
66/C2 Stiens, Neth.
159/J4 Stigler, Ok,US
151/M4 Stikine (riv.), BC,Can
166/C2 Still Creek (res.), Pa,US
157/K4 Stillwater, Mn,US
158/C3 Stillwater (range), Nv,US
159/H3 Stillwater, Ok,US
166/C1 Stillwater (lake), Pa,US
159/J4 Stilwell, Ok,US
56/D1 Stinchar (riv.), Sc,UK
162/C3 Stinnett, Tx,US
82/F5 Štip, Macd.
69/F5 Stiring-Wendel, Fr.
71/G4 Stírka (peak), Czh.
116/K6 Stirling, Austl.
117/G2 Stirling, Austl.
117/M9 Stirling, Austl.
116/C4 Stirling (peak), Austl.
54/C4 Stirling, Sc,UK
116/C5 Stirling Range Nat'l Park, Austl.
78/C3 Stirone (riv.), It.
61/D3 Stjørdal, Nor.
54/B4 Stob a' Choin (mtn.), Sc,UK
54/B3 Stob Choire Claurigh (mtn.), Sc,UK
77/F2 Stockach, Ger.
59/E4 Stockbridge, Eng,UK
65/J4 Stockerau, Aus.
71/E2 Stockheim, Ger.
62/H2 Stockholm (cap.), Swe.
63/S7 Stockholm (inset) (cap.), Swe.
76/D4 Stockhorn (peak), Swi.
146/E2 Stockon (plat.), Tx,US
131/B4 Stockpoort, SAfr.
57/F5 Stockport, Eng,UK
57/F4 Stocks (res.), Eng,UK
57/G5 Stocksbridge, Eng,UK
70/C3 Stockstadt am Main, Ger.
165/M11 Stockton, Ca,US
159/J3 Stockton (lake), Mo,US
162/C4 Stockton (plat.), Tx,US
57/G2 Stockton-on-Tees, Eng,UK
109/D3 Stoeng Treng, Camb.
58/B6 Stoke (pt.), Eng,UK
57/F5 Stoke-on-Trent, Eng,UK
119/B4 Stokes (pt.), Austl.
116/D5 Stokes Nat'l Park, Austl.
82/C4 Stolac, Bosn.
69/F2 Stolberg, Ger.
89/P2 Stolbovoy (isl.), Rus.
132/K10 Stompneuspunt (pt.), SAfr.
57/F6 Stone, Eng,UK
104/D3 Stone Forest, China
54/D3 Stonehaven, Sc,UK
59/E4 Stonehenge (ruins), Eng,UK
58/D3 Stonehouse, Eng,UK
54/C5 Stonehouse, Sc,UK
157/J3 Stonewall, Mb,Can
54/C5 Stoneyburn, Sc,UK
161/Q9 Stoney Creek, On,Can
157/J2 Stony (pt.), Mb,Can
165/F6 Stony (cr.), Mi,US
166/B3 Stony (cr.), Pa,US
167/E2 Stony Brook, NY,US
165/F6 Stony Creek (lake), Mi,US
157/J3 Stony Mountain, Mb,Can
167/E1 Stony Point, NY,US
88/K3 Stony Tunguska (riv.), Rus.
160/D1 Stooping (riv.), On,Can
153/S7 Stor (isl.), NW,Can
67/G1 Stör (riv.), Ger.
62/D2 Stora Le (lake), Swe.
61/F2 Stora Sjöfallets Nat'l Park, Swe.
61/F2 Storavan (lake), Swe.
62/A2 Stord (isl.), Nor.
62/D4 Store Bælt (chan.), Den.
61/D3 Støren, Nor.
79/G1 Štorje, Slov.
119/C4 Storm (bay), Austl.
157/K5 Storm Lake, Ia,US
56/C2 Stormont, NI,UK
55/H7 Stornoway, Sc,UK
59/F5 Storrington, Eng,UK
168/B2 Storrs, Ct,US
55/H8 Storr, The, Sc,UK
62/G1 Storsjön (lake), Swe.
61/F1 Storsteinsfjellet (peak), Nor.
62/D4 Storstrøm (co.), Den.
59/G3 Stort (riv.), Eng,UK
61/F2 Storuman, Swe.
157/G3 Story, Wy,US
143/J7 Stosch (isl.), Chile
59/F2 Stotfold, Eng,UK
77/G2 Stötten, Ger.
157/H3 Stoughton, Sk,Can
168/C1 Stoughton, Ma,US
58/D5 Stour (riv.), Eng,UK
59/E2 Stour (riv.), Eng,UK
59/H3 Stour (riv.), Eng,UK
59/H4 Stour (riv.), Eng,UK
58/D2 Stourbridge, Eng,UK
59/G4 Stour, Great (riv.), Eng,UK
58/D2 Stourport on Severn, Eng,UK
54/D5 Stow, Sc,UK
166/C5 Stow (cr.), NJ,US
168/F5 Stow, Oh,US
59/G2 Stowmarket, Eng,UK
59/E3 Stow on the Wold, Eng,UK
55/H9 Strabane, NI,UK
56/A2 Strabane (dist.), NI,UK
54/D2 Strachan, Sc,UK
54/A4 Strachur, Sc,UK
78/C2 Stradella, It.
66/D6 Straelen, Ger.
71/G4 Strakonice, Czh.
83/H4 Straldzha, Bul.
64/G1 Stralsund, Ger.
132/B4 Strand, SAfr.
56/C3 Strangford, NI,UK
56/C3 Strangford Lough (inlet), NI,UK
84/C4 Strängnäs, Swe.
117/G2 Strangways (peak), Austl.
56/B1 Stranocum, NI,UK
56/C2 Stranraer, Sc,UK
157/G3 Strasbourg, Sk,Can
76/D1 Strasbourg, Fr.
160/D3 Stratford, On,Can
115/R10 Stratford, NZ
168/A3 Stratford, Ct,US
167/L7 Stratford (har.), Ct,US
167/E1 Stratford (pt.), Ct,US
166/C4 Stratford, NJ,US
59/E2 Stratford upon Avon, Eng,UK
54/B5 Strathaven, Sc,UK
54/E1 Strathbeg (bay), Sc,UK
54/B5 Strathblane, Sc,UK
54/B5 Strathclyde (reg.), Sc,UK
54/C4 Strathearn (val.), Sc,UK
156/E3 Strathmore, Ab,Can
54/D3 Strathmore (val.), Sc,UK
54/B1 Strathpeffer, Sc,UK
54/C2 Strathspey (val.), Sc,UK
54/B4 Strathyre, Sc,UK
58/B5 Stratton, Eng,UK
71/F5 Straubing, Ger.
61/M6 Straumnes (pt.), Ice.
65/G2 Strausberg, Ger.
164/B2 Strawberry (peak), Ca,US
117/G5 Streaky (bay), Austl.
165/P15 Streamwood, Il,US
53/N7 Streatham, Eng,UK
59/E3 Streatley, Eng,UK
160/B3 Streator, Il,US
71/H3 Středočeská Žulová Vrchovina (mts.), Czh.
71/G2 Středočeský (reg.), Czh.
65/K4 Středoslovenský (reg.), Slvk.
58/D4 Street, Eng,UK
168/F5 Streetsboro, Oh,US
161/Q8 Streetsville, On,Can
83/F3 Strehaia, Rom.
116/D4 Streich (peak), Austl.
71/G3 Střela (riv.), Czh.
116/C2 Strelley Abor. Land, Austl.
84/H2 Strel'na (riv.), Rus.
57/F5 Stretford, Eng,UK
59/G2 Stretham, Eng,UK
70/D2 Streu (riv.), Ger.
71/G3 Stříbro, Czh.
54/D1 Strichen, Sc,UK
66/B5 Strijen, Neth.
81/H2 Strimón (gulf), Gre.
81/H2 Strimónas (riv.), Gre.
54/A5 Striven (inlet), Sc,UK
143/K7 Strobel (lake), Arg.
81/G4 Strofádhes (isls.), Gre.
80/D3 Stromboli (isl.), It.
55/J8 Stromeferry, Sc,UK
62/D2 Strømmen, Nor.
55/N13 Stromness, Sc,UK
62/D2 Strömstad, Swe.
61/E3 Strömsund, Swe.
77/E6 Strona (riv.), It.
168/F5 Strongsville, Oh,US
65/J3 Stronie Śląskie, Pol.
55/N13 Stronsay, Sc,UK
55/N13 Stronsay Firth (inlet), Sc,UK
71/H5 Stropnice (riv.), Czh.
58/D3 Stroud, Eng,UK
55/H8 Struan, Sc,UK
62/C3 Struer, Den.
82/E5 Struga, Macd.
132/C4 Struisbaai (bay), SAfr.
56/A2 Strule (riv.), NI,UK
81/H2 Struma (riv.), Bul., Gre.
58/A2 Strumble Head (pt.), UK
82/F5 Strumica, Macd.
168/G5 Struthers, Oh,US
61/C3 Stryn, Nor.
65/J3 Strzegom, Pol.
65/H2 Strzelce Krajeńskie, Pol.
117/J4 Strzelecki (cr.), Austl.
117/G2 Strzelecki (peak), Austl.
119/D4 Strzelecki (peak), Austl.
65/J3 Strzelin, Pol.
65/L4 Strzyżów, Pol.
156/B2 Stuart (lake), BC,Can
156/B2 Stuart (riv.), BC,Can
163/H5 Stuart, Fl,US
160/E4 Stuarts Draft, Va,US
65/G1 Stubbenkammer (pt.), Ger.
59/E5 Studland, Eng,UK
59/E2 Studley, Eng,UK
65/J4 Stupava, Slvk.
84/H5 Stupino, Rus.
78/A4 Stura di Demonte (riv.), It.
78/A2 Stura di Lanzo (riv.), It.
157/J3 Sturgeon (bay), Mb,Can
160/B1 Sturgeon (lake), On,Can
160/D2 Sturgeon (riv.), On,Can
160/C2 Sturgeon Bay, Wi,US
160/E2 Sturgeon Falls, On,Can
160/C3 Sturgis, Mi,US
157/H4 Sturgis, SD,US
58/D5 Sturminster Newton, Eng,UK
59/H4 Sturry, Eng,UK
117/J4 Sturt (des.), Austl.
119/B1 Sturt (peak), Austl.
117/M8 Sturt (riv.), Austl.
119/B1 Sturt Nat'l Park, Austl.
132/D4 Stutterheim, SAfr.
70/C5 Stuttgart, Ger.
162/F3 Stuttgart, Ar,US
163/F3 Stuttgart, Ar,US
86/C2 Styr (riv.), Ukr.
73/L3 Styria (prov.), Aus.
141/D1 Suaçui Grande (riv.), Braz.
127/D5 Suakin (arch.), Sudan
130/B2 Suam (riv.), Kenya
138/C3 Suárez (riv.), Col.
110/C5 Subang, Indo.
105/F3 Subao (mtn.), China
80/C1 Subasio (peak), It.
123/W18 Subayṭilah, Tun.
96/C4 Subei, China
110/C3 Subi (isl.), Indo.
82/D2 Subotica, Yugo.
166/D2 Succasunna-Kenvil, NJ,US
78/D4 Succiso, Alpe di (peak), It.
83/H2 Suceava, Rom.
83/G2 Suceava (co.), Rom.
65/L3 Suchedniów, Pol.
60/B3 Suck (riv.), Ire.
136/E7 Sucre (cap.), Bol.
138/C2 Sucre (dept.), Col.
138/A5 Sucre, Ecu.
139/F2 Sucre (state), Ven.
138/B5 Sucúa, Ecu.
136/G5 Sucunduri (riv.), Braz.
141/B2 Sucuriú (riv.), Braz.
53/T10 Sucy-en-Brie, Fr.
84/H4 Suda (riv.), Rus.
125/L5 Sudan
124/H5 Sudan (phys. reg.), Afr.
160/D2 Sudbury, On,Can
59/G2 Sudbury, Eng,UK
168/C1 Sudbury, Ma,US
67/H2 Sude (riv.), Ger.
65/H3 Sudeten (mts.), Czh., Pol.
130/C5 Sudi, Tanz.
66/D5 Südlohn, Ger.
129/H5 Sud-Ouest (prov.), Camr.
125/L6 Sue (riv.), Sudan
75/E3 Sueca, Sp.
83/G4 Süedinenie, Bul.
91/C4 Suez (can.), Egypt
91/C5 Suez (gulf), Egypt
91/C5 Suez (As Suways), Egypt
91/D3 Sūf, Jor.
167/D1 Suffern, NY,US
59/G2 Suffolk (co.), Eng,UK
168/C1 Suffolk (co.), Ma,US
167/F2 Suffolk (co.), NY,US
160/E4 Suffolk, Va,US
159/K2 Sugar (riv.), Il, Wi,US
168/F6 Sugar (cr.), Oh,US
168/H5 Sugar (cr.), Pa,US
165/P14 Sugar (cr.), Wi,US
162/E4 Sugar Land, Tx,US
115/J6 Sugarloaf (pt.), Austl.
58/C3 Sugar Loaf (mtn.), Wal,UK
163/H2 Sugarloaf (peak), Ky,US
112/C4 Sugbai (passg.), Phil.
92/C2 Suğla (lake), Turk.
112/B4 Sugut (riv.), Malay.
112/B4 Sugut, Tanjong (cape), Malay.
96/F1 Sühbaatar, Mong.
70/D1 Suhl, Ger.
92/B2 Şuhut, Turk.
109/B4 Şui (pt.), Thai.
137/H6 Suia-Missu (riv.), Braz.
97/L2 Suibin, China
107/K2 Suichuan, China
97/L3 Suifenhe, China
97/K2 Suihua, China
104/D2 Suijiang, China
97/K2 Suileng, China
103/D4 Suining, China
104/E2 Suining, China
103/C4 Suiping, China
68/D5 Suippe (riv.), Fr.
60/C5 Suir (riv.), Ire.
100/D2 Suishō (isl.), Rus.
165/K10 Suisun (bay), Ca,US
165/K10 Suisun (cr.), Ca,US
165/K10 Suisun City, Ca,US
99/L10 Suita, Japan
166/B6 Suitland-Silver Hill, Md,US
103/D4 Suixi, China
105/F4 Suixi, China
103/C4 Sui Xian, China
105/E3 Suiyang, China
76/B2 Suize (riv.), Fr.
103/E2 Suizhong, China
105/G2 Suizhou, China
106/B2 Sūjāngarh, India
110/C5 Sukabumi, Indo.
110/C4 Sukadana, Indo.
110/C4 Sukadana (bay), Indo.
99/G2 Sukagawa, Japan
108/B2 Sukheke, Pak.
86/E1 Sukhinichi, Rus.
63/N1 Sukhodol'skoye (lake), Rus.
84/J4 Sukhona (riv.), Rus.
109/B2 Sukhothai, Thai.
109/B2 Sukhothai (ruins), Thai.
87/G4 Sukhumi, Geo.
95/J3 Sukkur, Pak.
98/C4 Sukumo, Japan
105/G3 Sul (riv.), China
111/G4 Sula (isls.), Indo.
85/L2 Sula (riv.), Rus.
95/J3 Sulaimān (range), Pak.
111/E4 Sulawesi (Celebes) (isl.), Indo.
127/B4 Sulb Temple (ruins), Sudan
56/D3 Sulby (riv.), IM,UK
65/H2 Sulechów, Pol.
65/H2 Sulęcin, Pol.
65/L2 Sulejówek, Pol.
67/F3 Sulingen, Ger.
96/D4 Sulin Gol (riv.), China
61/F2 Sulitjelma (peak), Nor.
144/A2 Sullana, Peru
60/A6 Sullane (riv.), Ire.
156/F3 Sullivan (lake), Ab,Can
160/C4 Sullivan, In,US
160/E1 Sullivan Mines, Qu,Can
58/C4 Sully, Wal,UK
80/C1 Sulmona, It.
159/J4 Sulphur (riv.), Ar, Tx,US
162/E4 Sulphur, La,US
159/H4 Sulphur, Ok,US
159/G4 Sulphur Spring Draw (cr.), NM, Tx,US
162/E3 Sulphur Springs, Tx,US
165/D2 Sultan (cr.), Wa,US
130/C3 Sultan Hamud, Kenya
112/D4 Sultan Kudarat, Phil.
112/C4 Sulu (sea), Malay., Phil.
112/C4 Sulu (arch.), Phil.
92/C1 Suluova, Turk.
125/K1 Sulūq, Libya
69/G2 Sülz (riv.), Ger.
71/E4 Sulz (riv.), Ger.
70/D4 Sulzach (riv.), Ger.
70/B6 Sulz am Neckar, Ger.
69/G5 Sulzbach, Ger.
71/F6 Sulzbach (riv.), Ger.
71/E4 Sulzbach-Rosenberg, Ger.
113/P Sulzberger (bay), Ant.
113/Q Sulzberger Ice Shelf, Ant.
77/F3 Sulzfluh (peak), Aus.
82/E3 Šumadija (reg.), Yugo.
112/B4 Sumangat, Tanjong (cape), Malay.
138/C4 Sumapaz Nat'l Park, Col.
110/B4 Sumatra (isl.), Indo.
71/G4 Šumava (uplands), Czh.
110/E5 Sumba (isl.), Indo.
111/E5 Sumba (str.), Indo.
87/L5 Sumbar (riv.), Trkm.
110/E5 Sumbawa (isl.), Indo.
111/E5 Sumbawa Besar, Indo.
130/A4 Sumbawanga, Tanz.
126/B3 Sumbe, Ang.
96/F2 Sümber, Mong.
55/P13 Sumburgh Head (pt.), Sc,UK
151/M4 Sumdum (mtn.), Ak,US
140/C2 Sumé, Braz.
82/C2 Sümeg, Hun.
110/D5 Sumenep, Indo.
87/J4 Sumgait, Azer.
57/G3 Summer Bridge, Eng,UK
156/D3 Summerland, BC,Can
161/J2 Summerside, PE,Can
160/D4 Summersville, WV,US
163/G3 Summerville, Ga,US
163/H3 Summerville, SC,US
166/D2 Summit, NJ,US
168/F5 Summit (co.), Oh,US
165/C3 Sumner, Wa,US
98/D3 Sumoto, Japan
65/J4 Šumperk, Czh.
163/H3 Sumter, SC,US
86/E2 Sumy, Ukr.
86/E2 Sumy Obl., Ukr.
104/B4 Sun (peak), Burma
156/E4 Sun (riv.), Mt,US
100/B2 Sunagawa, Japan
108/C2 Sunām, India
99/M9 Sunami, Japan
119/C3 Sunbury, Austl.
166/B2 Sunbury, Pa,US
59/F4 Sunbury on Thames, Eng,UK
101/D5 Sunch'ŏn, SKor.
158/D4 Sun City, Az,US
164/C3 Sun City, Ca,US
161/G3 Suncook, NH,US
90/J10 Sunda (isls.), Indo.
110/B5 Sunda (str.), Indo.
157/G4 Sundance, Wy,US
106/E3 Sundarbans (reg.), Bang., India
106/D3 Sundargarh, India
108/D2 Sundarnagar, India
132/D4 Sundays (riv.), SAfr.
57/G2 Sunderland, Eng,UK
67/F6 Sundern, Ger.
119/D1 Sundown Nat'l Park, Austl.
156/E3 Sundre, Ab,Can
61/F3 Sundsvall, Swe.
63/R7 Sundyberg, Swe.
110/B4 Sungaipenuh, Indo.
110/B2 Sungai Petani, Malay.
92/C1 Sungurlu, Turk.
103/C3 Suning, China
164/F7 Sunland, Ca,US
162/B4 Sunland Park, NM,US
61/D3 Sunndalsøra, Nor.
62/E2 Sunne, Swe.
59/F4 Sunninghill, Eng,UK
165/K12 Sunnyvale, Ca,US
99/H8 Su-no-saki (cape), Japan
160/B3 Sun Prairie, Wi,US
166/D1 Sunrise (mtn.), NJ,US
119/B2 Sunset Country (reg.), Austl.
158/E4 Sunset Crater Nat'l Mon., Az,US
119/F5 Sunshine, Austl.
89/P3 Suntar-Khayata (mts.), Rus.
67/G4 Süntel (mts.), Ger.
164/F7 Sun Valley, Ca,US
97/K2 Sunwu, China
129/E5 Sunyani, Gha.
130/A5 Sunzu (peak), Zam.
98/B4 Suo (sea), Japan
109/D1 Suoi Rut, Viet.
63/L1 Suomenlinna, Fin.
61/H3 Suomenselkä (reg.), Fin.
109/D4 Suong, Camb.
144/B3 Supe, Peru
160/C2 Superior (lake), Can., US
158/E4 Superior, Az,US
156/E4 Superior, Mt,US
160/A2 Superior, Wi,US
160/B2 Superior (upland), Wi,US
109/C3 Suphan Buri, Thai.
111/J4 Supiori (isl.), Indo.
101/C2 Sup'ung (res.), China, NKor.
101/C2 Sup'ung (dam), NKor.
93/F4 Sūq ash Shuyūkh, Iraq
91/E2 Şuqaylabīyah, Syria
103/D4 Suqian, China
143/F3 Sur (pt.), Arg.
69/E4 Sûr (riv.), Belg.
71/F7 Sur (riv.), Ger.
158/B3 Sur (pt.), Ca,US
87/H1 Sura (riv.), Rus.
110/D5 Surabaya, Indo.
106/D4 Surada, India
62/G2 Surahammar, Swe.
110/D5 Surakarta, Indo.
101/G6 Suraksan (mtn.), SKor.
112/D4 Surallah, Phil.
108/G3 Sūramangalam, India
76/B5 Suran (riv.), Fr.
65/K4 Šurany, Slvk.
106/B3 Surat, India
106/B2 Suratgarh, India
109/B4 Surat Thani, Thai.
69/G6 Surbourg, Fr.
143/J7 Sur, Campo de Hielo (glacier), Chile
82/E3 Surčin, Yugo.
82/F4 Surdulica, Yugo.
69/E4 Sûre (riv.), Belg., Lux.
106/B3 Surendranagar, India
72/C3 Surgères, Fr.
88/H3 Surgut, Rus.
106/E3 Sūri, India
75/F2 Súria, Sp.
112/D3 Surigao, Phil.
109/C3 Surin, Thai.
139/G3 Suriname
102/A4 Surkhob (riv.), Taj.
166/B6 Surrattsville (Clinton), Md,US
156/C3 Surrey, BC,Can
53/M8 Surrey (co.), Eng,UK
76/E3 Sursee, Swi.
124/J1 Surt, Libya
61/D3 Sur-Trøndelag (co.), Nor.
91/D3 Şūr (Tyre), Leb.
140/D2 Surubim, Braz.
92/D2 Sürüç, Turk.
99/F3 Suruga (bay), Japan
139/F4 Surumu (riv.), Braz.
117/F3 Surveyor General's Corner, Austl.
53/T9 Survilliers, Fr.
139/F3 Surwakwima (falls), Guy.
123/X18 Sūsah, Tun.
123/X17 Sūsah (gov.), Tun.
98/C4 Susaki, Japan
93/G4 Süsangerd, Iran
158/B2 Susanville, Ca,US
92/D1 Suşehri, Turk.
103/B4 Sushui (riv.), China
71/G4 Sušice, Czh.
151/J3 Susitna (riv.), Ak,US
103/D5 Susong, China
99/F3 Susono, Japan
160/E3 Susquehanna (riv.), US
166/B5 Susquehanna Nat'l Wild. Ref., Md,US
161/H2 Sussex, NB,Can
166/C6 Sussex (co.), De,US
166/D1 Sussex (co.), NJ,US
59/F4 Sussex, Vale of (val.), Eng,UK
77/E4 Sustenhorn (peak), Swi.
77/E4 Sustenpass (pass), Swi.
66/C6 Susteren, Neth.
89/Q3 Susuman, Rus.
92/B2 Susurluk, Turk.
118/H9 Sutherland, Austl.
82/D4 Sutjeska Nat'l Park, Bosn.
108/B2 Sutlej (riv.), India, Pak.
165/L9 Sutter (co.), Ca,US
57/H6 Sutterton, Eng,UK
53/N7 Sutton, Eng,UK
53/N7 Sutton (bor.), Eng,UK
168/C1 Sutton, Ma,US
57/J6 Sutton Bridge, Eng,UK
59/E1 Sutton Coldfield, Eng,UK
57/G5 Sutton in Ashfield, Eng,UK
57/J5 Sutton on Sea, Eng,UK
57/H5 Sutton on Trent, Eng,UK
63/K2 Suur (str.), Est.
132/D4 Suurberge (mts.), SAfr.
120/G6 Suva (cap.), Fiji
99/F2 Suwa, Japan
65/M1 Suwałki, Pol.
65/M2 Suwałki (prov.), Pol.
163/H4 Suwannee (riv.), Fl,US
100/K6 Suwanose (isl.), Japan
121/J6 Suwarrow (atoll), Cookls.
91/D3 Şuwaylih, Jor.
101/D4 Suwŏn, SKor.
76/D3 Suze (riv.), Swi.
103/D4 Suzhou, China
103/E5 Suzhou, China
101/C2 Suzi (riv.), China
99/E2 Suzu, Japan
98/E3 Suzuka, Japan
99/M10 Suzuka (range), Japan
99/M10 Suzuka (riv.), Japan
99/E2 Suzu-misaki (cape), Japan
79/D3 Suzzara, It.
88/C2 Svalbard (arch.), Nor.
63/U9 Svalöv, Swe.
63/R7 Svartsjölandet (isl.), Swe.
71/F2 Svatava (riv.), Czh.
109/D4 Svay Rieng, Camb.
62/F2 Svealand (reg.), Swe.
62/D4 Svendborg, Den.
153/S7 Svendsen (pen.), NW,Can
62/E3 Svenljunga, Swe.
85/P4 Sverdlovsk (Yekaterinburg), Rus.
153/S7 Sverdrup (chan.), NW,Can
153/R7 Sverdrup (isls.), NW,Can
88/H2 Sverdrup (isl.), Rus.
86/D1 Svetlogorsk, Bela.
87/G3 Svetlograd, Rus.
82/E4 Svetozarevo, Yugo.
61/P7 Svíahnúkar (peak), Ice.
82/E3 Svilajnac, Yugo.
83/H5 Svilengrad, Bul.
83/G4 Svishtov, Bul.
65/J4 Svitavy, Czh.
97/K1 Svobodnyy, Rus.
83/F4 Svoge, Bul.
61/E1 Svolvær, Nor.
89/Q2 Svyatyy Nos (cape), Rus.
59/E1 Swadlincote, Eng,UK
59/G1 Swaffham, Eng,UK
118/D3 Swain (reefs), Austl.
163/H3 Swainsboro, Ga,US
121/H5 Swains Island (atoll), ASam.
126/C2 Swa-Kibula, Zaire
126/B5 Swakopmund, Namb.
57/G3 Swale (riv.), Eng,UK
59/H4 Swalecliffe, Eng,UK
59/G4 Swale, The (chan.), Eng,UK
66/D6 Swalmen, Neth.
117/G2 Swan (peak), Austl.
116/K7 Swan (riv.), Austl.
156/D2 Swan (hills), Ab,Can
157/H2 Swan (riv.), Mb, Sk,Can
149/F2 Swan (isls.), Hon.
165/F7 Swan (cr.), Mi,US
59/E5 Swanage, Eng,UK
119/B2 Swan Hill, Austl.
156/E2 Swan Hills, Ab,Can
53/P7 Swanley, Eng,UK
59/G4 Swanley Hextable, Eng,UK
165/F7 Swan, North Branch (cr.), Mi,US
157/H2 Swan River, Mb,Can
53/P7 Swanscombe, Eng,UK
58/C3 Swansea, Wal,UK
58/C3 Swansea (bay), Wal,UK
168/C2 Swansea, Ma,US
166/C4 Swarthmore, Pa,US
132/D3 Swart Kei (riv.), SAfr.
166/D1 Swartswood (lake), NJ,US
165/E6 Swartz (cr.), Mi,US
65/J2 Swarzędz, Pol.
71/E2 Swarzenbach an der Sächsischen Saale, Ger.
132/B2 Swarzrand (mts.), Namb.
166/B3 Swatara (cr.), Pa,US
56/B2 Swatragh, NI,UK
59/E5 Sway, Eng,UK
133/E2 Swaziland
61/E3 Sweden
156/C4 Sweet Home, Or,US
164/D5 Sweetwater (res.), Ca,US
162/C3 Sweetwater, Tx,US
156/F5 Sweetwater (riv.), Wy,US
132/C4 Swellendam, SAfr.
65/J3 Świdnica, Pol.
65/M3 Świdnik, Pol.
65/H2 Świdwin, Pol.
65/J3 Świebodzice, Pol.
65/H2 Świebodzin, Pol.
65/K2 Świecie, Pol.
156/G3 Swift Current, Sk,Can
55/H9 Swilly, Lough (inlet), Ire.
167/D3 Swimming River (res.), NJ,US
59/E3 Swindon, Eng,UK
57/H6 Swineshead, Eng,UK
60/B2 Swinford, Ire.
65/H2 Świnoujście, Pol.
57/G5 Swinton, Eng,UK
76/D4 Swiss (plat.), Swi.
69/F2 Swist Bach (riv.), Ger.
76/D4 Switzerland
60/D3 Swords, Ire.
84/G3 Syamozero (lake), Rus.
65/J3 Syców, Pol.
119/D2 Sydney, Austl.
161/J2 Sydney, NS,Can
118/H8 Sydney (inset), Austl.
121/H5 Sydney (Manra) (atoll), Kiri.
161/J2 Sydney Mines, NS,Can
67/F3 Syke, Ger.
85/L3 Syktyvkar, Rus.
163/G3 Sylacauga, Al,US
61/E3 Sylarna (peak), Swe.
107/F3 Sylhet, Bang.
64/E1 Sylt (isl.), Ger.
85/N4 Sylva (riv.), Rus.
160/D3 Sylvania, Oh,US
165/F6 Sylvan Lake, Mi,US
77/H2 Sylvenstein-Stausee (lake), Ger.
81/L6 Syntagma Square, Gre.
167/E2 Syosset, NY,US
113/C Syowa, Ant.
159/G3 Syracuse, Ks,US
160/E3 Syracuse, NY,US
80/D4 Syracuse (Siracusa), It.
88/G5 Syrdar'ya (riv.), Asia
92/D3 Syria
107/G4 Syriam, Burma
92/D3 Syrian (des.), Asia
85/L3 Sysola (riv.), Rus.
59/E1 Syston, Eng,UK
87/J1 Syzran', Rus.
82/E1 Szabolcs-Szatmár-Bereg (co.), Hun.
65/J2 Szamotuły, Pol.
82/E2 Szarvas, Hun.
82/D2 Százhalombatta, Hun.
65/H2 Szczecin, Pol.
65/H2 Szczecin (prov.), Pol.
65/J2 Szczecinek, Pol.
65/L2 Szczytno, Pol.
82/E2 Szeged, Hun.
82/E2 Szeghalom, Hun.
82/E2 Szegvár, Hun.
82/D2 Székesfehérvár, Hun.
82/D2 Szekszárd, Hun.
82/D2 Szentendre, Hun.
82/E2 Szentes, Hun.
82/E1 Szerencs, Hun.
65/M1 Szeskie (peak), Pol.
84/D5 Szeskie Wzgorza (peak), Pol.
82/C2 Szigetvár, Hun.
82/E2 Szolnok, Hun.
82/C2 Szombathely, Hun.
65/H3 Szprotawa, Pol.
65/K2 Sztum, Pol.
65/J2 Szubin, Pol.
65/L3 Szydłowiec, Pol.

T

112/C2 Tabaco, Phil.
112/D3 Tabango, Phil.
93/J3 Ţabas, Iran
149/F4 Tabasara, Serranía de (range), Pan.
147/G5 Tabasco (state), Mex.
140/A3 Tabatinga (mts.), Braz.
130/D2 Tabda, Som.
124/E2 Tabelbala, Alg.
156/E3 Taber, Ab,Can
75/E3 Tabernes de Valldigna, Sp.
140/C2 Tabira, Braz.
120/G5 Tabiteuea (atoll), Kiri.
112/C2 Tablas (isl.), Phil.
112/C3 Tablas (str.), Phil.
60/D3 Table (mtn.), Ire.
132/B4 Table (bay), SAfr.
132/L10 Table (peak), SAfr.
159/J3 Table Rock (lake), Ar, Mo,US
74/B1 Taboada, Sp.
71/H4 Tábor, Czh.
130/B4 Tabora, Tanz.
130/B4 Tabora (prov.), Tanz.
128/D5 Tabou, IvC.
93/F2 Tabrīz, Iran
121/K4 Tabuaeran (Fanning) (atoll), Kiri.
112/C1 Tabuk, Phil.
92/D4 Tabūk, SAr.
140/C2 Tabuleiro do Norte, Braz.
120/F6 Tabwemasana (mtn.), Van.
63/S6 Täby, Swe.
148/C3 Tacaná (vol.), Mex.
149/G4 Tacarcuna (mtn.), Pan.
102/D2 Tacheng, China
105/J3 Tachia (riv.), Tai.

223
Tachi – Teres

98/A4 **Tachibana** (bay), Japan
99/F3 **Tachikawa,** Japan
71/F7 **Tachinger See** (lake), Ger.
138/C2 **Táchira** (state), Ven.
71/F3 **Tachov,** Czh.
112/D3 **Tacloban,** Phil.
144/D5 **Tacna,** Peru
165/C3 **Tacoma,** Wa,US
144/D5 **Tacora** (vol.), Chile
75/X16 **Tacoronte,** Canl.,Sp.
143/G1 **Tacuarembó,** Uru.
143/G2 **Tacuarembó** (dept.), Uru.
112/D4 **Tacurong,** Phil.
139/F4 **Tacutu** (riv.), Braz., Guy.
99/F2 **Tadami** (riv.), Japan
99/L10 **Tadaoka,** Japan
57/G4 **Tadcaster,** Eng,UK
124/F2 **Tademaït** (plat.), Alg.
106/D4 **Tādepallegūdem,** India
121/V12 **Tadine,** NCal.
59/E4 **Tadley,** Eng,UK
92/D3 **Tadmur,** Syria
99/M9 **Tado,** Japan
101/C5 **Tadohae Hasang Nat'l Park,** SKor.
98/C3 **Tadotsu,** Japan
106/C5 **Tādpatri,** India
124/H2 **Tadrart** (mts.), Alg., Libya
53/N8 **Tadworth,** Eng,UK
101/D2 **T'aebaek** (mts.), NKor., SKor.
101/E4 **T'aebaek,** SKor.
101/F7 **Taebudo** (isl.), SKor.
101/D4 **Taech'ŏn,** SKor.
101/C4 **Taech'ŏng** (isl.), SKor.
101/D3 **Taedong** (riv.), NKor.
101/D3 **Taegang-got** (pt.), NKor.
101/E5 **Taegu,** SKor.
101/E5 **Taegu-Jikhalsi** (prov.), SKor.
101/C5 **Taehŭksan** (isl.), SKor.
101/D4 **Taejŏn,** SKor.
101/C2 **Taeryŏng** (riv.), NKor.
58/B3 **Taf** (riv.), Wal,UK
74/E1 **Tafalla,** Sp.
58/C3 **Taff** (riv.), Wal,UK
135/C2 **Tafí Viejo,** Arg.
93/H4 **Taft,** Iran
112/D3 **Taft,** Phil.
95/H3 **Taftān** (mtn.), Iran
99/M9 **Taga,** Japan
86/F3 **Taganrog,** Rus.
86/F3 **Taganrog** (gulf), Rus., Ukr.
128/C2 **Tagant** (reg.), Mrta.
93/J2 **Tagarav** (peak), Trkm.
98/B4 **Tagawa,** Japan
112/C3 **Tagbilaran,** Phil.
78/A5 **Taggia,** It.
124/E1 **Taghit,** Alg.
112/F6 **Tagig,** Phil.
151/M3 **Tagish,** Yk,Can
79/G1 **Tagliamento** (riv.), It.
68/D5 **Tagnon,** Fr.
112/C3 **Tagolo** (pt.), Phil.
112/D3 **Tagoloan,** Phil.
149/G1 **Taguasco,** Cuba
140/A4 **Taguatinga,** Braz.
112/C1 **Tagudin,** Phil.
120/E6 **Tagula** (isl.), PNG
112/D4 **Tagum,** Phil.
85/P4 **Tagun** (riv.), Rus.
74/C3 **Tagus** (Tajo) (riv.), Sp.
74/B3 **Tagus** (Tejo) (riv.), Port.
110/B3 **Tahan** (peak), Malay.
99/N10 **Tahara,** Japan
124/G3 **Tahat** (peak), Alg.
123/R16 **Tahat, Oued et** (riv.), Alg.
97/J1 **Tahe,** China
121/L6 **Tahenea** (atoll), FrPol.
92/E2 **Tahir** (pass), Turk.
121/L6 **Tahiti** (isl.), FrPol.
63/K2 **Tahkuna** (pt.), Est.
162/E3 **Tahlequah,** Ok,US
151/J3 **Tahneta** (pass), Ak,US
158/C3 **Tahoe** (lake), Ca, Nv,US
162/C3 **Tahoka,** Tx,US
129/G3 **Tahoua,** Niger
129/G3 **Tahoua** (dept.), Niger
156/B3 **Tahsis,** BC,Can
127/B3 **Tahtā,** Egypt
144/D3 **Tahuamanu** (riv.), Peru
121/L6 **Tahuata** (isl.), FrPol.
111/G3 **Tahulandang** (isl.), Indo.
165/B3 **Tahuyo** (riv.), Wa,US
103/L8 **Tai** (lake), China
101/B2 **Tai'an,** China
121/X15 **Taiarapu** (pen.), FrPol.
96/F5 **Taibai** (peak), China
103/C3 **Taibai Shan** (mtn.), China
96/H3 **Taibus Qi,** China
103/E5 **Taicang,** China
105/J3 **Taichung,** Tai.
103/C3 **Taigu,** China
103/C3 **Taihang** (mts.), China
103/C4 **Taihe,** China
103/D5 **Taihu,** China
103/C4 **Taikang,** China
100/C2 **Taiki,** Japan
97/J2 **Tailai,** China
99/L10 **Taima,** Japan
54/B1 **Tain,** Sc,UK
105/J4 **Tainan,** Tai.
81/H4 **Taínaron, Ákra** (cape), Gre.
128/D5 **Taï Nat'l Park,** IvC.
140/B4 **Taiobeiras,** Braz.
121/L5 **Taiohae,** FrPol.
105/J3 **Taipei** (cap.), Tai.
103/D5 **Taiping,** China
97/J2 **Taiping** (peak), China
110/B3 **Taiping,** Malay.
140/D2 **Taipu,** Braz.
98/C3 **Taisha,** Japan
105/G4 **Taishan,** China
99/L10 **Taishi,** Japan
105/H3 **Taishun,** China
142/B5 **Taitao** (pen.), Chile
130/B2 **Taiti** (peak), Kenya
105/J3 **Taiwan**
105/H4 **Taiwan** (str.), China, Tai.
103/E4 **Tai Xian,** China
103/E4 **Taixing,** China
81/H4 **Taíyetos** (mts.), Gre.
103/C3 **Taiyuan,** China
103/D4 **Taizhou,** China
103/E2 **Taizi** (riv.), China
110/C4 **Tajam** (peak), Indo.
124/H3 **Tajarhī,** Libya
88/H6 **Tajikistan**
99/F2 **Tajima,** Japan
99/E3 **Tajimi,** Japan
99/L10 **Tajiri,** Japan
148/D3 **Tajmulco** (vol.), Guat.
74/C3 **Tajo** (Tagus) (riv.), Sp.
93/G3 **Tajrīsh,** Iran
74/D2 **Tajuña** (riv.), Sp.
109/B2 **Tak,** Thai.
99/G2 **Takahagi,** Japan
98/D3 **Takahama,** Japan
98/C3 **Takahashi,** Japan
98/C3 **Takahashi** (riv.), Japan
99/G2 **Takahata,** Japan
99/L10 **Takaishi,** Japan
98/D3 **Takamatsu,** Japan
99/M10 **Takami-yama** (peak), Japan
98/B4 **Takanabe,** Japan
100/B3 **Takanosu,** Japan
99/E2 **Takaoka,** Japan
115/R10 **Takapuna,** NZ
99/L10 **Takarazuka,** Japan
121/L6 **Takaroa** (isl.), FrPol.
99/F2 **Takasaki,** Japan
99/M9 **Takashima,** Japan
99/L10 **Takatori,** Japan
98/D3 **Takatsuki,** Japan
130/C3 **Takaungu,** Kenya
99/E2 **Takayama,** Japan
98/E3 **Takefu,** Japan
98/C3 **Takehara,** Japan
93/G2 **Tākestān,** Iran
98/B4 **Taketa,** Japan
99/M10 **Taketoyo,** Japan
109/D4 **Takev,** Camb.
107/H4 **Ta Khli,** Thai.
125/R2 **Takht-e Jamshīd** (Persepolis) (ruins), Iran
99/M10 **Taki,** Japan
152/E2 **Takijuq** (lake), NW,Can
100/B2 **Takikawa,** Japan
99/K10 **Takino,** Japan
159/J2 **Takio** (cr.), Ia,US
156/B2 **Takla** (lake), BC,Can
102/D4 **Takla Makan** (des.), China
129/E5 **Takoradi,** Gha.
123/V17 **Takouch** (cape), Alg.
91/B4 **Talā,** Egypt
130/C3 **Tala,** Kenya
57/E5 **Talacre,** Wal,UK
108/B1 **Talagang,** Pak.
142/Q9 **Talagante,** Chile
106/B3 **Talāja,** India
129/G2 **Talak** (reg.), Niger
149/F4 **Talamanca, Cordillera de** (range), CR
126/C2 **Tala Mugongo,** Ang.
110/B4 **Talang** (peak), Indo.
148/E3 **Talanga,** Hon.
69/F5 **Talange,** Fr.
76/A3 **Talant,** Fr.
144/A2 **Talara,** Peru
102/B3 **Talas** (riv.), Kaz.
92/C2 **Talas,** Turk.
111/G3 **Talaud** (isls.), Indo.
74/C3 **Talavera de la Reina,** Sp.
106/D6 **Talawakele,** SrL.
125/M5 **Talawdī,** Sudan
74/C3 **Talayuela,** Sp.
114/D2 **Talbot** (cape), Austl.
116/E3 **Talbot** (peak), Austl.
166/B6 **Talbot** (co.), Md,US
142/C2 **Talca,** Chile
142/B3 **Talcahuano,** Chile
106/E3 **Tālcher,** India
102/C3 **Taldy-Kurgan,** Kaz.
72/C4 **Talence,** Fr.
76/C4 **Talent** (riv.), Swi.
77/H4 **Talfer** (Talvera) (riv.), It.
88/H5 **Talgar,** Kaz.
58/C3 **Talgarth,** Wal,UK
111/F4 **Taliabu** (isl.), Indo.
112/C4 **Talipaw,** Phil.
125/M6 **Tali Post,** Sudan
112/D3 **Talisayan,** Phil.
111/E5 **Taliwang,** Indo.
91/B4 **Ţalkhā,** Egypt
163/G3 **Talladega,** Al,US
92/E2 **Tall 'Afar,** Iraq
163/G4 **Tallahassee** (cap.), Fl,US
163/F3 **Tallahatchie** (riv.), Ms,US
91/G8 **Tall 'Āsūr** (Ba'al Hazor) (mtn.), WBnk.
116/B4 **Tallering** (peak), Austl.
166/C4 **Talleyville,** De,US
63/L2 **Tallinn** (cap.), Est.
91/E2 **Tall Kalakh,** Syria
93/E2 **Tall Kayf,** Iraq
168/F5 **Tallmadge,** Oh,US
163/H3 **Tallulah** (falls), Ga,US
163/F3 **Tallulah,** La,US
125/N5 **Talo** (peak), Eth.
106/B3 **Taloda,** India
95/J1 **Tāloqān,** Afg.
146/D4 **Talpa,** Mex.
71/F1 **Talsperre Pöhl** (res.), Ger.
135/B2 **Taltal,** Chile
152/E2 **Taltson** (riv.), NW,Can
109/C4 **Talumphuk** (pt.), Thai.
77/H4 **Talvera** (Talfer) (riv.), It.
108/C2 **Talwāra,** India
99/H7 **Tama,** Japan
99/H7 **Tama** (riv.), Japan
112/A5 **Tama Abu** (range), Malay.
99/H6 **Tamagawa,** Japan
99/M10 **Tamaki,** Japan
129/E4 **Tamale,** Gha.
138/B3 **Tamana** (peak), Col.
120/G5 **Tamana** (atoll), Kiri.
122/C2 **Tamanghasset,** Alg.
129/F1 **Tamanghasset** (wilaya), Alg.
166/C2 **Tamaqua,** Pa,US
58/B5 **Tamar** (riv.), Eng,UK
100/H8 **Tamara** (isl.), Japan
138/C3 **Tamar, Alto de** (peak), Col.
148/E4 **Tamarindo Nat'l Wild. Ref.,** CR
77/E5 **Tamaro, Monte** (peak), Swi.
82/D2 **Tamási,** Hun.
146/E5 **Tamazula,** Mex.
147/F4 **Tamazunchale,** Mex.
99/L9 **Tamba,** Japan
99/L9 **Tamba** (hills), Japan
130/B2 **Tambach,** Kenya
128/B3 **Tambacounda,** Sen.
128/B3 **Tambacounda** (reg.), Sen.
128/C3 **Tambaoura, Falaise de** (escarp.), Mali
131/D3 **Tambara,** Moz.
110/C3 **Tambelan** (isls.), Indo.
144/C3 **Tambo** (riv.), Peru
144/C4 **Tambo Colorado** (ruins), Peru
144/A2 **Tambo Grande,** Peru
144/D4 **Tambopata** (riv.), Bol., Peru
77/F5 **Tambo, Pizzo** (peak), Swi.
111/E5 **Tambora** (peak), Indo.
140/B2 **Tamboril,** Braz.
119/C3 **Tamboritha** (peak), Austl.
87/G1 **Tambov,** Rus.
87/G1 **Tambov Obl.,** Rus.
74/A1 **Tambre** (riv.), Sp.
125/L6 **Tambura,** Sudan
59/E1 **Tame** (riv.), Eng,UK
74/B2 **Támega** (riv.), Port.
129/H2 **Tamgak** (peak), Niger
128/B3 **Tamgue, Massif du** (reg.), Gui., Sen.
147/F4 **Tamiahua,** Mex.
148/B1 **Tamiahua** (lag.), Mex.
108/F3 **Tamil Nadu** (state), India
91/B5 **Ţāmiyah,** Egypt
109/E3 **Tam Ky,** Viet.
109/D2 **Tam Le,** Viet.
166/C2 **Tammany** (mtn.), NJ,US
63/K2 **Tammisaari** (Ekenäs), Fin.
163/H5 **Tampa,** Fl,US
108/H4 **Tampalakamam,** SrL.
63/K1 **Tampere,** Fin.
147/F4 **Tampico,** Mex.
139/H4 **Tampoc** (riv.), FrG.
110/A3 **Tampulonanjing** (peak), Indo.
147/F4 **Tamuín,** Mex.
148/B1 **Tamuín** (riv.), Mex.
119/D1 **Tamworth,** Austl.
59/E1 **Tamworth,** Eng,UK
101/D5 **Tamyang,** SKor.
107/K3 **Tan** (riv.), China
125/N5 **Tana** (lake), Eth.
130/D3 **Tana** (riv.), Kenya
61/H1 **Tana** (riv.), Nor.
98/D4 **Tanabe,** Japan
141/B2 **Tanabi,** Braz.
61/J1 **Tanafjorden** (fjord), Nor.
151/C6 **Tanaga** (isl.), Ak,US
151/C6 **Tanaga** (vol.), Ak,US
80/D2 **Tanagro** (riv.), It.
99/G2 **Tanagura,** Japan
109/C5 **Tanah Merah,** Malay.
114/E3 **Tanami** (des.), Austl.
117/F2 **Tanami Desert Wild. Sanct.,** Austl.
109/D4 **Tan An,** Viet.
151/J3 **Tanana** (riv.), Ak,US
130/B4 **Tanangozi,** Tanz.
130/D3 **Tana River Primate Nat'l Rsv.,** Kenya
78/B3 **Tanaro** (riv.), It.
103/D4 **Tancheng,** China
146/E5 **Tancitaro, Pico de** (peak), Mex.
106/C2 **Tānda,** India
106/D2 **Tandā,** India
128/D3 **Tanda** (lake), Mali
112/D3 **Tandag,** Phil.
125/M5 **Tandaltī,** Sudan
83/H3 **Ţăndărei,** Rom.
142/F3 **Tandil,** Arg.
108/B2 **Tāndliānwāla,** Pak.
95/J3 **Tando Ādam,** Pak.
95/J3 **Tando Allāhyār,** Pak.
95/J3 **Tando Muhammad Khān,** Pak.
119/B2 **Tandou** (lake), Austl.
56/B3 **Tandragee,** NI,UK
98/B5 **Tanega** (isl.), Japan
104/C5 **Tanem** (range), Burma, Thai.
124/E3 **Tanezrouft** (des.), Alg., Mali
103/C3 **Tang** (riv.), China
103/C4 **Tang** (riv.), China
130/C4 **Tanga,** Tanz.
130/C4 **Tanga** (prov.), Tanz.
133/H8 **Tangainony,** Madg.
130/A4 **Tanganyika** (lake), Afr.
137/G6 **Tangará da Serra,** Braz.
151/G1 **Tangent** (pt.), Ak,US
64/F2 **Tangerhütte,** Ger.
123/M13 **Tanger** (Tangier), Mor.
102/E5 **Tanggula** (mts.), China
102/F5 **Tanggula Shankou** (pass), China
103/C4 **Tanghe,** China
123/M13 **Tangier** (Tanger), Mor.
165/B3 **Tanglewilde-Thompson Place,** Wa,US
168/A1 **Tanglewood,** Ma,US
102/E5 **Tangra** (lake), China
103/D3 **Tangshan,** China
112/C3 **Tangub,** Phil.
105/F2 **Tangyan** (riv.), China
103/C4 **Tangyin,** China
97/K2 **Tangyuan,** China
140/B4 **Tanhaçu,** Braz.
104/C2 **Taniantaweng** (mts.), China
111/H5 **Tanimbar** (isls.), Indo.
112/C3 **Tanjay,** Phil.
110/A3 **Tanjungbalai,** Indo.
110/C5 **Tanjungkarang-Telukbetung,** Indo.
110/C4 **Tanjungpandan,** Indo.
110/A3 **Tanjungpura,** Indo.
108/A1 **Tānk,** Pak.
120/F6 **Tanna** (isl.), Van.
99/L9 **Tannan,** Japan
102/F1 **Tannu-Ola** (mts.), Mong., Rus.
129/E5 **Tano** (riv.), Ghana, IvC.
147/F4 **Tanquián,** Mex.
140/C3 **Tanquinho,** Braz.
125/M1 **Tantā,** Egypt
91/B4 **Ţanţā,** Egypt
124/C2 **Tan-Tan,** Mor.
147/F4 **Tantoyuca,** Mex.
106/D4 **Tanuku,** India
112/E7 **Tanza,** Phil.
130/B3 **Tanzania**
99/H7 **Tanzawa-yama** (peak), Japan
105/G3 **Tao** (riv.), China
109/B4 **Tao** (isl.), Thai.
97/J2 **Tao'er** (riv.), China
96/F4 **Taole,** China
97/J2 **Taonan,** China
80/D4 **Taormina,** It.
159/F3 **Taos,** NM,US
124/E3 **Taoudenni,** Mali
123/N13 **Taourirt,** Mor.
107/K2 **Taoyuan,** China
105/J3 **Taoyuan,** Tai.
63/L2 **Tapa,** Est.
148/C3 **Tapachula,** Mex.
139/H5 **Tapajós** (riv.), Braz.
139/H4 **Tapanahoni** (riv.), Sur.
148/C2 **Tapantatepec,** Mex.
136/F5 **Tapauá,** Braz.
136/E5 **Tapauá** (riv.), Braz.
112/C3 **Tapaz,** Phil.
141/B4 **Tapejara,** Braz.
141/B4 **Tapes,** Braz.
144/C2 **Tapiche** (riv.), Peru
104/C3 **Taping** (riv.), Burma
110/B3 **Tapis** (peak), Malay.
129/F3 **Tapoa** (prov.), Burk.
82/C2 **Tapolca,** Hun.
54/D2 **Tap O'Noth** (hill), Sc,UK
160/E4 **Tappahannock,** Va,US
167/K7 **Tappan** (lake), NJ, NY,US
167/E1 **Tappan,** NY,US
168/F7 **Tappan** (dam), Oh,US
168/F7 **Tappan** (res.), Oh,US
167/E1 **Tappan Zee** (reach), NY,US
100/B3 **Tappi-zaki** (pt.), Japan
165/C3 **Tapps** (lake), Wa,US
106/B3 **Tāpti** (riv.), India
112/C4 **Tapul** (isls.), Phil.
127/B5 **Taqab,** Sudan
127/D5 **Taqātu' Hayyā,** Sudan
141/B4 **Taquara,** Braz.
141/B4 **Taquari,** Braz.
137/G7 **Taquari** (riv.), Braz.
141/B2 **Taquaritinga,** Braz.
141/B2 **Taquarituba,** Braz.
144/B1 **Taquil,** Ecu.
79/G2 **Tar,** Cro.
60/B5 **Tar** (riv.), Ire.
102/B3 **Tar** (riv.), Kyr.
82/D4 **Tara** (riv.), Bosn., Yugo.
88/H4 **Tara,** Rus.
131/B3 **Tara,** Zam.
129/H4 **Taraba** (riv.), Nga.
91/D2 **Ţarābulus** (Tripoli), Leb.
124/H1 **Ţarābulus** (Tripoli) (cap.), Libya
60/D2 **Tara, Hill of,** Ire.
56/B4 **Tara, Hill of** (hill), Ire.
111/E3 **Tarakan,** Indo.
100/E2 **Taraku** (isl.), Rus.
74/D2 **Tarancón,** Sp.
130/C3 **Tarangire Nat'l Park,** Tanz.
80/E2 **Taranto,** It.
80/E3 **Taranto** (gulf), It.
144/B2 **Tarapoto,** Peru
72/F4 **Tarare,** Fr.
72/F5 **Tarascon,** Fr.
144/D3 **Tarauacá,** Braz.
144/D2 **Tarauacá** (riv.), Braz.
121/M7 **Taravai** (isl.), FrPol.
120/G4 **Tarawa** (atoll), Kiri.
74/E2 **Tarazona,** Sp.
74/E3 **Tarazona de la Mancha,** Sp.
102/D2 **Tarbagatay** (mts.), Kaz.
130/D2 **Tarbaj,** Kenya
54/C1 **Tarbat Head** (pt.), Sc,UK
55/K8 **Tarbat Ness** (pt.), Sc,UK
95/K2 **Tarbela** (res.), Pak.
54/A5 **Tarbert,** Sc,UK
72/D5 **Tarbes,** Fr.
54/B6 **Tarbolton,** Sc,UK
163/J3 **Tarboro,** NC,US
82/A2 **Tarcento,** It.
72/E3 **Tardes** (riv.), Fr.
72/D4 **Tardoire** (riv.), Fr.
97/M2 **Tardoki-Jani** (peak), Rus.
119/E1 **Taree,** Austl.
123/V18 **Tarf** (lake), Alg.
127/C2 **Ţarfā', Wādī al** (dry riv.), Egypt
127/B4 **Tarfâwi, Bîr** (well), Egypt
56/D2 **Tarf Water** (riv.), Sc,UK
167/E2 **Target Rock Nat'l Wild. Ref.,** NY,US
124/H1 **Tarhūnah,** Libya
144/B1 **Tarifa,** Ecu.
74/C4 **Tarifa,** Sp.
136/F8 **Tarija,** Bol.
111/J4 **Tariku** (riv.), Indo.
111/J4 **Tariku-taritatu** (plain), Indo.
96/B4 **Tarim** (basin), China
102/D3 **Tarim** (riv.), China
130/B3 **Tarime,** Tanz.
95/J2 **Tarin** (riv.), Afg.
111/J4 **Taritatu** (riv.), Indo.
86/E3 **Tarkhankut, Mys** (cape), Ukr.
129/E5 **Tarkwa,** Gha.
112/C2 **Tarlac,** Phil.
54/D2 **Tarland,** Sc,UK
144/C3 **Tarma,** Peru
72/D5 **Tarn** (riv.), Fr.
96/E2 **Tarna** (riv.), Mong.
95/J2 **Tarnak** (riv.), Afg.
63/T9 **Tårnby,** Den.
65/L3 **Tarnobrzeg,** Pol.
65/L3 **Tarnobrzeg** (prov.), Pol.
65/L3 **Tarnów,** Pol.
65/L3 **Tarnów** (prov.), Pol.
108/C2 **Tarn Tāran,** India
102/D5 **Taro** (lake), China
78/D3 **Taro** (riv.), It.
100/B4 **Tarō,** Japan
105/J3 **Taroko Nat'l Park,** Tai.
124/D1 **Taroudannt,** Mor.
163/H4 **Tarpon Springs,** Fl,US
57/F5 **Tarporley,** Eng,UK
80/B1 **Tarquinia,** It.
75/F2 **Tarragona,** Sp.
75/F2 **Tàrrega,** Sp.
130/D2 **Tarri,** Som.
167/E1 **Tarrytown,** NY,US
91/D1 **Tarsus,** Turk.
91/D1 **Tarsus** (riv.), Turk.
135/D1 **Tartagal,** Arg.
79/E2 **Tartaro** (riv.), It.
63/M2 **Tartu,** Est.
91/D2 **Ţarţūs,** Syria
91/D2 **Ţarţūs** (dist.), Syria
99/M9 **Tarui,** Japan
98/B5 **Tarumizu,** Japan
109/B5 **Tarutao Nat'l Park,** Thai.
96/D2 **Tarvagatay** (mts.), Mong.
57/F5 **Tarvin,** Eng,UK
164/E7 **Tarzana,** Ca,US
109/D3 **Ta Seng,** Camb.
102/E2 **Tashanta,** Rus.
88/F5 **Tashauz,** Trkm.
87/L4 **Tashauz Obl.,** Trkm.
93/H4 **Ţashk** (riv.), Iran
102/A3 **Tashkent** (cap.), Uzb.
102/B3 **Tash-Kumyr,** Kyr.
110/C5 **Tasikmalaya,** Indo.
91/C1 **Taşkent,** Turk.
92/C1 **Taşköprü,** Turk.
119/C4 **Tasman** (pen.), Austl.
115/R11 **Tasman** (bay), NZ
51/S7 **Tasman** (sea)
119/C4 **Tasman Head** (cape), Austl.
119/C4 **Tasmania** (state), Austl.
82/F2 **Tăşnad,** Rom.
92/D1 **Taşova,** Turk.
147/K6 **Tasquillo,** Mex.
63/T9 **Tåstrup,** Den.
82/D2 **Tata,** Hun.
124/D2 **Tata,** Mor.
130/A2 **Tata,** Zaire
82/D2 **Tatabánya,** Hun.
160/D2 **Tatachikapika** (riv.), On,Can
121/M6 **Tatakoto** (isl.), FrPol.
96/D4 **Tatalin** (riv.), China
97/N2 **Tatar** (str.), Rus.
85/L5 **Tatar Aut. Rep.,** Rus.
88/H4 **Tatarsk,** Rus.
124/H1 **Tatāwīn,** Tun.
99/F3 **Tateyama,** Japan
99/E2 **Tate-yama** (mtn.), Japan
152/E2 **Tathlina** (lake), NW,Can
128/B2 **Tatilt** (well), Mrta.
152/G3 **Tatnam** (cape), Mb,Can
129/H3 **Tatokou,** Niger
65/K4 **Tatranský Nat'l Park,** Slvk.
65/K4 **Tatrzański Nat'l Park,** Pol.
53/P8 **Tatsfield,** Eng,UK
99/E3 **Tatsuno,** Japan
57/H5 **Tattershall,** Eng,UK
92/E2 **Tatvan,** Turk.
140/B2 **Tauá,** Braz.
141/H8 **Taubaté,** Braz.
70/C3 **Tauber** (riv.), Ger.
70/C3 **Tauberbischofsheim,** Ger.
73/K3 **Tauern, Hohe** (mts.), Aus.
71/F6 **Taufkirchen,** Ger.
70/C1 **Taufstein** (peak), Ger.
159/K3 **Taum Sauk** (peak), Mo,US
104/B4 **Taungdwingyi,** Burma
104/C4 **Taunggyi,** Burma
104/B3 **Taungthonlon** (peak), Burma
104/B5 **Taungup** (pass), Burma
108/A2 **Taunsa,** Pak.
161/S8 **Taunton,** On,Can
58/C4 **Taunton,** Eng,UK
168/C2 **Taunton,** Ma,US
168/C2 **Taunton** (riv.), Ma,US
70/B2 **Taunus** (range), Ger.
70/B2 **Taunusstein,** Ger.
115/S10 **Taupo,** NZ
115/S10 **Taupo** (lake), NZ
63/K4 **Tauragė,** Lith.
115/S10 **Tauranga,** NZ
72/D3 **Taurion** (riv.), Fr.
91/B1 **Taurus** (mts.), Turk.
74/E2 **Tauste,** Sp.
72/C2 **Taute** (riv.), Fr.
121/X15 **Tautira,** FrPol.
120/E5 **Tauu** (isls.), PNG
158/E3 **Tavaputs** (plat.), Ut,US
163/H4 **Tavares,** Fl,US
92/B2 **Tavas,** Turk.
85/Q4 **Tavda** (riv.), Rus.
59/H1 **Taverham,** Eng,UK
53/S9 **Taverny,** Fr.
130/C3 **Taveta,** Kenya
121/Z17 **Taveuni** (isl.), Fiji
74/B4 **Tavira,** Port.
58/B5 **Tavistock,** Eng,UK
109/B3 **Tavoy,** Burma
109/B3 **Tavoy** (pt.), Burma
97/L3 **Tavrichanka,** Rus.
92/B2 **Tavşanlı,** Turk.
58/B5 **Tavy** (riv.), Eng,UK
58/B4 **Taw** (riv.), Eng,UK
99/L10 **Tawaramoto,** Japan
160/D2 **Tawas City,** Mi,US
111/E3 **Tawau,** Malay.
58/C3 **Tawe** (riv.), Wal,UK
108/C1 **Tāwi** (riv.), India
130/C5 **Tawi,** Tanz.
112/B4 **Tawi-tawi** (isl.), Phil.
127/D5 **Ţawkar,** Sudan
124/G1 **Ţawzar,** Tun.
147/F5 **Taxco,** Mex.
147/K8 **Taxco de Alarcón,** Mex.
108/B1 **Taxila,** Pak.
108/B1 **Taxila** (ruins), Pak.
102/C4 **Taxkorgan Tajik Zizhixian** (Taxkorgan), China
102/C4 **Taxkorgan** (Taxkorgan Tajik Zizhixian), China
54/C4 **Tay** (firth), Sc,UK
54/C4 **Tay** (riv.), Sc,UK
148/D2 **Tayasal,** Guat.
54/B3 **Tay, Loch** (lake), Sc,UK
159/H2 **Taylor,** Ne,US
160/B4 **Taylorville,** Il,US
89/L2 **Taymyr** (isl.), Rus.
88/K2 **Taymyr** (pen.), Rus.
88/K2 **Taymyr** (riv.), Rus.
88/J2 **Taymyr Aut. Okr.,** Rus.
109/D4 **Tay Ninh,** Viet.
54/D4 **Tayport,** Sc,UK
138/C2 **Tayrona Nat'l Park,** Col.
88/K4 **Tayshet,** Rus.
54/C3 **Tayside** (reg.), Sc,UK
112/B3 **Taytay,** Phil.
88/J3 **Taz** (riv.), Rus.
123/M13 **Taza,** Mor.
100/B4 **Tazawako,** Japan
123/M13 **Tazekka** (peak), Mor.
163/H2 **Tazewell,** Tn,US
160/D4 **Tazewell,** Va,US
125/K2 **Tāzirbū** (oasis), Libya
148/D3 **Tazumal** (ruins), ESal.
87/H4 **Tbilisi** (cap.), Geo.
126/B1 **Tchibanga,** Gabon
124/H6 **Tcholliré,** Camr.
65/K1 **Tczew,** Pol.
139/E5 **Tea** (riv.), Braz.
57/H5 **Tealby,** Eng,UK
115/Q12 **Te Anau,** NZ
115/Q12 **Te Anau** (lake), NZ
167/D2 **Teaneck,** NJ,US
147/G5 **Teapa,** Mex.
115/S10 **Te Araroa,** NZ
115/S10 **Te Aroha,** NZ
115/S10 **Te Awamutu,** NZ
110/B4 **Tebak** (peak), Indo.
123/W18 **Tébessa,** Alg.
123/V18 **Tébessa** (gov.), Alg.
123/W18 **Tebessa** (mts.), Alg., Tun.
129/F2 **Tebesselamane** (well), Mali
135/E2 **Tebicuary** (riv.), Par.
110/A3 **Tebingtinggi,** Indo.
87/H4 **Tebulos-mta** (peak), Rus.
146/E5 **Tecalitlán,** Mex.
147/M8 **Tecamachalco,** Mex.
75/G1 **Tech** (riv.), Fr.
83/J3 **Techirghiol,** Rom.
142/C4 **Tecka** (riv.), Arg.
63/U9 **Teckomatorp,** Swe.
147/F4 **Tecolutla,** Mex.
148/B1 **Tecolutla** (riv.), Mex.
146/E5 **Tecomán,** Mex.
147/K6 **Tecozautla,** Mex.
146/D4 **Tecuala,** Mex.
83/H3 **Tecuci,** Rom.
165/G7 **Tecumseh,** On,Can
160/D3 **Tecumseh,** Mi,US
159/H2 **Tecumseh,** Ne,US
95/H1 **Tedzhen,** Trkm.
88/G6 **Tedzhen** (riv.), Trkm.
57/G2 **Tees** (bay), Eng,UK
57/G2 **Tees** (riv.), Eng,UK
136/F4 **Tefé,** Braz.
136/E4 **Tefé** (riv.), Braz.
110/C5 **Tegal,** Indo.
66/D6 **Tegelen,** Neth.
124/H2 **Tegheri** (well), Libya
56/E6 **Tegid, Llyn** (lake), Wal,UK
129/H3 **Tégouma** (wadi), Niger
148/E3 **Tegucigalpa** (cap.), Hon.
152/G2 **Tehek** (lake), NW,Can
93/G3 **Tehrān** (cap.), Iran
93/G2 **Tehrān** (gov.), Iran
102/C5 **Tehri,** India
147/F5 **Tehuacán,** Mex.
148/C3 **Tehuantepec** (gulf), Mex.
147/G5 **Tehuantepec** (isth.), Mex.
148/C2 **Tehuantepec** (riv.), Mex.
147/M8 **Tehuipango,** Mex.
75/X16 **Teide** (peak), Canl.,Sp.
58/B2 **Teifi** (riv.), Wal,UK
58/B2 **Teifiside** (vall.), Wal,UK
125/L4 **Teiga** (plat.), Sudan
58/C5 **Teignmouth,** Eng,UK
71/F7 **Teisendorf,** Ger.
54/B4 **Teith** (riv.), Sc,UK
74/B3 **Tejo** (Tagus) (riv.), Port.
159/H2 **Tekamah,** Ne,US
115/R9 **Te Kao,** NZ
147/H4 **Tekax,** Mex.
102/C3 **Tekeli,** Kaz.
102/D3 **Tekes** (riv.), China
94/C6 **Tekezē Wenz** (reg.), Eth.
125/N5 **Tekezē Wenz** (riv.), Eth., Sudan
102/D4 **Tekiliktag** (peak), China
83/H5 **Tekirdağ,** Turk.
92/A1 **Tekirdağ** (prov.), Turk.
106/D4 **Tekkali,** India
92/D1 **Tekkeköy,** Turk.
115/S10 **Te Kuiti,** NZ
106/D3 **Tel** (riv.), India
148/E3 **Tela,** Hon.
123/Q16 **Télagh,** Alg.
87/H4 **Telavi,** Geo.
91/D3 **Tel Aviv** (dist.), Isr.
91/D3 **Tel Aviv-Yafo,** Isr.
128/E2 **Télé** (lake), Mali
102/G2 **Telem** (lake), Mong.
141/B3 **Telemaco Borba,** Braz.
62/C2 **Telemark** (co.), Nor.
111/E3 **Telen** (riv.), Indo.
83/G4 **Teleorman** (co.), Rom.
124/G3 **Telertheba** (peak), Alg.
137/G5 **Teles Pires** (riv.), Braz.
58/D1 **Telford,** Eng,UK
77/H3 **Telfs,** Aus.
67/E5 **Telgte,** Ger.
148/E3 **Telica,** Nic.
128/B4 **Télimélé,** Gui.
148/B2 **Telixtlahuaca,** Mex.
91/G8 **Tel Jericho Nat'l Park,** WBnk.
156/B2 **Telkwa,** BC,Can
123/Q16 **Tell Atlas** (mts.), Alg.
160/C4 **Tell City,** In,US
108/E3 **Tellicherry,** India
158/F3 **Telluride,** Co,US
91/G6 **Tel Megiddo Nat'l Park,** Isr.
96/D2 **Telmen** (lake), Mong.
110/B3 **Telok Anson,** Malay.
147/F5 **Teloloapan,** Mex.
102/E1 **Telotskoye** (lake), Rus.
63/K4 **Telšiai,** Lith.
65/G2 **Teltow** (reg.), Ger.
129/E5 **Tema,** Gha.
160/D2 **Temagami** (lake), On,Can
132/E2 **Tembisa,** SAfr.
126/C2 **Tembo,** Zaire
131/D2 **Tembue,** Moz.
58/D2 **Teme** (riv.), Eng,UK
164/C4 **Temecula,** Ca,US
82/D3 **Temerin,** Yugo.
110/B3 **Temerloh,** Malay.
102/B1 **Temirtau,** Kaz.
161/F1 **Témiscamie** (riv.), Qu,Can
160/E2 **Témiscaming,** Qu,Can
96/E1 **Temnik** (riv.), Rus.
121/M7 **Temoe** (isl.), FrPol.
158/E4 **Tempe,** Az,US
80/A2 **Tempio Pausania,** It.
162/D4 **Temple,** Tx,US
56/B2 **Templepatrick,** NI,UK
119/G5 **Templestowe,** Austl.
65/G2 **Templin,** Ger.
147/F4 **Tempoal,** Mex.
148/B1 **Tempoal** (riv.), Mex.
148/B1 **Tempoal de Sanchez,** Mex.
126/C3 **Tempué,** Ang.
86/F3 **Temryuk,** Rus.
68/D1 **Temse,** Belg.
142/B3 **Temuco,** Chile
115/R11 **Temuka,** NZ
138/B5 **Tena,** Ecu.
167/K8 **Tenafly,** NJ,US
124/D5 **Tena Kourou** (peak), Burk.
106/D4 **Tenāli,** India
147/F3 **Tenamaxtle,** Mex.
147/F5 **Tenancingo,** Mex.
147/K7 **Tenango,** Mex.
148/B2 **Tenango,** Mex.
147/F5 **Tenango de Río Blanco,** Mex.
109/B3 **Tenasserim** (range), Burma
109/B4 **Tenasserim** (Thanintharyi) (div.), Burma
66/D2 **Ten Boer,** Neth.
58/D2 **Tenbury,** Eng,UK
58/B3 **Tenby,** Wal,UK
78/A4 **Tenda, Colle di** (pass), It.
125/P5 **Tendaho,** Eth.
99/G1 **Tendō,** Japan
76/C4 **Tendre** (peak), Swi.
124/G3 **Ténéré du Tafassasset** (des.), Niger
129/H2 **Ténéré, 'Erg du** (des.), Niger
75/X16 **Tenerife** (isl.), Canl
123/R15 **Ténès,** Alg.
75/L6 **Tenes** (riv.), Sp.
104/C4 **Teng** (riv.), Burma
104/C3 **Tengchong,** China
111/E4 **Tenggarong,** Indo.
96/E4 **Tengger** (des.), China
102/A1 **Tengiz** (lake), Kaz.
138/B5 **Tenguel,** Ecu.
103/D4 **Teng Xian,** China
73/G4 **Tenibres** (peak), It.
135/D1 **Teniente Enciso Nat'l Park,** Par.
76/D1 **Teningen,** Ger.
82/D3 **Tenja,** Cro.
108/F4 **Tenkāsi,** India
129/E4 **Tenkodogo,** Burk.
158/D4 **Tenmile** (cr.), Az,US
163/F2 **Tennessee** (riv.), US
163/G3 **Tennessee** (state), US
142/C2 **Teno,** Chile
61/H1 **Tenojoki** (riv.), Fin.
147/H5 **Tenosique,** Mex.
99/L10 **Tenri,** Japan
99/E3 **Tenryū,** Japan
99/E3 **Tenryū** (riv.), Japan
59/G4 **Tenterden,** Eng,UK
109/B2 **Ten Thousand Buddhas, Cave of,** Burma
111/F3 **Tentolomatinan** (peak), Indo.
130/B2 **Tenus** (peak), Kenya
74/A1 **Teo,** Sp.
146/E4 **Teocaltiche,** Mex.
147/N7 **Teocelo,** Mex.
141/A2 **Teodoro Sampaio,** Braz.
141/D1 **Teófilo Otoni,** Braz.
130/A2 **Te'Okutu,** Ugan.
149/H4 **Teorama,** Col.
147/L7 **Teotihuacán** (ruins), Mex.
146/E5 **Tepalcatepec,** Mex.
147/L8 **Tepalcingo,** Mex.
146/E4 **Tepatitlán,** Mex.
147/M7 **Tepatlaxco de Hidalgo,** Mex.
147/F5 **Tepeaca,** Mex.
147/F5 **Tepeapulco,** Mex.
147/K7 **Tepeji del Río,** Mex.
71/F2 **Tepelská Plošina** (mts.), Czh.
147/M8 **Tepexi de Rodríguez,** Mex.
146/D4 **Tepic,** Mex.
71/F2 **Teplá** (riv.), Czh.
71/G5 **Teplá Vltava** (riv.), Czh.
65/G3 **Teplice,** Czh.
146/B2 **Tepoca, Cabo** (cape), Mex.
121/L6 **Tepoto** (isl.), FrPol.
147/Q9 **Tepotzotlán,** Mex.
147/K8 **Tepoztlán,** Mex.
146/E4 **Tequila,** Mex.
75/G1 **Ter** (riv.), Sp.
129/F3 **Téra,** Niger
74/B1 **Tera** (riv.), Sp.
66/B4 **Ter Aar,** Neth.
121/K4 **Teraina** (Washington) (atoll), Kiri.
80/C1 **Teramo,** It.
92/E2 **Tercan,** Turk.
75/S12 **Terceira** (isl.), Azor.,Port.
142/E2 **Tercero** (riv.), Arg.
83/K2 **Terderovsk** (bay), Ukr.
83/K2 **Terderovsk** (spit), Ukr.
87/H4 **Terek** (riv.), Rus.
138/D2 **Terepaima Nat'l Park,** Ven.
140/B2 **Teresina,** Braz.
141/L7 **Teresópolis,** Braz.

224

Tergn – Tongc

68/C4 **Tergnier,** Fr.
96/D4 **Tergun Daba** (mts.), China
66/B5 **Terheijden,** Neth.
84/G1 **Teriberskiy, Mys** (pt.), Rus.
66/C2 **Terkaplesterpoelen** (lake), Neth.
83/H5 **Terkirdağ** (prov.), Turk.
77/H4 **Terlan** (Terlango), It.
95/J1 **Termez,** Uzb.
80/C4 **Termini Imerese,** It.
147/H5 **Términos** (lag.), Mex.
158/B2 **Termo,** Ca,US
80/D1 **Termoli,** It.
58/D1 **Tern** (riv.), Eng,UK
111/G3 **Ternate,** Indo.
66/A6 **Terneuzen,** Neth.
80/C1 **Terni,** It.
72/F3 **Ternin** (riv.), Fr.
68/B3 **Ternoise** (riv.), Fr.
86/C2 **Ternopol',** Ukr.
86/C2 **Ternopol' Obl.,** Ukr.
97/N2 **Terpeniya** (bay), Rus.
97/N2 **Terpeniya** (cape), Rus.
156/A2 **Terrace,** BC,Can
160/C1 **Terrace Bay,** On,Can
80/C2 **Terracina,** It.
161/Q8 **Terra Cotta,** On,Can
80/A3 **Terralba,** It.
140/B4 **Terra Nova,** Braz.
140/C3 **Terra Nova,** Braz.
161/L1 **Terra Nova Nat'l Park,** Nf,Can
75/G2 **Terrassa,** Sp.
72/D4 **Terrasson-la-Villedieu,** Fr.
161/N6 **Terrebonne,** Qu,Can
161/N6 **Terrebonne** (co.), Qu,Can
163/G2 **Terre Haute,** In,US
118/H8 **Terrey Hills,** Austl.
59/G1 **Terrington Saint Clement,** Eng,UK
77/F4 **Terri, Piz** (peak), Swi.
157/G4 **Terry,** Mt,US
102/A1 **Tersakkan** (riv.), Kaz.
66/C2 **Terschelling** (isl.), Neth.
75/E2 **Teruel,** Sp.
109/B5 **Terutao** (isl.), Thai.
83/H4 **Tervel,** Bul.
73/K3 **Terza Grande** (peak), It.
96/C1 **Tes,** Mong.
96/D2 **Tes,** Mong.
72/D5 **Tescou** (riv.), Fr.
151/G1 **Teshekpuk** (lake), Ak,US
100/D2 **Teshikaga,** Japan
100/B1 **Teshio,** Japan
100/C1 **Teshio** (riv.), Japan
100/C2 **Teshio-dake** (mtn.), Japan
96/D2 **Tesiyn** (riv.), Mong.
96/C1 **Tes-Khem** (riv.), Rus.
82/C3 **Teslić,** Bosn.
152/C3 **Teslin** (lake), BC,Can
151/M3 **Teslin,** Yk,Can
152/C2 **Teslin** (riv.), Yk,Can
129/G3 **Tessaoua,** Niger
69/E1 **Tessenderlo,** Belg.
59/E4 **Test** (riv.), Eng,UK
75/G1 **Têt** (riv.), Fr.
58/D3 **Tetbury,** Eng,UK
131/D3 **Tete,** Moz.
131/D2 **Tete** (prov.), Moz.
76/D1 **Tête de Faux** (peak), Fr.
73/G4 **Tête de l'Estrop** (peak), Fr.
76/C6 **Tête du Torraz** (peak), Fr.
147/L8 **Tetela del Volcán,** Mex.
147/M7 **Tetela de Ocampo,** Mex.
76/D5 **Tête Ronde** (peak), Swi.
62/E5 **Teterow,** Ger.
83/G4 **Teteven,** Bul.
57/H5 **Tetford,** Eng,UK
121/L6 **Tetiaroa** (isl.), FrPol.
69/F5 **Teting-sur-Nied,** Fr.
151/K3 **Tetlin Nat'l Wild. Ref.,** Ak,US
156/F4 **Teton** (riv.), Mt,US
123/M13 **Tétouan,** Mor.
82/E4 **Tetovo,** Macd.
77/F2 **Tettnang,** Ger.
75/N9 **Tetuan,** Sp.
71/F4 **Teublitz,** Ger.
135/D1 **Teuco** (riv.), Arg.
80/A3 **Teulada** (cape), It.
157/J3 **Teulon,** Mb,Can
100/B1 **Teuri** (isl.), Japan
67/F4 **Teutoburger Wald** (for.), Ger.
79/F5 **Tevere** (Tiber) (riv.), It.
91/D3 **Teverya** (Tiberias), Isr.
54/D6 **Teviot** (riv.), Sc,UK
54/D6 **Teviotdale** (vall.), Sc,UK
118/D4 **Tewantin-Noosa,** Austl.
58/D3 **Tewkesbury,** Eng,UK
162/E3 **Texarkana,** Ar, Tx,US
162/C4 **Texas** (state), US
162/E4 **Texas City,** Tx,US
147/L7 **Texcoco de Mora,** Mex.
147/R9 **Texcoco, Lago del** (lake), Mex.
66/B2 **Texel** (isl.), Neth.
66/B3 **Texelstroom** (chan.), Neth.
159/G3 **Texoma,** Ok,US
84/J4 **Teykovo,** Rus.
147/F5 **Teziutlán,** Mex.
147/F5 **Tezoatlán,** Mex.
147/L7 **Tezontepec,** Mex.
104/B3 **Tezpur,** India
109/C1 **Tha** (riv.), Laos
152/G2 **Tha-anne** (riv.), NW,Can
132/E3 **Thabana-Ntlenyana** (peak), Les.
133/E2 **Thabankulu** (peak), SAfr.
132/D2 **Thabazimbi,** SAfr.
109/B3 **Tha Chin** (riv.), Thai.
109/B4 **Thaen** (pt.), Thai.
109/D1 **Thai Binh,** Viet.
109/C3 **Thailand**
109/C4 **Thailand** (gulf), Thai.
109/D1 **Thai Nguyen,** Viet.
108/A1 **Thal,** Pak.
108/A2 **Thal** (des.), Pak.
109/C5 **Thaleban Nat'l Park,** Thai.
77/E3 **Thalwil,** Swi.
94/E6 **Thamar, Jabal** (mtn.), Yem.
59/F3 **Thame,** Eng,UK
59/F3 **Thame** (riv.), Eng,UK
160/D3 **Thames** (riv.), On,Can
115/S10 **Thames,** NZ
53/P7 **Thames** (riv.), Eng,UK
53/P7 **Thames Barrier,** Eng,UK
106/B4 **Thāna,** India
59/H4 **Thanet, Isle of** (isl.), Eng,UK
107/J5 **Thang Duc,** Viet.
109/D2 **Thanh Hoa,** Viet.
107/J4 **Thanh Lang Xa,** Viet.
109/D4 **Thanh Phu,** Viet.
109/D4 **Thanh Tri,** Viet.
109/B4 **Thanintharyi** (Tenasserim) (div.), Burma
108/G3 **Thanjavur,** India
76/D2 **Thann,** Fr.
76/C1 **Thaon-les-Vosges,** Fr.
95/J3 **Thar** (des.), India, Pak.
106/B3 **Tharād,** India
104/B5 **Tharrawaddy,** Burma
81/J2 **Thásos** (isl.), Gre.
59/E4 **Thatcham,** Eng,UK
109/D1 **That Khe,** Viet.
104/C5 **Thaton,** Burma
104/B3 **Thaungdut,** Burma
107/H4 **Tha Uthen,** Thai.
59/G3 **Thaxted,** Eng,UK
65/H4 **Thaya** (riv.), Aus.
104/B5 **Thayetmyo,** Burma
104/C4 **Thazi,** Burma
59/E4 **Theale,** Eng,UK
127/C3 **Thebes** (ruins), Egypt
162/C3 **The Caprock** (cliffs), NM,US
60/D3 **The Curragh,** Ire.
156/C4 **The Dalles,** Or,US
119/B3 **The Grampians** (mts.), Austl.
117/F2 **The Granites** (peak), Austl.
66/B4 **The Hague** (s'-Gravenhage) (cap.), Neth.
119/C3 **The Lakes Nat'l Park,** Austl.
152/F2 **Thelon** (riv.), NW,Can
56/B2 **The Loup,** NI,UK
108/F4 **Theni-Allinagaram,** India
117/F2 **Theo** (peak), Austl.
157/H3 **Theodore,** Sk,Can
158/E4 **Theodore Roosevelt** (lake), Az,US
157/G4 **Theodore Roosevelt Nat'l Park,** ND,US
157/H2 **The Pas,** Mb,Can
68/B5 **Thérain** (riv.), Fr.
131/C3 **The Range,** Zim.
81/H3 **Thermaic** (Salonika) (gulf), Gre.
81/H3 **Thermopílai** (Thermopylae) (pass), Gre.
156/F5 **Thermopolis,** Wy,US
81/H3 **Thermopylae** (Thermopílai) (pass), Gre.
53/U9 **Thérouanne** (riv.), Fr.
160/D2 **Thessalon,** On,Can
81/H2 **Thessaloníki** (Salonika), Gre.
81/H3 **Thessaly** (reg.), Gre.
55/H8 **The Storrs,** Sc,UK
59/G2 **Thet** (riv.), Eng,UK
59/G2 **Thetford,** Eng,UK
161/G2 **Thetford Mines,** Qu,Can
69/E2 **Theux,** Belg.
53/T9 **Thève** (riv.), Fr.
59/G1 **The Wash** (bay), Eng,UK
59/G4 **The Weald** (reg.), Eng,UK
162/E4 **The Woodlands,** Tx,US
58/D1 **The Wrekin** (hill), Eng,UK
53/P7 **Theydon Bois,** Eng,UK
53/T10 **Thiais,** Fr.
81/G3 **Thíamis** (riv.), Gre.
163/F4 **Thibodaux,** La,US
157/J3 **Thief River Falls,** Mn,US
76/C4 **Thielle** (riv.), Swi.
156/C5 **Thielsen** (peak), Or,US
79/E1 **Thiene,** It.
109/D4 **Thien Ngon,** Viet.
72/E4 **Thiers,** Fr.
53/T9 **Thiers-sur-Thève,** Fr.
128/A3 **Thiès,** Sen.
128/A3 **Thiès** (reg.), Sen.
104/E4 **Thiet Tra,** Viet.
130/C3 **Thika,** Kenya
106/E2 **Thimphu** (cap.), Bhu.
61/N7 **Thingvellir Nat'l Park,** Ice.
69/F5 **Thionville,** Fr.
81/J4 **Thíra** (isl.), Gre.
127/B5 **Third Cataract** (falls), Sudan
57/E2 **Thirlmere** (lake), Eng,UK
57/G3 **Thirsk,** Eng,UK
116/D5 **Thirsty** (peak), Austl.
62/C3 **Thisted,** Den.
61/P6 **Thistilfjördhur** (bay), Ice.
117/G5 **Thistle** (isl.), Austl.
151/L3 **Thistle** (mtn.), Yk,Can
121/Z18 **Thithia** (isl.), Fiji
81/H3 **Thívai,** Gre.
61/N7 **Thjórsa** (riv.), Ice.
152/G2 **Thlewiaza** (riv.), NW,Can
131/C4 **Thohoyandou,** SAfr.
109/D4 **Thoi Binh,** Viet.
76/A5 **Thoissey,** Fr.
66/B5 **Tholen,** Neth.
66/B5 **Tholen** (isl.), Neth.
69/G5 **Tholey,** Ger.
166/B6 **Thomas** (pt.), Md,US
168/A2 **Thomaston,** Ct,US
163/G3 **Thomaston,** Ga,US
163/G4 **Thomasville,** Al,US
163/H4 **Thomasville,** Ga,US
163/H3 **Thomasville,** NC,US
115/G4 **Thompson** (riv.), Austl.
156/C3 **Thompson** (riv.), BC,Can
157/J2 **Thompson,** Mb,Can
168/C2 **Thompson,** Ct,US
159/J2 **Thompson** (riv.), Ia, Mo,US
156/E4 **Thompson Falls,** Mt,US
156/D3 **Thompson, North** (riv.), BC,Can
165/B3 **Thompson Place-Tanglewilde,** Wa,US
152/E1 **Thomsen** (riv.), NW,Can
118/A4 **Thomson** (riv.), Austl.
163/H3 **Thomson,** Ga,US
109/C3 **Thon Buri,** Thai.
107/J4 **Thon Cam Lo,** Viet.
109/B2 **Thongwa,** Burma
109/E4 **Thon Lac Nghiep,** Viet.
76/C5 **Thonon-les-Bains,** Fr.
109/E4 **Thon Song Pha,** Viet.
158/E4 **Thoreau,** NM,US
156/E2 **Thorhild,** Ab,Can
53/U10 **Thorigny-sur-Marne,** Fr.
165/Q16 **Thorn** (cr.), Il,US
57/G2 **Thornaby-on-Tees,** Eng,UK
58/D3 **Thornbury,** Eng,UK
57/H4 **Thorne,** Eng,UK
161/R8 **Thornhill,** On,Can
54/B4 **Thornhill,** Sc,UK
56/E1 **Thornhill,** Sc,UK
57/G2 **Thornley,** Eng,UK
57/G3 **Thornthwaite,** Eng,UK
57/E4 **Thornton Cleveleys,** Eng,UK
57/H3 **Thornton Dale,** Eng,UK
161/R9 **Thorold,** On,Can
161/R9 **Thorold South,** On,Can
53/M7 **Thorpe,** Eng,UK
59/H3 **Thorpe le Soken,** Eng,UK
57/G2 **Thorpe Thewles,** Eng,UK
72/C3 **Thouars,** Fr.
72/C3 **Thouet** (riv.), Fr.
164/B2 **Thousand Oaks,** Ca,US
130/C3 **Thowa** (riv.), Kenya
86/C4 **Thracian** (sea), Gre., Turk.
165/E6 **Thread** (cr.), Mi,US
156/F4 **Three Forks,** Mt,US
151/L4 **Three Guardsmen** (mtn.), BC,Can
156/E3 **Three Hills,** Ab,Can
119/C4 **Three Hummock** (isl.), Austl.
115/R9 **Three Kings** (isls.), NZ
166/B3 **Three Mile** (isl.), Pa,US
109/B3 **Three Pagodas** (pass), Burma
129/E5 **Three Points** (cape), Gha.
160/C3 **Three Rivers,** Mi,US
162/D3 **Throckmorton,** Tx,US
116/E3 **Throssell** (lake), Austl.
58/B5 **Thrushel** (riv.), Eng,UK
58/D2 **Thruxton,** Eng,UK
109/D4 **Thu Dau Mot,** Viet.
109/D4 **Thu Duc,** Viet.
68/D3 **Thuin,** Belg.
72/E5 **Thuir,** Fr.
70/C2 **Thulba** (riv.), Ger.
153/T7 **Thule Air Base,** Grld.
112/B3 **Thumb** (peak), Phil.
76/D4 **Thun,** Swi.
160/B1 **Thunder Bay,** On,Can
76/D4 **Thunersee** (lake), Swi.
109/C2 **Thung Salaeng Luang Nat'l Park,** Thai.
77/E2 **Thur** (riv.), Swi.
77/F2 **Thurgau** (canton), Swi.
71/E1 **Thüringer Schiefergebirge** (mts.), Ger.
70/D1 **Thüringer Wald** (for.), Ger.
64/F3 **Thuringia** (state), Ger.
59/E2 **Thurlaston,** Eng,UK
60/C4 **Thurles,** Ire.
55/K7 **Thurso,** Sc,UK
113/T **Thurston** (isl.), Ant.
165/A3 **Thurston** (co.), Wa,US
113/S **Thwaites Iceberg Tongue,** Ant.
131/D3 **Thyolo,** Malw.
136/E7 **Tiahuanco** (ruins), Bol.
151/M5 **Tian** (pt.), BC,Can
103/D4 **Tianchang,** China
105/E4 **Tiandeng,** China
107/J3 **Tian'e,** China
140/B1 **Tianguá,** Braz.
103/D3 **Tianjin,** China
103/D3 **Tianjin** (prov.), China
107/J3 **Tianlin,** China
103/C5 **Tianmen,** China
103/K9 **Tianmu** (mts.), China
88/H5 **Tian Shan** (range), Asia
96/F5 **Tianshui,** China
103/C5 **Tiantangzhai** (mtn.), China
107/J3 **Tianyang,** China
103/C2 **Tianzhen,** China
105/F3 **Tianzhu,** China
123/R16 **Tiaret,** Alg.
123/R16 **Tiaret** (wilaya), Alg.
121/S9 **Tiavea,** WSam.
141/B3 **Tibagi,** Braz.
141/B2 **Tibaji** (riv.), Braz.
124/H6 **Tibati,** Camr.
57/F6 **Tibberton,** Eng,UK
63/R7 **Tibble,** Swe.
128/C4 **Tibé, Pic de** (peak), Gui.
80/C1 **Tiber** (riv.), It.
91/D3 **Tiberias** (Sea of Galilee) (lake), Isr., Syria
91/D3 **Tiberias** (Teverya), Isr.
79/F5 **Tiber** (Tevere) (riv.), It.
124/J3 **Tibesti** (mts.), Chad, Libya
90/H6 **Tibet** (reg.), China
104/B2 **Tibet** (Xizang) Aut. Reg., China
75/L7 **Tibidabo** (peak), Sp.
124/H1 **Ţīb, Ra's aţ** (Cape Bon) (cape), Tun.
62/F2 **Tibro,** Swe.
57/G5 **Tibshelf,** Eng,UK
138/B3 **Tibugá, Ensenada de** (gulf), Col.
149/H2 **Tiburon** (cape), Haiti
146/B2 **Tiburón** (isl.), Mex.
149/G4 **Tiburón** (cape), Pan.
165/K11 **Tiburon,** Ca,US
59/G4 **Ticehurst,** Eng,UK
165/P14 **Tichigan** (lake), Wi,US
128/C2 **Tîchît, Dhar** (hills), Mrta.
124/C3 **Tichla,** WSah.
78/C2 **Ticino** (riv.), It.
77/E5 **Ticino** (canton), Swi.
77/E5 **Ticino** (riv.), Swi.
57/G5 **Tickhill,** Eng,UK
160/F3 **Ticonderoga,** NY,US
147/H4 **Ticul,** Mex.
62/E2 **Tidaholm,** Swe.
57/G5 **Tideswell,** Eng,UK
124/F2 **Tidikelt** (plain), Alg.
128/C2 **Tidjikdja,** Mrta.
78/C3 **Tidone** (riv.), It.
111/G3 **Tidore** (isl.), Indo.
128/A2 **Tidra** (isl.), Mrta.
75/X16 **Tiede Nat'l Park**
66/C5 **Tiel,** Neth.
97/K2 **Tieli,** China
101/B1 **Tieling,** China
75/N9 **Tielmes,** Sp.
68/C1 **Tielt,** Belg.
69/D2 **Tielt-Winge,** Belg.
128/D4 **Tiemba** (riv.), IvC.
102/E3 **Tiemen Guan** (pass), China
69/D2 **Tienen,** Belg.
105/H3 **Tieniu** (pass), China
90/H5 **Tien Shan** (range), China
109/D1 **Tien Yen,** Viet.
109/D2 **Tien Yen,** Viet.
124/J3 **Tieroko** (peak), Chad
62/G1 **Tierp,** Swe.
158/F3 **Tierra Amarilla,** NM,US
147/F5 **Tierra Blanca,** Mex.
143/L8 **Tierra del Fuego** (isl.), Arg., Chile
143/L8 **Tierra del Fuego,** Antártida e Islas del Atlántico Sur (prov.), Arg.
143/K8 **Tierra del Fuego Nat'l Park,** Arg.
138/B4 **Tierradentro** (ruins), Col.
74/C2 **Tiétar** (riv.), Sp.
141/B2 **Tietê** (riv.), Braz.
124/C2 **Tifariti,** WSah.
160/D3 **Tiffin,** Oh,US
163/H4 **Tifton,** Ga,US
121/V12 **Tiga** (isl.), NCal.
139/G4 **Tiger** (falls), Guy., Sur.
54/A6 **Tighvein** (hill), Sc,UK
124/H6 **Tignère,** Camr.
143/S12 **Tigre,** Arg.
144/C1 **Tigre** (riv.), Peru
139/F2 **Tigre** (riv.), Ven.
93/F4 **Tigris** (riv.), Asia
124/J4 **Tigui** (well), Chad
129/G2 **Tiguidit, Falaise de** (escarp.), Niger
62/C3 **Tihøje** (peak), Den.
147/F4 **Tihuatlán,** Mex.
61/J3 **Tiilikkajärven Nat'l Park,** Fin.
128/B1 **Tijirît** (reg.), Mrta.
141/K8 **Tijuca Nat'l Park,** Braz.
141/B3 **Tijucas,** Braz.
141/B1 **Tijuco** (riv.), Braz.
148/D2 **Tikal** (ruins), Guat.
148/D2 **Tikal Nat'l Park,** Guat.
106/C3 **Tīkamgarh,** India
151/G3 **Tikchik** (lakes), Ak,US
121/L6 **Tikehau** (atoll), FrPol.
86/G3 **Tikhoretsk,** Rus.
84/G4 **Tikhvin,** Rus.
93/E3 **Tikrīt,** Iraq
81/H2 **Tikveš** (lake), Macd.
66/C5 **Tilburg,** Neth.
53/Q7 **Tilbury,** Eng,UK
162/D4 **Tilden,** Tx,US
166/B6 **Tilghman** (isl.), Md,US
54/D5 **Till** (riv.), Eng,UK
57/H5 **Till** (riv.), Eng,UK
156/C4 **Tillamook,** Or,US
76/B3 **Tille** (riv.), Fr.
54/C4 **Tillicoultry,** Sc,UK
62/D3 **Tilst,** Den.
54/C3 **Tilt** (riv.), Sc,UK
142/Q9 **Tiltil,** Chile
92/B5 **Ţimā,** Egypt
85/L2 **Timan** (ridge), Rus.
115/R11 **Timaru,** NZ
86/F3 **Timashevsk,** Rus.
140/D2 **Timbaúba,** Braz.
157/H4 **Timber Lake,** SD,US
140/B2 **Timbiras,** Braz.
141/B3 **Timbó,** Braz.
128/E2 **Timbuktu** (Tombouctou), Mali
111/H4 **Timbuni** (riv.), Indo.
81/G3 **Timfristós** (peak), Gre.
123/V18 **Timgad** (ruins), Alg.
124/F2 **Timimoun,** Alg.
128/A2 **Timiris** (cape), Mrta.
82/E3 **Timiş** (co.), Rom.
82/E3 **Timiş** (riv.), Rom.
82/E3 **Timişoara,** Rom.
129/G2 **Ti-m-Mershoï** (wadi), Niger
160/D1 **Timmins,** On,Can
160/B2 **Timms** (hill), Wi,US
140/B2 **Timon,** Braz.
166/B5 **Timonium,** Md,US
114/D2 **Timor** (sea), Austl.
111/F5 **Timor** (isl.), Indo.
141/D1 **Timóteo,** Braz.
89/N4 **Timpton** (riv.), Rus.
61/F3 **Timrå,** Swe.
163/G3 **Tims Ford** (lake), Tn,US
132/E3 **Tina** (riv.), SAfr.
112/D4 **Tinaca** (pt.), Phil.
138/D2 **Tinaco,** Ven.
106/C5 **Tindivanam,** India
124/D2 **Tindouf,** Alg.
74/B1 **Tineo,** Sp.
105/H3 **Ting** (riv.), China
118/F7 **Tingalpa** (cr.), Austl.
118/F7 **Tingalpa** (res.), Austl.
119/D3 **Tingaringy Nat'l Park,** Austl.
124/H2 **Tinghert** (upland), Libya
128/C4 **Tingi** (mts.), Gui., SLeo.
151/F2 **Tingmerkpuk** (mtn.), Ak,US
144/C3 **Tingo María,** Peru
142/C2 **Tinguirrica** (vol.), Chile
137/L6 **Tinharé,** Braz.
140/C4 **Tinharé** (isl.), Braz.
109/D2 **Tinh Gia,** Viet.
120/D3 **Tinian** (isl.), NMar.
166/C4 **Tinicum Nat'l Env. Ctr.,** Pa,US
159/H4 **Tinker A.F.B.,** Ok,US
128/C4 **Tinkisso** (riv.), Gui.
165/Q16 **Tinley Park,** Il,US
135/C2 **Tinogasta,** Arg.
81/J4 **Tínos** (isl.), Gre.
68/C5 **Tinqueux,** Fr.
124/G2 **Tinrhert** (plat.), Alg.
124/D1 **Tinrhir,** Mor.
104/B3 **Tinsukia,** India
58/B5 **Tintagel,** Eng,UK
58/B5 **Tintagel Head** (pt.), Eng,UK
58/D3 **Tintern Abbey,** Wal,UK
74/B4 **Tinto** (riv.), Sp.
54/C5 **Tinto** (mtn.), Sc,UK
167/D3 **Tinton Falls** (New Shrewsbury), NJ,US
57/G5 **Tintwistle,** Eng,UK
144/B3 **Tinyahuarco,** Peru
124/F4 **Ti-n-Zaouâten,** Alg.
157/H3 **Tioga,** ND,US
110/B3 **Tioman** (isl.), Malay.
123/S15 **Tipaza,** Alg.
123/R15 **Tipaza** (wilaya), Alg.
60/C4 **Tipperary** (co.), Ire.
59/G3 **Tiptree,** Eng,UK
106/C5 **Tiptūr,** India
121/L6 **Tiputa,** FrPol.
140/A1 **Tiracambu** (mts.), Braz.
127/C2 **Tiran** (str.), Egypt
92/C5 **Tīrān** (isl.), SAr.
81/F2 **Tiranë** (cap.), Alb.
127/C3 **Tiran, Jazīrat** (isl.), Egypt
77/G5 **Tirano,** It.
117/H4 **Tirari** (des.), Austl.
83/J2 **Tiraspol',** Mol.
92/A2 **Tire,** Turk.
86/F4 **Tirebolu,** Turk.
55/H8 **Tiree** (isl.), Sc,UK
129/F1 **Tirest** (well), Mali
83/G3 **Tîrgovişte,** Rom.
83/H3 **Tîrgu Bujor,** Rom.
83/F3 **Tîrgu Cărbuneşti,** Rom.
83/H2 **Tîrgu Frumos,** Rom.
83/F3 **Tîrgu Jiu,** Rom.
83/F2 **Tîrgu Lăpuş,** Rom.
83/G2 **Tîrgu Mureş,** Rom.
83/H2 **Tîrgu Neamţ,** Rom.
83/H2 **Tîrgu Ocna,** Rom.
83/H3 **Tîrgu Secuiesc,** Rom.
95/K1 **Tirich Mīr** (mtn.), Pak.
83/G2 **Tîrnava Mare** (riv.), Rom.
83/G2 **Tîrnava Mică** (riv.), Rom.
83/G2 **Tîrnăveni,** Rom.
81/H3 **Tírnavos,** Gre.
77/G3 **Tirol** (prov.), Aus.
141/C1 **Tiros,** Braz.
58/C1 **Tir Rhiwiog** (mtn.), Wa,UK
71/F3 **Tirschenreuth,** Ger.
80/A2 **Tirso** (riv.), It.
108/F3 **Tiruchchendūr,** India
108/G3 **Tiruchchirāppalli,** India
108/G4 **Tiruchendūr,** India
108/F4 **Tirumangalam,** India
108/F4 **Tirunelveli,** India
106/C5 **Tirupati,** India
108/G3 **Tiruppattūr,** India
108/F3 **Tiruppūr,** India
108/E3 **Tirūr,** India
108/G3 **Tirutturaippūndi,** India
108/F4 **Tiruvalla,** India
106/C5 **Tiruvannāmalai,** India
86/B2 **Tisa** (riv.), Eur.
83/G1 **Tisa** (riv.), Ukr.
58/D4 **Tisbury,** Eng,UK
157/G2 **Tisdale,** Sk,Can
159/H4 **Tishomingo,** Ok,US
123/R16 **Tissemsilt,** Alg.
123/R16 **Tissemsilt** (wilaya), Alg.
63/T8 **Tisvilde,** Den.
82/E2 **Tisza** (riv.), Hun.
82/E2 **Tiszaföldvár,** Hun.
82/E2 **Tiszafüred,** Hun.
82/E2 **Tiszakécske,** Hun.
82/E1 **Tiszalök,** Hun.
82/E2 **Tiszavasvári,** Hun.
79/F5 **Titano, Monte** (peak), SMar.
112/C4 **Titay,** Phil.
82/E3 **Titel,** Yugo.
144/D4 **Titicaca** (lake), Bol., Peru
168/A3 **Titicus** (mtn.), Ct,US
76/E2 **Titisee Neustadt,** Ger.
106/D3 **Titlagarh,** India
77/E4 **Titlis** (peak), Swi.
82/D4 **Titograd,** Yugo.
82/D4 **Titovo Užice,** Yugo.
82/E5 **Titov Veles,** Macd.
82/E5 **Titov vrh** (peak), Macd.
117/G2 **Ti-Tree Abor. Land,** Austl.
53/P8 **Titsey,** Eng,UK
83/G3 **Titu,** Rom.
163/H4 **Titusville,** Fl,US
130/C3 **Tiva** (riv.), Kenya
128/A3 **Tivaouane,** Sen.
82/D4 **Tivat,** Yugo.
58/C5 **Tiverton,** Eng,UK
168/C2 **Tiverton,** RI,US
63/T9 **Tivoli Gardens,** Den.
144/B1 **Tixán,** Ecu.
147/L7 **Tizayuca,** Mex.
147/H4 **Tizimín,** Mex.
123/T15 **Tizi Ouzou,** Alg.
123/T15 **Tizi Ouzou** (wilaya), Alg.
95/L1 **Tiznap** (riv.), China
124/D2 **Tiznit,** Mor.
66/C3 **Tjeukemeer** (lake), Neth.
62/D3 **Tjorn** (isl.), Swe.
147/M7 **Tlachichuca,** Mex.
148/B2 **Tlacolula,** Mex.
147/P8 **Tlacotalpan,** Mex.
147/R10 **Tláhuac,** Mex.
146/E3 **Tlahualilo de Zaragoza,** Mex.
147/K6 **Tlahuelilpa de Ocampo,** Mex.
146/E4 **Tlajomulco,** Mex.
147/N8 **Tlalixcoyan,** Mex.
147/R10 **Tlalmanalcó de Valásquez,** Mex.
147/Q9 **Tlalnepantla,** Mex.
147/K7 **Tlalnepantla de Galeana,** Mex.
147/Q10 **Tlaloc** (mtn.), Mex.
147/Q10 **Tlalpan,** Mex.
147/K8 **Tlaltizapan,** Mex.
147/F5 **Tlapa,** Mex.
147/R10 **Tlapacoya** (ruins), Mex.
147/F5 **Tlapacoyan,** Mex.
146/E4 **Tlaquepaque,** Mex.
147/K8 **Tlaquiltenango,** Mex.
147/M7 **Tlatlauquitepec,** Mex.
147/E5 **Tlatlaya,** Mex.
147/F5 **Tlaxcala,** Mex.
147/F5 **Tlaxcala** (state), Mex.
147/L7 **Tlaxcala de Xicohténcatl,** Mex.
147/K6 **Tlaxcoapan,** Mex.
147/L7 **Tlaxco de Morelos,** Mex.
147/L8 **Tlayacapan,** Mex.
123/Q16 **Tlemcen,** Alg.
123/Q16 **Tlemcen** (wilaya), Alg.
131/B5 **Tlokweng,** Bots.
124/J2 **Tmassah,** Libya
149/F4 **Toabré,** Pan.
83/G2 **Toaca** (peak), Rom.
138/B4 **Toachi** (riv.), Ecu.
123/G6 **Toamasina,** Madg.
133/J7 **Toamasina** (prov.), Madg.
165/B2 **Toandos** (pen.), Wa,US
121/L6 **Toau** (atoll), FrPol.
156/B3 **Toba** (inlet), BC,Can
96/D5 **Toba,** China
110/A3 **Toba** (lake), Indo.
99/E3 **Toba,** Japan
150/F5 **Tobago** (isl.), Trin.
95/J2 **Toba Kākar** (range), Pak.
74/E3 **Tobarra,** Sp.
108/B2 **Toba Tek Singh,** Pak.
78/B3 **Tobbio, Monte** (peak), It.
56/B2 **Tobermore,** NI,UK
117/H2 **Tobermorey,** Austl.
55/H8 **Tobermory,** Sc,UK
100/B2 **Tōbetsu,** Japan
140/C3 **Tobias Barreto,** Braz.
112/C3 **Tobias Fornier,** Phil.
116/E2 **Tobin** (lake), Austl.
157/H2 **Tobin** (lake), Sk,Can
161/H2 **Tobique** (riv.), NB,Can
99/M9 **Tobishima,** Japan
85/Q4 **Tobol** (riv.), Kaz., Rus.
88/G4 **Tobol'sk,** Rus.
125/K1 **Tobruk,** Libya
166/C1 **Tobyhanna** (cr.), Pa,US
166/C1 **Tobyhanna** (lake), Pa,US
166/C1 **Tobyhanna Saint Park,** Pa,US
85/L2 **Tobysh** (riv.), Rus.
137/J5 **Tocantinópolis,** Braz.
140/A2 **Tocantins** (riv.), Braz.
140/A3 **Tocantins** (state), Braz.
163/H3 **Toccoa,** Ga,US
77/E5 **Toce** (riv.), It.
99/F2 **Tochigi,** Japan
99/F2 **Tochigi** (pref.), Japan
147/L8 **Tochimilco,** Mex.
99/F2 **Tochio,** Japan
74/C4 **Tocina,** Sp.
135/B1 **Tocopilla,** Chile
149/G4 **Tocumen,** Pan.
138/D2 **Tocuyito,** Ven.
138/D2 **Tocuyo** (riv.), Ven.
99/H7 **Toda,** Japan
106/C2 **Toda Bhīm,** India
59/F3 **Toddington,** Eng,UK
130/B1 **Todenyang,** Kenya
80/C1 **Todi,** It.
77/E4 **Tödi** (peak), Swi.
57/F4 **Todmorden,** Eng,UK
101/C5 **Todohae Hasang Nat'l Park,** SKor.
140/C4 **Todos os Santos** (bay), Braz.
167/J9 **Todt Hill,** NY,US
60/A7 **Toe Head** (pt.), Ire.
139/G3 **Toekomstig** (res.), Sur.
156/E2 **Tofield,** Ab,Can
61/E3 **Töfsingdalens Nat'l Park,** Swe.
121/H6 **Tofua** (isl.), Tonga
128/C2 **Togba** (well), Mrta.
77/F3 **Toggenburg** (val.), Swi.
151/G4 **Togiak Nat'l Wild. Ref.,** Ak,US
101/D2 **Togno** (riv.), NKor.
129/F4 **Togo**
99/N9 **Tōgō,** Japan
103/B2 **Togtoh,** China
101/D5 **Tŏgyu-san Nat'l Park,** SKor.
158/E4 **Tohatchi,** NM,US
166/C3 **Tohickon** (cr.), Pa,US
121/X15 **Tohivea** (peak), FrPol.
100/B3 **Tōhoku** (dist.), Japan
99/F2 **Tōhoku** (prov.), Japan
99/F3 **Toi,** Japan
99/M9 **Tōin,** Japan
158/C3 **Toiyabe** (range), Nv,US
98/C3 **Tojō,** Japan
99/L10 **Tōjō,** Japan
100/C2 **Tokachi** (riv.), Japan
99/E3 **Tōkai,** Japan
99/F2 **Tōkamachi,** Japan
127/D5 **Tokar,** Sudan
100/K6 **Tokara** (isls.), Japan
127/D5 **Tokar Game Rsv.,** Sudan
92/D1 **Tokat,** Turk.
92/D1 **Tokat** (prov.), Turk.
101/C4 **Tŏkchŏk** (arch.), SKor.
50/A6 **Tokelau** (isls.), NZ
121/H5 **Tokelau** (terr.), NZ
99/N9 **Toki,** Japan
99/N9 **Toki** (riv.), Japan
99/H6 **Tokigawa,** Japan
99/M10 **Tokoname,** Japan
100/D1 **Tokoro,** Japan
100/C2 **Tokoro** (riv.), Japan
115/S10 **Tokoroa,** NZ
99/F3 **Tokorozawa,** Japan
96/B2 **Toksun,** China
102/B3 **Toktogul** (res.), Kyr.
100/K7 **Tokuno** (isl.), Japan
100/K7 **Tokunoshima,** Japan
98/D3 **Tokushima,** Japan
98/C4 **Tokushima** (pref.), Japan
98/B3 **Tokuyama,** Japan
131/C3 **Tokwe** (riv.), Zim.
99/H7 **Tokyo** (bay), Japan
99/F3 **Tōkyō** (cap.), Japan
99/F3 **Tōkyō** (pref.), Japan
99/H7 **Tōkyō Disneyland,** Japan
99/H7 **Tōkyō** (inset) (cap.), Japan
148/E4 **Tola,** Nic.
123/G7 **Tôlanäro,** Madg.
83/H4 **Tolbukhin,** Bul.
135/F1 **Toledo,** Braz.
112/C3 **Toledo,** Phil.
74/C3 **Toledo,** Sp.
74/C3 **Toledo** (mts.), Sp.
160/D3 **Toledo,** Oh,US
162/E4 **Toledo Bend** (dam), La,US
162/E4 **Toledo Bend** (res.), La, Tx,US
80/C1 **Tolentino,** It.
142/C3 **Tolhuaca Nat'l Park,** Chile
102/D2 **Toli,** China
133/G8 **Toliara,** Madg.
133/H8 **Toliara** (prov.), Madg.
138/C4 **Tolima** (dept.), Col.
138/C3 **Tolima, Nevado del** (peak), Col.
111/F3 **Tolitoli,** Indo.
60/D3 **Tolka** (riv.), Ire.
168/B2 **Tolland,** Ct,US
168/B2 **Tolland** (co.), Ct,US
168/A1 **Tolland Saint For.,** Ma,US
82/A2 **Tolmezzo,** It.
82/D2 **Tolna,** Hun.
82/D2 **Tolna** (co.), Hun.
111/F4 **Tolo** (gulf), Indc.
55/P13 **Tolob,** Sc,UK
74/D1 **Tolosa,** Sp.
101/D5 **Tolsan** (isl.), SKor.
165/D2 **Tolt** (res.), Wa,US
165/D2 **Tolt** (riv.), Wa,US
142/B3 **Toltén,** Chile
142/B3 **Toltén** (riv.), Chile
165/D2 **Tolt, North Fork** (riv.), Wa,US
165/D2 **Tolt, South Fork** (riv.), Wa,US
138/C2 **Tolú,** Col.
147/K7 **Toluca,** Mex.
148/B2 **Toluca,** Mex.
147/Q10 **Toluca de Laredo,** Mex.
148/B2 **Toluca, Nevado de** (peak), Mex.
87/J1 **Tol'yatti,** Rus.
88/J4 **Tom'** (riv.), Rus.
160/B3 **Tomah,** Wi,US
100/B2 **Tomakomai,** Japan
100/B1 **Tomamae,** Japan
120/G6 **Tomanivi** (peak), Fiji
74/A3 **Tomar,** Port.
81/G3 **Tómaros** (peak), Gre.
92/C2 **Tomarza,** Turk.
65/M3 **Tomaszów Lubelski,** Pol.
65/L3 **Tomaszów Mazowiecki,** Pol.
54/C2 **Tomatin,** Sc,UK
136/G6 **Tombador** (mts.), Braz.
125/M6 **Tombe,** Sudan
163/F4 **Tombigbee** (riv.), Al, Ms,US
126/B2 **Tomboco,** Ang.
103/B4 **Tomb of Qinshihuang,** China
124/E4 **Tombouctou,** Mali
128/E2 **Tombouctou** (Timbuktu), Mali
158/E5 **Tombstone,** Az,US
126/B4 **Tombua,** Ang.
142/B3 **Tomé,** Chile
72/B2 **Tomé** (isl.), Fr.
62/E4 **Tomelilla,** Swe.
74/D3 **Tomelloso,** Sp.
111/F4 **Tomini** (gulf), Indo.
74/A2 **Tomiño,** Sp.
54/C2 **Tomintoul,** Sc,UK
99/H7 **Tomiura,** Japan
99/F3 **Tomiyama,** Japan
89/N4 **Tommot,** Rus.
138/D3 **Tomo** (riv.), Col.
160/C4 **Tompkinsville,** Ky,US
167/D3 **Toms** (riv.), NJ,US
88/J4 **Tomsk,** Rus.
167/D4 **Toms River,** NJ,US
91/D1 **Tömük,** Turk.
151/K3 **Tom White** (mtn.), Ak,US
148/C2 **Tonalá,** Mex.
77/G5 **Tonale, Passo del** (pass), It.
156/D3 **Tonasket,** Wa,US
161/S9 **Tonawanda,** NY,US
161/S9 **Tonawanda** (cr.), NY,US
161/S9 **Tonawanda Ind. Res.,** NY,US
53/P8 **Tonbridge,** Eng,UK
139/G3 **Tonckens** (falls), Sur.
99/L10 **Tondabayashi,** Japan
111/F3 **Tondano,** Indo.
62/C4 **Tönder,** Den.
108/G4 **Tondi,** India
125/K6 **Tondou** (mts.), CAfr.
99/J7 **Tone,** Japan
99/G3 **Tone** (riv.), Japan
58/C4 **Tone** (riv.), Eng,UK
93/G2 **Tonekābon,** Iran
60/D3 **Tonelagee** (mtn.), Ire.
96/F5 **Tong** (riv.), China
121/H7 **Tonga**
105/H3 **Tong'an,** China
121/K5 **Tongareva** (Penrhyn) (atoll), CookIs.
121/H7 **Tonga-tapu** (isl.), Tonga
103/C4 **Tongbai,** China
101/G6 **Tongbu,** SKor.
105/G2 **Tongcheng,** China

159/G5 **Twin Buttes** (res.), Tx,US
156/E5 **Twin Falls,** Id,US
131/C1 **Twingi,** Zam.
166/D3 **Twin Rivers,** NJ,US
168/F5 **Twinsburg,** Oh,US
67/G6 **Twiste** (riv.), Ger.
67/F3 **Twistringen,** Ger.
115/R11 **Twizel,** NZ
159/G3 **Two Buttes** (riv.), Co,US
119/D3 **Twofold** (bay), Austl.
157/L4 **Two Harbors,** Mn,US
156/F2 **Two Hills,** Ab,Can
160/C2 **Two Rivers,** Wi,US
59/E1 **Twycross,** Eng,UK
59/F4 **Twyford,** Eng,UK
58/C1 **Twymyn** (riv.), Wal,UK
56/D2 **Twynholm,** Sc,UK
104/B4 **Tyao** (riv.), Burma, India
100/E1 **Tyatya Gora** (mtn.), Rus.
65/K3 **Tychy,** Pol.
59/G1 **Tydd Saint Giles,** Eng,UK
160/E2 **Tyendinaga,** On,Can
163/H3 **Tyger** (riv.), SC,US
57/F4 **Tyldesley,** Eng,UK
162/E3 **Tyler,** Tx,US
97/N1 **Tymovskoye,** Rus.
73/L2 **Týn,** Czh.
159/H2 **Tyndall,** SD,US
54/B4 **Tyndrum,** Sc,UK
57/F2 **Tyne** (riv.), Eng,UK
54/D5 **Tyne** (riv.), Sc,UK
57/G2 **Tyne & Wear** (co.), Eng,UK
57/G1 **Tynemouth,** Eng,UK
92/C3 **Tyre,** Leb.
62/H2 **Tyresö,** Swe.
63/S7 **Tyresta** (reg. park), Swe.
91/D3 **Tyre** (Şūr), Leb.
62/D1 **Tyrifjorden** (lake), Nor.
97/L2 **Tyrma** (riv.), Rus.
87/G4 **Tyrnyauz,** Rus.
119/B2 **Tyrrell** (cr.), Austl.
119/B2 **Tyrrell** (lake), Austl.
80/B2 **Tyrrhenian** (sea), It.
62/A2 **Tysnesøy** (isl.), Nor.
166/A6 **Tysons Corner,** Va,US
87/J3 **Tyub-Karagan** (pt.), Kaz.
87/J3 **Tyulen'i** (isls.), Kaz.
87/H3 **Tyuleniy** (isl.), Rus.
85/Q4 **Tyumen',** Rus.
85/Q4 **Tyumen' Obl.,** Rus.
102/C3 **Tyup,** Kyr.
58/B3 **Tywi** (riv.), Wal,UK
58/B1 **Tywyn,** Wal,UK
131/C4 **Tzaneen,** SAfr.

U

112/C2 **Uac** (mtn.), Phil.
121/M5 **Ua Huka** (isl.), FrPol.
54/B4 **Uamh Bheag** (mtn.), Sc,UK
121/L5 **Ua Pou** (isl.), FrPol.
139/G5 **Uatumã** (riv.), Braz.
140/C3 **Uauá,** Braz.
139/E5 **Uaupés,** Braz.
138/D4 **Uaupés** (riv.), Braz.
147/H5 **Uaxactún,** Guat.
148/D2 **Uaxactún** (ruins), Guat.
82/E3 **Ub,** Yugo.
141/D2 **Ubá,** Braz.
69/F2 **Übach-Palenberg,** Ger.
85/Q5 **Ubagan** (riv.), Kaz.
140/C4 **Ubaíra,** Braz.
140/C4 **Ubaitaba,** Braz.
140/B1 **Ubajara,** Braz.
140/B1 **Ubajará Nat'l Park,** Braz.
125/J7 **Ubangi** (riv.), Zaire
140/C4 **Ubatã,** Braz.
138/C3 **Ubaté,** Col.
141/H8 **Ubatuba,** Braz.
112/D3 **Ubay,** Phil.
73/G4 **Ubaye** (riv.), Fr.
66/C5 **Ubbergen,** Neth.
98/B4 **Ube,** Japan
74/D3 **Úbeda,** Sp.
136/G7 **Uberaba** (lake), Bol.
141/C1 **Uberaba,** Braz.
69/F5 **Überherrn,** Ger.
141/B1 **Uberlândia,** Braz.
77/F2 **Überlingen,** Ger.
77/F2 **Überlingersee** (lake), Ger.
111/J4 **Ubia** (peak), Indo.
109/D3 **Ubon Ratchathani,** Thai.
74/C4 **Ubrique,** Sp.
126/E1 **Ubundu,** Zaire
144/C3 **Ucayali** (dept.), Peru
144/C2 **Ucayali** (riv.), Peru
64/C3 **Uccle,** Belg.
85/N5 **Uchaly,** Rus.
85/X8 **Uchinskoye,** Rus.
100/B2 **Uchiura** (bay), Japan
64/F2 **Uchte** (riv.), Ger.
89/P4 **Uchur** (riv.), Rus.
69/F5 **Uckange,** Fr.
65/G2 **Uckermark** (reg.), Ger.
59/G5 **Uckfield,** Eng,UK
156/B3 **Ucluelet,** BC,Can
96/F1 **Uda** (riv.), Rus.
106/B3 **Udaipur,** India
108/F3 **Udamalpet,** India
108/G4 **Udankudi,** India
62/D2 **Uddevalla,** Swe.
54/B5 **Uddingston,** Sc,UK
61/F2 **Uddjaure** (lake), Swe.
66/C5 **Uden,** Neth.
66/C5 **Udenhout,** Neth.
106/C4 **Udgīr,** India
108/C1 **Udhampur,** India
79/G1 **Udine,** It.
79/G1 **Udine** (prov.), It.
106/B5 **Udipi,** India
85/L4 **Udmurt Aut. Rep.,** Rus.
109/C2 **Udon Thani,** Thai.
65/H2 **Ueckermünde,** Ger.
99/F2 **Ueda,** Japan
125/K7 **Uele** (riv.), Zaire
67/H3 **Uelzen,** Ger.
98/E3 **Ueno,** Japan
99/F3 **Uenohara,** Japan
67/G1 **Uetersen,** Ger.
67/H4 **Uetze,** Ger.
85/M5 **Ufa,** Rus.
85/N5 **Ufa** (riv.), Rus.
59/E3 **Uffington,** Eng,UK
130/A4 **Ugalla,** Tanz.
130/A4 **Ugalla** (riv.), Tanz.
130/A4 **Ugalla River Game Rsv.,** Tanz.
130/B1 **Uganda**
81/F3 **Ugento,** It.
54/E1 **Ugie** (riv.), Sc,UK
73/G4 **Ugine,** Fr.
97/N2 **Uglegorsk,** Rus.
84/H4 **Uglich,** Rus.
73/L4 **Ugljan** (isl.), Cro.
86/E1 **Ugra** (riv.), Rus.
96/F2 **Ugtaaltsaydam,** Mong.
130/C3 **Ugweno,** Tanz.
65/J4 **Uherské Hradiště,** Czh.
70/C5 **Uhingen,** Ger.
71/G4 **Úhlava** (riv.), Czh.
71/F3 **Úhlavka** (riv.), Czh.
140/B3 **Uibaí,** Braz.
55/H7 **Uig,** Sc,UK
55/H8 **Uig,** Sc,UK
126/C2 **Uíge,** Ang.
101/D4 **Ŭijŏngbu,** SKor.
87/K2 **Uil** (riv.), Kaz.
132/L11 **Uilkraal** (riv.), SAfr.
87/G4 **Uilpata, Gora** (peak), Rus.
158/E2 **Uinta** (mts.), Ut,US
140/C2 **Uiraúna,** Braz.
101/E4 **Ŭisŏng,** SKor.
132/D4 **Uitenhage,** SAfr.
66/B3 **Uitgeest,** Neth.
66/B4 **Uithoorn,** Neth.
120/F4 **Ujae** (atoll), Mrsh.
120/F4 **Ujelang** (atoll), Mrsh.
82/E2 **Újfehértó,** Hun.
99/L10 **Uji,** Japan
99/L10 **Uji** (riv.), Japan
130/A4 **Ujiji,** Tanz.
99/L10 **Ujitawara,** Japan
106/C3 **Ujjain,** India
111/E5 **Ujung Pandang,** Indo.
130/B3 **Ukara** (isl.), Tanz.
130/B3 **Ukerewe** (isl.), Tanz.
85/M3 **Ukhta,** Rus.
158/B3 **Ukiah,** Ca,US
63/L4 **Ukmergė,** Lith.
86/D2 **Ukraine**
91/C2 **U.K. Sovereign Base Area** (mil. res.), Cyp.
130/B5 **Ukwama,** Tanz.
96/F2 **Ulaanbaatar** (cap.), Mong.
96/C2 **Ulaangom,** Mong.
96/B2 **Ulaanhus,** Mong.
96/F1 **Ulan-Burgasy** (mts.), Rus.
97/J2 **Ulanhot,** China
103/B2 **Ulansuhai** (salt lake), China
96/F1 **Ulan-Ude,** Rus.
102/F5 **Ulan Ul** (lake), China
165/L10 **Ulatis** (cr.), Ca,US
130/C4 **Ulaya,** Tanz.
101/E4 **Ulchin,** SKor.
82/D5 **Ulcinj,** Yugo.
96/G2 **Uldz** (riv.), Mong.
62/C2 **Ulefoss,** Nor.
97/H2 **Ulgain** (riv.), China
106/B4 **Ulhāsnagar,** India
96/D2 **Uliastay,** Mong.
125/L8 **Ulindi** (riv.), Zaire
120/D3 **Ulithi** (atoll), Micr.
74/A1 **Ulla** (riv.), Sp.
119/D2 **Ulladulla,** Austl.
55/J8 **Ullapool,** Sc,UK
144/D4 **Ulla Ulla Nat'l Rsv.,** Bol.
61/F1 **Ullsfjorden** (fjord), Nor.
57/F2 **Ullswater** (lake), Eng,UK
98/B2 **Ullŭng** (isl.), SKor.
70/C6 **Ulm,** Ger.
63/S7 **Ulnasjön** (lake), Swe.
131/D2 **Ulonguè,** Moz.
62/E3 **Ulricehamn,** Swe.
101/E5 **Ulsan,** SKor.
70/C1 **Ulster** (riv.), Ger.
56/A3 **Ulster** (reg.), Ire.
56/A2 **Ulster American Folk Park,** NI,UK
148/E3 **Ulua** (riv.), Hon.
92/B2 **Uluborlu,** Turk.
92/B1 **Uludağ, Tepe** (peak), Turk.
93/F2 **Uludoruk** (peak), Turk.
130/C4 **Uluguru** (mts.), Tanz.
148/D2 **Ulumal,** Mex.
96/B2 **Ulungur** (lake), China
96/B2 **Ulungur** (riv.), China
117/F3 **Uluru** (Ayers Rock) (peak), Austl.
117/F3 **Uluru Nat'l Park,** Austl.
102/A2 **Ulutau, Gora** (peak), Kaz.
57/E3 **Ulverston,** Eng,UK
119/C4 **Ulverstone,** Austl.
63/J1 **Ulvila,** Fin.
63/P2 **Ul'yanovka,** Rus.
162/C2 **Ulysses,** Ks,US
147/H4 **Umán,** Mex.
86/D2 **Uman',** Ukr.
112/D3 **Umanum** (pt.), Phil.
140/C2 **Umarizal,** Braz.
106/D4 **Umarkot,** India
95/L2 **Umāsi La** (pass), India
120/D5 **Umboi** (isl.), PNG
77/G4 **Umbrailpass** (pass), Swi.
77/G4 **Umbrail, Piz** (peak), Swi.
80/C1 **Umbria** (reg.), It.
79/F5 **Umbro-Marchigiano, Appennino** (mts.), It.
131/C5 **Umbuluze** (riv.), Moz., Swaz.
88/B3 **Ume** (riv.), Swe.
131/C3 **Ume** (riv.), Zim.
61/G3 **Umeå,** Swe.
61/F2 **Umeälv** (riv.), Swe.
133/E3 **Umfolozi** (riv.), SAfr.
131/C3 **Umfuli** (riv.), Zim.
133/E3 **Umgeni** (riv.), SAfr.
95/F4 **Umm as Samīm** (salt dep.), Oman
125/M4 **Umm Durmān** (Omdurman), Sudan
91/D3 **Umm el Fahm,** Isr.
127/C4 **Umm Hibal, Bi'r** (well), Egypt
125/M5 **Umm Ruwābah,** Sudan
151/E5 **Umnak** (isl.), Ak,US
151/E5 **Umnak** (passg.), Ak,US
131/C3 **Umniati,** Zim.
131/C3 **Umniati** (riv.), Zim.
156/C5 **Umpqua** (riv.), Or,US
132/E3 **Umtata,** SAfr.
135/F1 **Umuarama,** Braz.
132/E3 **Umzimvubu** (riv.), SAfr.
131/C4 **Umzingwani** (riv.), Zim.
82/B3 **Una** (riv.), Bosn., Cro.
140/C4 **Una,** Braz.
115/R11 **Una** (peak), NZ
140/A5 **Unaí,** Braz.
151/E5 **Unalaska** (isl.), Ak,US
92/D3 **'Unāzah, Jabal** (mtn.), SAr.
158/E3 **Uncompahgre** (plat.), Co,US
131/C2 **Undaunda,** Zam.
62/F2 **Unden** (lake), Swe.
157/H4 **Underwood,** ND,US
121/Z17 **Undu** (pt.), Fiji
86/E1 **Unecha,** Rus.
151/F4 **Unga** (isl.), Ak,US
130/D3 **Ungama** (bay), Kenya
153/K3 **Ungava** (bay), Qu, Can
153/J2 **Ungava** (pen.), Qu,Can
86/C3 **Ungeny,** Mol.
140/B2 **União,** Braz.
141/B3 **União da Vitória,** Braz.
140/C3 **União dos Palmares,** Braz.
151/E4 **Unimak** (isl.), Ak,US
151/E5 **Unimak** (passg.), Ak,US
139/F5 **Unini** (riv.), Braz.
54/C5 **Union** (can.), Sc,UK
159/K3 **Union,** Mo,US
167/D2 **Union,** NJ,US
167/D2 **Union** (co.), NJ,US
166/C5 **Union** (lake), NJ,US
156/D4 **Union,** Or,US
166/A2 **Union** (co.), Pa,US
163/H3 **Union,** SC,US
167/D3 **Union Beach,** NJ,US
165/K11 **Union City,** Ca,US
167/D2 **Union City,** NJ,US
163/F2 **Union City,** Tn,US
167/L9 **Uniondale,** NY,US
149/F1 **Unión de Reyes,** Cuba
146/D5 **Unión de Tula,** Mex.
148/C2 **Unión Hidalgo,** Mex.
163/G3 **Union Springs,** Al,US
160/E4 **Uniontown,** Pa,US
161/R8 **Unionville,** On,Can
159/J2 **Unionville,** Mo,US
94/F4 **United Arab Emirates**
55/* **United Kingdom**
167/K8 **United Nations,** NY,US
101/E5 **United Nations Mem. Cemetery,** SKor.
152/* **United States**
153/T6 **United States** (range), NW,Can
156/F2 **Unity,** Sk,Can
162/D4 **Universal City,** Tx,US
147/Q10 **University City,** Mex.
168/F5 **University Heights,** Oh,US
164/G8 **Univ. of California-Irvine,** Ca,US
164/F7 **Univ. of California-Los Angles,** Ca,US
164/F7 **Univ. of Southern California,** Ca,US
106/B3 **Unjha,** India
117/M8 **Unley,** Austl.
67/E5 **Unna,** Ger.
106/D2 **Unnão,** India
60/B1 **Unshin** (riv.), Ire.
55/P12 **Unst** (isl.), Sc,UK
64/F3 **Unstruct** (riv.), Ger.
77/F2 **Unterargen** (riv.), Ger.
70/D3 **Unterpleichfeld,** Ger.
71/E6 **Unterschleissheim,** Ger.
77/E2 **Untersee** (lake), Ger., Swi.
76/E4 **Unterwalden** (canton), Swi.
92/D1 **Ünye,** Turk.
98/A4 **Unzen-Amakusa Nat'l Park,** Japan
98/B4 **Unzen-dake** (mtn.), Japan
85/K4 **Unzha** (riv.), Rus.
99/E2 **Uozu,** Japan
140/C2 **Upanema,** Braz.
139/F2 **Upata,** Ven.
126/E2 **Upemba** (lake), Zaire
126/E2 **Upemba Nat'l Park,** Zaire
54/C5 **Uphall,** Sc,UK
112/D4 **Upi,** Phil.
132/C3 **Upington,** SAfr.
130/B5 **Upiriwombe,** Zam.
106/B3 **Upleta,** India
53/P7 **Upminster,** Eng,UK
154/U10 **Upolu** (pt.), Hi,US
121/H6 **Upolu** (isl.), WSam.
158/C2 **Upper** (lake), Ca,US
167/D2 **Upper** (bay), NJ, NY,US
163/H1 **Upper Arlington,** Oh,US
156/D3 **Upper Arrow** (lake), BC,Can
71/H6 **Upper Austria** (prov.), Aus.
166/C4 **Upper Darby,** Pa,US
139/G3 **Upper Demerara-Berbice** (reg.), Guy.
59/G5 **Upper Dicker,** Eng,UK
129/E4 **Upper East** (reg.), Gha.
77/F5 **Upper Engadine** (val.), Swi.
115/S11 **Upper Hutt,** NZ
159/J2 **Upper Iowa** (riv.), Ia,US
156/C5 **Upper Klamath** (lake), Or,US
56/B2 **Upperlands,** NI,UK
60/C1 **Upper Lough Erne** (lake), NI,UK
160/C2 **Upper Peninsula** (pen.), Mi,US
157/L5 **Upper Peoria** (lake), Il,US
157/K3 **Upper Red** (lake), Mn,US
165/F7 **Upper Rouge** (riv.), Mi,US
167/J7 **Upper Saddle River,** NJ,US
139/G4 **Upper Takutu-Upper Essequibo** (reg.), Guy.
59/E3 **Upper Thames** (val.), Eng,UK
129/E4 **Upper West** (reg.), Gha.
59/F1 **Uppingham,** Eng,UK
62/G2 **Upplands-Väsby,** Swe.
62/G2 **Uppsala,** Swe.
62/G1 **Uppsala** (co.), Swe.
151/D3 **Upright** (cape), Ak,US
118/B2 **Upstart** (bay), Austl.
118/B2 **Upstart** (cape), Austl.
157/G4 **Upton,** Wy,US
58/D2 **Upton upon Severn,** Eng,UK
93/F4 **Ur** (ruins), Iraq
138/B2 **Urabá** (gulf), Col.
103/B2 **Urad Qianqi,** China
99/H7 **Uraga** (chan.), Japan
100/C2 **Urahoro,** Japan
140/A1 **Uraim** (riv.), Braz.
100/C2 **Urakawa,** Japan
88/F3 **Ural** (mts.), Rus.
88/F5 **Ural** (riv.), Rus., Kaz.
87/J2 **Ural'sk,** Kaz.
87/J2 **Ural'sk Obl.,** Kaz.
130/B4 **Urambo,** Tanz.
140/B4 **Urandi,** Braz.
152/F3 **Uranium City,** Sk,Can
139/F4 **Uraricoera** (riv.), Braz.
100/J7 **Urasoe,** Japan
99/F3 **Urawa,** Japan
88/G3 **Uray,** Rus.
99/H7 **Urayasu,** Japan
70/C5 **Urbach,** Ger.
160/B3 **Urbana,** Il,US
160/D3 **Urbana,** Oh,US
149/G1 **Urbano Noris,** Cuba
140/B1 **Urbano Santos,** Braz.
79/F5 **Urbino,** It.
77/E3 **Urdorf,** Swi.
57/G3 **Ure** (riv.), Eng,UK
158/E5 **Ures,** Mex.
99/M10 **Ureshino,** Japan
92/D2 **Urfa,** Turk.
92/D2 **Urfa** (prov.), Turk.
67/G6 **Urft** (riv.), Ger.
88/G5 **Urgench,** Uzb.
78/C1 **Urgnano,** It.
61/H1 **Urho Kekkosen Nat'l Park,** Fin.
77/E4 **Uri** (canton), Swi.
138/D3 **Uribante** (riv.), Ven.
54/D2 **Urie** (riv.), Sc,UK
136/F2 **Urimáan,** Ven.
139/F3 **Urimán,** Ven.
146/D3 **Urique** (riv.), Mex.
77/E4 **Uri-Rotstock** (peak), Swi.
63/K1 **Urjala,** Fin.
66/C3 **Urk,** Neth.
92/A2 **Urla,** Turk.
83/H3 **Urlaţi,** Rom.
108/C2 **Urmar,** India
97/L2 **Urmi** (riv.), Rus.
93/F2 **Urmia** (lake), Iran
57/F5 **Urmston,** Eng,UK
77/E4 **Urnersee** (lake), Swi.
82/E4 **Uroševac,** Yugo.
56/E1 **Urr Water** (riv.), Sc,UK
147/N7 **Úrsulo Galván,** Mex.
137/J6 **Uruaçu,** Braz.
146/E5 **Uruapan,** Mex.
144/C3 **Urubamba** (riv.), Peru
139/G5 **Urubu** (riv.), Braz.
140/C1 **Uruburetama,** Braz.
140/C4 **Uruçuca,** Braz.
140/A2 **Uruçuí,** Braz.
140/A3 **Uruçuí** (mts.), Braz.
140/A5 **Uruçuí** (riv.), Braz.
140/A3 **Uruçuí Prêto** (riv.), Braz.
135/E2 **Uruguaiana,** Braz.
135/E3 **Uruguay**
135/E2 **Uruguay** (riv.), SAm.
96/B3 **Ürümqi,** China
140/B1 **Uruoca,** Braz.
89/R5 **Urup** (isl.), Rus.
141/B4 **Urussanga,** Braz.
130/A4 **Uruwira,** Tanz.
97/H1 **Uryumkan** (riv.), Rus.
87/G2 **Uryupinsk,** Rus.
83/H3 **Urziceni,** Rom.
53/R9 **Us,** Fr.
96/C1 **Us** (riv.), Rus.
98/B4 **Usa,** Japan
53/J2 **Usa** (riv.), Rus.
130/B3 **Usagara,** Tanz.
92/B2 **Uşak,** Turk.
92/B2 **Uşak** (prov.), Turk.
126/C5 **Usakos,** Namb.
143/N7 **Usborne** (peak), Falk.
166/D6 **U.S.C G. Receiving Ctr.,** NJ,US
166/A5 **U.S. Dept. of Energy,** Md,US
130/A4 **Usevia,** Tanz.
130/B3 **Ushashi,** Tanz.
130/B4 **Ushetu,** Tanz.
98/B4 **Ushibuka,** Japan
99/J7 **Ushiku,** Japan
130/A3 **Ushirombo,** Tanz.
102/C2 **Ushtobe,** Kaz.
143/K8 **Ushuaia,** Arg.
108/F4 **Usilampatti,** India
130/A4 **Usinge,** Tanz.
70/B2 **Usingen,** Ger.
53/H3 **Usinsk,** Rus.
58/D3 **Usk,** Wal,UK
58/D3 **Usk** (riv.), Wal,UK
83/J5 **Üsküdar,** Turk.
67/G5 **Uslar,** Ger.
71/G4 **Úslava** (riv.), Czh.
86/F1 **Usman',** Rus.
166/B6 **U.S. Naval Academy,** Md,US
150/E3 **U.S. Naval Res.,** PR
164/F8 **U.S. Nav. Weap. Sta., Seal Beach,** Ca,US
130/B4 **Usoke,** Tanz.
96/E1 **Usol'ye-Sibirskoye,** Rus.
112/C2 **Uson,** Phil.
142/C2 **Uspallata** (pass), Arg., Chile
154/W13 **U.S.S. Arizona Mem.,** Hi,US
72/E4 **Ussel,** Fr.
70/D5 **Ussel** (riv.), Ger.
76/C5 **Usses** (riv.), Fr.
130/B4 **Ussure,** Tanz.
97/L2 **Ussuri** (Wusuli) (riv.), Rus., China
97/L3 **Ussuriysk,** Rus.
77/E3 **Uster,** Swi.
80/C3 **Ustica** (isl.), It.
89/L4 **Ust'-Ilimsk,** Rus.
65/H3 **Ústí nad Labem,** Czh.
65/J1 **Ustka,** Pol.
89/S4 **Ust'-Kamchatsk,** Rus.
102/D2 **Ust'-Kamenogorsk,** Kaz.
89/L4 **Ust'-Kut,** Rus.
96/E1 **Ust'-Ordynskiy,** Rus.
65/M4 **Ustrzyki Dolne,** Pol.
85/K3 **Ust'ya** (riv.), Rus.
87/K4 **Ustyurt** (plat.), Kaz., Uzb.
102/D3 **Usu,** China
98/B4 **Usuki,** Japan
148/D3 **Usulután,** ESal.
148/C2 **Usumacinta** (riv.), Guat., Mex.
158/E3 **Utah** (state), US
158/D2 **Utah** (lake), Ut,US
131/D2 **Utale,** Malw.
99/L10 **Utano,** Japan
100/C2 **Utashinai,** Japan
159/G3 **Ute** (cr.), NM,US
63/L4 **Utena,** Lith.
130/B5 **Utengule,** Tanz.
71/G3 **Uterský** (riv.), Czh.
130/C4 **Utete,** Tanz.
109/C3 **Uthai Thani,** Thai.
160/F3 **Utica,** NY,US
74/E3 **Utiel,** Sp.
157/K2 **Utik** (lake), Mb,Can
156/E2 **Utikuma** (lake), Ab,Can
148/E2 **Utila** (isl.), Hon.
140/B4 **Utinga,** Braz.
120/G3 **Utirik** (atoll), Mrsh.
120/G5 **Utiroa,** Kiri.
117/G2 **Utopia Abor. Land,** Austl.
106/D2 **Utraulā,** India
66/C4 **Utrecht,** Neth.
66/C4 **Utrecht** (prov.), Neth.
74/C4 **Utrera,** Sp.
99/F2 **Utsunomiya,** Japan
108/F4 **Uttamapālaiyam,** India
109/C2 **Uttaradit,** Thai.
102/C5 **Uttarkashi,** India
106/C2 **Uttar Pradesh** (state), India
57/G6 **Uttoxeter,** Eng,UK
63/R7 **Uttran** (lake), Swe.
150/E3 **Utuado,** PR
120/F6 **Utupua** (isl.), Sol.
121/K6 **Uturoa,** FrPol.
50/B6 **Uturoa** (isl.), FrPol.
96/G2 **Uulbayan,** Mong.
96/E1 **Üür** (riv.), Mong.
96/C1 **Üüreg** (lake), Mong.
96/C1 **Uus** (lake), Mong.
63/J1 **Uusikaupunki,** Fin.
63/L1 **Uusimaa** (prov.), Fin.
138/D4 **Uva** (riv.), Col.
162/D4 **Uvalde,** Tx,US
85/K4 **Uval, Northern** (hills), Rus.
71/H2 **Uvaly,** Czh.
87/G2 **Uvarovo,** Rus.
130/A4 **Uvinza,** Tanz.
130/A3 **Uvira,** Zaire
149/F4 **Uvita** (pt.), CR
102/F1 **Uvs Nuur** (lake), Mong.
98/C4 **Uwajima,** Japan
125/L6 **Uwayl,** Sudan
53/M7 **Uxbridge,** Eng,UK
168/C1 **Uxbridge,** Ma,US
103/B3 **Uxin Qi,** China
147/H4 **Uxmal** (ruins), Mex.
85/P5 **Uy** (riv.), Kaz., Rus.
96/E2 **Uyanga,** Mong.
96/C2 **Üyench,** Mong.
104/B3 **Uyu** (riv.), Burma
136/E8 **Uyuni,** Bol.
88/G5 **Uzbekistan**
86/B2 **Uzhgorod,** Ukr.
86/F1 **Uzlovaya,** Rus.
92/D2 **Üzümlü,** Turk.
83/H5 **Uzunköprü,** Turk.
77/F3 **Uzwil,** Swi.

V

132/C3 **Vaal** (riv.), SAfr.
132/E2 **Vaaldam** (res.), SAfr.
69/F2 **Vaals,** Neth.
69/E2 **Vaalsberg** (hill), Neth.
131/C5 **Vaalwater,** SAfr.
61/G3 **Vaasa** (prov.), Fin.
61/G3 **Vaasa** (Vasa), Fin.
66/C4 **Vaassen,** Neth.
82/D2 **Vác,** Hun.
165/K10 **Vaca** (mtn.), Ca,US
165/K10 **Vaca** (mts.), Ca,US
141/B4 **Vacaria,** Braz.
165/L10 **Vacaville,** Ca,US
149/H2 **Vache** (isl.), Haiti
153/J2 **Vachon** (riv.), Qu,Can
78/B4 **Vado Ligure,** It.
77/F4 **Vadret, Piz** (peak), Swi.
62/F2 **Vadstena,** Swe.
77/F3 **Vaduz** (cap.), Lcht.
84/J3 **Vaga** (riv.), Rus.
82/B3 **Vaganski vrh** (peak), Cro.
85/R4 **Vagay** (riv.), Rus.
62/F3 **Vaggeryd,** Swe.
65/J4 **Vah** (riv.), Slvk.
121/M6 **Vahitahi** (isl.), FrPol.
54/B1 **Vaich, Loch** (lake), Sc,UK
70/B5 **Vaihingen an der Enz,** Ger.
95/K5 **Vaijāpur,** India
108/F4 **Vaikam,** India
159/F3 **Vail,** Co,US
68/C5 **Vailly-sur-Aisnes,** Fr.
167/J9 **Vailsburg,** NJ,US
76/B1 **Vair** (riv.), Fr.
53/T10 **Vaires-sur-Marne,** Fr.
120/G5 **Vaitupu** (isl.), Tuv.
86/F4 **Vakfıkebir,** Turk.
88/J3 **Vakh** (riv.), Rus.
95/K1 **Vākhān** (mts.), Afg.
95/J1 **Vakhsh** (riv.), Trkm.
76/D5 **Valais** (canton), Swi.
79/G2 **Valalta,** Cro.
62/G1 **Valbo,** Swe.
66/C5 **Valburg,** Neth.
79/E1 **Valdagno,** It.
84/G4 **Valdai** (hills), Rus.
79/E5 **Valdarno** (val.), It.
69/F6 **Val-de-Bide,** Fr.
74/C3 **Valdecañas** (res.), Sp.
79/E6 **Val d'Elsa, Colle di,** It.
53/T10 **Val-de-Marne** (dept.), Fr.
62/G2 **Valdemarsvik,** Swe.
75/M8 **Valdemorillo,** Sp.
74/D3 **Valdepeñas,** Sp.
74/C2 **Valderaduey** (riv.), Sp.
142/E4 **Valdés** (pen.), Arg.
138/B4 **Valdez,** Ecu.
142/B3 **Valdivia,** Chile
79/F1 **Valdobbiadene,** It.
68/A5 **Val-d'Oise** (dept.), Fr.
160/E1 **Val d'Or,** Qu,Can
163/H4 **Valdosta,** Ga,US
74/A1 **Valdoviño,** Sp.
156/D5 **Vale,** Or,US
156/D2 **Valemount,** BC,Can
141/K7 **Valença,** Braz.
140/B2 **Valença do Piauí,** Braz.
72/F4 **Valence,** Fr.
138/B5 **Valencia,** Ecu.
55/F11 **Valencia** (isl.), Ire.
112/D3 **Valencia,** Phil.
112/D4 **Valencia,** Phil.
75/E3 **Valencia,** Sp.
75/E3 **Valencia** (aut. comm.), Sp.
75/F3 **Valencia** (gulf), Sp.
138/E2 **Valencia,** Ven.
74/B3 **Valencia de Alcántara,** Sp.
68/C3 **Valenciennes,** Fr.
83/H3 **Vălenii de Munte,** Rom.
140/C3 **Valente,** Braz.
76/C3 **Valentigney,** Fr.
140/B2 **Valentim** (mts.), Braz.
159/G2 **Valentine,** Ne,US
162/B4 **Valentine,** Tx,US
53/T10 **Valenton,** Fr.
78/B2 **Valenza,** It.
112/E6 **Valenzuela,** Phil.
138/D2 **Valera,** Ven.
63/M3 **Valga,** Est.
141/G7 **Valhinos,** Braz.
72/D5 **Valier** (mtn.), Fr.
80/A2 **Valinco** (gulf), Fr.
82/D3 **Valjevo,** Yugo.
63/K1 **Valkeakoski,** Fin.
63/M1 **Valkeala,** Fin.
69/E2 **Valkenburg,** Neth.
66/C6 **Valkenswaard,** Neth.
147/H4 **Valladolid,** Mex.
74/C2 **Valladolid,** Sp.
75/E3 **Vall de Uxó,** Sp.
138/B5 **Valle,** Ecu.
165/L11 **Valle** (arroyo), Ca,US
75/N9 **Vallecas,** Sp.
78/A5 **Vallecrosia,** It.
78/A1 **Valle d'Aosta** (prov.), It.
78/A1 **Valle d'Aosta** (reg.), It.
147/E5 **Valle de Bravo,** Mex.
138/B3 **Valle de Cauca** (dept.), Col.
139/E2 **Valle de la Pascua,** Ven.
75/M8 **Valle de los Caídos,** Sp.
147/E4 **Valle de Santiago,** Mex.
138/C2 **Valledupar,** Col.
136/F7 **Vallegrande,** Bol.
147/F3 **Valle Hermoso,** Mex.
75/X16 **Vallehermoso,** Canl.,Sp.
66/C4 **Valleikanaal** (can.), Neth.
165/K10 **Vallejo,** Ca,US
135/B2 **Vallenar,** Chile
69/G3 **Vallendar,** Ger.
63/S6 **Vallentuna,** Swe.
63/S6 **Vallentunasjön** (lake), Swe.
80/D5 **Valletta** (cap.), Malta
157/J4 **Valley City,** ND,US
167/E1 **Valley Cottage,** NY,US
160/D2 **Valley East,** On,Can
168/C2 **Valley Falls,** RI,US
161/M7 **Valleyfield,** Qu,Can
166/C3 **Valley Forge Nat'l Hist. Park,** Pa,US
167/E2 **Valley Stream,** NY,US
150/F3 **Valley, The,** Angu.
156/D2 **Valleyview,** Ab,Can
79/F3 **Valli Bertuzzi** (lag.), It.
79/F3 **Valli di Comacchio** (lag.), It.
76/B4 **Vallière** (riv.), Fr.
142/E3 **Vallimanca** (riv.), Arg.
63/R7 **Vällingen** (lake), Swe.
75/F2 **Valls,** Sp.
77/G3 **Valluga** (peak), Aus.
156/G3 **Val Marie,** Sk,Can
75/M8 **Valmayor** (res.), Sp.
67/F6 **Valme** (riv.), Ger.
63/L3 **Valmiera,** Lat.
53/S9 **Valmondois,** Fr.
81/F2 **Valona** (bay), Alb.
108/F3 **Vālpārai,** India
142/C2 **Valparaíso,** Chile
142/C2 **Valparaíso** (reg.), Chile
146/E4 **Valparaíso,** Mex.
163/G4 **Valparaiso,** Fl,US
160/C3 **Valparaiso,** In,US
76/D6 **Valpelline** (riv.), It.
82/D3 **Valpovo,** Cro.
72/F4 **Valréas,** Fr.
132/D2 **Vals** (riv.), SAfr.
106/B3 **Valsād,** India
147/L8 **Valsaquillo** (res.), Mex.
132/B4 **Valsbaai** (bay), SAfr.
76/B5 **Valserine** (riv.), Fr.
77/F4 **Valserrhein** (riv.), Swi.
77/G4 **Valsura** (riv.), It.
77/F5 **Valtellina** (vall.), It.
86/F2 **Valuyki,** Rus.
108/H4 **Valvedditturai,** SrL.
74/B4 **Valverde del Camino,** Sp.
63/K1 **Vammala,** Fin.
93/E2 **Van,** Turk.
93/E2 **Van** (lake), Turk.
93/E2 **Van** (prov.), Turk.
63/K1 **Vanajavesi** (lake), Fin.
121/L7 **Vanavaro** (isl.), FrPol.
162/E3 **Van Buren,** Ar,US
161/H2 **Van Buren,** Me,US
159/K3 **Van Buren,** Mo,US
159/H3 **Vance A.F.B.,** Ok,US
167/K8 **Van Cortlandt Park, New York City,** NY,US
116/C5 **Vancouver** (cape), Austl.
156/C3 **Vancouver,** BC,Can
156/B3 **Vancouver** (isl.), BC,Can
156/C4 **Vancouver,** Wa,US
151/L3 **Vancouver** (mtn.), Yk,Can, Ak,US
113/L **Vanda,** Ant.
160/B4 **Vandalia,** Il,US
159/K3 **Vandalia,** Mo,US
158/B4 **Vandenberg A.F.B.,** Ca,US
132/D2 **Vanderbijl Park,** SAfr.
167/E2 **Vanderbilt Museum,** NY,US
156/B2 **Vanderhoof,** BC,Can
114/F3 **Vanderlin** (isl.), Austl.
114/E2 **Van Diemen** (cape), Austl.
114/E2 **Van Diemen** (gulf), Austl.
69/F6 **Vandoeuvre-lès-Nancy,** Fr.
62/E2 **Vänern** (lake), Swe.
62/E2 **Vänersborg,** Swe.
130/C4 **Vanga,** Kenya
133/H8 **Vangaindrano,** Madg.
66/C2 **Van Harinxmakanaal** (can.), Neth.
109/D1 **Van Hoa,** Viet.
162/B4 **Van Horn,** Tx,US
153/R7 **Vanier** (isl.), NW,Can
120/F6 **Vanikoro** (isl.), Sol.
76/D4 **Vanil Noir** (peak), Swi.
111/K4 **Vanimo,** PNG
97/N2 **Vanino,** Rus.
61/F3 **Vännäs,** Swe.
72/E2 **Vanne** (riv.), Fr.
72/B3 **Vannes,** Fr.
109/E3 **Van Ninh,** Viet.
164/B2 **Van Norman** (lakes), Ca,US
164/F7 **Van Nuys,** Ca,US
73/G4 **Vanoise Nat'l Park,** Fr.
132/E3 **Vanreenenpas** (pass), SAfr.
111/J4 **Van Rees** (mts.), Indo.
62/F1 **Vansbro,** Swe.
153/H2 **Vansittart** (isl.), NW,Can
63/L1 **Vantaa,** Fin.
120/G6 **Vanua Levu** (isl.), Fiji
120/F6 **Vanuatu**
53/S10 **Vanves,** Fr.
160/C3 **Van Wert,** Oh,US
109/D1 **Van Yen,** Viet.
73/G5 **Var** (riv.), Fr.
78/C4 **Vara** (riv.), It.
62/E2 **Vara,** Swe.
149/F1 **Varadero,** Cuba
93/G3 **Varāmīn,** Iran
106/D2 **Vārānasi,** India
61/J1 **Varangerfjorden** (fjord), Nor.
61/J1 **Varangerhalvøya** (pen.), Nor.
80/D2 **Varano** (lake), It.
82/C2 **Varaždin,** Cro.
78/B4 **Varazze,** It.
62/E3 **Varberg,** Swe.
81/G2 **Vardar** (riv.), Gre.
82/E5 **Vardar** (riv.), Macd.
62/C4 **Varde,** Den.
67/F2 **Varel,** Ger.
161/P6 **Varennes,** Qu,Can
68/A4 **Varennes** (riv.), Fr.
53/T10 **Varennes-Jarcy,** Fr.
72/E3 **Varennes-Vauzelles,** Fr.
82/D3 **Vareš,** Bosn.
78/B1 **Varese,** It.
78/B1 **Varese** (prov.), It.
140/C3 **Vargem** (riv.), Braz.
141/G6 **Vargem do Sul,** Braz.
140/B1 **Vargem Grande,** Braz.
141/H6 **Varginha,** Braz.
62/A2 **Varhaug,** Nor.
81/L7 **Vari,** Gre.
61/H3 **Varkaus,** Fin.
108/F4 **Varkkallai,** India
63/T9 **Værløse,** Den.
63/S7 **Värmdo,** Swe.
63/S7 **Värmdolandet** (isl.), Swe.
62/E2 **Värmeln** (lake), Swe.
62/E2 **Värmland** (co.), Swe.
83/H4 **Varna,** Bul.
83/H4 **Varna** (reg.), Bul.
62/F3 **Värnamo,** Swe.
82/D2 **Várpalota,** Hun.
92/E2 **Varto,** Turk.
60/D3 **Vartry** (res.), Ire.
60/D3 **Vartry** (riv.), Ire.
140/C2 **Várzea Alegre,** Braz.
141/C1 **Várzea da Palma,** Braz.
137/G7 **Várzea Grande,** Braz.
140/A4 **Varzelândia,** Braz.
84/H2 **Varzuga** (riv.), Rus.
82/C2 **Vas** (co.), Hun.
140/C3 **Vasa Barris** (riv.), Braz.
65/M4 **Vásárosnamény,** Hun.
61/G3 **Vasa** (Vaasa), Fin.
85/K2 **Vashka** (riv.), Rus.
165/C3 **Vashon** (isl.), Wa,US
86/D2 **Vasil'kov,** Ukr.
83/H2 **Vaslui,** Rom.
83/H2 **Vaslui** (co.), Rom.
160/D3 **Vassar,** Mi,US
62/B2 **Vassdalsegga** (peak), Nor.
81/G4 **Vassés** (Bassae) (ruins), Gre.
141/K7 **Vassouras,** Braz.
62/G2 **Västerås,** Swe.
61/F2 **Västerbotten** (co.), Swe.
62/E1 **Västerdalälven** (riv.), Swe.
62/H2 **Västerhaninge,** Swe.
61/F3 **Västernorrland** (co.), Swe.
62/G3 **Västervik,** Swe.
62/G1 **Västmanland** (co.), Swe.
84/C3 **Vastmanland** (co.), Swe.
80/D1 **Vasto,** It.
62/E2 **Västra Silen** (lake), Swe.
71/E6 **Vaterstetten,** Ger.
80/C2 **Vatican City**
61/P7 **Vatnajökull** (glac.), Ice.
83/G2 **Vatra Dornei,** Rom.
62/F2 **Vättern** (lake), Swe.
121/Y18 **Vatukoula,** Fiji
76/C4 **Vaud** (canton), Swi.

227

Vaud – Wadd

161/M7 Vaudreuil, Qu,Can
161/M7 Vaudreuil (co.), Qu,Can
161/Q8 Vaughan, On,Can
159/F4 Vaughn, NM,US
76/A6 Vaulx-en-Velin, Fr.
138/D4 Vaupés (comm.), Col.
138/D4 Vaupés (riv.), Col.
72/F5 Vauvert, Fr.
68/D4 Vaux (riv.), Fr.
156/E3 Vauxhall, Ab,Can
53/R9 Vaux-sur-Seine, Fr.
68/B3 Vaux-Vraucourt, Fr.
121/H6 Vava'u Group (isls.), Tonga
108/H4 Vavuniva (dist.), SrL.
108/H4 Vavuniya, SrL.
63/S7 Vaxholm, Swe.
62/F3 Växjö, Swe.
53/J2 Vaygach (isl.), Rus.
141/C1 Vazante, Braz.
141/G8 Vázea Paulista, Braz.
84/G5 Vazuza (res.), Rus.
66/D4 Vecht (riv.), Neth.
67/F3 Vechta, Ger.
67/E4 Vechte (riv.), Ger.
82/D2 Vecsés, Hun.
78/B1 Vedano Olona, It.
108/G3 Vedāranniyam, India
83/G3 Vedea (riv.), Rom.
142/E2 Vedia, Arg.
66/D2 Veendam, Neth.
66/C4 Veenendaal, Neth.
66/A5 Veersedam (dam), Neth.
66/A5 Veerse Meer (res.), Neth.
61/D2 Vega (isl.), Nor.
151/B6 Vega (pt.), Ak,US
61/D2 Vegafjorden (fjord), Nor.
63/U8 Vegeån (riv.), Swe.
66/C5 Veghel, Neth.
81/G2 Vegoritis (lake), Gre.
156/E2 Vegreville, Ab,Can
63/M1 Vehkalahti, Fin.
142/E2 Veinticinco de Mayo, Arg.
70/C3 Veitshöchheim, Ger.
62/C4 Vejen, Den.
74/C4 Vejer de la Frontera, Sp.
62/C4 Vejle, Den.
62/C4 Vejle (co.), Den.
76/D6 Vélan, Monte (peak), Swi., It.
75/S12 Velas, Azor,Port.
138/B5 Velasco Ibarra, Ecu.
66/E6 Velbert, Ger.
73/L3 Velden am Wörthersee, Aus.
66/C6 Veldhoven, Neth.
66/D5 Velen, Ger.
82/B2 Velenje, Slov.
138/C3 Vélez, Col.
74/C4 Vélez-Málaga, Sp.
74/D4 Vélez-Rubio, Sp.
141/C1 Velhas (Araguari) (riv.), Braz.
82/C3 Velika Gorica, Cro.
82/E3 Velika Plana, Yugo.
63/N3 Velikaya (riv.), Rus.
63/P3 Velikiye Luki, Rus.
53/H2 Velikiy Ustyug, Rus.
83/G4 Veliko Tŭrnovo, Bul.
83/G4 Velingrad, Bul.
53/S10 Vélizy-Villacoublay, Fr.
65/J4 Velké Meziříčí, Czh.
65/K4 Veľký Krtíš, Slvk.
71/F3 Velký Zvon (peak), Czh.
108/G3 Vellār (riv.), India
80/C2 Velletri, It.
67/G6 Vellmar, Ger.
75/N8 Vellón (res.), Sp.
106/C5 Vellore, India
84/J3 Vel'sk, Rus.
66/C4 Veluwe (reg.), Neth.
66/C4 Veluwemeer (lake), Neth.
66/C4 Veluwezoom Nat'l Park, Neth.
157/H3 Velva, ND,US
108/F3 Vembādi Shola (peak), India
108/F4 Vembanād (lake), India
63/T9 Ven (isl.), Swe.
54/B4 Venachar, Loch (lake), Sc,UK
147/L6 Venados, Mex.
142/E2 Venado Tuerto, Arg.
80/D2 Venafro, It.
139/F3 Venamo (peak), Ven.
141/A4 Venâncio Aires, Braz.
168/H5 Venango (co.), Pa,US
78/A2 Venaria, It.
73/G5 Vence, Fr.
141/B2 Venceslau Brás, Braz.
74/A3 Vendas Novas, Port.
72/D3 Vendôme, Fr.
75/F2 Vendrell, Sp.
79/F2 Veneta (lag.), It.
79/E1 Veneto (reg.), It.
79/F2 Venezia (gulf), It.
79/F1 Venezia (prov.), It.
79/F2 Venezia, Po di (riv.), It.
79/F2 Venezia (Venice), It.
139/E3 Venezuela
138/D2 Venezuela (gulf), Ven.
106/B4 Vengurla, India
151/G4 Veniaminof (vol.), Ak,US
163/H5 Venice, Fl,US
79/F2 Venice (Venezia), It.
72/F4 Vénissieux, Fr.
62/E1 Venjansjön (lake), Swe.
106/C5 Venkatagiri, India
66/D6 Venlo, Neth.
62/B2 Vennesla, Nor.
62/C3 Veno (bay), Den.
76/C4 Venoge (riv.), Swi.
80/D2 Venosa, It.
77/G4 Venosta (vall.), It.
66/C5 Venray, Neth.
63/J3 Venta (riv.), Lat., Lith.
74/C2 Venta de Baños, Sp.
121/L6 Vent, Iles du (isls.), FrPol.
121/K6 Vent, Iles sous le (isls.), FrPol.
78/A5 Ventimiglia, It.
59/E5 Ventnor, Eng,UK
166/D5 Ventnor City, NJ,US
63/J3 Ventspils, Lat.
139/E3 Ventuari (riv.), Ven.
164/A2 Ventura (co.), Ca,US
164/A2 Ventura (riv.), Ca,US
164/A2 Ventura (San Buenaventura), Ca,US
80/B1 Venturina, It.
140/C3 Venturosa, Braz.
121/X15 Vénus (pt.), FrPol.
148/C2 Venustiano Carranza, Mex.
135/D2 Vera, Arg.
147/F5 Veracruz, Mex.
147/F5 Veracruz (state), Mex.
141/B4 Veranópolis, Braz.
106/B3 Verāval, India
78/B1 Verbania, It.
78/B2 Vercelli, It.
78/B2 Vercelli (prov.), It.
76/C3 Vercel-Villedieu-le-Camp, Fr.
161/P6 Verchères (co.), Qu,Can
61/D3 Verdal, Nor.
141/B1 Verdão (riv.), Braz.
142/E3 Verde (bay), Arg.
141/H6 Verde (riv.), Braz.
146/D3 Verde (riv.), Mex.
147/E4 Verde (riv.), Mex.
135/E1 Verde (riv.), Par.
124/B5 Verde (cape), Sen.
158/E4 Verde (riv.), Az,US
78/A5 Verde, Capo (cape), It.
74/B1 Verde, Costa (coast), Sp.
140/B4 Verde Grande (riv.), Braz.
112/C2 Verde Island (chan.), Phil.
67/G3 Verden, Ger.
159/J3 Verdigris (riv.), Ks, Ok,US
141/B1 Verdinho (riv.), Braz.
72/F5 Verdon (riv.), Fr.
164/F7 Verdugo (mts.), Ca,US
161/N7 Verdun, Qu,Can
69/E5 Verdun-sur-Meuse, Fr.
132/D2 Vereeniging, SAfr.
79/E1 Verena, Monte (peak), It.
85/M4 Vereshchagino, Rus.
65/M4 Veretskiy Pereval (pass), Ukr.
128/B4 Verga (cape), Gui.
74/D1 Vergara, Sp.
161/F2 Vergennes, Vt,US
81/H2 Vergina (ruins), Gre.
74/B2 Verin, Sp.
70/C6 Veringenstadt, Ger.
141/B1 Veríssimo, Braz.
84/F1 Verkhnetulomskiy (res.), Rus.
89/N3 Verkhoyansk (range), Rus.
67/F5 Verl, Ger.
68/C4 Vermand, Fr.
140/A3 Vermelho (riv.), Braz.
78/A4 Vermenagna (riv.), It.
156/F2 Vermilion, Ab,Can
156/F2 Vermilion (riv.), Ab,Can
159/K2 Vermilion (riv.), Il,US
168/E5 Vermilion, Oh,US
168/E5 Vermilion (riv.), Oh,US
157/K4 Vermillion (range), Mn,US
157/J5 Vermillion, SD,US
159/H2 Vermillion (riv.), SD,US
161/F2 Vermont (state), US
158/E2 Vernal, Ut,US
72/D2 Verneuil-sur-Avre, Fr.
53/R10 Verneuil-sur-Seine, Fr.
132/C3 Verneukpan (salt pan), SAfr.
76/C5 Vernier, Swi.
156/D3 Vernon, BC,Can
68/A5 Vernon, Fr.
168/B2 Vernon, Ct,US
162/D3 Vernon, Tx,US
165/Q15 Vernon Hills, Il,US
166/D1 Vernon Valley/Great Gorge & Action Park, NJ,US
53/R10 Vernouillet, Fr.
69/F5 Verny, Fr.
163/H5 Vero Beach, Fl,US
81/H2 Véroia, Gre.
79/D2 Verona, It.
79/D1 Verona (prov.), It.
167/J8 Verona, NJ,US
76/C6 Verres, Pointe des (peak), Fr.
53/S10 Verrières-le-Buisson, Fr.
78/B3 Versa (riv.), It.
53/S10 Versailles, Fr.
160/C4 Versailles, Ky,US
53/S10 Versailles, Chateau de, Fr.
86/E2 Verskla (riv.), Rus., Ukr.
67/F4 Versmold, Ger.
76/C5 Versoix, Swi.
74/E1 Vert (riv.), Fr.
73/J3 Vertana (peak), It.
77/G4 Vertana, Cima (peak), It.
76/C6 Verte, Aiguille (peak), Fr.
53/T11 Vert-le-Grand, Fr.
53/T11 Vert-le-Petit, Fr.
72/C3 Vertou, Fr.
53/T11 Vert-Saint-Denis, Fr.
69/E2 Verviers, Belg.
59/E5 Verwood, Eng,UK
58/B6 Veryan (bay), Eng,UK
77/E5 Verzasca (riv.), Swi.
77/E5 Verzasca (Gerra), It.
78/A2 Verzel, Punta (peak), It.
69/F2 Vesdre (riv.), Belg.
71/H4 Veselí nad Lužnicí, Czh.
87/G3 Veselyy (res.), Rus.
63/L1 Vesijärvi (lake), Fin.
68/D5 Vesle (riv.), Fr.
76/C2 Vesoul, Fr.
62/B2 Vest-Agder (co.), Nor.
62/D2 Vestby, Nor.
61/E1 Vesterålen (isls.), Nor.
52/E2 Vestfjorden (bay), Nor.
61/E2 Vestfjorden (fjord), Nor.
62/C2 Vestfold (co.), Nor.
62/D4 Vest-Sjælland (co.), Den.
61/E1 Vestvågøya (isl.), Nor.
82/C2 Veszprém, Hun.
82/C2 Veszprém (co.), Hun.
82/E2 Vészto, Hun.
132/D3 Vet (riv.), SAfr.
62/F3 Vetlanda, Swe.
85/K4 Vetluga (riv.), Rus.
80/C1 Vetralla, It.
72/D3 Veude (riv.), Fr.
68/B1 Veurne, Belg.
76/C5 Vevey, Swi.
69/F2 Veybach (riv.), Ger.
76/B5 Veyle (riv.), Fr.
72/D4 Vézère (riv.), Fr.
92/C1 Vezirköprü, Turk.
136/E7 Viacha, Bol.
78/D3 Viadana, It.
140/A1 Viana, Braz.
74/B1 Viana del Bollo, Sp.
74/A2 Viana do Castelo, Port.
74/A2 Viana do Castelo (dist.), Port.
66/C5 Vianen, Neth.
109/C2 Viangchan (Vientiane) (cap.), Laos
74/C4 Viar (riv.), Sp.
78/D5 Viareggio, It.
53/T9 Viarmes, Fr.
72/E4 Viaur (riv.), Fr.
62/C3 Viborg, Den.
62/C3 Viborg (co.), Den.
80/E3 Vibo Valentia, It.
75/G2 Vic, Sp.
74/D3 Vícar, Sp.
144/A2 Vice, Peru
164/F8 Vicente (pt.), Ca,US
146/E4 Vicente Guerrero, Mex.
143/S12 Vicente López, Arg.
79/E1 Vicenza, It.
79/E1 Vicenza (prov.), It.
77/H6 Vicenza (state), It.
138/D3 Vichada (comm.), Col.
138/D3 Vichada (riv.), Col.
84/J4 Vichuga, Rus.
72/E3 Vichy, Fr.
163/F3 Vicksburg, Ms,US
163/F3 Vicksburg Nat'l Mil. Park, Ms,US
80/C1 Vico (lake), It.
140/C3 Viçosa, Braz.
141/D2 Viçosa, Braz.
140/B1 Viçosa do Ceará, Braz.
81/G3 Vicou Gorge Nat'l Park, Gre.
68/C5 Vic-sur-Aisne, Fr.
69/F6 Vic-sur-Seille, Fr.
130/B3 Victoria (lake), Afr.
142/E2 Victoria, Arg.
114/E3 Victoria (riv.), Austl.
119/C3 Victoria (state), Austl.
148/D2 Victoria (peak), Belz.
104/B4 Victoria (peak), Burma
156/C3 Victoria (cap.), BC,Can
152/E1 Victoria (isl.), NW,Can
152/F2 Victoria (str.), NW,Can
161/Q8 Victoria, On,Can
142/B3 Victoria, Chile
105/G4 Victoria (cap.), HK
112/C2 Victoria, Phil.
112/B3 Victoria (peak), Phil.
83/G3 Victoria, Rom.
162/D4 Victoria, Tx,US
131/B3 Victoria (falls), Zam.
131/B3 Victoria Falls, Zim.
113/L Victoria Land (reg.), Ant.
130/B2 Victoria Nile (riv.), Ugan.
112/G3 Victorias, Phil.
161/G2 Victoriaville, Qu,Can
146/E4 Víctor Rosales, Mex.
164/C1 Victorville, Ca,US
133/F3 Vidal (cape), SAfr.
163/H3 Vidalia, Ga,US
163/F4 Vidalia, La,US
141/B3 Videira, Braz.
83/G3 Videle, Rom.
71/G4 Vidhošt (peak), Czh.
106/C3 Vidisha, India
162/E4 Vidor, Tx,US
62/F3 Vidöstern (lake), Swe.
72/E5 Vidourle (riv.), Fr.
72/C3 Vie (riv.), Fr.
71/F4 Viechtach, Ger.
142/E4 Viedma, Arg.
143/J7 Viedma (lake), Arg.
71/H5 Viehberg (peak), Aus.
74/C1 Vieja (mtn.), Sp.
162/B4 Vieja (mts.), Tx,US
144/B2 Viejo (peak), Peru
69/E3 Vielsalm, Belg.
67/H5 Vienenburg, Ger.
166/A6 Vienna, Va,US
160/D4 Vienna, WV,US
65/J4 Vienna (Wien) (cap.), Aus.
72/F4 Vienne, Fr.
72/D3 Vienne (riv.), Fr.
109/C2 Vientiane (Viangchan) (cap.), Laos
150/E3 Vieques (isl.), PR
69/D6 Viere (riv.), Fr.
66/D5 Vierlingsbeek, Neth.
70/B3 Viernheim, Ger.
69/E4 Vierre (riv.), Fr.
66/D6 Viersen, Ger.
77/E3 Vierwaldstättersee (Lucerne) (lake), Swi.
72/E3 Vierzon, Fr.
80/E2 Vieste, It.
109/D2 Vietnam
109/D1 Viet Tri, Viet.
68/C3 Vieux-Condé, Fr.
150/F4 Vieux Fort, StL.
54/B5 Viewpark, Sc,UK
76/C5 Vieze (riv.), Swi.
112/D2 Viga, Phil.
112/C1 Vigan, Phil.
78/B2 Vigevano, It.
137/J4 Vigia, Braz.
78/B1 Vigliano Biellese, It.
80/C2 Viglio (peak), It.
72/C5 Vignemale (mtn.), Fr.
53/T10 Vigneux-sur-Seine, Fr.
79/E4 Vignola, It.
74/A1 Vigo, Sp.
79/E2 Vigonza, It.
69/F5 Vigy, Fr.
95/K2 Vihāri, Pak.
63/L1 Vihti, Fin.
61/H3 Viitasaari, Fin.
106/D4 Vijayawada, India
81/F2 Vijosë (riv.), Alb.
62/C2 Vikersund, Nor.
83/F5 Vikhren (peak), Bul.
156/F2 Viking, Ab,Can
108/F4 Vikramasingapuram, India
120/F6 Vila (cap.), Van.
75/G2 Viladecans, Sp.
75/V14 Vila de Porto Santo, Madr.,Port.
131/D3 Vila de Sena, Moz.
74/A2 Vila do Conde, Port.
75/T13 Vila do Porto, Azor,Port.
75/K7 Vilafranca del Penedès, Sp.
74/A3 Vila Franca de Xira, Port.
75/T13 Vila Franca do Campo, Azor.,Port.
72/B3 Vilaine (riv.), Fr.
133/H7 Vilanandro (cape), Madg.
131/D4 Vilanculos, Moz.
74/A2 Vila Nova de Gaia, Port.
75/F2 Vilanova i la Geltrù, Sp.
75/K7 Vilanova i la Geltru, Sp.
74/B2 Vila Real, Port.
74/B2 Vila Real (dist.), Port.
74/B4 Vila Real de Santo António, Port.
141/D2 Vila Velha Argolas, Braz.
83/F3 Vîlcea (co.), Rom.
61/F2 Vilhelmina, Swe.
136/F6 Vilhena, Braz.
63/M4 Viliya (riv.), Bela.
63/L2 Viljandi, Est.
83/K2 Vil'kitsogo (str.), Rus.
142/Q9 Villa Alemana, Chile
150/D3 Villa Altagracia, DRep.
135/D2 Villa Ángela, Arg.
112/D3 Villaba, Phil.
74/E1 Villaba, Sp.
74/B1 Villablino, Sp.
138/D2 Villa Bruzual, Ven.
142/E2 Villa Cañas, Arg.
74/D3 Villacañas, Sp.
78/D1 Villa Carcina, It.
135/D3 Villa Carlos Paz, Arg.
74/D3 Villacarrillo, Sp.
73/K3 Villach, Aus.
142/E2 Villa Constitución, Arg.
146/C3 Villa Constitución, Mex.
74/A1 Villa de Cruces, Sp.
139/E2 Villa de Cura, Ven.
74/C4 Villa del Río, Sp.
135/C3 Villa Dolores, Arg.
77/E5 Villadossola, It.
148/C2 Villa Flores, Mex.
74/B3 Villafranca de los Barros, Sp.
79/D2 Villafranca di Verona, It.
74/A1 Villagarcía, Sp.
162/E4 Village Mills, Tx,US
143/F3 Villa Gesell, Arg.
142/F1 Villaguay, Arg.
147/G5 Villahermosa, Mex.
149/J2 Villa Jaragua, DRep.
75/E3 Villajoyosa, Sp.
74/B1 Villalba, Sp.
74/B2 Villalcampo (res.), Sp.
142/E2 Villa María, Arg.
74/C4 Villamartín, Sp.
136/F8 Villa Montes, Bol.
77/H4 Villandro, Monte (peak), It.
138/C2 Villanueva, Col.
148/D3 Villa Nueva, Guat.
148/E3 Villanueva, Hon.
148/E3 Villanueva, Nic.
74/A1 Villanueva de Arosa, Sp.
74/C3 Villanueva de Córdoba, Sp.
74/D3 Villanueva del Arzobispo, Sp.
74/C3 Villanueva de la Serena, Sp.
74/D3 Villanueva de los Infantes, Sp.
147/Q10 Villa Obregon, Mex.
79/G1 Villa Opicina, It.
164/C3 Villa Park, Ca,US
165/Q16 Villa Park, Il,US
142/D3 Villa Regina, Arg.
138/C3 Villa Rosario, Col.
75/E3 Villarreal de los Infantes, Sp.
142/B3 Villarrica, Chile
142/B3 Villarrica (lake), Chile
142/C3 Villarrica (vol.), Chile
135/E2 Villarrica, Par.
142/C3 Villarrica Nat'l Park, Chile
74/D3 Villarrobledo, Sp.
74/D3 Villarrubia de los Ojos, Sp.
166/D5 Villas, NJ,US
149/E3 Villa Sandino, Nic.
142/F2 Villa San José, Arg.
78/C1 Villasanta, It.
136/F7 Villa Serrano, Bol.
135/C2 Villa Unión, Arg.
138/C3 Villavicencio, Col.
74/C1 Villaviciosa, Sp.
75/N9 Villaviciosa de Odon, Sp.
136/E8 Villazón, Bol.
53/T10 Villecresnes, Fr.
53/S10 Ville-d'Avray, Fr.
72/E4 Villefranche-de-Rouergue, Fr.
72/E4 Villefranche-sur-Saône, Fr.
53/T10 Villejuif, Fr.
53/T10 Villemomble, Fr.
75/E3 Villena, Sp.
68/C2 Villeneuve-d'Ascq, Fr.
53/S10 Villeneuve-la-Garenne, Fr.
53/U10 Villeneuve-le-Comte, Fr.
53/T10 Villeneuve-le-Roi, Fr.
72/F5 Villeneuve-lès-Avignon, Fr.
68/B6 Villeneuve-Saint-Georges, Fr.
72/D4 Villeneuve-sur-Lot, Fr.
72/D5 Villeneuve-Tolosane, Fr.
53/R10 Villennes-sur-Seine, Fr.
53/T10 Villeparisis, Fr.
53/T10 Villepinte, Fr.
162/E4 Ville Platte, La,US
53/S10 Villepreux, Fr.
68/B4 Villers-Bocage, Fr.
68/C5 Villers-Cotterêts, Fr.
69/F6 Villers-lès-Nancy, Fr.
68/C3 Villers-Outreaux, Fr.
69/E5 Villerupt, Fr.
76/A6 Villeurbanne, Fr.
53/T10 Villevaudé, Fr.
53/T9 Villiers-le-Bel, Fr.
53/T10 Villiers-sur-Marne, Fr.
70/B6 Villingen-Schwenningen, Ger.
70/B2 Villmar, Ger.
108/G3 Villupuram, India
63/L4 Vilnius (cap.), Lith.
61/H3 Vilppula, Fin.
71/E4 Vils (riv.), Ger.
71/F6 Vilsbiburg, Ger.
71/G5 Vilshofen, Ger.
68/D2 Vilvoorde, Belg.
89/M3 Vilyuy (range), Rus.
89/N3 Vilyuy (riv.), Rus.
78/C1 Vimercate, It.
74/B1 Vimianzo, Sp.
62/F3 Vimmerby, Swe.
78/C2 Vimodrone, It.
71/G4 Vimperk, Czh.
68/B3 Vimy, Fr.
124/H6 Vina (riv.), Camr.
142/C2 Viña del Mar, Chile
73/G5 Vinaigre (mtn.), Fr.
75/F2 Vinaroz, Sp.
113/H Vincennes (bay), Ant.
53/T10 Vincennes, Fr.
53/U10 Vincennes (res.), Fr.
160/C4 Vincennes, In,US
164/B1 Vincent, Ca,US
138/B5 Vinces, Ecu.
61/F2 Vindeln, Swe.
161/R9 Vineland, On,Can
166/C5 Vineland, NJ,US
161/R9 Vineland Station, On,Can
168/D3 Vineyard (sound), Ma,US
109/D2 Vinh, Viet.
141/G8 Vinhedo, Braz.
109/D4 Vinh Long, Viet.
109/D2 Vinh Moc, Tunnels of, Viet.
109/D4 Vinh Quoi, Viet.
109/E3 Vinh Thanh, Viet.
109/D1 Vinh Yen, Viet.
82/F5 Vinica, Macd.
159/J3 Vinita, Ok,US
82/F3 Vînju Mare, Rom.
82/D3 Vinkovci, Cro.
86/D2 Vinnitsa, Ukr.
86/D2 Vinnitsa Obl., Ukr.
86/B2 Vinogradov, Ukr.
78/A3 Vinovo, It.
50/E9 Vinson (peak), Ant.
112/C1 Vintar, Phil.
53/R9 Viosne (riv.), Fr.
79/G1 Vipava, Slov.
112/D2 Virac, Phil.
92/D2 Viranşehir, Turk.
106/B4 Virār, India
157/H3 Virden, Mb,Can
72/C2 Vire, Fr.
126/B4 Virei, Ang.
62/F2 Viren (lake), Swe.
140/B5 Virgem da Lapa, Braz.
135/C7 Vírgenes (cape), Arg.
161/R9 Virgil, On,Can
150/E3 Virgin (isls.), UK, US
158/D3 Virgin (riv.), US
150/E3 Virgin Gorda (isl.), BVI
160/E5 Virginia (state), US
157/K4 Virginia, Mn,US
160/F4 Virginia Beach, Va,US
158/C3 Virginia City, Nv,US
53/M7 Virginia Water, Eng,UK
150/E3 Virgin Islands Nat'l Park, USVI
109/D3 Virochey, Camb.
53/S10 Viroflay, Fr.
68/D3 Viroin (riv.), Belg.
160/B3 Viroqua, Wi,US
82/C3 Virovitica, Cro.
69/E4 Virton, Belg.
144/B3 Virú, Peru
108/F4 Virudunagar, India
130/A3 Virunga, Zaire
130/A3 Virunga Nat'l Park, Zaire
53/T10 Viry-Châtillon, Fr.
80/D1 Vis (isl.), Cro.
106/D4 Visākhapatnam, India
158/C3 Visalia, Ca,US
112/C3 Visayan (sea), Phil.
67/F3 Visbek, Ger.
62/H3 Visby, Swe.
141/D2 Visconde do Rio Branco, Braz.
153/R7 Viscount Melville (sound), NW,Can
69/E2 Visé, Belg.
82/D4 Višegrad, Bosn.
74/B2 Viseu, Port.
74/B2 Viseu (dist.), Port.
83/G2 Vişeu de Sus, Rom.
85/L3 Vishera (riv.), Rus.
85/N3 Vishera (riv.), Rus.
132/B4 Vishoek, SAfr.
106/B3 Visnagar, India
82/D3 Višnjevac, Cro.
82/D4 Visoko, Bosn.
76/D5 Visp, Swi.
67/G3 Visselhövede, Ger.
164/C4 Vista, Ca,US
81/J2 Vistonís (lake), Gre.
86/B2 Vistula (riv.), Pol.
65/K2 Vistula (Wisła) (riv.), Pol.
83/G4 Vit (riv.), Bul.
157/J3 Vita, Mb,Can
73/J5 Vitalba (peak), It.
78/D6 Vitalba, Monte (peak), It.
63/P4 Vitebsk, Bela.
63/N4 Vitebsk Obl., Bela.
80/C1 Viterbo, It.
109/D4 Vi Thanh, Viet.
120/G6 Viti Levu (isl.), Fiji
96/G1 Vitim (plat.), Rus.
96/G1 Vitim (riv.), Rus.
71/H5 Vítkuv Kamen (peak), Czh.
141/D2 Vitória, Braz.
74/D1 Vitoria, Sp.
140/B4 Vitória da Conquista, Braz.
140/D3 Vitória de Santo Antão, Braz.
140/A1 Vitória do Mearim, Braz.
140/A2 Vitorino Freire, Braz.
83/F4 Vitosha Nat'l Park, Bul.
72/C2 Vitré, Fr.
72/F5 Vitrolles, Fr.
68/D6 Vitry-le-François, Fr.
53/T10 Vitry-sur-Seine, Fr.
130/A3 Vitshumbi, Zaire
76/B1 Vittel, Fr.
80/D4 Vittoria, It.
73/K4 Vittorio Veneto, It.
72/F4 Vivarais (mts.), Fr.
74/B1 Vivero, Sp.
78/A2 Viverone (lake), It.
146/B3 Vizcaíno, Sierra de (mts.), Mex.
83/H5 Vize, Turk.
85/K2 Vizhas (riv.), Rus.
106/D4 Vizianagaram, India
79/G2 Vižinada, Cro.
66/B5 Vlaardingen, Neth.
82/F2 Vlădeasa (peak), Rom.
53/H4 Vladikavkaz, Rus.
53/H3 Vladimir, Rus.
84/J5 Vladimir Obl., Rus.
86/C2 Vladimir-Volynskiy, Ukr.
97/L3 Vladivostok, Rus.
67/E2 Vlagtwedde, Neth.
83/G2 Vlăhiţa, Rom.
82/E4 Vlajna (peak), Yugo.
82/D3 Vlasenica, Bosn.
65/H4 Vlašim, Czh.
82/F4 Vlasotince, Yugo.
71/G3 Vlastec (hill), Czh.
66/B2 Vlieland (isl.), Neth.
66/C2 Vliestroom (chan.), Neth.
66/C5 Vlijmen, Neth.
66/A6 Vlissingen, Neth.
81/F2 Vlorë, Alb.
67/F4 Vlotho, Ger.
71/H2 Vltava (riv.), Czh.
71/G6 Vöcklabruck, Aus.
84/H3 Vodlozero (lake), Rus.
71/H4 Vodňany, Czh.
79/G3 Vodnjan, Cro.
66/D5 Voerde, Ger.
70/C1 Vogelsberg (mts.), Ger.
78/C3 Voghera, It.
77/E5 Vogorno, Pizzo di (peak), Swi.
82/D4 Vogošća, Bosn.
71/E2 Vogtland (reg.), Ger.
121/U12 Voh, NCal.
71/F3 Vohenstrauss, Ger.
133/H9 Vohimena (cape), Madg.
133/G7 Vohipeno, Madg.
77/G1 Vöhringen, Ger.
130/C3 Voi, Kenya
165/C3 Voight (cr.), Wa,US
54/B4 Voil, Loch (lake), Sc,UK
72/F4 Voiron, Fr.
72/D2 Voise (riv.), Fr.
153/K3 Voisey (bay), Nf,Can
68/B5 Voisne (riv.), Fr.
82/D5 Vojosë (riv.), Alb.
82/D3 Vojvodina (aut. prov.), Yugo.
69/F5 Völklingen, Ger.
79/E3 Volano, Po di (riv.), It.
149/F4 Volcán Barú Nat'l Park, Pan.
120/C2 Volcano (isls.), Japan
149/E4 Volcán Poás Nat'l Park, CR
130/A3 Volcans Nat'l Park, Rwa.
63/Q1 Volchiy Nos (cape), Rus.
61/C3 Volda, Nor.
66/C4 Volendam, Neth.
53/H4 Volga (riv.), Rus.
84/H3 Volga-Baltic Wtwy., Rus.
53/H4 Volgodonsk, Rus.
87/H2 Volgograd, Rus.
87/H2 Volgograd (res.), Rus.
87/G2 Volgograd Obl., Rus.
70/D3 Volkach, Ger.
70/D3 Volkach (riv.), Ger.
66/B5 Volkerakdam (dam), Neth.
73/L3 Völkermarkt, Aus.
77/E3 Volketswil, Swi.
63/Q2 Volkhov, Rus.
84/F4 Volkhov (riv.), Rus.
64/D4 Völklingen, Ger.
67/G6 Volkmarsen, Ger.
65/N2 Volkovysk, Bela.
133/E2 Volksrust, SAfr.
69/G5 Volmunster, Fr.
84/H4 Vologda, Rus.
84/J3 Vologda Obl., Rus.
76/C1 Vologne (riv.), Fr.
81/H3 Vólos, Gre.
81/H3 Volos (gulf), Gre.
78/A2 Volpiano, It.
53/H3 Vol'sk, Rus.
129/E4 Volta (lake), Gha.
129/F5 Volta (reg.), Gha.
129/F5 Volta (riv.), Gha.
141/J7 Volta Redonda, Braz.
79/D6 Volterra, It.
80/D2 Volturno (riv.), It.
123/M13 Volubilis (ruins), Mor.
81/H2 Vólvi (lake), Gre.
71/G4 Volyňka (riv.), Czh.
85/L5 Volzhsk, Rus.
53/H4 Volzhskiy, Rus.
151/H3 Von Frank (mtn.), Ak,US
72/D3 Vonne (riv.), Fr.
66/B4 Voorburg, Neth.
66/B5 Voorne (isl.), Neth.
66/B4 Voorschoten, Neth.
66/D4 Voorst, Neth.
77/F4 Vorab (peak), Swi.
77/F3 Vorarlberg (prov.), Aus.
70/C4 Vorbach (riv.), Ger.
71/G7 Vorchdorf, Aus.
66/D4 Vorden, Neth.
77/E4 Vorderrhein (riv.), Swi.
72/F4 Voreppe, Fr.
53/K2 Vorkuta, Rus.
63/K2 Vormsi (isl.), Est.
87/G1 Vorona (riv.), Rus.
53/G3 Voronezh, Rus.
86/F1 Voronezh (riv.), Rus.
87/G2 Voronezh Obl., Rus.
63/Q1 Voronov (cape), Rus.
84/G1 Voron'ya (riv.), Rus.
69/E1 Vorst, Belg.
63/L2 Vörts (lake), Est.
63/M3 Võru, Est.
76/C1 Vosges (dept.), Fr.
76/C2 Vosges (mts.), Fr.
84/H5 Voskresensk, Rus.
62/B1 Voss, Nor.
113/V Vostock (cape), Ant.
113/H Vostok, Ant.
121/K6 Vostok (isl.), Kiri.
53/J3 Votkinsk, Rus.
85/M4 Votkinsk (res.), Rus.
141/C2 Votorantim, Braz.
141/B2 Votuporanga, Braz.
74/B2 Vouga (riv.), Port.
76/B5 Vouglans (lake), Fr.
76/B5 Vouglans, Barrage de (dam), Fr.
81/H5 Voúxa, Ákra (cape), Gre.
157/K3 Voyageurs Nat'l Park, Mn,US
113/J Voyeykov Ice Shelf, Ant.
85/M3 Voy-Vozh, Rus.
84/H3 Vozhe (lake), Rus.
86/D3 Voznesensk, Ukr.
76/B1 Vraine (riv.), Fr.
83/H3 Vrancea (co.), Rom.
90/S2 Vrangelya (isl.), Rus.
82/E4 Vranje, Yugo.
65/L4 Vranov nad Teplou, Slvk.
83/F4 Vratsa, Bul.
82/C3 Vrbas (riv.), Bosn.
82/D3 Vrbas, Yugo.
71/H4 Vrchy (peak), Czh.
132/E2 Vrede, SAfr.
66/D4 Vreden, Ger.
132/B4 Vredenburg, SAfr.
73/L4 Vrhnika, Slov.
108/G3 Vriddhāchalam, India
66/D2 Vries, Neth.
66/D4 Vriezenveen, Neth.
64/B5 Vrin (riv.), Fr.
106/C2 Vrindāban, India
82/E4 Vrnjačka Banja, Yugo.
82/E3 Vršac, Yugo.
79/G2 Vrsar, Cro.
132/D2 Vryburg, SAfr.
133/E2 Vryheid, SAfr.
65/K4 Vsetín, Czh.
151/E5 Vsevidof (mtn.), Ak,US
63/P1 Vsevolozhsk, Rus.
65/K4 Vtáčnik (peak), Slvk.
82/E4 Vučitrn, Yugo.
66/C5 Vught, Neth.
82/D3 Vukovar, Cro.
156/E3 Vulcan, Ab,Can
83/F3 Vulcan, Rom.
80/D3 Vulcano (isl.), It.
83/F4 Vŭlchedrŭm, Bul.
80/B1 Vulci (ruins), It.
109/D2 Vu Liet, Viet.
109/D4 Vung Tau, Viet.
120/G7 Vunisea, Fiji
63/M1 Vuohijärvi (lake), Fin.
63/N1 Vuoksa (lake), Rus.
84/E1 Vuotso, Fin.
130/C3 Vuria (peak), Kenya
83/F4 Vŭrshets, Bul.
130/B5 Vwawa, Tanz.
106/B3 Vyāra, India
53/H3 Vyatka, Rus.
85/L4 Vyatka (riv.), Rus.
85/L4 Vyatka Obl., Rus.
85/L4 Vyatskiye Polyany, Rus.
97/L2 Vyazemskiy, Rus.
84/G5 Vyaz'ma, Rus.
63/N1 Vyborg, Rus.
63/N1 Vyborg (bay), Rus.
85/N2 Vychegda (riv.), Rus.
65/H3 Východočeský (reg.), Czh.
65/L4 Východoslovenský (reg.), Slvk.
84/G3 Vygozero (lake), Rus.
65/M4 Vyhorlat (peak), Slvk.
84/J5 Vyksa, Rus.
85/L3 Vym' (riv.), Rus.
58/C1 Vyrnwy (riv.), Wal,UK
84/G4 Vyshniy Volochek, Rus.
65/J4 Vyškov, Czh.

W

129/E4 Wa, Gha.
66/C5 Waal (riv.), Neth.
66/C6 Waalre, Neth.
66/C5 Waalwijk, Neth.
68/C1 Waarschoot, Belg.
156/E2 Wabasca, Ab,Can
152/E3 Wabasca (riv.), Ab,Can
160/C4 Wabash (riv.), Il, In,US
160/C3 Wabash, In,US
67/G6 Wabern, Ger.
157/K3 Wabigoon (lake), On,Can
157/J2 Wabowden, Mb,Can
65/K2 Wąbrzeźno, Pol.
103/D4 Wabu (lake), China
101/G6 Wabu, SKor.
99/L9 Wachi, Japan
68/C1 Wachtebeke, Belg.
66/D6 Wachtendonk, Ger.
70/C2 Wächtersbach, Ger.
168/C1 Wachusett (res.), Ma,US
162/D4 Waco, Tx,US
162/D3 Waconda (lake), Ks,US
157/K4 Waconia, Mn,US
99/J7 Wada, Japan
119/D3 Wadbilliga Nat'l Park, Austl.
124/J2 Waddān, Libya
66/C2 Waddenzee (sound), Neth.

Wadd – West

156/B3 **Waddington** (mtn.), BC,Can
57/F4 **Waddington**, Eng,UK
57/H5 **Waddington**, Eng,UK
66/B4 **Waddinxveen**, Neth.
118/D4 **Waddy** (pt.), Austl.
58/B5 **Wadebridge**, Eng,UK
157/H3 **Wadena**, Sk,Can
157/K4 **Wadena**, Mn,US
77/E3 **Wädenswil**, Swi.
69/F4 **Wadern**, Ger.
67/F5 **Wadersloh**, Ger.
69/F5 **Wadgassen**, Ger.
59/G4 **Wadhurst**, Eng,UK
91/D4 **Wādī As Sīr**, Jor.
127/B4 **Wādī Ḩalfā'**, Sudan
166/D4 **Wading** (riv.), NJ,US
125/M5 **Wad Medanī**, Sudan
65/K4 **Wadowice**, Pol.
168/F5 **Wadsworth**, Oh,US
101/E5 **Waegwan**, SKor.
103/D3 **Wafangdian**, China
130/B2 **Wagagai** (peak), Ugan.
67/F3 **Wagenfeld-Hasslingen**, Ger.
66/C5 **Wageningen**, Neth.
152/G2 **Wager** (bay), NW,Can
119/C2 **Wagga Wagga**, Austl.
70/B4 **Waghäusel**, Ger.
71/F7 **Waginger See** (lake), Ger.
77/E3 **Wägitalersee** (lake), Swi.
140/B4 **Wagner**, Braz.
65/J2 **Wągrowiec**, Pol.
95/K2 **Wāh**, Pak.
111/G4 **Wahai**, Indo.
127/B4 **Wāḩat Salīmah** (well), Sudan
154/V12 **Wahiawa**, Hi,US
159/H2 **Wahoo**, Ne,US
157/J4 **Wahpeton**, ND,US
158/D3 **Wah Wah** (range), Ut,US
106/B4 **Wai**, India
154/V13 **Waianae**, Hi,US
103/D2 **Waibamiao**, China
73/L3 **Waidhofen an der Ybbs**, Aus.
111/H3 **Waigeo** (isl.), Indo.
111/E5 **Waikabubak**, Indo.
115/R11 **Waikari**, NZ
154/T10 **Wailuku**, Hi,US
115/R11 **Waimate**, NZ
154/V12 **Waimea** (falls), Hi,US
161/R10 **Wainfleet**, On,Can
57/J5 **Wainfleet All Saints**, Eng,UK
106/C3 **Waingangā** (riv.), India
111/F5 **Waingapu**, Indo.
139/G2 **Waini** (riv.), Guy.
156/F2 **Wainwright**, Ab,Can
154/V13 **Waipahu**, Hi,US
154/U10 **Waipio**, Hi,US
115/S11 **Waipukurau**, NZ
115/S10 **Wairoa**, NZ
115/R10 **Waitara**, NZ
115/R10 **Waitemata**, NZ
121/Z17 **Waiyevu**, Fiji
99/E2 **Wajima**, Japan
130/D2 **Wajir**, Kenya
111/G4 **Waka** (cape), Indo.
98/D3 **Wakasa**, Japan
98/D3 **Wakasa** (bay), Japan
157/G2 **Wakaw**, Sk,Can
98/D3 **Wakayama**, Japan
98/D4 **Wakayama** (pref.), Japan
120/F3 **Wake** (isl.), PacUS
162/D2 **Wakeeney**, Ks,US
57/G4 **Wakefield**, Eng,UK
160/B2 **Wakefield**, Mi,US
168/C3 **Wakefield-Peacedale**, RI,US
104/B5 **Wakema**, Burma
98/D3 **Waki**, Japan
100/B1 **Wakkanai**, Japan
99/H7 **Wakō**, Japan
100/B4 **Wakuya**, Japan
160/D1 **Wakwayowkastic** (riv.), On,Can
130/B4 **Wala** (riv.), Tanz.
83/G3 **Walachia** (range), Rom.
83/G3 **Walachia** (reg.), Rom.
116/D2 **Walagunya Abor. Land**, Austl.
131/C2 **Walamba**, Zam.
65/J3 **Wałbrzych**, Pol.
65/J3 **Wałbrzych** (prov.), Pol.
59/E4 **Walbury** (hill), Eng,UK
77/H2 **Walchensee** (lake), Ger.
66/A5 **Walcheren** (isl.), Neth.
68/D3 **Walcourt**, Belg.
65/J2 **Wałcz**, Pol.
77/E3 **Wald**, Swi.
71/H6 **Waldaist** (riv.), Aus.
69/G2 **Waldbröl**, Ger.
70/B5 **Waldbronn**, Ger.
67/G6 **Waldeck**, Ger.
159/F2 **Walden**, Co,US
70/C5 **Waldenbuch**, Ger.
156/G2 **Waldheim**, Sk,Can
70/A6 **Waldkirch**, Ger.
71/F4 **Waldmünchen**, Ger.
71/F3 **Waldnaab** (riv.), Ger.
71/F3 **Waldsassen**, Ger.
77/E2 **Waldshut-Tiengen**, Ger.
70/C5 **Waldstetten**, Ger.
73/L2 **Waldviertel** (reg.), Aus.
167/J7 **Waldwick**, NJ,US
111/F4 **Walea** (str.), Indo.
111/F4 **Waleabahi** (isl.), Indo.
77/F3 **Walensee** (lake), Swi.
153/H2 **Wales** (isl.), NW,Can
55/J10 **Wales**, UK
168/G6 **Walford** (Bessemer), Pa,US
113/T **Walgreen** (coast), Ant.
71/F4 **Walhalla**, Ger.
157/J3 **Walhalla**, ND,US
163/H3 **Walhalla**, SC,US
168/E7 **Walhonding** (riv.), Oh,US
126/E1 **Walikale**, Zaire
132/L11 **Walker** (bay), SAfr.
158/C3 **Walker** (lake), Nv,US
158/C3 **Walker** (riv.), Nv,US
54/C5 **Walkerburn**, Sc,UK
131/D2 **Walkers Ferry**, Malw.
160/D2 **Walkerton**, On,Can
166/D1 **Walkill** (riv.), NJ, NY,US
156/E4 **Wallace**, Id,US
165/H6 **Wallaceburg**, On,Can
116/D1 **Wallal Downs**, Austl.
57/E5 **Wallasey**, Eng,UK
156/D4 **Walla Walla**, Wa,US
70/B4 **Walldorf**, Ger.
70/C3 **Walldürn**, Ger.
165/F6 **Walled** (lake), Mi,US
101/G7 **Walled City**, SKor.
165/F6 **Walled Lake**, Mi,US
67/F4 **Wallenhorst**, Ger.
68/C3 **Wallers**, Fr.
71/G7 **Wallersee** (lake), Aus.
59/E3 **Wallingford**, Eng,UK
168/B3 **Wallingford**, Ct,US
167/J8 **Wallington**, NJ,US
121/H6 **Wallis** (isls.), Wall.
120/G6 **Wallis & Futuna** (terr.), Fr.
77/E3 **Wallisellen**, Swi.
156/D4 **Wallowa** (mts.), Or,US
55/P12 **Walls**, Sc,UK
57/G2 **Wallsend**, Eng,UK
57/E3 **Walney, Isle of** (isl.), Eng,UK
164/C2 **Walnut**, Ca,US
158/E4 **Walnut Canyon Nat'l Mon.**, Az,US
165/K11 **Walnut Creek**, Ca,US
164/F8 **Walnut Park**, Ca,US
163/F2 **Walnut Ridge**, Ar,US
165/G6 **Walpole I. Ind. Res.**, On,Can
116/C5 **Walpole-Nornalup Nat'l Park**, Austl.
151/F4 **Walrus** (isls.), Ak,US
58/E1 **Walsall**, Eng,UK
153/K2 **Walsingham** (cape), NW,Can
59/G1 **Walsingham**, Eng,UK
67/G3 **Walsrode**, Ger.
77/G2 **Waltenhofen**, Ger.
163/H3 **Walterboro**, SC,US
166/C1 **Walter, F. E.** (res.), Pa,US
163/G4 **Walter F. George** (res.), Al, Ga,US
168/C1 **Waltham**, Ma,US
53/P6 **Waltham Abbey**, Eng,UK
53/N7 **Waltham Forest** (bor.), Eng,UK
59/G3 **Waltham Holy Cross**, Eng,UK
57/F4 **Walton-le-Dale**, Eng,UK
59/F4 **Walton on Thames**, Eng,UK
59/H3 **Walton on the Naze**, Eng,UK
67/E5 **Waltrop**, Ger.
126/B5 **Walvis Bay**, Namb.
165/P14 **Walworth** (co.), Wi,US
116/C4 **Walyahmoning** (peak), Austl.
116/L6 **Walyunga Nat'l Park**, Austl.
126/C3 **Wama**, Ang.
130/C2 **Wamba**, Kenya
125/L7 **Wamba**, Zaire
66/C5 **Wamel**, Neth.
130/C4 **Wami** (riv.), Tanz.
57/E2 **Wampool** (riv.), Eng,UK
156/G5 **Wamsutter**, Wy,US
103/D5 **Wan** (riv.), China
115/Q11 **Wanaka**, NZ
167/D1 **Wanaque**, NJ,US
167/D1 **Wanaque** (res.), NJ,US
97/L2 **Wanda** (mts.), China
130/A2 **Wandi**, Ugan.
104/C3 **Wanding**, China
53/N7 **Wandsworth** (bor.), Eng,UK
109/B2 **Wang** (riv.), Thai.
115/S10 **Wanganui**, NZ
119/C3 **Wangaratta**, Austl.
103/C3 **Wangdu**, China
77/F2 **Wangen**, Ger.
67/E1 **Wangerooge** (isl.), Ger.
111/F6 **Wanggamet** (peak), Indo.
101/A2 **Wanghai Shan** (peak), China
109/B4 **Wang Hip** (peak), Thai.
103/D5 **Wangjiang**, China
97/K2 **Wangkui**, China
104/E3 **Wangmo**, China
103/E5 **Wangpan** (bay), China
97/K3 **Wangqing**, China
111/F4 **Wani** (peak), Indo.
139/H3 **Wanica** (dist.), Sur.
77/H2 **Wank** (peak), Ger.
131/B3 **Wankie** (Hwange) Nat'l Park, Zim.
107/K4 **Wanning**, China
99/M9 **Wanouchi**, Japan
103/C2 **Wanquan**, China
102/D5 **Wanquan** (lake), China
105/F5 **Wanquan** (riv.), China
103/B4 **Wanrong**, China
57/G1 **Wansbeck** (riv.), Eng,UK
53/P7 **Wanstead**, Eng,UK
59/E3 **Wantage**, Eng,UK
167/L9 **Wantagh**, NY,US
105/F2 **Wanxian**, China
69/E2 **Wanze**, Belg.
112/D4 **Wao**, Phil.
160/C3 **Wapakoneta**, Oh,US
157/G2 **Wapawekka** (lake), Sk,Can
156/D2 **Wapiti** (riv.), Ab, BC,Can
111/J4 **Wapoga** (riv.), Indo.
159/K3 **Wappapello** (lake), Mo,US
157/K5 **Wapsipinicon** (riv.), Ia,US
166/B1 **Wapwallopen** (cr.), Pa,US
99/H7 **Warabi**, Japan
106/C4 **Warangal**, India
59/F2 **Warboys**, Eng,UK
67/G6 **Warburg**, Ger.
117/H3 **Warburton** (cr.), Austl.
108/B2 **Warburton**, Pak.
117/E3 **Warburton** (Central Australia) Abor. Rsv., Austl.
117/E3 **Warburton Range Abor. Rsv.**, Austl.
69/F3 **Warche** (riv.), Belg.
115/R11 **Ward**, NZ
59/G4 **Warden** (pt.), Eng,UK
67/F2 **Wardenburg**, Ger.
106/C3 **Wardha**, India
57/F3 **Ward's Stone** (mtn.), Eng,UK
59/F3 **Ware**, Eng,UK
168/B1 **Ware**, Ma,US
168/B1 **Ware** (riv.), Ma,US
68/C2 **Waregem**, Belg.
58/D5 **Wareham**, Eng,UK
168/D2 **Wareham**, Ma,US
69/E2 **Waremme**, Belg.
64/G2 **Waren**, Ger.
67/E5 **Warendorf**, Ger.
59/F3 **Wargrave**, Eng,UK
109/D3 **Warin Chamrap**, Thai.
56/B3 **Waringstown**, NI,UK
57/F1 **Wark**, Eng,UK
65/L3 **Warka**, Pol.
115/R10 **Warkworth**, NZ
58/D2 **Warley**, Eng,UK
53/N8 **Warlingham**, Eng,UK
157/G2 **Warman**, Sk,Can
132/E2 **Warmbad**, SAfr.
67/G6 **Warmebach** (riv.), Ger.
67/H5 **Warme Bode** (riv.), Ger.
65/K1 **Warmia** (reg.), Pol.
58/D4 **Warminster**, Eng,UK
166/C3 **Warminster**, Pa,US
158/B2 **Warner** (mts.), Ca,US
163/H3 **Warner Robins**, Ga,US
64/G2 **Warnow** (riv.), Ger.
66/D4 **Warnsveld**, Neth.
117/G2 **Warrabri Abor. Land**, Austl.
117/G2 **Warramunga Abor. Land**, Austl.
117/H3 **Warrandirinna** (lake), Austl.
119/G5 **Warrandybe**, Austl.
118/B4 **Warrego** (range), Austl.
115/H5 **Warrego** (riv.), Austl.
116/C5 **Warren** (riv.), Austl.
151/M2 **Warren** (pt.), NW,Can
162/E3 **Warren**, Ar,US
165/F6 **Warren**, Mi,US
157/J3 **Warren**, Mn,US
166/D2 **Warren**, NJ,US
166/C1 **Warren** (co.), NJ,US
168/G5 **Warren**, Oh,US
160/E3 **Warren**, Pa,US
168/C2 **Warren**, RI,US
56/B3 **Warrenpoint**, NI,UK
159/J3 **Warrensburg**, Mo,US
168/F5 **Warrensville Heights**, Oh,US
132/D3 **Warrenton**, SAfr.
160/E4 **Warrenton**, Va,US
165/P16 **Warrenville**, Il,US
57/F5 **Warrington**, Eng,UK
163/G4 **Warrington**, Fl,US
119/B3 **Warrnambool**, Austl.
157/K3 **Warroad**, Mn,US
119/D1 **Warrumbungle Nat'l Park**, Austl.
160/C3 **Warsaw**, In,US
159/J3 **Warsaw**, Mo,US
65/L3 **Warsawa** (prov.), Pol.
65/L2 **Warsaw** (Warszawa) (cap.), Pol.
65/H5 **Warscheneck** (peak), Aus.
57/G5 **Warslow**, Eng,UK
57/G5 **Warsop**, Eng,UK
67/F6 **Warstein**, Ger.
65/L2 **Warszawa** (Warsaw) (cap.), Pol.
65/H2 **Warta** (riv.), Pol.
118/D5 **Warwick**, Austl.
59/E2 **Warwick**, Eng,UK
168/C2 **Warwick**, RI,US
59/E2 **Warwickshire** (co.), Eng,UK
158/E2 **Wasatch** (range), Ut,US
158/C4 **Wasco**, Ca,US
157/K4 **Waseca**, Mn,US
152/F1 **Washburn** (lake), NW,Can
57/G4 **Washburn** (riv.), Eng,UK
157/M3 **Washi** (lake), On,Can
57/H5 **Washingborough**, Eng,UK
57/G2 **Washington**, Eng,UK
156/C4 **Washington** (state), US
166/A6 **Washington** (cap.), DC,US
160/B3 **Washington**, Il,US
160/C4 **Washington**, In,US
163/J3 **Washington**, NC,US
161/G2 **Washington** (mtn.), NH,US
166/D2 **Washington**, NJ,US
160/D3 **Washington**, Pa,US
168/G7 **Washington** (co.), Pa,US
168/C2 **Washington** (co.), RI,US
165/C2 **Washington** (lake), Wa,US
160/C2 **Washington** (isl.), Wi,US
160/D4 **Washington Court House**, Oh,US
121/K4 **Washington** (Teraina) (atoll), Kiri.
159/H4 **Washita** (riv.), Ok, Tx,US
165/E7 **Washtenaw** (co.), Mi,US
59/G1 **Wash, The** (bay), Eng,UK
65/M2 **Wasilków**, Pol.
93/F3 **Wāsiţ** (gov.), Iraq
160/E1 **Waskaganish** (Rupert House), Qu,Can
151/G4 **Waskey** (mtn.), Ak,US
66/B4 **Wassenaar**, Neth.
66/D6 **Wassenberg**, Ger.
71/F6 **Wasserburg am Inn**, Ger.
70/C2 **Wasserkuppe** (peak), Ger.
154/C4 **Wassuk** (range), Nv,US
57/E3 **Wast Water** (lake), Eng,UK
160/E1 **Waswanipi** (lake), Qu,Can
111/E4 **Watampone**, Indo.
99/M10 **Watarai**, Japan
99/F2 **Watarase** (riv.), Japan
99/G1 **Watari**, Japan
58/C4 **Watchet**, Eng,UK
59/E3 **Watchfield**, Eng,UK
168/C3 **Watch Hill** (pt.), RI,US
167/H9 **Watchung** (mts.), NJ,US
59/G2 **Waterbeach**, Eng,UK
131/B5 **Waterberge** (mts.), SAfr.
168/A2 **Waterbury**, Ct,US
161/Q9 **Waterdown**, On,Can
163/H3 **Wateree** (dam), SC,US
163/H3 **Wateree** (lake), SC,US
163/H3 **Wateree** (riv.), SC,US
60/C5 **Waterford**, Ire.
60/C5 **Waterford** (co.), Ire.
60/D5 **Waterford** (har.), Ire.
165/F6 **Waterford**, Mi,US
58/A6 **Watergate** (bay), Eng,UK
157/J2 **Waterhen** (lake), Mb,Can
156/F2 **Waterhen** (riv.), Sk,Can
68/D2 **Waterloo**, Belg.
160/D3 **Waterloo**, On,Can
159/J2 **Waterloo**, Ia,US
160/B4 **Waterloo**, Il,US
68/D2 **Waterloo Battlesite**, Belg.
166/D2 **Waterloo Village**, NJ,US
59/E5 **Waterlooville**, Eng,UK
68/D2 **Watermael-Boitsfort**, Belg.
156/E3 **Waterton Lakes Nat'l Park**, Ab,Can
168/A2 **Watertown**, Ct,US
168/C1 **Watertown**, Ma,US
160/F3 **Watertown**, NY,US
157/J4 **Watertown**, SD,US
160/B3 **Watertown**, Wi,US
133/E2 **Waterval-Bo**, SAfr.
161/G2 **Waterville**, Me,US
156/C4 **Waterville**, Wa,US
53/M7 **Watford**, Eng,UK
157/H4 **Watford City**, ND,US
116/B4 **Watheroo Nat'l Park**, Austl.
57/G5 **Wath-upon-Dearne**, Eng,UK
150/C1 **Watling** (San Salvador) (isl.), Bahm.
59/F3 **Watlington**, Eng,UK
109/B2 **Wat Mahathat**, Thai.
159/H4 **Watonga**, Ok,US
111/G3 **Watowato** (peak), Indo.
104/D5 **Wat Phra Si Ratana Mahathat**, Thai.
109/D3 **Wat Phu**, Laos
157/G3 **Watrous**, Sk,Can
130/A2 **Watsa**, Zaire
160/C3 **Watseka**, Il,US
152/D2 **Watson Lake**, Yk,Can
158/B3 **Watsonville**, Ca,US
73/J3 **Wattens**, Aus.
68/C2 **Wattignies**, Fr.
59/G1 **Watton**, Eng,UK
68/C2 **Wattrelos**, Fr.
164/F8 **Watts**, Ca,US
77/F3 **Wattwil**, Swi.
168/C2 **Watuppa** (pond), Ma,US
109/C2 **Wat Xieng Thong**, Laos
163/H5 **Wauchula**, Fl,US
165/P15 **Wauconda**, Il,US
116/D2 **Waukarlycarly** (lake), Austl.
165/Q15 **Waukegan**, Il,US
165/P13 **Waukesha**, Wi,US
165/P14 **Waukesha** (co.), Wi,US
58/C3 **Waun Fâch** (mtn.), Wal,UK
58/C1 **Waun Oer** (mtn.), UK
160/B3 **Waupun**, Wi,US
159/H4 **Waurika**, Ok,US
160/B2 **Wausau**, Wi,US
160/C3 **Wauseon**, Oh,US
165/P13 **Wauwatosa**, Wi,US
59/H2 **Waveney** (riv.), Eng,UK
57/E2 **Waver** (riv.), Eng,UK
119/G5 **Waverly**, Austl.
163/G2 **Waverly**, Tn,US
68/D2 **Wavre**, Belg.
68/B2 **Wavrin**, Fr.
125/L6 **Wāw**, Sudan
160/C2 **Wawa**, On,Can
149/E3 **Wawa** (riv.), Nic.
160/E1 **Wawagosic** (riv.), Qu,Can
149/E3 **Wawasang** (mtn.), Nic.
167/H7 **Wawayanda Saint Park**, NJ,US
162/D3 **Waxahachie**, Tx,US
69/F3 **Waxweiler**, Ger.
163/H4 **Waycross**, Ga,US
168/C1 **Wayland**, Ma,US
165/F7 **Wayne**, Mi,US
165/F7 **Wayne** (co.), Mi,US
159/H2 **Wayne**, Ne,US
167/D2 **Wayne**, NJ,US
168/F6 **Wayne** (co.), Oh,US
166/C1 **Wayne** (co.), Pa,US
163/H3 **Waynesboro**, Ga,US
163/F4 **Waynesboro**, Ms,US
160/E4 **Waynesboro**, Pa,US
160/E4 **Waynesboro**, Va,US
159/J3 **Waynesville**, Mo,US
163/H3 **Waynesville**, NC,US
68/C3 **Waziers**, Fr.
108/C1 **Wazīrābād**, Pak.
99/L10 **Wazuka**, Japan
64/K2 **Wda** (riv.), Pol.
129/F3 **W du Niger Nat'l Park**, Afr.
110/A2 **We** (isl.), Indo.
59/G4 **Weald, The** (reg.), Eng,UK
57/G2 **Wear** (riv.), Eng,UK
57/F2 **Wear Head**, Eng,UK
159/H4 **Weatherford**, Ok,US
162/D3 **Weatherford**, Tx,US
57/F5 **Weaver** (riv.), Eng,UK
158/B2 **Weaverville**, Ca,US
162/D3 **Webb A.F.B.**, Tx,US
168/C1 **Webster**, Ma,US
168/C1 **Webster** (lake), Ma,US
157/J4 **Webster**, SD,US
157/K5 **Webster City**, Ia,US
130/B2 **Webuye**, Kenya
113/W **Weddell** (sea), Ant.
143/M7 **Weddell** (isl.), Falk.
119/C2 **Weddin Mountains Nat'l Park**, Austl.
67/G1 **Wedel**, Ger.
67/G3 **Wedemark**, Ger.
58/D4 **Wedmore**, Eng,UK
58/D1 **Wednesbury**, Eng,UK
58/D1 **Wednesfield**, Eng,UK
131/C3 **Wedza**, Zim.
158/B2 **Weed**, Ca,US
59/E2 **Weedon Bec**, Eng,UK
167/J8 **Weehawken**, NJ,US
163/H4 **Weeki Wachee Springs**, Fl,US
58/B5 **Week Saint Mary**, Eng,UK
66/D4 **Weerselo**, Neth.
66/C6 **Weert**, Neth.
66/C4 **Weesp**, Neth.
66/D6 **Wegberg**, Ger.
65/L1 **Węgorzewo**, Pol.
65/M2 **Węgrów**, Pol.
76/D2 **Wehr**, Ger.
76/D2 **Wehra** (riv.), Ger.
67/G6 **Wehre** (riv.), Ger.
70/B2 **Wehrheim**, Ger.
97/H4 **Wei** (riv.), China
97/H3 **Weichang**, China
64/G3 **Weida**, Ger.
71/F3 **Weiden**, Ger.
103/D3 **Weifang**, China
166/B4 **Weigelstown**, Pa,US
101/B4 **Weihai**, China
70/C4 **Weikersheim**, Ger.
70/B2 **Weil** (riv.), Ger.
70/B2 **Weilburg**, Ger.
70/B5 **Weil der Stadt**, Ger.
69/F2 **Weilerswist**, Ger.
77/H2 **Weilheim**, Ger.
70/C5 **Weilheim an der Teck**, Ger.
70/B2 **Weilmünster**, Ger.
64/F3 **Weimar**, Ger.
77/F2 **Weinfelden**, Swi.
70/B4 **Weingarten**, Ger.
77/F2 **Weingarten**, Ger.
70/B3 **Weinheim**, Ger.
70/C4 **Weinsberg**, Ger.
70/C5 **Weinstadt**, Ger.
65/J4 **Weinviertel** (reg.), Aus.
168/G7 **Weirton**, WV,US
156/D4 **Weiser**, Id,US
156/D4 **Weiser** (riv.), Id,US
103/D4 **Weishan**, China
103/D4 **Weishan** (lake), China
103/C4 **Weishi**, China
69/F4 **Weiskirchen**, Ger.
163/G3 **Weiss** (lake), Al,US
70/B5 **Weissach**, Ger.
71/F2 **Weisse Elster** (riv.), Ger.
71/E4 **Weisse Laber** (riv.), Ger.
70/D4 **Weissenburg im Bayern**, Ger.
64/F3 **Weissenfels**, Ger.
70/D6 **Weissenhorn**, Ger.
76/D3 **Weissenstein** (mtn.), Swi.
69/G3 **Weissenthurm**, Ger.
71/E2 **Weisser Main** (riv.), Ger.
71/F4 **Weisser Regen** (riv.), Ger.
69/F3 **Weisser Stein** (peak), Ger.
76/D5 **Weisshorn** (peak), Swi.
77/G4 **Weisskugel** (Palla Bianca) (peak), Aus., It.
76/D5 **Weissmies** (peak), Swi.
65/H3 **Weisswasser**, Ger.
70/B3 **Weiterstadt**, Ger.
107/G2 **Weixi**, China
103/C3 **Wei Xian**, China
107/J2 **Weixin**, China
96/E4 **Weiyuan**, China
104/D4 **Weiyuan** (riv.), China
73/L3 **Weiz**, Aus.
105/F4 **Weizhou** (isl.), China
65/K1 **Wejherowo**, Pol.
166/A3 **Welch** (hill), Pa,US
160/D4 **Welch**, WV,US
125/N5 **Weldiya**, Eth.
59/F2 **Weldon**, Eng,UK
125/M6 **Welel** (peak), Eth.
59/E4 **Welford**, Eng,UK
53/N6 **Welham Green**, Eng,UK
106/D6 **Weligama**, SrL.
69/E2 **Welkenraedt**, Belg.
132/D3 **Welkom**, SAfr.
161/R10 **Welland**, On,Can
161/R10 **Welland** (can.), On,Can
59/F1 **Welland** (riv.), Eng,UK
161/R10 **Wellandport**, On,Can
69/E2 **Wellen**, Belg.
114/F3 **Wellesley** (isls.), Austl.
168/C1 **Wellesley**, Ma,US
59/F2 **Wellingborough**, Eng,UK
119/C3 **Wellington** (inlet), Austl.
153/S7 **Wellington** (chan.), NW,Can
143/J7 **Wellington** (isl.), Chile
115/R11 **Wellington** (cap.), NZ
132/B4 **Wellington**, SAfr.
58/C5 **Wellington**, Eng,UK
58/D2 **Wellington**, Eng,UK
162/D2 **Wellington**, Ks,US
162/C3 **Wellington**, Tx,US
116/D3 **Wells** (lake), Austl.
156/C2 **Wells**, BC,Can
58/D4 **Wells**, Eng,UK
156/E5 **Wells**, Nv,US
59/G1 **Wells-next-the-Sea**, Eng,UK
160/D4 **Wellston**, Oh,US
71/H6 **Wels**, Aus.
77/H5 **Welshnofen** (Nova Levante), It.
58/C1 **Welshpool**, Wal,UK
67/E5 **Welver**, Ger.
59/F3 **Welwyn**, Eng,UK
59/F3 **Welwyn Garden City**, Eng,UK
70/C5 **Welzheim**, Ger.
57/F6 **Wem**, Eng,UK
130/B4 **Wembere** (riv.), Tanz.
156/D2 **Wembley**, Ab,Can
53/N7 **Wembley Stadium**, Eng,UK
58/B6 **Wembury**, Eng,UK
153/J3 **Wemindji**, Qu,Can
68/D2 **Wemmel**, Belg.
54/B5 **Wemyss Bay**, Sc,UK
156/C4 **Wenatchee**, Wa,US
105/F5 **Wenchang**, China
105/J3 **Wencheng**, China
129/E5 **Wenchi**, Gha.
67/H4 **Wendeburg**, Ger.
69/G2 **Wenden**, Ger.
101/B4 **Wendeng**, China
59/F3 **Wendover**, Eng,UK
158/D2 **Wendover**, Nv,US
58/A6 **Wendron**, Eng,UK
107/K3 **Wengyuan**, China
58/D2 **Wenlock Edge** (ridge), Eng,UK
67/F6 **Wenne** (riv.), Ger.
67/G4 **Wennigsen**, Ger.
57/F3 **Wennington**, Eng,UK
107/H3 **Wenshan**, China
103/D4 **Wenshang**, China
103/C3 **Wenshui**, China
57/F3 **Wensleydale** (val.), Eng,UK
59/H1 **Wensum** (riv.), Eng,UK
57/G4 **Went** (riv.), Eng,UK
103/B4 **Wenxi**, China
103/C4 **Wen Xian**, China
105/J3 **Wenzhou**, China
131/A5 **Werda**, Bots.
64/G3 **Werdau**, Ger.
125/Q6 **Werdēr**, Eth.
67/E6 **Werdohl**, Ger.
66/B5 **Werkendam**, Neth.
67/E5 **Werl**, Ger.
67/E3 **Werlte**, Ger.
67/E6 **Wermelskirchen**, Ger.
70/C3 **Wern** (riv.), Ger.
67/E5 **Werne an der Lippe**, Ger.
70/D3 **Werneck**, Ger.
67/H5 **Wernigerode**, Ger.
119/D2 **Werong** (peak), Austl.
67/G6 **Werra** (riv.), Ger.
67/F4 **Werre** (riv.), Ger.
119/E1 **Werrikimbe Nat'l Park**, Austl.
57/F5 **Werrington**, Eng,UK
67/E5 **Werse** (riv.), Ger.
70/D6 **Wertach** (riv.), Ger.
70/C3 **Wertheim**, Ger.
167/F2 **Wertheim Nat'l Wild. Ref.**, NY,US
67/F4 **Werther**, Ger.
70/D5 **Wertingen**, Ger.
66/C3 **Wervershoof**, Neth.
68/C2 **Wervik**, Belg.
70/B3 **Weschnitz** (riv.), Ger.
66/D5 **Wesel**, Ger.
67/E5 **Wesel-Datteln-Kanal** (can.), Ger.
67/F2 **Weser** (riv.), Ger.
67/G4 **Wesergebirge** (ridge), Ger.
162/D5 **Weslaco**, Tx,US
132/D2 **Wes-Rand**, SAfr.
114/F2 **Wessel** (cape), Austl.
114/F2 **Wessel** (isls.), Austl.
58/D4 **Wessex** (reg.), Eng,UK
157/J4 **Wessington Springs**, SD,US
119/C4 **West** (pt.), Austl.
165/C2 **West** (pt.), Wa,US
117/G5 **Westall** (pt.), Austl.
165/P13 **West Allis**, Wi,US
163/H3 **West Augusta**, Ga,US
167/E2 **West Babylon**, NY,US
91/D3 **West Bank** (occ. zone)
54/D5 **West Barns**, Sc,UK
160/B3 **West Bend**, Wi,US
106/E3 **West Bengal** (state), India
59/G3 **West Bergholt**, Eng,UK
168/C1 **West Boylston**, Ma,US
160/C2 **West Branch**, Mi,US
168/F5 **West Branch Saint Pk.**, Oh,US
168/C1 **West Bridgewater**, Ma,US
57/G6 **West Bridgford**, Eng,UK
59/E1 **West Bromwich**, Eng,UK
58/D4 **Westbury**, Eng,UK
167/E2 **Westbury**, NY,US
149/H1 **West Caicos** (isl.), Trks.
54/C5 **West Calder**, Sc,UK
167/H8 **West Caldwell**, NJ,US
116/C5 **West Cape Howe Nat'l Park**, Austl.
167/E1 **Westchester** (co.), NY,US
166/C4 **West Chester**, Pa,US
165/P16 **West Chicago**, Il,US
130/C3 **West Chyulu Game Consv. Area**, Kenya
53/M8 **West Clandon**, Eng,UK
58/B3 **West Cleddau** (riv.), Wal,UK
163/H3 **West Columbia**, SC,US
57/G2 **West Cornforth**, Eng,UK
164/C2 **West Covina**, Ca,US
58/C5 **West Dart** (riv.), Eng,UK
66/A6 **Westdorpe**, Neth.
52/F3 **West Dvina** (riv.), Eur.
162/B2 **West Elk** (mts.), Co,US
66/D3 **Westerbork**, Neth.
53/P8 **Westerham**, Eng,UK
67/E4 **Westerkappeln**, Ger.
64/E1 **Westerland**, Ger.
69/D1 **Westerlo**, Belg.
168/C3 **Westerly**, RI,US
91/A5 **Western** (des.), Egypt
129/E5 **Western** (reg.), Gha.
130/B2 **Western** (prov.), Kenya
128/B4 **Western** (area), SLeo.
130/A2 **Western** (prov.), Ugan.
131/A2 **Western** (prov.), Zam.
116/D3 **Western Australia** (state), Austl.
132/C4 **Western Cape** (prov.), SAfr.
131/A3 **Western Caprivi Game Park**, Namb.
98/A3 **Western Channel** (str.), Japan, SKor.
88/C4 **Western Dvina** (riv.), Lat., Rus.
106/B4 **Western Ghats** (mts.), India
124/B3 **Western Sahara**
121/R9 **Western Samoa**
96/C1 **Western Sayan** (mts.), Rus.
66/A6 **Westerschelde** (chan.), Neth.
67/E2 **Westerstede**, Ger.
160/D3 **Westerville**, Oh,US
66/C5 **Westervoort**, Neth.
69/G2 **Westerwald** (for.), Ger.
67/F4 **Westfalica, Porta** (pass), Ger.
143/M8 **West Falkland** (isl.), Falk.
157/J4 **West Fargo**, ND,US
120/D4 **West Fayu** (isl.), Micr.
168/B1 **Westfield**, Ma,US
168/B1 **Westfield** (riv.), Ma,US
167/D2 **Westfield**, NJ,US
68/B2 **West Flanders** (prov.), Belg.
160/B4 **West Frankfort**, Il,US
66/C2 **West Frisian** (isls.), Neth.
58/C3 **West Glamorgan** (co.), Wal,UK
59/F1 **West Glen** (riv.), Eng,UK
53/P7 **West Ham**, Eng,UK
168/B2 **West Hartford**, Ct,US
168/B3 **West Haven**, Ct,US
167/E1 **West Haverstraw**, NY,US
167/C2 **West Hazleton**, Pa,US
163/F3 **West Helena**, Ar,US
167/L9 **West Hempstead**, NY,US
54/D2 **Westhill**, Sc,UK
164/F7 **West Hollywood**, Ca,US
53/Q7 **West Horndon**, Eng,UK
53/M8 **West Horsley**, Eng,UK
57/F4 **Westhoughton**, Eng,UK
161/Q8 **West Humber** (riv.), On,Can
113/F **West Ice Shelf**, Ant.
115/J4 **West Islet** (isl.), Austl.
167/E2 **West Islip**, NY,US
158/E2 **West Jordan**, Ut,US
54/B5 **West Kilbride**, Sc,UK
53/P8 **West Kingsdown**, Eng,UK
168/C3 **West Kingston**, RI,US
57/E5 **West Kirby**, Eng,UK
54/D3 **West Knock** (mtn.), Sc,UK
168/F5 **Westlake**, Oh,US
164/B2 **Westlake Village**, Ca,US
165/F7 **Westland**, Mi,US
54/C5 **West Linton**, Sc,UK
156/E2 **Westlock**, Ab,Can
131/B2 **West Lunga** (riv.), Zam.
131/B2 **West Lunga Nat'l Park**, Zam.
60/C3 **Westmeath** (co.), Ire.
163/F3 **West Memphis**, Ar,US
59/G3 **West Mersea**, Eng,UK
59/E2 **West Midlands** (co.), Eng,UK
168/H7 **West Mifflin**, Pa,US
167/D1 **West Milford**, NJ,US
164/B3 **Westminster**, Ca,US
166/B4 **Westminster**, Md,US
53/N7 **Westminster Abbey**, Eng,UK
53/N7 **Westminster, City of** (bor.), Eng,UK
165/Q16 **Westmont**, Il,US
166/C4 **Westmont** (Haddon), NJ,US
57/F3 **Westmoreland** (reg.), Eng,UK
161/N7 **Westmount**, Qu,Can
54/C3 **Westmuir**, Sc,UK
167/D2 **West New York**, NJ,US
131/C4 **West Nicholson**, Zim.
168/A3 **Weston**, Ct,US
168/C1 **Weston**, Ma,US
159/J3 **Weston**, Mo,US
160/D4 **Weston**, WV,US
132/P13 **Westonaria**, SAfr.
58/D4 **Weston-super-Mare**, Eng,UK
58/D4 **Weston Zoyland**, Eng,UK
167/D2 **West Orange**, NJ,US
168/B1 **Westover A.F.B.**, Ma,US
163/H5 **West Palm Beach**, Fl,US
167/J8 **West Paterson**, NJ,US
53/Q8 **West Peckham**, Eng,UK
163/G4 **West Pensacola**, Fl,US
159/K3 **West Plains**, Mo,US
163/G3 **West Point** (lake), Al, Ga,US
163/F3 **West Point**, Ms,US
159/H2 **West Point**, Ne,US
167/D1 **West Point** (mil. res.), NY,US
115/R11 **Westport**, NZ
167/E1 **Westport**, Ct,US
55/N13 **Westray** (isl.), Sc,UK
156/B2 **West Road** (riv.), BC,Can
165/L9 **West Sacramento**, Ca,US
161/S10 **West Seneca**, NY,US
88/H3 **West Siberian** (plain), Rus.
168/B1 **West Springfield**, Ma,US
59/F4 **West Sussex** (co.), Eng,UK
53/P7 **West Thurrock**, Eng,UK
158/E2 **West Valley City**, Ut,US
156/C3 **West Vancouver**, BC,Can
168/G6 **West View**, Pa,US

160/D4 West Virginia (state), US
58/B4 Westward Ho!, Eng,UK
168/C2 West Warwick, RI,US
54/D3 West Water (riv.), Sc,UK
168/C1 Westwood, Ma,US
167/D2 Westwood, NJ,US
131/C2 Westwood, Zam.
57/G4 West Yorkshire (co.), Eng,UK
162/B2 Wet (mts.), Co,US
111/G5 Wetar (isl.), Indo.
111/G5 Wetar (str.), Indo.
156/E2 Wetaskiwin, Ab,Can
130/C4 Wete, Tanz.
160/E1 Wetetnagami (riv.), Qu,Can
57/F2 Wetheral, Eng,UK
57/G4 Wetherby, Eng,UK
119/B2 Wetherell (lake), Austl.
168/B2 Wethersfield, Ct,US
67/E6 Wetter, Ger.
70/B2 Wetter (riv.), Ger.
70/C2 Wetterau (reg.), Ger.
68/C1 Wetteren, Belg.
76/E4 Wetterhorn (peak), Swi.
77/E3 Wettingen, Swi.
67/E4 Wettringen, Ger.
77/E3 Wetzikon, Swi.
71/E2 Wetzstein (peak), Ger.
68/C2 Wevelgem, Belg.
120/D5 Wewak, PNG
159/H4 Wewoka, Ok,US
60/D5 Wexford, Ire.
60/D5 Wexford (co.), Ire.
60/D5 Wexford (har.), Ire.
53/M8 Wey (riv.), Eng,UK
59/H1 Weybourne, Eng,UK
53/M7 Weybridge, Eng,UK
157/H3 Weyburn, Sk,Can
117/G5 Weyland (pt.), Austl.
58/D5 Weymouth, Eng,UK
58/D5 Weymouth (bay), Eng,UK
168/D1 Weymouth, Ma,US
115/S10 Whakatane, NZ
57/G5 Whaley Bridge, Eng,UK
168/D2 Whaling Museum, Ma,US
57/F4 Whalley, Eng,UK
55/P12 Whalsey (isl.), Sc,UK
115/R10 Whangarei, NZ
57/G3 Wharfe (riv.), Eng,UK
162/D4 Wharton, Tx,US
157/G5 Wheatland, Wy,US
59/E3 Wheatley, Eng,UK
165/P16 Wheaton, Il,US
58/D1 Wheaton Aston, Eng,UK
166/A5 Wheaton-Glenmont, Md,US
166/C5 Wheaton Village, NJ,US
163/G3 Wheeler (lake), Al,US
159/F3 Wheeler (peak), NM,US
158/D3 Wheeler (peak), Nv,US
154/V13 Wheeler A.F.B., Hi,US
165/Q15 Wheeling, Il,US
160/D3 Wheeling, WV,US
57/F3 Whernside (mtn.), Eng,UK
57/G2 Whickham, Eng,UK
117/G5 Whidbey (pt.), Austl.
165/B1 Whidbey (isl.), Wa,US
60/A6 Whiddy (isl.), Ire.
117/F3 Whinham (peak), Austl.
158/B2 Whiskeytown-Shasta-Trinity Nat'l Rec. Area, Ca,US
57/G2 Whitburn, Eng,UK
54/C5 Whitburn, Sc,UK
161/S8 Whitby, On,Can
57/H3 Whitby, Eng,UK
57/F6 Whitchurch, Eng,UK
59/E4 Whitchurch, Eng,UK
59/F3 Whitchurch, Eng,UK
58/C4 Whitchurch, Wal,UK
113/D White (isl.), Ant.
117/F2 White (lake), Austl.
161/K1 White (bay), Nf,Can
160/C1 White (lake), On,Can
84/H2 White (sea), Rus.
151/L4 White (pass), Ak,US
163/F3 White (riv.), Ar,US
158/E2 White (riv.), Co, Ut,US
160/C4 White (riv.), In,US
159/J5 White (lake), La,US
159/K4 White (riv.), La, Mo,US
165/E6 White (lake), Mi,US
159/G2 White (riv.), Ne, SD,US
158/D3 White (riv.), Nv,US
162/C3 White (riv.), Tx,US
160/D4 White (peak), Va,US
165/D3 White (riv.), Wa,US
165/P14 White (riv.), Wi,US
54/D5 Whiteadder Water (riv.), Sc,UK
161/K1 White Bear (riv.), Nf,Can
157/G3 White City, Sk,Can
54/C6 White Coomb (mtn.), Sc,UK
156/E2 Whitecourt, Ab,Can
166/A1 White Deer (cr.), Pa,US
54/C6 White Esk (riv.), Sc,UK
157/K4 Whiteface (riv.), Mn,US
57/F4 Whitefield, Eng,UK
160/C2 Whitefish (bay), On,Can, Mi,US
156/E3 Whitefish, Mt,US
151/L2 Whitefish Station, Yk,Can
58/B3 Whiteford (pt.), Wal,UK
157/G2 White Fox, Sk,Can
55/N13 Whitehall, Sc,UK
156/E4 Whitehall, Mt,US
166/C2 Whitehall (Fullerton), Pa,US
56/E2 Whitehaven, Eng,UK
56/C2 Whitehead, NI,UK
54/D1 Whitehills, Sc,UK
151/L3 Whitehorse (cap.), Yk,Can
59/E3 Whitehorse (hill), Eng,UK
166/B5 White Marsh, Md,US
166/D2 White Meadow Lake, NJ,US
151/J2 White Mountains Nat'l Rec. Area, Ak,US
157/K3 Whitemouth (riv.), Mb,Can
125/M5 White Nile (riv.), Sudan
166/B5 White Oak, Md,US
160/A1 White Otter (lake), On,Can
167/E1 White Plains, NY,US
160/C1 White River, On,Can
158/E4 Whiteriver, Az,US
162/B3 White Rock, NM,US
158/F4 White Sands, NM,US
158/F4 White Sands Nat'l Mon., NM,US
143/K8 Whiteside (chan.), Chile
156/F4 White Sulphur Springs, Mt,US
160/D4 White Sulphur Springs, WV,US
163/J3 Whiteville, NC,US
129/E4 White Volta (riv.), Burk., Gha.
157/L3 Whitewater (lake), On,Can
166/C2 Whitewater Kingdom/ Dorney Park, Pa,US
165/D3 White, West Fork (riv.), Wa,US
157/H3 Whitewood, Sk,Can
56/D2 Whithorn, Sc,UK
54/A6 Whiting Bay, Sc,UK
58/B3 Whitland, Wal,UK
57/G1 Whitley Bay, Eng,UK
168/D1 Whitman, Ma,US
158/C3 Whitney (mtn.), Ca,US
159/H4 Whitney (lake), Tx,US
58/B6 Whitsand (bay), Eng,UK
59/H4 Whitstable, Eng,UK
115/H4 Whitsunday (isl.), Austl.
118/C3 Whitsunday I. Nat'l Park, Austl.
164/B3 Whittier, Ca,US
119/G5 Whittlesea, Austl.
59/F1 Whittlesey, Eng,UK
57/G5 Whitwell, Eng,UK
57/F4 Whitworth, Eng,UK
152/F2 Wholdaia (lake), NW,Can
117/H5 Whyalla, Austl.
109/B2 Wiang Ko Sai Nat'l Park, Thai.
160/D2 Wiarton, On,Can
130/B2 Wiawer, Ugan.
68/C2 Wichelen, Belg.
159/H3 Wichita, Ks,US
159/H4 Wichita (mts.), Ok,US
159/H4 Wichita (riv.), Tx,US
162/D3 Wichita Falls, Tx,US
55/K7 Wick, Sc,UK
158/D4 Wickenburg, Az,US
59/G3 Wickford, Eng,UK
119/C3 Wickham (cape), Austl.
59/H2 Wickham Market, Eng,UK
168/F4 Wickliffe, Oh,US
60/D4 Wicklow (co.), Ire.
60/D4 Wicklow (mts.), Ire.
60/D3 Wicklow Gap (pass), Ire.
56/C6 Wicklow Head (pt.), Ire.
67/F4 Wickriede (riv.), Ger.
57/F5 Widnes, Eng,UK
69/G2 Wied (riv.), Ger.
67/G2 Wiedau (riv.), Ger.
67/F2 Wiefelstede, Ger.
67/F4 Wiehengebirge (ridge), Ger.
69/G2 Wiehl, Ger.
65/L4 Wieliczka, Pol.
68/C2 Wielsbeke, Belg.
65/K3 Wieluń, Pol.
65/J4 Wien (prov.), Aus.
65/J5 Wiener Neustadt, Aus.
65/J4 Wien (Vienna) (cap.), Aus.
73/L2 Wienwald (reg.), Aus.
65/M3 Wieprz (riv.), Pol.
66/D4 Wierden, Neth.
66/B3 Wieringermeerpolder (polder), Neth.
66/C3 Wieringerwerf, Neth.
65/K3 Wieruszów, Pol.
70/B2 Wiesbaden, Ger.
76/D2 Wiese (riv.), Ger.
88/H2 Wiese (isl.), Rus.
70/B1 Wieseck (riv.), Ger.
70/E3 Wiesent (riv.), Ger.
70/B4 Wiesloch, Ger.
67/E2 Wiesmoor, Ger.
67/E3 Wietmarschen, Ger.
67/G3 Wietze, Ger.
67/G3 Wietze (riv.), Ger.
65/K1 Wiezyca (peak), Pol.
57/F4 Wigan, Eng,UK
163/F4 Wiggins, Ms,US
59/E5 Wight, Isle of (isl.), Eng,UK
63/K5 Wigry (lake), Pol.
59/E1 Wigston, Eng,UK
57/E2 Wigton, Eng,UK
56/D2 Wigtown, Sc,UK
56/D2 Wigtown (bay), Sc,UK
66/C5 Wijchen, Neth.
66/D4 Wijhe, Neth.
66/C5 Wijk bij Duurstede, Neth.
125/N5 Wik'ro, Eth.
77/F3 Wil, Swi.
159/H2 Wilber, Ne,US
118/G8 Wilberforce, Austl.
57/H4 Wilberfoss, Eng,UK
168/D2 Wilbur (pt.), Ma,US
156/D4 Wilbur, Wa,US
159/J4 Wilburton, Ok,US
88/G1 Wilczek (isl.), Rus.
70/B5 Wildbad im Schwarzwald, Ger.
70/B5 Wildberg, Ger.
132/E4 Wild Coast (reg.), SAfr.
166/C2 Wild Creek (res.), Pa,US
67/F3 Wildeshausen, Ger.
161/Q8 Wildfield, On,Can
77/G3 Wildgrat (peak), Aus.
76/D5 Wildhorn (peak), Swi.
164/C3 Wildomar, Ca,US
157/J4 Wild Rice (riv.), Mn,US
77/G4 Wildspitze (peak), Aus.
76/D5 Wildstrubel (peak), Swi.
166/B6 Wild World, Md,US
132/E2 Wilge (riv.), SAfr.
168/G5 Wilhelm (res.), Pa,US
113/F Wilhelm II (coast), Ant.
139/G4 Wilhelmina (mts.), Sur.
66/C5 Wilhelminakanaal (can.), Neth.
67/G2 Wilhelmsburg, Ger.
67/F1 Wilhelmshaven, Ger.
166/C1 Wilkes-Barre, Pa,US
163/H2 Wilkesboro, NC,US
113/J Wilkes Land (reg.), Ant.
156/F2 Wilkie, Sk,Can
113/V Wilkins (sound), Ant.
168/H7 Wilkinsburg, Pa,US
151/N4 Will (mtn.), BC,Can
165/P16 Will (co.), Il,US
156/C4 Willamette (riv.), Or,US
119/C2 Willandra Nat'l Park, Austl.
156/B4 Willapa (bay), Wa,US
57/F5 Willaston, Eng,UK
158/E4 Willcox, Az,US
67/G5 Willebadessen, Ger.
68/D1 Willebroek, Belg.
150/D4 Willemstad (cap.), NAnt.
53/N7 Willesden, Eng,UK
119/B3 William (peak), Austl.
116/C5 William Bay Nat'l Park, Austl.
158/D4 Williams, Az,US
160/C4 Williamsburg, Ky,US
167/K9 Williamsburg, NY,US
160/E4 Williamsburg, Va,US
156/C2 Williams Lake, BC,Can
160/D4 Williamson, WV,US
166/A1 Williamsport, Pa,US
119/F5 Williamstown, Austl.
166/D4 Williamstown, NJ,US
161/S10 Williamsville, NY,US
66/D6 Willich, Ger.
168/B2 Willimantic, Ct,US
166/D3 Willingboro, NJ,US
57/G2 Willington, Eng,UK
57/G6 Willington, Eng,UK
162/E4 Willis, Tx,US
115/J3 Willis Islets (isls.), Austl.
156/C2 Williston (lake), BC,Can
163/H4 Williston, Fl,US
157/H3 Williston, ND,US
167/L8 Williston Park, NY,US
58/C4 Williton, Eng,UK
158/B3 Willits, Ca,US
157/K4 Willmar, Mn,US
168/F4 Willoughby Hills, Oh,US
156/C2 Willow (riv.), BC,Can
156/D4 Willow (cr.), Or,US
164/F8 Willowbrook, Ca,US
165/Q16 Willowbrook, Il,US
157/G3 Willow Bunch, Sk,Can
166/C3 Willow Grove, Pa,US
166/C3 Willow Grove Nav. Air Sta., Pa,US
117/G2 Willowra Abor. Land, Austl.
156/C2 Willow River, BC,Can
158/B3 Willows, Ca,US
114/D4 Wills (lake), Austl.
76/D1 Willstätt, Ger.
165/Q15 Wilmette, Il,US
53/P7 Wilmington, Eng,UK
164/F8 Wilmington, Ca,US
166/C4 Wilmington, De,US
163/J3 Wilmington, NC,US
160/D4 Wilmington, Oh,US
163/H4 Wilmington Island, Ga,US
57/F5 Wilmslow, Eng,UK
69/H2 Wilnsdorf, Ger.
108/G4 Wilpattu Nat'l Park, SrL.
66/B6 Wilrijk, Belg.
67/G2 Wilseder Berg (peak), Ger.
153/H2 Wilson (cape), NW,Can
164/B2 Wilson (mtn.), Ca,US
163/J3 Wilson, NC,US
161/S9 Wilson, NY,US
166/C2 Wilson, Pa,US
115/H7 Wilsons Promontory (pen.), Austl.
119/C3 Wilsons Promontory Nat'l Park, Austl.
59/E4 Wilton, Eng,UK
168/A3 Wilton, Ct,US
59/E4 Wiltshire (co.), Eng,UK
53/N7 Wimbledon, Eng,UK
58/E5 Wimborne Minster, Eng,UK
68/A2 Wimereux, Fr.
130/B3 Winam (gulf), Kenya
132/D3 Winburg, SAfr.
58/D4 Wincanton, Eng,UK
59/E3 Winchcombe, Eng,UK
59/G5 Winchelsea, Eng,UK
59/E4 Winchester, Eng,UK
168/A2 Winchester, Ct,US
160/C4 Winchester, Ky,US
163/G3 Winchester, Tn,US
160/E4 Winchester, Va,US
165/L12 Winchester Mystery House, Ca,US
165/P14 Wind (lake), Wi,US
156/F5 Wind (riv.), Wy,US
77/G2 Windach (riv.), Ger.
157/G5 Wind Cave Nat'l Park, SD,US
163/H3 Winder, Ga,US
57/F3 Windermere, Eng,UK
57/F3 Windermere (lake), Eng,UK
168/B2 Windham, Ct,US
168/B2 Windham (co.), Ct,US
126/C5 Windhoek (cap.), Namb.
157/K5 Windom, Mn,US
158/E4 Window Rock, Az,US
156/F5 Wind River (range), Wy,US
59/E3 Windrush (riv.), Eng,UK
118/G8 Windsor, Austl.
161/L1 Windsor, NF,Can
161/H2 Windsor, NS,Can
165/F7 Windsor, On,Can
161/G2 Windsor, Qu,Can
59/F4 Windsor, Eng,UK
168/B2 Windsor, Ct,US
168/B1 Windsor (dam), Ma,US
168/B2 Windsor Locks, Ct,US
149/H2 Windward (passg.), Cuba, Haiti
150/F4 Windward (isls.), NAm.
156/D3 Winfield, BC,Can
159/H3 Winfield, Ks,US
59/F3 Wing, Eng,UK
57/G2 Wingate, Eng,UK
68/C1 Wingene, Belg.
161/R10 Winger, On,Can
59/H4 Wingham, Eng,UK
116/D2 Winifred (lake), Austl.
157/M2 Winisk, On,Can
157/M2 Winisk (lake), On,Can
157/M2 Winisk (riv.), On,Can
157/J3 Winkler, Mb,Can
129/E5 Winneba, Gha.
160/B3 Winnebago (lake), Wi,US
158/C2 Winnemucca, Nv,US
70/C5 Winnenden, Ger.
157/J5 Winner, SD,US
165/Q15 Winnetka, Il,US
156/F4 Winnett, Mt,US
162/E4 Winnfield, La,US
116/B2 Winning, Austl.
157/J3 Winnipeg (cap.), Mb,Can
157/J2 Winnipeg (lake), Mb,Can
157/K3 Winnipeg (riv.), Mb, On,Can
157/J3 Winnipeg Beach, Mb,Can
157/J3 Winnipegosis, Mb,Can
157/H2 Winnipegosis (lake), Mb,Can
162/F3 Winnsboro, La,US
163/H3 Winnsboro, SC,US
161/Q9 Winona, On,Can
157/L4 Winona, Mn,US
66/E2 Winschoten, Neth.
58/D4 Winscombe, Eng,UK
57/F5 Winsford, Eng,UK
58/D4 Winsley, Eng,UK
59/F3 Winslow, Eng,UK
158/E4 Winslow, Az,US
168/A2 Winsted, Ct,US
163/H2 Winston-Salem, NC,US
66/D2 Winsum, Neth.
67/F6 Winterberg, Ger.
132/D4 Winterberge (mts.), SAfr.
58/D3 Winterbourne, Eng,UK
163/H4 Winter Haven, Fl,US
70/C6 Winterlingen, Ger.
163/H4 Winter Park, Fl,US
166/B4 Winters Run (riv.), Md,US
77/F3 Winterstaude (peak), Aus.
66/D5 Winterswijk, Neth.
77/E2 Winterthur, Swi.
166/C4 Winterthur Museum and Gardens, De,US
168/D1 Winthrop, Ma,US
161/G2 Winthrop, Me,US
165/Q15 Winthrop Harbor, Il,US
76/D1 Wintzenheim, Fr.
64/F3 Wipper (riv.), Ger.
67/H2 Wipperau (riv.), Ger.
67/E6 Wipperfürth, Ger.
57/G5 Wirksworth, Eng,UK
57/E5 Wirral (pen.), Eng,UK
59/G1 Wisbech, Eng,UK
76/D1 Wisches, Fr.
160/B2 Wisconsin (state), US
160/B2 Wisconsin Rapids, Wi,US
70/E1 Wisenta (riv.), Ger.
54/C5 Wishaw, Sc,UK
157/J4 Wishek, ND,US
65/K4 Wisła, Pol.
63/H4 Wiślany (lag.), Pol.
65/K2 Wisła (Vistula) (riv.), Pol.
65/L4 Wisłok (riv.), Pol.
65/L4 Wisłoka (riv.), Pol.
64/F2 Wismar, Ger.
69/G5 Wissembourg, Fr.
69/G2 Wissen, Ger.
59/G1 Wissey (riv.), Eng,UK
132/E2 Witbank, SAfr.
132/A2 Witberg (peak), Namb.
59/G3 Witham, Eng,UK
57/H5 Witham (riv.), Eng,UK
58/C5 Witheridge, Eng,UK
57/J4 Withernsea, Eng,UK
151/J3 Witherspoon (mtn.), Ak,US
163/H4 Withlacoochee (riv.), Fl, Ga,US
57/F4 Withnell, Eng,UK
117/G3 Witjira Nat'l Park, Austl.
132/D3 Wit Kei (riv.), SAfr.
65/J2 Witkowo, Pol.
59/E3 Witney, Eng,UK
65/H2 Witnica, Pol.
76/D2 Wittelsheim, Fr.
69/E2 Wittem, Neth.
67/E6 Witten, Ger.
77/F3 Wittenbach, Swi.
64/G3 Wittenberg, Ger.
64/F2 Wittenberge, Ger.
76/D2 Wittenheim, Fr.
59/F1 Wittering, Eng,UK
67/H3 Wittingen, Ger.
69/F4 Wittlich, Ger.
67/E1 Wittmund, Ger.
65/G1 Witton (pen.), Ger.
64/G2 Wittstock, Ger.
130/D3 Witu, Kenya
132/P12 Witwatersrand (reg.), SAfr.
67/G6 Witzenhausen, Ger.
58/C4 Wiveliscombe, Eng,UK
115/J5 Wivenhoe (lake), Austl.
59/G3 Wivenhoe, Eng,UK
165/E6 Wixom, Mi,US
139/H3 W. J. van Blommenstein (lake), Sur.
65/L2 Wkra (riv.), Pol.
65/K1 Władysławowo, Pol.
65/K2 Włocławek, Pol.
65/K2 Włocławek (prov.), Pol.
65/K2 Włocławskie (lake), Pol.
65/M3 Włodawa, Pol.
65/K3 Włoszczowa, Pol.
58/C1 Wnion (riv.), Wal,UK
130/B2 Wobulenzi, Ugan.
59/F3 Woburn Abbey, Eng,UK
59/F2 Woburn Sands, Eng,UK
119/C3 Wodonga, Austl.
65/K4 Wodzisław Śląski, Pol.
66/B4 Woerden, Neth.
69/G6 Woerth, Fr.
66/C3 Wognum, Neth.
77/E3 Wohlen, Swi.
76/D4 Wohlen bei Bern, Swi.
164/D4 Wohlford (lake), Ca,US
69/F5 Woippy, Fr.
111/H5 Wokam (isl.), Indo.
97/K2 Woken (riv.), China
53/M8 Woking, Eng,UK
59/F4 Wokingham, Eng,UK
101/D5 Wŏlch'ul-san Nat'l Park, SKor.
168/B2 Wolcott, Ct,US
161/S9 Wolcottsville, NY,US
53/N8 Woldingham, Eng,UK
120/D4 Woleai (atoll), Micr.
144/J6 Wolf (isl.), Ecu.
144/J7 Wolf (vol.), Ecu.
151/H2 Wolf (mtn.), Ak,US
165/R16 Wolf (lake), In,US
168/F5 Wolf (cr.), Oh,US
159/G3 Wolf (cr.), Ok, Tx,US
168/G5 Wolf (cr.), Pa,US
160/B2 Wolf (riv.), Wi,US
70/B6 Wolfach (riv.), Ger.
151/F3 Wolf Creek (mtn.), Ak,US
156/E4 Wolf Creek, Mt,US
64/G3 Wolfen, Ger.
67/H4 Wolfenbüttel, Ger.
70/B2 Wölfersheim, Ger.
67/G6 Wolfhagen, Ger.
157/G3 Wolf Point, Mt,US
77/H2 Wolfratshausen, Ger.
67/H4 Wolfsburg, Ger.
77/F3 Wolfurt, Aus.
65/G1 Wolgast, Ger.
65/H2 Woliński Nat'l Park, Pol.
152/E2 Wollaston (pen.), NW,Can
152/F3 Wollaston (lake), Sk,Can
143/L8 Wollaston (isl.), Chile
59/F2 Wollaston, Eng,UK
119/D2 Wollemi Nat'l Park, Austl.
119/D2 Wollongong, Austl.
132/D2 Wolmaransstad, SAfr.
73/J3 Wolnzach, Ger.
124/C6 Wologizi (range), Libr.
65/L2 Wołomin, Pol.
65/J3 Wołów, Pol.
132/L10 Wolseley, SAfr.
57/G2 Wolsingham, Eng,UK
65/J2 Wolsztyn, Pol.
68/D2 Woluwé-Saint-Lambert, Belg.
66/D3 Wolvega, Neth.
58/D1 Wolverhampton, Eng,UK
59/F2 Wolverton, Eng,UK
160/D2 Woman (riv.), On,Can
60/B6 Womanagh (riv.), Ire.
58/D1 Wombourne, Eng,UK
57/G4 Wombwell, Eng,UK
165/P15 Wonder (lake), Il,US
131/C2 Wonder Gorge, Zam.
71/F3 Wondreb (riv.), Ger.
119/C1 Wongalarroo (lake), Austl.
101/D4 Wŏnju, SKor.
119/C3 Wonnangatta-Moroka Nat'l Park, Austl.
101/D3 Wŏnsan, NKor.
116/C3 Wonyulgunna (peak), Austl.
157/H2 Wood (lake), Sk,Can
156/G3 Wood (mtn.), Sk,Can
151/K3 Wood (mtn.), Yk,Can
161/Q8 Woodbridge, On,Can
59/H2 Woodbridge, Eng,UK
168/A3 Woodbridge, Ct,US
167/D2 Woodbridge, NJ,US
152/E2 Wood Buffalo Nat'l Park, Ab, Yk,Can
161/Q9 Woodburn, On,Can
56/C2 Woodburn, NI,UK
156/C4 Woodburn, Or,US
166/C4 Woodbury, NJ,US
60/B4 Woodcock (hill), Ire.
165/Q16 Wood Dale, Il,US
118/D4 Woodgate Nat'l Park, Austl.
57/H5 Woodhall Spa, Eng,UK
165/F7 Woodhaven, Mi,US
165/L9 Woodland, Ca,US
164/F7 Woodland Hills, Ca,US
159/F3 Woodland Park, Co,US
120/E5 Woodlark (isl.), PNG
166/B5 Woodlawn, Md,US
59/F4 Woodley, Eng,UK
167/E2 Woodmere, NY,US
165/P16 Woodridge, Il,US
167/J8 Wood-Ridge, NJ,US
117/F3 Woodroffe (peak), Austl.
165/D2 Woods (cr.), Wa,US
57/F6 Woodseaves, Eng,UK
117/M8 Woodside, Austl.
161/H2 Woodstock, NB,Can
59/E3 Woodstock, Eng,UK
168/C2 Woodstock, Ct,US
165/P15 Woodstock, Il,US
160/E4 Woodstock, Va,US
163/F4 Woodville, Ms,US
162/E4 Woodville, Tx,US
159/H3 Woodward, Ok,US
58/D5 Wool, Eng,UK
58/D4 Woolavington, Eng,UK
54/E5 Wooler, Eng,UK
57/G1 Woolsington, Eng,UK
53/P7 Woolwich, Eng,UK
117/G4 Woomera Prohibited Area, Austl.
116/L6 Woonoloo (brook), Austl.
168/C1 Woonsocket, RI,US
159/H1 Woonsocket, SD,US
118/C4 Woorabinda Abor. Community, Austl.
116/B3 Wooramel (riv.), Austl.
57/F6 Woore, Eng,UK
168/F6 Wooster, Oh,US
59/E3 Wootton Basset, Eng,UK
76/D4 Worb, Swi.
132/B4 Worcester, SAfr.
58/D2 Worcester, Eng,UK
168/C1 Worcester, Ma,US
168/C1 Worcester (co.), Ma,US
58/D2 Worcester & Birmingham (can.), Eng,UK
168/C3 Worden (pond), RI,US
73/K3 Wörgl, Aus.
56/E2 Workington, Eng,UK
57/G5 Worksop, Eng,UK
156/G4 Worland, Wy,US
50/* World
167/J9 World Trade Ctr., New York City, NY,US
66/B4 Wormer, Neth.
53/N6 Wormley, Eng,UK
70/B3 Worms, Ger.
70/D5 Wörnitz (riv.), Ger.
67/F2 Worpswede, Ger.
70/B3 Wörrstadt, Ger.
70/B2 Worsbach (riv.), Ger.
57/G4 Worsbrough, Eng,UK
165/Q16 Worth, Il,US
70/B4 Wörth am Rhein, Ger.
59/F5 Worthing, Eng,UK
157/K5 Worthington, Mn,US
70/E6 Wörthsee (lake), Ger.
120/F3 Wotho (atoll), Mrsh.
120/G4 Wotje (atoll), Mrsh.
58/D3 Wotton under Edge, Eng,UK
66/C4 Woudenberg, Neth.
66/C5 Woudrichem, Neth.
149/F3 Wounta (lag.), Nic.
66/B5 Wouw, Neth.
111/F4 Wowoni (isl.), Indo.
57/H5 Wragby, Eng,UK
89/T2 Wrangel (isl.), Rus.
151/A5 Wrangell (cape), Ak,US
151/K3 Wrangell (mts.), Ak,US
151/K3 Wrangell-Saint Elias Nat'l Park & Prsv., Ak,US
57/J5 Wrangle, Eng,UK
55/J7 Wrath (cape), Sc,UK
159/G2 Wray, Co,US
53/M7 Wraysbury, Eng,UK
53/M7 Wraysbury (res.), Eng,UK
57/H6 Wreake (riv.), Eng,UK
115/K4 Wreck (reef), Austl.
132/B3 Wreck (pt.), SAfr.
58/D1 Wrekin, The (hill), Eng,UK
57/F5 Wrenbury, Eng,UK
168/C1 Wrentham, Ma,US
57/F5 Wrexham, Wal,UK
157/G5 Wright, Wy,US
59/G3 Writtle, Eng,UK
65/J3 Wrocław, Pol.
65/J3 Wrocław (prov.), Pol.
53/P8 Wrotham, Eng,UK
152/D1 Wrottesley (cape), NW,Can
58/D1 Wroxeter, Eng,UK
59/H1 Wroxham, Eng,UK
65/J2 Września, Pol.
65/J3 Wschowa, Pol.
105/F3 Wu (riv.), China
105/G3 Wu (riv.), China
103/C3 Wu'an, China
116/C4 Wubin, Austl.
103/C5 Wuchang, China
103/C5 Wuchang (lake), China
103/D3 Wucheng, China
105/H3 Wuchiu (isl.), Tai.
103/B2 Wuchuan, China
97/K2 Wudalianchi, China
105/F1 Wudang (mts.), China
105/F1 Wudang Shan (mtn.), China
103/D3 Wudi, China
103/B3 Wuding (riv.), China
103/B5 Wufeng, China
105/G3 Wugong (mts.), China
96/F4 Wuhai, China
103/C5 Wuhan, China
103/D4 Wuhe, China
103/D5 Wuhu, China
96/F3 Wujia (riv.), China
103/E5 Wujiang, China
66/E6 Wülfrath, Ger.
103/D4 Wulian, China
104/D3 Wulian (mts.), China
104/D4 Wuliang (mts.), China
105/F2 Wuling (mts.), China
107/J2 Wulong, China
129/H5 Wum, Camr.
104/D3 Wumeng (mts.), China
67/F2 Wümme (riv.), Ger.
106/C3 Wŭn, India
130/C3 Wundanyi, Kenya
116/L7 Wungong (brook), Austl.
116/L7 Wungong (res.), Austl.
67/F5 Wünnenberg, Ger.
71/F2 Wunsiedel, Ger.
67/G4 Wunstorf, Ger.
158/E4 Wupatki Nat'l Mon., Az,US
67/E6 Wupper (riv.), Ger.
67/E6 Wuppertal, Ger.
103/B3 Wuqi, China
102/C4 Wuqia, China
103/C3 Wuqiang, China
103/D3 Wuqiao, China
77/H1 Würm (can.), Ger.
69/F2 Würm (riv.), Ger.
71/E6 Würm (riv.), Ger.
129/G3 Wurno, Nga.
69/F2 Würselen, Ger.
70/C3 Würzburg, Ger.
97/H5 Wushan (lake), China
105/G2 Wusheng Guan (pass), China
102/C3 Wushi, China
67/G6 Wüstegarten (peak), Ger.
97/L2 Wusuli (Ussuri) (riv.), China, Rus.
77/E2 Wutach (riv.), Ger.
103/C3 Wutai, China
103/C3 Wutai Shan (peak), China
128/C4 Wuteve (peak), Libr.
70/D1 Wutha-Farnroda, Ger.
66/B6 Wuustwezel, Belg.
103/D5 Wuwei, China
103/E5 Wuxi, China
105/H2 Wuxi (riv.), China
103/C3 Wuxiang, China
103/C5 Wuxue, China
103/C4 Wuyang, China
103/C3 Wuyi, China
105/H3 Wuyi (mts.), China
96/F3 Wuyuan, China
97/K2 Wuyur (riv.), China
103/B3 Wuzhai, China
103/C4 Wuzhi, China
105/F5 Wuzhi (mts.), China
105/F5 Wuzhi Shan (peak), China
105/F4 Wuzhou, China
167/M8 Wyandanch, NY,US
165/F7 Wyandotte, Mi,US
165/F7 Wyandotte Nat'l Wild. Ref., Mi,US
119/D2 Wyangale (dam), Austl.
167/D1 Wyckoff, NJ,US
58/D3 Wye (riv.), UK
131/C4 Wyllie's (pass), SAfr.
58/D4 Wylye (riv.), Eng,UK
57/G6 Wymeswold, Eng,UK
59/H1 Wymondham, Eng,UK
163/F3 Wynne, Ar,US
118/F6 Wynnum, Austl.
157/G3 Wynyard, Sk,Can
156/F5 Wyoming (state), US
160/C3 Wyoming, Mi,US
156/F5 Wyoming (peak), Wy,US
158/E2 Wyoming (range), Wy,US
166/C3 Wyomissing, Pa,US
119/B2 Wyperfeld Nat'l Park, Austl.
116/D5 Wyralinu (peak), Austl.
57/F4 Wyre (riv.), Eng,UK
65/L2 Wyszków, Pol.
160/D4 Wytheville, Va,US

X

109/D4 Xa Binh Long, Viet.
148/B3 Xadani, Mex.
102/E5 Xainza, China
106/E2 Xaitongmoin, China
131/D4 Xaiva, Moz.
131/D5 Xai-Xai, Moz.
104/E4 Xam (riv.), Laos
109/D1 Xam Nua, Laos
109/D3 Xan (riv.), Viet.
66/D5 Xanten, Ger.
81/J2 Xánthi, Gre.
141/B3 Xanxerê, Braz.
125/Q7 Xarardheere, Som.
109/E4 Xa Song Luy, Viet.
126/C3 Xassengue, Ang.
109/D3 Xa Tho Thanh, Viet.
137/J6 Xavantes (mts.), Braz.
141/B2 Xavantes (res.), Braz.
109/D4 Xa Vo Dat, Viet.
102/D3 Xayar, China
147/J4 Xel-há (ruins), Mex.
160/D4 Xenia, Oh,US
109/D2 Xeno, Laos
131/B4 Xhumo, Bots.
103/E2 Xi (lake), China
101/A2 Xi (riv.), China
104/D3 Xiaguan, China
103/C3 Xiajin, China
105/H3 Xiamen, China
103/B4 Xi'an, China
103/B5 Xianfeng, China
105/G3 Xiang (riv.), China
96/G5 Xiangcheng, China
103/C4 Xiangfan, China
103/B4 Xiangfen, China
103/D3 Xianghe, China
105/G3 Xianghua (mtn.), China
109/C2 Xiang Khoang (plat.), Laos
103/B4 Xiangning, China
97/H5 Xiangshui, China
105/G2 Xiangtan, China
105/G3 Xiangtan, China
104/D3 Xiangyun, China
105/J2 Xianju, China
103/C5 Xianning, China
104/D2 Xianshui (riv.), China
103/C5 Xiantao, China
105/H2 Xianxia (mtn.), China
96/F5 Xianyang, China
103/C3 Xiao (riv.), China
104/D3 Xiao (riv.), China
105/F3 Xiao (riv.), China
97/J1 Xiaobole (peak), China
103/C5 Xiaogan, China
97/K2 Xiao Hinggang (mts.), China
104/D2 Xiaojin (riv.), China
105/G3 Xiaomei (pass), China
103/D3 Xiaoqing (riv.), China
103/L9 Xiaoshan, China
103/C3 Xiaowutai Shan (peak), China
103/D4 Xiao Xian, China
103/B3 Xiaoyi, China
148/D2 Xiatil, Mex.
103/D4 Xiayi, China
107/F2 Xibaxa (riv.), China
103/C4 Xicheng Shan (mtn.), China
107/H3 Xichou, China
103/B4 Xichuan, China
147/F4 Xicohténcatl, Mex.
147/F4 Xicotepec, Mex.
105/J2 Xidongting (mtn.), China
103/C4 Xifei (riv.), China
96/F4 Xifeng, China
97/J3 Xifeng, China
106/E2 Xigazê, China
96/E5 Xihan (riv.), China
103/B3 Xihekou, China
103/C4 Xihua, China

230
Xijir – Zhang

102/F4 **Xijir Ulan** (lake), China
103/E2 **Xiliao** (riv.), China
107/J3 **Xilin**, China
104/C4 **Ximeng Vazu Zizhixian**, China
105/H2 **Xin** (riv.), China
103/C4 **Xin'an**, China
103/D5 **Xin'an** (riv.), China
105/H2 **Xin'anjiang** (res.), China
131/D5 **Xinavane**, Moz.
97/H2 **Xin Barag Zuoqi**, China
101/C2 **Xinbin**, China
103/C4 **Xincai**, China
105/J2 **Xinchang**, China
103/C3 **Xincheng**, China
107/K3 **Xinfeng**, China
105/G4 **Xinfengjiang** (res.), China
105/F3 **Xing'an**, China
103/E2 **Xingcheng**, China
126/C2 **Xinge**, Ang.
103/D4 **Xinghua**, China
102/D3 **Xingjiang Uygur Aut. Reg.**, China
97/L3 **Xingkai** (lake), China
103/D2 **Xinglong**, China
103/B5 **Xingshan**, China
103/C3 **Xingtai**, China
137/H4 **Xingu** (riv.), Braz.
103/C4 **Xingyang**, China
104/E3 **Xingyi**, China
103/E3 **Xinhe**, China
105/F3 **Xinhuang Dongzu Zizhixian**, China
96/E4 **Xining**, China
90/K6 **Xining Shi**, China
103/C3 **Xinji**, China
103/B4 **Xinjiang**, China
90/J5 **Xinjiang** (reg.), China
101/A3 **Xinjin**, China
103/C3 **Xinle**, China
101/B2 **Xinmin**, China
104/D3 **Xinping Yizu**, China
105/F3 **Xinshao**, China
103/D4 **Xintai**, China
103/C4 **Xinxiang**, China
103/C4 **Xinyang**, China
103/C4 **Xinye**, China
103/D4 **Xinyi**, China
105/G3 **Xinyu**, China
102/D3 **Xinyuan**, China
103/C4 **Xinzheng**, China
103/C5 **Xinzhou**, China
103/D3 **Xiong Xian**, China
103/C4 **Xiping**, China
96/E5 **Xiqing** (mts.), China
140/B3 **Xique-Xique**, Braz.
107/J2 **Xishui**, China
103/E5 **Xitang**, China
105/H2 **Xitianmu** (peak), China
105/G2 **Xiu** (riv.), China
103/D5 **Xiuning**, China
107/J2 **Xiuwen**, China
103/C4 **Xiuwu**, China
101/B2 **Xiuyan**, China
106/E2 **Xixabangma** (peak), China
104/D2 **Xixi** (riv.), China
103/B4 **Xixia**, China
104/E4 **Xiyang** (riv.), China
104/B2 **Xizang** (Tibet Aut. Reg.), China
103/E3 **Xizhong** (isl.), China
147/K8 **Xochicalco** (ruins), Mex.
147/Q10 **Xochimilco**, Mex.
147/M8 **Xochitlán**, Mex.
105/H3 **Xu** (riv.), China
103/B5 **Xuan'en**, China
103/C2 **Xuanhua**, China
104/E3 **Xuanwei**, China
103/C4 **Xuchang**, China
125/P7 **Xuddur** (Oddur), Som.
104/C3 **Xue** (mts.), China
103/E5 **Xuedou** (peak), China
96/D4 **Xugin Gol** (riv.), China
103/B4 **Xun** (riv.), China
105/F4 **Xun** (riv.), China
97/K2 **Xunke**, China
103/C4 **Xun Xian**, China
103/B4 **Xunyang**, China
105/F4 **Xuwen**, China
103/D4 **Xuyi**, China
104/E2 **Xuyong**, China
103/D4 **Xuzhou**, China

Y

104/D2 **Ya'an**, China
124/G7 **Yabassi**, Camr.
125/N7 **Yabēlo**, Eth.
96/F1 **Yablonovyy** (ridge), Rus.
150/E3 **Yabucoa**, PR
99/G2 **Yabuki**, Japan
112/D3 **Yacgam** (mtn.), Phil.
104/E3 **Yachi** (riv.), China
99/J7 **Yachiyo**, Japan
99/K9 **Yachiyo**, Japan
141/A4 **Yacuí** (riv.), Braz.
136/F8 **Yacuiba**, Bol.
138/D2 **Yacumbu Nat'l Park**, Ven.
106/C4 **Yādgīr**, India
100/G8 **Yaeyama** (isl.), Japan
99/L9 **Yagi**, Japan
124/J5 **Yagoua**, Camr.
96/D4 **Yagradagzê** (peak), China
148/E3 **Yaguale** (riv.), Hon.
142/G3 **Yaguarón** (riv.), Uru.
144/D1 **Yaguas** (riv.), Col., Peru
149/J2 **Yague del Sur** (riv.), DRep.
99/N10 **Yahagi** (riv.), Japan
146/E4 **Yahualica de Gonzalez Gallo**, Mex.
92/C2 **Yahyalı**, Turk.
99/F2 **Yaita**, Japan
99/F3 **Yaizu**, Japan
91/E1 **Yakacık**, Turk.
97/J2 **Yakeshi**, China
156/C4 **Yakima**, Wa,US
156/C4 **Yakima** (riv.), Wa,US
100/B1 **Yakishiri** (isl.), Japan
129/E3 **Yako**, Burk.
125/K7 **Yakoma**, Zaire
83/F4 **Yakoruda**, Bul.
98/B5 **Yaku** (isl.), Japan
98/B5 **Yaku-Kirishima Nat'l Park**, Japan
100/B2 **Yakumo**, Japan
99/K9 **Yakuno**, Japan
151/K4 **Yakutat** (bay), Ak,US
89/N3 **Yakut Aut. Rep.**, Rus.
89/N3 **Yakutsk**, Rus.
109/C5 **Yala**, Thai.
148/E1 **Yalahua** (lag.), Mex.
117/F4 **Yalata Abor. Land**, Austl.
148/D2 **Yalbac** (hills), Belz.
116/B5 **Yalgorup Nat'l Park**, Austl.
159/K4 **Yalobusha** (riv.), Ms,US
124/J6 **Yaloké**, CAfr.
104/D2 **Yalong** (riv.), China
83/J5 **Yalova**, Turk.
86/E3 **Yalta**, Ukr.
97/J3 **Yalu** (riv.), China, NKor.
92/B2 **Yalvaç**, Turk.
100/B4 **Yamada**, Japan
98/B4 **Yamaga**, Japan
99/G1 **Yamagata**, Japan
99/F1 **Yamagata** (pref.), Japan
98/B3 **Yamaguchi**, Japan
98/B3 **Yamaguchi** (pref.), Japan
88/G2 **Yamal** (pen.), Rus.
88/G3 **Yamal-Nenets Aut. Okr.**, Rus.
99/F3 **Yamanashi** (pref.), Japan
118/B2 **Yamanie** (falls), Austl.
118/B2 **Yamanie Falls Nat'l Park**, Austl.
88/F4 **Yamantau** (peak), Rus.
85/N5 **Yamantau, Gora** (peak), Rus.
99/N9 **Yamaoka**, Japan
116/D3 **Yamarna Abor. Rsv.**, Austl.
116/D4 **Yamarna Abor. Rsv.**, Austl.
99/L10 **Yamashiro**, Japan
99/F2 **Yamato**, Japan
99/L10 **Yamato** (riv.), Japan
99/L10 **Yamato-Kōriyama**, Japan
98/D3 **Yamatotakada**, Japan
99/M10 **Yamazoe**, Japan
125/L7 **Yambio**, Sudan
83/H4 **Yambol**, Bul.
104/C4 **Yamethin**, Burma
111/K4 **Yamin** (peak), Indo.
118/A4 **Yamma Yamma** (lake), Austl.
99/G1 **Yamoto**, Japan
128/D5 **Yamoussoukro** (cap.), IvC.
158/F2 **Yampa** (riv.), Co,US
106/C2 **Yamuna** (riv.), India
108/D2 **Yamunānagar**, India
107/E2 **Yamzho Yumco** (lake), China
103/B3 **Yan** (riv.), China
108/H4 **Yan** (riv.), SrL.
89/P3 **Yana** (riv.), Rus.
98/B4 **Yanagawa**, Japan
98/C4 **Yanai**, Japan
85/M4 **Yanaul**, Rus.
107/H2 **Yanbian**, China
103/C4 **Yancheng**, China
103/E4 **Yancheng**, China
116/B4 **Yanchep Nat'l Park**, Austl.
121/T12 **Yandé** (isl.), NCal.
116/C2 **Yandeearra Abor. Rsv.**, Austl.
104/B5 **Yandoon**, Burma
125/K7 **Yangambi**, Zaire
104/C3 **Yangbi** (riv.), China
103/C4 **Yangcheng**, China
103/L8 **Yangcheng** (lake), China
105/H3 **Yangdang** (mts.), Laos
101/D2 **Yanggang-do** (prov.), NKor.
103/C2 **Yanggao**, China
103/C3 **Yanggu**, China
101/D3 **Yanggu**, SKor.
105/F4 **Yangjiang**, China
101/A4 **Yangma** (isl.), China
105/F3 **Yangming** (peak), China
104/C5 **Yangon** (Rangoon) (cap.), Burma
103/C3 **Yangqu**, China
103/C3 **Yangquan**, China
107/K3 **Yangshan**, China
107/K3 **Yangshuo**, China
104/C3 **Yangtouyan**, China
105/H2 **Yangtze** (Chang) (riv.), China
104/D3 **Yangtze** (Jinsha) (riv.), China
125/P5 **Yangudi Rassa Nat'l Park**, Eth.
103/D3 **Yangxin**, China
105/G2 **Yangxin**, China
101/E3 **Yangyang**, SKor.
103/C2 **Yangyuan**, China
103/D4 **Yangzhong**, China
103/D4 **Yangzhou**, China
97/K3 **Yanji**, China
103/C4 **Yanjin**, China
104/E2 **Yanjin**, China
129/H4 **Yankari Game Rsv.**, Nga.
167/K8 **Yankee Stadium, New York City**, NY,US
157/J5 **Yankton**, SD,US
103/C4 **Yanling**, China
103/C3 **Yanmen Guan** (pass), China
103/D3 **Yanshan**, China
103/C4 **Yanshi**, China
97/K2 **Yanshou**, China
103/E3 **Yantai**, China
104/E2 **Yanting**, China
103/C2 **Yantong Shan** (mtn.), China
119/G5 **Yan Yean** (res.), Austl.
104/D3 **Yanyuan**, China
103/D4 **Yanzhou**, China
98/D3 **Yao**, Japan
107/H2 **Yao'an**, China
103/B3 **Yaodian**, China
124/H7 **Yaoundé** (cap.), Camr.
120/C4 **Yap** (isls.), Micr.
139/E4 **Yapacana Nat'l Park**, Ven.
111/J4 **Yapen** (isl.), Indo.
111/J4 **Yapen** (str.), Indo.
167/F2 **Yaphank**, NY,US
146/C3 **Yaqui**, Mex.
146/C2 **Yaqui** (riv.), Mex.
59/E5 **Yar** (riv.), Eng,UK
149/G1 **Yara**, Cuba
138/D2 **Yaracuy** (state), Ven.
92/C1 **Yaralıgöz** (peak), Turk.
111/J4 **Yaramaniapuka** (mtn.), Indo.
85/K4 **Yaransk**, Rus.
91/B1 **Yardımcı** (pt.), Turk.
166/D3 **Yardville-Groveville**, NJ,US
59/H1 **Yare** (riv.), Eng,UK
138/C4 **Yarí** (riv.), Col.
99/E2 **Yari-ga-take** (mtn.), Japan
83/J5 **Yarımca**, Turk.
138/D2 **Yaritagua**, Ven.
102/C4 **Yarkant** (riv.), China
161/H3 **Yarmouth**, NS,Can
84/H4 **Yaroslavl'**, Rus.
84/H4 **Yaroslavl' Obl.**, Rus.
119/G5 **Yarra** (riv.), Austl.
119/G5 **Yarra Glen**, Austl.
138/C3 **Yarumal**, Col.
120/G6 **Yasawa Group** (isls.), Fiji
86/C1 **Yasel'da** (riv.), Bela.
100/B4 **Yashima**, Japan
99/H7 **Yashio**, Japan
99/K10 **Yashiro**, Japan
87/L2 **Yasnyy**, Rus.
109/D3 **Yasothon**, Thai.
94/F4 **Yas, Sir Bani** (isl.), UAE
99/M9 **Yasu**, Japan
99/M10 **Yasu** (riv.), Japan
98/C3 **Yasugi**, Japan
92/D1 **Yasun** (pt.), Turk.
138/B5 **Yasuni Nat'l Park**, Ecu.
99/G2 **Yatabe**, Japan
92/B2 **Yatağan**, Turk.
58/D3 **Yate**, Eng,UK
59/F4 **Yateley**, Eng,UK
129/E3 **Yatenga** (prov.), Burk.
159/J3 **Yates Center**, Ks,US
152/G2 **Yathkyed** (lake), NW,Can
99/M9 **Yatomi**, Japan
99/E2 **Yatsuo**, Japan
98/B4 **Yatsushiro**, Japan
130/C3 **Yatta** (plat.), Kenya
91/D4 **Yaṭṭah**, WBnk.
58/D4 **Yatton**, Eng,UK
144/C4 **Yauca** (riv.), Peru
150/E3 **Yauco**, PR
147/K7 **Yautepec**, Mex.
144/C2 **Yavari** (riv.), Peru
144/C2 **Yavarí Mirim** (riv.), Peru
106/C3 **Yavatmāl**, India
88/H2 **Yavay** (pen.), Rus.
148/C2 **Yaveo**, Mex.
139/E4 **Yávita**, Ven.
149/G4 **Yaviza**, Pan.
91/F8 **Yavne**, Isr.
92/D2 **Yavuzeli**, Turk.
99/J7 **Yawahara**, Japan
99/L10 **Yawata**, Japan
98/C4 **Yawatahama**, Japan
148/D2 **Yaxchilán** (ruins), Mex.
59/F2 **Yaxley**, Eng,UK
91/E2 **Yayladağı**, Turk.
93/H4 **Yazd**, Iran
93/H3 **Yazd** (gov.), Iran
163/F3 **Yazoo** (riv.), Ms,US
163/F3 **Yazoo City**, Ms,US
71/H7 **Ybbs** (riv.), Aus.
62/C3 **Yding Skovhøj** (peak), Den.
109/B3 **Ye**, Burma
57/G4 **Yeadon**, Eng,UK
58/B6 **Yealmpton**, Eng,UK
109/C4 **Yeay Sen** (cape), Camb.
102/C4 **Yecheng**, China
75/E3 **Yecla**, Sp.
147/N7 **Yecuatla**, Mex.
92/B1 **Yedigöller Nat'l Park**, Turk.
93/M6 **Yedikule**, Turk.
86/F1 **Yefremov**, Rus.
87/G3 **Yegorlak** (riv.), Rus.
147/M8 **Yehualtepec**, Mex.
91/F7 **Yehud**, Isr.
125/M7 **Yei**, Sudan
85/P4 **Yekaterinburg Obl.**, Rus.
85/P4 **Yekaterinburg** (Sverdlovsk), Rus.
100/E1 **Yekateriny** (chan.), Rus.
85/M5 **Yelabuga**, Rus.
87/G2 **Yelan'**, Rus.
86/F1 **Yelets**, Rus.
89/Q4 **Yelizavety** (cape), Rus.
89/R4 **Yelizovo**, Rus.
55/P12 **Yell** (isl.), Sc,UK
123/R16 **Yellel**, Alg.
97/J4 **Yellow** (sea), Asia
163/G4 **Yellow** (riv.), Al, Fl,US
168/G6 **Yellow** (cr.), Oh,US
166/A3 **Yellow Breeches** (cr.), Pa,US
157/G3 **Yellow Grass**, Sk,Can
97/H4 **Yellow** (Huang) (riv.), China
152/E2 **Yellowknife** (cap.), NW,Can
152/E2 **Yellowknife** (riv.), NW,Can
168/G6 **Yellow, North Fork** (cr.), Oh,US
157/G4 **Yellowstone** (riv.), Mt,US
156/F4 **Yellowstone** (lake), Wy,US
156/F4 **Yellowstone Nat'l Park**, Wy,US
162/E2 **Yellville**, Ar,US
58/B6 **Yelverton**, Eng,UK
96/D4 **Yema** (riv.), China
94/E5 **Yemen**
86/F2 **Yenakiyevo**, Ukr.
104/B4 **Yenangyaung**, Burma
109/D1 **Yen Bai**, Viet.
129/E4 **Yendi**, Gha.
102/C4 **Yengisar**, China
86/E4 **Yenice** (riv.), Turk.
83/J5 **Yenişehir**, Turk.
88/J3 **Yenisey** (riv.), Rus.
88/K4 **Yeniseysk**, Rus.
109/D1 **Yen Minh**, Viet.
116/E3 **Yeo** (lake), Austl.
58/D5 **Yeo** (riv.), Eng,UK
95/K4 **Yeola**, India
116/E3 **Yeo Lake Nature Rsv.**, Austl.
58/D5 **Yeovil**, Eng,UK
118/C3 **Yeppoon**, Austl.
81/H3 **Yerakovoúni** (peak), Gre.
68/A4 **Yères** (riv.), Fr.
87/H4 **Yerevan** (cap.), Arm.
158/C3 **Yerington**, Nv,US
92/C2 **Yerköy**, Turk.
102/C1 **Yermak**, Kaz.
88/H4 **Yermentau**, Kaz.
91/D4 **Yeroḥam**, Isr.
72/D2 **Yerre** (riv.), Fr.
53/T10 **Yerres**, Fr.
53/U11 **Yerres** (riv.), Fr.
144/B3 **Yerupaja** (peak), Peru
91/D4 **Yerushalayim** (Jerusalem) (cap.), Isr.
104/B4 **Yesagyo**, Burma
101/D4 **Yesan**, SKor.
102/A1 **Yesil'**, Kaz.
92/C2 **Yeşilhisar**, Turk.
86/F4 **Yeşilırmak** (riv.), Turk.
91/E1 **Yeşilkent**, Turk.
101/D3 **Yesŏng** (riv.), NKor.
87/G3 **Yessentuki**, Rus.
54/D5 **Yetholm**, Sc,UK
58/D5 **Yetminster**, Eng,UK
72/B3 **Yeu** (isl.), Fr.
106/B3 **Yevla**, India
87/H4 **Yevlakh**, Azer.
86/E3 **Yevpatoriya**, Ukr.
103/D3 **Ye Xian**, China
86/G3 **Yeya** (riv.), Rus.
86/F3 **Yeysk**, Rus.
103/C4 **Yi** (riv.), China
143/G2 **Yi** (riv.), Uru.
81/H2 **Yiannitsá**, Gre.
81/J4 **Yiaros** (isl.), Gre.
104/E2 **Yibin**, China
103/B5 **Yichang**, China
103/B4 **Yicheng**, China
103/C5 **Yicheng**, China
103/C4 **Yichuan**, China
105/G3 **Yichun**, China
107/K2 **Yifeng**, China
105/H3 **Yihuang**, China
97/K2 **Yilan**, China
92/D1 **Yıldız** (peak), Turk.
92/D2 **Yıldızeli**, Turk.
93/N6 **Yildiz Park**, Turk.
97/J1 **Yilehuli** (mts.), China
104/E3 **Yiliang**, China
104/B3 **Yima**, China
104/D3 **Yimen**, China
97/J2 **Yimin** (riv.), China
96/F3 **Yin** (mts.), China
103/D4 **Yinan**, China
96/F4 **Yinchuan**, China
116/D4 **Yindarlgooda** (lake), Austl.
103/C4 **Ying** (riv.), China
105/G2 **Yingcheng**, China
107/K3 **Yingde**, China
101/B2 **Yingkou**, China
103/C5 **Yingshan**, China
103/D4 **Yingshang**, China
105/H2 **Yingtan**, China
102/D3 **Yining**, China
104/B2 **Yi'ong** (riv.), China
125/M6 **Yirol**, Sudan
105/F3 **Yishan**, China
103/D4 **Yishui**, China
103/F2 **Yitong** (riv.), China
96/C3 **Yiwu**, China
103/D5 **Yixing**, China
103/C4 **Yiyang**, China
105/G2 **Yiyang**, China
103/D3 **Yiyuan**, China
107/K2 **Yizhang**, China
103/D4 **Yizheng**, China
56/E6 **Y Llethr** (mtn.), Wal,UK
63/K1 **Ylöjärvi**, Fin.
62/G2 **Yngaren** (lake), Swe.
162/D4 **Yoakum**, Tx,US
101/D5 **Yŏch'ŏn**, SKor.
98/D3 **Yodo** (riv.), Japan
89/P4 **Yoduma** (riv.), Rus.
112/D2 **Yog** (pt.), Phil.
124/J4 **Yogoum** (well), Chad
110/D5 **Yogyakarta**, Indo.
156/D3 **Yoho Nat'l Park**, BC,Can
100/B2 **Yoichi**, Japan
148/D3 **Yojoa** (lake), Hon.
124/J7 **Yokadouma**, Camr.
98/E3 **Yōkaichi**, Japan
98/D3 **Yokawa**, Japan
98/E3 **Yokkaichi**, Japan
99/F3 **Yokohama**, Japan
99/H7 **Yokohama** (inset), Japan
99/F3 **Yokosuka**, Japan
100/B4 **Yokote**, Japan
124/H6 **Yola**, Nga.
149/E4 **Yolaina, Serranías de** (range), Nic.
165/L9 **Yolo** (co.), Ca,US
109/C2 **Yom** (riv.), Thai.
126/B1 **Yombi**, Gabon
105/F4 **Yon** (riv.), China
72/C3 **Yon** (riv.), Fr.
98/C3 **Yonago**, Japan
100/G8 **Yonaguni** (isl.), Japan
100/K7 **Yonaha-dake** (peak), Japan
100/B3 **Yoneshiro** (riv.), Japan
99/G2 **Yonezawa**, Japan
105/H3 **Yong'an**, China
105/F3 **Yong'an** (pass), China
96/E4 **Yongchang**, China
103/D4 **Yongcheng**, China
101/E5 **Yŏngch'ŏn**, SKor.
107/G3 **Yongde**, China
103/H7 **Yongding** (riv.), China
101/E4 **Yŏngdŏk**, SKor.
101/F6 **Yongdungpo**, SKor.
107/J3 **Yongfu**, China
103/B3 **Yonghe**, China
101/D3 **Yŏnghŭng** (riv.), NKor.
103/B4 **Yongji**, China
101/F6 **Yŏngjong** (isl.), SKor.
101/E4 **Yŏngju**, SKor.
101/D4 **Yongmun-san** (mtn.), SKor.
103/C3 **Yongnian**, China
109/E1 **Yongning**, China
103/D3 **Yongqing**, China
103/H7 **Yongqing**, China
107/H2 **Yongren**, China
101/D5 **Yŏngsan** (riv.), SKor.
104/D2 **Yongshan**, China
105/D3 **Yongsheng**, China
107/J2 **Yongshun**, China
101/E4 **Yŏngwŏl**, SKor.
107/K2 **Yongxin**, China
105/F3 **Yongzhou**, China
167/E2 **Yonkers**, NY,US
72/E2 **Yonne** (riv.), Fr.
99/H7 **Yono**, Japan
102/C4 **Yopurga**, China
164/C3 **Yorba Linda**, Ca,US
114/G2 **York** (cape), Austl.
114/C2 **York** (sound), Austl.
161/R8 **York**, On,Can
161/Q8 **York** (co.), On,Can
161/H1 **York** (riv.), Qu,Can
57/G4 **York**, Eng,UK
163/G4 **York**, Al,US
159/H2 **York**, Ne,US
166/B4 **York**, Pa,US
166/B3 **York** (co.), Pa,US
163/H3 **York**, SC,US
160/E4 **York** (riv.), Va,US
117/H5 **Yorke** (pen.), Austl.
157/J1 **York Landing**, Mb,Can
57/G4 **York Minster**, Eng,UK
57/F3 **Yorkshire Dales Nat'l Park**, Eng,UK
57/H3 **Yorkshire Wolds** (hills), Eng,UK
157/H3 **Yorkton**, Sk,Can
167/E1 **Yorktown Heights**, NY,US
57/G3 **York, Vale of** (val.), Eng,UK
148/E3 **Yoro**, Hon.
99/M9 **Yōrō**, Japan
99/J7 **Yōrō** (riv.), Japan
99/M10 **Yoroi-zaki** (pt.), Japan
100/K7 **Yoron** (isl.), Japan
96/F2 **Yöröö**, Mong.
57/F6 **Yorton**, Eng,UK
129/F4 **Yorubaland** (plat.), Nga.
158/C3 **Yosemite Nat'l Park**, Ca,US
98/C4 **Yoshida**, Japan
98/D3 **Yoshii** (riv.), Japan
99/H7 **Yoshikawa**, Japan
98/D3 **Yoshimo** (riv.), Japan
99/L10 **Yoshino**, Japan
99/L10 **Yoshino** (riv.), Japan
98/E3 **Yoshino-Kumano Nat'l Park**, Japan
85/L4 **Yoshkar-Ola**, Rus.
101/D5 **Yŏsu**, SKor.
100/B2 **Yōtei-san** (mtn.), Japan
99/J7 **Yotsukaidō**, Japan
105/G3 **You** (peak), China
105/E4 **You** (riv.), China
105/F2 **You** (riv.), China
60/C6 **Youghal** (bay), Ire.
119/D2 **Young**, Austl.
143/F2 **Young**, Uru.
165/C3 **Youngs** (lake), Wa,US
161/R9 **Youngstown**, NY,US
168/G5 **Youngstown**, Oh,US
107/J2 **Youyang**, China
97/L2 **Youyi**, China
139/E3 **Yovi** (peak), Ven.
92/C2 **Yozgat**, Turk.
165/E7 **Ypsilanti**, Mi,US
56/D6 **Yr Eifl** (mtn.), Wal,UK
158/B2 **Yreka**, Ca,US
68/B2 **Yser** (riv.), Fr.
62/E4 **Ystad**, Swe.
58/C3 **Ystalyfera**, Wal,UK
58/C3 **Ystradgynlais**, Wal,UK
58/C3 **Ystrad Mynach**, Wal,UK
58/C2 **Ystwyth** (riv.), Wal,UK
54/D2 **Ythan** (riv.), Sc,UK
62/A1 **Ytre Sula** (isl.), Nor.
107/J3 **Yu** (riv.), China
105/J4 **Yü** (peak), Tai.
103/C5 **Yuan** (lake), China
105/F2 **Yuan** (riv.), China
105/G3 **Yuan** (riv.), China
103/B5 **Yuan'an**, China
105/F3 **Yuanbao** (mtn.), China
103/C3 **Yuanping**, China
103/B4 **Yuanqu**, China
104/D4 **Yuan** (Red) (riv.), China
103/C3 **Yuanshi**, China
103/C4 **Yuanyang**, China
158/B3 **Yuba City**, Ca,US
100/B2 **Yūbari**, Japan
100/C1 **Yūbetsu**, Japan
100/C2 **Yūbetsu** (riv.), Japan
164/C2 **Yucaipa**, Ca,US
148/E1 **Yucatan** (chan.), Cuba, Mex.
148/D2 **Yucatan** (pen.), Mex.
148/D1 **Yucatán** (state), Mex.
158/D4 **Yucca**, Az,US
103/C4 **Yucheng**, China
103/D3 **Yucheng**, China
103/C3 **Yuci**, China
105/G3 **Yudu**, China
104/E2 **Yuechi**, China
105/G2 **Yuelu** (mtn.), China
117/F2 **Yuendumu Abor. Land**, Austl.
105/J2 **Yueqing**, China
105/H2 **Yuexi**, China
104/D2 **Yuexi** (riv.), China
105/G2 **Yueyang**, China
85/K3 **Yug** (riv.), Rus.
85/P1 **Yugorskiy** (pen.), Rus.
82/D3 **Yugoslavia**
103/L9 **Yuhang**, China
105/G3 **Yuhua** (mtn.), China
105/J2 **Yuhuan**, China
99/F2 **Yūki**, Japan
152/B2 **Yukon** (riv.), Can., US
151/K2 **Yukon-Charley Rivers Nat'l Prsv.**, Ak,US
151/L3 **Yukon Crossing**, Yk,Can
151/F3 **Yukon Delta Nat'l Wild. Ref.**, Ak,US
151/J2 **Yukon Flats Nat'l Wild. Ref.**, Ak,US
152/C2 **Yukon Territory** (terr.), Can.
93/F2 **Yüksekova**, Turk.
98/B4 **Yukuhashi**, Japan
117/F3 **Yulara**, Austl.
105/F4 **Yulin**, China
103/B3 **Yulin** (riv.), China
103/D5 **Yuling Guan** (pass), China
104/D3 **Yulongxue** (peak), China
158/D4 **Yuma**, Az,US
159/G2 **Yuma**, Co,US
117/G4 **Yumbarra Consv. Park**, Austl.
130/A2 **Yumbe**, Ugan.
142/B3 **Yumbel**, Chile
126/E1 **Yumbi**, Zaire
138/B4 **Yumbo**, Col.
96/D4 **Yumen**, China
102/D2 **Yumin**, China
103/C5 **Yun** (riv.), China
92/B2 **Yunak**, Turk.
103/B4 **Yuncheng**, China
103/C4 **Yuncheng**, China
103/C2 **Yungang Caves**, China
136/E7 **Yungas** (reg.), Bol.
142/B3 **Yungay**, Chile
144/D5 **Yunguyo**, Peru
105/F4 **Yunkai** (mts.), China
117/F2 **Yunkanjini Abor. Land**, Austl.
107/G2 **Yunlong**, China
104/D3 **Yunnan** (prov.), China
103/D4 **Yuntai Shan** (peak), China
103/D2 **Yunwu Shan** (peak), China
103/B4 **Yunxi**, China
103/B4 **Yun Xian**, China
104/D3 **Yun Xian**, China
104/D3 **Yunyan** (riv.), China
103/B3 **Yunyanzhen**, China
103/C3 **Yunzhong Shan** (mtn.), China
107/J2 **Yuping**, China
103/H7 **Yuqiao** (res.), China
98/D3 **Yura** (riv.), Japan
144/B2 **Yuracyacu**, Peru
88/J4 **Yurga**, Rus.
100/E2 **Yuri** (isl.), Rus.
144/B2 **Yurimaguas**, Peru
139/F3 **Yuruari** (riv.), Ven.
102/C4 **Yurungkax** (riv.), China
85/N5 **Yuryuzan'** (riv.), Rus.
105/J4 **Yushan Nat'l Park**, Tai.
103/C3 **Yushe**, China
103/D4 **Yutai**, China
103/D3 **Yutian**, China
69/F5 **Yutz**, Fr.
103/C3 **Yu Xian**, China
103/C4 **Yu Xian**, China
105/J2 **Yuyao**, China
100/A4 **Yuza**, Japan
100/B4 **Yuzawa**, Japan
100/D1 **Yuzhno-Kuril'sk**, Rus.
97/N2 **Yuzhno-Sakhalinsk**, Rus.
86/D2 **Yuzhnyy Bug** (riv.), Ukr.
53/R10 **Yvelines** (dept.), Fr.
76/C4 **Yverdon**, Swi.
53/S10 **Yvette** (riv.), Fr.
69/D3 **Yvoir**, Belg.
72/E3 **Yzeure**, Fr.

Z

104/C1 **Za** (riv.), China
123/N13 **Za** (riv.), Mor.
66/B4 **Zaandam**, Neth.
70/C4 **Zaber** (riv.), Ger.
65/L2 **Ząbki**, Pol.
65/J3 **Ząbkowice Śląskie**, Pol.
95/H2 **Zābol**, Iran
65/J4 **Zábřeh**, Czh.
65/K3 **Zabrze**, Pol.
148/D3 **Zacapa**, Guat.
147/M7 **Zacapoaxtla**, Mex.
147/E5 **Zacapú**, Mex.
146/E4 **Zacatecas**, Mex.
146/E3 **Zacatecas** (state), Mex.
148/D3 **Zacatecoluca**, ESal.
147/K8 **Zacatepec**, Mex.
147/M7 **Zacatlán**, Mex.
163/F4 **Zachary**, La,US
148/D3 **Zaculeu**, Guat.
82/B3 **Zadar**, Cro.
109/B4 **Zadetkyi** (isl.), Burma
96/D5 **Zadoi**, China
74/B3 **Zafra**, Sp.
65/H3 **Żagań**, Pol.
123/X17 **Zaghwān'**, Tun.
123/W17 **Zaghwān'** (gov.), Tun.
82/B2 **Zagorjeob Savi**, Slov.
82/C3 **Zagreb** (cap.), Cro.
93/F2 **Zagros** (mts.), Iran
102/E5 **Za'gya** (riv.), China
95/H3 **Zāhedān**, Iran
106/C4 **Zahirābād**, India
91/D3 **Zaḩlah**, Leb.
94/D5 **Zahrān**, SAr.
122/E5 **Zaire**
122/E4 **Zaire** (Congo) (riv.), Zaire
82/F4 **Zaječar**, Yugo.
131/C4 **Zaka**, Zim.
96/E1 **Zakamensk**, Rus.
93/E2 **Zākhū**, Iraq
81/G4 **Zákinthos**, Gre.
81/G4 **Zákinthos** (isl.), Gre.
65/K4 **Zakopane**, Pol.
125/J5 **Zakouma Nat'l Park**, Chad
81/J5 **Zakro** (ruins), Gre.
82/C2 **Zala** (co.), Hun.
82/C2 **Zala** (riv.), Hun.
82/C2 **Zalaegerszeg**, Hun.
74/C3 **Zalamea de la Serena**, Sp.
97/J2 **Zalantun**, China
82/C2 **Zalaszentgrót**, Hun.
82/F2 **Zalău**, Rom.
124/J2 **Zaltan** (well), Libya
66/C5 **Zaltbommel**, Neth.
99/H7 **Zama**, Japan
126/F4 **Zambezi** (riv.), Afr.
131/A2 **Zambezi**, Zam.
131/D3 **Zambézia** (prov.), Moz.
131/B3 **Zambezi Escarpment** (cliff), Zam., Zim.
131/B2 **Zambia**
112/C4 **Zamboanga City**, Phil.
65/M2 **Zambrów**, Pol.
75/P11 **Zambujal de Cima**, Port.
129/G3 **Zamfara** (riv.), Nga.
109/B3 **Zami** (riv.), Burma
144/B2 **Zamora**, Ecu.
144/B1 **Zamora** (riv.), Ecu.
74/C2 **Zamora**, Sp.
144/B2 **Zamora-Chinchipe** (prov.), Ecu.
146/E5 **Zamora de Hidalgo**, Mex.
65/M3 **Zamość**, Pol.
65/M3 **Zamość** (prov.), Pol.
74/D3 **Záncara** (riv.), Sp.
102/C5 **Zanda**, China
66/A5 **Zandkreekdam** (dam), Neth.
66/B4 **Zandvoort**, Neth.
163/H2 **Zanesville**, Oh,US
103/C3 **Zanhuang**, China
93/G2 **Zanjān**, Iran
93/G2 **Zanjān** (gov.), Iran
130/C4 **Zanzibar**, Tanz.
130/C4 **Zanzibar** (isl.), Tanz.
130/C4 **Zanzibar North** (prov.), Tanz.
130/C4 **Zanzibar South** (prov.), Tanz.
130/C4 **Zanzibar West** (prov.), Tanz.
130/B3 **Zanzui** (hill), Tanz.
103/C3 **Zaoqiang**, China
99/G1 **Zaō-san** (mtn.), Japan
103/C4 **Zaoyang**, China
103/D4 **Zaozhuang**, China
97/N2 **Zapadno-Sakhalin** (mts.), Rus.
71/G3 **Západočeský** (reg.), Czh.
65/J4 **Západoslovenský** (reg.), Slvk.
142/C3 **Zapala**, Arg.
135/C1 **Zapaleri** (peak), Arg.
149/F1 **Zapata** (pen.), Cuba
162/D5 **Zapata**, Tx,US
138/C3 **Zapatoca**, Col.
138/C2 **Zapatosa, Ciénaga de** (lake), Col.
71/H4 **Záplatský Rybnik** (lake), Czh.
84/F1 **Zapolyarnyy**, Rus.
86/E3 **Zaporozh'ye**, Ukr.
86/E3 **Zaporozh'ye Obl.**, Ukr.
138/B5 **Zapotal**, Ecu.
82/B3 **Zaprešić**, Cro.
92/D2 **Zara**, Turk.
138/C3 **Zaragoza**, Col.
147/E2 **Zaragoza**, Mex.
75/E2 **Zaragoza** (Saragossa), Sp.
129/H4 **Zaranda** (hill), Nga.
142/F2 **Zárate**, Arg.
74/D1 **Zarauz**, Sp.
139/E2 **Zaraza**, Ven.
93/G3 **Zard** (mtn.), Iran
93/H4 **Zargān**, Iran
129/G4 **Zaria**, Nga.
95/H2 **Zarmast** (pass), Afg.
83/G3 **Zărneşti**, Rom.
93/F2 **Zarrīneh** (riv.), Iran
93/G3 **Zarrin Shahr**, Iran
65/J4 **Záruby** (peak), Slvk.
144/B1 **Zaruma**, Ecu.
144/A1 **Zarumilla**, Peru
65/H3 **Żary**, Pol.
138/B3 **Zarzal**, Col.
74/A1 **Zas**, Sp.
95/L2 **Zāskar** (range), India
71/G2 **Žatec**, Czh.
68/D2 **Zaventem**, Belg.
82/D3 **Zavidovići**, Bosn.
97/K1 **Zavitinsk**, Rus.
131/D5 **Závora** (pt.), Moz.
65/K3 **Zawadzkie**, Pol.
131/C3 **Zawi**, Zim.
65/K3 **Zawiercie**, Pol.
96/D6 **Zaya** (riv.), China
102/D2 **Zaysan**, Kaz.
102/D2 **Zaysan** (lake), Kaz.
104/C2 **Zayü**, China
104/C2 **Zayü** (riv.), China
149/G1 **Zaza** (riv.), Cuba
65/H2 **Zbąszyń**, Pol.
65/H4 **Žd'ár nad Sázavou**, Czh.
65/K3 **Zduńska Wola**, Pol.
142/C5 **Zeballos** (peak), Arg.
123/R16 **Zeddine** (riv.), Alg.
68/C1 **Zedelgem**, Belg.
66/A5 **Zeeland** (prov.), Neth.
160/C3 **Zeeland**, Mi,US
132/D2 **Zeerust**, SAfr.
66/C4 **Zeewolde**, Neth.
91/D3 **Zefat**, Isr.
65/L2 **Zegrzyńskie** (lake), Pol.
65/G2 **Zehdenick**, Ger.
117/G2 **Zeil** (peak), Austl.
66/C4 **Zeist**, Neth.
64/G3 **Zeitz**, Ger.
68/D1 **Zele**, Belg.
85/L5 **Zelenodol'sk**, Rus.
63/N1 **Zelenogorsk**, Rus.
87/G3 **Zelenokumsk**, Rus.
66/D4 **Zelhem**, Neth.
70/D1 **Zella-Mehlis**, Ger.
76/E1 **Zell am Harmersbach**, Ger.
73/K3 **Zell am See**, Aus.
71/G7 **Zellersee** (lake), Aus.
77/E2 **Zellersee** (lake), Ger.
76/D2 **Zell in Wiesental**, Ger.
65/K3 **Zelów**, Pol.
82/B2 **Zeltweg**, Aus.
68/C1 **Zelzate**, Belg.
80/B4 **Zembra** (isls.), Tun.
125/J6 **Zemio**, CAfr.
123/R16 **Zemmora**, Alg.
147/N7 **Zempoala**, Mex.
147/Q10 **Zempoala** (mtn.), Mex.
148/C2 **Zempoaltepec, Cerro** (mtn.), Mex.
68/D2 **Zemst**, Belg.
158/B2 **Zenia**, Ca,US
82/C3 **Zenica**, Bosn.
165/C3 **Zenith**, Wa,US
70/D3 **Zenn** (riv.), Ger.
157/H2 **Zenon Park**, Sk,Can
98/C3 **Zentsūji**, Japan
82/D3 **Žepče**, Bosn.
123/S15 **Zeralda**, Alg.
123/L13 **Zerga** (lake), Mor.
86/G3 **Zernograd**, Rus.
152/F1 **Zeta** (lake), NW,Can
67/E2 **Zetel**, Ger.
67/G2 **Zeven**, Ger.
66/D5 **Zevenaar**, Neth.
66/B5 **Zevenbergen**, Neth.
97/K1 **Zeya**, Rus.
97/K1 **Zeya** (res.), Rus.
97/K1 **Zeya** (riv.), Rus.
97/K1 **Zeya-Bureya** (plain), Rus.
74/A3 **Zêzere** (riv.), Port.
91/D2 **Zghartā**, Leb.
65/K3 **Zgierz**, Pol.
65/H3 **Zgorzelec**, Pol.
97/K2 **Zhan** (riv.), China
103/B5 **Zhang** (riv.), China
105/G3 **Zhang** (riv.), China
103/C5 **Zhangdu** (lake), China
97/K3 **Zhangguangcai** (mts.), China
103/C2 **Zhanghei**, China
103/C2 **Zhangjiakou**, China

Acknowledgements

Several years ago, we saw an opportunity to create a radically new map-making system. Advances in technology put within our grasp a means of producing maps more efficiently and more accurately than ever before. At the heart of our plan was a computerized geographic database – one which would enable maps to be created and changed at whim.

This world atlas is one of the first products of our new system. Behind it hums another world, a bustling, close-knit family of talented and innovative cartographers, researchers, editors, artists, technicians and scholars. In the five years it has taken to create our new system, their world has seen almost as many upheavals as our own planet. For their constancy and faith in a project which sometimes seemed so daunting, for their patience and creativity to explore new technologies, and for the teamwork which enabled us to realize such an ambitious goal, we are deeply grateful.

We are especially grateful for the support of our many contributors, whose efforts made this volume better. In particular, we wish to thank Mitchell Feigenbaum, a brilliant scientist and dear friend, whose illumination of the world around him extends to the art – and science – of cartography. His genius is ever-present in this atlas, from his revolutionary map projection to his pioneering software, which was crucial to the success of our computer mapping system.

At last, a map-making system that moves as fast as the world is changing. As new technology continues to redefine what is possible, we will continue to push the envelope, to pioneer a better way. We are committed to maintaining the highest level of quality – in accuracy and timeliness, in design and printing, and in service to our clients and readers. It is our goal to ensure that you can always turn to Hammond for the very best in map and atlas design and geographic information.

C. Dean and Kathleen Hammond

COMPUTERIZED CARTOGRAPHIC ADVISORY BOARD

Mitchell J. Feigenbaum, Ph.D
Chief Technical Consultant
Toyota Professor, The Rockefeller University
Wolf Prize in Physics, 1986
Member, The National Academy of Sciences

Judson G. Rosebush, Ph.D
Computer Graphics Animation
Producer, Director and Author

Gary Martin Andrew, Ph.D
Consultant in Operations Research,
Planning and Management

Warren E. Schmidt, B.A.
Former U.S. Geological Survey,
Chief of the Branch of Geographic
and Cartographic Research

HAMMOND PUBLICATIONS ADVISORY BOARD

UNITED STATES AND CANADA
Daniel Jacobson
Professor of Geography and Education,
Adjunct Professor of Anthropology,
Michigan State University

LATIN AND MIDDLE AMERICA
John P. Augelli
Professor and Chairman,
Department of Geography-Meteorology,
University of Kansas

WESTERN AND SOUTHERN EUROPE
Norman J. W. Thrower
Professor, Department of Geography,
University of California, Los Angeles

NORTHERN AND CENTRAL EUROPE
Vincent H. Malmstrom
Professor, Department of Geography,
Dartmouth College

SOUTH AND SOUTHEAST ASIA
P. P. Karan
Professor, Department of Geography,
University of Kentucky

EAST ASIA
Christopher L. Salter
Professor and Chairman,
Department of Geography,
University of Missouri

AUSTRALIA, NEW ZEALAND
& THE PACIFIC AREA
Tom L. McKnight
Professor, Department of Geography,
University of California, Los Angeles

POPULATION AND DEMOGRAPHY
Kingsley Davis
Distinguished Professor of Sociology,
University of Southern California
and Senior Research Fellow,
The Hoover Institution,
Stanford University

BIBLICAL ARCHAEOLOGY
Roger S. Boraas
Professor of Religion,
Upsala College

FLAGS
Whitney Smith
Executive Director,
The Flag Research Center,
Winchester, Massachusetts

LIBRARY CONSULTANT
Alice C. Hudson
Chief, Map Division,
The New York Public Library

SPECIAL ADVISORS

DESIGN CONSULTANT
Pentagram

CONTRIBUTING WRITER
Frederick A. Shamlian

HAMMOND INCORPORATED

Charles G. Lees, Jr., V.P.
Editor in Chief, Cartography

William L. Abel, V.P.
Graphic Services

Phil Giouvanos
Director, Computer Cartography

Michael E. Agishstein, Ph.D
Director, Research and Development

Ernst G. Hofmann
Manager Emeritus, Topographic Arts

Martin A. Bacheller
Editor in Chief, Emeritus

Joseph F. Kalina, Jr.
Managing Editor

ALASKA
151

CANADA
152

GREENLAND

NORTH AMERICA
145

ICELAND 61

EUROPE
52

NOR

United States
154

156

160

167
Metropolitan
New York

London
53

Par
53

Metropolitan Los Angeles
164

158

162

Azores 75

Madeira 75

MOROCCO

NORTHERN
AFRICA
124

Canary Is. 75

ALGERI

154
HAWAII

Oahu
154

146
MEXICO

Distrito
Federal
147

Mexico City — Veracruz
CUBA
JAMAICA
HAITI
150
BAHAMAS

DOM.
REP.

150

MAURITANIA

MALI

SEN.

128

NIC

GUINEA

B.F.

LIBR.

CÔTE
D'IV.

CHANA

BEN

TO

AFRICA
122

GA

CENTRAL
PACIFIC OCEAN
120

121
Samoa

121
Tahiti

GUA.
HON.
NICAR.
COSTA RICA

PANAMA

148

VENEZUELA

138

COLOMBIA

SUR.
GUYANA

Fr. Guiana

CAPE VERDE 122

NORTHERN
SOUTH AMERICA
136

144
Galapagos Is.

ECU.

144
PERU

BRAZIL

140

SOUTHER
AFRICA
126

SOUTH AMERICA
134

BOLIVIA

PAR.

141
São Paulo —
Rio de Janiero
141

142
Santiago
Valparaíso

ARGENTINA

UR.
143

Río de la
Plata
142

SOUTHERN
SOUTH AMERICA
135

CHILE

143

UNITED STATES/CANADA

CANADA

AB.

SK.

MB.

BC

156

Seattle
Tacoma
165

WA.

MT.

ND

MN.

ON.

QU.

Montréal
161

Chicago
Milwaukee
165

Toronto
Buffalo
161

OR.

ID.

WY.

SD

IA.

WI.

Detroit
165

MI.

NB

ME.

NS

NV.

UT.

CO.

NE.

IL.

IN.

OH.

168

NY

168

PA.

166

CA.

158

AZ.

NM

KS.

MO.

UNITED STATES

OK.

AR.

KY.

WV

VA.

TN.

NC

SC

Sacramento
San Francisco
San Jose
165

TX.

MS.

AL.

GA.

LA.

FL.

MEXICO

KEY TO ATLAS MAPS

1:14,000,000 ASIA 90
AND SMALLER SCALES

1:7,000,000 162

1:1,170,000 165

1:10,500,000 106

1:3,500,000 100

1:587,000 • London 53

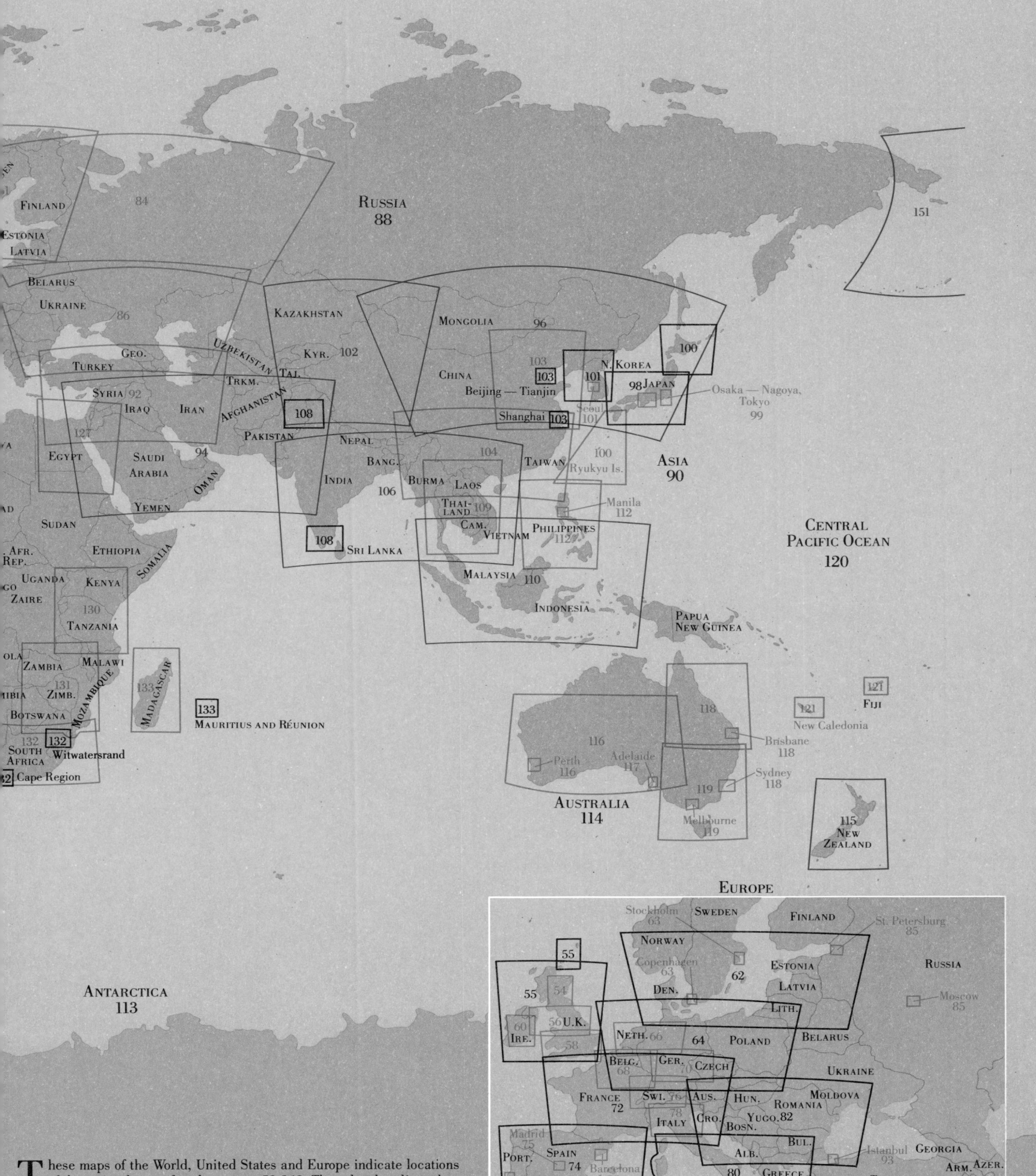

These maps of the World, United States and Europe indicate locations of the regional maps found on pages 52-168. The colored outlines show the scale of each map (per the accompanying legend) and the extent of each map's coverage. Page numbers of the same color are found in the center of each outline. Large scale map insets are noted by outline, name and page number. Small scale maps of continents and large countries are indicated by name and page number only. A map of the world appears on pages 50-51.